THE SOCIONOMIC THEORY OF FINANCE

Socionomics — The Science of History
and Social Prediction, Volume 3

by

Robert R. Prechter

Socionomics Institute Press

Printed in the United States of America

First Printing, 2016

ISBN: 978-0-9776112-5-6
Library of Congress Catalog Card Number: 2016916930

Publisher: Socionomics Institute Press
Gainesville, Georgia USA

The Socionomics Institute

www.socionomics.net

Address for comments: institute@socionomics.net

CONTENTS

Foreword vii

PART I: The Absence of Exogenous Cause in Financial Markets

Chapter 1: The Myth of Shocks. 3
Robert R. Prechter

Chapter 2: The Conventional Error of Exogenous Cause and Rational
Reaction in Finance 23
Robert R. Prechter

Chapter 3: Central-Bank Policy Does Not Control Interest Rates;
It's the Other Way Around 73
Alan Hall, Mark Galasiewski and *Robert Prechter*

Chapter 4: Stocks' Rise After the Charlie Hebdo Attack Was Anything But
a "Rational Reaction". 81
Brian Whitmer

Chapter 5: Time for a New Model. 85
Robert R. Prechter

PART II: Socionomic Theory

Chapter 6: The Structure of Socionomic Theory. 109
Robert R. Prechter

Chapter 7: Sociometers and Their Application 131
Robert R. Prechter

Chapter 8: Socionomics and the Elliott Wave Model Provide a Framework for
Projecting the Lag Time of News. 149
Alan Hall

Chapter 9: Did U C New Studies? Tweets N Blogs Predict Equity Prices . . 169
Euan Wilson

Chapter 10: From Observation to Prediction. 173
Robert R. Prechter

Chapter 11: Socionomics Satisfies the Criteria of Falsifiability and
Predictability 195
Robert R. Prechter

PART III: The Socionomic Theory of Finance

Chapter 12: The Financial/Economic Dichotomy 203
Robert R. Prechter

Chapter 13: Fundamentals of STF, in Contrast to Those of Economics 235
Robert R. Prechter

Chapter 14: The Economic-Socionomic Spectrum of Markets 265
Robert R. Prechter

Chapter 15: The Financial/Economic Dichotomy in Social Behavioral
Dynamics: The Socionomic Perspective 273
Robert R. Prechter and *Wayne D. Parker*

PART IV: Herding and Social Mood

Chapter 16: Unconscious Herding Behavior as the Psychological Basis of
Financial Market Trends and Patterns 325
Robert R. Prechter

Chapter 17: Financial Herding is Universal and Fractal 337
Robert R. Prechter

Chapter 18: The Awesome Power of Exogenous-Cause Mythology and
Consensus Thinking to Hijack Investors' Minds 361
Robert R. Prechter

Chapter 19: On Mood, Herding and Alternative Hypotheses 375
Robert R. Prechter

Chapter 20: Are Crowds Really Wise? Study Confirms that Herding
Undermines the Wisdom-of-Crowds Effect 415
Alan Hall

PART V: STF vs. Conventional Thinking

Chapter 21: Linear Extrapolation vs. Fractal Extrapolation 421
Robert R. Prechter

Chapter 22: Elliott Waves vs. Supply and Demand: The Oil Market 457
Robert R. Prechter

Chapter 23: Popular Bubble Theories vs. the Elliott Wave Model 503
Robert R. Prechter

Chapter 24: Contrasting STF with Certain Tenets of the Austrian School . . . 525
Robert R. Prechter

Chapter 25: Contrasting STF with Keynesian and Monetarist Technocratic
Theories 539
Robert R. Prechter

PART VI: The Primacy of Social Mood in Financial-Market Causality

Chapter 26: Social Mood Impels Feelings of Certainty and Uncertainty 549
  Alan Hall
Chapter 27: Social Mood Influences Aggregate Opinions about Inflation and
  Deflation Irrespective of Pertinent Data.................... 557
  Wayne Gorman
Chapter 28: Social Mood Governs the Tone of Federal Reserve Board
  Meetings.. 569
  Alan Hall
Chapter 29: Skepticism about "Potent Directors" Can Set You Apart from the
  Crowd.. 577
  Brian Whitmer
Chapter 30: A Proposed Relationship between Collective Approach-Avoidance
  Motivation and Social Mood 581
  Kenneth Olson
Chapter 31: Social Mood and Financial Economics 585
  John R. Nofsinger

PART VII: Metatheory and STF's Relationship to Other Theories

Chapter 32: The Metatheoretical Foundation of Socionomics 621
  Wayne D. Parker
Chapter 33: Socionomics: A New and Metatheoretically Consistent Social
  Science Paradigm................................... 631
  Wayne D. Parker
Chapter 34: Herding: An Interdisciplinary Integrative Review from a
  Socionomic Perspective 655
  Wayne D. Parker
Chapter 35: A Literature Review of Social Mood.................... 667
  Kenneth R. Olson
Chapter 36: The Socionomic Theory of Finance and the Institution of Social
  Mood: Pareto and the Sociology of Instinct and Rationalization 691
  Wayne D. Parker
Chapter 37: Methodological Individualism vs. Methodological Holism and
  Their Resolution in Socionomic Theory 721
  Wayne D. Parker
Chapter 38: Socionomics Theorist Wayne D. Parker, PhD, Dies at 61 731

PART VIII: And for Dessert...

Chapter 39: Brain Teaser: Discounting Theory vs. Socionomic Theory 735
    Robert R. Prechter

Chapter 40: Using Socionomics To Predict Trends in the Popularity of
    Financial Theories 745
    Robert R. Prechter

Chapter 41: Setting the Record Straight about Socionomics. 757
    Mark Almand and *Matt Lampert*

Chapter 42: A Well-Known Scholar Embraces Socionomics 773
    Dave Allman and *John Casti*

Chapter 43: Two Popular Science Magazines Review the Socionomic
    Hypothesis 777
    Chuck Thompson

Chapter 44: An Interview with Robert Prechter on the Origin and Future of
    Socionomics. 779

Appendix: Key Events in Socionomics. 791

List of Illustrations 801
Index 807

The Authors

Robert Prechter is President of the Socionomics Institute, the Socionomics Foundation and Elliott Wave International.

Wayne Parker, PhD served as Executive Director of the Socionomics Foundation.

Alan Hall, Euan Wilson and Chuck Thompson are researchers at the Socionomics Institute, where Matt Lampert is Director of Research. Wayne Gorman and Mark Almand are board members of the Socionomics Foundation.

Brian Whitmer is editor of *The European Financial Forecast*, Mark Galasiewski is editor of *The Asian-Pacific Financial Forecast*, and Dave Allman is a senior analyst, at Elliott Wave International.

Kenneth Olson is Professor Emeritus of Psychology, Fort Hays State University; John Nofsinger is William H. Seward Endowed Chair in International Finance, University of Alaska; and John Casti, PhD (mathematics) is head of X-Center Vienna.

Prominently featured writers include Steven Hochberg and Peter Kendall, editors of *The Elliott Wave Financial Forecast*, and Steven Craig, editor of *Energy Pro Service* and contributor to *Global Market Perspective*, all of which are publications of Elliott Wave International.

FOREWORD

The socionomic theory of finance (STF) is a subset of the larger field of socionomics. Two of my previous books concentrated on socionomic theory overall, whereas this book focuses mainly on STF.

To put this volume in perspective: It is not just another book challenging conventional economic theory on the subjects of finance and macroeconomics; it is a book about what should replace it. It is not another book updating the age-old observation that investors are emotional; it is a book about the origin of those emotions. It is not another book about occasional investor irrationality; it is a book about contexts accommodating rational or impulsive thought. It is not another technical analysis book about interpreting financial market sentiment; it is a book about why there is even such a thing as financial market sentiment. It is not another book about market psychology; it is a book about psychology's role in financial and social causality. It is not a how-to book about the craft of social futurism; it is a book about the primary cause of the social future.

Part I of this book dispenses with the ideas of exogenous cause and rational reaction in financial pricing. Parts II through V introduce socionomic theory and explain the fundamentals of STF. Parts VI through VIII expand the scope of the discussion. When pertinent, headers provide original composition dates for contributors' chapters previously published elsewhere. I have edited them to fit smoothly into this book.

Quotations from news articles are excerpted and sometimes re-arranged for conciseness; ellipses are sometimes omitted for ease of reading. Parts of quoted publications are underlined or italicized for emphasis. All sources are cited if you want to access the originals.

With deepest gratitude, I would like to acknowledge Wayne Parker, Kenneth Olson, Alan Hall, Mark Galasiewski, Brian Whitmer, Wayne Gorman, Chuck Thompson, John Nofsinger, Euan Wilson and Dave Allman for their contributions to this book. Special thanks go to Matt Lampert for his contribution and for playing economists' advocate, prompting an expansion of Chapter 12, and to Mark Almand for his contribution, editing suggestions and the initial idea for Chapter 39. Thanks also to Angela Hall for charts and production, Sally Webb for production and layout, Ohki Komoto for the rear flap photo and Pam Greenwood for collaborating on the dust jacket design. My co-authors and I are deeply indebted to the valiant souls who have stepped forward publicly to endorse this effort. Without their courageous support, the book may not be afforded the opportunity to find an audience.

Work on this book began in 2003. Early versions of many chapters appeared in my monthly publication, *The Elliott Wave Theorist*. Writing was completed by the end of 2015. Some chapters written for the book were subsequently published to subscribers. Updating the 240 charts, figures and tables, creating the endnotes, confirming internal and external references and editing the text lasted throughout the first quarter of 2016. During that time, Chapter 22 was expanded to reflect Q1 2016 data, and three new references were added. The layout, indexes, chart normalization and production processes lasted through Q2, after which I inserted a late note into Chapter 18. In Q3, we sent the book to academics and professionals for pre-publication comments, designed the jacket and made final tweaks. It is scheduled to go to the printer in early November. Two more books—on socionomic causality in culture and politics—are in the works for publication in early 2017.

If you are short on time and wish to access only the key nuggets of material, I suggest Chapters 1, 2, 6, 8, 12, 13, 14, 17, 19, 22 and 23. These are only one fourth of the chapters, constituting three eighths of the text, but they will give you a solid grounding in how the socionomic theory of finance differs from conventional views. Be sure also to read our upcoming book, *Socionomic Causality in Politics* (2017), which dispenses with the ubiquitous notion that politics are a major determinant of financial prices, replacing that notion with socionomic causality.

Socionomics is not a dismal science. It is fresh, fun, fascinating, informative, exhilarating and inspiring.

I tried to make this book a good read, so I hope you will take your time and read Parts I-V straight through. There is a lot to absorb, though, so you might want to limit yourself to a chapter or two at a time.

What you have here is the best that I can do. I welcome critiques that may lead me to amend any errors I or my co-authors have committed. If you wish to communicate, please write to institute@socionomics.net.

—Robert Prechter

Part I:

THE ABSENCE OF
EXOGENOUS CAUSE IN
FINANCIAL MARKETS

Chapter 1

The Myth of Shocks

Robert R. Prechter

Few people find a new theory accessible until they first see errors in the old way of thinking. Part I of this book challenges the universally accepted paradigm under which humans' rational reactions to exogenous (external, or externally generated) causes purportedly account for financial market behavior.

The current chapter explores whether dramatic news events affect financial markets. Chapter 2 investigates the supposed effects of economic, financial, monetary and political conditions on financial markets. A bit later, Chapter 12 will examine the relationship between company-valuation measures and stock prices. Chapters 12 and 22 assess whether supply and demand regulate financial prices. Once you see that nothing of the sort explains the behavior of financial markets, you may be open to accepting a whole new paradigm that does explain it.

Testing Financial-Market Reaction under Perfect Conditions

In the physical world of mechanics, action is followed by reaction. When a bat strikes a ball, the ball changes course.

Most financial analysts, economists, historians, sociologists and futurists believe that society works the same way. They typically say, "Because so-and-so has happened, it will cause such-and-such reaction." This mechanics paradigm is ubiquitous in financial commentary. The news headlines in Figure 1 reflect what economists tell reporters: Good economic news makes the stock market go up; bad economic news makes it go down. But is it true?

Good economic news propels markets
—*USA Today*, January 15, 2004

Bad economic news is chilling investors
—*The New York Times*, July 15, 2012

Figure 1

In the second half of the 1990s, a popular book made a case for buying and holding stocks forever. In March 2004, after several terrorist attacks had occurred, the author told a reporter, "Clearly, the risk of terror is the major reason why the markets have come down. We can't quantify these risks; it's not like flipping a coin and knowing your odds are 50-50 that an attack won't occur."[1]

In other words, he accepts the mechanics paradigm of exogenous cause and effect with respect to the stock market but says he cannot predict a major cause part of the equation. The first question is, if one cannot predict causes, then how can one write a book predicting effects? A second question is far more important: Is there any evidence that dramatic news events that make headlines, including terrorist attacks, political events, wars, natural disasters and other crises, are causal to stock market movement?

Suppose the devil were to offer you historic news a day in advance, no strings attached. "What's more," he says, "you can hold a position in the stock market for as little as a single trading day after the event or as long as you like." It sounds foolproof, so you accept.

His first offer: "The president will be assassinated tomorrow." You can't believe it. You are the only person in the world who knows it's going to happen.

The devil transports you back to November 22, 1963. You quickly take a short position in the stock market in order to profit when prices fall on the bad news you know is coming. Do you make money?

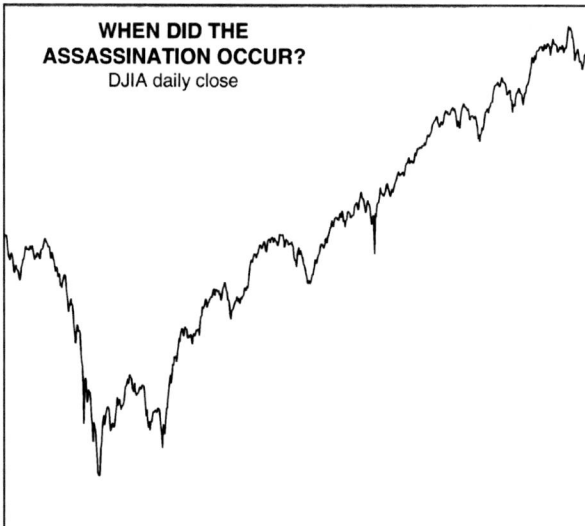

Figure 2

Figure 2 shows the DJIA around the time when President John F. Kennedy was shot. First of all, can you tell by looking at the graph exactly when that event occurred? Maybe before that big drop on the left? Maybe at some other peak, causing a selloff?

The first arrow in Figure 3 shows the timing of the assassination. The market initially fell, but by the close of the next trading day, it was above where it was at the moment of the event, as you can see by the position of the second arrow. The devil had said that you could hold as briefly as one trading day after the event, *but not less*. You can't cover your short sales until the following day's up close. You lose money.

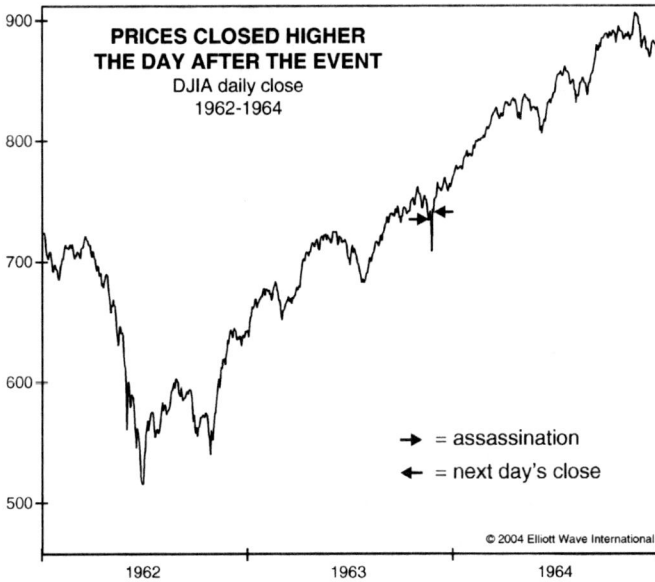

Figure 3

You aren't really angry because, after all, the devil delivered on his promise. Your only error was to believe that a presidential assassination would dictate the course of stock prices. So, you vow to bet only on things that will directly affect the economy.

The devil pops up again, and you explain what you want. "I've got just the thing," he says, and announces, "The biggest electrical blackout in the history of North America will occur tomorrow." Wow. Billions of dollars of lost production. People stranded in subways and elevators. The last time a blackout occurred, there was a riot in New York City, causing extensive property damage. "Sold!" you cry. The devil transports you back to August 2003.

Figure 4 shows the DJIA around the time of the blackout. Does the history of stock prices make it evident when that event occurred? After all, if market prices change due to action and reaction, then this surprise economic loss should show up unmistakably, shouldn't it? There are two big drops on the graph. Maybe it happened just before one of them.

WHEN DID THE BLACKOUT OCCUR?
DJIA daily close

Figure 4

The arrow in Figure 5 shows the timing of that event. Not only did the market fail to collapse, *it gapped up the next morning.* You sit all day with your short sales and cover the following day with another loss.

"Third time's the charm," says the devil. "Forget it," you reply. "I don't understand why the market isn't reacting to these causes. Maybe these events you're giving me just aren't strong enough. What I need is a real *shock.*"

The devil leans into your ear and whispers, "Terrorists will detonate two bombs in London, leveling landmark buildings and killing 3,000 people. Another bomb planted at Parliament will misfire, merely blowing the side off the building. The planners will vow to continue their attacks until England is wiped off the map." He promises that you can sell short on the London Stock Exchange ten minutes before it happens and even offers to remove the one-day holding restriction. "Cover whenever you like," he says. You agree. The devil then transports you to a parallel universe where New York is London, the Pentagon is Parliament and the DJIA is the LSE. It's a replay of September 11, 2001.

Figure 5

Figure 6 shows the DJIA around that time. Study it carefully. Can you find an *anomaly* on the graph? Is there an obvious time when the shocking events of 9/11 show up? If markets react to exogenous shocks, as baseballs do, there would be something obviously *different* on the graph at that time, wouldn't there? But there isn't.

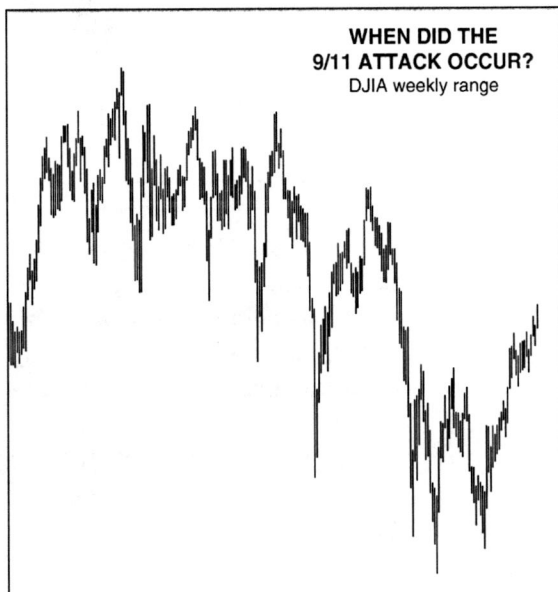

Figure 6

Authorities closed the stock market for four and a half trading days after the 9/11 attack, and it stayed closed over the following weekend. Was it certain that the market would re-open on the downside? No. Some popular radio talk-show hosts and administration officials advocated buying stocks on the opening just to "show 'em." You sit with your short position, and you are nervous. But you are also lucky. The market opens down, continuing a decline that had already been in force for 17 weeks. You cheer. You're making money now! Well, you do for five days, anyway. Then the market leaps higher, and somewhere between one and six months later (see Figure 7) you become disgusted and confused and finally cover your shorts at a loss.

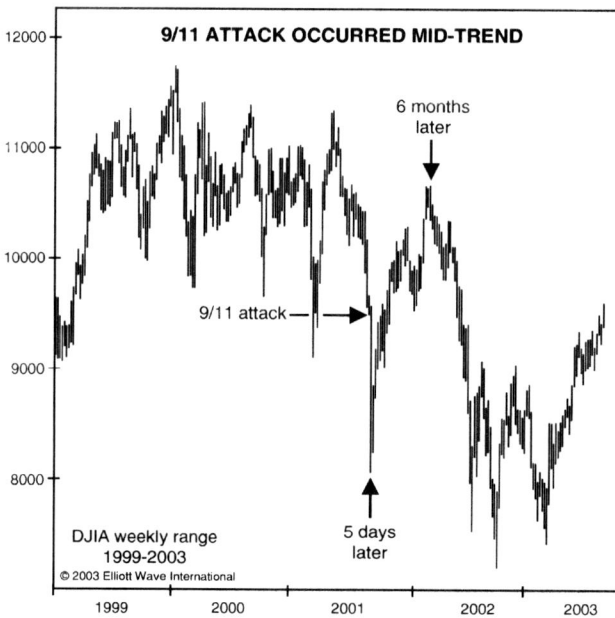

Figure 7

The devil spreads his hands in apology. "Wait! You saw how it worked for a few days! I can't help it if you held on too long." You start to walk away. He gives it one last shot. "I know. You need something that's going to work long term. How would you like to take a long term trade that's guaranteed in print?"

You hesitate. He says, "I happen to know of a devastating event that future historians will describe as 'the costliest natural disaster in the history of the United States.'[2] Does that sound promising?" You're not sure. "Where is it going to hit?" "New Orleans will get the worst of it." "Forget it. I can't short New Orleans." The devil smiles slyly. "No, but you can buy oil futures contracts. Hang on. Just read this future description of the effects of the event, which will be available on the Internet *ten years after the fact.*" He hands you this report:

> Katrina shut down 95% of crude production and 88% of natural gas output in the Gulf of Mexico. This amounted to a quarter of total U.S. output. About 735 oil and natural gas rigs and platforms had been evacuated due to the hurricane. The price of oil fluctuated greatly. According to [a spokesman on the scene], "half billion dollars a day of oil and gas is unavailable. Hurricane Katrina will impact oil and gas infrastructure, not just short term but *long term* as well." The storm interrupted oil production, importation, and refining in the Gulf, thus having a *major effect on fuel prices.*[3]

"C'mon!" he says. "You can't get a better guarantee than that!"

You think, "He's right. It's there in black and white: 'a long term impact...a major effect on fuel prices.'" This is the trade you've been look- ing for. You agree to go for it. The devil transports you back to the early morning of August 29, 2005, the day Hurricane Katrina hit shore. As soon as the market opens, you buy an armload of oil futures contracts. You sit back and wait for the outcome future historians had described.

Figure 8 shows the day you placed your all-out bullish bet: August 29, 2005, right at a top in oil prices and just before a three-month slide of

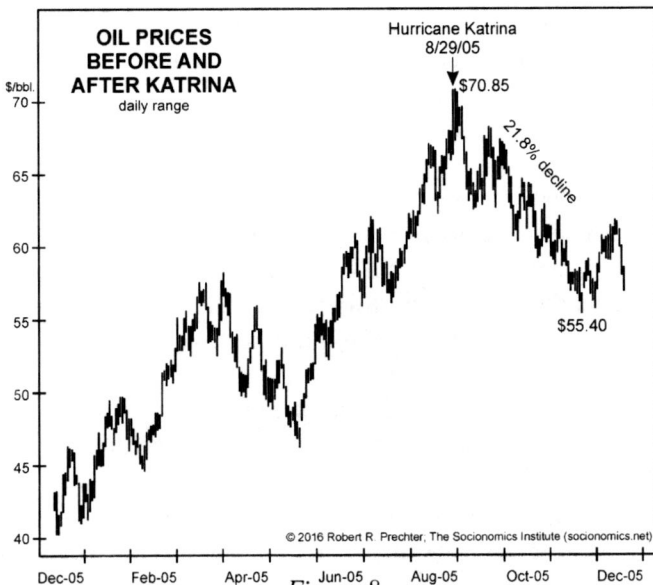

Figure 8

over 20%. You are stunned. A record-breaking, *surprise* disruption in the supply of oil failed to make oil prices zoom. On the chart, it even looks as if somehow *the event made prices fall*. You are bewildered. You took Econ 101 in college, and the market's reaction makes no sense. You finally sell out, taking a loss.

You look into the history of the matter and come across a footnote on Wikipedia saying that President G.W. Bush had released oil from the U.S. Strategic Petroleum Reserve in the wake of Katrina. Maybe that was the devil's secret! But, no. The U.S. was consuming 21 million barrels of oil a day at the time,[4] and the Reserve over a period of weeks released only half a day's worth.[5]

You pull out a historical chart of oil and discover that even in late August 2007, *two years after the event*, its price was exactly the same as it was on the day you had bought, even though oil was in the middle of a monstrous bull market in which its price soared over 1300% from 1998 to 2008. Somehow your purchase caught one of the few setbacks within it.

You do a Google search, and there it is—the passage the devil had read. The historians lied. They must have figured that a disaster of such magnitude simply *had* to have a major effect on oil prices, so they just *said* it did. Their devotion to exogenous-cause logic obscured their perception of history.

You take a day off to do some research and come across an exhaustive, 40-year study of the impact of 177 large earthquakes on the returns of stock market indices in 35 different countries from January 1973 to August 2013. You read that despite limiting the earthquakes under study to those causing at least 1,000 fatalities or a minimum of $25 million in property damage, the authors were able to identify "No systematic effect of earthquakes on aggregate stock market indices, either directly or through the control variables."[6] Then you realize: This must go for assassinations, blackouts, terrorist attacks and hurricanes, too.

If you are an everyday thoughtful person, you decide that events are irrelevant to markets and begin a long process of educating yourself on why markets move as they do. If you are a conventional economist, you don't bother.

Now think about this: In real life, *you don't get to know about dramatic events in advance*. Investors who sold stocks upon hearing of the various events cited above did so because they believed that events cause changes in stock values. *They all sold the lows or bought the highs*. I chose bad news for these exercises because it tends to be more dramatic, but the same irrelevance attaches to good news.

Exogenous-Cause Claims Lead to Perverse Conclusions

Economists often say that an unexpected "shock" would cause them to re-evaluate their bullish stock market forecasts. It does seem logical that a scary event such as a destructive terrorist attack, particularly one that implies more attacks to come, would be bearish for stock prices.

Take a moment to study Figure 6 again. Surely all of those exceptionally dramatic swings in the DJIA must have been caused by equally dramatic news: bad news at each of the peaks and good news at each of the bottoms. At least that's what the exogenous-cause model would have us believe.

As it happens, there was a lot of scary news during this time. Aside from the 9/11 terrorist attack on the World Trade Center and the Pentagon, there was also a slew of mailings of deadly anthrax bacteria, which killed several people, prompted Congress to evacuate a session and wreaked havoc lasting months. Where on the graph of stock prices in Figure 6 would you guess the anthrax mailings happened?

If you guessed, "the very day of a rally high and all through a four-month stock-price collapse," befitting exogenous-cause theory, Figure 9 would vindicate you. It shows that the first anthrax attack occurred precisely

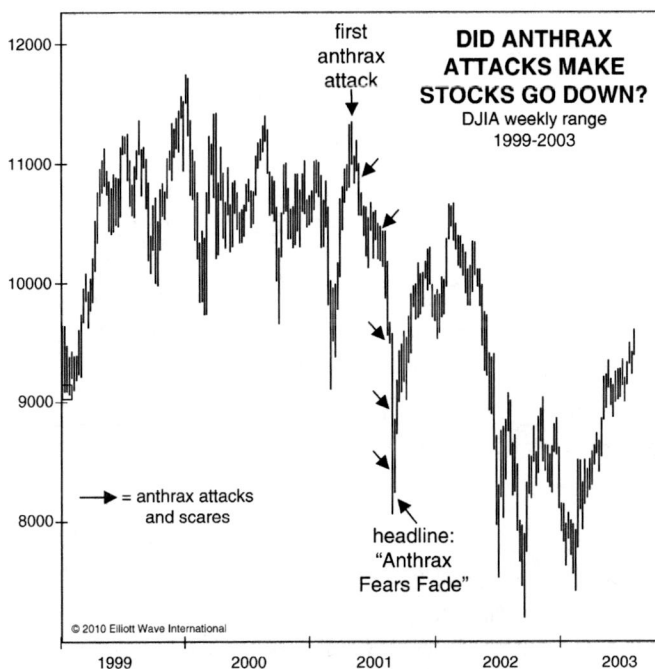

Figure 9

on the top day of a rocketing advance that appeared destined to take the
Dow to a new all-time high. The stock market reversed sharply and then
fell throughout the period of attacks. When the attacks stopped, the decline
stopped, and the market turned on a dime and soared. Good for you and
exogenous cause theory!

The only problem with your case is that Figure 9 is a lie.

Figure 10 tells the truth. The first anthrax attack actually occurred on
the very day of the low for the year, after a dramatic, 18-month decline in
the Dow. Afterward, despite six more attacks and public concern that more
were in the works, the stock market rallied for six months. These attacks,
deaths and scares, moreover, occurred throughout *the strongest rally on
the entire graph*. To put it more starkly, the market bottomed the day the
attacks started and topped out as soon as people realized they were over.

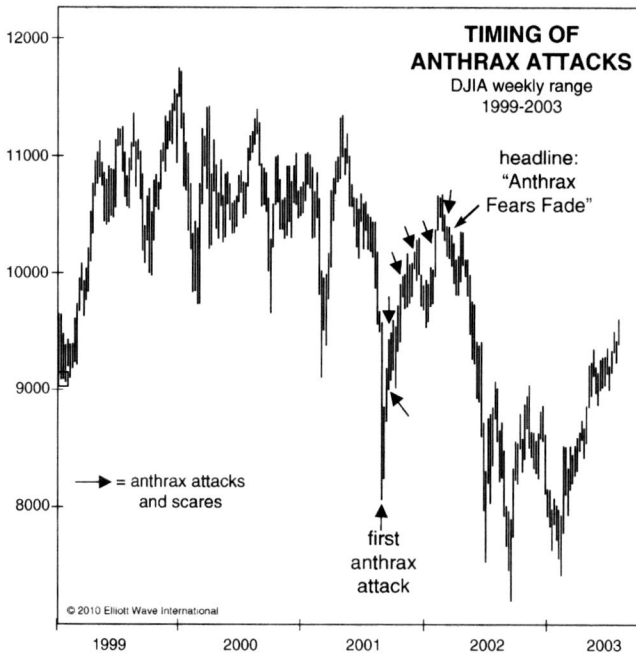

Figure 10

Figures 7 and 10 reveal an irrefutable fact: *Terrorist attacks do not make
the stock market go down*. The assumption behind economists' repeated
implications that terrorist attacks would constitute an "exogenous shock"
that would serve to drive down stock prices is simply wrong.

Since even possessing advance secret knowledge of highly dramatic, surprise events provides no advantage for speculating, guessing about coming events is an utter waste of time. There can be no causes related to external events that even the most prescient person could exploit.

It gets worse. From the viewpoint of exogenous cause, Figures 3, 5, 7, 8 and 10 make it appear as if the assassination of President Kennedy was bullish, the New York City blackout contributed to a rally, Hurricane Katrina caused oil prices to drop, and terrorist attacks made stock prices soar. These conclusions are discordant and perverse.

Can you imagine a way to make perfect sense of Figure 10? As we will discover in Part II and Chapter 19, a fundamentally different theory of social causality accounts for the chronology of events in Figure 10 so as to turn discordant perversity into harmonic compatibility.

Retrospective Data-Fitting is Easy

We have seen that even the most dramatic news is irrelevant to the stock market. How, then, can the media frequently explain a day's market action by the news? The answer is, *There is a lot of news every day*. Commentators don't write their cause-and-effect stories before all the news comes out but afterward. Much of the time it's no trick to fit news to the market after the fact.

Rationalized Data-Fitting: "News Shocks" That Aren't

Nevertheless, it is surprising how often commentators are unable to get the news to fit a day's market action, prompting them to resort to convoluted reasoning. Consider this example: The news at 8:30 a.m. on April 13, 2004 was *good*: a "stronger-than-expected," 1.8% jump in March retail sales. But the market had a big down day. How, then, did analysts interviewed for the next morning's newspaper, searching for some sort of external cause and effect, explain the presumed reaction? A common headline read, "Rising-Rates Scenario Sends Stocks Reeling."[7] This and other articles presented the following ex-post-facto explanation for the fall: Investors decided that the *good news* that the economy is "starting to accelerate" *might* mean a future rise in interest rates, which would *presumably* compete with stock dividends for investors' dollars, which *would* be bearish for stocks *if* it happened. This contrived reasoning is further suspect given the fact that the stock market opened higher on the day in question, nicely in concert with the standard view that an increase in retail sales should be bullish. There was no more big news that day. Had there been some bad news immediately after the opening, no one would have bothered to concoct the interest-rate explanation. The bad news would have provided a direct reason for the rout.

An even less defensible version of this rationalization appeared just a week later. On the morning of April 20, 2004, the stock market rallied for half an hour, peaked at 10:00 a.m. and sold off for the rest of the day. Almost every newspaper and wire service claimed that the market fell because "Greenspan told Congress that the nation's banking system is well prepared to deal with rising rates, which the market interpreted as a new signal the Fed will tighten its policy sooner rather than later."[8]

Greenspan's Hint on Rate Jolts Markets
—*The Wall Street Journal,* April 21, 2004

Possible rate increase sends stocks reeling
—*Atlanta Journal-Constitution,* April 21, 2004

Is this explanation plausible? No. Consider these points:

Point #1: Greenspan began speaking around 2:30, but the market had already peaked, at 10:00.

Point #2: Greenspan said something *favorable* about the banking system, not unfavorable about rates. A caption in *The Wall Street Journal* read, "Greenspan smiles, markets don't."[9] The real story here is that the market went down *despite* his upbeat comments, not because of them.

Point #3: Greenspan's speech was not the only news available. Most of the other news that day was good as well. As the AP reported, data on corporate profits were good, and "most economists don't expect the Fed to raise rates at its next meeting."[10] If news were causal, then on balance the market should have risen.

Point #4: Greenspan *did not say* that the Fed would raise its rates.

Point #5: Contrary to popular belief, the Fed's interest rate changes *lag* the market's interest rate changes (see Chapter 3). Interest rates on freely traded Treasury bills had moved higher for months. Even if Greenspan had stated (which he didn't) that the Fed would raise its rates immediately, it simply would have followed an interest-rate trend already in progress.

Point #6: No one offered data on the history of stock market movement following mere *implications* of possible rate rises, which means there were no data on which commentators could justifiably base an explanation of the market's movement following such an implication, if in fact there was one.

Point #7: The simultaneously reported item that "most economists don't expect the Fed to raise rates at its next meeting" contradicts the argument for why investors sold stocks. If economists don't expect it, why should investors?

Point #8: As Chapter 2 will show in detail, *there is no evidence that a rise in interest rates makes the stock market go down.* In 1992, the federal funds rate was 3%. In December 1999, it was 5.5%. The Dow didn't go down during that time; it *tripled*. Rates also rose from the late 1940s to the late 1960s, during which time there was a huge bull market. Ned Davis Research found that in the 22 instances of an initial rate hike since 1917, "the Dow was always *higher*...whether three months, six months, one year or two years later."[11] In other words, if interest rates truly cause the stock market to move, a rate rise at that time would have been unequivocally *bullish*. According to Davis, it takes a series of four to six rate increases to hurt the market, and that's if one allows the supposed effect to appear up to twelve months after the supposed cause. Accepting the widely promulgated explanation for the market's action would require believing that investors had to read into Greenspan's optimistic comment on the banking system a whole series of four to six rate rises, a year after which *maybe* the market would go down!

So why did so many people conclude that Greenspan's speech made the market go down? They did *not* "conclude" it from any applicable data; *they just made it up.* They *rationalized* it. The range of mental errors required for people to concoct such "analysis" is immense, from an inapplicable chronology to contradictory facts to a lack of confirming data to a false underlying theory. Yet it happened. All year long it happens.

Quiz: What does this sentence from the AP article mean? "Worries that interest rates will rise sooner rather than later have distracted investors from profit reports this earnings season."[12] Answer: It simply means, "The market went down today." There is no other meaning in all those words.

Had the stock market instead *risen* on April 13, 2004, commentators would have cited the numerous optimistic statements in Greenspan's address as the reason for the rise. He said, "deflation is no longer an issue," "pricing power is gradually being restored," "inflation is reasonably contained" and labor productivity is "still impressive." There were, in fact, no—none, zero—negative statements about markets, the economy or the monetary climate in his address, which is why commentators—consistently with their belief that news causes changes in stock prices—had to resort to such an elaborate rationalization to explain stocks' net decline that day.

There's more to the story. The stock market went up the next day. Let's see what the popular explanation was for that event:

> Appearing this time before the Joint Economic Committee of Congress, Greenspan reiterated that interest rates "must rise at some point" to prevent an outbreak of inflation. But he added that "as yet," the Fed's policy of keeping interest rates low "has not fostered an

environment in which broad-based inflation pressures appear to be building." Analysts took that to mean the Fed might not be in such a hurry to raise short-term rates, <u>the opposite of their reaction</u> to his testimony to the Senate Banking Committee on Tuesday.
—*The Atlanta Journal-Constitution*, April 22, 2004[13]

So, Greenspan "reiterated" his comments; in other words, he said essentially the same thing as he did the day before, yet investors' "reaction" to the statements was "the opposite" of what it was the day before.

We can know for certain that this explanation, too, is utterly false. How? By once again taking time to look at the data.

Figure 11 is a ten-minute bar graph of the S&P 500 index for both days in question, which I published in the wake of these events. On it are marked both times Greenspan spoke. Observe that the market *fell* throughout both of his speeches, and it rallied on the second day only after he was done. So, his speech did not make the market close up on the second day. It's no good saying that there was a "delayed positive reaction," because that's not what happened the day before when stocks fell throughout the speech *and* for the rest of the day.

Ex-post-facto rationalization is common but rarely based on verifiable facts and often inconsistent with past explanations. The cited causes conveniently morph as occasions demand. Why does it happen? The conventional presumption of action and reaction in financial markets requires that analysts identify an external force that propelled the market's movements, and they often manage either to find or to manufacture one. An article that put the two days' events side by side reveals how silly such causal arguments are:

Stocks ended higher Wednesday despite Federal Reserve Chairman Alan Greenspan's acknowledgment that short-term interest rates will have to be raised at some point. The gains came a day after stocks had sold off sharply when Greenspan said pricing power was improving for U.S. companies, sparking inflation fears.
—*USA Today*, April 22, 2004[14]

Attesting to analysts' ex-post-facto employment of financial-market rationalization is the fact that there is virtually never any evidence that people bought or sold stocks *for the reasons cited*. The idea that people actually sent stock prices lower one day and higher the next day because of these long chains of reasoning is dubious at best. Had you asked investors during the rout and the rally why they were buying or selling, would they have cited either of these convoluted arguments? I doubt it.

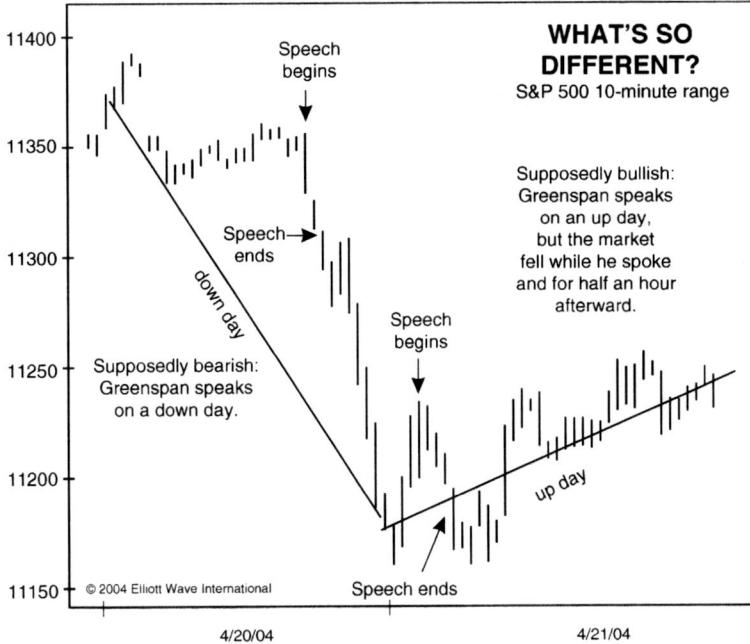

Figure 11

Read again carefully the newspaper excerpts quoted above. If at some point you begin laughing, you're halfway to enlightenment.

Those offering external-cause arguments for stock-market movement include Wall Street analysts, market strategists and professional economists, people who spend their professional lives studying the stock market, interest rates and the economy. Yet even these experts barrel ahead on nothing but intuition, sans valid data, sans principle and sans correlation. Their explanations *seem* to make sense, because most people's minds resort to the mechanical notion of action and reaction when analyzing financial and social events. When we take the time to examine the results of applying that causal view, however, we find it useless for consistently explaining market behavior.

This lack of explanatory power extends to papers by academic economists claiming to have identified exogenous shocks to the stock market. Such claims in fact do nothing but affirm the consequent. One representative study[15] proceeded first by locating times over the past 50 years when volatility among S&P indexes (measured by VIX and VXO) leaped over a period of weeks and then by scouring the news archives for shocking events that might account for the commotion. Whenever it found a compatible event, it cited it as a shock. When no event fit—which was often—it nevertheless declared that one did. For example, it ascribed the high volatility of February

2003 to "Gulf War II," although the war didn't start until the third week of March. It ascribed the jump in volatility of March 1980 to the Iran hostage crisis, even though the crisis had begun four months earlier and continued for another ten months thereafter. Ironically, Wikipedia's page[16] on the 444-day hostage crisis chronicles 25 crisis-related events occurring nearly every month of the period *except* March 1980. One shock the paper listed to explain the high volatility of July-September 2002 is "Enron," but the Enron scandal in fact unfolded throughout the stock market's *advance* of November 2001 to March 2002—negating any possible implication of a shock—and ended with a House of Representatives resolution in April, two days before the Value Line Arithmetic Index peaked for the year. (You can see a detailed chart of the timing of these events in Chapter 31 of *Pioneering Studies in Socionomics*.) The study credited the high VIX of August-October 1982 to a "monetary cycle turning point," but the monetary cycle had unequivocally turned earlier, as indicated by the long term reversals in precious metals prices (see Figure 18 in Chapter 2), commodities prices (see Figure 20 in Chapter 2) and interest rates (see Figure 2 in Chapter 18) in 1980-1981. It ascribed the earlier volatility of August 1966 to a "Vietnam War buildup," but the Vietnam War had been ongoing since 1955; the well-documented buildup lasted from March 1965 to November 1968, not just one particular month; and there was no jump in VIX even when the U.S. lost the war in April 1975. It ascribed the biggest VIX of all, that of October 1987, to "Black Monday," for which economists nearly unanimously agree (see Chapter 2) there was no causal news. It is not accurate to call such a method data-fitting, because too many of the data don't fit. All these examples do, however, comfortably suit our label of *rationalized* data-fitting. Properly vetted, studies like this actually augment the case that shocks to overall stock prices are a myth.

The intent here is not to single out any particular study but to illustrate a widespread theoretical bias among economists. Type "exogenous shocks stock market" into an Internet search engine, and a slew of links to comparable papers comes up. The methodological problem with all such studies is that they categorically presume the existence of shocks, thereby just as categorically presuming away any possibility of endogenous (internal, or internally generated) market volatility, such as proposed in Chapters 6 and 23 of this book. To maintain their supposition, researchers avoid looking carefully at the data and eschew identifying any consistency or predictability in the nature of particular types of news and their effects on markets, and for good reason. As Chapter 2 will show, there are no such things.

A Shocking Revelation

What's happening is this: Observers' job, as they see it, is simply to identify which external events caused whatever price changes occur. When news seems to coincide sensibly with market movement, they presume a causal relationship. When news doesn't fit, they attempt to devise a cause-and-effect structure to make it fit. When they cannot even devise a plausible way to twist the news into justifying market action, they chalk up the market's move to "psychology," which means that, despite the plethora of news and numerous inventive ways to interpret it, their imaginations aren't prodigious enough to concoct a credible causal story.

Most of the time it is easy for observers to believe in news causality. Financial markets fluctuate constantly, and news comes out constantly, and sometimes the two elements coincide well enough to reinforce commentators' mental bias towards mechanical cause and effect. When news and the market fail to coincide, they shrug and disregard the inconsistency. Those operating under the mechanics paradigm in finance never seem to see or care that these glaring anomalies exist.

Irrelevance Applies to Fed "Shocks," Too

Actions taken by the Federal Reserve provide a good basis for our exposé, because nearly everyone involved in financial markets believes that the most powerful banking monopoly on earth is capable of delivering shocks to financial markets. That is why Fed meetings, Fed minutes and Fed member speeches inspire such breathless commentary. Let's look at three examples when emotions ran especially high.

On March 18, 2015, a national newspaper, echoing other media outlets, ran an article titled, "Market Reaction Hinges on One Word: *'PATIENT'*."[17] It wondered aloud whether or not the Fed at that day's meeting would use that crucially important word again regarding the urgency of any intent to raise its discount rate and/or its federal funds rate. That's how minute the parsing of the Fed's language had become. Numerous market commentators weighed in on the question: Would the Fed drop the "patient" language and hint of an imminent rate hike? Would it drop the "patient" language and hint of a delayed rate hike? Or would it leave the "patient" language in, suggesting an even longer delay? Analysts proposed specific market reactions for each scenario. I forget what the Fed said that day, but it didn't matter. The session does not stand out on a chart; it occurred in the middle of an 8-trading-day bounce shortly after the start of a 4½-month sideways trend. One could hardly identify a day of less import. All that ink for nothing.

The Fed's irrelevance to the stock market applies even on volatile days. Consider what happened on October 28, 2015. The stock market closed up on the day, and headlines[18] attributed the rise to investors' bullish reaction to the Fed's post-meeting announcement, issued at 2:00 p.m. ET.

Figure 12 negates that claim. It shows that the S&P futures contract gapped up on the opening, rose until the very minute of the announcement, plunged 23.5 points immediately thereafter, and then rose until the close. Extrapolating the pre-announcement trend from the peak of the opening one-minute bar to the peak at 2:00 p.m. takes it exactly to the session's closing price. One can better describe the day, then, as naturally rising but with a temporary interruption due to a *bearish* reaction to the Fed announcement. If *that's* what happened, then one must conclude that the most powerful financial institution in the world had no more effect on stock prices than an 18-minute midday disruption with no net effect on the trend. But wait. If speculators reacted bearishly to the "shock" of the Fed's announcement, what news made the market rise thereafter? No one cited any. Exogenous cause *still* doesn't explain the day's action.

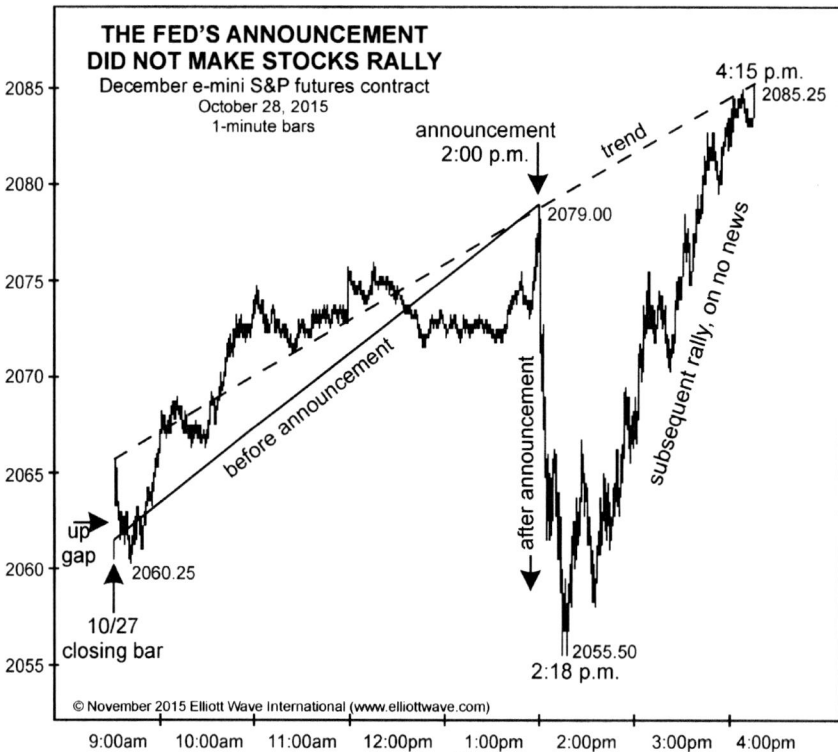

Figure 12

While concluding this book in December 2015, I find nothing has changed. As the Fed's mid-month meeting approached, the media called its looming decision on whether to tweak its interest rate *"Historic and momentous."*[19] A strategist at a major money-center bank, echoing the consensus, opined, "Where markets go from here depends to a large extent on the Fed." Many reasons were given. Many brows were furled. Many hands were wrung. Many fingers on keyboards twitched. Many breaths were held. Many foreheads perspired. Pins and needles edged up through chair seats. A few hours later the Fed—historically and momentously—raised both its discount rate and its federal funds rate, by 1/4 point, for the first time in 9½ years. Yet nothing historic or momentous happened in stocks or any other financial market. At year's end, the major stock averages (see Figure 13) were quietly trading at the same levels they were the day before the announcement. Had the markets done something dramatic, the media would have cited the rate change as the obvious reason. For yet another time, however, the "shock" meant nothing.

CAN YOU SPOT THE "HISTORIC AND MOMENTOUS" RATE HIKE? NEITHER CAN I

Figure 13

People object, "You can't tell me news doesn't move the market. I see it happen every day!" But they don't see any such thing, and it takes careful study to reveal that they don't. Consider: If the market's moves and the tenor of news were independently random, the two types of events would still fit each other half the time, wouldn't they? That's more or less what people see, and they expand those coincidences into what they *think* they see.

As this chapter shows, the notion that exogenous shocks change market trends is highly suspect. Chapter 2 will broaden the scope of our investigation into exogenous causes of financial pricing.

NOTES AND REFERENCES

[1] Shell, Adam, "Fear of Terrorism Jolts Stock Market," *USA Today*, March 23, 2004.

[2] Wikipedia, "Hurricane Katrina."

[3] Wikipedia, "Strategic Petroleum Reserve."

[4] "United States Crude Oil Production and Consumption by Year," *Index Mundi*, indexmundi.com.

[5] Wikipedia, "Strategic Petroleum Reserve (United States)."

[6] Ferreira, Susana and Berna Karali, "An Assessment of the Impact of Earthquakes on Global Capital Markets," Annual Meeting of the Agricultural and Applied Economics Association. Minneapolis, MN. July 27-29, 2014.

[7] Walker, Tom, "Rising Rates Scenario Sends Stocks Reeling," *The Atlanta Journal-Constitution*, April 14, 2004.

[8] Associated Press, "Possible Rate Increase Sends Stocks Reeling," *The Atlanta Journal-Constitution,* May 21, 2004.

[9] *The Wall Street Journal*, April 21, 2004.

[10] Associated Press, "Interest Rate Fears Brings Stocks Down," *The Ledger,* April 24, 2004.

[11] Walker, Tom, "Stocks Plunge on Greenspan's Rate-boost Hint," *The Atlanta Journal-Constitution*, April 21, 2004.

[12] Associated Press, "Markets Tumble After Comments by the Fed Chairman," *The New York Times,* April 21, 2004.

[13] Walker, Tom, "Greenspan Soft-pedals on Rates; Market Rebounds," *The Atlanta Journal-Constitution,* April 22, 2004.

[14] Shell, Adam, "Greenspan Calms Jittery Investors," *USA Today,* April 22, 2004.

[15] Bloom, Nicholas, "The Impact of Uncertainty Shocks," *Econometrica*, Vol. 77, No. 3, pp. 623-685, May 2009.

[16] "Iran Hostage Crisis," Wikipedia.

[17] Shell, Adam, "When It Comes to Fed-Rate Talk, Market Reaction Hinges on One Word: Patient," *USA Today*, March 18, 2015, p. 1B.

[18] For example: Mahmudova, Anora, "Stocks Rise After Fed Signals Possible December Rate Hike." *MarketWatch*, October 28, 2015.

[19] Shell, Adam, "Markets Brace for Historic Fed Move," *USA Today,* December 16, 2015.

Chapter 2

The Conventional Error of Exogenous Cause and Rational Reaction in Finance

Robert R. Prechter

We have seen that even the most dramatic news does not account for changes in stock prices. What about bedrock business, economic, financial, monetary and political conditions? Do they determine stock prices? In this chapter, we will further examine the validity of the reigning mechanics paradigm of financial causality.

A Fundamental Assumption behind Conventional Financial and Macroeconomic Theories

Conventional financial and macroeconomic theories rely upon the seemingly sensible, if not imperative, ideas of exogenous cause and rational reaction. Modern academic papers on social motivation—in the fields of finance, economics, politics, history and sociology—begin with these ideas, whether they are stated explicitly or not. Studies are packed with discussions of and conjecture about "information flows," "fundamentals," "input," "optimization," "reactions," "shocks," "catalysts" and "triggers." Even hypotheses of stock market pricing that make room for mass psychology embrace ideas such as "positive feedback loops" in which events are causal. Papers that allow for bouts of non-rational financial behavior (see Chapters 19 and 23) treat such instances as temporary exceptions or departures from a normal state of rationality, objectivity, utility maximization and market equilibrium, all of which are characteristic of neoclassical economics' exogenous-cause, rational-reaction paradigm. The efficient market hypothesis (EMH) and its variants in academic financial modeling as well as in professionally applied economics rely upon this paradigm. As far as I can determine, however, no evidence supports its premises, and, as the ensuing discussion will show, all relevant evidence contradicts them.

How Financial Prices Would Look under the Exogenous-Cause Model

The reigning theory of stock market pricing, deriving from neoclassical economic theory and EMH, proposes that as new information enters the marketplace, rational, fully informed investors revalue stocks accordingly. If this claim were true, company share prices and the overall stock market would trend mostly sideways, with near-vertical jumps and drops to new planes of stability whenever crucial information came out. In such a world, the overall stock market would have a price history looking something like the illustration shown in Figure 1. It would fluctuate narrowly around equilibrium as minor bits of news on individual companies mostly canceled each other out. Then important events affecting market valuation would serve as shocks causing investors to adjust prices to a new level, reflecting that new information. One would see these reactions in real time, and investigators of market history would face no difficulties in identifying precisely what new information caused the changes in stock prices.

Figure 1 is an idealized representation showing what would be the presumed effects on overall stock prices of a sudden slew of bad earnings reports, an unexpected terrorist attack implying many more to come, a large "economic stimulus" program, a major contraction in GDP, a government program to bail out at-risk banks, a declaration of peace after a time of war

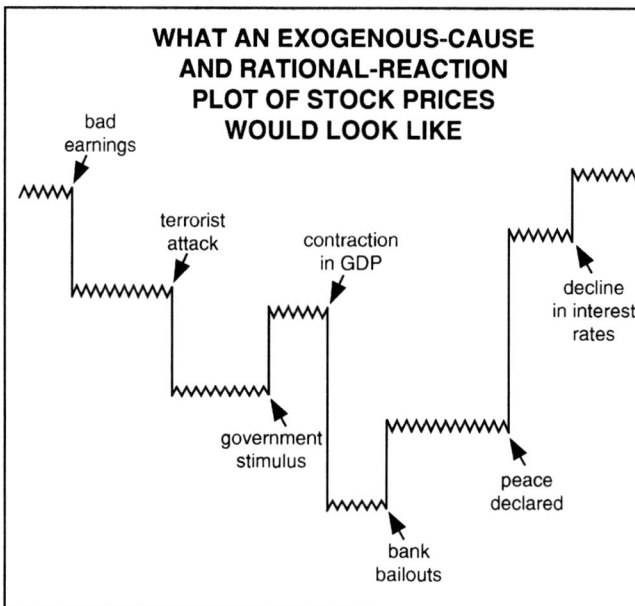

Figure 1

and a significant decline in interest rates. Under this causal model, such events would—rationally and objectively—effect a change in overall stock prices.

The problem is, this depiction does not match empirics. That is *not* how overall stock prices behave. They run wildly up and down every second, minute, hour, day, week, month, year and decade.

An idea such as exogenous cause is easy to test. But almost no one tests its ubiquitous assertions, much less with a critical eye.

The following pages challenge thirteen widely accepted claims about causal relationships between changes in economic, political and monetary variables and subsequent changes in financial market prices. Our illustrations are not statistically rigorous, but in *refuting* a theory, statistical rigor is unnecessary. If someone says, "All leaves are green," all one need do is find a red one to refute the claim. I hope when we are done with our survey, you will see that the claims we challenge are more akin to economists saying "All leaves are made of iron." We will be unable to find a single example from nature that agrees.

Testing Exogenous Cause from Economic Conditions

Claim #1: "Interest rates drive stock prices."

Economic theory holds that bonds compete with stocks for investment funds. The higher the yield investors can get from bonds, the less attractive is a set rate of dividend payout from stocks; conversely, the less yield investors can get from bonds, the more attractive is a set rate of dividend payout from stocks.

This explanation appears sensible. And it would be, if it applied to the field of *economics*. For example, "Rising prices for beef make chicken a more attractive purchase." This statement is simple and true. But in the field of *finance*, such statements fly directly in the face of evidence.

Figure 2 shows a history of the four biggest stock market declines of the past hundred years. The graphs display routs of 54% to 89%. In all four cases, interest rates *fell*, and in two of those cases they went all the way to zero. At the same time, stocks' dividends hardly changed, so their dividend yield rose throughout the bear market in every case. Under economic theory, investors should have traded all of their falling-payout debt instruments for rising-payout stocks. But they didn't; instead, they sent stock prices lower. What is it about the relative value of interest payments and dividends that investors fail to understand? Don't they get it?

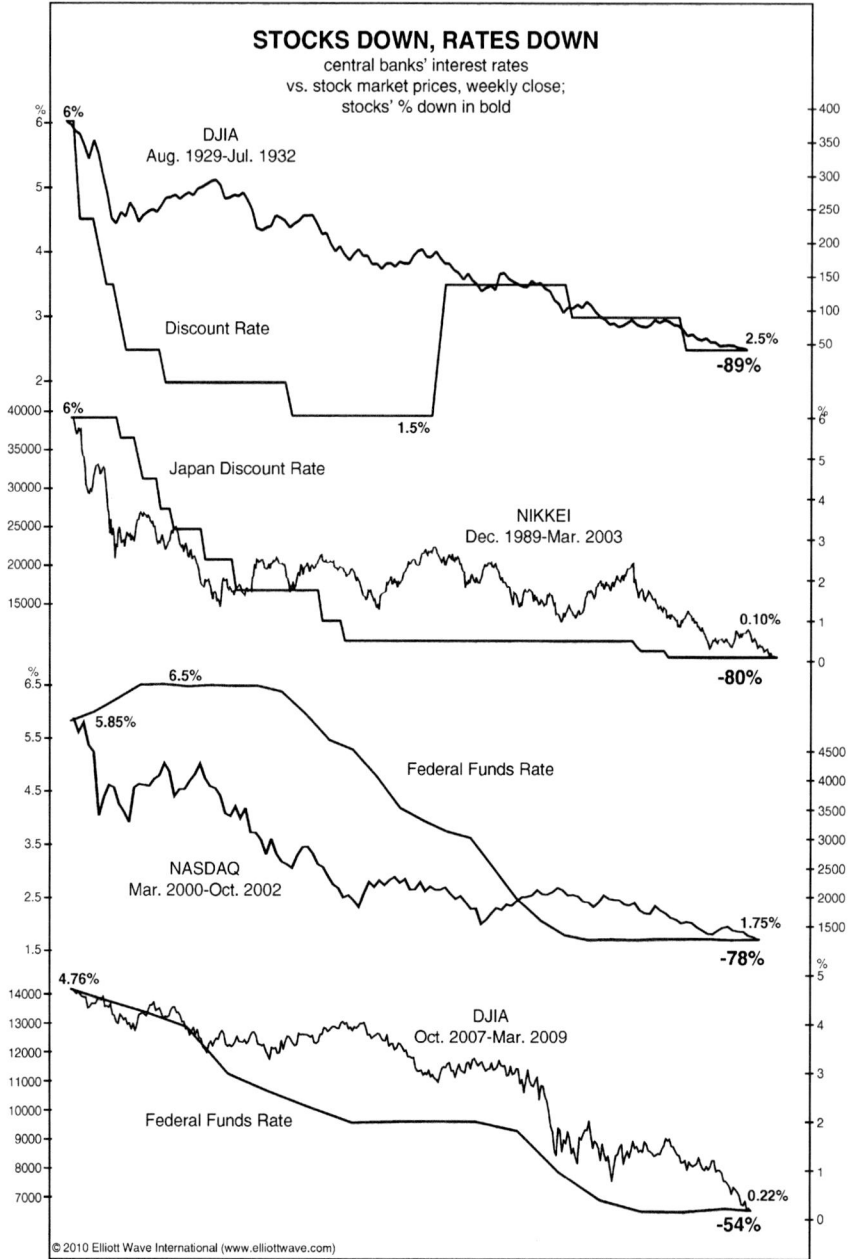

STOCKS DOWN, RATES DOWN
central banks' interest rates
vs. stock market prices, weekly close;
stocks' % down in bold

DJIA
Aug. 1929-Jul. 1932

6%

Discount Rate

2.5%
-89%

1.5%

Japan Discount Rate

6%

NIKKEI
Dec. 1989-Mar. 2003

0.10%
-80%

6.5%

5.85%

Federal Funds Rate

NASDAQ
Mar. 2000-Oct. 2002

1.75%
-78%

4.76%

DJIA
Oct. 2007-Mar. 2009

Federal Funds Rate

0.22%
-54%

© 2010 Elliott Wave International (www.elliottwave.com)

Figure 2

As with most claims based on exogenous cause, one can argue just as effectively the opposite side of the claim. It is easy to sound sensible when saying this: "When an economy contracts, corporate values fall, depressing the stock market. At the same time, demand for loans falls, depressing interest rates. In other words, when the economy contracts, stock prices and interest rates move down together. Conversely, when the economy expands, both of these trends move up together. This is why interest rates and stock prices go *in the same direction*." This explanation is just as rational and sensible in posing precisely the opposite relationship between the two variables. On this basis, suddenly the examples in Figure 2 make sense. So do the converse examples in Figure 3. Is this new explanation valid?

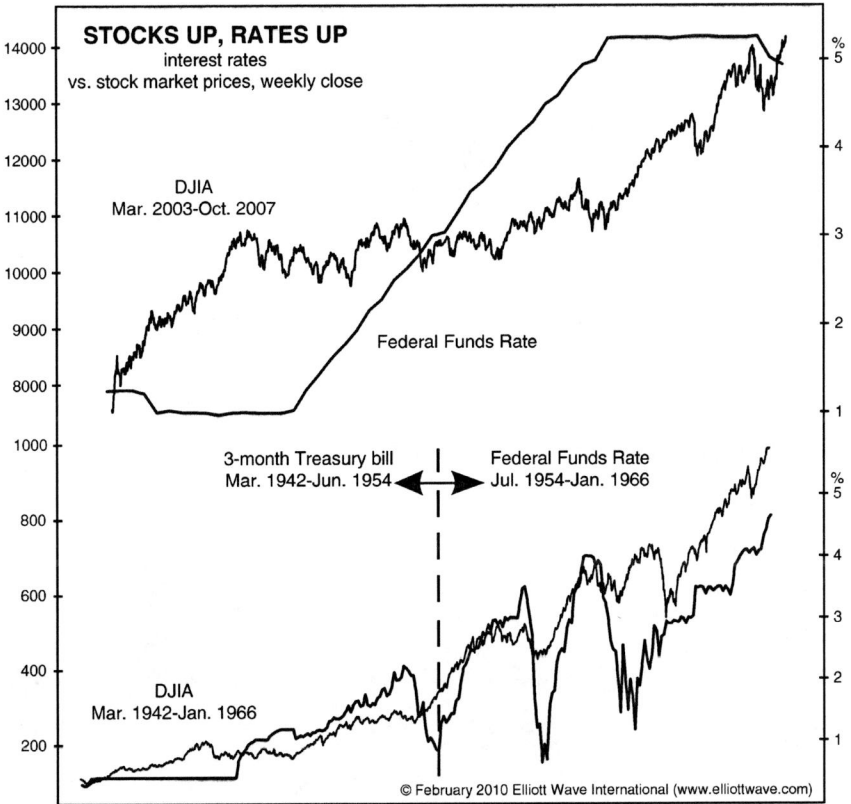

Figure 3

No, it can't be valid, because, in line with the first version of the claim, there have been plenty of times when the stock prices rose and interest rates fell. It happened, for example, in the period from 1984 to 1987, when stock indexes more than doubled while interest rates fell by half. There have also been times when stocks fell and interest rates rose, as in 1973-1974 when stock indexes dropped nearly in half as interest rates doubled. Figures 4 and 5 show these and two more examples.

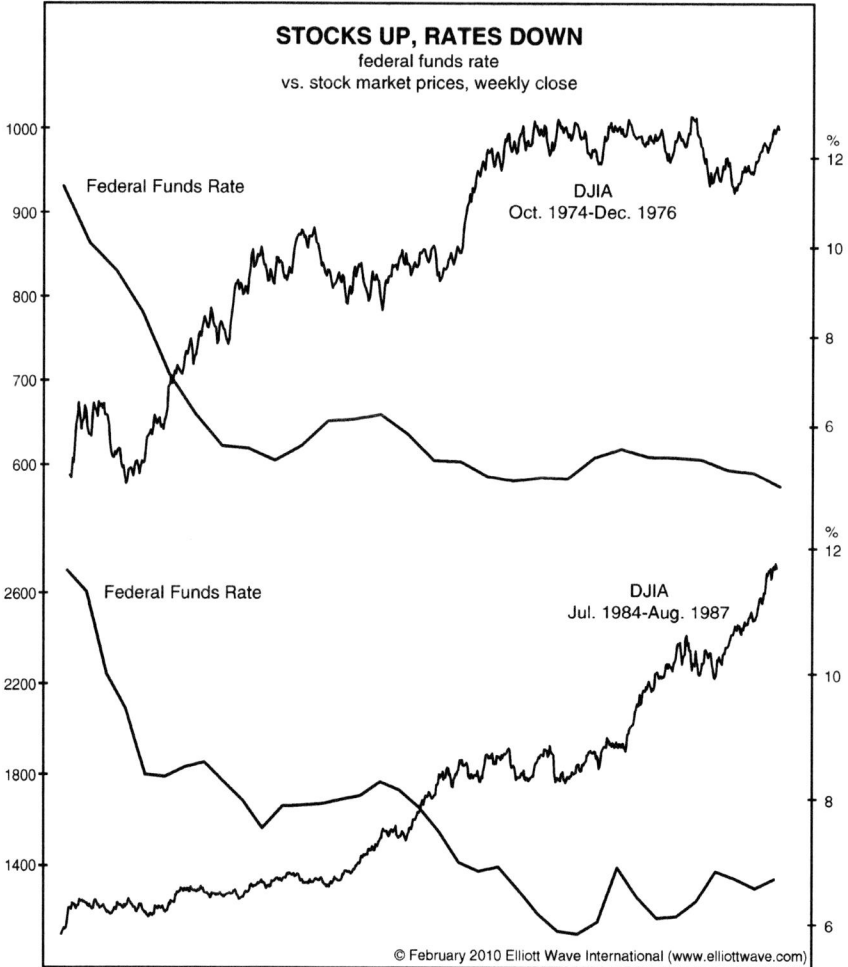

STOCKS UP, RATES DOWN
federal funds rate
vs. stock market prices, weekly close

Federal Funds Rate

DJIA
Oct. 1974-Dec. 1976

Federal Funds Rate

DJIA
Jul. 1984-Aug. 1987

© February 2010 Elliott Wave International (www.elliottwave.com)

Figure 4

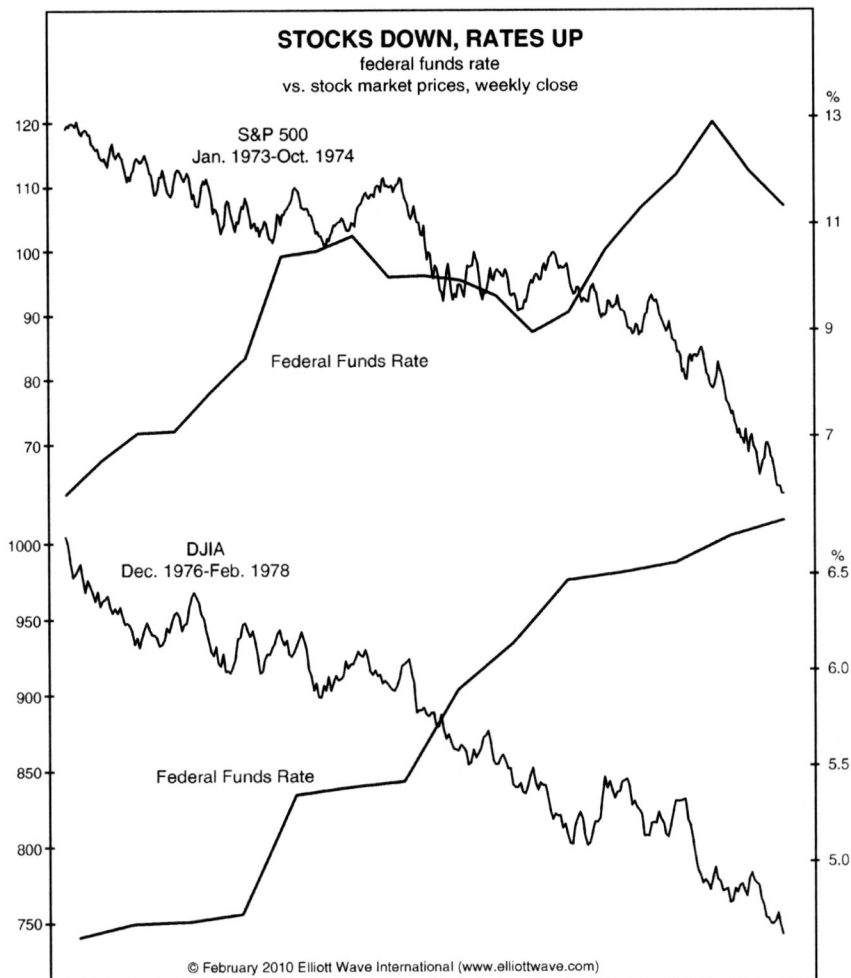

Figure 5

One cannot accept either causal explanation, because these histories refute each of them. Neither can one believe both of them at the same time, because they contradict each other. For some reason, sensible-sounding statements about utility-maximizing behavior (per the first explanation) and about mechanical relationships in finance (per the second explanation) fail to capture what is going on.

Claim #2: "Rising oil prices are bearish for stocks."

It would take months to collect all the statements that economists have made to the press over the past forty years to the effect that rising oil prices are "a concern" or that an unexpected (they're always unexpected) "oil price shock" would force them to adjust or rescind their bullish outlook for stocks and the economy. Academic papers supporting this claim are legion.

For many economists, the underlying assumption about causality in this case stems from the experience of 1973-1974 after the Arab Oil Embargo, when stock prices went down as oil prices went up. That juxtaposition appeared to fit a sensible story of causation regarding oil prices and stock prices, to wit: Rising oil prices increase the cost of energy and therefore reduce corporate profits and consumers' spending power, thus putting drags on stock prices and the economy. These headlines are compatible with this claim:

Earnings, Lower Oil Prices Rally Stocks—*USA Today,* April 8, 2006

Surging Oil Prices Pull Stocks Lower—*ABC News,* July 14, 2006

Is the claim valid?

In response to these very headlines, the July 25, 2006 issue of *The Elliott Wave Theorist* offered Figure 6, showing the preceding three-year market environment. Examine it and see if you can discern any indication whatsoever that lower oil prices make stocks rise or vice versa. As I said at the time, "Oil and stocks have trended *mostly in the same direction* for more than three years, so these headlines are backwards."

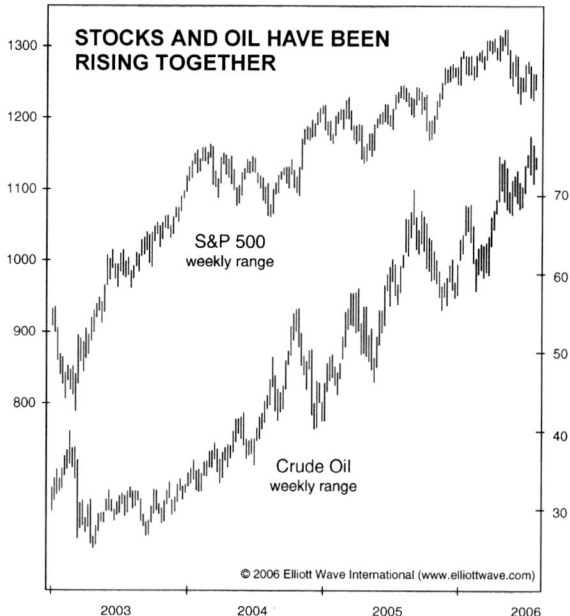

Figure 6

Switching to forecasting mode, that issue added, "A falling oil price probably won't be bullish for stocks, either. When deflation takes hold, they will probably both go down together." That's exactly what happened two years later, as you can see on the left-hand side of Figure 7.

One of the most revealing headlines of this period occurred a month into oil's crash:

It's hard to lose betting on stocks as oil falls

—*USA Today,*
August 12, 2008

The accompanying article offered a 20-year study that predicted how much each stock sector would rise during a bear market in oil. An economist and chief portfolio manager explained, "If oil prices are falling, a key cost for both consumers and businesses is also falling. It acts as a benefit for the stock market overall." A fellow money manager agreed, saying, "Nothing bad happens if oil prices keep falling. But if oil prices turn up, uh oh."[1] The causal case could hardly have been clearer. As it turns out, the very next trading day capped a three-week stock market rally, after which the Dow began to accelerate downward in its biggest bear market in three generations, all while plunging oil prices were providing their supposed benefit to consumers, businesses and the stock market.

As published on March 18, 2011

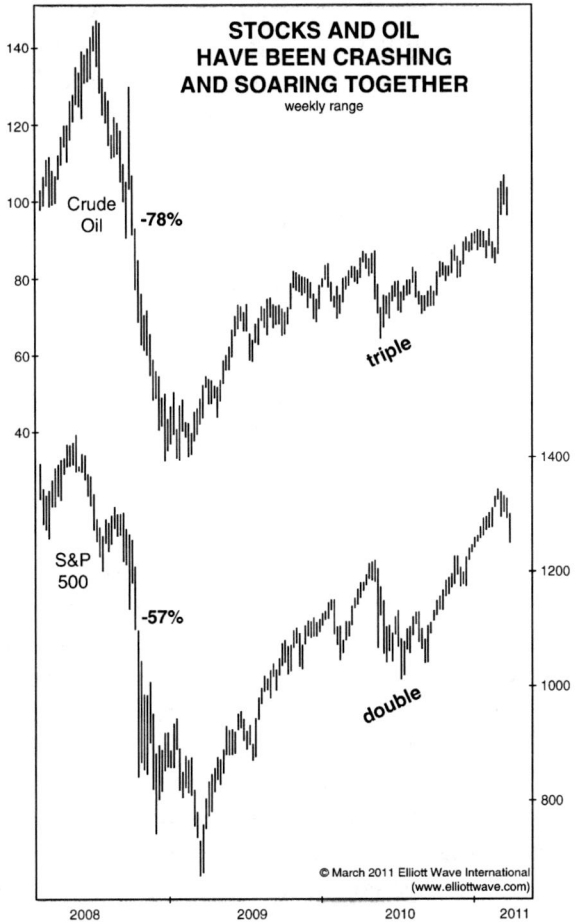

Figure 7

On February 21, 2011, the price of oil rose for a day (ostensibly on unrest in the Middle East), and U.S. stocks fell. The media once again quoted many economists warning that an "oil-price shock" would be bearish for stocks and the economy. At least three world-class news publications[2] ran lead editorials detailing the financial and economic damage said oil price shock might cause. Those assertions prompted our publication of Figure 7. Observe that as oil prices crashed 78% in five months, stock prices were cut in half; and then, as oil tripled, stocks doubled. These are not minor moves that one could dismiss as being anomalous. They include the biggest, fastest decline in oil prices ever along with the deepest stock market decline in 76 years, and the fastest oil-price-tripling on record along with the fastest two-year stock market rise in 72 years. Consider also that during most of the *decline* in both markets a *recession* was in progress, and during most of the *rise* in both markets an economic *recovery* was in progress. These are palpable refutations of economists' causal hypothesis.

No one looking at these histories could wrest from them the idea that rising oil prices "shock" the stock market into a decline and the economy into a contraction and vice versa. Only those *not* looking at data who are married to their causal explanation and who routinely ignore evidence could tell reporters in February 2011 that a one-day rise in the oil price was bearish for stocks and that further rises in its price would wreak havoc on the stock market and the economy. Yet dozens of experts did just that, in dozens of articles.

As with our interest-rates example, an economist could account for the evidence in Figure 7 *and* stay true to his exogenous-cause model by reversing the direction of his exogenous-cause argument—as we did earlier with respect to the stock market and interest rates—to postulate that an expanding economy makes stock prices and oil prices rise and fall together. He could offer the following logic: As the economy expands, business picks up, so stock prices rise; and as businesses operate at higher capacity, demand for energy rises, pushing up the price of oil. That's why prices for stocks and oil go up together. That makes sense, too, doesn't it?

An economist who made that case, however, would have to tell the media that the one-day rise in the oil price was bullish and that a falling oil price would jeopardize the stock market and the economy. Would economists ever say such a thing?

Claim #3: "Falling oil prices are bearish for stocks."

They would. Here in December 2015, articles have been quoting dozens of economists and market strategists making precisely the opposite exogenous-cause claim as before. Now they say that *falling* oil prices are bearish for stocks. Observe how sensible the reverse argument sounds:

A rout in crude oil prices hammers stock market
Report sends energy shares down, sparking sell-off that spans globe
A slump in oil prices sparked a global sell-off in financial markets on Friday with losses spreading from Asia to Europe to the U.S., where stocks fell sharply to cap their worst week since the summer. The selling was broad, with all 10 sectors of the Standard and Poor's 500 index ending down. Investors worry the sharp fall in the price of oil and other commodities is a sign of weakness in the global economy, especially China, and that that will cut into profits at big energy companies and suppliers of raw materials as well as other companies.
—The Associated Press, December 12, 2015[3]

Stocks rose? Look for a shock. Stocks fell? Look for a shock. Oil rose? That was a shock. Oil fell? That was a shock. Why look for shocks? Because we believe in shocks.

As we are beginning to see, one can reverse the causality asserted in any exogenous-cause claim and sound perfectly logical either way. Economists continually do just that. No one seems to notice; and until now no one has offered a theoretical and empirical challenge to the practice.

As is typically the case with such dual lines of reasoning, neither causal formulation explains the data. Figure 8 shows that for the past 21 years there has been no consistent relationship between the trends of oil prices and stock prices on a 52-week basis. Sometimes it is positive, and sometimes it is negative; sometimes stock and oil prices go in the same direction, and sometimes they go in opposite directions. From the graphs in Figure 8, we can isolate numerous examples of all four pairs of coincident trends: up/up, up/down, down/up and down/down. This non-relationship, moreover, is fractal. Pick any duration—52 hours, 52 days, 52 weeks, 52 months, 52 years—and you will find the same picture. In the end, we can determine no consistent causal relationship whatsoever between the two price series.

These histories contradict economists' claims that an "oil shock"—consisting of either rising or falling prices—would hurt the stock market and the economy. Upon examining all these data, an honest economist would have no choice but to admit that the "oil price shocks" upon which his profession's forecasts depended are imaginary.

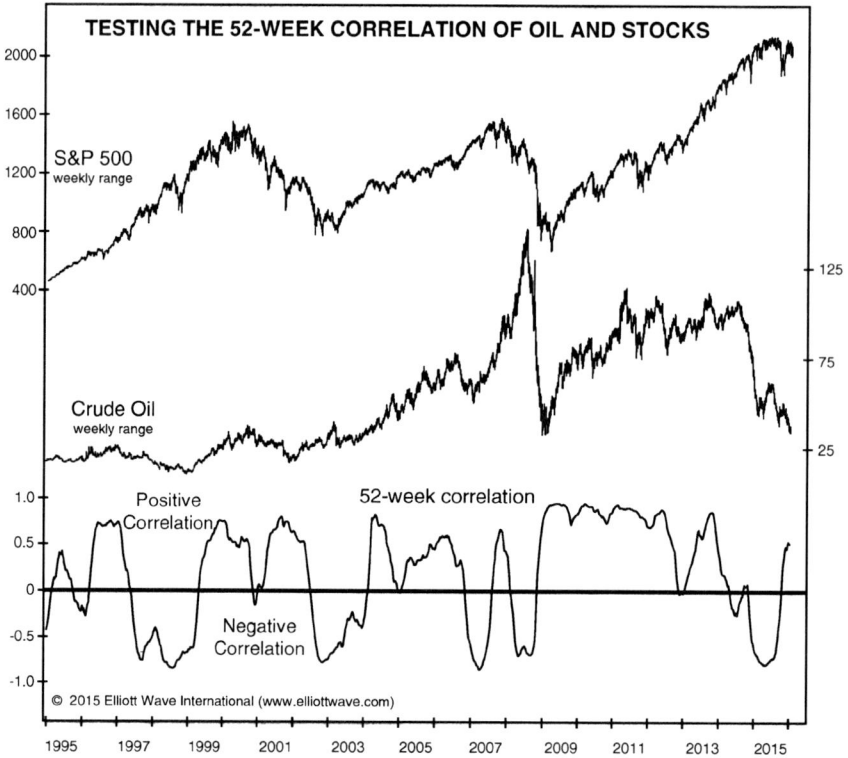

Figure 8

Claim #4: "An expanding trade deficit is bad for a nation's economy and therefore bearish for stock prices."

Over the past four decades, hundreds of articles have quoted economists' expressions of worry whenever the U.S. trade deficit expands and expressions of relief when it contracts. All their assessments were wrong, sometimes remarkably so. Here are just a few examples, with the context added in brackets:

> March 29, 1979
> The Commerce Department reported yesterday that the $1.3 billion US trade deficit last month was the smallest since May 1977. Government economists said they were delighted with the news. "The news figures are terrific," said one Commerce Department economist; "Hopefully, it's the start of a trend."[4] [The first recession in five years lay seven months ahead.]

March 28, 1981

On a somewhat brighter note for the economy, the Commerce Department also reported yesterday the nation's balance of trade deficit had improved in February.[5] [The second of back-to-back recessions began just five months later.]

March 1, 1984

"While the domestic economy continues to be strong, the trade deficit is an economic disaster," said [   ], chief economist for the National Association of Manufacturers.[6] [An eight-year boom was just getting going.]

April 12, 1985

The secretary of state said, "We can break the back of the trade deficit only through...a stronger worldwide recovery...."[7] [Precisely the opposite was true; the trade deficit *rose* during the strong worldwide recovery.]

May 26, 1990

The better-than-expected trade performance sent many economists scurrying to revise their trade forecasts for the year.[8] [A recession started a month later.]

February 22, 2002

The Commerce Department reported that the nation's trade deficit narrowed by 11.4 percent in December to $25.3 billion, its best showing since September. This unexpectedly large improvement sent economists scurrying to upwardly revise their estimates for overall economic activity in the fourth quarter.[9] [The stock market was peaking and collapsed to new lows in October. The economy contracted but was not officially declared to be in recession.]

January 23, 2005

After the November report of a record trade deficit was released, economists rapidly reduced their forecasts of fourth-quarter economic activity.[10] [A terrific boom was underway and still had three years to go.]

February 15, 2008

[   ], Chief US economist at High Frequency Economics, said that the smaller December trade deficit will help to boost overall economic growth from the final three months of last year from the initial estimate of a mere 0.6 percent expansion.[11] [The second-worst financial

crash and economic contraction in a hundred years were already underway.]

It is hard to overstate the frequency with which such pronouncements appear. Here is a sample of counterproductive comments from a single four-week period in the summer of 2010 in the early stages of an economic expansion that so far has lasted nearly seven years:

- "Rising trade deficit could <u>drag down</u> U.S. recovery."
  —*USA Today*, July 14, 2010

- "Sagging exports and a rise in imports pushed the U.S. trade deficit up sharply in June—an <u>unwelcome development</u> during an already-weak economic recovery."
  —*The Christian Science Monitor*, August 11, 2010

- "In the United States, the Commerce Department said the trade deficit had widened 18.8 percent, to $49.9 billion—a figure so large it sent economists scrambling to <u>revise their growth forecasts</u> for the quarter and predicting that <u>unemployment may increase</u> later in the year. —*The Washington Post*, August 12, 2010

Yet the recovery continued, growth expanded and unemployment shrank.

My staff collected articles from 1975 to the present in which economists attached positive value terms—including *good, better, best, terrific, improve, improving, improvement, bolster, lift, boost, better-than-expected, strength, reprieve, good news* and *a good thing*—to a falling trade deficit and negative value terms—including *bad, fear, danger, disappointing, disturbing, an economic disaster, break the back, culprit, a drag on the economy, sucking the strength out of the economy, worse, worst, worsen, worsening* and *worse-than-expected*—to a rising trade deficit.

Figure 9 reveals that had economists reversed their statements and expressed relief whenever the trade deficit began to expand and concern whenever it began to shrink, they would have quite accurately negotiated the ups and downs of the stock market and the economy over the past 40 years. The relationship, if there is one, is precisely the opposite of the one they believe is there. Over the span of these data, there has been a consistently positive—not negative—correlation among the stock market, the economy and the trade deficit. So, the trade deficit's widely presumed effect is 100% wrong. Once again, economists have made claims that are inconsistent with the data, and they have neglected to consult the data to see if their claims are accurate.

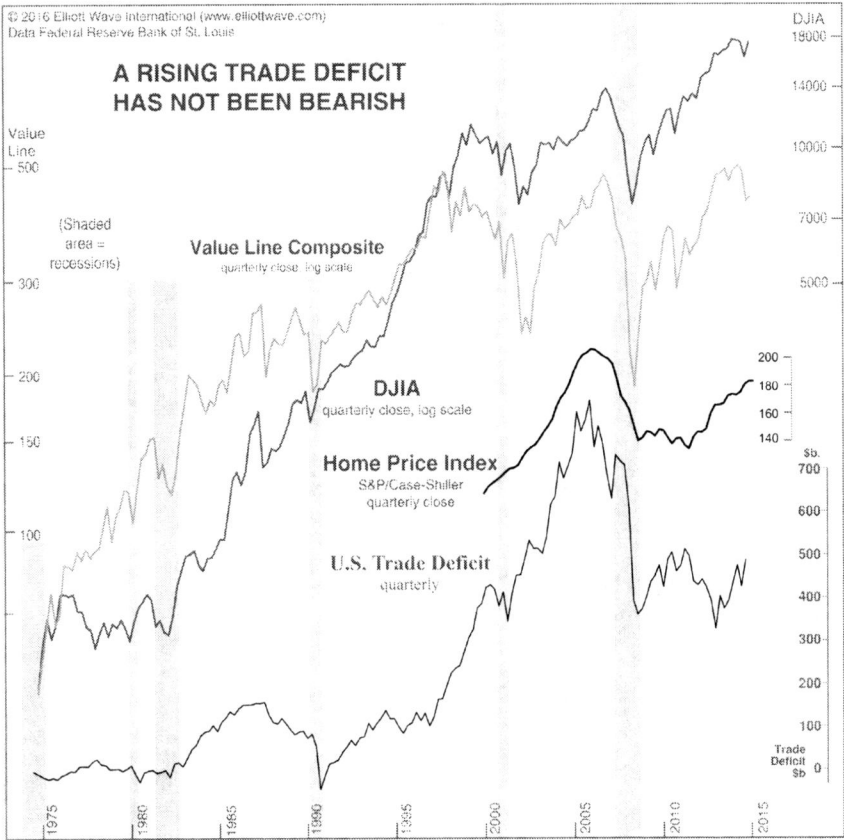

Figure 9

It is no good saying, "Well, an expanding trade deficit will bring on a problem *eventually*." Anyone who can see the relationship shown in Figure 9 would be far more successful saying that once the trade deficit starts *shrinking*, it will portend a problem (as we did; see Chapter 10). Whether or not one assumes that these data indicate a causal relationship between economic health and the trade deficit, it is clear that the "sensible" causal assumption upon which most economists have relied throughout this time is invalid.

The falling national savings rate has been another oft-cited bugaboo throughout these decades. Yet the U.S. savings rate has followed nearly the same path as the U.S. trade balance, whereby a negative trend has proved to be more a companion of economic expansions than contractions.

Around 1998, articles began quoting a minority of economists who started arguing the opposite claim. Consistent with our examples so far, they were easily able to reverse the exogenous-cause argument and have it sound just as plausible. It goes like this: In the past thirty years, when the U.S. economy has expanded, consumers have used money and credit to purchase goods from overseas in greater quantity than foreigners were purchasing goods from the U.S. Prosperity brings more spending, and recession brings less. So, a rising U.S. economy coincides with a rising trade deficit, and vice versa. Voila! Exogenous cause still applies, albeit now in the opposite way.

But once again there is a problem. If you examine the graph closely, you will see that peaks in the trade deficit *preceded* recessions in every case, sometimes by years, so one cannot blame recessions for declines in the deficit. Something is still wrong with the conventional style of reasoning.

We are still not done revealing the errors with which exogenous-cause claims are riddled. Consider the fact that while the trade balance's relationship to the stock market and the economy during this period was consistently negative for the U.S., it was mostly *positive* for China. As with our previous examples, we can observe both of these directly opposed explanations working—in this case simultaneously—which means that neither one stands as a statement of principle.

Claim #5: "Corporate earnings drive stock prices."

The belief that corporate earnings drive stock prices has long powered a vast bulk of research on Wall Street. Numerous analysts try to forecast corporate earnings so they can in turn forecast stock prices. The presumed exogenous-cause basis for this research is clear: Corporate earnings reflect the success and thus the value of companies; therefore, if you can forecast earnings, you can forecast stock prices.

Suppose you knew that corporate earnings would rise strongly for the next six quarters straight. Would you buy stocks?

Figure 10 shows that in 1973-1974, earnings per share for S&P 500 companies soared for six quarters in a row, during which time the same companies' stock prices suffered their largest collapse since 1937-1942. This is not a small departure from the expected relationship but a history-making departure. Moreover, the S&P bottomed in early October 1974, and earnings per share then turned *down* for twelve straight months, just as the S&P turned up! A speculator with foreknowledge of these earnings trends would have made two perfectly incorrect decisions, buying near the top of the market and selling at the bottom. Such glaring exceptions to the idea of a causal relationship between corporate earnings and stock prices pose a challenge for conventional economic theory.

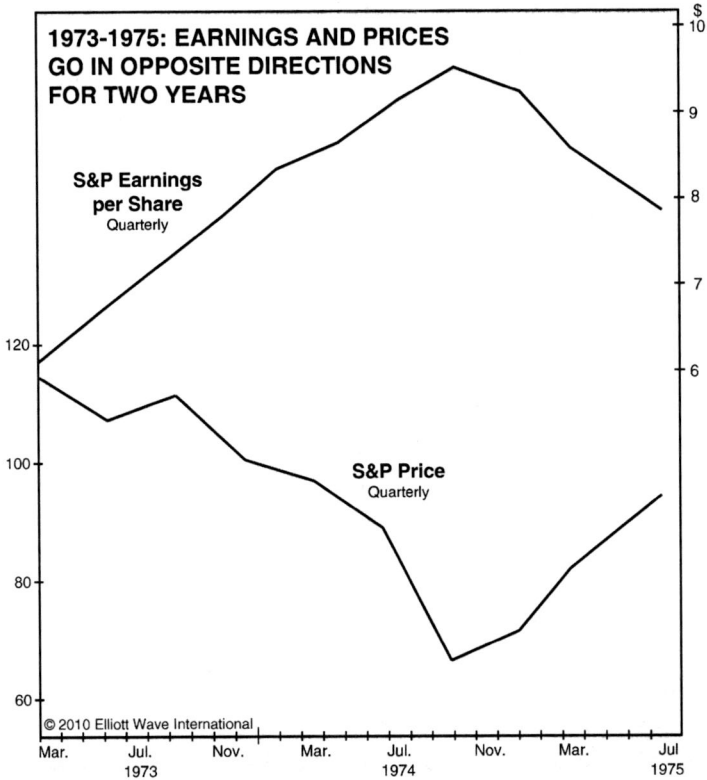

1973-1975: EARNINGS AND PRICES GO IN OPPOSITE DIRECTIONS FOR TWO YEARS

S&P Earnings per Share
Quarterly

S&P Price
Quarterly

© 2010 Elliott Wave International

Figure 10

In real life, no one knows what earnings will do, so no one would have made such bad decisions on the basis of foreknowledge. Unfortunately, the basis that investors actually use is *estimated* earnings, which incorporate analysts' lagging trend-extrapolation bias (see Chapters 17 and 21), making their investment decisions often even worse timed than advance knowledge of earnings would allow.

Claim #6: "Jobs drive stock prices."

In July 2009, economists expected that approximately 320,000 Americans would lose their jobs that month. When the Labor Department released the numbers in early August, it turned out that the economy had lost "only" 247,000 jobs. The unemployment rate fell one tenth of one percentage point, its first decline in more than a year. The day those figures were reported, the Dow Jones Industrial Average and S&P 500 rose 1.23% and 1.34% respectively. Here are two representative examples of conventional analysts' end-of-session market commentary:

July Jobs Data Lifts Stock Indexes

Stocks rallied on Friday, pushing the Standard & Poor's 500 to a 10-month high as the July jobs report was less bleak than feared and underpinned hopes the economy was on track for recovery.

—Reuters, August 7, 2009

U.S. Stocks End Higher on Jobs Report

Major stock indexes barreled higher by more than 1 percent Friday after the government said the U.S. unemployment rate unexpectedly fell in July for the first time in 15 months and that employers cut fewer jobs.   —Associated Press, August 7, 2009

Such analysis is based on an exogenous-cause understanding of markets. The idea is that the jobs report acted like a rock that whacked traders on the head and caused them to re-value share prices upward. Yet the fact is that people were still *losing jobs* at a rapid rate. Shouldn't the mechanics paradigm have required investors to bid stocks *lower* but at a commensurately slower rate? Apparently not; simply the change toward the less bad, they said, was sufficient to justify pricing stocks higher. Let's investigate this logic.

To establish a causal relationship, it is necessary (though not sufficient) for the cause to precede the effect. If changes in jobs data caused the market to rise and fall, the unemployment rate should have improved coincidentally with the market's five-month rally. But in fact the rate had worsened for 15 months, and the stock market had trended higher for the last five of them. The chronology was the reverse of what logic demands, so the case for causality collapses. During the rally from March through July 2009, there were no headlines that read, "Rising Unemployment Rate Sends Stocks Higher," because such a statement would have made no sense. Analysts simply sought out other news to explain the market's action.

Further, since employment trends lag the stock market (as shown in Figure 18 of Chapter 21), there is no reason to believe that any *present* jobs report indicates *future* gains or losses in the stock market. So, even the idea that the report should have changed *expectations* among rational, informed investors is invalid.

Claim #7: "GDP drives stock prices."

Surely the stock market reacts to changes in the nation's Gross Domestic Product. The level of aggregate corporate success shows up as changes in GDP. Stocks are shares in corporations. How could their prices not follow the ebb and flow of GDP?

Suppose you knew for certain that GDP would be positive *every single quarter* for the next 3¾ years and that one of those quarters would surprise economists in sporting the strongest quarterly rise in GDP over a half-century span. Would you buy stocks?

If you had acted on such knowledge in March 1976, you would have owned stocks for four years in which the DJIA fell 22%. Near the end of Q1 1980, had you realized that both the current and the next quarter's GDP would be negative, and you thought that development would be bearish, you would have sold stocks at the bottom.

Suppose you possessed guaranteed knowledge that the next quarter's GDP would be the strongest over a span of 15 years. Would you buy stocks?

Had you anticipated precisely this event for Q4 1987, you would have owned stocks for the biggest stock market crash since 1929. GDP, moreover, was in the middle of an extended period of expansion, turning in a positive

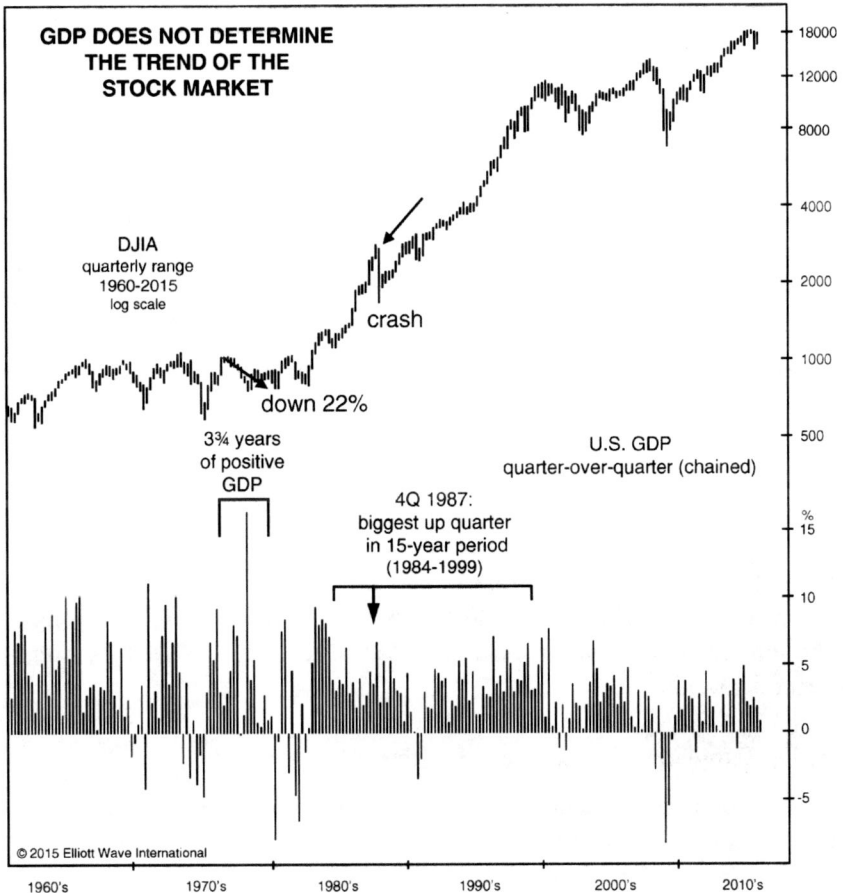

Figure 11

performance every quarter for thirty straight quarters—twenty before the crash and ten thereafter. But the market crashed anyway. Three years after the start of Q4 1987, stock prices were still below their level of that time despite ten more uninterrupted quarters of rising GDP.

Figure 11 shows these two events. It seems that there is something wrong with the idea that investors rationally value stocks according to expansions and contractions in GDP.

Much of the time, GDP and stock prices are allied. But if exogenous causality reigned in this realm, they would always be allied. They aren't. In fact, they are often diametrically opposed.

The Irrelevance of Economic News and Events: A Confirming Study

I can find no economic data that seem to be important, or even relevant, to explaining stock price changes. But you need not trust only me and your own eyes. Consider a statistical study that is stunning for its boldness in actually checking basic premises. Cutler, Poterba and Summers in a paper for the *Journal of Portfolio Management* in 1989 meticulously investigated the stock market's action immediately following major economic news as well as other types of news. They built 53 models using various combinations of financial and macroeconomic variables in an attempt to predict the stock market retrospectively. Some models accounted for as little as 2% of past stock price movement. (Models earning the highest scores cheated; see discussion in Chapter 8.) In the end, the authors concluded, "Macroeconomic news bearing on fundamental values…explains only about one fifth of the movement in stock prices."[12] This dismal showing challenges the presumption of exogenous causality from GDP, corporate earnings, jobs, trade figures or any other measure of economic performance.

Even the conclusion that macroeconomic news explains one fifth of the movement in stock prices is suspect. The stock market has persistent trends, and the economy has persistent trends. Sometimes the trends coincide. Any presumed causality is tenuous at best.

If the stock market is not reflecting economic realities, what else might it be doing? What about political forces? Maybe political events trump economic events.

Testing Exogenous Cause from Political Conditions

It is common for economists to offer a forecast for the stock market yet add a caveat to the effect that "If a war shock occurs, then I would have to modify my outlook." For such statements to have any validity, there must be a relationship between war and peace on the one hand and the stock market on the other. Let's explore this notion.

Claim #8: "Wars are bullish/bearish for stock prices."

Observe in the form of this claim that once again the exogenous-cause paradigm permits two diametrically opposed claims. Economists have in fact presented both sides of this argument. Some have held that war stimulates the economy, because in wartime the government spends money furiously, inducing companies to gear up for the production of war materials. That depiction seems to make sense. Others have argued that war hurts the economy because it diverts resources from productive enterprise, not to mention that it usually ends up destroying cities, factories and capital goods. That position

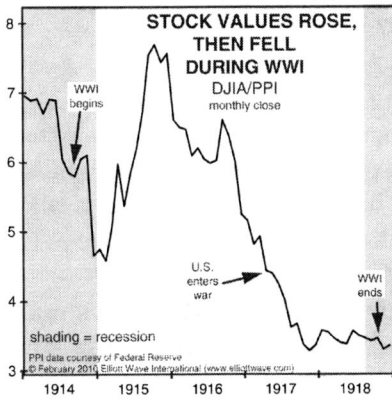

Figure 12

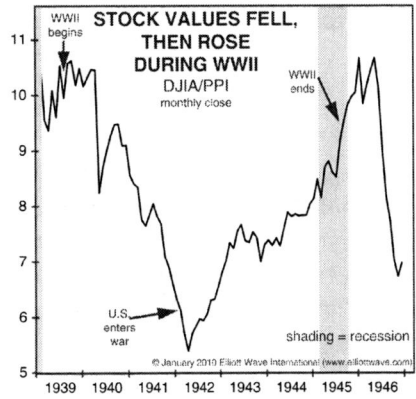

Figure 13

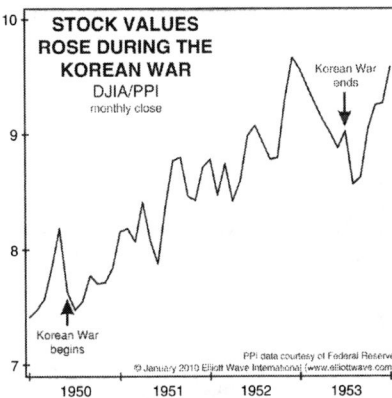

Figure 14

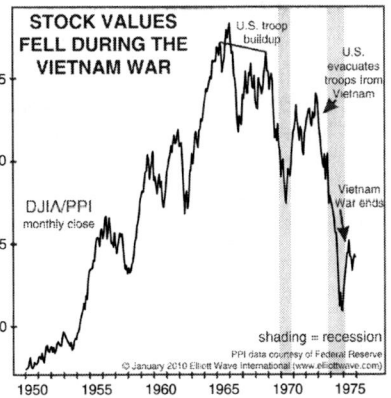

Figure 15

seems to make sense, too. Apparently the way that a new war would affect an economist's stock market outlook depends upon which version of the exogenous-cause argument he believes, or, more probably, which way a particular economy was going during a particular war he studied.

We can negate both sides of the case by looking at a few charts. Figure 12 shows a time of war when stock prices (normalized for inflation) rose, then fell; Figure 13 shows a time when they fell, then rose; Figure 14 shows a time when they rose throughout; and Figure 15 shows a time when they fell throughout the hottest half (1965-1975) of a twenty-year conflict. Who wins the war doesn't seem to matter. A group of allies won World War I as stock values reached fourteen-year lows; and nearly the same group of allies won World War II as stock values neared fourteen-year highs. Given such conflicting relationships, how do economists expect the *next* war to affect the stock market and the economy? There's no telling.

Claim #9: "Peace is bullish for stocks."

Most economists would probably agree that peace is bullish for stock prices. It would seem sensible to say that peace allows companies to focus on manufacturing, providing services, innovating and competing, all of which are activities that boost the overall economy. But does peace in fact have anything to do with determining stock prices?

Figure 16 provides an example from the 1920s in which stock prices seemingly benefited from peaceful times. The Dow rose over 500% in just eight years as peace mostly reigned around the globe.

Figure 16

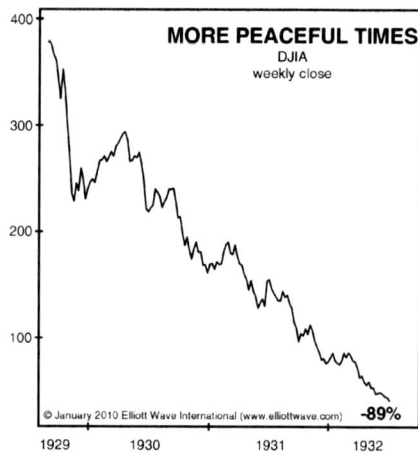

Figure 17

Figure 17, however, shows that in the three years immediately thereafter, peace likewise mostly reigned around the globe yet stock prices fell more than they had risen in the preceding eight years! It seems that we cannot count upon any consistent relationship between peaceful times and stock prices.

The Socionomic Institute's study of U.S. presidential election outcomes[13] shows that the party elected has no reliable effect on stock prices, either. Apparently, political events and conditions, like economic events and conditions, have no consistent causal relationship to the overall rise and fall of stock prices. Happily, we are not entirely alone in making this observation, either.

The Irrelevance of Political News and Events: A Confirming Study

The aforementioned study by Cutler et al. also tested the value of political events—such as presidential election results, military interventions, assassinations of leaders and the naming of new Fed chairmen—in forecasting the stock market. They began with a list of "Important World Events" from 1941 to 1987, as published in the *World Almanac*. From it they culled only those events that were featured in a lead story in *The New York Times* and which the *Times'* Business Section specifically reported as having affected investors. Despite this promising input, the authors concluded about stock prices, "There is a surprisingly small effect [from] big news [of] political developments…and international events."[14] Their conclusion is indeed surprising, at least to devotees of the mechanical, exogenous-cause paradigm.

Testing Exogenous Cause from Monetary and Fiscal Policy

Claim #10: "Inflation makes gold and silver go up."

This one seems like a no-brainer. Most economists, analysts and investors are certain that inflation makes gold and silver prices rise. They reason that an expanding supply of fiat dollars—termed *inflation*—reduces the value of each dollar, so the price of gold will rise in proportion to the rise in inflation.

Once again, it doesn't happen that way. Let's examine the history of inflation and precious metals prices since the low of the Great Depression.

Inflation occurred relentlessly from 1934 to 1970, yet gold and silver remained unchanged over that entire time. Granted, the U.S. government in 1934 had fixed the price of gold at $35/oz. But markets are more powerful than any government, and if the market had wanted precious metals prices higher, it would have set them higher. We know this to be true because in 1968 investors began forcing the price of gold beyond the official level, and the Treasury was powerless to stop them. They could just as well have done so anytime between 1934 and 1968, but they didn't.

Had you held gold during the inflationary period of 1934-1968, you would have held the worst investment item on the board. Investors in the stock market from 1934 to 1968, meanwhile, made ten times their money through capital gains and fifteen times their money when incorporating a 4% (non-reinvested) dividend. Bond investors made nearly as much money through compound interest. Yet gold was dead in the water.

Inflation continued during the decade from 1970 to 1980, and gold and silver soared. Inflation was all in the news, so people credited inflation for making precious metals' prices rise. They also predicted that their rise would not stop, because inflation was not going to stop. They were right about the inflation part.

Inflation continued from January 1980 to April 2001, during which time the money supply nearly tripled. But gold and silver lost a stunning 83% of their combined value during those 21 years, as shown in Figure 18. Investors who held precious metals during that time were once again stuck in the worst investment items available, but this time the result was far more devastating, as precious metals and commodities constituted the only major investment sectors that lost dollar value during those decades. Real estate went up, stocks went up, and bonds had a positive return. Yet at the end of this period, a hoard of gold and silver was worth only 17 cents (in inflated-dollar terms, no less) for each dollar that it was worth in January 1980. The exogenous-cause expectation that prices would rise commensurately with the money supply failed by a whopping factor of sixteen. In terms of CPI purchasing power, the result was even worse, as the value of these metals fell to about *six pennies* per 1980 dollar. Stock prices over the same period rose 13 times in terms of dollars and 45 times in terms of gold.

People who feared inflation in January 1980 were *right*. Yet gold and silver investors lost dollar value for two decades, lost even more buying power because the dollar itself was losing value against goods and services, and lost even more wealth in the form of missed opportunities in other markets. Gold and silver's bear market produced a 94% loss in terms of these metals' purchasing power of goods and services, and even more in terms of homes and corporate shares. How is such an outcome possible during a time of inflation? The path to the answer begins with the recognition that financial markets are not a matter of action and reaction; the mechanics paradigm of financial markets is wrong.

Inflation continued from 2001 forward, and gold and silver had a huge bull market into 2011. Since then they have lost over half their combined value through 2015, all while inflation has persisted. Thus, out of a total history of 82 years of persistent monetary inflation, gold and silver rose for 20 of them. For 62 of those years, they went sideways or down.

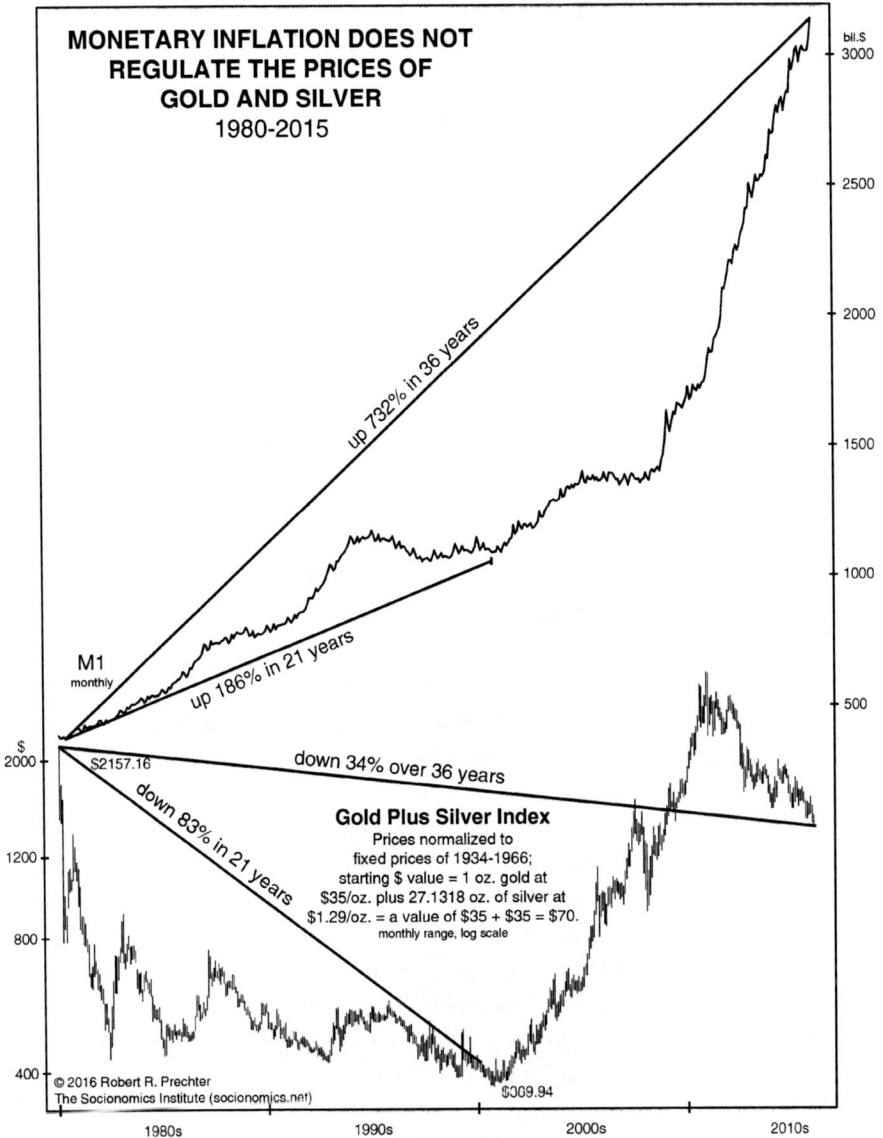

Figure 18

Consider also that despite the past 36 years of relentless inflation, despite an 8.3-times multiple in the M1 measure of the money supply, despite a thirteen-fold increase in the amount of dollar-denominated credit outstanding, despite central banks promising unlimited credit at zero interest, and despite the Fed creating $4 trillion of new base money, the combined value of gold and silver at year-end 2015 is below its high of 1980, as shown in Figure 18.

It does no good to say—as we sometimes hear from those attempting to rescue the mechanics paradigm in finance—that gold will follow the money supply "eventually." Billiard balls on an endless plane do not *eventually* return to a straight path after wandering all over the place, including in the reverse direction from the way they were hit. The fact remains that in 1934, had a speculator possessed clairvoyant knowledge that inflation would persist for the next eighty-plus years, he would have been unable to predict the volatile paths of gold and silver.

According to the mechanics paradigm, prices for gold and silver should have adjusted sensibly to the amount of inflation month by month and year by year. But nothing akin to that scenario happened.

More theoretically speaking, what mechanics-minded investor can be certain that gold should follow the money supply rather than vice versa? Is it unquestionable which element in the picture should be presumed to be the cause and which the effect? After all, a higher gold price increases the value of central banks' gold reserves, supporting more lending throughout the banking system. As we have already seen, cause-and-effect arguments are highly manipulable when using the mechanics paradigm.

Claim #11: "Quantitative easing (QE) makes financial prices rise."

Surely a concentrated effort by central banks to expand the base money supply would make prices of everything rise, right? Figures 19 through 22 do not support this claim.

As the stock market moved upward for 75 years, from 1932 to 2007, there was mostly a steady rise in the amount of debt the Fed was monetizing. As a benchmark, its rate of money creation from 1992 through August 2008 averaged 6.4% annually. Then, over just six years from September 2008 through 2014, the Fed's "quantitative easing" policies caused the base money stock to soar nearly 30% annually until it quintupled. Surely stock prices should have risen commensurately to reflect this dramatic change. But they didn't. From July 7, 1932 to September 12, 2008, the DJIA rose 27,609% without a QE policy. From the beginning of the QE policy on September 12, 2008 to its end on October 27, 2014 (see Figure 19), the DJIA rose only 47%, coming nowhere close to reflecting the Fed's five-fold inflating of its base money supply.

From these data, economists have wrested a case that QE caused the rise in the stock market that did occur. But such a case must rely on the assumption that QE produced a general inflation that would have caused all prices—not just stock prices—to rise; otherwise the claim is just data-fitting.

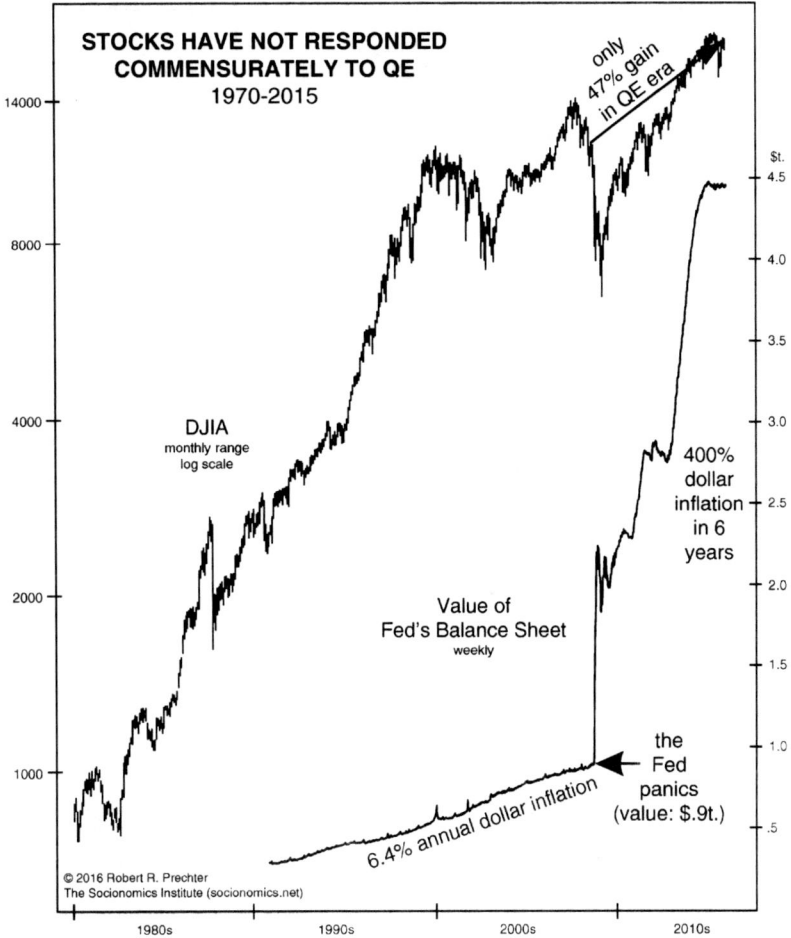

Figure 19

Figure 20 dispels any notion that QE worked as advertised. As with stock prices, commodity prices rose from 1932 to 2008 without a QE program. Then, in July 2008, just two months prior to the onset of QE, commodity prices started their biggest bear market since 1932, from which they have yet to emerge. Anyone applying exogenous-cause thinking to these data would have to conclude that QE worsened the collapse in commodity prices.

The observation of QE's impotence with respect to moving market prices is not just a retrospective observation. A socionomist applied it prospectively at the precise moment of all-time maximum QE heat. On December 12, 2012, the Fed announced that it would more than double its

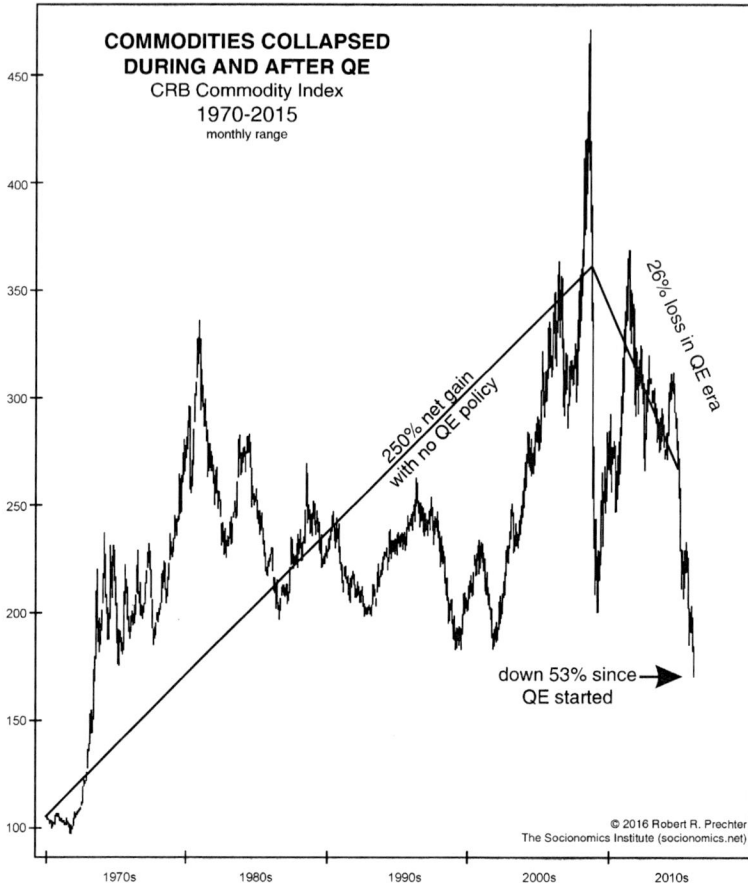

Figure 20

three-month-old program of purchasing $40 billion worth of mortgages per month by purchasing an additional $50 billion worth of Treasury bonds per month, *with no time limit.* During the hour of 1:30 to 2:30, right as the Fed's chairman was holding a press conference about the decision, I was on the phone doing an interview with GoldSeek radio, saying this:

> The Fed has probably played its last QE card today. People who have been arguing for more inflation got the Fed to do exactly what they've been predicting. The Fed has tripled its balance sheet, and it still can't get these markets to new highs. Since top investment banks are calling for $2,000 gold, I think you can bet against those ideas.[15]

The second arrow in Figure 21 shows that the exact timing of that commentary.

As published on December 30, 2012

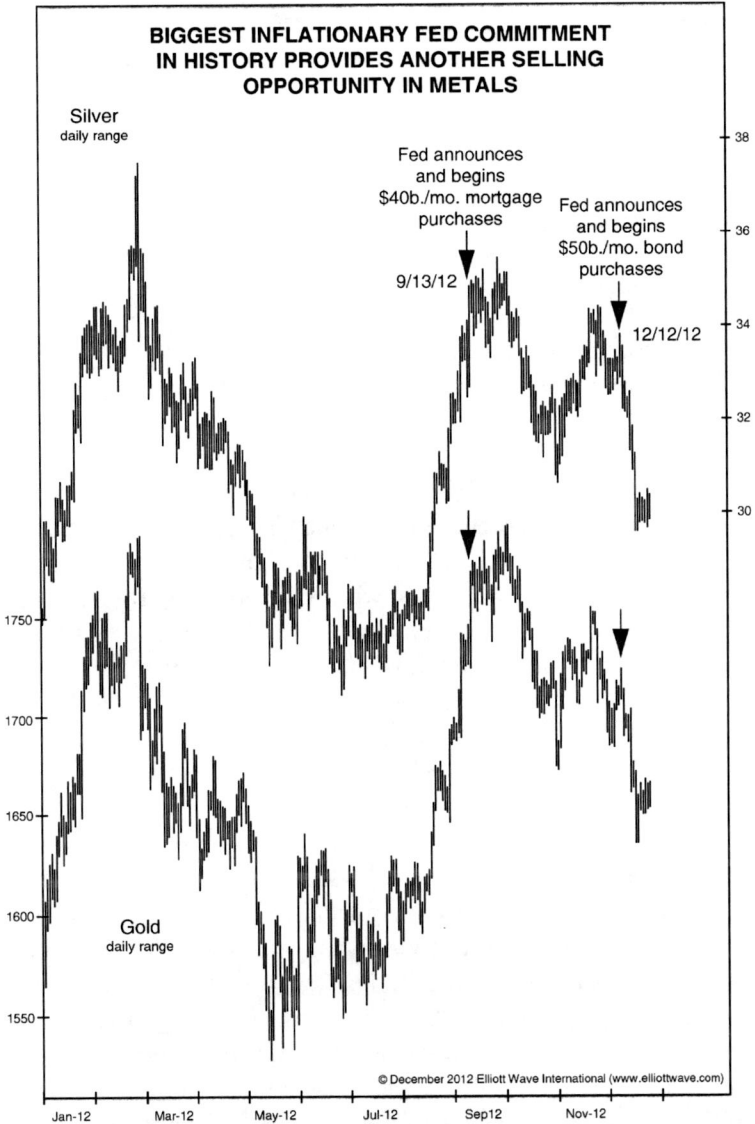

Figure 21

The December 30, 2012 issue of *The Elliott Wave Theorist* followed up on that conviction by publishing Figure 21 with the following text:

Precious Metals

Speaking of paradox, gold and silver peaked on Fed day, December 12, at a *lower* high. I haven't seen any commentary about that amazing event. This wasn't any old Fed day, either. It was the day the Fed promised to inflate the money supply indefinitely at the rate of over $1 trillion per year, the most aggressively inflationary policy—by many multiples—in its 99-year history.

This chart [Figure 21] shows gold and silver prices for the past year along with the dates of the Fed's unprecedented announcements. Both times, metals bulls got everything they hoped for and feared. Yet both markets peaked shortly after the first announcement, and they fell hard from a lower peak starting the *very hour* that Ben Bernanke confirmed the rest of his program.

Think about the headline I placed on that chart. It reads, "Biggest Inflationary Fed Commitment in History Provides another Selling Opportunity in the Metals." It does not say "Buying Opportunity," as nearly everyone thought it would be and as the standard model of exogenous cause and rational reaction unequivocally dictated. Once you bring yourself to think socionomically about markets, you will find that such seemingly paradoxical statements are in fact fully logical. Part II of this book will explain why.

Throughout the next two years, while the Fed's massive inflating program was in force, gold and silver slid lower. During its downtrend, *The Economist* noted, "Many of the most enthusiastic buyers of gold believed that QE would ultimately lead to rapid consumer inflation. *So far that has not come to pass.*"[16] Why? Because financial markets and overall economies do not obey the rules of mechanics. Figure 22 updates the picture through 2015.

In the famous "invisible gorilla" experiment,[17] subjects directed to count the number of times people in a video pass a basketball back and forth tend to miss the fact that a gorilla strolls across the court. Evidence of QE's total irrelevance to precious-metals pricing has likewise paraded boldly across observers' field of vision as these metals have declined for the duration of the Fed's program and past it, but almost no one sees it. In the cited experiment, about 50% of observers miss the gorilla. In finance, close to 100% of observers miss the gorilla. Figures 20 and 22 are gorillas that theoretical economists don't see. They are too busy concentrating on identifying whatever exogenous causes seem to fit their paradigm.

Had gold *risen* for the duration of the Fed's program from September 2012 through October 2014, commentators would have declared with steel-trap conviction how obvious it was that QE fueled the rise. Since the

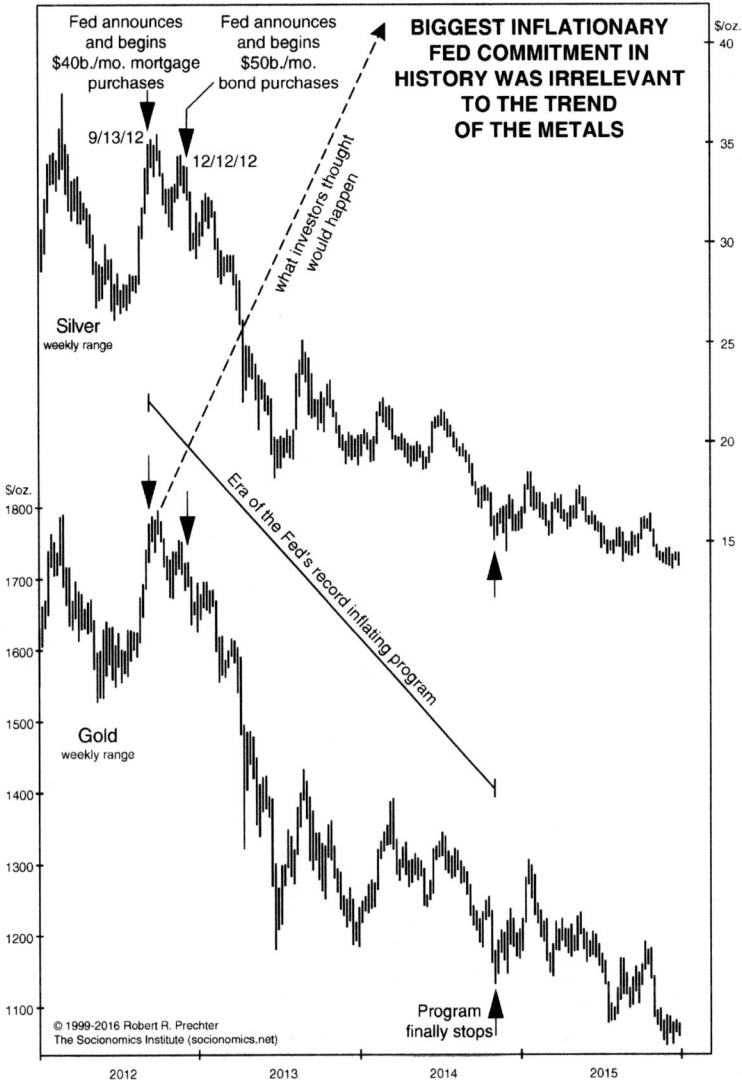

Figure 22

timing of things makes it appear as if QE made gold and silver *fall*—another perverse, nonsensical conclusion—they have avoided the subject. When markets coincide sensibly with external events, observers assume the events are causal to market action. When the complete opposite happens, they evade the contradiction. They have yet to figure out that in neither case are events causal to the market's price changes.

Testing Exogenous Cause from Direct Intervention in Markets

Claim #12: "Targeted central-bank buying and selling moves markets."

Economists and laymen alike would surely agree that direct, heavy central-bank buying or selling of an investment item should cause its price to rise or fall. Figure 23 certainly seems to justify this belief. It shows that central-bank buying of gold pushed prices higher from 2001 to 2011, and then central-bank selling caused the deep bear market that followed. Pure cause and effect, right?

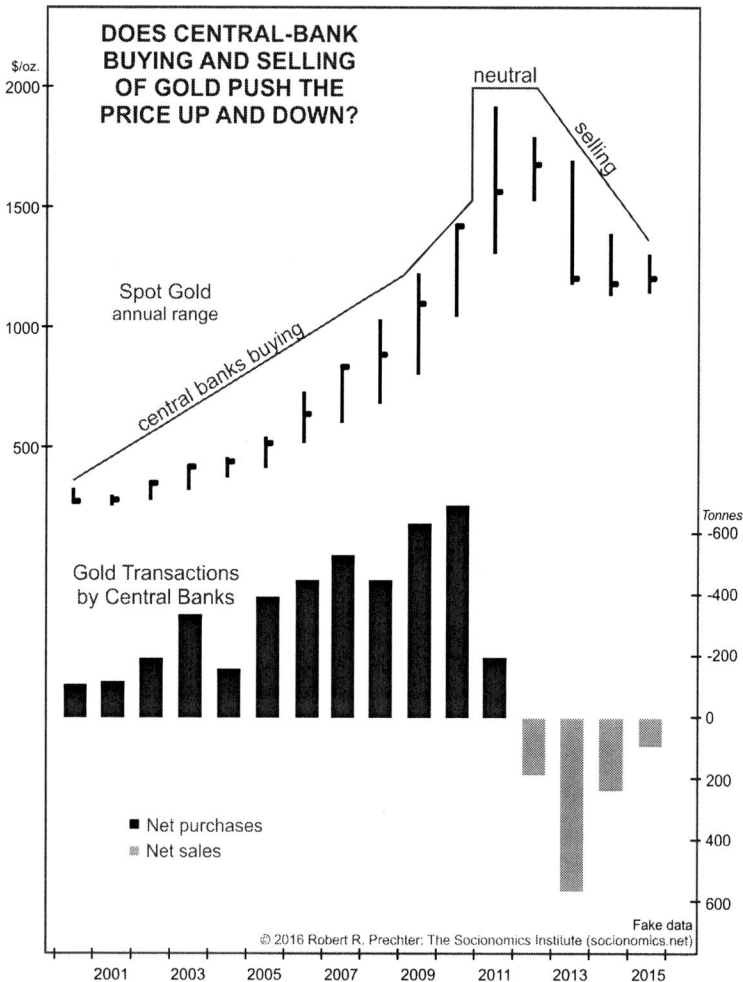

Figure 23

Not exactly, because Figure 23 is another lie. I just made up the data to show you what it would look like if exogenous cause worked. Study it carefully, because it shows you exactly what most everyone would have expected to see.

Figure 24 displays the actual data, offering another stunning case in point. Despite the huge and theoretically unlimited buying power of governments' money-creating monopolies, their buying and selling of gold has in fact been *inversely* related to the metal's price trend. Central banks' persistent selling of gold from 2000 through 2009 occurred as the metal rose five times in value; their neutral stance of 2009-2010 saw gold double;

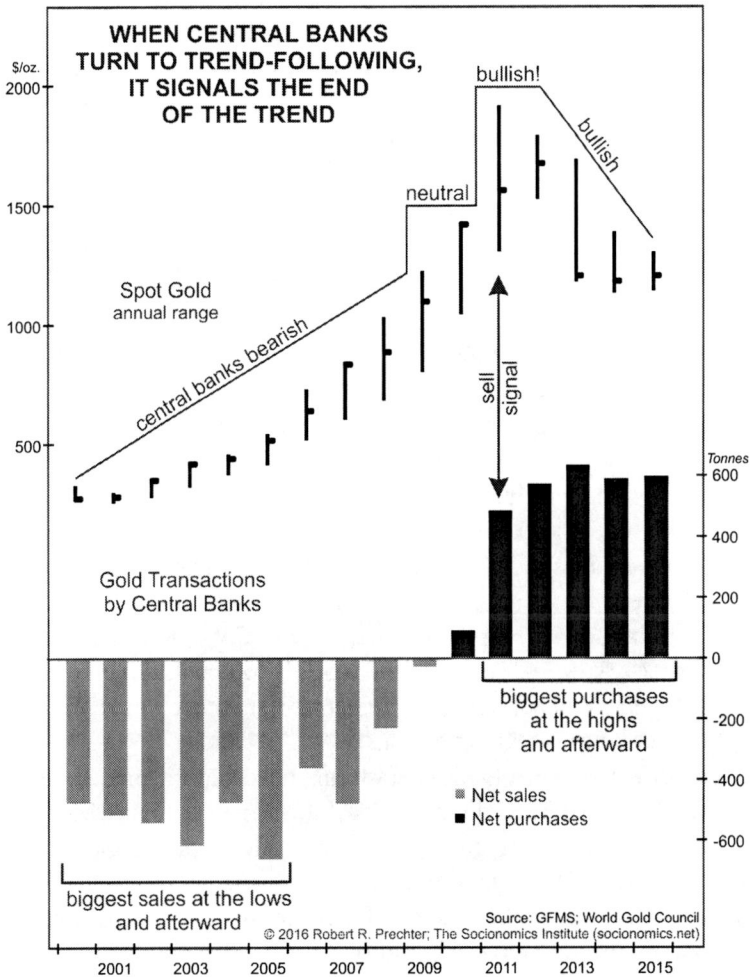

Figure 24

their rush to buy in 2011 caught the top of the market; and their persistent buying has continued throughout the bear market to date. It's amazing, isn't it? Even the directly administered investment policies of central banks fail as an exogenous cause of gold-price movement. If central banks can't move gold around, no institution can move any market around.

As a market analyst, I have no trouble explaining this picture. As you can see from the headline in Figure 24, originally published in April 2015, I simply observed that central bankers are lousy investors. They act as naïve odd-lotters, who fight a trend until it ends and then join it. It's that simple. Since we can count on them to do the wrong thing almost continuously, their behavior is an excellent long term market-timing tool. Like all such tools it is best used in the opposite of the common-sense way.

The common-sense conviction that direct, heavy central-bank buying or selling of an asset would force its price to rise or fall is flat-out wrong. In real life, sometimes central banks' interventions are in harmony with market trends and sometimes they aren't. When the latter condition applies, central banks' ineffectiveness is on stark display.

Claim #13: "Authorities can boost the stock market and prevent recessions and depressions."

Virtually everyone believes this statement. Chapter 19 of *The Wave Principle of Human Social Behavior* (1999) made a case that governmental and monetary authorities are powerless to control markets or the economy, so there is no need to recount that argument here. But you might find the most recent example of hubris and impotence instructive.

In 2007-2008, the U.S. government announced that it would fully back the debt of the mortgage companies it had created, Fannie Mae and Freddie Mac. It pledged to use unlimited amounts of money to fund banks that it deemed "too big to fail." It pledged that the FDIC would fund shortfalls at all other banks. At the same time, the world's top central bankers offered banks unlimited credit at near-zero interest rates, in other words, free money. All of these policies remain in effect.

According to the mechanics paradigm, these historic pledges and bail-outs should have had immediate results. Take a look at Figure 25. Can you tell where on this graph of stock prices authorities took these actions? According to the action-reaction model, the only logical place for them to have taken place would be at the bottom of the market. The day the authorities began flooding the market with liquidity is the day it should have turned up.

Figure 26 reveals that none of the many official actions during this period caused stock prices to turn up. On the contrary, the market kept falling,

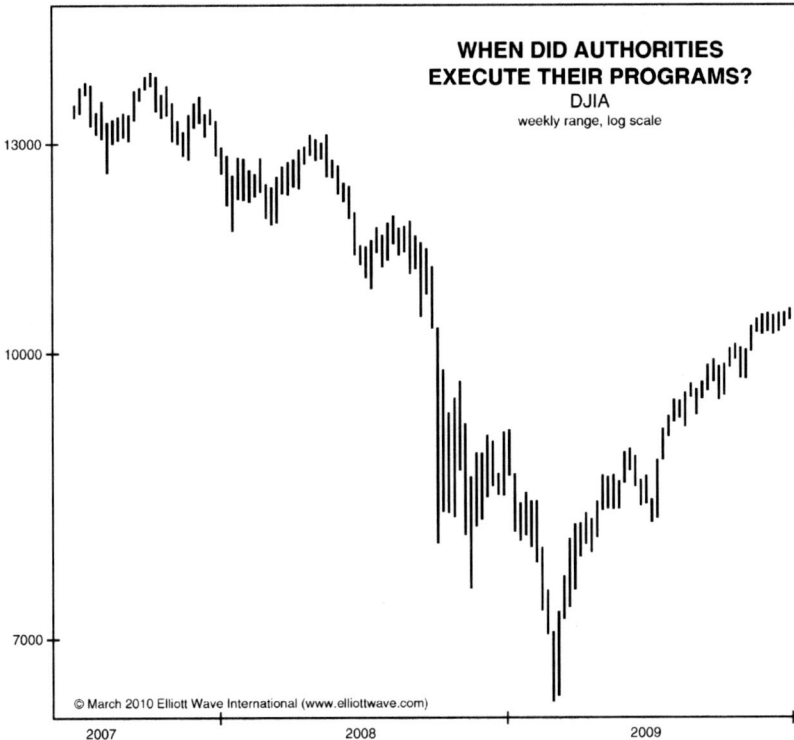

**WHEN DID AUTHORITIES
EXECUTE THEIR PROGRAMS?**
DJIA
weekly range, log scale

© March 2010 Elliott Wave International (www.elliottwave.com)

Figure 25

for seventeen months. The authorities did not act to prevent anything; they *re*acted, all the way down. Ultimately, the presumably in-control Fed presided over the second-biggest plunge in financial prices and the second-biggest economic contraction of its century-long tenure.

The Fed and the U.S. government have since claimed that their actions are the reason the bear market eventually ended. Had they begun their rescue programs in, say, February 2009, one might be justified in thinking their actions positively impacted the market. But their first program—that of lowering interest rates—began in September 2007, *a month before the stock market topped and three months before the recession began.* In fact, as Figure 27 shows in far greater detail, every time after the Fed or the government took action during the worst of the bear market, the market plummeted again. I kept this real-time record only through my publication date of October 21, 2008, but the authorities kept doing big things. Shortly after they stopped doing big things, in the first quarter of 2009, the S&P finally bottomed, at 667.

By this chronology, an exogenous-cause advocate should conclude that these authorities caused the worst bear market in 76 years, continually

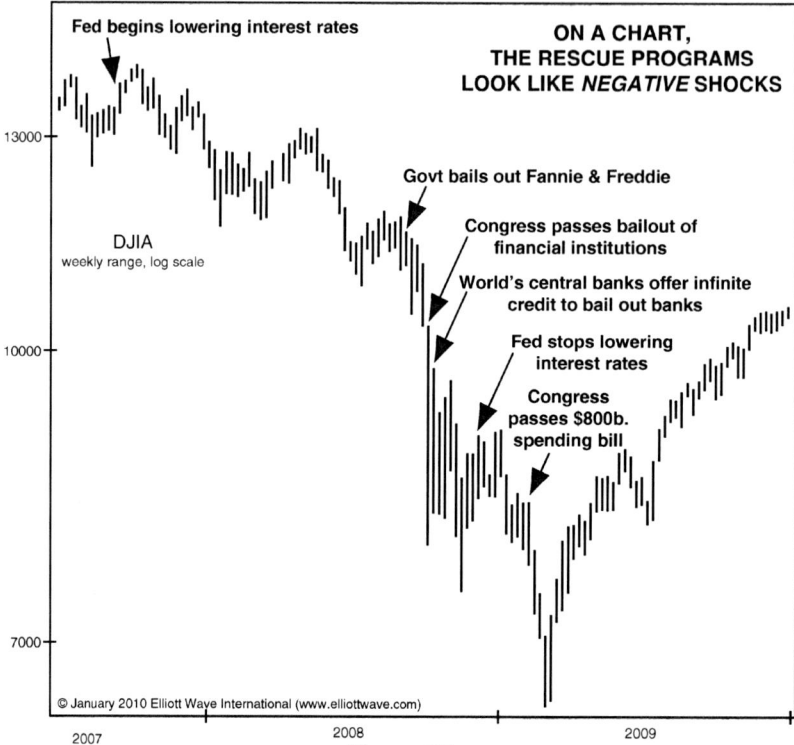

Figure 26

worsened it with every policy they announced or enacted and finally allowed it to end when they stopped. But we prefer to hypothesize that the market did what it did, the authorities responded by frantically pressing buttons, and the stock market eventually found a bottom on its own.

Again, it is no good to claim that these actions had results *eventually*. Any future turn in the stock market—no matter how long delayed—would serve such a contention. Such reasoning is tautological, because the market fluctuates.

Nevertheless, thanks to the subsequent recovery and people's unshakeable loyalty to the exogenous-cause paradigm, the belief in governments' and central banks' power to move markets remains entrenched.

U.S. institutions are not the only beneficiaries of this belief. Read this respectful snippet about the People's Bank of China (PBOC), as reported on October 23, 2015: "China stepped up monetary easing with its sixth interest-rate cut in a year to combat deflationary pressures and a slowing economy."[18] According to the article, the Chinese central bank has been acting and combatting. But it hasn't; it has been reacting and acquiescing. In those months, it took part in the trend toward deflation and recession

As published on October 21, 2008

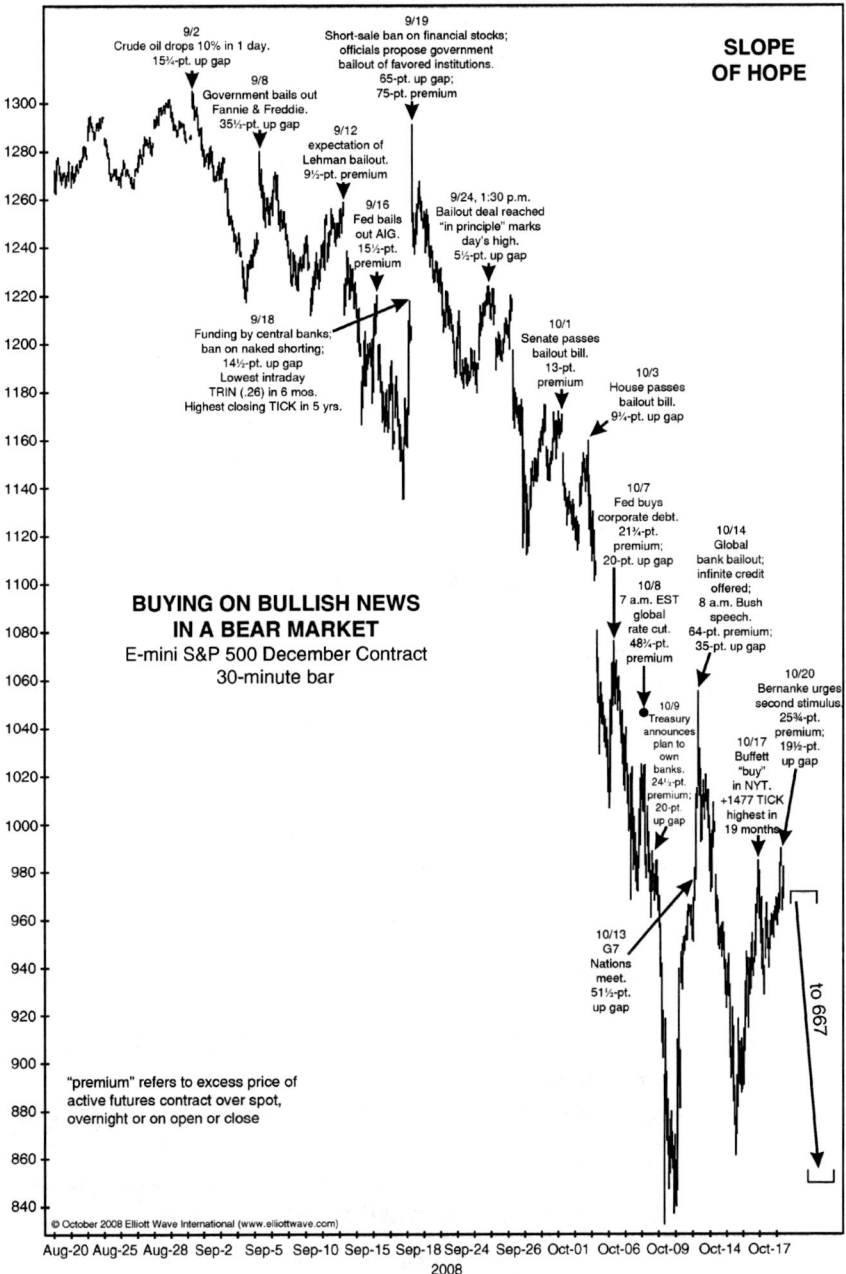

Figure 27

by lowering the price of borrowing money, just as Beijing cart vendors lowered the price of fried rice. After all, if cutting interest rates were some sort of cure, wouldn't the Chinese economy already have strengthened after a full year of such cuts? The article offers another unintended revelation: "Meantime, consumer inflation is at about half the government's target." If the authorities have a target, doesn't that mean they control the inflation rate? Clearly not. If the trend continues down, the PBOC will be powerless to stop it. If an uptrend emerges, the PBOC will likely claim credit for it, just as the Fed did in the U.S.

Lost in a Maze

While working toward completing this book in October 2015, I saw an article on *The Wall Street Journal*'s website demonstrating the lengths to which proponents will go to accommodate the ideas of exogenous cause and rational reaction while simultaneously undermining their own case. Here are the key passages:

> **Price of the precious metal fluctuates with expectations on when Fed will raise rates**
>
> The price of gold, which typically swings with political, economic and inflationary threats, these days moves in step with a different force: the Federal Reserve. Traders and analysts say <u>the precious metal's role as a haven investment in times of turmoil has waned recently,</u> with <u>the price more likely to fluctuate because of shifting expectations about when the Fed will raise interest rates</u>. Higher rates, when they occur, are widely expected to undermine future demand for gold, which doesn't pay interest so becomes less competitive against investments that do.
>
>   <u>Historically, gold has reacted to political and financial upheaval</u>. <u>But</u> this August, when fears about China's economic health triggered a 17% collapse in oil prices and an 11% plunge in the S&P 500 stock index, gold gained just 5.9% before falling back. The pattern has been repeated throughout 2015, with events such as Russia's involvement in the separatist war in Ukraine and in Syria moving oil markets but barely affecting gold. "It's not been doing well on the geopolitical side," said [   ], who oversees $11.5 billion at Fiduciary Trust. "<u>People have looked at gold and expected it to act as a safe haven, and it hasn't</u>," said [   ], who heads commodities research at Barclays.
>
>   <u>While rates have always influenced gold prices, the Fed's last period of rate increases, in 2006, did little</u> to knock gold off a 10-year

rally to a record of $1,888 in August 2011. Lately, gold prices have closely shadowed the short-dated Treasury market. The impact rarely has been as pronounced as now. Gold's <u>new trading pattern</u> reflects a world in which <u>financial markets are waiting for the Fed to act</u> after a record period of keeping borrowing costs near zero. That waiting game is <u>drowning out other market influences</u>.

An extended period of low rates could be good for gold. Some investors say that the ultra-loose monetary policies in place since the financial crisis will finally begin to stoke inflation. <u>Then</u>, investors will flock to gold again to protect themselves against rising prices, said [ ], a billionaire Canadian investor and former mining executive.[19]

Let's summarize these conflicting claims: (1) "Gold typically goes up during times of political turmoil, except that it hasn't done so for years." (2) "Because debt competes with gold as an investment, gold goes down when interest rates rise, except that gold didn't go down during the last big run of interest-rate increases." (3) "Alternatively, gold might in fact rise when interest rates rise, if low rates produce inflation." In this expression of exogenous-cause theory, a cause can affect or not affect a market, and an effect can be either falling or rising prices.

None of the article's fundamental claims of causality are true. The traditional view that gold acts as a "crisis hedge" is mythical. Money is a crisis hedge, and gold is sometimes money; but when it is not, the claim fails. Nearly a century of statistics[20] reveal that the price of gold has risen more often when the economy is expanding than when it is contracting, and when a huge financial crisis hits it tends to fall. During the financial collapse and Great Depression of 1929-1932, the government fixed the price of gold, so it couldn't fall; but its freely traded cousin, silver, plummeted 50% to complete an 81% bear market from its 1920 peak. Silver began rising in December 1932, and the government revalued gold higher in 1934, both events occurring during the powerful bull market in stocks of 1932-1937. Gold and silver soared from 1970 to 1980 but collapsed in 1980 when a recession hit, then sold off further in 1981-1982 when a second recession hit. During the credit meltdown and Great Recession of 2008, gold managed to go *down* 34% in its biggest seven-month decline since 1980, even though for a dozen years surrounding 2008 it was in a major bull market. Most crises in fact prompt people to *sell* gold, because their goal is to get money. The only monetary condition under which people reliably—and quite sensibly—prefer gold over money is hyperinflation.

What about the article's core idea that interest rates compete with gold for investment dollars? Figure 28 dispels the notion that gold prices and interest rates are reliably related in any discernible way. As our *Elliott Wave Financial Forecast* commented in December 2015,

> One commonly accepted notion is that rising interest rates are bearish for gold prices. The seeming logic behind this view is that since gold does not pay interest or dividends, rising interest rates provide competition for gold prices. This next chart dramatically contradicts this claim.[21]

Indeed, the 16-year history in Figure 28 progressively shows times when interest rates rose as gold fell, rates plummeted as gold rose, rates soared as gold rose, rates plunged as gold rose and then fell, rates held near zero as gold soared and then plummeted, and, finally, rates rose as gold fell. There is no consistent relationship between the two variables. Any hypothesis of dependence derived from a portion of these data can only be ad hoc.

As published in December 2015, with data updated to year's end

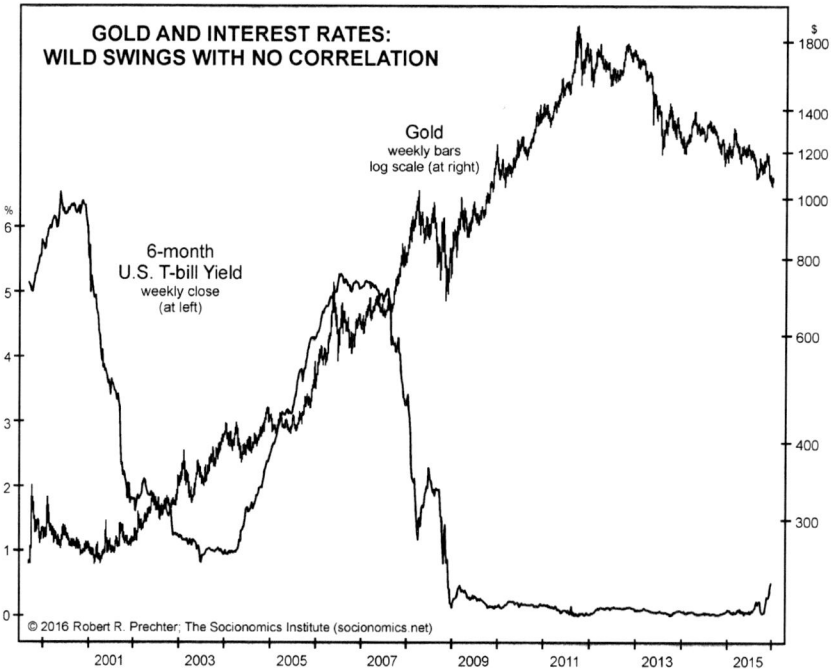

Figure 28

To be thorough, we also checked gold's relationship to *real* interest rates by dividing the six-month T-bill rate by the year-over-year change in the Personal Consumption Expenditure Core Price Index, which is the Fed's go-to formula for real rates. But since nominal rates were by far the more volatile component, the picture looks little different from that of nominal rates depicted in Figure 28. Once again, sensible economic thinking fails to apply to financial markets.

What about in 1970-1981, when interest rates rose to their highest levels in U.S. history? Did those rising interest rates compete with gold? Did gold fall as investors moved their portfolios into bonds, notes and bills? On the contrary, it rose in its biggest bull market ever.

Maybe the extremely positive inflation rate of that period, as evidenced by the rapidly rising PPI and CPI, is a reliable cause of rising gold prices. No, it isn't, because such was not the case from 2001 to 2011, when gold had its second-biggest bull market in modern history despite one of the lowest inflation rates on record. Forget it. You can't formulate exogenous-cause and rational-reaction explanations in any consistent, reliably applicable way.

Those Copious Numbers

Speculators' focus on economic statistics—relating to GDP, the trade balance, unemployment, jobless claims, the PPI, the CPI, construction spending, manufacturing output, factory orders, home sales, etc.—commonly called "the numbers," is a waste of time. Traders of stock market futures tend to get nervous just before and after each such bit of information is released, typically at 8:30, 9:15, 10:00 and 2:00 ET, and futures prices sometimes jump around contemporaneously. But overall one cannot identify specific numbers that consistently matter, nor can one identify from graphs of stock averages when economic numbers have had an effect on market prices.

I do recognize (see Figure 27 and Chapter 19) that news sometimes coincides with heightened emotional states among traders, which coincide with increases in market volatility lasting from a few seconds to a few minutes. But exogenous cause is not vindicated even here, because no specifically described cause produces a *consistent* reaction. A type of event that seems to affect stock prices one way in the present, when investigated in the past, often seems to have had the opposite effect or no effect at all. Just as often, even volatility doesn't budge.

Summary So Far

Over the preceding pages, we have seen that interest rates, oil prices, the trade balance, corporate earnings, employment trends, changes in GDP, periods of warring, peaceful times, inflation, central-bank monetary policy, direct central-bank investing and even targeted government programs have no reliable effect on financial market prices. I have tested as many exogenous-cause assumptions and statements as I can, and so far none of them holds up under scrutiny. Claims that seem inescapably reasonable, even compelling, fail the test of moderately rigorous investigation.

Many exogenous-cause claims contradict others, as we have seen throughout this discussion. Proponents often adopt one explanation and then the other, to fit market events. Chapter 19 expands our list of seemingly sensible but completely contradictory exogenous-cause explanations to over two dozen examples. While each such claim seems reasonable on an ad-hoc basis, I challenge exogenous-cause proponents to make any principled statement about any financial-market cause that holds up consistently throughout the historical record.

Seventy-five years ago, a financial modeler named Ralph Nelson Elliott, after observing markets for some time, concluded, "Current news and political developments are of only incidental importance, soon forgotten; their presumed influence on market trends is not as weighty as is commonly believed."[22] According to our investigation, Elliott was too generous. Aside from occasionally appearing to prompt fleeting emotional reactions, news and politics appear to carry no weight at all.

Reasoning in Reverse, from Market Actions to Prior Causes

We have investigated whether one can find any consistent cause of financial market price changes by looking at events and conditions and trying to tie them to resulting market movements. What if one flips the investigation and looks for dramatic price changes *first* and then tries to fit them to causal conditions and events?

In their 1989 paper, Cutler et al. investigated just such situations. They identified the fifty largest one-day changes in the S&P Composite Index from 1946 through 1987 and scoured the *The New York Times* for plausible explanations for them. Their conclusion is stunning: "many of the largest market movements in recent years have occurred on days when there were no major news events."[23] "On several of these days," they added, *"The New York Times* actually reported that there were no apparent explanations for the market's rise or decline."[24]

None other than the chairman of the Federal Reserve weighed in on this very topic in testimony before Congress. The morning after a one-day, 3.3% swoon in the DJIA in 2007, "The nation's top central banker said he could not identify 'a single trigger' that caused Tuesday's dramatic drop."[25] This is a remarkable admission for a macroeconomic mechanist who advocates "financial engineering." More recently, August 20, 2015 sported the biggest down day in 18 months for stock prices, yet reporters admitted there was a "lack of major U.S. economic news"[26] to explain it.

Rarely, in fact, has there been any news sufficiently striking to explain times when the stock market leaped or plummeted more than usual. As discussed in Chapter 1, it cannot even account for the biggest volatility spikes on record. Such barren results occur despite the fact that news pours forth all the time, providing substantial opportunity for some news event to appear causal. The lack of identifiable causes in such a generous environment deeply challenges the mechanics paradigm.

Perhaps longer-term market trends are trumping daily news. Surely the most dramatic price changes lasting *months* have clear causes. Or do they?

What was the cause in August 1982 of the start of the strongest one-year rally in stocks since 1942-1943? Was it the bad news of the ongoing recession? No, that doesn't make sense.

What was the cause in October 1987 of the biggest stock market crash since 1929? Was it because Q4 1987 had the strongest quarterly GDP expansion in over four years? No, that doesn't make sense, either.

The crash of 1987 has mystified economists. They are sure that the crash was a reaction, so external events must have caused it. *They can't find any.* In a 1991 paper, published four years after the fact, William Brock studied economists' commentaries and concluded, "In my opinion, no satisfactory explanation has been found [for] the most recent crash...Black Monday, October 19, 1987."[27] Fully a dozen years later, an article titled "Identifying Sell-off Trigger Difficult"[28] reported that despite careful research of all possible causal particulars, scholars in the field of economics remain at a loss to explain why the stock market crashed in 1987. There are as many explanations as there are economists arguing over them.

Can you imagine physicists endlessly debating the cause of avalanches? Physicists know why avalanches occur because they are operating under the proper paradigm of physics, which incorporates the laws and properties of matter and physical forces. Economists are mystified over the causes of market declines and economic contractions because they are using a mechanical model in the realm of finance, where it doesn't apply.

A decade later, in 1997, another dramatic event occurred. Is that one explicable by exogenous cause? Apparently not. According to a Nobel-prize-winning economist, "The truth is that nobody really imagined that something like the Asian financial crisis was possible, and even after the fact there is no consensus about why and how it happened."[29] It's the same refrain.

When an economist does offer an ad-hoc rationalization, it doesn't hold water. Let's briefly review two examples.

One causal hypothesis[30] offered for the crash of 1987 is that a Congressional committee was preparing a bill to limit interest deductions for debt used to finance corporate takeovers. For such a claim to be valid, it must derive from a principled statement that consistently holds true, such as, "Whenever Congressional committees contemplate doing something financially restrictive, the stock market crashes," or "Whenever Congressional committees craft rules hindering corporate takeovers, the stock market crashes." An exhaustive study of Congressional mullings is unlikely to reveal any such reliable causality. This singular, retrospective choice of causes was simply mined from the data.

Along the same lines, a retrospective reason[31] given for the stock market's five-year rise beginning in late 2002 was that Congress lowered the capital-gains tax rate in May 2003. Yet in 2008 Congress lowered the capital-gains tax rate again, for low-income individuals, and the stock market collapsed that year anyway. In 2013, after stock prices had risen for four years, Congress raised the capital-gains tax rate for people in the top income bracket rate right back to where it had been before May 2003,[32] yet stock prices not only failed to return immediately to their May 2003 levels but kept moving higher. The absence of commensurate reactions upon these further instances neuters the original argument.

What about the most devastating economic event of the 20th century, the Great Depression and the collapse in stock prices that preceded it? The Winter 1999 issue of the Federal Reserve Bank of Minneapolis' *Quarterly Review* observed, "Economists and policymakers are still studying and debating what caused this catastrophic economic event."[33]

Dissatisfied with this state of affairs, the Minneapolis Fed "decided to find out what caused this event."[34] So, in October 2000, it held a conference titled "Great Depressions of the Twentieth Century." It invited 56 noted economists, including a Nobel laureate, the subsequent chairman of the Federal Reserve, economists from various Federal Reserve banks, and professors from the University of Chicago, U.C. Berkeley, Carnegie Mellon, Brown, Penn, Stanford and other top schools, to offer their analyses.[35]

Here are excerpts from the Minneapolis Fed's report, each summarizing a different paper presented from the podium:

> [P]roductivity shocks (or sudden changes in productivity) are the starting point; that is, the first question asked is how much can productivity shocks explain. In this case, the authors show, productivity shocks don't tell the story; rather, changes in institutional and market regulation are more likely culprits for the depth and duration of the French depression.

[T]he authors found that productivity shocks can't explain the persistence of the U.K. depression in the 1920s. The standard explanation for the 1920s decline, that a deflationary monetary policy and an inordinately high fixed exchange rate were the prime factors, does not conform to the evidence either. According to the authors: "The most promising candidate shock is a substantial increase in unemployment benefits that began in the early 1920s." As for the worsening of the depression in the 1930s United Kingdom, lower world income and productivity are likely answers.

[The] authors suggest that productivity changes may have been crucial in Germany, but they "do not have a story which can account for these changes." However, this paper evaluates the role of fiscal policy and real wages in the depression and recovery in Germany, and finds that fiscal policy had a limited effect on the economy, but that the behavior of real wages might have been an important factor.

[T]he authors claim that the post-1929 slowdown in Italy cannot be explained solely by productivity shocks, but that other factors—namely, trade restrictions and wage rigidities—are to blame.

What happened [in Argentina] in the 1980s? The authors don't present definitive answers; rather, their intention is to present economic evidence within the framework of the neoclassical growth model.

Neoclassical theory predicts that following a slump, the economy should recover strongly and with low real wages—precisely opposite of what occurred from 1934-1939 in the United States, generally noted as the recovery years from the Great Depression, but cited by the authors as a continuation of the depression. The authors find that New Deal cartelization policies (National Industrial Recovery Act and its heirs) are an important factor in the post-1933 depression, and that the key depressing factor of New Deal policies was...the link between paying high wages and collusion.

As the title ["A Dual Method"] suggests, this paper was as much about the usefulness of the neoclassical model as it was about using this model to shed light on the Great Depression. Suffice to say that the former point garnered much discussion but would offer little insight to the general reader; on the latter point, the author challenges the neoclassical approach to explain why the marginal product of labor and the marginal value of leisure diverged so much and why that wedge persisted.[36]

Two months later, the Minneapolis Fed's *Quarterly Review* filed its report on these presentations. Here are the pertinent excerpts:

> A guiding premise of the conference was to apply neoclassical growth theory (discussed later) to events that occurred over 60 years ago, in the hopes of shedding light on one of the most vexing questions in economics. ...As one economist said in the middle of his presentation: "And then, in 1933, something unanticipated happened." The task of those gathered in Minneapolis was to explain how those unanticipated events caused these economic depressions.
>
> Although many causes have been suggested for the Great Depression, economists have yet to agree on a uniform explanation. The standard approach of the profession since the 1940s has been to try to determine the causes of the depression by searching for relationships or correlations in the data. But since the Great Depression was so unique, there is no basis for comparison and, therefore, empirical analyses always come up short.
>
> In the end, if the Great Depression is, indeed, a story, it has all the trappings of a mystery that is loaded with suspects and difficult to solve, even when we know the ending; the kind we read again and again, and each time come up with another explanation.[37]

The article added, "It may strike some as odd to describe economists as storytellers, but it's a term they use when discussing themes and ideas."

The claim that the Great Depression was unique, by the way, is false. Economies have fluctuated violently from time to time since the dawn of human societies.

These commentaries are dated December 2000, 68 years after the bottom of the Great Depression. Economists today have had even more time, over eight decades, to extract something of value out of their exogenous-cause model, only to find that it offers no useful answers and no causal explanation upon which its proponents can agree.

In this case, we are not asking economists of the 1920s to have *predicted* the Great Depression. We seek today only a consensus on a *retrospective* explanation of the event, and 56 top economists can't provide one. A more damning indictment of the mechanics paradigm can hardly be imagined.

Two decades after Cutler et al.'s finding that macroeconomic and political news fails to explain 80% of stock-price movement, Joulin et al.[38] confirmed and expanded upon those results. They examined both the biggest news events and the biggest stock market moves, searching for cause and effect. Finding none, they devastated the reigning causal paradigm in no uncertain terms. As *New Scientist* reported in 2008,

> Earlier this year, physicist Jean-Philippe Bouchaud and colleagues at Capital Fund Management in Paris studied the news feeds produced by Dow Jones and Reuters that provide real-time reports of items of potential interest to investors. Looking at more than 90,000 news items relevant to hundreds of stocks over a two-year period, they studied how "jumps" in stock prices—sudden, large movements— were linked to news items. <u>They weren't. Most such jumps weren't directly associated with any news at all, and most news items didn't cause any jumps.</u>[39]

Given that 40% of statistical results reported in peer-reviewed economics papers cannot be replicated,[40] this is a noteworthy confirmation of Cutler et al.'s earlier findings.

These two studies are not just incidental curios. They offer fundamental challenges to the status quo of economic theory. They should have changed the entire basis of financial market analysis and reporting. They have been almost entirely ignored.

Conclusion

We have shown that the phrases, "interest-rate shock," "oil-price shock," "trade-balance shock," "earnings shock," "GDP shock," "war shock," "peace shock," "terrorism shock," "inflation shock," "monetary shock," "fiscal shock," "Fed policy shock" and "government action shock" offer no value for analyzing the behavior of financial markets. On the contrary, they are distracting and misleading, so their value is negative.

Shining a light on contradictions between belief and reality with the graphs in this chapter makes one realize how powerfully humans are im-pelled to use exogenous-cause logic when tasked with predicting financial market trends. Not even the most blatant contrary evidence has been able to shake it.

Exogenous-cause claims contradict evidence and have no useful ap-plication. Still, in economics, such arguments are the coin of the realm. With them you can buy your way into any financial discussion, and you can be assured respect as well. But you can't help anybody.

If you are brilliant, your mind is rational, your logic is sound, and yet your conclusions are continually wrong or inadequate, then there is only one explanation: Your premise is false.

One might try to argue that the problem is one of complexity. Perhaps a web of interrelationships among many exogenous causes simultaneously operating and interacting explains the non-correlations we have uncovered. But if no individually tested condition or event is reliably causal, it is a stretch to claim that combinations of them would be reliably causal. Nor has any economist employed any such causal web successfully to forecast any financial market or trends in the economy. Quantitative ("quant") researchers have spread a broad net, especially during the past two decades, trying to identify combinations of economic, intermarket and intramarket variables that reliably predict financial prices. There seems to be little evidence that they have succeeded, whereas failures have been widely reported. Since financial markets' price changes exhibit a fractal form, which is independent of quantitative causality, I suspect the quant quest will prove quixotic. Nevertheless, we are open to evidence and await a demonstration. In the meantime, we will hold to our observation that, for conventional economists, markets are what happen when you are busy misinterpreting other things.

To summarize our findings up to this point:

(1) No type of exogenous event leads to a consistent result in stock market movement.

(2) The biggest and most dramatic stock market movements have no clear exogenous causes even in retrospect.

(3) There are no consistent correlations or relationships between supposed exogenous causes and stock market results.

So, events and conditions do not make speculators behave in any reliable way that has been identified.

Sherlock Holmes said, "There is nothing more deceptive than an obvious fact."[41] We can add: There is nothing more deceptive in finance than an obvious cause.

Bouchaud et al. mused on the implications of their study:

> Bouchaud's evidence says that, in fact, markets have <u>unruly internal dynamics all their own</u>, with rallies and crashes emerging <u>seemingly from nowhere</u>. "<u>Jumps seem to occur for no identifiable reason</u>," Bouchaud says.[42]

Parts II and III of this book will propose that financial-market price changes in fact emerge from *somewhere* for *an identifiable reason* based on internal market dynamics that are substantially *ruly*. But we are still a few chapters away from that revelation.

NOTES AND REFERENCES

[1] Shell, Adam, "It's Hard to Lose Betting on Stocks as Oil Falls," *USA Today*, August 12, 2008.

[2] "Oil Pressure Rising," *The Economist Online*, February 23, 2011; Rich, Motoko, Catherine Rampell and David Streitfeld. "Rising Oil Prices Pose New Threat to U.S. Economy," *The New York Times*, February 24, 2011; "Our view: Mideast Oil Shock Threatens U.S., Again,' *USA Today*, February 25, 2011.

[3] Condon, Bernard, Associated Press, as published in *The Atlanta Journal-Constitution*, December 12, 2015.

[4] "Trade Deficit Falls as Oil Imports Drop," *The Pittsburgh Press*, March 29, 1979, p. A20.

[5] *The Palm Beach Post*, March 28, 1981.

[6] "U.S. Trade Deficit Record $9.5 Billion," *The Spokesman-Review* (Spokane, Washington), March 1, 1984, p. 11.

[7] "Schultz Discusses Trade," *The Victoria Advocate*, April 12, 1985, p. 7B.

[8] Associated Press, "U.S. Trade Deficit Shrinks in 1st quarter," *Gainesville Sun*, May 26, 1990, p. 4B.

[9] Crutsinger, Martin, "Recession Might Be Finished,"Associated Press, as published in the *Lakeland Ledger*, February 22, 2002, p. E1.

[10] Ratajczak, Donald, "If Trade Deficit Improves, Dollar Could Stabilize," *Atlanta Journal-Constitution*, January 23, 2005.

[11] Crutsinger, Martin, (AP), "U.S. Trade Deficit Declined in 2007" *Eugene Register-Guard*, February 15, 2008, p. B3.

[12] Cutler, David M., James M. Poterba, and Lawrence H. Summers. "What Moves Stock Prices?" *Journal of Portfolio Management*, 15, 3, Spring, (1989), pp. 4-12.

[13] "A Democrat or Republican in the White House: Which is Better for Stocks and the Economy?" *The Socionomist*, October 2012. Reprinted in *Socionomic Causality in Politics*, 2017.

[14] Cutler, David M., James M. Poterba, and Lawrence H. Summers. "What Moves Stock Prices?" *Journal of Portfolio Management*, 15, 3, Spring, (1989), pp. 4-12.

[15] Prechter, Robert, excerpt of interview on GoldSeek radio, www. GoldSeek.com, December 12, 2012, 1:30-2:30 p.m. E.T.

[16] Buttonwood, "Like Chess, Only Without the Dice," *The Economist,* April 20, 2013.

[17] Chabris, Christopher and Daniel Simons, " The Invisible Gorilla: And Other Ways Our Intuitions Deceive Us," *Harmony,* May 18, 2010.

[18] "China Cuts Interest Rates as Policy Divergence With U.S. Widens," *Bloomberg News*, October 23, 2015.

[19] "Gold's Role as Safe-Haven Investment Wanes," *The Wall Street Journal*, October 19, 2015.

[20] Prechter, Robert. *The Elliott Wave Theorist*, March 14, 2008.

[21] Hochberg, Steven and Peter Kendall. *The Elliott Wave Financial Forecast*, December 4, 2015.

[22] Elliott, R.N., "The Basis of The Wave Principle, October 1, 1940." Reprinted in *R.N. Elliott's Masterworks*, ed. Robert R. Prechter (New Classics Library, 1980/1994), pp. 188-196.

[23, 24] Cutler, David M., James M. Poterba, and Lawrence H. Summers. "What Moves Stock Prices?" *Journal of Portfolio Management*, 15, 3, Spring, (1989), pp. 4-12.

[25] Geewax, Marilyn, "Bernanke Calms Market," *The Atlanta Journal-Constitution*, March 1, 2007.

[26] Sweet, Ken, "Stock Market Endures Worst Day in 18 Months," Associated Press, August 21, 2015.

[27] Brock, William A., "Causality, Chaos, Explanation and Prediction in Economics and Finance," Social Systems Research Institute, No. 387, 1991.

[28] Walker, Tom, "Identifying Sell-off Trigger Difficult," *The Atlanta Journal-Constitution,* August 6, 1998.

[29] Krugman, Paul, "Analytical Afterthoughts on the Asian Crisis," Massachusetts Institute of Technology, www.mit.edu.

[30] Mark L. Mitchell and Jeffry M. Netter, "Triggering the 1987 Stock Market Crash—Antitakeover Provisions in the Proposed House Ways and Means Tax BHI?" *Journal of Financial Economics*, Vol. 24, 1989, pp. 37-68.

[31] Sources of this idea are numerous. As but one example, see Moore, Stephen, and Tyler Grimm, NCPA Policy Report No. 307, "The Bush Capital Gains Tax Cut After Four Years: More Growth, More Investment, More Revenues," *National Center for Policy Analysis*, January 2008.

[32] Wikipedia, "Capital Gains Tax in the United States," accessed November 15, 2015.

[33] Federal Reserve Bank of Minneapolis *Quarterly Review*, Vol. 23, No. 1, Winter 1999. http://www.minneapolisfed.org.

[34] Fettig, David, Ed., "Something Unanticipated Happened," *The Region*, December 2000, http://www.minneapolisfed.org.

[35] You can review the list of speakers at https://www.minneapolisfed.org.

[36, 37] Fettig, David, Ed., "Something Unanticipated Happened," *The Region*, December 2000, http://www.minneapolisfed.org.

[38] Joulin, Armand, Augustin Lefevre, Daniel Grunberg, and Jean-Philippe Bouchaud. "Stock price jumps: news and volume play a minor role." ArXiv:0803.1769v1, December 2, 2008.

[39] Buchanan, Mark, "Why Economic Theory is Out of Whack," *New Scientist*, July 19, 2008.

[40] Colin F. Camerer et al., (March 25, 2016). "Evaluating Replicability of Laboratory Experiments in Economics." *Science*. Vol. 351, No 6280. 1433-1436.

[41] Doyle, Arthur Conan, "The Boscombe Valley Mystery," *The Adventures of Sherlock Holmes*, 1891.

[42] Buchanan, Mark, "Why Economic Theory is Out of Whack," *New Scientist*, July 19, 2008.

Chapter 3

Central-Bank Policy Does Not Control Interest Rates; It's the Other Way Around

Alan Hall, Mark Galasiewski and Robert Prechter

Most economists and financial-market observers believe that central banks set interest rates. This notion is false. For more than two decades, socionomists have been tracking the relationship between interest rates set by the marketplace and interest rates set by the U.S. Federal Reserve, the European Central Bank, the Bank of England and the Reserve Bank of Australia. The link we have long identified—that the market *leads* and central banks *follow*, not the reverse—continues to hold.

The Market Leads the U.S. Federal Reserve

Let's begin with an update of EWI's chart from 2007[1] showing the three-month U.S. Treasury bill yield set by the market and the federal funds rate set by the Fed. This history shows that the T-bill market moves first and the Fed's interest-rate changes follow. Chapter 19 of *The Wave Principle of Human Social Behavior* described the result: No one monitoring the Fed's decisions can predict when T-bill rates will change, but anyone monitoring the T-bill rate can predict with fair accuracy when the Fed's rates will change. We demonstrated this ability in August 2007 by predicting that the Fed was about to lower its federal funds rate dramatically. Our prediction is quoted on Figure 1, and the aftermath is shown in Figure 2.

This relationship maintained even during the dramatic period of double-digit rates in the late 1970s and early 1980s. Figure 3 plots T-bill rates and the effective federal funds rate (a weighted average of the federal funds rate across all banking transactions) from 1978 to 1984. T-bill rates peaked four times in 1980-1982. Each of those peaks occurred a month or more before subsequent and reactive peaks in the federal funds rate. The Fed's rate also lags at bottoms, as depicted on the chart at the lows of 1980, 1981 and 1982-3. That interest rates were in a relentless upward

EWI's Analysis in September 2007

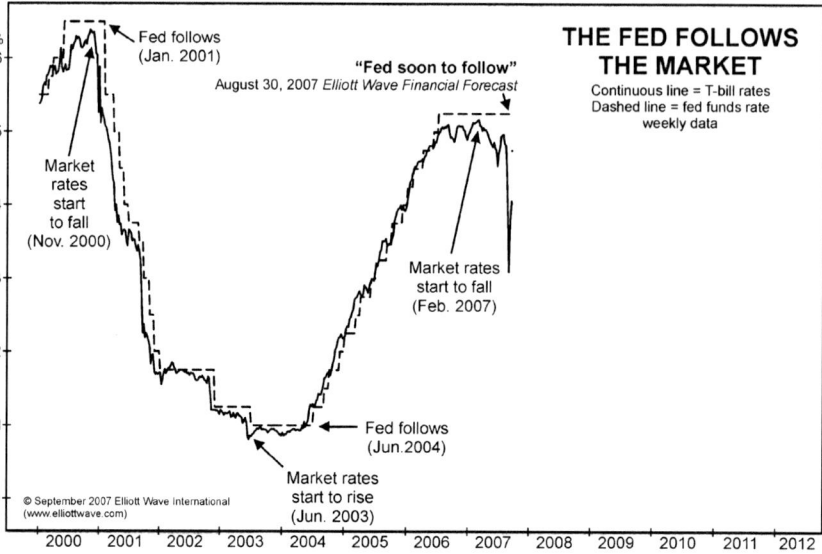

Figure 1

Aftermath

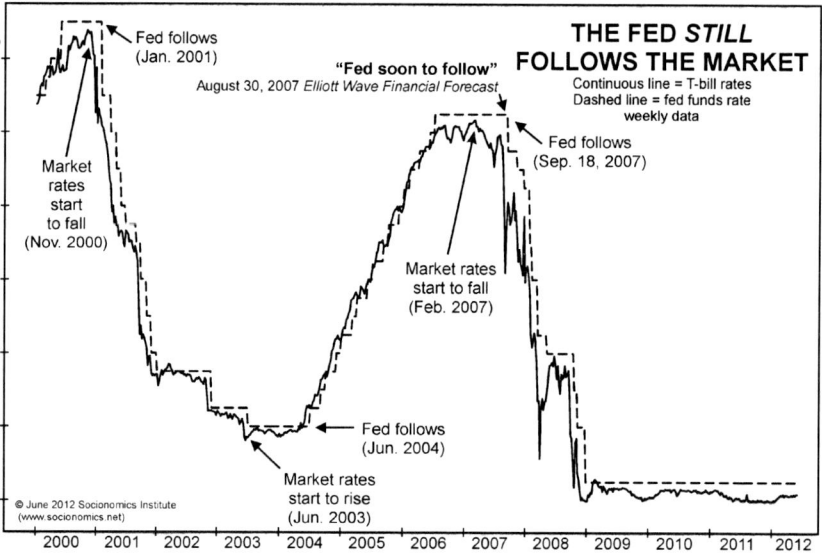

Figure 2

trend during the entire decade of the 1970s and that they have been stuck at zero since 2008—in both cases despite the Federal Reserve's contrary desires—is powerful evidence reinforcing the point that the Fed is not in control of interest rates.

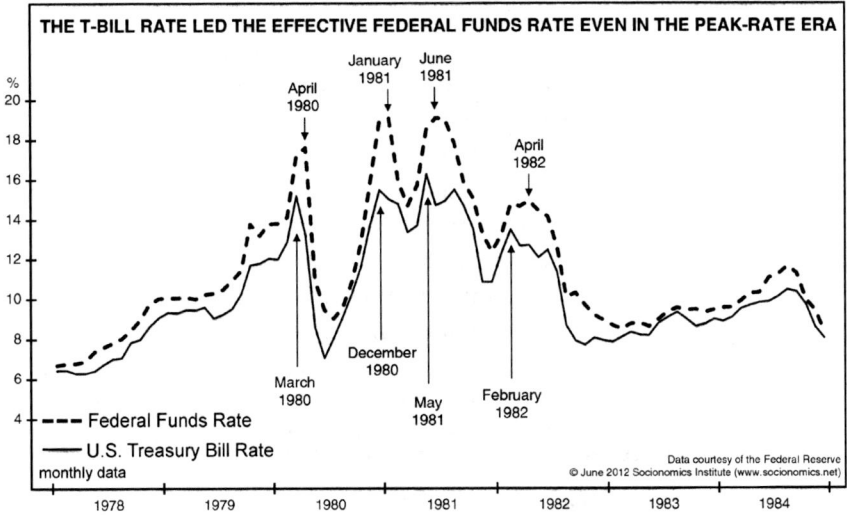

Figure 3

The Market Leads Central Banks' Actions in Europe and the U.K.

The same dynamic rules interest rates in the European Union and the United Kingdom. Figure 4 plots monthly data for the interest rate of the freely-traded, 3-month euro generic government bond versus the European

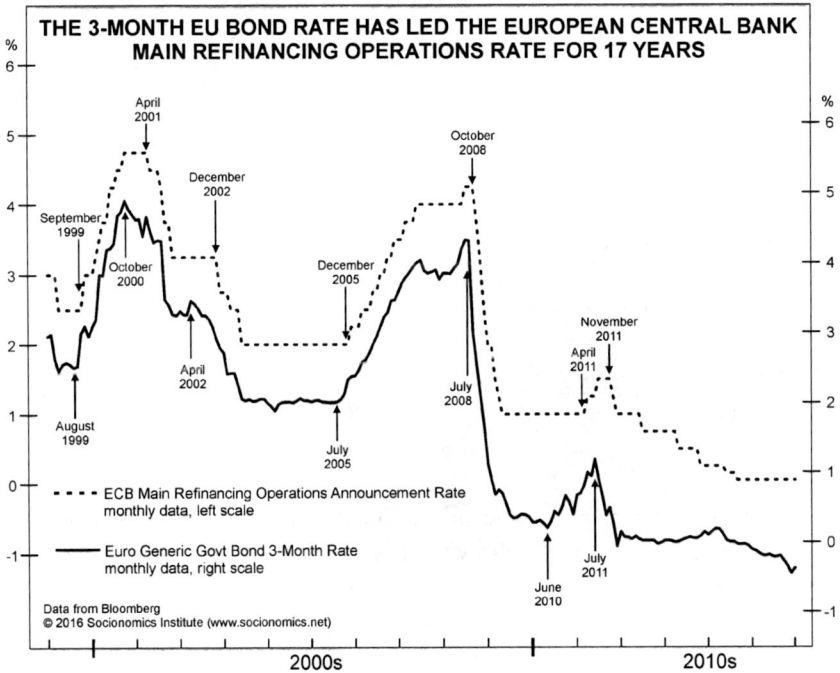

Figure 4

Central Bank's (ECB's) main refinancing operations rate, which is Europe's equivalent to the U.S. federal funds rate. As these graphs show, rate-setting actions by the ECB have lagged the freely traded debt market at all seven major turning points in interest rates since 1999. The lags vary from one to ten months, and the average lag is 5.3 months.

The same story is evident for an even longer time in the U.K. Figure 5 plots interest rates on the U.K.'s freely-traded, 3-month government bond against the Bank of England's (BOE's) official daily bank-lending rate. These lines show that the BOE's rate-setting actions have lagged the freely traded debt market at all twelve major turning points in rates since 1993. The lags vary from two to nine months, and the average lag is 4.8 months.

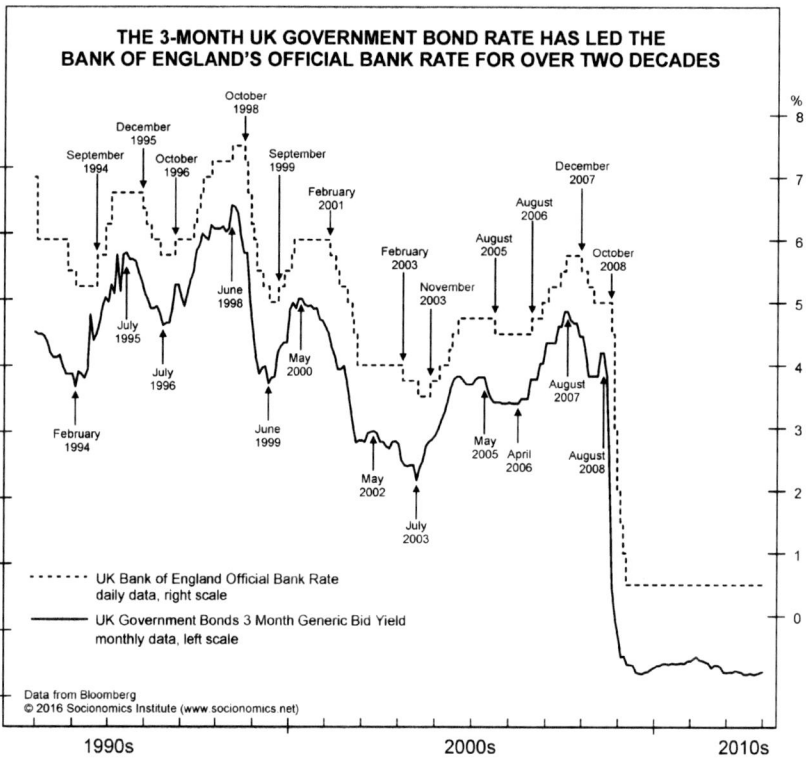

Figure 5

Central banks' interest-rate decisions are not proactive but reactive. Central bankers continually follow the market because they lack any other useful guide.

The Same Principle Holds for Australia

Conventional wisdom holds that central banks are able not only to set interest rates but also to direct other financial markets and even economies by manipulating interest rates. Take, for example, this assertion from an article in a weekly economics magazine: "Part of the aim of central banks in driving down interest rates is to encourage a greater risk appetite among investors."[2] Two key assumptions underlie that statement: (a) central banks determine interest rates; and (b) lower interest rates will increase society's appetite for risk.

This chapter has so far challenged the first assumption with charts of interest rates for the U.S., Europe and Great Britain. We can augment the case with graphs of Australian data, which show that movements in the cash "target" rate set by Australia's central bank, the Reserve Bank of Australia (RBA), almost always follow those in 3-month Australian Treasury bills. As in the previously cited instances, the proper conclusion to draw is not that the RBA *directs* changes in interest rates but that it *responds* to them.

The insight that central banks' rate decisions follow movements in the 3-month Treasury bill market helped us forecast the RBA's "surprising" rate increase in early October, 2009. At the time, the bank's cash rate target was only 3%, while the market rate was already 3.28%, so on September 28 we specifically predicted, on a televised interview,[3] a move up to 3.25% in the bank's cash rate target. A week later, with T-bill rates surging even higher, the RBA announced its decision to become the first major central bank to raise interest rates—to 3.25%—in the wake of the previous year's global financial crisis. Later that month, the October 30, 2009 issue of *The Asian-Pacific Financial Forecast* published Figure 6 noting the still-widening gap between the two data series and predicted another move up in the cash target rate. That forecast worked out, too. Figure 7 updates the history.

As published on October 30, 2009

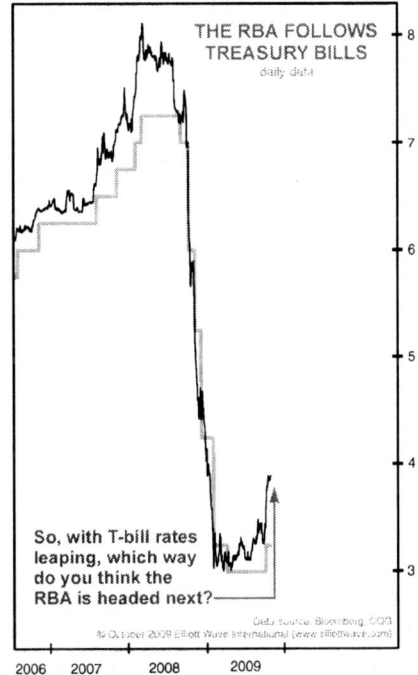

THE RBA FOLLOWS TREASURY BILLS
daily data

So, with T-bill rates leaping, which way do you think the RBA is headed next?

Data source: Bloomberg, CQG
© October 2009 Elliott Wave International (www.elliottwave.com)

Figure 6

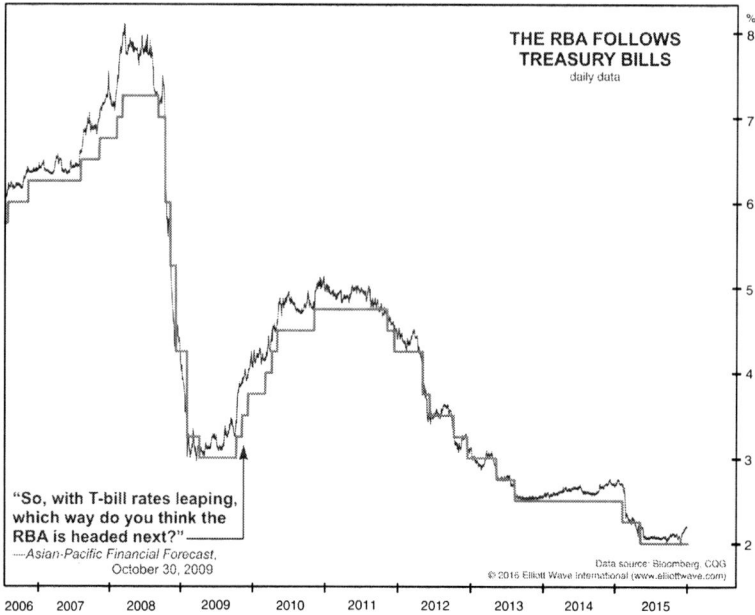

Figure 7

Shortly after the RBA's first rate increase, a global bank's chief economist exclaimed, "What you're seeing is the new monetary policy orthodoxy, that central banks should actually raise rates to prevent an asset bubble from inflating. Australia is at the vanguard of this new thinking."[4] But there was no "vanguard," no "new thinking" and no "new monetary policy." The RBA did what central banks always do: It followed the market.

Now let's look at the second assumption behind the earlier cited quote, namely that lower interest rates increase society's appetite for risk, thereby encouraging investment. Figure 8 offers evidence that this assumption is false. After the 1987 crash, the ASX All Ordinaries index rallied for two years on *rising* rates and then sold off through 1990 on *falling* rates. Stocks then rose in 1991 on continued falling rates and sold off in 1992 on even lower rates. Keep following the graphs to the right and you will see that there is no consistent relationship between the direction of interest rates and that of the stock market. Chapter 2 found the same lack of reliable correlation between corresponding U.S. markets over the past century. If interest rates did determine risk-taking in the stock market, all these graphs would show a consistent, inverse relationship between the two sets of data; but they don't.

The same principles hold for the Bank of Canada, the Swiss National Bank and no doubt every other central bank on the planet. They are all followers, not leaders. Markets matter to them, but they don't matter to markets.

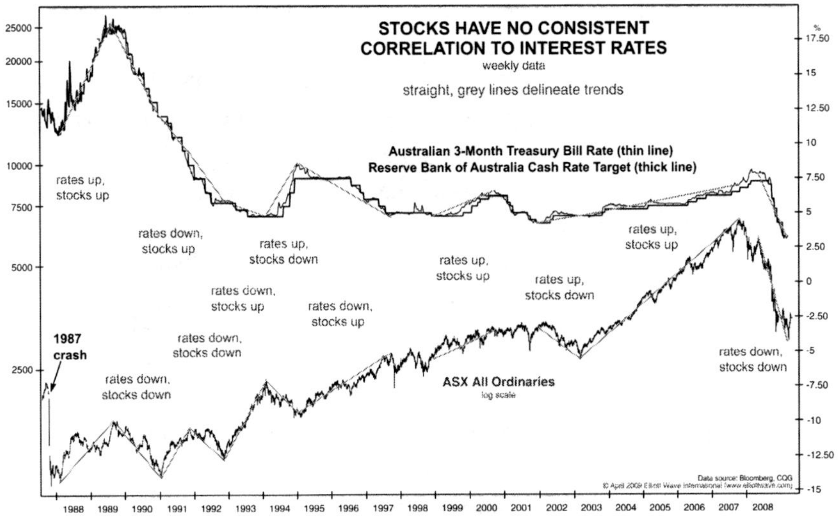

**STOCKS HAVE NO CONSISTENT
CORRELATION TO INTEREST RATES**
weekly data

straight, grey lines delineate trends

Australian 3-Month Treasury Bill Rate (thin line)
Reserve Bank of Australia Cash Rate Target (thick line)

rates up,
stocks up

rates down,
stocks up

rates up,
stocks down

rates up,
stocks up

rates up,
stocks down

rates up,
stocks up

rates down,
stocks up

rates down,
stocks up

**1987
crash**

rates down,
stocks down

rates down,
stocks down

rates down,
stocks down

ASX All Ordinaries
log scale

Data source: Bloomberg, CQG
© April 2008 Elliott Wave International (www.elliottwave.com)

Figure 8

Time to Adopt a New Perspective

The myths of central bank potency and interest-rate causality are so pervasive that conventional analysts cannot imagine a better explanation for trends in financial markets and the overall economy. But the interest-rate market is the dog wagging the central-bank tail, and neither of them determines risk preferences, stock prices or trends in the economy.

For most people, the idea that markets guide the decisions of central bankers rather than the other way around is counterintuitive. But no data show that financial prices change in reaction to administrative directives. On the contrary, these data expose the fact that administrators constantly monitor markets to decide what actions they should take.

Some theorists might try to argue that speculators in government debt are successfully anticipating central banks' policy moves and adjusting market rates on government bills ahead of central-bank announcements. This is a variation of discounting theory, which Chapters 7 and 39 heartily challenge with respect to stocks and the economy. With respect to interest rates, which scenario is more likely: that central banks follow the market with approximately a five-month lag, or that investors follow central banks' directives five months in advance? The latter claim would seem detached from reality on at least two counts: Prior to central-bank meetings, market observers and even trained economists typically express not foreknowledge but pervasive uncertainty about possible rate actions; and there is no evidence that central bankers know five months in advance what they themselves are going to do.

Our thesis also challenges some charges made by the Fed's detractors. Economists have widely embraced the claim that a minor rate increase by the Fed helped cause the U.S. economy's plunge in 1937.[5] This causal conclusion is ridiculous in the context of the full history of interest rates, where rates typically rise for years as the economy booms. All the Fed did in 1937 was follow T-bill rates, which had edged upward near the peak of an economic expansion. Its timing only seemed to be a cause; in fact it was a result. One should not credit *or* blame the Fed for rate changes.

As a theoretical clarification, our observation does not necessarily mean that interest rates have been the same as they would have been without a central bank. Markets have been setting interest rates in the context of central banks' existence. Were there no central banks doling out new money and credit, the context would differ, and rates may have differed as well.

Nor do we argue, as many theorists do, that rates would *necessarily* have differed absent central banking. Financiers could well have built credit-issuing structures of equal import even in the absence of state-endorsed monopolies called central banks. What we do say is that central banks cannot, and do not, *set* or *control* interest rates; they follow rates set by the market.

In sum, the market—not the Fed, the ECB, the BOE, the RBA or any other central bank—sets interest rates. After the market sets rates, central banks follow. Central banks' interest-rate decisions, therefore, are never critical, crucial, pivotal, historic or momentous. They are mostly irrelevant.

Realizing that central bankers are not in charge of interest rates has immense benefits. Rather than waiting in a state of uncertainty for central bankers to announce their rate changes, we simply monitor market rates to anticipate what central bankers will do.

For an example of the benefits that derive from disbelieving in the power of central bankers to set currency exchange rates, see Chapter 29. For an example relating to gold, see Chapter 2.

REFERENCES
[1] Published by Elliott Wave International in *The Elliott Wave Financial Forecast*, August 30, 2007.

[2] Buttonwood, "Searching for Value: Where Might the Bottom for Shares Prove to be?" *The Economist*, March 26, 2009.

[3] Interview of Mark Galasiewski by Haslinda Amin, Bloomberg TV Asia, September 28, 2009, 8:31 a.m.

[4] Petrie, Dan and Sarah McDonald, "Australia Shuns Greenspan for 'New Wave' Plan," Bloomberg News, October 15, 2009.

[5] See "Eggertsson, Gauti, and Benjamin Pugsley, "The Mistake of 1937: A General Equilibrium Analysis," *Monetary and Economic Studies (Special Edition)*, December 2006, as well as numerous essays available on line.

Chapter 4

Stocks' Rise After the Charlie Hebdo Attack Was Anything But a "Rational Reaction"

Brian Whitmer

Talk about irony and paradox. Did you notice what failed to happen during "France's worst terrorist attack in a generation"[1]?

On the morning of January 7, 2015, Islamic terrorists stormed the Paris office of *Charlie Hebdo*, a satirical French magazine, murdered the company's editor and eleven other people and then escaped. Within 30 minutes, officials put Paris on its highest state of alert, panic descended on the city, and a massive three-day manhunt began. The massacre made front-page headlines around the world, and news of a second attack—the murder of a police trainee—broke just as French financial markets opened on January 8.

Yet, not only did France's CAC 40 stock index fail to plunge as fear swelled and the terrorist threat intensified, it actually *gapped higher* that morning (see Figure 1). The CAC 40 was still higher at 10:30 a.m., when news erupted that two suspects were driving around the area with assault rifles and rocket launchers. The index accelerated higher at that point and closed the day up more than 3.5%, *its largest daily gain in nearly two years*.

Meanwhile, U.S. markets opened at 2:30 p.m. Paris time, just as panic over the event was reaching a zenith. Both the Dow and S&P 500 also gapped higher, with the Dow scoring its second-largest up day in more than three years.

On January 8, a major world news organization confessed, "There was some bewilderment around here yesterday about the reaction in stock markets to the slaughter of 12 people at or around the Paris offices of Charlie Hebdo."[2]

This quote reveals the lengths to which people will go to maintain the theory that stock prices react to events: Observers referred to "the reaction in stock markets" even though there was no such thing. They would sooner accept the implication of widespread human depravity—the celebration of slaughter—than question news causality under the mechanics paradigm.

Other pundits, when contacted by the reporter, evaded this perverse conclusion by offering a string of rationalizations:

"The market…has become numb to this type of thing."

"The idea that this attack is somehow connected to a larger threat to the West, that it is somehow imminent that it is going to have an effect on business or finance, would be far-fetched, and in that sense it makes sense that the markets haven't reacted."

"The one thing everybody knows about France is that its security is fantastic and water-tight. The fact that these guys got through to what was actually probably a pretty soft target is absolutely no indication, I don't think, of any sort of larger vulnerability."

"I think, in a bizarre sense, this incident has made it less probable that these people will be able to fuel anti-Islamic extremism, because the dignity and sympathy and humanism of the reaction of the French, who have gone out in the streets."

"People are just focusing on these other events right now: lower oil, the good U.S. economy and buying on the dip."[3]

A few financial reporters, unable to make sense of stock markets' "reaction" to the event, simply ignored it. As Bloomberg noted of its own coverage, "The killings weren't mentioned at all in the Bloomberg global markets wrap."[4] Had the French stock market plunged 3.5% that day, you can bet the media would have employed extra-large type in blaming the terrorist attacks for the swoon.

The market's "bewildering" behavior continued the next day. The terrorists resurfaced just minutes after trading began on Friday, January 9. As they hijacked a car and drove it into an industrial complex, French stocks again failed to turn down. In fact, the CAC 40 rallied at the open and was still rising fifty minutes later, when the news broke that a shootout was in progress on the N2 motorway.

The CAC 40 didn't peak until 9:16 a.m. on January 9. As the terrorist threat wound down, share prices began to decline. When Paris police closed in on the suspects at 11:30, stocks were down almost 1% from their earlier highs. By 2:30, police had publicly identified two of the suspects, and the CAC 40 proceeded to plunge 2%. The news that police had killed three of the four suspects broke around 5:15 p.m., 45 minutes after European shares

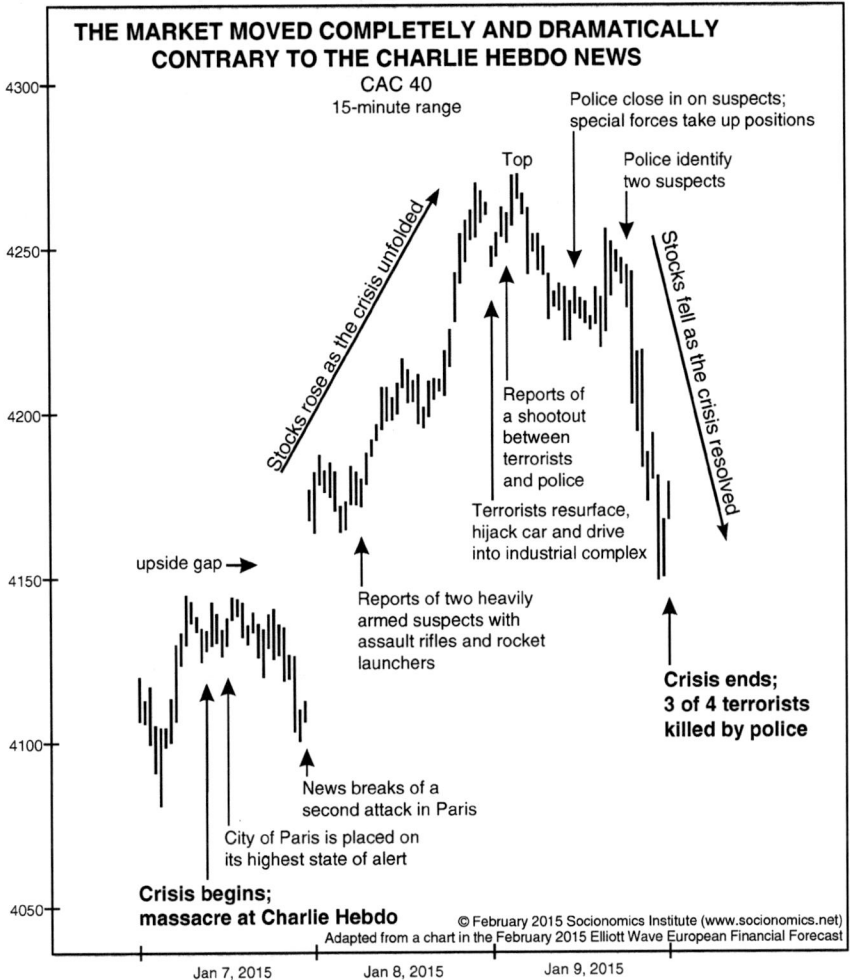

THE MARKET MOVED COMPLETELY AND DRAMATICALLY CONTRARY TO THE CHARLIE HEBDO NEWS

CAC 40
15-minute range

Police close in on suspects; special forces take up positions

Police identify two suspects

Top

Stocks rose as the crisis unfolded

Stocks fell as the crisis resolved

Reports of a shootout between terrorists and police

Terrorists resurface, hijack car and drive into industrial complex

upside gap →

Reports of two heavily armed suspects with assault rifles and rocket launchers

Crisis ends; 3 of 4 terrorists killed by police

News breaks of a second attack in Paris

City of Paris is placed on its highest state of alert

Crisis begins; massacre at Charlie Hebdo

© February 2015 Socionomics Institute (www.socionomics.net)
Adapted from a chart in the February 2015 Elliott Wave European Financial Forecast

Jan 7, 2015   Jan 8, 2015   Jan 9, 2015

Figure 1

closed for trading. An hour earlier, the CAC 40 had ended the day down 1.7%, with other European bourses falling 3% to 4%.

No headlines attributed the French stock market's big jump on January 8 to an outbreak of terrorism in the capital city. Nor did any headlines attribute stocks' subsequent selloff to the return of peace and safety. You can be sure, however, that had European stock markets *fallen* 4% as the crisis unfolded and then *rallied* 2% as it ended, every mainstream paper on the planet would have connected the two events.

Don't be fooled when commentators connect events to market moves. The mechanics paradigm of exogenous cause is false.

REFERENCES

[1] "France's worst terrorist attack in a generation leaves 12 dead," *The Telegraph* U.K., January 7, 2015.

[2] Thompson, C. and Laurence Arnold, "French Terror Spawns Theories on Markets, Humanity: Opening Line," Bloomberg, January 8, 2015.

[3] *Ibid.*

[4] *Ibid.*

Chapter 5

Time for a New Model

Robert R. Prechter

Why the Invalidity of Economists' Explanations Is Not Often Apparent

Most of the time, the stock market rises and the economy expands. During such periods, economists confidently cite numerous exogenous causes to explain the growth that is occurring. Their explanations are either tautological ("the increase in jobs has fueled a pickup in GDP") or refutable in every case by showing a single historical graph.

When the trends of the stock market and the economy are rising in parallel, no discernible cognitive dissonance occurs among economic theoreticians or practicing economists and their clients. Bull markets and economic expansions make all these people feel comfortable, so they accept the adequacy of the explanations despite insufficient evidence of their validity. But during bear markets and economic contractions, people are *uncomfortable*, so they begin to seek valid explanations, which do require sufficient evidence. This is the only time they bother to investigate economists' theories, methods and explanations, and they are always found wanting. Every time there is a recession, observers grumble about economists' forecasting methods. The deeper the recession, the louder the grumbling. Economic forecasters as a group never anticipate the economy's trend changes, but consumers of their commentary do not notice this inability until recessions occur, because that is the only time everyone can feel the pain that economists' failed methods have caused. Their methods are just as useless when times are good, but during such times no one bothers to check.

In the long run, the complaints never stick. Once the economy begins expanding again, people forget about them. The media resume quoting economists, and people are once again satisfied that their analyses make perfect sense. It happens, over and over, and it will probably never cease.

Take, for example, this detailed forecast from a noted university economist and head of an academic think-tank, as reported on August 24, 2006:

[   ] discounted odds of a downturn. "You'd have to give me a mondo inflation problem that would make the Fed more aggressive and have them raising rates again," he said. If interest rates were to climb further, the added burden might tip the economy into recession, [   ] said. But that is unlikely since the Fed is likely to take the opposite route: "They won't let it turn into a recession. They will do a rate cut." While the price of oil has tripled since early 2002, the worst of the economic damage done by oil and gas prices may also be over, he said. Unless there is a dramatic disruption in supplies—an accident, terror attack or perhaps a replay of the 1970s—the U.S. economy can handle current prices. According to [him,] oil prices will neither soar nor drop dramatically.

[H]ousing is slowing [but] the soft-landing scenario is at center stage, [   ] said. "I call it orderly moderation," he said. "In the local economy, there has been no bubble."[1]

Every snippet of this forecast was wrong, from theoretical causality to practical utility. Let's review: The only way he can imagine a downturn in the economy is if inflation heats up. But the downturn in real estate that was already several months old and the downturns in stocks and the economy that began the following year all occurred in a deflationary environment, not an inflationary one, as commodities crashed across the board. He says if the Fed were to raise interest rates it could trigger a recession. But the Fed had been raising its discount rate aggressively for two years, from 2% to 6.25%, and the economy expanded throughout that time. The Fed's program of *lowering* rates, which began a year later, preceded the onset and accompanied the acceleration of the Great Recession; and stocks, the economy and interest rates all went down together until rates hit zero. He says the Fed won't let a recession happen. It did let a recession happen, and it was the deepest economic contraction since 1933. He says the Fed will prevent recession with a rate cut. The Fed made twelve rate cuts in sixteen months, from mid-September 2007 to mid-December 2008, yet the recession occurred anyway. Deeply contrary to his entire causal presumption, the recession started four months *after* the first rate cut and extended six months *past* the final one. He describes the preceding four-year rise in oil prices as having inflicted economic damage. On the contrary, the stock market was rising and the economy was expanding throughout the entire time. He says the worst of that damage may be over and calls for a moderation of that damage if oil prices stop rising. When the price of oil finally fell, however, the stock market and the economy fell with it, and neither of them recovered until several months after oil prices turned back up. The succession of upturns was opposite to his causal model, too: Oil bottomed in December 2008, the stock market in March 2009 and the economy in June 2009. He says oil prices and the economy will remain stable unless there is a dramatic disruption in oil supplies caused by an accident, a terrorist attack or perhaps a replay of the problems of the 1970s. No such event occurred, yet oil prices soared over the next year and a half. He predicts that oil prices will neither soar nor drop dramatically, yet they did both in succession, first tripling in two years and then plunging 78% in five months. He predicts the housing market will have a soft landing because house prices are merely undergoing an orderly moderation. In fact, the housing market had just started its biggest implosion since 1926. He asserts there has been no bubble in local real estate, yet his home city was one of the hardest hit over the next six years until there was a record amount of empty office space.

The point is not just that he was wrong about the future. Every forecaster, myself often included, has been wrong about the future. The point is that every single one of at least ten stipulated causes and effects failed to apply, even to the point of numerous opposite outcomes.

The identity of this economist is irrelevant, as he spoke for the profession. Respected colleagues ranging from academics to bankers to money managers to Federal Reserve Board members pretty much agreed with him. In August 2006, the president of the Federal Reserve Bank of Dallas said, "there is no recession in sight."[2] In September 2006, the president of the Federal Reserve Bank of Boston said, "One of the more striking features of the current economic outlook...is how relatively benign it is. The forecast for the next couple of years seems quite optimistic."[3] Observe that she considered the outlook *so benign* that it was *striking*. Observe the words *outlook* and *forecast*, representing projections that turned out to be not just wrong but backwards. Consider finally that conditions in fact were anything but benign. The massive indebtedness of the time, when finally stressed by a contractionary trend, led to the biggest financial implosion since 1929-1932. Prices for real estate, the most credit-infused market, had already been falling for several months, and stocks, commodities and the economy were the next areas to join in the decline. On March 1, 2007, an article reported, "Federal Reserve Chairman Ben Bernanke assured Congress on Wednesday that he is sticking by his optimistic economic outlook and that financial markets are 'working well.'"[4] On July 23, 2007, the Treasury Secretary of the United States said the housing slump appeared to be "at or near the bottom." On July 25, 2007, the president of the New York Fed told the Forum on Global Leadership, "Financial markets outside the United

States are now deeper and more liquid than they used to be."[5] On July 31, 2007, *The Wall Street Journal* ran an editorial titled, "The Best Economy Ever," in which the chairman of an economic consultancy argued that a slew of economic factors, for reasons carefully explained, had "set the stage for extraordinary economic growth."[6] The Dow Jones Composite Index had peaked at an all-time high twelve days earlier, foreshadowing what proved rather to be an extraordinary economic setback. Economists polled at the time by *The Wall Street Journal* and Bloomberg were unanimous in calling for further expansion.

On September 18, 2007, the Fed cut its discount rate by half a point, the first in a long series of cuts. The cut was twice as large as economists had predicted. Experts explained—based on exogenous cause—what it would surely mean:

> Hopes for keeping the U.S. economy growing soared Tuesday.... Consumers should see immediate benefits from the rate cut. ...Even more important, home owners will get a break. [They will] pay less for carrying debt on credit cards and home-equity loans. ...NAHB President [ ] issued a statement saying the rate cut would help "ensure that the economy keeps moving ahead and the housing market regains its strength." [ ], the U.S. Chamber of Commerce's chief economist, also cheered the moves to loosen the credit environment. Fed policy makers "made the right decision to move more aggressively at this time," he said. [ ], a wealth adviser at Merrill Lynch in Atlanta, said it's good for the economy if businesses can borrow for less. "If their cost of capital has decreased, you'd expect that saving to drop to the bottom line," he said. "So earnings will increase," he said, and that will send stock prices higher.[7]

Not one of these predictions came true, because not one of the causal claims is valid. All that really happened is that the Fed, responding to deflationary pressures, lowered the rental cost of its money. It wasn't "stimulating" anything (see Chapter 25), despite widespread statements to the contrary. Economists took the supposed stimulation so seriously that in typical exogenous-cause fashion they feared inflationary consequences. As the media reported, "the Fed's rate cuts also raised the fear that inflation will rear its ugly head [to] spark a period of rising prices [and] further wage gains."[8] The presumed causality was only imagined, the proof being that as rates were repeatedly cut over ensuing months, wages, commodity prices, the Producer Price Index and even the Consumer Price Index all fell. On September 17, 2007, *USA Today* headlined, "Greenspan Predicts Double-

Digit Rates." That very date marked the last day of the highest Fed discount rate since 2000. Fifteen months later, the discount rate was at 0.5% and the federal funds rate was stuck between 0.25% and zero.

On Friday, October 19, 2007, the 20th anniversary of the crash of 1987, reporters conducted interviews with numerous financial experts, money managers and economists. Our city paper began with this comment:

> It was 20 years ago today that the stock market suffered its worst crash in history. That's worth noting now, with two important stock indexes hovering near all-time highs…. Which is not to imply that anyone thinks another "meltdown"—as officials of the New York Stock Exchange called the crash then—is on the horizon. <u>No one does</u>.[9]

"Everyone" was right: A crash was not "on the horizon." It was an inch from their faces. The Dow had registered an all-time high just eight days earlier, from which it plummeted 57% in eighteen months. It was the second-biggest stock market decline in 150 years, and corporate earnings (see Figure 26 in Chapter 21) suffered their biggest crash in the 140-year history of the data.

One rationale for economists' optimism was assurances from the Fed. On August 31, 2007, the chairman of the Fed told a Jackson, Wyoming audience that the Fed "will act as needed"[10] to keep the economy strong. On October 21, 2007, a governor of the Federal Reserve, addressing the Institute of International Bankers, declared, "The Federal Reserve will do whatever is necessary to prevent damage to the economy…. The Federal Reserve will continue to monitor developments in financial markets and act as needed to support the effective functioning of these markets and to foster sustainable economic growth and price stability."[11] The stock market was already ten days into a year-and-a-half period of what he surely would have called price *in*stability (actually just a bear market), and the economy was weeks away from a turn from moderate expansion to rapid contraction. On November 27, 2007, an article titled "Fed keeps cash pipeline flowing" quoted the chief economist at an advisory firm saying, "The Fed wants to make absolutely certain that nobody thinks they are going to drop the ball."[12] The Fed certainly succeeded in making people *think* that it would not drop the ball. But since the Fed doesn't hold any metaphoric ball in the first place, the whole vision is a fantasy. As related in Chapter 2, the stock market and the economy collapsed from that very point despite a flood of historically radical Fed actions that began even before the recession did.

All of these people are really smart. They're just working from the wrong premise.

Fifteen months later, the unanticipated meltdown was nearing its end, but by then the consensus "outlook" appeared anything but "strikingly benign." On February 24, 2009, an AP article quoted an equity trader saying, "There's nowhere to hide anymore"; a chief investment strategist saying, "This proverbial lack of clarity is damaging market psychology"; and a financial advisor saying, "People left and right are throwing in the towel."[13] Ten days later, the stock market bottomed; then it tripled.

The inability of economists to predict trend changes in financial markets and the economy did not emerge suddenly in 2007. It has been consistent since the dawn of the profession. An IMF report from 2000 testified, "Earlier U.S. recessions were also missed by forecasters, as Victor Zarnowitz, an expert in the assessment of economic forecasts, pointed out in a 1986 paper."[14] Fourteen years after that time, the IMF concluded, "the record of failure to predict recessions is virtually unblemished."[15] A decade after that, "A repeat of the study found that exactly *zero* economic forecasters saw the 2009 recession coming.[16] This is a staggering degree of failure. Economists cannot see around corners, yet they keep telling us what they think lies around the corner.

Economists don't miss just big changes. Their errors are fractal. In June 2011, Pundit Press put together a compilation of headlines about economic news that included the word *unexpected*. They found 25 of them in the first five months of that year, an average of more than one per week.[17]

Futurists who are this thoroughly wrong about causes and effects might be using an inappropriate model of causality. At the very least, we can say that the extent to which reality—in every nuanced way—has continually contradicted both their expectations and their rationales is in neat accord with our case that the mechanics paradigm is misapplied to finance and macroeconomics.

Unrest within the Profession

Economists' failure to anticipate the economic contraction of 2002 and especially that of 2007-2009 prompted not only bitter criticism from outside the profession but also intense soul-searching within it.

On October 6, 2002, Paul Samuelson, a co-founder of modern economics and popularizer of the economics profession through textbooks and *Newsweek* magazine articles, decried his profession's half-century flirtation with terminology of "false precision." He admitted, "We are at a loss for words. If nothing else, *this baffling economy has defeated the vocabulary of economics*."[18] (The vocabulary of socionomics—introduced in Part II of this book—can fix the problem.) Samuelson's statement is deeply true. He was unaware at the time, however, that his passionate expression of perplexity appeared just three days from the daily closing low for the 2½-year bear market. Economists are not cognizant of what motivates them to express such sentiments near stock-market lows, but socionomics uniquely explains their timing, as we will see in Chapters 17, 18 and 22.

Samuelson's declaration of exasperation was just a prequel. Seven years later, as the stock market and the economy headed into their lows of 2009, scores of economists began criticizing their profession's performance and in some cases even questioning its fundamental ideas. Here are some of the most revealing commentaries:

January 9, 2009, *PBS News Hour:*

Economists Explain Why Hints of the Economic Crisis Eluded Them

Some of the nation's brightest economists failed to predict the foreclosure crisis and economic recession that followed. No one connected the dots in time to warn the public.

Paul Solman, interviewer: "The convention itself was packed with top-flight economists, holding forth to peers and newly minted PhDs. But many didn't warn us. Why were so many blindsided?"

Alan Blinder, Princeton University: "I think the fair answer is nobody thought that this might happen. The number of things that have gone wrong and the ferocity with which they have gone wrong, I think, was beyond the imagination of almost everyone."

Frank Levy, Massachusetts Institute of Technology: "I think part of the reason that many people didn't know is that the people who were issuing all these derivatives had big incentives to keep what they were doing secret."

Ken Arrow, Stanford University: "We [had] no reason to distrust their intelligence in the investment banks, so we took it for granted these people protect themselves. We were wrong, obviously."

Joseph Stiglitz, Columbia University: "People wanted to believe that markets were self-regulating. And if that was the case, you couldn't have a bubble, because if there was a bubble, you needed to have somebody do something about it."

William Darity, Duke University: "There is not much of a tendency to hire economists who think outside of the box."

George Akerlof, University of California, Berkeley: "I think the major thing was that people simply were too trusting. They trusted that they could buy mortgages and things like that which simply were not going to pay off. They should have been much more careful."

Laura Tyson, University of California, Berkeley: "A central lesson is that this is a kind of Greek tragedy, where the explanation of the tragedy is human failings deep within what it means to be human."

Robert Shiller, Yale University: "The basic problem I would say is that we became overconfident, and then we discovered that it was built on faulty premises, and now our confidence is crashing."

Andrew Lo, Massachusetts Institute of Technology: "Neuroscientists have shown that financial gain triggers the exact same reward circuitry in the brain that cocaine does; it makes you relax and be a lot less concerned about risk."[19]

The psychology-oriented economists in the final three comments skated closest to the mark, but the profession still needs a comprehensive theoretical framework within which their observations can fit.

January-February 2009, *Foreign Policy*:

The financial crisis has killed the claim that economics deserves to be treated as a science. The measure of a science is its capacity to explain, predict, and prescribe. And most economists not only failed to anticipate the nature and evolution of the catastrophe, but their conflicting recommendations on how to stabilize the situation exposed the unreliability of their knowledge.

Policy gyrations and faulty calls have revealed that economics itself is in crisis: The experts simply have no idea what to do. The fault lies…with the accumulated body of economic knowledge that failed miserably to equip policymakers with more reliable tools to anticipate and navigate the crisis.[20]

February 2009, The Kiel Institute:

The Financial Crisis and the Systemic Failure of Academic Economists
The global financial crisis has made clear a systemic failure of the economics profession. In our hour of greatest need, societies around the world are left to grope in the dark without a theory.

It is not enough to put the existing model to one side, observing that one needs "exceptional measures for exceptional times." <u>What we need are models capable of envisaging such "exceptional times."</u> On the macroeconomic level, <u>it would be desirable to develop early warning schemes that indicate the formation of bubbles.</u> Indeed, analysis of these issues would require <u>a different type of mathematics</u> than that which is generally used now by many prominent economic models.

The implicit view behind standard models is that markets and economies are inherently stable and that they only temporarily get off track. The confinement of macroeconomics to models of stable states that are perturbed by limited external shocks and that neglect the intrinsic recurrent boom-and-bust dynamics of our economic system is remarkable.

Many economic models are built upon the twin assumptions of "rational expectations" and a representative agent. The "representative agent" aspect of many current models in macroeconomics (including macro finance) means that modelers subscribe to the most extreme form of <u>conceptual reductionism</u> (Lux and Westerhoff, 2009): by assumption, all concepts applicable to the macro sphere (i.e., the economy or its financial system) are fully reduced to concepts and knowledge for the lower-level domain of the individual agent. The major problem is that despite its many refinements, this is not at all an approach based on, and confirmed by, empirical research. The corner stones of many models in finance and macroeconomics are rather maintained <u>despite all the contradictory evidence discovered in empirical research.</u> Much of this literature shows that human subjects act in a way that <u>bears no resemblance to the rational expectations paradigm</u> and also have problems discovering "rational expectations equilibria" in repeated experimental settings. What we are arguing is that as a modeling requirement, <u>internal consistency must be complemented with external consistency.</u> It is highly problematic to insist on a specific view of humans in economic settings that is irreconcilable with evidence.

"Rational expectations" forces individuals' expectations into harmony with the structure of the economist's own model. This concept can be thought of as merely a way to close a model. Thus, even when applied economics research or psychology provide insights about how individuals actually form expectations, these insights cannot be used within RE models.

Yet, financial economists gave little warning to the public about the fragility of their models; even as they saw individuals and businesses build a financial system based on their work. The majority of economists thus failed to warn policy makers about the threatening system crisis and ignored the work of those who did.

Paradoxically self-reinforcing feedback effects within the profession may have led to the dominance of a paradigm that has no solid methodological basis and whose empirical performance is, to say the least, modest. Moreover, the current academic agenda has largely crowded out research on the inherent causes of financial crises.[21]

The rest of this book will offer a fresh, new perspective that fulfills the authors' requirements for a new model. It is a fundamental re-thinking of economics and finance, it is compatible with reality, it can be used to anticipate bubbles, and it is consistent with a different type of mathematics—not the mathematics pertaining mostly to machines but the mathematics pertaining mostly to life forms (see *The Wave Principle of Human Social Behavior*).

February 21, 2009, former Fed Chairman Paul Volcker on the economy:

"It's broken down in the face of almost all expectation and prediction. Even the experts don't quite know what's going on."[22]

May 2009, Wharton Business School:

[W]hat about economists? Of all the experts, weren't they the best equipped to see around the corners and warn of impending disaster? "It's not just that they missed it, they positively denied that it would happen," says Wharton finance professor Franklin Allen, arguing that many economists used mathematical models that failed to account for the critical roles that banks and other financial institutions play in the economy. Over the past 30 years or so, economics has been dominated by an "academic orthodoxy" which says economic cycles are driven by players in the "real economy"—producers and consumers of goods and services, while banks and other financial institutions have been assigned little importance.

As computers have grown more powerful, academics have come to rely on mathematical models to figure how various economic forces will interact. But many of those models simply dispense with certain variables that stand in the way of clear conclusions, says Wharton management professor Sidney G. Winter. <u>Commonly missing are hard-to-measure factors like human psychology and people's expectations about the future</u>, he notes. Clearly, he says, <u>rational behavior is not that dependable</u>, or else people would not do self-destructive things like taking out mortgages they could not afford, a key factor in the financial crisis. Nor would completely rational executives at financial firms invest in securities backed by those risky mortgages, which they did.[23]

<u>July 16, 2009, *The Economist*:</u>

Of all the economic bubbles that have been pricked, few have burst more spectacularly than the reputation of economics itself. Barry Eichengreen, a prominent American economic historian, says the crisis has "cast into doubt much of what we thought we knew about economics." Add these criticisms together and <u>there is a clear case for reinvention, especially in macroeconomics.</u>[24]

<u>Nobel laureate Myron J. Scholes in the same issue of *The Economist*:</u>

"To say something has failed, <u>you have to have something to replace it, and so far we don't have a new paradigm to replace efficient markets.</u>" The trouble with behavioural economics, he adds, is that "it really hasn't shown in aggregate how it affects prices."[25]

<u>September 2009, *The New York Times*:</u>

The real failure, according to finance experts and economists, was in the quants' mathematical models of risk that suggested the arcane stuff was safe. <u>What they didn't sufficiently take into account was human behavior.</u>[26]

<u>February 2010, Stanford University economist Russ Roberts in *The Wall Street Journal*:</u>

Is the Dismal Science Really a Science?
There is no consensus on the cause of the crisis or the best way forward. [M]ost sciences make progress. But in economics, theories that were once discredited surge back into favor. Which paradigm is the "right" way to think about the boom and the bust? Or are they all wrong?

I once thought econometrics—the application of statistics to economic questions—would settle these disputes and the truth would out. But I've come to believe there are too many factors we don't have data on, too many connections between the variables we don't understand and can't model or identify. I've started asking economists if they can name a study that applied sophisticated econometrics to a controversial policy issue where the study was so well done that one side's proponents had to admit they were wrong. I don't know of any. Perhaps what we're really doing is confirming our biases.

Nearly all economists accept the fundamental principles of microeconomics—that incentives matter, that trade creates prosperity—even if we disagree on the implications for public policy. But the business cycle and the ability to steer the economy out of recession may be beyond us.[27]

Roberts' last paragraph is as direct as a laser beam: Economists understand what they call microeconomics very well, but they have no clue about so-called macroeconomic trends. To understand that causality requires a new field of study, one that the rest of this book describes.

June 17, 2010, *The Wall Street Journal*:

Nearly three years after the crisis began, business school academics are sifting through the wreckage of long-held theories and developing new ideas. Certainties about the healthy functioning of always-efficient, rational markets were shattered by the upheaval. Central tenets like the law of one price, which holds that markets will always ensure two similar assets have similar prices, were called into question by the crisis and the bubbles that preceded it, says Denis Gromb, finance professor at INSEAD business school in Fontainebleau, France. The overvaluation of many stocks during the boom years and then widespread undervaluation as markets sank in 2008 and 2009 both pose big challenges to standard theories that hold that an asset's price reflects its fundamental value, he says. "This really calls for a big change in the paradigm." The big task now is to find the patterns in what can look like chaos and build new models that do a better job of reflecting the realities of markets.[28]

September 24, 2010, *Marketwatch*:

Federal Reserve Board Chairman Ben Bernanke [speaking at an economics conference at Princeton University] on Friday defended new Keynesian economic models even though they failed to predict the financial crisis. Bernanke said the failure of the economic models did not mean that they were irrelevant or significantly flawed. Bernanke said the financial system and regulators took for granted that some financial assets could always be sold at prices close to their fundamental values. Three areas of research he recommended were human behavior in times of panic, the role of liquidity in markets and how asset bubbles are created and pop. Bernanke said that more work is needed about instances when decision makers are so uncertain that they cannot fathom what might happen next.[29]

As we will see, there is a method that proves useful in all four of these areas: human behavior in times of panic (and times of calm, and times of euphoria), the role of liquidity in markets (and why it waxes and wanes), how asset bubbles arise and pop (not as an exception to the rule but within a consistent model) and decision-making in times of uncertainty (which in finance is always).

October 16, 2010, *The New York Times*:

Why do economists argue at all? Why isn't a right answer self-evident?[30]

December 20, 2010, *The San Francisco Chronicle*:

Unlike physics, in which atoms consistently follow discernible rules, economic models seek to predict the aggregate outcome of events that depend on individual or institutional behaviors that remain, so far, unpredictable. "Economics can be thought of as physics with strategic atoms who keep trying to foil any efforts to understand them," Colander said.[31]

November 29, 2012, *Bloomberg Businessweek*:

Where Coase and Wang see too little demand for new ideas, Sims sees too little supply.

The financial crisis forced economists to confront the limitations of their profession. Former Federal Reserve Chairman Alan Greenspan admitted as much when he told Congress in October 2008 that markets might not regulate themselves after all.[32]

But markets *do* regulate themselves, as the rest of this book will show.

August 24, 2013, two professors of the philosophy of science in *The New York Times*:

> It's easy to understand why economics might be mistaken for science. It uses quantitative expression in mathematics and the succinct statement of its theories in axioms and derived "theorems," so economics looks a lot like the models of science we are familiar with from physics. The trouble with economics is that it lacks the most important of science's characteristics—a record of improvement in predictive range and accuracy. In fact, when it comes to economic theory's track record, there isn't much predictive success to speak of at all.
>
> Moreover, many economists don't seem troubled when they make predictions that go wrong. What is economics up to if it isn't interested enough in predictive success to adjust its theories the way a science does when its predictions go wrong?[33]

The answer to this mystery is that conventional economists adhere to bedrock assumptions of rational reactions to exogenous causes and of equilibrium punctuated by shocks, and they simply *cannot imagine* any alternative to it.

In June 2009, a champion of the random walk model defended the reigning causal model: "It's ridiculous," he said, to blame the financial crisis on the efficient market hypothesis. "If you are leveraged 33-1, and you're holding long-term securities and using short-term indebtedness, and then there's a run on the bank—which is what happened to Bear Stearns—how can you blame that on efficient market theory?"[34] It is true that the efficient market hypothesis is not responsible for the crisis per se, but it is responsible for its adherents' blindness to its precursory signals, one being precisely the exceptional level of optimism and complacency implied by speculators' financing long term speculations with short term debt at 33-to-1 leverage.

The Profession Failed, but Will It Change?

After the Great Recession ended in June 2009, a handful of the world's most prominent economists admitted that their profession is unequipped for macroeconomic forecasting. In July 2009, Harvard Professor of Economics Gregory Mankiw conceded, "Fluctuations in economic activity are largely unpredictable."[35] In January 2010, Eugene Fama, father of EMH and (refreshingly) a proud non-macroeconomist, told *The New Yorker*, "I'd love to know more about what causes business cycles. I used to do macroeconomics, but I gave [it] up long ago. Economics is not very good at explaining swings in economic activity. We don't know what causes recessions. We've never known."[36] This report came out the same month:

Downturn a learning experience for economists
Though some believe forecast methods won't change

The turbulence has been historic: a plunge in home values, a surge of foreclosures, a tidal wave of layoffs. More than 7.2 million jobs swept away.... The Wall Street crisis cascaded through the economy, washing the nation into the deepest, longest downturn in seven decades. As the economic storm of the past two years approached, most economists badly underestimated its intensity—or didn't see it coming at all. Yet even now, the experts differ about what lessons they have learned from this episode, if any.

"The issue is, what should we do to not let that happen again?" said [ ], director of research at the Federal Reserve Bank of Atlanta. "Certainly, you can't go through an event like this and not spend some serious time reconsidering the framework in which you are operating."

Yet forecaster [ ] bristles at the charge that economists misread the signals and must revise their approach. The economy was tipped from modest growth to deep and painful recession in a series of turning points that simply were not predictable, he said. Housing, for instance, did not have to deflate the way it did, said [ ], director of the Economic Forecasting Center at [ ]. "And you can never predict when a bubble will burst, because by definition, a bubble is nonfundamental. And you can't see a nonfundamental shock coming." Collapse of the big financial firms was in many ways like an old-fashioned bank run, he said. "I don't think we were moving toward the abyss until after the Lehman collapse. Bank runs are not predictable."

"Even moderate recessions tend to be anomalous events that you don't see coming," said the Fed's [ ]. ...the world of practical economics has not yet caught up, [ ] said. "There hasn't been much change from economic forecasters. They are still using the same historic patterns to try and predict the future. The way I look at it, we really haven't learned much."[37]

The third paragraph above quotes the same economist who offered the faulty analysis we reviewed from 2006. He says *all* of the spectacular events of the previous three years "simply were not predictable." Indeed they were not, at least with the mechanics paradigm's methods. Yet he still "bristles at the charge that economists misread the signals." If they did not misread the signals, shouldn't they reconsider the validity of the signals?

His comment, "*You* can never predict when a bubble will burst," actually means, "*I* can't predict when a bubble will burst," implying, "since I can't do it, nobody can." As related in Chapter 23, most economists agree with him. On the other hand, the guys who famously shorted subprime mortgages and loaded up on bearish credit default swaps in 2006 did a pretty good job of it, probably because not one of them was an economist.[38]

His comment, "you can't see a *non*fundamental shock coming," implies that "fundamental" shocks are somehow predictable, about which the writer of the article cogently observed, "But economists disagree. What is a shock? If something is an economic 'shock,' it is, almost by definition, impossible to account for it in making predictions."

In the end, honest economists admitted—sometimes testily—that their tools failed to anticipate the most dramatic economic event since 1929-1933. Yet the same economists went right back to predicting the economy every quarter thereafter, and the media have continued to quote them.[39] The rebound in the economy since June 2009 allowed clients to relax and economists to return to business as usual. This quite natural transition puzzled writers at *The Telegraph*: "2009 ought to have been the year that economists well and truly fell from grace. But bizarrely enough, it hasn't happened."[40] The bankruptcy of conventional methods for predicting trends in the macroeconomy has not gone away, though; it's just hiding again.

Obviously, the first article's subhead was right: "forecast methods won't change." Eugene Fama agreed. When asked, "Will there be big changes?" he replied, "I don't see any."[41] The January 6, 2011 issue of *Oxford Analytica* explained why:

> **Paradigm shift?** It is premature to conclude that there is some fundamental change in economic thinking at work. Paradigms are not discarded unless there is another paradigm to replace them—as emphasised by Hungarian philosopher of science Imre Lakatos. A superior paradigm should not only resolve anomalies that have arisen—in this case the origins and persistence of the economic and financial crisis—but also address the same broad array of issues and problems of the paradigm that it is to replace. While it may be possible to suggest revisions to this paradigm at the margins, there is little evidence that an alternative paradigm to understand the economic world is gaining widespread credibility among mainstream

economists. Although the crisis has exposed serious weaknesses in the neoclassical synthesis, no alternative paradigm is likely to eclipse it in the short term. Moreover, there are strong intellectual and social pressures that work to hold the paradigm in place.[42]

At the bottom of the next economic contraction, people will again agree that economic theory is worthless for anticipating economic change. Then, in the recovery—unless there is a fundamental shift in theoretical perspective (which may be unlikely over the long run; see Chapter 40)—they will go back to relying on economists' forecasts.

In any other field of endeavor, repeated failures would prompt a restatement of fundamental principles. Not so in economics. At least, not yet.

Calls for a New Model

Briefly after the crash of 1987, conventional economics came under attack from a small band of behavioral economists. During the far larger 2008 financial crisis, a broader array of thinkers began to realize that something is amiss with respect to the entire edifice of neoclassical economic theory as it applies both to finance and to the economy as a whole. As early as July 2008, physicist and science writer Mark Buchanan declared in *New Scientist*,

> Everything from observations of irrationality in traders to the statistics of market fluctuation is telling us something is wrong with received wisdom and a growing band of researchers has formed the view that <u>we desperately need to develop a new theory of economics</u>.[43]

We *do* desperately need a new theory of economics but not in its entirety. Economics, properly defined as what is now called microeconomics (see Chapter 13), is mostly fine. The disaster area for economists is the accepted paradigm purporting to explain fluctuations in financial markets and in the overall economy.

After the dust had cleared, some fringe thinkers pledged in 2010 to try developing new models:

Economists' Grail: A Post-Crash Model

<u>Physicist</u> Doyne Farmer thinks we should analyze the economy the way we do epidemics and traffic. <u>Psychoanalyst</u> David Tuckett believes the key to markets' gyrations can be found in the works of Sigmund Freud. <u>Economist</u> Roman Frydman thinks we can never forecast the economy with any accuracy.

For decades, most economists, including the world's most powerful central bankers, have supposed that people are rational enough, and the working of markets smooth enough, that the whole economy can be reduced to a handful of equations. They assemble the equations into mathematical models that attempt to mimic the behavior of the economy.

In the wake of a financial crisis and punishing recession that the models failed to capture, a growing number of economists are beginning to question the intellectual foundations on which the models are built. Researchers, some of whom spent years on the academic margins, are offering up a barrage of ideas.... The Institute for New Economic Thinking…so far has approved funding for more than 27 projects…aimed at developing new ways to model the economy. Some of academia's most authoritative figures say the new ideas are…still very far from producing a model that demonstrably improves on the status quo.

[Four academic] economists are hoping to involve dozens of experts on the behavior of consumers, investors and firms in a massive model-building project. Inputs could include everything from historical data to interviews.

Many economists think the next big idea will more likely come from the ranks of younger PhD candidates, who are producing reams of work examining the financial crisis.

Mr. Farmer says he thinks the traditional models will always be useful for certain types of analysis, but isn't optimistic they'll provide the whole solution. "Economic forecasts have never been very good, and it's not clear that if we stick with the methods we're pursuing we'll do any better," he says. "We need to try something new."[44]

Physics and psychoanalysis have provided some valuable insights into financial market behavior. But I don't think people working in these disciplines can model it. The last line says it all: *We need to try something new.*

When should we do it? Roger Farmer of UCLA observed that the field is ripe for a paradigm shift *now*: "The time is absolutely right for new ideas to come in, much as they did in the 1930s and the 1970s."[45] In an article titled, "Economists Debate Why They Blew It,"[46] three comments stand out:

(1) A Nobel-prize winning economist is quoted as saying, "<u>Virtually no one</u> saw...how fragile the system had become."

The key word here is *virtually*. A handful of observers did see it coming. What were *their* tools and perspectives? Shouldn't the profession investigate and test their methods and, if proved out, adopt them?

(2) The article says, "Now economists debate whether they <u>lacked the right tools</u> or <u>needed a different perspective</u>."

The answer is: *both*.

(3) Robert Shiller of Yale rightfully stated, "We want to have <u>a beautiful and elegant model</u>."

Yes, we do.

The socionomic theory of finance is not only beautiful and elegant but also true. That is the subject of the rest of this book.

The Answer to the Mystery

How can it be that events, conditions and authorities' actions have no impact on the stock market? The answer is: They are not causes but *results*. No wonder they don't cause anything.

Results of what? Read on.

NOTES AND REFERENCES

[1] Kanell, Michael E., "Forecaster Sees 'Soft Landing' for Economy," *The Atlanta Journal-Constitution*, August 24, 2006.

[2] "Dallas Fed president: No Recession in Sight," *USA Today*, August 17, 2006.

[3] Cathy Minehan, as quoted in Geewax, Marilyn, "Forecasters, Voters Differ in Viewpoint," *The Atlanta Journal-Constitution*, September 17, 2006.

[4] Geewax, Marilyn, "Bernanke Calms Market," *The Atlanta Journal-Constitution*, March 1, 2007.

[5] As quoted in Morgenson, Gretchen, "The Bank Run We Knew So Little About," *The New York Times*, April 2, 2011.

[6] Hale, David, "The Best Economy Ever," *The Wall Street Journal*, July 31, 2007.

[7] Geewax, Marilyn, "Fed Acts to Encourage Growth," *The Atlanta Journal-Constitution*, September 19, 2007.

[8] Waggoner, John, "Inflation Lurking? Adjust Portfolio, Just in Case," *USA Today*, September 21, 2007.

[9] Hendrick, Bill, "'87 Crash Crew Crowd to Wall Street," *The Atlanta Journal-Constitution*, October 19, 2007, p. G2.

[10] Bernanke, Ben. Remarks at a symposium sponsored by the Federal Reserve Bank of Kansas City, Jackson Hole, Wyoming, August 31, 2007.

[11] Aversa, Jeannine, "Fed Official: Bank Will Protect Economy," Associated Press, October 22, 2007.

[12] Hagenbaugh, Barbara, *USA Today*, November 27, 2007.

[13] Keith Springer, as quoted in Paradis, Tim, "Major Stock Indexes Fall to 1997 Levels," The Associated Press, February 24, 2009.

[14] Loungani, Prakash, "The Arcane Art of Predicting Recessions," *Views and Commentaries*, International Monetary Fund, December 18, 2000.

[15] *Ibid.*

[16] "Economists and Economics," Evanson Asset Management, September 2015.

[17] Adding insult to injury, "University of Michigan economist Edward Gramlich, who went on to serve on the Federal Reserve's board of governors, noted in the early 1980s that UM's national survey of consumers seemed to be a more accurate inflation predictor than the Fed's long-running survey of economists' forecasts."* Everyday people, it seems, are better at forecasting than the professionals.

*Grantham, Russell, "Expert Predictions Often Off the Mark," *The Atlanta Journal-Constitution*, February 6, 2010.

[18] Samuelson, Paul, "Recovery or Recession?" *Newsweek*, written "On October 6, 2002 at 8:00 p.m."

[19] Solman, Paul, "Economists Explain Why Hints of the Economic Crisis Eluded Them," *PBS News Hour*, January 9, 2009.

[20] Naím, Moisés, "An Intellectual Bailout: We Must Add Another Field to the List of Those in Need of Rescuing–Economics Itself," *Foreign Policy*, January-February 2009.

[21] Colander, David and Hans Föllmer, Armin Haas, Michael Goldberg, Katarina Juselius, Alan Kirman, Thomas Lux and Brigitte Sloth, "The Financial Crisis and the Systemic Failure of Academic Economics," *Kiel Working Papers*, Kiel Institute for the World Economy, No. 1489, February 2009.

[22] Connelly, Eileen, "Volcker Sees Crisis Leading to Regulation," Associated Press, February 21, 2009.

[23] "Why Economists Failed to Predict the Financial Crisis," Knowledge at Wharton, May 13, 2009.

[24] "How the discipline should change to avoid the mistakes of the past," *The Economist*, July 16, 2009.

[25] "Efficiency and beyond," *The Economist*, July 16, 2009.

[26] Lohr, Steve, "Wall Street's Math Wizards Forgot a Few Variables," *The New York Times*, September 12, 2009.

[27] Roberts, Russ, "Is the Dismal Science Really a Science?" *The Wall Street Journal*, February 26, 2010.

[28] Gardiner, Beth, "Back to School: Economists Rethink Theories in Light of Global Crisis," *The Wall Street Journal*, June 17, 2010.

[29] Robb, Greg, "Bernanke Defends Economic Models that Missed Crisis," *MarketWatch*, September 24, 2010.

[30] Segal, David, "The X Factor of Economics: People," *The New York Times*, October 16, 2010.

[31] Abate, Tom, "After Calamity, Economics Leaders Rethink Strategy," *The San Francisco Chronicle*, December 20, 2010, p. D10.

[32] "Urging Economists to Step Away from the Blackboard," Bloomberg *Businessweek*, November 29, 2012.

[33] Rosenberg, Alex and Tyler Curtain, "What Is Economics Good For?" *The New York Times*, August 24, 2013.

[34] Nocera, Joe, "Poking Holes in a Theory on Markets," *The New York Times*, June 6, 2009.

[35] Mankiw, N. Gregory, "That Freshman Economics Course Won't be Quite the Same," *St. Petersburg Times*, July 22, 2009.

[36] Cassidy, John, "Interview with Eugene Fama," *The New Yorker*, January 13, 2010.

[37] Kanell, Michael E., "Downturn a Learning Experience for Economists—Though Some Believe Forecast Methods Won't Change," *The Atlanta Journal-Constitution*, January 29, 2010.

[38] Their professions were doctor (Burry), lawyer (Eisman), teacher (Lippman), banker (Hockett) and businessman (Paulsen).

[39] See for example Chapman, Dan, "Atlanta's Economy: 'Quasi-growth' Ahead," *The Atlanta Journal-Constitution*, August 25, 2010; Chapman, Dan, "Economists predict slow-moving recovery," *The Atlanta Journal-Constitution*, November 18, 2010; and Kanell, Michael E., "State economy builds steam," *Atlanta Journal-Constitution*, May 30, 2014.

[40] Conway, Edmund, "The Economic 'Experts' Who Stopped Making Sense," *The Telegraph*, December 31, 2009.

[41] Cassidy, John, "Interview with Eugene Fama," *The New Yorker*, January 13, 2010.

[42] "Global Crisis Fails to End Paradigm," *Oxford Analytica*, January 6, 2011.

[43] Buchanan, Mark, "Why Economic Theory is Out of Whack," *New Scientist*, July 19, 2008.

[44] Whitehouse, Mark, "Economists' Grail: A Post-Crash Model," *The Wall Street Journal*, November 30, 2010.

[45] Coy, Peter, "What Good Are Economists Anyway?" *Business Week*, April 27, 2009.

[46] Kanell, Michael E., "Economists Debate Why They Blew It," *Atlanta Journal Constitution*, January 6, 2010.

Part II:

SOCIONOMIC THEORY

Chapter 6

The Structure of Socionomic Theory

Robert R. Prechter

The causal paradigm on which modern macroeconomics depends is fallacious. One reason it has nevertheless remained dominant is that mainstream economists have evaded validating their ideas through empirical observation. As Noah Smith commented,

> Economics is a theory-centric field. Until the last decade or so, theory dominated the literature and empirics took a back seat. In the world of engineering and practical application, that is a recipe for trouble. Theories that have not been rigorously tested against data may get papers published and may win Nobel prizes, but they will not necessarily work when you try to apply them.[1]

Socionomic theory evolved differently. Socionomics is based on empirics, which led to the induction of hypotheses, which coalesced into a theory.

The perspective presented in this chapter began with numerous observations that financial market movements substantially adhere to a model of fractal fluctuation called the Wave Principle, which Ralph Nelson Elliott derived empirically in the 1930s. It progressed with dozens more observations that exogenous-cause claims fail time and again to account reliably for any aspect of financial market behavior. It coalesced with another empirical observation, that changes in the character of social conditions seem to track changes in the trend of the stock market. The drive to explain these singular perceptions led to the conclusion that they all resulted from the same cause. From there, it remained to acquire statistical support for the theory, rebut challenges to it, refine its ideas and conduct studies in its defense. (For some of the early details, see Chapter 44.)

The empirically driven approach to the study of economics has been rare since the days of Adam Smith. Modern economists have instead proceeded substantially by way of theoretical constructs, mathematical equations and *ceteris paribus* ("all else remaining constant") clauses (see Chapter 33). There is not a single *ceteris paribus* clause in this book. All of its arguments and conclusions are based on real-world data.

In further contrast to most tomes on economics, this book is full of charts. A striking study[2] from 2012 showed that when academic economists from leading universities worldwide looked for truth in a chart, they came up with wrong answers only 3% of the time. When researchers granted their requests to see statistical data as well, their frequency of being "spectacularly wrong" leaped to 61%; and when they had only the statistical data from which to work it rose to 72%. You can understand a lot from charts, and you can miss a lot without them.

I have decided to introduce socionomics not in the same order it was developed but with a presentation of its theoretical framework. With that basis established, each time you encounter a new point you can slide it into the right theoretical compartment. This seems to be a good approach for keeping a multi-faceted theory as simple as possible to understand.

The Wave Principle of Human Social Behavior and the New Science of Socionomics (1999) and *Pioneering Studies in Socionomics* (2003) provide a grounding in socionomic theory. Part II of this book both condenses and expands upon previous observations. The first two chapters of this section are fairly dense. Once you get through them, the book will resume its easy flow.

Mechanical Social Causality vs. Socionomic Causality

The foregoing chapters have described, with respect to financial and macroeconomic theory, what we may designate as the *mechanics paradigm*, with its causal hypotheses of exogenous cause and rationally motivated reaction. We will now investigate the *socionomics paradigm*, with its causal hypotheses of endogenous cause and pre-rationally motivated action.

It may seem presumptuous to describe socionomics as a paradigm, but it offers an explanation of social causality differing to that great a degree from the standard view. Socionomics is not in the least derivative of the reigning paradigm. Mechanics and socionomics describe two different worlds, each with its own laws of causality.

In the fields of economics, finance, history and sociology, the paradigm of mechanical causality is rarely stated but almost always implicit, probably because theorists see no alternative explanation. In the field of socionomics, the causal formulation is always explicit, because we see, understand and reject the alternative explanation.

Starting Point

In terms of the social aggregate, the mechanical presumption is that how people act is the primary cause of how people feel. Socionomics proposes that how people feel is the primary cause of how people act. More concisely, the mechanical presumption is that *social actions motivate social mood*. Socionomics proposes that *social mood motivates social actions*.

Definitions

Mood

While dictionaries' first definition of *mood* is usually "state of mind or feeling," the original Old English word meant *disposition*, which means *inclination*. The definition most compatible with the hypothesis of socionomic causality is that mood is an unconscious state of mind inclining a person to bring to consciousness certain types of emotions, which in turn foster attitudes and prompt actions expressing those emotions. Mood differs from emotions, which can have external causes and always have external referents. For a discussion of mood vs. emotions, see Chapter 19.

Herding

Herding is the process of participating in coordinated actions with other people. It can involve small or large groups. Herding can be consciously and rationally motivated (see Chapter 19), but more often it is unconsciously and pre-rationally motivated. Socionomic causality involves the latter version.

Social Mood

Social mood is an unconsciously shared mental disposition that arises in humans when they interact socially. It arises independently from events and is endogenously regulated. It is also unremembered. Social mood predisposes members of society toward feeling and expressing through action certain characteristic sets of emotions. Humans' impulses to herd in contexts of uncertainty allow social mood free rein to regulate social actions. Social mood does not spread by contagion or propagation. It is not imparted by leaders, nor is it imposed by authorities. It arises from mutual interaction—the way an economic marketplace does—although in this case the cooperation is only mental. Choices of *foci* for social mood expression—such as which investment to own, which pop star to idolize or which enemy to attack—do seem to spread via the contagion/propagation model (see Chapter 19).

Waves of Social Mood

Social mood fluctuates constantly between "positive" and "negative" poles. Fluctuations in social mood take the form of a self-affine, hierarchical fractal denoted the Wave Principle (WP) and described by the Elliott wave model (EW). WP's fundamental structures are called *waves*. Social attitudes and actions impelled by waves of social mood reflect the mood's direction (positive or negative), extremity and position in the fractal form.

Mood Sharing

Mood sharing is the process whereby interacting people communicate unconsciously in a feedback system of mutually causal signaling so as to participate in waves of social mood.

Socionomic Actions

Socionomic actions are actions of social aggregations that express social mood. Socionomic actions result from decision-making in a social context of significant uncertainty (as in financial markets, business and politics) or arbitrariness (as with fads and fashions). Under conditions of uncertainty, human minds default to pre-rationally motivated herding, which social mood regulates.

Socionomic actions differ from shared actions taken entirely for practical reasons, for example when people rush to take advantage of a sale or to evacuate an area ahead of a tsunami. When people possess undisputed facts and clear options in a context of certainty, they usually act rationally to meet a desired goal, and occasionally conditions are such that they do so in concert. This description applies to economic markets for utilitarian goods and services (see Part III), where objective factors such as price and utility matter.

Social actions that are not primarily socionomic actions are rare. Many social actions that most people *think* are rational responses to external stimuli are not so at all. Aggregate voting results (see *Socionomic Causality in Politics*, 2017), for example, are due primarily not to rational behavior but to socionomic behavior. Trends in the economy also ebb and flow with social mood.

It makes a difference how far one goes to investigate underlying causes. Although one would be inclined to classify mass flight from an erupting volcano as a non-socionomic social action, people's original decision to settle at the base of a volcano may have had a socionomic cause whereby they complacently ignored its dangers because of shared optimism resulting from an elevated social mood. If so, the later mass flight would ultimately have had a socionomic cause.

Direction, Extremity, Tenor, Character and Speed

Social mood has two primary aspects: *direction* (positive or negative) and *extremity*. Combined expressions of direction and extremity such as "mildly positive," "extremely negative" and "neutral" convey the *tenor* of social mood and its manifestation in the sum of social actions. Elliott wave designations (see *Elliott Wave Principle*, 1978) provide a basis for far more specific descriptions of past, current and future tenors of social mood (see Chapter 23 for an example).

Character refers to the emotional attributes of social attitudes and actions that express social mood. They populate polar constructs, such as optimistic/pessimistic, confident/fearful, forbearing/angry, etc. (For a list, see Chapter 14 of *The Wave Principle of Human Social Behavior*.)

Speed is the rate of mood change. A stock market crash or "melt-up" records a high-speed condition; a subdued trading range or sluggish trend records a low-speed condition. The Appendix to Chapter 13 explains some conditions under which changes in the speed of mood change are predictable under the Elliott wave model.

Predicting a wave of a certain degree in the positive or negative direction is to forecast tenor. Predicting an increase in social expressions of benevolence or anger is to forecast character. Predicting an increase or decrease in the rate of mood change is to forecast speed.

Socionomics

Socionomics (*so-shee-o-nom'-ics* or *so-see-o-nom'-ics*) is the study of social mood and its influence over social attitudes and actions. It provides a basis for explaining the genesis of past social events and for anticipating future ones, thereby offering a new science of history and social prediction.

Socionomist

A socionomist (*so-she-on'-o-mist* or *so-see-on'-o-mist*) is a specialist in the study and application of socionomics.

Sociometer

A sociometer (*so-she-om'-i-ter* or *so-see-om'-i-ter*) is a measure comprising data on social actions that express social mood. For details, see Chapter 7.

The Socionomic Hypothesis

The socionomic hypothesis is that waves of social mood regulate the tenor and character of social attitudes and actions.

One who accepts this hypothesis is said to have achieved the *socionomic insight.*

Socionomic Theory

Socionomic theory proposes that endogenous waves of social mood, impelled at the individual level by unconscious herding impulses and regulated at the aggregate level by a self-affine, hierarchical fractal designated the Wave Principle (see upcoming discussion), determine the tenor and character of social attitudes and actions in contexts of uncertainty.

The Socionomic Theory of Finance

The socionomic theory of finance (STF), a subset of socionomic theory, proposes that speculators' spontaneous commands, impelled unconsciously at the individual level by herding impulses and mood sharing and regulated at the aggregate level by waves of social mood fluctuating in accordance with the Wave Principle, determine prices in financial markets.

Primary Components of Socionomic Theory

Figure 1 displays the major hypotheses of socionomics. As shown at the center of the diagram, the two fundamental bases of socionomic theory are:

(1) **The Socionomic Hypothesis**: Social mood motivates social actions. Fluctuations in social mood regulate the tenor and character of social actions.

(2) **The Wave Principle (WP) and the Elliott wave model (EW)**: Social mood fluctuates according to a robust (as defined in Chapter 3 of *The Wave Principle of Human Social Behavior*), self-affine, hierarchical fractal governed by a compounded 5-3 (Fibonacci) relationship, as described by Ralph N. Elliott in 1938 and 1940.[3] This form, called the Wave Principle (WP), regulates fluctuations in sociometers such as the stock market as well as the varying tenor of other mood-induced social actions. The Elliott wave model (EW) comprises all available knowledge of WP.

Although the second tenet is an integral part of socionomic theory, one may investigate socionomic causality irrespective of the validity of the Wave Principle. If you are resolutely against it, ignore it.

STRUCTURE OF SOCIONOMIC THEORY

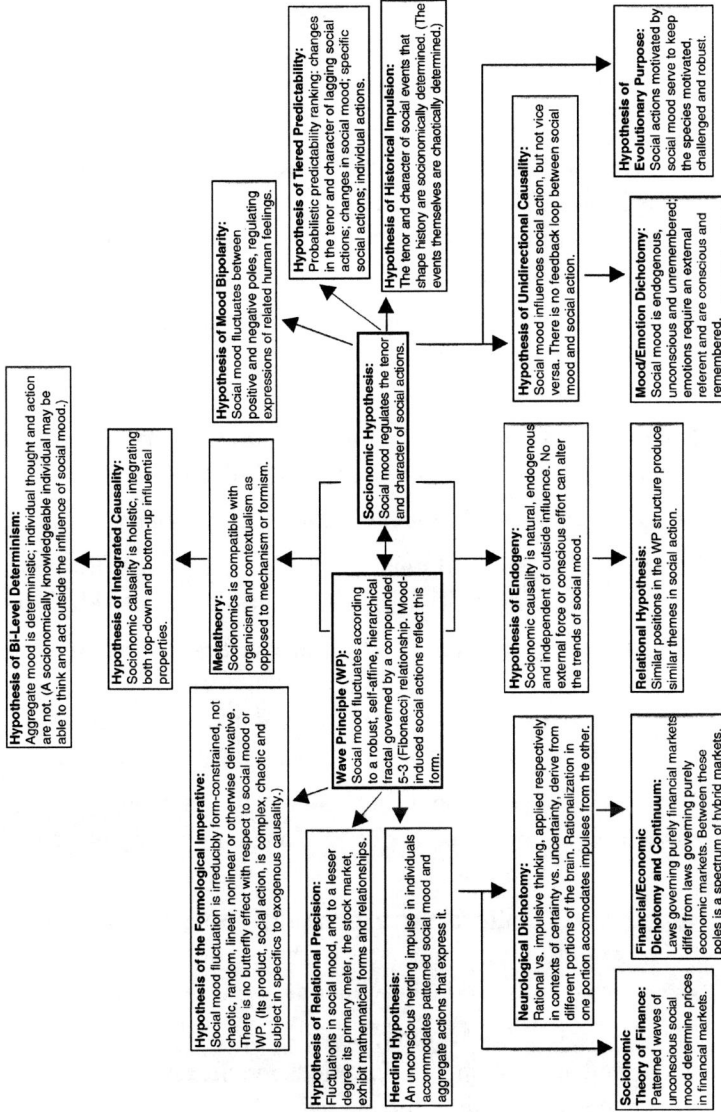

Hypothesis of Bi-Level Determinism:
Aggregate mood is deterministic; individual thought and action are not. (A socionomically knowledgeable individual may be able to think and act outside the influence of social mood.)

Hypothesis of Integrated Causality:
Socionomic causality is holistic, integrating both top-down and bottom-up influential properties.

Metatheory:
Socionomics is compatible with organicism and contextualism as opposed to mechanism or formism.

Hypothesis of Mood Bipolarity:
Social mood fluctuates between positive and negative poles, regulating expressions of related human feelings.

Hypothesis of Tiered Predictability:
Probabilistic predictability ranking; changes in the tenor and character of lagging social actions; changes in social mood; specific social actions; individual actions.

Hypothesis of Historical Impulsion:
The tenor and character of social events that shape history are socionomically determined. (The events themselves are chaotically determined.)

Socionomic Hypothesis:
Social mood regulates the tenor and character of social actions.

Hypothesis of Unidirectional Causality:
Social mood influences social action, but not vice versa. There is no feedback loop between social mood and social action.

Hypothesis of Evolutionary Purpose:
Social actions motivated by social mood serve to keep the species motivated, challenged and robust.

Mood/Emotion Dichotomy:
Social mood is endogenous, unconscious and unremembered; emotions require an external referent and are conscious and remembered.

Wave Principle (WP):
Social mood fluctuates according to a robust, self-affine, hierarchical fractal governed by a compounded 5-3 (Fibonacci) relationship. Mood-induced social actions reflect this form.

Hypothesis of the Formological Imperative:
Social mood fluctuation is irreducibly form-constrained, not chaotic, random, linear, nonlinear or otherwise derivative. There is no butterfly effect with respect to social mood or WP. (Its product, social action, is complex, chaotic and subject in specifics to exogenous causality.)

Hypothesis of Relational Precision:
Fluctuations in social mood, and to a lesser degree its primary meter, the stock market, exhibit mathematical forms and relationships.

Herding Hypothesis:
An unconscious herding impulse in individuals accommodates patterned social mood and aggregate actions that express it.

Hypothesis of Endogeny:
Socionomic causality is natural, endogenous and independent of outside influence. No external force or conscious effort can alter the trends of social mood.

Relational Hypothesis:
Similar positions in the WP structure produce similar themes in social action.

Neurological Dichotomy:
Rational vs. impulsive thinking, applied respectively in contexts of certainty vs. uncertainty, derive from different portions of the brain. Rationalization in one portion accommodates impulses from the other.

Financial/Economic Dichotomy and Continuum:
Laws governing purely financial markets differ from laws governing purely economic markets. Between these poles is a spectrum of hybrid markets.

Socionomic Theory of Finance:
Patterned waves of unconscious social mood determine prices in financial markets.

© 2004-2016 Robert R. Prechter Jr.
The Socionomics Institute (www.socionomics.net)

Figure 1

From these two bases spring five sub-hypotheses of socionomics:

(1) **Metatheory**: Socionomics is compatible metatheoretically with organicism and contextualism as opposed to mechanism or formism (Pepper, 1942[4]). See Chapters 32 and 33.

(2) **Hypothesis of Integrated Causality**: Socionomic causality is compatible with integrated holism, in which both top-down and bottom-up properties contribute to causality. See discussion below and Chapter 37.

(3) **Hypothesis of Bi-Level Determinism**: Social mood is deterministic; individual thought and action are not. A socionomically knowledgeable individual may be able to think and act outside the influence of social mood.

(4) **Hypothesis of Endogeny**: Socionomic causality is natural, endogenous and independent of outside influence. No external force or conscious effort can alter waves of social mood.

(5) **Relational Hypothesis**: Similar positions in the Elliott wave structure produce similar themes in social action.

The socionomic hypothesis alone leads to these formulations:

(1) **Hypothesis of Mood Bipolarity**: Social mood fluctuates between positive and negative poles, regulating expressions of related emotions.

(2) **Hypothesis of Tiered Predictability**: Predictability, always probabilistic, is highest for changes in the tenor and character of lagging social actions, less for changes in social mood, still less for specific social actions, and least for individual actions.

(3) **Hypothesis of Historical Impulsion**: The tenor and character of social events that shape history are socionomically determined. (The events themselves are chaotically determined.)

(4) **Hypothesis of Unidirectional Causality:** Social mood influences social actions, but not vice versa. There is no feedback loop between social mood and social actions.

(5) **Mood/Emotion Dichotomy**: Social mood is endogenous, unconscious and unremembered. Emotions require an external referent and are conscious and remembered.

(6) **Hypothesis of Evolutionary Purpose**: Social actions motivated by social mood serve to keep the human species motivated, challenged and robust.

The Wave Principle, to which fluctuations in social mood adhere, leads to these formulations:

(1) **Hypothesis of the Formological Imperative**: Social mood fluctuation is irreducibly form-constrained, not chaotic, random, linear, nonlinear or otherwise derivative. There is no butterfly effect with respect to social mood. (In contrast, its product, social action, is complex, chaotic and subject in specifics to feedback and exogenous causality.)

(2) **Hypothesis of Relational Precision**: Fluctuations in social mood —and to a lesser degree its primary meter, the stock market— exhibit quasi-geometrical forms and mathematical relationships.

(3) **Herding Hypothesis**: An unconscious herding impulse in individuals facilitates mood-sharing and accommodates the macro-level constraint of patterned social mood and the aggregate actions that express it.

The herding hypothesis leads to these formulations:

(1) **Neurological Dichotomy**: Rational vs. impulsive thinking (including economic vs. financial thinking), applied in contexts of relative certainty vs. uncertainty respectively, derive from different portions of the brain. Rationalization in one portion also accommodates impulses from the other. See Chapter 13.

(2) **Financial/Economic Dichotomy and Continuum**: Laws governing purely financial markets, which are subject to socionomic causality, are fundamentally different from laws governing purely economic markets. See Chapters 12 and 13. Between these poles is a spectrum of hybrid markets. See Chapter 14.

(3) **The Socionomic Theory of Finance (STF)**: Financial speculators' spontaneous commands, impelled unconsciously at the individual level by herding impulses and mood sharing and regulated at the aggregate level by waves of social mood fluctuating in accordance with a self-affine, hierarchical fractal designated the Wave Principle, determine prices in financial markets.

The socionomic theory of finance (STF) is a subset of socionomic theory. Aside from this chapter and Chapter 10, the primary focus of this book is on the STF-related boxes in Figure 1.

The diagram in Figure 1 and these lists are hardly inclusive of all the thoughts and ideas attending socionomic theory, but they do show its main aspects and their derivations. Socionomics literature discusses all these aspects and more.

How Socionomic Causality Differs from the Mechanics Paradigm

The underlying idea of causality that social sciences have heretofore borrowed inappropriately from mechanics is that the tenor and character of social actions—portrayed as events and characterized as physical shocks—cause reactive changes in social mood. In contrast, the socionomic hypothesis of social causality is that endogenously regulated waves of social mood determine the tenor and character of social actions. Here is an example of the fundamental difference between socionomic causality and the standard view: Economists typically argue that a strengthening economy causes consumers and business people to become optimistic. A socionomist proposes that increasingly optimistic consumers and business people generate a strengthening economy. Indeed, how could it be otherwise? An improvement in the economy is not a causeless event. Economic expansion must arise from more optimistic decision-making by consumers and business people. Otherwise, optimism would have to result from expansionary actions taken for no reason. Changes in the economy are an eventual *result* of social mood change, not a *cause* of social mood change. Table 1 offers contrasting views of social causality in a variety of areas.

It seems common-sensical to most people that increased aggregate joblessness would produce a negative social mood. That is why our work showing this belief to be false is so important. Socionomics' claim is the opposite: Negative social mood causes joblessness. (It is important not to confuse social mood with personal emotions; see Chapter 19.) This inversion of widely presumed cause and effect is akin to challenging the common-sense conclusion that the sun moves around the earth. It took time to invalidate that cosmological notion, but meticulous testing did it. As our elections study[5] showed, we can meticulously test our claims, too.

Unidirectional Causality: No Feedback Loop between Social Mood and Social Actions

Social mood arises from human interaction. Exactly what signals humans use to communicate unconsciously in regulating social mood is presently unknown. They may communicate by way of sight, sound and

MECHANICAL CAUSALITY (exogenous cause) *Social events determine the tenor and character of social mood.*	SOCIONOMIC CAUSALITY (endogenous cause) *Social mood determines the tenor and character of social events.*
Examples "Recession causes business people to be cautious." "Talented leaders make the population happy." "A rising stock market makes people increasingly optimistic." "Scandals make people outraged." "The availability of derivatives fosters a desire to speculate." "War makes people fearful & angry." "Epidemics cause society to be fearful and depressed." "Happy music makes people smile." "Nuclear bomb testing makes people nervous." "The success of financial television spurred excitement among investors." "An expanding economy puts people in a good mood." "Falling markets make investors fearful." "Good news makes stocks rise, and bad news makes them fall."	*Examples* "Cautious business people cause recession." "A happy population makes leaders appear talented." "Increasingly optimistic people make the stock market rise." "Outraged people seek out scandals." "A desire to speculate fosters the availability of derivatives." "Fearful and angry people make war." "A depressed and fearful society is susceptible to epidemics." "People who want to smile choose happy music." "Nervous people test nuclear bombs." "Excited investors spurred the success of financial television." "People in a good mood generate an expanding economy." "Fearful investors make markets fall." "Not so. These events just coincide sometimes."

Table 1

smell, involving, for example, facial expressions,[6] timbres of voice and pheromones. Mood sharing relies on feedback, as each interacting person's mood-signals and mood-receptors must cooperate with those of others in the aggregate process. This feedback system is limited only to the purpose of initiating, maintaining and regulating social mood.

Chaos and complexity theorists would likely presume another feedback loop of mutual causation between social actions and social mood whereby actions affect mood, which in turn affects actions, and so on, ad infinitum. Yet Chapters 1 and 2 of this book and several chapters in *Pioneering Studies in Socionomics*[7] show that even the most dramatic social actions and events have no effect on investors' moods, neutering the case for a feedback loop of mutual causality between them. All our studies (see Chapters 8 and 10) lead to the conclusion that social mood induces social actions, period. Social actions are results, not causes, placing them outside the system of mental cooperation that causes social mood to fluctuate. That social actions immediately expressing social mood (see Chapter 7) fluctuate according to the Wave Principle (see below) is compatible with this conclusion.

Social activity is nevertheless rich in the production of specific responsive and counter-responsive actions, producing the complex social dynamic in which events cause events, to which feedback does apply. Specific social events produce chains of other specific social events, stemming from the exercise of both rational and non-rational choices. For example, if negative social mood were to lead one government to attack another's territory, the target government would respond, other governments would choose sides, soldiers would be drafted, families would become fatherless, and so on. The assumption of power by authoritarian governments in a time of extremely negative social mood might have local consequences with respect to freedom of expression, travel and commerce for decades. Such indirect, or secondary, results of social mood can be ironic. A positive trend in social mood leads to more employment, higher incomes and an adventuresome spirit, prompting more people to drive, which leads to more traffic deaths, and vice versa. So, more people die on the highways when social mood is positive than when it is negative.[8] Social mood does not regulate these changes directly, but it eventually results in them. Thus, the ultimate effects of social mood trends and the social actions they induce are wide-ranging and chaotic. None of these subsequent events, however, feeds back to affect the endogenously and autonomously regulated fluctuations in social mood.

Always a Mix of Actions

At no time does society produce social actions whose character is entirely one-sided in expressing positive or negative mood. The balance among them is always changing, creating a net expression of overall mood. Figure 1 in Chapter 8 illustrates the idea of social mood's fractal fluctuation and the net tenor of social attitudes and actions it induces.

One must be careful not to confuse a positive or negative trend in social mood with a positive or negative mood per se. A move away from a positive extreme is a new negative *trend*, but a net positive *mood* and actions expressing it still prevail for a while. Likewise, a move away from a negative extreme is a new positive trend, but a net negative mood and actions expressing it still prevail for a while. The balance shifts at the midpoint of the wave structure, as explained in Chapter 8.

The Wave Principle and the Elliott Wave Model

Most academic economists believe that price changes in financial markets follow an essentially random distribution, whether Gaussian or martingale, whether constrained by fat tails or power laws, or whether described as an indefinite fractal or a multifractal. Their agreed-upon claim is that—aside from volatility clustering[9]— one could re-arrange records of net price changes in a financial market on any particular time scale (say, daily) in a thousand ways, and the properties of the resulting plots would be indistinguishable from those of the actual financial price changes.

STF need not incorporate a model of financial price change. Its primary claim is that aggregate stock prices change in accordance with social mood, however it may fluctuate.

Nevertheless, there is a better model than full or substantial randomness. In 1938, Ralph N. Elliott described a specifically patterned, self-affine, hierarchical fractal of financial market price fluctuation that he called the Wave Principle. He observed that stock market movements in the direction of the one-larger trend subdivide into five waves of a certain description, while movements in the opposite direction subdivide into three waves or multiples thereof. The numbers of waves in iterations of this unifying expression accord with the Fibonacci sequence, tying together three of nature's common forms: spirals, waves and branching systems (see *The Wave Principle of Human Social Behavior*). Socionomic theory, on the bases of empirical observation (see Chapter 22) and theoretical compatibility (see Figure 1), holds that fluctuations in social mood and aggregated herding impulses conform to the Wave Principle, which in turn regulates price fluctuations in the stock market as well as in numerous other social activities.

Elliott's detailed description of the Wave Principle, which has since been augmented (see Frost and Prechter, *Elliott Wave Principle*), is called the Elliott wave model. As there is probably more to learn about the Wave Principle, we find it useful to differentiate between Elliott waves in actuality and Elliott waves as Elliott and his successors[10] have modeled them. We use the Wave Principle (WP) for the former designation and the Elliott wave model (EW) for the latter. An overview of the Elliott wave model is available in Chapters 1 and 2 of *The Wave Principle of Human Social Behavior* (1999), and details are provided in *Elliott Wave Principle* (1978).

Figure 2 depicts a simple, idealized Elliott wave at increasing degrees of detail. Each more complex expression serves to depict either subdivisions of, or further development of, the earlier wave.

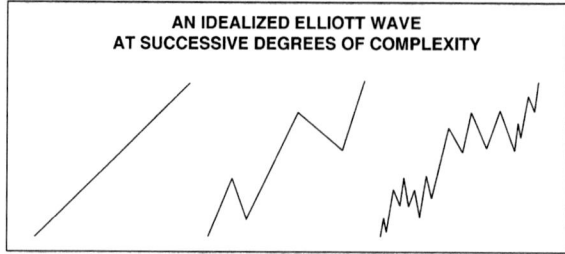

Figure 2

Figure 3 displays the same wave at five degrees of iteration. In order to clarify the underlying idea, these illustrations depict a self-identical fractal rather than one with the varied self-similarity of actual Elliott waves. Even with that restraint, Figure 3 fairly well depicts the "look" of a real financial market, perhaps because—as evidence in Chapters 21, 22 and 23 suggests—it derives from the proper model.

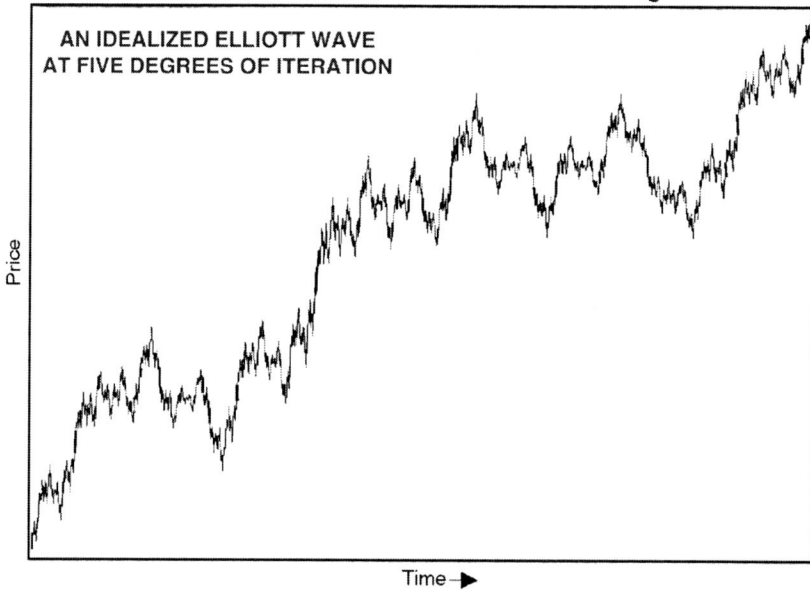

Figure 3

The Wave Principle's hierarchical structure is akin to the hierarchical structure of branching systems found throughout nature. Branches of trees may be all sizes, but they aren't randomly so. A one-degree-narrower branch emerges from its parent, which emerges in the same way from *its* parent. One can categorize the trunk as being of the first degree, branches emerging from the trunk as of the second degree, branches from those branches as of the third degree, and so on, much as R.N. Elliott categorized waves hierarchically in the stock market. Elliott waves and branching systems—as discussed in Chapter 3 of *The Wave Principle of Human Social Behavior*—are natural growth patterns and may in fact be two expressions of the same process.

When delineating waves of social mood, one must take degree into account. Fractal fluctuation means that the stock market might be in a small rising wave within a larger rising wave within a larger falling wave within a larger rising wave, each wave reflecting a positive or negative trend in social mood at its degree. Extremes of social mood—and therefore optimism or pessimism in the stock market—arrive when waves of mood in the same direction reach their terminus at several successive degrees. The higher the degrees involved, the greater the extreme in mood (see Figure 2 in Chapter 21).

The Elliott wave model provides a template of quite specific designations for the tenor of social mood. Recognizing, for instance, that the stock market is in Minor wave 1 of Intermediate wave (3) of Primary wave ⑤ conveys a lot of information about the current state and probable future trends of social mood. Details are beyond the scope of this book, although Chapter 22 offers some details and a good example of the model's application.

Decades after Elliott, Benoit Mandelbrot[11] confirmed mathematically the fractal fluctuation of financial market prices. Although he denied[12] that prices form specific patterns or possess hierarchical degrees of fluctuation, his identification of fractals in financial prices and throughout nature nevertheless provided seminal support for the validity of the Wave Principle.

The persistence of WP is consistent with socionomic theory's conclusion that social actions are effects, never causes, of endogenously regulated social mood. Financial-market prices relentlessly trace out this fractal form regardless of what else is going on. That's why—as explored in Chapter 2—even dedicated exogenous-cause proponents are so often unable to reach any kind of consensus on exogenous causes of even the most radical market behavior.

A Holistic System

Do herding impulses *produce* Elliott waves, or do they *conform* to Elliott waves? This is a metatheoretical question, to which we apply Pepper's[13] metatheoretical constructs. Under the worldview of mechanism, only the first answer can be right, and under the worldview of formism only the second answer can be right. From our viewpoint of organicism, the answer to the question is "both at once." Socionomic causality is holistically inter-connected, with both micro and macro facets cooperating in an integrated system. Chapters 32, 33 and 37 provide further discussion.

The same perspective pertains to the idea of social mood. If someone were to ask, "What causes social mood to change?" we could answer, "El-liott waves," implying that form is in charge.[14] If someone were to ask, "What causes Elliott waves?" we could answer, "changes in social mood," implying that participating individuals are in charge. Since the interplay between participants and form is irreducible, however, neither answer is exclusively correct. Once again, the more complete answer is: "Individual participants both contribute to and conform to Elliott waves of social mood." Under organicism, macro-level behaviors do not either emerge from or cause micro-level behaviors. Macro and micro-level behaviors interact in a mutually causal, organic whole.

Since both the individual and aggregate levels of financial vs. economic behavior (see Chapters 12 and 13) depend upon whether the context for ac-tion is one primarily of certainty or uncertainty (see Chapter 13), and since both the motivation for and the meaning of an individual's action depend upon that context, socionomic theory also contains elements to which the worldview of contextualism applies (see Chapters 32 and 33).

Some mechanists have expressed the impression that top-down cau-sality strikes them as being akin to magic. But the claim of progressive reducibility—by which the properties of subatomic particles explain all causes, properties and structures in the universe while even smaller compo-nents must explain their properties, and so on—makes bottom-up causality sound no less magical. The universe is a wondrous place, and no one can know the superior or correct conceptual view of ultimate causality.

Socionomists nevertheless assert that the organicist and contextualist viewpoints have two advantages: They allow one to conceive of what is hap-pening socionomically more swiftly than the mechanistic viewpoint allows; and they provide for more successful prediction. Based simply on the idea that Elliott waves will continue to manifest no matter what happens otherwise in the world (see Chapters 21, 22 and 23), we have been able to make highly useful forecasts of trend change that—as evidenced throughout Part I and in Chapters 22 and 23—chronically elude mechanistically minded futurists. Elliott waves of social mood and global herding patterns provide excellent bases for prediction, and no available knowledge of individuals' behavior or patterns of behavior can bring one to the same level of efficacy. Such "formological" thinking, as I term it, is a direct route to useful conclusions and an efficient basis for sweeping away what doesn't matter when it comes both to understanding human social behavior and to predicting aspects of it.[15]

After decades of dominance by bottom-up reductionist thinking about causality in all kinds of scientific fields, the trend is beginning to turn toward a more balanced view. Cosmologist George Ellis—co-author with Stephen Hawking of *The Large Scale Structure of Space-Time* (1973)—recently declared,

> It has become clear to me how ubiquitous and important top-down causation is. It is also a counter to strong reductionist ideas, which I believe misrepresent the way causation works in the real world. Top-down causation provides a foundation for genuine emergence. Critics are thinking in terms of the billiard-ball model; [but] lower-level entities are not unchanging; context affects their nature and shapes how they behave. And what about the way that social influences act on the brain?[16]

Socionomics has incorporated this view for four decades, and the Elliott wave model has suggested it for eight decades.

Despite our viewpoint, we strive to be open-minded. If someday mechanists were to discover a chain of causality by which quarks, bosons and atoms combine in human bodies to give individual human beings attributes that in a social setting inalterably produce Elliott waves of social mood and financial-market pricing—or even to establish a different pattern or none at all—we would be all ears. In the meantime, our striving for a thorough integration of micro and macro socionomic ideas at the theoretical level coupled with practical demonstrations of the predictive power of the top-down aspect of socionomics' proposed causal structure should serve to illustrate the relative utility of our holistic point of view.

Compatible Terminology

Working with a holistic system, socionomists tend to avoid using unconditional and unidirectional terms of causality such as *compel, control, demand, determine, dictate, drive, force, impact* and *propel*, which fit the metatheoretical viewpoint of mechanism. Causal terms such as *accommodate, affect, arise, conform, constrain, govern, guide, impel, influence, inform, limit, motivate, participate, prompt, regulate* and *restrict* better fit our metatheoretical viewpoint of organicism. Nevertheless, under the theory's contextualist aspect, socionomists use the former terms when the context requires.

It seems prudent also to eschew using the term *agent* to indicate individual participants in the holistic process. One of Merriam-Webster's[17] definitions of the word is "a person who acts on behalf of another," which is inappropriate to our purposes. Another definition is "a person or thing that causes something to happen," a meaning that pertains only to bottom-up causality. "Agent-based" computer modelers use the term in that way to refer to units programmed with particular rules of behavior with the aim of discovering emergent behavior at the aggregate level, an approach that proceeds under the mechanistic assumption of unidirectional, bottom-up causality. (To simulate real-world socionomic behavior, one would instead construct a computer model requiring agents' aggregate behavior to conform to Elliott waves while otherwise setting individual agents free to act within that global constraint. Such a model would not be agent-based but form-*and*-agent-based, which is the structure we are after.) In sociology, the term *agency* specifically refers to "the capacity of individuals to act independently and to make their own free choices."[18] Since under socionomics the degree of people's employment of this capacity is highly dependent upon the social context involved (see Chapter 12), this definition cannot serve general socionomic application. Another widely cited definition of *agent*, which is compatible with socionomics, is "one that acts," and many sociological studies do use the term simply to mean *actor*. In our previously published papers—kept intact (except where noted) for this book—we used the term *agent* in that sense.

A final comment on terminology pertains to related theories. Elliott waves of social mood and herding patterns may be termed "emergent" properties of human social interaction or characterized as properties of a "complex system." The literature on emergence and complexity is compatible with socionomic causality when it recognizes the importance of symbiotic interaction between entities and the global properties that their aggregations display, especially when it asserts the irreducibility of those properties. Yet some discussions in those fields attribute emergence and complexity only to bottom-up causality. Those areas of study, moreover, apply to inanimate matter as well. While inanimate matter shares with animate matter certain properties pertinent to our field of study (as noted in *The Wave Principle of Human Social Behavior*), freedom of choice for individual entities does not appear to be one of them. Socionomic causality applies to human aggregations, and it recognizes that each individual is at least somewhat free to act apart from what is required of society to maintain the global properties of social mood and aggregate herding patterns. So, while socionomics may sit quite comfortably under the umbrellas of emergence and complexity—or for that matter those of evolutionary psychology, self-organizing systems and other conceptual frameworks—it seems best at this stage simply to express our ideas in our own terms without explicitly hitching to others' established posts. Socionomics is open to further explication from any field of study.

Why Do Waves of Social Mood Exist?

Environmental stresses keep animal and plant species resilient. Humans, however, have conquered many environmental stresses. Waves of social mood probably serve an evolutionary purpose in imposing stresses and rewards upon humans at fractal intervals, thus keeping individuals repeatedly challenged yet hopeful and motivated to strive. Periods of positively trending social mood motivate constructive social behaviors, whereas periods of negatively trending social mood motivate destructive social behaviors. By the system's simultaneous regulation of humans' aggregate levels of optimism and pessimism, changes in social trends are impeccably counter-intuitive to people ignorant of the Wave Principle, which is nearly everyone, so they are caught off guard in both directions time and again. It can be very tough on individuals at times, but by impelling humans unwittingly to construct, deconstruct and reconstruct civilization ultimately to thrive, it is probably good for the resilience and longevity of the species.

We may take yet another step in line with Ellis, who further observed, "But things are even more radical than this. Sometimes the lower-level entities only exist because of the nature of the higher-level structures." He cited "Cooper pairs" of electrons as an example of when the organizational aspect of a system is crucial to the existence of an entity. His point could well apply to socionomics' identification of an organizing principle for human society. Were there no top-down organizational principle behind waves of social mood to imbue humans with constant motivation, perhaps our species would not have succeeded.

The Promise of Socionomic Theory

Scientists widely recognize that a new theory, to be worth considering, must be both internally and externally consistent; it must be more elegant, natural and parsimonious than competing theories; it must account for anomalies in the reigning paradigm; it must explain a range of behavior in different contexts; and it must generate new ideas for conducting empirical inquiry. Socionomics is and does all of these things. Socionomic theory is free of contradictions; it is consistent with reality; it is simple and elegant; it explains data that the reigning mechanics paradigm cannot; it accounts for behaviors across a wide spectrum of social activity; it throws open doors for further inquiry; and it has the added bonus of being counter-intuitive, which is often a good sign. Whether it is correct is another matter. The purpose of this book is to answer that question in the positive.

A Gap to be Filled in Socionomic Theory

Fractals, branching systems and Fibonacci-related structures and processes characterize brain and nervous-system physiology and activity as well as aspects of many other natural growth systems, among which Elliott waves of human social behavior quite comfortably reside (see Chapters 10 through 12 in *The Wave Principle of Human Social Behavior*). Differences in conscious and unconscious circuits in the human brain (see Chapters 13 and 16) also well account for economic vs. socionomic causality, respectively (see Chapters 12 and 13). But to date there remains a missing component to the full picture: precise details of the neurological, physiological and endocrinal processes involved in mood-sharing and impulsive herding. Social-mood fluctuations could activate, or derive from activation within, certain parts of the brain that regulate when risk-taking appears unconsciously to be more or less attractive.[19] Perhaps mood-sharing regulates certain hormone levels, providing an intangible reward. Perhaps hormone levels regulate impulses to herd.[20] We don't know. Neurological studies may someday reveal the mental and physiological features governing herding and mood-sharing, an as-yet-unresolved aspect of socionomic theory. Chapter 19 extends this discussion.

James A. Warren[21] pointed out that when Charles Darwin[22] conceived of evolution through natural selection, when Alfred Wegener[23] hit upon the idea of continental drift, and when J. Thomas Looney[24] figured out who Shakespeare really was, all of them lacked the means to discover the precise details involved in the processes they proposed. It was only after later scientists discovered genetics in the 1920s and plate tectonics in the 1970s that the first two theories fully won people over. Socionomics, as with the third aforementioned theory, is gaining ground but still faces this gap of knowledge.

Such knowledge, however, is surely forthcoming. I am confident that future research will clear up this question.

NOTES AND REFERENCES

[1] Smith, Noah, "The World's Smartest Bad Investors," *Bloomberg View*, December 9, 2015.

[2] Soyer, Emre, and Robin M. Hogarth, "The Illusion of Predictability: How Regression Statistics Mislead Experts," *International Journal of Forecasting*, 2012; available on SSRN.com.

[3] Elliott, Ralph Nelson, *The Wave Principle* (1938) and "The Basis of the Wave Principle" (1940). Republished: (1980/1994). *R.N. Elliott's Masterworks—The Definitive Collection.* Prechter, Robert. (Ed.). Gainesville, GA: New Classics Library.

[4] Pepper, Stephen C., *World Hypotheses: A Study in Evidence,* Berkeley, California: University of California Press, 1942.

[5] Prechter, Robert R., Deepak Goel, Wayne D. Parker and Matthew Lampert, "Social Mood, Stock Market Performance, and U.S. Presidential Elections: A Socionomic Perspective on Voting Results," *SAGE Open*, October 2012. Republished in *Socionomic Causality in Politics*, The Socionomics Institute, 2017. This paper is publicly available at http://papers.ssrn.com.

[6] See Alan Hall's socionomic study, "Social Mood Can Be Evident in Facial Expressions," *The Socionomist*, December 2013. Reprinted in *Socionomic Studies of Society and Culture* (2017).

[7] Namely, "The Socionomic Insight vs. the Assumption of Event Causality," "Challenging the Conventional Assumption about the Presumed Sociological Effect of Terrorist News" and "Social Behavior During Blackouts," comprising Chapters 31, 32 and 12 of *Pioneering Studies in Socionomics* (2003).

[8] Wilson, Euan, "Roads and Recessions: A Socionomic Analysis of Cars and Travel," *The Socionomist*, September 2009, pp. 1-4.

[9] Mandelbrot, Benoit, "The Variation of Certain Speculative Prices," *The Journal of Business*, Vol. 36, No. 4, 1963, pp. 394-419.

[10] Following Elliott's death in 1948, A. Hamilton Bolton, Charles J. Collins, A.J. Frost and Richard Russell successively published material on the Wave Principle through 1974, keeping Elliott's work from falling into obscurity. All Elliott wave material issued by R.N. Elliott and the first four of his successors has been republished in book form. See list at www.elliottwave.com/books. Their key stock market calls are summarized in *Understanding the Extraordinary Value of the Elliott Wave Model* (DVD), 2010.

[11] Mandelbrot, Benoit, *The Fractal Geometry of Nature*, New York: W.H. Freeman and Co., 1982.

[12] See Chapters 37 through 42 of *Pioneering Studies in Socionomics.*

[13] Pepper, Stephen C., *World Hypotheses: A Study in Evidence,* Berkeley, California: University of California Press, 1942.

[14] For more on the Wave Principle as a constraint, see pp. 399-400 of *The Wave Principle of Human Social Behavior*, 1999.

[15] Chapters 22 and 23 provide powerful evidence for the determinism attending Elliott waves. But the only certainly deterministic aspect of waves is aspects of their form, not necessarily their absolute extents and durations, which vary substantially. It is not clear whether the top-down or bottom-up aspect of patterned herding is responsible for the quantitative variation among waves. One possibility is that what we perceive as quantitative variability actually derives from an as-yet-undiscovered, non-variable function of the top-down, formological system. Another possibility is that top-down causality assures only that fluctuations in social mood will adhere to the qualitative aspects (called *rules* within EW) of WP's wave forms, whereas robust causality welling from bottom up determines their quantitative aspects in current time. Future Elliotticians may well discover reliable aspects of waves of which we are currently unaware, in which case our predictions based on them can only get better.

[16] Ellis, George, "Time to Turn Cause and Effect on Their Heads," *New Scientist*, August 21, 2013.

[17] http://www.merriam-webster.com/dictionary/agent.

[18] Wikipedia, "Agent (sociology)"

[19] See, for example, Kuhnen, Camelia M. and Brian Knutson, 2005, "The Neural Basis of Financial Risk Taking," *Neuron*, Vol. 47, pp. 763-770.

[20] See, for example, Coates, J.M. and J. Herbert, "Endogenous Steroids and Financial Risk Taking on a London Trading Floor," *Proceedings of the National Academy of Sciences* (PNAS), Vol. 104, No.16, The National Academy of Sciences, April 22, 2008.

[21] Warren, James A., "Oxfordian Theory, Continental Drift and the Importance of Methodology," *The Oxfordian*, Vol.17, 2015, pp. 193-221.

[22] Darwin, Charles, *The Origin of Species*. London: John Murray, 1859.

[23] Wegener, Alfred, *The Origin of Continents and Oceans*, New York: Methuen & Co., 1915, 1928.

[24] Looney, J. Thomas, *Shakespeare Identified*. London: Cecil Palmer, 1920.

Chapter 7

Sociometers and Their Application

Robert R. Prechter

A socionomist analyzes social mood by way of sociometers. A socio-meter records aggregate actions expressing fluctuations in overall social mood, or, in the case of specialized sociometers (see discussion below), herding and/or mood-sharing dynamics narrower in scope. The ideal soci-ometer would record mood changes from within people's minds, but such a tool is (currently) unavailable. Since there are delays between changes in social mood and the various actions it impels, all available sociometers lag changes in social mood.

A sociometer that most reliably measures overall social mood is termed a *benchmark sociometer*. A benchmark sociometer has, relative to all other available sociometers, (1) the most data, (2) the cleanest data, (3) the most immediately reported data, (4) the longest history of data, (5) the briefest lag time between mood changes and the actions that express them, (6) a bi-directional construct, (7) a quality of reflecting overall social mood and (8) broad representation of the society under study. These traits make the soci-ometer a good one for plotting, analysis, forecasting and decision-making.

The stock market is our benchmark sociometer for the United States over the past two centuries and for the U.K. over the past three centuries, because the data produced by this auction market satisfy these criteria far better than any other measure. The stock market offers the virtues of vo-luminous data with actions recorded daily and even intraday, meticulous records, immediate reporting, a long history of data, an ability to express social mood immediately, a polar construct relating to emotions (optimism/pessimism), exceptional service as a proxy for social mood (for evidence, see Chapter 8 as well as *Socionomic Studies of Society and Culture* and *Socionomic Causality in Politics,* 2017), fairly widespread participation and even a direct tie to human progress in being society's (unconscious) valuation of its own productive capability. The initiation of data collection on this uniquely human passion some 300 years ago is the very reason we have been able to construct graphs displaying magnificent pictures of Elliott waves of social mood, which were heretofore hidden from human perception.

The monthly report of Gross Domestic Product (GDP) covers a broader subset of society than the stock market, better satisfying the eighth criterion listed above, but GDP is not a benchmark sociometer because (1) it provides sparse data compared to the stock market (nothing weekly, daily or intraday), (2) it lags social mood more than the stock market does (see Chapter 8), and (3) there is a substantial time lag in data reporting. Point #2 especially trumps the breadth of the GDP measure, as shown in Chapters 8 and 10 and as we demonstrated statistically in our paper on predicting elections (reprinted in *Socionomic Causality in Politics,* 2017).

A Range of Scope

Sociometers range from *broad* to *narrow* in scope. These terms refer to the number of people participating in the activity being measured. GDP is a broad sociometer. The number of people engaging in break-dancing or attending extreme-fighting events is a narrow sociometer.

Even narrow sociometers that lack the ideal qualities of a benchmark sociometer can reflect overall social mood very well. Only a small subset of society may intermittently engage in a fad or fashion such as wearing mini-skirts, buying yellow cars or enjoying bubble-gum, teeny-bopper or boy-band music, but strong sales for such clothing, cars and music nevertheless serve as societal sociometers by recording expressions of extremely positive social mood.

A sociometer can fluctuate in scope from narrow to broad. In the 19th century, few people speculated in stocks, whereas in the late 20th century many people did. The stock market is nevertheless a consistent sociometer, because stock speculators express changes in social mood whatever the percentage of the population they may be, as shown in Chapter 10 and in our elections study (reprinted in *Socionomic Causality in Politics*, 2017).

Classes of Sociometers

There are two classes of sociometers: *societal* and *specialized.* A societal sociometer records changes in the overall mood of a society. A specialized sociometer records changes in a social activity involving herding and/or mood-sharing that has a dynamic of its own which is substantially unrelated or only peripherally or temporarily related to overall social mood.

Examples of societal sociometers are the stock market, consumer sentiment polls, human conception rates (see Chapter 10) and GDP. These measures fluctuate in response to changes in overall social mood.

Examples of specialized sociometers are the total number of participants who have engaged in smoking, belonged to a labor union or were involved in the African slave trade.[1] The trends in these activities must derive from mood-sharing and/or herding behavior, because they have fluctuated in Elliott waves. But they appear to be activities isolated from overall social mood, since their trends have been independent of trends in societal sociometers. As with activities such as snuff taking, goldfish eating, phone-booth stuffing and guild membership, they simply appeared and mostly disappeared. Many financial markets trace out Elliott waves but do not track the stock market. Waves in commodities and precious metals have had a mostly inverse relationship to waves of overall social mood for at least the past century (see discussion in Chapter 19), but among all financial markets the stock market is the only consistently reliable societal sociometer.

Design of Sociometers

Sociometers are *bounded* or *unbounded*. These terms relate to their design.

Bounded sociometers fluctuate between fixed extremes, such as 0 to 100%. Examples include certain measures of optimism and pessimism toward the future, such as the Consumer Confidence Index (CCI), the University of Michigan's Consumer Sentiment Index (CSI), the percentage of a population participating in the stock market, the percentage of advisors who are bullish or bearish on a financial market, the percentage of commitment to the long or short side among various classes of futures traders, etc. Such measures are common in the realm of technical market analysis, and some, such as the CCI, are popular among economists. Most conventional economists apply such measures backwards, however, for example by citing a high CCI reading as portending good times and vice versa, the opposite of its true implications.

Unbounded sociometers incorporate potentially endless trends of growth or decay. They also trace out Elliott waves. Examples are stock market indexes and commodity prices. These data are unbounded by their composition and can fluctuate freely to whatever higher or lower levels social mood and herding speculators may carry them.

Leading and Lagging Sociometers

Socionomically motivated social actions fall along an open-ended continuum of delay following the initial influence of social mood. Delays range from *immediate* (pertaining, for example, to changes in stock prices and emotional expressions via social media) through *intermediate* (as with changes in styles of popular entertainment) to *eventual* (pertaining to economic and political trends and the climate for peace and war). The term *eventual* does not mean final, as one might always be able to observe or postulate yet later consequences of socionomically motivated social actions, although the effects of past social moods dissipate with time. Chapter 8 expands upon this theme.

The terms *leading* and *lagging* define the temporal position of societal sociometers relative to each other. Leading sociometers portend the paths of lagging ones, which is the source of their utility.

The most immediate consequence of mood is to induce emotions, attitudes, decisions and actions. Thereafter lies a continuum of durations relating to the actions taken as a consequence of those initial emotions, attitudes, decisions and actions.

Lagging social actions result from decisions made earlier that expressed social mood. People may decide to propose marriage or to agree to get married as immediate expressions of social mood, but the marriages take place months later. People decide to have sex or to have children, but conceptions lag these decisions, and births lag even more. Writers conceive of ideas for films and TV shows, but it takes months or years to produce them. Company managers may decide to expand or contract their businesses on the very same day that others decide to take action in the stock market, but expanding or contracting business activities often takes months to actualize. It takes time to meet with directors, execute plans, hire or fire employees, obtain new bank loans or pay off old ones, purchase materials or cancel orders, design or wind down advertising campaigns, rent new space or withdraw from a lease, etc. It likewise takes time for newly optimistic consumers to carry out spending decisions: to shop for a new car or boat, find a new home, arrange a mortgage, plan a more ambitious vacation, and so on, and for newly pessimistic consumers to extricate themselves from such possessions, debts and plans. Politicians may decide to offer new legislation, but it takes weeks to vet it, drum up support for it and get a legislature to pass or reject it. Leaders may express social mood by deciding to go to war, but thereafter it takes time to gather advisors, gain intelligence, accumulate supplies and mobilize troops. The full follow-through on the initial decision takes so much time that a planned action, such as an attack, may not take place until months later. In each set of cases, people make decisions when the mood strikes, but the eventual results take time to effect. Political actions in particular significantly lag social mood trends.

Decisions to take social actions rarely make news. *Actualizing* those decisions, which takes varying amounts of time, often does. This is why economic and political news lags the stock market. News is therefore useless for predicting the stock market, whereas the stock market is an excellent predictor of the tenor and character of social actions later reported as news.

An analogy from meteorology should serve to clarify this point. A suddenly wet sidewalk is an immediate indicator of rain, while water runoff is an intermediate, lagging indicator of rain, and river level is an eventual, lagging indicator of rain. Each of the first two indicators is a leading indicator of what follows.

From a socionomic perspective, conventional economists' use of economic data to forecast the stock market is akin to meteorologists using river fluctuations to predict rain. If they did, rain would surprise meteorologists as much as recessions surprise economists.

There is a good reason for using the term *sociometer* for any social-mood indicator along the entire continuum from immediate to eventual. When various types of socionomic data of roughly equivalent quality are available, one would choose the most leading sociometer to make socionomic assessments and predictions. The stock market would be *the* sociometer for all occasions, except that for many areas of the world at various times in history no stock data are available. An archeologist studying an ancient civilization, for example, may possess data only on fluctuations in production activity based upon the strata of scrap around the site of a copper mine or the layers of commercial debris in the sediment of a harbor. Yet if he understands that business activity expands and contracts as a lagging indicator of social mood, he may be able to make all kinds of tentative presumptions about kindred social actions preceding, accompanying and following the known times of expansion and contraction in economic activity for those civilizations. He may have a lagging sociometer, but he has a sociometer nevertheless.

Although specialized sociometers do not reflect overall social mood, the terms *leading*, *lagging*, *immediate*, *intermediate* and *eventual* still apply to them. The popularity of smoking (see *Socionomic Studies of Society and Culture*, 2017) has lagging results in the incidence of lung cancer. Fluctuations in the price of oil (see Chapter 22) affect producers' searches for new supplies and alternative energy sources.

Categorizing Sociometers: Examples

—The stock market is a broad, societal, unbounded, immediate sociometer.

—In peacetime,[2] approval ratings for a leader and the percentage of total votes cast for an incumbent leader (see *Socionomic Causality in Politics*, 2017) are broad, societal, bounded, immediate sociometers.

—GDP is a broad, societal, unbounded, eventual sociometer.

—The percentage of nations at war is a broad, societal, bounded, eventual sociometer.

—The record of bubble-gum music sales is a narrow, societal, unbounded, intermediate sociometer.

—The audience share of westerns on television is a narrow, societal, bounded, intermediate sociometer.

—The average length of hemlines for dresses sold by retailers is a broad, societal, bounded, immediate sociometer.

—The total number of people dying from epidemic disease is a narrow, societal, unbounded, eventual sociometer.

—The percentage of the population belonging to a labor union is a narrow, specialized, bounded sociometer.

—The number of cigarette smokers is a narrow, specialized, unbounded sociometer.

Some indicators may be inherently immediate but structurally intermediate. The Consumer Confidence Index would constitute an immediate sociometer if data were instantly available, but it must be treated as an intermediate sociometer due to the delay in data reporting.

A single activity can yield several types of sociometers. For example, the number of new skyscrapers planned is a narrow, societal, unbounded, intermediate sociometer; whereas the number of new skyscrapers completed is a narrow, societal, unbounded, eventual sociometer (see *Socionomic Studies of Society and Culture*, 2017). Similarly, the total number of conceptions in a society (had we the data nine months earlier than we do) would be a broad, societal, unbounded, nearly immediate sociometer; the ratio of conceptions to total population (see Chapter 10) would be a broad, societal, bounded, nearly immediate sociometer; the total number of births in a society is a broad, societal, unbounded, eventual sociometer; and the birth rate is a broad, societal, bounded, eventual sociometer.

Data Impurity

I think it is valid to use absolute terms such as *always* and *never* when talking about aspects of the inferred fractal pattern of social mood. We cannot use these terms in reference to the wave action of sociometers, though, because they are a step removed from mood.

No sociometer (yet) comprises purely socionomic data. Sociometers are indirect gauges, because they record social actions, not mood per se.

Certain individuals' specific actions included in the makeup of a sociometer may have an entirely rational motive disconnected from mood. For instance, a D.J. might choose to play a particular song due to a financial incentive, a criminal might kick a dog without provocation to impress a sadistic companion, a clown might use certain facial expressions to generate a response in an audience, a non-citizen might marry to obtain a green card, and an investor might sell stock to pay for an expensive medical procedure.

Such data impurity, by the way, goes both ways: Trends in payola, sadism, entertainment, citizenship restriction and human health—as demonstrated or implied in studies cited in this book and in our 2017 books—all ebb and flow with social mood, so even the actions cited above may well be subject to socionomic influence and not rationally pristine.

When the primary motivation for social action is socionomic, the net influence of individual, rational—as opposed to rationalized—actions on the socionomic dynamic is negligible, leaving socionomic trends and patterns intact. This observation extends even to rational investment decisions that take crowd behavior into account (see Chapter 19).

The formula for a sociometer can change, too. From time to time, custodians replace the components of their stock indexes. It might seem that substitutions would have to alter an index's behavior, but there is little evidence of such an effect. Investors simply jettison one stock and adopt another, keeping the index and its progression of Elliott waves intact.

Random impediments to action can affect very short term fluctuations in a sociometer. A speculator who wants to buy or sell an investment item might be too occupied at work to act, or he might find his communication device or trading platform temporarily out of service, and so on. A change toward positive mood lasting a minute might prompt a few active day traders to buy immediately, but during that same minute a broker might be executing sales for clients who had called earlier while he was in a meeting. Order delays can produce qualities of randomness at the smallest degrees in a sociometer.

Brief emotional responses to news do not affect social mood, but they may contribute short term noise to immediate sociometers such as those based on stock transactions and social-media messages (see Chapter 9). Such noise, however, may pertain to brief bouts of volatility more so than to meaningful net changes in the measures (see Chapter 19).

At smaller scales, then, say minute-to-minute, interference between mood-motivated impulses and speculators' actions can obscure in a sociometer the Elliott wave form to which social mood likely adheres. Fortunately, such noise never disturbs the trends and patterns at the higher degrees that pertain to socionomic analysis.

No Perfect Sociometer

Social mood regulates trends in the stock market because society's valuation of stock certificates is highly dependent upon people's attitudes toward the future, which derive from feelings of optimism and pessimism, which in the aggregate are regulated by fluctuations in social mood. We have not, however, determined whether any particular measure of stock prices is superior to others for recording social mood. No stock index is as precisely appropriate to the task of valuing the stock market as a thermometer is to gauging temperature. One may quote the value of a stock market index in terms of dollars, real money (gold), the Producer Price Index (PPI), indexes of commodities or some other basis. Over the years we have found that the Dow/PPI ratio, i.e. the Dow Jones Industrial Average priced in things, usually fits data on cultural changes better than does the nominal Dow, as you can see in charts throughout Chapter 10.

Since nominal stock indexes have been highly inflated due to currency debasement and especially to credit expansion, one might be tempted to charge that they have been distorted, making them unsuitable for recording social mood. Yet the nominal indexes remain highly relevant, because society-wide credit expansion requires optimism, and elevated nominal stock indexes have captured that consequence of a long term positive trend in social mood, which also accounts for conditions such as loose lending policies and record-low junk bond yields. A major shift toward negative mood will reverse these manifestations. Certain long term price and time relationships that Elliotticians seek out[3] seem to show up better in nominal prices, too.

The tenor and character of some socionomic events conform well to the Dow/gold ratio (for examples, see Figure 13 in Chapter 10 and Figure 1 in Chapter 26). Before 1933, the nominal Dow and Dow/gold were identical, because gold was money. Since then, these measures have diverged mightily. Perhaps one day society will re-adopt stable money, allowing a single monetary measure for the DJIA.

The Dow is hardly the only stock market index, either. In the U.S. alone, stock indexes include the Dow Jones Industrial Average, the Dow Jones Transportation Average, the Dow Jones Utility Average, the Dow Jones Composite Average, the S&P 500 index, the S&P 400 Industrial index, the S&P 100 (big-cap) index, the S&P MidCap 400 index, the S&P SmallCap 600 index, the Value Line Composite Geometric Index (to which "Value Line Composite" and "VLC" refer throughout this book), the Value Line Composite Arithmetic Index, the Wilshire 5000 Total Market index, the NASDAQ Composite index, the NASDAQ 100 index and the NYSE

Composite index, not to mention scores of sectors, groups and the recently created exchange-traded funds, of which 4396 are in existence at the end of 2015.[4] Many of these measures are constructed in ways that differ mathematically. Some are price averages, some are capitalization weighted, and others are based on the daily percentage changes in their components. This panoply of indicators is substantially a result of socionomic causality: As a long term, maturing trend toward positive social mood has induced a desire to speculate, interest in the stock market has grown, and so has the number of its measures.

These multiple measures tend to trend roughly together, but their precise turn dates often differ, both complicating and enriching socionomic analysis. Multiple gauges provide more information, which can lead to useful insights. For example, when they act in concert, the trend of social mood is clear; when they diverge, the trend is either pausing or maturing.

One can rightfully charge that multiple stock market gauges give socionomists leeway to make their claims fit better. We do avail ourselves of differences among benchmark sociometers when displaying correlations to other sociometers. But the differences are nonsignificant at the theoretical level. A measure that tracks DJIA, Dow/PPI, Dow/gold or VLC exquisitely will track the other measures well enough, so our cases still stand.

Sociometers lack universal applicability. As noted earlier, not all societies in history had a stock market. We have records of birth data for some nations, but nations are not static entities; their boundaries change and occasionally disappear. We have data on the annual number of nuclear bomb tests worldwide, but those data extend back only to the 1940s, when nuclear bombs were invented.

In every case, then, socionomic data are impure, inexact, changeable and/or limited. It is a universal problem.

For the record, economists have far worse problems with their data, including more limited histories, larger time lags, selective reporting times and charges of political manipulation (of the CPI and the unemployment rate, for example). It's still better to be a socionomist.

Force Can Ruin a Sociometer, but It Cannot Change Social Mood

Socionomists do not say that all social activity arises non-mechanically. We say there are no mechanical, exogenous causes of social mood fluctuations and unconscious herding patterns. Sociometers record social activities, not mood per se, so they can be ruined by exogenous causes. For instance, when social mood becomes very positive in a country run by religious fundamentalists, many young people may want to hold dance parties; but they don't, because the government might order them to be jailed, whipped or executed. So, exogenous interference obliterates what might otherwise be a useful sociometer: the popularity of dance parties. The government's attitude in such a case may have stemmed from a progression of events that had a socionomic origin, but at the end of the string of causes, the proximate cause of low numbers of dance parties had effectively become mechanical and exogenous.

The German hyperinflation of the early 1920s was mechanically caused by the government's use of a printing press, rendering nominal stock prices useless as a sociometer. That cause, however, had a socionomic origin: The government printed currency at a furious rate in order to neuter a punishing treaty, which stemmed from a war, which erupted as an expression of negative social mood. By the time the string of causes led to the money-printing decision, the proximate cause of the rapid rise in stock prices was, practically speaking, exogenous.

If intensely negative social mood were to lead to a despot's achieving power, he may act to outlaw the stock market or even to engineer the destruction of most productive enterprises, as happened in Mao's China, Pol Pot's Cambodia and the Kims' North Korea. In such a case there wouldn't *be* a stock market to serve as a sociometer, even if social mood were to shift toward the positive during the time of the restrictive program.

Despite this caveat, it is striking how rarely exogenous causes interfere with sociometers and their Elliott wave patterns. Even a national credit-issuing monopoly does not disrupt them. In the context of a century's worth of officially sanctioned currency debasement in the U.S., the price of oil has faithfully traced out Elliott wave structures of exceptional clarity, as described in Chapter 22. Both nominal and inflation-adjusted measures of aggregate stock prices have reflected Elliott waves of social mood during the same period (as illustrated respectively in Figure 3 of Chapter 23 and Figure 6 of Chapter 19). As demonstrated dramatically in 2007-2009 (see Chapters 2 and 5), social mood, not the central bank, is in charge of swings in stock prices and the economy. As shown in Chapter 3, central banks don't even control interest rates; the market does. As shown in Chapter 28, social mood is even in charge of the Federal Reserve Board's emotional states. It takes a draconian measure—such as a deadly political climate or deliberate hyperinflation—to destroy a sociometer. Even events such as those do not derail socionomic analysis. If authorities ruin one sociometer, all one need do is find another. No force can manipulate social mood, and its traces always show up somewhere.

Applying Sociometers to Forecasting

There are five bases for socionomic forecasting:

(1) Leading sociometers predict the tenor and character of social actions to be registered in lagging sociometers.

(2) Lagging sociometers provide a basis for hypothesizing about the earlier behavior of leading ones.

(3) Lagging sociometers help confirm trend changes in leading ones.

(4) A bounded sociometer's extremes help predict its own changes as well as changes in related unbounded sociometers.

(5) Elliott wave patterns in unbounded sociometers can help predict their own changes as well as the tenor and character of social actions due to accompany and follow those changes.

All of these forecasting abilities are probabilistic.

Here follow general discussions of each approach. Chapters 21 and 22 will offer specific examples of real-time application.

(1) Leading Sociometers Predict Lagging Ones

At the near end of the leading-lagging spectrum are swiftly executable mood-expressing actions such as using a tone of voice, making a facial expression, choosing the content of an utterance or message, selecting a type of song to listen to, singing spontaneously, driving aggressively, calling a friend to chat, laughing, crying, cursing, starting an argument, and acting to buy or sell stocks. While emotional reactions to stimuli can prompt such actions individually, social mood regulates their occurrence in the aggregate.

Toward the far end of the spectrum are social actions resulting from mood-induced decisions made much earlier. They include expanding or contracting businesses, initiating labor strikes, producing movies, getting married, bearing children, organizing mass protests, negotiating peace treaties, getting legislation passed and starting or ending wars.

Between these two extremes are intermediate social actions of every imaginable type, such as adopting fashions, buying musical recordings, choosing films or sporting events to see, attending concerts, proposing marriage, conceiving children, creating new business plans, styling products and drafting legislation. Many qualities of popular songs (including tone, mode, register, length, speed, lyrical content, melody range, arrangement complexity and amount of noise) could constitute intermediate sociometers. Unfortunately, data for such measures are difficult to come by.

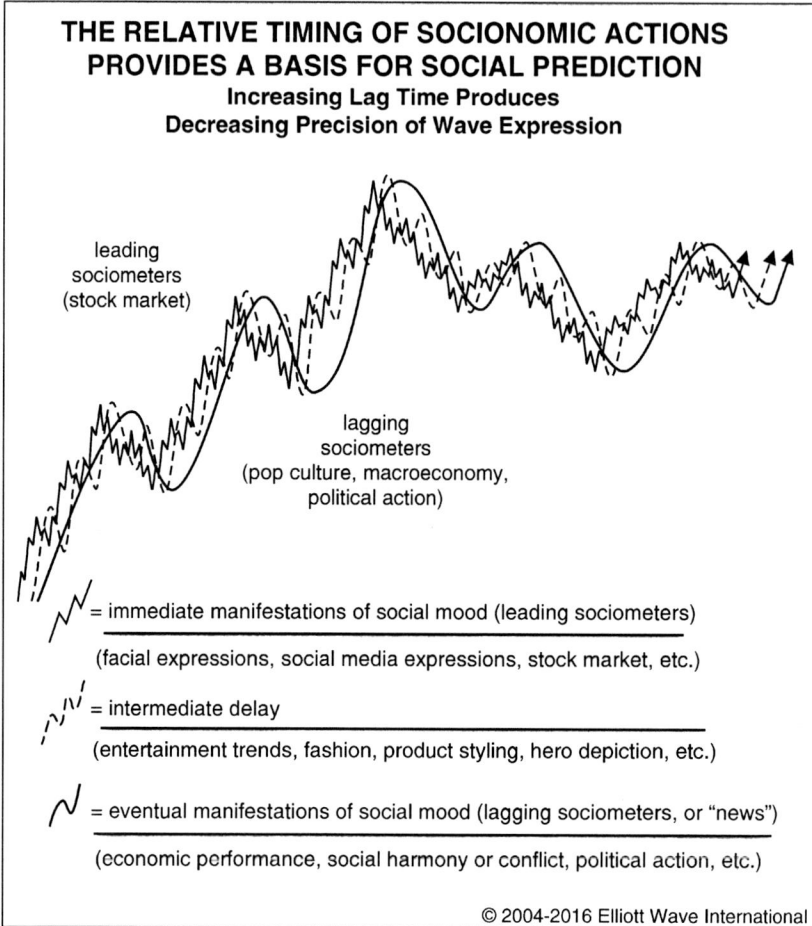

**THE RELATIVE TIMING OF SOCIONOMIC ACTIONS
PROVIDES A BASIS FOR SOCIAL PREDICTION**
**Increasing Lag Time Produces
Decreasing Precision of Wave Expression**

leading
sociometers
(stock market)

lagging
sociometers
(pop culture, macroeconomy,
political action)

= immediate manifestations of social mood (leading sociometers)

(facial expressions, social media expressions, stock market, etc.)

= intermediate delay

(entertainment trends, fashion, product styling, hero depiction, etc.)

= eventual manifestations of social mood (lagging sociometers, or "news")

(economic performance, social harmony or conflict, political action, etc.)

© 2004-2016 Elliott Wave International

Figure 1

Figure 1 presents a diagram of the temporal relationships between immediate social actions, which constitute the best sociometers, and lagging
social actions, which often constitute news. The left-most line in Figure 1
represents actions that people can take immediately in response to social
mood. The dashed line in the middle depicts social actions that take a bit more
time to manifest. The solid line to the right represents social actions that take
substantial time to manifest. If the chart were to depict social mood per se, it
would lie to the left of the left-most line, so close as nearly to touch it. Because fluctuations in the stock market, an immediate sociometer, conform to
Elliott waves, it seems reasonable to postulate that its regulator, social mood,
fluctuates in Elliott wave form as well, and that's how we would depict it.

Socionomic causality as represented here both explains why and predicts that the stock market will turn down before recessions begin and turn up before they end, and that peace or war will usually break out well after the beginning of the trend in social mood that brought it about. It also accounts for the diminishing detail within of the fractal form over the continuum of delay. Lagging social actions, such as changes in the overall economy, show no reliable Elliott wave patterns on daily, weekly or monthly charts, because the lags between individual decisions and ultimate actions vary in length, reducing the specificity of aggregate fluctuation. Yet since varying lags of a week to a quarter don't obscure trends lasting years or decades, Elliott waves do show up in the longer term trends of lagging sociometers. That's why the lines in Figure 1 are progressively smoother.

I have positioned these waves to reflect a fact that Elliotticians have long observed: The best news appears up to one rising wave of relatable size past the stock market's top, and the worst news appears up to one declining wave past the stock market's bottom. An example of the former type of event is the historic achievement of the Apollo 11 moon landing in July 1969, a few weeks after the Dow peaked just below its all-time high. An example of the latter type of event is the occurrence of the Great Depression's broadest unemployment in the first quarter of 1933, as stocks were making a higher low seven months after the bottom. (See fuller discussion in Chapter 8.)

By observing the swiftest consequences of social mood, a socionomist can predict the tenor and character of social actions that take longer to effect. He can do this because he knows that people have made decisions not only to buy or sell stocks but also to do other things whose tenor and character will reflect the same mood. If people are revaluing stocks upward, reflecting an increasingly positive social mood, they are also deciding to expand businesses, cooperate with others, propose marriage, conceive children, buy happy music, exercise more, dress with brighter colors and less fabric, get along with their neighbors, remove obstacles to trade, celebrate heroes and support leaders. If people are revaluing stocks downward, reflecting an increasingly negative social mood, they are also deciding to contract businesses, engage in conflict, delay proposals, delay conceptions, buy somber music, exercise less, dress with duller colors and more fabric, attack their neighbors, restrict trade, celebrate antiheroes and withdraw support for leaders. The *consequences* of these decisions will become manifest in ensuing months. Once a socionomist observes the tenor of immediate social actions, he can predict social actions that will express a compatible character with respect to cooperation or conflict, economic expansion or contraction, social tolerance or repression, centrism or polarization of political opinion, cultural ebullience or malaise, and so on. (For a list of polar characteristics, see Chapter 14 in *The Wave Principle of Human Social Behavior*.)

(2) Lagging Sociometers Provide a Basis from which to Hypothesize about Previous Leading Ones and Subsequent Lagging Ones

While lagging sociometers may not be ideal for analysis, they are nevertheless useful. As noted earlier, an archaeologist using layers of harbor debris as a benchmark sociometer for an ancient civilization could work backwards from those data to hypothesize about earlier socionomic trends and conditions. For example, he might postulate that the tone of popular music became increasingly energetic and joyous before the peak of commercial activity and that a decline in local property values preceded the nadir of commercial activity. Such considerations could help date structures, artworks and surviving scraps of music or literature from the period.

When immediate sociometers are unavailable, it is helpful to know that lagging sociometers such as economic performance precede more-lagging ones such as peace and war. Euan Wilson's review of civil wars in Spain and China, reprinted in *Socionomic Causality in Politics* (2017), provides an example of applying lagging sociometers to historical studies.

(3) Lagging Sociometers Can Help Confirm Presumed Trend Changes in Leading Ones

If a socionomist is anticipating or has recognized a change in the long term trend of social mood, the passage of a major new financial law (a narrow, societal, unbounded, eventual sociometer) can serve to confirm it. (For a record of such laws, see Figure 8 in Chapter 17; for an example of application, see Chapter 21.) If he has tentatively identified an extreme in negative social mood and a stock market bottom, a consensus among economists (a broad, societal, bounded, eventual sociometer) that a recession is in force can help confirm that the stock market bottom has occurred and that the recession is nearly over.

Successful application of such lagging sociometers requires knowing the typical lag times of different types of social actions. It also helps to have an understanding of the socionomic effects of various aspects of Elliott waves such as wave number and degree. Different wave numbers have different effects. Different degrees produce correspondingly larger and longer-lasting, or smaller and briefer, effects. At Primary degree, positive mood will typically lead to an economic expansion, negative mood a recession; at Supercycle degree, positive mood will foster an extended economic boom, negative mood a depression; at Millennium degree, positive mood will bring on a golden age, negative mood a dark age.

(4) A Bounded Sociometer's Extremes Can Help Predict Its Own Changes and Changes in Related Sociometers

When a bounded sociometer approaches an extreme, a socionomist may begin to anticipate a trend reversal simply on the grounds that social mood fluctuates. If, for example, records reveal that a vast majority of speculators in a particular financial market are bullish, one may deduce that the market is probably closer to a top than a bottom.

A very large-degree trend in an unbounded sociometer will produce a long duration of extreme readings in a related bounded sociometer. (Chapter 21 offers an example.) Therefore, bounded sociometers are best recorded and plotted over multiple durations—such as daily, weekly, monthly and annually—and analyzed according to the Elliott wave position of the unbounded sociometer.

Even eventual sociometers have some predictive value for their own changes. When the best of times or worst of times appears to exist with respect to eventual sociometers (such as the economic and political climate), a socionomist can anticipate change based simply on the famous advice of the king's page: "This, too, shall pass." This anticipation, however, must be grounded in knowledge of the largest operative wave degrees, which regulate the duration and extremity of good and bad times.

(5) An Unbounded Sociometer's Elliott Wave Patterns Can Help Predict Its Own Changes and thus Changes in the Tenor and Character of Social Actions

Social mood is endogenous and self-regulating, so it has no preceding, mechanical cause that may be analyzed to predict its changes. Furthermore, nothing requires socionomists to predict fluctuations in social mood or in any of its immediate manifestations, such as changes in stock prices. It would be asking too much of analysts in any field to forecast correctly the path of their own indicators. Predicting changes in sociometers is a probabilistic craft that any person—socionomist or not—can choose to ignore or pursue.

With these points established, you may still aspire to become an Elliott wave analyst, or Elliottician. Because Elliott waves are patterned, a careful analysis of developing wave patterns in an immediate, unbounded sociometer offers probabilistic knowledge of its future path. Unbounded sociometers with clear Elliott wave patterns announce their own reversals. When an unbounded sociometer completes an Elliott wave of a certain degree, an Elliottician may anticipate a reversal at corresponding degree.

A projection of wave form not only predicts changes in social mood but also forecasts the tenor and character of immediate, intermediate and eventual social actions. A good Elliottician can analyze wave structures to predict—at times and on a probabilistic basis—likely changes in wave form, and therefore in social mood, and therefore in social events, well in advance of a sociometer's trends. For demonstrations, see Chapters 21 and 22.

Five things affect the utility of Elliott wave analysis: the probabilistic nature of potential wave paths, the degree of clarity in the waves, the analyst's degree of competence, biases of the analyst, and analysts' own impulses to herd in contexts of uncertainty. Dealing with these difficulties takes immense effort. Most people don't do it well, and many people can't do it at all. No one does it well all the time. Some good news on this front is that a project we started years ago is nearing its goal of computerizing Elliott wave analysis, which will at least sidestep the problems of incompetence, bias and herding.

The highly probabilistic nature of Elliott wave forecasting is a far cry from the far easier and more dependable craft of socionomic forecasting. Returning to our analogy from meteorology, the forecasting value of Elliott wave formations is similar to the rain-forecasting value of cloud formations. Each formation is only a probabilistic indicator of the future. Once the market moves or the rain begins, however, one may attach more certainty to forecasts of lagging indicators. While clouds are only a *tentative* predictor of rain, rain is a more reliable predictor of water runoff, and both rain and runoff are reliable predictors of even-more-lagging river levels. Similarly, while the apparent positions of Elliott wave patterns are only tentative predictors of socionomic behavior, the manifest trends of leading sociometers are more reliable predictors of the tenor and character of lagging ones.

All of these forecasting formulas have valuable practical applications. Chapter 21 presents a dozen real-time examples.

How News Fools Investors

The temporal offset between trends of social mood and eventual socionomic actions reported as news fools investors in two ways.

First, news confounds investors in a subtle and systematic way. From Figure 1, you can see why it is so easy for investors to believe that news causes stock market trends: For much of a social mood trend, the tenor of the news is parallel to that of the stock market. News of intermediate and eventual socionomic actions is not disassociated from stock trends; it simply lags them. The tenor of the news aligns with the stock market particularly well in the middle and final waves of a trend. During those waves, stocks are rising and news is mostly good, or stocks are falling and news is mostly bad. At such times, economists, investors and the media are flush with certainty about the news' causality of market trends. Thus, the *compatibility* of news and market action in the latter half of a major trend misleads investors at the theoretical level.

Second, news confounds investors in a dramatic and occasional way. The decoupling of waves and news comes at the turns. News of eventual sociomonic actions stays very good or gets better after a stock market peak has passed and stays very bad or gets worse after a stock market low has passed. Thus, the *opposition* of news to market action in the initial waves of a new major trend misleads investors at the practical level. The dramatic crashes of 1929 and 1987 took place amidst a strong economy and rosy forecasts. The rapid stock market advances of 1932-1933, August-October 1982 and March-June 2009, which were the initial waves of bull markets, took place during a depression, a recession and a great recession respectively, taking economists and the investing public by surprise. The stock market downturns of 2000 and 2007 came while news was good, as revealed by economists' optimistic assessments of those times, as quoted in Chapter 2. The fuller treatment in Chapter 8 should make this dynamic crystal clear to you.

It is important to realize that news' opposition to mood changes comes at turns of every degree. Because news of intermediate and eventual social actions always lags stock market turns, investors see many news-related reasons to take the wrong actions and few news-related reasons to take the right ones. When multiple degrees of trend are culminating together, the general conviction among speculators that the trend will continue reaches its zenith, which means that it happens at precisely the wrong time, over and over. The subtlest mood changes induce buying and selling at the margin, creating the trend changes we see in the stock market. Thereafter each speculator takes a turn ignoring, resisting, joining and then embracing the newly evolving trend.

Socionomics Offers Direct Causality, Forward in Time

Economic theorists account for the lagging nature of economic news by proposing that investors see into the future and "discount" it by buying or selling ahead of it. The discounting hypothesis is an attempt to maintain the error of exogenous cause and rational reaction by placing the exogenous cause in the future. There is no such thing as reverse-temporal causality. If discounting occurred, people wouldn't be surprised by social events, but they are, all the time. There is no evidence that speculators see around corners and ample evidence (see Chapters 17 and 22) that they don't. When extending the notion of stock-market discounting to socionomic actions such as fashion trends and audiences' film preferences (see Chapter 10), it devolves into incoherence. Chapters 3 and 39 in this book and Chapter 43 in *Pioneering Studies in Socionomics* dispense with this magical notion. Socionomic causality, in contrast, is non-magical, coherent and empirically and theoretically consistent in offering a direct cause as to why the stock market leads trend changes in the economy, politics and culture.

A Rewarding Exercise

Socionomic analysis is worth the effort. Successfully predicting the tenor of financial, economic, cultural and political news can be highly rewarding to planning the course of an enterprise or even one's life. If you can anticipate price changes in financial markets, you can take advantage of opportunities and avoid disastrous losses. If you can anticipate changes in the economy, you can expand your business at the right time, choose a good time to buy a house, know when to ask for a long term contract or know when to sell your land. If you can anticipate changes in the culture, you can choose the right film to produce, know which band is likely to succeed or put your firm on the cutting edge of fashion trends. If you can anticipate changes in the political climate, you can choose the best time to run for office, know when to put the most money and effort behind your candidate of choice or decide when to think of leaving a country before its borders close. And so on.

Inexact though it may be, there is no science of social prediction outside socionomics. If you wish to forecast the social future, you must begin here.

NOTES AND REFERENCES

[1] See *Socionomic Studies of Society and Culture*, 2017.

[2] Wartime leaders can be popular despite negative social mood. Declarations of war tend to coincide with brief but strong jumps in presidential popularity. G.H.W. Bush and G.W. Bush both benefitted briefly from this connection, as their popularity zoomed to above 90% when they went on the attack. Sociometers such as the stock market do not shift in what they represent, but it is clear that pre-rationally motivated support for a leader in times of war shifts what leaders' popularity polls represent. Social mood drives this sociometer in two opposing ways: During peacetime people take their anger out on the leader, whereas in wartime the leader champions that anger.

[3] See, for example, Prechter, Robert, *Beautiful Pictures from the Gallery of Phinance*, New Classics Library, 2003.

[4] "Number of Exchange-Traded Funds (ETFs) Worldwide from 2003 to 2015," statista.com.

Chapter 8

Socionomics and the Elliott Wave Model Provide a Framework for Projecting the Lag Time of News

Alan Hall

One of the most important things to understand about the stock market is its relationship to social news. Most social news results from trends in social mood, which manifest in social actions with various lag times. This chapter uses real-world data to demonstrate the idea that we can use knowledge of these lag times to anticipate the tenor and character of social actions that make news.

Figure 1, from Prechter's presentation to the Socionomics Summit of April 2011, illustrates the idea that there is always a mix of positive and negative social events, which vary in quantity and extremity in expressing social mood. The horizontal bar in Figure 1 fluctuates up and down in fractal form, conforming to WP. Chapter 6 noted that when social mood turns toward the positive following a major negative extreme, mood is not suddenly positive but just a bit less negative; and vice versa. This chapter will show precisely when transitions from net positive to net negative mood, and vice versa, take place within the Elliott wave structure.

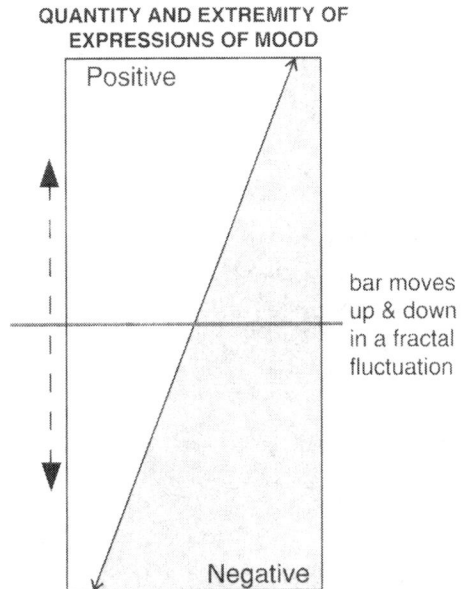

QUANTITY AND EXTREMITY OF EXPRESSIONS OF MOOD

Positive

Negative

bar moves up & down in a fractal fluctuation

Figure 1

PIVOT POINTS IN IDEALIZED ELLIOTT WAVES

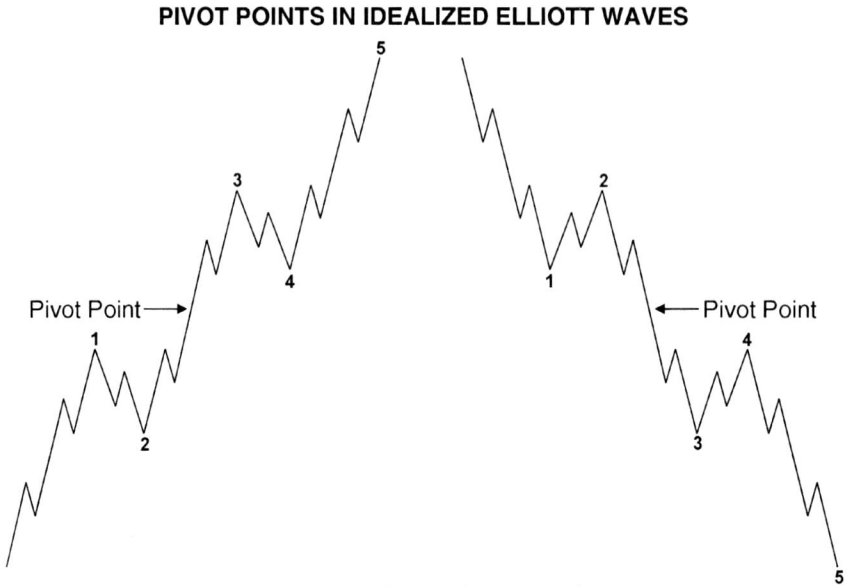

Figure 2

Figure 2 shows an idealized five-wave structure from the Elliott wave model, in both the up and down direction. Each diagram is marked with the point of most rapid change in the move toward positive or negative social mood. Each of these "pivot points," as we call them, occurs at the structural center of the largest third wave. Within a positive trend, it marks the point at which people on balance shift from fearing the worst to hoping for the best. Within a negative trend, it marks the point at which people on balance shift from hoping for the best to fearing the worst. In corrective waves, the shift comes at the center of wave three of C. (For a labeled diagram, see Figure 6 in Chapter 22.)

After social mood passes the pivot point, lagging actions that express social mood tend to begin flooding more one-sidedly in the direction of the trend. They become starkly one-sided at and after the end of the final fifth wave.

The Stocks vs. News Progression of 1929-1933

Figure 3 imposes Figure 1 over a graph of the Dow Jones Industrial Average for the period of April 1930 to July 1932. It includes the long-established Elliott wave labeling as published in past issues of *The Elliott Wave Theorist*.

The smooth descending line in Figure 3 is our "lag line," a six-month moving average of the DJIA shifted six months into the future. It is designed

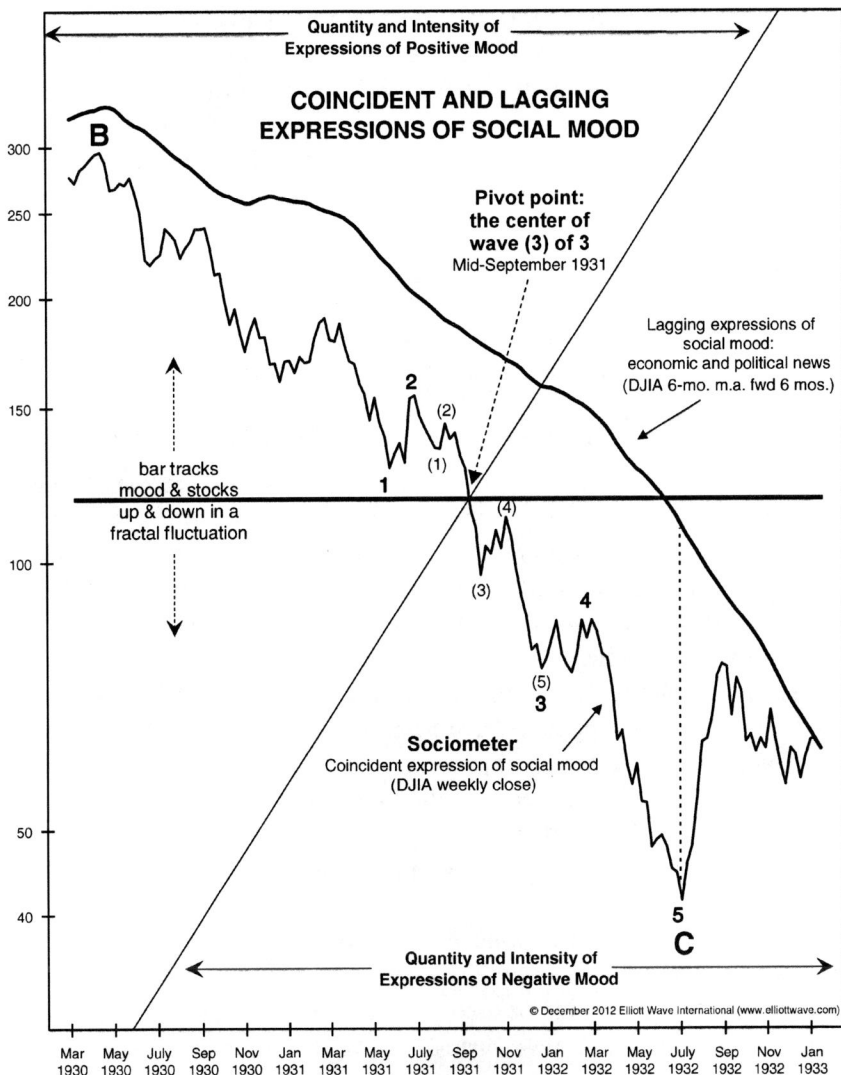

Figure 3

to approximate the timing of eventual expressions of social mood such as economic and political news. At major trend extremes of the past century, it has turned roughly nine months after stock prices. One should think of this lag line as the approximate centerline of a broad swath of probability, much as volatility bands are designed to contain most of the price action in graphs of stock prices.

In a slight departure from the norm, the economy began weakening concurrently with the Dow in 1929, but it did so well after the highs in most stocks as indicated by the peak in the advance-decline line in 1928.

Pessimism became the dominant stock market sentiment at the pivot point of mid-September, 1931. But notice that the lag line representing news of social actions did not reach the price level of the pivot point until near the time of the end of wave C. The bottom in stocks actually marked the *beginning* of the flood of reports expressing the worst economic, political and social news of the decade. In other words, the stock market indicated what was happening with respect to social mood months before the media reported news of its economic and political consequences.

Lagging Expressions of Social Mood: Social, Economic and Political

I had a memorable experience while searching on-line archives. Google News handily provides images of old newspaper pages with one's search term highlighted. For one article, I wanted a screen-capture of a clean, non-highlighted image. So, I entered a search for a headline that I knew appeared on an adjoining page, "500,000 Chicagoans." As expected, it led me back to the same two-page spread, but it also turned up a second usage of this unusual phrase. One of the stories was from 1931 and the other from 1932, on dates that happen to have been respectively four months before and nine months after the pivot point within wave C.

At the top of the next page is the first of the two articles, issued on May 14, 1931 by the Associated Press. Keep in mind that the celebration it recounts occurred almost halfway through the biggest collapse of stock prices in U.S. history.

This story describes a public gathering packed so tightly that "several score of persons were overcome, so great was the press of the crowd."[1] One person died and many needed first aid, but not because of violence; on the contrary, the crowd was festive and well behaved, according to the cheery reporter.

Read about the upbeat unity of the crowd, reported near the end of the article. Social mood had been trending negatively for 21 months—since September 1929—and the country was suffering financially. But the critical psychological threshold—the September 1931 center of wave C—still lay ahead. Note, too, that the hero of the crowd was not a military officer or a politician but a Chamber of Commerce president. Society, though less optimistic, was still clinging to hopes of a business resurgence.

The crowd in Chicago that day knew nothing of what lay ahead. Social mood and economic conditions were about to worsen drastically.

500,000 Chicagoans Revel

Merrymakers Turn Downtown District into Circus at All-Chicago Trade Jubilee

[By The Associated Press]

Chicago, May 14.—State St., one of the world's busiest thoroughfares, capitulated last night to half a million merrymakers.

Seemingly, all Chicago converged on the famous street, in celebration of the All-Chicago trade jubilee. Men, women and children packed the street from the Chicago River to Van Buren St., a distance of 10 blocks, giving the police what they described as their "biggest assignment."

An army of more than 2,500 policemen was on the job to preserve order as Chicago held mardi gras, but the crowd was orderly for the most part.

Several score of persons were overcome, so great was the press of the crowd. They were given first aid at stations set up along the street.

One policeman carried away so many fainting women that he himself was overcome.

One man died of heart disease. He was Dennis Sullivan, a barber, caught in the crush at State and Madison Sts.

Six Ring Circus

While huge search lights swept the skies and ticker taps showered down, the carnival held sway for three hours along State St., gaily festooned and converted into a six ring circus. A half dozen orchestras on as many platforms situated in the center of street intersections pepped the crowd up, while radio stars, vaudeville actors and other professional entertainers did their stuff.

Approximately 2,000 persons attended a banquet held by the Chamber of Commerce, preceding the celebration, in honor of the delegates to the recent International Chamber of Commerce convention at Washington. Business men from 36 nations were present.

The retiring president of the International Chamber, M. Georges Theunis, former Prime Minister of Belgium, brought thundering shouts of "no" from the assemblage when he introduced a three word resolution: "are we downhearted," which he said had been omitted from the Washington meeting.

The celebration was broadcast by radio.

Pessimism became dominant in society when stock prices plummeted through the pivot point. Here is the second article, from June 3, 1932. It came out a year after the previous article and a month before the bottom in stock prices.

As you can see, this second story is starkly different, and so are the next two articles, which were adjacent to it on the same page of the newspaper.

STARVATION FACING 500,000 CHICAGOANS

Illinois Commission Seeks Frantically for Way to Feed Them.

By United Press.

CHICAGO, June 3.—Starvation faced 500,000 persons today as the Illinois emergency relief commission worked frantically to obtain funds to continue relief activity.

Funds upon which 110,000 families in Cook county have depended for food will be exhausted Saturday and relief work suspended unless the empty coffers are replenished.

Leaps Into Volcano Pit With Fiancee in His Arms

By DAN CAMPBELL,
United Press Staff Correspondent.

HILO, T. H. June 3.—The body of his sweetheart in his arms, Sylvester Nunes, sturdy young Hawaiian, followed ancient tradition and leaped to death in the Kilauea volcano, investigators reported today.

Nunes, before jumping to death on the rocks close to the fiery pit, shot and killed his 17-year-old high school sweetheart, Margaret Enos. His auto was found parked near the edge of the crater, an automatic pistol on the floor and bloodstains on its cushions.

"Ten minutes to eight," a note left in the car read. "Margaret died instantly. She did not suffer. Now I must pay."

Police prepared today to lower a man 1200 feet into the pit to recover the bodies. The task was a considerable one, since heat and smoke from molten lava, the height from which operations must be carried on and the sharp rocks made the slightest mishap perilous.

National Park Superintendent Leavitt awaited word from Washington, D. C., as to whether his men should carry on the recovery attempt. The crater is located in a national park and is under federal administration.

The bodies were sighted by park rangers with the aid of powerful binoculars. Miss Enos, clad in a red kimono, was seen on a ledge about 900 feet below the crater's rim, while Nune's body lay sprawled on a heap of rocks just above her. The youthful islander had taken the girl from her home this morning after shooting her sister, Mrs. Manuel Furtado, thru the hand when the sister attempted to resist his commands to Margaret that she follow him.

Waving a revolver, Nunes compelled the young girl to leave the house with him.

Kilauea is famed in island history and legend as the home of Madam Pele, goddess of fire. Many stories are told of the custom of sacrifices being thrown into the smoking pit, known as Alemaumau.

These two suicide stories bring to life the grim statistics on U.S. suicide rates,[2] which reached their all-time high—still never exceeded—as darkening social mood carried the stock market to its 1932 bottom.

Figure 4 marks the timing of representative news items relating to that bear market. The numbers along the lag line refer to notable

DOCTOR IS SUICIDE

Authority on Diabetes, Holder of Honor Medal Shoots Self.

PHILADELPHIA, June 3 — Dr. Orlando H. Petty, holder of the congressional medal of honor awarded for bravery as a marine in the world war, shot and killed himself last night.

He was a leading authority on diabetes.

anecdotal expressions of prevailing sentiment, listed in chronological order on the pages that follow.

Our lag line peaked nine months after the Dow, in 1930, illustrating the persistent but waning evidence of post-peak optimism that helps explain investors' tendency to hold on to losing stocks during the initial stages of major declines. Observe how the tone of social expression changed after stocks passed the pivot point (indicated on the chart with an asterisk).

A few public protests and brief riots occurred during the first portion of the decline in 1930 and 1931, but expressions of the increasingly negative mood became broader and more intense following the pivot point and especially after the low in stock prices. Peter Dreier, a professor of politics at Occidental College in Los Angeles, recently wrote, "Civil disobedience takes place when people are *hopeful*. Riots occur when people are *hopeless*."[3] (Emphasis added.) Socionomic causality explains the difference, and the Elliott wave model can help predict the shift: People tend to abandon hope after the wave structure passes the pivot point. Our lag line finally bottomed in 1933, eight months after the Dow's low and coincident with the worst economic and political news of the period.

The consequences of trends in unconscious social mood never manifest in exactly the same way, but their lagging nature is highly reliable. Another reliable dynamic is that positive mood and positive news fool people after tops, and negative mood and negative news fool people after bottoms.

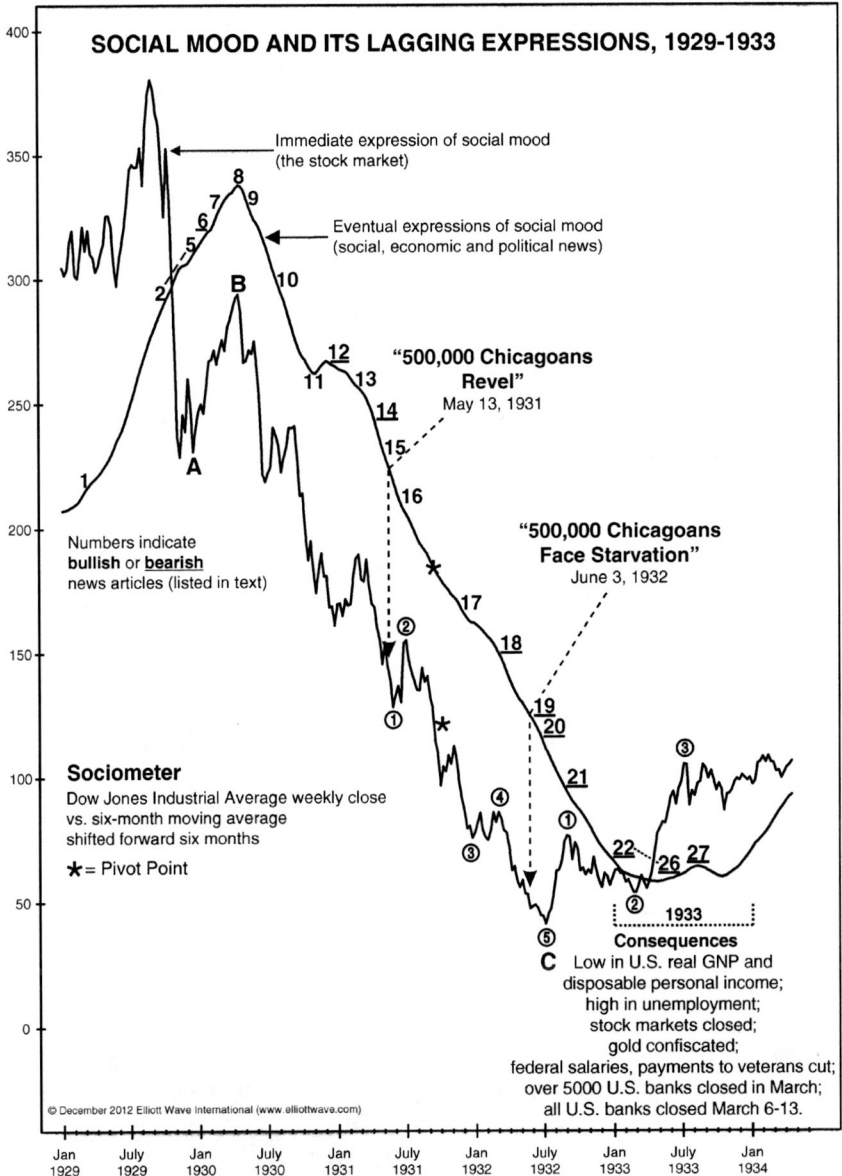

SOCIAL MOOD AND ITS LAGGING EXPRESSIONS, 1929-1933

Immediate expression of social mood
(the stock market)

Eventual expressions of social mood
(social, economic and political news)

"500,000 Chicagoans
Revel"
May 13, 1931

Numbers indicate
bullish or **bearish**
news articles (listed in text)

"500,000 Chicagoans
Face Starvation"
June 3, 1932

Sociometer
Dow Jones Industrial Average weekly close
vs. six-month moving average
shifted forward six months

★ = Pivot Point

© December 2012 Elliott Wave International (www.elliottwave.com)

1933
Consequences
Low in U.S. real GNP and
disposable personal income;
high in unemployment;
stock markets closed;
gold confiscated;
federal salaries, payments to veterans cut;
over 5000 U.S. banks closed in March;
all U.S. banks closed March 6-13.

| Jan | July | Jan | July | Jan | July | Jan | July | Jan | July | Jan |
| 1929 | 1929 | 1930 | 1930 | 1931 | 1931 | 1932 | 1932 | 1933 | 1933 | 1934 |

Figure 4

News Stories Numbered in Figure 4

The first of these stories is an excerpt from John Kenneth Galbraith's book, *The Great Crash 1929*, in which the author described the prevailing optimism of the time and a prescient exception to it. The rest of these stories represent typical Google News Archive search returns for "economic outlook."

Stock market top: September 1929

1. In November 1929, a few weeks after the crash, the Harvard Economic Society gave, as a principal reason why a depression need not be feared, its reasoned judgment that business in most lines has been conducted with prudence and conservatism. [But] the fact was that American enterprise in the twenties had opened its hospitable arms to an exceptional number of promoters, grafters, swindlers, imposters, and frauds...a kind of flood tide of corporate larceny.

In November, it said firmly that a severe depression like that of 1920-21 is outside the range of probability. We are not facing protracted liquidation. This view the Society reiterated until it was liquidated.

However there were exceptions. One was Paul M. Warburg of the International Acceptance Bank, whose predictions...were remarkably prescient. In March of 1929 (#1 in Figure 4), he called for a stronger Federal Reserve policy and argued that if the present orgy of "unrestrained speculation" were not brought promptly to a halt there would ultimately be a disastrous collapse. This he suggested, would be unfortunate not alone for the speculators. It would "bring about a general depression involving the entire country...." As the market went up and up, his warnings were recalled only with contempt.
—John Kenneth Galbraith, *The Great Crash 1929*

2. *Stock prices have reached what looks like a permanently high plateau....* I believe the principle of the investment trusts is sound and the public is justified in participating in them.... [I expect] to see the stock market a good deal higher than it is today, within a few months.
—Irving Fisher, Yale economist,
Milwaukee Journal, October 16, 1929

3. [Nearly] all of the standard railroad stocks are cheap and the industrial list is filled with stocks selling at real bargain prices. ... Prudent investors are now buying stocks in huge quantities and will profit handsomely when this hysteria is over...my friends and I are all buying stocks.

—John J. Raskob, "one of the country's leading industrial and political leaders," in *The New York Times*, October 30, 1929

4. I am convinced that through these measures we have reestablished confidence.   — President Herbert Hoover, December 1929

5. Editors Report to Hoover; Heads of Trade Organs Says Business Outlook is Good   —*The New York Times*, December 17, 1929

6. Opinion is Doubtful on Our 1930 Outlook; London Not Reassured by Trade Returns   —*The New York Times*, January 27, 1930

7. Hardware Outlook Good; Orders Booked in Week Indicate Feeling of Optimism   —*The New York Times*, February 5, 1930

8. [The] intensity of the speculative boom which reached its climax in the crash of last fall was as great or greater than that of "any of our major manias before," but...the intensity of the slump which followed it was greatly diminished by the efforts put forth to prevent it.... There has been no significant bank or industrial failure. That danger, too, is safely behind us.
        —Herbert Hoover, *The Evening Independent*, May 1, 1930

9. Advertisers Optimistic   —*The New York Times*, May 7, 1930

10. Guaranty Survey Sees Slow Upturn
        —*The New York Times*, July 28, 1930

11. European Outlook in Trade Improves
        —*The New York Times*, October 22, 1930

12. Hoover Urges Congress to Economize as He Presents Record Peace Budget; 4,860,000 Now Idle in Nation.... Warning Congress to avoid embarking on any new or enlarged ventures....
        —*The New York Times*, December 4, 1930

13. Bright Realty Outlook   —*The New York Times*, March 8, 1931
14. Tax Collections Continue to Fall
        —*The New York Times*, March 25, 1931
15. Economic Recovery in Sight
        —*The New York Times*, June 7, 1931
16. Depression Losing Grip.... Forget Gloom, Banish Fears....
        —Herbert Hoover, *The Milwaukee Journal*, June 16, 1931

* Pivot Point: Mid-September, 1931

17. J.E. Allen Hopeful on Realty Outlook
        —*The New York Times*, December 24, 1931

18. Unemployed autoworkers demonstrated in The Ford Hunger March from Detroit to Dearborn. Authorities shot and killed five workers and injured 60, many by gunshot.[4]
—Maurice Sugar (1980), *The Ford Hunger March*, March 7, 1932

19. We are likely to have a complete economic collapse in Europe within the next few months.
— L.S. Amery, British House of Commons,
in *The New York Times*, May 27, 1932

20. July brought violent deaths among the Bonus Army, 43,000 World War I veterans and their families who occupied areas of Washington for over a month to demand immediate payment of government-promised compensation for wartime service. After police shot and killed two of the veterans, troops commanded by General Douglas MacArthur and Major George Patton used bayonets and poison gas to drive the rest of the protesting vets out of the city.
—"Bonus Army Spectacle, U.S. Capital, 1932: What Really Happened," July 28, 1932

Stock market bottom: July 1932

21. Striking farmers now fight hunger. Several clashes with deputies occur—tear gas disperses big mob.[5]
—*The Montreal Gazette*, August 25, 1932

22. Famine Widespread In Quebec Region—10,000 people on the verge of starvation and another 60,000 faced with an acute shortage of provisions....[6]
—*The Rochester Evening Journal*, December 8, 1932

23. Unemployment Soars to New Record Mark
Unemployment has reached an "all time peak" with more than 11,600,000 persons now out of work in this country, according to President William Green of the American Federation of Labor....
"We are experiencing the worst unemployment crisis in our history," the labor leader said. "Those out of work are in greater need than ever before, for after three years of depression their resources are exhausted. Mental and physical wreckage caused by depression is driving families to seek relief in constantly growing numbers."
—United Press, January 7, 1933

24. Hoarders in Fright Turn in $30,000,000; Gold Pours Into Banks and the Federal Reserve as Owners Act to Avoid Penalty. Names

Taken Off List; Even Christmas Coins Help to Swell Week's Recovery of Metal to $65,000,000. Spurred by fear of public exposure and the threat of fines and imprisonment, gold hoarders scurried back to the Federal Reserve Bank and its member institutions yesterday to redeposit the yellow coins that they had lately stampeded to withdraw... little piles of gold pieces brought in by frightened individuals.... The repentant hoarders displayed a good deal of agitation, but they were received courteously by the guards of the Reserve Bank and came out with an evident air of relief when they had disposed of their dangerous treasure. The drastic character of the proposed law against gold hoarding frightened even those who had not thought of themselves as hoarders, but who suddenly recalled a few odd coins left over from Christmas presents which had not been spent because they were too "pretty".... The importance of the return-flow of gold to the Federal Reserve bank was emphasized by bankers, who pointed out that the $65,000,000 recovered so far this week could be used as the basis for the issuance of $162,500,000 of Federal Reserve notes or a very much larger amount of the new currency.

—*The New York Times*, March 10, 1933

25. Prolonged Illness Found Among Idle; Survey Shows 40% of Sick on Relief Rolls in State Have Been Ailing for Year. Others Average 25 Days   —*The New York Times*, April 16, 1933

26. There is a deeper feeling of pessimism among many of the delegations tonight regarding the...World Economic Conference than there has been since it assembled.

—*The New York Times*, June 21, 1933

27. Gas Bombs Close Stock Exchange at Noon
        — "A Chronological Survey of the Outstanding Financial Events of the Past Year," *The New York Times*, August 4, 1933

As indicated in Figure 4, lagging expressions of negative social mood reached a climax in 1933, producing the worst economic conditions of the century. As a thought experiment, imagine if you had been among investors who still owned stocks at that low. Consider how challenging it would have been to continue holding them while reading the news items listed at the bottom right of Figure 4. Most people would not have been able to resist the urge to abandon their holdings, even as a few speculators, expressing a slightly less negative social mood, were bidding up stocks at the margin.

Had you incorporated the socionomics model of immediate and lagging social actions at that time, you would have understood that the bad news was irrelevant to your investment decision-making. Had you employed the Elliott wave model, you might have been motivated to buy stocks, while others, stuck with the natural human default of assigning social-mood change to external causes such as economic and political news, would have despaired—as always—near the low.

The Stocks vs. News Progression of 1972-1975

Figure 5 shows the timing of news events relating to the 1973-1974 decline in the DJIA, the largest and steepest decline in the grueling 16-year bear market of 1966-1982. (That bear market is especially visible in inflation-adjusted measures such as the Dow/PPI, as depicted in charts throughout Chapter 10.) As happened in April 1930, the lagging event-line peak of late 1973 coincided with a B-wave (intra-correction) peak in stock prices.

Once again, the low in our lag line roughly coincides with the worst economic and political news of 1974-1975. In 1975, some five to nine months after the stock market low, U.S. unemployment hit a 33-year high, the federal deficit reached a 32-year high, U.S. investment and disposable income hit lows, and Saigon fell to the communists, giving them victory in the Vietnam War.

Headlines from The New York Times *Article Archive*

Here are some of the *Times'* representative news reports from July 1972 to December 1974. They express then-current perceptions and expectations about the future. All of them came up in internet searches for "economic outlook."

Reserve Chief Optimistic on the Economy   —July 27, 1972

Economic Seers Preview '73 as Another Bumper Year for Business
                                                 —August 7, 1972

Continued Economic Growth is Predicted for 1973
                                                 —September 28, 1972

* Stock market top: January 1973

Heartening Signals Sighted   —May 6, 1973

The Astonishing Boom...   —August 29, 1973

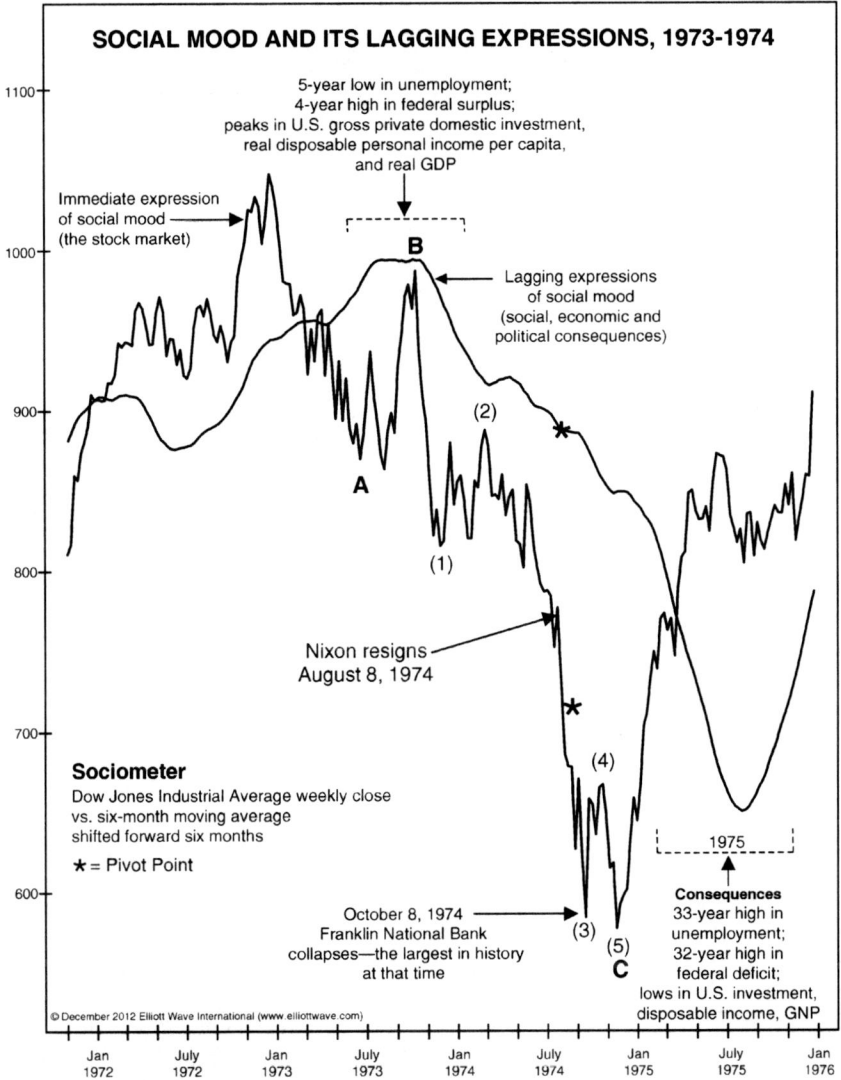

SOCIAL MOOD AND ITS LAGGING EXPRESSIONS, 1973-1974

5-year low in unemployment;
4-year high in federal surplus;
peaks in U.S. gross private domestic investment,
real disposable personal income per capita,
and real GDP

Immediate expression
of social mood
(the stock market)

B

Lagging expressions
of social mood
(social, economic and
political consequences)

(2)

A

(1)

Nixon resigns
August 8, 1974

Sociometer
Dow Jones Industrial Average weekly close
vs. six-month moving average
shifted forward six months

★ = Pivot Point

(4)

1975

October 8, 1974
Franklin National Bank
collapses—the largest in history
at that time

(3)
(5)
C

Consequences
33-year high in
unemployment;
32-year high in
federal deficit;
lows in U.S. investment,
disposable income, GNP

© December 2012 Elliott Wave International (www.elliottwave.com)

| Jan 1972 | July 1972 | Jan 1973 | July 1973 | Jan 1974 | July 1974 | Jan 1975 | July 1975 | Jan 1976 |

Figure 5

Western Industrial Nations Are Experiencing Their Greatest Economic Boom in More Than Two Decades. Economists See a 'Soft Landing' When Boom Ends   —September 2, 1973

Forecasts' Tone Improves   —October 21, 1973

Some Signs Point to the Right Path; The Economy, The Nation
                                            —November 4, 1973

World's Business Slowing.... Evidence is Mounting that the Worldwide Economic Boom of 1972-73 Has Cooled Off and that a Less Frantic Period of Economic Growth Has Set In.
                                            —November 18, 1973

Business is Optimistic on Economy   —December 10, 1973

Economic Outlook Gets Gloomier   —February 13, 1974

It's Still Early, But Economy May Have Seen the Worst
                                            —March 24, 1974

Economic Storm   —May 31, 1974

The Sky is Falling   —June 30, 1974

* Pivot Point: August 23, 1974

A Bundle of Economic Dilemmas   —September 5, 1974

S&P bottom: October 1974

It's a Recession, All Right   —October 27, 1974

A Nation in Deep Gloom   —November 24, 1974

DJIA bottom: December 1974

The Economic Threat...The Year is Ending With Much of the Nation in a State of Deep Anxiety Over the Course of the Economy. There Has Been Nothing Like the Present Degree of Apprehensiveness—or Confusion—about the Business Outlook Since 1930....
                                            —December 29, 1974

As explained in Chapter 26, expressions of "confusion," "uncertainty" and "unpredictability"—such as articulated immediately above—simply mean that a negative mood trend has been in force for some time. As in all our examples, negative economic news culminated months after the low and well into the next stock market advance, as noted at the bottom right of Figure 5.

The Stocks vs. News Progression of 2007-2012

Figure 6 shows the bear market of 2007-2009 and part of the subsequent advance. As you can see from the notes on the chart, a number of positive economic consequences lagged the October 2007 peak in the stock market. Likewise, negative economic consequences lagged the March 2009 bottom in the stock market, as bad economic news flooded the media for several months thereafter. Fitting socionomic causality, the National Bureau of Economic Research reported that the Great Recession officially began in December 2007, two months after the stock market peaked, and ended in June 2009, three months after the stock market bottomed.

Economists pay lip service to the fact that the stock market is a leading indicator, but they don't use it. When predicting corporate earnings for Q4 2008, the consensus among economists—even as late as the final week of December—was for quite a positive report. Following the stock market's collapse into October, corporations in fact turned in their worst performance in 140 years' worth of data: their first outright loss (see Figure 26 in Chapter 21). As some articles pointed out, it was the economic profession's biggest earnings-prediction error ever. Had economists been attuned to socionomic causality, they would not have been so optimistic.

On a cultural note, sociologists have traced the genesis of the rebellious Tea Party movement to CNBC commentator Rick Santelli's rant of February 19, 2009, in which he called out the moral hazard of the Fed and the government's bank and mortgage bailouts and proposed hosting a "Chicago tea party." Jenny Beth Martin advanced the cause by organizing a protest at the Georgia state capitol on February 27, 2009. On April 15, a month after the bottom in stocks, protesters demonstrated around the country, and on September 12, "a half-million people descended on Washington for a '9/12' tax protest organized by Fox News personality Glenn Beck."[7] These were lagging consequences of the trend toward negative social mood.

The stock market began advancing in 2009, but the lagging consequences of the turn toward positive social mood didn't begin pouring out until 2½ years after the rally started. The November 2011 issue of *The Elliott Wave Financial Forecast* listed a number of them:

- Industrial production rose in October at the fastest pace in three months at the nation's factories, utilities and mines.

- Factory output, the largest component of industrial production, increased a solid 0.5%. It was the fourth straight monthly gain.

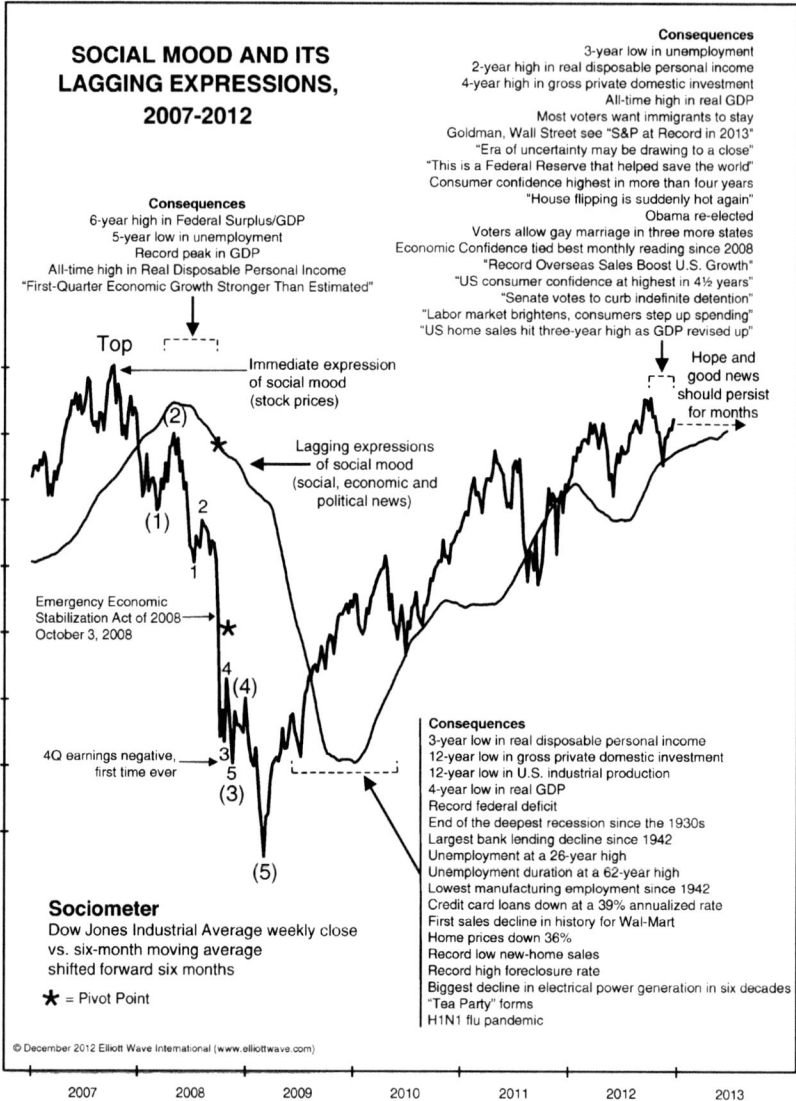

SOCIAL MOOD AND ITS LAGGING EXPRESSIONS, 2007-2012

Consequences
3-year low in unemployment
2-year high in real disposable personal income
4-year high in gross private domestic investment
All-time high in real GDP
Most voters want immigrants to stay
Goldman, Wall Street see "S&P at Record in 2013"
"Era of uncertainty may be drawing to a close"
"This is a Federal Reserve that helped save the world"
Consumer confidence highest in more than four years
"House flipping is suddenly hot again"
Obama re-elected
Voters allow gay marriage in three more states
Economic Confidence tied best monthly reading since 2008
"Record Overseas Sales Boost U.S. Growth"
"US consumer confidence at highest in 4½ years"
"Senate votes to curb indefinite detention"
"Labor market brightens, consumers step up spending"
"US home sales hit three-year high as GDP revised up"

Consequences
6-year high in Federal Surplus/GDP
5-year low in unemployment
Record peak in GDP
All-time high in Real Disposable Personal Income
"First-Quarter Economic Growth Stronger Than Estimated"

Top

Immediate expression of social mood (stock prices)

Hope and good news should persist for months

Lagging expressions of social mood (social, economic and political news)

Emergency Economic Stabilization Act of 2008 → October 3, 2008

4Q earnings negative, first time ever

Consequences
3-year low in real disposable personal income
12-year low in gross private domestic investment
12-year low in U.S. industrial production
4-year low in real GDP
Record federal deficit
End of the deepest recession since the 1930s
Largest bank lending decline since 1942
Unemployment at a 26-year high
Unemployment duration at a 62-year high
Lowest manufacturing employment since 1942
Credit card loans down at a 39% annualized rate
First sales decline in history for Wal-Mart
Home prices down 36%
Record low new-home sales
Record high foreclosure rate
Biggest decline in electrical power generation in six decades
"Tea Party" forms
H1N1 flu pandemic

Sociometer
Dow Jones Industrial Average weekly close
vs. six-month moving average
shifted forward six months

★ = Pivot Point

© December 2012 Elliott Wave International (www.elliottwave.com)

2007   2008   2009   2010   2011   2012   2013

Figure 6

- The auto industry has rebounded to drive most of the growth in factory output. Production of motor vehicles and parts rose 3.1% in October, the fourth straight monthly gain. Light trucks were the biggest contributor.

- Retail sales last month were higher than analysts had expected, rising 0.5%, according to the Commerce Department.

- Wal-Mart, the country's biggest retailer, said it had posted a quarterly increase in sales after nine consecutive quarters of declines.

Even better economic news came out later that year. Reuters reported on December 22 that Toyota forecast a 20% jump in global sales. On the same day, *The New York Times* described such "unexpected" results of the new trend toward positive social mood and, naturally, treated them as new causes:

> In recent weeks, a broad range of data—like reports on new residential construction and small business confidence—have beaten analysts' expectations. As the fourth quarter draws to a close, a spate of unexpectedly good economic data suggests that it will have some of the fastest and strongest economic growth since the recovery started in 2009, causing a surge in the stock market and cheering economists, investors and policy makers.[8]

Among political consequences, President Obama got a lift in the polls in November 2011, and he was re-elected a year later amidst even more optimism, confidence and bonhomie. His rise in popularity during this time was another expression of the positive trend in social mood (see *Socionomic Causality in Politics*, 2017).

Our charts also demonstrate why people remember news as having caused the market's moves. During the early stages of a new trend, emotions are subdued and the market/news alignment is weak. But in the months of maximum emotion, such as the final years of the 1990s advance and the final months of the 2007-2009 decline, news powerfully aligns with the trend. People connect the two conditions and "remember" news being causal.

We are unaware of any study demonstrating any type of social action or natural event, or combination thereof, as a consistent, reliable precursor of trends and changes in social mood as reflected by the stock market. On the other hand, trends and changes in social mood as reflected by the stock market are consistent, reliable precursors of compatible social actions.

Investors constantly ask what event will cause a bull or bear market to end. But as shown in Figures 4 through 6, news is best at and after a market top, which is the opposite of a negative shock, and news is worst at and after a major market bottom, which is the opposite of a positive shock. Those expecting exogenous conditions to signal trend reversals are always left behind at the turns.

A Confirming Report

A report from 2012 on Gallup's "Daily Negative Emotions" tally is chock full of socionomic statements:

> The U.S. was in the top quartile for daily negative emotions in 2011, scoring a 32 with increases in sadness, worry, and physical pain since 2007. Americans' negative emotions were at their lowest in 2007, with an index score of 23, the year before the economic downturn.
>
> Major world events did not necessarily affect the daily negative emotions in some countries. Japan's score of 21 on the index was exactly the same three months after the massive earthquake in 2011 as it was the year before. The trend was similar in earthquake-ravaged Haiti, where the level of negative emotions did not change between December 2008 and June 2010.
>
> Countries and territories with the highest negative emotions have been struck with economic hardship, riots, and revolutions. In some cases, such as Egypt and Bahrain, negative emotions were running high well before the unrest.[9]

Socionomics makes sense of every one of these observations: (1) A peak in positive social mood in 2007 coincided with a major top in the stock market and the lowest readings in negative emotions; (2) a negative state of social mood in 2011, the year of the first stock market low following the 2009 bottom, the year of the low in the Dow/gold ratio and a few months before the March 2012 bottom in real estate, fostered an outpouring of negative emotions; (3) major world events such as earthquakes have no effect on social mood even in the countries where they occur; and (4) areas reporting the most negative emotions later suffer extreme social events, such as economic hardship, riots and revolution. All of these statements conform to the socionomic case that social mood is not a result of current natural or social events but rather a primary cause of current and future social events.

Socionomic Causality Explains These Real-World Results

The charts in this chapter are real-world versions of the theoretical diagram presented as Figure 1 in Chapter 7. They show socionomic causality at work.

The same causality accounts for other researchers' results, heretofore unexplained. Take, for example, the Cutler et al. study of 1989, cited in Chapter 2, which included a departure from usual procedure. In searching for a model under which financial, political and economic events would predict aggregate stock prices, the authors built versions that included future information unavailable to investors in real time. Mixed models that included these variables managed to account for as much as 53% of the variance in aggregate stock prices. The delay of many socionomically motivated actions, as explained in Chapter 7 and detailed here, elegantly explains why that approach succeeded: News available only in the future did not predict past stock market movement; social mood regulating real-time stock market movement determined the tenor and character of future news. That study, which contributed immensely to the cause of challenging the mechanics paradigm, also modeled socionomic causality, albeit without realizing it.

Socionomic theory explains why it is ultimately futile for investors, politicians, economists and other futurists to base their decisions on present social events and conditions. Scouring the news and economic data for hints of what they "mean" for stock prices is an utter waste of time. The more aware you become of the socionomic dynamic, the more you can save yourself trouble and think independently of the crowd.

There is an even greater value to the socionomic perspective: By making the future much less unknown, it offers a substantial measure of serenity. As an email to us put it, "Ever since I started reading about socionomics (and subscribing to you guys), life has begun to resemble a movie based on a book I've already read."[10]

REFERENCES

[1] "500,000 Chicagoans Revel: Merrymakers Turn Downtown District Into Circus at All-Chicago Trade Jubilee," *Youngstown Vindicator*, May 14, 1931.

[2] Luo F., Florence C.S., Quispe-Agnoli M., Ouyang L., Crosby A.E. "Impact of Business Cycles on US suicide rates, 1928–2007." *American Journal of Public Health*. 2011; 101(6):1139-46.

[3] Dreier, P. "Protests? Yes. Riots? No." *Huffington Post*, September 20, 2011.

[4] "Ford Hunger March," Wikipedia.

[5] "Striking Farmers Now Fight Hunger. Several Clashes with Deputies Occur—Tear Gas Disperses Big Mob," *The Montreal Gazette*, August 25, 1932.

[6] "Famine Widespread in Quebec Region," *Rochester Evening Journal*, December 8, 1932.

[7] Davis, Mark, "Jenny Beth Martin: The Head Tea Party Patriot," *Atlanta Journal-Constitution*, May 9, 2010.

[8] Lowrey, Annie, "Signs Point to Economy's Rise, but Experts See a False Dawn," *The New York Times*, December 21, 2011

[9] Clifton, Jon, "Middle East Leads World in Negative Emotions," *Gallup World*, June 6, 2012.

[10] Scott, Fred, email, May 17, 2005.

Chapter 9

Did U C New Studies? Tweets N Blogs Predict Equity Prices

Euan Wilson

February 4, 2011[1]

Recently published as well as preliminary work from researchers at four universities indicates that expressions of social mood as displayed in social media can be useful in predicting price moves in the stock market. These results challenge conventional economic and financial theory but are compatible with the socionomic hypothesis that changes in social mood motivate and therefore precede changes in social actions that express them.

The researchers used data from two social media platforms: Twitter and Live Journal. Twitter is an online service that enables each user to post to followers, on a personal page, text with a 140-character limit. Twitter currently processes 65 million posts (called "tweets") per day from an estimated 175 million users. LiveJournal is an online journal, or blog, a platform that accepts more lengthy posts than Twitter. Its history is longer than Twitter's, so it has produced a longer-term data set. Academics and market professionals are increasingly viewing these data as a source of real-time information about what users are thinking and feeling. Such data, it seems, may prove to be an even more immediate sociometer than the stock market.

Twitter Paper: "Twitter Mood Predicts the Stock Market"

Johan Bollen et al.[2] were the first researchers to assess the relationship between Twitter posts and stock-market movements. Operating under the assumption that movements in the stock market would buffet people's emotions, the researchers were surprised to find that aggregate expressions of emotional states *preceded* stock market changes. NPR reported,

As Bollen explains, when he began his study, he expected that the mood on Twitter would be a reflection of up and down movements in the stock market. He never imagined it would be a precursor....

"And then [my co-author] said, 'There's one more thing you should know. I had to shift the mood curve forward in time by three or four days.'"

That's when Bollen knew: It wasn't that the Dow Jones could be used to predict the mood on Twitter—it was that Twitter could be used to predict the Dow Jones.[3]

To test their data, the research team set up a three-day, preceding-value indicator as a control. Then they assessed nine million tweets over a span of nine months in 2008 using a program to comb the tweets for words expressing six different emotional states: Calm, Alert, Sure, Vital, Kind and Happy. They created a seventh category designating each tweet as positive or negative and designed a model that would predict the direction of the stock market based on the prevalence of each emotion.

The most effective indicator was Calm (an indication of low or high anxiety), which improved upon the control by 13.4 percentage points. Positive spikes in Calm portended advances in the Dow, and negative spikes in Calm portended declines in the Dow. These results fit the socionomic proposition that calm certainty and anxious uncertainty are expressions of positive and negative social mood, respectively.

LiveJournal Paper: "Widespread Worry and the Stock Market"

Gilbert and Karahalios[4] created a program that searches LiveJournal posts for words associated with fear and anxiety to build what they called an Anxiety Index. The program assessed 20 million entries that bloggers posted over a nine-month period in 2008, a pace of roughly 74,000 declarations of emotion per day.

The authors then compared trends in the posts to movements in the stock market. They likewise discovered that spikes in expressions of worry *preceded* stock market declines, in this case by two days.

The authors stated that their study has several limitations. For example, they cited a paper finding that bloggers tend to be younger than the general population. They also noted that some LiveJournal bloggers speak not only of their own emotions but also of those of the people around them. For socionomists, both points in fact offer advantages. The mood of the young often reflects more passionately the mood of society at large, and reporting on friends' emotions increases the size of the representative group.

MIT Study in Progress

Peter Gloor and colleagues[5] randomly sampled Twitter posts and searches for the emotive keywords *hope*, *fear* and *worry*. Initial results have shown that increases in the use of the three words corresponded, with a brief lead time, positively to the S&P 500's volatility measure (VIX) and negatively to stock prices.

The team's findings also fit one of socionomic theory's subtler observations. Wall Street considers hope and fear to be opposites. Gloor's results suggest that hope and fear both reflect negative mood. This inference corresponds to socionomists' understanding that a feeling of uncertainty—which prompts both fear and hope—is an emotional manifestation of negative social mood (see Chapter 26). Prechter has long described bear markets as proceeding along a Slope of Hope. Gloor expressed similar sentiments:

> To put this in simple words, when the emotions on Twitter fly high, that is when people express a lot of hope, fear, and worry, the Dow goes down the next day. When people have less hope, fear, and worry, the Dow goes up. It therefore seems that just checking on Twitter for emotional outbursts of any kind gives a predictor of how the stock market will be doing the next day.[6]

Gloor cautioned that much work remains before his team verifies the hypothesis scientifically. But to date, their results align with socionomic theory.

What These Studies Mean for Socionomics

Contrary to expectations based on the mechanics paradigm, these three studies independently found that stock price changes did not *precede* but rather *followed*, by one to three days, aggregate verbal expressions of emotions on social media. Socionomic theory explains why: People can tweet about their moods faster than they can express those moods by making stock trades, one reason being that stock markets are often closed and unavailable for trading until hours later.

These researchers' efforts may lead to new, more sensitive sociometers. If society does express its mood via social media more swiftly than via the stock market, and if researchers are able to distill their data into an unbounded sociometer, we may be able to add a line to Figure 1 in Chapter 7 that lies slightly to the left of the line representing the stock market.

REFERENCES

[1] Adapted from Wilson, Euan, "Did U C New Studies? Tweets N Blogs Predict Equity Prices," *The Socionomist*, February 4, 2011.

[2] Bollen, Johan, Huina Mao, and Xiao-Jun Zeng, "Twitter Mood Predicts the Stock Market," *Journal of Computational Science*, 2011, Vol. 2, No. 1. pp. 1-8.

[3] "Need stock tips? Read your tweets." National Public Radio, October 24, 2010.

[4] Gilbert, Eric, and Karrie Karahalios. "Widespread Worry and the Stock Market." Fourth International Association for the Advancement of Artificial Intelligence Conference on Weblogs and Social Media, Washington, D.C. May 23-26, 2010.

[5] Zhang, Xue, Hauke Fuehres, and Peter A. Gloor. "Predicting Stock Market Indicators Through Twitter: 'I Hope It Is Not As Bad As I Fear.'" *Procedia—Social and Behavioral Sciences*, 2011, Vol. 26. pp. 55-62.

[6] Gloor, P.A. "Predicting Stock Market Indicators Through Twitter 'I Hope It Is Not as Bad as I Fear,'" Swarm Creativity Blog, August 5, 2010.

Chapter 10

From Observation to Prediction

Robert R. Prechter

A Prefacing Note On Statistics and Anecdotal Evidence

Professional economists rely on weak, ad hoc anecdotal evidence to a stunning degree. They see news; they see the market move; they call it cause and effect. Their use of statistics isn't ideal, either. As noted in Chapter 2, a staggering 40% of statistical results published in peer-reviewed economics journals cannot be replicated. Sometimes researchers select convenient time periods for testing that will yield a statistically significant result. (See, for example, Matt Lampert's review of claims that the party elected affects the performance of the economy.[1]) The old "damn lies" joke has some truth behind it.

Scientists favor statistics over anecdotal evidence, which is fine. But they typically dismiss anecdotal evidence as worthless. Both types of evidence, however, can be valid or invalid. Socionomists respect properly vetted statistics, and we conduct statistical studies when data are sufficient to support them. But with the real world as a lab, we are also comfortable taking certain anecdotal evidence into account. Sometimes anecdotal evidence is pregnant with meaning, while statistics are barren.

Here's an example: I was sitting at a trading desk in New York on the afternoon of January 21, 1980, when my office buddy came back from lunch to tell me about an experience he had just had. He had been visiting a pal in the coin business when a customer rushed in with a briefcase full of cash. He plopped the cash on the counter—$50,000 worth—and said to the proprietor, "Turn that money into silver." The dealer said, "I'll have to call for a quote, and I will have to charge you a fee of $4 an ounce because of the volatility." The man responded, "I don't care! Turn that money into silver!" The customer walked away with an order confirmation for a shipment of 943 ounces of silver, for which he paid $53 an ounce. When he finished telling his story, my buddy and I both exclaimed, "Silver has got to be near a top." As it turned out, that session's close was the peak in the silver mania. It's been 35 years now, and still the metal's price has never been higher. Including the fee, the customer's purchase price turned out to be $3 higher than the highest price ever reported for spot silver.

What could statistics have told you on that day about the future price trend for silver? Not much. Events such as this, on the other hand, are not only evidence of current and future market conditions but very good evidence.

In most cases, the anecdotal evidence we discern to be valuable implies statistical significance. With respect to the above example, I had never seen any such thing happen; my colleague, who had been in the business 25 years by then, hadn't seen it; and the coin dealer, who had been in business for 20 years, had never experienced such an incident in his shop. Considering that the event took about ten minutes and that our combined professional experiences covered 13,000 working days, each with 48 ten-minute periods, the customer's silver buy was a once-in-a-624,000-period event. A statistician might be able to measure the validity of the evidence by polling a representative sample of coin dealers in the country to get back data on their experiences, compile it and test it against aggregate prices for silver; but if we lack the substantial resources required to conduct such a survey, is it really necessary that we discard the evidence we do have?

With socionomics still in its early stages of validation, socionomists have avoided dogmatically dismissing anecdotal evidence. As data and statistics become available, we will use them. In the meantime, we have tried to apply wisdom to the task of discerning the difference between high-quality and low-quality evidence of any type, whether statistical or anecdotal. You will find instances of both types in this chapter and in Chapter 21.

Socionomic Causality Explains and Predicts

Socionomics' utility derives from both its explanatory power and its predictive power. It accounts for a plethora of past events and can be applied to anticipate higher or lower probabilities for many types of future events.

Issues of *The Elliott Wave Theorist* from 1979 onward, a special report titled "Popular Culture and the Stock Market" (1985)[2] and *The Wave Principle of Human Social Behavior* (1999) introduced a number of textual and graphic observations of compatibility between stock prices and other records of social actions. According to socionomics, the causation involved does not issue from among any of these variables but from a hidden variable, social mood.

It is true that "correlation is not causation." On the other hand, as demonstrated in Part I, exogenous-cause claims with respect to finance fail to provide *any* causally consistent correlations, which is a far more serious challenge to overcome. That socionomics can identify numerous correlations is a significant achievement.

Observed Correlations Have Become Successful Predictions

Socionomics has made numerous successful predictions. The past 12 to 36 years have provided a substantial amount of out-of-sample data. This period includes four shifts at Primary degree from positive to negative social mood or vice versa, and three shifts at even higher degree as recorded in measures of stock prices adjusted by PPI or gold. In every case, social changes occurred pretty much as socionomic causality suggested they should. The following list and accompanying illustrations extend the records of a dozen of these originally proposed relationships, with data updated through 2015.

(1) *Major trend changes in the stock market lead trend changes in prosperity and depression.* I made this observation in *The Elliott Wave Theorist* in August 1979.[3] Shortly after the inflation-adjusted Dow (Dow/PPI) (plotted in Figure 4) bottomed in 1982, the economic malaise of the preceding dozen years yielded to an economic boom.

Ever since the real-money value of stocks (Dow/gold; plotted in Figure 13) peaked in 1999, the trend toward increasing prosperity has given way to a trend toward decreasing prosperity. But with nominal prices (per Figure 1) and PPI-adjusted prices (see Figure 4) both having achieved new highs, the economy has avoided depression—so far.

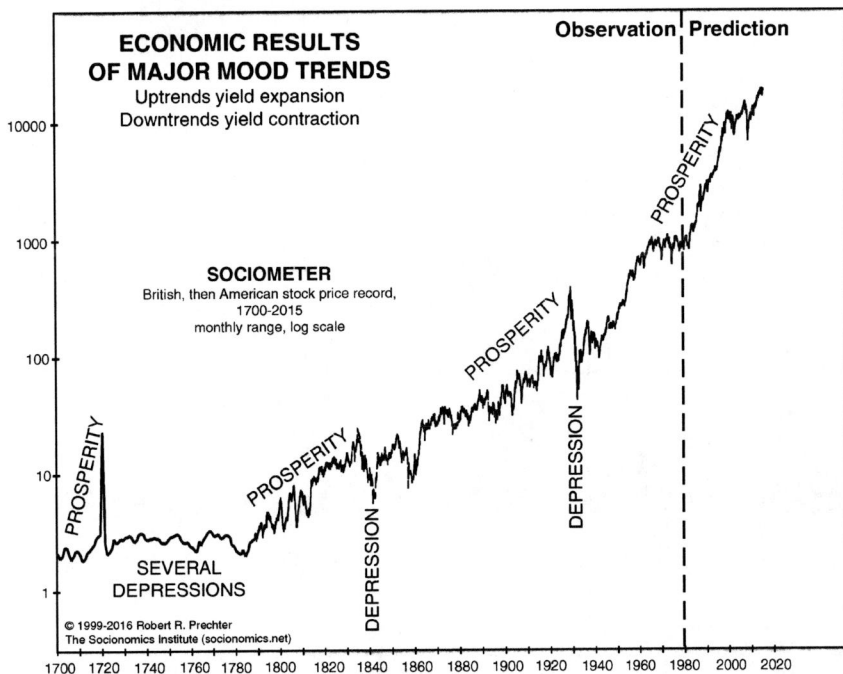

Figure 1

(2) *The stock market leads GDP*. As the stock market fell in Q1 1980 and again in 1981-1982, back-to-back recessions developed. As the stock market rose from 1982 to 1987, an economic boom occurred. After stock prices went sideways to down from 1987 to 1990, a recession developed. As stock prices resumed rising, the economy resumed expanding. As the stock market fell in 2000-2001, a recession developed. As the stock market recovered in 2002-2007, an economic expansion occurred. As the stock market fell in 2007-2009, a recession developed, and it was commensurate with the size of the drop: The largest stock market decline since 1929-1932 led to the deepest recession since 1929-1933. As the stock market has recovered since 2009, an economic expansion has developed. In all cases but one, the stock market either turned down before the recession began or turned up before the expansion began. The lone exception was in 2002, when the Dow made a new low after the official end of the recession in 2001. Data show that a setback in GDP growth into that later bottom just barely missed creating a recessionary quarter. (It is important to understand

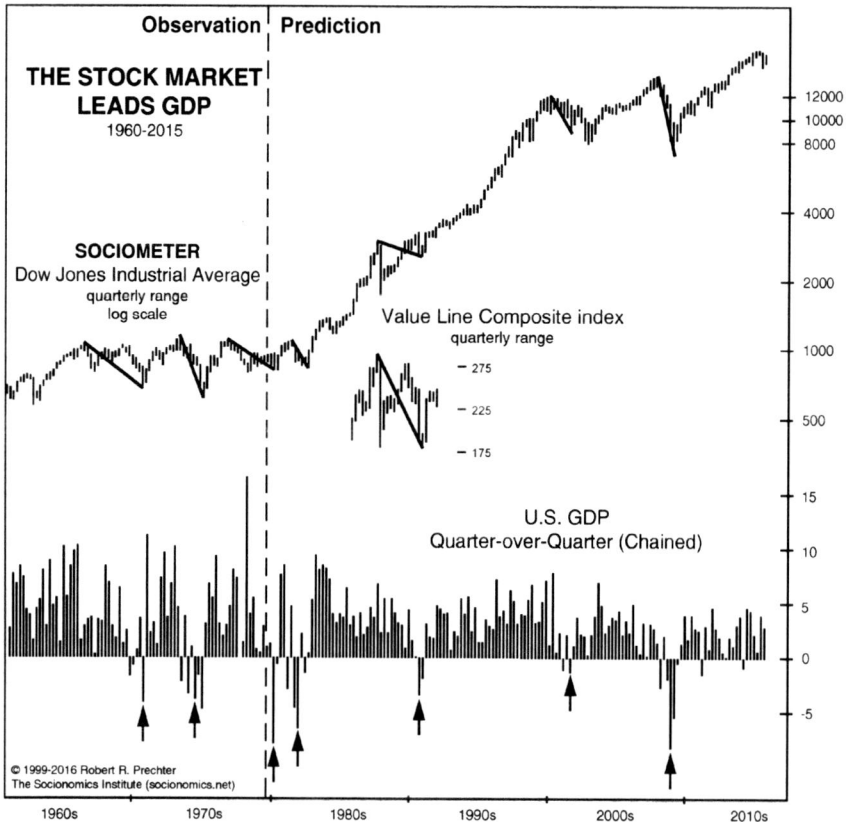

Figure 2

that socionomic causality does not predict that each stock market decline will produce an official recession as defined by the NBER; it predicts that stock market declines and advances will reliably lead rather than follow whatever official recessions and recoveries do occur.[4])

(3) *The stock market leads trends in the number of patents granted.* Since the *Theorist* made this observation in 2004,[5] the trends in patents granted have continued to reflect the trends in stock prices, with a fairly consistent lag reflecting the long time it takes to proceed from coming up with a novel idea to registering a patent. The causality here is counter-intuitive. One might think that people would come up with more inventions when they were unemployed and had more time to tinker in the basement, but such is not the case. Social mood regulates the incentive to be inventive.

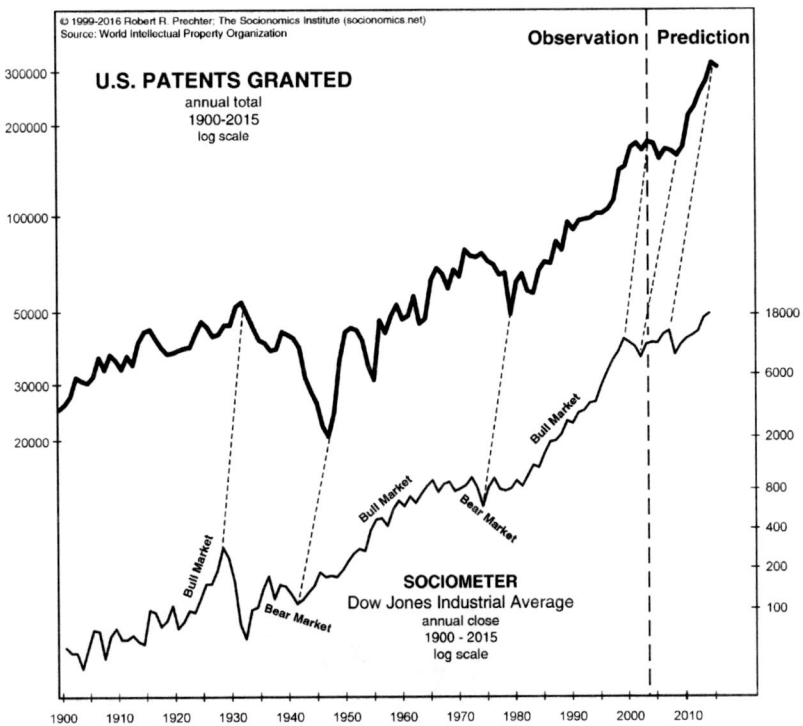

Figure 3

(4) *Rising stock prices coincide positively with the quality and popularity of Disney's animated fairy-tale films, and falling stock values coincide positively with the originality and popularity of horror movies.* I made the horror movie connection in 1985 and the Disney film connection in 1999.

Disney studios was asleep at the wheel for six years after the 1982 bottom in the Dow/PPI, but the company finally caught on to the positive trend in social mood and issued *The Little Mermaid* in 1989, kicking off a new string of family-oriented, animated tales. After the stock market's real value peaked in 1999 and a ten-year bear market began, horror movies

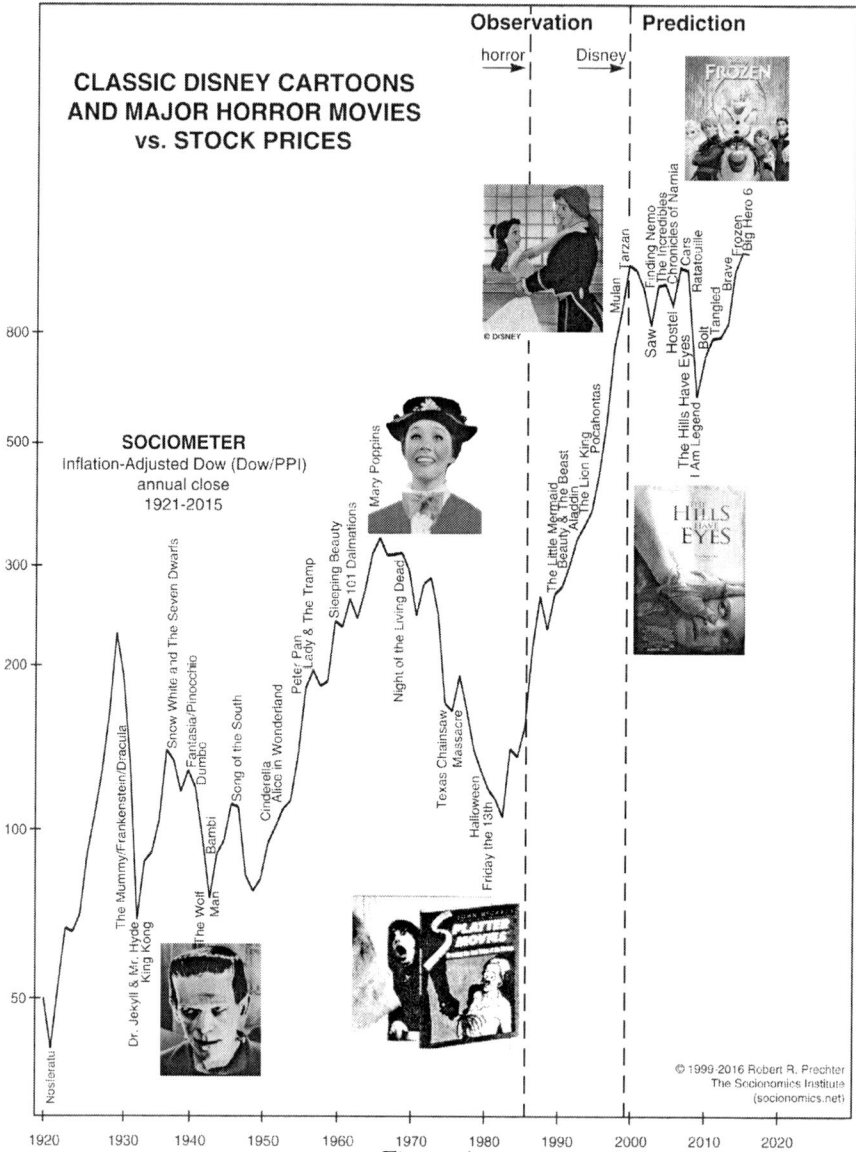

Figure 4

became a theater staple and filmmakers found a new way to shock people, with "torture porn" films, led by *Saw* (2004) and *Hostel* (2005). Disney's animated films continued in production as slipping stock values nevertheless held near all-time highs, but 2009's *The Princess and the Frog*, issued near a major stock market bottom, was so poorly attended that the studio announced on November 20, 2010 that, though it had completed work on *Tangled*, it had canceled its other fairy-tale projects "for the foreseeable future."[6] As stock prices resumed rising, however, the company quickly resumed producing fairy-tale films. In 2014, with the stock market at all-time highs, Disney's *Frozen* became the highest-grossing animated film ever. It was also a critical success, winning two Academy Awards. Although horror movies have remained in production during this time, their box-office success has lessened and none of them has been thematically ground-breaking. Their intensity has softened, too, as exemplified in the 2011 headline, "Blood and Guts Give Way to Subtler Film Frights at Box Office."[7] As exemplars of the slide in quality, *I, Frankenstein* (2014) was rated only 1½ stars ("based on 87 reviews, the general consensus is 'Loud, incoherent, and dramatically listless'..."[8]) and *Victor Frankenstein* (2015) suffered a grade of "D" and even more dismal reviews ("a mashed-up mess...tedious...unintentionally amusing...you have to suffer through...will be quickly forgotten"[9]). Our thesis retained its predictive value for both genres. *Socionomic Studies of Society and Culture* (2017) offers another dozen examples of popular entertainment's reflection of social mood.

Pop quiz: What tenor of social mood would accommodate pictures of smiling monster families?

If you guessed, "a major extreme in positive mood," you're correct. The two television series featuring these characters ran from 1964 to 1966, right as the Dow/PPI was heading into its major top of 1966. The subjects' smiles are almost as big as Mary Poppins' in Figure 4.

As long as the current bull market continues in both nominal and real-money terms, Disney's animated tales should continue to enjoy great popularity and horror moves should be fewer and less impressive. In the next bear market, the horror genre will plunge human minds into new depths of depravity, and Disney will curtail or cease its production of family-oriented, animated fairy-tale features.

(5) *Trends in the stock market correlate positively with human concep-tion rates.* This is a very long term correlation and is not expected to coincide with year-by-year trends. Nevertheless, in the sixteen years following this observation,[10] the conception rate has continued to track leading sociom-eters. It rose into the peak of the biggest U.S. investment mania ever, that of real estate, into 2006. That's why in 2007 more babies were born than in any other year in U.S. history. A drop in births followed the same leading sociometer downward into a century-low birth rate in 2009 and persisted for four years, reflecting the fall in real estate prices that lasted into 2012.

Sociologists, working in the paradigm of exogenous cause, blamed the reversal in births from 2007 to 2009 on the Great Recession, with this reasoning: "When the economy is bad and people are uncomfortable about their financial future, they tend to postpone having children."[11] This explanation fails, however, because people don't decide at the last minute whether or not to let the baby out of the womb; it's too late by then. Birth rates are a proxy for conception rates. When the annual data are plotted a year earlier, roughly adjusting for the human gestation period, the data show that the highest number of conceptions occurred in 2006, after which there was a decline in 2007 and a plunge in 2008. These years are a perfect match with the peak in real estate prices in 2006 and the plunges in stock and property prices in 2007-2008. When social mood was elevated, people initiated more babies, and as it shifted toward the negative, they initiated fewer, in both cases ahead of the lagging economic data. That's why births in 2009 were low. The causality change was not a response to economic conditions but an expression of social mood, of which birth rates and the trend of the economy are both lagging results.

(On a technical note, we had to abandon the cumulative advance-decline line as our sociometer when stocks went to decimal pricing, skewing the data. This is another example of the data impurity problem broached in Chapter 7. Figure 5 substitutes real estate prices and the Dow from that time forward, but they are not likely to fit as well. Conceptions have closely tracked stock market momentum indicators, which turn down before stock

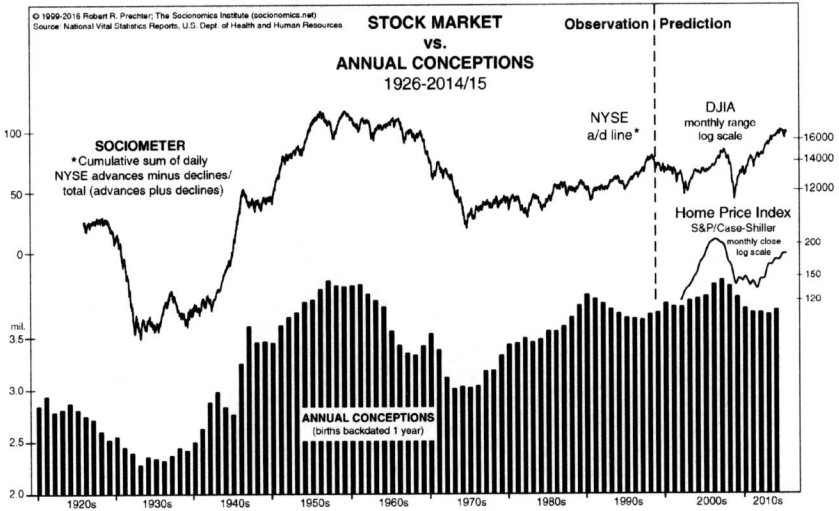

Figure 5

averages do. Current and future rising trends in conception rates should continue to turn down before the stock market does. For further discussion, see Chapter 9 of *Pioneering Studies in Socionomics*.)

(6) *Stock market trends correlate with the height of fashionable women's hemlines.* The University of Pennsylvania's George Taylor in 1926, Ralph Rotnem in the 1960s and Paul Montgomery in the early 1990s demonstrated that women's hemlines have risen and fallen with the stock market. In August 1985, "Popular Culture and the Stock Market," which was condensed for an article in *Barron's*,[12] offered an explanation for the correlation: "A rise in both hemlines and stock prices reflects a general increase in friskiness and daring among the population, and a decline in both, a decrease."[13] In other words, a trend toward positive social mood induces speculators to bid up stock prices and prompts women to wear frisky clothes, whereas a trend toward negative social mood induces speculators to offer down stock prices and prompts women to wear somber clothes. In September, someone wrote to *Barron's* protesting that one would think Prechter is saying it's better to pay attention to *"Women's Wear Daily* than *The Wall Street Journal* [and] *Billboard* instead of...Financial News Network." As I responded in *Prechter's Perspective*,[14] "That's exactly what I'm saying."

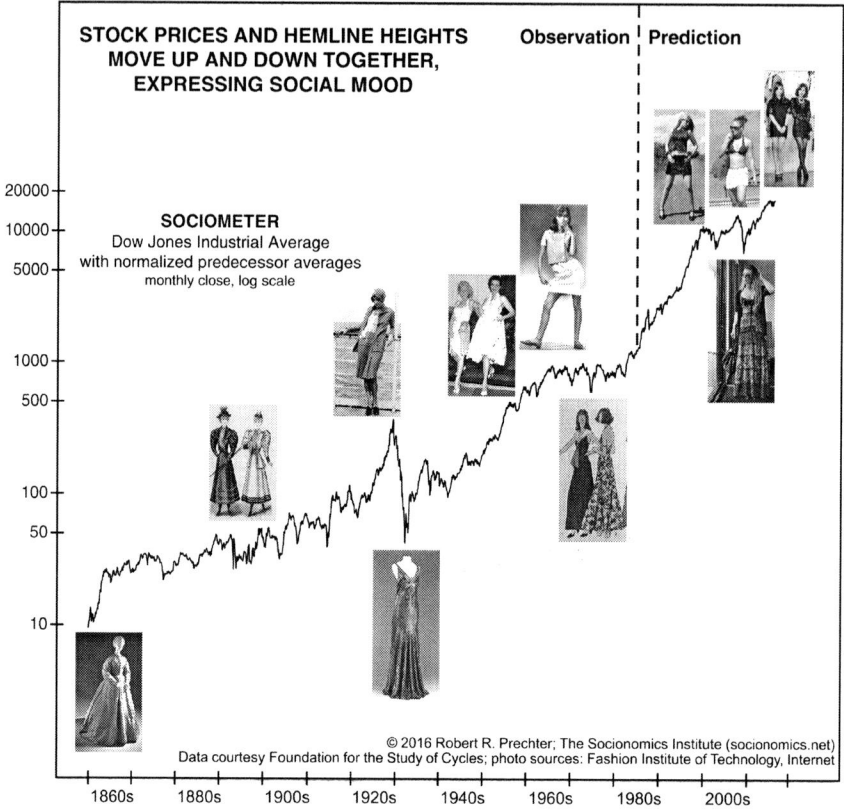

Figure 6

Figure 6 displays representative photographs from the Fashion Institute of Technology and the Internet characterizing skirt fashions of the past 150 years. Figure 7 displays related news headlines near the latest peaks and troughs in the stock market. Once again, a socionomic observation has led to multiple successful predictions. Early in the bull market, my 1985 report quoted a fashion model saying about skirts of the day, "they're real cute *as long as they're not too short*." As social mood headed toward a positive extreme in the late 1990s, mini-skirts became widely popular for the first time since the late 1960s. Following a lull during the stock market setback of the early 2000s, mini-skirts dominated fashion again near the stock market peak of 2007, when a headline advised, "The Mini-Skirt is Back, So Get Those Legs in Shape." When stock markets around the world plunged from that year into 2009, fashions returned to the "maxi-skirt" look popular at the bear-market low of 1974. In April 2014, after the Dow Jones Industrial Average had risen all the way back to a new all-time high, *The Wall Street Journal* noted that skirt styles had progressed from "shin-length confections" in 2011 to "the shortest in years"[15] at the spring 2014 fashion shows. In November 2014, *The New York Post*[16] highlighted an array

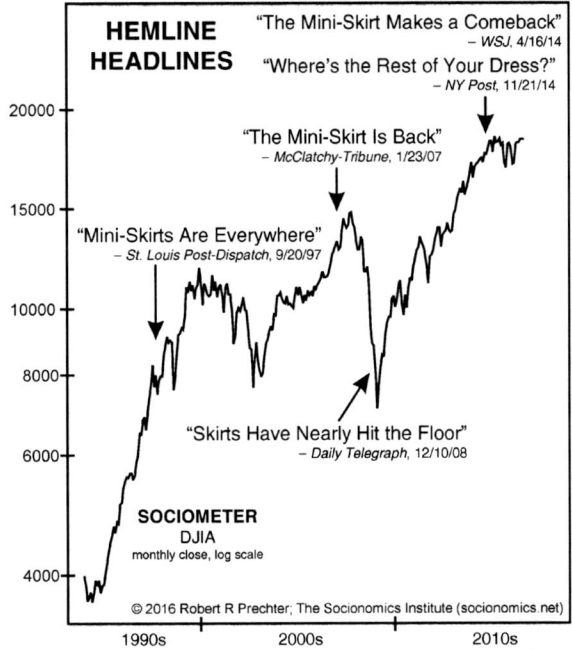

HEMLINE HEADLINES

"The Mini-Skirt Makes a Comeback"
 – *WSJ, 4/16/14*

"Where's the Rest of Your Dress?"
 – *NY Post, 11/21/14*

"The Mini-Skirt Is Back"
 – *McClatchy-Tribune, 1/23/07*

"Mini-Skirts Are Everywhere"
 – *St. Louis Post-Dispatch, 9/20/97*

"Skirts Have Nearly Hit the Floor"
 – *Daily Telegraph, 12/10/08*

SOCIOMETER
DJIA
monthly close, log scale

© 2016 Robert R Prechter; The Socionomics Institute (socionomics.net)

1990s   2000s   2010s

Figure 7

of celebrities sporting ultra-short skirts. As the Dow continued climbing to another new all-time high in May 2015, the roster of celebrity mini-skirt sightings grew notably longer, as recorded by photographs in *People* and *Us* magazines. It appears, then, that the tendency of young women to express degrees of friskiness or somberness by the height of their hemlines has continued along socionomic lines.

(7) *Stock market trends provide a basis for predicting the reelection or rejection of incumbents.* The Socionomics Institute's peer-reviewed paper[17] on using stock market trends to predict reelection outcomes demonstrated a highly significant statistical relationship between the two sets of data presented in Figure 8. Our correlation, originally published in *The Wave Principle of Human Social Behavior* in 1999, has made two successful pre-dictions. In 2004, incumbent George W. Bush faced reelection. The stock market had bottomed two years earlier and had eked out a slight gain by election time. In accordance, Bush eked out a slight reelection win in terms of electoral votes. In 2012, incumbent Barack Obama faced reelection. The stock market had risen into Election Day on a 1-year, 2-year, 3-year and 4-year basis. Obama handily won the reelection with 61.7% of the electoral vote.

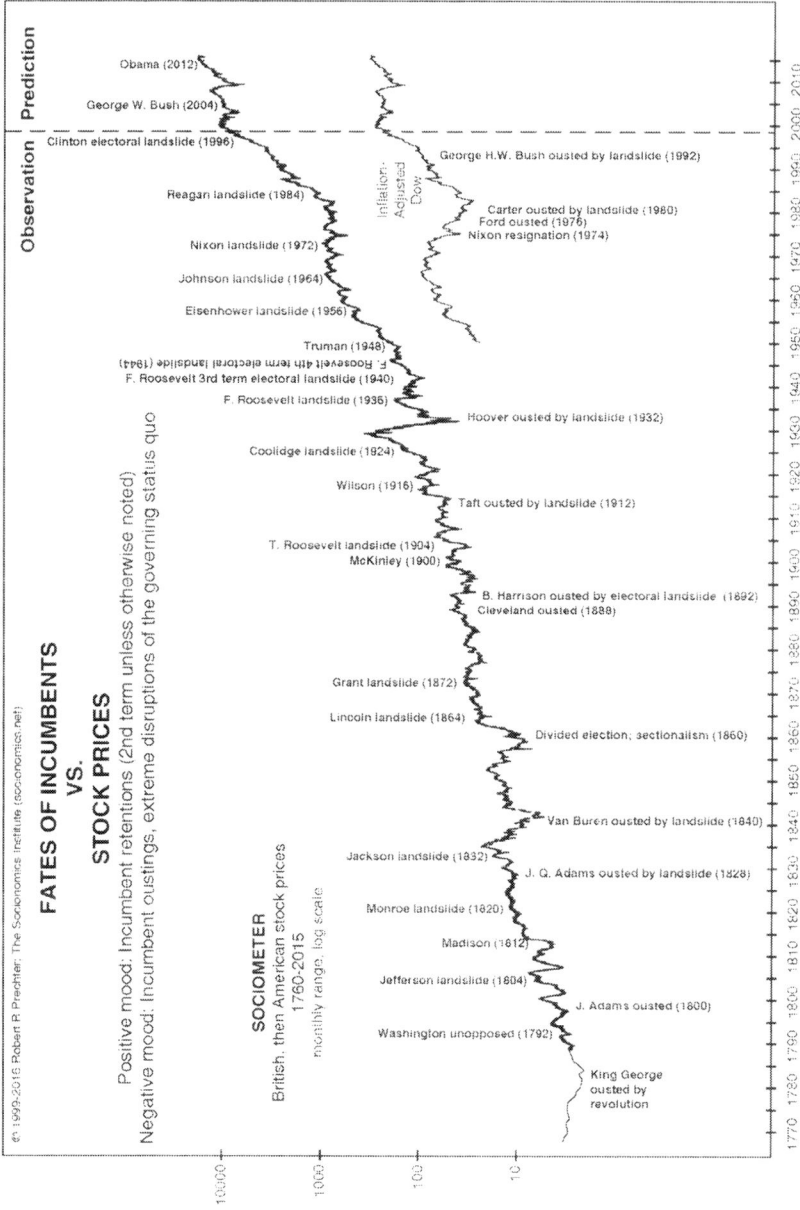

Figure 8

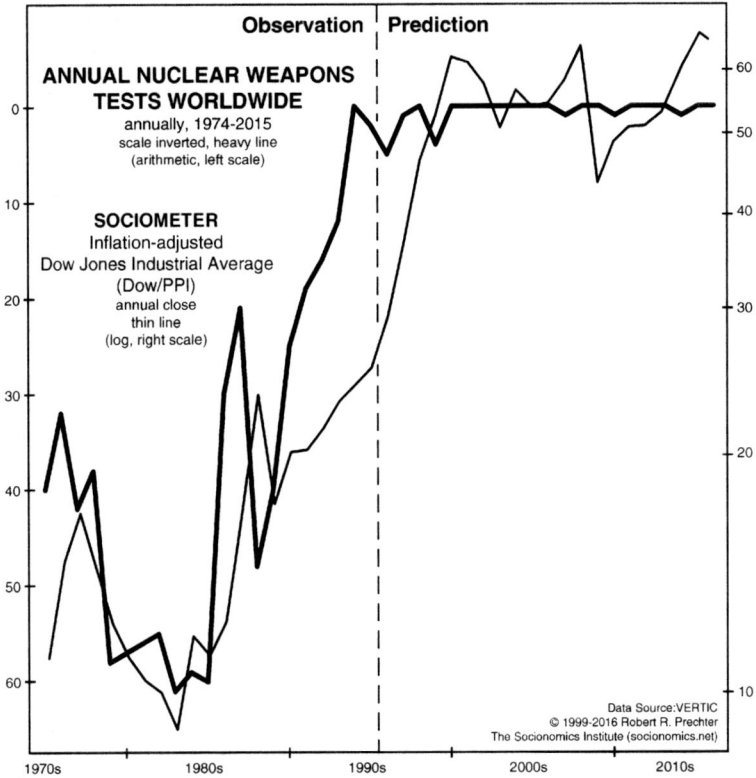

Figure 9

(8) *Stock market trends correlate with trends in nuclear weapons testing.* The first version of Figure 9—which begins at the start of the data—was published in *The Elliott Wave Theorist* in June 1995. Twenty years have passed since then, and the trends have continued to coincide. Matt Lampert has run statistics on these data. The correlation (r) of the raw nuclear test data to the log of annual closes for the DJIA is -0.92, with a one-tailed p-value $< 10^{-6}$. Detrended data produce a correlation (r) of -0.71, with a one-tailed p-value $< 10^{-6}$. These results are highly statistically significant. This is another very long term relationship, and it has been predictive. With the stock market holding near historically high prices and valuations since the late 1990s, nuclear weapons tests have remained at or near zero.

(9) *Long term bull markets in stocks precede mostly peaceful times, and long term bear markets precede significant wars.* I introduced this theme in the October 1982 issue of *The Elliott Wave Theorist* by predicting that there would be "No international war for at least ten years." Most of the globe did

enjoy peaceful times throughout the bull market that carried through 2000.
The only significant skirmish involving the U.S. during that time was the
Gulf War of 1991, which compatibly with socionomic causality followed
the stock market's Primary-degree correction of 1987-1990, as manifest
clearly in the path of the Value Line indexes, per Figure 3 of Chapter 41.
The *Theorist* published the first version of Figure 10 in February 1989, and
its implications have held true over the quarter-century since then.

Three years after the major stock market top of 2000, the U.S. became
mired in its longest war ever. The 9/11 attacks of 2001 occurred after eighteen months of decline in the S&P following its peak in March 2000. After
two and a half years of increasingly negative social mood, on October 10,
2002, the very day of a multi-year low in the Dow Jones Industrial Average,
the U.S. Congress passed a resolution to attack Iraq. The attack itself took
place on March 19, 2003, just seven days after a multi-year low in the World
Stock Index and the second low of a double bottom in the Dow. (Figure 4
of Chapter 41 graphs these events.) Suggesting rationalization at work, the
U.S. government's stated reason for starting the war was that Iraq possessed

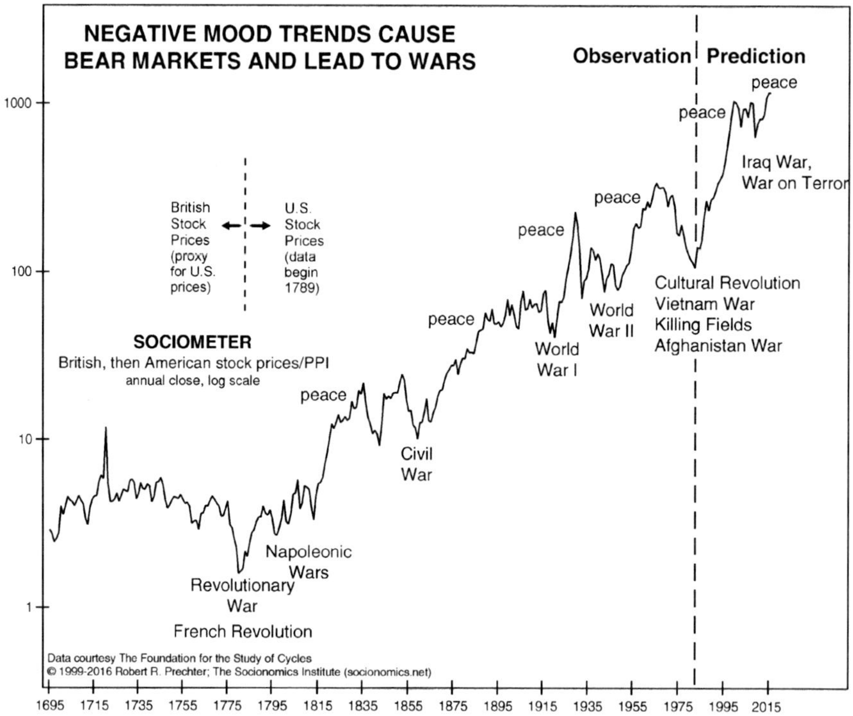

Figure 10

weapons of mass destruction, which turned out not to exist. Hostilities escalated in Afghanistan, where the number of U.S. troops soared during the bear market of 2007-2009, and in 2011 fighting spread to Libya and Syria. U.S. troop deployment in the Middle East peaked in 2011, coincidentally with the low in the Dow/gold ratio (plotted in Figure 13) and the last full year of the downtrend in U.S. real estate prices. Exquisitely reflecting the ensuing positive trend in social mood, the number of U.S. troops deployed in the region then fell by over 90% as most nominal stock market indexes rose to new all-time highs. The government's focus has shifted to helping fight ISIS, but with social mood having trended positively, U.S. involvement has been restrained and U.S. casualties have remained low. For additional coverage of the connection between social mood and armed conflict around the world, see *Socionomic Causality in Politics* (2017).

(10) *Social mood affects the national trade balance more than the trade balance affects the economy.* Recall from Chapter 2 the errors of thought and forecasting that economists have committed over the past 40 years when trying to use the trade balance to predict changes in the economy. A socionomic orientation has yielded better results. *The Wave Principle of Human Social Behavior* offered the idea that an increasingly positive social mood had been propelling the stock market, the economy, consumer spending and the U.S. trade deficit higher in concert, as ebullient U.S. consumers used credit to purchase more goods from abroad. The February 11, 2005 issue of *The Elliott Wave Theorist* added, "The irony stemming from economists' improper premise will continue in the [upcoming] bear market. When the trade deficit begins shrinking again, economists will assign it a bullish value when in fact this time it will go hand in hand with the onset of a depression." The accompanying chart (see Figure 11) boldly declared, "When the Trade Deficit 'Improves,' the Stock Market Will Tank."

Figure 12 shows how well this outcome played out. The trade deficit began shrinking in 2006. Economists, echoing similar expressions quoted in Chapter 2, hailed it as a bullish improvement. But in line with our prediction, the real-estate boom ended simultaneously, stocks and GDP peaked the following year, and all four measures plummeted together during the Great Recession of 2007-2009. It was the biggest stock market decline since 1929-1932, the deepest real-estate bear market since the bust of 1926, the deepest recession since the Great Depression, *and the deepest retrenchment in the trade deficit on record*, a combination precisely opposed to economists' expectations but compatible with ours. When the trend in social mood reversed from negative to positive in 2009, stocks, the trade deficit, the economy and (eventually) real estate all turned back up.

As published in February 2005

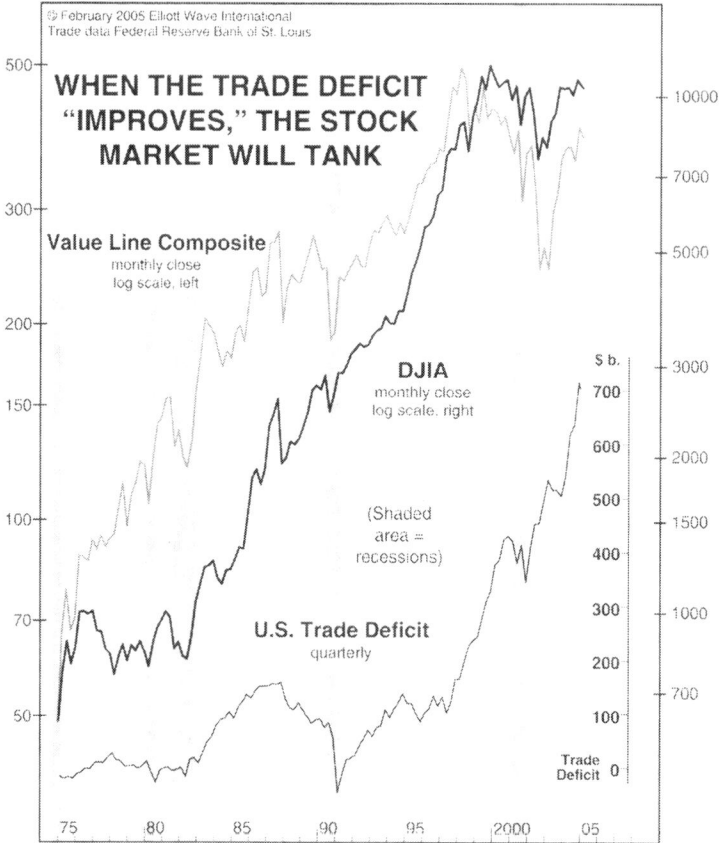

Figure 11

Take a moment to ruminate over the fact that no economist any-where—as far as we can determine—made the forecast we did. Knowledge of socionomics wasn't even necessary. Anyone who examined the data in Figure 11 could have come to the same conclusion. The entire economics profession must be doing something wrong, while socionomists must be doing something right.

For the record, the lengthy negative relationship between social mood and the U.S. trade balance illustrated here is not permanent. As noted in Chapter 2, the trade balance is not a universally applicable sociometer but a measure that has been tracking social mood differently in different countries over a certain period of time. One day these data sets could shift to a different relationship or none at all.

Outcome

THE TRADE DEFICIT "IMPROVED," AND THE STOCK MARKET TANKED

© September 2009 Elliott Wave International
Trade data Federal Reserve Bank of St. Louis

Value Line Composite
monthly close
log scale, left

DJIA
monthly close
log scale, right

(Shaded area = recessions)

U.S. Trade Deficit
quarterly

Figure 12

(11) *Bear markets portend outbreaks of epidemic disease, and bull markets their lack.* The March 18, 1994 issue of *The Elliott Wave Theorist* made this observation: "For whatever reason, disease sometimes plays a prominent role in major corrective periods, with some Cycle and Supercycle degree corrections containing epidemics and larger ones pandemics." This observation was also a prediction in suggesting that the relationship would continue to hold for newly conducted historical research as well as in real-time experience. It has indeed held well on both bases over the ensuing 21 years, as shown in Alan Hall et al.'s multi-national study of stock markets and epidemics, reprinted in *Socionomic Studies of Society and Culture* (2017).

(12) *Generally speaking, the character of social trends of all kinds will change in line with the tenor of social mood as recorded by the stock*

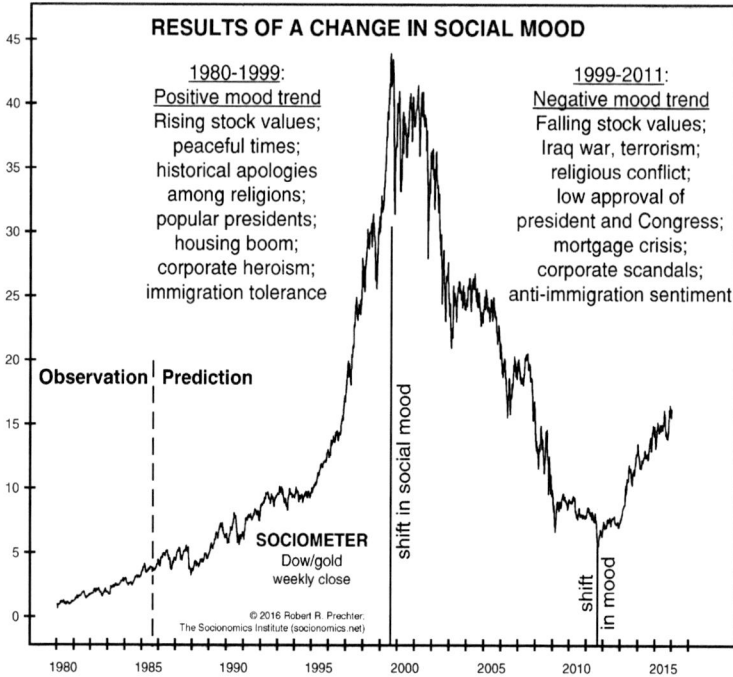

Figure 13

market. Figure 13 dramatizes the shift in social mood that occurred in 1999 by showing the Dow priced in terms of real money (gold). The list of events on the left side is quite in contrast to the list on the right side. If history had no socionomic cause, social changes would not bunch like this. But they do.

And Much More

Socionomists have observed correlations between trends in the stock market and over fifty types of social actions. Our list includes shifts in prosperity vs. depression, GDP, patents granted, Disney's animated films, horror movies, procreation rates, incumbents' re-election outcomes, nuclear weapons testing, peace and war, political and social alliances, political and religious apologies, presidential popularity, immigration tolerance, corporate heroism vs. scandals, credit and debt creation, secessionism, authoritarianism, epidemic disease, employment, film ratings, film earnings, television programming, accounting practices, collectibles prices, baby names, social-media sentiment, sports-car horsepower, automobile styling, pop stardom, popular musical styles, skyscraper construction, roller-coaster construction, drug prohibition, rates of imprisonment, the popularity of eugenics, attitudes toward education, expressions of uncertainty, government benefits, artists' styles, globalization, financial regulation, space exploration, suicide rates, mass shootings, protest movements, state aggression, the activity of serial killers, meat consumption, sugar consumption, commercial and industrial fatalities, central bankers' emotional states, ladies' hemlines, facial expressions in crowds and society's focus on heroes or anti-heroes. All of these treatments were reported in our monthly periodicals, *The Elliott Wave Theorist* and *The Socionomist*, from which selected studies are included in *Socionomic Studies of Society and Culture* (2017) and *Socionomic Causality in Politics* (2017). These correlations have endured in subsequent, out-of-sample data, and we are confident that they will continue to do so.

Waves of social mood even regulate things such as what kinds of studies behavioral psychologists are doing, what courses college students take, what kinds of rulings come out of the courts, what kinds of recreational drugs are popular, the nature and number of state-sponsored atrocities, what kind of art is going through a revival, what types of financial theories are dominant (see Chapter 40) and even what questions pollsters ask. Waves of social mood explain why in the 1950s parents sent their kids to summer camp to learn survival skills whereas in the late 1990s parents sent their kids to summer camp to learn stock-trading skills. If you take the time to study the history of your own profession, you will see how mightily waves of social mood—as indicated by trends in the stock market—account for many of its trends and changes. Trends and events in many people's individual lives fit these waves as well.

Three Possible Explanations

There are three ways to explain the numerous historical correlations we have found between our primary leading sociometer—the stock market—and data from the economy, politics, health and culture:

(1) *It's all coincidence.* It could be. But the number of data series correlating not only to the stock market but also to each other renders this position untenable.

(2) *Each correlation is an isolated case in which A causes B or B causes A.* Economists can get away with this formulation when dealing with the economy and the stock market by offering the notion (challenged in Chapter 39 of this book and in Chapter 43 of *Pioneering Studies in Socionomics*) that speculators are divining future trends in the economy. But no one can argue that those testing nuclear bombs are doing so in reaction to human conception rates, no one would assert that fashion designers are adjusting skirt heights as an inverse expression of the popularity of horror movies, and no one would propose that those designing sports cars are doing so in response to fluctuations in epidemic disease.

(3) *There is a hidden variable C, an anterior common cause.* Our candidate is waves of social mood. This explanation is simple, direct, efficient and elegant.

Evidence in Favor of Explanation #3

(1) *Quantity of correlations*: We have produced dozens of graphs displaying correlations between stock prices and other social data series that we anticipated on the basis of socionomic theory. Exogenous cause models lack such evidence, as demonstrated in Part I.

(2) *Chronology within the correlations*: In all our data, trends in the stock market either *precede* or *coincide with* the other social trends and events. There are no instances in which other social trends and events reliably precede stock market movements. This chronology fits socionomic causality and no other theory of which we are aware.

(3) *Temporal spread in the timing of correlations*: Only socionomics explains why certain types of social trends lag the stock market by comparatively little time (as with fashion styles and popular entertainment) and why others do by months or years (as with GDP, employment, peace and war, and grants of patents).

(4) *Bunching of correlations*: We have shown the preceding set of graphs individually, but we could stack all of our observations on top of one another from floor to ceiling to demonstrate that we are observing not dozens of isolated instances of cause and effect but one (hidden) cause with dozens of effects.

(5) *Lack of contrary evidence*: Although occasional minor disparities appear in the data (such as the lack of an official recession in 2002), we have found no long term data series that persistently contradict socionomic causality.

(6) *No data mining:* In Part I we tested all exogenous-cause claims for financial markets of which we are aware, and in this chapter we listed dozens of socionomic relationships that we have correctly anticipated. We have not cherry-picked these data series while excluding others, and we did not apply an electronic spreadsheet to the task of retrofitting variables—as financial-market modelers typically do—to manufacture patterns from random data. As every data-miner discovers, fabricated correlations typically fail as soon as the in-sample period ends. This has not been the case with socionomics. The post-introduction maintenance of the correlations shown in Figures 1 through 13 has continued to reflect socionomic causality.

(7) *Predictive power with respect to the past*: Socionomic theory allows us to figure out that we should be looking for certain unusual types of

relationships in the first place. Nearly every time we have posited a correlation between two data series based on social-mood causality—even ones that would appear strange to most people—it has worked out as expected. So, socionomic theory is a good predictor of correlations between sets of previously untested data.

(8) *Predictive power with respect to the future*: Socionomically informed correlations, once demonstrated, have predictive power with respect to future, out-of-sample data.

For the record, the high quantity of correlations we have proposed and identified subsumes the possibility that a few of our observed correlations may in fact be coincidence. In the majority of cases, theory and data are tightly wedded, but the validity of socionomic theory does not rest upon whether or not trends in, say, patent grants result primarily from trends in social mood or from sociological causes. Given the breadth of our investigation, occasional errors of causal presumption in specific cases seem more likely than an error of theory.

Conclusion

Financial analysts search for causality in macroeconomics and politics. Macroeconomists search for causality in politics and finance. Political analysts search for causality in finance and macroeconomics. All of them believe that someone else's A is causing their B. The result is the equivalent of three dogs chasing each other's tails. Instead of looking at each other's fields for causes, all three types of analysts—along with sociologists and historians—might consider joining socionomists in finding ultimate causality in variable C—waves of unconscious social mood.

A program of statistically validating more of our graphic correlations is underway. My statistically minded colleagues have already obtained highly significant p-values and/or correlations (r) for five relationships: those between the DJIA/PPI and nuclear-bomb tests (as reported in this chapter); the DJIA and U.S. presidential reelection outcomes (in a published, peer-reviewed paper[18]); the DJIA and sugar consumption in the U.S. ("Sweet Correlations," 2007); the DJIA and U.S. aircraft accidents ("Social Mood and Aircraft Accidents," 2007); and the DJIA/PPI and the U.S. Index of Social Health ("Exploring Socionomic Causality in Social Health and Epidemics," 2016, a paper currently under submission to an academic journal and posted at ssrn.com). The latter three studies are to be included in *Socionomic Studies of Society and Culture* (2017). The not-for-profit Socionomics Foundation (socionomics.org) funds work in this field entirely from tax-deductible donations.

NOTES AND REFERENCES

[1] Reprinted in *Socionomic Studies of Society and Culture*. Prechter, Robert (Ed.). Gainesville, GA: Socionomics Institute, 2017.

[2] Prechter, Robert R. "Popular Culture and the Stock Market," August 22, 1985, reprinted in *Pioneering Studies in Socionomics*, 2003.

[3] *The Elliott Wave Theorist*, August 3, 1979. Quoted in Chapter 1 of *Pioneering Studies in Socionomics*.

[4] At least one official recession occurs within each correction of Primary or Cycle degree. In the bear markets of 1937-1942 and 1960-62, recessions (in 1937-8 and 1960-1) followed the A waves but not the ensuing C waves. When the A wave does not produce a recession (as in 1966, 1978 and 1987), the ensuing C wave does (as in 1969-70, 1980 and 1990-91). At higher degrees, corrective-wave declines always produce economic contractions.

[5] *The Elliott Wave Theorist*, October 15, 2004. Republished as Chapter 11 in *Pioneering Studies in Socionomics*.

[6] Chmielewski, Dawn C. and Claudia Eller, "Disney Animation is Closing the Book on Fairy Tales," *Los Angeles Times*, November 21, 2010.

[7] White, Michael, "Blood and Guts Give Way to Subtler Film Frights at Box Office," Bloomberg, January 26, 2011.

[8] Wikipedia, "I, Frankenstein," accessed December 30, 2015.

[9] Rodriguez, Rene, "*Frankenstein* is a Mashed-up Mess of a Film," *Miami Herald*, November 26, 2015.

[10] Prechter, Robert R. "A Socionomic View of Demographic Trends, or Stocks and Sex," *The Elliott Wave Theorist*, September 24, 1999. Reprinted in *Pioneering Studies in Socionomics*, 2003.

[11] Marchione, Marilynn, "Recession May Have Pushed US Birth Rate To New Low," Associated Press, August 27, 2010.

[12] Prechter, Robert R. "Elvis, Frankenstein and Andy Warhol." *Barron's*, September 9, 1985.

[13] Prechter, Robert R. "Popular Culture and the Stock Market," August 22, 1985, reprinted in *Pioneering Studies in Socionomics*, 2003.

[14] Prechter, Robert R. *Prechter's Perspective*, New Classics Library, 1996, pp. 180-181.

[15] Brinkley, Christina, "The Mini-Skirt Makes a Comeback," *The Wall Street Journal*, April 16, 2014.

[16] "Where's the Rest of Your Dress?" *New York Post*, November 21, 2014.

[17, 18] Prechter, Robert R., Deepak Goel, Wayne D. Parker and Matthew Lampert, "Social Mood, Stock Market Performance, and U.S. Presidential Elections: A Socionomic Perspective on Voting Results," *SAGE Open*, October 2012. Republished in *Socionomic Causality in Politics*, The Socionomics Institute, 2017. This paper is publicly available at http://papers.ssrn.com.

Chapter 11

Socionomics Satisfies the Criteria of Falsifiability and Predictability

Robert R. Prechter

Falsifiability

For any theory to be scientific, it must be falsifiable. In other words, it must generate hypotheses that someone could test to see if they are false. Examples of non-falsifiable theories are (1) Nostradamus' predictions are accurate if you interpret them properly; (2) people have souls, which live on after their bodies die; (3) aliens will someday return to earth and take the progeny of their spawn back to their planet; (4) certain illuminati arrange global economic and political trends to suit them. These theories are non-falsifiable, because there is no way to disprove them so that proponents would jettison their beliefs.

Socionomics is Falsifiable

Socionomic theory's hypotheses are thoroughly falsifiable. Here are some of its testable claims:

(1) The tenor of multi-year stock market trends is more often positively than negatively correlated with the tenor of economic and political events that follow. (Examples: Changes from economic contraction to expansion are more likely to follow upward stock market reversals of Primary or larger degree than downward ones, and vice versa. An incumbent is more apt to be re-elected than rejected if the stock market rose during his term than if it fell, and vice versa. Socionomists have done this study. See *Socionomic Causality in Politics*, 2017.)

(2) Preceding trends in the stock market predict election results, wars, peace and trends in the economy better than election results, wars, peace and the trends in the economy predict ensuing trends in the

stock market. (Examples: Recessions should follow stock market declines of Primary or larger degree more often than they precede them. Changes in the employment rate should follow changes in the stock market of Primary or larger degree more often than they precede them. Figure 18 in Chapter 21 speaks to this claim. The stock market should be a better predictor of election outcomes than election outcomes are of the stock market. We have done this study; see *Socionomic Causality in Politics*, 2017.)

(3) Social actions that take time to mobilize tend to lag social actions that express social mood more immediately. (Example: Stock price trends should lead commensurate trends in the economy and initiations of peace or war.)

(4) Claims and assumptions favoring exogenous causes of stock market trends will fail to survive testing. (We set the stage for testing this claim throughout Chapters 1 and 2.)

(5) When both endogenous-cause and exogenous-cause, rational-reaction explanations for social action are tested simultaneously, the endogenous-cause explanation will usually better fit the data. (Examples: The stock market should be a better predictor than jobs-related legislation of employment trends; the stock market should be a better predictor than economic statistics of reelection results. Socionomists have completed part or all of these two studies; see Chapter 22 in this book and our elections paper in *Socionomic Causality in Politics*, 2017.)

(6) Because the herding impulse drives most participants in financial markets to buy investment items at higher prices than they sell them, most speculators' decision-making in the financial marketplace tends eventually to result in losses. (See Chapter 17 for evidence supporting this hypothesis.)

(7) Different cognitive processes are involved in economic vs. financial decision-making. (fMRI studies could confirm or refute this expectation; see Chapter 13 for preliminary evidence supporting this assertion.)

(8) The volume of transactions in investment items will be positively correlated with those items' prices more consistently than the volume of transactions in economic items will be positively correlated with those items' prices. (See Figure 9 in Chapter 12.)

(9) Actual stock market data will adhere to the Elliott wave model better than will randomized stock market data. (My colleagues and I hope to test this claim with our computer program, EWAVES.)

(10) The closer a social or financial trend comes to termination, the more certain most forecasters will become that the trend and conditions accompanying it will continue.

If these claims were falsified, I would abandon socionomic theory. If these statements are false, so is the theory.

Other socionomic hypotheses, harder to test but still subject to falsification, might include the following:

(1) Positive changes or negative changes—defined before testing—in stock prices, incumbent leaders' popularity, international relations, conception rates, tone and theme of popular music, films, games and sports, flamboyance of clothing, and other aggregate actions that would seem to express social mood are more often positively correlated with each other than negatively correlated.

(2) Producers and consumers mostly reason, whereas financial speculators mostly rationalize. (See Chapters 12 and 19).

(3) Price changes for speculatively traded items bought and sold in a financial setting will adhere to the Elliott wave model more closely than will price changes for goods and services bought and sold in an economic setting. (See Chapters 12 and 13.) (EWAVES equips us to test this claim.)

(4) Financial markets will adhere to the Elliott wave model more closely than to any predictive model based on supply and demand. (See Chapter 22 for evidence favoring this expectation).

(5) Most speculators do not objectively calculate either value or risk before buying or selling an investment item.

Testing these five ideas would be difficult. For example, how would one go about distinguishing between reasoning and rationalizing? Although I believe one can detect changes in the emotional tone of popular music, which we have demonstrated aurally,[1] what exactly is emotional tone, and how would one measure it?

We may have solved the latter research problem by narrowing our focus only to the margins. With respect to the popularity of film genres, we contrasted only extreme expressions of positive and negative social mood, respectively, as evidenced by the success of Disney's animated fairy tales vs. horror films (see Figure 4 in Chapter 10). We also investigated animated features that include graphic sex and/or vulgar language and images and found that they have occurred almost exclusively in periods of negative social mood as evidenced by bear markets in stocks.[2] A similar approach of testing extreme expressions at the margin might work with regard to other modes of social-mood expression.

The Non-Falsifiability of Conventional Economic Practice

Economists continually speak as if their exogenous-cause paradigm is useful. They make highly specific, after-the-fact statements of causality, such as, "When the oil price moved, the stock market reacted," or "the stock market celebrated because party X got elected." Our simple graphs have falsified every theoretical generalization derivable from the commonest of such statements, as detailed in Part I and in studies republished in *Pioneering Studies in Socionomics* (2003) and *Socionomic Causality in Politics* (2017). We also expect to be able to falsify any similar claims we may encounter in the future. If data fail to confirm any general statement that a theory makes, hasn't the theory been falsified? I think so.

As explored in Chapters 24 and 25, Keynesian, monetarist and Austrian economic theories have non-falsifiable aspects. Multiple failures of theory-driven interventionist policies in the U.S., Europe and Japan suggest that their proponents have avoided establishing clear parameters for falsifiability. Yet universities embrace and teach those ideas.

As detailed in Chapters 2 and 19, exogenous-cause claims in finance and macroeconomics are endlessly self-contradictory. One economist will explain why an increasing trade deficit will hurt stocks and the economy; another will explain why it indicates an active consumer and therefore a healthy economy. One economist says *rising* oil prices will hurt stocks and the economy; another says that *falling* oil prices will hurt them. One says a Democrat's win will help stocks and the economy; another says it will hurt. One says that a tsunami in Japan will damage that country's economy; another says it will spur economic activity. Taken together, such claims are a shambles.

A theory whose proponents routinely accept and defend conflicting hypotheses is non-falsifiable. A theory that routinely *generates* conflicting hypotheses must be false.

Chapter 33 cites other researchers who have challenged aspects of neoclassical economic theory as both empirically inconsistent and non-falsifiable. Yet economists have maintained the mechanics paradigm of exogenous cause anyway, by default, because they have been unable to conceive of anything to replace it. Socionomics offers an alternative.

History shows that once bad ideas become accepted, status-quo bias fosters a double standard with respect to judging evidence and falsifying theories. The accepted theory gets many passes, while the challenging theory is given high hurdles. Some people say this is good science, but I don't think so. Evidence and objectivity should always rule judgment.

Successful Prediction is Crucial to Theoretical Validation

Falsifiability is hardly the only requirement for establishing a valid scientific theory. Sokal and Bricmont explained:

> The Popperian scheme—falsifiability and falsification—is not a bad one, if it is taken with a grain of salt. But numerous difficulties spring up as soon as one tries to take falsificationist doctrine literally. [H]is solution, taken literally, is a purely negative one: we can be certain that some theories are false, but never that a theory is true or even probable.

> Obviously, every induction is an inference from the observed to the unobserved, and no such inference can be justified using solely deductive logic. [A]t least <u>one of the roles of science is to make predictions on which other people…can reliably base their activities, and all such predictions rely on some form of induction</u>.

> There are always experiments or observations that cannot be fully explained, or that even contradict the theory, which are put aside awaiting better days. [But] <u>the history of science teaches us that scientific theories come to be accepted above all because of their successes</u>.[3]

Socionomic theory satisfies this elevated criterion. It is falsifiable, which is good, but it is also uniquely successful at social prediction. It has allowed us to predict that the stock market would be a better predictor of election outcomes than would economic data (see *Socionomics Studies of Society and Culture*, 2017), that governments' testing of nuclear bombs would track the stock market (see Chapter 10), that trend changes in employment would lag trend changes in the stock market rather than be leading or coincident (see Chapter 21), that the 1980s would be free of international warring (see Chapter 10), that the price of oil would trace out Elliott waves (see Chapter 22) and dozens of other outcomes. All of these predictions came from the logical application of the socionomic theory of causality. The mechanics paradigm's exogenous-cause theories, in contrast, have not offered—and cannot offer—any general statements useful for financial and social prediction. I am confident that rigorous testing of both sets of claims will prove out in socionomics' favor.

NOTES AND REFERENCES

[1] See *History's Hidden Engine* (DVD) Prechter, Robert and David E. Moore. The Socionomics Institute, March 2006.

[2] Wilson, Euan, "Of Mice and Mood: Animation's History Through a Socionomic Lens," *The Socionomist*, August 24, 2010. Also, Euan Wilson, "Of Mice and Mood, 1969-Present: Part Two of a Study on Animation and Socionomics." *The Socionomist*, February 4, 2011. Republished in *Socionomic Studies of Society and Culture*, The Socionomics Institute, 2017.

[3] Sokal, Alan, and Jean Bricmont, *Fashionable Nonsense: Postmodern Intellectuals' Abuse of Science*, 1998, New York, NY: Picador USA, pp. 62, 63, 67.

Part III:

THE SOCIONOMIC THEORY
OF FINANCE

Chapter 12

The Financial/Economic Dichotomy

Robert R. Prechter

Neoclassical economic theory posits that fully informed, utility-maximizing agents with static valuation methods who react rationally and consistently to external stimuli produce a stable, equilibrium-seeking, mean-reverting system of pricing, values and trade, regulated by the laws of supply and demand. It applies this description equally to economic and financial settings. While capturing, in my view, key aspects of individuals' economic behavior, neoclassical economic theory does not offer a useful model of finance or the behavior of economies. Not so well known is what model should replace it. Before answering that question, we need to recognize five key differences between economic behavior and financial behavior, each one of which incorporates numerous component differences.

Difference #1: Financial Prices Have No Reliable Standards of Value

In economic markets, prices serve as mutual benchmarks of value. Knowing the price of one good or service allows one to estimate the price of another. Goods and services—whether grains vs. meats or house-cleaning services vs. car-repair services—are priced consistently sensibly relative to each other in the minds of both producers and consumers. Even when relative values change due to unusual conditions, such as war or famine, price changes are sensible in light of people's objectively determined needs and values at the time.

Economists believe that financial markets operate the same way: "The standard theory of financial markets...is founded on the idea that the prices of stocks and other securities should tend toward their proper values."[1] While the term "proper values" is elusive, economists generally agree that stock prices derive from rational considerations of objective criteria such as present and/or future corporate earnings, dividends, book values and dividend payouts relative to interest payments from bonds. This idea makes perfect sense. It is also perfectly wrong.

NO RELIABLE STANDARDS OF VALUE FOR THE STOCK MARKET

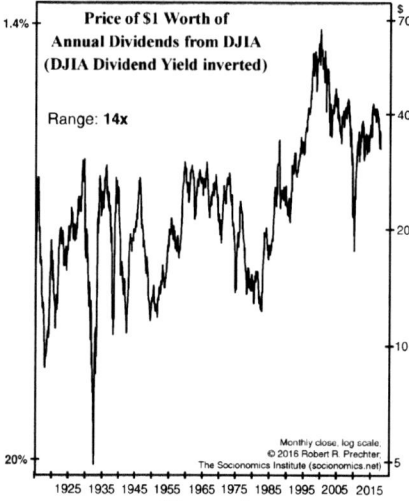

Figure 1

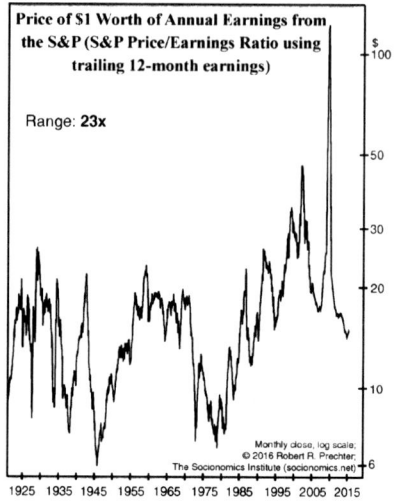

Figure 2

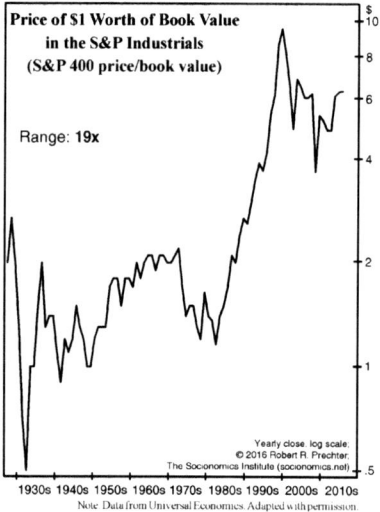

Figure 3

Figure 4

In financial markets, nothing serves as a reliable standard of value. Prices for stock shares do not consistently reflect any objective value standards, in either absolute or relative terms. Figures 1 through 4 reveal that over the past century (through Q4 2015), the price that investors have been willing to pay for a dollar of dividends from the DJIA has fluctuated by 14 times; the price for a dollar of S&P earnings has fluctuated by 23 times; the price for a dollar's worth of S&P 400 corporate book value has fluctuated by 19 times; and the price of a dollar of yield from S&P 400 stock dividends in terms of yield from corporate bonds *issued by the same companies* has fluctuated by 21 times. In other words, even given perfect foreknowledge of dividends, earnings, book value and bond yields, you still wouldn't know whether the market would price the entire S&P stock index at 50 or 1,000 or somewhere in between.

These graphs do not even come close to revealing the full measure of stocks' independence from traditional value standards. All four of these measures involve slow-moving annual averages, and they pertain to entire stock indexes, containing 30 to 500 stocks. The only reason the P/E ratio in Figure 2 is listed as fluctuating "only" by a factor of 23 is that the graph smooths the data over four quarters. In Q4 2008, earnings were negative, so P/E was infinite. With respect to individual stocks, every one of these ratios' denominators can be—and often has been—zero. So, ranges for P/E, P/D, P/book value and bond yield/dividend yield stretch from single digits (even less in terms of the last two ratios) to infinity. Measures that can fluctuate between one and infinity do not make useful benchmarks.

A rational-valuation theorist would view dividends, earnings, book values and relative yields as something very important with respect to what stocks are supposedly worth. But *markets* don't care what they are. If they did, each of the lines in Figures 1 through 4 would be more or less horizontal, befitting a good benchmark. Instead, they seem to depict a bear market followed by a bull market followed by another bear market (which is exactly what they do).

Now let's take a further step and discuss such indicators in terms of economic theory. Ask an economist: "All else being equal, if a company raised its dividend, would the price of the stock rise or fall?" The answer would be, "The price would rise." That's economic valuation.

Next ask: "All else being equal, if the yield from dividends of a company's stock rose *relative to the yield from bonds issued by the same company*, would the stock's price rise or fall?" The answer would be the same: "The price would rise." Once again, that's economic valuation.

So, wouldn't it make perfect sense for overall stock prices to rise as dividend payouts rise, and wouldn't it make perfect sense for overall stock prices to go up as the ratio of dividend yields to bond yields goes up? Of course it would. But that is not the norm.

For a bit of geographical variety, I have selected Figure 5 to show the history of stock prices and dividend payouts as they played out in Japan

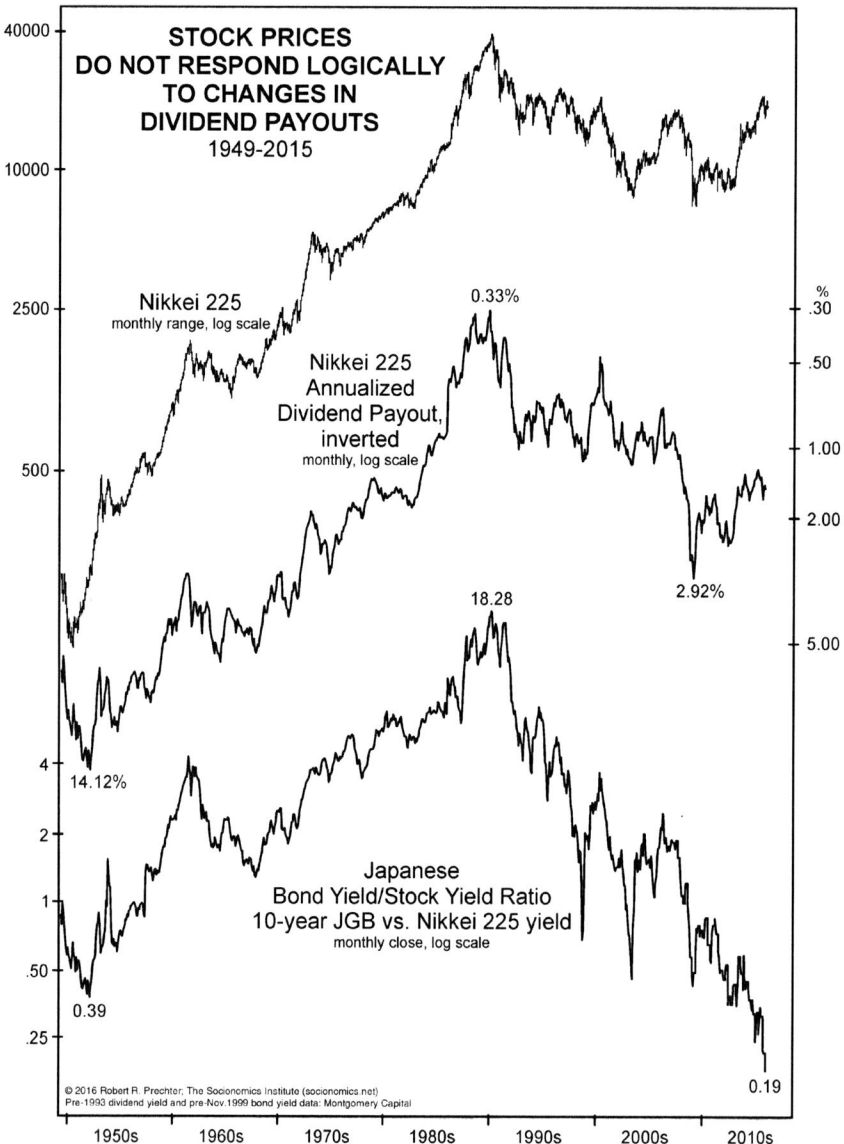

Figure 5

over the past six decades. The same relationship holds for the U.S. over the past century's worth of data, and everywhere else as well. The history in Figure 5 is clear: As absolute and relative dividend payouts persistently fell, investors bid stock prices relentlessly *higher*, and as dividend payouts persistently rose, they offered stock prices relentlessly *lower*. When the dividend payout was 14% and 2½ times what bonds paid, stock prices were low; and when the dividend payout was only 1/3 of 1% and less than 1/18 of what bonds paid, stock prices were high. The relationship of stock prices to both absolute and relative dividend payouts is the *exact opposite* of what makes economic sense. Think about it: If the two lower graphs on this chart were inverted, wouldn't economists consider the relationship between prices and payouts to be perfectly logical? If so, why don't they recognize that the one that actually exists is perfectly illogical?

It is easy to rationalize the relationship. One can say, for instance, that stocks' "capital gains potential" based on companies' "future prospects" justifies high stock prices and low dividend payouts, and vice versa. That is in fact just what speculators do say in real time to excuse their habit of paying high prices for small dividend payouts and low prices for large ones. Such rhetoric evades the glaring valuation anomalies in Figure 5. After all, the single most important value to consider rationally is dividends, the only assured benefit to investors; and it is self-evidently false that the risk of capital loss falls as the market rises and rises as the market falls. The edifice of the argument collapses, exposing its basis in rationalization.

Because stock prices consistently rise as both absolute and relative dividend payouts fall, and vice versa, such payouts are clearly *not* providing speculators with benchmarks for valuation. The same observation pertains to earnings and book values.

The absence of an economic relationship between dividend payouts and stock prices extends also to volatility. From a century of data, Shiller[2] concluded that stock price volatility has been five to thirteen times greater than news relating to dividends could possibly justify. In other words, someone who espouses the dividend-discount model of stock pricing can cook up a story to account for only 1/13 to 1/5 of market volatility, a miniscule amount. Socionomic theory—which attributes stock market volatility to Elliott waves operating independently of supposed fundamental causes—is luxuriously comfortable with this result.

The data graphed in Figures 1 through 5 make *no economic sense*, but they make *perfect socionomic sense*. Waves of unconscious social mood induce optimism and then pessimism in speculators. When investors bid stocks higher, they rationalize that stocks hold an increasing likelihood of capital gains, thereby reducing or eliminating in their minds the detriment of lower dividends, lower P/Es and lower book values; and when they offer stocks lower, they rationalize that stocks hold an increasing risk of capital losses, thereby reducing or eliminating in their minds the advantage of higher dividends, higher P/Es and higher book values. Succinctly put, Figures 1 through 5 actually depict nothing but long term sentiment indicators. Chapter 17 shows eight more.

Socionomic causality accounts for the absence—indeed the inversion—of economic valuation in the stock market, and WP accounts for the wild (non) relationship between stock prices and all such valuation measures. These traits attend every stock market in the world and have done so as far back in history as we can go.

When prices in financial markets reach a level at which they appear nonsensical by traditional standards, speculators just invent new ones. In at least two mania eras, when corporate earnings were insufficient to justify high stock prices, optimistic valuers shifted to focusing not on the level of earnings but on their *trend*—whether they increased or decreased in the latest quarter, even if by only a penny per share. In a rarely read chapter,[3] Graham and Dodd related that this shift in focus occurred toward the end of the stock mania of the 1920s. I republished their chapter in the October 1999 issue of *The Elliott Wave Theorist*, pointing out that investors in the stock mania of the late 1990s were resorting to "the same superficially plausible rationalization." In those and comparable market environments, such as in 1720, 1968 and 1999, companies with no earnings, no dividends, few assets, a negative cash flow, mounds of debt and no market share were often priced higher than venerable, reliable, successful companies producing desirable goods and services. By late 1999, certain Internet stocks were priced so far beyond traditionally purported benchmarks of value that speculators justified their purchases by postulating that companies with higher "burn rates" of venture capital were more desirable to own. In other words, they valued these companies more highly not by the rate they made money but by the rate they blew through it. This radical shift in focus was amusing anecdotal evidence of the extent to which value standards are irrelevant to pricing. Socionomists who saw it happen knew in real time that the proposed new benchmark was merely cover for expressing extreme optimism, and transparently thin cover at that. In May 2000, Dave Allman, host of EWI's podcast, *Wall Street Uncut*, interviewed Michael Wolff about his book *Burn Rate* and discussed with him the delusional accounting being used to justify sky-high "dot-com" stock prices at the time. Needless to say, the value standards of 1999 did not work out well for those adopting them, as the ensuing decade was the worst ever for U.S. stocks, with technology stocks falling the most.

The data in Figures 1 through 5 make—and have always made—a mockery of the claim that stocks are priced rationally and objectively. On the contrary, they are priced capriciously with respect to every purported standard of value. Economic theory works only in textbooks; socionomic theory is compatible with real life.

Difference #2: The Relationship between Price and the Motivation to Buy

Economic theory offers two opposing causal relationships between price and the motivation to buy. It asserts that a rising price for a good or service makes the motivation to buy it go down, yet a rising motivation to buy a good or service—in the short run—makes its price go up; and conversely that a falling price for a good or service makes the motivation to buy it go up, yet a falling motivation to buy a good or service—in the short run—makes its price go down. (They illustrate the first parts of these statements by showing shifts in the supply curve along the demand curve's downward slope, and the second parts by showing shifts in the demand curve along the supply curve's upward slope.) Thus, economists claim that price and the motivation to buy are related in opposite ways *simultaneously* depending upon whether the primary driver of change is a shift in price or a shift in demand.

No such duality exists in finance. Price and the motivation to buy move in the same direction *all the time*.

To establish this difference, we will first explore the influence of price on the actions of consumers in the economic marketplace vs. speculators in the financial marketplace and then investigate the influence of their respective actions on prices.

The Influence of Price on Demand

In economics, lower prices for a good or service tend to prompt consumers to purchase a larger quantity of that good or service. An example is the fact that consumers are buying more computers today at $500 apiece than they did at $5,000 25 years ago or at $1 million half a century ago, and more people own them, and those who own them possess more of them. Conversely, a rise in prices tends to curtail purchases. For example, when gasoline prices go up, some people carpool, take public transit or behave in other ways that cut back on the purchase and consumption of gasoline. (These observations pertain to real and relative prices, not necessarily to overall price changes due to monetary inflation or deflation.)

Figure 6 displays a history of the price regulator at work with respect to demand in utilitarian economic transactions, in this case involving

PRICE CORRELATES NEGATIVELY TO
CUSTOMERS' HOLDINGS OF PCs

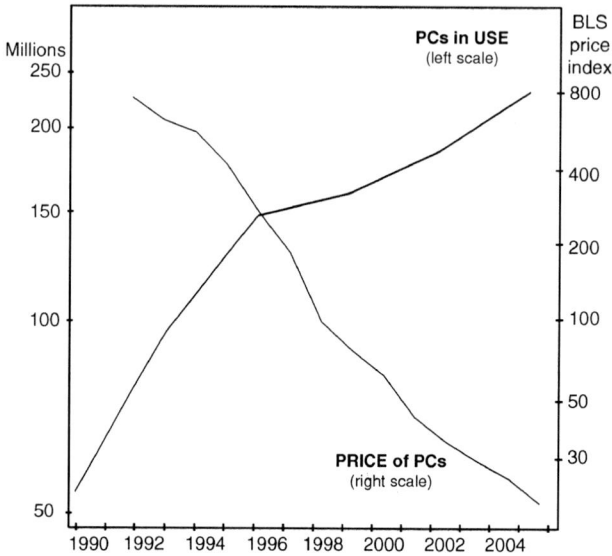

The Socionomics Institute, 2007. Data from the Survey of Consumer Finances
and the Bureau of Labor Statistics. Adapted with permission.

Figure 6

computers. The lower prices for computers went, the more people bought and owned them.

Price differences relate to demand in this way because people, who are almost universally motivated to survive and thrive, apply their conscious reason to the task of maximizing the utility of their money. "If I spend too much on jewelry," thinks a rich person, "I may not have enough to pay for my beach condo." A poor person thinks, "If I spend too much on clothes, I may not be able to eat." When people violate this guide to behavior by wasting their money, those with a lot of money may fail to thrive and those with little money may fail to survive. Maximizing the utility of money is economically advantageous for people of limited means, which is everybody.

In finance, prices do not regulate behavior in this manner. Figure 7 shows that lower prices for stocks do not prompt a greater percentage of the population to buy, and rising prices do not prompt a greater percentage of the population to avoid buying. On the contrary, higher prices for stocks correspond with more owners, and lower prices correspond with fewer owners.

Moreover, when prices fall, investors do not increase the percentage of household assets invested in stocks; they decrease it. Conversely, as prices

**PRICE CORRELATES POSITIVELY WITH
THE NUMBER OF STOCK OWNERS**

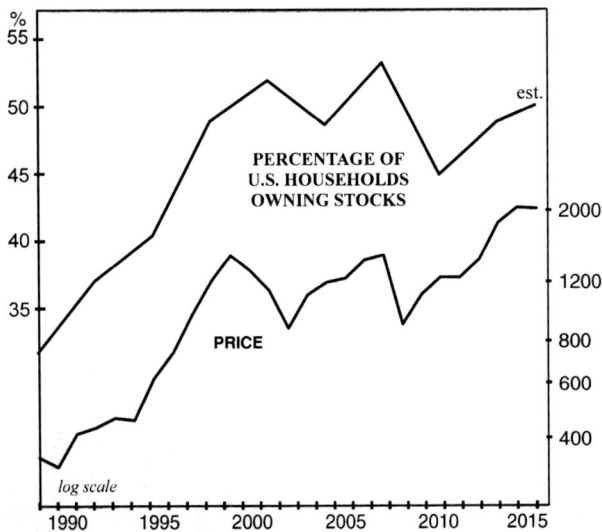

The Socionomics Institute, 2007. Respondents were limited to individuals who are heads of household or married to heads of household. Data from the Survey of Consumer Finances. Adapted with permission. Percentage data are available only every three years, which likely obscures an even tighter fit than shown.

Figure 7

rise, investors do not reduce the percentage of household assets invested in stocks; they increase it. Figure 8 illustrates this fact in depicting the relative value of the U.S. public's holdings of stocks against the prices at which those stocks have sold. Granted, much of the change in ownership percentage is due to changes in stock prices relative to other assets rather than positive or negative rates of share acquisition; but the point remains: If investors were behaving economically by buying when prices are low and selling when prices are high, their ownership trends would be the opposite of what they are.

Consider further that in the marketplace for goods and services, the volume of transactions almost always moves inversely to prices. High prices prompt consumers to reduce the volume of transactions, and a "liquidation sale" prompts consumers to increase the volume of transactions. The transaction volume in the marketplace for investment items, however, tends to fluctuate in the same direction as price. As prices rise, volume tends to rise, and as prices fall, volume tends to fall. Speculators do not shun high prices and rush in to buy bargains but rather tend to transact more as prices rise and stand aside when bargains are available. Figure 9 shows this tendency over an 80-year period.

PRICE CORRELATES POSITIVELY WITH
EXTENT OF STOCK OWNERSHIP

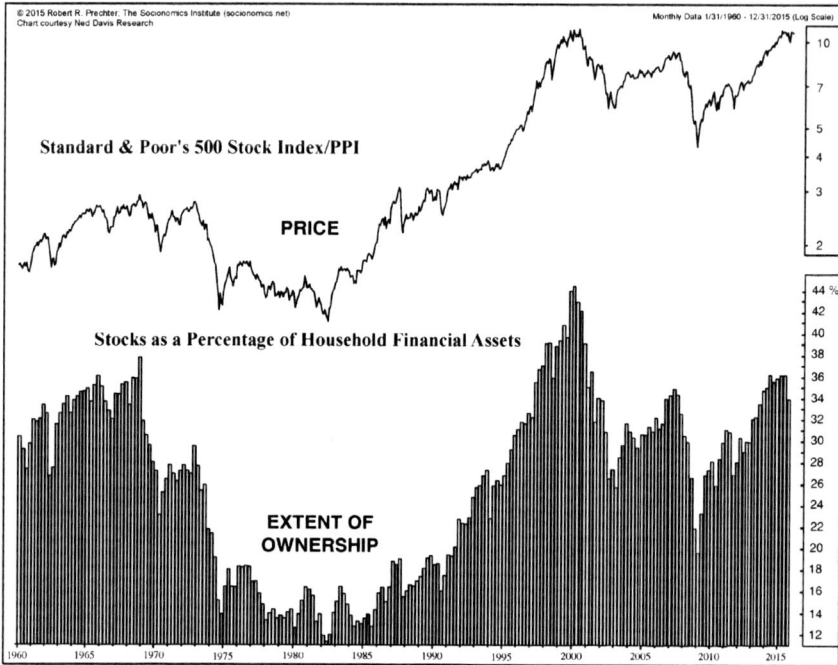

Figure 8

We have calculated correlations, *t*-statistics and *p*-values for the relationships depicted in Figures 7, 8 and 9. They are reported in Table 1 and Figures 10, 11 and 12 in Chapter 15.

The difference in psychology between these situations is palpable: When prices for goods are low due to a sale, consumers are excited, whereas when prices for investment items are low, speculators are defensive. Conversely, when prices rise, speculators are excited whereas consumers are defensive.

In these four fundamental ways—the number of owners vs. price, the extent of ownership vs. price, the volume of transactions vs. price and the emotions related to price change—conditions in the financial marketplace are the opposite of those in the economic marketplace. This is a striking fact.

**PRICE CORRELATES POSITIVELY WITH
TRADING VOLUME**

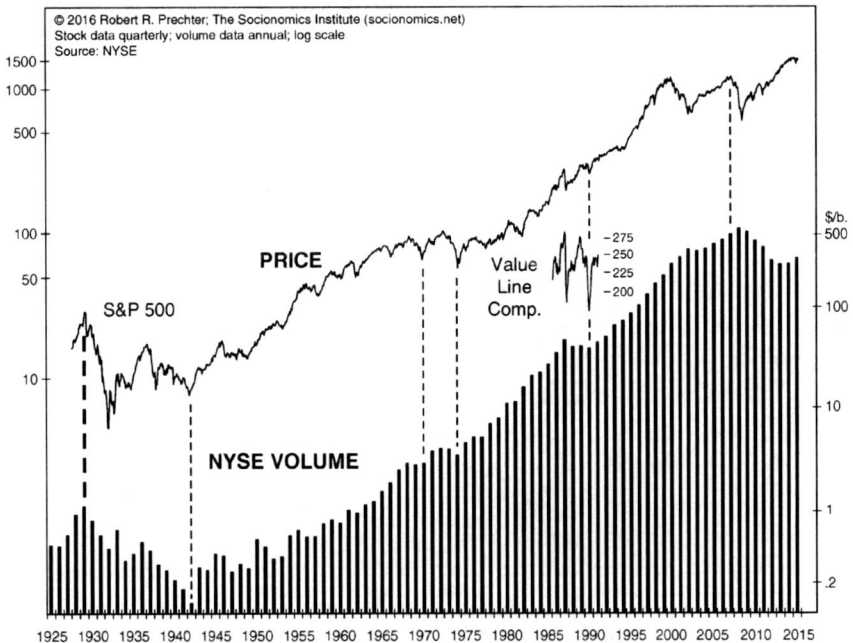

Figure 9

The data in Figures 7 through 9 reveal the fundamental truth that most participants in financial markets do not act reasonably to maximize the utility of their money. People in their role as speculators have the same motivation to survive and thrive as they do in their role as consumers. But if they were applying their reasoning capacity to the task of maximizing the utility of their money, then *one of the two graphs in each of Figures 7, 8 and 9 would be inverted.* People would act to own more stock at a bottom and less at a top, and get rich in the process. But that is not what they do; it is the opposite of what they do.

The Influence of Demand on Price

Over the short run in economics, a sudden increase in demand from consumers can lead to higher prices, and a sudden decrease in demand from consumers can lead to lower prices. For example, if a diet guru recommends a certain food and demand for it suddenly soars, sellers of that food might be prompted to raise its price until supplies expand; the food is thereby allocated according to the greatest demand. This short-run relationship is depicted by shifting a downward-sloping demand curve to the right along an upward-sloping supply curve.

Yet as implied in Figure 6, over the long run an increase in demand from consumers encourages more production, and large-scale production efficiencies lead to lower prices. So, in economic markets the ultimate result of increasing demand is lower prices. When economists shift their supply and demand curves, they can capture this essential relationship secondarily, but our Figure 10 makes it explicit.

In contrast, in financial markets, an increase in the motivation to buy leads to higher prices, while a decrease in the motivation to buy leads to lower prices, *over every span of time.* A greater desire among speculators to buy and own stocks never leads to lower prices, because there are no large-scale production efficiencies to exploit. Figure 11 expresses this consistency.

We can state the difference another way: While over the short run an overall increase in participants' desire to buy and own an item has the same effect in economic and financial markets, over the long run its effects are the opposite.

Figures 10 and 11 summarize the following observations: In economics, over the long run, the motivation to buy goods and services moves in the *opposite* direction from price, whereas in finance, the motivation to buy and the desire to own investment items always moves in the *same* direction as price. We explore the reason for this consistency below.

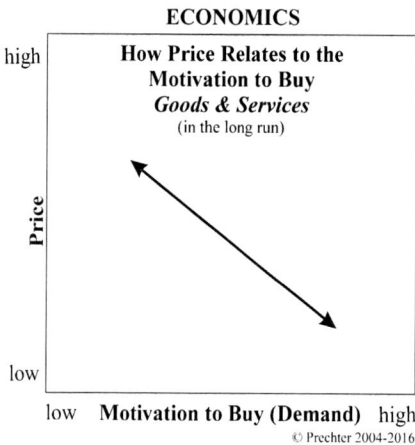

Figure 10

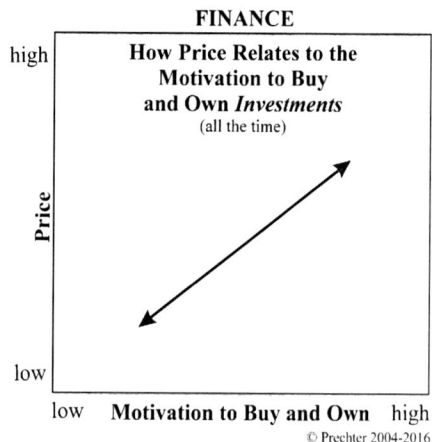

Figure 11

Prices Per Se Matter to Producers and Consumers,
but Only the Direction and Extent of Price Change Matter to Speculators

Prices are an important causal factor in economic decision-making because they express precisely the amount of resources producers and consumers respectively must expend relative to the benefit they are to receive from transacting. In contrast, financial prices have no relationship to cost, effort or utility, so speculators have no basis for caring what prices are.

From empirics as shown in our graphs, and from theory in the form of our hypotheses and models (presented more fully in Chapter 13), it is clear that financial prices do not regulate speculators' buying and selling decisions. A rising desire to own stocks, motivated by the herd's waxing optimism, produces rising prices, and a falling desire to own stocks, motivated by the herd's waxing pessimism, produces falling prices. That's all there is to it. The speculating herd does not derive any meaning from prices per se. Prices are simply an epiphenomenon of the herd's unconscious, endogenously regulated impulses to buy and sell.

In economic markets, specific prices are powerful in determining producers' and consumers' buying and selling decisions. In financial markets, specific prices are irrelevant to speculators' buying and selling decisions. It is easy to say, "Sorry, $500 is too much to pay for a truck tire." But nobody knows if a stock price of $5, $50 or $500 for XYZ Corporation is too high or too low in terms of its future direction. Its specific price, even relative to other stocks' specific prices, can't tell you if the stock is going to go up or down, so it cannot indicate its value *to you*.

Producers and consumers' orientation to price is completely different from that of speculators. Producers and consumers make rational decisions based on what the prices *are*; speculators make impulsive decisions based on the belief, hope or fear that prices will *change*. Each speculator cares only about the future *direction* and *extent* of price change, not its present *level*.

Difference #3: Opposed Heterogeneous Participants vs. Unopposed Homogeneous Participants

Traditionally, economists have talked about buyers and sellers of stocks as if in those roles they are different groups of people akin to consumers and producers in economic markets. They're not. Opposition between buyers and sellers of investment items does not endure but appears only at the instant a buyer and seller transact; the next instant could see a reverse transaction between the very same individuals. Sometimes a buyer in the morning becomes a seller in the afternoon. A trader can buy one moment and sell six seconds later. An arbitrageur might simultaneously buy one investment item and sell another. This unity of role also applies to institutional speculators such as hedge funds and mutual funds. Speculators share a single goal: to make money speculating. To that end they must buy *and* sell, or they could not profit. They form a single, unopposed, homogeneous group, whose members are continuously doing the same thing: expressing fleeting changes in desire for ownership that manifest as price. To conclude, during trading in economic markets, two heterogeneous entities play opposing roles, whereas in financial markets homogeneous entities play one role.

A Qualitatively Consistent Term for Financial-Market Participants

What shall we call the participant in financial markets? The terms *trader* and *investor* are typically linked to vaguely quantitative holding periods, i.e. short term and long. A proper label, however, serves a qualitative purpose. The word *trade*, moreover, is used all the time in economic markets, such as in "foreign trade" and "the carpet trade"; and the word *invest* is misused in economic markets in such comments as "You should invest in a new car." The term *speculator*—as we have applied it numerous times so far—seems especially useful for designating the participant in a financial market. All participants in financial markets, no matter what their time horizons, are speculators. Speculators assume *risk* upon buying investment items. Producers and consumers generally do the opposite: They increase their *security* upon buying what they want and need. Producers and consumers take some risks, but their aim is primarily to maximize the utility of their resources, not primarily to guess the future. So, *speculator* seems a good financial word to use opposite the economic terms *producer,* a.k.a. *supplier,* and *consumer,* a.k.a. *demander.*

Suppliers and Demanders vs. Speculators

We can elucidate this dichotomy further by asking two questions. Using the terms of economics,

(1) With respect to soft drinks, is the Coca-Cola company a supplier or a demander?

(2) With respect to stocks, is the Berkshire Hathaway company a supplier or a demander?

Answering the first question is easy: Coca-Cola is a supplier. Its entire reason for operating is to supply soft drinks to consumers, i.e. demanders. The Coca-Cola company doesn't have a program for buying Coca-Colas; it just produces them and sells them. Consumers don't produce Cokes in their basements; they just buy them and drink them. Suppliers and demanders of Cokes are distinct groups, each with its own agenda.

Answering the second question has led financial theorists astray for a century. Many people would say that investment company Berkshire Hathaway is both a supplier and a demander. It "supplies" stock when it sells shares of a company and "demands" stock when it buys shares of a company. This is the way most people attempt to apply the law of supply and demand to the stock market.

But there is a crucial distinction between such behavior and that of participants in economic markets. Does Coca-Cola switch from being a supplier of soft drinks to being a demander of them? No, it *never* changes its role in regard to its product. It has spent over a century of effort and billions of dollars on perfecting and maintaining its role as one thing: a supplier of soft drinks. But with simple changes of mind, Berkshire Hathaway routinely switches roles as a so-called "supplier" or "demander" of stock.

Sometimes companies that issue stock become net buyers of their own stock. But they never turn into net buyers of their own *products*. So, distinct entities only buy or only sell Coca-Cola *products*, but no distinct entities only buy or only sell Coca-Cola *stock*. There must be something fundamentally different between the supposed "supplying" and "demanding" that those who trade investment items practice as against such actions by those who trade in goods and services.

The correct answer is that Berkshire Hathaway is neither a supplier nor a demander, because it is not a producer or consumer; it is a *speculator*. A speculator is a different type of transactor. A producer wants to sell a good or service; a consumer wants to buy a good or service; a speculator wants to make money buying and selling investment items. These are three distinct roles: two heterogeneous roles in economics and one homogeneous role in finance. The differing nature of these roles negates any claim that buyers and sellers of stock are equivalent to demanders and suppliers in economic markets.

Homogeneity of Motivation

Under the socionomic model, participants in financial markets are a homogeneous group also in terms of their motivation. Aside from two exceptions, discussed in Chapter 17, there is no fundamentally important qualitative difference in herding behavior pertaining to the widely asserted qualitative dichotomies between various classes of speculators (such as traders vs. investors), as listed in Chapter 17 and discussed further in Chapter 19. The terms involved do not in fact relate to dichotomies but to continua, so the distinctions are suspect to begin with, if not spurious. Be that as it may, differences in herding tendencies among participants are quantitative, not qualitative. Some people herd more or less often than others; some herd sooner or later than others; some herd more or less intensely than others; and some may be smarter and more knowledgeable than others. But in the end everyone herds to some degree.

Difference #4: Supply and Demand Operate in Economics but Not in Finance

One can attempt to use the terms *supply* and *demand* in a financial context, as we saw in our discussion of Coca-Cola and Berkshire Hathaway. Economic theorists and practitioners do it all the time. But doing so is misleading, because the supply-demand model is inappropriate for describing what happens in financial markets. To reach this conclusion requires several trains of thought that go well beyond the homogeneity issue.

A Semantic Illusion

Economists' use of the terms *supply* and *demand* when discussing financial markets makes financial markets appear equivalent to economic markets. This appearance comes not from actual equivalence but from semantics.

Semantic illusion can trick even the best minds. Consider a common argument from theologians that runs like this: "Everything that came into existence has a cause; the universe exists, so it had a cause." They elaborate, "A car came into existence, and someone made it; a river came into existence, and natural forces made it; the universe exists, so someone/something made it." These statements sound perfectly logical. Yet the logic depends upon an illusion in which the same words hide non-equivalent meanings. In the formula, the phrase "came into existence" means two different things. In the first case, it means to re-arrange matter, and in the second case it means to bring matter into being from nothing. So, the claim really is: "Because matter can be re-arranged, it must be true that a supernatural being made matter from nothing." While the latter claim may turn out to be true, its veracity cannot derive from such non-sequiturs.

Similarly, using the terms *supply* and *demand* in both financial and economic contexts fools people into thinking their meanings are identical when they are not. The trick works only by incorporating into the concept of *supply* two fundamentally different types of offering: producers' offering an item to be consumed and speculators' offering an item to be owned temporarily on a bet; and by incorporating into the concept of *demand* two fundamentally different desires: consumers' desire to consume an item and speculators' desire to own an item temporarily while *not* consuming it. In the economic context, moreover, the two terms have important connotations involving management, labor, effort, production, distribution, consumption, scarcity, abundance, want, need and sustenance, whereas in the financial context they have no such connotations. One can speak of the *heart* of an artichoke, but the term lacks all the important connotations it has when applied to an animal, such as pumping blood, distributing oxygen and sustaining life. Economists use the terms *supply* and *demand* just as indiscriminately. Conflating their meanings may well serve a theoretical construct, but doing so obscures a seminal distinction. That distinction encompasses a number of specific observations, as outlined below.

The Term "Supply" is Inapplicable to Financial Markets

Here are some specific reasons why the term *supply* does not pertain to financial markets:

- In economics, the term *supply* as a noun means the amount of a specific good or service available to consumers and as a verb means to provide a specific good or service. Stock is not a good or service to be utilized or consumed; stock is simply traded.

- Goods and services are produced and consumed, after which they are gone. As goods and services are consumed, more must be produced. Stock shares, once created and sold, are not consumed but stay in existence.

- Services once sold to a consumer cannot change hands, and goods once sold to a consumer rarely change hands. Once stock is initially sold, it remains at large and constantly changes hands.

- Sellers of goods and services expend productive effort, which provides economic value. Manufacturers create goods; wholesalers create a service to retailers; retailers create a service to consumers; and service providers create services for all kinds of people. Sellers of existing stock do not expend any productive effort, so they provide no economic value.

- The cost required to produce a good or service provides a utility-based benchmark of value for that good or service. Stockholders' costs—the widely varying amounts each owner originally paid for the stock—provide no benchmark of value.

- A good or service has personal value to people. An investment item has no personal value to people.

- Owners of stock behave differently from suppliers in economic markets. At any given instant the vast majority of stock owners are simply holding their shares, unwilling to sell at the prevailing market price. Producers and store owners do not hoard their wares; they typically sell them as fast as they can, whatever the prevailing market price. The latter entities are active sellers of goods and services in an economic marketplace, whereas the vast bulk of stockholders are passive holders—and thus only *potential* sellers—of investment items in the financial marketplace. Thus, there is a qualitative difference between the two types of owners.

- Surpluses of supply can occur in economic markets. When farmers overproduce a crop, consumers will not consume it all at the normally prevailing price. To motivate consumers to buy more, producers must lower the price. Prices can fall so low that the farmers are ruined. Prices could fall to zero and still leave an abundance of produce rotting in the fields. None of these dynamics pertain to the stock market, because—since stock is not an item to be used or consumed—there is no such thing as a surplus of stock. The amount of stock is pretty much constant week to week, and it is always desirable at a price.

- Shortages of supply can occur in economic markets. When a natural or man-made disaster prevents shipments of goods into a city, there is a shortage of supply. Consumers in the area might use up all the available food or gasoline. The curtailment of supply during a famine can be so severe that prices for food reach infinity, and no one will part with supply at any price. None of these dynamics pertain to the stock market because—since stock is not an item necessary for surviving and thriving—there is no such thing as a shortage of stock. The amount of stock is pretty much constant week to week, and it is always available at a price.

  To elaborate on this point, if it happened that there were only 100 potatoes left in a field during a famine or only 100 working computers left on the planet after a neutron-bomb explosion, these goods would sell for a king's ransom. But if most public corporations went private and there were only 100 shares of stock left for the public to own, they would not be priced highly due to shortage. They would simply represent certain portions of a few companies, and they would be priced in that context, not in a context of shortage.

- In the economic marketplace, a higher price for a specific good or service encourages producers to supply more of it, but higher prices for all goods (for example due to inflation) does not encourage more supply. In financial markets, a high price for a specific company's stock does not encourage a greater supply of that stock (the company is what it is, regardless of the number of shares into which it is divided), but higher prices for all stocks do encourage financiers to create new supplies of stock in the form of initial public offerings (IPOs) of stock in new corporations.

- In economic markets, more supply encourages lower prices, but in the stock market there is no such dynamic. On rare occasions when a new company issues stock to the public, the total amount of stock available has increased. Economists equate such events with increases in "supply." Yet participants in the stock market do not offer down all stocks in response. So, new stock cannot be supply in the economic sense. On the contrary, participants in the stock market tend to bid up prices not only for IPOs but also for the rest of the market around the same time. This behavior makes no economic sense, but it does make socionomic sense: When optimistic speculators' impulsive bidding for stock makes prices rise to high levels, financiers exploit the opportunity by selling new stock to an excited public. The new "supply" doesn't push prices lower. On the contrary, IPOs issued in environments of waxing optimism typically enjoy voracious bidding.

To conclude, one cannot honestly apply the economic term *supply* to any aspect of finance.

Using the Term "Supply" in Finance Misleads Theorists and Modelers

Employing economic terms in a financial context allows people to fool themselves in subtle ways. Many economists, corporate analysts and company managers—thinking they are applying the law of supply and demand to the stock market—believe that when a publicly owned company buys back some of its issued shares, its act has the effect of "reducing supply"[4] of the stock, which makes the price go up. Initially, the matter does seem to be one of simple math: Remove half the stock of a company, and supply has been cut in half, right? What could be more obvious? Although this claim seems self-evidently valid to many people, it is absurd. Let's discuss this idea both logically and practically.

A company engaging in stock buybacks can proceed in either of two ways: It can cancel the acquired shares so that the remaining shares still represent the whole company, or it can hold the acquired shares as a non-dividend-paying investment (so-called "treasury shares"). In neither case is there a reduction in supply. In the former case the company has done nothing but re-portion itself, so that each portion of the company is in, say, one basket instead of two, while the total value of its shares remains the same. In the latter case, the company has simply joined the investment pool, and each share still represents exactly the portion of the company it did before, making it no more valuable than it was before. Even if the company pledged never to re-issue its purchased shares, the total remaining publicly traded shares would *still* not be worth more than before, because they would still represent a smaller portion of the company.

Now let's bring the discussion into the real world. Suppose you own stock representing 1% of a company that has $1 billion in cash in the bank. The company decides to buy back and cancel half its stock in order to jack up its stock price by reducing "supply." Its program will cost $2 billion. The company's assets are valuable, so a big bank is willing to lend it $1 billion for the project. At the end of this scheme, does your share of the company represent twice its previous value? Hardly. Instead of owning 1% of a company holding $1 billion in cash, you own 2% of a company that is strapped with $1 billion in debt. The economic value of your share of the company (irrespective of its financial value) may leave you worse off than before.

Gregory King around 1700 is credited with being the first statistician to demonstrate that the price of corn fluctuates with the extent of harvests. If corn production shrinks, the price of corn rises, and vice versa. Advocates of the idea that removing stock from the marketplace raises the value of the remaining stock are applying King's Law of Prices to stock shares. They reflexively equate the number of stock shares available with the economic term *supply*. But stock is not corn. The substance of a fresh ear of corn is static, so its value fluctuates with supply. The substance of a corporate share, however, changes with a company's very act of buying back its stock.

Why, then, do stocks tend to be rising in price when companies buy back their own shares? The socionomic answer is simple and elegant: The waxing optimism driving the bull market prompts some companies to join the herd by bidding up their own stocks' prices.

That is why in the above discussion I used the term *value*, not *price*, in reference to the deterioration in your share of the company after a buyback program. The price of the stock may well hold up or rise even as the value of the share of the company it represents becomes worth objectively less.

Stock shares are impulsively priced, and during times of extreme optimism speculators giddily price stocks highly with no care about objectively calculable corporate values.

Recent studies (see Chapter 17) have shown that companies that buy back their own stock have significantly worse returns on their investment than is provided by the market as a whole. This result stems from two causes: the socionomic fact that companies tend to buy their own shares *after* they are highly priced and vulnerable to falling, and the economic fact that such buying impoverishes the companies that do it.

When thinking about financial markets, one must jettison the whole idea of supply. It gets in the way of proper thinking.

The Term "Demand" is Either Inapplicable to Financial Markets or Has a Different Meaning

Now we will explore some specific reasons why the term *demand* as used in economic theory does not properly pertain to finance:

- In economics, the term *demand* as a noun means consumers' desire to acquire a specific good or service at a price and as a verb means the act of paying to acquire a specific good or service. Stock is not a good or service to be utilized or consumed; stock is simply traded.

- Consumers' purchases of goods and services support life and enhance the experience of life. Speculators' purchases of investment items perform neither function. The buyer of an investment item may view his acquisition as a potential means toward one of those ends, but it is not the end itself. Ironically, more often than not, financial speculation ultimately leads to a reduction in speculators' quality of life.

- Demanders of goods and services operate in a context of relative certainty about how those goods and services will benefit them. Buyers of investment items operate in a context of uncertainty about whether others' future actions will transfer value to them or from them. These contexts for decision-making are worlds apart.

- Nearly everyone must participate in the economic marketplace in order to survive and thrive. An individual can avoid participating in the financial marketplace and suffer no negative impact on his or her quality of life. Rather, since most speculators lose money (see Chapter 17), the impact of opting out of financial markets is more likely to be positive than negative.

- Once consumers buy and use a good or service, the money spent is substantially if not wholly irretrievable, so the buying decision is more or less final. Since stock is not consumed, buying decisions are not final. A buyer can nearly always retrieve some multiple of his or her money on command.

- In economic markets, a higher price reduces the quantity of a good or service that consumers demand, and a lower price increases it, so the motive to buy moves in the opposite direction from price. In financial markets, by all measures on all time scales (see Figures 7, 8 and 9), the motive to buy and own investment items moves in the same direction as price. Financial buyers must be exercising something other than utilitarian demand.

To conclude, one cannot honestly apply the economic term *demand* to any aspect of finance. To avoid using the same word to mean different things in these opposing contexts, Chapter 13 will offer an alternative.

The Supply-Demand Model Does Not Apply to Finance

Individually considered, then, supply and demand—as used in the field of economics—are absent from financial markets. What about the very law of supply and demand? Can we not envisage the stock market under this umbrella?

It seems so obvious: Sellers "supply" stock, and buyers "demand" stock. When sellers "supply" more stock, prices fall, and when buyers "demand" more stock, prices rise. What's to object?

A careful consideration of this formula reveals that the key terms are simply substitutes for the terms *sell* and *buy* and are devoid of any additional meaning. In similar fashion, the common phrase, "there is a lot of demand for stock," simply means "speculators have become more bullish"; and "a lot of supply is coming into the market" simply means "speculators have become more bearish." If the terms *demand* and *supply* are simply substitutes for variations of *buy* and *sell* or *bullish* and *bearish*, what is the point of using them? By employing sophisticated terms from economics, people feel they are elevating the discussion, but in fact they are mucking it up.

In economics, the two terms have useful meanings. Suppliers don't just sell goods and services; they *make* them. Demanders don't just buy goods and services; they *use* them and *use them up*.[5] In other words, a supplier is a *producer*, and a demander is a *consumer*. Since in the economic marketplace all suppliers are producers and all demanders are consumers, we can equate each pair of terms in the realm of economics. But nobody equates them in finance. People throw around the terms *supply* and *demand* in finance all the time, but they never use the essentially identical terms *produce* and *consume* or *production* and *consumption* in finance, because the inapplicability of these terms is too obvious. Speculators don't produce or consume stock, which means they don't supply or demand it, either.

Speculators do unintentionally create a sort of economic value by providing market liquidity so that new companies can sell shares easily. But such value is secondary to, and different from, economic production. One cannot escape the essential point that a dichotomy exists, because in finance buyers and sellers *both* produce this liquidity and *no one* consumes it.

An advocate of the supply-demand model in finance might work to give the terms roughly equivalent meanings in economic and financial markets by carefully defining *supply* and *demand* as, say, "the quantities of items that market participants wish to buy and to sell at various prices at any particular instant." A meticulously chosen set of words such as this does describe an identifiable aspect of both economic and financial markets. But every other aspect of the two situations differs, so we are left with a narrow theoretical construct that has no real-world utility. For further discussion, see the Appendix to Chapter 13.

In economics, the terms *supply* and *demand* mean more than just items people desire to sell or buy. They refer to identifiable causes. In economics, one can often discern whether prices are moving because of a change in demand or supply. For example, if prices for a certain type of electronic gadget are falling, one might observe that consumers are reducing their consumption of those gadgets in favor of new technology (less demand) or that manufacturers overseas have overproduced the gadgets and shipped them all to market (more supply). Prices are going only one way (down), yet there is a qualitative difference between the two possible causes. In the stock market, there are no such distinctly different causes of falling—or rising—prices, because there are no producers or consumers.

Stock market commentators often reflexively say such things as, "An increase in demand made prices go up" or "An increase in supply made prices go down." But such statements convey no more information than saying, "Prices went up" and "Prices went down." The extra words are superfluous. They offer nothing at all in the way of comprehension, much less causality. In such cases, people are using price changes to presume the cause, not any observable cause to explain the price changes. Since employing these extra terms doesn't *explain* anything, the causal claim is retrospective and tautological.

The Laws of Supply and Demand are Separately Inapplicable to Finance

Even taken separately, the law of supply and the law of demand do not apply to finance. According to their definitions, "the law of supply states that the quantity of a good supplied rises as the market price rises, and falls as the price falls. Conversely, the law of demand says that the quantity of a good demanded falls as the price rises, and vice versa."[6] The first definition does not apply consistently to economics, because, as shown earlier in this chapter, falling prices for goods (such as computers) often accompany rising supply, especially over the long run. And the second definition doesn't apply to finance, because, as shown in Figures 7, 8, 9 and 11, the actual relationship between price and the desire to own an investment item is the opposite of that stated.

Toward a More Concise Statement of the Law of Supply and Demand

The widely disseminated definitions cited above are incomplete and problematic. Their veracity depends entirely upon the direction of causality, as the converses of the two definitions are false: It is *not* true that price rises because the quantity of a good supplied rises and falls because the quantity supplied falls, nor that price rises because the quantity of a good demanded falls and falls because the quantity demanded rises. So, the first law is true if price rises first but false if supply rises first; and the second law is true if price rises first but false if demand rises first. Economists, then, have a dualistic theory in which supply and demand can move prices, and prices can move supply and demand, in opposite directions. The way they express it is substantially incoherent. They typically need a substantial amount of text and a half-dozen diagrams to describe what they think is going on. My reply is, "Can't you at least find a concise way to state your model that is universally true?"

One can in fact summarize economic theorists' proposed relationships among supply, demand and price in a single statement:

A concise expression of the laws of supply and demand:

When shifts in demand affect price, the change in the quantity supplied moves in the *same* direction as price (producing a positive correlation); and when shifts in supply affect price, the change in the quantity demanded moves in the *opposite* direction as price (producing a negative correlation).

This is a neater and clearer formulation of economists' statements of causality, it is always applicable, and it produces no contradictions in relationships among the three variables. But I have never seen an economic text state its law in this unambiguous way.

With respect to that concise formulation, socionomics recognizes an opposing truth pertaining to financial markets: Price *always* moves in the same direction as so-called "demand," defined as the motivation to buy and own investment items. Supply is irrelevant.

As hinted above, the foregoing discussion is not necessarily meant to sanction economists' supply-demand model as complete or even a valid representation of what happens in the economic marketplace. Under the mechanics paradigm of discreet objects and forces, economists' mix of reciprocally inconstant relationships among supply, demand and price seem problematic to their causal claims. I would propose a holistic process of interaction among supply, demand and price. Choose which formulation you prefer. Regardless, the key point remains that there is a stark contrast in the supply-demand model's basic applicability to each type of market, to the point that it is inappropriate for representing what happens in the financial marketplace.

Difference #5: Equilibrium, Mean-Reversion and Price Stability vs. Constant Dynamism

Long-Run Equilibrium in Economic Markets but Not in Financial Markets

Producers and consumers share the same basic goals—to survive and thrive—and both sets of transactors use reason to maximize the utility of their resources. But their desires regarding price are diametrically opposed. Producers of goods and services desire to obtain as much money as they can for their product, while consumers of goods and services desire to obtain as much product as they can for their money. Equilibrium describes a state in which an economic market, through competition, establishes a price at which the utility of resources (involving money, time and effort) is maximized for both groups combined. At that price, the quantity of a good or service producers are willing to supply is equal to the quantity of that good or service consumers are willing to consume. A state of equilibrium in an economic market implies that price has arbitrated the opposing desires of producers and consumers so that they are balanced on the buy and sell sides of the transactions. As illustrated in Figure 12, the result is a reliable, long-run state of equilibrium. Although this condition may be interrupted or shifted from time to time, it always quickly returns.

ECONOMICS:
Opposition between producers and consumers,
deriving from conscious utility maximization,
produces a tendency towards stability in the
pricing of utilitarian goods and services.

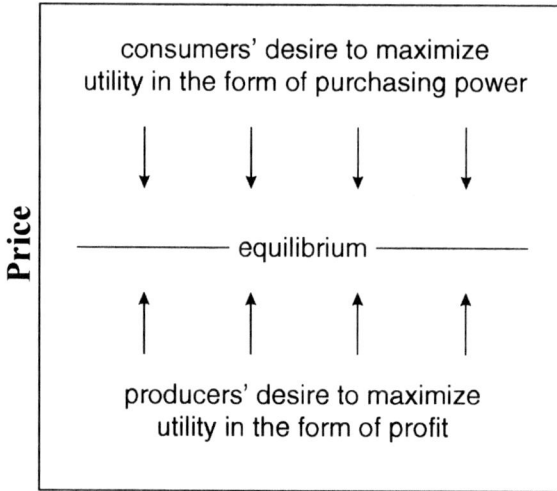

Figure 12

At equilibrium, the two opposing groups' efforts to thrive provide the maximum benefit to the maximum number of people. Adam Smith personified the process producing this outcome as the Invisible Hand.

In financial markets, there is no opposition of forces among producers and consumers. There is only an unopposed herd of speculators. Because financial prices have no basis for long-run equilibrium, no long-run equilibrium is possible in financial markets.

Economists sometimes force their equilibrium model onto finance by making inventive claims. I am aware of two of them.

One way economists have modeled volatile financial markets is to propose "multiple equilibria." According to one published example,[7] bonds will be stably priced if the economy is either locked into a consistent rate of expansion or mired in a depression, but not in between. Economists depict their idea with a snake-shaped curve for demand crossing a straight, upward-sloping line for supply at two or more points. The implication is that points in between the intersections are out of equilibrium, as if the transition period between prosperity and depression is a temporary pathway between two stable states. But the economy fluctuates in fractal form, so no such stable states exist. One era's point along the pathway is another era's peak or trough. Even considering theory alone, modelers can shift these lines in any direction, so depicted points of equilibrium are arbitrary. The claim of multiple equilibria eventually dissolves into an assertion of infinite equilibria, which means no equilibrium at all.

Another way economists have modeled volatile financial markets is to declare that every trade in a financial market implies instantaneous equilibrium at the price of each and every transaction. This idea of countless fleeting equilibria shifting by the millisecond in financial markets is quite different from the long-run equilibrium characteristic of economic markets. Each "equilibrium" is only of the moment. Asserting a new equilibrium at every instant may be a way for economists to make their model appear valid, but it does so only by evading the necessity of accounting for what is in fact ceaselessly dynamic price behavior. In the end, it amounts to nothing more than acknowledging that transactions occur. Ironically, the idea of instantaneous equilibrium at every price implies infinite equilibria, which is exactly the end result of the "multiple equilibria" claim. Again, it means the market has no state of equilibrium at all.

Both stances described above inherently concede that prices in financial markets are fundamentally dynamic and have no long-run equilibrium state. Wouldn't it therefore be better to employ a model that proposes dynamism, rather than equilibrium, as a fundamental aspect of financial market pricing? As Chapter 13 will show, that's exactly what STF does.

No Mean Reversion in Financial Markets

Many academic theorists contend that stock prices "revert to the mean." According to definition, "In finance, mean reversion is the assumption that a stock's price will tend to move to the average price over time."[8] But stocks do not even remotely behave according to this assumption. More often than not, when stock prices or values approach a mean, they careen right through it toward another extreme. Their behavior seems closer to mean-aversion than mean-reversion.

Reversion implies a return to some standard of usual conditions, such as the sea on non-stormy days, which is most days, or prices when mature economic markets are operating freely, which is most of the time. A hurricane at sea and the catastrophic disruption of supply in an economic market are temporary events, and in each case one can depend upon the system reverting to the mean. But there is no normal, stable state in finance, so applying the idea of mean reversion is invalid.

To which "average price" for a stock, by the way, does the above-quoted definition of mean reversion refer? Any calculated mean for stock prices is merely an artifact of whatever pricing has occurred in some selected portion of the past. There is no stock-price mean that isn't arbitrarily determined by the duration of the data or constantly changing due to new data. As a case in point, in recent decades stock prices have been so far away from all past-calculated means and values that some commentators have proposed that the market has established "a new mean" of higher valuation. Such discussions belie the very assumption on which they are based. Irving Fisher (see Chapter 40) said something similar in 1929, lived to regret it, and ended up changing his entire view of financial and macroeconomic causality.

Even more fundamentally, the idea of *prices* reverting to some average completely ignores the value of the underlying company. Since the value of each company constantly changes, the idea of a mean residing in price rather than value destroys the whole basis of economic valuation upon which conventional models depend.

Modelers of the efficient market hypothesis (EMH) understand this problem and mostly reject the idea of price-mean reversion. Yet proponents of all but the strongest version of EMH, including followers of Graham and Dodd (see Chapters 15 and 33), do embrace the idea of *value* reversion, whereby if stock prices temporarily diverge from properly representing the values of underlying companies, they will quickly return to their proper level. Socionomics, compatibly with the real-world data on prices and values as displayed in Figures 1 through 4, rejects both expressions of the reversion claim. STF recognizes that prices fluctuate independently of corporate valuation measures. That's why prices constantly wander both toward and away from supposed "proper values" and never settle upon them.

The idea of reversion to the mean is useful in physics and economics but irrelevant to finance. Stock prices have no systemically determined mean to which to revert. In fact, they have nothing constant—no mean, no values, no equilibrium, not even a set of multiple equilibria—to which to revert.

Stable vs. Dynamic Markets

The qualities of objective valuation, meaningful prices, heterogeneous opposition, equilibrium-seeking and mean reversion are constraints that produce a tendency toward price stability in economic markets. Financial markets do not possess any of these qualities. Being free from those constraints, the speculating herd is able to drive financial prices up and down at will. Speculators' overall motivation to own each investment item fluctuates impulsively, and prices follow. As a result, financial prices tend toward constant *dynamism*. Figures 13 and 14 illustrate a key aspect of this distinction.

Market empirics reflect the difference in these two models. The prices of sardines and toothpicks do not race up and down second by second, minute

**Conscious Reasoning among Members of
Two Heterogeneous, Opposing Groups
Produces Stability in Utilitarian Economics**

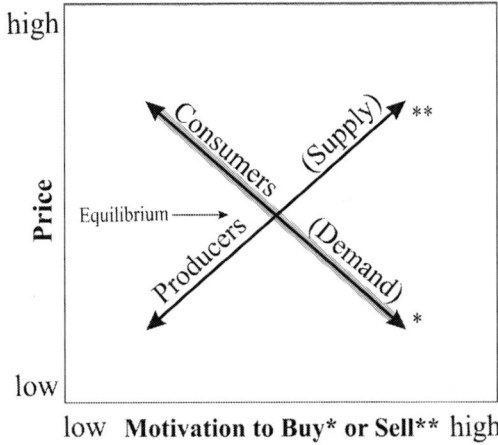

© Prechter 2004-2016

Figure 13

**Unconscious Herding among Members of
One Homogenous, Unopposed Group
Produces Dynamism in Finance**

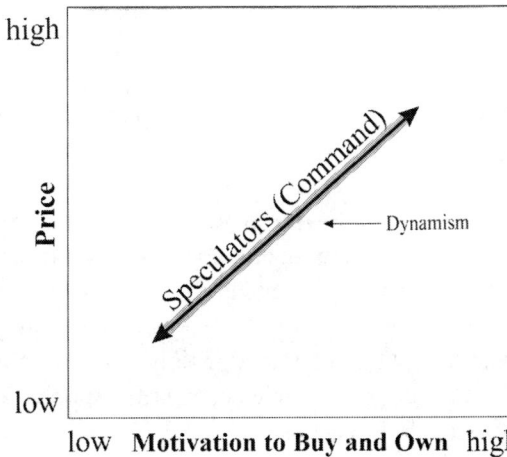

© Prechter 2004-2016

Figure 14

by minute, hour by hour, day by day or even week by week as stocks do. Nor do they routinely soar and crash; but the prices of stocks do, all the time, on all scales.

As established by R.N. Elliott empirically and Benoit Mandelbrot mathematically, financial prices fluctuate as a fractal, with a comparable style of movement on all time scales, from seconds to centuries. This is a model of a dynamic marketplace, not a stable one.

The equilibrium model and the Elliott wave model delineate the difference between economic and financial price movement. Economic pricing and financial pricing are both anchored, but to different things. Economic prices are anchored to equilibrium, making them relatively stable, while financial prices are anchored to Elliott waves, making them dynamic.

Stable vs. Dynamic Sentiment

The unceasing dynamism attending financial market prices extends to the psychology of its participants. According to neoclassical economic theory and its financial counterpart, EMH, there should be no changes in investors' optimism or pessimism, since prices are simply adjustments to present reality, communicating no reason to be bullish or bearish on future prices.

Socionomics differs in being acutely aware of yet another financial/economic dichotomy: Consumers' level of passion towards utilitarian goods—such as hammers, shoes and bread—hardly ever changes, which is why no one constructs active sentiment gauges for them. On the other hand, speculators' level of passion towards investment items (see Chapters 18, 21 and 22) changes radically all the time, often reaching astonishing extremes. The reason is that the herd's emotionally charged and constantly fluctuating desire to own investment items is what drives financial price changes in the first place.

The supply-demand model, with its attendant qualities of equilibrium, mean reversion, utility maximization and objective pricing, are so useful in the economic realm that they have seduced economists into inappropriately extending them to the financial realm. STF rejects the entire package.

Figures 10 through 14 depict crucial insights, because they reveal key differences between economics and finance, ones that supply-demand curves and equilibrium models fail to accommodate.

In sum, the qualitative difference between economic markets and financial markets is immense. One should not apply the same laws to both realms. Chapter 13 presents the discrete sets of laws that *do* apply.

NOTES AND REFERENCES

[1] Buchanan, Mark, "Why economic theory is out of whack," *New Scientist*, July 19, 2008.

[2] Shiller, Robert J. "Do Stock Prices Move Too Much to Be Justified by Subsequent Changes in Dividends?" *American Economic Review*, 1981, Vol. 71, No. 3. pp. 421-436.

[3] Graham and Dodd, *Security Analysis*, 1934. Later editors removed their highly informative chapter, probably on the premise that it was no longer relevant. Chapter 13 of *Market Analysis for the New Millennium* (2002) reproduces their chapter under the title, "The Rationalization of Value in a Mania."

[4] As reported in Investopedia, "Buyback." Type "stock buyback, reduction in supply" into Google search and you will find a dozen expressions of the same idea from myriad sources.

[5] This distinction is somewhat qualified with respect to naturally available, unproduced goods. Raw land, for example, may be supplied or demanded without being used or used up. It may even provide personal value, such as when an owner holds land as a privacy buffer. River water may be interrupted by a dam to provide energy, but the water is not used up. Nevertheless, each such good could be used for other purposes and used up in the process. The land could be stripped of its resources, and the water could be diverted upstream to irrigate farmland. Ultimately the land and water are valuable because they have aspects that may be utilized or used up. The same point would apply to consumer goods temporarily stored in a warehouse. Such technical discussions do not negate the essential point.

[6] Ehrbar, Al. "Supply." *The Concise Encyclopedia of Economics*, Library of Economics and Liberty, 2008.

[7] Source and diagram are available in Ip, Greg, "Multiple Equilibria," *The Economist* blog ("Free Exchange Economics"), October 7, 2011. Because supply and demand do not properly pertain to finance, supply-demand modelers often just make things up. Proof is in the disconnection between the model and reality. Contrary to a key assumption behind the construct in question, there is no evidence that investors' demand for bonds rises with yields in either "normal" or "abnormal" times as depicted in the dual-equilibrium model. On the contrary, sentiment indicators based on the market opinions of Treasury bond futures traders reveal that when bond prices fall (yields rise), investors become not increasingly purchase-happy but increasingly purchase-averse. Chapter 18 adds some anecdotal evidence to these statistics. The same perverse attitudes attend companies' dividend payouts, as shown in Figures 1, 4 and 5.

[8] Investopedia.

Chapter 13

Fundamentals of STF, in Contrast to Those of Economics

Robert R. Prechter

Economic and financial markets involve fundamental differences in causality. They are governed by different laws.

Multiple Interrelated Causes among Supply, Demand and Price in Economic Markets vs. a Single Unidirectional Cause of Price Change in Financial Markets

Under the supply-demand model of economic markets, related causal forces determine *supply*, *demand* and *price*, each of which is subject to change and each of which in fact continually does change. An economist asked to predict supply will speak of demand and prices; an economist asked to predict demand will speak of supply and prices; and an economist asked to predict price will speak of supply and demand. A change in any one of these three components is presumed mechanically to cause changes in both of the others: Demand affects price; price affects the quantity demanded; supply affects price; price affects the quantity supplied; demand affects the quantity supplied; and supply affects the quantity demanded. Although I prefer a holistic description whereby supply, demand and price are simultaneously, symbiotically intercausal, our purpose here is not to re-frame economic theory but to focus on contrasting economic and financial causality.

In financial markets, the complex relationships described above cannot exist. Supply and demand do not pertain to finance, and the law of supply, the law of demand, and the law of supply and demand do not operate in financial markets, so there can be no causal interrelationships among supply, demand and price within them. What causality is operating?

As explained in Chapter 12, new "supply" is an unimportant factor in financial markets. Among the three variables involved in economics, only price and some version of "demand" remain as possible causal variables in finance. The only causal options remaining, then, are that the motivation to buy or sell affects price, that price affects the motivation to buy or sell, or that both affect each other.

The latter formula cannot hold: If an increasing motivation among speculators to buy and own stocks caused stock prices to rise, and rising stock prices simultaneously caused an increase in speculators' motivation to buy and own stocks, there would be a positive feedback loop between prices and speculators' actions, and the market would move perpetually upward, or in the converse case, downward. Prices in fact fluctuate continually in fractal form, so there can be no self-reinforcing feedback loop and there-fore no dual positive causality. While rising prices do tend to attract more financial-market participants (see Chapters 6 and 19), the rising number of participants does not in turn cause rising prices. While one might be able to postulate a causal system based on some complex mix of positive and negative feedback, we would not presume to try.

We are left with two possible statements of causality: Price changes motivate participants to act, or participants' actions motivate price changes.

We know from Figures 7 through 9 of Chapter 12 that the price of stocks and the desire to own stocks fluctuate in the same direction. Which causes which?

The idea that rising stock prices motivate an increase, and falling prices a decrease, in the desire to own stocks is a popular notion. Intuitively it seems to make sense, since speculators' excitement about stocks does change as stocks rise and fall. But this fact is true regardless of the direction of causal-ity. It also holds for the opposing case that an increasing desire to buy and own stocks leads to rising prices, a decreasing desire leads to falling prices.

The idea that price motivates desire in finance is an unsound theoretical position, because it is incompatible with any coherent hypothesis regarding the cause of changing prices. One might try to make this idea work by tak-ing the position that stock prices respond positively to changes in corporate values, and speculators' desires to own stock then respond positively to the price changes. But neoclassical economists and proponents of EMH must and do reject this reasoning. A greater desire to own stock implies a greater hope of *future* price rise, and vice versa. But if stock prices were in fact fluctuating efficiently to reflect fundamental values, there would be no reason for speculators' desire to own stock to fluctuate positively with prices. The same analysis applies to commodities, bonds, real estate and every other financial asset. Under conventional finance theory, every price is always a fair price, never a price to indicate anything at all about the future, and therefore never a price to encourage or discourage buying or selling.

One might be able to retain the notion that changes in stock prices motivate changes in the desire to own stocks by asserting that stock price changes have no identifiable cause. But doing so would be to assert that any complete understanding of financial causality is impossible. Since socionomics does offer an explanation for it, such a nihilistic stance is unnecessary.

Only one causal option remains: *Changes in speculators' desire to own stocks motivate their actions to buy and sell, which cause changes in price.* According to socionomics, this is the only causal relationship that applies.

To remain rigorous, we must jettison the common expression that "buying" stocks makes prices go up and "selling" makes them go down. There is no such duality, because every purchase is simultaneously a sale. Every buyer buys from a seller, and every seller sells to a buyer. One could just as well say that selling stocks makes prices go up and buying them makes prices go down.

In truth there is but a single dynamic occurring, which is that active participants in the speculating herd—and even the inactive ones by their choices not to act—simply *agree*, albeit unconsciously, that a financial price should be higher, lower or unchanged from the previous price. They bring about these results by buying and selling simultaneously, that is, by transacting, *at a new price*. For more on this idea, see Chapter 17.

The last elements to explain are (1) What is the micro-level regulator of speculators' buying and selling actions, and what should we call it? (2) What is the macro-level regulator of speculators' buying and selling actions, and what should we call it? Answering these questions will give us a complete picture of financial price causality.

Spontaneous Commands at the Individual Level

Chapter 12 established that the mental orientation of a speculator buying and selling investment items is qualitatively different from the mental orientation of a producer selling, or a consumer buying, goods and services. Socionomic theory offers a hypothesis for codifying this difference: Because the motivation to own stock always fluctuates positively rather than negatively with price (see Chapter 12), because speculators constantly rationalize their decisions (see Chapter 19), because the vast majority of speculators eventually end up losing money (see Chapter 17), because there is evidence of unconscious herding among participants in financial markets (see Chapter 16), and because there is evidence that financial-market prices fluctuate according to the Wave Principle (see Chapters 22 and 23), socionomics proposes that speculators' desire and motivation to buy or sell derive not from reason but from impulse.

Formerly (as in Chapter 15, originally published in 2007) I had de-faulted to using the term *demand* in the context of finance in saying that financial prices change in response to shifts in speculators' demand. But I realized that doing so was yet another erroneous holdover from conventional economic thought, with which Chapter 12 has dispensed. I see no point in using the same word to mean two different things, especially when there is a more accurate term available. A word that signifies the impulsive nature of speculators' actions is *command*. The herd of speculators simply com-mands prices up and down to match participants' impulsively determined agreement on where prices should be.

The term *command* usually denotes a consciously motivated action, whereas under STF the herd's commands are unconsciously motivated. To capture this difference, we can expand the expression to say that the herd drives financial prices up and down by *spontaneous command*.

The market for eggs is a supply-and-demand market. The market for stocks is a spontaneous-command market.

The Law of Patterned Herding at the Aggregate Level

Conventional economic theory proposes that investment items are priced rationally according to the laws of supply and demand. In their stead, socionomics proposes the law of patterned herding (LPH), which states that investment items are priced pre-rationally (see below) according to a patterned herding dynamic that conforms to the Wave Principle, which is described by the Elliott wave model.

Combining the micro and macro levels of causality in the two opposing models produces the following formulation: Economic markets are regulated at the individual level by rationally motivated utility maximization and at the aggregate level by the laws of supply and demand. Financial markets are regulated at the individual level by pre-rationally motivated spontane-ous commands and at the aggregate level by the law of patterned herding.

Financial-Market Herding

Taking Paul Montgomery's lead, I often use the term *pre-rational* to describe herding impulses, because the unconscious, non-rational portion of the human mind, which evolved first, is not pathologically irrational but rather has a positive goal. The term *non-rational* is useful when discussing these impulses in contrast to *rational* mentation, and the term *irrational* is useful at times to describe pre-rational impulses' persistent counter-productivity in inappropriate contexts, such as finance. Since the portion of the mind that humans inherited from lower animals evolved substantially in a primitive environment, it improperly employs a blunt, pre-rational technique of self-preservation—herding—in the modern setting of finance, where it is leads to counterproductive, and therefore contextually irrational, actions. (For more on this topic, see Chapter 24.)

The motivation behind economic and financial behavior is the same as that for all evolved behaviors: to survive and thrive. In finance, however, people's minds are operating differently. Buyers in a rising market appear unconsciously to think, "The herd must know where the food is. Run with the herd and you will *prosper.*" Sellers in a falling market appear unconsciously to think, "The herd must know that there is a lion racing toward us. Run with the herd or you will *die.*"

Speculators are conscious only of the powerful emotions that attend their unconscious thoughts. If herding impulses and the rationales they foster were conscious, rational people would see through them, ignore the false reasoning and instead buy low, sell high and get rich. Herding speculators, however, cannot buy cheaply and sell dearly, because their very bidding higher makes prices rise, and their very offering lower makes them fall.

A Context of Uncertainty

Uncertainty prompts humans to herd. The utility of herding derives from the fact that sometimes other members of the herd know something you don't. At such times, herding can provide an advantage. In finance, there are no knowledgeable members of the herd, because no one knows the financial future. Herding thus offers speculators no advantage and in fact places them at a disadvantage.

All day long in finance, speculators are uncertain, and nothing can fix the problem. Even the most rational speculators cannot escape the fact that a fickle herd is in charge of price changes, which dooms them to a state of uncertainty about what the herd will do, thereby making them vulnerable to herding no matter how strongly they wish to avoid it.

Broadly speaking, socionomics proposes a theory of human decision-making in which context is crucial. To the degree that a context of relative certainty applies, humans avail themselves of conscious, independent reason. To the degree that a context of uncertainty applies, humans default to unconscious, dependent herding. STF therefore proposes the following dichotomy of decision-making in economic vs. financial contexts: In the economic marketplace, consumers are *knowledgeable* about their *own values*, producing relative *certainty*, so they can *reason*, whereas in the financial marketplace, speculators are *ignorant* of *others' future actions*, producing *uncertainty*, so they *herd*. Amidst the calm of conscious, rational thought, economic transactors make considered decisions; in the throes of unconscious, impulsive thought, financial transactors issue spontaneous commands.

Rational Valuation Creates Objective Pricing; Impulsive Valuation Creates Subjective Pricing

Rational valuation produces objective pricing, and objective pricing provides mutual benchmarks of value. Absent extraordinary circumstances, any competent person in an unfamiliar country with its own currency who knows the local cost of a loaf of bread can reliably estimate the local cost of a pound of butter or a pound of chicken. A simple formula gives the answers. But no one in that situation who knows the price of a share of stock in a local bread-producing company can reliably estimate the relative price of a share of stock in a local company producing butter or chicken. Such inability extends even to people who possess substantial knowledge of each of the companies. If the first company sells at $122 a share, what is the price per share of the other two companies? There is no telling. Who knows what seemingly reasonable or absurd value the market has placed on such shares? No formula can produce a reliable answer, because impulsive valuation produces subjective pricing, and subjective pricing provides no mutual benchmarks of value. Chapter 24 further explores this issue.

Rationalization Facilitates Herding

The reasoning and perhaps the perceptual portions of the brain play a secondary role in the herding process. Herding is an unconscious imperative that for eons has proved useful to self-preservation, so human nervous systems have evolved to accommodate it. When the impulse to herd motivates a speculator to act, cooperating mental circuits accommodate the action by rationalizing what the speculator does.

Mental circuits that apply reason to decision-making generally resist irrational actions in the service of achieving the host's goal of self-preservation. Herding overrides those circuits. Research shows (see Chapter 16) that unconscious impulses are fast and powerful and attached to emotional rewards. They developed through evolution because they kept countless species alive. Evolution has yet to result in the elevation of reason above herding in emotionally charged social contexts of uncertainty, such as financial markets.

To dissipate reason's potential resistance to herding impulses, human minds go through some of the motions of reasoning. They engage in rationalization, sometimes before taking the action and sometimes after. Without this service, the herding impulse would clash with reason to produce cognitive dissonance, which could initially bar the way to action or afterward dilute the action's powerful emotional reward, the feeling of relief. This system of internal mental cooperation evolved during a time when herding often sustained life. The reconciliation of conscious thought with unconscious impulse is itself an unconsciously directed effort to keep the person alive and thriving. Unfortunately, in finance, it is detrimental to success.

Although most speculators, money managers, economists and media commentators believe they are reasoning—at a high level, no less—rationalization unconsciously motivates most financial market commentary. When participants feel bullish, they perceive bullish events and make bullish arguments. When participants feel bearish, they perceive bearish events and make bearish arguments. The wondrous plasticity of exogenous-cause arguments (see Chapters 2 and 19) provides an ideal basis for facilitating the imperative to rationalize.

As illustrated in Chapters 1 and 2 of this book, speculators are afforded numerous referents every day that they can use to justify opinions and actions based on their moods and herding impulses. Virtually none of them matter. The demonstrated irrelevance of widely presumed causes reveals the immense power of the unconscious: It can impel a human being to spout nonsense about stock-market causality day after day without realizing it. Unconscious impulses and emotions are so strong, and rationalization is so comforting, that even when confronted with conflicting data, most people will go on believing their mechanistic causal assumptions to be valid.

Turn back to Figure 4 of Chapter 12 and take a good look at the extreme range of the bond yield/stock yield ratio for the S&P 400 over the past century. We can cite the rationalizations that investors were using at the all-time low and the all-time high: In the 1940s, when corporate stock dividends yielded more than two and a half times what the same companies' bonds did, investors declared, "This difference is reasonable; stocks have a *risk factor*." In 2000, when corporate stock dividends yielded only one ninth what the same companies' bonds did, they declared, "This difference is reasonable; stocks have *profit potential*." Both expressions of purportedly self-evident logic are in fact pure rationalization.

Sometimes people say, "I'm buying because it's a bull market." STF recognizes such statements as being just another example of rationalization, an excuse for people to do what their mood and impulses impel them to do. They actually have no idea whether the bull market will continue or has just ended.

When I gave a presentation on stocks and real estate to a small group of wealthy investors at the behest of their advisor in the summer of 2006, they seemed thoughtfully to consider and even to accept my bearish view of the stock market. But when I showed socionomic reasons why real estate prices were poised to turn down, the volume level in the room rose as they returned a barrage of counter-arguments: "They're not making any more real estate!" "Everyone has to live somewhere!" "My properties are in prime locations!" "There is a flood of immigrants, and they all need housing!" "Prices have been going up for 60 years!" "Don't you get it? It's all about location, location, location!" In accordance with socionomic theory, the present price of property was irrelevant to them; they didn't even mention it. I replied, "It's not about those things; it's about the extremes in borrowing, lending and prices, and the looming spectre of illiquidity."

I quickly figured out why I was getting such blowback on my outlook for property prices: *That's what they owned.* They had already gone through the rationalization process, so their minds were clamped shut and unreachable. They weren't committed to stocks, so they could listen to a case against owning them. Their reaction to my view of real estate was not calm, as if we were debating a tenet among Robert's Rules of Order; it was *emotional.* Herding provides emotional rewards. Attempting to stop it causes stress and emotional reactions. Their passion was another sign of a major peak in property prices. It turned out to be almost perfectly timed.

Rationalization permeates all speculatively traded markets. Chapters 18 and 22 are packed with additional real-world examples.

Economic theorists do not recognize the pervasive practice of rationalization in finance. They model financial markets as if they are equivalent to those for shoes. I wonder how an economist would react if he walked into a shoe store and the manager rushed up and told him to "double up" because prices had skyrocketed last week or if customers in the parking lot warned him to stay away because prices had been collapsing. What would he think if he attended a cocktail party (as Mr. B below) and got involved in the following conversation?

A: "Psst! Whaddaya think of shoes?"

B: "Huh?

A: "Are you buying or selling?"

B: "What do you mean?"

C (overhearing): "I'm bullish Hush Puppies, myself. The whole loafers sector looks good."

A: "Yeah? Well, I'm long wing-tips and sneakers. They're gonna fly!"

D (joining in): "Fine, but you gotta realize, if shoes are gonna go, socks are next."

A: "Good point! I'd better load up on socks."

D: "Yep, Argyles are set to run. Hey, what do you think, bub?"

B: "Huh?"

Thinking such as this derives from impulse and rationalization. Consumers do not behave in this manner, so they need not rationalize their decisions to buy shoes and socks. As *The Wave Principle of Human Social Behavior* put it, "Most investors can quickly rationalize selling an investment when its price is falling or buying it when its price is rising, but there is not a soul who desperately rationalizes doing with less bread because the price is falling or who drives his car twice as much because the price of gasoline has doubled."[1]

Herding Produces Losses

The difference in mental processing that attends economic vs. financial settings produces a dichotomy of result between the two types of markets. Economic transactions benefit both sellers and buyers. Financial transactions may temporarily benefit a buyer *or* a seller, but not both. Over time, they reliably work to the ultimate detriment of the vast bulk of speculators, as demonstrated in Chapter 17. Since speculators tend to buy at higher prices than they sell, it can be no other way.

Biology Accounts for Differences in Economic and Financial Thought

Figure 1 suggests possible differences in the mental origins of human behavior in an economic setting vs. a financial setting. It derives from Paul MacLean's conception that the human brain is the result of eons of development through the long process of animals' evolution (see further discussion in Chapter 16). Speaking of MacLean's model, Joseph LeDoux stated,

> [T]he notion that emotions involve relatively primitive circuits that are conserved throughout mammalian evolution seems right on target. Furthermore, the idea that cognitive processes might involve other circuits, and might function relatively independent of emotional circuits, at least in some circumstances, also seems correct.[2]

The neurological key to our proposed dichotomy is that the reasoning neocortex is substantially "independent of emotional circuits," which are more strongly attached to the "relatively primitive circuits"—however they are specifically delineated—which operate unconsciously. Socionomics embraces this crucial duality at the biological level to help account for the

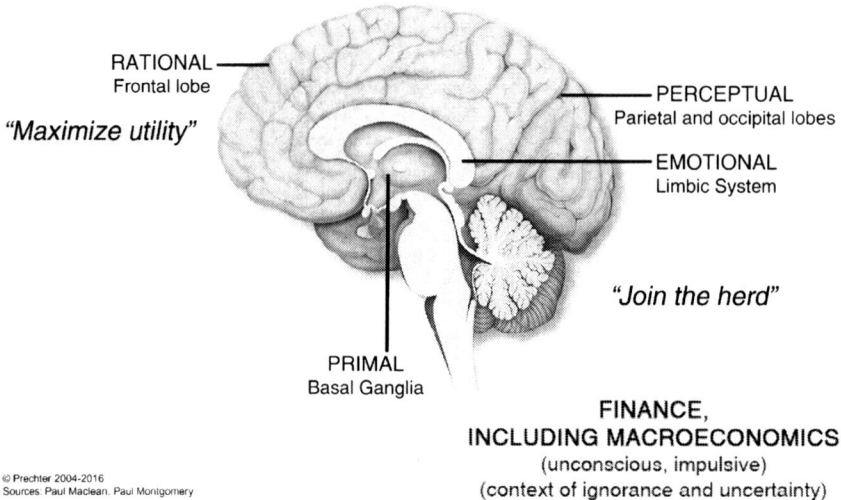

UTILITARIAN ECONOMICS
(conscious, reasoned)
(context of knowledge and certainty)

"Rationalize decisions to herd"

RATIONAL
Frontal lobe

"Maximize utility"

PERCEPTUAL
Parietal and occipital lobes

EMOTIONAL
Limbic System

"Join the herd"

PRIMAL
Basal Ganglia

FINANCE,
INCLUDING MACROECONOMICS
(unconscious, impulsive)
(context of ignorance and uncertainty)

© Prechter 2004-2016
Sources: Paul Maclean, Paul Montgomery

Figure 1

financial/economic dichotomy. Specifically, in an economic context, people are relatively knowledgeable and certain, so they can employ the conscious mental process of reasoning, handled primarily by the frontal lobe, whereas in a financial context, people are ignorant and uncertain, so they default to the unconscious mental process of herding, handled primary by the more impulsive, emotional and perceptual areas of the brain.

These areas of the brain cooperate with each other through constant mediation. The rational faculty at times accommodates pre-rational impulses by way of rationalization and at times curbs them by introspection and reason.

A Successful Lab Experiment

The idea that herding and reasoning derive from different parts of the brain made a successful forecast. Following several weeks of email exchange, in February 2003 Gordon Graham, the Socionomics Institute's first Director, and I met for three hours with Dr. Greg Berns, a neuroscientist from Emory University, in a private room at the Cherokee Country Club in Atlanta. Berns had access to an fMRI machine that a subscriber to *The Elliott Wave Theorist* had purchased for the school. In an email sent prior to the meeting, I applied information from Chapter 8 of *The Wave Principle of Human Social Behavior* and the 2001 paper reprinted as Chapter 16 in this book to come up with the following proposal:

> The idea is to test whether information about what a crowd is doing with respect to a task assigned to a subject influences which areas of the brain the subject employs to complete the task. The question is whether people have an impulsive drive to join a crowd and if so, where the origin of that impulse lies within the brain.
>
> Broad Hypothesis 1: When alone, a subject will calmly apply his cerebral cortex to a task involving mathematical calculation and deliver a predictable response. He will experience little or no pre-rational brain perturbation. When supplied with the information that a crowd disagrees with his initial conclusion, he will experience perturbation from the pre-rational portions of his brain, i.e., the limbic system and/or primitive brain stem, which will influence his ultimate response and cause him to adjust his answer in the direction of the crowd's conclusion.[3]

It is of course widely known that crowds influence people's opinions. But the idea that a person would access a *different part of the brain* when making decisions in the presence of an opinionated group is not a self-evident proposition. It could just as well be argued that a person given information about the opinions of others would use the reasoning portion of his mind to take those opinions into account, weighing them simply as a fact to be considered. Most academic economists (see Chapters 19 and 23) do in fact argue that herding is rational.

Berns and his colleagues designed an experiment to test the thesis, and the results bore out the essence of the prediction: When performing mental tasks, subjects accessed a different part of the brain when opinions of others were introduced into their deliberations. Here is a summary of their findings:

> Conformity was associated with functional changes in an occipital–parietal network, especially when the wrong information originated from other people. Independence was associated with increased amygdala and caudate activity, findings consistent with the assumptions of social norm theory about the behavioral saliency of standing alone. These findings provide the first biological evidence for the involvement of perceptual and emotional processes during social conformity.[4]

The amygdala is part of the limbic system, the caudate nucleus is a component of the basal ganglia, and the occipital and parietal lobes are at the rear of the brain. These areas process emotions, impulses, visualization and perception, respectively, more so than high reasoning. The researchers at Emory found that perturbation in these areas, suggesting a condition of stress, occurred when the subject disagreed with the crowd and decided not to go along. Subjects who capitulated to the crowd did not exhibit the same neurological activity. This finding suggests that joining a herd involves a stress-free path of mentation and that the impulsive areas of the brain issue alarms if an individual has opted, for the moment, not to join a herd. The subjects involved had no tangible stakes in the experiment, yet even so an independent stance perturbed them. Speculators who place bets in financial markets must have significantly higher levels of stress, because in that setting the stakes are high. One can imagine a speculator bravely staying independent of the crowd for only so long, until the pressure of signals from his amygdala and its partner structures impelling him to join the herd become so intense that all he wants is relief.

The study also hinted that the occipital and parietal lobes are involved in the rationalization process, since they were active when the subject went along with the crowd. These areas of the brain appear to ease their host's path to conformity by actually altering the host's perceptions. A *Forbes* article reported on the experience:

> Lemminglike, she usually went along with the majority view, even when it was wrong. Her brain scan shows why: A change in perceptual processing. [T]he group changed what the reporter perceived.[5]

A percept is so basic to cognition, as well as demonstrably alterable by unconscious influences (see Chapter 16), that the mental process leading to an alteration in perception must be substantially unconscious.

So, we can trace the reasoning vs. herding dichotomy in human behavior—which underlies the economic vs. financial dichotomy—all the way down to biology. Proponents of conventional economic theories would not have considered such a prediction. Proponents of socionomics did, and it was successful.

Features of the Financial/Economic Dichotomy

Figure 2 summarizes socionomic theory's proposed differences between economics and finance at both the individual (micro) level and the aggregate (macro) level. The left-hand column lists properties of economic markets, and the right-hand column lists properties of financial markets. STF incorporates all the aspects of the financial side of the financial/economic dichotomy. The paragraphs below briefly review the features of both types of markets.

Per the Socionomic Theory of Finance (STF), Economics and Finance are Two Separate Fields

ECONOMICS
(Markets for Utilitarian Goods and Services)

FINANCE
(Markets for Investment Items)

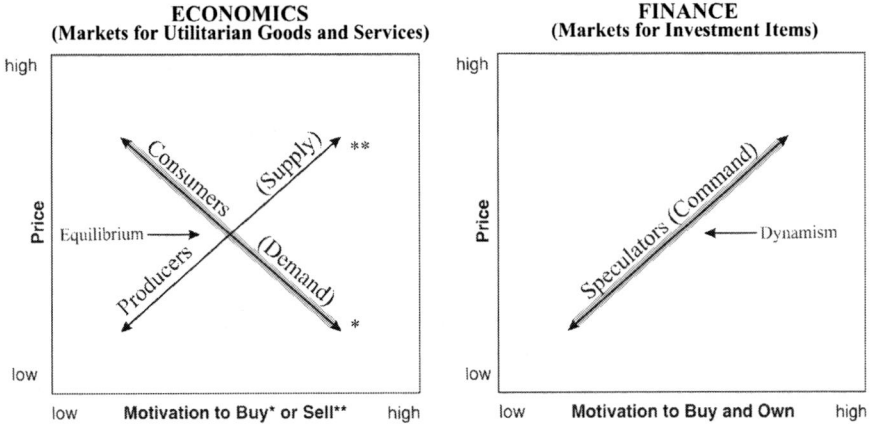

Features at the Individual (Micro) Level
Goal: Survival and Success
Participants: Opposed Producers and Consumers
Orientation to One's Own Values
Independent Decisions
Known present prices matter
Context: Knowledge and Certainty
Mental State: Conscious
Motivation: Maximize Utility
Means: Reason
Action: Considered Transactions
Ultimate Result: Survival and Success

Features at the Aggregate (Macro) Level
Reliable Standards of Value
Rational Valuation
Objective Values
Prices express information efficiently
Stability (Equilibrium and Mean Reversion)
Laws of Supply and Demand (S&D) regulate price
Motivation to buy moves in opposite direction from price
Price is a meaningful product
Explanatory Hypothesis: Neoclassical Theory and the Efficient Market Hypothesis (EMH)
Px Change Model: Statistically Random Responses to S&D
Product: Prosperity and Stability
Benefit: Short Term Survival of Individuals and Societies
Scholarly Domain: Economics

Features at the Individual (Micro) Level
Goal: Survival and Success
Participants: Unopposed Speculators
Orientation to Others' Future Actions
Dependent Decisions
Unknown future price changes matter
Context: Ignorance and Uncertainty
Mental State: Unconscious
Motivation: Join the Herd
Means: Impulse, Rationalization
Action: Spontaneous Commands
Ultimate Result: Losses and Failure

Features at the Aggregate (Macro) Level
No Reliable Standards of Value
Pre-Rational, Impulsive Valuation
Subjective Values
Prices express mood and herding efficiently
Dynamism
Law of Patterned Herding (LPH) regulates price
Price moves in same direction as motivation to buy
Price is a meaningless byproduct
Explanatory Hypothesis: Socionomic Theory of Finance (STF)
Price Change Model: Elliott Wave Principle
Product: Boom and Bust at All Degrees
Benefit: Long Term Survival of the Species
Scholarly Domain: Socionomics

© Prechter 2004-2016

Figure 2

Features at the Individual (Micro) Level
Identical Goals

Participants' goal in both types of markets—economic and financial—is survival and success. Everyone involved is acting so as to succeed at life. This is the only trait the two markets share. Everything else is different.

Participants: Heterogeneous Entities vs. One Homogeneous Group

Economic markets comprise two sets of heterogeneous role players: producers, who sell goods and services, and consumers, who buy goods and services. Financial markets comprise a homogeneous aggregation of speculators, who trade investment items back and forth.

In the economic marketplace, producers are trying to get the most money they can, while consumers are trying to get the most they can for their money. In the financial marketplace, speculators are presumably trying to achieve *both* of these ends—getting the most for their money and getting the most money they can.

Orientation: One's Own Actual Values vs. Others' Potential Future Actions

In the economic marketplace, the purchaser of a good or service is oriented to his or her *own actual values*. If you go into a store, you know what kind of food you like, or you know that you need to buy some lumber to build that shed out back. You are oriented to your own wants and needs, which derive from your own values.

In finance, the purchaser of an investment item is oriented to *others' potential future actions*. A stock certificate is not something one wants or needs, so one's personal values are irrelevant to the transaction. A speculator assumes the task of projecting how other speculators will value that certificate later. Speculators are oriented toward what *they think others will do*, not to what *they themselves presently want or need*.

An orientation towards others' unknown potential actions is an orientation to nothing. There are no personal values to weigh objectively.

A value-free item is not real to people. All it can represent is mental fantasies, typically of riches, but also of superior intelligence, higher social standing, alpha maleness or some other intangible benefit.

Independence vs. Dependence in Decision-Making

Economic decisions are highly independent from the thoughts, feelings and actions of others, whereas financial decisions are highly dependent on the thoughts, feelings and actions of others. This dependence ruins speculators' autonomy and therefore their ability to reason, inducing them to herd.

Focus on Known Present Prices vs. Unknown Future Price Changes

In economic markets, the price of a good or service matters greatly to producers' decisions about how much of it to produce and consumers' decisions about how much of it to consume. In financial markets, the price of an investment item is irrelevant to speculators' decisions to buy or sell it. Participants in economic markets care what prices are; participants in financial markets only believe, hope or fear that prices will change. Each producer and consumer cares about the known, present price of an item he may sell or buy, but each speculator cares only about the unknown, potential future direction and extent of price change for an item he may sell, buy or own.

Knowledge and Certainty vs. Ignorance and Uncertainty

The economic context is one of relative knowledge and certainty. Consumers know what they want, because they know what their values are, they know what their resources are, and they know what present prices are. So, they can be quite certain as to the correctness of their purchasing decisions relating to goods and services.

The financial context is one of ignorance and uncertainty. Speculators have no basis for valuing an investment item and no idea what future prices will be, so there is always uncertainty about the correctness of their buying, selling and holding decisions relating to investment items. This uncertainty is objectively real but not always conscious. When speculators feel certain, which can happen temporarily when their actions express an extreme in social mood, they tend to get into even more trouble than usual.

Conscious Utility Maximization vs. Unconscious Herding

Conscious and unconscious mental processes are always operating in the human mind, but context determines which process is dominant. When dealing in economic markets, producers and consumers consciously try to maximize the utility of their resources. In financial markets, speculators default to unconscious herding, because there is no basis for determining utility.

Reason vs. Impulse and Rationalization

When producers take their wares to market, and when consumers enter the marketplace to buy, they rely on reason for their decision-making. A seller reasons about how to make the most money, and a buyer reasons about how to save the most money.

In the financial marketplace, speculators' decisions are mostly impelled by pre-rational herding impulses. To accommodate these impulses, the reasoning and apparently even the perceptual portions of the brain provide the service of rationalization. Without it, the human organism might be paralyzed to act and barred from experiencing the feeling of relief that rewards the act of herding. Rationalization is nearly ubiquitous in financial analysis.

Considered Transactions vs. Spontaneous Commands

Conscious reason leads producers and consumers to make considered transactions. Unconscious herding leads speculators to issue spontaneous commands.

A Difference in Ultimate Result

Producers and consumers engage in mutually beneficial transactions. The ultimate result of producers and consumers' participation in economic markets is survival and success. Their actions produce nearly all the material wonders and many of the pleasurable experiences humans enjoy.

Speculators cannot create mutually beneficial transactions and usually end up creating mutually detrimental transactions. The ultimate result of speculators' participation in financial markets is losses and failure. Some speculators might be successful for a while, but nearly all speculators (see Chapter 17) ultimately end up with less money than they had at the start.

Features at the Aggregate (Macro) Level
Reliable Standards of Value vs. No Reliable Standards of Value

In economic markets, the price of one good or service provides a benchmark of value for other goods and services. Bread, butter and steak have all been at about the same relative prices for hundreds, if not thousands, of years. In financial markets, nothing reliably serves as an absolute or even a relative benchmark of value. Knowing one stock's price offers no guide to another stock's price. Knowing a company's earnings, its dividend payout, its book value and its dividend yield relative to its bond yield offers no reliable way to estimate the price of that company's stock.

Rational Valuation and Objective Values vs. Pre-Rational, Impulsive Valuation and Subjective Values

Economic markets allow rational valuation based on facts, making economic values objectively determined. Financial markets accommodate only impulsive valuation based on feelings, making financial values subjectively determined. For more on objectivity vs. subjectivity, see Chapter 24.

A Difference in Efficient Expression

Market efficiency vs. inefficiency is an unhelpful dichotomy. The question is not whether financial markets are efficient but what they are efficiently doing. In economic markets, prices express information efficiently. In financial markets, prices express social mood and herding impulses efficiently.

Stability vs. Dynamism

In economic markets, the two opposing groups of participants, in order to transact to their mutual benefit, must reach a truce as expressed by price. Rational utility maximization by both sets of participants pursuing their own values produces tendencies toward equilibrium and mean reversion. As a result, prices of utilitarian goods and services are fairly stable both in absolute terms and relative to each other.

In financial markets, the single, unopposed group of participants has no behavioral check, so prices of investment items fluctuate based on how speculators feel. Speculators' spontaneous commands produce dynamic price fluctuation in every financial market at every degree of trend, from intra-minute to intra-century, creating fractals of fluctuation in both the absolute and the relative pricing of investment items.

The Laws of Supply and Demand vs. the Law of Patterned Herding

Under the supply-demand model, the price regulator in economic markets is the interaction of the laws of supply and demand, whereby negotiation between producers and consumers determines price changes.

Under STF, the price regulator in financial markets is the law of patterned herding, whereby spontaneous commands issued by a herd of speculators conform in the aggregate to the hierarchical fractal designated the Wave Principle (WP) and described by the Elliott wave model (EW).

How Price Relates to the Motivation to Buy and Own an Item

In economic markets, price and the motivation to buy usually move in opposite directions. In financial markets, price always moves in the same direction as the motivation to buy.

Price as a Meaningful Result vs. a Meaningless Artifact

In economic markets, prices are meaningful products of the rationally motivated interplay between producers and consumers. In financial markets, prices are meaningless byproducts of speculators' pre-rationally motivated spontaneous commands to buy and sell.

Contrasting Explanatory Hypotheses

Neoclassical economic theory and EMH propose that knowledgable valuers determine financial prices objectively by rationally considering information. Socionomics recognizes that this description applies only to pricing in economic markets.

STF proposes that ignorant speculators determine financial prices subjectively by issuing spontaneous commands derived from pre-rational herding impulses.

Contrasting Models of Financial Price Change

Under the supply-demand model, economic prices change in response to substantially unpredictable shifts in supply and demand, which in a statistical sense occur randomly. Under STF, financial prices change substantially non-randomly according to a self-affine, hierarchical fractal designated WP and described by EW.

Contrasting Global Results

In both economic and financial behavior, ironies abound between individual motivation and global results. In neither role are individuals striving to bring about these results.

By engaging in economic activity, people act to further their own ends, and in doing so they bring prosperity and a measure of stability to society. This beneficial result is known as the Invisible Hand.

By engaging in financial activity, people likewise act to further their own ends, but in doing so they participate in a ceaselessly dynamic fractal of price movement, producing boom and bust at all degrees of fluctuation.

Rational utility maximization prompts reasonable individual actions. Impulsive herding prompts passionate social actions. The combination of these dynamics infuses the human social experience with a wondrous complexity.

Contrasting Benefits

Economic behavior is imperative for the survival and prosperity of individuals and societies. Socionomic behavior, which presents humans with rewards and challenges, may be necessary for the long-run survival, robustness and prosperity of the species (see Chapter 6).

Scholarly Domains: Distinctly Different Fields

The proper scholarly domain of economics is currently called microeconomics, the study of how individuals behave when faced with utilitarian decisions. The proper scholarly domain of finance is socionomics, the study of how society behaves when herding under the influence of waves of social mood.

Economic theory does *not* inform fields that economists have long incorporated by default: finance and so-called macroeconomics. Trends in financial markets and in the overall economy result from herding and social mood trends, placing them in the domain of socionomics.

The field of economics is properly much smaller than it purports to be. The field of socionomics owns the rest of the territory.

Economists are valuable when they stick to economics. They can explain, for example, why individuals' pursuit of self-interest in a free society is beneficial to others, why prices fall when production technology improves, why competition leads to lower prices, why cooperation leads to economic success, why sales attract customers, and how new laws will affect producers' and consumers' motives. Such knowledge is crucial to the survival of economies. On the other hand, if you want to understand financial market behavior, anticipate social changes or predict the expansion and contraction of the overall economy, seek out a socionomist.

Tables 1 and 2 add titles to all these dichotomies, providing a convenient reference.

Microeconomics and *Macroeconomics* are Inaccurate, Misleading Terms

How can it be that in the realm of *microeconomics* reason and utility maximization dominate, while in the realm of *macroeconomics* social mood and pre-rational herding dominate? Don't these terms denote different-sized versions of the same behavior?

Semantics are once again misleading. The very form of the words confuses the issue. One term is not a differently sized version of the other. The terms *microeconomic* and *macroeconomic* are inaccurate holdovers from the old paradigm and should be retired. Chapter 19 elaborates on the errors to which the additive thinking behind these terms leads.

The proper words to use are *economics* and *socionomics*. Reason governs economic behavior in contexts of relative certainty, while social mood and pre-rational herding govern socionomic behavior in contexts of uncertainty.

COMPONENTS OF THE FINANCIAL/ECONOMIC DICHOTOMY

Dichotomies at the Individual (Micro) Level	
Economic Markets (for goods and services)	**Financial Markets** (for investment items)
1. Participation Dichotomy	
Opposing heterogeneous groups of producers and consumers participate in economic markets.	An unopposed, homogeneous group of speculators participates in financial markets.
2. Orientation Dichotomy	
Consumers and producers are oriented toward their own actual values.	Speculators are oriented toward others' potential future actions.
3. Dependence Dichotomy	
In economic markets, decisions are substantially independent of group dynamics.	In financial markets, decisions are highly dependent upon group dynamics.
4. Price Relevance Dichotomy	
Known present prices matter to producers and consumers.	Only the direction and extent of unknown future price changes matter to speculators.
5. Knowledge and Certainty Dichotomy	
Consumers are mostly knowledgeable and certain about their own values and the goods and services they want and need.	Speculators are ignorant and chronically uncertain about what investment items to buy and sell and when to buy and sell them.
6. Dichotomy of Dominant Mental State	
Conscious thought dominates production and consumption decisions.	Unconscious thought dominates investment decisions.
7. Dichotomy of Motive	
In economic markets, a mental context of knowledge and certainty accommodates the rational motive to maximize utility.	In finance, a mental context of ignorance and uncertainty accommodates the pre-rational, impulsive motive to herd.
8. Means Dichotomy	
Producers and consumers primarily reason in the economic context..	Speculators primarily rationalize impulses in the financial context.
9. Action Dichotomy	
Producers and consumers engage in considered transactions.	Speculators issue spontaneous commands.
10. Dichotomy of Individual Result	
Economic activity mostly produces gains and success.	Financial activity mostly produces losses and failure.

Table 1

Dichotomies at the Aggregate (Macro) Level	
Economic Markets (for goods and services)	**Financial Markets** (for investment items)
A. Value Standards Dichotomy	
Prices for goods and services provide reliable standards of value for each other.	There are no reliable standards of value for pricing investment items.
B. Valuing Dichotomy	
Rational valuation produces objective pricing.	Pre-rational, impulsive valuation produces subjective pricing.
C. Efficiency Dichotomy	
Economic markets express information efficiently.	Financial markets express social mood and herding efficiently.
D. Volatility Dichotomy	
Economic markets tend toward equilibrium, mean reversion and stability.	Financial markets are dynamic.
E. Regulation Dichotomy	
In economics, supply, demand and price symbiotically regulate each other under the laws of supply and demand.	In finance, spontaneous commands of the herd regulate price under the law of patterned herding.
F. Direction Dichotomy	
Price and motivation to buy usually move in opposite directions.	Motivation to buy and price always move in the same direction.
G. Price Relevance Dichotomy	
In economic markets, prices are meaningful products of supply and demand.	In financial markets, prices are meaningless byproducts of impulses to buy and sell.
H. Explanatory Hypothesis Dichotomy	
Economic behavior conforms to the efficient market hypothesis (EMH).	Financial behavior conforms to the socionomic theory of finance (STF).
I. Price-Change Model Dichotomy	
Economics' model of price change is statistically random responses to supply and demand.	Socionomics' model of price change is the Wave Principle.
J. Dichotomy of Result	
Economic dynamics produce prosperity and stability, benefiting individuals and societies.	Financial dynamics produce boom and bust at all degrees, benefiting the species.

Table 2

Individuals participate in socionomic and economic behavior simultaneously all the time. Social mood and pre-rational herding by the group determine the ebb and flow of overall prosperity. Within that context, individuals generally exercise reason to maximize the utility of their resources. Their socionomic behavior is unconscious, while their economic behavior is conscious.

The idea that a mix of rational vs. pre-rational, conscious vs. unconscious, and individually motivated vs. group motivated behavior characterizes human society may be challenging to contemplate, but in the end it clears up what was heretofore a misconception of the human experience. Since it happens, we must strive to understand, explain and benefit from it.

The Two Fields Are Contextually, Not Intrinsically, Delineated

Humans are motivated to act economically and socionomically. Context determines which motivation dominates.

The difference between the financial and economic realms is not intrinsic to entities or actions. It is dependent upon participants' mental orientation, at both the individual and aggregate levels.

To an individual, a particular good is either an economic item or a financial item, depending upon whether his mind is oriented primarily to his own actual present valuation of it or to others' potential future valuation of it. A person could buy a leather jacket for warmth or because he thinks it will make others think he's cool. In the first instance, his relationship to the item is as a consumer to a good, which has a context of certainty in being based on his own actual values; in the second instance, his relationship to the item is as a speculator to an investment—in this case an investment in popularity—which has a context of uncertainty in being based on other people's potential future judgements. Chapter 14 discusses the difference between *clothing* and *fashion*.

In the marketplace as a whole, a consumer good becomes an investment item when the bulk of market participants changes its orientation from self-regarding to other-regarding, in which case impulsive pricing invades the economic sphere. At times, people have bid up the price of rare coins or baseball cards as collectors' items and the price of tulip bulbs or houses as investment items. From 1995 to 2006, many speculators built or bought housing and other properties in anticipation of higher prices, thereby treating formerly economic items as financial items. Market participants' shift in mental orientation from a producing or consuming mindset to a speculative mindset changed their behavior, resulting in a classic boom and bust (see Figure 3).

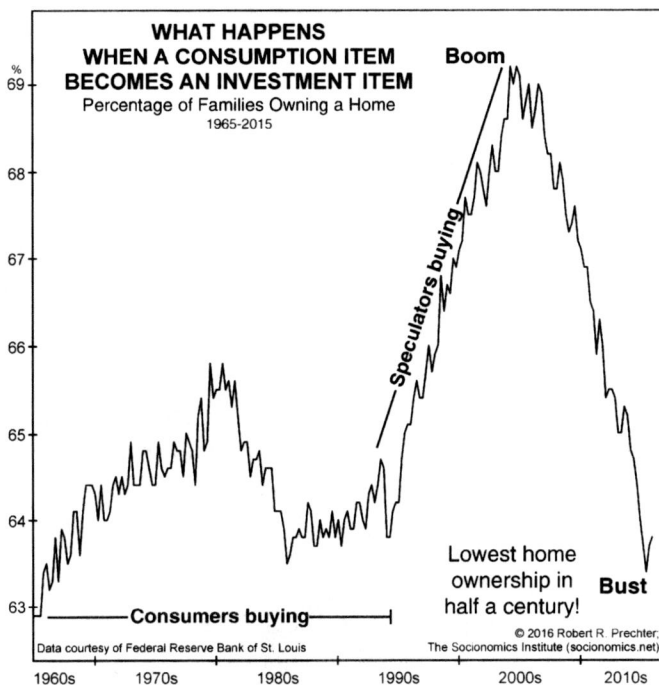

Figure 3

Conversely, rational utility maximization sometimes enters the financial sphere, as when manufacturing companies, such as the ones identified by the Commodity Futures Trading Commission as "Commercials," buy commodities for use in producing consumer goods. These buyers' mental orientation interprets items typically viewed as being in the financial realm as being in the economic realm, so their thinking and behavior differ from those of speculators. Their utility-maximizing mindset, unique among financial-market participants, also makes them the only consistently successful group among the CFTC's categories of futures transactors. (See further discussion in Chapter 17.)

Surprisingly, socionomic causality sometimes regulates consumers' and producers' behavior even in the economic realm. Alan Hall demonstrated in a 200-year study (reprinted in *Socionomic Studies of Society and Culture,* 2017) that U.S. per capita sugar consumption has ebbed and flowed not because of rational reactions to the price of sugar in the service of utility maximization but in concert with waves of social mood as recorded by the stock market. Furthermore, production has followed demand, so social mood has ultimately regulated the production of sugar as well. Chapter 22 provides a similar example with respect to oil production.

Even the market for stock shares sometimes serves economic motivations. Some people may buy shares of a publicly traded company in order to take it private, or sell shares of a privately owned company to the public, in each case to secure an economic benefit. In such cases, the buyers and sellers, respectively, are making an economic decision in which the company serves as a good to be demanded or supplied. Speculators do not think this way. That their shares represent a piece of a company is irrelevant to their goal. They simply want to trade pieces of paper at a profit.

Sometimes the application of knowledge can overcome the herding impulse in finance, for example when a speculator is well informed about his own moods, emotions and herding impulses as well as the impulsive nature of financial markets. For such a person, financial markets can become more like economic markets, in which he can employ reason to create positive personal outcomes. The exercise remains highly problematic, however, because the context of uncertainty still prevails, allowing even the most pristine reasoning to succeed only on a probabilistic basis. This observation, moreover, pertains only to individuals. In the aggregate, as long as financial markets exist and humans do not evolve to disregard their herding impulses, speculators, faced with uncertainty, will herd in a patterned way, and prices in financial markets will fluctuate accordingly.

The Initial Sale vs. Subsequent Sales Dichotomy in Financial Markets

Once we understand financial vs. economic behavior, we can fine-tune some contextual observations about the properties of markets. For example, the initial sale of a stock or bond is qualitatively different from subsequent sales. When people create a new company, their decision to sell shares or bonds is made in an economic context, since their purpose in raising money is to enable and ultimately to profit from the production of goods and/or services. The buyers of those stocks and bonds, in contrast, are speculators operating in a financial context. Once the stocks and bonds have been created and sold, both buyers and sellers of them thereafter are speculators making financial decisions.

There is no such dichotomy in economic markets. Producers who sell goods and services, retailers who buy them and re-sell them, consumers who buy them, and even consumers who re-sell them as used items, are always making economic decisions. In sum, all transactions in purely utilitarian economic markets are economically motivated, whereas all transactions in purely financial markets are financially motivated except for initial sales of financial items, in which case only the seller is economically motivated; stock purchases to take a company private, in which case only the buyer is economically motivated; and transactions between speculators and Commercials (see Chapter 17), in which only the Commercials are economically motivated. Chapter 14 describes a spectrum of markets that share both economic and financial aspects.

Contrasting Conventional Financial Theory with STF

Utilitarian economic transactions take place among knowledgeable, rational valuers who are maximizing the utility of their resources, an activity that produces objective values for goods and services in a market regulated by supply and demand and conducive to equilibrium-seeking, value reversion and relatively stable prices. Neoclassical economic theorists have tried

Contrasting Models of Finance	
Neoclassical Theory and EMH	**Socionomic Theory of Finance (STF)**
1. Objective, conscious, rational decisions to maximize utility determine financial values.	1. Subjective, unconscious, prerational impulses to herd determine financial values.
2. Financial markets tend toward stability (equilibrium) and revert to mean values.	2. Financial markets are dynamic and do not revert to anything.
3. Investors in financial markets typically use information to reason.	3. Investors in financial markets typically use information to rationalize mood-induced imperatives.
4. Investors' decisions are based on knowledge and certainty.	4. Investors' decisions are fraught with ignorance and uncertainty.
5. Exogenous variables determine most investment decisions.	5. Endogenous social processes determine most investment decisions.
6. Financial prices derive from individual decisions about value.	6. Financial prices derive from herding activity and trends in social mood.
7. Financial price changes are essentially random.	7. Financial prices adhere to an organizing principle at the aggregate level.
8. Financial prices are unpredictable; the character of news is unpredictable.	8. Financial prices are probabilistically predictable; so is the character of news.
9. Changing events presage changes in the values of associated financial instruments.	9. Changing values of financial instruments presage changes in associated events.
10. Economic principles govern finance.	10. Socionomic principles govern finance.

Table 3

to cram financial markets into this framework, and financial theorists have formalized this essential construction as the efficient market hypothesis (EMH). Researchers in the field of behavioral finance have poked some holes in this model and several related constructs, as discussed in Chapters 15 and 19. Socionomic theory is unique in both wholly rejecting the prevailing model of financial market behavior and in offering something with which to replace it, namely STF, which differs from every one of the shared particulars of neoclassical financial theory and EMH as listed in Table 3.

Item #10 reveals a curiosity that our dichotomy has uncovered: EMH substantially describes individuals' economic motivation, where it is not applied, but fails to describe financial motivation, where it is applied.

The efficient market hypothesis and the socionomic theory of finance are principled, extreme theories of aggregate financial pricing. The former proposes purely conscious, rational, reactive pricing, whereas the latter proposes purely unconscious, impulsive, proactive pricing. EMH is on one end of the rational/non-rational spectrum, and STF is on the other. Chapter 19 explores hypotheses that attempt to take a middle ground.

Summary

At a 19th-century medical conference, speakers proposed differing theories of the human stomach. A physician who had studied the stomach his whole professional life rose to the podium and responded to their ideas as follows: "Some physicologists will have it that the stomach is a mill; others, that it is a fermenting vat; others, again that it is a stewpan; but in my view of the matter, it is neither a mill, a fermenting vat nor a stew-pan, but a stomach gentlemen, a stomach."[6] Likewise, a few years ago a popular finance model was the physics of sand piles. More recently it has been evolving systems, based on macrobiology. Game theorists have offered their descriptions, and complexity theorists have offered theirs. Meanwhile, economists still equate financial markets to economic markets, central bankers still think the monetary system is a machine they can fine-tune, and EMH proponents still think financial price fluctuation is mostly or entirely random. But I would like to suggest that the stock market is not a random walk or chaos or billiard balls or a sand pile or a machine or an ecology or a game *or an economy*. It is a stock market, ladies and gentlemen, a stock market.

Appendix

ECONOMIC vs. SOCIONOMIC MODELING OF
PRICE AND VOLUME CHANGES IN FINANCIAL MARKETS

Two key variables in financial markets are price and volume. Economists could try to model these variables, but socionomic theory can both model them and occasionally predict them, a crucial difference when theories are judged on efficacy.

By using the carefully composed definitions of *supply* and *demand* by which these terms can apply to both economics and finance—as offered earlier in this chapter—an economist might try to model price and volume in financial markets in the following clever way: Buy and sell orders, both on the books and at market, represent demand and supply, respectively. On a day of rising stock prices, an increase in volume indicates that greater demand was the cause of the price rise, whereas a decrease in volume indicates that lower supply was the cause. Conversely, on a day of falling stock prices, an increase in volume indicates that greater supply was the cause of the price decline, whereas a decrease in volume indicates that lower demand was the cause.

This formulation offers only retrospective descriptions of changes in price and volume. To have any predictive capacity, it would have to incorporate a way of anticipating shifts in the supply and demand curves it assumes are operative. Economists list four factors that can shift the supply curve: prices of inputs used in production, production technology, the number of sellers, and expectations; and five factors that can shift the demand curve: the number of buyers, income (wouldn't wealth be a surer factor?), prices of related goods, tastes, and expectations.[7] As discussed in this chapter, production and consumption are irrelevant to the dynamics of the stock market. So are goods, but in the financial context modelers could substitute the term *investments*. As explained in this book, all five of the remaining factors—the numbers of buyers and sellers, buyers' income (in the aggregate), prices of related investments (which, as shown in Chapter 2, are irrelevant), tastes (to some degree), and expectations—are socionomically driven, not rationally and/or mechanically driven. Absent socionomic causality, economists cannot predict any of these factors, either within the suggested model or in real life.

One can use socionomic theory to model changes in price and volume in financial markets using only a single causal factor: patterned herding. That factor, moreover, is probabilistically predictable, making price and volume probabilistically predictable. Socionomics proposes that changes in aggregate herding impulses shift the balance of speculators' desires to bid up or offer down stock prices. Stronger actions among a larger number of speculators produce greater volume, and weaker actions among a smaller number of speculators produce lesser volume. When either the strength of actions or the number of speculators acting increases while the other decreases, the direction of volume change from one period to another depends upon the difference in the multiples of the two components.

We can model this socionomic idea mathematically. If S is the average number of shares each speculator buys and/or sells (measuring the *strength* of shifts in the motivation to act), B is the number of speculators trading (measuring the *breadth* of shifts in motivation to act) and V is volume, and considering that every buy is simultaneously a sell, then $(S \times B)/2 = V$. Given current restraints on access to data, only V is generally available. But the formula derived is not retrospective by necessity as the economic formulation is, because every financial-transaction firm could calculate its clients' S and B, and the data could be aggregated to determine V.

We can also postulate that if P is *price* and ΔP is *speed*, $\Delta P \times V$ would measure the *intensity*, denoted I, of net herding impulses, so that $I = \Delta P \times V$. To allow consistent historical comparisons, all three terms would be expressed in logs.

Because the Elliott wave model describes the pattern of aggregated herding impulses, and because that model has predictive aspects, Elliotticians at times can predict shifts in P, V and I. The Elliott wave model provides a basis for the probabilistic prediction of P, as demonstrated in Chapter 22, and often of ΔP and V, based on guidelines of price and volume fluctuation attending the model, as elucidated in *Elliott Wave Principle*. (For example, third waves typically sport faster price change and higher volume than first waves and, at lower degrees, fifth waves as well. Turn back to Figure 9 of Chapter 12 and you will see this tendency at two instances of high degree: 1936-1937 and 2010-2015.) Changes in I are a direct product of these changes. An Elliottician even predicted an increase in the variable B in 1983 when forecasting a stock mania with broad public participation, as detailed in Chapter 23. Since the Elliott wave model incorporates observations of simultaneous changes in ΔP and V at certain times (they are both relatively high in third waves), forecasting on that basis subsumes occasional predictions of ΔI. In sum, socionomists' modeling of price and volume is based on a full account of a single causal factor, whose changes are predictable within the model and at times predictable in real life.

This model and its attendant shifts in P, V and I are programmable. A project to do so is currently in development.

There are caveats to the idea that formulas involving V and I would change perfectly in accord with natural herding patterns. Long term changes in B and V could be due to population shifts and (theoretically, at least) to contagion-based shifts in the referents people choose to express social mood. So, while data on V and I might be analytically relatable over short periods of time, changes to B, V and I due to factors outside the Elliott wave model might render data for these expressions unsuitable for comparison over long periods of time. The most reliable indicator of market mood is the pattern of P alone. As discussed in Chapter 7, however, sometimes exogenous causes—such as hyperinflation—can ruin the utility even of stock prices as a sociometer.

Socionomists have a long way to go in terms of mathematically formulating their ideas. Economists' dubious history in this area suggests that the task will prove formidable. Social reality is and probably always will be less quantifiable than physics. But socionomic hypotheses and the Elliott wave model do provide a valid basis for the attempt.

NOTES AND REFERENCES

[1] See Chapter 20, *The Wave Principle of Human Social Behavior.*

[2] LeDoux, Joseph E. "Emotion Circuits in the Brain," *Annual Review of Neuroscience*, 2000, Vol. 23, pp. 155-184.

[3] Prechter, Robert, Memo to Dr. Gregory Berns, Associate Professor of Psychiatry and Behavioral Science, Emory University, and Jim Richards, January 30, 2003, emailed February 3, 2003.

[4] Berns, G.S., J.C. Chappelow, C.F. Zink, G. Pagnoni, M.E. Martin-Skurski, R. Richards, "Neurobiological Correlates of Social Conformity and Independence During Mental Rotation," *Biological Psychiatry*, 2005, 58:245-253.

[5] Wells, Melanie, "In Search of the Buy Button," *Forbes,* September 3, 2003.

[6] John Hunter, in *Principles and Practice of Medicine,* by John C. Peters and Frederick Snelling, New York: William Radde, 1863, pp. 64-65.

[7] Mankiw, N. Gregory. *Principles of Macroeconomics*, 3rd Edition, 2004. Mason, Ohio: Thomson South-Western, pp. 67-69; 73-75.

Chapter 14

The Economic-Socionomic
Spectrum of Markets

Robert R. Prechter

The two lists in Figure 2 of Chapter 13 present traits of theoretically pristine economic and financial markets. These conditions attend the far ends of a spectrum. Between these poles lies a wide variety of intermediary markets that share, to varying degrees, both economic and socionomic properties. Figure 1 endeavors to list these markets in order of their proportions of each set of properties.

At the top of the table is the ideal of quintessentially utilitarian goods and services, priced by participants in a mental state of pure rationality, applied to the goal of maximizing utility. At the bottom of the table is the ideal of non-utilitarian investment items and fads, priced by participants in a mental state of pure feeling, deriving from mood, emotion and whim.

Fashions and fads are not financial markets, but they are socionomically regulated. So, the spectrum's poles are properly designated as representing economics and socionomics. The latter category subsumes that of finance.

We can envision these markets as lying on a scale from 1 to 10, with 1 being a purely economic market and 10 being a purely socionomic market. Socionomists might adopt a habit of referring to different markets as being a "4" or an "8" on the scale. Perhaps someday these differences might be quantifiable. For now, a qualitative discussion will have to suffice.

Nearest the purely economic end of the spectrum is the market for *tools*, things with which people work. Examples are hammers, nails, wrenches, drills, pots, pans, machines used in manufacturing, etc. Producers and consumers apply reason in pricing tools so as to maximize the utility of their money. Granted, people might splurge on an expensive set of pots, but prices for such items typically relate reasonably to their quality. When there is a boom and bust in oil or real estate, prices for oil drilling or construction equipment may rise and fall accordingly due to high demand. Nevertheless, such items are never the focal point of fads or speculation.

THE ECONOMIC-SOCIONOMIC SPECTRUM OF MARKETS

UTILITARIAN GOODS & SERVICES
(PRICES ECONOMICALLY DETERMINED)
(knowledge; certainty; consciousness; reasoning; utility maximization; objectivity; independence; personal values; value benchmarks; stability)

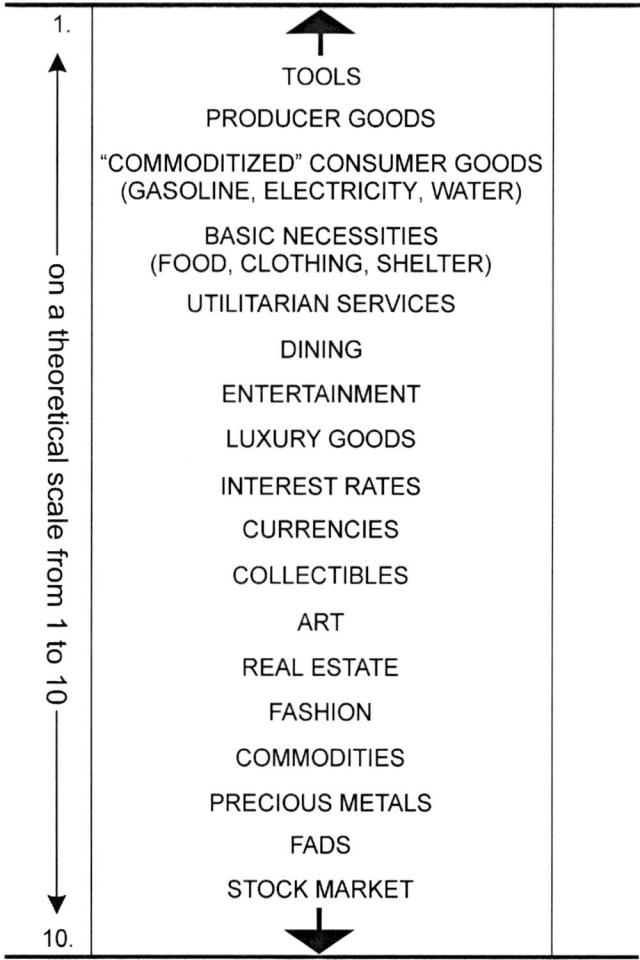

1.

on a theoretical scale from 1 to 10

TOOLS

PRODUCER GOODS

"COMMODITIZED" CONSUMER GOODS
(GASOLINE, ELECTRICITY, WATER)

BASIC NECESSITIES
(FOOD, CLOTHING, SHELTER)

UTILITARIAN SERVICES

DINING

ENTERTAINMENT

LUXURY GOODS

INTEREST RATES

CURRENCIES

COLLECTIBLES

ART

REAL ESTATE

FASHION

COMMODITIES

PRECIOUS METALS

FADS

STOCK MARKET

10.

FINANCIAL INVESTMENTS & FADS
(PRICES SOCIONOMICALLY DETERMINED)
(ignorance; uncertainty; unconsciousness; impulsion; herding; subjectivity; dependence; others' potential actions; no value benchmarks; dynamism)

Figure 1

They remain just tools. There are no booms and busts in hedge trimmers, and no sentiment gauges to measure how bullish or bearish speculators are on the price of cotter pins.

Next are **producer goods**, materials that manufacturers and service providers need to produce their finished goods and services. Examples are concrete, bricks, steel ingots, rubber mats, raw plastic, sheets of metal, dry-cleaning chemicals, massage oil, etc. They are produced not for consumption but for production. These items are essentially tools, too. But they also have a raw-material component, so their prices might fluctuate a bit because those for iron, rubber and oil do.

Next are **commoditized consumer goods**, such as gasoline, electricity and water. Nearly everybody uses these essentials to stay alive. But they're not *just* tools. People might use more gasoline near positive extremes in social mood because they're feeling flush so they buy sportier vehicles that get fewer miles per gallon. Some people might use more electricity at the same time because they built a mansion with a lighted tennis court and a heated swimming pool. Water is something people generally use as they need, but when incomes are up they may splurge to soak the entire lawn twice a week. So, these items are a bit further away from purely rational use and therefore purely rational pricing. (Numerous governments currently fix the price of water, however, disallowing natural pricing.)

Next are the oft-cited necessities of life: **food, clothing** and **shelter**. Everyone's got to have them. Relative values for such items are objective and reasonable most of the time. But people can treat these items as more than just necessities, so there is room for mood-based spending in terms of the specific choices people make in these areas. A family can buy a bigger house than it needs. People can buy steak and lobster instead of chicken and hot dogs. They can buy fitted slacks instead of a utilitarian pair of chinos.

Next we have **utilitarian services**, for example, house cleaning, lawn maintenance, food delivery, dry cleaning, and so on. There is a utilitarian component to such services, as they can free consumers to do more work. But there is also a luxury component. People can exceed the utilitarian aspect of personal services, say, by getting massages and pedicures twice a week.

Dining is a less utilitarian version of food. Zipping by the take-out window at a fast-food restaurant can have a utilitarian purpose in saving time. But people can also choose to buy an expensive bottle of wine for a negligible increase in pleasure over a lesser-priced bottle. In 1989, Japanese consumers (at their peak in social mood; see Figure 5 in Chapter 12) were sprinkling flakes of gold on their food. Restaurants go in and out of fashion, too. One year they're packed, and the next year there's a "For Lease" sign in the window. Social mood and faddism can bring about such changes.

With ***entertainment*** we're crossing the midpoint of the spectrum. Types of entertainment are generally fairly reasonably priced relative to the cost of production and with respect to each other, but shifting preferences, influenced by social mood, determine who gets the money. A singer who is really popular can charge top prices for tickets, whereas a few years later the same singer may be unable to fill the local coffee house. Social mood strongly influences what various entertainers can charge for their products and services.

Next in line are ***luxury goods***. Luxury goods can range from reasonably priced to faddishly priced. They tend to be popular at extremes in positive social mood, as the stock market and economic prosperity approach major peaks. They tend to go out of favor when these trends reverse.

Interest rates. Borrowed money is useful, so people should price it fairly objectively. Yet people often lend and borrow money for non-rational reasons, such as to facilitate real estate and stock market speculation. Social mood is substantially in control of such things as the quantity of junk bonds issued, bond-quality yield spreads, and the overall expansion and contraction of credit. Moreover, for centuries interest rates have traced out decades-long trends, which are not likely the result of rational assessments of daily economic conditions. (Government-created credit engines displace free-market pricing in this area as well.)

Currencies, especially fiat currencies, have ethereal values, which constantly fluctuate in Elliott waves due to speculation. Unlike stock shares, however, currencies have personal value to their owners, a factor supporting a strong measure of objective valuation. Currencies are subject to deliberate inflating, which interferes with stable pricing. Yet people respond rationally by devaluing them relative to goods and services.

Collectibles are an interesting category. Collectibles are utterly unnecessary for survival, and prices depend heavily upon subjective judgments. Yet rarity and quality are factors that lend some objectivity to their relative pricing. A pristine 1913 Liberty Head nickel of which only five were made is priced far higher than worn-out nickels of which 30,000 were made. The difference seems rational. But people buy these items for no utilitarian reason. They simply want them on a shelf, for amusement, which is a non-rational reason. Collectibles are also subject to fluctuations in popularity. Some extremely rare items don't sell for much money, because people don't care to collect them. Why? They just don't. A collectible item can be priced dearly in one decade and meanly in the next. Why? Reasons given tend to be based on feelings, not utility. As the May 28, 1990 issue of *The Elliott Wave Theorist* explained, "Coins are trophies to collectors and 'investments' to investors, both of which are bid up based upon amorphous desire in an environment of general affluence." The non-rational aspects of collecting require placing collectibles far away from utilitarian goods on our continuum.

Art is a type of collectible, so there is a component of objectivity in its pricing. A rare painting by a Renaissance genius will be priced reliably higher than a drawing by an average ten-year-old for a school art project. But such differential pricing is not consistent, because judging the value of art is a subjective exercise. In 2014, a white canvas sold for $15,000,000, proving that there is more than a wisp of non-rationality involved in art pricing. Art dealers wisely set up auction markets because they unleash people's herding impulses, which activate pre-rationally motivated bidding.

Real estate is a term people use when approaching land or shelter not objectively as a consumer good but subjectively as an investment item. It's the same item but considered from a different mental orientation. When people come to view real estate as an investment item, their brains shift the way they process price information relating to it. Instead of using reasoning circuits for bargain-hunting to maximize utility, they default to pre-rational mood circuits in deciding how much property to buy in hopes of selling it to others at higher prices. When the bulk of participants in the market are consumers who think of houses as shelter, prices are stable. When a significant portion of participants in the market are speculators who think of houses as investment items, prices soar and crash. Shelter is in the economic realm, whereas real estate is in the financial, and therefore socionomic, realm. I met a businessman in 2009 who was closing down his rather singular business, which was supplying an Ivy League endowment fund with Atlanta properties in which to invest. The fund managers' acquisition of those properties and their eventual divestiture were entirely apart from any desire for shelter. To them it wasn't shelter; it was real estate.

Fashion is to clothing as dining is to food and real estate is to shelter. But whereas the herd buys real estate in hopes of a capital gain, the herd buys fashions in hopes of a popularity gain. In some cases, an item of clothing may serve a utilitarian purpose such as keeping a person warm, but its look or label may determine whether the transaction price is X, 10X or 100X. Other fashion items are almost entirely frivolous, such as jewelry. Fashion items have some utility in attracting members of the opposite sex, but on the other hand sexual attraction is yet more behavior in the non-rational realm. One reason fashion is near the socionomic end of the spectrum is that fashion buyers are often oriented not to their own values but to what they think others' values are. As with financial markets, investing in fashion involves guessing others' future actions. The producer hopes his creations will catch on, and the consumer hopes for positive responses to his or her accoutrements. Another reason that fashion is near the socionomic end of the spectrum is that fashion expresses social mood, as illustrated in Figures 6 and 7 in Chapter 10. As a result, herding is ubiquitous in the fashion industry. A fashion that everyone wants to wear one year may be sitting on the rack at a thrift store the following year.

Commodities are useful goods. The cost to produce a commodity affects producers' motivation to supply it, thus tying prices ultimately to an economic factor that influences the range over which commodities trade. But when commodities are listed on exchanges, they become investment items, thereby transforming most participants' behavior towards them and thus these markets' behavior. Markets for exchange-traded commodities adhere to the law of patterned herding, so their prices fluctuate in Elliott waves (see Chapter 22).

Precious metals have a commodity component, since they are used in manufacturing. But they also have a monetary history (and perhaps such a future), imbuing them with a measure of grandeur, so speculators usually attach more powerful feelings to them than they do to other commodities. Booms in precious metals tend to be extraordinarily passionate, placing them far toward the socionomic end of the spectrum.

Fads have no utilitarian value aside from expressing mood and producing pleasure. Fads are a product of herding. Many people in society may participate in an activity for a time simply because they feel like it; then a few years later they don't participate in it, because they don't feel like it. When Cabbage Patch Kids were a fad, one parent sprang for a round-trip flight to London to buy one for his child for Christmas. Today, no one would do that. Chapter 21 recounts a real-time socionomic analysis of a fad.

The most socionomic market is the ***stock market***, because Elliott waves of social mood almost entirely determine aggregate stock prices. This is not to say that individual stocks always fit this mold. There may be rational reasons to price one stock above another. The market, however, mostly ignores them.

To conclude, we must consider not only the dichotomy between each type of market at the poles but also the continuum along which other types of markets reside. The next time you're involved in one of these markets, think about its portion of rationality versus impulsivity. Let me know if you have any additional suggestions.

Relationships of Certain Intermediary Markets to Overall Social Mood

Prices in some intermediary markets—notably those for art, real estate and fashion—tend to change in step with overall social mood. Art prices rise and fall roughly along with stock prices, indicating that speculators bid up artworks near extremes in positive social mood and let prices slide as social mood trends towards the negative. Real estate prices have a similar relationship to stock prices (see Chapter 19), partly because real estate sells mostly on credit, and social mood regulates when creditors and debtors feel optimistic or pessimistic. In fashion, expressions of flamboyance and friskiness (see Chapter 10) fluctuate with social mood. Prices for other intermediary markets—notably those for interest rates, currencies, commodities, precious metals and collectibles—seem quite independent of overall social mood. Chapter 19 nevertheless entertains the possibility that they are substantially allied in a complex manner.

Contextual Market Pricing Pertains also to Intermediary Markets

Chapter 13 proposed that producers and consumers care about present prices, whereas speculators care only about future price changes. These statements remain independently true for markets listed in Figure 1 that substantially share financial and economic aspects, such as those for real estate and certain commodities. For markets in which both economically and financially oriented participants are active, both sets of statements apply simultaneously: The price of a house or commodity is powerful in affecting the buy and sell decisions of producers and consumers of those items, but only anticipated price changes matter to the buy and sell decisions of speculators in them.

But which participants, exactly, are in charge of price changes in the overall markets for these items? The answer is: If speculators are dominant, they are in charge, and price fluctuations will adhere to the Wave Principle as participants herd. If speculators are mostly absent, producers and consumers are in charge, and the market will seek equilibrium as participants maximize utility. Figure 3 in Chapter 13 shows how this difference manifested recently in real estate. As for commodities, two types of oil provide cases in point: Crude oil is an exchange-traded commodity, so its price fluctuates dynamically in Elliott waves (see Chapter 22). Cooking oil is a grocery item, so its price fluctuates so little that no one wastes any time predicting it. The answer is that simple and that profound.

Price vs. Supply-and-Demand Causality across the Spectrum

For non-speculatively traded goods, supply, demand and price are either variously or symbiotically causal. For speculatively traded goods, spontaneous command is the primary determinant of price, and the resulting changes in price exert upward and downward pressures on supply and demand. This difference in primary causality is paramount to a proper understanding of market dynamics involving supply, demand, command and price.

Contrary to neoclassical economic theory, the cause of changes in the price and the supplied quantity of a speculatively traded commodity is substantially unidirectional: Herding speculators agree unconsciously on price changes and spontaneously command them to occur, thereby motivating producers to produce more or less of that commodity. Higher prices spur more production, and lower prices spur less production. So, while the price of a speculatively traded commodity is irrelevant to the decisions of investors, it is supremely causal to the decisions of producers.

These observations pertain to oil, as detailed in Chapter 22, as well as to speculatively traded agricultural commodities, in which changes in price encourage or discourage production via farming activity. They also pertain to booms and busts in the real estate market: Higher prices spur new construction, and lower prices curtail it. In all these cases, production is not mostly leading prices around; prices are mostly leading production around.

Some of the intermediary markets listed in Figure 1 do not fit these molds, because production is not involved. Examples are the markets for art by deceased artists, and collectibles. No one is making any more Picassos, Rembrandts, 1913 Liberty Head nickels or inverted Jenny stamps. No matter how high or low these prices go, there is no production to encourage or discourage.

Changes in prices for speculatively traded commodities also affect the quantity demanded by consumers, who tend to use more or less of products made from them in response. It can be difficult, however, to discern the effect, if any, of such actions on prices, because speculators are behaving in the opposite manner. Some consumers will cut back on heating oil and gasoline use when oil is expensive, and some consumers will shy away from expensive real estate near the peak of a boom, but in each case speculators are buying so much of the item that it's hard to tell. Manufacturers tend to curtail usage of an overpriced commodity for which substitutes are available at the same time that speculators are bidding it up. So, whereas the effects of price changes on production are clear-cut, those on consumption are often hidden, because speculators' spontaneous commands are dominating the marketplace. A careful socionomist can discern the difference.

The financial/economic dichotomy and the financial-economic spectrum provide socionomists with conceptual tools heretofore lacking in the traditional field of economics. With them, we can understand market causality better and formulate accurate descriptions of causal chains in the sometimes overlapping fields of finance and economics.

Chapter 15 is Prechter and Parker's paper on the Financial/Economic Dichotomy, published in 2007. Though it includes an earlier version of some of the material in Chapters 12 and 13, it also differs substantially by including a historical review, differing textual formulations and numerous citations.

Chapter 15

The Journal of Behavioral Finance
Vol. 8, No. 2, Summer 2007
Reprinted with permission

The Financial/Economic Dichotomy in Social Behavioral Dynamics: The Socionomic Perspective

Robert R. Prechter
Wayne D. Parker

Neoclassical economics does not offer a useful model of finance, because economic and financial behavior have different motivational dynamics. The law of supply and demand operates among rational valuers to produce equilibrium in the marketplace for utilitarian goods and services. The efficient market hypothesis (EMH) is a related model applied to financial markets. The socionomic theory of finance (STF) posits that contextual differences between economics and finance produce different behavior, so that in finance the law of supply and demand is irrelevant, and EMH is inappropriate. In finance, uncertainty about valuations by other homogeneous agents induces unconscious, non-rational herding, which follows endogenously regulated fluctuations in social mood, which in turn determine financial fluctuations. This dynamic produces non-mean-reverting dynamism in financial markets, not equilibrium.

Robert R. Prechter is Executive Director of the Socionomics Institute, Gainesville, Georgia.

Wayne D. Parker is Executive Director of the Socionomics Foundation, Gainesville, Georgia, and an adjunct faculty member, Department of Psychiatry, Emory University School of Medicine, currently on inactive status.

Introduction

This paper aims to present a fundamental idea about human behavior that may seem fairly simple: In uncertain social situations, people make decisions differently from the way they do either in isolation or in social situations where information relevant to a rational solution is readily available. Under conditions of certainty, people tend to reason consciously, while under conditions of uncertainty, people tend to herd unconsciously. One of the ideas proposed within this new paradigm of *socionomics* (see the appendix) is that, in the aggregate, economic decisions attend the former context, and financial decisions attend the latter.

In the first section, we review problems with various aspects of neoclassical finance theory. In the second section, we articulate the financial/economic dichotomy. The third section presents the socionomic *law of patterned herding* (LPH) as it relates to finance. The fourth section summarizes key differences between economic and finance models. The final section concludes.

Problems with Traditional Finance Theories and Their Relationship to the Socionomic Model

The pillars of neoclassical finance theory include the concept of market efficiency, utility and value theory, neoclassical asset pricing theory and business cycle theory. Research has uncovered serious problems with each of these ideas.

Efficient Market Hypothesis

Inquiry begins with a problem. The *efficient market hypothesis* (EMH)—the idea that security prices are rationally determined, "reflect all available information" (Fama [1991, p. 1575]) and seek equilibrium—has become a problem. It fails to explain financial market valuation, and, as studies in behavioral finance have demonstrated (see Smith [2003] for an overview), it fails to consider relevant aspects of human behavior. LeRoy's [1989] summary of the history and prehistory of EMH reviewed some of the evidence against it: variance-bound violations, mean reversion problems, excessive volatility, calendar-based "anomalies" such as the January effect, and other problems.

EMH is further confounded by internal disorder. Not only are there "weak, semi-strong, and strong versions" of the theory (Fama [1970]), but there are also different varieties because each theorist must pair his model of market efficiency with one of the many models of market equilibrium, creating a "joint hypothesis problem" that technically makes EMH untestable.

EMH has also depended on successive theories of aggregate pricing behavior, namely the random walk model (Cootner [1964]) and the martingale model (LeRoy [1989]), both of which have been criticized for unrealistic assumptions. Addressing the random walk model, Lo and MacKinlay [1999, p. 20] pointed out,

> Although the traditional random walk hypothesis restricts the [price increments] to be independently and identically distributed (IID) Gaussian random variables, there is mounting evidence that financial time series often possess time-varying volatilities and deviate from normality.

Samuelson [1965] and Mandelbrot's [1966, 1971] martingale model "assumed risk neutrality, whereas in fact people are risk-averse" (LeRoy [1989, p. 1603]). Despite inconsistencies in the martingale model, "the practice in the efficient capital markets literature is to speak of stock prices as following a martingale" (LeRoy [1989]). Because the martingale version asserts that stock prices incorporate the "rational expectation" (Muth [1961]) of discounted future dividends, the shift from the random walk to the martingale model forever wed EMH to rational choice theory. But behavioral finance has found that non-rational behavior in investors' future expectations undermines rational choice theory as well as the entire theoretical structure related to it.

Critics of EMH, such as Shiller [1984] and Lo and MacKinlay [1999], have become numerous. Evidence of what behavioral economists call "bounded rationality" has precipitated a crisis of sorts for the neoclassical version of finance theory in general and EMH in particular. In Kuhn's [1970] terms, when do enough anomalies in a paradigm pile up to necessitate a paradigm shift?

Even Mandelbrot [2003], one of the fathers of EMH, recently rejected the notion that economics and finance should have similar models:

> From the availability of the multifractal alternative [see Mandelbrot, 1972, 1997, for details of this model], it follows that, today, economics and finance must be sharply distinguished; FBM [fractional Brownian motion] may be arguably applicable to the former but not to the latter. (p. 603)

Socionomic theory has long been compatible with this conclusion (see Prechter [1999, chap. 20]).

Utility and Value Theory <1>

Neoclassical utility theory has supported EMH and shares its problems. Utility theory is based on rational choice theory, in which men of all social classes, education levels and degrees of wealth are assumed to act rationally in regard to all their financial decisions, even under highly uncertain and risky conditions. Although Friedman and Savage [1948] adopted Von Neumann and Morgenstern's [1947] assumption of rationality in their analysis of risky investment behavior, they acknowledged in passing,

> It does not, of course, follow that there will exist a utility function that will rationalize in this way the reactions of individuals to risk. It may be that individuals behave inconsistently. ...Further empirical work should make it possible to determine whether or not these implications conform to reality. (p. 282)

The authors further commented on people's capacity for non-rational financial behavior because of their "ignorance of the odds." They quoted Adam Smith's [1776/1994] remarks about men taking irrational financial risks due to "their absurd presumption in their own good fortune" as well as Alfred Marshall's [1890/1920] observation about the financial risk-taking of "young men of an adventurous disposition [who] are more attracted by the prospects of a great success than they are deterred by the fear of failure" (Friedman and Savage [1948, p. 280]). Yet they rejected these ideas in favor of pure rational choice, perhaps because it made for a simpler, more manageable model.

Other neoclassical studies of finance and speculation have likewise assumed difficult or anomalous conditions out of existence to make economists' most convenient statistical tools usable, because without those assumptions, the use of certain statistics is invalid. For example, Farrell's [1966] investigation of whether speculation could be reliably profitable began by assuming the statistical independence of stock price changes. This assumption automatically rules out any chance his model will capture the "fads and fashions" of Shiller [1981, 1984, 2000] or the herding dynamic described here, much less the occasional bubble, "rational" (Treynor [1998]) or otherwise. Under all of these hypothesized conditions, investor decision-making is highly dependent upon previous pricing.

Selective and restrictive assumptions have been nearly ubiquitous in neoclassical finance theory and can render it circular and tautological. Such assumptions allow neoclassical economists to avoid admitting that empirical research has falsified their theories. As Welty [1971] pointed out, difficult-to-model or "irrational" aspects of human behavior are often dismissed by the use of *ceteris paribus* clauses in neoclassical theory. When later empirical data do not confirm the theory, proponents invoke these same clauses to excuse the discrepancy. Ever since Marshall [1890/1920] attempted to formalize utility theory mathematically (per Welty [1971]), such assumptions have rendered neoclassical theory unfalsifiable and thus of dubious scientific merit.

Penrose [1953, p. 608] offered a similar criticism of the infamous *ceteris paribus* device in neoclassical theory, while Hodgson [2001, pp. 232-247] presented perhaps the most devastating critique of its non-falsifiability. Over the years, the long list of "anomalies" in neoclassical finance theory, such as those demonstrated by Kahneman and Tversky [1979], Kahneman, Slovic, and Tversky [1982], Loewenstein and Thaler [1989], and Camerer, Loewenstein, and Rabin [2004], has contradicted the basic assumptions on which the theory's use of certain analytical tools depends. As the anomalies multiplied, economists first began to challenge some of the theory's assumptions and then to call for more predictive models (see MacDougall [1974] and Leontief [1971]).

Some economists have announced theoretical breakthroughs challenging the neoclassical model of finance. But they have cautiously left its most basic assumptions unchanged: mechanistic causality, equilibrium, utility maximizing, rational choice, and the summing of individual agents to model aggregate dynamics. These researchers have essentially invited neoclassical theorists simply to add yet another factor to expand their equations, yielding little significant change in the fundamental underpinnings of finance theory or in its predictive ability.

Asset Pricing Theory

Asset pricing theory is a field in which modelers attempt to account for investment values. The dividend discount model (Gordon [1956]), for example, states that stock prices are entirely a function of the value of future dividends. This is simply a version of EMH in which the number of exogenous variables presumably affecting a stock's price is reduced to one. It therefore suffers from all the same problems (for critiques of this specific model, see Kleidon [1986] and Shiller [1986]).

Fama and French [2004] presented a devastating critique of the theoretical model of asset pricing most frequently taught in American business schools today: the capital asset pricing model (CAPM) of Sharpe [1964] and Lintner [1965]. To explain why CAPM does not work in the real world, Fama and French [2004] discussed evidence that some aspects of investor behavior are less than completely rational. While other economists have tried to salvage CAPM by adding more complexity to the model, Carhart [1997] acknowledged unresolved problems with "model bias" and admitted that due to the "joint hypothesis problem" mentioned earlier, "I interpret the results from these tests [of my modified CAPM model] with caution" (p. 76).

The idea of occasional non-rationality provides the basis for the most esteemed asset pricing theory within the neoclassical tradition, the "fundamental analysis" of stock prices, best represented by Graham and Dodd [1934]. The idea here is that an investor should be able to calculate a fair price for a stock by figuring out the underlying company's supposed "fundamental value" based on a number of objective features, such as the company's industry position, sales trends, profit margins and earnings, asset composition and liquidity, and its mix of financing (Gitman and Joehnk [1984]).

This version of asset pricing theory does not insist that the market always reflect such "fundamental" value, because emotional investors can cause values to deviate from what they "should" be. A fundamental analyst nevertheless makes two assumptions: (1) that other investors are only temporarily non-rational from time to time (thereby providing bargains and over-priced shares that the fundamental analyst exploits), and (2) that investors will be rational enough at some point to value stocks logically by asset pricing theory.

Because fundamental analysis (like behavioral finance) attributes only intermittent non-rationality to investors, it ultimately depends on equilibrium theory and the rational choice model. According to fundamental analysis, when prices deviate from rational value they will tend inherently to "revert to the mean." See Jegadeesh [1991] and Black [1990] for summaries of the literature.

LeRoy [1989, p. 1586] noted, however, "The only problem with fundamental analysis was that it appeared not to work." Cowles's [1933] study showed that fundamental analysts' forecasts actually yielded worse results than random choice. Stock price action over the past ten years has especially confounded fundamental analysts, who have watched share prices fluctuate wildly despite little change in traditional "fundamental value" (or in some cases despite no fundamental value at all).

Socionomics challenges not just the validity of fundamental-analysis valuation but also its underlying idea of inevitable reversion to the mean. We observe that every proposed stock price mean is changing or arbitrary, being a function of the time period chosen, so stock prices have nothing constant to which to revert.

Data on stock prices as they relate to "fundamental" values confirm this point: Over the past century, the prices that investors have been willing to pay for $1 of dividends from the DJIA has differed by fourteen times (see Figure 1); prices for $1 of annual S&P earnings have differed by eight times (see Figure 2) [in 2008, it expanded to a range of 23 times by this measure]; and prices for $1 worth of S&P 400 corporate book value have differed by over eighteen times (see Figure 3). Finally, the multiple for an annual percentage point of yield via S&P 400 stock dividends versus via the same companies' corporate bonds has differed by more than sixteen times (see Figure 4).

These data suggest that the stock market is blissfully unaware of the dividend discount model, the earnings discount model, corporate liquidation value, and the Fed's relative-yield pricing model. For the most part, moreover, these values rise and fall together, so dramatic differences are not the result of the market's summing various individual values to achieve an overall equilibrium value; a sum of these values swings just as wildly as its components.

Thus we assert that financial market prices are not stable but dynamic, and they are not dependent upon but rather substantially independent of supposedly related "fundamental" values. From the point of view of fundamental analysis, prices spend far more time deviating from means and values than reflecting them. This history seriously challenges the assumptions of traditional asset pricing theory.

Business Cycle Theory

Some neoclassical finance theories offer various conceptions of a "business cycle" to forecast the behavior of financial prices (see Lucas [1980], Plosser [1989] and Mankiw [1989] for overviews). All the diverse theorists—from Jevons [1866] to Schumpeter [1954] to the monetarists to Keynes [1936/1997]—share common assumptions, primarily that aggregate economic activity is attracted to equilibrium. Just as fundamental analysis presumes market oscillation around a value mean, neoclassical business cycle theory presumes economic oscillation around an activity mean, at which supply and demand are stable. Where business cycle theorists have gotten creative is in their diverse attempts to explain departures from equilibrium. There is usually no theoretical connection between their explanations for equilibrium and disequilibrium, because neoclassicists have simply taken the former as a theoretical given and the latter as an exception to the rule.

Researchers have found it difficult to find empirical evidence that supports innate equilibrium-seeking in the economy. Faced with data that do

Price of $1 Worth of Annual Dividends from the DJIA
(DJIA Dividend Yield inverted)

Figure 1

Price of $1 Worth of Annual Earnings from the S&P
(S&P Price/Earnings Ratio using trailing 12-month earnings)

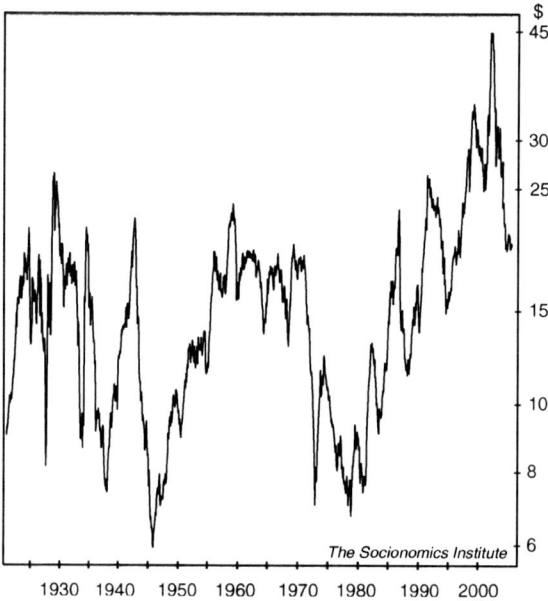

Figure 2

**Price of $1 Worth of Book Value in the S&P
(S&P 400 price/book value)**

1930s 1940s 1950s 1960s 1970s 1980s 1990s 2000s

Note. Data from Universal Economics. Adapted with permission.

Figure 3

**Bond-Yield Price of $1 in Dividends from the S&P Industrial
Companies (S&P 400 bond yields/stock yields**

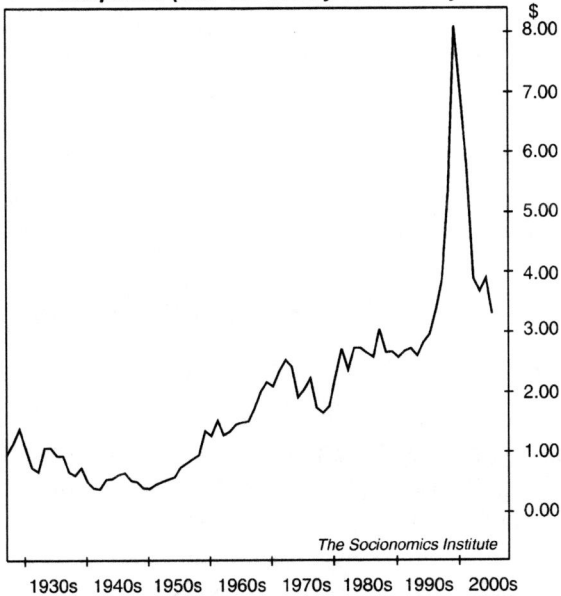

1930s 1940s 1950s 1960s 1970s 1980s 1990s 2000s

Note. Data from Universal Economics. Adapted with permission.

Figure 4

not fit the early versions of equilibrium theory, creative neoclassicists have invented ever-more-complicated theories of "multiple equilibria" [see also Chapter 12] to try to explain why the economy never seems to revert to its original mean (for examples, see Nielsen [1988], Debreu [1970], Durlauf [1993], and Bhushan, Brown, and Mello [1997]). None of these more complex versions of equilibrium theory has garnered universal acceptance.

Summary of Theoretical Review

Neoclassical finance theory—from its bedrock in EMH, rational choice, equilibrium theory and mean reversion to its various expressions relating to utility and value, asset pricing and business cycles—fails to explain convincingly the dynamics of investors' behavior and the aggregate results of their pricing decisions. Worse, the details are so underspecified that empirical research from this perspective seems close to useless when, as Hodgson [2001, p. 237] pointed out, "*any observed behaviour can be fitted into the theory*" (emphasis his). We would add to that already devastating remark that, absent *ceteris paribus* clauses, much observed behavior cannot consistently be fitted into the theory. We hope to offer a more useful alternative.

The Financial/Economic Dichotomy

Proponents of EMH and related theories assert that financial markets are no different from markets for such things as shoes and bread. Socionomists beg to differ. We wonder how a proponent of EMH would react if he walked into a shoe store and the manager rushed up and told him to "double up" on shoes because prices had skyrocketed, or if nervous customers warned him to postpone purchases of socks because prices had fallen by half. Such behavior never happens in a shoe store. Yet such behavior with respect to share prices happens all the time in a brokerage office. Both situations involve transactions between buyers and sellers, so why is there a difference? We propose that the difference derives from transactional contexts.

The Law of Supply and Demand

Prices for utilitarian goods and services are governed by the *law of supply and demand*, a theory developed and expanded by Cournot [1838/1897/1960], Walras [1874/1926/1954], Marshall [1890/1920], Pareto [1906/1927/1971] and others. The essential idea is that prices in economic markets result from the opposing desires of producers to sell dearly and of consumers to buy cheaply. The rational choices of producers and consumers achieve objective values for goods and services. The aggregate result of these opposing desires and rational choices is that markets seek equilibrium, making prices stable. EMH is an attempt to force the law of supply and demand into the realm of financial markets. Muth [1961] and Lucas and Prescott [1971] provided details of such attempts.

But even to a casual observer, price equilibrium is obviously absent from financial markets. If financial markets were efficient and participants were fully rational and knowledgeable, as EMH has proposed, financial price movements would look quite different. Company share prices, for example, would trend mostly sideways, with a near-vertical jump or drop to a new plane of equilibrium whenever new information came out. But actual financial prices run wildly in one direction and then the other, every minute, hour, day, week, month, year and decade. If the law of supply and demand were regulating financial markets, prices and relative values for investments would be as stable as those for shoes and bread.

Given this difference in market behavior, the theoretical underpinnings of the application of the law of supply and demand to finance are suspect. Ross [1987, p. 30] pointed out that, unlike what occurs in a microeconomic context,

> The demand curves [in finance] are perfectly elastic because of the implicit assumption that financial markets are filled with assets which are very close substitutes for one another.

As a result, Ross drew a sharp distinction between the domains of economics and finance. In finance,

> The forces of supply and demand have no meaning, since if the price is not the equilibrium price, then the difference between supply and demand is infinite. This is precisely what is meant by an arbitrage situation, and it is so qualitatively different from the economist's usual picture of demand and supply as to require a different approach.

Any new finance model must recognize the difference in price behavior between financial assets and utilitarian goods. Before presenting the socionomic model, we first explore a key difference in the relationship between price and demand that exists in these two types of markets.

Contrasting Economic and Financial Markets in Terms of Price versus Demand Behavior

For our purposes, we define "economic" markets as those for *utilitarian goods and services*, and "financial" markets as those for *investments and speculations.* Aside from differences in mathematics (per Mandelbrot [2003]) and form (per Frost and Prechter [1978/1998] and Prechter and Goel [2007]), a financial market differs fundamentally from an economic market in the relationship that exists between prices and demand. In economic markets, demand generally rises as prices fall and vice versa. In financial markets, demand generally rises as prices rise and vice versa. This difference is essential because the behavior of economic markets is compatible with the law of supply and demand, while the behavior of financial markets is not. Socionomics offers an explanation for these differences.

Neoclassical utility theorists postulate that price depends on the utility value of the goods or services in question. The perceived scarcity of goods and their relative "desiredness" (Pigou [1920/1932]) in turn determine utility value. Thus, in neoclassical economic theory, lower prices mean greater utility value to consumers per monetary unit expended, so lower prices tend to bring about an increase in demand. This observation holds true for transactions relating to utilitarian goods and services. For example, more computers are selling at $1,000 each today than sold at $5,000 a decade ago, or at $1 million half a century ago. As prices have fallen, sales have risen. Figure 5 shows this inverse correlation between price and demand.

Conversely, a rise in price tends to curtail sales. For example, when gasoline prices go up, some people carpool or take public transit to cut back on the purchase and consumption of gasoline. Again, there is an inverse correlation between price and demand.

Prices for utilitarian goods and services relate to demand this way primarily because people are motivated to survive and thrive, so they apply their conscious reason toward maximizing the utility of their money. Thus, as prices for a particular item rise in an economic setting, consumers tend to buy less of it; as prices fall, they tend to buy more. When people violate this guide to behavior by, for example, wasting their money, those with a lot of money may fail to thrive, and those with little money may fail to survive. Maximizing the utility of money is economically advantageous for people of limited means, a group comprising nearly everybody.

In finance, prices do not influence behavior in this manner. Figures 6-8 demonstrate a positive rather than negative correlation between price and demand over various durations. As Figure 6 shows, the volume of trading in the stock market, in contrast to that for goods and services, also tends to fluctuate in the same direction as price.

Poterba [2001] tabulated various types of data showing that between 1989 and 1998, a decade of nearly uninterrupted rise in stock prices, there was a "rapid growth of stock ownership" and "a broad increase in stock ownership across many different groups" (p. 1). Figure 7, constructed from these data, shows that the number of participants in the stock market tends to fluctuate in the same direction as price. Although some observers have argued that these results derive from external forces such as tax exemptions or age demographics, Poterba's [2001] data show a positive correlation between price and participation regardless of investor age bracket, level of education, annual income or taxable status of the account.

Finally, Figure 8 shows the U.S. public's relative stock holdings against the prices at which those stocks sold in terms of physical goods. Note that as real stock prices fall, investors actually decrease their percentage of stock holdings. Conversely, as real prices rise, investors increase their percentage of stock holdings.

One of the factors Poterba [2001] explored in order to "explain the rise in the number of stockholders" is the idea that "transaction costs associated with stock ownership have declined during the 1990s" (p. 6). Ironically, this explanation, which derives from economics, is utterly at odds with similar thinking about the stock market itself. No one explains the rise in stock ownership during the 1990s by noting that *stock* prices declined, because, contrary to economic logic, they actually soared. Yet it makes perfect sense, in the context of economic motivation, that computer ownership rose in the 1990s because computer prices persistently fell.

Figures 9-12 omit the time dimension from Figures 5-8 and display the same data on price and demand axes to conform to expressions of economic theory. Figure 9 shows the standard relationship taught in economics classes; Figures 10-12 show the opposite relationship. Table 1 lists the exceptionally high negative and positive statistical correlations that we find between price and demand in these economic and financial markets, respectively.

As these graphs and Table 1 show, the relationship between price and demand in finance is the opposite from what it is in economics. As prices rise in a financial setting, volume generally rises, more investors participate, and ownership of financial assets increases; as prices fall, the opposite happens.

If investors in the aggregate applied reason toward maximizing the utility of their money, then one of the two graphs in Figures 6-8 would be inverted, and the lines in Figures 10-12 would decline toward the right rather than rise. People would purchase more stock near a trough and less stock near a peak. But this is not what they do; it is the opposite of what they do.

One might claim that the mechanism behind price change is the same in both settings because increasing demand forces stock prices higher in the

**Economic Market: Prices Trend Inversely to Customers' Holdings
(Price of Personal Computers vs. Personal Computers in Use)**

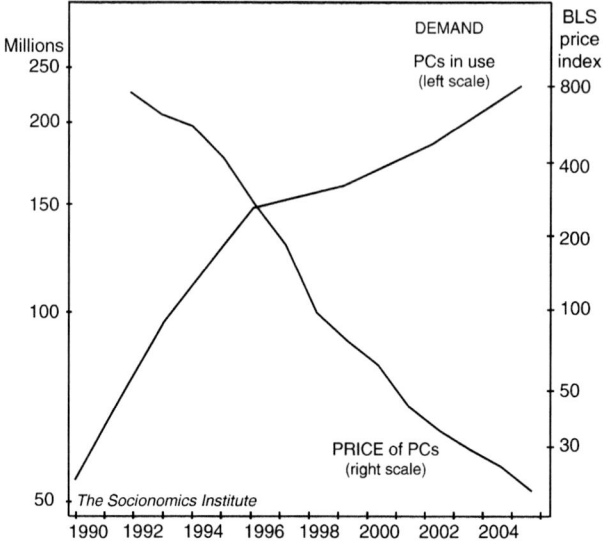

Note. Data from the Survey of Consumer Finances and the Bureau of
Labor Statistics. Adapted with permission.

Figure 5

**Financial Market: Prices Trend in the Same Direction as Volume
(S&P 500 vs. NYSE Volume)**

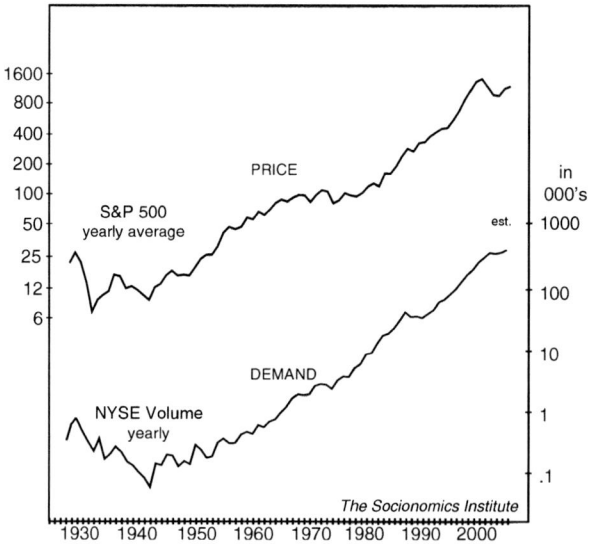

Figure 6

**Financial Market: Prices Trend in the Same Direction as the Number of Owners
(S&P 500 vs. Number of Annual Survey Respondents Who Own Stock)**

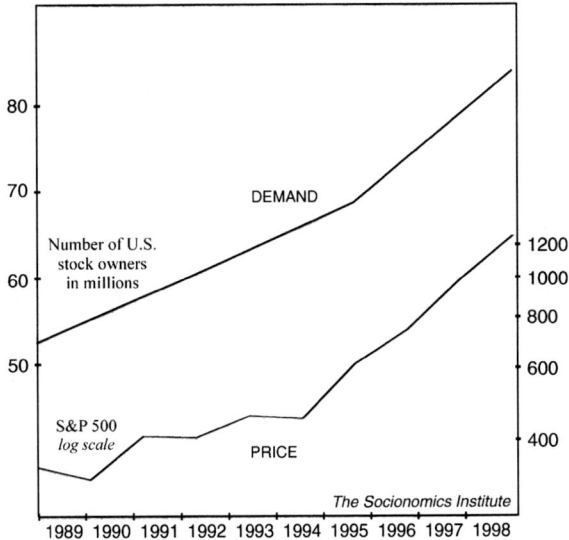

Note. Respondents were limited to individuals who are heads of
household or married to heads of household. Data from the Survey of
Consumer Finances. Adapted with permission.

Figure 7

**Financial Market: Prices Trend in the Same Direction as Investors' Relative Holdings
(S&P 500/PPI vs. Stocks as a Percentage of Household Financial Assets)**

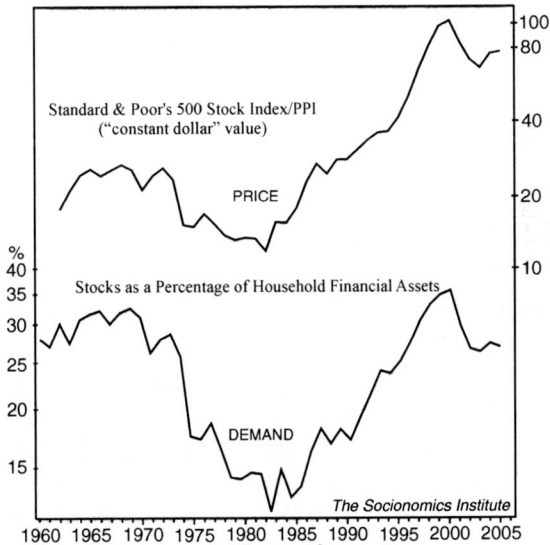

Figure 8

**Economic Market: Computer Prices Correlate Negatively with Customers' Holdings
(Price of PCs vs. PCs in Use, in Logs, 1991-2005)**

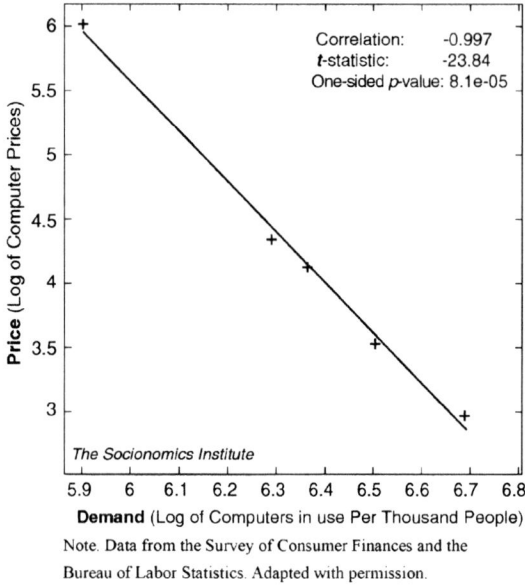

Correlation: -0.997
t-statistic: -23.84
One-sided *p*-value: 8.1e-05

The Socionomics Institute

Demand (Log of Computers in use Per Thousand People)

Note. Data from the Survey of Consumer Finances and the
Bureau of Labor Statistics. Adapted with permission.

Figure 9

**Financial Market: Prices Correlate Positively with Volume
(S&P 500 vs. NYSE Volume, in Logs, 1928-2005)**

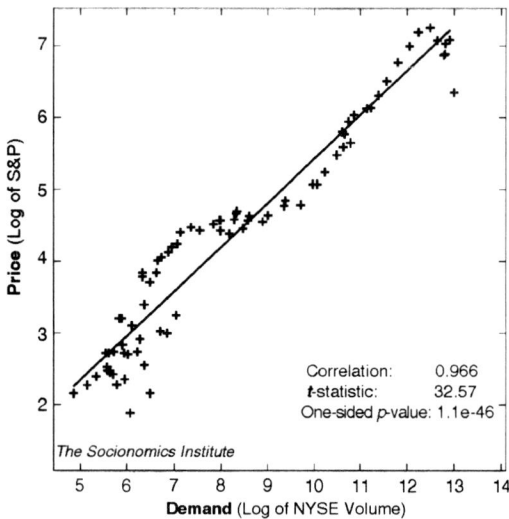

Correlation: 0.966
t-statistic: 32.57
One-sided *p*-value: 1.1e-46

The Socionomics Institute

Demand (Log of NYSE Volume)

Figure 10

Financial Market: Prices Correlate Positively with the Number of Owners
(S&P 500 vs. Number of Annual Survey Respondents Who Own Stock, in Logs, 1989-1998)

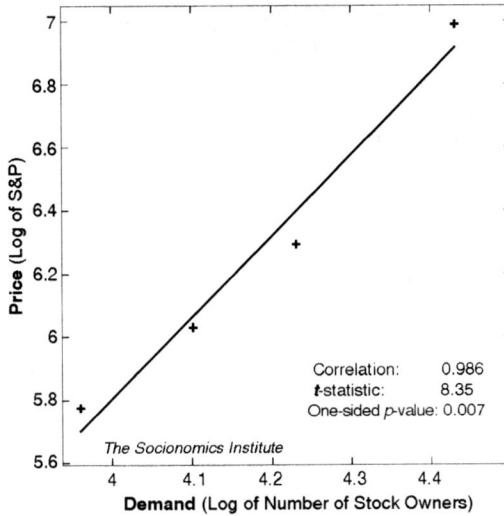

Figure 11

Financial Market: Prices Correlate Positively with Investors' Holdings
(S&P 500/PPI vs. Stocks as a % of Household Financial Assets, in Logs, 1962-2005)

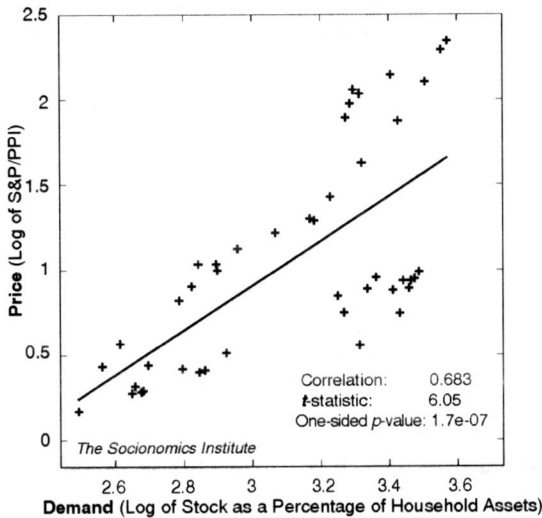

Figure 12

Table 1: Correlation Statistics for Figures 9-12

Type of Market	Comparison	Correlation Type	Correlation	t	p (one-sided)
Economic: Computers	Price vs. Ownership	Direct	-0.997	-23.8	10^{-5}
		Returns	-0.986	-8.3	0.007
Financial: Stocks	Price vs. Volume	Direct	0.966	32.6	10^{-46}
		Returns	0.570	6.0	10^{-8}
Financial: Stocks	Price vs. Participants	Direct	0.986	8.3	0.007
		Returns	0.967	6.2	0.05
Financial: Stocks	Price vs. Holdings	Direct	0.683	6.1	10^{-7}
		Returns	0.930	16.2	10^{-19}

Note: EMH theoretically allows independence of future prices from present prices. If value conditions were to change dramatically, so would price. Stock market statistics imply recent-value dependence (time-lagged self-correlation), as large fluctuations have occurred less often than small ones. Our table uses calculations to account for both views. "Direct" correlations refer to actual values and "Returns" refer to differences between adjacent data points. Figures 9 through 12 display "Direct" correlations of actual values.

The Socionomics Institute

way that a sudden increase in demand (for groceries prior to a hurricane, for example) might cause prices of any economic good to rise. Such a relationship in economics, however, can only be temporary; the law of supply and demand assures that the long-term trend is always toward lower demand at higher prices and higher demand at lower prices.

The main situation in which volume rises in a falling stock market is during a panic, as Figure 13 shows. This rise in volume, however, is not due to rising demand for stocks. It is due to the rising desire to disown stocks, which again is precisely the opposite of what occurs in the economic marketplace.

Balanced versus Unbalanced Market Dynamics

In the economic marketplace, the law of supply and demand accounts not only for the motivation of buyers but also for the opposing motivation of sellers. Producers of goods and services desire to get as much money as they can for their products. The higher a product's price climbs, the more actual and potential producers are motivated to produce it. Conversely, the lower a product's price goes, the more consumers are motivated to buy it.

**In Panics, Financial Prices Briefly Correlate Negatively with Volume
(S&P 500 vs NYSE Volume)**

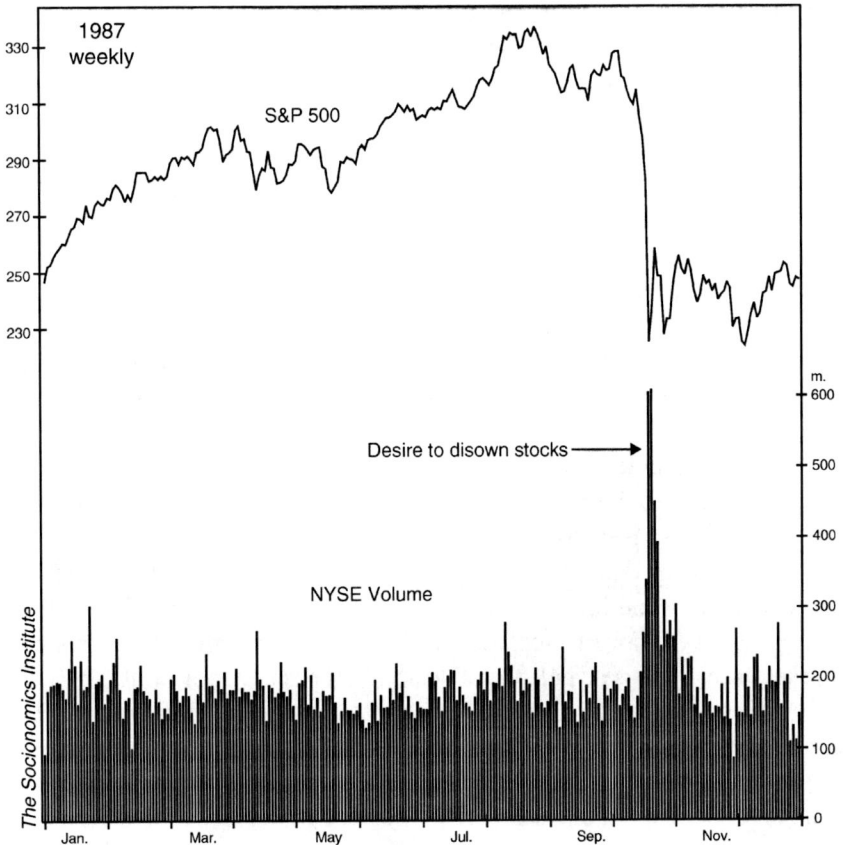

Figure 13

These conflicting desires create a dynamic balance, arbitrated by price. At some price, enough producers are motivated to produce enough of a product to satisfy demand from enough consumers to create a price for the product that is reasonable to both parties. Values are objective because both parties use reason to maximize the utility of their resources. The opposing desires of producers and consumers on the buy and sell sides of transactions create equilibrium in prices.

In finance, there is no such balance. It is a common fallacy among financial market professionals to equate those on the sell side of a stock transaction with "producers," and those on the buy side with "consumers," representing "supply" and "demand." But this is a spurious analogy. In the world of transactions for goods and services, producers (supply) and consumers (demand) are separate entities. In the stock market, a "supplier" on Tuesday could be a "demander" on Wednesday. Indeed, many traders buy and sell the same financial instrument continually all day long.

Producers of goods and services do not behave this way. A supplier does not routinely morph into a demander for the good or service he produces, and a demander does not routinely morph into a supplier of each good or service he desires. The fundamental error in equating economic and financial markets with respect to the law of supply and demand is that in financial markets buying and selling are two sides of the same coin, and that coin is demand. When a person's level of demand rises, he buys, and when it falls, he sells.

The stock market does have a few suppliers. Anyone who starts a new business venture and provides new shares of its stock to the marketplace is a supplier. Every investor from that time forward is a demander. Suppliers are rare, and their actions account for a negligible portion of daily volume. Thus, vacillating demanders make up virtually the entire market for stock shares. With respect to each transaction in the utilitarian marketplace, a producer sells and a consumer buys; in the financial marketplace, investors are on both sides of each transaction. In other words, economics has both suppliers and demanders, and finance—practically speaking—has only demanders.

Because the law of supply and demand does not regulate the financial marketplace, there is no balance of desires that prices can arbitrate. Without the governing influence of the law of supply and demand deriving from the conflicting purposes of producers and consumers, financial prices are free to rise or fall wherever investors' aggregate impulses take them. The result is not equilibrium but unceasing dynamism at all degrees of fluctuation. If any law is operating in finance, it must be something other than the law of supply and demand, and it must take into account actual market behavior.

The Law of Patterned Herding in Finance

As outlined briefly in the appendix, socionomics is a theory of social behavior that integrates a structural model of aggregate behavior with a model of individual agent participation. This paper relates primarily to a component of socionomic theory, the *law of patterned herding* (LPH). In brief, LPH states: *Social systems comprising homogeneous agents uncertain about other agents' valuations that are critical to survival and success provide a context in which an endogenously regulated aggregation of unconscious herding impulses constitutes a pattern of social mood, which in turn motivates social actions.*

In this section, we discuss the value of LPH in accounting for individuals' financial behavior within transactional systems as it relates to uncertainty, intentionality relative to valuation by self versus others, unconscious herding impulses, social mood, post hoc rationalization, and the homogeneity of agents.

Uncertainty Characterizes Financial Decision-Making

EMH claims that investors simply revalue markets rationally as new information becomes available, implying that investors are never uncertain about current values. But as Alan Greenspan [2003] said about central banking, "Uncertainty is not just an important feature of the monetary policy landscape, it is the defining characteristic of that landscape." If those with the power to dictate a national interest rate feel chronically uncertain, we can be sure that the average investor is less than perfectly informed, knowledgeable, and confident. Echoing Knight's [1921] and Keynes's [1921] claims back in the 1920s, socionomic theory argues that the role of uncertainty is vitally important to causality in financial markets.

Intentionality as it Relates to the Importance of Valuation by Self versus Others

The uncertain valuation of financial assets as opposed to economic goods is not intrinsic to certain things, because some items can serve as either economic goods or investments. For example, tulips in Holland in the 1630s began as goods and became investments. Beanie Babies in the 1990s began as toys and became investments, and, recently, homes have metamorphosed from economic goods into vehicles for speculation as people buy them to "flip" and trade options on their purchase.

The fundamental difference between a utilitarian good and an investment is an agent's intentionality regarding the item. If most owners and potential owners view it as something to be owned for production or pleasure or to be consumed, it is an *economic good*. If most owners and potential owners view it as something to be sold at a higher price to others (short-sellers buy money with stock), it is an *investment*.

When an item is generally viewed as a good to be used, it will have a certain value because individuals will know how to value it over time for their own purposes. When an item is generally viewed as an investment, it will have an uncertain value because individuals will not know how it will be valued over time by others. This distinction, deriving from the mental orientation of the majority of the valuers and the resulting uncertainty of others' valuations, appears to be the source of financial uncertainty. Shiller [1990], for example, found that investors in the heat of emotion during the 1987 crash were "reacting to each other...trying to fathom what other investors were likely to do," thus revealing the basis of their uncertainty.

This distinction can apply to any object. A work of art is an economic good to any person who buys it to enjoy. He knows its value to himself, and he pays a reasonable price in the economic context of certain value. A work of art is a financial asset to a person who buys it with the expectation of re-selling it at a higher price. He does not know its value to other people, and he pays a price that may or may not turn out to be useful in the financial context of uncertain value. The same thing applies to shares of stock. People who wish to buy a company in order to use its underlying assets for production are treating the company as a utilitarian good. They are often surprised that others, who may wish to buy shares of the company in order to sell at a higher price, do not share their view of the company's value. And even if a buyer's premise of value is valid in an economic context, it may be invalid in a financial context. We agree with Hogarth [2005] that "one of the major lessons of research in psychology over the last 50 years has been the importance of context" (p. 12). The contextualism of socionomic theory contrasts with the assumptions of neoclassical economics, where, as in physics, the context of agents' mental attitudes is assumed to be irrelevant (see Prechter and Parker [2004]).

This contextual duality between economics and finance does not appear to delineate poles of a continuum but a dichotomy. [We have since revised this notion. See Chapter 14.] Except for rare transitional periods, items are consistently priced in the aggregate either economically or financially. We do not fully understand yet what causes a transition from the aggregate intentionality to value something for one's own consumption to the intentionality to value something for speculative trading with others, or vice versa. What we do know is that applying financial thinking to economic goods does not work. And, as Figures 1-4 demonstrate, applying economic thinking to investing does not work, either. Chronic uncertainty about what the majority of other investors may do without regard for personal utility value is sufficient to destroy the efficacy of investing on that basis.

Herding Characterizes Decision-Making under Uncertainty

The existence of pervasive market uncertainty is vitally important to the financial/economic dichotomy. When people are certain about the relative utilitarian values of available options, they usually choose an action based on their own rational evaluation. We propose that when people are uncertain about the relative values of available options, they typically default to a herding impulse. In utilitarian economic settings, where certainty is the norm, people reason; in financial settings, where uncertainty is pervasive, they herd.

According to MacLean [1990], herding is an unconscious, impulsive behavior developed and maintained through evolution. Its purpose is to increase the chance of survival. When humans do not know what to do, they are impelled to act as if others know. Because sometimes others actually do know, herding increases the overall probability of survival. Unfortunately, when investors in a modern financial setting look to the herd for guidance, they do not realize that most others in the herd are just as uninformed, ignorant and uncertain as they are.

Differences in Neural Processing are Consistent with the Financial/ Economic Dichotomy

Cosmides and Tooby [1994, p. 327] declared that findings from "evolutionary psychology suggest that...explicit theories of the structure of the human mind can be made endogenous to economic models in a way that preserves and expands their elegance, parsimony, and explanatory power." In concordance with this inspiration, socionomics proposes that the neural origin of human behavior in economic settings is different from that in financial settings.

Montgomery [1983, 1985] was the first to relate MacLean's [1990] "triune brain" concept to herding in finance. Montgomery postulated that reason and herding are components of aggregate financial valuation. We differ from Montgomery in arguing that individuals' exercises in independent reasoning cancel each other out, making them ineffective in determining aggregate values and leaving herding as the sole determinant of financial price trends. We postulate that economic behavior is mediated primarily by the neocortex, which processes conscious ideas. Financial behavior, on the other hand, is mediated primarily by the limbic system and basal ganglia (see Prechter [1999, chap. 8]), which generate unconscious thoughts and emotions (according to MacLean [1990] and LeDoux [1989], among others).

While more recent research has revealed that both normal and pathological mood regulation involve complex interactions among the limbic system, reticular activating system, prefrontal cortex, sympathetic nervous system and possibly other neural structures, most researchers still credit the limbic system with the central role in coordinating mood regulation. We are also aware of the theoretical and empirical problems with the "limbic-cortical" distinction as a way of describing emotional versus cognitive aspects of mental activity and its neural correlates (see LeDoux [2000] for a detailed summary of these issues). But until a more adequate comprehensive neurological theory of emotion emerges, we use these short-hand designations to describe the relationship between areas of the brain that mediate affect and cognition.

Recent studies support our case that unconscious portions of the brain can motivate herding behavior even while conscious portions are unaware it is happening. In a research review, Camerer, Loewenstein, and Prelec [2004, pp. 7-9] provided a picture of the brain that has more modularity and independence among its neural systems than previously thought.

Bischoff-Grethe et al. [2001] provided neurophysiological evidence that the brain processes information differently in contexts of uncertainty versus certainty, a finding that fits our contextual case for a neurological basis for the financial/economic dichotomy.

A recent study by Shiv et al. [2005] supports this view. The authors found that patients with "chronic and stable focal lesions in specific components of a neural circuitry that has been shown to be critical for the processing of emotions" made investment decisions that "were closer to a profit-maximizing viewpoint" than control subjects. The brain-damaged patients responded less emotionally to other subjects' behavior and were thus better able to execute a logical investing strategy. The researchers noted that "decisions under uncertainty...draw upon different neural processes." They concluded: "Depending on the circumstances, moods and emotions can play useful as well as disruptive roles in decision making" (p. 428).

These studies showed no evidence that subjects in group situations were conscious of the nature of the social processes in which they were engaged. Banaji, Lemm, and Carpenter's [2001] review of recent studies illustrates the power and range of unconscious social processes. Over the past thirty-five years or so, social psychologists have found that unconscious dynamics affect memory, perceptual skills, self-concept and self-evaluation, and biases and stereotypes related to race, gender and political partisanship. Socionomics adds financial decision-making to this list.

Herding accounts for human behavior in the financial realm that is anomalous to neoclassical economic theory. The motivation of both types of behavior (financial and economic) is surely the same as that for all evolved behaviors: to survive and thrive. In finance, however, the mind is operating differently. Buyers in a rising market appear unconsciously to think, "The herd must know where the food is. Run with the herd and you will prosper." Sellers in a falling market appear to think, "The herd must know that there is a lion racing toward us. Run with the herd or you will die."

Investors must be aware only of the powerful emotions that attend these unconscious impulses and sometimes of the rationales for their consequent actions. If such motivating impulses were conscious, investors would recognize their inappropriateness for successful investing and use reason to buy low, sell high, and get rich. In the aggregate, however, investors always do the opposite, which is a strong indication that the impulses driving their behavior are unconscious. Even individually, most investors, despite years of his exposure to financial markets, do the opposite of what they should, again and again. The best way for an investor to change his behavior is to become aware of his herding impulses and counteract them. The rarity of successful investors speaks to the difficulty of success in this task.

Some may find it contradictory that an evolutionary instinct can be both good and bad for survival. But instincts developed in one environmental context can lose their survival value if the environment changes sufficiently. The herding impulse evolved millennia before the creation of speculative financial markets, a modern context in which participants are punished for moving with the herd. In other contexts, such as cultural fads and fashions, the herding impulse may continue to have advantages even in modern times (see Prechter [1999, Chapters 15-16]).

Social Mood as the Basis for Aggregate Financial Valuation

Because herds are ruled by the majority, financial market trends appear to be based on little more than investors' mood. The term "mood" as we use it is substantially similar to Russell's "prolonged core affect" (see Russell [2003] and Olsen [2003]). "Social mood" we postulate, is the net mood of the populace, shared through the herding impulse.

In light of the role of optimism and pessimism in asset valuation (see McNichols and O'Brien [1997], Easterwood and Nutt [1999], and Hirshleifer [2001]), socionomics posits that the huge differences in valuation exhibited in Figures 1-4 are due to one thing: people's opinion about the capital gain potential of stocks, in other words, the extent to which they are bullish or bearish. Thus, we believe that such valuations are a direct measure of investor optimism or pessimism about the valuations they believe others will place on stock prices.

The idea that affect influences financial decisions is not new (see Dreman [2003, 2004] for reviews of some of the relevant literature). What is new in socionomics is that (1) social mood trends are unconsciously determined by endogenous dynamics, not consciously determined by the rational evaluation of external factors, and (2) investors' unconsciously regulated moods are the primary determinant of the direction of stock prices. In socionomics, the ontology behind the financial markets is a psychological process—namely, valuing and desiring under the influence of an optimistic or pessimistic mood—rather than the ontology of value residing in an external object, waiting to be rationally calculated.

To put it more succinctly, investor moods, generated endogenously and shared via the herding impulse, motivate aggregate stock market values and trends. Moods are the basis upon which investors judge the way they expect other investors to value stocks in the future, so they motivate current buying and selling. Thus in finance there is no mean reversion to equilibrium. There is only the ceaseless dynamism of social mood waves, fluctuating between optimism and pessimism.

Bubbles are Consistent with Unconscious Risk Aversion, Not Rational Risk Assumption

The notion that investors are willing to take on more risk as prices rise is a real conundrum for utility value theory. Some theorists nevertheless have proposed explanations within that paradigm. Sornette [2003] postulated that investors participate in a bubble because of their rational acceptance of higher risk in exchange for the potential of higher rewards under the assumption that the bubble will probably continue.

Treynor [1998, p. 69] has argued, as have Blanchard [1979], Diba and Grossman [1988], and Froot and Obstfeld [1991], that "rational bubbles" exist in the stock market. Treynor defined a bubble as a "self-reinforcing, self-perpetuating mechanism that prevents successive security price changes from being random." His model proposes several qualitatively different classes of investors interacting in a way that translates the apparent irrationality of bubbles into rational behavior.

Such analyses have several logical problems. First, if stock prices were mean-reverting, it would be irrational for investors to buy more stock as prices rise further above some calculated mean, because mean reversion would imply a rational expectation that prices would retreat to that mean. Second, the appealing notion of explanation via interactions between heterogeneous investor types (whether fundamental analysts versus technicians, rich versus poor investors, long-term versus short-term traders, experienced traders versus novices, etc.) violates the mathematical assumptions of homogeneity and continuous distributions of price changes required by the statistical tools underlying EMH and equilibrium theory. Finally, there is something troubling about reconciling a bubble with rationality, because the very term "bubble" implies non-rationality.

Socionomics proposes that aggregate investor thought is not conscious reason but unconscious impulsion. The herding impulse is an instrument designed, however improperly for some settings, to reduce risk. As Gajdusek [1970], Janis [1972] and MacLean [1990] demonstrated, straying from the group induces feelings of danger and unease, while herding induces feelings of safety and well being. Therefore, investors in the aggregate—whether they are buying in uptrends or selling in downtrends—are always acting unconsciously to reduce risk, thanks to the emotionally satisfying impulse to herd.

Objectively, risk increases in both cases. But herding is not objective; it is impulsive, so greater risk is actually perceived as less risk. This paradox between reasonable and actual investor behavior accounts for—and indeed explains and predicts—the information in Figures 6-8. Investors who buy in uptrends are not acting consciously to increase risk; they are acting unconsciously to reduce risk by herding. Investors who habitually sell in downtrends are not acting consciously to increase their risk of losing money; they are acting unconsciously to reduce risk, again by herding.

This dichotomy between non-rational, unconscious mental activity in financial behavior and rational, conscious mental activity in economic behavior is what we believe underlies the financial/economic dichotomy. It also appears compatible with Kahneman [2003], who proposed two types of thinking, "System 1" and "System 2," and to Sloman's [1996] related dichotomy between the "associative system" and the "rule-based system" of reasoning.

Herding and Rationalization

If the conscious, rational neocortex is not evaluating risk, what is it doing? Bechara et al. [1997, p. 1293] offered neurophysiological evidence that in contexts of risk and uncertainty, "Overt reasoning is preceded by a nonconscious biasing step that uses neural systems other than those that support declarative knowledge."

In accordance with this observation, socionomics (see Prechter [1999, Chap. 8, 2001]) incorporates the idea that the areas of the brain mediating rational thought have a role in the herding process. They provide rationalization, generating plausible justification for an investor's unconsciously induced behavior.

Investors who are unaware of their unconscious motivations use the neocortex—often after the fact—to explain the actions that the herding impulse has impelled. LeDoux [1989] found neural pathways for emotional response that do not go through the neocortex and are faster than the neural processing in the neocortex. This finding is consistent with the socionomic theory that affective impulses (primarily from the limbic system) occur first in financial decision-making, followed later by rationalization (from the neocortex). Without support from rationalization, the herding impulse would encounter resistance from the dictates of reason.

Although most economists know the Italian economist Vilfredo Pareto [1901/1968/1991] for his early contributions to neoclassical equilibrium theory, he is less known for his later sociological theory concerning the basic motivations of human behavior. It features a similar distinction between unconscious drives and conscious rationalizations that people generate a posteriori to explain their own behavior. His postulation of an instinctive "sociability" suggests a herding impulse, and the mental "derivations" that he claimed people use to justify such behavior is akin to the idea of rationalization under socionomic theory (Parker and Prechter [2006]). Burnham [2005, p. 23] reviewed compatible laboratory studies and came to a similar conclusion:

> We are built to cover up the fact that the lizard brain influences us. When we think we have decided to take an action with our rational brain, we often have simply made up a story for the cause of action.

The contrast between economic behavior and financial behavior with respect to rationalization is stark. As stated in Prechter [1999, p. 393],

> Most investors can quickly rationalize selling an investment because its price is falling or buying it because its price is rising, but there is not a soul who desperately rationalizes doing with less bread because the price is falling or who drives his car twice as much because the price of gasoline has doubled.

Shiller's [1990] study of the stock market crash of 1987 provides a good example of the discrepancy between what investors say is the reason for a large market decline and what they actually do as they sell their stock. His survey revealed that the most frequent reasons cited for the crash were that the market was "overpriced" and that large institutional investors were selling when the market hit "stop-loss" points. These ideas sound calm, rational, and at least roughly related to fundamental analysis or rational trading techniques. Shiller's research, however, found that on the day of the big crash, an astounding 43% of his random sample of institutional investors experienced "unusual symptoms of anxiety (difficulty concentrating, sweaty palms, tightness in chest, irritability, or rapid pulse) regarding the stock market" (p. 58).

In contrast to the calm reasoning process that investors reported, Shiller [1990] found that these investors actually displayed "heightened attention and emotion," and were "falling back on intuitive models." The respondents' stated reasons for the huge stock market decline appear to be belated rationalizations for actions borne of panic.

Shiller's [1990] survey data revealed "no recognizable exogenous trigger for the crash." Walker [1998] confirmed, "scholars still debate the reason why" the 1987 crash occurred. Exogenous causes of the even more dramatic crash of 1929 have remained equally elusive for seven decades. The most widely cited explanations are those of Galbraith [1954] and Kindleberger [2000], both of whom explained the crash in terms of endogenous psychological factors such as "mania" and "fads."

White [1990] reviewed the literature by researchers attempting to find exogenous causes for the 1929 crash and found no compelling case for any such cause or combination of causes. He acknowledged that most scholars "treat the demise of the bull market as an endogenous collapse of expectations" (p. 78).

If economists cannot even retrospectively explain such historic market events in terms of exogenous causes, we should be highly suspicious of ubiquitous daily rationales for market action. Researchers have already demonstrated in laboratory settings that events outside the market are unnecessary for motivating the price movement of investments. Smith, Suchanek, and Williams's [1988] study and others reviewed by Porter and Smith [2003] revealed a boom and bust profile typical of financial herding despite the absence of news. Caldarelli, Marsili, and Zhang [1997] likewise found "a market which behaves surprisingly realistically…in spite of…the outright exclusion of economic external factors."

News may be more than unnecessary; it may actually be irrelevant. Cutler, Poterba, and Summers [1989, pp. 4-5] statistically tested the idea that the stock market adjusts to major news "bearing on fundamental values" (p. 9). They determined that "macroeconomic news…explains only about one fifth of the movement in stock prices" (p. 5). They found "a surprisingly small effect [from] big news [of] political developments…and international events" (p. 8). The authors, moreover, judged news as a cause and increased volatility as an effect in the positive cases without considering market direction or establishing causation. But because news is common, it may correlate with volatility in some individual cases simply by chance, causality being another matter.

Prechter [2004] examined eight of the most dramatic events of recent decades and demonstrated their lack of effect on aggregate stock prices despite media claims to the contrary. Data from these studies and others in socionomics (Prechter [1999, 2003, 2004]) suggest there is insufficient evidence to support adopting any opinion on the future direction of the stock market that relies on causes outside the market. In every case, the supposed cause failed to exhibit a reliable correlation with subsequent stock price movements.

Cutler, Poterba, and Summers [1989, pp. 4-5] supported this finding with "the observation that many of the largest market movements in recent years have occurred on days when there were no major news events." The inadequacy of exogenous forces to account for subsequent market actions applies to economic reports, election outcomes, wars and peace treaties, terrorism, corporate earnings, scandals, Fed actions, and the movements of other markets. We find no consistent leading or coincident relationship between these types of events and stock price movement, making them useless for explaining the behavior of the stock market. (To the extent that any relationship does exist, it is a lagging one due to social mood's inducing social actions. See Prechter [1999, Chapters 14-16], Table 2 and the appendix.)

Despite this plethora of evidence, however, the vast bulk of market commentary defaults to the theme of exogenous causes. Thus is revealed the immense power of the unconscious: It can impel people to appeal to faulty reasons for stock market movements day after day and not realize it. These unconscious impulses, moods and emotions are so strong that even when confronted with conflicting data, most investors continue to believe in their own particular explanation. They may justify their beliefs as "common sense." This assertion is correct in an ironic sense because humans commonly resort to rationalizing unconsciously motivated actions. In our judgment, rationalization accounts for virtually every external-cause explanation for stock market behavior.

The Result of Herding in an Inappropriate Setting

Herding behavior commonly leads to failure in a financial context because the ultimate result of buying high and selling low is loss. Most people don't know how consistently investors lose money in financial markets. They think that everyone else is getting rich. The only people who know the true extent of the public's financial losses are the IRS and those working in the back offices of brokerage firms. The CEO of a futures brokerage firm once confided to us off the record that, in the aggregate, the firm's customers had never once had a winning year. This experience is not likely an anomaly. Most people are too embarrassed to tell the truth, and brokers don't want investors to know. Neither do the authors of the tax code, which calls for taxing annual gains while forcing taxpayers to shoulder nearly the full brunt of accumulated losses.

Examining some numbers will tell the real story. Wolff's [2000] analysis of Federal Reserve data revealed that two-thirds of American households failed to increase their retirement wealth "at all" from 1983 to 1998, despite the fact that U.S. stocks enjoyed their biggest bull market ever during this period [and real estate values were in a record climb as well]. The retirement wealth of the median household during that time actually fell 13%.

Given such dismal performance during a historic bull market, one can imagine how poorly investors typically fare during a bear market. In 1917, a broker using the pseudonym Don Guyon wrote a small book called *One-Way Pockets* (Guyon [1917]). He recounted that after a full cycle of rise and fall in the market, when stocks were priced about the same as they were at the beginning, every one of his clients had lost money. In searching for an explanation, he found, in essence, moods and herding. His clients were fearful at the start of the bull market and tended to trade in and out constantly. At the market's peak, they felt confident and bullish, and held much more stock "for the long run." Like their modern counterparts in Figure 8, their moods dictated their behavior.

To conclude, LPH accounts for investors' aggregate results. The long-term result of herding behavior in a financial context is not thriving but failure. In rare cases, survival itself may be challenged: Some people go bankrupt from financial speculation, and a few commit murder or suicide.

Is herding therefore irrational? Taking Montgomery's [1985] lead, we use the term *prerational* as opposed to *irrational*, because our unconscious mind is not irrational; it is oriented toward a positive goal. The problem of inefficacy arises when the unconscious mind inappropriately uses this ancient, blunt instrument of self-preservation in a modern finance setting, where herding impedes success and threatens survival.

Do Prices Motivate Financial Behavior?

Although it may appear that rising prices in financial assets attract buyers [and that falling prices repel buyers], we argue that they do not (see also Prechter [2003, pp. 217-18]). If buying made prices go up and rising prices made people buy, [or if selling made prices go down and falling prices made people sell,] there would be a positive feedback loop between prices and investor actions. Because price trends continually stop and reverse, there can be no continuously reinforcing feedback loop.

It may be possible to construct a theory of feedback based on heteroge-neous agents who react either positively or negatively to price movements in order to explain fluctuations, but we remain skeptical that such a theory could explain why the values of "fundamentals" change so dramatically, as per Figures 1-4. We remain open-minded and welcome all contributions to socionomic theory, but we tentatively conclude that prices are irrelevant to the herding dynamic. Waxing optimism produces rising prices, and waxing pessimism produces falling prices. Aggregate prices are simply an epiphenomenon of unconscious, subjective impulses to buy and sell in accordance with fluctuations in social mood. This is why we are careful (see Figure 16) to discuss how prices *relate* to aggregate demand, not how prices *affect* aggregate demand.

To summarize, in economics, prices are powerful motivators of pro-ducer and consumer behavior; in finance, prices are irrelevant to motivating investor behavior. The primary question for investors, regardless of price, is, "Will someone else pay more?" Aggregate financial prices are merely a gauge of aggregate demand, which is a function of investor psychology deriving from social mood.

Homogeneous Agents

We have shown that heterogeneity among agents contradicts the un-derlying assumptions of EMH. But some researchers working in the EMH framework have used it to account for anomalies, thereby producing a theoretical contradiction. LPH is among the minority of herding theories that models the process with homogeneous agents (Parker and Prechter [2005]). We see, for example, no significant differences in action between the traditional classes of "smart money" and "dumb money" when it comes to herding.

Friedman [1984, pp. 507-508], referring to the pressures of social opinion, tackled the myth of "smart money" head on:

> There is simply no reason to believe that institutional investors are less subject to such social influences on opinion than other investors, and there are substantial grounds for thinking that they may be even more so. To begin, apart from a few lonely Warren Buffetts, insti-tutional investors exist in a community that is exceptionally closely knit by constant communication and mutual exposure. The familiar extent to which economists talk shop with one another, look at the same aspects of the world they study, read the same research, and congregate at [the same] meetings ... simply pales in comparison to the day-to-day activity of the typical institutional investor.

Olsen [1996] demonstrated that even professional money managers, in the aggregate, fail to beat the market. Sias [2004], Welch [2000], Graham [1999], Trueman [1994], and Scharfstein and Stein [1990] all provided evidence of herding in institutions, investment newsletter writers, brokers, financial analysts and money managers. Although Shiller's [1984, p. 482] model made a distinction between "smart money" and "ordinary investors," he acknowledged that "managers, like the public, are forecasting earnings and may become overly optimistic or pessimistic." Indeed, Figure 14 shows that at good prices for buying, money managers have high levels of cash, and at good prices for selling, they have low levels of cash, exactly the opposite of what they should be doing for maximum return. This outcome cannot be the result of reason, but it is compatible with the idea that professionals are herding, just like the rest of us.

Yet the mechanism of herding is complex and not just a matter of individual ignorance. Professional money managers with years of experience may, in fact, be less inclined to herd. But the demands of the herd drive managers to join market trends if they wish to remain in business;

**Evidence of Herding by Financial Professionals
(S&P 500 vs. Stock Mutual Funds' Cash/Assets Ratio)**

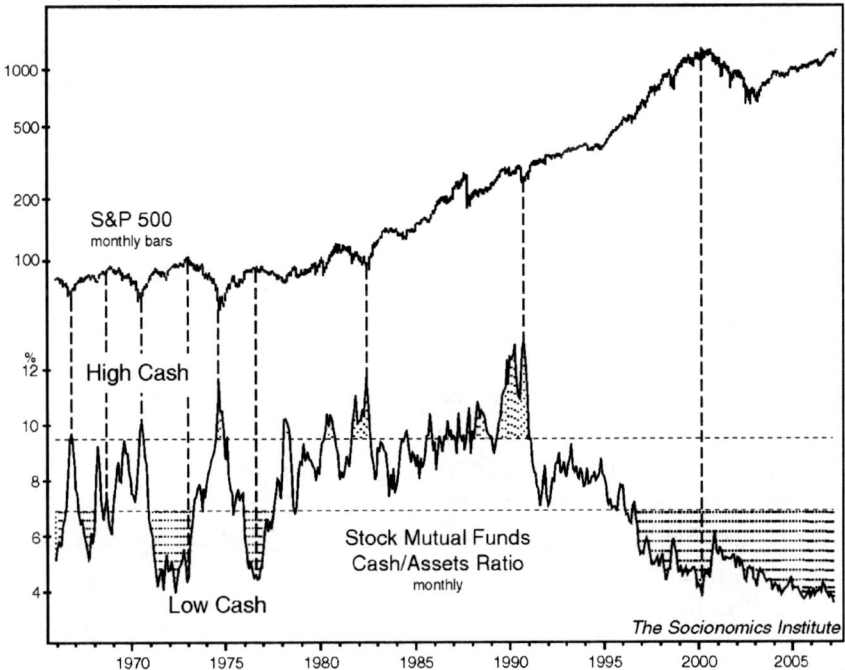

Note. Data from Investment Company Institute. Adapted with permission.

Figure 14

if they refuse, customers take their funds elsewhere. Even knowledgeable speculators who wish to profit from the herd may at times decide to buy in an uptrend or sell short in a downtrend. In any case, however, they are refraining from acting on economic valuation and implicitly acknowledging the dominance of the herd by joining it.

We believe that our concept of herding applies to nearly everyone despite—and ultimately because of—varying individual propensities to herd. For example, even Isaac Newton famously waited until the very peak of the South Sea Bubble to buy (Kindleberger [2000, p. 31]), but his personality did not change suddenly from a non-herder to a herder. Each person mentally plays his part in the herding process and then behaviorally joins—or refrains from joining—the herd's actions according to his own thresholds. When Newton was not buying, he was monitoring the crowd, thus participating in the process. He resisted buying for awhile, but he didn't resist the herding impulse.

The fact that some people act with the herd quickly and others do so slowly, tentatively or wholeheartedly is part of the dynamic that produces the aggregate movement. So our model accepts a quantitative heterogeneity of herding impulsivity at the individual level. But this fact is different from the model's assertion of qualitative homogeneity with regard to individual herding impulsivity. Quantitative heterogeneity provides our model with perpetual dynamism, while qualitative homogeneity provides our model with consistency: At the aggregate level, individuals form one homogeneous herd, even if individually their participatory actions differ.

Despite the socionomic assumption of agent homogeneity to explain aggregate financial market behavior, our theory does allow for a certain type of "smart money," which makes it uniquely compatible with real-world observations. We agree with Friedman [1984, p. 507] that "smart money ought to refer not to an advantage in assessing objective considerations but rather to the freedom, at least in comparison with other investors, from being subject to socially determined fads and fashions."

Under socionomics, smart money is managed by those rare investors and traders who (1) have learned to recognize aspects of herding that can be predictive, and (2) can overcome to some degree their own tendency to herd. Unlike EMH, which has no room for successful investors, socionomics accommodates the existence of a few consistently successful traders, investors and managers.

Proponents of the random walk theory have ascribed such success to luck, but successful investors profit far too consistently to be likened to lottery winners. The difficulty that the average person has in mastering his unconscious impulses assures that this type of "smart money" will remain rare. The number of talented investors is so minuscule when compared to the total number of investors that our model still views the herd as homogeneous.

The incorporation of homogeneous agents completes our outline of LPH as it relates to finance. Our review of herding theories (Parker and Prechter [2005]) demonstrates that LPH is unique: It is the only model of herding that eschews traditional assumptions of equilibrium and utility maximization while positing unconscious, prerational herding behavior derived from endogenous dynamics that have evolved in homogeneous groups of humans and which is applicable only in contexts of uncertainty.

Contrasting Models of Economics and Finance

Figures 15 and 16 express graphically the economic/financial dichotomy with respect to price behavior and the two separate models that account for it. Figures 17 and 18 contrast the different features of the regulator of economics, the law of supply and demand, with our proposed regulator of finance, LPH. They show that human motivation in a financial setting is the same as that in an economic setting, but the means and mechanisms are different. In the field of economics, the means are utility maximization, and the mechanism is conscious reason. In the field of finance, the means are herding, and the mechanism is unconscious impulsion.

In an economic setting, therefore, markets feature rational (utility-minded, conscious) valuation, equilibrium and objective values. In a financial setting, markets feature prerational (impulsive, unconscious) valuation, dynamism and subjective values. These different laws typically produce different results: success in the economic context, and failure in the financial context. The fields of finance and economics, we assert, are fundamentally different.

To complete our presentation of the financial/economic dichotomy, we have added notes to Figures 17 and 18 about the aggregate governors of these distinctly different fields. In both fields, global governors emerge without the knowledge or intention of individual agents. Economics has its dynamic of global constraint, the invisible hand (per Smith [1776/1994, p. 485], Andriopoulos [1999] and Rothschild [1994]). We believe that finance has its dynamic of global constraint, too: a robust, self-affine, hierarchical fractal called the Wave Principle (WP) (see Frost and Prechter [1978/1998] and Prechter [1999, Chapters 1-3]), whose pattern is the P in LPH.

In economics, people act to further their own ends. As a result, they bring cooperation, long-term prosperity and a steady reliability to social relationships, providing a measure of stability to society. In finance, people act to further their own ends as well. But in this case they create waves of affluence and ruin and bring a vacillating unreliability to social relationships, providing a measure of instability to society. In neither role are individuals consciously striving to bring about these results. The combination of these two sets of dynamics imbues society with a wondrous complexity.

Researchers in behavioral finance have made great headway in demolishing EMH, but their theoretical base is often still mired in the economic

Economics: How Price Relates to Aggregate Demand for Goods & Services

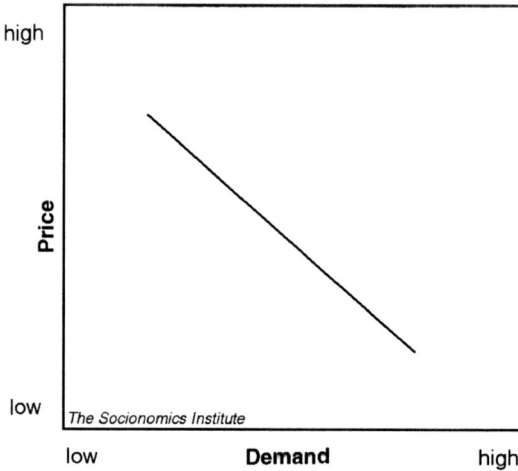

Figure 15

Finance: How Price Relates to Aggregate Demand for Investments

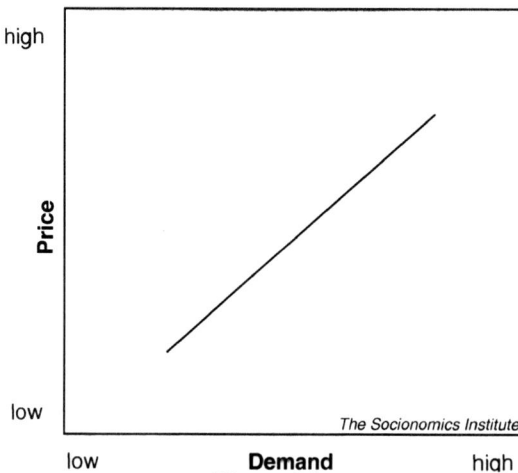

Figure 16

Economics: Law of Supply & Demand

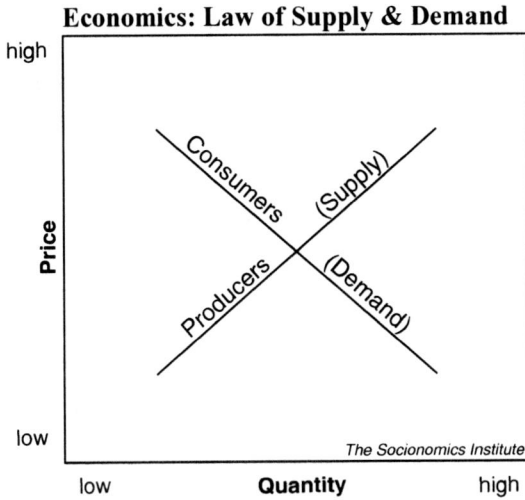

Field: Economics
Motivation (goal): Survival and Success
Means: Maximizing Utility
Mechanism: Conscious Reason
Result: Survival and Success
Features: Rational Valuation
       Equilibrium
       Objective Values
Aggregate Governor: The Invisible Hand

Figure 17

model of finance, so they propose anomalies to EMH due to human incon-sistencies in applying reason. Socionomic theory holds that just as humans in the aggregate are consistent in utilitarian economics, they are likewise consistent in finance. Economics produces a consistency of equilibrium motivated by reason and governed by the law of supply and demand. Finance produces a consistency of dynamism motivated by impulse and governed by LPH.

The reigning—if battered—model of financial markets, EMH, derives from economics. The model we propose as a better description and predic-tor of financial market behavior is the *socionomic theory of finance* (STF), which derives from socionomics.

Table 2 gives a list of the key differences between these two contrasting models. Points 1-6 in Table 2 are aspects of LPH as discussed here; points 7-9 refer to theoretical issues beyond the scope of this paper, one being aspects of WP and another being the *socionomic hypothesis*, as discussed in the appendix. Table 2 includes these latter points to facilitate an overall comparison of both theories.

Finance: Law of Patterned Herding

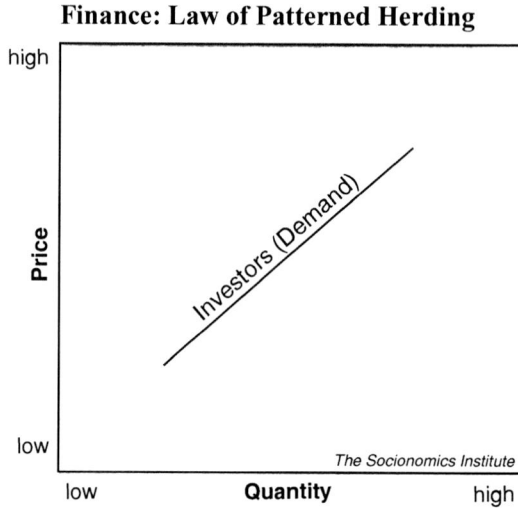

Field: Finance
Motivation (goal): Survival and Success
Means: Herding
Mechanism: Unconscious Impulsion
Ultimate Result: Losses
Features: Pre-Rational (Impulsive) Valuation
                Dynamism
                Subjective Values
Aggregate Governor: The Wave Principle

Figure 18

Conclusion: Socionomic Theory Resolves a Long-Standing Theoretical Conflict

Thanks to experiments in behavioral finance, economists have begun to recognize the importance of non-rational and instinctive aspects of human behavior. We propose a theoretical context in which to understand when traditional economic theory applies and when it doesn't. Noelle-Neumann [1993, p. 116] documented this long-running theoretical struggle:

> In the nineteenth and twentieth centuries, two views have repeatedly clashed—the view that stresses instinctual behavior and sees man as determined by herd instincts; and the view that assumes man reacts rationally to the experience of reality. ...From one historical perspective it can be said that behaviorism has supplanted two different instinct theories, the one by the British biologist Wilfred Trotter [whose 1916 book first popularized the term "herd instinct"]...and the other one by McDougall [whose 1920 book *The Group Mind* was a seminal text about social behavior].... The schools of thought that

Table 2: Contrasting Models of Finance

The Efficient Market Hypothesis (EMH)	The Socionomic Theory of Finance (STF)
1. Objective, conscious, rational decisions to maximize utility determine financial values.	1. Subjective, unconscious, pre-rational impulses to herd determine financial values.
2. Financial markets tend toward equilibrium and revert to the mean.	2. Financial markets are dynamic and do not revert to anything.
3. Investors in financial markets typically use information to reason.	3. Investors in financial markets typically use information to rationalize emotional imperatives.
4. Investors' decisions are based on knowledge and certainty.	4. Investors' decisions are fraught with ignorance and uncertainty.
5. Exogenous variables determine most investment decisions.	5. Endogenous social processes determine most investment decisions.
6. Financial prices derive from individual decisions about value.	6. Financial prices derive from trends in social mood.
7. Financial prices are random.	7. Financial prices adhere to an organizing principle at the aggregate level.
8. Financial prices are unpredictable.	8. Financial prices are probabilistically predictable.
9. Changing events presage changes in the values of associated financial instruments.	9. Changing values of financial instruments presage changes in associated events.
10. Economic principles govern finance.	10. Socionomic principles govern finance.

The Socionomics Institute

emphasized the rationality of man regarded imitation as a purposeful [conscious, rational] learning strategy. Because these schools clearly prevailed over the instinct theories, the subject of imitation [as instinctual herding]…fell into neglect.

The pendulum of history is beginning to swing in the other direction, but the correct view, we propose, is not an either/or matter. Socionomics provides a different solution: Neither reason nor herd instinct alone offers a full explanation for human social behavior. Humans apply reason in contexts of certainty and the prerational herding impulse in contexts of uncertainty. When certainty about personal valuation applies, people maximize utility and markets seek equilibrium. When uncertainty about others' valuations applies, people herd and markets are dynamic. The first state is common in markets for utilitarian goods and services; the second is common in markets for financial assets.

Socionomics proposes not only the segregation of finance and economics but also their re-integration into a contextual theory of human motivation as it relates to the challenge of survival. The financial/economic dichotomy thus brings to light a key underlying duality in the social experience, thereby enhancing the power of science to understand and predict certain aspects of social behavior. We are confident that the time is right for a new theory of finance. We welcome challenges to STF as well as assistance from colleagues to help pursue this line of research.

Acknowledgments

The authors gratefully acknowledge the comments of Robin Hogarth, Marco Novarese, Terry Burnham, John Nofsinger, Laurence Chud, Philipp Otto, and Gordon Graham on an earlier draft. They also thank Valeri Safonov for his help in obtaining the Russian materials cited in the appendix, Vadim Pokhlebkin for translating them, and Deepak Goel for his help with our statistical analysis. This paper derives in part from Prechter [1999, pp. 393-395] and from Prechter's presentation to professors and graduate students at MIT's Lab for Financial Engineering on September 12, 2003. Some of this material was presented in substantially different form in Prechter [2004] and Prechter and Parker [2004]. This research was supported in part by a grant from the Socionomics Foundation.

APPENDIX

THE SOCIONOMIC THEORY OF FINANCE (STF)

Socionomics is a comprehensive theory of social behavior that describes the causal relationship between social mood and social action. The main theoretical principles are that, in human, complex systems:

- Shared unconscious impulses to herd in contexts of uncertainty lead to mass psychological dynamics manifested as social mood trends.

- These social mood trends conform to a hierarchical fractal called the Wave Principle (WP) and therefore are probabilistically predictable.

- These patterns of human aggregate behavior are form-determined due to endogenous processes, rather than mechanistically determined by exogenous causes.

- Social mood trends determine the character of social actions and are their underlying cause.

The theory integrates a hypothesis of individual agent participation (LPH) with a principle of aggregate organization (WP). The socionomic theory of finance (STF) simply applies LPH and WP to transactional systems.

The body of this paper focuses on the LPH component. Using the language of LPH and adding the WP component, STF proposes that transactional systems comprising homogeneous agents uncertain about other agents' valuations that are critical to survival and success provide a context in which an endogenously regulated aggregation of unconscious herding impulses constitutes a pattern of social mood. Social mood in turn motivates social actions, one of which is buying and selling in financial markets, records of which manifest as a probabilistically predictable hierarchical fractal described by the Wave Principle. For a discussion of socionomics' metatheoretical context, see Prechter and Parker [2004].

Point #9 in Table 2 may require some clarification for those unfamiliar with socionomics. The socionomic hypothesis (see Prechter [1979/2003, 1985/2003, 1999]) is that social mood trends, which arise endogenously, motivate social action. This is a reversal of the accepted view that social actions—manifested as economic, political, or cultural events—cause changes in social mood.

As far as we know, our formulation is unique in Western thought, although we have found a Russian paper in which Toschenko [1998] proposed that "social mood comprises dominant characteristics of consciousness and behavior, thus allowing social analysts to foretell dynamics of social behavior." This comment is similar but not identical to our socionomic hypothesis.

REFERENCES

Andriopoulos, Stefan. "The Invisible Hand: Supernatural Agency in Political Economy and the Gothic Novel." ELH [English Literary History], 66, 3, (1999), pp. 739-758.

Arrow, Kenneth J., and Gerard Debreu. "Existence of an Equilibrium for a Competitive Economy." *Econometrica*, 22, 3, (1954), pp. 265-290.

Banaji, M.R., K.M. Lemm, and S.J. Carpenter. "Automatic and Implicit Processes in Social Cognition:' In A. Tesser and N. Schwartz, eds., *Blackwell Handbook of Social Psychology: Intraindividual Processes.* Oxford: Blackwell, (2001), pp. 134- 158.

Bechara, Antoine, Hanna Damasio, Daniel Tranel, and Antonio R. Damasio. "Deciding Advantageously Before Knowing the Advantageous Strategy." *Science*, 275, February 28, (1997), pp. 1293-1295.

Bhushan, Ravi, David P. Brown, and Antonio Mello. "Do Noise Traders 'Create Their Own Space?'" *Journal of Financial and Quantitative Analysis*, 32, 1, March, (1997), pp. 25-45.

Bischoff-Grethe, A., M. Martin, H. Mao, and G.S. Berns. "The Context of Uncertainty Modulates the Subcortical Response to Predictability." *Journal of Cognitive Neuroscience*, 13, 7, (2001), pp. 986-993.

Black, Fischer. "Mean Reversion and Consumption Smoothing." *Review of Financial Studies*, 3, 1, (1990), pp. 107-114.

Blanchard, Olivier Jean. "Speculative Bubbles, Crashes and Rational Expectations." *Economics Letters*, 3, (1979), pp. 387-389.

Buck, Ross. "The Biological Affects: A Typology." *Psychological Review*, 106, 2, April, (1999), pp. 301-336.

Burnham, Terry. *Mean Markets and Lizard Brains.* Hoboken: John Wiley & Sons, Inc., (2005).

Caldarelli, G., M. Marsili, and Y.C. Zhang. "A Prototype Model of Stock Exchange." *Europhysics Letters*, 40, 5, December 1, (1997), pp. 479-484.

Camerer, Colin F., George Loewenstein, and Drazen Prelec. "Neuroeconomics: Why Economics Needs Brains." Available at http://www.hss.caltech.edu, (2004).

Camerer, Colin F., George Loewenstein, and Matthew Rabin, eds. *Advances in Behavioral Economics.* Princeton: Princeton University Press, (2004).

Carhart, Mark M. "On Persistence in Mutual Fund Performance." *Journal of Finance*, 52, 1, March, (1997), pp. 57-82.

Cootner, Paul, ed. *The Random Character of Stock Market Prices.* Cambridge: MIT Press, 1964.

Cosmides, Leda, and John Tooby. "Better than Rational: Evolutionary Psychology and the Invisible Hand." *American Economic Review*, 84, 2, May, (1994), pp. 327-332.

Cournot, Augustin. *Recherches sur les Principes Mathematiques de la Theorie des Richesses (Researches into the Mathematical Principles of the Theory of Wealth)*. Paris: Hachette, 1838. English translation by N.T. Bacon published in *Economic Classics*, Macmillan, 1897, and reprinted in 1960 by Augustus M. Kelly. As quoted on website at http:/fhomepage. newschool.edu/ het/profiles/cournot.htm, 1838/1897/1960.

Cowles, Alfred. "Can Stock Market Forecasters Forecast?" *Econometrica*, 1, 4, July, (1933), pp. 309-324.

Cutler, David M., James M. Poterba, and Lawrence H. Summers. "What Moves Stock Prices?" *Journal of Portfolio Management*, 15, 3, Spring, (1989), pp. 4-12.

Debreu, Gerard. "Economies with a Finite set of Equilibria." *Econometrica*, 38, 3, May, (1970), pp. 387-392.

Debreu, Gerard. "The Mathematization of Economic Theory." *American Economic Review*, 81, 1, March, (1991), pp. 1-7.

Diba, Behzad T., and Hershel I. Grossman. "The Theory of Rational Bubbles in Stock Prices." *Economic Journal*, 98, 392, September, (1988), pp. 746-754.

Dreman, David. "Editorial Commentary: Bubble Jr." *Journal of Behavioral Finance*, 4, 4, (2003), pp. 188-190.

Dreman, David. "Editorial Commentary: The Influence of Affect on Investor Decision-Making." *Journal of Behavioral Finance*, 5, 2, (2004), pp. 70-74.

Durlauf, Steven N. "Nonergodic Economic Growth." *Review of Economic Studies*, 60, 2, April, (1993), pp. 349-366.

Easterwood, John C., and Stacy R. Nutt. "Inefficiency in Analysts' Earnings Forecasts: Systematic Misreaction or Systematic Optimism?" *Journal of Finance*, 54, 5, October, (1999), pp. 1777-1797.

Elliott, R.N. 1938/1993/2005. *The Wave Principle*. New York: Self-published. Reprinted in Prechter [1993/2005].

Elliott, R.N. 1946/1993/2005. *Nature's Law*. New York: Self-published. Reprinted in Prechter [1993/2005].

Fama, Eugene F. "Efficient Capital Markets: A Review of Theory and Empirical Work." *Journal of Finance*, 25, 2, (1970), pp. 383-417.

Fama, Eugene F. "Efficient Capital Markets II." *Journal of Finance*, 46, 5, December, (1991), pp. 1575-1617.

Fama, Eugene F., and Kenneth R. French. "The Capital Asset Pricing Model: Theory and Evidence." *Journal of Economic Perspectives*, 18, 3, Summer, (2004), pp. 25-46.

Farrell, M.J. "Profitable Speculation." *Economica*, New Series, 33, 130, May, (1966), pp. 183-193.

Friedman, Benjamin M. "Comments and Discussion," pp. 504-508. In Robert J. Shiller, Stanley Fischer, and Benjamin M. Friedman, "Stock Prices and Social Dynamics." Brookings Papers on Economic Activity, 2, (1984), pp. 457-510.

Friedman, Milton, and L.J. Savage. "The Utility Analysis of Choices Involving Risk." *Journal of Political Economy*, 56, 4, August, (1948), pp. 279-304.

Froot, Kenneth A., and Maurice Obstfeld. "Intrinsic Bubbles: The Case of Stock Prices." *American Economic Review*, 81, 5, December, (1991), pp. 1189-1214.

Frost, Alfred John, and Robert R. Prechter *Elliott Wave Principle—Key to Market Behavior*. Gainesville, GA: New Classics Library, 1978/1998.

Gajdusek, D.C. "Physiological and Psychological Characteristics of Stone Age Man." Symposium on Biological Bases of Human Behavior, *Eng. Sci.*, 33, (1970), pp. 26-33, 56-62.

Galbraith, John Kenneth. *The Great Crash 1929*. New York: Houghton Mifflin Company, 1954.

Gitman, Lawrence J., and Michael D. Joehnk. *Fundamentals of Investing*, 2nd ed. New York: Harper and Row, 1984.

Gordon, M.J., and Eli Shapiro, "Capital Equipment Analysis: The Required Rate of Profit." *Management Science*, 3, 1, October, (1956), pp. 102-110. [This reference replaces a reference to Modigliani and Miller in the original paper.]

Graham, Benjamin, and David Dodd. *Securities Analysis*. New York: McGraw-Hill, 1934.

Graham, John R. "Herding Among Investment Newsletters: Theory and Evidence." *Journal of Finance*, 54, 1, February, (1999), pp. 237-268.

Greenspan, Alan. Remarks at a symposium sponsored by the Federal Reserve Bank of Kansas City, Jackson Hole, Wyoming. Available at http://federalreserve.gov, 2003.

Guyon, Don. *One-Way Pockets: The Book of Books on Wall Street Speculation*. Wells, Vermont: Fraser Publishing Co., 1917/1965.

Hirshleifer, David. "Investor Psychology and Asset Pricing." *Journal of Finance*, 56, 4, August, (2001), pp. 1533-1597.

Hodgson, Geoffrey M. *How Economics Forgot History: The Problem of Historical Specificity in Social Science*. New York: Routledge, 2001.

Hogarth, Robin M. "The Challenge of Representative Design in Psychology and Economics." Working paper #751, Universitat Pompeu Fabra, Barcelona, Spain. Available at http://www.econ.upf.edu/leex/llista.php?id=p2047 &nom=Robin+Hogarth. Revised version published in *Journal of Economic Methodology*, 12,2, June, (2005), pp. 253-263.

Janis, Irving L. *Victims of Groupthink: A Psychological Study of Foreign-Policy Decisions and Fiascoes*. New York: Houghton Mifflin, 1972.

Jegadeesh, Narasimhan. "Seasonality in Stock Price Mean Reversion: Evidence from the U.S. and the U.K." *Journal of Finance*, 46, 4, September, (1991), pp. 1427-1444.

Jevons, W. Stanley. "On the Frequent Autumnal Pressure in the Money Market, and the Action of the Bank of England." *Journal of the Statistical Society of London*, 29, 2, June, (1866), pp. 235-253.

Kahneman, Daniel. "Maps of Bounded Rationality: Psychology for Behavioral Economics." *American Economic Review*, 27, 5, December, (2003), pp. 1449-1475.

Kahneman, Daniel, Paul Slovic, and Amos Tversky, eds. *Judgment under Uncertainty: Heuristics and Biases*. Cambridge: Cambridge University Press, 1982.

Kahneman, Daniel, and Amos Tversky. "Prospect Theory: An Analysis of Decision Under Risk." *Econometrica*, 47, 2, March, (1979), pp. 263-291.

Keynes, John M. *The Treatise on Probability*. London: Macmillan, 1921.

Keynes, John M. *The General Theory of Employment, Interest Rates, and Money*. New York: Prometheus Books, 1936/1997.

Kindleberger, Charles P. *Manias, Panics, and Crashes: A History of Financial Crises*, 4th ed. New York: Basic Books (originally published in 1978), 1978/2000.

Kleidon, Allan W. "Anomalies in Financial Economics: Blueprint for Change?" *Journal of Business*, 59, 4 (part 2), (1986), pp. S469-S499.

Knight, Frank H. *Risk, Uncertainty, and Profit*. New York: Houghton Mifflin, 1921.

Kuhn, T.S. *The Structure of Scientific Revolutions*, 2nd ed. Chicago: University of Chicago Press, 1970.

LeDoux, Joseph E. "Cognitive Emotional Interactions in the Brain." *Cognition and Emotion*, 3, (1989), pp. 267-289.

LeDoux, Joseph E. "Emotional Circuits in the Brain." *Annual Review of Neuroscience*, 3, (2000), pp. 155-184.

Leontief, Wassily. "Theoretical Assumptions and Non-Observed Facts." *American Economic Review*, 61, 1, March, (1971), pp. 1-7.

LeRoy, Stephen F. "Efficient Capital Markets and Martingales." *Journal of Economic Literature*, 27, December, (1989), pp. 1583-1621.

Lintner, John. "The Valuation of Risky Assets and the Selection of Risky Investments in Stock Portfolios and Capital Budgets." *Review of Economics and Statistics*, 47, 1, (1965), pp. 13-37.

Lo, Andrew W., and A. Craig MacKinlay. *A Non-Random Walk Down Wall Street*. Princeton: Princeton University Press, 1999.

Loewenstein, George, and Richard H. Thaler. "Anomalies: Intertemporal Choice." *Journal of Economic Perspectives*, 3, 4, Fall, (1989), pp. 181-193.

Lucas, Robert E. Jr. "Methods and Problems in Business Cycle Theory." *Journal of Money, Credit and Banking*, 12 (4, Part 2), November, (1980), pp. 696-715.

Lucas, Robert E. Jr., and Edward C. Prescott. "Investment Under Uncertainty." *Econometrica*, 39, September, (1971), pp. 659- 681.

MacDougall, Donald. "In Praise of Economics." *Economic Journal*, 84, 336, December, (1974), pp.773-786.

MacLean, Paul D. *The Triune Brain in Evolution: Role in Paleocerebral Functions.* New York: Plenum Press, 1990.

Mandelbrot, Benoit B. "Forecasts of Future Prices, Unbiased Markets and 'Martingale' Models." *Journal of Business*, 39, January, (1966), pp. 242-255.

Mandelbrot, Benoit B. "When Can Price Be Arbitraged Efficiently? A Limit to the Validity of the Random Walk and Martingale Models." *Review of Economics and Statistics*, 53, 3, August, (1971), pp. 225-236.

Mandelbrot, Benoit B. "Possible Refinements of the Lognormal Hypothesis Concerning the Distribution of Energy Dissipation in Intermittent Turbulence." In M. Rosenblatt and C. Van Atta, eds., *Statistical Models and Turbulence.* New York: Springer-Verlag, 1972.

Mandelbrot, Benoit B. "Global (long-term) Dependence in Economics and Finance." Virtual Selecta H30 from Fractal and Multifractal Finance: Crashes and Long Dependence. Open-ended web-book available at http://www.math.yale.edu/ mandelbrot/web_pdfs/9H30.pdf], 2003.

Mandelbrot, Benoit B., Adlai Fisher, and Laurent Calvet. "A Multifractal Model of Asset Returns." Cowles Foundation Discussion Paper #1164, available at http://www.econ.yale.edu/ ~fisher/papers.htm, 1997.

Mankiw, N. Gregory. "Real Business Cycles: A New Keynesian Perspective." *Journal of Economic Perspectives*, 3, 3, Summer, (1989), pp. 79-90.

Marshall, Alfred. *Principles of Economics*, 8th ed. London: Macmillan and Co., Ltd. (available at http://www.econlib.org/library /Marshall/marP.html), 1890/1920.

McNichols, Maureen, and Patricia C. O'Brien. "Self-Selection and Analyst Coverage." *Journal of Accounting Research*, 35, (1997), pp. 167-199.

Montgomery, Paul Macrae. "Classical Philosophy and the Bond Market." Universal Economics, October 1. Updated in Prechter [2002b] as "Classical Philosophy and the Capital Markets," (1983), pp. 115-124.

Montgomery, Paul Macrae. "Neurophysiology and Interest Rate Behavior." Universal Economics, April 12. Updated in Prechter [2002b] as "The Necessity of Accounting for Immaterial Mental States within Financial Analysis," (1985), pp. 79-112.

Muth, John F. "Rational Expectations and the Theory of Price Movements." *Econometrica*, 29, 3, July, (1961), pp. 315-335.

Nielsen, Lars Tyge. "Uniqueness of Equilibrium in the Classical Capital Asset Pricing Model." *Journal of Financial and Quantitative Analysis*, 23, 3, September, (1988), pp. 329-336.

Noelle-Neumann, Elisabeth. *The Spiral of Silence: Public Opinion—Our Social Skin*, 2nd ed. Chicago: University of Chicago Press, 1993.

Olsen, Robert A. "Implications of Herding Behavior." *Financial Analysts Journal*, 52, 4, July/August, (1996), pp. 37-41.

Olsen, Robert A. "Research Elsewhere: Review of 'Core Affect and the Psychological Construction of Emotion' by James A. Russell." *Journal of Behavioral Finance*, 4, 3, (2003), pp. 184-186.

Pareto, Vilfredo. "Un Applicazione di Teorie Sociologiche." *Rivista Italiana di Sociologia*, pp. 402-456. Reprinted in English as Pareto, Vilfredo, *The Rise and Fall of the Elites: An Application of Theoretical Sociology*. New Brunswick, NJ: Transaction Publishers, 1901/1991. Originally published in English in 1968 by Bedminster Press, Totowa, New Jersey, as cited in Zetterberg [1993], 1901.

Pareto, Vilfredo. *Manual of Political Economy* (1971 translation of 1927 edition). New York: Augustus. M. Kelley, 1906/1927/1971.

Parker, Wayne D., and Robert R. Prechter "Herding: An Interdisciplinary Integrative Review from a Socionomic Perspective." In Boicho Kokinov, ed., *Advances in Cognitive Economics: Proceedings of the International Conference on Cognitive Economics*, Sofia, August 5-8, 2005. Sofia, Bulgaria: NBU Press, pp. 271-280. Also available online at http://papers. ssrn.com/sol3/papers/cfm?abstract_id=2009898, 2005.

Parker, Wayne D., and Robert R. Prechter "The Socionomic Theory of Finance and the Institution of Social Mood: Pareto and the Sociology of Instinct and Rationalization." Paper presented at the meeting of the Association for Heterodox Economics, London, England, July 14-16, 2006. Available at http://www.socionomics.org/pdf/socionomics_pareto.pdf, 2006.

Penrose, Edith T. "Biological Analogies in the Theory of the Firm: Rejoinder." *American Economic Review*, 43, 4, September, (1953), pp. 603-609.

Pigou, A.C. *The Economics of Welfare*, 4th ed. London: Macmillan and Company, 1920/1932.

Plosser, Charles I. "Understanding Real Business Cycles." *Journal of Economic Perspectives*, 3, 3, Summer, (1989), pp. 51-77.

Porter, David P., and Vernon L. Smith. "Futures Contracting and Dividend Uncertainty in Experimental Asset Markets." *Journal of Business*, 68, 4, October, (1995), pp. 509-541.

Porter, David P., and Vernon L. Smith. "Stock Market Bubbles in the Laboratory." *Journal of Behavioral Finance*, 4, 1, (2003), pp. 7-20.

Poterba, James M. "The Rise of 'Equity Culture': U.S. Stock Ownership Patterns, 1989-1998." Working document available online at http://econ-www.mit.edu/facultynprof-id=poterba&type= paper, 2001.

Prechter, Robert R., Jr. "What's Going On?" *The Elliott Wave Theorist*, August 3. Reprinted in Prechter [2003, p. 1], 1979/2003.

Prechter, Robert R., Jr. "Popular Culture and the Stock Market." *The Elliott Wave Theorist*, August. Reprinted in Prechter [2003, pp. 3-46], 1985/2003.

Prechter, Robert R., Jr., ed. *R.N. Elliott's Masterworks*. Gainesville, GA: New Classics Library, 1993/2005.

Prechter, Robert R., Jr. *The Wave Principle of Human Social Behavior and the New Science of Socionomics*. Gainesville, GA: New Classics Library, 1999.

Prechter, Robert R., Jr. "Unconscious Herding Behavior as the Psychological Basis of Financial Market Trends and Patterns." *Journal of Psychology and Financial Markets (now Journal of Behavioral Finance)*, 2, 3, (2001), pp. 120-125. http://www.socionomics.org/pdf/Unconscious_herding.pdf, 2001.

Prechter, Robert R., Jr. *Conquer the Crash: You Can Survive and Prosper in a Deflationary Depression*. Gainesville, GA: New Classics Library, 2002a.

Prechter, Robert R., Jr., ed. *Market Analysis for the New Millennium*. Gainesville, GA: New Classics Library, 2002b.

Prechter, Robert R., Jr., ed. *Pioneering Studies in Socionomics*. Gainesville, GA: New Classics Library, 2003.

Prechter, Robert R., Jr. "The Stock Market is Not Physics—Parts I and II." *The Elliott Wave Theorist*, May 20 and June 21, 2004.

Prechter, Robert R., Jr., and Deepak Goel. "Idealized Elliott Waves, the Stock Market and Random Walk Tests." Working paper. Available at http://www.socionomics.org/pdf/randomness.pdf, 2007.

Prechter, Robert R., Jr., and Wayne D. Parker. "The Financial/Economic Dichotomy." In Heping Pan, Didier Sornette, and Kenneth Kortanek, eds., *Intelligent Finance—A Convergence of Mathematical Finance with Technical and Fundamental Analysis*. Melbourne, Australia: International Workshop on Intelligent Finance (University of Ballarat). Also available at http://www.socionomics.org/pdf/fin_econ_melbourne_us_REV.pdf, 2004.

Ross, Stephen A. "The Interrelations of Finance and Economics: Theoretical Perspectives." *American Economic Review*, 77, 2, May, (1987), pp. 29-34.

Rothschild, Emma. "Adam Smith and the Invisible Hand." *American Economic Review*, 84, 2, May, (1994), pp. 319-322.

Russell, James A. "Core Affect and the Psychological Construction of Emotion." *Psychological Review*, 110, 1, January, (2003), pp. 145-172.

Samuelson, Paul A. "Proof that Properly Anticipated Prices Fluctuate Randomly." *Industrial Management Review*, 6, Spring, (1965), pp. 41-49.

Scharfstein, David S., and Jeremy C. Stein. "Herd Behavior and Investment." *American Economic Review*, 80, 3, June, (1990), pp. 465-479.

Schumpeter, Joseph A. *History of Economic Analysis*. New York: Oxford University Press, 1954.

Sharpe, William F. "Capital Asset Prices: A Theory of Market Equilibrium under Conditions of Risk." *Journal of Finance*, 19, 3, (1964), pp. 425-442.

Shiller, Robert J. "The Use of Volatility Measures in Assessing Market Efficiency." *Journal of Finance*, 36, 2, May, (1981), pp. 291-304.

Shiller, Robert J. "Comment on Miller and on Kleidon." *Journal of Business*, 59, 1 (part 2), (1986), pp. S501-S505.

Shiller, Robert J. "Speculative Prices and Popular Models." *Journal of Economic Perspectives*, 4, 2, Spring, (1990), pp. 55-65.

Shiller, Robert J. *Irrational Exuberance*. Princeton: Princeton University Press, 2000.

Shiller, Robert J., Stanley Fischer, and Benjamin M. Friedman. "Stock Prices and Social Dynamics." *Brookings Papers on Economic Activity*, 2, (1984), pp. 457-510.

Shiv, Baba, George Loewenstein, Antoine Bechara, Hanna Damasio, and Antonio R. Damasio. "Investment Behavior and the Negative Side of Emotion." *Psychological Science*, 16, 6, June, (2005), pp. 435-439.

Sias, Richard W. "Institutional Herding." *Review of Financial Studies*, 17, I, Spring, (2004), pp. 165-206.

Sloman, Steven A. "The Empirical Case for Two Systems of Reasoning." *Psychological Bulletin*, 119, 1, January, (1996), pp. 3-22.

Smith, Adam. *The Wealth of Nations*. New York: Modern Library (Random House), 1776/1994.

Smith, Vernon L. "Constructivist and Ecological Rationality in Economics." *American Economic Review*, 93, 3, June, (2003), pp. 465-508.

Smith, Vernon L., G.L. Suchanek, and A.W. Williams. "Bubbles, Crashes, and Endogenous Expectations in Experimental Spot Asset Markets." *Econometrica*, 56, 5, September, (1988), pp. 1119-1151.

Sornette, D. "Critical Market Crashes." *Physics Reports*, 378, 1, (2003), pp.1-98.

Thaler, Richard H., and Eric J. Johnson. "Gambling with the House Money and Trying to Break Even: The Effects of Prior Outcomes on Risky Choice." *Management Science*, 36, 6, June, (1990), pp. 643-660.

Toschenko, Zhan Terent'evich. "Social Mood: A Phenomenon of Contemporary Sociological Theory." Russian, privately translated by Vadim Pokhlebkin. Sotsiologicheskie Issledovaniya, 25, 1, (1998), pp. 21-34.

Treynor, Jack. "Bulls, Bears, and Market Bubbles." *Financial Analysts Journal*, 54, 2, March/April, (1998), pp. 69-74.

Trueman, Brett. "Analyst Forecasts and Herding Behavior." *Review of Financial Studies*, 7,1, Spring, (1994), pp. 97-124.

Von Neumann, John, and Oskar Morgenstern. *Theory of Games and Economic Behavior*, 2nd ed. Princeton: Princeton University Press. 1947.

Walker, T. "Identifying Sell-Off Triggers is Difficult." *Atlanta Journal-Constitution*, August 6, (1998), p. F3.

Walras, Leon. *Elements of Pure Economics: Or the Theory of Social Wealth*. 1954 translation of 1926 edition. Homewood, IL: Richard Irwin, 1874/1926/1954.

Welch, Ivo. "Herding Among Security Analysts." *Journal of Financial Economics*, 58, 3, (2000), pp. 369-396.

Welty, Gordon A. "Giffen's Paradox and Falsifiability." *Weltwirtschaftliches Archiv*, 107, I, (1971), pp. 139-146.

White, Eugene N. "The Stock Market Boom and Crash of 1929 Revisited." *Journal of Economic Perspectives*, 4, 2, Spring, (1990), pp. 67-83.

Wolff, Edward. "Recent Trends in Wealth Ownership, 1983-1998." Working Paper No. 300, (May 2000), Jerome Levy Economics Institute, available at http://www.levy.org.

Zetterberg, Hans L. "Elites: Vilfredo Pareto." Chapter 3 in *European Proponents of Sociology Prior to World War I*, (1993). Web publication available at http://zetterberg.org/Books, accessed on April 11, 2005.

EDITOR'S NOTE

[1] The topics covered in this section and the next two sections are treated more extensively in Chapter 33.

Part IV:

HERDING AND SOCIAL MOOD

Chapter 16

The Journal of Psychology and Financial Markets
2001, Vol. 2, No. 3, pp. 120–125

Unconscious Herding Behavior as the Psychological Basis of Financial Market Trends and Patterns[1]

Robert R. Prechter

Human herding behavior results from impulsive mental activity in individuals responding to signals from the behavior of others. Impulsive thought originates in the basal ganglia and limbic system. In emotionally charged situations, the limbic system's impulses are typically faster than rational reflection performed by the neocortex. Experiments with a small number of naïve individuals as well as statistics reflecting the behavior of large groups of financial professionals provide evidence of herding behavior. Herding behavior, while appropriate in some primitive life-threatening situations, is inappropriate and counterproductive to success in financial situations. Unconscious impulses that evolved in order to attain positive values and avoid negative values spur herding behavior, making rational independence extremely difficult to exercise in group settings. A negative feedback loop develops because stress increases impulsive mental activity, and impulsive mental activity in financial situations, by inducing failure [should read "generating losses"—RP], increases stress.[2] The interaction of many minds in a collective setting produces super-organic behavior that is patterned according to the survival-related functions of the primitive portions of the brain. As long as the human mind comprises the triune construction and its functions, patterns of herding behavior will remain immutable.

Experimental research suggests that human beings possess biologically based psychological sources of unconscious emotional imperatives that cause a cooperative interaction on the part of financial market participants. If so, not only might mass emotional change be the primary mover of financial market prices, but we may also expect its operation to be immutable.

The Triune Brain

Paul MacLean, former head of the Laboratory for Brain Evolution at the National Institute of Mental Health, developed the concept of a "triune" brain, i.e., one that is divided into three basic parts: the brain stem, the limbic system and the neocortex.[3] While the neocortex processes ideas by reason, the more primitive portions of the brain control impulses and emotions that propel actions that are lifesaving or life-enhancing under most circumstances. Along with such matters as fighting, fleeing, hoarding, territorialism and breeding, the basal ganglia control *herding* behavior, while the limbic system produces emotions as a spur to further these objectives. The rational cortex cannot influence the impulses generated by these portions of the brain.

As a primitive tool of survival, emotional impulses from the limbic system impel a desire among individuals to seek signals from others in matters of knowledge and behavior and therefore to align their feelings and convictions with those of the group. The desire to belong to and be accepted by the group is particularly powerful in intensely emotional social settings, when it can overwhelm the higher brain functions.

Anatomically related studies (Ledoux, 1989) led to the discovery of neural pathways for emotional response that do not go through the neocortex and which are up to 40 milliseconds faster than the neocortex. Because the limbic system is quicker in response than the neocortex, emotions are often not reactions to considered *ideas* but immediate reactions to *perceptions* relayed by the senses. Herding behavior, because it derives from the same primitive portion of the brain, is similarly unreflective and impulsive.

When are individuals' herding impulses most likely to be activated, making people join together to produce collective agreement in thought and action? Dependence upon the behavior of others most easily substitutes for rigorous reasoning when knowledge is lacking or logic irrelevant. In a realm such as investing, where so few are knowledgeable, or in a realm such as fads and fashion, where logic is inappropriate and the whole point is to impress other people, the tendency toward dependence is pervasive. Trends in such activities are steered not by the rational decisions of individual minds but by the peculiar collective sensibilities of the herd.

Herding Psychology and Financial Markets

In the 1920s, Pigou connected cooperative social dynamics to booms and depression. His idea is that individuals routinely correct their own errors of thought when operating alone but abdicate their responsibility to do so in matters that have strong social agreement, regardless of the egregiousness of the ideational error. In Pigou's words,

> Apart altogether from the financial ties by which different business-men are bound together, there exists among them a certain measure of *psychological interdependence*. A change of tone in one part of the business world diffuses itself, *in a quite unreasoning manner,* over other and wholly disconnected parts. (Vittachi & Faber, 1998)

"Wall Street" certainly shares aspects of a crowd, and there is abundant evidence that herding behavior exists among stock market participants. Myriad measures of market optimism and pessimism[4] show that in the aggregate, such sentiments among both the public and financial professionals wax and wane concurrently with the trend and level of the market. This tendency is not simply fairly common; it is ubiquitous. Most people get virtually all of their ideas about financial markets from other people, through newspapers, television, tipsters and analysts, without checking a thing. They think, "Who am I to check? These other people are supposed to be experts." Many people are emotionally dependent upon the ticker tape, which simply reports the aggregate short-term decision-making of others. This dependence is nearly universal, even among long-term investors. They are driven to follow the herd because they do not have firsthand knowledge adequate to form an independent conviction, which makes them seek wisdom in numbers. The unconscious says: You have too little basis upon which to exercise reason; your only alternative is to assume that the herd knows where it's going. When a crowd is in command, participating individuals appear rational on the outside, but inside their impulses and emotions are in control.

Smith, Suchanek and Williams [1988] conducted sixty laboratory market simulations using as few as a dozen volunteers, typically economics students but in some experiments businessmen. The subjects received the same perfect knowledge of coming dividend prospects and then an actual declared dividend at the end of the simulated trading day, which could vary more or less randomly but which would average a certain amount. Despite this ideal environment of perfect knowledge, *the subjects in these experiments repeatedly created a boom-and-bust market profile.* The extremity of that profile was a function of the participants' lack of experience in the speculative arena. Head research economist Vernon L. Smith came to this conclusion: "Experienced subjects frequently produce a market bubble, but the likelihood is smaller than for inexperienced subjects. When the same group returns for a third market, the bubble disappears." In the real world, "these bubbles and crashes would be a lot less likely if the same traders were in the market all the time" (Bishop, 1987), but novices are always entering the market. While these experiments were conducted as if participants could actually possess true knowledge of coming events and so-called fundamental value, no such knowledge is available in the real world. The fact that participants create a boom–bust pattern *anyway* is overwhelming evidence of the power of the herding impulse.

The lower graph in Figure 1 shows the real-world result of the public's impulse to herd. As you can see, the general investing population commits more money to the market as it rises and less as it falls, behavior opposite from that which would generate profits.

It is not only novices and individual investors who fall in line. It is a lesser-known fact that the vast majority of professionals herd just like the naïve majority. The middle graph in Figure 1 shows the percentage of cash held at institutions. As you can see, this data series moves roughly together with the S&P 500 Composite index, showing that institutional portfolio managers herd in the market's direction for the most part right along with the public. [The charts in Figure 1 are updated in Figure 8 of Chapter 12 and Figure 4 of Chapter 17.]

Apparent expressions of cold reason by professional stock analysts follow herding patterns as well. Finance professor Robert Olsen [1996] conducted a study of 4,000 corporate earnings estimates by company analysts and reached this conclusion:

> Experts' earnings predictions exhibit positive bias and disappointing accuracy. These shortcomings are usually attributed to some combination of incomplete knowledge, incompetence, and/or misrepresentation. This article suggests that the human desire for consensus leads to herding behavior among earnings forecasters.

In that paper, Olsen showed that the greater the difficulty in forecasting earnings per share, which is a source of stress, *the more analysts' herding behavior increases.* Equally important, the more their herding behavior increases, *the greater the bias in their earnings estimates.* The greater an aggregate bias becomes, the less accurate are the aggregate forecasts. This is a self-reinforcing system with failure the motivator of further failure [and

Evidence of Herding Behavior in Stock Market Activity

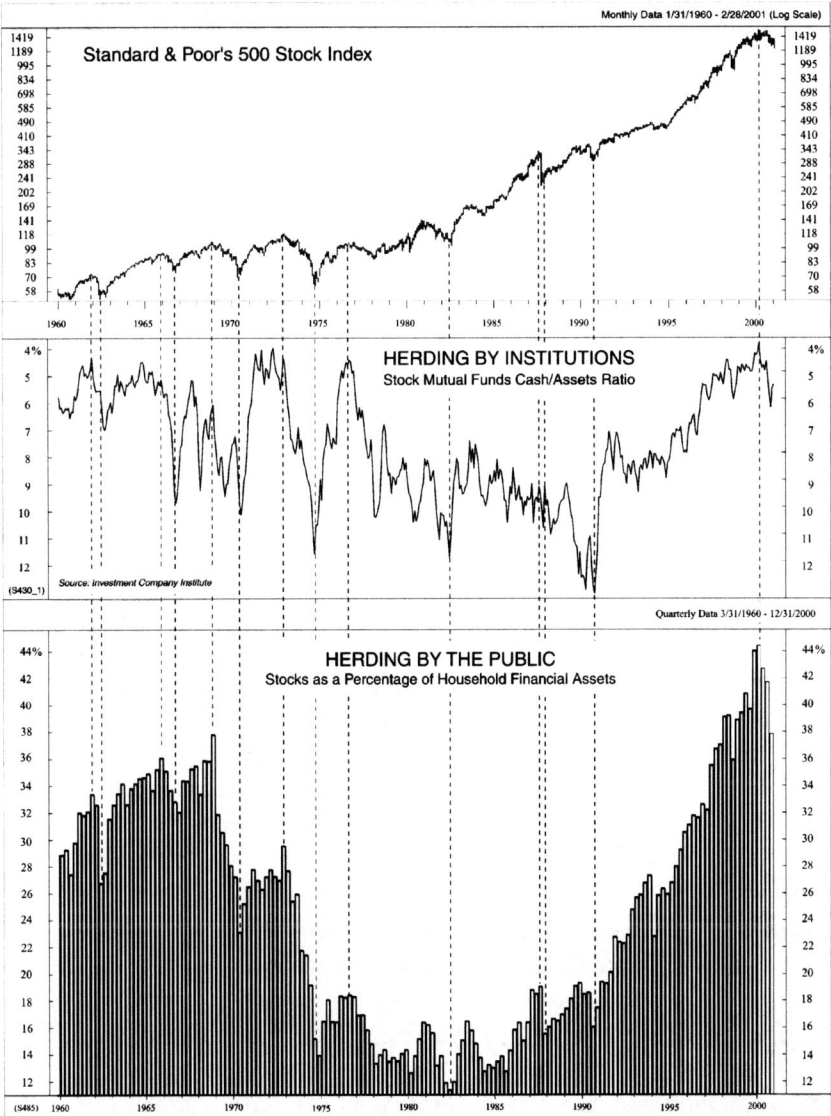

Monthly Data 1/31/1960 - 2/28/2001 (Log Scale)

Standard & Poor's 500 Stock Index

HERDING BY INSTITUTIONS
Stock Mutual Funds Cash/Assets Ratio

Source: Investment Company Institute

(S430_1)

Quarterly Data 3/31/1960 - 12/31/2000

HERDING BY THE PUBLIC
Stocks as a Percentage of Household Financial Assets

(S485)

chart courtesy Ned Davis Research

Figure 1

herding the motivator of further herding]. Available records (see Figure 7 in Chapter 17 and Figure 1 in Chapter 21) show that professional corporate analysts' opinions track the trend of the market, also in precisely the opposite fashion from that which would generate profits.

The reason forecasters' inaccuracy worsens with herding is that the net valuation of the stock market is the *result* of herding. To forecast on the basis of the current sentiments of the herd is to "forecast" the present mood, not future events. Success is simply a matter of whether the present mood maintains, which it usually does not.

How can seemingly rational professionals be so utterly seduced by the opinion of their peers to the effect that they will not only hold, but also *change* opinions collectively? MacLean [1990] explained, "the limbic system has the capacity to generate out-of-context, affective feelings of conviction that we attach to our beliefs *regardless of whether they are true or false.*" In other words, the neocortex is functionally disassociated from the limbic system. This means not only that feelings of conviction may attach to utterly contradictory ideas in different people, but also that they can do so *in the same person at different times.* In other words, a person may hold *opposite views* with equally intense emotion, depending upon the demands of survival perceived by the primitive portions of the brain. This fact relates directly to the behavior of financial market participants, who can be flushed with confidence one day and in a state of utter panic the next. As Robert Schiller put it in a *New York Times* article in 1989, "You would think enlightened people would not have firm opinions" about markets, "but they do, *and it changes all the time.*" (Passell) In each case, they are fully capable of explaining their new conviction, all such utterances being simply (yet sometimes superficially brilliant) rationalizations obediently generated by the neocortex. As market analyst Paul Macrae Montgomery [1991] explained, "to the limbic system, the phrase 'net present value of future cash flows' is meaningless because its *only sense of time is now and only value is pleasure or relief from stress.*" To relieve that stress without cognitive dissonance, the neocortex must generate "reasons" for a person's action, which justify the attendant emotional imperative. Throughout the herding process, whether the markets are real or simulated, and whether the participants are novices or professionals, the conviction of the *rightness* of stock valuation at each price level is powerful, emotional and impervious to argument.

Emotional Stress as the Limbic System's Herding Motivator

Falling into line with others for self-preservation involves not only the pursuit of positive values but also the avoidance of negative values, in which case the emotions reinforcing herding behavior are even stronger. Reptiles and birds harass strangers. A flock of poultry will peck to death any individual bird that has wounds or blemishes. Likewise, humans can be a threat to each other if there are perceived differences between them. It is an advantage to survival, then, to *avoid rejection by revealing your sameness.* D.C. Gajdusek [1970] researched a long-hidden Stone Age tribe that had never seen Western people and soon noticed that they mimicked his behavior; whenever he scratched his head or put his hand on his hip, the whole tribe did the same thing. Wrote MacLean, "It has been suggested that *such imitation may have some protective value by signifying, 'I am like you.'*" He added, "This form of behavior is phylogenetically *deeply ingrained.*" Thus, another advantage of herding behavior is the avoidance of seeming difference in order to defuse an excuse to attack.

This tendency toward mimicry is hardly confined to Stone Age tribes. Psychology professor Irving Janis [1972], after studying the dynamics of group decision making in the modern political setting, concluded, "In general, the greater the number of those in the decision maker's social network who are aware of the decision, the more powerful the incentive to avoid the social disapproval that might result from a reversal." What's more, "The greater the commitment to a prior decision, the greater the anticipated utilitarian losses, social disapproval and self-disapproval from failing to continue the present course of action and hence a greater degree of stress."

That is why, in financial markets, when the best time to buy or sell is at hand, *even the person who thinks he should take action experiences a strong psychological pressure to refrain from doing so.* He thinks, if only half consciously, "When my neighbor or advisor or friend thinks it's a good idea, then I'll do it, too. If I do it now, and I'm wrong, they will all call me a dope, *and I'll be the only dope.* I'll be singled out for ridicule, which is not only agonizing but dangerous." Pressure from, and influence by, peers, then, is at least one reason why most people cannot bring themselves to change from a bullish to bearish orientation or vice versa if to do so would go against the ideas of their associates and contacts. It also explains why a market or other social trend can continue for a long, long time and why financial valuations can become so extreme as to appear outrageous to those who believe that people ought to base their decisions rationally upon some calculable fundamental value.

The discomfort of being alone in one's convictions is so great that it involves physical reactions. "Emotional mentation," said MacLean, "represents the only form of psychological experience that, *by itself,* may induce pronounced autonomic activity" such as sweating, twitching, flushing, muscle tightening and hair standing on end. A person's reaction just *thinking* about taking an action apart from the herd can produce tenseness or even nausea. One knows from experience that anyone who shares a prevailing majority opinion on any subject, particularly one that is intensely attended by the emotions of the limbic system (such as politics, religion, wealth or sex), is treated with the respect due his obvious intelligence and morality. One who utters an opposing opinion is immediately punished by a chorus of deprecating smiles, cackling, mooing, snorting, nipping or outright hostility. It may sound funny, but if you are not used to verbal viciousness or rejection by the group, they are painful experiences, and most people cannot abide either.

Emotionally removed historians sometimes decry the lack of prescience among a population prior to a long-ago financial crisis or the lack of vocal critics in countries that are taken over by fascists, communists, inquisitors or witch-burners. Yet unless one is there, it is nearly impossible to imagine the social pressure to go along with the trend of the day. In many political and religious social settings, for example, "I am not like you" can mean death. The limbic system bluntly assumes that all expressions of "I am not like you" are infused with danger. Thus, herding and mimicking are preservative behavior. They are powerful because they are impelled, regardless of reasoning, by a primitive system of mentation that, however uninformed, is trying to save your life. In many cases, it does just that.

Unfortunately for humans in modern times, there are important exceptions to that benefit. Herding behavior is counterproductive to success in the world of modern financial speculation. If a financial market is soaring or crashing, the limbic system senses an opportunity or a threat and orders you to join the herd so that your chances for success or survival will improve. The limbic system produces emotions that support those impulses, including hope, euphoria, caution and panic. The actions thus impelled lead one inevitably to the *opposite* of survival and success, which is why the vast majority of people lose when they speculate.[5] In a great number of situations, hoping and herding can contribute to your well-being. Not in financial markets. In many cases, panicking and fleeing when others do cuts your risk. Not in financial markets. Moreover, because impulses and emotions result from rigid, "hard wired" thought processes, repeated failure in speculation and the attendant agony usually do little to deter the behavior.

From Individuals to Aggregates

We may not characterize these primitive impulses and emotions as rational, as they operate independently of reason. Yet neither may we label them irrational, because they have a purpose, no matter how ill applied in modern life. When the unconscious mind operates, it could hardly do so randomly, as that would mean no thought at all. It must operate in patterns peculiar to it. This is clearly the case among speculators, whose impulses produce the same patterns of aggregate behavior over and over. Can we link such patterns in individuals to the formation of a super-organic collective pattern? There is evidence to support this hypothesis as well.

Sornette and Johansen [1997] specifically connected the stock market to the primitive mentation of animals, including their occasional collective mentation: "Instead of the usual interpretation of the efficient market hypothesis in which traders extract and incorporate consciously (by their action) all information contained in market prices, we propose that the market as a whole can exhibit an 'emergent' behavior not shared by any of its constituent[s]. In other words, *we have in mind the process of the emergence of intelligent behavior at a macroscopic scale that individuals at the microscopic scale have no idea of.*" Biologists have made similar analogies with respect to ant colonies, bee swarms and other animal populations.

[I disavow this paragraph as originally written; some fixes are in brackets.—RP] To form such "emergent" behavior, individuals' impulses to herd must [both contribute and] relate to [subliminal] signals from the social environment Since all participants in a particular social setting share the same [social] environment, the combination of like minds produces global patterns of interactive dynamics in a social setting. This is particularly true of financial markets, where participants hear the same news [a better phrase: interact socially] and watch [should read: both generate and observe] the same price quotations, thus [issuing and] receiving substantially identical signals. Since the participants themselves generate many [actually all] of the signals [unconsciously], the result is a feedback loop of [subliminal] information and impulsivity. This process generates [shared moods and therefore] the trends and patterns of prices in financial markets.

The essential engine of the process is the mass interaction of numerous rigid, unreasoning basal ganglia and limbic systems. We may thus conclude that aggregate human interpersonal dynamics, and therefore the subset of speculative financial market dynamics, will remain immutable unless and until there evolves a change in the operation of the triune brain that constitutes the human mind.

NOTES

[1] [This paper derives substantially from Chapter 8 of *The Wave Principle of Human Social Behavior*.]

[2] [This idea differs from the idea of a positive feedback loop between social mood and the direction of the stock market, which socionomic theory rejects. Neither is my point that *acting* with the herd to buy or sell increases the feeling of stress, since in fact it provides a feeling of relief. The point here is that herding in financial markets tends to beget more herding.—RP]

[3] I would like to thank Paul Macrae Montgomery of *Universal Economics* for alerting me to MacLean's *The Triune Brain in Evolution* (1990). [While later research has challenged some specific aspects of MacLean's model—such as reptilian and mammalian origins of parts of the human brain—his basic description of an evolved brain and the several loci of primitive, unconscious impulses vs. logical thought has proved to be durable and useful. See Figure 15 of Chapter 13 for a visual depiction of these observations.—RP]

[4] Such measures include put and call volume ratios, cash holdings by institutions, index futures premiums, the activity of margined investors, and reports of market opinion from brokers, traders, newsletter writers and investors.

[5] There is a myth, held by nearly all people outside of back-office employees of brokerage firms and the IRS, that many people do well in financial speculation. Actually, almost everyone loses at the game eventually. The head of a futures brokerage firm once confided to me that never in the firm's history had customers in the aggregate had a winning year. Even in the stock market, when the public or even most professionals win, it is a temporary, albeit sometimes prolonged, phenomenon. The next big bear market usually wipes them out if they live long enough, and if they do not, it wipes out their successors. This is true regardless of today's accepted wisdom that the stock market always goes to new highs eventually. Aside from the fact that this very conviction is false (where was the Roman stock market during the Dark Ages?), what counts is *when* people act, and that is what ruins them.

REFERENCES

Bishop, Jerry E. "Stock Market Experiment Suggests Inevitability of Booms and Busts." *Wall Street Journal,* (November 17, 1987), p. 31.

Gajdusek, D.C. "Physiological And Psychological Characteristics of Stone Age Man." *Symposium on Biological Bases of Human Behavior, Eng. Sci.* 33, (1970), pp. 26–33, 56–62.

Janis, Irving L. *Victims of Groupthink.* Boston: Houghton Mifflin, 1972.

LeDoux, J.E. "Cognitive–Emotional Interactions in the Brain." *Cognition and Emotion,* 3, (1989), pp. 267–289.

MacLean, P. *The Triune Brain in Evolution: Role in Paleocerebral Functions.* New York: Plenum Press, 1990.

Montgomery, Paul Macrae. Speech. "Stocks and the Irrational: Possible Sub-Cortical Influences on Contemporary Equity Market Pricing." September 19, 1991.

Montgomery, Paul Macrae. Speech. "Capital Markets and the Irrational: Possible Non-Cortical Influences on the Price Structure of Investments." September 13, 1992.

Olsen, R. "Implications of Herding Behavior" *Financial Analysts Journal,* July/August, 1996, pp. 37–41.

Passell, Peter. "Dow and Reason: Distant Cousins?" *The New York Times,* August 25, 1989.

Pigou, Arthur C. The Economics of Welfare. London: F. Cass, 1920. Pigou, Arthur C. *Industrial Fluctuations.* London: F. Cass, 1927.

Smith, Vernon L., Gerry L. Suchanek and Arlington W. Williams."Bubbles, Crashes, and Endogenous Expectations in Experimental Spot Asset Markets." *Econometrica,* 56, (1988), pp. 1119–1151.

Sornette, Didier, and Andres Johansen. "Large Financial Crashes." *Physica A—Statistical and Theoretical Physics,* eds. Capel, H.W., B. Mulder, H. E. Stanley, and C. Tsallis, 245, (1997).

Vittachi, Nury and Marc Faber. *Riding the Millennial Storm: Marc Faber's Path to Profit in the Financial Crisis.* New York: John Wiley & Sons, 1998.

Chapter 17

Financial Herding is Universal and Fractal

Robert R. Prechter

Figures 1 through 8 show that nearly all subsets of financial market participants herd, including individual investors, futures traders, financial advisors, hedge fund managers, mutual fund managers, corporate insiders, Wall Street analysts and even government agencies. Herding permeates the investment world.

It is widely known that professional money managers, in the aggregate, fail to beat the market. The result is not, as some theorists say, because the market moves randomly. It is because most professionals are herding, right along with other speculators. Figure 4 updates a chart from Chapter 16 showing that at good prices for buying stock, mutual fund managers have high levels of cash, and at good prices for selling, they have low levels of cash. This record confirms that they consistently do the opposite of what they should be doing for maximum return.

Hedge fund managers, thought to be the smartest of all investors, herd too, as shown in Figure 5. In 2015, more hedge funds closed than in any year since 2009. It came as a direct consequence of their managers having invested together on the wrong side of the same markets.

Most people would be surprised to find out that even corporate insiders herd. It may seem that "inside information" should give company managers an advantage in deciding when to engage in buybacks of their own company's stock. On the contrary, their misperceptions are the same as everyone else's. When the stock market goes up for a long time, corporate health factors strengthen, and when it goes down, they weaken. Insiders misinterpret these indications of their company's *present* health as being the same as its *prospects*. Whenever their stock gets expensive, they think it's cheap, because they feel optimistic about the company's future. At such times they also tend to have more cash on hand to spend on investment. When managers get *really* optimistic, they may direct the company to borrow money to

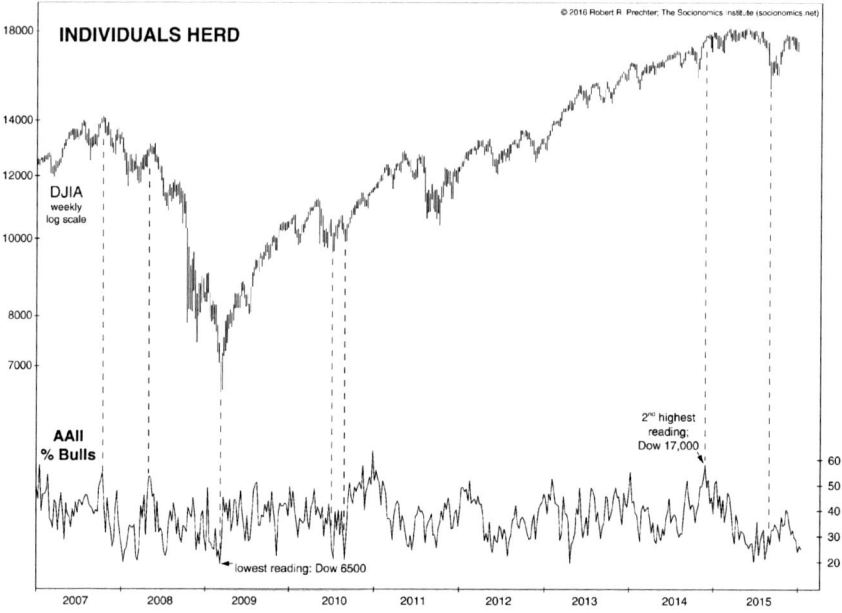

Figure 1

Figure 2

Figure 3

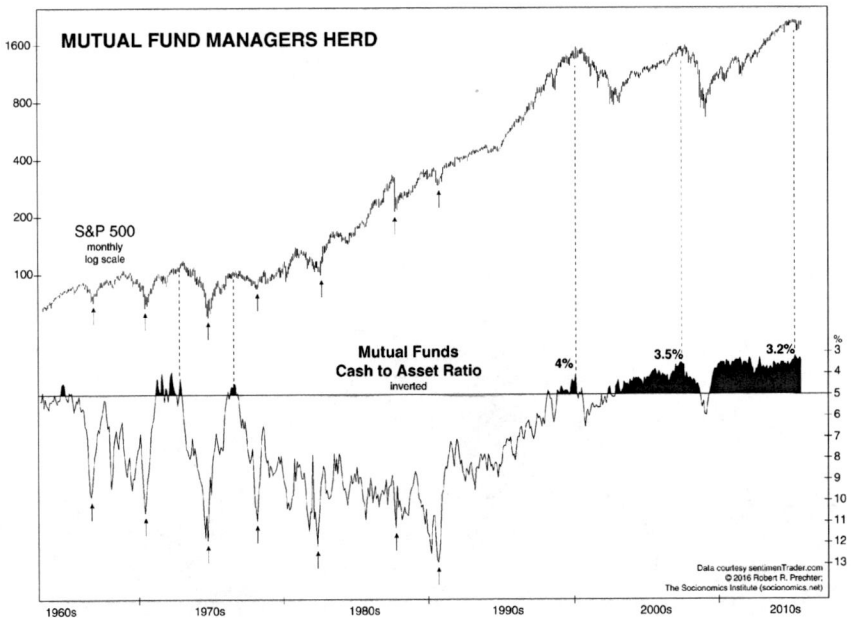

Figure 4

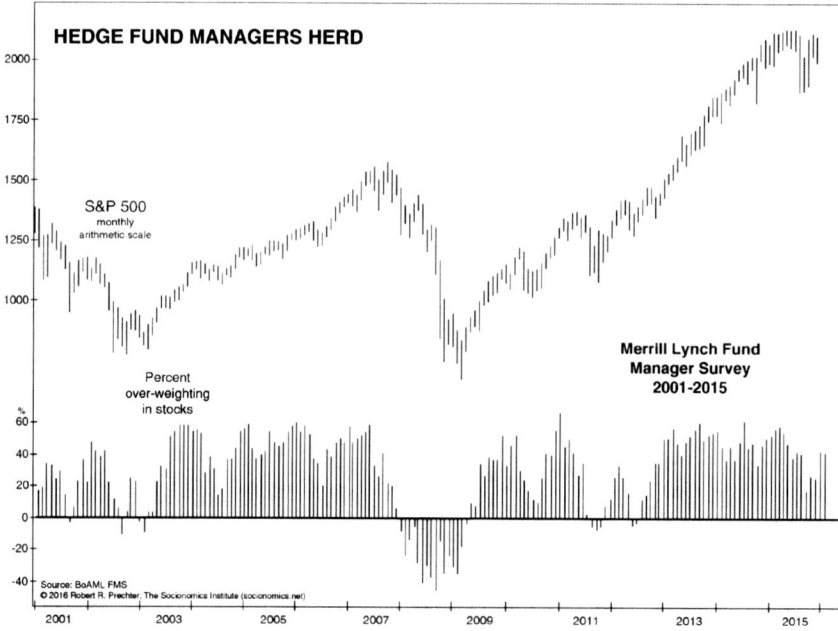

Figure 5

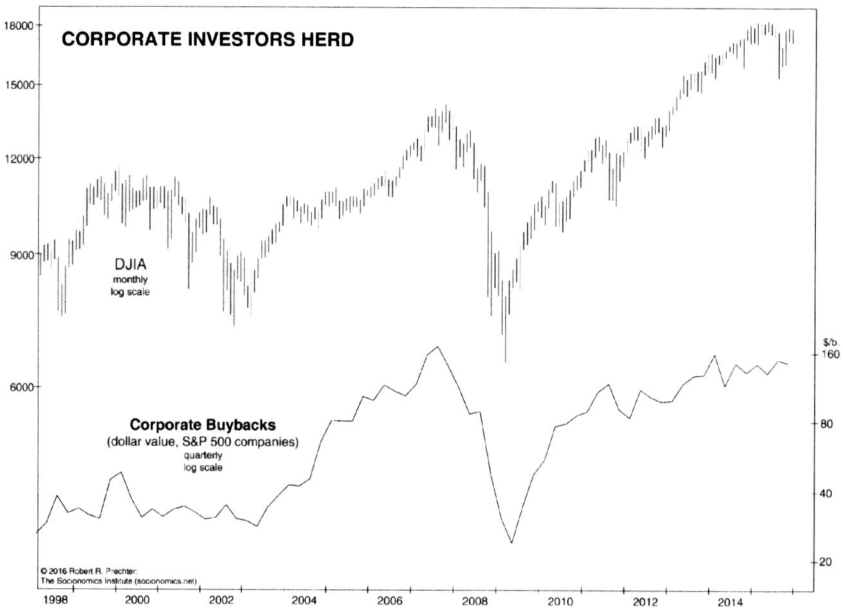

Figure 6

fund a stock-buyback program. This strategy has been standard practice in recent years. As Figure 6 shows, corporations buy back lots of stock near market tops and very little near market bottoms. If they did the opposite, they would thrive. They aren't rationally analyzing insider information; they're pre-rationally herding like all the other groups.

The waste of company cash in such endeavors, which could have gone into any number of better projects, is staggering. According to recent estimates,[1] corporations have lost 126 billion dollars investing in their own shares just from 2013 through 2015, even though the stock market was rising almost the whole time! As the S&P gained over 40%, corporations generated an estimated 15% loss on their buyback investments. That is a huge difference. These outsized losses are due primarily to two types of herding: on a company-by-company basis and on a timing basis. Managers of more flourishing companies are more prone to initiate buying programs, and they buy more stock near market highs of various degrees than near lows. Buyback programs can impoverish a company, as described in Chapter 12. Chapter 31 offers numerous additional examples of ways in which corporations act as a herd in expressing social mood.

Economists steeped in the mechanics paradigm of exogenous cause do not understand this dynamic. They think corporate buybacks should make a company's shares go up, and vice versa. A typical headline reads, "Bad sign: CEO's aren't buying stock in their companies."[2] A professor of accounting called that condition "a little disturbing," and a ranking university economist agreed, saying, "Clearly, it would be a favorable sign if insiders were actively buying their companies' stocks right now. The lack thereof is not good news." Examine Figure 6 and you will see that this sensible-sounding notion is exactly backwards.

A socionomist, in contrast, recognizes that trends in buybacks express social mood. Which interpretation is more useful? You tell me: The article just quoted is dated February 16, 2009. The stock market bottomed three weeks later, and shortly thereafter the economy joined it for one of the longest advances on record.

Figure 7 plots the average estimate for the year-ahead price per share of Apple Inc., as predicted monthly over the past ten years by analysts at 54 top Wall Street investment banks and brokerage firms. As the chart shows throughout its history, the average of their predictions is no more than the stock's present price plus a premium. When the stock price stays in an uptrend for more than a year, the forecasts catch up with prices and seem to be right for a while. At the turns, they are way off. The dashed line depicts analysts' forecasts against year-later prices so you can see how off the mark they are. These firms spend millions of dollars to pay analysts essentially to tell clients

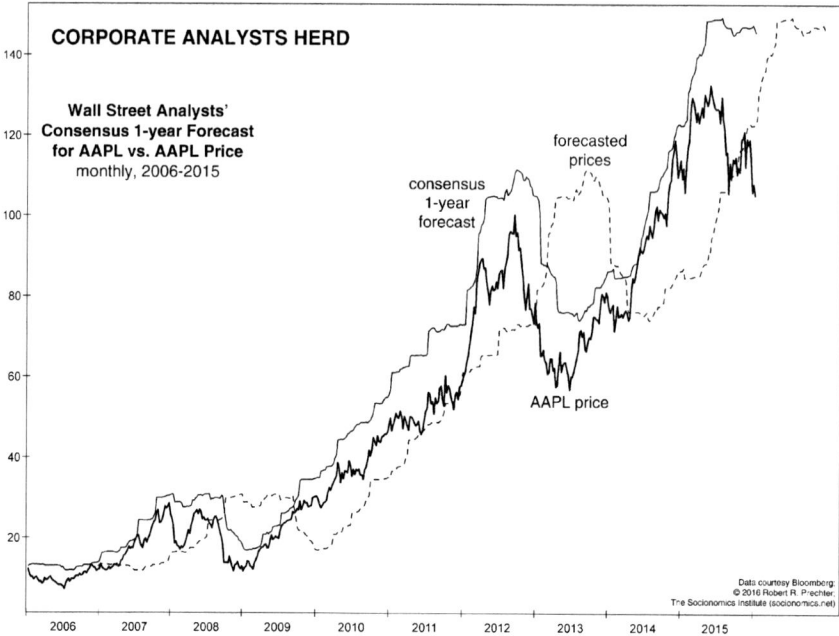

Figure 7

where the price of AAPL is now and to affirm that it will go up a few dollars in the coming year. This is a static stance, not informed predicting.

Governments aren't just part of the herd; they represent the herd. Government actions lag social mood substantially, because state institutions generally wait for a strong consensus to become motivated on an issue and then proceed slowly before finally taking action. A socionomic study by Nofsinger and Kim[3] from 2003 revealed that members of Congress, expressing the same extremes in social mood that speculators do, have passed lenient financial legislation near stock market tops and restrictive legislation near bottoms. Figure 8 updates the record.

Even behavioral economists who routinely warn against herding sometimes join the herd without realizing it. Professors at Harvard and Wharton figured out in 1998 how to use opt-out instead of opt-in criteria to manipulate employees into contributing to company-sponsored retirement plans and to maneuver them into buying stock funds instead of money market funds within them. They began implementing the idea in 1998 and published a paper on it in 2001.[4] No one would have recommended such a plan in 1974 or 1979, but after a quarter-century of rising stock prices, doing so seemed

GOVERNMENT REGULATORS HERD

The Socionomic Timing of
Major Investment
Legislation
DJIA
monthly range
log scale

Top Arrows: Expansive Legislation
Bottom Arrows: Restrictive Legislation

Financial Services
Regulatory Relief Act;
Pension Protection Act

Commodity Futures
Modernization Act

SEC Permits
"Crowd Funding"

* Financial Services
Modernization Act

Securities Litigation
Uniform Standards Act

Private Securities Litigation
Reform Act

Dodd-Frank
Wall Street
Reform Act

Public Company
Accounting Reform and
Investor Protection Act

Insider Trading and
Securities Fraud Enforcement Act

* Government agency
policy allows
commercial banks
to issue securities

Employee Retirement
Income Security Act

Securities Investor
Protection Act

Investment Company Act
and Investment Advisors Act

Banking Act and
Securities Exchange Act

* These laws combined commercial and investment banking.
They both occurred near the end of a Cycle degree wave V.
The law of 1999 repealed the Banking (Glass-Steagall) Act of 1933.

Data from Nofsinger and Kim (2003) and Peter Kendall
© 2016 Robert R. Prechter; The Socionomics Institute (socionomics.net)

Figure 8

perfectly sensible, even benevolent. Naturally, these techniques ended up encouraging novices to speculate in stocks at what turned out to be their most overvalued level in U.S. history in terms of dividend payout, the Dow/ gold ratio and other measures. The victims' immediate reward was a decade of negative returns. The professors' conviction that employees should own more stocks rested on the linear extrapolation of the past trend of stock prices. Even their conviction that funding a rule-laden retirement plan is better than not doing so was at least partially due to long term financial and political stability in the U.S. that may or may not continue.

By the time of the ensuing bull market peak, in 2007, paternalistic manipulation had morphed into plain force, initiated by government, promoted by investment firms, executed by companies and paid for by fees extracted directly from employees' accounts. On February 4, 2008, *The Wall Street Journal* reported on this development. I apologize for the length of this excerpt, but it is too entertaining to cut:

The Boss Lends a Hand

Encouraged by a new law, more employers are offering programs to help employees avoid investment blunders

Like many people, 24-year-old Erin Rendina didn't know quite what to do when it came to her 401(k) retirement plan, so she contributed—but did little else. For 14 months after she joined [her] company, the marketing assistant left her money parked in a "stable value fund," typically a safe but low-yielding investment option favored by investors nearing retirement.

But last August [2007], Ms. Rendina's 401(k) received an extreme makeover. Suddenly, she found her account spread among a diversified collection of six mutual funds, with 93% of her assets in stocks. Ms. Rendina didn't have a hand in any of this.

Her employer automatically made the changes for her—and increased her contribution to the plan—as part of a new effort to build retirement savings for employees who aren't doing it for themselves. [This company] is part of a wave of U.S. companies taking an activist role in 401(k)s and retirement planning.

Recent changes in federal law have limited potential liability from employers for advising employees and enrolling them in retirement plans, and companies are moving fast to take a more active role. Some companies are sending out alerts telling employees they're investing imprudently. Some are making financial advisers available, and offering one-on-one financial counseling for workers over the age of 55. Such hands-on help used to be considered "almost Big Brotherish," says [ ], director of 401(k) strategies at [a major broker] in San Francisco. Now it's viewed as "almost protective," she says.

The trend has been fueled largely by the Pension Protection Act [don't you love the titles they come up with?] of 2006, which is prodding U.S. employees to save for their futures as a way to reduce reliance on government subsidies in retirement. The law not only encourages employers to automatically enroll employees in retirement investment plans, but also to set their contribution amounts and help them decide which funds to select. The law limits employees' ability to sue their employers and plan administrators should that advice turn out to be bad.

Plan administrators, for their part, have been eager to get in on the advisory act, partly to cultivate relationships with workers who may elect to put their money elsewhere when they retire. [ ] says it has received a surge of calls from holders of these accounts since the recent market volatility began. "Many of these people have not had their money professionally managed or had access to investment advisers before," spokeswoman [ ] wrote in an email. "We let them know that we were monitoring the situation as well as their individual portfolios and reallocating if necessary." The company rebalances allocations as it sees fit.

Each employee in [ ]'s managed-account program pays an annual fee of as much as 0.40% of assets on top of the fees for the mutual funds in the participant's portfolio.

Some financial-services companies may have an inherent conflict in offering guidance if their 401(k) plans offer their own products. 11 of the 18 choices in the 401(k) are [ ]'s proprietary mutual funds. Two of four [of the] target-date funds offered rank in the bottom third of peers in returns over the past year and a third one ranks in the bottom half.

Unless they opt out, employees are automatically enrolled in the plan at an annual contribution of 3% of their pretax salaries. [The company] will automatically increase these contributions by one percentage point a year until the employee is contributing 12%. And unless they opt out, employees are enrolled in a managed account run by [ ].

Ms. Rendina, for one, likes having someone else take control. During the market's big sell-off in January, she did check her account. "Luckily, I've only taken a small hit to date," she says, adding that "as a result, I've placed my trust in [ ] that they will adjust my account allocations as needed."[5]

True to form, Congress passed its law—for which investment planning firms surely lobbied—in 2006, the very year of the all-time high in real estate, and the company finally took action on its employees' behalf in August 2007, a month after that year's high in the Dow Jones Composite Average and two months before the Dow and S&P peaked. Within just seventeen months, more than half the value of Ms. Rendina's retirement fund must have vanished. Considering that the plan's corporate administrator was already handling "a surge of calls" after "the big selloff" in January 2008, when it assuredly told callers not to panic, one can only imagine the heat of its phone lines in February and March 2009. Plan administrators, along with everyone else represented in Figures 1 through 8, have emotions, too, and any strategic reallocating they undertake is more likely to be timed to clients' detriment than to their advantage. This is not an insult; it's just the way it is.

Herding is manifest not only in the actions of buyers and sellers of investment items but also in the inaction of holders and non-holders. Some non-holders resist buying in an advance until their optimism becomes so intense they can't stand being out of the market. Some holders resist selling in a decline until their pessimism becomes so intense they can't stand being in the market. That's when their inaction turns to action. Their inaction was not an avoidance of herding; they were herding throughout the process.

As a corollary to this observation, financial advisors are almost always herding even when they advise against it. One of the commonest actions of herders is to deny a new trend in its early stages. At such times, seemingly sensible, cautionary advice not to "chase the rally" but to "sell the pop," or not to "join the panic" but to "buy the dip," reveals a misunderstanding of the intricate phenomenon of herding while simultaneously offering an example of it.

Advisors almost never recognize that rising prices are due to herding. They are happy to herd with a trend all the way up but caution against herding when prices turn down. This selectivity is non-rational. When market advisors recommend resisting the urge to sell in a down market, they can nevertheless sound sophisticated: "The selloff is a manifestation of herding behavior. Avoid following the herd. Use your independent, rational mind to combat the impulse to sell your stocks. Steel yourself against such unconscious fears and buy more. Stay focused on the long term." In fact, these advisors are telling everyone to do exactly what the majority has done throughout recorded time in the early stages of a bear market. The unison of voices proves the herding, and the larger, louder and more confident the chorus the deeper the eventual bear market tends to be.

Believing in external causality in finance dooms people to herd even when they are scientifically informed and dead-set against succumbing to the temptation. One accomplished neuroeconomist, echoing a widely shared opinion of the time, told a reporter[6] that the stock market decline up to late September 2008 was an illogical overreaction due to a herding mentality among investors (see Chapter 19 for a discussion of the over-reaction claim) and scolded a colleague for having sold stocks earlier. He said he had bought stocks because he perceived no evidence indicating an approaching depression. As related in Chapter 5, mainstream economists all agreed there was no evidence of an approaching depression, which is why the Great Recession blindsided them. The market started panicking two trading days later and suffered an additional 40% drubbing over the next six months. Investors who heeded the advice to avoid herding and hold onto their stocks were made highly vulnerable to capitulating with the herd at much lower prices.

Ironically, a later study by fellow neuroscientists examined reasons why "unrealistic optimism is maintained in the face of reality" and cited "an unrealistic assessment of financial risk" as a "contributing factor to the 2008 global economic collapse."[7] They added that learning can mitigate such errors. Each of the two neuroeconomic admonitions against human frailty cited here sounds wise when applied to finance, but like most trading adages—such as "Let profits run" and "You can't go broke taking a profit"— they are contradictory. "Don't panic with the herd" means *hold*, and "Don't be unrealistically optimistic" means *sell*. Intellectual independence is a tricky business.

It may be disappointing to learn that even trying to avoid herding rarely works out well. On the other hand, it is an improvement over the norm, since not realizing there is a herd never works out well.

As shown here, hard data are available on the activities of many subsets of financial market participants. Even when they are lacking, anecdotal evidence suggests that herding and mood-sharing, as noted in Chapter 12, permeate nearly every proposed qualitative dichotomy of speculators, including long term investors vs. short term traders, value investors vs. momentum investors, trend followers vs. contrarians, professionals vs. novices, fundamentalists vs. technicians, smart money vs. dumb money and scientists vs. laymen. Elliott wave analysts are subject to moods and herding, too. Wave interpretation involves substantial uncertainty, a necessary precondition of herding. Financial market participants may herd at different times, in different ways and to greater or lesser degrees, but nearly all of them do it.

Vernon Smith's 1988 study (see Chapter 16) showed that speculators herd even in the lab. Needless to say, the prodigious evidence of pre-rational herding in both the lab and real life is far from what mechanistic theories based on exogenous cause and rational reaction say should happen.

Herding Leads to Losses

When a bull market is raging and market chatter is at elevated volume, it may seem that many people are getting rich in the market. But one cannot take such a conclusion to the bank until a full cycle has played out. Even people who make money in a bull market tend to lose it by the end of the ensuing bear. At the end of March 2009, reports showed that a number of the best-performing fund managers during the stock market advance of 2002-2007 had become among the worst-performing managers during the decline of 2007-2009. Sometimes temporary outperformance is due simply to the ownership of high-beta investments or the use of leverage.

As Don Guyon's 1917 book first reported (see Chapter 15), investors are timid traders early in a bull market and confident long term holders at the peak. This is exactly how Isaac Newton behaved during the South Sea Bubble. He invested a little bit early in the trend and "wisely" took a small profit. Watching the trend continue, he finally bet heavily and "wisely" held on for the long run. He eventually sold out at a near-total loss. In the long run, *all* herders lose money.

Here is an even more terrible secret: Most investors don't make money even within a bull market. Edward Wolff's study (cited in Chapter 15) demonstrated this fact in no uncertain terms. How is it remotely possible that typical investors—most of whom never sell short—consistently lose money during huge bull markets? The answer is: because herding is fractal.

Herding Is Fractal

Read this report from *The Wall Street Journal*, dated December 31, 2009, the last day of the 2000s:

The decade's best performing U.S. diversified stock mutual fund [is] Ken Heebner's $3.7 billion CGM Focus Fund, which rose 18.2% annually and outpaced its closest rival by more than three percentage points.[8]

That's a gain of 18.2% annually, *compounded*, an amazing performance for a mutual fund, especially for a decade in which the S&P lost value.

Question: How much money did investors in this fund make over the full ten years?

Figure 9 shows the growth of an initial $100,000 investment in the CGM Focus Fund based on annual average growth of 18.2%. It more than quintupled in value to $532,000.

But this table does not answer the question I asked. It shows the growth of money in the fund, but I asked, "How

Growth of Investment over 10 Years	
Year	$100,000
1	$118,200
2	$139,712
3	$165,140
4	$195,195
5	$230,721
6	$272,712
7	$322,346
8	$381,013
9	$450,357
10	$532,322

Figure 9

much money did investors in this fund make?" The article provides the answer:

> The typical CGM Focus shareholder lost 11% annually in the 10 years ending Nov. 30, according to investment research firm MorningStar Inc.

Say what? Somehow, the experience of investors in the top-performing mutual fund was *an 11% annual loss, compounded.* Over the ten-year period during which the value of the fund was soaring, the average investor in CGM Focus Fund turned $100,000 into $31,200, for a loss of 68.8%. As depicted in Figure 10, this is *94% less* than the growth of money in the fund. How can this be? The answer is: *herding.* As the article explained,

Actual Comparative Returns over 10 Years

Year	Fund Value	Avg. Investor's Account
0	$100,000	$100,000
1	$118,200	$89,000
2	$139,712	$79,210
3	$165,140	$70,496
4	$195,195	$62,742
5	$230,721	$55,840
6	$272,712	$49,698
7	$322,346	$44,231
8	$381,013	$39,365
9	$450,357	$35,035
10	$532,322	$31,181

94% less ◄

Figure 10

> These investor returns incorporate the effect of cash flowing in and out of the fund. Shareholders often buy a fund after it has had a strong run and sell as it hits bottom.

As this history shows, investors and traders are herding non-rationally *all the time.* They are buying high and selling low, over and over again, at all degrees of fluctuation, whether day by day or long term. Some funds allow intraday trading, for speculators who want to lose money even faster.

Let's extrapolate this 10-year experience over an average lifetime of speculating, which we will estimate at 30 years. Figure 11 shows that if investors were to buy and sell an identically performing fund for 30 years, the fund would be up 150 times in value, turning $100,000 into $15 million, while the average investor's $100,000 would become $3,000, for a loss of 97%. The difference is 5,000 times; the amount left over is 99.98% less than it would have been for an untouched initial investment.

Projected Returns over 30 Years

Year	Fund Value	Avg. Investor's Account	Year	Fund Value	Avg. Investor's Account
0	$100,000	$100,000			
1	$118,200	$89,000	16	$14,517,09	$15,496
2	$139,712	$79,210	17	$1,715,920	$13,792
3	$165,140	$70,496	18	$2,028,217	$12,275
4	$195,195	$62,742	19	$2,397,353	$10,924
5	$230,721	$55,840	20	$2,833,671	$9,723
6	$272,712	$49,698	21	$3,349,399	$8,653
7	$322,346	$44,231	22	$3,958,990	$7,701
8	$381,013	$39,365	23	$4,679,527	$6,854
9	$450,357	$35,035	24	$5,531,201	$6,100
10	$532,322	$31,181	25	$6,537,879	$5,429
11	$629,205	$27,751	26	$7,727,773	$4,832
12	$743,720	$24,699	27	$9,134,228	$4,300
13	$879,077	$21,982	28	$10,796,658	$3,827
14	$1,039,069	$19,564	29	$12,761,649	$3,406
15	$1,228,180	$17,412	30	$15,084,270	$3,031

99.98% less ←

Figure 11

Now consider the fact that CGM Focus Fund was the best performing fund of that decade! How did investors in other funds do? Figure 12 shows the performance of the period's top and bottom funds. Investors in Frontier MicroCap Fund lost 35.6% per year, compounded, *if they did not touch the money.* If they traded the fund, no doubt their losses were even greater.

	Fund	Category	10-year annualized total return
	The Best- and Worst-Performing U.S. Diversified Stock Mutual Funds, 2000-2009		
Best	CGM Focus	Large cap growth	+18.2% ←
Worst	Frontier MicroCap	Small cap blend	-35.6% ←

Source: Morningstar   Data through Dec. 29, 2009. Excludes leveraged funds.

Figure 12

Financial markets are not a zero-sum game, because speculators have to pay transaction costs, which drain money from accounts. Many advocates for investing say that in the long run stock prices go up, making it a positive-sum game. But in actuality every stock could, and eventually does, go to zero. To make investing work, you have to buy and sell. Regardless, these facts don't much matter. Speculators typically rack up losses far larger than transaction costs and well before the stocks they own go to zero.

Opposed Transactors are Both Herding

Not every financial herder buys on up—or sells on down—moments, hours, days, weeks, months or years in the market. Such cannot be the case, because for every buyer at a higher price there is a seller on the other side of the trade, and for every seller at a lower price there is a buyer on the other side of the trade.

Some bubble theorists have been unable to reconcile the role of the seller in each transaction at a higher price during a rising market. The seller, they muse, must not be herding, because after all he is selling, not buying. But of course the seller is herding, because—as explained in Chapter 13— the process of propelling prices higher requires cooperating participants on both sides of the transaction to agree on the higher price. The seller had waited for the present price because he was more bullish than those who sold before him at lower prices. At the moment of each higher transaction, the buyer is slightly more optimistic than the seller, but, by agreeing on the higher price, both transactors expresses more optimism than the *preceding* buyer and seller at the lower price. Each of these transactors is then immediately free to return to the marketplace and agree, on *either side* of future transactions, upon higher prices still.

Financial "Learning" is a Mirage

Actual learning about the physical world differs utterly from apparent learning in the ethereal world of financial markets. People learn from past experience that if a river flows downhill today, it is likely to flow downhill tomorrow. This learning is real, because it is objective; it is economic, because it serves to enhance survival and success; and it is dependable, because it is based on physical laws. Changes in aggregate financial opinion, however, only *seem* to involve learning. They are in fact fluid rationalizations regulated subjectively by mood-sharing and herding impulses. It may appear that speculators become bullish after a long market rise because they have "learned" that the trend is up, and vice versa. But an extended past trend is never the reason for their opinion, whatever they might say; their positive or negative mood is the reason. When speculators resort to citing a past trend as a reason for its continuation, they are merely offering an impulsive and temporary rationalization for their optimism or pessimism. At whatever degrees of trend speculators are motivated, it takes a proportional shift in social mood in the opposite direction to prompt the rationalization process to justify a reversal of their former opinion. Unlike real learning, such rationalizations are subjective, undependable and counterproductive to success. They derive not from the laws of physics but of socionomics. If speculators in the aggregate ever did learn anything, they would abandon their naïve default to linear extrapolation as they figured out that markets fluctuate. Yet the bias persists, helping to keep speculators exquisitely wrong at all degrees of trend. Figure 1 of Chapter 21 depicts this mental default visually.

One of my favorite headlines, from 2005, is "Investors Have Learned Not to Panic."[9] Mood had waxed positive for the previous fifteen years, so the market's trend had been mostly up, and setbacks had been moderate. It may have seemed that investors had learned not to panic, but we know this claim to be false, because three years later they panicked. The Elliott wave form required it. Learning was not involved; it only appeared to be involved.

If herding, rationalization and social-mood ignorance were instantly deadly in financial settings, humans would have evolved away from these traits. But their negative effects tend to be spread over time. This saving grace is also a tragic curse, as it allows most people to repeat their financial experiences without learning anything. Learning is possible once one understands socionomic causality, but in that case one is engaged not in subjective, mood-regulated, apparent learning but in objective, non-mood-influenced, reality learning, which puts it on an entirely different plane.

A Tapestry of Herding

Nearly all speculators' actions fit into the collective herding dynamic. Only their styles of herding differ, based on their levels of sophistication. A novice may buy immediately as a market is rising, whereas a more seasoned trader might pride himself on waiting for pullbacks to buy. His moods and rationalization still ruin him: A positive trend in mood persists until he convinces himself the future trend is up, so he waits for a pullback to buy. The market pulls back. He buys. The market bounces briefly, making him feel temporarily right, and then continues lower. Mood eventually reaches a point at which he becomes convinced that the future trend is down, so he sells his position and waits for a bounce to sell short. The market bounces. He sells short. The market slips downward briefly, making him feel temporarily right, and then continues higher. And so it goes. Each time his mood induces him to perceive a new trend, he joins it, in a disciplined way on a countertrend move, only to find that the trend has changed. An even more sophisticated speculator might train himself always to sell into extended rallies and buy into extended declines. But he is still at the market's mercy. When a trend eventually continues past his entry point, losses will mount until he capitulates. Since sophistication levels vary, herding behavior goes on at every degree of fluctuation, in both directions, throughout the progress of a trend.

Even the most talented investors are ultimately at the mercy of the market. Speculators have famously shorted gambling stocks, tech stocks or the market as a whole, only to find that the trend they had bet against was so persistent that they had no choice but to cover their shorts—that is, to join the herd by buying into an advance—or go bankrupt.

Speculators can't sidestep the herd by using stops, either. On the contrary, stops are orders to buy or sell into the heat of market moves and thus to join the herd time and again. In the context of STF, stops designate prices at which speculators have to admit the herd beat them.

Figures 13 through 16 suggest templates for how various types of speculators behave. I put them together based on observation and introspection. All these behavioral styles weave together to form the tapestry of the herding process.

Observe that all of the strategically minded speculators depicted in Figures 14, 15 and 16 are profitable at times. Yet, try as they might, they

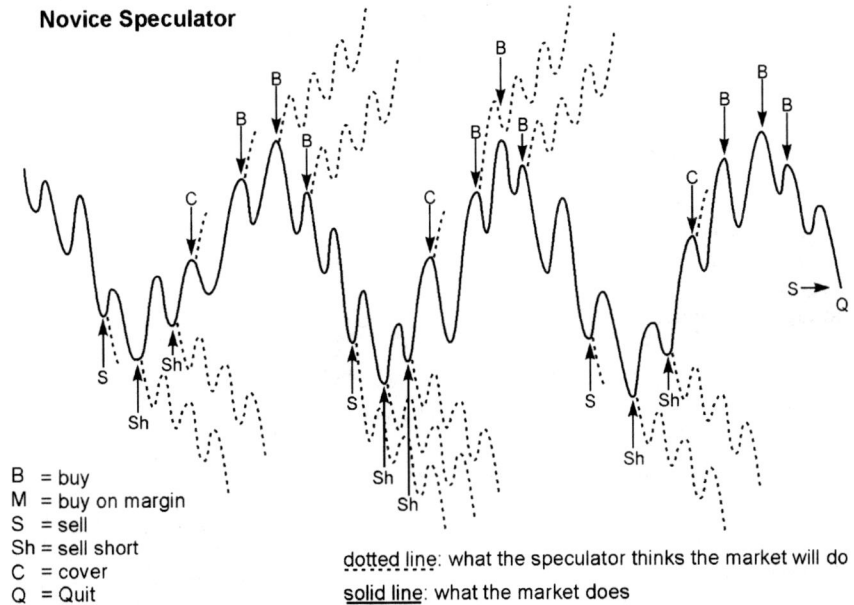

Novice Speculator

B = buy
M = buy on margin
S = sell
Sh = sell short
C = cover
Q = Quit

dotted line: what the speculator thinks the market will do
solid line: what the market does

Figure 13

Seasoned Speculator

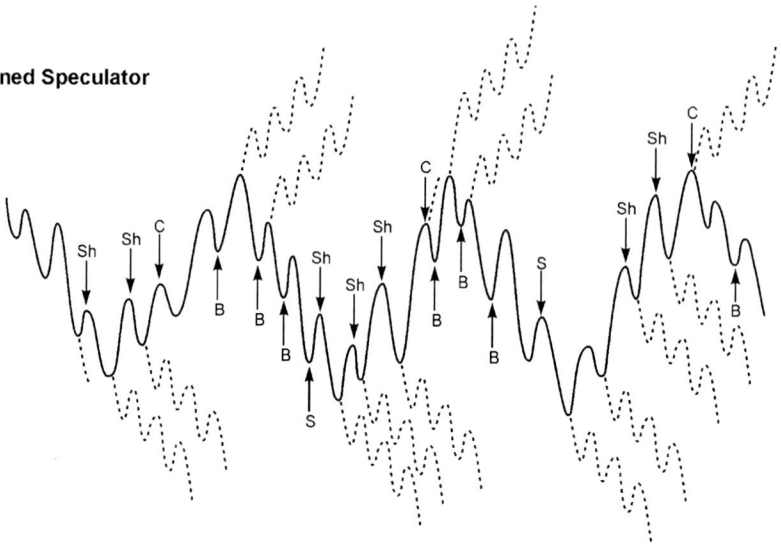

Figure 14

Sophisticated Speculator

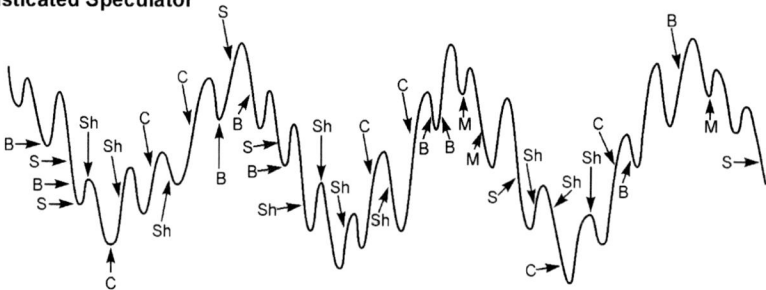

Figure 15

Contrarian Speculator

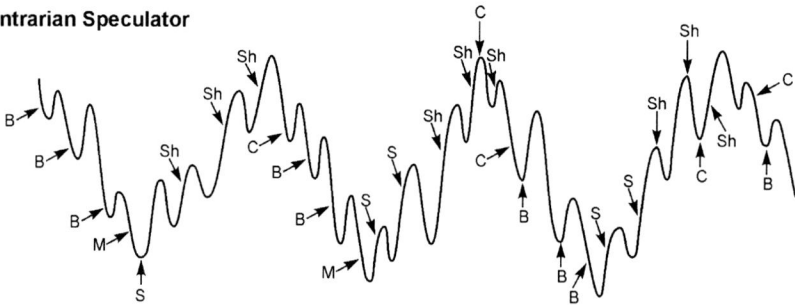

Figure 16

lose money in the end, because all of them herd—either by choice or necessity—at some points along the way. See if you can find yourself among these narratives.

Brilliance Has Nothing To Do With It

An article titled "The World's Smartest Bad Investors" cited six brilliant scientists and professors, including Nobel prize winners, who suffered dismal experiences in financial markets. The writer exclaimed, "These are some of the top finance and economics professors in history. Their deep and penetrating research has revolutionized the world of academic finance. To call them brilliant would be an understatement. So why have they stumbled...?"[10]

Socionomic theory easily explains why the smartest people on the planet typically lose money speculating. It has nothing to do with IQ, which is an attribute mostly of the rational neocortex. It has to do with most speculators' inappropriate assumption of exogenous causality coupled with an inability to curb their own pre-rational herding impulses while dealing with market capriciousness generated by *others'* herding.

The article also mentions two academics who have made fortunes managing money. Neither one of them is an economist.

The Distribution of Speculators' Returns Provides More Evidence that Price Change is Not Random but Systematic

If the market's price changes were statistically random, as would be the case were they responsive to events, speculators across the board would mostly break even. They would be more or less lucky on a random basis, producing a bell-curve distribution of individual speculators' returns. But that is not what we find. *By far* most speculators lose money, and they lose lots of it. Impulsive speculators buy high and sell low, or short low and cover high, again and again, producing the market's fractal form. Accordingly, the distribution of speculators' returns over a full cycle in the stock market does not conform to a bell curve but rather is mightily skewed toward major losses for nearly all speculators, with gains for an infinitesimal few, specifically those who learn to operate to some degree independently of the herd.

Exceptions to the Rule

There are two exceptions to the rule that all groups of financial-market participants herd. Each one of them has a delightful socionomic explanation.

The Commodity Futures Trading Commission follows the activity of three distinct groups of participants in the commodity markets: Small Speculators, Large Speculators and Commercials. Small Speculators are typically on the wrong side of the market at the turns. You might think that Large Speculators, because they have a lot more money, are right a lot, but they are likewise usually wrong at the turns. Commercials are the only participants in commodity markets who generally buy low and sell high. As noted in Chapter 13, our financial/economic dichotomy explains the reason: Commercials are in the business of manufacturing, not speculating, so they think economically rather than financially. They do not perceive commodities as investment items, so they are not participating in the herd. They perceive commodities as economic goods, so they search out bargains, just as a consumer does in the store. They want to buy commodities cheaply, not to re-sell to a greater fool but so that their company can use them profitably to manufacture retail goods. In short, Commercials are *consumers* of commodities, not *investors* in them. As a result, they are comfortable taking the other side of a trade from speculators at market extremes. If they think a price is exceptionally low, they might even buy futures contracts to lock in the current price, and they may sell excess contracts later at a high price. Such behavior derives from economic thinking, not financial thinking.

Another exception to the rule is competent market technicians. A recent study of 2600 investment recommendations made by technicians and fundamentalists on financial television and the Internet came to a striking conclusion: "Technicians display stock-picking skills, while fundamentalists reveal no value. In particular, technicians overwhelmingly outperform fundamentalists in predicting returns over horizons of three to nine months and moreover they produce large alpha with respect to the Fama and French (1993) and momentum benchmarks."[11]

The authors, reasoning within the exogenous-cause paradigm, attributed these results to the possibility that technicians can detect insider buying and selling by observing chart activity, allowing them to exploit hidden market "inefficiencies." How anyone could possibly discern insiders' buying and selling from other people's buying and selling by looking at a chart was left undemonstrated and unexplained. To me such a feat seems impossible.

The results of the study seem more compatible with socionomic theory, which suggests that while all analysts share an impulse to herd, those who focus properly on market behavior have a significant edge over those who focus improperly on external conditions and events. Wall Street's company analysts also tend to talk to each other and may therefore be more prone to herding than the more independent technicians.

The authors additionally reported, however, that "both schools of recommendation generate poor forecasts" when it comes to predicting overall trends in equity market indexes, Treasury bonds and commodities. The authors attributed this result to efficient markets.

This equal-performance outcome may seem to challenge the socionomic explanation for technicians' superiority at stock picking. But market conditions during the time period of the study could easily have skewed the results. The study took place from November 8, 2011 through December 31, 2014, a three-year period of such persistently rising stock prices that it lacked even a single setback in the Dow of 10% or more. Fundamentalists are widely known to have a bullish bias, and technicians are widely acknowledged to be more successful than fundamentalists during bear markets and trading ranges. Had the study in question been able to access data from 1966 to 1982 or from 2000 through 2010, its results may well have favored technicians in the category of overall market forecasting. Given the persistent rise in stock prices during the time of the test, it is impressive that technicians' at-times bearish recommendations for individual stocks worked out so well.

Socionomic theory would be fine with any ultimate finding that technicians analyzing overall markets herd as much as fundamentalists. But having been fairly observant in this business for forty years, and considering the consistently successful forecasting of a commodity by Elliotticians detailed in Chapter 22, which will never be matched by a fundamental analyst, I would suspect that more thorough studies will reveal that technicians have a consistent edge in overall market timing, too, at least in certain market environments.

Elliotticians have numerous, excellent opportunities to escape the herding trap (see Chapters 21, 22 and 23). Nevertheless, they can be uncertain about the proper interpretation of one or another wave degree for substantial periods of time, thereby putting them in danger of herding. When an Elliott wave is complete, however, it brings striking clarity to the market's position in the wave structure and therefore its likely future direction. Such junctures offer complete independence from the herd, and those times tend to be highly rewarding.

How valuable is independence? In late 2008, we received an email from a subscriber saying, "The day the market had its biggest down day in points ever was one of the most serene days of my life." He had gotten out of stocks two years earlier, when signs of enthusiasm and overvaluation were legion; he acted rationally and independently; he did not herd. As a reward, he was financially safe and personally unemotional at a time when those who had held stocks were experiencing mental anguish and increasingly amplified impulses to sell. At the same time, he was able to monitor the market objectively for signs of a buying opportunity.

STF Accommodates Rare Winners

Unlike the random walk model and EMH, socionomic theory, as noted in Chapters 13 and 15, can account for the existence of successful speculators. Because financial markets are patterned, some people can figure out enough about them to speculate profitably. The number of people who learn enough about markets to make money consistently from them, however, constitute a miniscule minority of all participants. Paul Tudor Jones, Marty Schwartz and Dick Diamond[12] made a lot of money consistently by trading options and futures contracts. Although random-walk proponents have claimed that successful traders are merely outliers on a bell curve, this claim fails statistically. It is not the number of successful speculators that matters but the number of successful decisions they make. When they make tens of successful decisions every day, week or month to produce a positive return eleven out of twelve months every year as Dick Diamond did, allowing him to trade markets as a profession for 40 years, their success is too far beyond the end of the bell curve to be within statistical norms. They transact way too often to be called lucky winners of a random lottery. STF, in contrast to the random-walk model, allows that rare individuals can learn enough about the market's patterned herding behavior to profit from it.

One might ask, "If almost everyone is losing money, who is making money?" Answer: Some of it goes to cheaters and front-runners, but most of it goes to financial service providers and peddlers of investment items. It costs a lot of money to run the system, and all of the fees come out of investors' and traders' accounts. A handful of successful speculators take the rest.

Successful Speculation is Just a Stone's Throw Away
(Good Luck with That)

The craft of making money via financial speculation is a challenge many times removed from both socionomics and market analysis. The aim of this book is to teach readers something about financial market causality, not about making money through speculation. There are other books to serve that purpose. Nevertheless, a few comments seem appropriate, if only to deter you from the attempt.

Although humans are hard-wired to herd, a portion of our brains—the neocortex—is independent enough to be able to understand that the hard-wiring is there. It can therefore attempt to deal with it. This is what successful financial speculation requires. Most brains can't do it well. Some can. Even for them, avoiding the herding trap isn't easy. Human minds are well suited to working out logical problems, but they are poorly equipped for guessing the future course of crowds. Human brains evolved to *participate* in crowds, not analyze them.

A plague will tend to kill 99.9% of rabbits, because 0.1% of them will have a trait that makes them immune. The percentage of humans who can learn to beat their own hard-wiring often enough to profit consistently from financial speculation is probably smaller than that. Learning is a requisite, because there is no such thing as a "born trader." People are born—or learn very early—to respect the laws of mechanics. This respect is so strong that they apply these laws even in inappropriate settings. When defaulting to the mechanics paradigm, people unconsciously perceive the market as a physical system. Under that illusion, buying during rallies is as natural as plucking fruit off a tree, and selling during declines is as natural as ducking when a rock is flying toward your face. People's natural default of unconsciously interpreting financial price movement as physical rewards and threats is what ruins them. The immense difficulty in overriding this default explains why successful speculators are so rare and why they are so immensely rewarded for their skills.

To be a successful speculator, you must learn to do something that almost no one else can do. You must sell near the emotional extremes of rallies and buy near the emotional extremes of declines. The mental discipline required to initiate a position by buying near a low or selling short near a high is akin to that required to walk away from a tree full of delicious fruit when you are hungry or to stand still when you see a rock hurtling toward your head. In the former situation, you must imagine the fruit to be poisonous. In the latter situation, you must be able to think, "I'm betting that the rock will *veer away* at the last moment *of its own accord*." To think in this manner, you must ignore the laws of mechanics to which your mind naturally defaults. In the physical world, this would be insane behavior; in finance, *ducking* is insane. Standing pat can make you rich. Unfortunately, the task is not that simple, because sometimes the rock does not veer. It smacks you in the head. All you have to rely upon is probability. You can know from long study under what circumstances the rock coming at you will veer away *most* of the time, but you must also take the consequences when it doesn't. The emotional fortitude required to stand in the way of a hurtling stone that will sometimes hit you is immense, and few people possess it. It is, of course, a great paradox that people who can't perform this feat endure serious stonings time and again in financial markets. Many great truths about life are paradoxical, and so is this one.

NOTES AND REFERENCES

[1] Condon, Bernard, "Companies lose billions buying back their own stock," Associated Press, February 9, 2016.

[2] Krantz, Matt, "Bad sign: CEO's aren't buying stock in their companies," *USA Today*, February 16, 2009.

[3] Nofsinger, John and Kenneth Kim, *Infectious Greed: Restoring Confidence in America's Companies*, Financial Times Prentice Hall, 2003. Study reprinted in Chapter 33 of *Pioneering Studies in Socionomics*.

[4] Choi, James J., David Laibson, Brigitte C. Madrian and Andrew Metrick, "Defined Contribution Pensions: Plan Rules, Participant Choices and the Path of Least Resistance," NBER, prepared for Tax Policy and the Economy, 2001; revised for 2004 as "Saving for Retirement on the Path of Least Resistance."

[5] Levitz, Jennifer, "The Boss Lends a Hand," *The Wall Street Journal*, Febr

[6] Dunham, Will and Jackie Frank, "Herd mentality rules in financial crises," Reuters, September 30, 2008.

[7] Sharot, Tali, Christopher W. Korn, and Raymond J. Dolan, "How Unrealistic Optimism is Maintained in the Face of Reality," *Nature Neuroscience*, November 2011, pp. 1475, 1479.

[8] Laise, Eleanor, "Best Stock Fund of the Decade: CGM Focus," *The Wall Street Journal*, December 31, 2009.

[9] Shell, Adam, "Investors Have Learned Not to Panic," *USA Today*, July 8, 2005.

[10] Smith, Noah, "The World's Smartest Bad Investors," *Bloomberg View*, December 9, 2015.

[11] Avramov, Doron, Guy Kaplanski, Haim Levy, "Talking Numbers: Technical versus Fundamental Recommendations," working paper, accessed August 20, 2015. *Late Note*: The paper has been posted on SSRN.com.

[12] Schwartz wrote a book about his experiences, and Diamond wrote a book about his method:
Schwartz, Martin, *Pit Bull*, Harper Business, 1998.
Diamond, Dick, *Trading as a Business*, John Wiley & Sons, 2015.

Chapter 18

The Awesome Power of Exogenous-Cause Mythology and Consensus Thinking to Hijack Investors' Minds

Robert R. Prechter

Consensus regarding the future course of financial-market prices has an awesome power to become ossified in the wrong direction at markets' major turning points. Let's review two striking examples.

A Historic Consensus on Interest Rates

Read the following analysis from the July 11, 1984 issue of *The Elliott Wave Theorist*:

> The background of investor psychology is very suggestive of an important bond market low. In fact, if this were the only measure I followed, it would appear that bonds are the buy of a lifetime. The news media, which all but ignored the rise in interest rates until May 1984, have been gushing out "higher interest rate" stories. Most of them came out, in typical fashion, *after* the May low, which was tested in June. During second waves, investors typically re-live the fears which existed at the actual bottom [even though] the worst has passed. The last five weeks have demonstrated this phenomenon vividly.
>
> On June 11, a WSJ headline read, "Fed Move to Tighten Credit is Expected during the Summer by Many Economists." On June 18, two full articles, including a front page feature, focused on the prospects for higher interest rates: "Cooler Economy Seen Failing to Stem Further Rise in Interest Rates This Year" and "Interest Rates Begin to Damp Economy; Many Analysts See Further Increases." On June 22, the WSJ featured an incredible *five-page* in-depth report titled "World Debt in Crisis," complete with a picture of falling dominoes

and quotes such as these: from a Congressman, "I don't think we're going to make it to the 1990's"; from a V.P. at Citicorp, "Let's be clear—nobody's debts are going to be repaid"; and from a former assistant secretary of state for economic affairs, "We are living on borrowed time and borrowed money." On July 2, the WSJ reported, without saying so, that economists have panicked. Their forecasts for higher rates now extend halfway into next year! The headline reads, "Higher Interest Rates Are Predicted for Rest of Year and Further Rises Are Seen for 1985's First 6 Months." Says the article, "Some say it would take a miracle for rates to fall." The WSJ is not alone in taking the pulse of economists. *Financial World* magazine's June 27 poll listed the forecasts of 24 economists against their beginning-of-year predictions. *Every single one of them* has raised his forecast, in a linear-logic reaction to the rise in rates that has already occurred. They are using the same type of thinking that led them to a "lower interest rates ahead" conclusion a year ago, at the bottom. This overwhelming consensus based on fundamental analysis is no guarantee that rates have peaked, but history shows that this type of analysis will rarely result in market profits. I prefer to bet on an overlooked theory which recognizes that market patterns repeat themselves over and over again because people are people.

Figure 1 is a long term chart of U.S. interest rates showing where this intense and broad consensus among economists took place. You can see that economists' conviction in June 1984 that interest rates would continue rising (and bond prices would continue falling) derived from linear extrapolation of a trend that had persisted since the 1940s. That trend had already ended in 1981. But economists' passion relating to the old trend was so strong that when rates headed back up in 1984 the only direction that felt right to them was up.

A consensus on a market usually entails both a psychological extreme and widespread exogenous-cause rationales, a combination that produces agreement on the "fundamental factors" that will drive prices higher or lower. The more convincing the arguments seem, the surer one can be that a consensus is signaling a turn in the other direction.

It seems unnecessary to take space to argue why economists' thinking in this case was in fact rationalization. Figure 2 says it *must* have been, as their reasoning and expectations were *strikingly* erroneous. Just look at the dramatic plunge in interest rates over precisely the twelve-month period that they predicted they would rise and the downtrend's relentless continuation ever since. Herding is a good explanation—and a respectful one—for an error that large and conviction that perfectly mistimed.

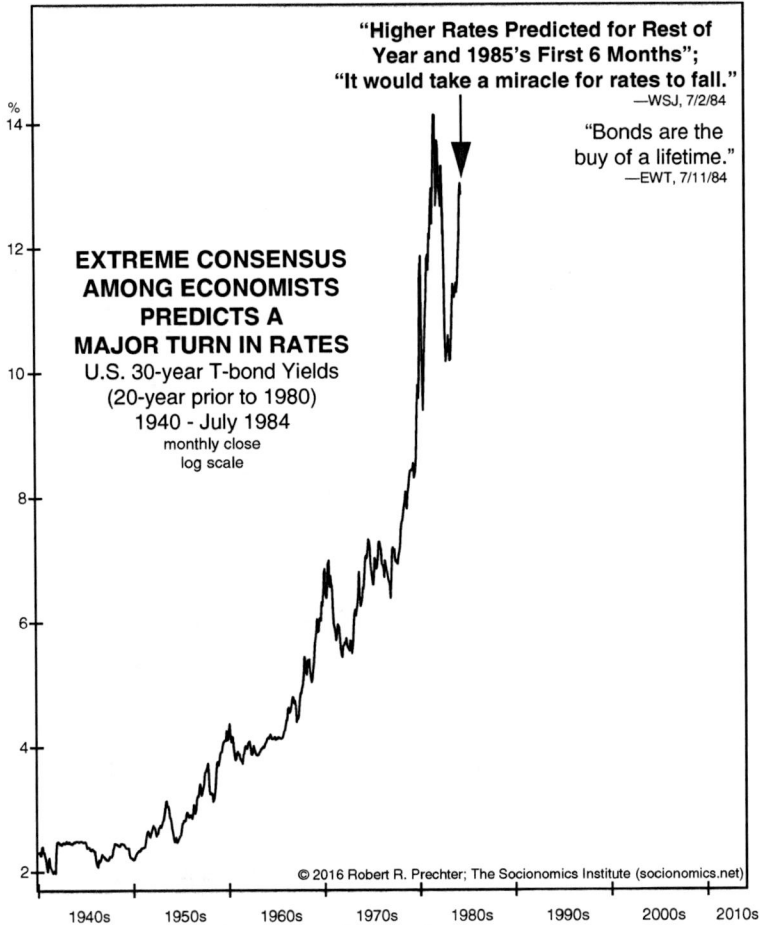

"Higher Rates Predicted for Rest of
Year and 1985's First 6 Months";
"It would take a miracle for rates to fall."
—WSJ, 7/2/84

"Bonds are the
buy of a lifetime."
—EWT, 7/11/84

**EXTREME CONSENSUS
AMONG ECONOMISTS
PREDICTS A
MAJOR TURN IN RATES**
U.S. 30-year T-bond Yields
(20-year prior to 1980)
1940 - July 1984
monthly close
log scale

© 2016 Robert R. Prechter; The Socionomics Institute (socionomics.net)

Figure 1

Generally speaking, such one-sidedness is as rare as a black swan. But at major market turns it is as common as a white one.

Post-production insert: Today the mechanistic paradigm offers the same type of logic today that it did 32 years ago, but in reverse. On July 13, 2016, *The Wall Street Journal* ran an article titled "Why Ultralow Interest Rates Are Here to Stay."[1] Glancing at the chart, it seems we can hardly go wrong with our usual construction, which is that the sentiment conveyed in the headline indicates a market "more likely near a bottom than a top."

The article declares, "Central-bank bond buying is the proximate cause for the plunge this month of the 10-year U.S. Treasury yield to its all-time low of 1.366%." STF's perspective is poles apart: As Figure 24 of Chapter

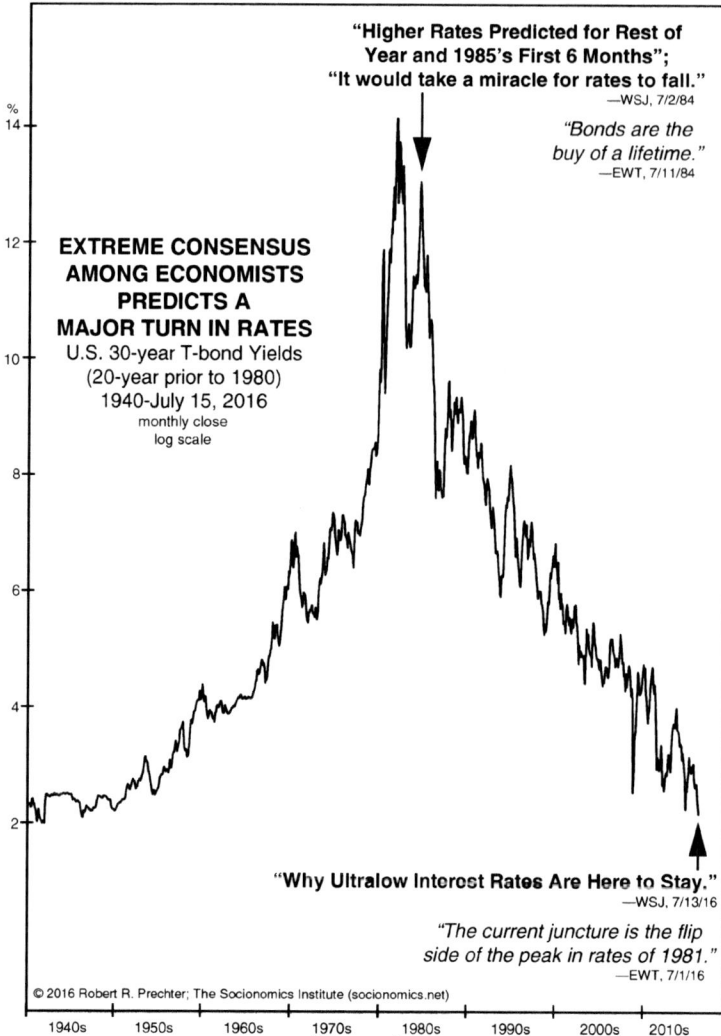

**"Higher Rates Predicted for Rest of
Year and 1985's First 6 Months";
"It would take a miracle for rates to fall."**
—WSJ, 7/2/84

*"Bonds are the
buy of a lifetime."*
—EWT, 7/11/84

**EXTREME CONSENSUS
AMONG ECONOMISTS
PREDICTS A
MAJOR TURN IN RATES**
U.S. 30-year T-bond Yields
(20-year prior to 1980)
1940-July 15, 2016
monthly close
log scale

"Why Ultralow Interest Rates Are Here to Stay."
—WSJ, 7/13/16

*"The current juncture is the flip
side of the peak in rates of 1981."*
—EWT, 7/1/16

© 2016 Robert R. Prechter; The Socionomics Institute (socionomics.net)

Figure 2

2 demonstrates, central-banks' gold dealings have been irrelevant to gold prices, and since central bankers lost money trading gold, they will probably lose money in their bond investments.

I have updated Figure 2 in order to note on it the timing of this article and to take the risk of quoting from an in-house study of Elliott waves in the bond market from two weeks ago. Whatever happens to rates going forward, at least we can see that endogenous cause and fractal extrapolation continue to provide an orientation to extreme market pricing that differs entirely from the one offered by exogenous cause and linear extrapolation.

Historic Consensuses on Gold

In 1970, gold was off investors' radar. In 1971, when President Nixon closed the gold window to halt foreigners' dollar redemptions, one prominent economist said he thought that gold was a relic and that the price would go down.

Ten years later, after gold had risen 24 times in value, it was America's favorite investment, and the annual hard-money conference in New Orleans was drawing crowds of 4,000 people, all of whom were bullish on the outlook for precious metals prices. As we will see in Chapters 21 and 22, Elliott wave and socionomic analysis often fosters independence from the crowd, and this time was no exception. The January 1980 issue of *Commodities* magazine,[2] published the month of the high, covered my prediction for major tops in the metals and declines that would take gold down to $282.50 and silver as low as $4. Their ultimate lows were $252.50 in 1999 and $3.51 in 1993, respectively.

Two decades later, after gold had fallen by 70% and silver by 93%, investors shunned the metals, and the hard money conference was down to 280 attendees.[3] In February 2001, at the start of the very week of the best buying opportunity for gold since 1970, the U.S.'s premier financial weekly reported the results of its interviews with participants in the gold market. As you can read in Figure 3, interviewees were as confident and one-sided about gold in February 2001 as economists were about interest rates in July 1984. Mired in the mechanics paradigm of exogenous cause, they searched everywhere for "a new catalyst to boost prices" but could detect "nothing positive on the horizon...that will make gold prices to up."

A decade later, at seven times the price, conventional economic thinkers found countless reasons why gold would continue higher. On June 15, 2011, a think tank issued a 68-page report meticulously analyzing the production rates of 345 gold mines throughout the world and concluded, "With the supply-demand balance so out of kilter, we see the gold price potentially going to $5,000/oz."[4] (The mention of a supply-demand imbalance was gratuitous, as Chapter 22 will confirm.) The report recommended the purchase of physical gold, exchange-traded gold funds and shares in secondary gold mining companies. Within days of gold's all-time high on September 6, 2011 at $1921.50/oz., the percentage of bulls among gold-futures traders reached 98%, everyday people polled by Gallup cited gold as "the best long term investment," and global investment bank Societe Generale issued a report[5] saying that the "fair value" of gold was $10,000/oz.

BARRON'S • MARKET WEEK   February 12, 2001

COMMODITIES CORNER
Tarnished!
Nobody expects gold prices to turn up soon.

Its difficult to find any positive news in the depressed gold market. At around $260 an ounce, the metal continues to trade near its cost of production, and almost no one believes it will rally soon.

"There doesn't seem to be anything on the horizon that will make gold prices go up."

And as if that weren't enough bad news for one week, on the same day, Tuesday, Anglogold announced that it would continue to hedge half of all of its production for the next five years.

"We are an industry incapable of realizing good returns for our shareholders," says Dippenaar.

Brokerage houses seem to agree. In another sign of the times, ABN Amro gold analyst Todd Hinrichs threw in the towel and stopped covering the industry a few weeks ago.

"There is nothing positive. It's as bad as it gets."

Another problem: As the stock-market value of gold companies has shrunk, along with their profits, mutual-fund managers no longer want to own them.

Commodity Futures Trading Commission statistics show that bearish bets are at their highest level in years.

"The shorts have a good thing going," says Hinrichs.

Even the ever-bullish World Gold Council, an industry group sponsored by the gold companies themselves, is finding it tough to come up with a new catalyst to boost prices.

"Unfortunately there is nothing positive on the horizon," says Dippenaar.

Figure 3

Socionomists treat such reports not as analyses but as market-mood indicators. True to form, gold was approaching a major top. Over the next four years (see Figure 4), gold fell nearly in half, silver slid 72%, and gold mining shares plummeted 80%.

When an Elliott wave reaches its final subdivision, numerous degrees of trend culminate, and opinion crystallizes—in the wrong direction. When both laymen and representatives across an entire profession agree passionately on the future trend of a market, it's a signal that powerful unconscious

"Gallup Poll Ranks Gold Best Long-Term Investment"
"Fair Value at $10,000"—Societe Generale
"Gold Fever Sweeps Criminal Underworld"
"SPDR Gold ETF Surpasses Value of S&P 500 ETF"
98% Bulls among Gold Futures Traders

CRYSTALLIZATION OF OPINION AT MAJOR TURNS IN GOLD
1980-2015
monthly range

Gold conference swells to 4000 attendees

Gold conference attendance down 93%.
"Nobody expects gold prices to turn up soon."
"There is nothing positive on the horizon."
"Bearish bets are at their highest level in years."

© 2016 Robert R. Prechter; The Socionomics Institute (socionomics.net)

Figure 4

impulses have overwhelmed their minds. This timing is inevitable and reliable. Conventional economic theory cannot explain why it happens; on the contrary, it says it should never happen. Socionomics explains why it happens and predicts this same result time and again.

Endless Paradox and Irony

Financial market behavior is saturated with paradox and irony. They are the inevitable results of herding, rationalization and the erroneous application of the mechanics paradigm's exogenous-cause, rational-reaction model to financial pricing. Here are some more classic, two-sided examples:

—When U.S. Treasury bills sported double-digit interest rates in 1979-1984, investors saw no reason to abandon their high-yielding T-bills for stocks. It turned out to be the greatest stock-buying opportunity in two generations. Heading into 2016, with the Dow priced 23 times higher, investors argue that the near-zero yield on T-bills makes them a bad investment choice and stocks highly attractive.

—When long term bonds and notes yielded 15% in 1981, investors were afraid to buy U.S. Treasury bonds, which were about to embark on their greatest bull market ever. Today's low and even negative interest rates put bond investors' wealth at tremendous risk, but they seem oblivious to it. On the contrary, bonds are the world's most popular investment sector. With conviction nearly equal to that of their counterparts in 1981, pundits are declaring that interest rates are sure to stay low, go lower and get *more* negative, with no end in sight. Naturally their conviction is based on "economic fundamentals." Predicting the continuation of a 35-year trend that in 5000 years of human history has never gone so far is linear extrapolation at its laziest and most dangerous. The probability of an approaching upturn in long term rates and downturn in bond prices as significant as the reversal of 1981 seems exceptionally high.

—When oil was $10.35 a barrel in 1998, analysts did not argue that world supplies were running out. When it was 6 to 14 times more expensive in 2006-2008, dozens of books passionately embraced the idea that global oil supplies would soon be depleted. Today, with oil prices down over 70%, supply-demand analysts say the world will never run out of oil. For details, see Chapter 22.

—In 1999, economists' optimism was so entrenched that several polls conducted at the most significant stock market peak in 70 years showed not one dissenter calling for an economic contraction or a major bear market. Economists were proclaiming a "New Economy" and a "Goldilocks Economy"—"not too hot and not too cold but just right." This attitude crystallized just prior to a decade-long period of negative stock market returns, culminating in the Great Recession. On March 2, 2009, the Daily Sentiment Index for S&P futures recorded only 2% bulls, its lowest reading ever, and on March 3 the media reported that a world-famous investor adored for his long term optimism had joined the swelling chorus of pessimists in declaring, "We're certain that the economy will be in shambles throughout 2009—and, for that matter, probably well beyond."[6] Three days later, the stock market turned around and shot upward in its fastest rally in 76 years, and the economy recovered.

—The more investors are convinced of coming inflation, the less likely they are to make money from inflation hedges. Chapters 2 and 21 cover examples relating to gold and the U.S. Dollar Index, respectively. An article dated March 10, 2008 provides another example, this one from the debt market:

> Bond investors have <u>never been so sure</u> that the Federal Re-serve will lose control of inflation. They're so convinced that they're giving up yields just to buy debt securities that protect against rising consumer prices.
>
> The yield on the five-year Treasury Inflation-Protected Security due in 2012 has been negative since February 29, and traded today at minus 0.17 percent. The notes, which were first sold in 1997, had never before traded below zero. Even so, firms from Deutsche Asset Management to Vanguard Group Inc., the second-biggest U.S. mutual fund company, say <u>TIPS are a bargain</u>.[7]

Well, *of course* the most expensive TIPS in history were a bargain. How else could investors have justified paying record high prices for them? The day this article came out, EWI's Steven Hochberg emailed it to the company's analytical team under the header, "Psychological extreme?" It was indeed, as yields on five-year TIPS bottomed on that exact day, at 0.21%. Their rates rose to 3.19% by October 28, 2008, providing in just seven months stunning losses of over 20% (more than 30% in the two-year TIPS) for investors in these supposedly super-safe government notes. Buyers on March 10 had locked in a negative yield based on fear of inflation just before deflation slammed financial markets. TIPS became a true bargain in October-November 2008, but it is unlikely that anyone said so, because by then investors were afraid of *de*flation and so had no use for TIPS. That's why they were a true bargain.

—At the peak of the housing market in 2006, forecasters were confi-dent that supply and demand factors would keep prices going higher. In Q1 2012, right at the low in national home prices to date, an analyst echoed the consensus in saying, "No one is able to confidently predict where the housing market is going to go in 2012. There's just too much noise in the data."[8] Translation: Prices are down, so we can no longer recommend buying.

And so on.

Rationalization attending financial markets is compatible with trends of the past and proceeds without a clue as to changes that have recently begun. By the time investors adopt convictions in tune with a maturing trend, the herd is ready to go in the other direction. Lagging social actions (see Chapters 7 and 8) justify previously formulated rationales about the stock market, interfering with a proper change of market opinion.

Market analysts' opinions tend to lag market trends in proportion to their duration. Once aggregate opinion crystallizes in line with a long-established trend, it doesn't shift to its opposite for a long time. It's hard to believe now, but even though stocks had bottomed in 1974/1982 (depending on the measure), analysts remained pessimistic pretty much through 1985, three years after the stock market had soared to new all-time highs and three years into an eight-year economic boom. Social mood had been negative throughout the 1970s and early 1980s, and though it had become less negative it had yet to cross the threshold to become net positive. (Chapter 8 offers our model of that threshold.) Following a minor stock market pullback in the third week of September 1985, with prices just below recent all-time highs, the Bullish Consensus reported the lowest percentage of advisory services bullish since the 1982 bottom. The service's data compiler, Peter Hackstedde, told me that if it weren't for the bullish outlooks of the monthly *Elliott Wave Theorist* and its short term hotline (which he counted separately), his firm's tally of the percentage of bulls on the outlook for stocks, for the first time ever, would have been zero. From there, the Dow more than doubled in just two years.

A financial author famously reported, "Some academics have gone so far as to suggest that a blindfolded monkey throwing darts at the stock listings could select a portfolio that would do just as well as one selected by the experts."[9] This formulation is in the right spirit, but statistically it is off the mark. Over a full market cycle, even most experts do not do as well as random selection. Extreme consensus opinions near market turns—even among experts, as shown in Chapter 17—are not the result of randomness but of herding, and herding leads to bad investment decisions.

Jam Yesterday and Jam Tomorrow, but Never Jam Today

When I address investment conferences, I sometimes show graphs of times in the past when extreme sentiment preceded major market reversals, up and down. I show how each and every time, be it in stocks, commodities, gold, oil, tech stocks, penny stocks, "Nifty Fifty" stocks, mining stocks, real estate (as recounted in Chapter 13) or whatever, there was *always* an airtight "fundamental" argument for a continuation of the trend as it neared its end.

I explain why airtight fundamental arguments in favor of trend continuation and widespread acceptance of them are key signs of an approaching reversal.

I also mention that even an extreme consensus can become larger (see Figure 25 of Chapter 21 for an example), so a consensus is not a pinpoint signal. It just warns that change is more likely than not. The consensus could in fact grow even stronger and larger. But if a speculator won't get out of the way of a large consensus, he will surely stand pat given a huge one. Recognizing a strong and widespread conviction about the future trend of a financial market doesn't mean you must take the risk of speculating in the opposite direction, but it is a good guide for determining when you should avoid speculating in the same direction.

People in audiences often heartily agree that my presentation is logical and a great guide to investing. But the agreement ends abruptly when I show them markets sporting extreme sentiment *now*. These are the markets that many investors in the audience succumbed to buying after years of inaction as their mood-sharing finally induced them to adopt rationales as to why the past trend would continue. Suddenly the logic of my case evaporates in their minds. They respond, "But X *has* to continue going up/down because...." They think I'm logical about the historical evidence but simply wrong *in this case*. They think I'm sadly blind to the obvious *forces* in play. They judge the other speakers—who explain with exogenous-cause arguments why the trend in market X must continue—to be as just as logical as I am but with the difference that they are right, *this time*. They crowd around the advocates, because their every word supports the overwhelming intensity of their own unconscious conviction with respect to the market in question. Audience members can *hear* what I say, but they cannot *feel* it. Because they share the mood of the herd, they are impervious to my words. Since they don't feel the argument, they won't act on it. Time after time, they concede that sentiment extremes have worked in the past, and they concede that they will assuredly work in the future, but they never agree that they will work today.

And they never will. This dynamic is immutable.

Trying to help non-socionomically educated people near major mood extremes is a hopeless endeavor. The reason is that it is nearly impossible for people to process statements that contradict their most powerful feelings. No one can successfully warn people to get out of investments at market peaks, encourage them to invest at market bottoms, suggest that they do or do not start a major new property development, convince them that inflation or deflation is coming, advise them to refrain from promoting a peace initiative or war effort or ask them to do *anything* contrary to the prevailing mood. They may hear your voice wafting on the air, but really listening, much less believing, is psychologically akin to denying reality. They will politely ignore you, make a joke, insult you or argue with you. As soon as you stop talking, their minds will return to perceiving reality as befits their mood.

All these statements are true with respect to aggregates. With a thoughtful individual, you have a chance at persuasion. I've seen it happen.[10]

Do Markets Make Sense?

Many people resist the idea of socionomic causality because it defies common sense. Indeed, that's exactly what it does. Socionomics argues that markets fail to make sense—common sense, anyway—not just sometimes but all the time.

Under the mechanics paradigm, markets sometimes seem to make sense and sometimes not. When they don't, observers often exclaim, "This market doesn't make sense." But such instances rarely seem to motivate them to challenge their premises.

The exceptions are exhilarating. One of our refutations of common sense, regarding the Enron scandal,[11] motivated John Casti, science writer and author of *Mood Matters*, to embrace socionomics (see Chapter 42). Bollen and Mao (see Chapter 9) courageously trusted their evidence on the timing of mood expressions on Twitter relative to stock market action even though it ran counter to common-sense expectations. They ultimately became interested in socionomics as a theoretical framework for understanding and explaining their research results, which they presented at our first annual Socionomics Summit. It is a glorious thing when evidence overturns common sense and leads to a revelatory moment.

Sometimes dramatic events occur for non-socionomic reasons, such as a leader falling ill, a storm hitting a populated shoreline, or an insane person shooting up a school. Emotions erupt in response, but because such events do not affect social mood, markets continue on their way as if nothing had happened. Chapter 4 presents a striking example. Such non-responses flummox the exogenous-cause mind. Socionomists realize they're normal.

Under STF, *financial markets always make perfect (non) sense*. STF accommodates a world in which gold can make a new ten-year high, suggesting runaway inflation, at the same time that real estate makes a new five-year low on deflating credit, as happened in 2011. It accommodates a world in which gold can have a big bull market while interest rates on T-bills soar to double digits, as happened in the 1970s, and then have another big bull market while interest rates on T-bills collapse to zero, as occurred in 2006-2011. When such "crazy" things happen, analysts working under the wrong paradigm are vulnerable to existential angst.

You can escape that angst. Anytime you hear something like, "With bond rates so low, stocks are an attractive alternative," or "The currency that yields the most will attract the most buyers," or "With all the manufacturing going on in China, commodities should remain in a bull market," or "With world politics heating up, investors are going to run to gold," or "Tight supplies of oil will lead to higher prices," or "The currency of that country is strong, so its stocks are more attractive to foreigners," or "Because interest rates are rising, investors will want to own more bonds," just ignore it. Such expressions are misapplications of rational, logical economic valuation to non-rational, illogical financial markets. Logical arguments that work in economic markets don't work in financial markets. Despite seemingly impeccable reasons why one should invest in item X instead of Y, the typically presumed causes simply do not apply.

Fortunately, the fact that financial markets are illogical in no way bans a logical understanding of them. Each financial market is akin to a person with OCD or bipolar disorder in that its behavior is patterned but not rational. In the context of the malady, the behavior of people suffering from such disorders makes perfect sense. It may even be fairly predictable. Financial market behavior likewise makes perfect sense *within the socionomic context*, and it is likewise fairly predictable by reference to unconscious herding impulses regulated by Elliott waves. One must therefore approach the task of market analysis not as a calculator of reasonable relationships but as a psychologist tasked with predicting the actions of OCD and bipolar patients. Such people share with speculators the trait of being impulsively and emotionally active in a relentlessly patterned way as opposed to rationally and serenely reactive in a statistically random way. This qualitative difference is crucial to a proper understanding of financial market behavior, and it is necessary for any chance at long-run success in dealing with it.

To an uninitiated person, conventional economic thinking feels right even though it's wrong, and socionomic causality feels wrong even though it's right. To begin your journey out of that mindset, you must learn to accept and then embrace irony and paradox, at least as humans are unconsciously wired to interpret things. Once you recognize that social mood and patterned herding are independent, primary causes that have consequences in social action, once you get used to the world of socionomic causality, the irony and paradox will melt away, and everything the markets do will make sense. Rather than appearing unfathomable, market action will become completely normal, somewhat predictable and wonderfully entertaining.

NOTES AND REFERENCES

[1] "Barr, Colin, ""Why Ultralow Interest Rates Are Here to Stay," *The Wall Street Journal*, July 13, 2016.

[2] "Elliott counts suggest bear moves," *Commodities* (now *Futures*) magazine, Vol. IX, No. 1, January 1980, p.64. The text is reprinted on page 5 of *How to Forecast Gold & Silver Using the Wave Principle* (2006).

[3] The host company considered retiring its venerable conference, but I (along with other speakers no doubt) encouraged the organizer to hang on for friendlier times waiting just around the corner. By 2006, total attendance was back above 1000. Needless to say, socionomics explains why attendance trends are the opposite of what they should be for attendees' maximum financial success.

[4] Chen, Yan, as quoted in Wenzel, Robert, "Standard Chartered: Limited New Production Will Result in $5,000 Per Ounce Gold," *Economic Policy Journal*, June 15, 2011.

[5] Grice, Dylan, a global strategist at Societe Generale SA, as quoted in Wilson, David, "Gold-Backed Dollar Signals $10,000 Metal Price: Chart of the Day," Bloomberg, September 14, 2011.

[6] Buffett, Warren, Berkshire Hathaway *Annual Report*, February 2009, p. 4.

[7] Hernandez, Sandra and Deborah Finestone, "TIPS' Yields Show Fed Has Lost Control of Inflation," Bloomberg, March 10, 2008.

[8] Williams, Misty, "Free Fall in Home Prices," *The Atlanta Journal-Constitution*, February 1, 2012.

[9] Malkiel, Burton, *A Random Walk Down Wall Street*, W.W. Norton & Co., 1973 (2015 edition), p.160. This comment is perennially misquoted so as to attribute the idea to the author, but he clearly stated that he was reporting a comment from others.

[10] Alastair Macdonald's account is a fun example: http://www.social-moodconference.com/2016/03//

[11] See Chapter 29 of *Pioneering Studies In Socionomics* (2003).

Chapter 19

On Mood, Herding and Alternative Hypotheses

Robert R. Prechter

Rational Economic Herding vs. Pre-Rational Financial Herding

Some herding is rational. Going with friends to a mall to take advantage of a sale is a rational act. So is queuing up for rationed gasoline or evacuating a disaster area. Decisions such as those derive from economic and social contexts of relative certainty.

Pre-rational herding prevails in contexts of uncertainty, such as fashions, fads, business, politics and financial markets. Socionomics is primarily concerned with this version of herding.

Mood vs. Emotion

Mood differs from emotions. Socionomists' use of these terms fits most widely available definitions. For purposes of elucidation in the field of socionomics, our formulation is that *emotions* are exogenously referred, consciously experienced feelings, regulated by a combination of mood, conditions and events, whereas *mood* is a non-referred, unconscious, affective, evaluative, future-oriented, global disposition towards experiencing certain emotions and taking compatible actions. Mood influences mental processes (thoughts) involving emotions, perceptions, wishes, desires, attitudes, beliefs, impulses, aspirations and decisions, which lead to compatible physical activity (actions) expressing mood.

As examples: Adoration and anger are emotions. "This singer is captivating" and "This president is a disaster" are beliefs. "I wish I could embrace this singer" and "I wish I could get rid of this incumbent" are wishes. "I have to go to that concert" and "I need to join the march on the capitol" are aspirations. And so on. All these aspects of mentation can spur actions.

Mood affects emotions, but emotions do not affect mood. A person translates mood into emotions when choosing a particular referent to justify the conscious expression of an emotion that is compatible with his unconscious mood. A positive mood might impel a person to seek a referent—such as sunshine, a song or a musical group—to justify an expression of joy; whereas a negative mood might impel a person to seek another referent—such as a traffic event, a political leader or people perceived as different—to justify an expression of anger. Mood can even dispose a person to express different emotions at different times relating to the same referent. A snippet of news overheard from a passing source could justify an angry outburst or a laugh from the same person, depending on his mood. When unconscious mood produces conscious emotions tied to external referents, the root cause—mood—generally goes unrecognized.

Events independent of mood can cause emotional reactions. A surprise win for the home team can trigger joy, and the unexpected death of a loved one can trigger grief. Even experiences such as these may not be entirely independent of socionomic influence, however, since mood can predispose a person to emote with more or less intensity and/or over a longer or shorter duration than otherwise would have been the case.

Rationalization of Mood-Induced Emotions

People choose referents to rationalize mood-induced emotions. Rationalization is pervasive among stock speculators, purveyors of fashions, swing voters in elections, and every other aggregation expressing social mood.

Referents are always available to serve as excuses for people's feelings. When people spot compatible referents, their feelings become conscious. In 1963-1964, society was in an increasingly positive mood of high degree, and when the Beatles showed up, greater numbers of people thought, "*They* make me happy." A decade later, in 1973-1974, society was in an increasingly negative mood of equal degree, and when President Nixon transgressed, greater numbers of people agreed, "*He's* why I'm annoyed."

A recent example of rationalizing mood is the about-face in global sentiment toward immigrants. Immigrants are visible by way of their differentness and thus make a handy referent for changes in social mood. During the positive mood trend of the 1990s, immigrants were more or less welcomed around the world. During and for a time after the bear market in stocks of 2007-2009—and perfectly encapsulating the time of the bear market in real estate of 2006-2012—immigrants were mostly vilified, to the point that U.S. states passed 164 anti-illegal-immigration laws in 2010-2011.[1] Negative social mood motivated that switch in attitude, and people resorted to rationalization to justify it. When they felt magnanimous, they welcomed immigrants as contributors to society. When they felt angry and fearful, they rejected immigrants as a menace to society. Usually about the same mix of good and bad attends immigration overall, so the key factor that changes is people's inclusionary and exclusionary feelings (see Chapter 14 of *The Wave Principle of Human Social Behavior*), which social mood regulates.

As noted in Chapter 16, unconscious impulses operate faster than conscious thought. Speculators often think and then act, but sometimes they act and then think. It is as if the neocortex stands ready either way to serve the action: "My host is about to—or just did—buy 100 shares of XYZ stock at $30 a share. I need to provide a reason for his doing so." For more on this theme, see Chapter 32.

Rational-market theorists don't buy this idea. They think stock market pricing is determined by people who calculate the worth of companies. Chapter 13 showed that there is no such calculation and not even a reliable basis for it. Empirical observation is enough to establish the fact that most speculators have no idea what a company is worth or how to determine it. Nor, generally speaking, do they care. Most investors trade on emotion and impulsively chosen advice. Millions of Chinese investors pick stocks and prices to buy on numerology and superstition. Such people are not just fringe players, either, as "numerology is a basic trading strategy in China."[2] Many speculators there look for stock codes that contain the day of the month of their birthdays, or the lucky number 8, especially in clusters. Folk advisors suggest wearing red clothes, eating beef and avoiding numbers with unlucky homonyms. Socionomists are perfectly comfortable with this information and even find reports of it useful. Theoretically speaking, we recognize that numerology and superstition are methods of rationalizing social-mood imperatives; they are just easier to see through than the methods economists and professional futurists use. Practically speaking, we identified *The Wall Street Journal*'s page-one article on the practices of Chinese investors as an indicator of an approaching top in China's stock market. The Shanghai Composite made its all-time high five months later, and it still stands.

The Plasticity of Exogenous-Cause Thinking Aids Rationalization

As suggested throughout Chapters 1, 2 and 22, the exogenous-cause mindset is perfectly suited to providing a broad template for rationalization. It doesn't matter what the facts are; one can use them in various contradictory ways to excuse emotions and actions that express either a positive or negative mood.

Any exogenous cause can be cited to justify either optimism or pessimism toward a financial market. Here's a particularly fun example: On Friday, June 5, 2009, the stock market rose for a while and then slipped. I captured these headlines, issued less than an hour apart:

U.S. Stocks Surge as Jobs Report Spurs Optimism on Economy
June 5, 2009; 13:39 GMT (Bloomberg)
U.S. stocks rose, sending the Dow Jones Industrial Average higher for 2009, after data showing employers cut fewer jobs than forecast last month boosted optimism the recession is ending.

Markets Slide on Jobless News
June 5, 2009; 14:31 GMT (UPI)
U.S. markets fell early Friday after the Labor Department said the unemployment rate jumped 0.5 percentage points to 9.4 percent.

Comical as such flips may be, they are common. The rarity in this case is that the flip was swift. Similar flips occur all the time from week to week, month to month, year to year and era to era. People don't recognize them for what they are because of the long duration between flips and the seeming sensibleness of each ad-hoc argument at the time it is made.

Below I have placed some examples of explanatory flips side by side, so you will see them for what they are. Every one of the exogenous-cause arguments in the following sets of contradictory claims is entirely sensible and entirely useless:

- A weak dollar is bullish for stocks because inflation makes stock prices go up.
- A weak dollar is bearish for stocks because it raises businesses' cost of purchasing raw materials from overseas.

- A strong dollar is bullish for stocks because it makes U.S. stocks attractive to foreigners.
- A strong dollar is bearish for stocks because it makes our goods more expensive for foreigners to buy, curbing our exports.

- Democrats are bullish for stocks because they tend to pursue inflationary policies.
- Democrats are bearish for stocks because they tend to restrict business through regulation.

- Republicans are bullish for stocks because they tend to be more laissez-faire towards business.
- Republicans are bearish for stocks because since 1928 stocks have done worse during Republican administrations.

- Rising oil prices are bearish for stocks because they raise costs to businesses and consumers.
- Rising oil prices are bullish for stocks because they indicate a robust economy with strong demand for energy.

- Falling oil prices are bullish for stocks because businesses and consumers thrive on cheap energy.
- Falling oil prices are bearish for stocks because they cause a contraction in the oil industry, a major market sector.

- Inflation is bullish for stocks because it causes all prices to rise.
- Inflation is bearish for stocks because it raises the cost of production and causes a misallocation of resources.

- Deflation is bullish for stocks because it lowers the cost of raw materials involved in production and lowers prices for consumers, giving them more purchasing power.
- Deflation is bearish for stocks because it indicates a contraction in credit, which squeezes businesses and consumers.

- A rising trade deficit is bearish for stocks because it means U.S. production is weak relative to other countries.
- A rising trade deficit is bullish for stocks because it indicates elevated demand from U.S. consumers.

- Government regulation is bullish for stocks because it levels the playing field.
- Government regulation is bearish for stocks because it hampers business.

- "Cash for clunkers" will be bullish for stocks because it will stimulate business by incentivizing people to buy new cars.
- "Cash for clunkers" will be bearish for stocks because it will destroy millions of dollars' worth of perfectly good transportation and force people to waste money maintaining their status quo.

- Higher interest rates are bearish for stocks because they raise the cost of borrowing.
- Higher interest rates are bullish for stocks because they indicate a robust economy with an increasing demand for credit.

- Lower interest rates are bullish for stocks because they lower the cost of borrowing.
- Lower interest rates are bearish for stocks because they indicate a slackening economy with a shrinking demand for credit.

- Full employment is bullish for stocks because it means that everyone is working.
- Less than full employment is bullish for stocks because it means there is room to grow.

- Full employment is bearish for stocks because businesses can't find the help they need and have to pay up for labor.
- Less than full employment is bearish for stocks because more unemployment checks and food stamps are a drag on the economy.

- A new tax will be bearish for stocks because it will take money away from business and consumers.
- A new tax will be bullish for stocks because it will pay for new infrastructure.

- Government subsidies for business are bullish for stocks because they keep productive enterprises going.
- Government subsidies for business are bearish for stocks because they waste resources on unproductive enterprises.

- Bank bailouts are bullish for stocks because they keep the financial system from collapsing.
- Bank bailouts are bearish for stocks because they create a moral hazard that will ultimately cause the financial system to collapse.

- Central banks are bullish for stocks because they keep credit flowing throughout the system, keeping the economy expanding.
- Central banks are bearish for stocks because they encourage system-wide indebtedness, which is a drag on the economy.

- Recessions are bearish for stocks because business contracts.
- Recessions are bullish for stocks because they cause businesses to get lean.

- Corporate buy-backs are bullish for stocks because they indicate confidence among business owners and managers.
- Corporate buy-backs are bearish for stocks because they load up companies with debt that has to be repaid later.

- War is bullish for stocks because it causes governments to spend money, stimulating the economy.
- War is bearish for stocks because it diverts investment capital, destroys capital goods, and kills young people who would have contributed to the economy.

I could go on, but you get the idea. As George Orwell might say, some of these claims are more equally invalid than others, but no matter. Economists will trot out any of these arguments to bolster their outlooks. If you haven't been exposed to many of these conflicting claims, you haven't been reading enough financial commentary.

Socionomics does not fall into that trap. It says that social mood regulates the tenor and character of social actions. There is no converse causal logic.

Economists' mechanistic view of objective news *causality* and socionomics' contextual view of subjective news *interpretation* are worlds apart. We address this point in Chapter 32.

As detailed in Chapter 19 of *The Wave Principle of Human Social Behavior*, stock investors experience serial passions favoring one exogenous cause or another. Although their pet explanations change continually, they believe them just as strongly each time. Investors have focused intently for a time on bond yields, the unemployment rate, the money supply, home sales, the trade deficit, the oil price, the gold price, the inflation rate and Fed meetings. All of these data simply serve rationalization. The proof is that while each factor has its time in the sun, the rest of the time investors ignore it.

Rationalization can even manifest in the form of suddenly abandoning previously established beliefs about causality. Consider one illustrative example. Recall from Chapter 2 that economists have doggedly deemed a rising trade deficit bearish for stocks and the economy and a falling trade deficit bullish. As depicted in Figures 11 and 12 of Chapter 10, we had observed the opposite historical relationship. Accordingly, the trade deficit and the stock market led the economy downward in 2006-2009. These trends bottomed respectively in January, March and June, 2009. On March 12 of that year, three days after low tick in the stock market, the Associated Press issued this report:

> The U.S. trade deficit plunged in January to the lowest level in six
> years. The Commerce Department said Friday the trade imbalance
> dropped to $36 billion in January, a decline of 9.7 percent from Decem-
> ber and the lowest level since October 2002. While the improvement
> was better than the $38 billion deficit that economists had expected,
> they did not see the development as good news for the economy.[3]

This was a perfect time for economists to say something bullish. They had
just observed an "improvement" in the trade deficit to even "better" than
they had forecast. It had reached its lowest level in over six years. In fact,
it was at the lowest level since the very month of the preceding major stock
market bottom. Yet, incredibly, "*they did not see the development as good
news for the economy.*" They offered a few excuses for maintaining a bearish
stance, but their logic is irrelevant. Social mood was at a negative extreme,
and economists simply invented reasons to maintain their newly adopted
pessimism, even in the face of news that they themselves had formerly used
as a basis for optimism. The last sentence of the above report should astound
you with its inconsistency. It doesn't surprise a socionomist. Rationalization
is a financial-market imperative.

No Memory for Mood as Opposed to Emotions

People in the aggregate are on a never-ending roller coaster of buying
high and selling low in financial markets, lending too much money and then
calling it in, borrowing too much money and then defaulting, electing one
political party and then another, and vacillating between negotiating peace
and demanding war. Why? Are they not smart enough to recognize a mood
reprise and its implications?

The answer must be that the brain has no storage mechanism for social
mood, at least not one that it accesses. Social mood, it seems, is *unconscious, transient* and *unremembered*, existing only for the moment. Humans
remember objects, events and stories well, but social mood changes are
detached from external referents, so there are no objects, events or stories
linking mood to memory. Without a referent, people have no ready basis
to credit or blame mood for prompting their feelings and actions. They do
remember emotions and their referents, however, so their default is to credit
or blame events for causing their feelings and actions.

Furthermore, no one experiences the mood of an isolated society of
which he is not a member. If the negative mood of one society were to prompt
a violent social act against a neighboring society in a positive mood, the

victims would not share the feelings that created the event; all they would experience is the event and the emotions it provoked.

People can recall some emotions for life. They remember just how they felt and even where they were at the time of the Kennedy assassination, the moon landing and the 9/11 attack. Ask them what their mood was for weeks after these events, and they will say it was compatibly positive or negative. But immediately following all of these events, the stock market moved for months in precisely the opposite direction of their emotional memory, because mood, not emotion, propelled it.

If you ask people how they felt when their first child was born or when a beloved pet died, they can tell you. If you ask your old war buddy, "Remember how scared we were in the trenches?" he will say, "I will never forget it my whole life." But if you ask investors to relate their mood at the last market top or bottom to the present situation, they won't be able to do it. They often think any fool could have recognized what good opportunities to sell or buy investment items the previous times afforded while still believing that today is different. They do not recognize being in the same mood because they are unable to remember the mood that impelled their past behavior. Thus, they have no basis upon which to judge the danger they are courting by acting or by failing to act when they are later in an identical mood. Benjamin Graham famously said, "Wall Street people learn nothing and forget everything."[4] Now we know why: They remember nothing, because they can't, and they learn nothing because they remember nothing.

People were unable to introspect and blame market mood and herding dynamics for their self-destructive optimism in 2000 toward stocks, in 2006 toward real estate, in 2007 toward stocks, in 2008 toward commodities and in 2011 toward gold and silver, despite the fact that all five of these investment manias peaked in the short span of a dozen years. They were likewise unable to introspect and blame moods and herding impulses for their self-destructive pessimism in 1974 toward stocks, in 1993 toward silver, in 1998 toward oil and in 2001 toward gold. They repeat the same behavior endlessly because they have no memory of what caused them to feel and behave as they did. They keep a razor-sharp lookout for events that will change market trends, which is a complete waste of time. They work hard to stay informed, which keeps them uninformed. They are unaware that the trend change will begin unconsciously in their own heads and that compatible events will follow. The dual disabilities of unremembered mood and misplaced focus on irrelevant events keeps people acting on their impulses without realizing it.

The Contagion Model of Herding vs. Mirroring and Mimicking

Psychological-contagion studies (see Chapter 34) typically claim that attitudes spread through society as diseases do. An example is "Catching Rudeness Is Like Catching a Cold."[5] This idea does not appear to be very well vetted. If rudeness can spread, then courtesy can spread, too, so in society the influence of all individuals' attitudes would produce a symbiotic mix quite different from the result of contagion. Contagion is a one-way process, from the sick to the well, or from the informed to the uninformed, but social attitudes arise from a process in which two or more participants interact. One disease does not negate another, either, but one attitude (such as courtesy) can negate another (such as rudeness) quite readily. In most cases, the contagion model is inadequate and misleading when applied to studies of how attitudes arise in society.

A better model for a group's adoption of moods and attitudes is mutual mimicking, because two or more mimickers can produce a behavioral compromise that none of the participants fully expressed at the start. The biological component of such behavior may be mirror neurons, which facilitate a cooperative system that enhances learning, socialization and empathy. Contagion does not involve mimicking and mirroring, but shared mood probably does. Contagion, moreover, is a mechanical process, whereas socionomics' metatheoretical lens of organicism (see Chapters 6, 32 and 38) promotes the understanding that human herding is due not to a mechanistic, unidirectional mental directive to "copy other people" but to an organic, omnidirectional process of "let's agree." Under socionomics, such agreement extends to opinions during positive-mood periods, but it more universally pertains to emotional attitudes, whereby people can unconsciously agree to be either courteous and cooperative or rude and antagonistic to each other. In the latter case it seems they are not agreeing, but emotionally they are.

Mood Arises, but Rationales Spread

As noted in Chapter 6, socionomics differentiates between the holistic arising of social mood and the mechanistic spreading of knowledge about referents for social-mood expression. Both systems are constantly operative.

People do not universally share referents for expressing mood as they share mood itself. Social mood is a simple motivator, but rationales for acting upon it and the actions people take to express it are highly variable and inventive. The chain of causality is: Social mood arises; people are induced to express it; they identify referents and invent rationales that accommodate mood-induced feelings and justify mood-induced actions; those referents and rationales spread by contagion.

Soaring house prices and rising pop stars do not create optimism; social mood does. But soaring house prices and ecstatic crowds do make news, which spreads knowledge of referents by which some optimistic people have been expressing their positive mood, thereby providing other optimistic people with ideas for potential referents to express the positive mood they are experiencing at the same time. Some may choose one of them, some may choose another, and some may refrain from acting, but spreading knowledge offers options, and options compatible with people's proclivities spur ideational contagion. The same thing happens in times of negative mood. The socionomic idea that referents and rationales spread in the service of social mood is both theoretically and empirically superior to the pure contagion model, under which attitudes spread for any reason or for no reason.

Extent of Participation Does Not Drive Mood

One might think that broadening participation in a financial market would cause rising prices, but it could just as easily produce falling prices. One might think that widening attention paid to a pop star would cause his or her fortunes to rise, but it could just as easily cause them to fall. So, these presumed causes fail. In each case, the fundamental cause is not the number of people involved but the mood of the participants. The number of participants does not regulate mood; mood regulates the number of participants.

Stock market speculators are simply a subset of society that expresses social mood in a certain way; the size of the subset is irrelevant. Ten thousand speculators can produce the same percentage gain or loss in a stock index as a hundred million speculators. We see this result across more populous and less populous countries, such as India and Iceland, respectively. The widely differing breadth of participation in the U.S. stock market over a 200-year period has had no effect on the fractal form of the market or on the market's relationship to Presidential reelection outcomes (see *Socionomic Causality in Politics,* 2017). Social mood determines the agreed-upon rises and falls in the stock market regardless of how many people participate.

Summing Individual Economic Behavior Will Not Simulate Socionomic Behavior

One reason *The Wave Principle of Human Social Behavior* cited Smith et al.'s 1988 study of boom-and-bust behavior in the lab and Caldarelli et al.'s 1997 study finding normal market-pricing behavior absent exogenous input is that they properly addressed the behavior of aggregations. Their results are problematic to mainstream economic theory, which holds the mechanistic view that macroeconomics is simply summed microeconomics.

I ran into this reductionist assumption in 2003 when I had the privilege of participating (albeit at the extreme periphery) in a conference of top researchers in neuroeconomics. One of the presenters espoused the idea that he would be able to extrapolate the results of brain experiments on single individuals in a lab to come to an understanding of human behavior in the aggregate. I thought, "Has this person been to a pop concert?" If a researcher were to play a film of a musical group to a teenaged girl in a lab, would she weep, scream, wail, bury her head in her hands and faint? Not likely; but hundreds of girls might do so in a crowd near an extreme in positive social mood. If a researcher were to show a film of an Adolf Hitler speech to a middle aged man in a lab, would he bellow "Heil Hitler" and run out to smash storefronts? No, but thousands of men in a nighttime crowd might do so near an extreme in negative social mood. Could any lab experiment induce an isolated person to yank his pants down or her shirt up? I doubt it, but "flashing" happens all day and night on Bourbon Street during Mardi Gras. Simple activities such as listening to music and walking down the street (see Figures 1 through 4) can look quite different depending upon whether participants are individually or collectively motivated, because crowds create a context that induces people to access a different part of their brains (see Chapter 13), resulting in different behavior.

Lab experiments on individuals are unlikely to capture this difference. Because the top-down influence within the holistic herding dynamic would be missing, a researcher could not observe or even deduce the existence of Elliott waves of social mood from individuals' behavior in isolation.

The macroeconomic formula[6] displayed in Figure 5 is a typical example of neoclassical economists' attempts to sum individual behavior to predict macro behavior. This attempt at modeling takes inputs that motivate rational individuals and sums them to predict the economy. Naturally, it contains a *ceteris paribus* provision, and it expressly omits "consumers' moods" as a factor. Because waves of social mood—not microeconomic factors—regulate the expansion and contraction of the overall economy, and because summing individual economic motivations cannot capture collective socionomic motivation, such formulas can't work; and they don't.

Some critics of such models have charged that the very notion that mathematics can forecast human behavior is erroneous.[7] Socionomists and Elliotticians, however, suspect that economists are simply using the wrong basis for their math. Fractals have mathematical properties, and a self-affine, hierarchical fractal has predictive properties. The mathematics attending Elliott waves, to the limited degree of our understanding, may not give answers nearly as reliably as celestial mechanics, but it serves better than economists' models of summed micro-motivations.

Individual Behavior   **Collective Behavior**

Figure 1

Figure 2

Individual Behavior   **Collective Behavior**

Figure 3

Figure 4

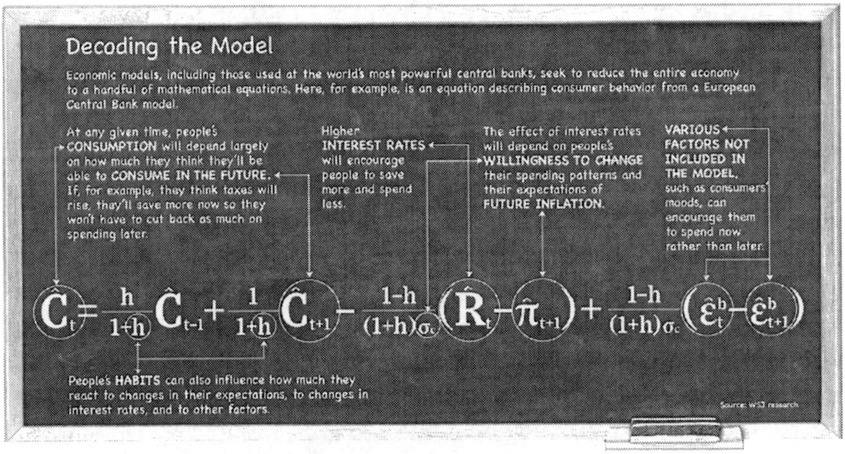

Figure 5

Socionomics' holistic model of social causality is incompatible with the mechanistic reductionism evident in Figure 5. Instead, its organicist viewpoint presumes an interactive relationship between the participatory qualities of individual human beings and an organizing principle governing the mood fluctuations of human aggregations. Individuals' personal moods may differ, and they may possess different and differing quantities of mood-related traits—including herding impulses, feelings of uncertainty, mimicking behavior, dopamine levels, oxytocin levels, testosterone levels and cortisol levels—but they cooperate with each other in simultaneously producing and experiencing fluctuations in social mood that comply with the Wave Principle. As philosophy professor Michael Green observed in 2001,[8] WP is non-mechanistic and impervious to reductionism. That's why Elliott called it a *principle* in the first place.

Induced Mood?

Some academic studies purport to have conducted experiments inducing mood by various means. Such claims might seem to challenge the socionomic idea that events are acausal to social mood. The studies we have perused, however, seem reasonably explicable within the bounds of socionomic theory.

When researchers say they have induced mood by showing subjects photographs of human faces with expressions of, say, elation or depression, we would concede that they may have tapped into one of the unconscious modes of communication that are involved in maintaining social mood. One study[9] in this regard—covered by both *New Scientist* (4/09) and *Scientific American* (7/09 and 4/10)—was funded by the Socionomics Foundation. Julie L. Hall and colleagues at the University of Michigan demonstrated that subtle social-mood cues, notably facial expressions, induced greater or lesser desires among subjects to choose an investment in risky stocks over safe bonds. Some of the facial cues were subliminal. This is an important aspect of the study, because socionomists infer from people's obliviousness to the existence of social mood that mood-sharing cues are subtle.

Hall et al.'s results support the socionomic hypothesis that positive social mood has impelled higher stock prices and lower savings rates, and vice versa. Most intriguingly, the study reported, "the expressions that had the *greatest effect* on both risk taking and the activity of the nucleus accumbens were the ones that *people could not consciously process*, suggesting that mood-altering cues that matter most to our bank accounts—and the stock market—are not obvious ones like the weather but rather *those that buffet our emotions beneath our awareness.*"[10] Hall's work seems to have identified one of the loci of mood and herding, since "the nucleus accumbens not only parallels a person's propensity for positive thinking but also is the neural barometer of financial risk taking."[11]

On the other hand, when studies suggest that events, actions or blatant manipulation affect people's mood, we first suspect that the result may be due to a temporary emotional response. In some studies, subjects are shown an evocative film or directed to recall a past event that made them feel a certain way, after which they are led to take a seemingly unrelated action that turns out to express the same feeling. These results seem to stem from sustained emotion, not induced mood.

A more subtle causality may attend studies that show, for example, that when a national sports team wins a major competition, that country's stock market tends to rise. If the claim is valid, and depending on the data involved in the claim, we would first investigate whether both events were due to an already-existing, positive state of social mood that would have impelled both the winning team to excel and the country's investors to buy stocks, a connection implied by Kendall's 75-year socionomic study of the sport of basketball.[12] Socionomic theory also allows (see below) that a temporary surge of emotion can prompt a brief perturbation of stock prices; but in such cases any market movement would sustain only if the trend had been underway already or was on the cusp of change anyway.

Does the Level of Emotion Determine the Amount of Herding?

Some researchers have concluded that people in an emotional state of mind are herding more so than people who are calm. But their tests may have detected different emotional states of herds rather than different amounts of herding. People in a state of high emotion may agree that the stock market is fascinating and worthy of attention. People in a state of low emotion may agree that the stock market is boring and unworthy of attention. The degree of emotion doesn't change the amount of agreement or the amount of herding. There are simply different intensities of emotion and varieties of action attached to the subject about which the herd agrees. Consider a group of gazelles on a savannah. If they begin to panic and run, are they suddenly herding more? No, the herd is simply moving from one emotional state to another. In the first case they were cueing each other to be calm, and in the second case they were cueing each other to be afraid.

The Idea of Rational Risk Assumption Is Inapplicable to Financial Markets, in which Speculators Are Actually Herding Pre-Rationally in an Attempt to Reduce Risk and Augment Reward

Some researchers have suggested that shifting risk preferences explain financial market behavior. Mired in the wrong context—that of utilitarian economics—they have postulated that buying and selling financial assets derives from conscious, rational decisions to take on more or less risk. The popular expression of this idea is the presumption of "risk on/risk off" changes in speculators' mindset as markets fluctuate. But since speculators take on more risk when prices are high and shed risk when prices are low, they are simply herding. The rational way to make money in financial markets is to do the opposite: take on more risk when prices are low and less risk when prices are high.

Just as with the terms *supply* and *demand* (see Chapter 12), the verbiage of risk preferences is unnecessary; it gives only an illusion of understanding bullish and bearish attitudes. In most discourses about speculators supposedly "accepting risk" and "rejecting risk," one could simply replace those terms with *bidding prices higher* and *offering prices lower* and end up with a more accurate statement. "Risk on/risk off" means the same thing as "bullish/bearish." The risk lingo offers no useful information, and, worse, the information it purports to offer is wrong.

Throwing all this risk talk into limbo is the fact that no one can actually calculate investment risk. One can calculate fairly reliably the statistical risk of flying commercial airlines, but no one can reliably calculate the risk of losing money on a financial speculation. The very fact that a speculator is considering a particular bet may be a function of social mood, herding and contagion, in which case the risk of making the bet is far greater than any statistics will reveal. Socionomics' primary objection to standard risk theory, however, is not on technical grounds but on fundamental grounds.

Socionomic theory holds that financial-market fluctuations are inconsistent with *rational risk assumption* but entirely consistent with *non-rational risk aversion*. Speculators are constantly herding, and herds act to *gain sustenance* and *avoid danger*. A herd of gazelles may lope toward the water hole and its vegetation to gain sustenance or dash from predators to avoid danger. The goal of both types of actions is to reduce the risk of death. Speculators exhibit the same unconsciously motivated behavior as if their decisions were a life-and-death matter. They bid prices higher during market advances as if herding will help them gain sustenance, and they offer prices lower during market declines as if herding will help them avoid danger. Ironically, the result is wholly the opposite: In the former case, acting with the herd leads them into danger due to taking on the risk of holding investment items at the wrong time, and in the latter case acting with the herd leads them away from sustenance due to jettisoning the risk of holding investment items, again at the wrong time.

The socionomic perspective explains what is really going on. In neither case—bidding prices higher or offering them lower—is there truly any thought whatsoever of taking on more risk, rationally or otherwise. In both cases, speculators in the aggregate are unconsciously acting to reduce risk, thanks to the emotionally satisfying impulse to herd. In a rising market, the herd thinks it is approaching reward, and in a falling market, the herd thinks it is avoiding danger. The law of patterned herding controls the vacillating emotions of optimism and pessimism that shift the herd's orientation between these two unconscious goals.

A standard assumption among theoretical economists is that the longer and further a market trend carries, the more it attracts risk-seekers. A socionomist identifies the opposite dynamic: The longer and further a market trend carries, the more it attracts the risk-*averse*.

Objectively, the risk of experiencing negative returns increases when speculators buy high and sell low. But herding is not objective, considered, conscious and rational; it is subjective, impulsive, unconscious and pre-rational. Subjectively, *herding speculators perceive greater risk as less risk and less risk as greater risk.* This is the source of all financial misery.

The discrepancy between objective levels of risk and speculators' subjective assessments of risk explains at least three things: the paradox between beneficial and actual speculator behavior (see Chapter 17); statistics demonstrating that speculators become more bullish the higher prices go and more bearish the lower prices go (see Figures 7, 8, 9, 11 and 14 of Chapter 12 and Figures 1 through 8 of Chapter 17); and powerful evidence that most speculators lose money (see Chapter 17).

Investors often claim to be assessing risk. They don't mean it. Most risk talk serves rationalization.

Economists who model risk preferences don't seem to consider how speculators feel. The vast majority of speculators, who buy when prices are elevated and sell when the market falls, do not feel nervous and fearful upon acting; they feel *relieved*. They do not know they have actually increased their chances of losing or reduced their chances of gaining, because unconsciously they have acted to reduce the discomforting feeling of missing out on gains or risking losses. Because their risk actually increases by both sets of actions, we may confidently conclude that such behavior is non-rational.

If you want to meet speculators who consciously take on risk, seek out the few who buy when others are panicking or sell short when the crowd is giddy. On taking the action, they will be nervous if not downright fearful, because the conscious portion of their minds understands they are taking on risk, and the unconscious portion is screaming at them not to do it.

Compatibly with the socionomic view of risk-taking, one study[13] in particular upset the idea that humans assess risk rationally. The authors concluded, "passing mood can profoundly alter 'rational decisions'"[14] about risk. Specifically, humans' attitude toward "loss aversion waxes and wanes in flexible ways, depending on whether or not the person is experiencing different fundamental motivational states, such as self-protection or looking for a mate."[15] According to socionomics, however, social mood is *the* "fundamental emotional state," and it heavily regulates supposedly causal desires such as "looking for a mate" and its ultimate results such as marriages, pregnancies and births (see Figure 5 of Chapter 10). It also heavily regulates levels of desire for "self-protection," as the very occurrence of stock market declines is due to the maladaptive impulse to flee with the herd as a means of self-protection.

The literature claiming that speculators practice conscious risk assumption and that bidding prices higher in uptrends and offering them lower in downtrends is rational needs to be scrapped. The socionomic perspective accounts for speculators' behavior in one neat causal explanation. For more on this topic, see Chapter 23.

Does the Market Ever React to News?

Part I of this book and Figures 1 through 5 in Chapter 12 essentially prove that the stock market is not priced according to external conditions, values or events. Nevertheless, speculators do sometimes at least *seem* momentarily to react to news.

At the theoretical level, socionomics has no trouble accommodating the possibility of brief, emotional reactions to news even with respect to stock indexes. News reactions, if they occur, create perturbations of mood-regulated pricing for only a few seconds or minutes, following which prices return as a cork in water to their mood-regulated level, as suggested by Figure 12 in Chapter 1. This potential, minor concession that mood-regulated pricing may be occasionally perturbed by emotional interference is akin to pragmatic economists' model of rational pricing occasionally perturbed by emotional interference, except that their primary regulator is rationally considered fundamental values and ours is waves of unconscious social mood.

On the other hand, evidence for even temporary emotional reactions in markets is surprisingly suspect. All market observers have seen futures prices gyrate more intensely for a few seconds or minutes before and/or after an announcement perceived as major news. As Chapters 1 and 4 demonstrate, however, ensuing market movement may be totally opposite to the tenor of such news, even when it is a total surprise. Then there are the numerous times (Chapter 2 offers two examples) when market participants are on the edge of their seats awaiting a dramatic market response to scheduled news, and *nothing happens*. The only thing we are fully comfortable conceding, then, is that volatility sometimes—but not always—increases briefly around news events. But since market volatility often increases quite suddenly *absent* any news events, we hardly feel compelled to make a case for any degree of reliable mechanical causality from news.

While stimulus-and-response is one way to account for the occasional coinciding of news and market volatility, there are two socionomically informed reasons why these coincidences may occur. One pertains to anticipated news, the other to unanticipated news. First, when observers are awaiting news—such as an economic number, a political address or a central-bank announcement—increased volatility immediately surrounding the event may be due to some speculators having held their mood-induced impulses at bay for a time (say, an hour or two) while waiting for news to come out, at which time they rush to push buy and sell buttons pretty much as they would have done anyway. Instead of flowing in a natural sequence, the orders come out first sparsely and then in a rush. Second, sometimes a correlation between dramatic, unexpected news and volatility may be due to the fact that when social mood is either at the center or on the cusp of rapid change, the emotions it fosters lead to increased market volatility while simultaneously prompting a social action that makes news. Figures 7 and 10 in Chapter 1 offer examples of news coinciding respectively with a wave center and a cusp. Consider also Figures 26 and 27 in Chapter 2. It *looks* as if each of some 21 news reports of authorities' actions made the stock market jump upward for a day or so in the middle of an extended market collapse. But one can just as well interpret the picture socionomically: At each temporary wave low, the authorities became so fearful that they rushed to announce some new program. In that case, the coincidence of news and jumps in the market were natural rather than due to mechanistic cause and effect. Supporting this version of events are three facts: (1) Sometimes authorities act and the market does not move; (2) bear market rallies are often sharp, news or no news; and (3) the entire decline traced out clear Elliott waves, which EWI labeled all the way down in real time.

It may seem that draconian news about a specific company sometimes impacts the price of its stock. Lawsuits pertaining to asbestos, for example, ruined Johns Manville, reducing its stock price to zero. But the lawsuits themselves had a socionomic cause, as they poured forth in 1982, the year of the bottom in a 16-year bear market in the Dow/PPI. The company filed for bankruptcy on August 26, seventeen days after that era's intraday low in the Dow and S&P. Chapter 29 of *Pioneering Studies in Socionomics* details a similar history pertaining to the Enron Corporation. In both cases, the companies were at risk for objective reasons, but it took a negative social mood to prompt social actions that brought them down.

Even investors who habitually buy and sell individual stocks on news may have no effect on overall stock prices. They can simply shift the composition of their overall holdings—for example by selling one stock while buying another—thus keeping stock market indexes at a level compatible with social mood.

Does the Market Overreact and Underreact to News?

Markets' constant dynamism and their pesky deviations from expected rational reactions to news challenge the mechanics paradigm. One response among theorists has been to add a dollop of non-rationality to the formula. Instead of exogenous cause and rational reaction, a widely proffered formulation proposes exogenous cause and *inappropriate* rational reaction.

One version[16] of this construct attempts to explain *fluctuations* in stock prices by postulating that speculators continually *overreact* to news after which prices revert to where they should have been; and to explain *trends* in stock prices by postulating that speculators continually *underreact* to news after which they figure out that they should have reacted more strongly, so they bring prices slowly and belatedly to their proper level.

In my view, these narratives are hindsight-driven, content-free, tautological and self-negating. Like purported changes in "supply" and "demand" in financial markets (see Chapter 12), these explanations can pertain only after the fact and have no substance themselves. They depend upon a pure presumption that markets ultimately find their proper level based on values. Proponents offer no evidence relating to proper values, and they cannot do so, because there isn't any. Another problem is that they do not specify the interaction between their two completely opposing mechanisms. Markets constantly trend and fluctuate at different degrees simultaneously, so are speculators overreacting at some degrees while simultaneously underreacting at others? If so, how do we know aside from simply observing that the market is fluctuating at some degrees and trending at others? Finally, since stock price changes are a fractal covering all scales, as Mandelbrot proved mathematically, what really is the difference between trending and fluctuating? In the sense that a fractal is an infinitely subdivided object, there is none.

Socionomics' explanation differs: The detachment between news and subsequent stock market prices that researchers have observed is real, but it is not due to speculators continually misjudging the meaning of news. It is due to patterned herding operating independently of news.

As related in Chapter 2, virtually everyone concurs that the crash of 1987 took place in the absence of causal news. Thus, there was no news to which investors could overreact. To maintain the overreaction model in the face of such contrary evidence, one study, while admitting that "little fundamental news about security values" attended the crash, resorted to the idea of *endogenously* generated news: "One interpretation of the crash is that investors overreacted to the news of panic selling by other investors...."[17] The choice of words here—"*news* of panic selling"—is an attempt to maintain the exogenous-cause model in the face of its negation. If markets operate this way all the time, with speculators copying each other for no exogenously caused reason, we end up right where we should: at pure herding, with actual news being irrelevant.

Socionomics dispenses with hypotheses of overreaction and underreaction to news. Since the stock market does not react to news in the first place (as demonstrated in Chapters 1, 2 and 4), it cannot overreact or underreact to it.

Are Financial Markets Priced According to a Mix of Fundamental Values and "Psychology"?

Many treatises assert that stock prices are anchored to fundamental values but repeatedly depart from them—often for years—for various psychological reasons, after which they revert to their proper level. Value investors in the tradition of Graham and Dodd (see Chapter 33), professional economists, market commentators and even most technicians seem to agree that stock prices are determined by a mix of fundamentals and emotions. This view supposedly accounts for the observation that stocks are priced sometimes near and sometimes far from various standards of value; reason presumably governs in the first case and emotions in the second.

This explanation has the earmarks of an ad-hoc formulation: Fundamentals determine prices except when they don't; emotions drive buying and selling except when they don't. The thesis of mixed causality has inspired edifying behavioral-finance studies on certain errors of human thought, but it has not led to a coherent theory of financial pricing, nor is it likely to do so.

Socionomic theory explains more neatly what is going on: Speculators impulsively command prices up and down. As a byproduct of this activity, stock prices seem reasonably related to corporate values at some times and unreasonably cheap or expensive at other times. When values appear reasonable, it looks as if the rational assessment of fundamentals is determining them, and when values appear cheap or expensive, it looks as if psychology is in charge. But the differences are merely artifacts resulting from the market's natural dynamic, not results of qualitatively varying causes.

The widely unrecognized independence of financial-market price movement from news has had a confounding effect upon economists' thinking. Keynes wrote, "day-to-day fluctuations in the profits of existing investments, which are obviously of an ephemeral and nonsignificant character, tend to have an altogether excessive, and even an absurd, influence on the market."[18] Exasperation is just what a socionomist would expect from a keen market observer lamentably anchored to exogenous cause. Think about it: If a bit of news is "obviously insignificant," why would there be any influence on the market at all, much less an absurd one? The trouble is not with the market but with Keynes' formulation. All such misconceptions melt away under the socionomic perspective: The market does not alternate inconsistently from sanity to madness in reacting to news; its pre-rational dynamic operates consistently apart from news.

The hypothesis of mixed causality is quite plastic in its application. The stock market seems to regulate whether market observers will point to fundamental or psychological causes on any particular day.

Socionomic causality is steadfast. Rather than offering a model in which rationality and non-rationality jointly or alternately characterize purely financial markets, socionomic theory observes a more accurate and useful dichotomy in which rationality characterizes purely economic markets and non-rationality characterizes purely financial markets.

Another Bogus Qualitative Distinction, between Up and Down

Market commentators often speak as if they consider uptrends to be normal and downtrends to be aberrant. This belief is based on the idea that uptrends and downtrends have qualitatively different psychological origins. Observers often describe market rises as resulting from investors rationally weighing fundamentals and market declines as resulting from traders panicking due to "mob psychology." Although widely applied, this formulation is incoherent. The same error of qualitative duality attaches to the idea of aberrant uptrends under traditional bubble theory (see Chapter 23). Socionomics differs in recognizing both rises and declines in markets as components of a single, unified process.

A Variant on Rationality-Plus-Psychology in which Direction Matters

The "Fractal Market Hypothesis" (FMH)[19] incorporates rationality, dual agency, investor psychology and a fundamental difference between uptrends and downtrends in financial markets into a single model. FMH is another middle-ground construction in which financial-market agents rationally process information except when they don't.

FMH recognizes (along with Elliott and Mandelbrot) that financial-market fluctuations lasting days look similar to fluctuations lasting months. It attempts to explain this fact by proposing that speculators process information differently due to their different time horizons: Short term traders evaluate information for its near term implications, creating small fluctuations in the market, while long term investors evaluate information for its long term implications, creating big fluctuations in the market. An exogenous "shock" in the form of news, for instance, might cause traders to sell but investors to buy.

This formulation is simply EMH with the added component of hetero-geneous agency in the form of traders and investors. The idea of a trader/investor dichotomy has been around for a hundred years. While seemingly reasonable, speculators in fact operate over a wide continuum of infinitely different and constantly shifting time horizons, so the proposed dual-agency distinction is spurious.

To keep its formulation viable, FMH proposes yet another dichotomy, delineating normal market behavior from panics. It asserts that its heteroge-neous system is normally operative but becomes "broken"[20] during market panics, at which time heterogeneity disappears and all participants suddenly become short-term oriented, causing the market to become "unstable and inefficient."[21] In other words, the heterogeneous system explains things except when it doesn't, in which case there must be a homogeneous system.

Ironically, the very existence of the market's fractal form negates this fractal-hypothesis claim. Market prices decline—sometimes swiftly—on all time scales, not just during the few panics that modelers feel a need to explain. To account for all sharp price drops by proposing agents' shifts from dual to single mindedness abandons the model's bedrock idea of heterogeneous-agent causality and seems to transform the overall hypothesis into a clever but ad-hoc pretext for market dynamism.

STF rejects all four of FMH's key ideas—rational information processing, heterogeneous agency, the idea of heterogeneous/homogeneous shifts, and the idea of an up/down dichotomy—as being fundamentally causal to financial market movement. Pre-rational herding accounts for financial market swings; the Wave Principle is never "broken"; financial-market participants are a homogeneous group; there is no fundamentally important, qualitative difference between sharp declines and other times; markets are never "unstable" but always dynamic at the level of experience while simultaneously being metastable at the system level; and socionomic theory never has to replace waves of social mood temporarily with something else to account for market trends.

Is the Market Reflexing, Feeding Back, Adapting or Evolving?

Theories of financial causality involving reflexivity, feedback, adaptation and evolution have in common the assumption that all market causality resides in individual agents. Although advocates advance these theories to oppose the static model of neoclassical economics, they share its metatheoretical base of mechanistic reductionism (see Chapter 6). Under these theories of inconstant agency, financial markets are viewed as qualitatively mutable and variable, whereas under WP they are understood to be qualitatively immutable and only quantitatively variable. We will briefly review two versions of the idea of self-referential, infinitely mutable markets.

Reflexivity Theory

In *The Alchemy of Finance*,[22] famed investor George Soros proposed what he called "the principle of reflexivity," under which "investors['] belief[s] will change the way they invest, and that in turn will change the nature of the markets they are observing."[23] He identified two feedback loops, one between investors' subjective beliefs and market action, and another between market action and external conditions. Both loops at times can be self-fulfilling or self-negating. Beliefs can run the gamut from faith in efficient markets to supposing that a particular exogenous cause will impact a market in a certain way. The idea is that beliefs cause actions, which change the market, which changes perceptions, which causes new actions, which change exogenous conditions, which change perceptions, which change the market, and so on ad infinitum. All of these interactions presumably cause markets to evolve, often in unpredictable ways. Soros charged that because fallibility undermines fundamental analysis, because subjectivity rules pricing, and because reflexivity causes uncertainty, there can be no laws of finance. He nevertheless saw a "need for a new paradigm in social science"[24] based on the conviction that none of the social sciences can be on the same level of precision as the physical sciences.

Socionomics agrees that financial pricing is subjective, that non-rational beliefs are involved in the financial pricing process, that attitudes change economic and social conditions, and that social science differs from physical science in terms of precision and predictability. Soros got all this right because he is not a conventional economist but an observant trader dealing in the real world.

Socionomics, however, does not embrace reflexivity. Soros complained, "My critics say that I am merely stating the obvious."[25] But socionomics holds that what seems obvious to all these market observers in this self-referential mechanistic stew is just as wrong as the conventional view.

Under socionomics, beliefs about future market prices do not arise from misinterpreting exogenous causes (from whatever theoretical base) but from fluctuations in social mood. Speculators subjectively (mis)interpret exogenous causes all the time, but it is not because their logic is fallible; it is because their premise of exogenous cause is invalid. Their beliefs about specific exogenous causes, moreover, are not fundamental determinants of market behavior but only a transitory phase in the service of rationalizing their optimism or pessimism. There are no feedback loops between beliefs and market actions or between market actions and social conditions; the cause is unidirectional, from mood to beliefs to actions, which create conditions. Financial markets thus remain ruled by pre-rational herding and do not evolve. The Wave Principle of human social behavior is a product of evolution, and WP is probably even a governor of evolution (see Chapter 13 of *The Wave Principle of Human Social Behavior*), but WP itself does not evolve from one form to another. Changes in "the nature of markets" that *seem* like evolution are merely shifts in the tenor of markets and economic conditions, which are prompted by fluctuations in social mood. Finally, socionomics holds that subjective pricing per se is in no way an impediment to science. Rather, understanding it finally allows us to discern the true laws of finance, therefore offering a basis for eventually turning the field into a science.

Adaptation Theory

The Adaptive Markets Hypothesis (AMH) is a model of financial markets incorporating economic motivation, heterogeneous agency, reactive agents and evolutionary adaptation. Its roots extend to Alchian's evolutionary finance theory, proposed in 1950 (see Chapter 33). AMH proposes the existence of "distinct groups of market participants"—including retail investors, market makers, hedge funds and pension funds—who compete for "profit opportunities" as if they were different species competing for resources such as "food and water."[26] It proposes that these groups' investing strategies evolve through learning by way of "positive and negative reinforcement" with the goal of achieving financial survival in an environment that constantly changes due to participating agents' own actions, which feed back into the system as new environmental causes, just as reflexivity theory has it. AMH aims to reconcile EMH and behavioral finance (see next section) with ideas of evolution and natural selection and by equating financial behavior to economic behavior.

STF—as detailed in Chapter 12—differs from this depiction on several counts. Under STF, financial markets comprise no heterogeneous groups that one can attach to a multiple-species metaphor. Speculators are not members of qualitatively different groups but of a single species, motivated by pre-rational herding, whose investment behaviors do not fit into distinct categories but fall along continua. Financial and economic markets, moreover, are fundamentally different and cannot be equated, even metaphorically. Producers and consumers on one hand and speculators on the other perform two distinctly different behavioral roles. Competing for resources does help people to thrive in economic markets, but the best way for most people to thrive when it comes to financial markets is to avoid them. Furthermore, it is difficult to see how profit opportunities can be considered scarce resources to be exploited or fought over, because no one uses up the store of profit opportunities; they are, in fact, perpetually available. Finally, while nature produces many successful species, no "species" of speculator (see Chapter 17) learns anything reliable or achieves long-run financial success, so there must be no process of adaptation, natural selection or evolution going on among such groups. Even the captains of America's top investment banks, which had been in business for a hundred years, proved they had learned little about capturing profit opportunities when they went bankrupt—either officially or unofficially (to be saved by non-free-market bailouts)—in 2008. Under STF, financial markets cannot evolve, because no group of speculators escapes the primitive dynamic of pre-rational herding.

AMH incorporates and aims to explain the longstanding proposition that the dynamics of financial markets shift in response to temporarily profitable investment strategies—such as value investing and momentum investing—so that they are continually thwarted. STF differs in viewing vicissitudes in strategic success merely as epiphenomena. WP's natural dynamism shifts market environments on its own schedule, which incidentally alters, at fractal intervals, various investment strategies' degrees of success and failure. Speculators do not control shifts in the experience of waves; waves control shifts in the experiences of speculators.

MIT finance professor Andrew Lo, who formulated AMH, also conducted a seminal study[27] statistically validating the famous head and shoulders pattern (H&S) in financial markets. H&S is a function of normal price and volume development under EW,[28] which is why the pattern is real as well as timeless. It would seem, however, that if markets did adapt to, and evolve away from, profit opportunities, then H&S, which signals a profit opportunity, could not be a consistent phenomenon but would have to be merely an occasional one, to be obliterated repeatedly, if not permanently, by adaptation and evolution. In other words, it would appear that one can attach either H&S or AMH directly to causality, reliability and predictability but not both. STF, in its quest to be metatheoretically consistent, is on the side of H&S.

Could Reflexive, Adapting, Evolving Markets Dissolve the Wave Principle?

The idea that markets adapt to the actions of individual agents has long led to a charge that if everyone started applying EW to speculating, WP would self-destruct. This view likewise derives from the mechanistic view of markets, under which reductionistic, bottom-up causality is the only operative influence. Since that is the wrong theoretical paradigm, we may be sure there is no chance the proposed outcome would happen. Practical thinking leads—as it must under any valid theory or philosophy—to the same conclusion, for numerous reasons: First, the robust nature of waves makes them only probabilistically predictable, leaving substantial leeway for alternative outcomes and opinions at every degree of analysis. Second, it takes study and practice to achieve success in market analysis and specula-tion, which a significant number of people will never achieve. Third, to alter Elliott waves in a financial market, individuals would have to bet on them en masse identically, and that will never happen because of points one and two. Fourth, such betting would have to be done emotionlessly and sans errors of laziness, greed and stupidity, which will also never happen un-less humans turn into Spocks. We might personify the issue by saying that Elliott waves are more in control of their own behavior than participating individuals are of theirs. Fifth, whenever a financial market enters a major corrective period, predictive accuracy at all but the highest wave degrees recedes, pushing the potential for widespread agreement even further out of reach. By the time a correction induces people to give up on reading Elliott waves, an impulse emerges and waves become clearer again. Ultimately, the organic nature of the social-mood system assures that humans in the aggregate will never dominate, outsmart or eliminate Elliott waves.

Behavioral Finance and Economics—A Middle Ground

Behavioral economics (BE) and behavioral finance (BF) have so far taken a middle ground between the ideas of rational and non-rational markets. Studies conducted under the banner of behavioral finance have been extremely beneficial toward chipping away at the edifice of neoclassical economic theory and EMH. Whether elucidating ownership bias, the house money effect, the sunk cost fallacy, the disposition effect, the endowment effect or the use of heuristics to make decisions, studies in this field have identified exceptions to rational decision-making in both economic and financial contexts.

Researchers in these fields generally accept rationality as the primary determinant of both economic and financial pricing, in which case their identified non-rational biases account only for departures from that norm. While psychological quirks may be extremely important to understanding nuances of economic behavior, they cannot be used to explain financial markets' deviations from a rational norm if there isn't one; and there isn't one. With respect to finance, BF formulations may turn out to describe aspects or artifacts of the pre-rational herding dynamic.

R.N. Elliott Anticipated Behavioral Finance

R.N. Elliott anticipated behavioral finance in 1938. He stated, "Those who have attempted to deal with the market's movements have failed to recognize the extent to which the market is a psychological phenomenon."[29] In 1943 he added, "The study of psychology in economics is not only interesting but highly enlightening. A liaison would increase their utility and explain effectively any abnormal behavior of markets. …How far booms and depressions are due to purely economic events or to exaggeration of temperament would be hard to define, of course. Yet there is more to it than, at first thought, one might suppose."[30]

Chapter 2 of *The Wave Principle of Human Social Behavior* quotes Elliott extensively to show that he laid the foundation for the discovery of socionomic causality. Yet as the above comments show, he did not fully understand that his Wave Principle discovery had wiped out such ideas as "abnormal behavior of markets" and changes in prosperity due to "purely economic events." He was still mixing psychological and mechanical causality, as do modern proponents of behavioral finance and conventional bubble theories (see Chapter 23).

Socionomics makes no such concessions. It is principled, radical and purist. Fluctuations in stocks and the economy are *results*, not causes. "Temperament," to use Elliott's term, is their only cause. Social mood drives social actions, period.

The Socionomic Theory of Herding Fosters a Richer Comprehension of Social Trends

Socionomic ideas open the door to a deeper understanding of all kinds of social trends and events. Consider this enlightened discussion from physicist Mark Buchanan, quoting academic economist Brad DeLong, from mid-2008:

> The crisis also illustrates another shortcoming of equilibrium thinking: a tendency to underestimate the likelihood of sudden large events. …Failure to appreciate this has led to a number of big losses by "quant" hedge funds, which use complex mathematical algorithms to analyse the markets. "They said things like, 'Our strategy was fine,

we were just hit by a 16-standard-deviation event,'" he says. This reflects erroneous equilibrium thinking that assumes the tail of the curve is slender. "Tails are fat," says DeLong.[31]

Mandelbrot's observation from 1963[32] that price changes in financial markets have fat-tailed distributions became widespread after the 1987 crash and remains accurate. But fat tails do not explain why many quant funds failed so soon after coming into being. They geared up for big wins but imploded in a very short time. (Chapter 40 cites an example.) Why is that?

Socionomics provides insight into this question. It is true that the financial system did not experience a once-in-a-million years event in 2008, but even if a fat tail were to render the likelihood of such a crisis to be, say, once in fifty or a hundred years, it still wouldn't account for why these quants lost money so quickly after formulating their strategies. Socionomics uniquely recognizes that the very models they constructed were the product of a mindset shaped by social mood, herding, ideational contagion and linear projection. The quarter-century-long trend toward positive social mood and the incessant news of rising stock and bond prices eventually prompted mathematically inclined people to search for treasure in financial markets. That same period provided the skewed market data on which they based their analyses, and as appliers of linear as opposed to fractal projection they were not attuned to the fact that the longer a trend goes on, the more likely it is to change. These quants, simply put, joined the herd after a long trend toward positive social mood that led people to spread awareness about finance and which also produced a seemingly reliable investment environment. These two conditions regulated the timing of quants' decisions to try to figure how to make money from financial markets. Their propensity for projecting long-lasting conditions linearly into the future sealed their doom. By the time their strategies became fully operational, old trends and conditions had matured to the point that new ones were due to emerge. Emerge they did. That's why these funds went under so quickly.

In 2009, two political scientists[33] reported that fat tails are also characteristic of distributions of data on the intensity of geopolitical events. Socionomics explains why: Fat tails in both finance and politics derive from exactly the same source: the WP structure of fluctuations in social mood.

The Mechanics Paradigm Leads to Immoral Policy Prescriptions; Socionomics is Morally Good

Chapter 1 showed that the anthrax attacks of 2001-2002 began on the exact day of a significant low in the stock market in September 2001 and continued until shortly after an equally significant peak in March 2002, from which point the stock market plummeted to new lows. Socionomic theory suggests that the year-and-a-half trend toward negative social mood finally prompted the attacker to act, and positive mood likely induced him to quit.[34] In other words, the attacks were not causes of mood change but results. As noted in that chapter, the mechanics paradigm under which terrorist attacks are causes of market behavior would force a person to conclude that anthrax attacks are bullish for the stock market and that ceasing them is bearish. Stock markets' behavior during and after the Charlie Hebdo attack (described in Chapter 4) leads to the same type of conclusion. Figure 10 in Chapter 1 and Figure 1 in Chapter 4 would thereby have implications for public policy, whereby authorities should encourage crazed people to shoot up newspaper offices and send deadly packages to prominent citizens in order to get the stock market to go up.

Laugh if you will, but exogenous-cause logic demands this immoral policy prescription. Such a plan would not be as evil as advocating war to get the economy rolling, an idea that has no doubt surfaced in the private chambers of more than one U.S. president, thanks to economists who promulgate the perverse idea that war stimulates an economy. As recently as 2009, one of the most prominent economists of the Ivy League declared, "The only way we got out of the Great Depression was a full-scale war."[35]

Socionomics wipes this wicked idea off the map. A socionomist can explain the true causality: Two results of the high-degree trend toward negative social mood that began in 1929 were the Great Depression and ultimately a full-scale war, which broke out in the final month of a second economic contraction and lasted through the beginning of the ensuing recovery. The timing of these events fooled economists into thinking that government spending on the war caused the recovery. Spending on the war was not a cause; it was a result.

Do not listen to anyone who recommends war or government spending as a way to generate prosperity. Such advice stems from the exogenous-cause mindset, which is blind to the true motivator of social change. War and government spending are wasteful and destructive. Economies recover not because of them but despite them. This truth attends all technocrats' policy prescriptions for governments and central banks, as discussed in Chapter 25.

Socionomic analysis can warn individuals ahead of time when war and terrorist attacks are likely, thereby helping them avoid these dangers. Ultimately, socionomic knowledge leads to life instead of death. Socionomics is morally good because it is both practical and true.

Are Specialized Sociometers Independent of Overall Social Mood?

We infer from patterns in stock market prices that society's overall mood fluctuates in accordance with Elliott waves. We also observe that prices in speculatively traded markets that do *not* track overall social mood also fluctuate in accordance with Elliott waves. Certain non-financial social activities, some of which are described in *Socionomic Studies of Society and Culture* (2017), do so as well. Is the difference between these two classes of herding qualitative or merely quantitative? Do people share multiple mood processes when they participate in multiple herds, or is herding an autonomous process that pertains to many activities but which social mood only sometimes guides?

To date, socionomic theory has been meticulous in differentiating between the patterned pricing observable in myriad financial markets and the dynamic of overall social mood, which reliably regulates fluctuations only in the stock market. There are four reasons for this stance:

- Cultural trends correlate consistently with the stock market, as shown in Chapter 10. I am unaware of cultural trends correlating well with trends in financial markets that move independently of the stock market.

- Price changes in bonds, precious metals, commodities and currencies do not track those in the stock market, suggesting a substantial degree of independence from the stock market.

- Trends in many financial markets seem quite independent of each other. I have found so-called intermarket analysis—"If market X does this, market Y should do that"—to be unreliable. Markets may trend in the same or opposite directions for a while, but such correlations (aside from those between married first cousins, such as gold and silver) always evaporate eventually. (See, for example, Figure 8 in Chapter 2.) Whenever I find my mind slipping toward the mental default that two markets should "make sense" with respect to each other, I slap my face to sober up. Of course, I can almost always formulate a story to fit; that's what everyone does.

- Fluctuations in other types of social activities also seem independent of each other. As noted in Chapter 7, separate Elliott wave dynamics have regulated the aggregate activity of people who smoke cigarettes, join unions or trade slaves. They undoubtedly regulate many other social activities as well.

The combination of these empirical observations leads to the conclusion that herding and/or mood-sharing can occur apart from fluctuations in overall social mood and its meter, the stock market.

Nevertheless, we might at least entertain the possibility that there exists a complex interrelationship among all these sets of waves, coordinated by subtle attributes of overall social mood that we have yet to discover. Supporting this possibility is the fact that certain investment items—such as commodities—have tended to lie dormant during upward impulse waves (i.e. bull markets as opposed to bear market rallies) in the stock market and rise during corrective waves in the stock market. Occasionally they fall hard during declines at the start or end of stock market corrections. The prices of the Dow/PPI and oil have followed this description for over a century, as depicted in Figure 6. The interplay between these two markets is not due to a shock system, as no rule governs the two markets' price directions on any scale of measurement. It is a dance between two Elliott waves.

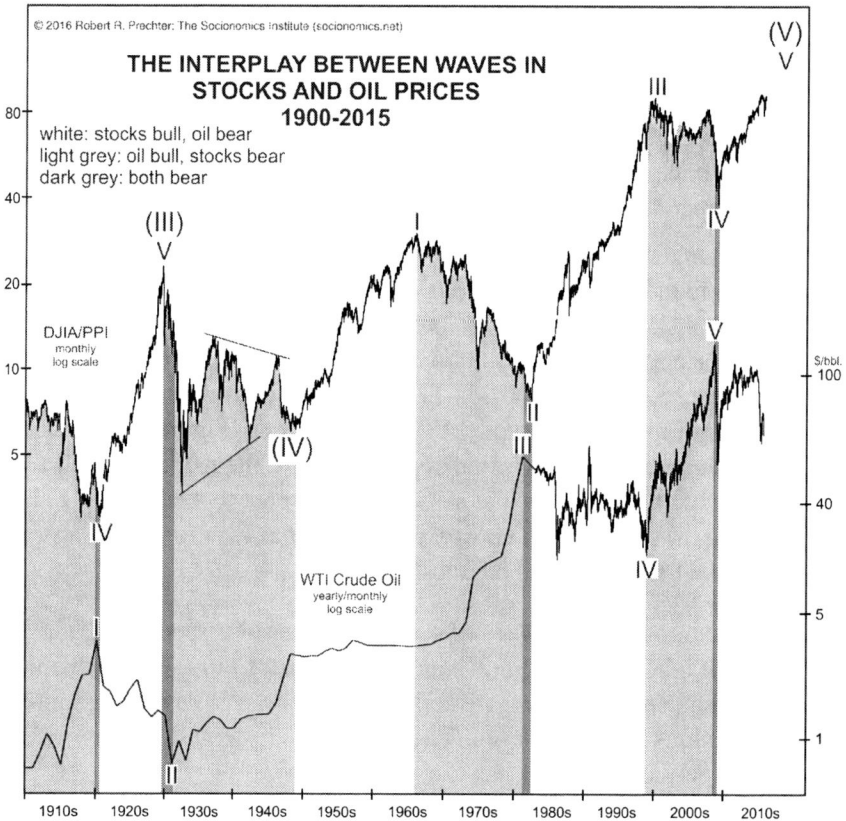

Figure 6

Precious metals have tended to move in concert with commodities, but not perfectly. In their previous major bull market, the two sectors peaked at different times, in 1980 and 1981, respectively. More recently, commodities topped in 2008, while the metals resumed rising into 2011. Yet, somewhat harmonically, the metals did top in the final full year of decline in real estate prices and the same year that the DJIA bottomed in the first decline within its new uptrend. Those two markets indicated that social mood at that time was near the negative extreme it had reached at the 2009 bottom.

Regarding another alternative investment, it happens that the two largest real estate booms of the past century ended at nearly the same time within the stock market's wave pattern. A nationwide land boom famously topped and reversed in 1925-6, and the more recent national real estate mania topped and reversed in 2005-6. In both cases, the reversal took place between the peak of wave ③ and the end of wave ④ within a larger wave V in the stock market. (Not shown; but you can infer the position of these wave labels by examining Figure 3 in Chapter 23.)

The question is, do all Elliott waves of social activity involve independent herding and/or mood-sharing dynamics, or does overall social mood somehow regulate the interplay among them? The latter thought leads to deep contemplation but not necessarily to the truth.

Challenging the notion of a single causal source is the observation that contradictory nuances of behavior among these markets appear at lesser degree. For example, within stocks' bear markets, sometimes commodities have fluctuated mostly negatively with stocks' subwaves, as happened during the 1970s, and sometimes they have fluctuated mostly positively with them, as happened in 2002-2011. This difference could be due to some reliably shifting relationship of which we are unaware. But Occam's razor requires that we default, for now, to ascribing it to the two sectors' substantial independence.

Detailing various markets' possible interrelationships at ever-lower degrees would become increasingly complex in fractal fashion. Attempting to delineate fully any such grand formula is beyond the scope of this book and may not even be a valid exercise. Perhaps a future socionomist will take up the challenge. Until such time, the most parsimonious theoretical statement, which also affords the cleanest way to anticipate market trends, remains that each social activity or financial market that displays Elliott waves is dynamically independent and should be analyzed according to its own waves. For an excellent example of just such an exercise, see Chapter 22.

Since financial markets, for the most part, fluctuate according to Elliott waves just as stocks do, something identical must be in charge of each market's fluctuations. The remaining question is whether that something is herding, mood-sharing or a combination of the two. As conceded at the end of Chapter 6, we remain ignorant of the precise details of the cognitive processes involved in herding and mood-sharing. But we can entertain some conjectures.

Animal vs. Human Herding

A dog will repeatedly looks at its owner, constantly looking for cues of what to do. The owner is the leader, and the dog is a pack animal. Participants in financial markets are doing something similar. They constantly watch their fellows, alert for cues of what to do. Since no leaders actually set the course of markets, however, followers are cueing off each other in a guidance void, allowing social mood to arise as an attribute of the group.

Human mood-sharing and financial herding differ from herding in animals. Animals herd, but only a few animal species seem to share mood, and presumably no groups of animals change in a fractal pattern how they express moods or value things. The Elliott wave pattern of social mood fluctuation also regulates human societies' periods of technological progress and regress, which animals do not experience.

The integrity of socionomic theory does not rest on the idea of herding as it pertains to animal populations. It is not socionomics' starting point, nor would socionomic theory be negated if herding as animals do were someday shown to be unrelated to human mood-sharing. The herding to which socionomics refers is whatever social actions derive from social mood and/ or fluctuate in Elliott waves.

Two Evolutionary Possibilities

How did evolution produce socionomic causality? I can think of two possibilities.

One possibility is that humans evolved in such a way that our animal ancestors' impulses to herd *morphed into* an impulse to participate in mood-sharing, with the added property of fractal fluctuation. Under this option, the single process of mood-sharing governs all socionomic causality.

The other possibility is that humans inherited animals' primitive herding impulses but evolved to develop an *independent* mood-sharing capacity, which began regulating the herding impulses. Under this option, the two capacities work together in the process of socionomic causality.

If, as we would suspect, animals do not participate in Elliott waves of social mood, such participation must have come about only during human evolution, not before. Since by both of these suggested evolutionary paths mood-sharing came late in the evolutionary process, it must be mood-sharing, not herding, that initiates humans' participation in Elliott waves.

The presence of Elliott waves in all of the above-cited instances in turn suggests that all humans are able to participate in multiple, separate, mood-sharing processes simultaneously. The terms "group mood" and "market mood" can thus apply separately to all types of uncorrelated social trends and financial markets. By this chain of logic, overall social mood would have to differ only quantitatively, not qualitatively, from more narrowly shared moods. The term "social mood" can still refer to the mood of an entire society, but it must termed "overall social mood" at times when we discuss it along with lesser examples of group mood or market mood whose fluctuations are differently timed.

The idea that *Elliott waves of shared moods*—not just an animal-like herding dynamic—are the mental drivers and primary shapers of multiple sets of social actions explains why people embraced so maniacally the bullish case for real estate in 2005-2006 (see Figure 3 in Chapter 13), for oil in 2006-2008 (see Figure 27 in Chapter 22) and gold in 2009-2011 (see Figure 4 in Chapter 18). The extremity of speculators' bullish zeal at these markets' peaks does not fit simple herding attending advances of merely a few years' duration but well fits three markets that were culminating mood trends lasting nearly a century, which is what our Elliott wave analysis (see Chapter 22) had long indicated. In other words, it took mood-sharing of peak, Supercycle-degree extremity to bring about the lofty level of passion in evidence toward the end of those long bull markets. Herding alone— especially as it pertains to animals—does not seem to account for these quantitative extremes.

It may seem strange that a person could share multiple mood states at once, with more than one group. But the effects of this ability appear all the time, as when a single speculator aggressively buys one market and shorts another while expressing equally passionate positive and negative feelings respectively towards them.

It may also seem strange that people can participate fully in social mood trends that began before they were born. But as an article about a sports team quoted at the outset of Chapter 13 in *The Wave Principle of Human Social Behavior* so poetically demonstrated, people can absorb long-lasting cultural trends and histories from others as if they had lived them. Under socionomics' holistic causal structure (see Chapters 6 and 37), it makes perfect sense that they do.

Modeling the Single-Process Version

In elucidating socionomic causality, we currently use the term *herding impulse* to refer to mental motivation, *patterned mood-sharing* to refer to its

regulator, and *herding* to refer to resulting physical activity. If socionomic causality is ever proven to involve only one process that came about when herding
in animals evolved into mood-sharing in humans, socionomic theory would
shift to using only the term *patterned mood-sharing* for the mental motivational
aspect of socionomic causality and *herding* for its action aspect.

The idea that mood-sharing *is* herding in humans is theoretically neat.
On the other hand, the idea of two independent but integrated processes, a
new one built aside the old, seems more compatible with the messy way that
evolution typically progresses. Perhaps future neurological studies on animals
and humans will resolve this question. To complete our discussion, Kenneth
Olson offers his ideas on the theoretical attributes of the second option:

Modeling the Dual-Process Version (by Kenneth R. Olson)

Herding and social mood are two central constructs in socionomics.
Both are unconscious, non-rational, endogenously determined processes
that operate continually.

The exact relationship between herding and social mood currently
entails some ambiguity. Conceptual clarity would result from considering
that neither social mood nor herding causes or predisposes the other but,
instead, they are two independent processes that interact to produce patterns
of society-wide behavior.

The process of herding assures that people will act in concert but by itself
does not produce social mood or determine the tenor and character of behavior. Social mood is the rudder that steers the direction of herding behavior.

Herding is always present, whether in animals who join together in
packs or in humans that exhibit collective action. But the specific actions of
the herd vary, as a pack of animals may calmly graze together and then stam-
pede in terror. Similarly, social mood is always present, yet its tenor varies.

Social mood likely varies along two primary dimensions that have been
found in studies of individuals' mood. Evidence has supported an influential
two-dimensional model of emotion (Russell, 1980; Feldman Barrett & Russell, 1998, 1999). One dimension is *valence:* pleasure versus displeasure,
or pleasant versus unpleasant feelings (also referred to as hedonic value).
The other dimension is *level of arousal:* high versus low, or activated versus
deactivated. This dimension reflects the degree of affective intensity and
energy. According to Russell (2003), the combination of the valence and
arousal dimensions, called core affect, describes mood and is always present.

Thus, the valence of social mood determines the direction (positive or
negative) of social mood, while the level of arousal determines the intensity
of social mood. For example, mood with negative valence plus high arousal
would be characteristic of a crashing financial market.

The Elliott wave pattern present in so many forms of collective behavior may emerge from the interaction of social mood and herding. Another possibility is that the Elliott wave form attends only social mood and not herding. Thus, the valence and intensity of mood alone may determine how herding is expressed. Future research is needed to explore these possibilities.

It might be possible to test the relationship between herding and mood in a group of individuals in a controlled experiment. Herding by individuals has been measured in lab settings (Smith, Suchanek & Williams, 1988), and self-report measures of mood, such as the widely used Positive Affect and Negative Affect Schedule (PANAS), are available. Expanding upon this research would help us learn if and how these two processes interact to produce the rich, multifarious dimensions of the human social experience.

Applying Socionomics in a Herding World

Socionomists expect that humanity will always rationalize unconscious moods and herding impulses, yet we hold a seemingly contradictory hope that people will get it and change their ways. We think, simultaneously, "It can be no other way," and "Let us show people how to think differently." These thoughts, however, do resolve under socionomic theory: Society can never learn and change, but an individual can.

Socionomic thinking is invaluable for an individual pursuing his or her goals. It may even be helpful to small organizations. My organizations comprise about 80 people, a number of whom understand the socionomic point of view, and we operate with it in mind. It is possible, then, to influence, and perhaps even to saturate, a small organization with this type of thinking. Even so, there is no escaping the influence of social mood, which permeates every aspect of society. It is a triumph occasionally to mitigate it.

Educating society to behave differently would be a pipe dream. For the vast majority of people, not only are mood impulses unperceived and irresistible but they also produce rationalizations that obscure the very fact that they are taking actions to express mood.

People have asked me, "Why don't you advise the government what it ought to be doing to avoid bubbles and crises?" No such thing is possible, because society's presumed leaders are actually followers, who act at the behest of the crowd. When people want action, politicians oblige. There is no way to get masses of people to stop what they have been feeling, thinking and doing unconsciously since the dawn of humanity, and there is no way to convince a committee or a congress to commit political suicide by doing something responsible in opposition to the social mood of the day. It is theoretically possible to convince a wise *individual* leader to do so, but succeeding at the endeavor would be an exceptionally rare event.

Socionomic forecasting as a profession is just a matter of analyzing and advising, so it's a viable option. Your main problem will be that when you are right few will embrace your vision, whereas the wronger you are, the more support you will have. You can't fix it. People in the aggregate buy and sell advice just as they do stocks.

Because socionomists get more strident in calling for change precisely when the crowd is most strident in calling for the trend to continue, socionomic forecasters can appear as Cassandras, predicting change that few can imagine following from present circumstances. The more extreme and important an approaching turn, the more your vision of change will be ignored. And, they will remind you, you were wrong the last time. When change does come to pass, increasing numbers of people will claim to have predicted it, based on "fundamentals." Observers will hang onto the words of those who belatedly explain, with exogenous-cause arguments that people can easily understand and readily accept, why the change toward the positive or negative trend now well underway was inevitable. They will attach prescience to people who become *more* passionate in embracing the trend as it proceeds while you seem oblivious because your passion is cooling and you are beginning to look for signs of the trend's reversal.

It is much safer to be a trend-following forecaster, because people will change their opinions right along with you, and they will think you are talking sense all the time. This is why economists are almost always treated with respect. Go into the field of socionomic forecasting only if you can stand it.

REFERENCES FOR OLSON'S SECTION

Feldman Barrett, L. & Russell, J. A. (1998). Independence and bipolarity in the structure of current affect. *Journal of Personality and Social Psychology*, 74, pp. 967-984.

Feldman Barrett, L. & Russell, J.A. (1999). The structure of current affect: Controversies and emerging consensus. *Current directions in psychological sciences*, 8, pp. 10-14.

Russell, J. A. (1980). A circumplex model of affect. *Journal of Personality and Social Psychology*, 39, pp. 1161-1178.

Russell, J.A., (2003). Core affect and the psychological construction of emotion. Psychological Review, 110, pp. 145-172.

Smith, Suchanek & Williams. (1988). Bubbles, crashes, and endogenous expectations in experimental spot asset markets. *Econometrica*, 56, no. 5, p. 1149.

NOTES AND REFERENCES

[1] Gordon, Ian, and Tasneem Raja, "164 Anti-Immigration Laws Passed Since 2010? A Mojo Analysis," *Mother Jones*, March/April 2012.

[2] Areddy, James T., "Chinese Investors Crunching Numbers Are Glad to See 8s," *The Wall Street Journal*, May 4, 2007, p. A1.

[3] Crutsinger, Martin, "US Trade Deficit Plummets to 6-year Low," The Associated Press, March 14, 2009.

[4] Butler, Hartman L. "An Hour With Mr. Graham." Occasional Paper Number 5, The Financial Analysts Research Foundation, March 6, 1976.

[5] Foulk, Trevor, Andrew Woolum and Amir Erez, "Catching Rudeness Is Like Catching a Cold: The Contagion Effects of Low-Intensity Negative Behaviors," *Journal of Applied Psychology*, June 29, 2015.

[6] Whitehouse, Mark, "Economists' Grail: A Post-Crash Model," *The Wall Street Journal*, November 30, 2010.

[7] Philips, Matthew, "Revenge of the Nerd," *Newsweek*, June 8, 2009.

[8] Green, Michael K. "R.N. Elliott's Fundamental Challenge to Mechanistic Social Models," 2001, presented to the Fifth Congress of the International Society for the Interdisciplinary Study of Symmetry. Reprinted as Chapter 1 of *Market Analysis of a New Millennium*, 2002.

[9] Hall, J., R. Gonzalez, and O. Schultheiss, "Put Your Money Where Your Heart Is: Affective Influences on Financial Investment Decisions." Presented at the annual convention of the Society for Psychophysiological Research, Austin, TX, 2008. Abstract published in *Psychophysiology*, 45, S40; and subsequent conferences in 2008-2010.

[10, 11] Wickelgren, Ingrid, "Subliminal Cues Can Empty Wallets," *Scientific American*, April 20, 2010.

[12] Kendall, Peter, "Basketball and the Bull Market," *The Elliott Wave Theorist* Special Report, December 16, 1996. Republished in *Pioneering Studies in Socionomics*, Chapter 17.

[13] Li, Yexin Jessica et al., "Economic decision biases and fundamental motivations: How mating and self-protection alter loss aversion," *Journal of Personality and Social Psychology*, March 2012.

[14, 15] "New study shows passing mood can profoundly alter 'rational decisions'," *MedicalXpress*, October 20, 2011.

[16] Daniel, Kent, David Hirschleifer, and Avanidhar Subrahmanyam, "Investor Psychology and Security Market Under- and Overreactions," *Journal of Finance*, Vol. 53, No. 6, 1998, pp. 1839-1885; Barberis, Nicholas, Andrei Shleifer and Robert Vishny, "A Model of Investor Sentiment," *Journal of Financial Economics*, Vol. 49, No. 3, 1998, pp. 307-343.

[17] Barberis et al. *Ibid*, p. 333.

[18] Keynes, John M., *The General Theory of Employment, Interest and Money*, London: Harcourt Brace Jovanovich, 1936, pp. 153-154.

[19] Peters, Edgar E., *Chaos and Order in the Capital Markets*, John Wiley and Sons, 1991; and *Fractal Market Analysis,* John Wiley and Sons, 1994.

[20] Anderson, Nicola, and Joseph Noss, "The Fractal Market Hypothesis and its Implications for the Stability of Financial Markets," *Vox*, September 3, 2013.

[21] "Fractal Market Hypothesis (FMH)." Investopedia.

[22] Soros, George, *The Alchemy of Finance,* John Wiley & Sons, 1987.

[23] Soros, George, "Fallibility, Reflexivity, and the Human Uncertainty Principle," *Journal of Economic Methodology*, January 13, 2014.

[24] *Ibid.*

[25] *Ibid.*

[26] Lo, Andrew (2004). "The Adaptive Markets Hypothesis: Market Efficiency from an Evolutionary Perspective," *Journal of Portfolio Management*. Vol. 5, No. 30, pp. 15–29.

[27] Lo, Andrew W., Harry Mamaysky, and Jiang Wang, "Foundations of Technical Analysis: Computational Algorithms, Statistical Inference, and Empirical Implementation," *The Journal of Finance*, Vol. 55, No. 4, August 2000, pp. 1705-1765

[28] See Frost and Prechter, *Elliott Wave Principle* (1978), Chapter 7; and Robert Prechter, "Does the Wave Principle Subsume All Valid Technical Chart Patterns?" *Journal of Technical Analysis*, Fall/Winter 2009, No. 66, Market Technicians Assoc., Inc., New York, NY, pp. 28-50.

[29] Elliott, Ralph Nelson. (1938). *The Wave Principle*. Republished: (1980/1994). *R.N. Elliott's Masterworks — The Definitive Collection*. Prechter, Robert. (Ed.). Gainesville, GA: New Classics Library.

[30] Elliott, R.N., April 20, 1943, "Educational Bulletin Q," reprinted in *R.N. Elliott's Masterworks*, p. 182.

[31] Buchanan, Mark, "Why Economic Theory is Out of Whack," *New Scientist*, July 19, 2008.

[32] Mandelbrot, Benoit, "The Variation of Certain Speculative Prices," *The Journal of Business*, Vol. 36, No. 4, pp. 394-419.

[33] Bremmer, Ian, and Preston Keat, *The Fat Tail: The Power of Political Knowledge for Strategic Investing*, Oxford University Press, 2009.

[34] See Chapter 32 of *Pioneering Studies in Socionomics* on the anthrax attacks as well as *Socionomic Studies of Society and Culture* (2017) on the timing of serial killers' activities.

[35] Lassila, Kathrin Day, "Q&A: Rick Levin—Once an Economist, Always an Economist," *Yale Alumni Magazine*, May/June 2009, p. 28.

Chapter 20

Are Crowds Really Wise?
Study Confirms that Herding Undermines the Wisdom-of-Crowds Effect

Alan Hall

The True Nature of the Wisdom-of-Crowds Effect

In 1907, Francis Galton made an observation that author James Surowiecki would eventually say demonstrates "the wisdom of crowds." At a county fair, 787 people each paid to guess the weight of an ox. In what amounted to a secret ballot, individual participants handed in their estimates on stamped and numbered cards. The average of the estimates proved far more accurate than any individual guess, coming to within one pound of the correct weight of 1,198 pounds. What Galton observed were *independent, individual* assessments, not *dependent, collective* assessments. He wrote, "The judgments were unbiased by passion and uninfluenced by oratory and the like."[1] Surowiecki likewise clearly delineated three requirements of a wise "crowd": diversity of opinion, independence from others and decentralization of knowledge.[2] So, to be precise, the "wisdom-of-crowds" effect describes the tendency for the average of independent estimates of individuals to be more accurate than any individual expert's estimate.

The wisdom-of-crowds effect is real, but its name is a misnomer because it implies that the individuals involved are interacting. A less catchy but more precise name would be the "aggregated independent estimates" effect.

Crowds Are Not Wise

William H. Whyte in 1952 coined the term "groupthink," which he described as "rationalized conformity—an open, articulate philosophy which holds that group values are not only expedient but right and good as well."[3] In 1972, Yale psychologist Irving Janis[4] tied groupthink to a number of

American foreign policy disasters and other faulty decisions in history. He concluded that groupthink suppresses both the expression and subsequent evaluation of non-core views.

A recent study, "How social influence can undermine the wisdom of crowd effect," by Lorenz et al.,[5] has confirmed these observations and provided important support for socionomic theory.

The authors demonstrated that "even mild social influence" is sufficient to undermine the utility of the wisdom-of-crowds effect. They found that social interaction among the participants produces convergent opinions, less accurate opinions and higher confidence in those opinions. These results support the socionomic observations that crowds are prone to herding and that in certain settings doing so is unwise.

Procedure

Lorenz and colleagues asked participants various questions, each with a factual answer. One question was, "How many murders were registered

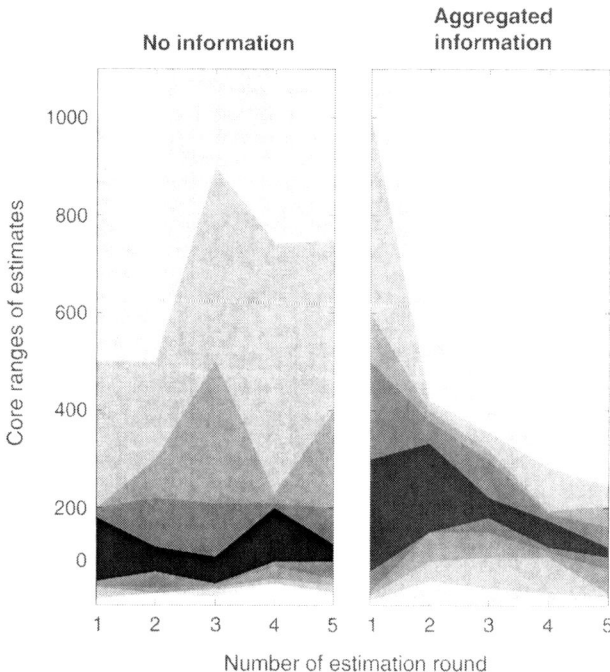

Social Influence Leads to Opinion Convergence: Sample results from the Lorenz et al. study. Individuals in the group on the left were given no information about other participants' answers. The group on the right was told the range of answers of the group from the preceding round. The shaded blocks display the "core ranges" of the answers in each round, with light gray the largest and black the narrowest range. Note how the diversity of opinions narrowed in the group on the right but not in the group on the left.

Figure 1

in Switzerland in 2006?" The participants were divided into three groups: those who were given no information about past answers, those who were informed of participants' answers from the preceding round, and those who were informed of the trajectory of participants' answers from all prior rounds.

The study led to several socionomically important conclusions:

1. The crowd became no better at determining the correct answer when it had information about others' answers. Sometimes it became worse.

2. When participants were informed of other participants' estimates, the range of their estimates narrowed dramatically. (See Figure 1.)

3. Finally, as participants gained information about others' estimates, they became more confident of their own.

The authors concluded, "As social influence among human group members may trigger individuals to revise their estimates, it can have a substantial impact on the statistical wisdom-of-crowd effect in societies. [T]he wisdom-of-crowds indicator tends to decline over time under conditions of social influence. This effect is substantial and statistically significant for all questions."[6]

The degradation of the wisdom-of-crowds effect occurred even though the survey questions had a factually correct answer. The authors mused, "Presumably, herding is even more pronounced for opinions or attitudes for which no predefined correct answers exist." We wholeheartedly agree with that statement. In "The Financial/Economic Dichotomy in Social Behavioral Dynamics: The Socionomic Perspective" (2007) (see Chapter 15), Prechter and Parker posited that people default to herding under conditions of uncertainty. Conditions of uncertainty include being faced with questions whose answers one doesn't know or cannot know, such as, "will the price of this financial item go up or down?" At such times, humans herd, because they evolved to conform to others' behavior in uncertain situations as a primal survival tactic.

What This Study Means for Socionomics

The undermining of the wisdom-of-crowds effect under social influence supports the socionomic premise that unconscious, non-rational herding drives human behavior in contexts where interaction and uncertainty are pervasive. Wisdom is possible only from independent minds, not crowds.

REFERENCES

[1] Galton, F., "Vox populi," *Nature*, 1907, 75:7.

[2] Surowiecki, James, *The Wisdom of Crowds*, Doubleday, 2004, p. 22.

[3] Whyte, Jr. William H., "Groupthink," *Fortune*, March 1952, pp. 114-117, 142, 146.

[4] Janis, Irving L., *Victims of Groupthink*, Boston: Houghton Mifflin, 1972.

[5] Lorenz, J., H. Rauhut, F. Schweitzer and D. Helbing, "How Social Influence Can Undermine the Wisdom of Crowd Effect," *Proceedings of the National Academy of Sciences*, 2011.

[6] *Ibid.*

Part V:

STF VS. CONVENTIONAL THINKING

Chapter 21

Linear Extrapolation vs. Fractal Extrapolation

Robert R. Prechter

In March 2004, I asked an audience at the London School of Economics these four questions:

(1) In 1950, a good computer cost $1 million. In 1990, it cost $5,000. Today it costs $1,000. **Question: What will a good computer cost 50 years from today?**

(2) Democracy as a form of government has been spreading for centuries. In the 1940s, Japan changed from an empire to a democracy. In the 1980s, the Soviet system collapsed, and now Russia holds multi-party elections. In the 1990s, China adopted free-market reforms. In March of this year, Iraq, a former dictatorship, celebrated a new democratic constitution. **Question: Fifty years from today, will a larger or smaller percentage of the world's population live under democracy?**

(3) In the decade from 1983 to 1993, there were ten months of recession in the U.S.; in the subsequent decade from 1993 to 2003, there were 8 months of recession. In the first period, expansion was underway 92% of the time; in the second period, it was 93%. **Question: What percentage of the time will economic expansion take place during the decade from 2003 to 2013, and from 2013 to 2023?**

(4) In 1971, Reserve Funds kicked off the hugely successful money market fund industry. In 1973, the CBOE introduced options on stocks. In 1977, Michael Milken invented junk bond financing. In 1982, stock index futures and options on futures began to trade. In 1983, options on stock indexes became available. Keogh plans, IRAs and 401k's have brought tax breaks to the investing public.

The mutual fund industry, a small segment of the financial world in the late 1970s, has attracted the public's invested wealth to the point that there are more mutual funds than there are stocks on the NYSE. Futures contracts on individual stocks have just begun trading. **Question: Over the next 50 years, will the number and sophistication of financial products and services increase or decrease?**

Observe that I asked an economic question, a political question, a socionomic question and a financial question.

Linear Trend Extrapolation

Most responders extrapolated their answers linearly from the trends of previous data. They expected cheaper computers, more democracy, economic expansion 93% of the time, and an increase in financial sophistication.

People think it is sensible to answer such questions by linear extrapolation because they default to the mechanics paradigm when predicting social trends. They think, "The social trajectory will remain constant unless impacted by an outside force, and I don't perceive any outside forces that could change these trajectories." This mode of thought, which is the basis for standard social science, is deeply embedded in our minds because it has tremendous evolutionary advantages. When Og threw a rock at Ug back in the cave days, Ug *ducked*. He ducked because his mind understood the consequences of the Law of Conservation of Momentum, which is that an object will maintain its trajectory unless acted upon by an outside force. The rock heading towards him would not veer off course because there was nothing between the two men to act upon it, and rocks do not have minds of their own. Earlier animals that evolved to have an intuitive understanding of the laws of physics lived; those that didn't died, and their inabilities were weeded out of the gene pool. Knowledge of physics makes possible our modern technological world. People rely on it every day in handling objects. But social trends are not physical entities. As Paul Montgomery of Universal Economics explained, the Law of Conservation of Momentum is inapplicable to predicting social change, because the "rocks" in this case—people—*do* have minds of their own.

Viewing social trends as if they were physical objects in motion perpetuates two fallacies:

(1) extrapolating current trends into the future, and
(2) believing that an event must happen to change a trend's direction.

The fallacies of trend extrapolation and exogenous causality lie behind all the forecasting failures of conventional futurists.

For most people in most circumstances, the proper answer to each of the above questions is, "I don't know." (Fractal projection and knowledge of socionomic causality, however, can give you an edge in social prediction, as we will soon see.)

To get a feel for how useless—even counterproductive—linear extrapolation can be in social forecasting, consider these circumstances:

(1) It is 1886. Project the future of the American railroad industry.
(2) It is 1975. Project the future of China.
(3) It is 1963. Project the cost of medical care in the U.S.
(4) It is 1969. Project the future of the U.S. space program.
(5) It is 100 A.D. Project the future of Roman civilization.

In 1886, a futurist would have envisioned a landscape combed with rail lines connecting every city, town and neighborhood. Small trains would roll around to your home to pick you up, and a network of rail lines would help deliver you to your destination efficiently and cheaply. Super-fast trains would make cross-country runs. You could eat, work, read or sleep along the way.

Is that what happened? Would anyone have predicted—*did* anyone predict—that trains in 2015 would often be going slower than they did in 1886, that they would occasionally jump the tracks, that they would be inefficient, that they would have little food and few sleeper cars, and that the equipment would be old and worn out?

In 1975, the Communist party was entrenched in China. Over 35 million people were being slaughtered in the Cultural Revolution of 1966-1976, when Chinese youths helped exterminate people just because they were intellectual, successful or capitalist. Would anyone have imagined that China's economic production, in just over a single generation, would rival that of the United States, the world's premier industrial giant?

In 1963, medical care was cheap and accessible. Doctors made house calls for $20. They treated indigent patients for free. Hospitals were so accommodating that new mothers typically stayed up to a week before being sent home, and the stay and the care were affordable. Would anyone have guessed that in 2015 pills would sell for $2, $20, $200 and even $1,000 apiece, a surgical procedure and a week in the hospital would cost one-third of an annual wage, and people would have to take out expensive insurance policies just in case they got sick?

In the space of just 30 years in the mid-20th century, rockets had gone from the experimental stage to such sophistication that one of them brought men to the moon and back. In 1969, many people projected that the U.S. space program by the century's end would include colonies on the moon and trips to Mars. After all, it was only sensible, wasn't it? By linear extrapolation, it was. But in the decades since 1969, the space program has relentlessly regressed.

In 100 A.D., would you have predicted that the most powerful state in the world—the Roman Empire—would be reduced to rubble in a bit over three centuries? Few people of the day imagined that outcome.

Futurists—including economists, political strategists and business-trend predictors—nearly always extrapolate past trends linearly, and they are nearly always wrong, especially when trends are maturing. *The most certain aspect of social history is dramatic change.* Although rocks cannot change trajectories on their own, societies can and do change direction on their own, all the time. You cannot use linear extrapolation to predict social changes, because a straight line doesn't change direction.

Wondering what event will "shock" or "impact" the current trend to change it is a related error. Futurists generally try to identify cutting-edge events that might change the old trend or start a new one. But events predict nothing. Each new event could be the only time something of its kind ever happens. Or it could be the first event of a short-lived trend that's over in three months. Or it might be the start of a long term trend. *Conventional futurists don't know.* If they claim a new trend has begun, they are simply extrapolating a newly perceived line, but really they have no idea.

Linear Forecasting in Financial Markets and the Economy

Financial speculators and economists are futurists, and most of them extrapolate trends in markets and the economy in linear fashion. Decades of history for dozens of financial-market sentiment indicators (some of which are displayed in Chapter 17) and data from polls of economists' opinions uniformly demonstrate that aggregate optimism toward a financial market or an economy increases persistently during uptrends and decreases persistently during downtrends. Since optimism is future-oriented, we may safely conclude from these data that the longer trend continues, the greater is the number of people—experts and laymen alike—who extrapolate its continuation, and the further they extrapolate it. Since patterned herding creates both trends *and* reversals, linear extrapolation of a financial market or an economy is doomed to be exquisitely wrong when it matters.

Futurists even extrapolate sideways trends linearly. As two examples, one investment strategist asserted, "The S&P 500 could be stuck in [its] recent price range for a while,"[1] and a global market strategist at a money-center bank stated, "I suspect that this choppiness in the markets is something we are going to be seeing for some time to come."[2] These are linear projections. The market had been going sideways, so observers predicted it would continue going sideways. This is brain-dead forecasting.

Wall Street's corporate analysts, many of whom are trained economists, are notorious at this practice. They review data from the recent past and "predict" that the trend in effect will continue. Figure 1 displays the history of actual earnings of S&P companies vs. analysts' predictions of those companies' earnings. It shows that analysts' forecasts have lagged actual earnings by about a year. The extreme lag is due to their prediction model, which involves the linear extrapolation of delayed data. James Montier, who published this chart, commented, "The chart makes it transparently obvious that analysts lag reality. They only change their minds when there is irrefutable proof they were wrong, and then they change their minds very slowly."[3] In other words, there is no anticipation, just lagging linear extrapolation.

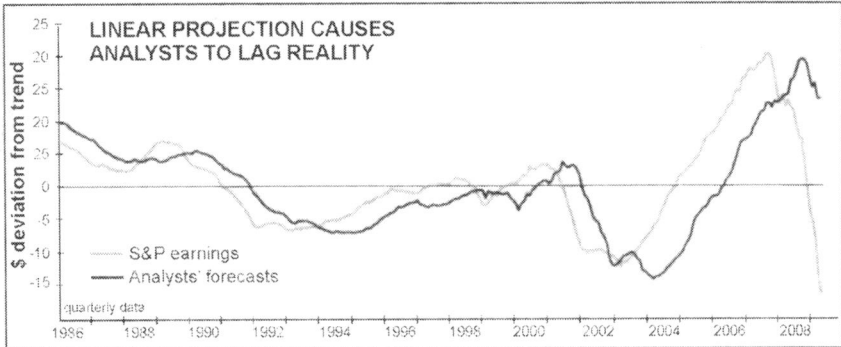

Figure 1

This approach is ubiquitous throughout the economics profession. Some observers have recognized the essence of the game:

Rearview Mirror Is Where Economists See Future
by Caroline Baum—Bloomberg, Sep 15, 2010
Every month, 60 respondents (on average) in the Bloomberg News economic survey provide forecasts for <u>various indicators, including real gross domestic product, the consumer price index and the</u>

<u>unemployment rate, and interest rates, such as the federal funds
rate and 10-year Treasury note yield</u>, for the next few quarters and
two years out.

As U.S. economic indicators started to sputter over the summer,
economists duly marked down their forecast for third-quarter real GDP
growth to 1.9 percent in the September survey from 2.5 percent in
August, 2.8 percent in July and 3 percent in June. <u>"Hindcast" would
be a more apt description for what these folks do</u>.

"It's really an indictment of the forecasting business," says Bob
Barbera, chief economist at Mt. Lucas Management Co., a New York
hedge fund, and himself a forecaster. That doesn't mean extrapolating
from one quarter to the next is a bad strategy. "Allowing the pace of
economic growth in the last three to six months to dictate the next
three to six months beats most forecasts—<u>except when it matters</u>,"
Barbera says.

And when does it matter? It matters at the turns. When you're a linear
forecaster, you can't detect any turns.

A sensible model must incorporate continual change naturally. Thankfully, there is a whole new way of looking at the idea of extrapolation.

Extrapolating Social Trends Using a Fractal Model

To explain and predict social change, socionomic theory rejects the
paradigm of *linear progression* and *exogenous disruption* and replaces it with
fractal progression and *endogenous consistency*. Instead of extrapolating
straight lines, Elliotticians extrapolate a different form: a robust, self-affine,
hierarchical fractal called the Wave Principle. Briefly stated, Elliotticians
extrapolate Elliott waves.

The Elliott wave model has an 80-year history of useful application.
By its very nature it incorporates both trends *and* trend changes, at all wave
degrees. It applies to financial-market herding and even more crucially to
social mood and its immediate consequences in social action.

By orienting to a fractal form rather than a straight line, Elliotticians
and socionomists have a method of anticipating change before any hint of
the new trend is manifest. When others are at peak excitement to extrapolate
linearly, we are at peak excitement to extrapolate a turn in the other direction. It is a completely different mindset.

Figure 2 depicts the fractal movements of the stock market as described
by an idealized version of the Elliott wave model. The arrows show how
conventional futurists approach forecasting. Because they project trends

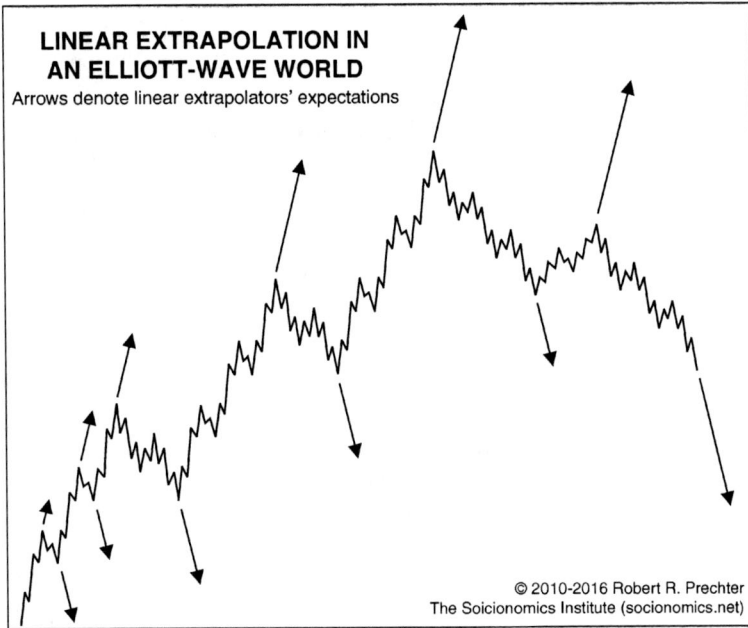

**LINEAR EXTRAPOLATION IN
AN ELLIOTT-WAVE WORLD**
Arrows denote linear extrapolators' expectations

© 2010-2016 Robert R. Prechter
The Soicionomics Institute (socionomics.net)

Figure 2

linearly, they are most convinced of an old trend's continuation at the very time when waves at several degrees of trend are culminating. The longer and further a trend has gone in the same direction, the stronger are futurists' expectations that it will continue, as depicted by the longer arrows. In between the points where the arrows are, their opinions morph from the direction of the first arrow to the direction of the second. The socionomic approach to social prediction incorporates this fractal model, so for us (ideally) the arrows go in the opposite direction.

A fractal model is not a panacea. It can dispose a futurist to look for too many turns. Being patient while an Elliott wave plays out can be challenging for a mind bent on looking for evidence of change. But at least Elliotticians are not *doomed* to miss every turn. They may be early or late, but they are not inevitably, pathologically late, as linear extrapolators are.

Intimate knowledge of the Elliott wave model greatly enhances one's ability to forecast the social future. Nevertheless, an analyst can apply socionomic thinking without employing EW. As outlined in Chapter 7, there are five bases for socionomic forecasting. The rest of this chapter covers five subsets of those approaches. Only the first two methods require detailed knowledge of the Elliott wave model. The rest of them do not. We will review each of these methods in turn.

(1) Extrapolating Trends Using the Elliott Wave Model

Chapter 22 details over two decades of Elliott-wave-based forecasts for the price of a representative of the commodity markets, oil. This section augments that history with a pair of examples—out of hundreds available—representing two other types of markets: individual stocks and currencies.

On October 27, 2000, Steven Hochberg and Peter Kendall, who write *The Elliott Wave Financial Forecast*, published Figure 3, showing a completed Elliott wave in GE stock. This quarter-century pattern portended a major reversal. Figure 4 shows what happened thereafter.

Observations such as this are valuable beyond investing. The CEO of General Electric might have made some different decisions, for example to get his company out of the finance business. Or, he might have resigned at the top and gone out in glory.

As published on October 27, 2000

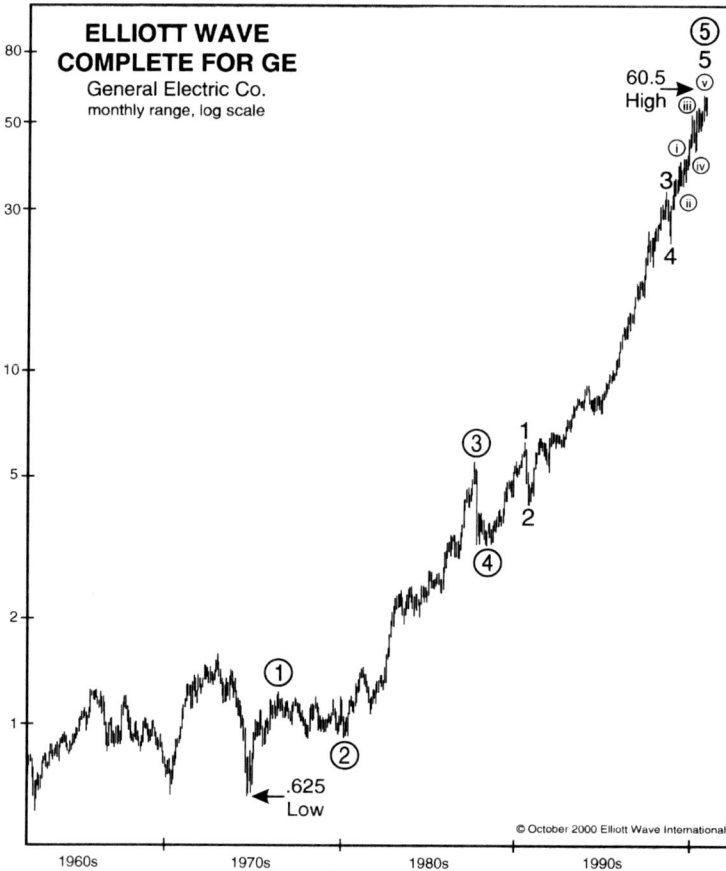

Figure 3

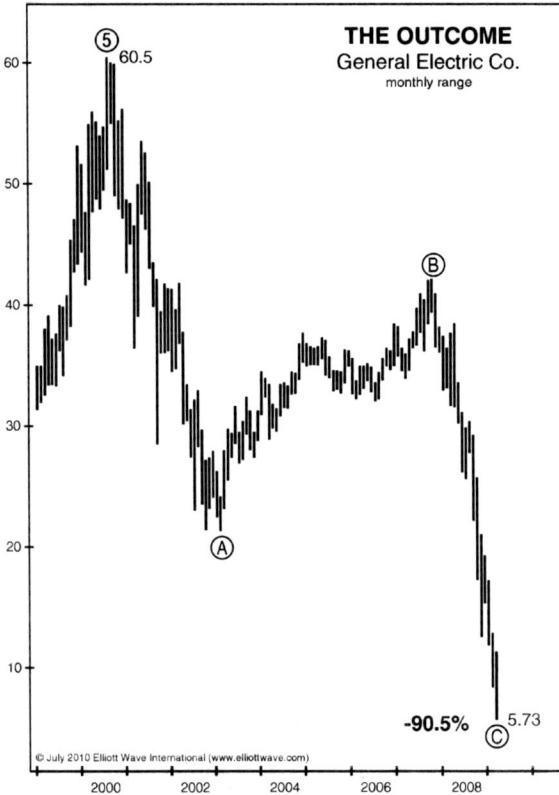

THE OUTCOME
General Electric Co.
monthly range

© July 2010 Elliott Wave International (www.elliottwave.com)

Figure 4

The Elliott wave model is useful for predicting currency values, too. The U.S. dollar had fallen a long way against other currencies during most of the decade of the 2000s. At each of the major lows of 2008, 2009 and 2011, the media and the Internet were awash in commentaries on the demise of the dollar. In one of the most delicious of ironies, the Dollar Index—which prices the dollar against a basket of other currencies—bottomed in March 2008, six months *before* the Federal Reserve began its policy of creating four trillion new dollars through multiple "quantitative easing" programs (see Chapter 2). Utterly ignoring these supposedly bearish exogenous-cause "fundamentals," the Dollar Index held above its 2008 low during the entire period of historic QE inflating. Speculators holding inflation-hedge investments were mystified. They were sure the Fed's actions were exogenous forces that would drive the dollar lower and foreign currencies higher. Socionomics, as usual, reverses the causality: The onset of declines in financial markets and the economy drove the Fed to adopt a QE policy. That is the only causality that makes sense of the data.

On May 16, 2011, QE was poised to accelerate at a historic rate with no scheduled time limit, and the Daily Sentiment Index[4] was recording percentages of bulls among Dollar-Index futures traders as low as 4%. That's when *The Elliott Wave Theorist* published Figure 5 and the following commentary:

As published on May 16, 2011

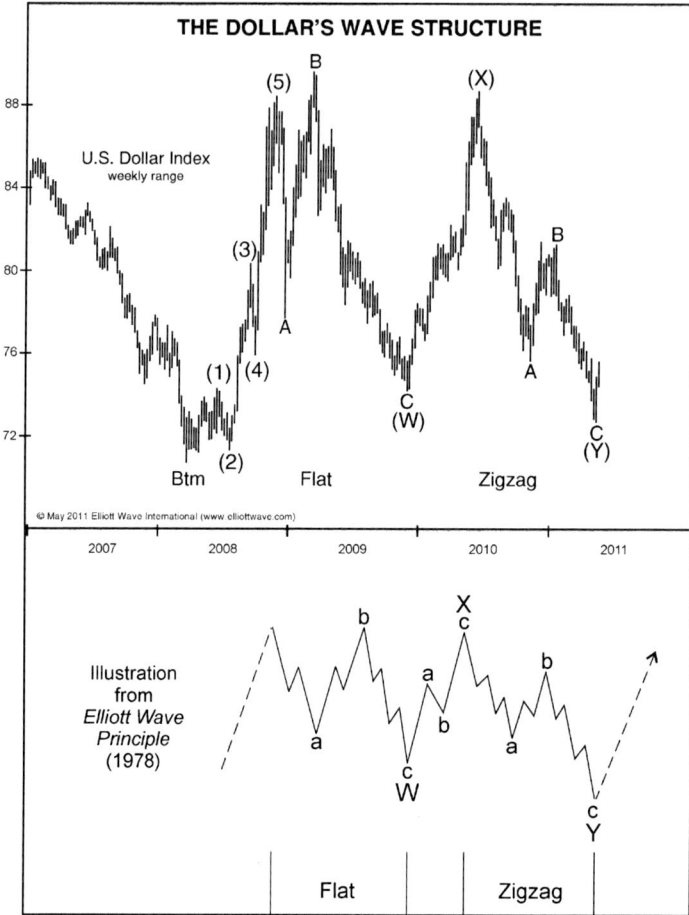

Figure 5

The chart shows the wave labeling for a completed bear market, a double three, labeled as a flat-X-zigzag along the lines of Figure 1-48 from *Elliott Wave Principle*, reproduced here. I think the dollar is starting a five-year bull market, which will coincide with a bear market in everything else.

Thereafter the Dollar Index took off on the upside, while commodities, precious metals and foreign currencies fell to the point of making headlines.

By March 2015, the Dollar Index had risen from 70.70 to 100.39, a gain of 42%. The Daily Sentiment Index reported readings of 98% bulls among Dollar Index traders on January 5, 2015, 96% on March 9 and 97% on March 10 and 11. The crowd that had hated the dollar now loved it. On

March 13, the day of the high that month, *The Elliott Wave Theorist* issued the following assessment:

> It was a long time coming, but the U.S. Dollar Index—in line with our forecast—has finally returned to par. After slipping as low as 70.70 in March 2008, it hit 100.39 today. The latest surge has been the fastest one-year rise in the Dollar Index since the early 1980s. The Dollar Index debuted at par in 1973. After a wild 42 years, it's back where it started.

Figure 6 places the bullish pattern identified in 2011 within a larger context. As of the close of 2015, the forecasted five years of rise—as opposed to, say, five weeks or five months—appears to have been a fairly good estimate of the dollar's potential at the low of 2011. How waves (4) and (5) resolve remains to be seen.

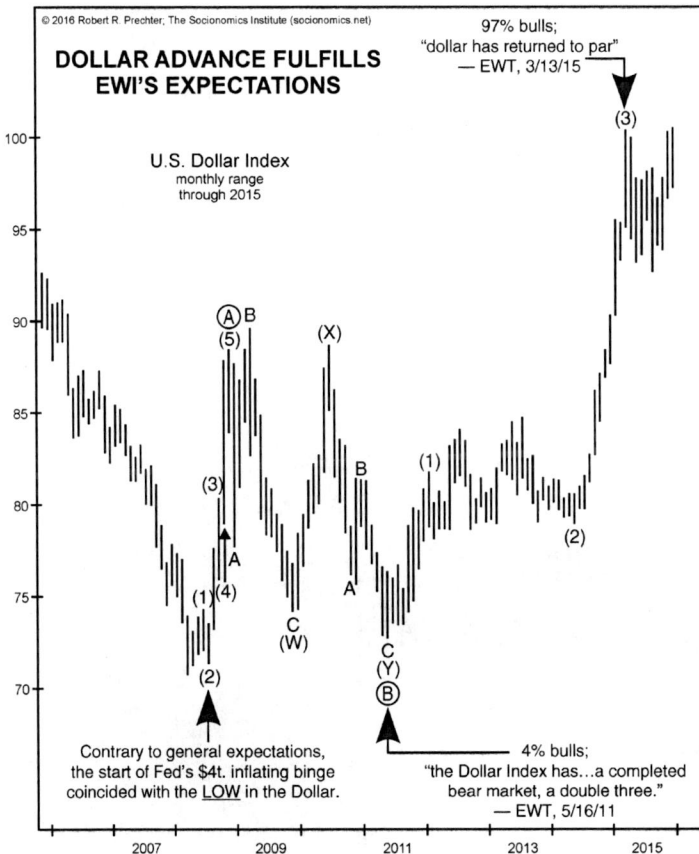

Figure 6

(2) An Elliott-Wave-Based Stock Market Outlook Implies Changes in Other Financial and Social Trends

If you can predict changes in stock market patterns using the Elliott wave model, you can predict the tenor and character of many other types of social-mood expression. Conventional economists and futurists try to forecast such things, too, but their tool is a straight line. Let's contrast the two approaches.

From 1966 to 1982, the nominal stock market went sideways (see Figure 7), while inflation-adjusted measures such as Dow/PPI and S&P/PPI (see Figure 4 in Chapter 10 and Figure 8 in Chapter 12, respectively), were going down throughout that period. Toward the end of that trend, what kind of books do you think people wrote? Would they tell you that a financial and economic boom lay directly ahead? No. They linearly extrapolated the aging downtrend and put out all kinds of bearish books, 20 of which are displayed in Figure 8 along with a bullish outlier, *Elliott Wave Principle*. What all these bearish futuristic books actually expressed was the *present* social mood, which was negative.

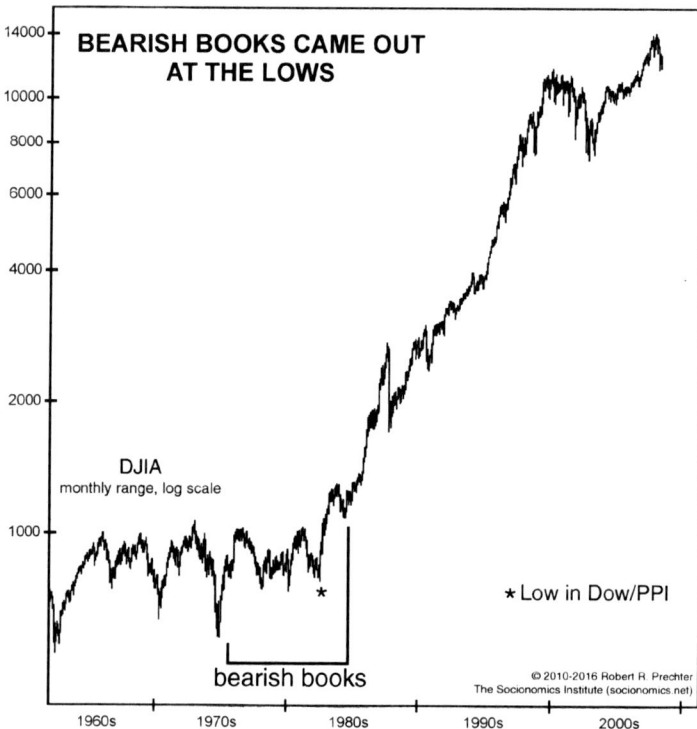

Figure 7

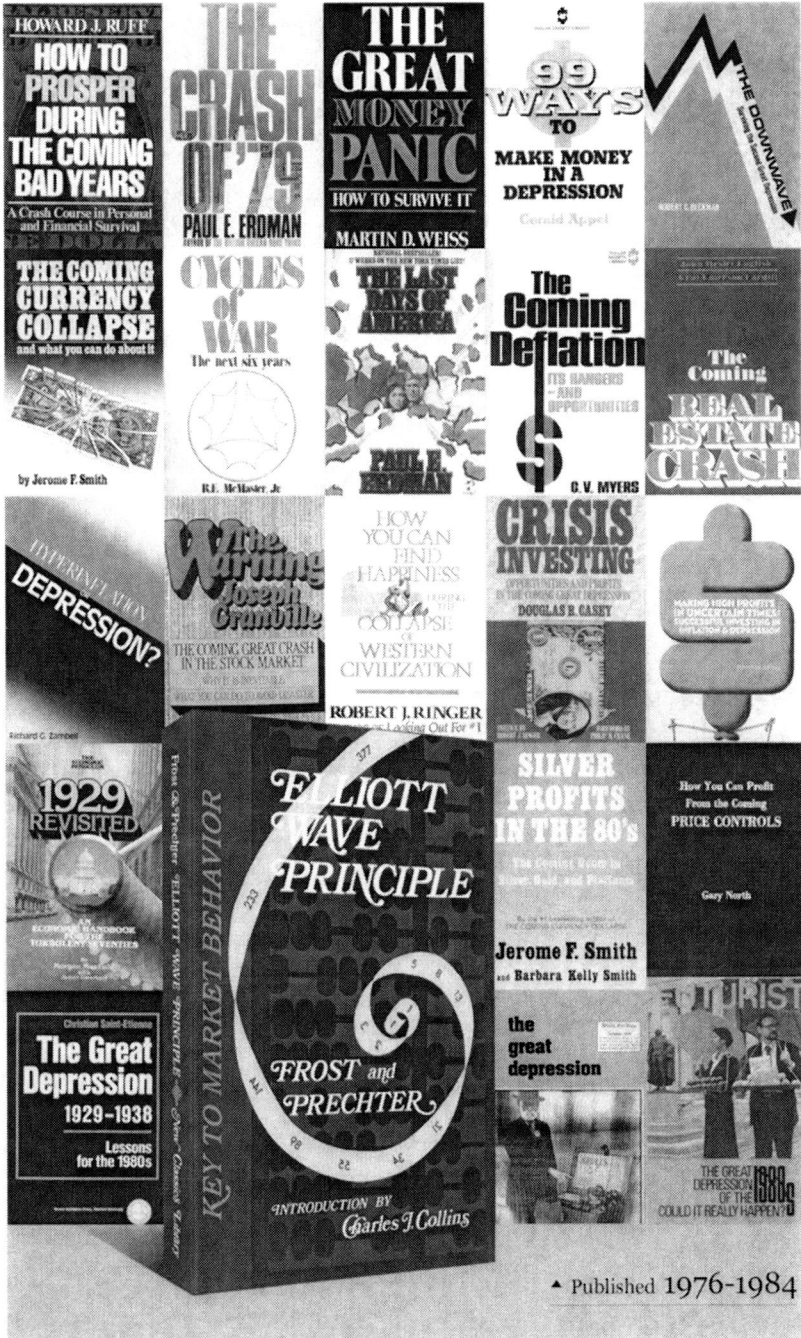

Figure 8

The image at the bottom right of Figure 8 shows the cover of a magazine called *The Futurist*. The headline at the bottom says, "The Great Depression of the 1980s: Could it Really Happen?" It would have happened if trends followed straight lines. But in the real world of fractal change, the opposite outcome occurred.

About that time, two Elliott wave analysts went about the same task of projection using a fractal model. In 1978, A.J. Frost and I wrote *Elliott Wave Principle*, which called for a 1920s-style boom. That's not extrapolating a straight line; that's looking around the corner. On October 6, 1982, as the boom began, *The Elliott Wave Theorist* made its first socionomic forecast, calling for "No international war for at least ten years." Regarding the economy, the November 8 issue announced, "Recovery Beginning." The March 1983 issue called for an "Economic Boom" and advised, "Don't build bomb shelters. This is a time to focus on finance, expand your business or promote your career." This conclusion followed from the assessment based on the Elliott wave model that social mood had just begun a positive trend of major degree. The wave-based forecast for a rising stock market implied prosperous and peaceful social conditions as well.

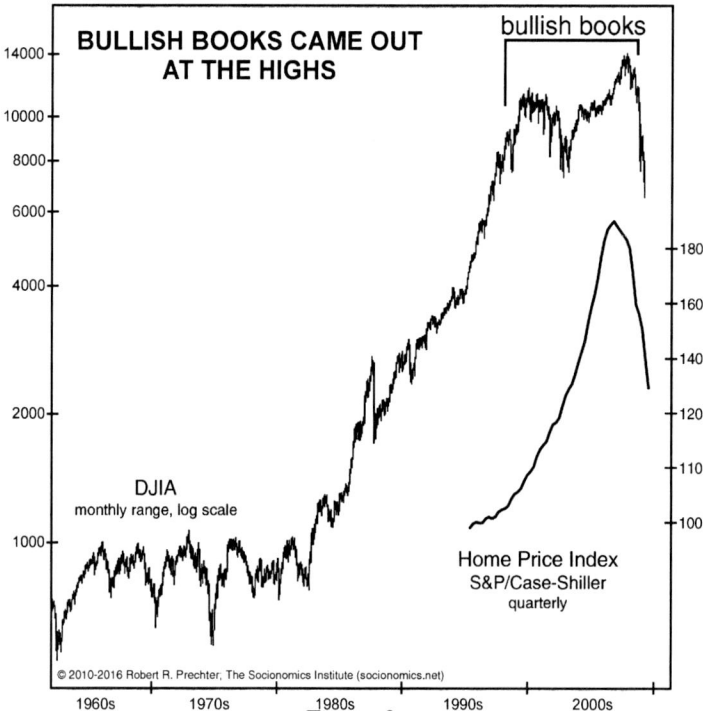

Figure 9

Let's look at the other end of the trend (see Figure 9). What kind of books did people write between 1998 and 2007, a period of historically extreme positive mood? Would authors tell you, "This is a great time to sell; stocks are overpriced, and property is at the peak of a debt-fueled bubble"? Of course not. Optimism permeated almost everyone's thinking, and their forecasts reflected it. Figure 11 shows 36 super-bullish titles that came out between 1998, when the Value Line Composite index made its all-time high for the era, and 2008, two years after real estate made its all-time high and a few months after the Dow and S&P topped. On the left side are the stock-market titles, with forecasts ranging from *Dow 36,000* to *Dow 100,000*. At

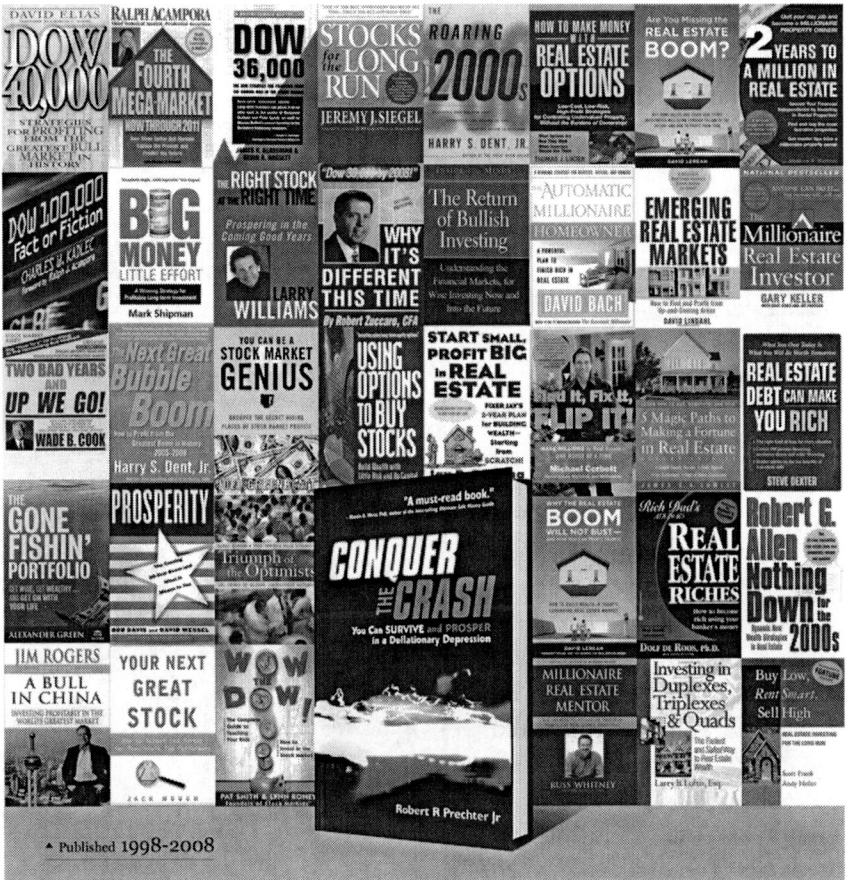

Figure 10

the time, EWI's Kendall called these and 30 new books on day-trading "an odd combination of dangerous and laughable."[5] On the right side are the real estate titles, including *Two Years to a Million in Real Estate* and *Real Estate Debt Can Make You Rich*. Reviewing that time years later, a financial columnist[6] listed ten public forecasts for the Dow made in and around 1999; linear extrapolations all, they ranged from 15,000 to 700,000. All these optimistic forecasts were products of a positive extreme in social mood.

We at Elliott Wave International were almost apoplectic looking at the extent of financial optimism during this period. Two years into the nine-year bear market, I got the nerve to put out a book called *Conquer the Crash* (shown in Figure 10). Its outlook wasn't (yet?) entirely accurate, but it saw dangers the other books didn't. It identified the conditions of a major stock market peak and forecast a debt crisis, based on socionomic causality: A positive mood trend had allowed incautious people to expand credits and debts to an extreme level, and negative mood would reverse that trend. The book called for a major decline in real estate prices at a time when the world believed that property was a fail-safe investment. It singled out the Federal National Mortgage Corporation (Fannie Mae) as a pending disaster. In the same month, Steven Hochberg and Peter Kendall of *The Elliott Wave Financial Forecast* added that Fannie Mae would get the "worst of the downturn" (see Figure 11). At that time, every mutual fund owned Fannie Mae stock. Investors figured that since Fannie Mae was a government-sponsored enterprise dedicated to financing the American dream and had been a staple of political promises for decades, it would never be allowed to implode. But it did implode, and the stock went virtually to zero, as shown in Figure 12. That's the kind of prediction you can make when you have a socionomic mindset and pay attention to what areas should be most affected by a change in social mood.

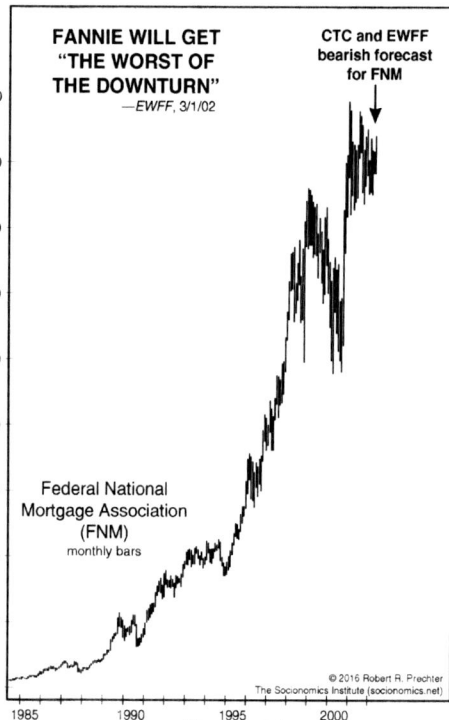

Figure 11

The extreme optimism of 2005 also prompted complacent investors to narrow the yield spread between junk bonds and 10-year U.S. Treasury notes. On March 4, 2005, Hochberg and Kendall in *The Elliott Wave Financial Forecast* published Figure 13 and stated, "If we were forced to make just one statement with respect to bonds for the rest of the bear market, it would be this: The yield spread between junk debt and U.S. Treasuries should widen to a record level. If you

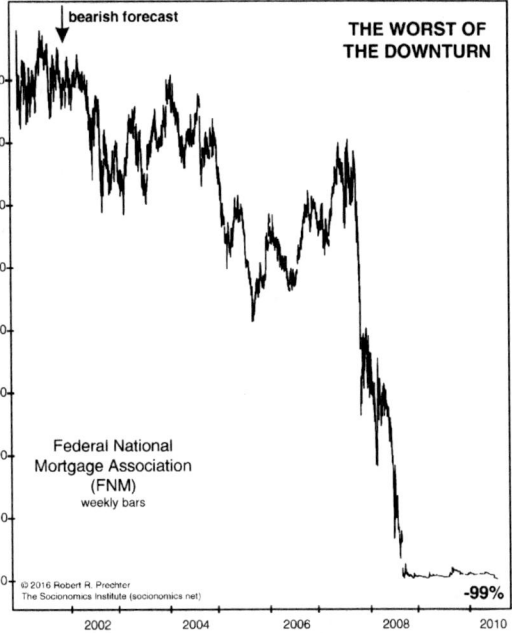

Figure 12

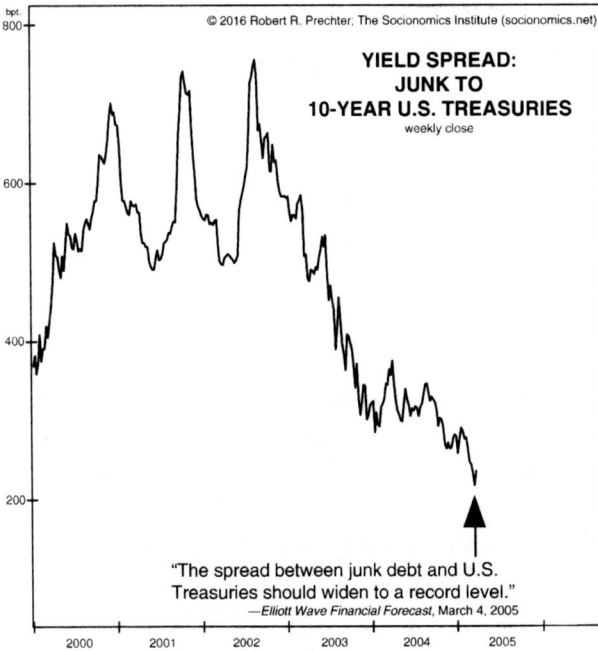

Figure 13

play that spread now, you'll probably make a lot of money." This outlook seemed crazy, because there was nothing in the "fundamentals" to worry about; the economy was in recovery, and housing was booming. As it happened, their comment caught the exact low in the spread. The stock market continued higher for another two years, so the spread hardly budged for a while. But in 2007-2008, it took off and went to its highest level since the early 1930s (see Figure 14). Again, that's looking around the corner.

Outcome

Figure 14

Let's examine a non-financial idea that's maybe a little closer to home for many people: the desire of human beings to stay fit. In 1985, I published a little table[7] (see Figure 15) based on my observation that in periods of positively trending social mood, people tend to practice and encourage physical fitness. During the 1980s and 1990s, an exercise craze took hold, and physical fitness centers became a booming business.

Read what tends to happen during the Falling Transition: "Fitness fanaticism wanes rapidly." In other words, when social mood turns negative, people don't want to work out as much as they did before. This was both an observation and a prediction.

Direction of Mood Trend				
AREA OF CULTURE	**RISING TRANSITION**	**PEAK POSITIVE MOOD**	**FALLING TRANSITION**	**PEAK NEGATIVE MOOD**
FITNESS/ HEALTH	Healthy lifestyle, physical fitness practiced, encouraged.	Body admired. Body building peaks. Smoking, "junk" foods taboo.	Fitness fanaticism wanes rapidly. Social concern replaces concern with self.	"Working out" is out of fashion.

Figure 15

During the boom years, a company called Bally's Total Fitness built and ran physical fitness centers. Figure 16 is a picture of the company's stock price near the peak and afterward, plotted against the Dow in terms of real money (gold). You can see that the stock's price followed the trend of the sociometer, falling from $30 per share all the way down until it was delisted. This collapse happened because social mood changed. During that period, people's increasingly negative mood kept them from wanting to go to the gym.

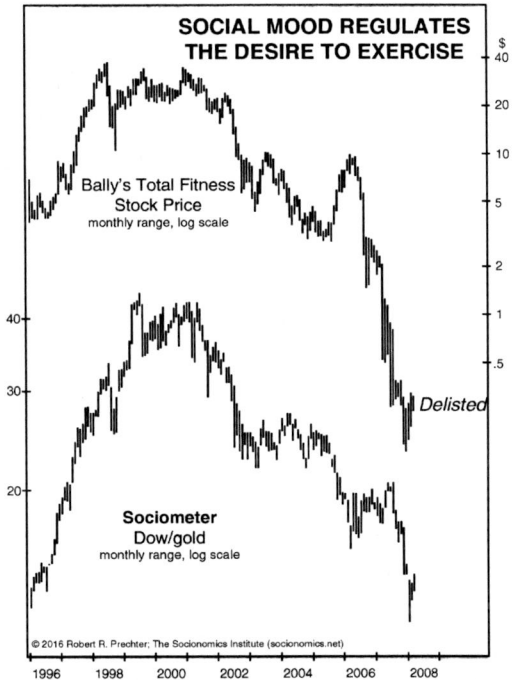

Figure 16

(3) Using Stock Market Trends—Without Applying the Elliott Wave Model—To Forecast Changes in Trends of Lagging Social Actions

The most reliable gift of the socionomic insight is that it offers a way to forecast vitally important social trends and events without having to predict financial prices. It is based on the time lag between some social actions and others. Chapter 8 offered numerous examples, to which three more are added here.

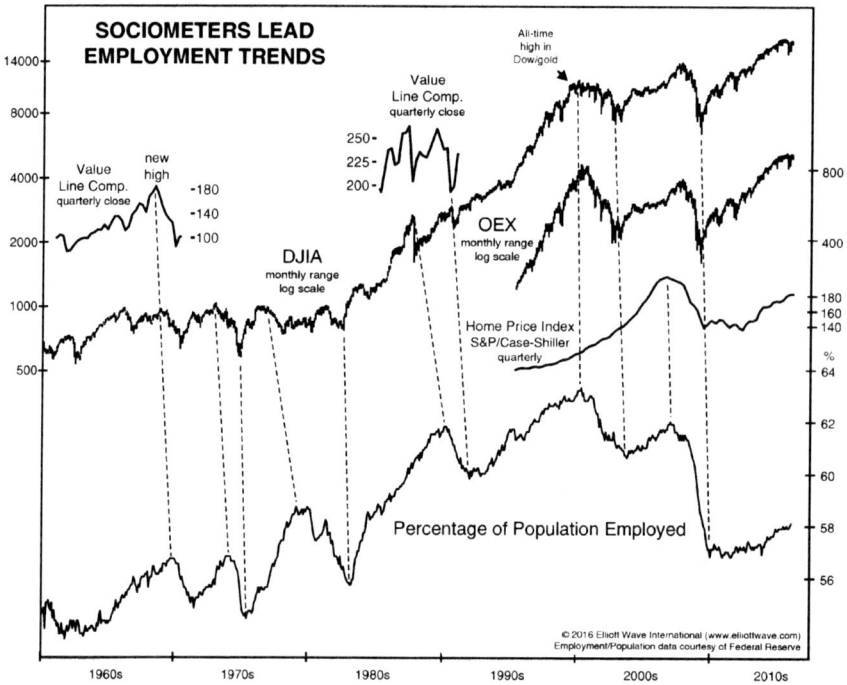

Figure 17

Major trend changes in economic variables are particularly easy to predict. The rightward slope of the dashed lines in Figure 17 show how reliably major trends in employment have lagged major turns in the leading sociometer. The leading sociometer is usually the stock market, but in 2006 the real estate market was the prime financial beneficiary of elevated social optimism, and that is where the reversal from positive mood first showed up. According to the history displayed on this chart, if you were to lag your forecasts for employment trends by one to three years at stock market tops of at least Primary degree and by three to eight months at commensurate stock market bottoms, you would be mostly right on both the trends and the turns.

If you simply want to be a step ahead of the economy most of the time, just change your outlook as the stock market moves. Thanks to the lag, there is no need to rush. Your record won't be perfect, but it will be the best possible.

Delays in social action allow the socionomist plenty of time to anticipate changes in politics, too. If the stock market has gone up for a long time, it portends incumbent reelections and peaceful times; if it has fallen a long way, it portends incumbents' oustings and times of internal and external conflict; and so on.

Recall from Chapter 1 that the 9/11 attacks offered conventional futurists no basis for stock market prediction. Neither did they have a basis for describing initial conditions under which such attacks would likely occur. Socionomic thinking did allow for a specific stock market prediction thereafter (see Chapter 41), and it had previously offered a basis for anticipating the social-mood environment that would encourage acts of terrorism. We had specifically predicted that in an upcoming bear market environment, "Foreigners will commit terrorist acts on U.S. soil. [A] few buildings…may be…bombed out of existence."[8] The eighteen-month stock market decline preceding 9/11 portended social actions of just such negative character.

It is more important to predict social environments when deadly political acts are likely than it is to predict the stock market. It is also easier; just let the trend of the averages tell you when social mood is becoming more positive or negative and to what degree. Political events will almost always follow, with compatible character and commensurate tenor. *Socionomic Causality in Politics* (2017) offers numerous additional examples of this reliable chronology from around the world.

Socionomic prediction is valuable with respect to periods of concord and opposition even within much smaller social units. In 1994, I had the privilege of addressing the Market Technicians Association at its annual conference. I applied socionomic causality to caution the organization as follows: "In the bear market, the MTA will become more…polarized. It will become more desirous of identifying an 'us' and a 'them.' This 'us vs. them' dynamic could show up ultimately in the tightening of the MTA's membership requirement. Or perhaps in secession by a regional affiliate. Or perhaps an east/west split of the entire organization."[9]

It took a while for this dynamic to manifest, but manifest it did. During the worldwide bear market of 2000-2003—after 30 years of cohesion—the MTA suffered extensive internal friction and ultimately a rebellion due to animosity over several issues, one of which was the looser standards for membership serving a policy of inclusionism that had reigned during the preceding 20-year period of positive social mood. A number of long-time members seceded to form a more restrictive organization, the American Association of Professional Technical Analysts, which was incorporated the following year.

If you are a futurist who doesn't want to learn the Elliott wave model—in fact, even if you disbelieve WP—this is an example of how you should approach your craft. Advise people about what the opportunities and risks will be depending upon the social mood environment as evidenced by stock market trends.

(4) Lagging Sociometers Confirm Extremities in Leading Ones

On November 1, 1999, 66 years after the low of the Great Depression, Kendall and Hochberg in *The Elliott Wave Financial Forecast* unequivocally conveyed the long term implication of Congress' latest financial law:

> "Government," *The Elliott Wave Theorist* has noted, "is the last sector of society to catch on to a trend. Usually it embraces a trend after it is over." The U.S. government may have just provided one of its greatest-ever demonstrations of this principle. On October 21, the Glass-Steagall Act, which purportedly had protected the financial infrastructure by separating the bank, insurance and brokerage industries, was effectively repealed. The Financial Services Act of 1999 "follows several failed efforts to do away with the Glass-Steagall Act over more than two decades."[10] The bill reopens the door to the securities business for banks and insurance firms. Glass-Steagall shut the door in 1933, the year after the bear market bottom in 1932. So, after totally missing the bear market it was supposed to prevent and protecting banks and insurance companies from six decades of rising [financial] prices, the U.S. government will free banks and insurers to take part in a financial consolidation that promises to be one of the biggest in history. In our opinion, this is once again perfect timing, one year after the top in most stocks and mutual funds. This long-term signal of the most entrenched, government-backed market consensus in at least 65 years [is] a long-term sell signal if ever there was one.[11]

It was an awesome call. The decade that followed provided a negative return for stock investors, a very rare event.

(5) Fractal Extrapolation from Behavioral Extremes Regardless of Elliott Waves, the Stock Market or Overall Social Mood

One can use the general idea of socionomic causality even without paying attention to overall social mood. Passionate, widely shared opinions and behavior constitute a reliable indicator of an impending reversal for any social trend. A prediction to that effect will appear uninformed, if not preposterous, to everyone else.

In 1989-1990, the market for collectible coins was hotter than ever. Over the previous decade, rare coins had risen in price more than any major investment. Prices were thirty times their level of 1974 and even three times their level of January 1980, when gold and silver had topped out. Brokerage firms were embracing rare coins as a new asset class, and they pledged a quarter of a billion dollars to buy coins for their newly created investment funds. In April 1990, high-grade coins made a new all-time high while medium-grade coins fell short of matching that feat, signaling (as noted in Chapter 7) a maturing trend. Based on these signs of peak zeal, *The Elliott Wave Theorist* on May 28, 1990 showed a chart of coin prices and cautioned, "The risk in this market now…is tremendous and increasing. A loss of 50%-90% would not be out of line. Any investor overly weighted in collector coins should strongly consider selling his collection at today's lofty prices."[12]

Coin prices drifted lower throughout the summer, and in September they crashed. By 1993, the value of brokerage firms' coin funds had plunged by more than half on their way to much lower prices, and the contents of several funds were liquidated at a no-minimum-bids auction. A long term price history later made available (see Figure 18) showed that a beautiful Elliott wave had ended in 1989-1990.

Remember the escalating talk about the "New Economy" in the late 1990s? The popular term in the late 1920s was "New Era." Impressed by the replay of such thinking, Kendall and Hochberg compiled data on the media's escalating use of the modern expression and predicted that it would lead to disappointment. In order to anticipate this outcome, they didn't need to study the stock market or apply Elliott waves; they needed only a socionomic mindset. *The Elliott Wave Financial Forecast* published Figure 19 in February 2000, one month before the peak of the dot-com bubble, which led to a bear market that ultimately culminated in the Great Recession of 2007-2009.

They did the same thing in the summer of 2005 with respect to real estate prices. Figure 21 shows that the S&P 500 Homebuilding Stock Index had risen 928% over the preceding five years. *Business Week*, having just polled a bevy of economists, reported in its June 22, 2005 issue that the profession was unanimous that housing prices were *not* "due to plunge." All but one of the economists polled concurred that the very idea of "a national

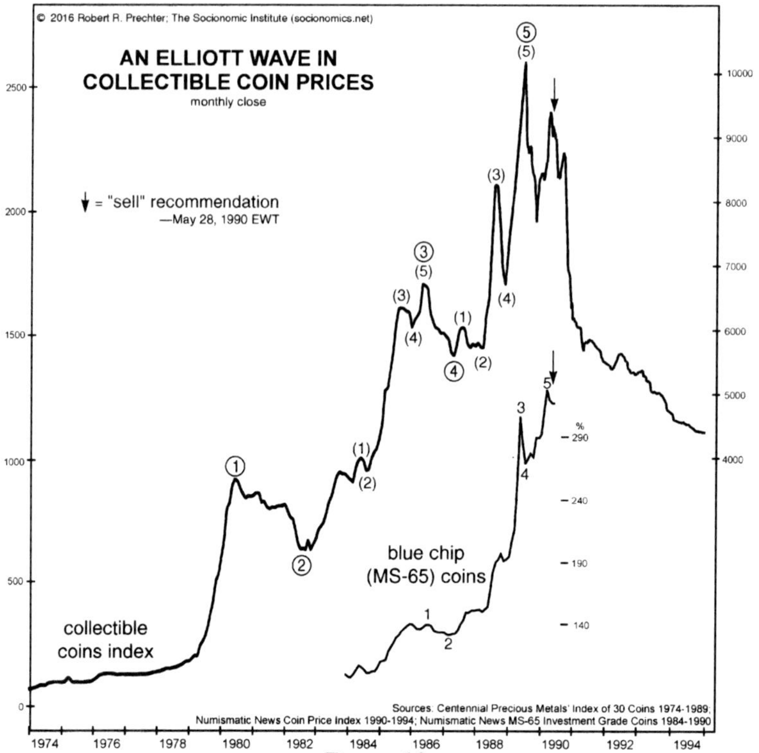

Figure 18

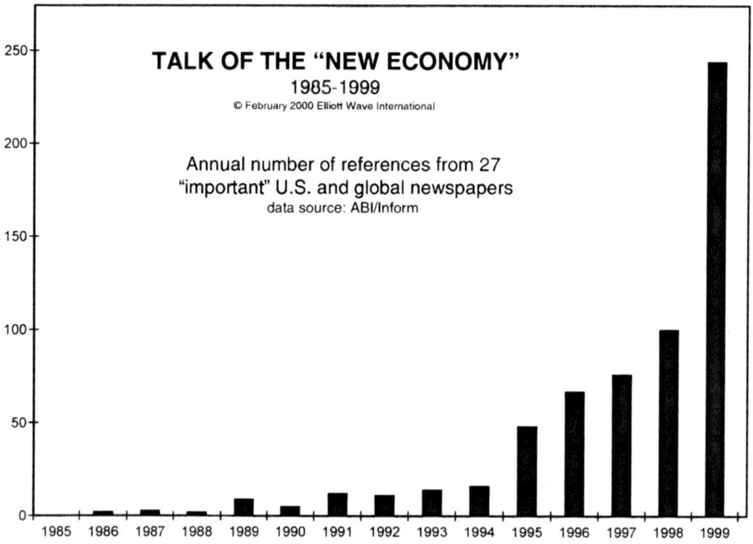

Figure 19

As published on September 2, 2005, with added notes

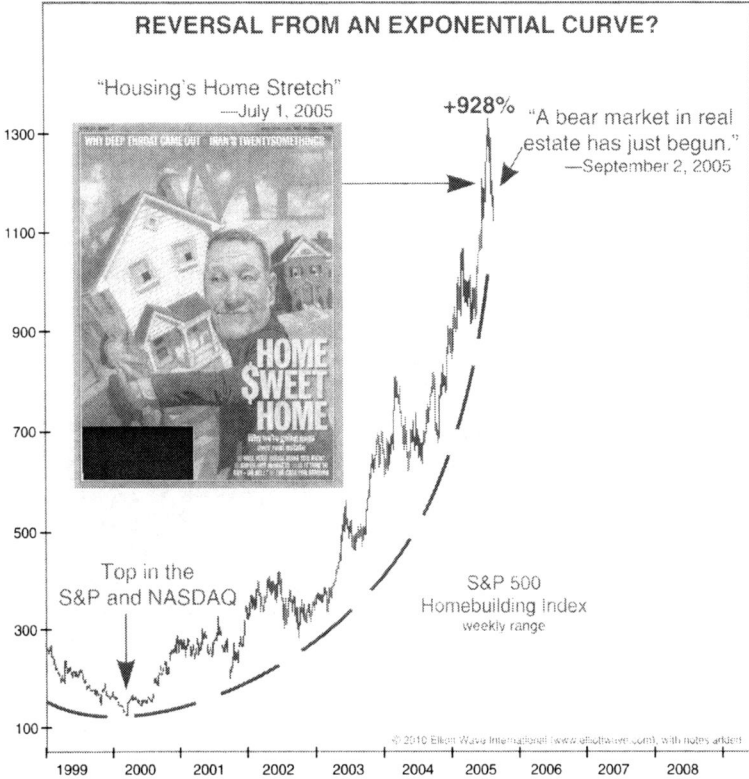

REVERSAL FROM AN EXPONENTIAL CURVE?

Figure 20

housing bubble is relatively silly." This was complacency at its smuggest. As Chapter 5 demonstrates and as Chapter 23 explains, experts' denial of a bubble is good evidence that one exists. A week later, *The Elliott Wave Financial Forecast* published a chart of the S&P Homebuilding Index along with a *Time* magazine cover titled "Home $weet Home" depicting an owner hugging his house. As Paul Montgomery demonstrated, the very appearance of a financial-market cover story in a general-interest magazine indicates an extreme in optimism or pessimism relating to the featured market. Kendall and Hochberg titled their chart "Housing's Home Stretch." On September 2 they issued an updated chart titled "Reversal of an Exponential Curve?" and confirmed, "We think a bear market in real estate has just begun." The reversal had occurred between those two assessments, in August. Figure 21 shows what happened to homebuilding stocks: a staggering 92% decline in just three years. Real estate prices followed, with an eight-month lag.

Outcome

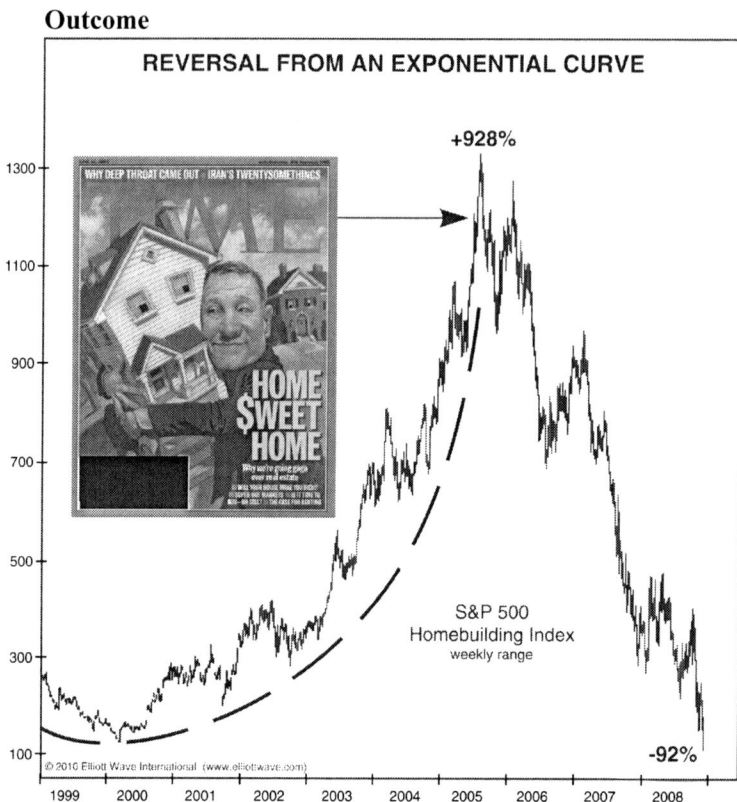

Figure 21

As noted earlier, governments herd, too, and their actions tend to lag substantially the trends in social mood. Kendall and Hochberg applied this observation in real time in June 2007. Their analysis offers a classic example of the difference between linear projection based on the mechanics paradigm and fractal projection based on the socionomics paradigm:

> The establishment of "sovereign wealth funds" is another sign that a downturn is falling into place and that governments are doing everything in their power to make the worst of it. These funds, which dozens of countries have established in recent weeks, invest a country's reserves and natural-resource earnings in global financial assets that are much riskier than the extra-safe bonds that governments have traditionally owned. Based on current rates of formation, projections show these investment pools rocketing from current levels of $1.5 trillion to $20 trillion over the next 20

years. On the basis of these forecasts, many Wall Street analysts now envision a "multi-trillion dollar industry" that will "transform the shape of the world economy and provide a massive boost for share prices in coming decades." Says one e-mailer to these offices, "Think of the vast sums of money that could flow into the U.S. stock market." But as we said last month with respect to one of the initial sovereign wealth fund investments—China's investment in Blackstone—these kinds of investments are not bullish; they are a "classic precondition to a reversal." They express how utterly conventional the drive into riskier financial instruments has become. With governments making the move, complacency toward risk has surely attained an extreme.[13]

This kind of prediction is strikingly counterintuitive to believers in exogenous cause. Yet true to socionomic form, just as investors prepared for "vast sums of money" to create "a massive boost for share prices," stock markets peaked worldwide, and commodities followed, plunging—along with these funds—more than at any time since the 1930s. As related in Chapter 2, speculators in gold made the same mistake three years later when, right at the top, they thought central banks' massive gold buying was bullish.

You can apply the same approach to predicting reversals of fortune for individuals who are public figures. Here is a quote from *The Elliott Wave Theorist* from March 29, 1991:

> On March 19th, Sony Corporation presented Michael Jackson the biggest contract ever awarded an entertainer. It would be reasonable to assume that the astounding value of the contract Mr. Jackson signed with Sony was a sign of a peak in his valuation.

Here we ascribed meaning to the fact that one of the biggest corporations in the world had decided to bet a billion dollars on a popular performer after he had had years of outsized success. We thought, "This looks like an extreme in society's valuation of Mr. Jackson's persona." Shortly thereafter, his image turned negative (see Figure 22), and Sony ended up rescinding its contract.

Four years earlier, I had come to a like conclusion about an approaching reversal in my own public persona. Being socionomically aware made it possible to recognize a professional peak as it happened and to brace myself for, and to temper, the negative experience that lay just around the corner. (For details, see *Prechter's Perspective*, 1996.) Michael Jackson could have sidestepped a lot of pain had he retired or gone on hiatus. Jerry Seinfeld did it

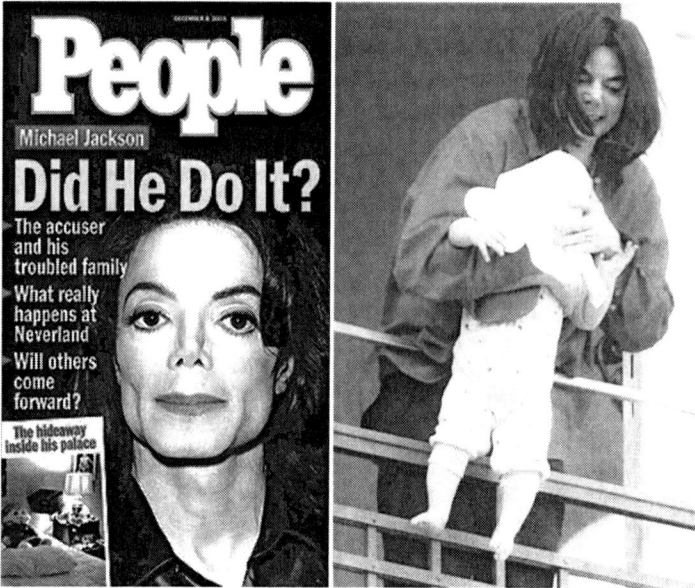

Figure 22

right. Taylor Swift might want to take a lesson. Socionomic thinking can provide real-time practical value to people who have a publicly determined image.

An extreme in social passion is a sign of trend termination in all kinds
of areas. By 2007, increasing concern over man-made global warming
had reached such a point. Dramatic depictions of future climate conditions—exemplified by the famous "hockey stick" graph—were based on
extrapolations of recent trends not with a modest straight line but with
something akin to a parabola. In 2004, a disaster flick, *The Day after Tomorrow*, presented an apocalyptic vision of the future due to man-made global
warming. In 2006, Al Gore's Oscar-winning documentary, *An Inconvenient
Truth*, and the kid-oriented cartoon film, *Ice Age: The Meltdown*, were in
theaters. The scope of mass global-warming activities continued to expand
into April 2007, when the "Largest-Ever Rally Against Global Warming"[14]
took place. It was one of the most intense episodes of public concern ever
recorded absent the threat of war. These manifestations prompted me to
forecast in June and July 2007 that people in general would not be worrying
about global warming to the same degree in the future, if at all:

> Advocates of man-made global warming may appear sober as judges
> individually, but they are participating in a mass movement, involving
> press releases, student rallies, pop concerts, movie documentaries and

an underlying tone of moral crusade.... There is powerful evidence of herding at the social level, and like all past social trends that were ending, there is a rush to extrapolate. Hysteria often signals the end of a trend.[15]

After issuing that analysis, I thought, "We need to get some data to see if this forecast works out." As it happens, the Gallup organization had created a specialized sociometer by regularly asking people if they thought the global warming argument was valid or understated vs. invalid or overstated. Figure 23 shows the data for ten years prior to the forecast and three years thereafter. The arrows on the chart show when I went to press.

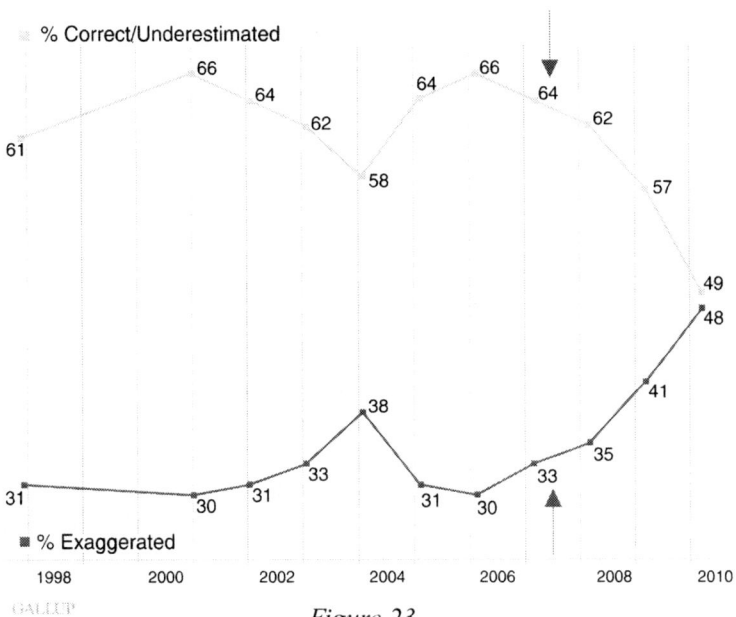

Figure 23

A report from the Pew Research Center confirmed a thorough reversal of public attitude. In its poll of Americans conducted in January 2013, the item titled "dealing with global warming," formerly the #1 concern, came in dead last in people's ranking of 21 issues on which government should focus its attention. I think we can label that 2007 forecast a success.

I do not recall any futurist making this prediction. Economists and sociologists typically wait until well after a trend has ended and then retrospectively come up with an exogenous-cause explanation for its reversal. This time was no different. An academic study from 2012 observed the decline in public interest over global warming and proposed that it was "driven by the economic insecurity caused by the Great Recession."[16] This is another "A caused B" mechanistic conclusion, which is not only useless for forecasting but also wrong. The public's passion over global warming began receding in 2006 or early 2007, well ahead of the supposed cause, negating the exogenous-cause argument. Though loosely tied to overall social mood, the global-warming movement receded substantially on its own internal dynamics. This is the only real-time socionomic analysis of a fad (referring to the cause as opposed to climate science per se) featured in this book.

Extremes in social mood show up not only in projections for the future but also in passionate assessments of present conditions. On December 18, 1964, after 32 years of rising real stock prices, President Lyndon Johnson declared, "These are the most hopeful times in all the years since Christ was born in Bethlehem."[17] Fourteen months later, the Dow/PPI started its deepest bear market since 1929-1932. Conversely, on July 15, 1979, after 13 years of declining real stock prices and rising inflation rates, President Jimmy Carter in a televised address memorably decried the country's "crisis of confidence...that strikes at the very heart and soul and spirit of our national will." Six months later, the Dow/gold ratio bottomed and took off on a 19-year run. The point is, you don't need the stock market to glean analytical value from public expressions of extremes in social mood.

The breadth of social mood's influence can hardly be understated. It permeates every area of social life. The extremity in positive mood that created the highest stock-market valuations of all time in 1999 simultaneously created, for example, the highest valuations for basketball franchises of all time. A retrospective analysis of the sport from 2011 noted,

> Owners in 1999 tolerated annual losses because so many were debt free and the values of their franchises were skyrocketing. The more recent [around 2007] buyers of NBA teams in some cases paid almost 20 times their predecessors—and in one case 500 times—taking on debt when the growth in franchise values is slowing."[18]

This is essentially the equivalent of saying,

> Tech-stock owners in 1999 tolerated dividend payouts of zero because the values of their stocks were skyrocketing. The more recent buyers of stocks in 2007 in some cases paid almost 20 times their predecessors—and in one case 500 times—increasing their margin debt when the uptrend slowed.

Exactly the same psychology is involved in both cases: There was no thought of losses or dividends, just dreams of capital gains. The ultimate result was the same, too. Stock owners suffered huge losses in 2008-2009, and team owners "contend they lost a combined $300 million"[19] in the 2010-2011 season.

So, even if you are unfamiliar with the Elliott wave model and do not follow the stock market, you can make useful forecasts simply by being attuned to extremes in social sentiment.

Socionomic Prediction is Counter-Intuitive

As this chapter shows, socionomists interpret the news in a way diametrically opposed to the way everyone else does. When we read that experts at a think tank have predicted rising energy prices for the next decade, we figure that energy prices are probably near a top. When we read that economists agree that a recession is in force, we see it as evidence that a recession is about over. And so on. By the time conditions, events and commentaries fully reflect a positive or negative mood trend of a particular degree, they can have predictive value in the opposite direction. Even absent detailed application of the Elliott wave model, such conclusions essentially derive not from linear extrapolation but from fractal extrapolation. Adopting such a mindset will set you far apart from the crowd.

Limits to Sentiment-Only Contrarianism

The unbounded nature of social mood fluctuations can make the bounded nature of most sentiment indicators problematic to forecasting. When waves of extremely high degree are in their late stages, bounded readings of optimism or pessimism can stay pinned near maximum levels for a long time. A striking example of this condition occurred from 1998 to 2007, as explained in the October 19, 2007 issue of *The Elliott Wave Theorist*:

Optimism in the Stock Market
The latest reading from Investors Intelligence shows 62% bulls among newsletter advisors, the second-highest reading over the past 21 years, a period that includes the tops of 1987 and 2000. And this is not the most extreme figure relating to investor sentiment. The *duration* of net optimism is the longest ever by many measures.

Figure [24] shows how the greatest tops of the 20th century compare on this basis. The X axis records the length of time that bulls consistently outnumbered bears for at least 50 out of 52 weeks in

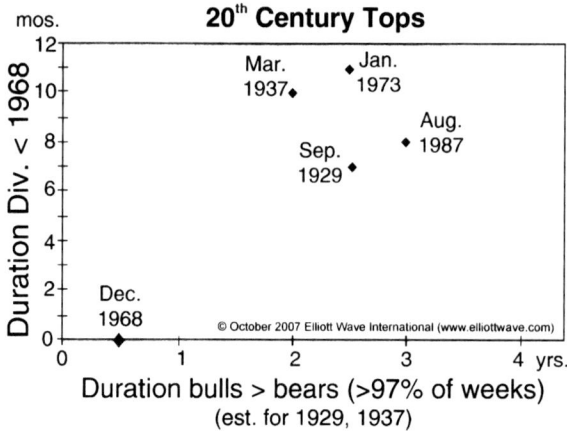

Figure 24

Investors Intelligence's weekly readings. (I estimate that at the tops in 1929 and 1937, bulls outnumbered bears continuously for about 2-2.5 years.) The Y axis records the length of time that the dividend yield from the Dow was less than it was at the 1968 top, the peak with the highest dividend payout among these five tops. As you can see, the other major tops cluster around an area of 2-3 years for a lopsided bullish consensus and only 7-11 months for extremely low dividend payout.

Now look at Figure [25]. This is the *same graph* but with two added data points representing the top of January 2000 and now. Compared to past market tops, the current juncture is nothing less than grotesque.

Let's use the peak reading of 1929, the greatest top of the 19th and 20th centuries, as a benchmark. At the 1987 high, bulls had reigned for three years, but just three months after the annual dividend yield from the DJIA fell below that of 1929, the market crashed. At the 2000 high, dividends had been below the 1929 level for a full six years, but the duration for a preponderance of bulls was only 1.25 years. That was enough for the S&P to fall in half and the NASDAQ to collapse 78%.

Here in October 2007, advisory bulls have consistently out-numbered bears for *9 years*, by an incredible 51/52 ratio of weekly readings, and the dividend yield has been below that of 1929 for *13 years*. Thus, optimism is not only historically extreme in terms of extent but also—by a huge amount—in duration, dwarfing all previous experiences.

Tops of the past 80 years

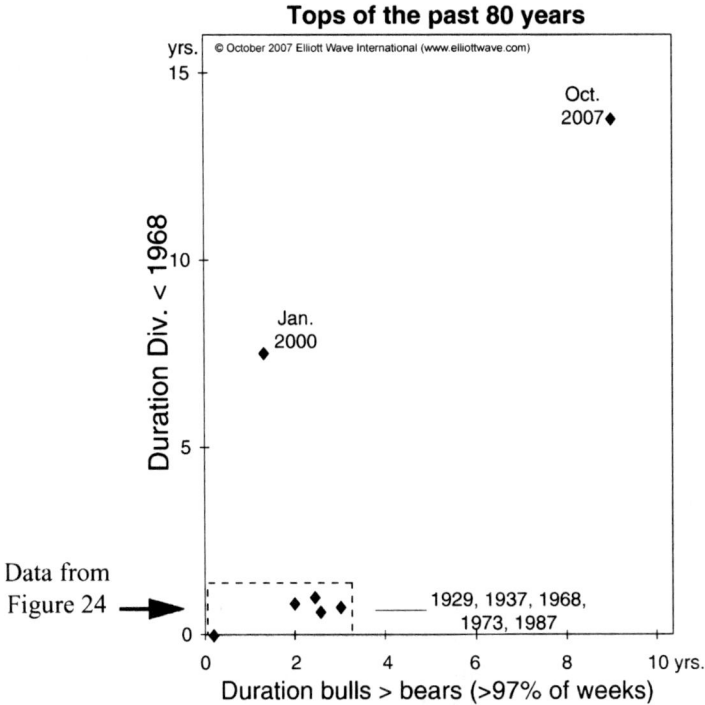

Figure 25

The condition described above had been troublesome, because it had kept me persistently bearish and wrong throughout the 2003-2007 intra-correction (B-wave) rally. The implication of these readings nevertheless prevented me from throwing in the towel and falling in with the herd at the top. The analysis quoted above was published eight days after the Dow's all-time high of 2007. Even as the biggest collapse in the stock market since the Great Depression took hold, net optimism among advisors persisted all the way into March 2008, adding another five months to the durations depicted by the data point in the upper right of Figure 25. When the optimists finally paid the piper, they did so commensurately with their preceding excess.

The ideal way to avoid being too early in expecting a trend change in the face of unrelenting optimism or pessimism recorded in sentiment indicators is to interpret the market's waves correctly. My coverage of the stock market during my career has provided several good examples of how it's not done. Chapter 22, covering Elliott Wave International's analyses of the oil market, offers a good example of how it is done.

Socionomic theory is unique in explaining why such sentiment extremes occur. In contrast to the exogenous-cause mindset, we understand that sentiment readings are results, not causes. They don't determine where the stock market goes; the mood driving the stock market determines where the sentiment indicators go. The higher the degree of the largest culminating wave, the greater the sentiment extreme will be.

Is Linear Projection Truly an Exercise in Prediction?

Linear forecasters are never actually right, because in fact *they are not forecasting*. Linear projections are merely descriptions of past trends and current conditions. Voicing them takes no special ability and has no value. It's just reading out loud.

Ironically, because economists are always predicting the past trend to continue, they can rightfully say, "We are right most of the time." This is because of the implication of Figure 1 in Chapter 7: Social conditions follow social mood closely, and social mood has *trends*. Therefore, once economists belatedly recognize a new trend, they will appear to be "right" as long as that trend remains in force.

Even though the practice of trend-following makes economists appear correct about the direction of the trend, say, 80% of the time, they are really never correct at all. We can understand this point more easily through analogy. Suppose there are two sets of forecasters on a train traveling through fog: a socionomist in the cab of the locomotive and a pack of economists in the caboose. Their job is to anticipate curves in the track so the engineer can slow the train in time to negotiate them. The economists are looking out the rear window saying, "The track is still straight as an arrow behind us, so we predict more of the same." Since curves in the track are few and far between, extrapolating past trends in linear fashion makes the economists appear correct most of the time, simply because the caboose is often going in the same direction as the locomotive. The socionomist in the cab can't see very well because of the fog, so he makes several cautious suggestions for naught, but when the curves arrive he can see them clearly. Although his forecasting record is imperfect, he is in no way condemned to miss all the turns as the economists are.

First question: Who is actually in the forecasting business? Who even has a *chance* to be right?

Second question: Who truly has the better track record? If the socionomist sees the curves in time to slow the train before it careens off the rails, he has provided an important service. Economists in the caboose cannot possibly anticipate any curves. For the task at hand, they are never right. When your life or livelihood depends upon advice, hind-casting is not an option. It is nothing.

In 2007 and early 2008—as detailed in Chapter 5—the most educated economists in the profession predicted that the macroeconomic "track" was still pointing straight ahead. Like their colleagues in the caboose, they were simply describing the state of the past while *marketing* it as a prediction. Figure 26 shows that people relying upon such statements suffered terrible injury when the train careened off the rails and crashed.

S&P Earnings, Inflation-Adjusted
Earnings/CPI
monthly

The old trend is not a reliable basis for forecasting.

Source: Standard & Poor's and Federal Reserve of St. Louis
© 2016 Robert R. Prechter; The Socionomics Institute (socionomics.net)

Figure 26

Consequences matter. In the real world, ill-timed business expansion can lead to corporate bankruptcy. Inordinate caution at the end of an economic contraction can lead to missed opportunity. Business people need timely warnings. They never get them from linear forecasters. Fractal forecasting is a more useful alternative.

NOTES AND REFERENCES

[1] Shell, Adam, "Tug of War Between Bulls and Bears Boxes in Stocks," *USA Today*, January 29, 2010.

[2] Rothwell, Steve, "Stocks Continue Last Week's Decline," *The Times*, April 8, 2014.

[3] Montier, James, "Asleep at the Wheel, or, How I Learned to Stop Worrying and Love the Bomb." InvestorsInsight.com, John Mauldin, Editor, April 7, 2008.

[4] A service of trade-futures.com.

[5] Kendall, Peter, *The Elliott Wave Financial Forecast*, July 30, 1999.

[6] Farrell, Paul B., "American Dream Died with Dow 49,200 Forecast," *MarketWatch*, February 16, 2013.

[7] "Popular Culture and the Stock Market," *The Elliott Wave Theorist*, August 22, 1985. Republished in *Pioneering Studies in Socionomics*.

[8] Prechter, Robert, *At the Crest of the Tidal Wave,* 1995, p. 435; and *The Wave Principle of Human Social Behavior*, 1999, p. 230.

[9] Prechter, Robert, "A Call to Arms," speech to Market Technicians Association annual conference, Wesley Chapel, Florida, May 1994, published in the *MTA Journal*, Summer/Fall 1994; republished in Prechter, Robert, Ed., *Market Analysis for the New Millennium*, New Classics Library, 2002.

[10] Schroeder, Michael, "Glass-Steagall Accord Reached After Last-Minute Deal Making," *The Wall Street Journal*, October 25, 1999.

[11] Hochberg, Steven and Peter Kendall, *The Elliott Wave Financial Forecast*, October 29, 1999, p. 5.

[12] You can read the full story in Prechter, Robert, *How To Forecast Gold and Silver Using the Elliott Wave Principle* (2006).

[13] Hochberg, Steven and Peter Kendall, *The Elliott Wave Financial Forecast*, June 28, 2007, p. 6.

[14] "Step It Up: Thousands Gather This Weekend for Largest-Ever Rally Against Global Warming," *DemocracyNow.org*, April 13, 2007.

[15] Prechter, Robert. *The Elliott Wave Theorist*, July 13, 2007, p. 4.

[16] Scruggs, Lyle and Salil Benegal, "Declining Public Concern About Climate Change: Can We Blame The Great Recession?" *Global Environmental Change*, February 2012.

[17] Johnson, Lyndon, "Remarks at the Lighting of the Nation's Christmas Tree," December 18, 1964.

[18] Soshnik, Scott, "Stern Finds New Owners Paying Too Much Show No Need of NBA Deal," Bloomberg, November 23, 2011.

[19] *Ibid.*

Elliott Waves vs. Supply and Demand: The Oil Market

Robert R. Prechter

Do Supply and Demand Regulate Oil Prices?

Nearly everyone reading that subhead would reply, "Of course supply and demand regulate oil prices! What else could regulate them? Consumers demand oil; producers supply oil; the price mediates their desires. What could be clearer?" It used to seem self-evident to me, too.

The correct answer, however, is no, they don't. In this chapter, I support my conclusion and demonstrate its value.

First question: Did shifts in supply and/or demand explain why the price of oil soared 1,300% in ten years, crashed over 78% in five months, tripled in 2½ years and then plunged 75% to date? From the limited data I have reviewed, it seems that economists would be hard pressed to demonstrate commensurately spectacular shifts in supply and/or demand that either preceded or coincided with these major changes in oil prices.

We already saw in Chapter 1 that the surprise curtailment of the U.S. oil supply due to the devastation wrought by Hurricane Katrina had no positive effect on oil prices. Let's examine a longer history of supply-demand data.

Consider Figure 1, which depicts worldwide oil production (upper time axis) and consumption (lower time axis), respectively. The letters placed on these graphs indicate major turning points in the price of oil. See if you can guess which way, and how far, prices went each time by studying these graphs. I can't do it. The list below the chart gives you the price changes.

One might wonder, since it has been illegal for U.S. oil producers to sell oil abroad, whether the ratio of consumption to production in North America might explain the swings in the oil price. Figure 2 displays this ratio along with oil-price extremes as noted on the graph. As you can see, there is no discernible connection there, either.

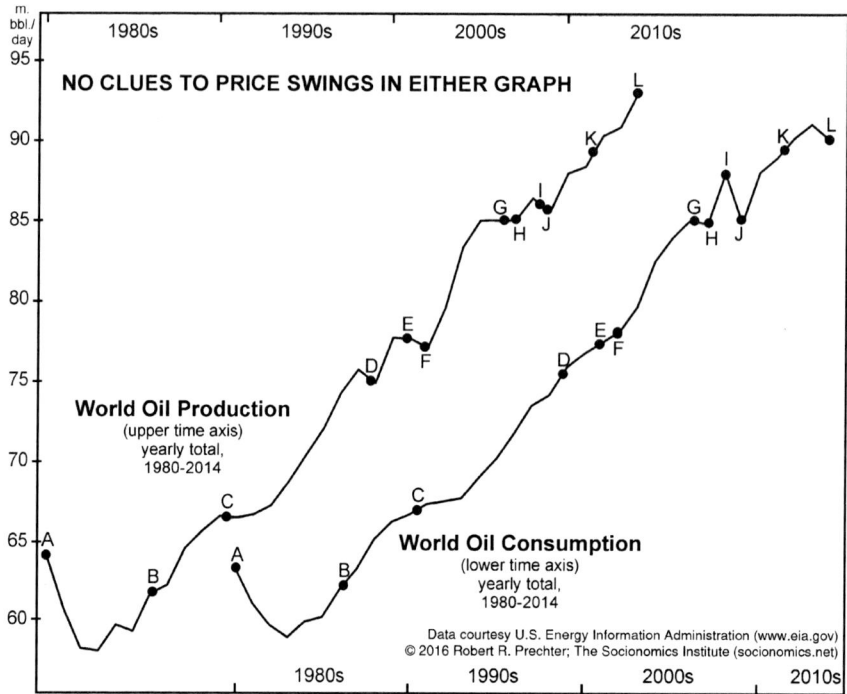

Figure 1

Changes in Oil Prices		Time Span
A to B:	75% drop	1980-3/86
B to C:	320% rise	3/86-6/90
C to D:	76% drop	6/90-12/98
D to E:	265% rise	12/98-11/00
E to F:	56% drop	11/00-11/01
F to G:	370% rise	11/01-7/06
G to H:	36% drop	7/06-1/07
H to I:	196% rise	1/07-7/08
I to J:	78% drop	7/08-12/08
J to K:	254% rise	12/08—5/11
K to L:	75% drop	5/11 thru 2015

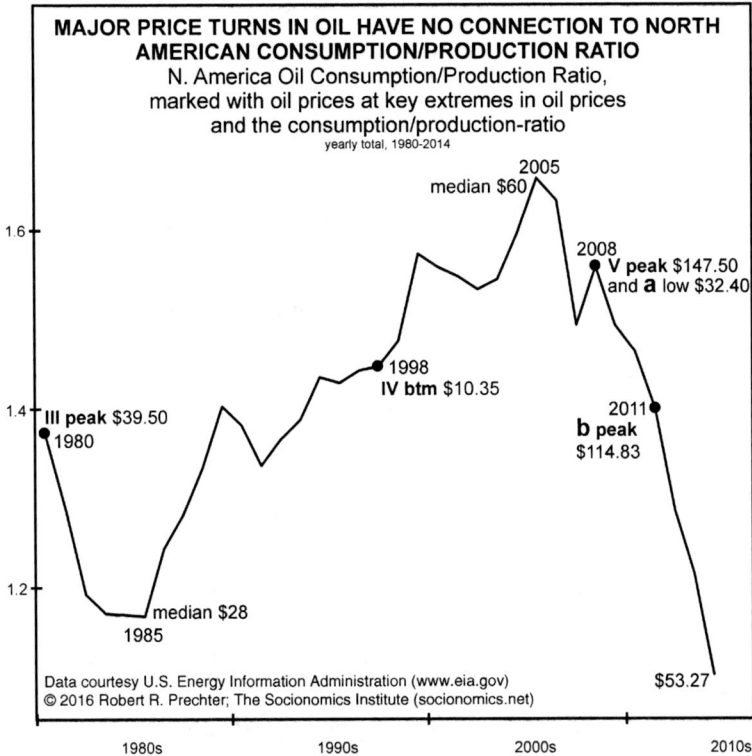

MAJOR PRICE TURNS IN OIL HAVE NO CONNECTION TO NORTH AMERICAN CONSUMPTION/PRODUCTION RATIO
N. America Oil Consumption/Production Ratio,
marked with oil prices at key extremes in oil prices
and the consumption/production-ratio
yearly total, 1980-2014

2005
median $60

2008
V peak $147.50
and **a** low $32.40

1998
IV btm $10.35

III peak $39.50
1980

2011
b peak
$114.83

median $28
1985

Data courtesy U.S. Energy Information Administration (www.eia.gov)
© 2016 Robert R. Prechter; The Socionomics Institute (socionomics.net)

$53.27

1980s   1990s   2000s   2010s

Figure 2

Without plausibly causative shifts, the claim for supply and demand causality is sorely pressed. We examine this issue further at the end of the chapter.

Second question: If supply and demand do regulate oil prices, one would think that shifts in supply and/or demand would have alerted economists to coming price changes. Did any of the 30,000 or so economists scattered over the earth use supply and demand analysis to forecast accurately the dramatic swings in oil prices over the past three decades? To my knowledge, none of them did.

Economists could argue (under what strikes me as a tautological model) that oil prices change simultaneously with shifts in supply and demand, making forecasting impossible, in which case their forecasting inability by itself would not prove that supply and demand do not regulate oil prices. If this hypothesis were true, we would all at least agree, for starters, that studying supply and demand in the oil market provides no basis upon which anyone can forecast oil prices.

Economists' unanimous helplessness with respect to forecasting the oil market establishes a benchmark for a test. If there is in fact a way to forecast oil prices, then economists must be wrong, either about the simultaneity of changes in supply-demand factors and the price of oil or about the very assumption that supply and demand regulate the price of oil.

Do Elliott Waves Regulate Oil Prices?

Now, if I were simply to show a history of oil prices with Elliott wave labels on it, few readers would concede it any theoretical validity. Even though being able to match historical prices to a specifically patterned model is in fact a substantial achievement favoring the model, skepticism about retrospective model-fitting would likely outweigh any claimed value. Perhaps this is as it should be. Fortunately, I can do much better than that.

Scientists agree (see Chapter 11) that successful prediction is a good sign that a model is valid. The supply-demand model can't help anyone forecast oil prices, but the Elliott wave model can and does. We will now review an extensive, real-time, 22-year history of oil-price forecasting over one of the most volatile histories for any commodity ever. It will offer a basis for comparing the predictive utility of the Elliott wave model to that of the supply-demand model.

In the early 1990s, Elliott Wave International launched a series of institutional services, one of which is a 100-page monthly publication titled *Global Market Perspective*. It includes coverage of the energy sector. Our review begins at that time.

Elliott Wave International's Oil-Price Forecasts from Inception to Present

Following a major peak at $39.50 per barrel in 1980, the price of crude oil gyrated up and down within a volatile sideways trend that included a spike to $40.40 a barrel in the summer of 1990 and then just as swift a plunge back into the teens by that year's end. In the midst of the chaos, Elliottician Peter DeSario kicked off the energy-markets section of our new service by offering two key insights about oil in the December 1993 issue:

> Price should fall into the general area of *$10.00* (to end a fourth wave move from 1980) before the final leg up takes prices into *new historical highs*.

Figure 3 shows where the market was at that time.

Forecast published in *Global Market Perspective,* November 25, 1993

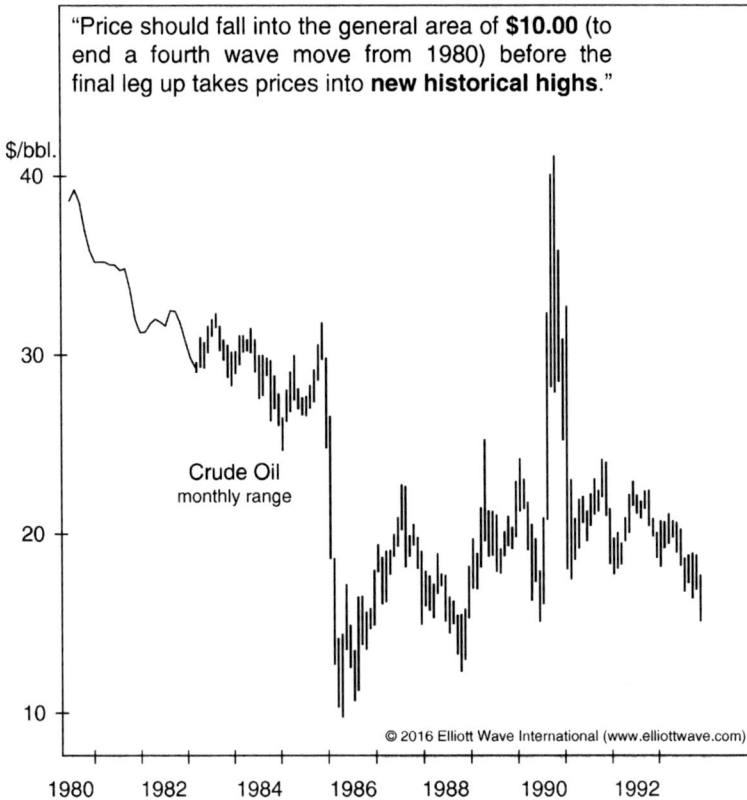

Figure 3

The very form of this forecast is rare. Market analysts are generally just bullish, bearish or neutral. Economists typically issue a slew of if/then statements. But the Elliott wave model's unique perspective provided a basis for a firm, complex, two-step forecast.

How could DeSario see all that coming? The answer is that oil prices had been following an Elliott wave form for over a hundred years, and he was confident they would continue to do so. Before we continue, take a look at Figure 4, which shows a plot of prices from the year of oil's discovery in 1859 through 1993. Reasons for predicting the next price moves are hardly evident when one looks at an unlabeled price graph, wouldn't you agree?

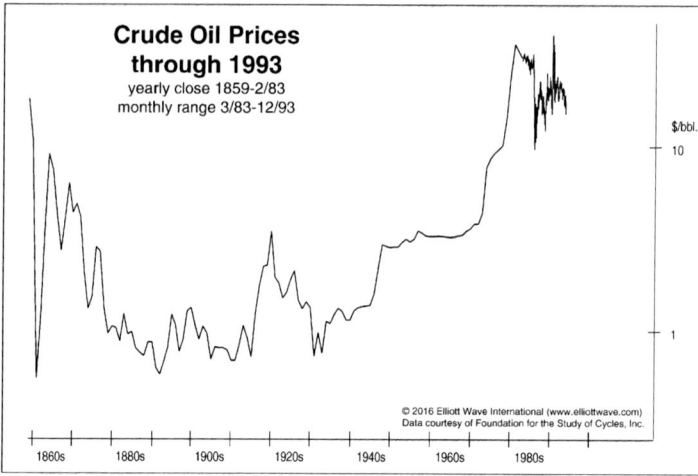

Figure 4

Figure 5 is the same graph with Elliott wave labels and pattern lines. It shows a corrective formation ending in 1910 and then a partially completed "impulse" of five waves. Our analyst had labeled waves I and II differently at the time, but the rest was the same, and so was the message of the model: Wave IV was still progressing, and wave V ultimately would trace out—in DeSario's words—"the final leg up" to finish off the pattern.

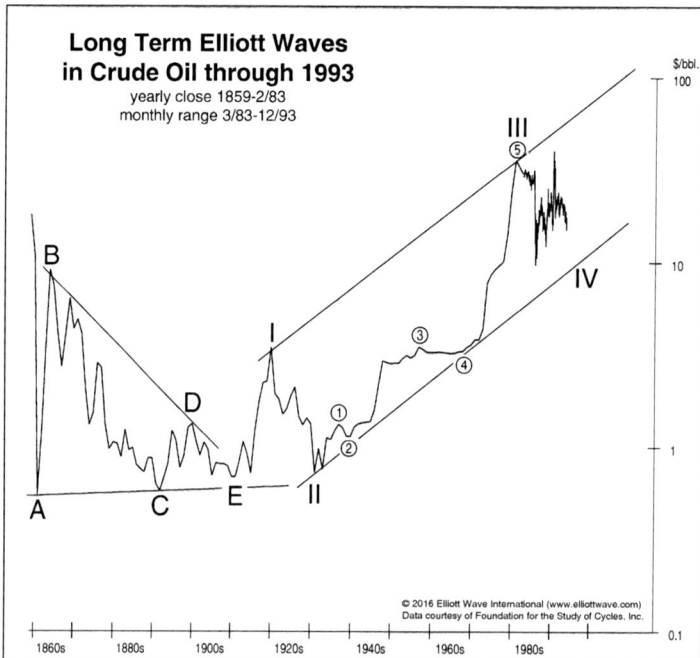

Figure 5

Figure 6 shows a simplified rendition of the Elliott wave model taken from Chapter 1 of *The Wave Principle of Human Social Behavior* (1999). It depicts a self-identical fractal comprising five waves in the direction of each wave of one larger degree and three waves (of two different shapes) in the opposite direction. Five-wave patterns, called impulses, are labeled with numbers one through five, and three-wave patterns, called corrections, are labeled with the letters A, B and C. The law of patterned herding—not supply and demand—motivates this pattern. Compare this schematic up to the arrow with the waves labeled with Roman numerals in Figure 5 and you will see the similarity between them. The dates added to Figure 6 depict the timing of compatible turns in oil prices from 1910 to 1980, and the arrow shows roughly (see *Elliott Wave Principle* for specific variations of corrective patterns) where our energy analyst believed the market was in 1993 with respect to the model. To create his forecast, he extrapolated waves from there.

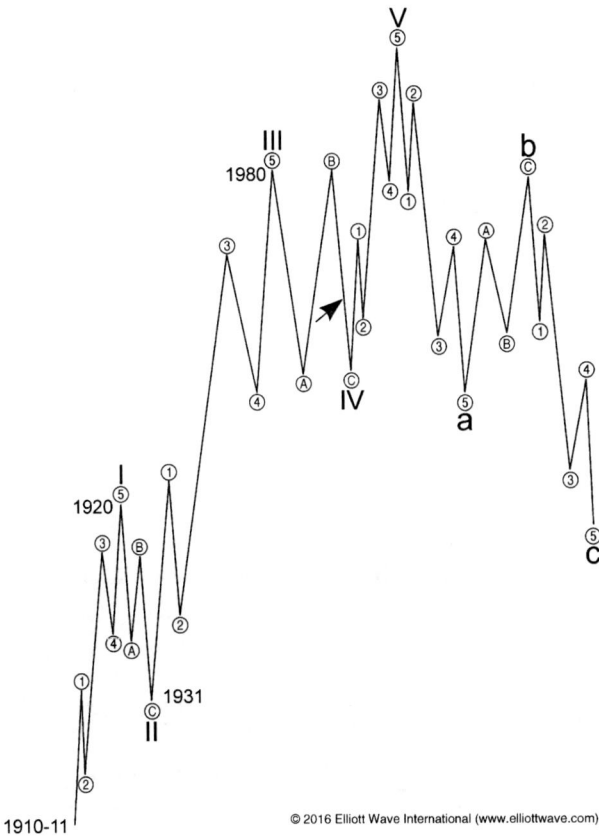

© 2016 Elliott Wave International (www.elliottwave.com)

Figure 6

Five years later, on December 21, 1998, oil finally entered "the general area of $10.00" when it reached $10.35 a barrel. Would it stop falling, turn up and make "new historical highs"? And did EWI's analysts recognize the bottom as it happened?

At the low in 1998, economists perceived supply and demand for oil to be quietly balanced. Analysts and speculators of the time generally felt that stocks were the only game worth playing, while oil near $10 a barrel wasn't worth their attention. EWI's Elliotticians, on the other hand, were in a state of high excitement over the prospects for oil prices.

As wave IV ground toward a close, Elliottician Al Graham took over writing the energy section of *Global Market Perspective*. Figure 7 shows his meticulous labeling of the sub-waves within wave IV right up to the price low in December 1998 and his forecast from there.

As you can see by the dashed lines on the chart, Graham's #1 scenario called for the market to generate four things: a bottom near $10, as DeSario had predicted; an initial rise not to new highs; a pullback not to new lows; and then a take-off to new all-time highs. Observe the very clear note on the chart: "Must hold $9.75 support," a requisite for his specific wave labeling. This was another multi-step forecast.

Forecast published in *Global Market Perspective*, December 4, 1998

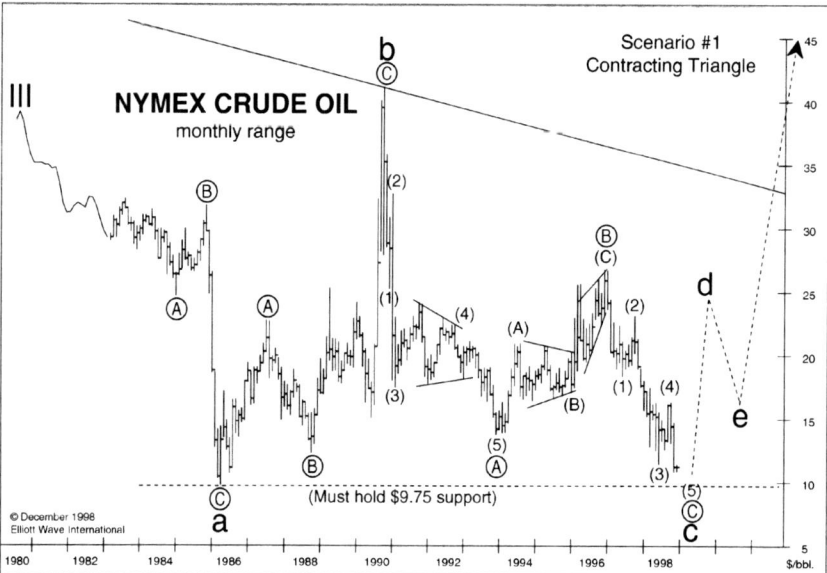

Figure 7

Oil did hold above $9.75, and after bottoming at $10.35 it more than tripled over the next two years. Would it stop rising shy of a new all-time high, pull back not to a new low and then go to an all-time high?

The Bull Market: Waves ①, ② and ③

In the December 2000 issue of *Global Market Perspective*, Peter Rehmer, the third Elliottician to provide the publication's energy analysis, identified the peak of the first rally, which occurred at $37.80, a few dollars below the all-time high. He shifted from counting a triangle for wave IV to the labeling shown in Figure 8, added two forecasting arrows and offered this commentary:

> Wave (IV) played out in the eighteen years into the 1998 low and has provided the foundation for a move to new all-time highs. The monthly chart...shows that crude oil has shot up 250% since late 1998. *We are soon likely to see a wave (C) [of ②] decline where oil tests the 50% retracement to the 19.13 level.* Once the...correction [into 1998] was over, crude exploded upward, and I expect the same outcome. One relatively conservative projection for fifth waves is equality with the corresponding first wave, in this case, a percentage move equal to that of 1933/1957 would take crude oil up to $61 per barrel in the coming years.

Forecast published in *Global Market Perspective*, December 4, 2000

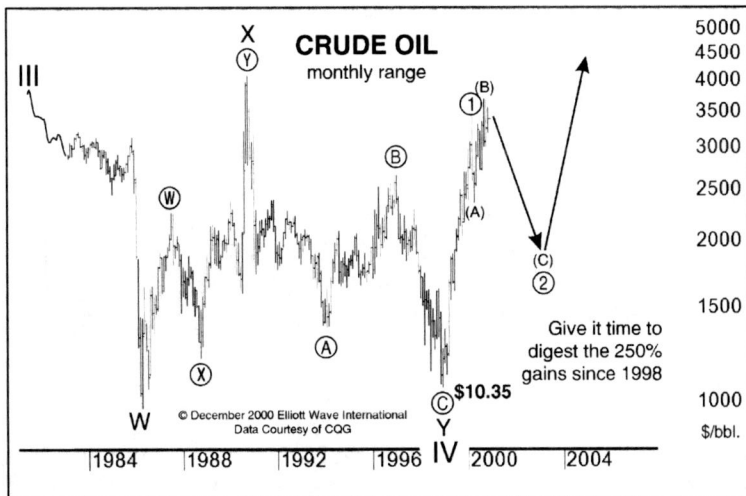

Figure 8

So, from the price just registered at $37.80, he was calling for an immediate drop of 50% into the teens and then a huge rise to at least $61 a barrel. This was another bold, complex forecast.

Oil plunged thereafter for an entire year. As it approached the forecasted decline of 50%, did Elliott waves signal the next low in real time, too?

The fourth analyst to take over EWI's energy analysis was Steven Craig. On October 26, 2001, three weeks before the bottom of wave ②, Craig published the detailed analysis shown in Figure 9. The waves were so clear that he was able to predict one last decline in weekly prices prior to a takeoff to the upside, a scenario he sketched on the chart. He explained his view as follows:

> Our downside targets have been met, but structurally the decline looks incomplete. The next significant targets on the continuation chart come at 16.97 and 14.29. If our count is on the mark, crude oil is in the final down leg of the longer-term correction from the October 2000 peak.

As published in *Global Market Perspective*, October 26, 2001

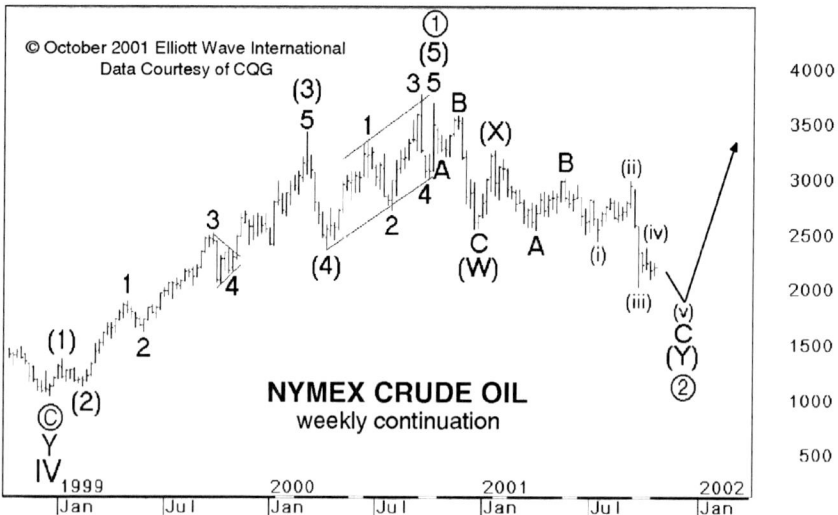

Figure 9

To keep readers oriented to the longer-term outlook, Craig added Figure 10 to his presentation. It reiterated our analysts' longstanding expectation that after wave ② ended, oil would trace out waves ③, ④ and ⑤ in carrying prices to new all-time highs.

As published on October 26, 2001

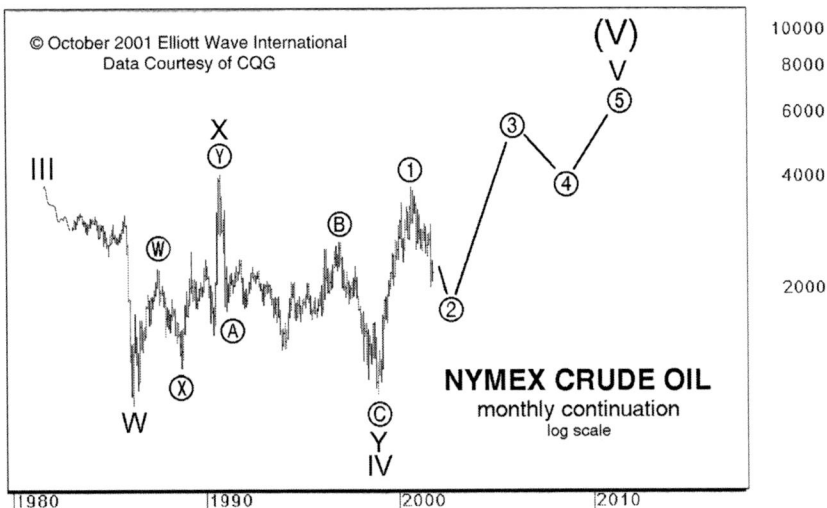

Figure 10

Three weeks later, on November 19, oil bottomed at $16.70, completing a 56% drop from the previous year's high. The intraday low occurred 29 cents under Craig's first target and $2.43 below the price Rehmer had forecasted when oil was trading at $37.80 the previous year.

Following the script, oil took off from the low of wave ② and soared more than 650% over the next five years. Along the way it achieved the "new historical highs" that DeSario, Graham, Rehmer and Craig had continually predicted.

In March 2006, while oil was climbing in wave ③, I was invited to address the Kenos Conference on oil in Vienna. My first slide was Figure 11, showing that wave ③ was not quite over. I had sketched out on log scale the likely path for the rest of oil's bull market. The Elliott wave model required a new high to complete wave ③, a pullback for wave ④, and a final run to a peak in wave ⑤. This hand-drawn estimate—based on the normal "look" of a wave—depicted an ultimate high at $135 per barrel.

Four months later, the subdivisions of wave ③ were complete. The July 25, 2006 issue of *The Elliott Wave Theorist*, published eleven days after that high, labeled the internal waves as shown in Figure 12 and unequivocally stated that an advance of Primary degree had completed "Five Waves Up from 2001."

Analysis and forecast from the Kenos Conference, March 16, 2006

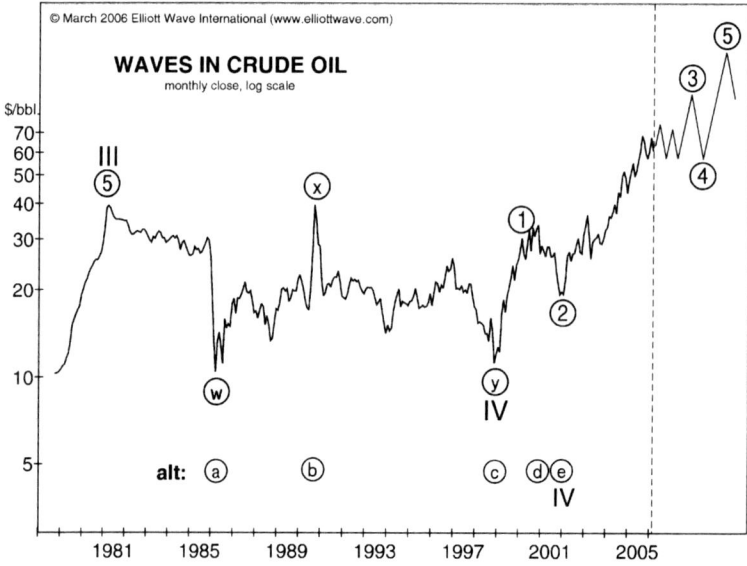

Figure 11

As published in *The Elliott Wave Theorist*, July 25, 2006

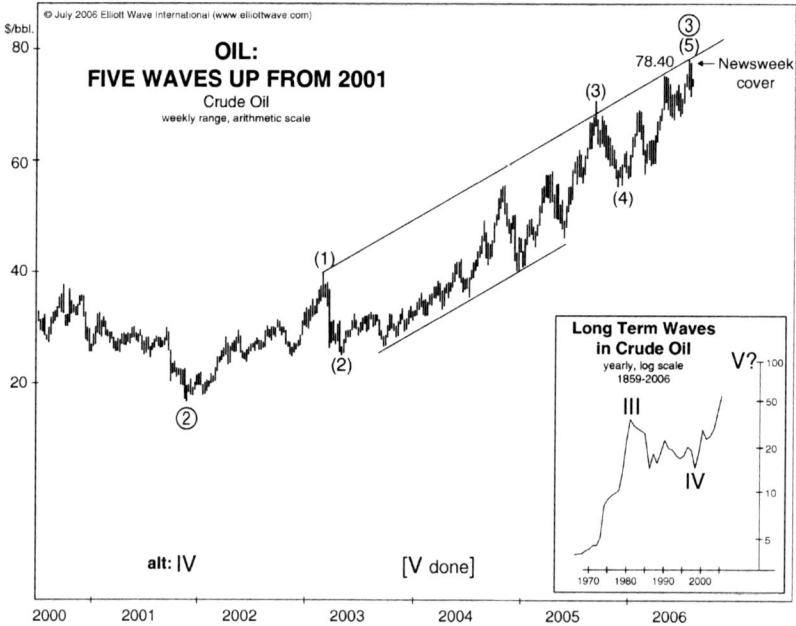

Figure 12

Psychological Environment

It is important to realize that the analysts quoted above were not afforded the luxury of making these predictions in a state of calm isolation. A mix of intense psychological pressures—most of them contrary to their outlook—pounded them from all sides during the entire time.

As the market passed the center of wave ③, psychology in the oil market—in line with the pivot point discussed in Chapter 8—switched to outright optimism, and people began competing with each other to extrapolate the upward trend higher. In 35 years of watching markets, I had never seen so many books written about a single commodity market, of which Figure 13 shows only nine. The theme of all these books was, "The world is running out of oil; the price is going to go to the moon; you're going to get rich if you invest in the oil market." There were no balancing, bearish books because no one wrote any. Meanwhile, the Internet became saturated with media outlets, independent websites, blogs, academics, economists and "Peak Oil" enthusiasts calling for rising, even infinitely rising, oil prices. In July 2005, the Bullish Consensus survey reported a whopping 96% bulls on oil among newsletter advisors. The August 22, 2005 cover of the tabloid *Weekly World News* blared, "NO MORE OIL! World Supply Will Be Gone in 6 Months—Economy Will Collapse!—Millions Will Starve!" On January 27, 2006, *Forbes* asked, "Ready for $262/barrel oil?" On February 11, 2006, a Princeton professor of geology, citing the "Hubbert peak" theory of depleted oil supplies, emphatically declared, "We passed the peak [of] world oil production...on December 16, 2005,"[1] and he showed a graph to prove it. On March 1, 2006, the venerable *New York Times* titled an article, "The End of Oil." The maturing Elliott wave of Supercycle degree in oil prices of nearly a century's duration accounts for this extreme social consensus.

The Elliott Wave Theorist of July 25, 2006 reported what it was like to take a contrary view in the heat of that moment:

> The oil price, which reached $78.40 intraday ($77.03 close) on Friday, July 14, is making headlines. A *Newsweek* cover (forward-dated to July 24) hitting newsstands that very weekend trumpets "Meltdown" in the Middle East and promises to tell us "What [It] Means for...The Price of Oil." The column quotes an analyst saying, "If another hurricane blows through the Gulf of Mexico and damages rigs and refineries, that will send prices way up." Never mind the incredibly low odds of such an occurrence. The fact is that the last time a hurricane blew through the Gulf of Mexico and damaged rigs, the event coincided with a top in prices, not a bottom [see Chapter 1].

Figure 13

There was no triggering event at the bottom, either; there never is. An elaborate direct-mail advertisement that reached my mailbox on July 13 (the day before the peak) spends the equivalent of 24 pages to convince its readers that a soaring oil price is *"In-ev-i-ta-ble."* One should pause, though, when the writer admits, "How did we NOT see this coming?" If someone didn't see it coming, should we rely on him to see it going? Today, right as we go to press, what may be the shrillest report yet about oil in the mainstream press has appeared in a mainstream magazine. Our local newspaper reported on it:

A world without oil—the doomsday scenario

What will life be like when we finally run out of oil? **Harpers** (August), citing an environmental group called Peak Oil, paints a nightmarish picture of such a world — the global economy in endless decline, cars becoming luxury items for the rich, suburbanites living in isolation from food and goods, agriculture withering, international trade halting, an end to air conditioning and the emergence of extreme political movements fighting to preserve the last resources. People will be forced to gather in small, self-sustaining and defensive communities to survive.

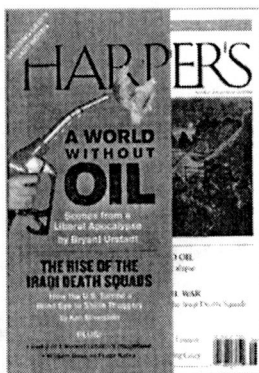

Bryant Urstadt, who wrote the article, says Peak Oil's outlook is an example of the kind of apocalyptic scenario "Americans seem born to love." But he also says the Peak Oilers "cannot be dismissed as madmen in sandwich boards," since petroleum is in fact a limited resource that will peak someday. Alternative energy sources have their own problems as well, whether coal, hydroelectric, solar, wind or nuclear power. But, writes Urstadt, the end-of-oil scenario has generated at least one growth industry — doom-and-gloom books such as Peak Oil's "The Party's Over: Oil, War and the Fate of Industrial Societies."

—The Atlanta Journal-Constitution, July 25, 2006

The *Theorist* pointed out that it had been a century and a half since Americans felt such extreme fear over a depleted energy source when on November 12, 1857 a headline in *The Boston Globe* read, "Whale Blubber Scarce—World to Go Dark." The world didn't go dark, of course, because high prices spur a search for alternatives, and people found one.

The *Theorist* also noted that record volume in oil futures contracts had just prompted the New York Mercantile Exchange to announce a pricey $250 million IPO of its own stock, which was enthusiastically received. That issue concluded, "myriad signs point strongly to a selling opportunity in oil." It takes years of practice to translate everyone else's excitement about an outcome into your own excitement for the opposite outcome, but, as you can see, one can learn this skill.

End of the Bull Market: Waves ④ and ⑤

The July 25, 2006 issue of the *Theorist* closed with this forecast:

[A] setback of at least Primary degree, if not a multi-year bear market, is due now. [If] months from now the waves imply another rally,
you will hear about it on our Energy Specialty [now Pro] Service.

Over the next six months, the price of oil slid 36.5% to $49.90 a barrel.

Steven Craig had since taken over EWI's Energy Pro Service and was
still writing the energy section of *Global Market Perspective*. On January
31, 2007 he presented Figure 14 and wrote the following analysis:

Crude extended its sell-off from last summer's record high to a
19-month low and reversed.... The three-wave structure from the top
fits my outlook for a corrective decline. I've adjusted the count to
show the decline as zigzag wave (A) of Primary wave ④. A strong
wave (B) advance would be the norm. Given the depth of the decline
(i.e., >38.2% retracement of the wave ③ advance), a strong alternate
is that wave ④ is complete.

As published in *Global Market Perspective*, January 31, 2007

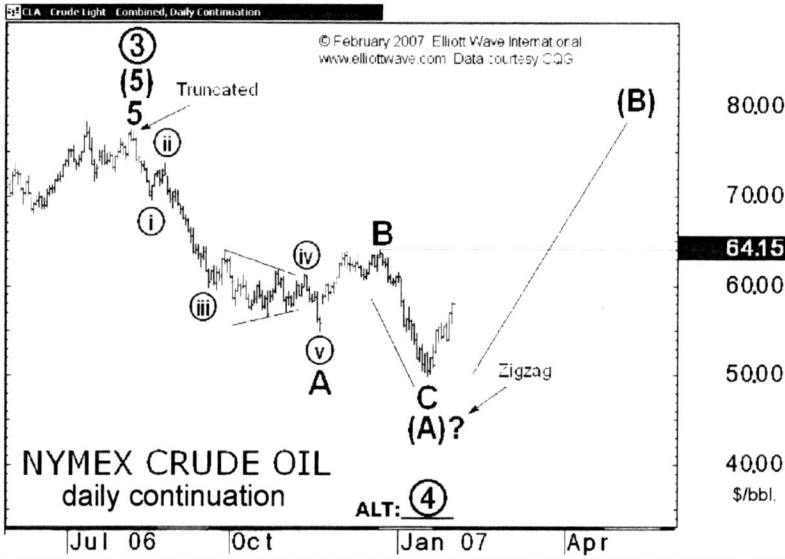

Figure 14

At that time, oil was just ten trading days past the low of wave ④. Wave ⑤ was underway, and it would last eighteen months.

In the first half of 2008, as oil passed $100 per barrel, the advance accelerated. Economists cited supply and demand as the reason for the advance, and a bullish frenzy once again gripped speculators. Price pullbacks became rare, lasting no more than a day or two.

At mid-year, *The Elliott Wave Theorist* stepped in front of that bus. The June 8, 2008 issue published the wave labels in Figure 15 depicting a nearly finished wave ⑤ and offered these emphatic comments:

The Top of Wave ⑤ in Crude Oil Is Fast Approaching

I am publishing this issue a bit early in order to alert you to an opportunity developing in the oil market. Bull markets in commodities virtually always end with an extended fifth wave, as explained in Chapter 6 of *Elliott Wave Principle* (p. 173). So, *one of the greatest commodity tops of all time is due very soon.* Ideally, crude oil should end on a *violent spike high* in the $160-$189 range.

I got no reaction from readers, and no news organization mentioned the call. Most people must have thought that comment was as disconnected from reality as predicting that the earth will run out of oxygen tomorrow.

Supply-demand theorists not only failed to envision the possibility of a major peak in oil prices but also fully embraced the upward trend at the very pinnacle of the bull market. On July 1, 2008, when oil was just $7 away from registering its all-time high, a national newspaper ran a cover story featuring one of the most revealing condemnations of supply-demand analysis you will ever read:

Efficient market purists...cite the Economics 101 concept of supply and demand as the main reason a barrel of oil has surged above $140, up nearly 50% in 2008. [The] senior market analyst at [ ] sums up this thesis best: "<u>You can argue that the economic fundamentals for oil are as strong as they have ever been in mankind's history.</u>" He cites robust demand from emerging economies around the world, a growing belief that future oil supplies will be tight, and the ability of foreigners to buy oil cheaply because of the steep drop in the value of the U.S. dollar.[2]

Later in the article, the president of an energy consulting firm repeated the same arguments.

As published in *The Elliott Wave Theorist* on June 9, 2008[3]

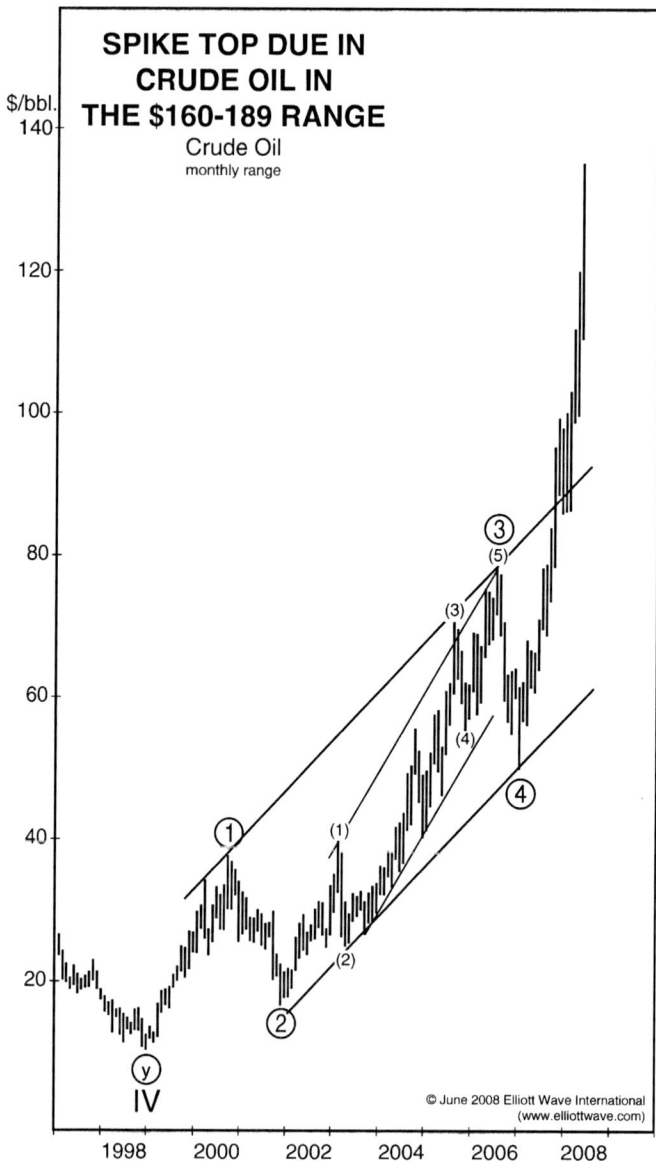

Figure 15

That passionately optimistic analysis came out at the very pinnacle of the century-long bull market. On July 11, 2008, oil registered its final high at $147.50. (That price was $12.50 above my original projection and $12.50 below my later one.)

For the record, even the sub-waves of wave ⑤, a seemingly unbridled moon shot, adhered to the Elliott wave model, as shown in Figure 16, right up to the top day on July 11. That evening, a reporter at the *Toronto Star* typed up a story that his editor would title, "Higher Gas Prices Here to Stay." It hit the stands on the morning of July 12.

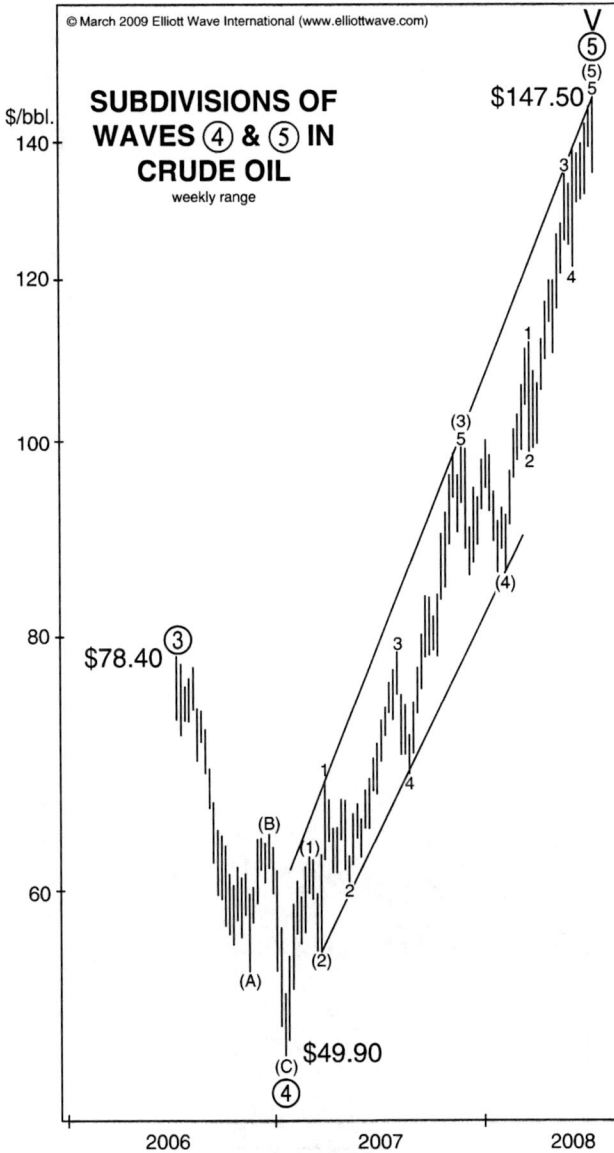

Figure 16

RedRed

The Bear Market: Waves **a**, **b** *and* **c**

Figure 17 shows the immediate aftermath of this set-up. If you know markets, you've never seen anything like it in your life: a breathtaking 78% crash in five months. The only faster commodity decline that I know of took place in frozen orange juice in the movie *Trading Places*.

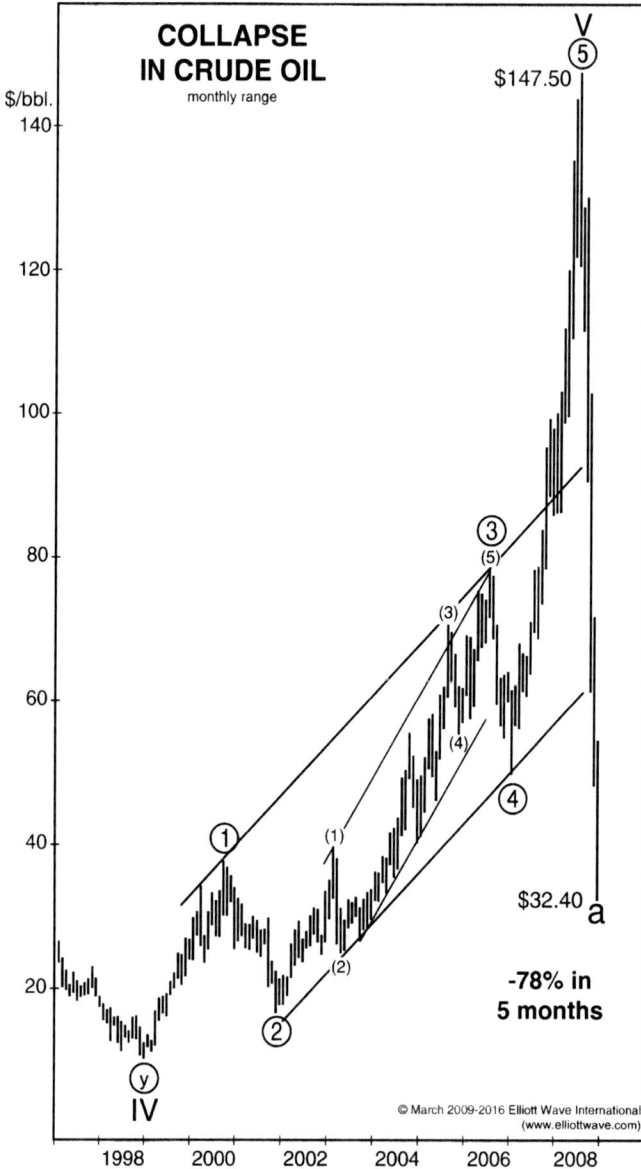

Figure 17

Only someone extrapolating an Elliott wave could see that "one of the greatest commodity tops of all time" lay dead ahead. Those using supply-demand arguments and linear extrapolation, including all the authors of the aforementioned books and articles, were in the wrong place at the wrong time. Those who got caught on margin were ruined.

How many people suffered? On July 2, 2008, nine days before oil topped out, the Daily Sentiment Index reported 97% bulls among oil-futures traders. Near the low it was 4%.

You may think that a collapse as dramatic and relentless as that for oil in 2008 would have no discernible wave structure. But it does. Figure 18 displays the daily-range detail of the decline. It shows a clear five waves, within which waves ② and ④ are nearly equal heights on log scale.

As the chart shows, oil bottomed at $32.40 on December 19, 2008 and completed the required five waves down at a slightly higher price of $32.70 on January 20, 2009. Two days later, on January 22, *The Elliott*

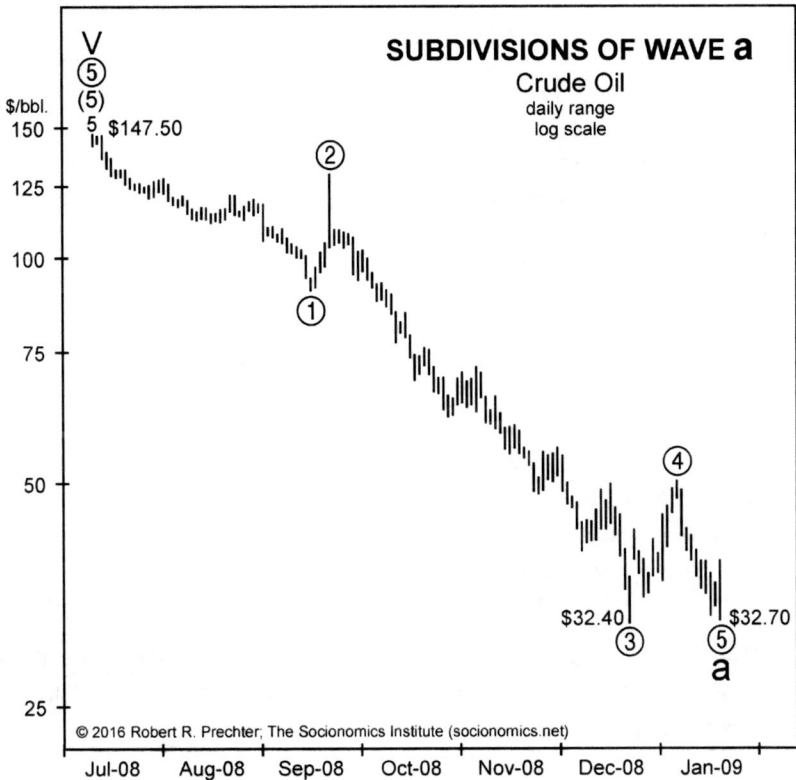

Figure 18

Wave Theorist published this commentary on the difference in usefulness between supply-and-demand analysis and Elliott waves:

Read this:

> Friday, January 16, 2009
> LONDON (Reuters)—<u>World oil demand will contract sharply in</u>
> <u>2009</u> as global economic slowdown further erodes consumption, the International Energy Agency (IEA) said on Friday. The Paris-based agency <u>joined the ranks of forecasters predicting</u>
> <u>a fall in global oil demand</u> this year, revising its previous 2009 estimate down by 940,000 barrels per day (bpd) to 85.3 million bpd—a 500,000 bpd year-on-year fall. <u>In its previous report</u>, the IEA forecast global oil demand would...<u>grow</u> by 440,000 bpd in 2009, based on the resilience of emerging economies.

If you were to wait for economists to figure out financial and macroeconomic trend changes before [acting, you would go broke.] All the reports of oil-related "fundamentals" coming out today were forecast by the simple number "V" anticipated on our charts. For any company making long-term decisions based on the price of oil, the Elliott wave label was nothing less than life-saving information.

People who based bullish forecasts on such things as "the resilience of emerging economies" found out the forecasting value of such lagging conditions, which is zero to negative. It's zero as long as the conditions maintain and negative when they change. Clear Elliott waves anticipate change. Knowing in the final $50 run-up that a peak was imminent was far more useful than hearing now—after oil prices have plummeted 78% in six months—that there will be a "fall in global oil demand."

[Actually,] economists have no reliable basis for predicting further slackening in oil demand; maybe the recession ended yesterday. Even if demand for oil were to slacken further, *prices may already have bottomed.* Economists have no way of knowing. But with Elliott waves you at least have a shot at knowing.

Wave ⑤ ended as I wrote those comments. It bottomed slightly above the low of wave ③, a rare condition called a truncation. As EWT allowed, "prices may already have bottomed."

That crash was not the end of the bear market. Under the Elliott wave model, a bear market requires (at minimum) three waves, labeled A, B and C, so the crash—as noted in Figure 18—had to be only wave **a**. The five-wave structure of the decline confirmed this analysis, leaving no alternative. The message was unequivocal that the ensuing recovery would be a bear-market rally, wave **b**.

The Elliott wave model also allowed Elliotticians to recognize the peak of wave **b** two years later. Upon request, I wrote an article on oil for the April 2011 issue of *Market Technician*, the journal of the U.K.'s Society of Technical Analysts, and concluded with this statement:

> We labeled the early 2009 low near $33 as wave A of a large A-B-C corrective pattern. Oil has since more than tripled to $107 and should be near the peak of wave B. Though the Federal Reserve has all but guaranteed that it will create inflation, this wave labeling implies that the dollar price of oil will fall below the 2009 low sometime this decade.[4]

Wave **b** ended that month just $7 higher, with a daily close of $113.93 on April 29 and an intraday high of $114.83 on May 2. On May 16, 2011, *The Elliott Wave Theorist* published the graph reprinted here as Figure 19 and confirmed that the top was in: "The zigzag form of the rally [in the CRB Commodities Index] adhered nicely to a trend channel. The biggie among the commodities—oil—counts as an ABC rally as well."

Oil fell right away, but over the next three years it made three lunges back toward wave **b**'s high, during which time speculators and economists became increasingly bullish.

The supply-demand theorists were especially vocal during this time. Were they helpful in calling for a trend change? On the contrary, they were competing amongst themselves to predict much higher oil prices. On April 26, 2011, three days before the wave **b** peak, a physicist published a detailed projection of supply and demand for the next five years and concluded, "oil prices will go through the roof."[5] Two months later, on July 4, 2011, the cover of *Barron's* declared, "Get Ready for $150 Oil." The arguments it offered for a new record high in price were based on an analysis of supply and demand. Hundreds of like articles appeared in 2011-2014 as oil floated just under its 2011 high. Here is a representative sample of supply-demand arguments relating to oil and gasoline, culled from that time over a mere six weeks:

Oil prices increase to near highs
Associated Press, February 25, 2012
Investors are snapping up oil contracts in case fighting breaks out in the heart of one of the world's biggest oil-producing regions. "Everyone's pricing in the potential for war now," independent

As published in *The Elliott Wave Theorist* on May 16, 2011

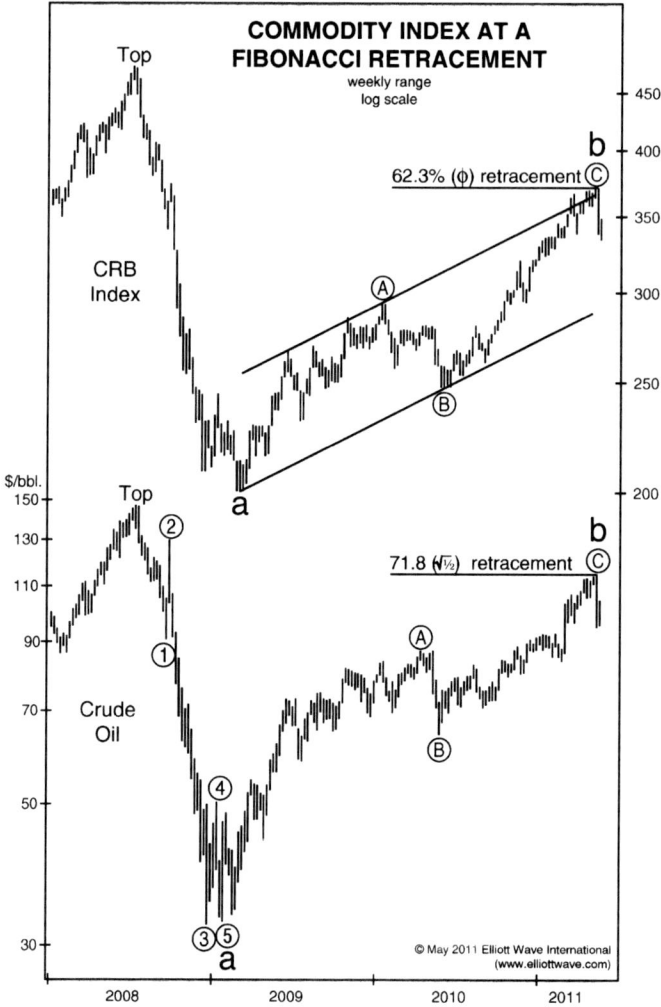

Figure 19

analyst [   ] said. "Without a concrete resolution, <u>nobody knows how high this can go</u>." <u>It looks like they'll keep climbing</u>.

Demand for gas has fallen, yet prices keep rising

Time magazine, March 19, 2012 (p. 12)

...in the long term, <u>global demand for oil will increase</u>, driven by developing countries. Which means that <u>someday soon, $4 gas is going to look cheap</u>.

Oil Prices at $200 a Barrel? Some Think It's Coming
Market Insider, March 21, 2012
Signs that crude futures may hit much higher levels are converging, say oil traders and analysts, some of whom predict that Brent crude could reach $200 a barrel within the next 12 months. The biggest issue, they say, is that global crude supply remains uncommonly tight—a scenario that's unlikely to be alleviated any time soon.

Energy experts say gas could hit $8 if Iran closes strait
USA Today, March 23, 2012
Gas prices could double if Iran acts to close the Strait of Hormuz to oil-tanker traffic near the beginning of next year, cutting global economic growth by more than 25%, a leading energy-consulting firm says. Brent crude oil prices could briefly hit $240 a barrel in the first quarter of 2013, said [ ], senior research director for Global Economics at [ ].

Gasoline prices about to pinch
Atlanta Journal-Constitution, March 31, 2012
Gas prices are still rising, and the pinch will get worse, said [ ], director of the Economic Forecasting Center at [ ] University. "As we come into a warm summer—even a normal summer—once the air conditioner comes on, there will be no relief for the pocketbook," [ ] said. "And if it's a hot summer, we will feel it even more."

T. Boone Pickens: Oil Could Hit $148 Per Barrel
CNBC.com, April 3, 2012
Tightening oil production worldwide could mean prices hitting $148 per barrel this summer, Texas billionaire investor T. Boone Pickens said Tuesday.

With exquisite irony, when the very threat that analysts warned about on March 23 loomed for real in July, oil prices tumbled 3.6% in a single day. As AP reported, "The price of oil fell this week even though Iran staged missile tests and *renewed threats to block key oil shipments out of the Persian Gulf.*"[6] The outcome was the complete opposite of economists' expectation. The article excused it by proposing that investors had shifted focus to "the bigger picture."

That same year, an economist educated at Oxford and Harvard published a late addition to the roster of "peak oil" books. In a tome "replete with illuminating facts and figures," she predicted that underground oil supplies would be exhausted within 46 years and that "an emerging global short-age of key commodities, including oil," would cause prices to "skyrocket to permanently higher levels."[7] Such arguments remained alive and well throughout this period, as commentators flush with bullish fever completely ignored the new crude oil production coming out of North Dakota.

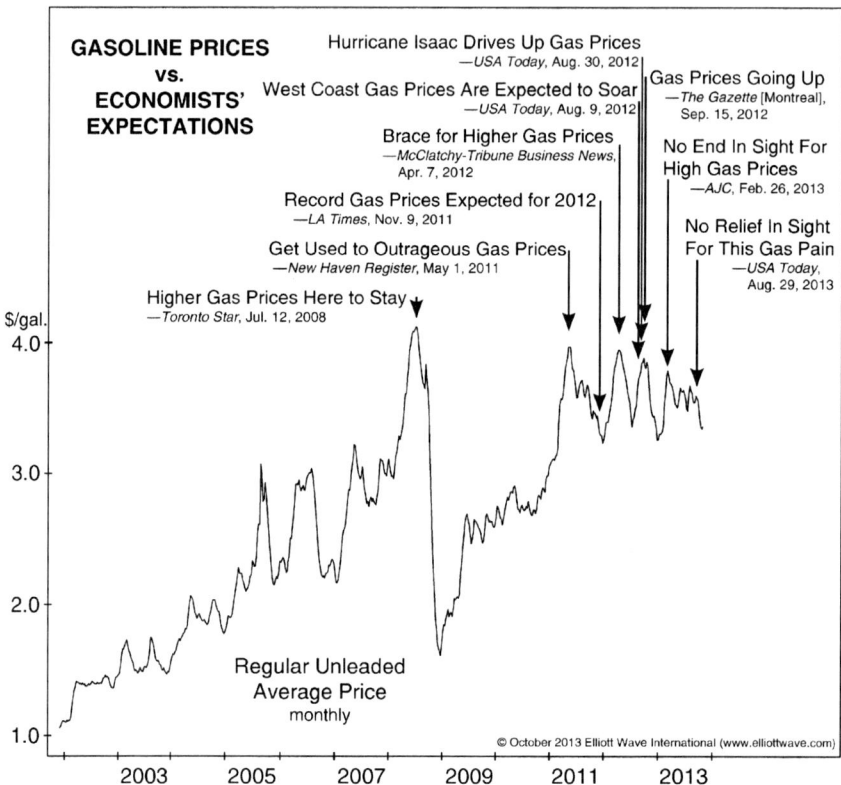

Figure 20

Figure 20 displays representative headlines on the outlook for gasoline prices from that period. Needless to say, they introduced articles offering supply-demand arguments for why gasoline prices were doomed to go ever upward. Here is but one example:

Record gas prices expected for 2012

If you think gasoline is expensive now, just wait until next year: A combination of <u>growing global demand</u> and rising U.S. fuel exports <u>could send gasoline prices to record highs in 2012, analysts say</u>.

"We are at the highest fuel prices ever for this time of year, even though they have dropped a bit in recent weeks," said [   ], chief oil analyst for the Oil Price Information Service. "I think we will see prices in 2012 that will break...records."

The primary reason for the stubbornly high prices is growing demand in Latin and South America, which is driving record U.S. exports of fuel to those parts of the world, particularly in the form of diesel.[8]

Elliotticians know from experience that the rally *after* a major market peak is typically a time of extreme conviction among commentators that the old uptrend has resumed. The most widely disseminated opinions of that time fit this expectation perfectly. (For another classic example, see Chapter 18 on bonds.) Socionomists attribute such arguments to rationalization. For this treatment, however, let's respectfully take economists at their word that they rigorously applied their supply-demand model to forecasting. Once again, it won't work out well.

As economists and speculators' expectations for a continuation of the old bull market reached near certainty, *The Elliott Wave Theorist's* expectation for a resumption of the bear market reached near certainty. The May 16, 2014 issue showed the chart reproduced here as Figure 21 and explained why the wave development and the psychological setup formed a "Deadly combination":

As published in *The Elliott Wave Theorist*, May 16, 2014

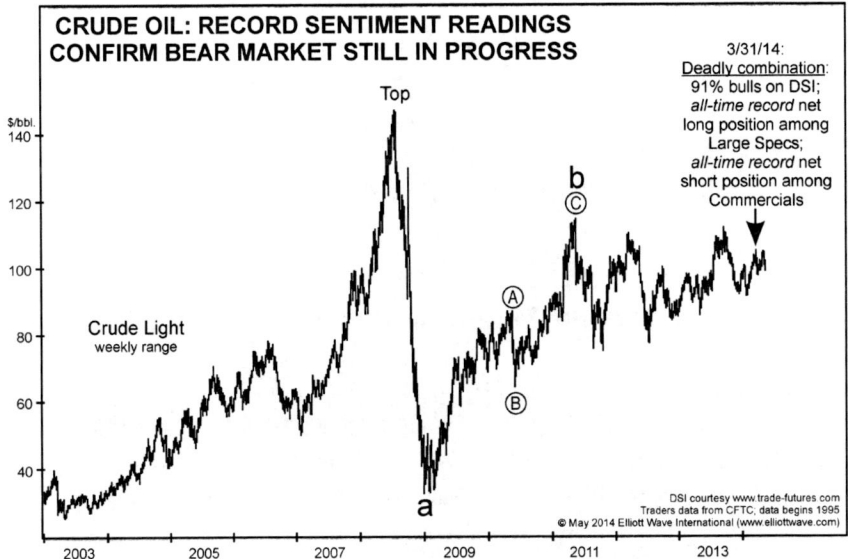

Figure 21

Investors are betting that commodity prices are poised to *soar*. As of March 31, Large Speculators in commodity futures, a sector of traders monitored by the CFTC, have amassed an all-time record net long position (with data going back to 1995) in the CRB Commodity Index. Only extreme optimism could prompt such buying, and the Daily Sentiment Index confirms this suspicion with an extremely high reading of 95% bulls on February 20. This huge amount of increasingly bullish conviction has generated only a small rally in commodity prices in 2014.

In crude oil futures, there is not only an all-time record net long position among Large Specs but also an all-time record net short position among Commercials, who have a history of being mostly on the right side of the markets they trade. Markets cannot stand such a high level of optimism among commodity investors (and pessimism among commodity users) for long. Whatever happens to oil prices in coming weeks, the multi-year outlook is for much lower prices.

One month later, both oil and overall commodity prices peaked and started to plunge. Figure 22 shows what happened over the next twenty months, as the bear market resumed with a degree of persistence just a bit less than that displayed in 2008. This subtle difference fulfills the Elliott wave observation that in 5-3-5 formations, C waves generally have a lesser slope than A waves.

Late Update—Q1 2016: The End of Wave ③ of c

On January 11, 2016, oil broke below the low of wave **a**. On the very next day, the global head of energy analysis at the Oil Price Information Service declared, "It's a meltdown. It's beyond hyperbole. *All bets are off on where prices are going*."[9] In other words, he had become so bearish he could no longer even imagine a stopping point for the decline.

In mid-February, attendees at a gigantic oil industry conference in London declared nothing but gloom:

The Oil Industry Got Together and Agreed <u>Things May Never Get Better</u>
No Hope—Prices will stay low for up to a decade.
<u>The thousands of attendees seeking reasons for optimism didn't find them</u> at the annual International Petroleum Week. Instead they were greeted by a <u>cacophony of voices</u> from some of the largest oil producers, refiners and traders <u>delivering the same message</u>: "There

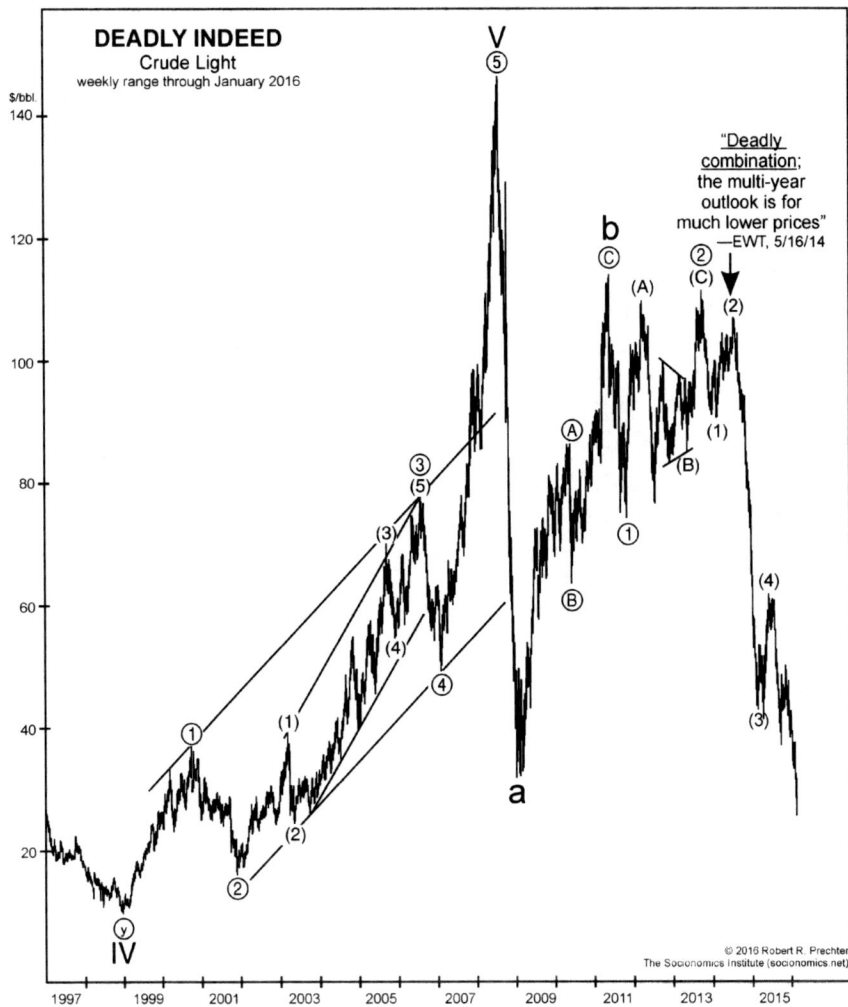

Figure 22

are few reasons for optimism. The world is awash with oil. The market is overwhelmingly bearish. Supply exceeds demand by as much as 1.7 million barrels a day. The BP Plc boss described himself as "very bearish" and joked that the surplus is so extreme that people will soon be filling swimming pools with crude.[10]

There it is in black and white: The same supply-demand approach that had industry analysts looking for higher prices when oil was $147 and $107 had them looking for lower prices at $26. In 2012, conventional analysts had looked up into the sky and said to reporters, "Nobody knows how high this can go," and in 2015 they looked down into the abyss and told them, "All bets are off on where prices are going." These comments expose the linear-extrapolation mindset, applied to different directions, exactly as depicted in Figure 2 of Chapter 21.

These sentiments, moreover, turned out to yet be another perfectly timed example of the spectacular disvalue of supply-demand analysis. Wave ③ of **c** ended at $26.05 on February 11, the very day of that conference.

An approach to market analysis and forecasting this counterproductive could not be invented deliberately if geniuses put their minds to the task. If this history isn't evidence of unconscious herding, I don't know what is.

Wave analysts at EWI did not succumb to such emotions. While conventional analysts were reaching their point of maximum despair, EWI's energy analyst Steven Craig had been preparing for the approaching end of wave ③. In the January 8 issue of *Global Market Perspective*, five weeks before

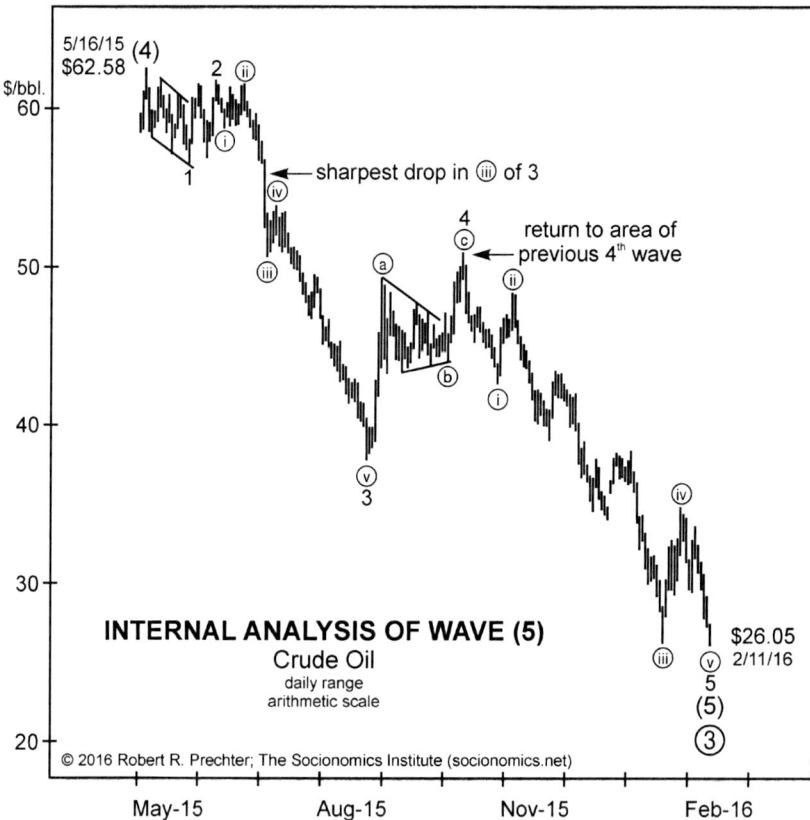

Figure 23

the low, he cautioned, "Further downside potential still exists to complete the final leg." In the February 5 issue, he stepped up to the plate: "A five-wave decline into new low territory would give wave ③ enough subwaves to count it as complete. At a minimum, the selloff should carry prices below $26.19." Figure 23 shows how Craig was labeling the subwaves as they progressed within wave (5).

The low of $26.05, which was 14 cents below Craig's minimum target, occurred six days later. In the next monthly issue, dated March 4, Craig presented the chart reproduced here as Figure 24 and affirmed, "*Primary wave ③ has run its course.*"

This comment brings our real-time commentary to a close, although as you can see in Figure 24, Craig's latest forecast arrow suggests that a normal outcome would be a bear-market rally in which oil would approximately double. He added, "Since wave ② lasted nearly two full years, wave ④ could be a time-consuming affair," implying that the projected peak might finish only wave (A) of ④. Whether that scenario and the anticipated remainder of the pattern play out remains to be seen.

As published in *Global Market Perspective*, March 4, 2016

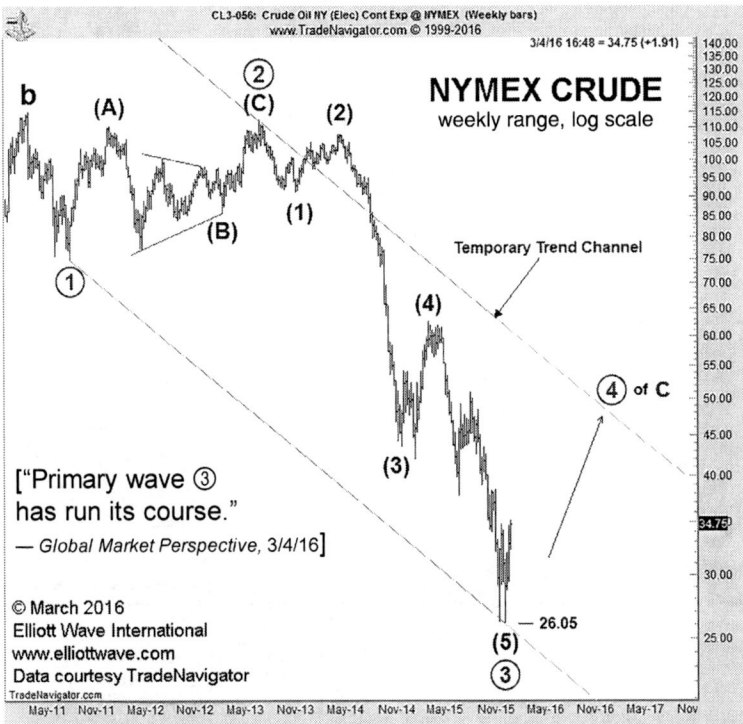

Figure 24

Review

Figure 25 displays the extreme prices associated with EWI's oil-market calls since 1993. Figure 26 places the turn dates on our idealized schematic.

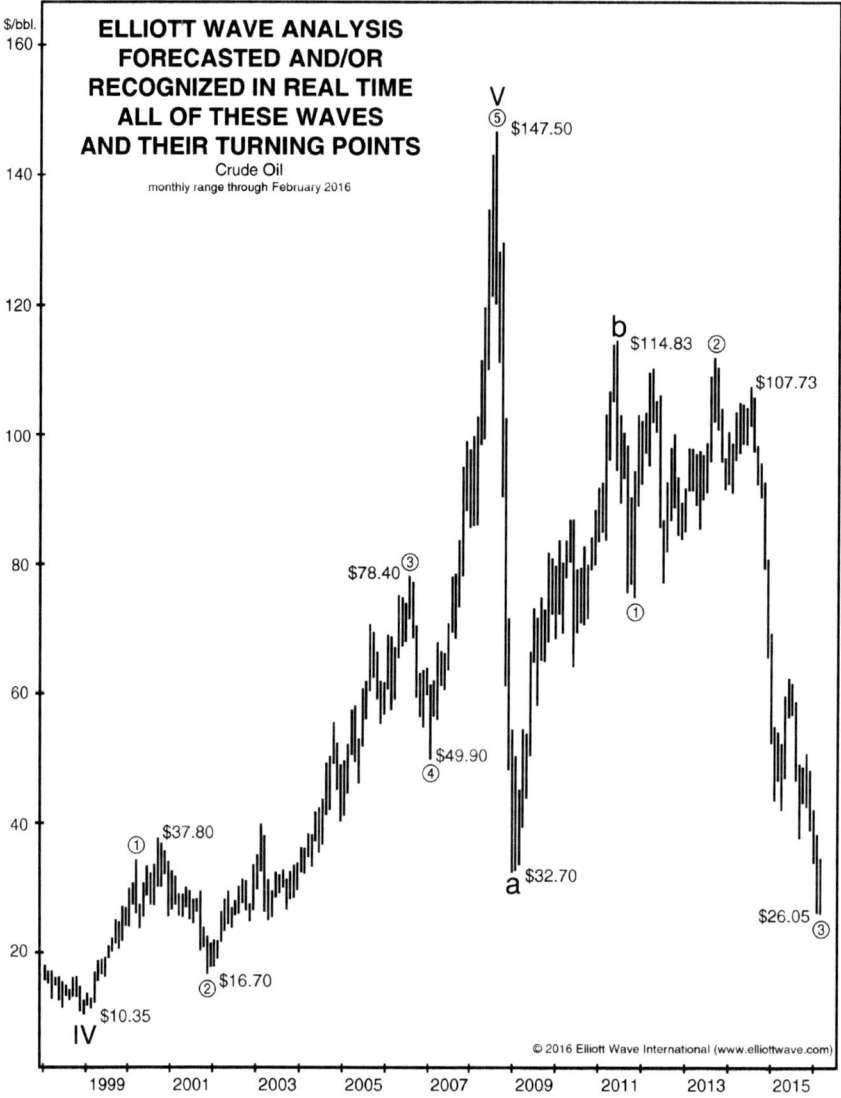

Figure 25

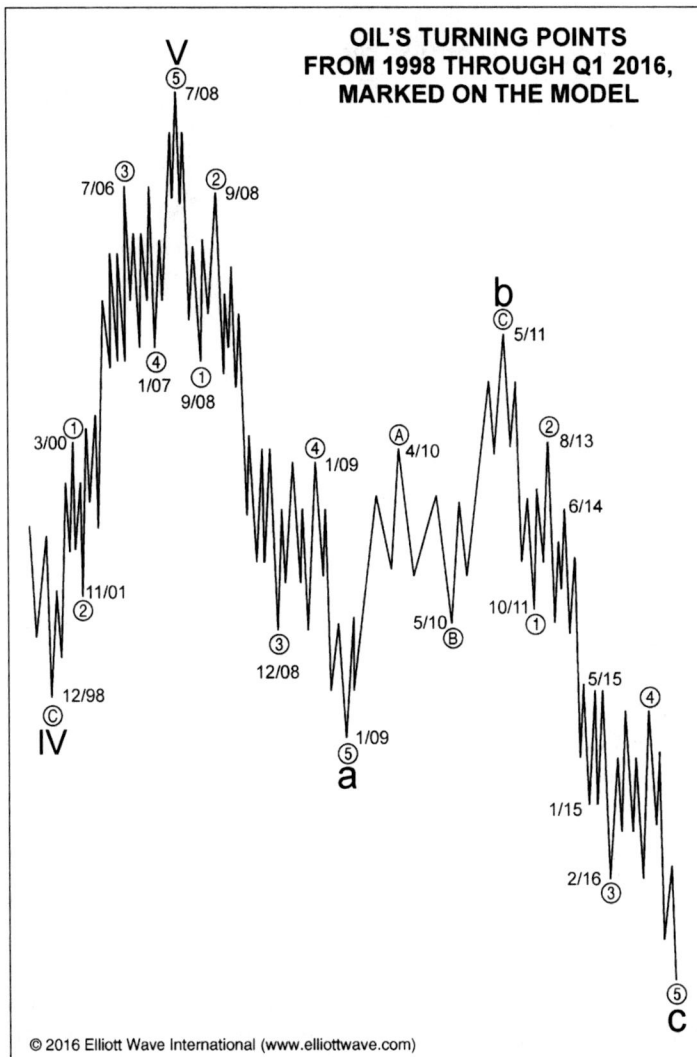

OIL'S TURNING POINTS
FROM 1998 THROUGH Q1 2016,
MARKED ON THE MODEL

Figure 26

Figure 27 updates the historical context. It depicts a half-century bear market followed by a full-century bull market followed by the onset of a new bear market of corresponding degree. Turn back a few pages, and you will see that Figure 6, constructed in 1999 from R.N. Elliott's observations made in 1938, offered a pretty good template for Figure 27.

That wave V exceeded the upper channel line, by the way, is a normal development that Elliott called a throw-over (see Chapter 2 of *Elliott Wave Principle*). A reversal of the surge indicates exhaustion of the larger trend.

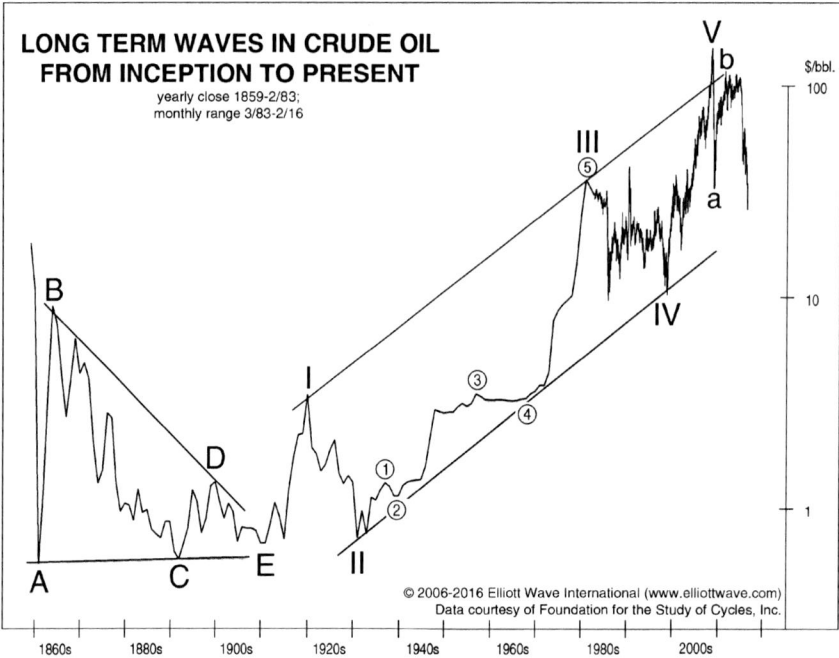

Figure 27

Markets do not always trace out Elliott waves this flawlessly. Such a degree of accuracy is possible only at certain times within wave structures. Given the real-time clarity of the waves in oil for the past 22 years, though, it seems we should be able to recognize the upcoming low for wave **c** as well.

A Valid Model Accounts for These Results

Analysts using the Elliott wave model created a detailed narrative for oil prices *in prospect* over a period of 22 years. The foregoing text depicts eight (potentially nine) terrific market calls in a row, all issued in the face of intense consensus opposition.

No one realizes how good an accurate market call truly is, for two reasons: Humans have a well-documented hindsight bias, whereby they retrospectively think an outcome should have been obvious or even that they or many others had recognized it, when no such thing is true. Market observers also retrospectively judge market calls based only on subsequent market action rather than in contrast to the diametrically opposed outlooks and actions of the majority of experts and laymen at the time, which is the proper benchmark for how investors would have done otherwise. A "good call" in that context is revealed in fact to be an awesome call. Not many people can do it.

These forecasts were not the product of a special individual, either, but of five different analysts. The one constant has been the template from which they worked, and that's what made them all special.

To counter the evidence for Elliott wave causality presented here, random-walk theorists would have to charge that Elliott Wave International's series of calls in the oil market was due to luck. For randomness to apply, however, one must demonstrate that it did apply. If our success were due to a one-in-a-thousand chance outcome, then some 30 of the 30,000 economists in the world should have done equally well. We are unaware, however, of any comparable series of forecasts among economists. Given their habitual trend-extrapolation approach to forecasting, we don't expect to see one.

Until someone can produce a handful of matching records from economists, thereby demonstrating that random chance could even remotely account for these market calls, the only sensible conclusion to draw is that Elliott waves—not supply and demand—regulate oil prices. When the price of oil bottomed in 1998, we did not argue that a change in demand would cause prices to rise, and when the price of oil completed five waves up over a decade of rising prices, we did not argue that a change in supply would cause prices to fall. We stated that prices would rise, and then fall, period. A week after the bottom a headline read, "Oil Is Now So Cheap Pirates Aren't Even Stealing It Anymore."[11] No economist at the highs of 2011-2014 saw *that* coming. But we did. If supply and demand were in charge of oil-price changes, we would have been unable to produce this long string of successful forecasts.

Not Supply and Demand

Supply-demand theorists could try to create a retrospective narrative involving tales of hedgers who continually bought and sold oil futures contracts based on anticipating future trends in supply and demand. I tried but couldn't make it work. The idea of financial market prices "discounting" the future is a myth, anyway, as addressed in Chapters 3, 7 and 39. I think Figure 21 in this chapter flat-out disproves discounting theory all by itself.

Difficult as it may be to accept, the price of oil is not determined primarily by changes in storage capacity, air conditioning use, heating oil use, production from Russia, demand from China, OPEC's strategies, war fears, the average mileage of automobiles, hurricanes damaging offshore drilling platforms, monetary policies, protesters blocking pipelines, the extent of new oil discoveries, shifts in production and consumption, or any combination of such factors. Herding speculators determine the price of oil, and all of these cited factors are either results or incidentals.

Nor is there the slightest indication in Figures 25 and 27 of any such thing as an equilibrium price, which the forces of supply and demand are supposed to provide. We know why: Supply and demand do not regulate oil prices, so there is no equilibrium price. Yet in the midst of these wild swings economists still made such statements as, "the oil market is trying to figure out an equilibrium price."[12]

Spontaneous commands from an impulsive herd well account for the dramatic and volatile swings in the price of oil over the past 35 years, and only the Elliott wave model could have aided analysts in predicting these swings. While we have missed our share of market moves over the years, results such as those detailed here are just not possible from analyses of supply and demand. Economists' track record at turns proves it. Choose any major high or low in the price of any speculatively traded commodity and review what economists were saying about supply and demand at the time. They will have been exquisitely wrong; there is no other possibility.

We have already covered what economists were saying at the key turns in oil from 1998 to Q1 2016. To bookend this history, let's examine two more striking examples, one from earlier and another more recent.

As the great inflationary decade of the 1970s brought wave III in oil prices to a peak, the February 25, 1980 issue of *U.S. News and World Report* quoted Charles W. Duncan, the U.S. Secretary of Energy under President Jimmy Carter, saying, "One thing is for certain: prices will continue to rise."[13] Duncan was one of countless voices saying the same thing. Werner Meyer collected over forty such quotes from economic and political luminaries and posted them at http://www.fortfreedom.org/b16.htm. Reading them provides a fifteen-minute education more impactful to understanding financial markets than a world-class economics degree. Since Duncan's remark expressed an extremity of market mood, the "one thing" he was sure would happen "for certain" was far surer *not* to happen. Accordingly, oil prices in late 1980 began a six-year slide from $39 to $9.75 a barrel, kicking off a bear market that lasted eighteen years. In June 1981, just a year and a half after Duncan's prediction, *The New York Times* and *Time* magazine reported on a global "glut" in oil.

Recall that as oil's bull market matured in 2006-2008, supply-demand analysts declared that world supplies were running out. Flash forward to the present. With the price of oil having fallen through most of wave **c**, what kind of statements would you expect to see about the future availability of oil? On October 13, 2015, the Chief Economist of British Petroleum echoed the new consensus when he told a conference of economists in London, "it is increasingly unlikely that the world's reserves of oil will ever be exhausted."[14] Now they tell us.

Recently an article quoted an economist saying that the slide in oil prices since 2014 has "obviously" been the result of an increase in the supply of oil resulting from the Parshall oil-field discovery in North Dakota. The authoritative tone of such assertions is hilarious in light of economists' virtually unanimous citation of bullish supply-demand factors heading into the peaks of 2008, 2011, 2012, 2013 and 2014. Only *after* the price of oil has fallen for more than seven years are economists somehow able to announce with a straight face that the reason for lower prices, which utterly escaped both them and the wealthiest futures traders in America in the spring of 2014, is obvious. According to the Elliott wave model, and as argued in Chapter 14, and as the next section will establish in detail, they are not even retrospectively right.

Perfect mistiming among supply-demand analysts is not confined to the oil market. It is ubiquitous across all speculatively traded markets, as evidenced in Chapter 18.

Supply-demand theory as applied to finance is not merely an approach that doesn't work. It is one that delivers exquisitely wrong answers, making it way worse than a method that simply doesn't work. Socionomists know why such is the case. A method that doesn't work condemns its practitioners to a state of extreme uncertainty, the very condition that prompts people to herd. In the service of herding, they must also rationalize their market opinions. This imperative explains why in 2014 supply-demand analysts failed to cite the bearish supply factor of massive new production coming out of North Dakota (see Figure 28) and instead invented bullish causes such as tightening production, war fears, air conditioning use and expected demand from developing countries. In delightful contrast, the Elliott wave model—as demonstrated by the history presented in this chapter—offers analysts a basis for completely conquering the impulse to herd, thereby negating the necessity to rationalize.

Amazingly yet predictably, hardly anyone learns anything in the aftermath of such failed analyses. Academics maintain exogenous-cause theories, economists take supply-demand causality for granted, the media continue to consult economists, and historians never think to compile the mounds of evidence that supply-demand analysis in fact blinds its practitioners to coming changes in markets. The mental default to mechanics is that strong.

Rational-valuation theorists perennially argue that even if price action eventually implies that a past price was high or low, it was reasonable *at the time* with respect to knowledge of supply and demand. It usually seems so; that's what traps speculators at the highs and lows. But how does one reconcile this claim of current-time reasonableness with the record bullishness among economists and Large Speculators in oil at the high price of $114.83 in May 2014 in the face of a six-year surge in the domestic oil supply with no end in sight? There are three possible reasons for investors' myopia: Either all these people were ignorant of the new source of supply; they didn't care to consider it; or they both knew about it *and* considered it but defaulted to rationalizing their bullish outlook with substitute, bogus supply-demand arguments. Any of these explanations ruins every version of rational-valuation theory. Socionomics is quite comfortable with all of them. Mood-sharing and herding impulses lead speculators to ignore or excuse such information, and that's exactly what they did.

Levels of certainty and uncertainty among economists concerning the very validity of their own causal model also wax and wane with market trends. When prices are exceptionally dynamic or extreme, economists become so confused and distraught that they sometimes take the embarrassing step of abandoning their bedrock belief in supply-demand causality. In the first quarter of 1980, at the peak of wave III, Energy Secretary Duncan justified his outlook for continuously rising oil prices by asserting, *"Traditional criteria of supply and demand don't apply."*[15] In other words, we all believe in supply and demand unless we are so emotional we can't think straight. In May 2008, near the peak of wave V, members of Congress used almost exactly the same language in charging that crude oil prices "are *no longer justified by traditional forces of supply and demand.*"[16] Proponents once again forsook their own theory right at the peak. They were briefly right in doing so but remain chronically unaware that supply and demand are never in charge of oil prices.

This practice is as old as markets. In November 1931, the stock market's two-year decline so disturbed a supply-demand thinker that he blamed chartists for the "unwarranted" setback. Under the header, "Down with Charts," the *Montreal Gazette* reported,

> One leading banker deplores the growing use of charts by professional stock traders and customers' men, who, he says, are causing unwarranted market declines by purely mechanical interpretation of a meaningless set of lines. It is impossible, he contends, to figure values by plotting prices based on supply and demand; but, he adds, if too many persons play with the same set of charts, they tend to create the very unbalanced supply and demand which upsets market trends. In his opinion, all charts should be confiscated, piled up at the intersection of Broad and Wall and burned with much shouting and rejoicing."[17]

It is a stunning admission for a supply-demand devotee to complain that economic valuation and equilibrium aren't strong enough to overcome "a meaningless set of lines."

As a last-ditch effort to maintain supply-demand causality in the oil market, one might try to postulate that the interaction of supply and demand somehow produces Elliott waves in oil prices. No formal hypothesis could make sense of this idea, and there is plenty of evidence against it. If the interaction of supply and demand were to create Elliott waves in oil prices, Elliott waves would also regulate prices for screwdrivers, grass seed and frozen pizzas, where supply and demand most certainly rule. But they don't. They show up only in speculatively traded markets.

It does not escape our notice that the century-long bull market in oil got going just two years before Congress created the Federal Reserve System. Monetary debasement obviously contributed substantially to the rise in the dollar price of oil along with the prices of everything else. The Fed's inflating of the base money supply, however, did not proceed in Elliott waves. It rather rose quite steadily most of the time—until September 2008, when the Fed panicked (see Figure 19 in Chapter 2), but that was after oil's bull market was over! Yet the oil market did fluctuate in Elliott waves, so clearly as to be predictable. The reason is that oil provides a basis for financial speculation, which creates a context of uncertainty that prompts herding, and herding progresses in Elliott waves.[18]

As we saw in Chapter 5, breathtaking swings in financial markets, especially when they go down, tend to call attention—if only briefly and retrospectively—to the failure of conventional analytical approaches. This time has been no different. In late 2015, some people finally began realizing that the peak-oil story of the preceding decade was a myth. We had said it was a myth back in 2006, in the heart of the boom. On December 30, 2015, *The Wall Street Journal* declared, "It's clear what threw prognosticators and policy makers for the biggest loop with their economic forecasts for 2015: oil."[19] But it's only oil *this time*. Next time it will be whatever other market is the most volatile. Since the herd is in charge of financial markets and supply and demand are not, it can be no other way.

Because socionomists recognize that supply and demand do not regulate price changes in financial markets (see Chapter 12), that "fundamentals" lag markets (see Chapter 8) and that humans rationalize their herding impulses (see Chapter 19), we can even predict what economists will be saying at each stage of wave development. As shown above, when oil was making highs in waves ③, ⑤ and **b**, high-profile supply-demand theorists asserted that the world's oil supplies were nearly depleted. Today, late in wave **c**, they are proclaiming an endless glut. I can absolutely guarantee that the recently emerging bearish stance toward oil prices based on the "fundamentals" of supply and demand will wane during rallies within wave ④. Near their peaks, the Daily Sentiment Index will record around 90% bulls and Large Speculators will have built a heavy long position. Later, when oil is at the ultimate bottom of wave ⑤ of **c**, we will see evidence of despair deeper than today's, to the point that few will care about forecasting oil prices or holding conferences on the outlook for oil. When wave **c** ends, the public's interest will reach a minimum, Large Speculators' downside bets will reach a maximum, economists' bearish supply-demand arguments will sound convincing if not irrefutable, the financial world will be focused on other things, and oil prices will turn up.

Rather than a Change in Supply Causing a Change in Price, a Change in Price Caused a Change in Supply

As shown throughout this chapter, economists quoted in financial media typically focus on the power of supply and demand to affect prices for speculatively traded commodities rather than focusing on a key element of their own theory—that higher prices spur greater supply. Socionomists are not sidetracked by the first formulation, because we know that the herd—not supply and demand—is in charge of the price movement. So, rather than stress the power of changes in supply and demand to affect the prices of speculatively traded commodities, a socionomist stresses the power of changes in the prices of speculatively traded commodities to affect both supply and demand as it relates to them.

In the case of oil, demand is fairly inelastic. Although rising oil prices did motivate some consumers to carpool, travel less, buy more fuel-efficient cars and switch to natural-gas heat, consumption rose steadily throughout oil's great bull market, as shown in Figure 1. Even record prices did little to curb consumption. Producers, on the other hand, became highly motivated to seek more oil, and they found it. They discovered the Parshall Oil Field in North Dakota in 2006, eight long years after the start of wave V up in oil prices. As Figure 28 shows, it took another two years, until September 2008, for U.S. oil companies to begin stepping up oil production, after which it rose furiously for six years.

Supply-demand theorists glance at this graph and declare that the trend toward more U.S. oil production caused oil's price to fall. But the claim does not bear scrutiny. How does one get a 14-times rise in the price of oil out of

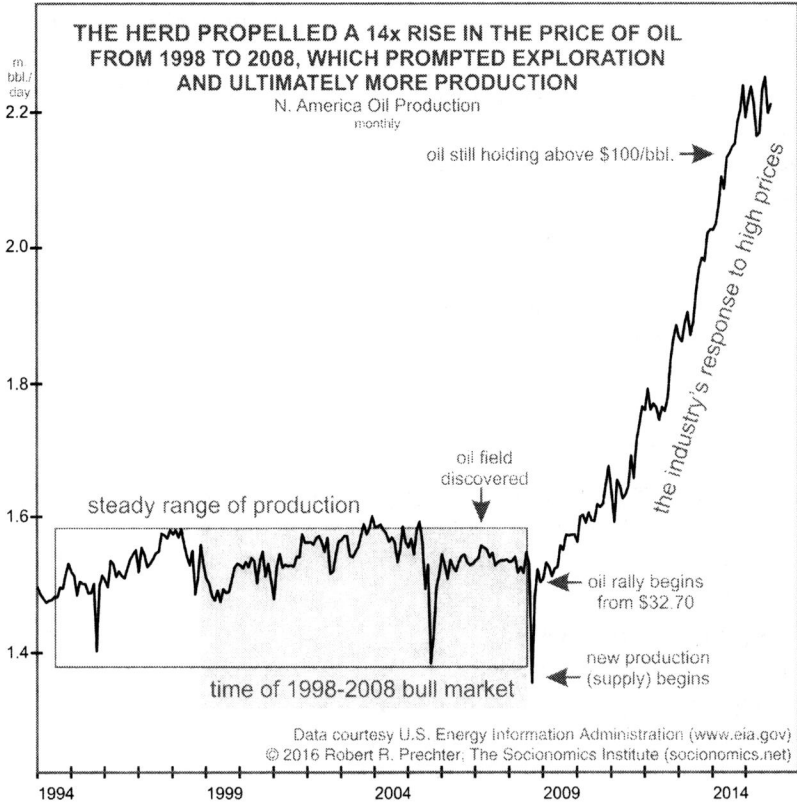

Figure 28

the perfectly sideways production trend from 1998 to 2008? It seems a bit extreme. Oil prices then crashed *before* the volume of production emerged from its historical range, an event that doesn't fit the mechanics paradigm. Finally, it is outright impossible to account for the fact that oil prices *tripled* as production surged from December 2008 to May 2011 and held up for three years thereafter (see details in Figure 21) as production continued to expand. This history of behavior mercilessly mocks the ubiquitous assumption that changes in the supply of oil determine changes in its price. Yet no one seems to notice.

Rather than a change in supply dictating a change in price, Figure 28 shows one thing unequivocally: that a change in price ultimately encouraged the discovery of a new source of supply. The huge, 14-times rise in the price of oil from 1998 to 2008 prompted U.S. oil producers to step up exploration, which ultimately led to new production.

Since oil prices have fallen in wave **c**, exploration has receded. We can predict that the bear market will eventually bring about a rash of bankruptcies among recently created, debt-financed, oil-related businesses. The next big bull market will again encourage exploration and production and/or the development of alternative energy sources. And so on. Speculators are moving oil's price up and down, and producers are responding, *not* vice versa.

This proposed orientation has predictive value. An Elliottician can probabilistically predict not only trends in the price of a commodity but also trends in its production. Economists' supply-demand observations are deleterious to planning and recipes for investment disaster and business failure. The socionomic point of view is *useful*.

Devil's Advocate

If any economist were able to apply the supply-demand model to predict oil prices successfully, it would be news. But forget prediction. Trying as hard as possible, can we find any way at all to use supply and demand data to explain *past* changes in the price of oil?

My efforts at the outset of this chapter failed, but in further service of the quest, I put together Figure 29. It shows the annual ratio between consumption and production worldwide. If you squint your eyes a bit, you can see by the three dashed lines that the ratio had a net decline during the 1980-1998 bear market in oil prices, a net advance during the 1998-2008 bull market in oil prices, and since then has mostly declined in line with the latest bear market in oil prices.

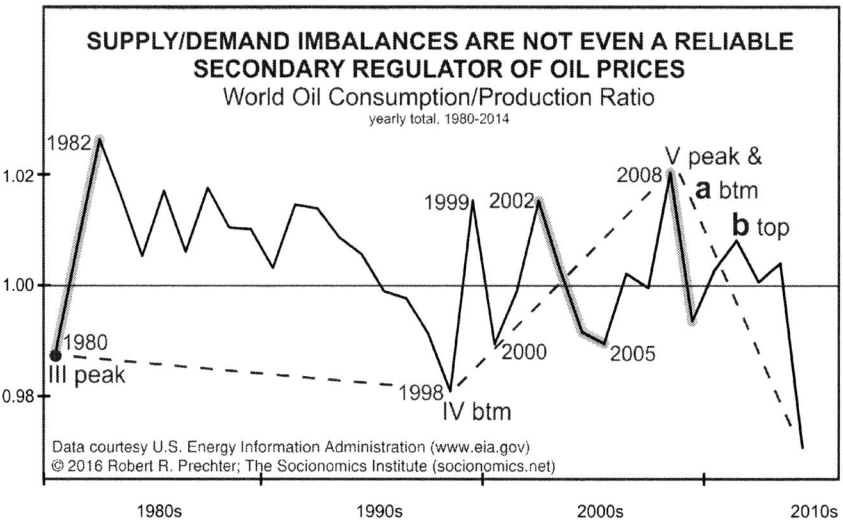

Figure 29

From this history, one might wonder if supply and demand might serve as a *secondary* regulator of oil prices. The answer is: They don't, because much of the history fails to fit. Take a look at the three shaded trends on the graph. The huge surge in the ratio between 1980 and 1982—the biggest rise on the chart—did not cause the price of oil to rise; rather, it fell, *a lot*. Nor did the large decline in the ratio between 2002 and 2005 cause the price of oil to fall; rather, it rose, *a lot*. And the rapid plunge in the ratio during 2009 did not cause the price of oil to fall; rather, it *tripled*. These extreme anomalies render the proposed causality spurious. Our attempt at a retrospective fit has proved as fruitless as economists' retrospective attempts to identify exogenous causes of the Great Depression, as detailed in Chapter 2.

Social Mood Regulates the Production/Consumption Ratio

As it happens, there is a data series that correlates much better with oil's consumption/production ratio, and it conforms to socionomic causality. Figure 30 inverts the ratio from Figure 29 and plots it along with the Value Line Composite index of stock prices. These data serve as global proxies, because the bull and bear markets depicted here were worldwide in scope.

Figure 30 shows that *declines* in oil production relative to consumption took place over three periods: from 1980 to 1982, during which time there was a bear market in stocks; from 1998 to 2002, during which time there was a bear market in stocks; and from 2005 to 2009, during which time there was a bear market first in homebuilding stocks, next in real estate and finally in the overall stock market. Conversely, *rises* in oil production relative to consumption took place over three periods: from 1982 to 1998, during most of which time there was a monstrous bull market in stocks (interrupted by a setback into 1990, during which time oil production compatibly fell relative to consumption); from 2002 to 2005, as stocks rose; and since 2009 as stocks have once again risen.

We may conclude from these congruent trends that Elliott waves of social mood, as reflected in stock prices, regulate feelings of optimism and pessimism among producers, alternately motivating them to overproduce and then underproduce oil relative to contemporaneous consumption. Their optimism makes them believe business will expand, so they produce more; and their pessimism makes them believe business will contract, so they produce less. This depiction of causality accounts quite well for the rises and falls in oil's production/consumption ratio. At the very least, it does so far better than changes in that ratio (per Figure 29) account for the rises and falls in the price of oil.

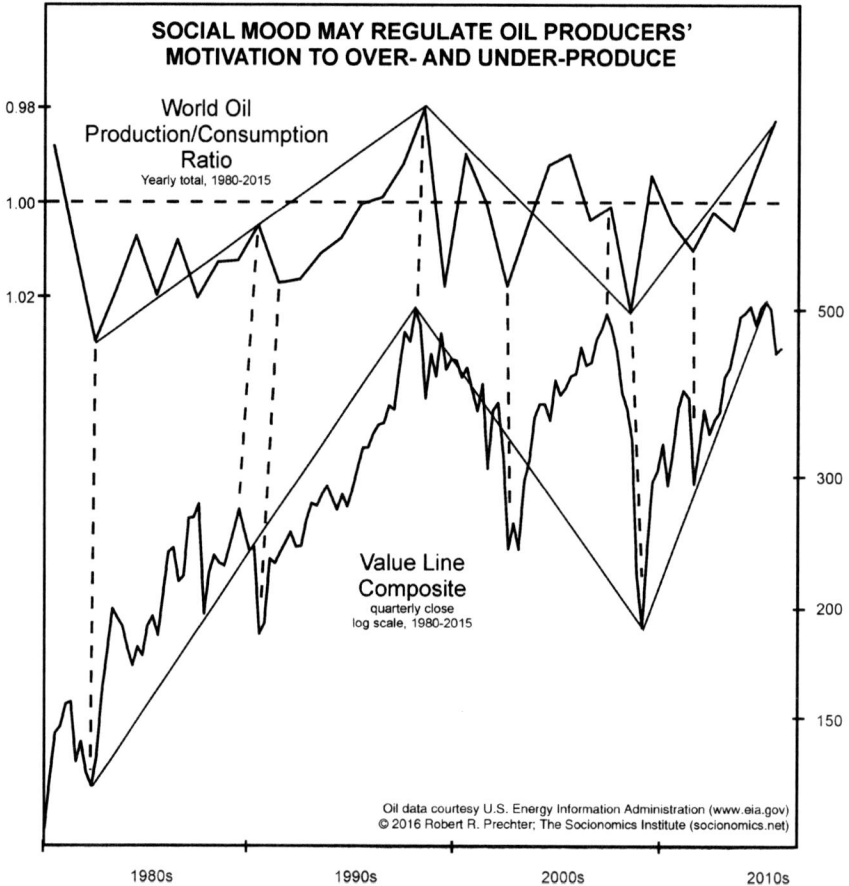

Figure 30

So, not only do Elliott waves regulate fluctuations in oil prices, but they also regulate fluctuations in overall social mood, which in turn are regulating changes in the production/consumption ratio for oil. This is a revealing pair of insights.

Summary

To conclude, Elliott waves, not supply and demand, regulate oil prices, and Elliott waves in overall social mood explain fluctuations in the production/consumption ratio for oil better than the production/consumption ratio for oil explains fluctuations in oil prices. Changes in the supply and demand for oil, then, are far more a result of prices than a cause of them.

NOTES AND REFERENCES

[1] Deffeyes, Kenneth S., *Current Events*, online newsletter, February 11, 2006.

[2] Shell, Adam, "Are Big Bets by Speculators Driving Up Oil?" *USA Today*, July 1, 2008.

[3] With added channel lines and the Intermediate degree wave labels already shown in Figure 12.

[4] Prechter, Robert, "Oil—A Real Time Application of the Elliott Wave Model," *Market Technician*, Issue 69, April 2011, pp. 10-12.

[5] Staniford, Stuart, "Gross World Product Will Not Grow at 4%+ for Five Years," *Early Warning*, April 26, 2011.

[6] Kahn, Chris, "Price of Oil Falls 3 Percent on Signs of Trouble," Associated Press, July 7, 2012.

[7] Moyo, Dambisa, in "Winner Take All: China's Race for Resources and What it Means for the World," as quoted in Rosen, Jon, "Economist Sees Gloomy Future of Frightening Scarcity," *USA Today*, September 11, 2012.

[8] White, Ronald D., "Record Gas Prices Expected for 2012," *The Los Angeles Times*, November 9, 2011.

[9] Krantz, Matt, "Oil in a 'Meltdown' as Prices Hit '03 Levels," *USA Today*, January 13, 2016.

[10] Hoffman, Andy et al., "The Oil Industry Got Together and Agreed Things May Never Get Better," Bloomberg, February 12, 2016.

[11] "Oil is now so cheap even pirates aren't stealing it anymore," Quartz (qz.com), February 18, 2016.

[12] Salvo, Mac, "Goldman Sachs Advisor Says 'Too Much Physical Oil' Could Send Prices Plummeting," *Market Daily News*, February 12, 2015.

[13] Charles W. Duncan, the U.S. Secretary of Energy under President Jimmy Carter, as quoted in *US News and World Report*, February 25, 1980.

[14] Schaps, Karolin, "Climate Qualms Mean Oil Will Never Be Used Up: BP," Reuters, October 13, 2015.

[15] Charles W. Duncan, the U.S. Secretary of Energy under President Jimmy Carter, as quoted in *US News and World Report*, February 25, 1980.

[16] The United States Senate, "Statements on Introduced Bills and Joint Resolutions," *The Congressional Record*, May 20, 2008.

[17] "Down with Charts," *Montreal Gazette*, November 23, 1931.

[18] Elliott waves of social mood are also ultimately in charge of long term trends of credit inflation and deflation. Bouts of deflation brought about by changes in social mood have taken place, and should continue to take place, regardless of preventative efforts by governments and central banks.

[19] "What Economic Forecasters Got Right, and Wrong, in 2015," *The Wall Street Journal*, December 30, 2015.

Chapter 23

Popular Bubble Theories
vs. the Elliott Wave Model

Robert R. Prechter

No Such Thing as Bubbles?

Advocates of the idea that financial markets are priced rationally do not believe in bubbles. They believe that every price reflects fundamental values. In a typical expression of this view, a bond-fund manager asserted that the idea of a bubble "is a falsehood. As long as demand exceeds or equals supply, there's no bubble."[1] Such formulations define bubbles out of existence. The supply and demand language is gratuitous (see Chapter 22), inappropriate (see Chapter 12) and irrelevant to whether bubbles occur.

In June 1999, an economist published an article titled "The Myth of Market 'Bubbles,'"[2] in which he argued that the Dutch tulip bulb mania of the early 1600s was "factually based."[3] An Ivy League economist agreed, contending that the episode exhibited "normal pricing behavior in bulb markets and cannot be interpreted as evidence of market irrationality."[4] It would seem, however, that something must have diverged from utility maximization and economic valuation, since in the aftermath of that credit-driven episode even the savvy *sellers* of tulip-bulb futures contracts suffered, receiving only 3½ cents on the dollar on their *correct* bets.[5]

The first economist mentioned above extended his argument to the stock market of 1999, saying, "current stock market levels are [not] at all excessive" because they "reflect profit rates expected in the future."[6] Socionomists agree with the latter part of this statement. Speculators were projecting outsized profit rates into the infinite future. That is how they rationalized paying fifteen times 1982 prices for stocks and five times 1982 prices for dividends.

As Chapter 40 will demonstrate, financial theories advocating full rationality are popular during trends toward more positive social mood, especially near their peaks, and this instance was no exception. The biggest stock market overvaluation in U.S. history culminated the following March. According to rational-valuation theorists, the events of 1999, including the thousand-percent run-ups in tech stocks over a matter of weeks, the astronomical prices paid for start-up companies, the massive amount of cash and credit extended to money-losing tech firms, the shift of valuation benchmarks from traditional measures to "burn rates" and a Dow dividend yield half of what it was on the top day in 1929 were all rationally driven.

That a stock mania was culminating is not just a retrospective observation. A seasoned observer recognized what was happening. On March 20, 2000, Barton M. Biggs wrote an issue of *Global Strategy* for his firm, Morgan Stanley Dean Witter, titled "Tulips in the Tech." The piece is a great read; I have culled only a few nuggets:

> Last week I went to Morgan Stanley Dean Witter's Millennium Conference. For two full days and one night I soaked in the New Economy. The great technology companies are the most magnificent growth machines in the world. There is no question about that. The issue is whether their shares are good investments at these prices.
>
> Since most [technology, media and telecommunications (TMT)] companies are still either losing money or burning cash, they need to sell more equity regularly. An increasing amount of infrastructure equipment is vendor-financed. Buying the startup that has the tech[nology] that might obsolete you makes sense, but some of the prices being paid are wild. The whole tech culture is built on rising stock prices.
>
> There are many conceptually oriented, momentum investors in TMT, and they are *fearless*. Virtually all of those attending had at least 50% of their portfolios in TMT and were happy with it. The investors I talked with were focused on the upside potential of the stocks. No one spoke of risk. Risk is not a factor in their investment religion.
>
> Managements were optimistic and extremely confident. A few were downright arrogant. Most were hard pressed to respond when asked what could go wrong. I listened to some great companies, but I am afraid I didn't come away with any great stocks.[7]

Did you appreciate the distinction made in that last line? Biggs was aware of the difference between *companies* and *stocks*. A good company, he implied, can sell at a bad price. Socionomics explains why: A company is an economic item, whereas a share of its stock is a financial item. In human minds, the two items are independent of each other.

As it happened, the celebratory conference and Biggs' coverage of it occurred right at peak prices for tech shares. The NASDAQ Composite index, which is heavily weighted toward tech stocks, had in fact just topped out, on March 10, and the blue-chip NASDAQ 100 index made its all-time high on March 24. Over the next 2½ years, these indexes tumbled 78.4% and 83.5%, respectively, on no discernibly causal news. Only a theorist who understands that bubbles exist can warn readers that one is culminating, whereas a theorist who thinks they do not exist lets his followers remain fully invested in one. Which one is more valuable to your investment success?

It may seem rational for speculators to base their actions on "profit rates expected in the future," but such is not the case if those very expectations are impulsively generated. Socionomics recognizes that speculators have no way of knowing the future, so they guess at it; they have no rational basis for guessing, so they default to herding; and they rationalize their decisions to make them appear as if they are based on judiciously considered criteria such as "profit rates expected in the future."

Bubbles

Definitions of bubbles run the gamut, but most of them do not relate properly to the term. The term *bubble* implies something inflated. It should pertain to times when speculators inflate prices through the use of credit. A more widely applicable term is *mania*, which dispenses with the bubble metaphor. Since *bubble* is currently the popular term, however, I use it in this chapter.

Credit can fuel bubbles in the prices of stocks, real estate, tulip bulbs, canal companies, farms, college educations and many other things. Some bubbles are inflated with the help of force (for example, the U.S.-government-sponsored real estate and college-education bubbles), while others are not. Speculators—and the lenders who back them, who are also speculating—drive financial bubbles. Consumers who purchase housing on credit in a bubble environment may not be speculating on future price gains but simply buying shelter at a less-than-ideal time. The brokers and credit providers will nevertheless tell them they are "making a good investment."

A Critique of Extant Bubble Theories

Theorists have variously proposed that participants in bubbles express either full rationality (the premier academic view), temporary departures from normal, rational behavior (the traditional view) or the mechanistic properties of sandpiles (the econophysics view). Let's discuss each of these hypotheses.

(1) Academic Bubble Theory: Pure Rationality

Some academic papers[8] have made the claim—already challenged more generally in Chapter 19—that chasing bubbles involves a conscious assumption of risk based on rational risk assessment. Working under the paradigm of mechanical causality, rational-bubble papers treat bubbles as if they are events to which humans react by joining, either voluntarily or because they are "forced"[9] by rational considerations to do so. There is little attempt to explain why bubbles happen in the first place. The usual vague description involves some sort of rare investment conditions incited by an unexplained introduction of easy credit into the system.

Specifically, rational-bubble advocates propose that speculators weigh their options and rationally decide that the risk of buying high to sell even higher is worth it. But a bubble is propelled by new buyers and by increasingly bullish conviction among those already invested. Few of the bubble-joiners have a basis for anticipating the bubble's bursting, so instead of buying high and selling higher, most of them do only the first part. Read Biggs' description again to see how participants in bubbles actually think. In the end, the vast majority of bubble buyers hold through the high and limp away one by one after finally bailing out at much lower prices.

Curiously, rational-bubble advocates never seem to consider the idea that buying after an extended *downtrend* should be considered a rational assumption of risk. It certainly better qualifies as such, since rational utility maximization should guide speculators toward buying low and selling high. No doubt they view selling in a panic as a rational shedding of risk, too, even though selling after an extended uptrend better qualifies as such.

Academic descriptions of "rational bubbles" convey no perception that the market participants described are in fact a vast, bug-eyed pack of speculators buying investment items on swelling amounts of margin and trading with increasing frequency as prices rise toward the peak of a mania. I think the assertion of rational bubbles is as irrational as bubble buying. Nearly all speculators suffer huge losses in bubbles and their aftermath. Self-destruction is not rational, so the "rational bubble" idea can't be right.

(2) Traditional Bubble Theory: Temporary Irrationality

Most books and professional literature relating to financial bubbles take a middle ground. They assert that market participants are *usually* rational, but every so often they become susceptible to a financial mania, after which everything returns to normal. By this narrative, bubbles are special circumstances akin to temporary insanity. For various proposed reasons, a financial market becomes the focus of speculation, and people abandon rationality to chase impossible dreams of riches. Irrationality spreads by contagion until it reaches fever pitch. Then an event triggers a reversal, and reality imposes itself on the proceedings, causing a reversal. Values collapse, causing financial ruin. Eventually, investors sober up and return to their natural state of rationality. From Mackay to Kindleberger, this is the most widely accepted version of bubbles.

Figure 1 illustrates this idea. Consistent with theory, it does not illustrate market prices per se but market prices relative to objective standards of value. It depicts investors pricing investment items rationally and consistently according to value standards while every now and then departing from that normal behavior. Somewhat along the lines of the "punctuated equilibrium" that Stephen J. Gould suggested for evolution (another model WP challenges; see Figure 13-2 in *The Wave Principle of Human Social Behavior*), financial markets are presumably near equilibrium most of the time with respect to objective measures of value but occasionally depart from it to undergo a boom and a bust.

What Financial Valuations Would Look Like under Traditional Bubble Theory

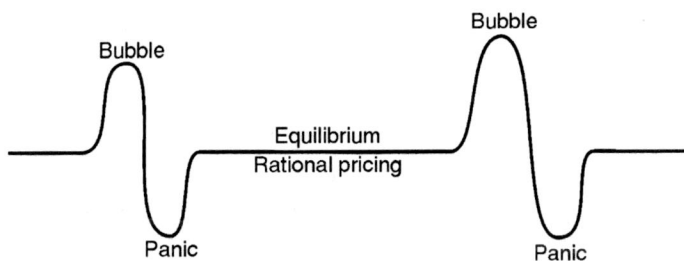

Figure 1

The first problem with this position is that there is no demonstrable norm of objective pricing. Figures 1 through 5 in Chapter 12 show that the stock market never attaches to any standards of value but rather is ceaselessly dynamic with respect to all of them. Since there is no evidence of consistent pricing around a valuation equilibrium, there can be no *departures* from such an equilibrium. Traditional bubble theory, therefore, does not fit the data.

The second problem with traditional bubble theory is that there is no evidence that speculators' behavior ever fundamentally changes. Yet descriptions of bubble conditions always assert qualitative shifts in the behavior of financial-market participants. Keynes, for example, held that "In *abnormal times* in particular…the market will be subject to waves of optimistic and pessimistic sentiment…"[10] whereas the rest of the time fundamentals and rationality presumably rule. A more recent economist echoed him, saying, "In normal times, psychology doesn't matter much. It reflects economic conditions. But in *abnormal times*, it's the reverse. Psychology determines economic conditions."[11] Though it is a popular notion (see Chapter 19) that economic conditions drive market pricing except when psychology drives bubbles, no one has in fact demonstrated any such qualitative difference.

According to socionomics, the psychology of the herd constantly drives financial prices, so they are always—not just occasionally—non-rationally determined. Under WP, the same qualitative behaviors occur at all degrees of fluctuation, so there are no abnormal times, either, just differently sized expressions of the same dynamics. Quantitative properties alone seem to determine when traditional theorists (usually in retrospect) elect to identify a rising wave as a bubble. More precisely—as will be shown below—Elliott wave structure and degree determine such times.

(3) A Mechanical Model of Shocks, Triggers, Catalysts and Tipping Points

Proponents of mechanical models of financial market behavior rarely offer ideas about how and why bubbles form, but they do offer a hypothesis of why they burst. Economists and traditional bubble theorists have posited for financial markets and social trends a system of mostly serene advances punctuated by "shocks" and "Minsky moments" set off by "triggers" and "catalysts" acting on "critical states" that have reached "tipping points."

Under the tipping-point hypothesis, a social trend of long duration reaches some point of critical fragility from which it "tips" in the other direction, as if it were a mountainside of snow finally giving way under the weight of one last snowflake or a tree leaning over and finally falling due to one last gust of wind. Kindleberger embraced the view that bubble reversals are exogenously prepped and triggered. He wrote,

> *Causa remota* of the crisis is speculation and extended credit; *causa proxima* is some incident which snaps the confidence of the system, makes people think of the dangers of failure, and leads them to move from commodities, stocks, real estate, bills of exchange—whatever it may be—back into cash. In itself, *causa proxima* may be trivial: a bankruptcy, suicide, a flight, a revelation, a refusal of credit to

some borrower, some change of view that leads a significant actor to unload. Prices fall. Expectations are reversed. The movement picks up speed."[12]

All this talk of causes must seem self-evident to many observers, since variations of it appear everywhere. But from the socionomic point of view, Kindleberger identified no causes, just results. The "causa remota" of speculation and credit expansion are results of an extended positive trend in social mood, and whatever "causa proxima" happens to occur is simply the first noticeable result of the ensuing negative trend in social mood.

Like all mechanistic formulations, Kindleberger's view that falling prices cause expectations to be reversed is backwards; rather, a reversal of expectations causes prices to fall. The same thing goes for such claims for bubbles as, "Increasing volatility leads to more emotionally based decision-making."[13] Socionomists, as always, flip the causality to say, "More emotionally based decision-making leads to increasing volatility." As stated in Chapter 6, there is no reconciling these two points of view. They are causal opposites.

Some financial historians have asserted that the failure of Creditanstalt bank in Austria in May 1931 was a "shock" that "triggered" the financial and economic contraction known as the Great Depression. An initial question is: How could a bank failure spark a global economic contraction that in fact had begun nearly two years earlier? Financial institutions, moreover, fail individually all the time. Why are twenty individual bank failures not systemic shocks but one is? The conclusion comes from affirming the consequent: A bubble burst; we can identify an early event; the event must have been a trigger, because we believe in triggers.

Economists and money managers express such causal claims all the time, even in the short run. Over a few days in June and July 2015, dozens of articles worldwide proclaimed that a drop in Chinese stocks had "triggered" stock declines elsewhere. Conclusions of this type rely on a simple formula: Whichever market falls first, or whichever bank fails first, must have caused the later events.

Mechanics-minded theorists blame "excess credit" for a bubble and a "debt crisis" for causing the ensuing crash. But this statement doesn't really explain anything. Where did the excess credit come from, and why did it shrink?

Trigger claims, like all exogenous-cause arguments, derive from ad hoc reasoning. Economists can see the credit expansion and contraction, so they cite them as remote causes. They can see the bank failures, so they assume that the first event of that type is a proximate cause of the rest. They can't see the hidden variable, social mood, so they are unaware of its fundamentally causal role.

Socionomic Causality Accounts for These Events

Socionomics explains the entire process without resorting to mechanics or leaving behind mysteries. A trend toward positive social mood at high degree induces optimism, which prompts expansive behavior among three groups: creditors, who begin supplying more credit on the belief that they will receive both interest and the return of their principal; debtors, who begin taking on more debt on the belief that they will make enough money to service and ultimately repay their debts; and speculators, who begin judging an increasingly wider range of IOUs to be low-risk investments. As these participants in the process cooperate with each other, loans balloon to a high level. The ensuing, natural trend toward negative social mood, at whatever point it begins, induces pessimism, which motivates lenders to call in loans and participants in the economy to curtail expansionary activity, which reduces income flows, causing weak borrowers to default. Defaults lead to the failure of the most affected bank. That first bank failure is a result, not a cause. If mood were to turn positive right at that moment, other banks may not fail.

Even when banks are systemically interdependent, any rash of failures is due not to the first bank's failure but to the reversal away from the positive mood that induced banks to become interdependent in the first place. Positive social mood at very high degree sets up a portion of the *system* to fail. Which bank fails first depends only on balance-sheet minutiae, which from a systemic point of view may as well be due to chance. To return to the famous example, Creditanstalt's substantial extension of credit in the 1920s was one of the results of a trend toward positive social mood culminating a wave of very high degree, and the bank's failure was one of countless results—many of which had already occurred—of a trend toward negative social mood at very high degree.

A socionomist can successfully predict when bank failures will become more likely. A reversal from extremely positive social mood, indicated by the onset of a declining wave of high degree in the stock market, signals an increased likelihood of bank failures. At the other end of the process, proponents of the mechanical model are devoid of a theoretical basis for anticipating when bank failures will lessen and cease. They believe that the first failure is the cause of subsequent failures, so what's to stop the process? Socionomics has this question covered, too. The failures will stop—as demonstrated throughout Chapter 8—shortly after social mood turns back toward the positive.

STF Accounts for Bubbles Quantitatively, Not Qualitatively

STF rejects the causal claims of all three forms of bubble theory discussed above. In their place it offers a comprehensive explanation for bubbles and crashes and humans' participation in them, *all as aspects of normal financial behavior.*

The practice among bubble theorists of describing only the final stage of a trend as having bubble characteristics hinders a full understanding of the process. Socionomic theory tracks it all the way. Consider the history behind the most recent bubble experience:

The credit-fueled financial bubble that reached peak inflation in 2006-2007 began decades before the period that bubble theorists describe as problematic. The degradation in U.S. banks' balance sheets—in the form of shedding Treasuries in favor of mortgages—began as far back as the late 1940s. Financiers are in the business of facilitating transactions, so the greater the degree of clients' optimism, the more creative they become in order to satisfy demands from all parties. As a trend toward positive social mood progresses, effects of the attendant optimism become increasingly intense. Over time, financiers and investors move from warily providing credit on substantial collateral (as with home loans in the 1950s) to loosely providing credit on slim collateral (as with home loans the 1990s) to incautiously providing more credit than the collateral can cover (as with the 100%+ home loans of 2004-2006) to rashly providing credit on nearly worthless collateral (such as used cars and home furnishings, widely collateralized in 2005 and again presently) to recklessly using debt as collateral for more credit (as when hedge funds use their portfolios of IOUs as collateral for issuing more IOUs to get more money for speculation) to pathologically using debt as collateral for issuing derivatives leveraged 100-to-1, and so on, ultimately carrying to whatever heights of leverage human minds are capable of justifying at the highest degree of positive social mood. Bubble theorists call the early part of the process normal and the latter part abnormal. But the difference in the earlier and later stages is not qualitative. It's quantitative. The question is not *what* but simply *how much.*

When social mood turns negative after a major extreme in positive mood, the sequence of events described above retraces its steps in reverse order until such time as social mood turns toward the positive again. These changes are likewise not qualitative but quantitative.

The progression outlined above for mortgage loans has also characterized the expansion of U.S. auto loans over substantially the same period.
Since credit trends are socionomically regulated, what form do you think
the expansion has taken? Examine Figure 2, and you will see that the
total value of auto loans has
traced out a clear Elliott wave
since the 1940s. Observe how
smooth the line is, much like
the rightmost line in the idealized diagram shown as Figure
1 of Chapter 7. Because borrowing decisions and loan
applications take varying
times to process, the Elliott
wave influence shows up best
in long-term data, such as
quarterly.

The only time socio-
nomic theory recognizes a
qualitative shift in market
participants' behavior is when
a non-speculatively traded
item becomes a speculatively
traded item. In such cases, the
traditional bubble description

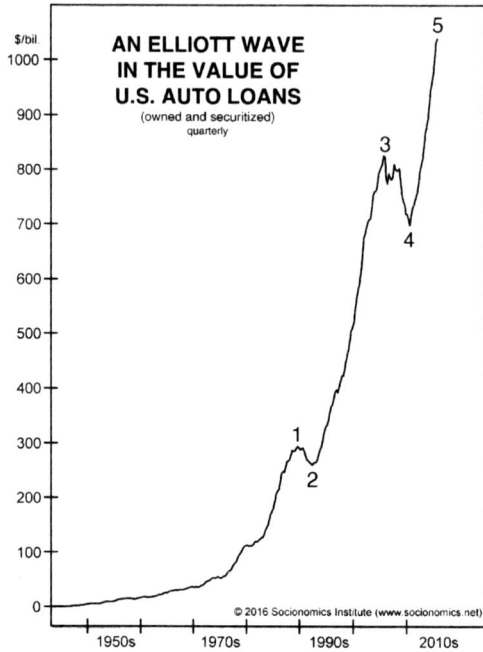

Figure 2

does capture, if only intuitively, an aspect of the dynamic involved. When
people's perception shifts so as to view a consumer good—such as a tulip
bulb or a Beanie Baby—as an investment item, their thought process shifts
from having a rational, economic orientation to having a pre-rational, financial orientation, which reverts as soon as the new perception dissolves.
Although this twofold swing in mental orientation may seem equivalent to
temporary insanity, socionomic theory offers a more careful description of
the thought processes involved. Real estate pricing—as depicted above—
always possesses latent bubble characteristics due to lending, leverage,
speculative property development and investment, all of which are subject
to mood-regulated swings between optimism and pessimism, under which
behavioral changes are only quantitative. Nevertheless, since housing is
also, and fundamentally, a consumption item, it is subject to significant,
qualitative shifts in many participants' mental orientation from producer

or consumer to speculator and back, as depicted in Figure 3 of Chapter 13. In markets that are normally speculatively traded, however, such as those for stocks and exchange-traded commodities, the mental orientation of participants is inalterably financial. In those cases, the "insanity" to which bubble theorists attest—which socionomics recognizes as consisting of pre-rational herding—is not occasional but always present, assuring that behavioral changes are only quantitative. The next section models this view.

The Wave Principle Naturally Subsumes Bubbles and Crashes

Under the Wave Principle, there is no such thing as abnormal financial-market behavior. Instances of extremely high pricing are natural and occur during fifth waves of large degree. Since fifth waves are followed by the largest bear markets since the five-wave sequence began, the "bubble" is naturally followed by a severe retrenchment, as illustrated multiple times in Figure 3. That's all there is to it. When it happens at Minor, Intermediate or Primary degree, people hardly notice. But when it happens at Cycle and especially Supercycle degree, they think it's a new animal.

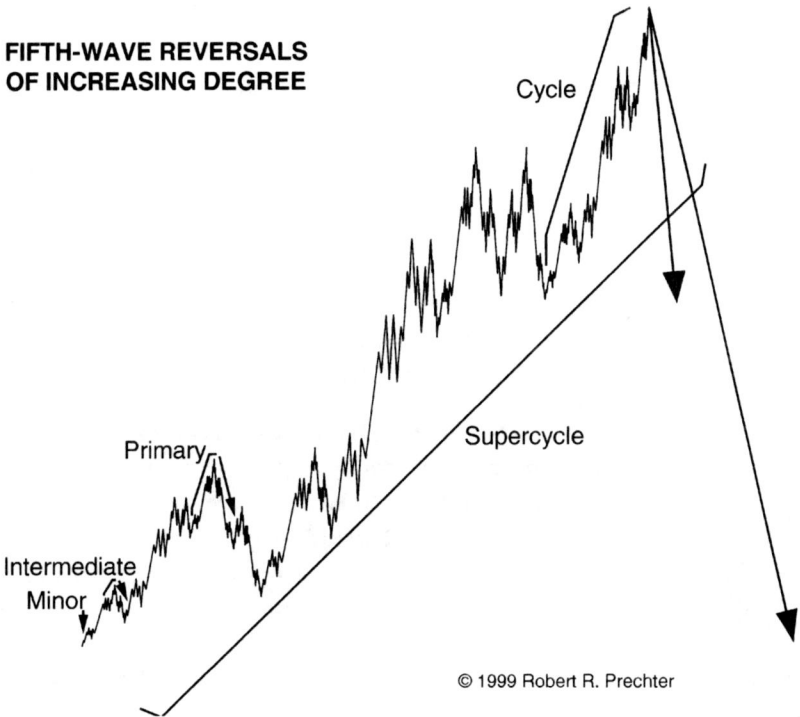

FIFTH-WAVE REVERSALS OF INCREASING DEGREE

Cycle

Primary

Intermediate

Minor

Supercycle

© 1999 Robert R. Prechter

Figure 3

The Wave Principle is a system of constant fluctuation that regulates changes in social mood and social actions, including financial pricing. WP has nothing to do with rational risk assessments, fundamental shifts in human psychology, perturbations of equilibrium, destabilization from "critical states" or reactions from tipping points. No *shocks, triggers* or *catalysts* impact Elliott waves.

In WP's hierarchical-fractal system, as reflected in real world market activity, financial prices change direction every second, so nearly every moment is akin to a point of criticality, or tipping point. Since all trend reversals imply critical moments, the tipping-point model breaks down. Proponents' only resort is to emulate the supply-demand theorists who postulate infinite equilibria by postulating infinite tipping points, which means none at all.

A recent study by Preis, Schneider and Stanley captures an aspect of the qualitative consistency implied by the Elliott wave model. The authors' findings are in perfect accord with socionomics' depiction of bubbles as being only quantitatively different from other waves:

> Financial market fluctuations are characterized by many abrupt switchings creating upward trends and downward trends, on time scales ranging from macroscopic trends persisting for hundreds of days to microscopic trends persisting for a few minutes. ...We find striking scale-free behavior of the transaction volume after each switching. Our findings can be interpreted as being consistent with time-dependent collective behavior of financial market participants.

> We suggest that the well-known catastrophic bubbles that occur on large time scales—such as the most recent financial crisis—may not be outliers but single dramatic representatives caused by the formation of increasing and decreasing trends on time scales varying over nine orders of magnitude from very large down to very small.[14, 15]

This study supports R.N. Elliott's empirical observations of eighty years ago.

Ignoring the fractal aspect of markets, conventional bubble theorists arbitrarily select only a certain range of extremes as representing bubbles. While they may choose deliberately to disregard countless small trend reversals, large ones lasting decades or centuries simply escape their notice. When Rome's fortunes topped out over a period of three centuries, "bubble" behaviors occurred, but the trends involved were of such large degree that bubble historians can't see the trees for the forest. WP's fractal system incorporates trend changes of all degrees and relates them to each other in the proper, quantitative way.

All three types of conventional bubble theorists are further selective in confining their observations almost exclusively to changes in trend from up to down. Proponents rarely consider shifts from down to up in the same light.[16] The Elliott wave model encompasses both directions of trend change in a natural way. Once you see the fractal graphically, it's clear: The market and the social mood behind it move in orderly fashion according to the Wave Principle, not sporadically in response to rational risk assessment, qualitative shifts in psychology or exogenous triggers.

The Wave Principle explains why financial markets have no reliable exogenous causes (see Chapters 1 and 2); why markets have no reliable benchmarks of price or value (see Chapter 12); why markets avoid equilibrium and are ceaselessly dynamic (see Chapter 12); and why financial price changes are sometimes strikingly dramatic, *as if* reacting to shocks. WP provides its own drama, which includes bubbles and crashes.

The Elliott wave model is dynamic even with respect to its own dynamism. Fluctuations in social mood produce volatility clustering (see Chapter 6), a statistically verified aspect of stock market behavior. At times—especially in third waves—the market gets more volatile simply because (as noted in the Appendix to Chapter 13) it adheres to WP. This fact accounts both for why people are motivated at such times to look for evidence of catalysts *and* for why their ad-hoc identifications never produce a reliable formula.

The Mechanics Paradigm and the Assumption of Rational Pricing Make It Impossible for Economists to Identify, Much Less Predict, Bubbles

Mainstream economists almost never identify bubbles in the midst of their inflation. On the contrary, they typically deny their existence at the time. Consider just two comments, delivered near the peak of the greatest housing bubble in U.S. history: On June 27, 2005, "Top officials at the Federal Deposit Insurance Corp…dismissed fears that rising home prices nationwide reflect a speculative bubble ready to burst."[17] The S&P Homebuilding Index (see Figure 21 in Chapter 21) peaked two months later. On September 19, 2005, one month after the start of a 92% collapse in homebuilding stocks and seven months prior to the onset of the biggest property bear market in 80 years, a pair of professors of real estate at the universities of Columbia and Wharton wrote an editorial for *The Wall Street Journal* to argue, "The market sure feels like a bubble. Yet basic economic logic suggests that this apparent evidence of a bubble is anything but."[18] The rest of the article carefully spelled out, with "basic economic logic," why housing was "anything but" in a bubble. The immediately preceding 928% rise in homebuilding stocks in just five years did not figure into their analysis. The easiest mortgage credit in history, which allowed many people to leverage their money up to infinity to buy a house, which in turn allowed speculators to buy multiple properties on margin—well fitting our definition of a bubble—was not one of the authors' considerations, either. The only caveat the writers offered to their bullish outlook was that "an unanticipated rise in real mortgage rates could cause appreciable declines in house prices." Their lone concern proved to be entirely backwards, as mortgage rates fell to unprecedentedly low levels while house prices plunged right along with them. As observed in Chapters 18 and 22, "basic economic logic" doesn't merely fail to work in finance and macroeconomics; it leads practitioners to exquisitely wrong conclusions. Paradoxically, socionomists have been successful in using widespread denials of the existence of a bubble as an excellent indicator that one exists. It's the very reason people feel a need to deny it.

It would have been useful—and a pleasant surprise—had any of these analysts said, "Wake up, people. You have less than a year to sell your real estate investments at good prices." Some people did say that, but they were mostly independent of academia and the economics profession, a rare exception being Yale's Robert Shiller. Elliott Wave International also said it, as recounted in Chapter 21.

A valid theory should be able to predict, but conventional economic theory is powerless to identify bubbles, so it can't anticipate their deflation. Eugene Fama, father of EMH, said just that. He conceded that bubbles might exist but cautioned, "They have to be predictable phenomena. I don't think any of this [the 2008 meltdown] was predictable."[19] All neoclassical economists (another is quoted in Chapter 5) agree on this point.

Even more assuredly, no one in the economics profession has ever predicted the *onset* of an asset bubble. Fed chairmen Alan Greenspan (see Chapter 25) and Ben Bernanke have said there is no way to do it. Nobel laureate Shiller concurred, saying, "It is impossible for anyone to predict bubbles accurately. And, because big bubbles last for many years, predicting them means predicting many years in the future."[20] Princeton professor and random-walk proponent Burton Malkiel agreed, saying, "I do think bubbles exist," but "the problem with bubbles is that you cannot recognize them in advance."[21] An article in the *Harvard Business Review*, "Why Asset Bubbles Will Always Surprise Us,"[22] echoed the consensus: "It would be nice if we could predict bubbles; even nicer if we could prevent them." Economists rarely agree on anything, but they unanimously agree that there is no basis upon which anyone could possibly forecast a bubble.

The Elliott Wave Model Allows for the Prediction of Asset Bubbles

Under the Elliott wave model, not only is the *bursting* of bubbles sometimes predictable (as demonstrated in Chapters 18, 21, 22 and 23), but the *onset* of bubbles is sometimes predictable as well. We can even provide an example of how it's done.

In late 1982 and early 1983, the stock market's position within the Elliott wave model prompted *The Elliott Wave Theorist* to forecast the biggest asset bubble in U.S. history, as the following excerpts demonstrate:

November 1982: Make no mistake about it. The next few years will be profitable beyond your wildest imagination. Make sure you make it while the making is good. Tune your mind to 1924.[23]

April 1983: In 1982 the DJIA finished a correction of very large degree. The evidence for this conclusion is overwhelming.... The advance following this correction will be a much bigger bull market than anything seen in the last two decades. ...Given the technical situation, what might we conclude about the psychological aspects of wave V? The 1920s' bull market was a fifth wave of a third Supercycle wave, while Cycle wave V is the fifth wave of a fifth Supercycle wave. Thus, as the last hurrah, it should be characterized at its end by an almost unbelievable institutional mania for stocks and a public mania for stock index futures, stock options, and options on futures. In my opinion, the long term sentiment gauges will give off major trend sell signals two or three years before the final top, and the market will just keep on going. In order to set up the U.S. stock market to experience the greatest crash in its history, which, according to the Wave Principle, is due to follow wave V, investor mass psychology should reach manic proportions, with elements of 1929, 1968 and 1973 all operating together and, at the end, to an even greater extreme.[24]

August 1983: With sentiment, momentum, wave characteristics and social phenomena all supporting our original forecast, can we say that the environment on Wall Street is conducive to developing a full-blown speculative mania? In 1978, an Elliott analyst had no way of knowing just what the mechanisms for a wild speculation would be. "Where's the 10% margin which made the 1920s possible?" was a common rebuttal. Well, to be honest, we didn't know. But now look! The entire structure is being built as if it were planned. Options on hundreds of stocks (and now stock indexes) allow the speculator to deal in thousands of shares of stock for a fraction of their value.

Futures contracts on stock indexes, which promise to deliver nothing, have been created for the most part as speculative vehicles with huge leverage. Options on futures carry the possibilities one step further. And it's not stopping there. Major financial newspapers are calling for the end of any margin requirements on stocks whatsoever. "Look-back" options are making a debut. S&Ls are leaping into the stock brokerage business, sending flyers to little old ladies. And New York City banks are already constructing kiosks for quote machines so that depositors can stop off at lunch and punch out their favorite stocks. Options exchanges are creating new speculative instruments—guess the C.P.I. and win a bundle! In other words, the financial arena is becoming the place to be. And, as if by magic, the media are geometrically increasing coverage of financial news. New financial newsletters and magazines are being created every few months. Financial News Network is now broadcasting 12 hours a day, bringing up-to-the-minute quotations on stocks and commodities via satellite and cable into millions of homes. Remember, this is just the set-up phase.... At the peak of the fifth wave, the spectacle could rival Tulipomania and the South Sea Bubble.[25]

What followed was a relentless climb to the greatest stock market overvaluation in U.S. history by all measures by a wide margin (see Figures 1 through 4 in Chapter 12). Along with them came a new all-time high in margin debt as a percentage of available funds, widespread speculative investing by formerly conservative pension funds and insurance companies, a bloated mutual-fund industry, a booming hedge-fund industry, a philosophy of index-fund investing whereby profits are presumably effortless, around-the-clock futures trading, the invention of exchange-traded funds, and what socionomist Peter Kendall called an "equity culture," which permeated society from cartoonists' references to tavern owners' choice of financial stations instead of sports stations for customers' TV viewing.

Only the Elliott wave model offered a basis both for recognizing the onset of a record-breaking asset bubble and for describing in advance what its maturity would look like. As far as we know, this is the only instance of such a forecast in the history of financial and economic commentary.

How was it possible? Figure 4 shows the basis of the forecast: Fifth waves of Cycle degree produce manias. The upturn in 1982[26] launched wave V of (V), and Elliotticians were equipped to know it.

Observe from Figure 4 that as the two-century-long wave ⒺⒾⒾ advanced, each "wave V" asset mania was larger, lasted longer and involved more asset

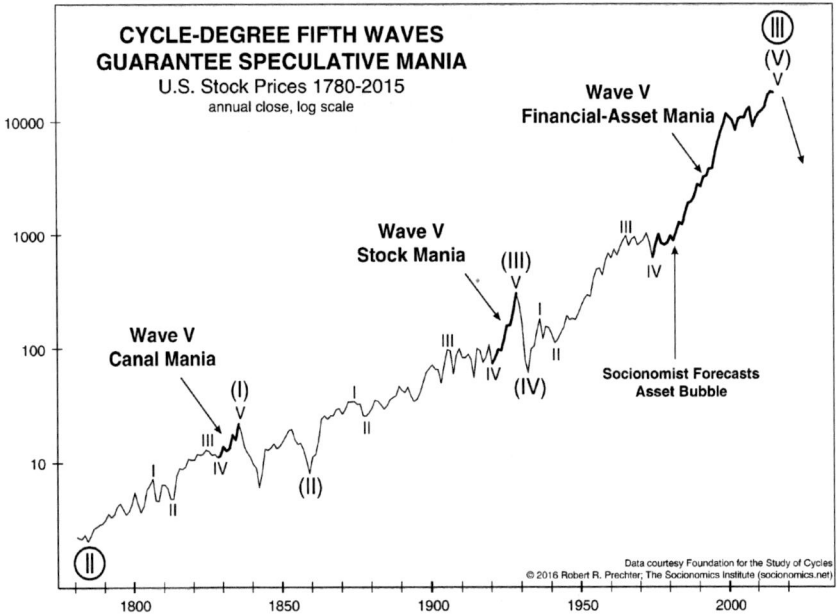

Figure 4

classes than the one before. This progression indicates successively more extreme expressions of positive social mood, reflecting the approach of a peak of even higher degree, that of wave Ⓘ. Anticipating that yet-greater extremity prompted the passionate prose of the prediction.

The coherence of this model is a remarkable thing. While some economists concede that bubbles exist, and while a precious few of them might be able to recognize a bubble in progress, and while a lone representative might be able to identify the maturation of an existing bubble, none of them has a basis upon which even to *imagine* that someone could predict a bubble's coming into existence with nary a hint from present conditions. WP takes bubbles in stride.

Using a theory to make a forecast that advocates of other theories deem impossible speaks to the validity of the theory successfully employed. If one can forecast a bubble using a hierarchical fractal model, then it is likely that the stock market adheres to a hierarchical fractal. If one can forecast a bubble using a model based on qualitatively uniform behavior among investors, then it is likely that investors' behavior is qualitatively uniform.

Bubbles in Bubble Theories (by Alan Hall)

A perusal of bubble literature reveals that conventional theorists typically address bubbles only after one has receded. Following the all-time high for stocks priced in real money (gold) in 1999, and especially after the reversal in real estate prices in 2006, economists herded in presenting hypotheses about bubbles. Vogel[27] listed some seventeen theories of bubbles and crashes in existence at the end of 2009. One is tempted to quip that deflating bubbles prompt bubbles in bubble theories. Since then, as the stock market has risen and the economy has expanded, the urge to theorize about bubbles has receded. Socionomists see all this belated activity as natural.

The socionomic perspective keeps practitioners way ahead of that curve. *The Elliott Wave Theorist*'s essay "Bulls, Bears and Manias,"[28] came out in the heat of the stock mania in 1997, not after it was over in 2009.

Can Authorities Prevent Bubbles? (by Alan Hall)

In 2011, four to five years after the latest bubble peaks and two years after the washout ended, the *Harvard Business Review* (HBR) weighed in on the discussion of asset bubbles and took the additional step of proposing five ways to prevent them. The author counseled,

- Make sure public leverage does not become excessive.
- Identify sources of "hidden leverage."
- Impose shorter term limits on certain public officials, for example the chairman of the Federal Reserve.
- Develop methods to recapitalize the financial system more quickly.
- Develop better corporate governance protocols.[29]

Socionomic causality implies that none of the article's well-intentioned suggestions can work. Even if tools to temper bubbles existed, authorities would never use them as theoretically intended. During the late stages of a positive trend in social mood, CEOs, politicians, regulators and ratings agencies are not motivated to investigate excessive or hidden leverage, limit the term of a central-bank maestro, investigate financial fraud, rein in bankers' speculations, set aside capital as deflation insurance or tighten corporate governance. Social mood works to *prevent* such pre-emptive solutions. As shown in Figure 8 of Chapter 17, restrictive regulation simply does not happen when social mood is at a positive extreme. Legislatures never enact financial regulation until after a bear market is over, which is too late to do any good. To his credit, the author of the HBR article gave a good reason why:

> No system can be perfectly self-conscious. The kind of immediate social awareness that would prevent bubbles from forming or bursting is a physical and mathematical impossibility.

This statement is in perfect accord with the formological imperatives of WP and socionomic causality.

Social policies can never control unconsciously regulated herding behavior. All segments of society, including authorities, participate in it.

Bubbles and their bursting are a natural part of the fractal fluctuation of WP. Authorities cannot prevent bubbles, but Elliotticians and socionomists can sometimes predict them; and, as individuals, we can employ them to our advantage rather than allow them to blindside us.

Summary

Socionomics does not echo popular bubble theories in relying on fore-ordained rationality, inexplicable departures from a psychological norm or mechanical causality. Under socionomics, non-rational pricing in finance *is* the norm; speculators are herding *all the time*, not just during bubbles and crashes; and the entire process is endogenously, holistically regulated. In large fifth waves, there is no sudden, anomalous seizure of "animal spirits" apart from some rational norm. Moderate or extreme, the market's mood is always determined by the law of patterned herding.

To conclude, investors do not value stocks *entirely* rationally, as the majority of academic bubble theorists claim; nor *mostly* rationally apart from certain errors of thought as proponents of behavioral economics and behavioral finance seem generally to assume (see Chapter 19); nor *usually* rationally while departing from normal behavior for mysterious reasons from time to time, as traditional bubble theorists assert; nor in response to mechanical forces. The consistent picture of unconscious, patterned herding offered by STF and its Elliott wave model is the one most compatible with the evidence. It is the only one useful for prediction.

NOTES AND REFERENCES

[1] Kapadia, Reshma, "A Bond Manager Finds the Silver Lining," *Barron's*, December 30, 2013.

[2] Salsman, Richard, "The Myth of Market 'Bubbles'," *Economic Education Bulletin*, American Institute for Economic Research, June 1999, pp. 2,6. A recorded speech of the same name was issued in July 2000.

[3] Salsman, p. 6. This author wrote from an intellectual foundation of Objectivism. But Alan Greenspan, in speaking of Ayn Rand, said, "From her, I learned that the economy is driven by psychology, values, attitudes, trust and other often-irrational and immeasurable factors. One cannot understand society as a whole unless you deal with all of it."* Without consideration of such factors, she added, he would "miss a very large part of how human beings behaved."** Her depiction—as reported by Greenspan—is a far cry from espousing inalterable human rationality and denying the existence of bubbles.

*Greenspan, Alan, "Alan Greenspan: A 70 Minute Conversation," BMO Financial Group meeting in Calgary, Canada, October 6, 2006.

**Wolfe, Alexandra, "Alan Greenspan: What Went Wrong," *The Wall Street Journal*, October 18, 2013.

[4] Garber, Peter. "Tulipmania," *Journal of Political Economy*, Vol. 97, No. 3, June 1989, p. 536. Garber did concede, "Nevertheless, a less emphasized aspect of the mania, the speculation in common bulbs, does defy explanation." (Garber, p. 536) What he means is that it defies *economic* explanation.

[5] Per Garber, p. 556 fn.

[6] Salsman, pp. 2,6.

[7] Biggs, Barton M., "Tulips in the Tech," *Global Strategy*, Morgan Stanley Dean Witter, March 20, 2000, pp. 9-10.

[8] See Blanchard, Olivier Jean, "Speculative Bubbles, Crashes and Rational Expectations," *Economics Letters*, 1979, Vol. 3, No. 4, pp. 387-389; and Brooks, Chris and Apostolos Katsaris, "Rational Speculative Bubbles: An Empirical Investigation of the London Stock Exchange," *Bulletin of Economic Research*, 2003, Vol. 55, No. 4, pp. 319-346.

[9] Vogel, Harold and Richard A. Werner, "An Analytical Review of Volatility Metrics for Bubbles and Crashes," *International Review of Financial Analysis*, 2015, Vol. 38.

[10] Keynes, John M., *The General Theory of Employment, Interest, and Money*, London: MacMillan, 1936, p. 162.

[11] Samuelson, Robert J., "The Saving Mentality is Hurting the Economy's Recovery," *The Washington Post*, August 30, 2010.

[12] Kindleberger, Charles P., *Manias, Panics, and Crashes*, third edition, 1996, New York: John Wiley & Sons.

[13] Vogel, Harold and Richard A. Werner, "An Analytical Review of Volatility Metrics for Bubbles and Crashes," *International Review of Financial Analysis*, Vol. 38, 2015.

[14] Preis, Tobias, Johannes J. Schneider and Eugene Stanley, "Switching Processes in Financial Markets," *Proceedings of the National Academy of Sciences of the United States of America*, Vol. 108, No. 19, May 10, 2010.

[15] Some econophysicists have proposed qualitative differences between bubbles and other times but have nevertheless concluded that endogenous dynamics are involved in regulating bubbles and crashes. They include Sornette (2004 and 2014)* and Harmon et al. (2011 and 2015).** Sornette (see also Chapter 34) simultaneously described mechanical forces such as exogenous "triggers" and believed—along with bubble theorist Hyman Minsky—in authorities' power to "prevent bubbles"*** by passing the right laws. His several successful predictions, however, appear to be based on internal market dynamics, not shocks and legislation.

> *Sornette, Didier, *Why Stock Markets Crash: Critical Events in Complex Financial Systems*, Princeton University Press, 2004; and Sornette et al., "Financial Bubbles: Mechanisms and Diagnostics," Research Paper No. 14-28, Swiss Finance Institute, April 8, 2014.

> **Harmon, Dion, et al., "Predicting Economic Market Crises Using Measures of Collective Panic," New England Complex Systems Institute, February 13, 2011; and "Anticipating Economic Market Crises Using Measures of Collective Panic," *PLOS*, July 17, 2015.

> ***Sornette, Didier, "Nurturing Breakthroughs; Lessons from Complexity Theory," *Journal of Economic Interaction and Coordination*, 3, 165-181 (2008).

[16] In a rare exception, econophysicists Sornette and colleagues in several papers have used the term *antibubble* to characterize bear markets with certain mathematical properties.

[17] "FDIC Bursts Housing Bubble Theory," *The Atlanta Journal-Constitution*, June 28, 2005.

[18] Mayer, Chris and Todd Sinai, "Bubble Trouble? Not Likely." *The Wall Street Journal*, September 19, 2005.

[19] Cassidy, John, "Interview with Eugene Fama," *The New Yorker*, January 13, 2010.

[20] Shiller, Robert J., "Bubble Spotting," *Project Syndicate*, March 22, 2011.

[21] Nocera, Joe, "Poking Holes in a Theory on Markets," *The New York Times*, June 6, 2009.

[22] Posner, K., "Why Asset Bubbles Will Always Surprise Us," *Harvard Business Review*, June 16, 2010.

[23] Prechter, R., *The Elliott Wave Theorist*, November 1982, p. 3. Reprinted in the Appendix to *Elliott Wave Principle*.

[24] Prechter, R., "A Rising Tide: The Case for Wave V in the Dow Jones Industrial Average," *The Elliott Wave Theorist*, April 1983, pp. 2, 3, 6. Reprinted in the Appendix to *Elliott Wave Principle* and in *Conquer the Crash*.

[25] Prechter, R., "The Superbull Market of the '80s: Has the Last Wild Ride Really Begun?" *The Elliott Wave Theorist*, August 1983, pp. 3, 5. Reprinted in the Appendix to *Elliott Wave Principle*.

[26] Elliotticians have identified the end of wave IV in nominal prices as occurring in 1974, as marked in Figure 4, or in 1982. The year 1982 unequivocally marked the low in the inflation-adjusted DJIA (Dow/PPI), as shown in charts throughout this book.

[27] Vogel, Harold L., *Financial Market Bubbles and Crashes*, Cambridge University Press, 2009, pp. 94-5.

[28] Prechter, R., "Bulls, Bears and Manias," *The Elliott Wave Theorist* Special Report, May 21, 1997. Reprinted (2002) *View from the Top of the Grand Supercycle*, Gainesville, GA: New Classics Library, pp. 4-21.

[29] Posner, K., "Why Asset Bubbles Will Always Surprise Us," *Harvard Business Review*, June 16, 2010.

Chapter 24

Contrasting STF with Certain Tenets of the Austrian School

Robert R. Prechter

Chapters 13 and 19 of this book necessarily address theories that expressly relate to finance. There is little need for detailed critiques of various theories of economics, because they share the same grand error of equating economic and financial markets, an absolutist position of which Part III of this book aimed to dispose.

Some challenges to the socionomic theory of finance from proponents of the Austrian school of economic thought, however, have prompted the discussion in this chapter. They go like this: "Socionomics says that economic decisions are objective and financial decisions subjective, but the Austrian school teaches that both types of decisions are subjective." (In opposing disagreement, the efficient market hypothesis implies that all such decisions are objective.) "Socionomics says that economic decisions are rational and financial decisions are pre-rational, but Austrian economics holds that both types of decisions are rational." And finally, "Socionomics says that context matters to how human minds approach the pricing of markets, but Austrian economics says that psychology is irrelevant." My responses below are primarily intended not to challenge a venerable economic theory but to defend certain central socionomic concepts and hypotheses as they explicitly conflict, or appear to conflict, with that theory.

Points of Compatibility and Difference between the Austrian School and Socionomics

In concert with Austrian theorists, socionomists agree that humans are not exclusively reactive but substantially active organisms (see Chapters 32 and 33). We also agree (along with all modern economists) that values are not intrinsic to items. Most compatibly, socionomic theory augments Austrians' scholarly case that authoritarian meddling cannot improve economies. Socionomics holds that authorities have no control over waves of social mood; rather, waves of social mood substantially govern authorities' actions (see Chapters 3, 17, 23, 25 and 28).

On the other hand, the Austrian school makes at least three theoretical claims that are at odds with socionomic theory:

(1) All values, including economic and financial, are subjectively, not objectively determined.

(2) People's decisions and actions in pursuing economic and financial values are always rational.

(3) Psychology has no place in the discussion of economics.

Let's address these assertions one by one.

The Subjective Theory of Value

Austrians propose that individuals trade goods with each other to mutual advantage because their values differ. So far, so good. But then they declare that all individuals' needs and desires are subjective and assert that objective valuation is impossible.

Confusion arises from the fact that Austrian theorists equate *objective* with *intrinsic* and *subjective* with *personal*. They would say, for example, "It is objectively true that an item is shaped as a cube, but it is only subjectively true that the item is valuable to Jim." A socionomist would say, "It is intrinsically (and objectively) true that an item is shaped as a cube, and it is personally (and objectively) true that the item is valuable to Jim."

In one sense, the rift here is a matter of semantics. But semantics matter, because they can either aid or inhibit understanding.

Available definitions of the terms *objective* and *subjective* differ substantially. Some of them fit the Austrians' use of the former term as meaning intrinsic and the latter term as meaning non-intrinsic and/or personal. But most definitions get to the heart of the matter by defining subjectivity as a quality attaching to a judgment that is "based on feelings or opinions rather than facts" (Merriam-Webster, #2) and as a mental bias that interferes with assessing truth due to "placing excessive emphasis on one's own moods, attitudes, opinions, etc." (dictionary.com, #3). The most useful definition available with respect to formulating a theory of thought relating to economics and finance is the #1 definition offered at OxfordDictionaries.com: "*Objective*: of a judgment not influenced by personal feelings or opinions in considering and representing facts."

The same dictionary offers a slightly problematic definition of *subjective* as being "Based on or influenced by personal feelings, tastes, or opinions," which is incomplete compared to its definition of *objective* and clouds the picture by adding the term *tastes*, many of which are factual attributes uninfluenced by feelings. But the dictionary immediately corrects any misunderstanding of the term by relating its two usage examples precisely to the task of assessing facts. It offers these treatments: "his views are highly subjective" and "there is always the danger of making a subjective judgment." The term *highly* implies a deviation from facts, and the term *danger* explicitly places the dictionary's definition in the service of recognizing the value of a truth claim, compatibly with its definition of *objective*.

From these formulations, we may construct two consistent definitions:

Objective: of a judgment not influenced by personal feelings or opinions in considering and representing facts.

Subjective: of a judgment influenced by personal feelings or opinions in considering and representing facts.

In other words, being objective means *assessing facts without interference from feelings*, whereas being subjective means *allowing feelings to interfere with the assessment of facts*.

Austrians' use of the terms *subjective* and *objective* is internally consistent, but it confuses crucial issues. Socionomics' use of the terms is likewise internally consistent, and it *elucidates* crucial issues.

Robert Murphy[1] discussed an example offered by Murray Rothbard in *Man, Economy and State* (pp. 105-110) showing that a horse might be worth 100 fish to Smith but only 80 fish to Johnson. Therefore, he concluded, the values of the horse and the fish are subjective. By the best definition of the term, however, the values of the horse and fish, while personal, are not subjective. The statements, "This horse is worth 100 fish to Smith" and "The same horse is worth 80 fish to Johnson" are objectively true *facts* based on the utility of the horse to each person and perhaps the satisfaction that horse ownership brings to each person. In order for someone to maximize the utility of his resources—to maximize their usefulness to him in obtaining goals and achieving satisfaction—he makes an objective determination of an item's relative value to him and acts accordingly.

Murphy wrote, "Because economic value is *subjective*, it is possible for the men to exchange some of their property and both walk away with the 'more valuable' item."[2] It is better to say, "Because economic value is *personal*, it is possible for the men to exchange some of their property and both walk away with the 'more valuable' item." He added, "This would not be true for *objective, intrinsic* properties of goods." Observe the conflation of *objective* with *intrinsic*, as if they are synonyms or requisite cousins. They are not. By the most useful definitions, these terms have different meanings: Items possess intrinsic qualities, while a person makes objective judgments.

Simply musing on the above example reveals that subjectivity is not the determinant of value for either person. Suppose it is summertime and Smith and Johnson live in a remote area where there will be no cold storage or transport available for fish for a week. Now how much are the fish worth relative to the horse? The fish are worth virtually nothing, to each person, for an objective reason: The fish are doomed to spoil. Such facts change individuals' valuations without interference from feelings and opinions, fitting the very definition of objective.

The personal nature of values does not banish objectivity as defined above. Socionomics expressly recognizes (see Chapter 13) that *one's own values* provide a solid basis for objective decision-making in the economic marketplace. Using personal values to judge the attractiveness of various prices for goods and services allows a consumer to order his or her purchasing preferences objectively.

Personal, objective judgment is based not only on some calculable, practical utility to a person's survival needs but also on individual tastes. "John hates the taste of broccoli" is a *personal* judgment but also an *objective* judgment not influenced by emotions or opinions but rather determined objectively by the reaction of John's taste buds to broccoli.

Suppose Jim declares to the world, "Broccoli tastes good." His statement is neither *universally* true nor *intrinsically* true, which is the Austrians' point (as well as ours), but neither is it subjective. His statement is objectively true, because his emotions and opinions did not interfere with his assessment of a fact. His friend John's statement to the world, "Broccoli tastes bad," is equally objectively true. Does broccoli taste good? Yes. Does broccoli taste bad? Yes. These are facts.

At the aggregate level, the availability of broccoli and the market price for broccoli are objectively determined by the extent of some consumers' desire to eat it and some producers' opportunity to make a profit providing it. Since virtually all individuals judge goods and services this way, economic market prices are objectively determined. That's why they make sense relative to each other. It's also the reason they are stable.

One cannot say the same thing about statements influenced by feelings and opinions. "Jim communicates with the dead" and "John does not communicate with the dead" are not equally factual statements. Since no adequate evidence indicates that the living can communicate with the dead, feelings and opinions drive the first statement, making it, to use the language of the examples quoted above, highly and perhaps even dangerously subjective.

On the other hand, the statement, "Jim thinks he communicates with the dead," is a fact. It might be useful in helping a university administrator make an objective decision about whether to hire Jim as a physics professor.

Austrians assert that subjectivity is required for people to trade. What they mean is that people would not trade an item if it possessed a specific, intrinsic value that everyone recognized. Along with all modern economists, we agree on this point. People must have differing desires of ownership—in both economics and finance—in order to trade. Based on our more useful definitions, however, whether those differing desires are objective or subjective is irrelevant to whether trade can occur. Under socionomic theory, objective decision-making is paramount in economic valuation while subjective decision-making is paramount in financial valuation, yet trade occurs under both conditions. Individuals can value an item differently by either objective or subjective means and still agree to trade. Thus, neither objectivity nor subjectivity is a requisite for trading.

Applying the term *subjective* identically to economics and finance, as required under Austrian theory, obscures an important truth that socionomics brings to light: Economic valuing by producers and consumers is based on each person's known personal values, whereas financial valuing by speculators is based on guessing other people's unknown future actions. Socionomics' careful distinction between the mostly objective decision-making attending contexts of certainty vs. the mostly subjective decision-making attending contexts of uncertainty is a useful construct.

Nor can we equate the two contexts by proposing that unconscious impulses and social mood are facts that a rational decider takes into account. In the aggregate, decision-makers in financial markets never take them into account, so financial and economic pricing still fundamentally differ. Individual speculators who do take them into account fully admit to the subjectivity of aggregate pricing.

Another Questionable Claim of Pure Rationality

Austrians state categorically that the mere fact that humans act presupposes that each person employs an internal value scale.[3] Some people's highly variable actions indicate that they often fail to stick to any particular set of value relations, so Austrians hypothesize that value scales can change at any time, even moment to moment. An infinitely plastic individual value scale, however, seems indistinguishable from a non-existent one.

Mises argued[4] that all actions taken by a person are rational even if they routinely conflict with one another. He reasoned that because a person's actions cannot be simultaneous, his acting one way one minute and an opposing way the next can be considered consistently rational under the presumption that his value scale changed prior to each action. Mises was, in effect, saying, "You think he's not rational? Prove it. I say he is simply shifting his value scale." Like economists' declaration that every trade in a financial market occurs at equilibrium (see Chapter 12), this is a non-falsifiable claim. To maintain it, Austrians explicitly avoid addressing the question of why value scales shift. Socionomics resolves the problem by proposing the ultimately falsifiable claim (see Chapters 11, 12 and 13) that in contexts of certainty humans tend to judge values rationally, whereas in contexts of uncertainty they tend to shift their values non-rationally in accordance with herding dynamics and fluctuations in social mood.

Austrian theorists make another categorical claim: The very fact that humans act means that they act rationally, because every act implies a desire, and every act to fulfill a desire is rational. So, there is no such thing as irrational human action. Mises asserted, "To apply the concept of *rational* or *irrational* to the ultimate ends chosen is nonsensical."[5] According to the thesaurus, *nonsensical* is one of the synonyms for *irrational*. Under the Austrian construction, a person who insists on using the term *irrational* cannot be irrational; but he is nonsensical.

Mises did not address the question of whether *thoughts* that lead to action can be irrational. He left this question to the field of psychology. If thoughts can be irrational, then under Austrian theory irrational thoughts can lead to rational actions. If thoughts cannot be irrational, then under Austrian theory *rational* and *irrational* have no meaning. *Rational* simply means that a person acted, directly neutering the value of the first term and indirectly neutering the value of the second. In searching for some kind of meaning for the term *irrational*, Mises equated *irrational* with *inconceivable* and wrote, "The ultimate given may be called an irrational fact,"[6] thereby directly neutering the value of the term *irrational*. (The term as he used it can only mean *inconceivable*, as otherwise the construction, "irrational fact," would present a contradiction.) He used the term *rational* but avoided using the term *irrational* to refer to anything going on in the human mind or with respect to human action. Austrian economists' definitions of these words are not useful. They serve only to ban one of the terms and turn the other one into a tautology.

Though each human may take action for the purpose of fulfilling a desire, it is useful to distinguish qualitatively between rational actions taken after due consideration of their ramifications (errors in thought notwithstanding) and irrational actions taken on unconsidered whim or impulse that a modicum of consideration would have revealed as counter to the acting person's higher-ranking desires. Let's explore the usefulness of this distinction.

If a person were to choose to shoot as many people as possible in a movie theater without considering the ultimate ramifications, he would certainly be acting to satisfy a desire. We may infer from his later "not guilty" plea in court, however, that this momentary desire was contrary to his higher-ranking desire to live. Austrians would say that because he took the two actions at different times, both of them were rational, as each action aimed to satisfy the desire of the moment. In their terms, his "value scale" simply shifted. Thinkers operating outside this template, however, would discern the following nuance: If this person considered his entire value scale and consciously valued the personal satisfaction he thought his violent act would produce above the risk of his own death at the hands of the state, he acted rationally. If he acted impulsively, *without* considering his entire value scale, he acted irrationally because he neglected to act in accordance with his higher value: to stay alive.

Be that as it may, socionomic theory (thankfully) does not depend on such arguments and does not even enter this particular debate. It mostly avoids the term *irrational* with all its baggage. Socionomics does, however, differentiate between two fundamental types of motivation and behavior.

The terms we use to distinguish conscious choices from unconscious impulses are *rational* and *pre-rational*. Neither term is a substitute for simply thinking or simply acting. When we use these terms, we mean something important. The terms *rational* and *pre-rational* refer to the mental source of a person's motivation, whether that motivation arises primarily in the neocortex or in the more primitive areas of the brain. In the former case, the person is thinking consciously in a context of relative certainty, and his brain applies reason to a task. In the latter case, the person is thinking unconsciously in a context of relative uncertainty, and his brain applies impulsivity to a task. In the former case—while anyone can make mistakes—the person is employing *appropriate* means to the task. In the latter case, the person at times may be employing *inappropriate* means to the task, which is precisely the case in financial markets, where the herding impulse is counterproductive to ultimate success.

Rothbard correctly stated, "all action involves exchange—an exchange of one state of affairs, X, for Y, which the actor anticipates will be a more satisfactory one (and therefore higher on his value scale)."[7] It may seem, therefore, that a speculator who exchanges money for a bet that he *antici-pates* will bring him more money is acting rationally. If his anticipation has a pre-rational origin, however, he is acting non-rationally.

Mises argued that once a person chooses an end, on whatever basis, all decisions he makes toward attaining that end are unavoidably rational. He wrote, "Human action is necessarily *always rational*. ...However unfath-omable the depths may be from which an impulse or instinct emerges, the means which man chooses for its satisfaction are determined by a rational consideration of expense and success. ...The ultimate end of action is al-ways the satisfaction of some desires of the acting man."[8] This formulation applies fairly well to economics but not to finance. The desire a speculator wishes to satisfy is monetary gain or perhaps bragging rights, and herding leads to the satisfaction of neither desire. Few speculators (see Chapter 19) rationally consider expense and success, either. It is not that they do a bad job of it; they don't do it at all. As a result, speculating rarely achieves, especially over time, the rational end of the acting person (see Chapter 17). Speculators rarely reason but often rationalize feelings derived from shared moods and herding impulses, and the typical end of speculative ac-tion is expensive failure and psychic misery, which speculators inflict upon themselves time and again.

The Austrian school, in line with neoclassical economic theory and EMH, explicitly ascribes full rationality to financial actions. "When a specu-lator goes to the stock exchange," wrote Mises, he uses "his own judgment concerning the future development of prices. ...Whether or not he clings to [a] plan, his actions are rational [because] the speculator is firm in his intention to make profits and avoid losses."[9] Yet no matter how *firm* a specu-lator's intention is to succeed, and no matter how smart he is (see Chapter 17) or how diligently he pursues his goal, none of it helps him. He rarely figures out why success eludes him, because the reasons for his decisions and failures are imperceptible moods and herding impulses; and even with special knowledge of their existence he rarely avoids or overcomes them, and even if he manages to do so to a significant degree, he rarely conquers the puzzle of properly anticipating the results of others' pre-rational impulses so he can make money from them.

A rational consumer can use a set of facts, including personal tastes, to determine objectively his or her valuation of a good or service. But no speculator can apply such facts to determine objectively his or her valu-ation of a stock certificate, because the certificate has no personal utility to anyone and no ability to satisfy personal tastes. A rational producer or consumer can also use information objectively to determine an attractive or unattractive price for selling or buying, respectively, a good or service based on his or her own values. But no rational speculator can use information objectively to determine an attractive or unattractive price for a share of stock, because personal tastes are irrelevant to the task, and production costs, corporate earnings, dividends, book values, bond yield/stock yield ratios, supply, demand (properly defined; see Chapter 12) and the prices of other investment items have no consistent relationship to the price of stock shares, either individually or in the aggregate, leaving no basis for objective valuation. So, while producers and consumers may base their economic decisions on personal value scales, value scales are inapplicable to investment items, making speculators' decisions no more anchored than feathers in a hurricane. The inability of speculators to apply value scales objectively places them in a context of uncertainty in which they fall under the influence of herding and social mood, which produce only pre-rational, subjective valuation. Even for some intermediary markets, such as commodities (see Chapters 14 and 22), Elliott waves are the primary determinant of pricing; production costs are only secondarily relevant to pricing; supply and demand do not regulate price changes but respond to them; and such factors lag rather than lead prices; all of which indicate that pre-rational herding is in charge of the pricing process. To accommodate this process, individual speculators allow their impulses, moods, fears, hopes, whims, rationalizations, feelings, emotions and opinions to color their assessment of facts, perfectly fitting the most useful definition of the term *subjective.* Whereas "I should/should not buy broccoli" is an objective decision based on rational thought, "I should/should not buy stocks" is usually a subjective decision based on the rationalization of pre-rational thought.

Even if a speculator's decision-making is based on definite criteria, it is not necessarily rational. Definite criteria differ from objective criteria, because definite criteria can be arbitrary. Some advisors, for instance, recommend a 10% loss point as a stop on positions. It is a definite criterion, but it is completely arbitrary. Why is 9.9% irrelevant but 10% crucial? There is no objective answer. As another example, if a speculator were to employ a specific formula to determine absolute or relative P/E ratios among stocks (Mises' "plan") and use it as a basis for choosing among them, the market doesn't know or care about his reasoning, because reality does not conform to it. Other speculators may blithely ignore P/E, making it irrelevant; earnings reports lag the market, making that basis for valuation chronically late; *expected* earnings are especially subject to optimism, pessimism and herding; and speculators can abandon their previously selected criteria due to later impulses to herd; all of which can neuter supposedly definite bases for valuation.

Since using rationality to value stocks is impossible personally, it is impossible collectively. By default, prices of investment items in the financial marketplace are determined primarily by two non-rational factors—herding and social mood.

One might argue that the value of an investment item to a speculator is the expected return that the buyer attaches to it, making the act of speculation rational. In economic markets, this formulation works, because a specific good purchased by a consumer is intimately and rationally connected to the expectation of satisfaction that the consumer attaches to it. But when an expectation of satisfaction arises in a speculator's head as a manifestation of positive social mood, it does so pre-rationally and independently of the investment item he ultimately buys to express his positive mood. He simply looks around for a referent for his optimistic belief and finds one. Consumers' specific expectations, moreover, are routinely and quickly satisfied once they purchase a good or service. In contrast, once an optimistic speculator buys an investment item on the expectation that its price will rise, his expectation is rarely satisfied; it just keeps on existing. He believes it will go higher, he believes it will go higher, he hopes it will go higher, and he hopes it will go higher, until he stops believing and hoping. The reason for the difference is that the investment item has no personal value to the buyer that he can rationally pursue. Participants in the market are not shifting their value scales; there are no applicable value scales.

One might propose that a person conscious of the fact that he speculates because it gives him a pleasing thrill is behaving rationally. If this were unalterably true, then his decisions to speculate would be rational. But in real life it is never true. The goal of speculating is to make money, and making money provides a pleasing thrill. But most people lose money when they speculate (see Chapter 17), and losing money is a crushing event, making them feel terrible. Deciding repeatedly to speculate anyway is a non-rational act, propelled by unconscious herding impulses that misinterpret the financial market environment as one in which herding will continually lead toward sustenance or away from danger.

Rational *and* Subjective?

Austrians say that both economic and financial items are priced fully rationally and fully subjectively, and that while decisions to buy and sell these items are rational, no rational person can value anything objectively.

The idea of *rational subjectivity,* or *subjective rationality*, while internally consistent within Austrian theory, is more usefully viewed—under our preferred definitions—as a contradiction.

Neoclassical economic theory, EMH and Austrian theory all assert that both economic and financial decisions are rational, a claim socionomics vigorously challenges. Thereafter, the first two theories consider all economic and financial values to be objective, while Austrian theory considers all economic and financial values to be subjective. These are comparable errors, merely at opposite poles. Socionomics employs all four terms—*objective, subjective, rational* and *non-rational*—in a comprehensive construct that is more consistent, accurate and useful.

Is Psychology Inapplicable to the Field of Economics?

Neoclassical economists and proponents of EMH avoid the subject of psychology, as it doesn't factor into their mechanistic formulas. Austrian theorists go so far as to explicitly ban the topic of psychology from any discussion of economics. They limit the study of economics to praxeology, the study of human action as such, without considering motives. Mises wrote, "The field of our science is human action, not the psychological events which result in an action."[10] Rothbard confirmed, "a problem important in the field of psychology may have no significance in the realm of praxeology, to which economics belongs."[11] He summarized their point of view by saying that psychology is applicable only to "*Why* man chooses various ends,"[12] not *that* they do.

Mises took this stance partly because he was positioning praxeology as a counter to "instinct-psychology," which he defined as a school of thought alleging that all human actions are due to "innate forces, impulses, instincts, [urges] and dispositions which are not open to any rational elucidation."[13] Socionomics likewise dispenses with the point of view described by Mises, because it is another misguided attempt at absolutism. Being contextual in nature, socionomic theory recognizes that human beings have both a rational capacity and pre-rational impulses, and it postulates contexts in which each type of thinking tends to dominate. Contrary to Mises' strange assertion that non-rational impulses "are not open to any rational elucidation," socionomists most certainly do see them as open to rational elucidation, a purpose this book has striven to serve.

At the outset, it seems to me that banning psychology from the discussion is an arbitrary dictum. Ignoring psychology may help keep an economic theory neat, but psychology pertains mightily to the real world of human activity. Psychology may not apply—directly, anyway—to the fields of mathematics, physics and chemistry, but it does apply to human behavior, a roof under which finance and economics reside.

Further, it seems to me that Austrians' statements that economic transactions are rational and that psychology is irrelevant are contradictory, since rationality is a psychological disposition. They would surely dispute this depiction. But there is a bigger problem:

By expressly banning the discussion of psychology from economics and finance, Austrians have erected a blind that makes it impossible for them to distinguish between the differing bases for economic and financial pricing. A person's psychological orientation—which is dependent upon the context of relative certainty or uncertainty—creates the difference. As articulated in Chapter 13, the "end" of economic and financial transacting is the same: to survive and thrive (however one may personally define *thrive*). Psychology doesn't matter to that observation. Where psychology matters is in the means a person employs to achieve an end. Herding pre-rationally and unconsciously in financial markets differs substantially from maximizing personal satisfaction rationally and consciously in economic markets. Mises stated of praxeology, "The only standard which it applies is whether or not the means chosen are fit for the attainment of the ends aimed at."[14] But this is a layered standard. If one were to say, "The speculator's end is to obtain a bet on future prices," then the standard is met. On the other hand, if one were to say, "The speculator's end is to make money," then the standard is not met, because the means he uses are unfit for attaining the desired end and thus will ultimately fail him. Nor is the expression that meets the standard on equal footing with the one that doesn't. The former expression makes the standard tautological, whereas the latter tells us something useful.

Finally, Mises' use of the phrase, "the means *chosen*," assumes that choice is applicable to begin with. But the difference in the means employed in an economic vs. a financial context is not a matter of choice. Socionomics explicitly recognizes that herding in financial markets is impulsive and automatic, a mental default, not a chosen means to an end. Speculators do not choose to herd; on the contrary, they can't help herding. When a snake lunges at a squirrel, the squirrel's reflexes are so fast that it can often leap out of the way just in time. In the same way, when a human brain perceives a situation as requiring a herding response, it simply orders it. It is not a "means chosen," even by the brain. The unconscious mind considers no other options. Mises' standard is useful here, though, because the means employed by the brain thwart success in finance, making them emphatically *not* "fit for the ends aimed at." Rather, they consistently thwart the end's achievement. Both the reason and the conclusion are that the means are non-rationally determined.

Not just Austrian theory but all established theories of economics either explicitly equate or fail to distinguish between economic markets and financial markets. By incorporating psychology, socionomics is able to offer a more encompassing view of human behavior as it relates to economic and financial markets and more broadly to all types of decision-making. Psychology informs these observations and should not be banned from the discussion.

Mises wrote, "Whereas praxeology says that the goal of an action is to remove a certain uneasiness, instinct-psychology says it is the satisfaction of an instinctive urge."[15] Under socionomic theory, the first explanation applies better to economic decisions, while the second explanation applies better to financial decisions. Socionomics accommodates this more discriminating observation because it is contextual (see Chapter 32).

Is Reconciliation Possible?

A subscriber of mine and proponent of the Austrian school wrote to me as follows: "My own view is that socionomics and [Austrian theory] are completely compatible. Social mood determines a large part of human valuations, and rational actors strive to get what they desire." I understand the basis of this construction but do not accept it. When people get what they desire time and again by acting rationally in economic markets but careen towards destruction time after time in financial markets, it seems to me that in the latter context something other than rational striving is going on.

REFERENCES

[1] Murphy, Robert P., "Subjective-Value Theory," *Mises Daily*, May 30, 2011.

[2] *Ibid.*

[3] Rothbard, Murray N., *Man, Economy, and State*, Los Angeles: Nash Publishing, 1962/1970, pp. 260, 308.

[4] Mises, Ludwig von, *Human Action*, New Haven: Yale University Press, 1949; 3rd Revised Edition, Henry Regnery Company, Chicago, 1963, p. 884.

[5] Mises, pp. 102-103.

[6] Mises, p. 21.

[7] Rothbard, p. 20.

[8] Mises, p. 15.

[9] Mises, p. 104.

[10] Mises, p. 11.

[11] Rothbard, p. 308.

[12] Mises, p. 16

[13] Rothbard, p. 74.

[14] Mises, p. 21.

[15] Mises, p. 15.

Chapter 25

Contrasting STF with Keynesian and Monetarist Technocratic Theories

Robert R. Prechter

Inconsistency in Reigning Schools of Economic Thought

Keynesian and monetarist theories have been highly influential. Yet they fall short of being coherent due to internal inconsistencies.

As a seasoned speculator as much as an academic economist, John Maynard Keynes correctly recognized the importance of psychology to financial markets and wrote of financial markets' "instability" due to the "spontaneous optimism" and "pessimism"[1] of crowds and the resulting fragility of their convictions. On the other hand, as a technocratic thinker he championed the idea that if the government spent money and dictated low interest rates it could foster perpetually full employment. So, while acknowledging the existence of non-rational, non-mechanistic, "animal spirits,"[2] he also believed that his policy prescriptions could motivate rational reactions by mechanical means. While proposing humans to be unpredictably active organisms in his commentary, he proposed them as predictably reactive organisms in his prescriptions. These are incompatible ideas.

Central bankers are mired in the same mix of conflicting ideas. Speaking about financial markets, Alan Greenspan theorized, "Doubtless, valuations are shaped in part, perhaps in large part, by the economic process itself. But history suggests that they also reflect waves of optimism and pessimism that can be touched off by seemingly small exogenous events."[3] In other words, the "economic process" determines values *objectively*, except when it doesn't, in which case values are determined *subjectively* by "waves of optimism and pessimism," which are triggered *mechanically* by "exogenous events." He further jumbled the ideas of endogenous process vs. rational reaction to exogenous events when he offered this humorously self-contradictory assessment: "Bubbles have to run their course. Bubbles are functions of unchangeable human nature. The obvious question is how to manage them."[4] His successors (see Chapter 5) have offered similar assessments.

The widely accepted view of markets and economies—that they are a tangle of straightforward exogenous cause and rational reaction conflated with endogenously regulated, self-propelling processes that are nevertheless mechanically triggered and somehow manageable by authorities—does not present a coherent picture.

Employing similarly incompatible views, founding monetarist Milton Friedman courageously championed free markets in his game-changing "Free to Choose" book and television series, yet he simultaneously offered guidelines for how central bank monopolies, established and maintained by government force, should operate. If one holds the principle that free markets are beneficial, it is contradictory to endorse the idea that the market for money should be under authoritarian control.

Eclectic stances such as these make Keynes' general theory (see also Chapter 33) and the monetarists' body of work internally and metatheoretically inconsistent. Socionomics consciously strives to be internally, externally and metatheoretically consistent (see Chapters 32 and 33).

Socionomic Causality Interferes with Technocratic Prescriptions

Socionomic theory has two things to say about technocratic prescriptions: (1) They can't work. (2) Even if they could work, social mood would prevent authorities from using them consistently in the prescribed manner.

Monetarists believe that absent a fluctuating money supply the entire economy would be inherently stable and function at equilibrium. While manipulated shifts in the money supply do disrupt economies, their lack would hardly serve to eradicate dynamic trends in economic growth and contraction, for which waves of unconscious social mood are responsible.

Socionomics is consistent in observing that all societies, groups and organizations—including central banks and governments (see Chapters 3, 17 and 28)—are subject to waves of social mood and prone to herding. No amount of central planning or policy actions can neuter this fact or change it. On the contrary, such machinations tend to play right into the imperative of the waves.

Some Keynesian economists have charged that efficient-market theorists were responsible for the crisis of 2008 because their belief in perfect market rationality kept them from taking measures to prevent the implosion. Some Austrian economists, on the other hand, have accused Keynesians of being responsible for the crisis of 2008 because they championed easy credit and therefore encouraged the debt buildup that created the preconditions for a crisis in the first place. Socionomists have an entirely different perspective. We say that waves of social mood do what they do, and behaviors of authorities informed by various schools of economic thought fit right into them. Watching authorities' shenanigans from a socionomic perspective is somewhat like watching mice respond to manipulated conditions in a lab while under the illusion that they are in charge.

False Premises Underlie Technocrats' Economic Policy Prescriptions

Metatheoretical inconsistency and socionomic causality are not the only problems with technocratic ideas. They are based on some false premises as well.

Monetarists, for example, have proposed an optimum quantity of money and an optimum rate of monetary inflation. There are no such things. Prices naturally adjust to the quantity of money so that total goods match total accounting units. Perpetual base-money inflation causes resources to be wasted in continually making otherwise unnecessary price adjustments.

Many economic theorists claim that demand drives an economy. But demand is a given, and it is infinite. What drives economies is production and trade. These factors are not givens, and they are easily hampered, often in ways that technocratic program designers fail to consider.

Conventional economists also believe that credit fuels economic expansion, so they think using force to provide more of it is a good thing. This is an error that socionomic theory can elucidate. Economic growth and credit expansion go hand in hand when they happen naturally as a result of a positive trend in social mood; so do their joint contraction along with a negative trend in social mood. Economists have improperly inferred from the positive correlation between these two variables that credit change is a cause and GDP change is an effect. Put simply, they believe that expanding credit causes booms and that contracting credit causes busts. If that were so, they would be correct in assuming that using force to encourage the use of credit would produce perpetual economic growth.

But the true cause of the correlation between changes in the economy and credit is a hidden variable: social mood. As mood becomes more positive, some people expand their businesses while other people extend more credit or take on more debt, both sides feeling increasingly confident that the debt will be repaid. That is why the two trends go together. We made the same essential point with respect to stock market trends and reelection outcomes (see *Socionomic Causality in Politics*, 2017): It's not A causing B or vice versa but hidden variable C regulating them both.

Economies expand and contract naturally, with or without technocratic intrusion. From 1836 to 1921, the U.S. economy expanded, contracted and recovered a dozen times without government or central-bank intervention, and that period sported the nation's fastest overall economic growth.

The entire *stimulus* metaphor so popular among economists is an illusion. Authorities can play into waves of social mood, but they cannot augment them, dampen them or alter them. Nor can they stimulate an economy through any of the means available to them; only market-inspired production and trade can do that.

An economy may happen to expand naturally at the same time that technocrats are using force to manufacture credit and encourage indebtedness, but it will not expand because of it. Sometimes it appears that demand-stimulation policies are generating prosperity. It can happen for long periods of time during a trend toward more positive social mood. But in such cases the two activities are merely coincident. When mood turns toward the negative, the pretty word *credit* becomes the ugly word *debt*, and the economy contracts as it always has. The implosion of 2006-2009 is only the most recent example.

As related in Chapter 40, in a moment of despair the IMF outright admitted that its decades-long policy of lending to credit-poor governments and individuals had only made things worse. Such policies' doom to failure is not just a technical matter of authorities being unable to grasp labyrinthine complexities—known as the "calculation problem"—or being blind to negative effects and unintended consequences, although these are important aspects of the issue. The problem is a deeper one of theoretical error, which cannot be alleviated with smarter planners and faster computer processing.

The wrong paradigm—mechanics—and the wrong model—exogenous cause—have inspired strange claims. Keynesian economists deem currency debasement a stimulus, but it's not; it's just currency debasement, which benefits some people and harms others. Likewise they deem government spending a stimulus, but it's not; it merely forcibly transfers spending decisions from some people to others, for no net benefit. These economic theorists have even taken a practice that anyone can see is dangerous for an individual and reversed its implication for society to the point of elevating it to a panacea. They admit that their claim that heavy debt is bad for individuals but good for society is paradoxical. But whereas socionomics' exposure of numerous paradoxes is due to a fundamental insight, the claim of enlightened irony in this case is due to ignorance. You need not deconstruct the acrobatic reasoning behind their claim to see that it is false. Just witness the next black swan in the debt markets.

Because the theories underlying technocratic policies are principle-free and therefore incoherent, technocrats cannot predict the outcomes of their own policies. As a result, advocates for intervention keep resorting to ad-hoc shifts in strategy. The financial and economic meltdown of 2006-2009 revealed that the credit-pushers had no idea how much instability their programs had fostered. In 2014, economists at the Bank of International Settlements admitted as much by switching stances 180 degrees to argue that government should stop focusing on moderating the business cycle—since its failure to do so in 2008 was so obvious—and start focusing on "preventing excessive debt."[5] These technocrats are no less oblivious now to what the consequences of their policy prescriptions will be than they were before. Their proposal to make governments responsible for preventing excessive indebtedness would work about as well as hiring Bacchus to prevent excessive partying. Technocratic economists' eclectic theories lead them repeatedly to the bizarre position of ignoring psychology while simultaneously trying to control it.

Political Hearts, Not Economics Hearts

Many economists advocate policy interventions. Their arguments are mainly over which ones are preferable and how big the programs should be. Such advice is popular with politicians, who welcome an intellectual basis for striking a pose and a pretext for exercising power for their own benefit.

Because of the serial dominance of Marxist, Keynesian and monetarist ideas over the past century, "The rap on economists, only somewhat exaggerated, is that they are overconfident, unrealistic, and political."[6] Socionomists, in contrast, tend to be cautiously confident, realistic and apolitical. Like EMH, socionomics may even be considered anti-political.

Socionomics implies that the economy is not a machine as technocrats would have it, a garden as socialists would have it, or a resource to be plundered as crony capitalists and their partners in government would have it. It is an ecology. Any attempt to tinker with the machine, force a garden into place or plunder economic resources disturbs the human ecology's natural flourishing. Machines wear out, gardens disintegrate, and plundered resources are used up; these circumstances have no other end results. An ecology, in contrast, arises to endure. To thrive, it should be left alone.

The situation will remain bleak as long as economists believe that authorities can generate prosperity by twiddling credit dials and fabricating money spigots. Yet there is reason for hope.

Modern Technocratic Theories Are Lame Ducks

Technocratic theories are not seminal contributions to economic thought but mere policy prescriptions, applicable only so long as there are government-created banking monopolies. When central banks go away, so will these ideas.

The Second Bank of the United States was chartered in 1816, and it was dissolved in 1836. One must delve into archives and blow dust from book covers to locate the fervently argued rationales that sprang up first to justify and then to direct that institution. Who reads them now? Nobody.

As argued in Chapter 13 of *Pioneering Studies in Socionomics*, social mood trends seem to direct when central banks come into being. Social mood trends should likewise help usher some or all of them out of existence. When might it happen?

The influence of technocratic ideas is currently at its greatest ever, not only throughout the chambers of central banks and governments but also within the economics profession. Strictly based on the socionomic idea of fluctuating social trends (see Chapter 21), we can anticipate that the influence of such ideas will wane, probably to the point of being discredited. The emergence of virtual currencies and middleman-free lending online, along with traces of renewed respect for gold, may be early hints at a new future. The very notion of central banking may well be facing end-times.

Eternal economic truths endure, but policy prescriptions die with the institutions they serve. When central banks go away, there will be no need for books, papers and articles on the fine points of "managing" the money supply, "stimulating" growth, "adjusting" interest rates, "liquefying" the banking system or "fine-tuning" the economy. There will be no more passionate editorials on the proper speed at which central banks should raid people's savings or endless arguments among economists over whether central banks should raise or lower interest rates. All such discussions will become meaningless, and they will stop. Treatises on these subjects will morph from being symbols of sophisticated economic knowledge to being quaint tokens of a bygone era.

Socionomic theory is different. It is timeless, applying to the past, present and future.

REFERENCES

[1] Keynes, John M., *The General Theory of Employment, Interest and Money*, London: Macmillan, 1936, pp. 161-162.

[2] *Ibid*, p. 156.

[3] Greenspan, Alan, " New Challenges for Monetary Policy," speech to a symposium sponsored by the Federal Reserve Bank of Kansas City in Jackson Hole, Wyoming, August 27, 1999.

[4] Robb, Greg, "Greenspan Says Bubbles Can't Be Stopped Without 'Crunch'," *MarketWatch*, July 24, 2014.

[5] Samuelson, Robert J., "The Business Cycle, RIP?" *The Washington Post*, June 29, 2014.

[6] Coy, Peter, "What Good Are Economists Anyway?" *Business Week*, April 27, 2009.

Part VI:

THE PRIMACY OF SOCIAL MOOD
IN FINANCIAL-MARKET CAUSALITY

Chapter 26

Social Mood Impels Feelings
of Certainty and Uncertainty

Alan Hall

One might think that investors' feelings of certainty and uncertainty about the financial and economic future would be stable or perhaps wax and wane with the extremity of social mood regardless of direction. Prechter observed something different: Investors and market observers tend to perceive the stock market and the economy's future to be far more certain during positive-mood periods than during negative-mood periods. Mood extremity appears to determine the extent of conviction behind the certainty or uncertainty that prevails. As Prechter has put it, the more extreme the positive mood, the more certain investors are that the stock market and the economy's future trends are certain, and the more extreme the negative mood, the more certain they are that their future trends are uncertain.

The Wave Principle of Human Social Behavior (1999) postulated that terms such as *uncertain* and *unpredictable* in financial discussions are often simply code words for *down*.[1] You will observe a phrase pertinent to our observation within the following article, from February 2007:

Toll, Centex, Lennar Join 'Moron' Speculators in Land Grab Bust
In the last three months of 2006, the publicly traded homebuilders were forced to write down the value of their land, a practice mandated by accounting rules. When a company expects to lose money on a budget item such as land, it must account for the loss at that time rather than incurring the losses in the future.

Fort Worth, Texas-based D.R. Horton, the biggest U.S. homebuilder, took inventory impairments and land option write-downs of $270.9 million in fiscal 2006, up from the $17.1 million that it claimed during the prior year.

> Pulte, the second-biggest homebuilder, wrote down $350 mil-
> lion last quarter on the sliding value of land and deposits it won't
> exercise. <u>The unpredictable outlook for land prices is hurting Pulte's
> ability to plan ahead.</u>[2]

Translation: "A bear market began last year." Instead of simply saying so, people asserted that real estate prices had become "unpredictable," whereas before the price peak of 2006 they were presumably predictable. But obviously they weren't, because these analysts never saw the setback coming.

The future of markets—bull or bear—is always unpredictable, so the distinction is nonsense. Nevertheless, from the consistency of conditions under which people express feelings of certainty and uncertainty, we can deduce that, for whatever reason, most humans naturally see uptrends as normal and downtrends as abnormal. So, when the trend of a market or the economy is down, people feel lost, as if laws of the universe had been temporarily suspended.

This tendency reveals one of the great values of understanding the Wave Principle. Trends change at all degrees. Down is just as natural as up. If one can invest for an up market and an expanding economy, why can't one invest for a down market and a contracting economy? There should be no reason why people cannot "plan ahead" when the trend is down just as well as when it is up. Unfortunately, the impulsive adoption of feelings of uncertainty during times of negative social mood impedes people's ability to plan and act in accordance with downtrends and thus may even be among the secondary psychological causes of economic contractions. Understanding socionomics gives us an advantage. We can see that both directions are normal and negotiable, and we can use widespread expressions of certainty or uncertainty as indicators of social mood.

A key subtlety is that actual uncertainty about individuals' personal futures usually does rise when the trend of social mood is negative. As negative mood induces social actions that create stressful conditions, people become objectively less certain about whether they will hold their jobs or be laid off, have enough money to pay rent, be victims of a bank failure or live or die in a war. But these conditions have nothing to do with uncertainty over the future directions of the stock market and the economy.

Researchers have recently developed ways of quantifying people's feelings of uncertainty about the economy. Their statistical data enable us to link changes in the volume of expressions of uncertainty to trends in the stock market, both of which are propelled by changes in social mood.

Let's investigate two measures of perceived economic uncertainty, which, to reiterate, are substantially independent of objective measures of actual economic uncertainty.

1. *The New York Times* Uncertainty Index

Figure 1 plots the Dow Jones Industrial Average against the New York Times Uncertainty Index developed by Alexopoulos and Cohen in their 2009 paper, "Uncertain Times, Uncertain Measures."[3] The vertical black bars represent the total number of articles appearing each month in the *Times* that "contain references to uncertainty and the economy."

Times of positive social-mood trends, prompting rising stock prices, are in white, and times of negative social-mood trends, prompting falling stock prices, are shaded grey. As you can see, positive mood trends tend to coincide with lesser feelings of uncertainty, while negative trends tend to coincide with greater feelings of uncertainty.

More important, the authors confirmed that feelings of uncertainty *precede* economic decline:

> Within the year <u>following</u> [an] uncertainty shock, industrial production, and employment fall, as does our measure of business investment and consumption. ...Changes in the level of uncertainty—especially the type that affects both Main Street and Wall Street—are, in short, a key contributor to business cycles.[4]

Concerning causality, they wrote,

> Some may worry about the direction of causality and thus question the usefulness of our index. That is, do newspaper articles raise the level of uncertainty among the general population or do they merely reflect the temper of the times? We would argue that, for our purposes, the answer to this question is irrelevant. The newspaper index is nothing more than a representation of the degree of uncertainty felt by households, firms, consumers, and producers. While it may be interesting to know if the media is both the messenger and creator of the message, this knowledge has no effect on the quality of our index.[5]

Socionomics re-frames the answer: The perception of uncertainty does not cause recession, nor does recession cause perceptions of uncertainty. They both result from a trend toward negative social mood. Expressions of uncertainty appear first because they immediately reflect social mood, whereas recessions lag because contractionary business decisions take time to effect.

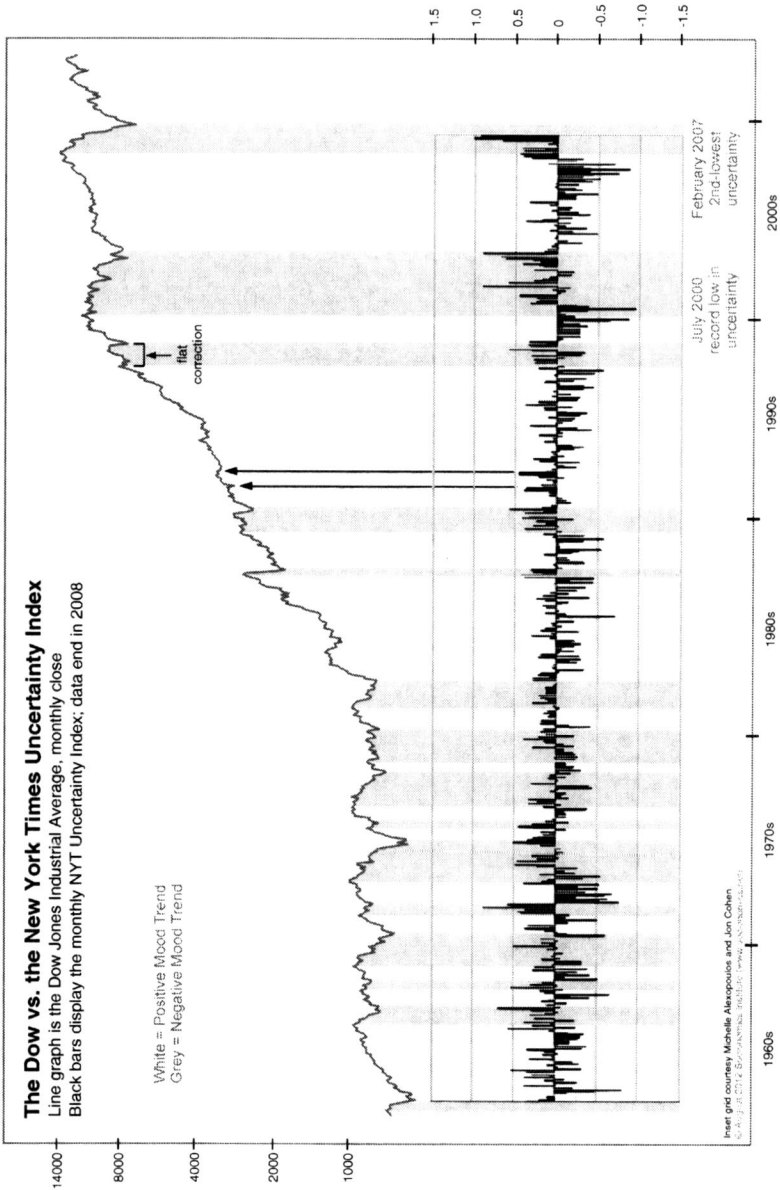

The Dow vs. the New York Times Uncertainty Index
Line graph is the Dow Jones Industrial Average, monthly close
Black bars display the monthly NYT Uncertainty Index; data end in 2008

White = Positive Mood Trend
Grey = Negative Mood Trend

flat correction

February 2007 2nd-lowest uncertainty

July 2000 record low in uncertainty

Inset grid courtesy Michelle Alexopoulos and Jon Cohen

Figure 1

2. Economic Policy Uncertainty

Economists Baker et al. developed an Index of Economic Policy Uncertainty in a February 2012 paper.[6] The authors used three measures to construct their index: (1) newspaper coverage of economic policy, (2) the number of federal tax code provisions set to expire and (3) the extent of disagreement among economic forecasters.

For our first display, we plot the authors' index against the monthly Dow Jones Industrial Average in terms of real money (gold). As you can see in Figure 2, the two overall trends coincide, and significant peaks and troughs in the uncertainty index correspond to significant lows and highs in Dow/gold and/or Dow/PPI. At the peak of Dow/gold in 1999, the uncertainty index reached its second-lowest level in nearly three decades. The negative trend in social mood from then until 2011 accompanied increasing expressions of uncertainty. The final peak moreover, is consistent with "wave two" psychology under the Elliott wave model (see quote at the start of Chapter 18) for the nominal Dow (plotted in Figure 4) and substantially in line with the end of the bear market in real estate (plotted in Figure 17, Chapter 21).

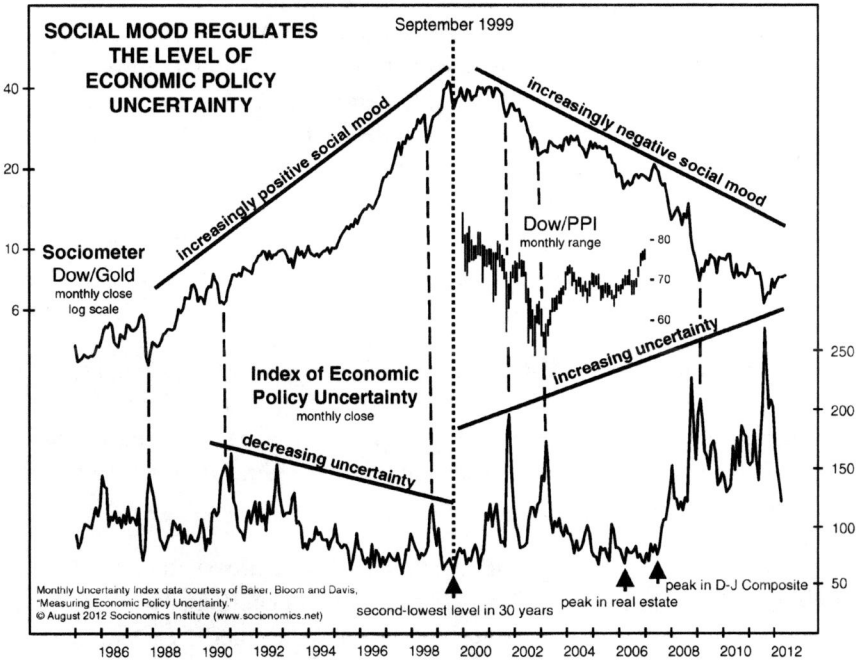

Figure 2

Figure 3 shows the authors' index along with contemporaneous news events attached to each significant peak, as published in their paper. The authors wrote, "The index spikes near consequential presidential elections and after major events such as the Gulf wars and the 9/11 attack." At first glance, one might think that these events—most of which are negative in character—caused the spikes in feelings of uncertainty. As related in Chapter 1, some of these events don't fit very well. For those that do, socionomists ask the critical question, "What generated the negative events?" We can also answer it.

Figure 4 plots the authors' index again, this time against the nominal Dow. As before, times of positive mood trends are in white, and times of negative mood trends are shaded grey. This shading makes it easy to discern a crucial observation: In every instance except that of 1986, multi-month downturns in the Dow and upturns in feelings of uncertainty *preceded* the events that the authors cited in Figure 3. The exogenous-cause explanation fails, whereas the exhibited chronology fits the socionomic case that negative social mood motivated both the feelings of uncertainty *and* ultimately the negative events.

The authors rightly connected the emotions of uncertainty and fear. One of their charts (not shown) illustrates a strong resemblance between their Uncertainty Index and measures of S&P indexes' volatility—primarily VXO, which traders commonly call the "Fear Index" since it tends to rise far more often in bear markets than in bull markets. The two measures' coincident trends reveal that fear does not result from the negative events; it develops beforehand and—according to socionomics—helps cause the events.

The authors confirmed Alexopolous and Cohen's results in finding strong evidence that feelings of uncertainty *precede* economic declines:

> VAR estimates show that an increase in policy uncertainty equal to the actual change between 2006 and 2011 <u>foreshadows</u> large and persistent declines in aggregate outcomes, with peak declines of 3.2% in real GDP, 16% in private investment and 2.3 million in aggregate employment.[7]

From this evidence they concluded, "Many measures of uncertainty rise in recessions and fall in recoveries, suggesting that uncertainty could play an important role in *driving* business cycles." (emphasis added) Socionomics, as usual, replaces this standard, A-causes-B mechanistic construction with the counterintuitive formulation that social mood simultaneously regulates aggregate feelings of uncertainty and overall fluctuations in business activity.

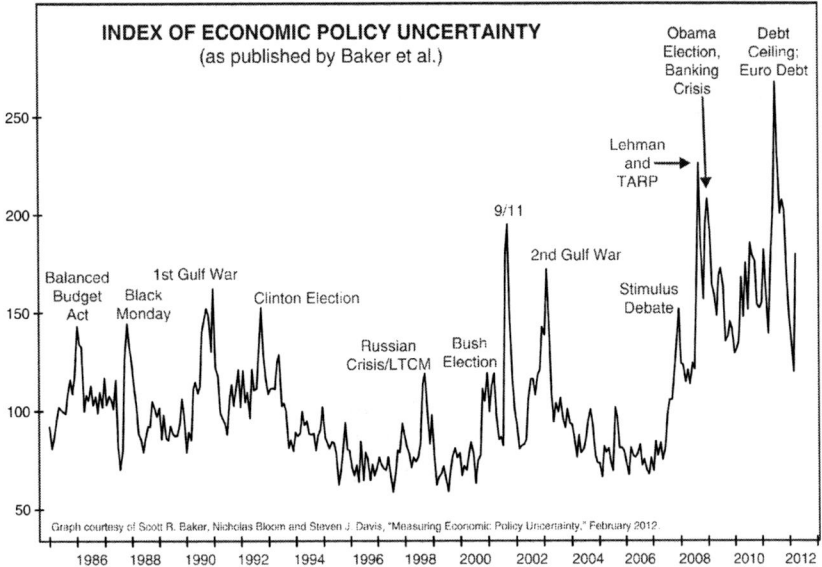

INDEX OF ECONOMIC POLICY UNCERTAINTY
(as published by Baker et al.)

Figure 3

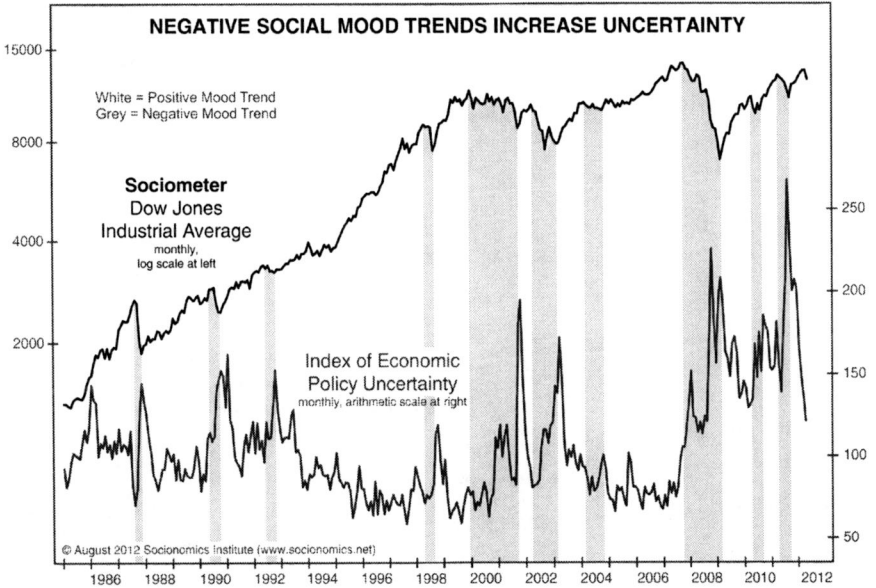

NEGATIVE SOCIAL MOOD TRENDS INCREASE UNCERTAINTY

Figure 4

REFERENCES

[1] Prechter, R., *The Wave Principle of Human Social Behavior,* New Classics Library, 1999, p. 343.

[2] Ivry, Bob, "Toll, Centex, Lennar Join 'Moron' Speculators in Land Grab Bust," Bloomberg, February 7, 2007.

[3] Alexopoulos, M., and J. Cohen, "Uncertain Times, Uncertain Measures," University of Toronto Department of Economics, Working Paper #352, February 24, 2009.

[4] Alexopoulos and Cohen.

[5] *Ibid.*

[6] Baker, Scott R., Nicholas Bloom and Steven J. Davis, "Economic Policy Uncertainty," working paper, February 2012. Scheduled for publication as "Measuring Economic Policy Uncertainty," *The Quarterly Journal of Economics*, 131:4, November 2016.

[7] *Ibid.*

Chapter 27

Social Mood Influences Aggregate Opinions about Inflation and Deflation Irrespective of Pertinent Data

Wayne Gorman

May 17, 2005[1]

One would expect economists to be concerned or relaxed about inflation and deflation in concert with trends in the Consumer Price Index. That's not what happens. Instead, economists have been expressing their concern in concert with prevailing social mood, often in opposition to the CPI's trends.

The Socionomic Perspective

Socionomics postulates that changes in social mood induce changes in attitudes towards all kinds of things. As social mood becomes increasingly positive or negative, people are respectively less or more likely to be fearful, whatever the referent for their feelings may be.

Confidence and fear may have a rational basis or a socionomic basis. In the latter case, people seek a referent to justify their feelings. Socionomic causality suggests that, irrespective of hard evidence, positive social mood trends will result in less fear of inflation and/or deflation, while negative social mood trends will lead to greater fear of inflation and/or deflation. Although statistical data on such fears are unavailable, we conducted an informal study of newspaper articles to determine whether experts' fears in this regard derive from hard facts or from social mood.

Figure 1 reports the results of our inquiry. The top graph shows the rate of change of the Consumer Price Index (CPI), revealing actual evidence of inflation and deflation. We added to it dates of 34 representative media reports of fear or complacency about the monetary outlook (see List of Articles, beginning three pages ahead). The bottom graph shows our sociometer, the Dow Jones Industrial Average (DJIA). We added to it dates and labels indicating when, based entirely on social mood, a socionomist would expect to see representative expressions of either fear or confidence.

Our tally indicates that periods of fear about the monetary outlook have coincided with major lows in the stock market, regardless of what was happening with the CPI. Additionally, periods of confidence in the monetary outlook coincided with major highs in the stock market, again regardless

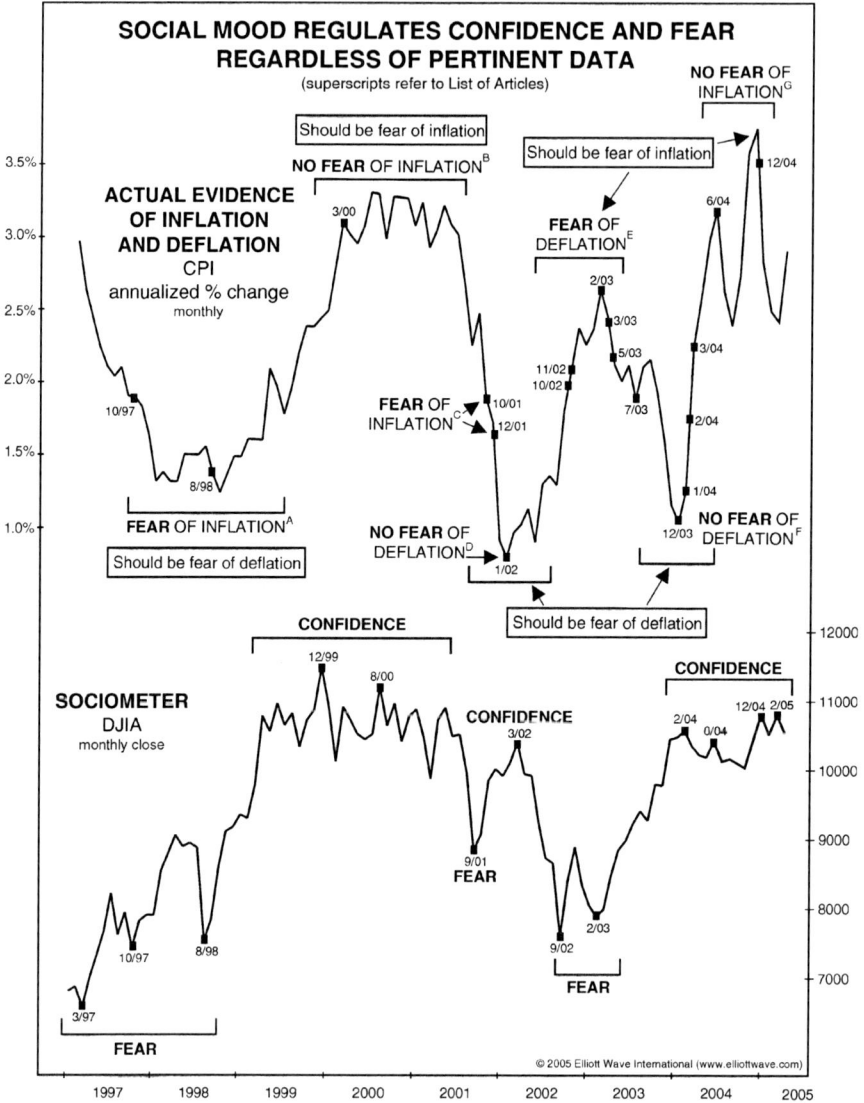

Figure 1

of what was happening with the CPI. In fact, experts' opinions about the prospects for inflation and deflation were often contrary to CPI data. For instance, from early 1999 to the first quarter of 2000, the rate of change in consumer prices rose dramatically, reaching its highest level since 1997, yet people's fear of inflation was subdued, in line with the positive social mood as evidenced by the elevated stock market of that time. In the first three quarters of 2001, the rate of change in the CPI fell precipitously, yet news sources reported great consternation over inflation. This fear corresponded with a trend toward negative social mood throughout the same period, as indicated by a falling stock market. If people's fears were evidence-based, however, they would have feared deflation. In the fourth quarter of 2001, the rate of change in consumer prices fell to its lowest level of the entire period. One would have expected experts to fear deflation, but the stock market rallied during that quarter, so, on balance they were complacent, reflecting the more positive social mood. As the stock market fell again from March 2002 to March 2003, experts increasingly expressed fears of deflation, yet the rate of change in consumer prices rose the entire time. From February to December 2003, the rate of change for consumer prices fell to its second-lowest level of the period, and the rate of change in M3 (not shown) was in negative territory for the only time during this entire eight-year period. Yet experts increasingly expressed a lack of fear about deflation. The reason appears to be that social mood, as represented by a rising stock market, was rapidly becoming more positive during that time. As stocks continued to rise thereafter, experts remained equally complacent despite a soaring rate of change for the CPI. Here in March 2005, the stock market is still rising, and economists and government officials have remained complacent, expressing no fears of either inflation or deflation.

One option is that these analysts are mostly guessing the future correctly in the face of contrary evidence, thereby offering a unique example of prescience. A better option is that social mood is more influential than hard data in regulating people's fear or complacency regarding monetary trends. Opinions' correspondence with our sociometer rather than the CPI corroborates socionomics' contention [see Chapter 19] that people's choice of referents when expressing social mood is substantially non-rational.

Socionomics offers a useful basis for both observing and predicting the beliefs and behavior of experts. Understanding the dynamic at work also equips socionomists to recognize real trends toward deflation or inflation based objectively on facts rather than subjectively on emotions. Sociono-mists try hard to maintain a gulf between emotions and data. Can we trust experts' opinions about the future? It would help if they were socionomists.

LIST OF ARTICLES
(superscripts refer to notes in Figure 1)

FEAR OF INFLATION [A]
(Despite a low rate of change in the CPI)

> *Los Angeles Times*, October 9, 1997
> The nation's central banker rained on Wall Street's parade again Wednesday by reviving inflation fears, sending the Dow Jones industrial average to its worst daily point loss in nearly a month.
> The average tumbled 83.25 points to 8,095.06 after Alan Greenspan, chairman of the Federal Reserve Board, warned that inflation might soon be pushed higher by rising wages and prices. The blue-chip measure finished above its worst levels of the day, however. It was down more than 120 points earlier in the session.
> Many analysts said Greenspan's comments contained no new information, and in fact many private economists already have been fretting about the prospect of higher inflation and its potential for hurting stock and bond prices.
> Federal Reserve Board Chairman Alan Greenspan said Wednesday that the U.S. economy has been on "an unsustainable track" and has not slowed enough to eliminate the threat of renewed inflation.[2]

> *The Washington Post*, October 9, 1997
> Greenspan described renewed inflation as 'without question, the greatest threat' to sustaining the surprising vigor of the current expansion, now in its seventh year.[3]

> *Denver Business Journal*, August 7, 1998
> *Business Week* magazine puts Hoenig, who heads the Federal Reserve Bank of Kansas City, into the camp of the inflation hawks.
> The hawks are concerned that upward pressure on wages and a growing money supply could trigger higher prices and inflation. They fear rapid growth more than an economic slowdown.[4]

NO FEAR OF INFLATION [B]
(Despite an elevated rate of change in the CPI)

> *Los Angeles Times*, March 18, 2000
> [   ], an economist at Boston's John Hancock Financial Services, said that while the higher energy prices would hurt consumers in the short-term— making driving to the beach this summer more expensive—the overall inflation picture remains subdued.

Despite February's higher-than-expected overall CPI figure, the inflation picture at the core level is still benign, with no signs of any broad-based inflationary pressures,' [   ] said.

Indeed, he added, there may be a silver lining in the higher energy prices for the Fed as it attempts to cool the rapidly expanding U.S. economy.[5]

Los Angeles Times, March 21, 2000
So far the Fed has been jacking up short-term interest rates to cool the economy, but it is as hot as ever and inflationary pressures do not appear to be building.[6]

FEAR OF INFLATION [C]
(Despite a falling rate of change in the CPI)

The Wall Street Journal, October 16, 2001
There is some good news coming from the bond market: The yield curve, or a comparison of the yields of various maturities of Treasury securities, has been steepening during recent months, meaning that yields on short-term bonds are falling much faster than yields on long-term bonds. During the past that has been a sure-fire sign that the economy is about to turn around, as bond investors dump long-term bonds amid a new fear of inflation.[7]

The Wall Street Journal, December 28, 2001
The gloomier perspective could lead the Fed to raise rates more quickly to avoid fueling inflation—or reinflating a bubble—with expectations of brisk growth.[8]

NO FEAR OF DEFLATION [D]
(Despite a low rate of change in the CPI)

Grand Forks Herald, January 24, 2002
The United States may be about to turn the corner on the deflation that has resulted in the devaluing of raw agricultural products, an agricultural economist says.[9]

FEAR OF DEFLATION [E]
(Despite an elevated rate of change in the CPI)

The Wall Street Journal, October 7, 2002
Of growing significance to some officials' thinking is the possibility that weak growth could eventually push inflation down to zero, perhaps to deflation, which would make it far harder for the Fed to stimulate the recovery. This may have been a factor for Dallas Fed President Robert McTeer, one

of the dissenters two weeks ago. "I don't know at what point welcome [declines in inflation] might morph into unwelcome deflation," he said last week, though he added, "I don't think we're there yet."[10]

The Wall Street Journal, November 6, 2002
Unsettling Scenario: Inside the Fed, Deflation Draws a Closer Look— Stumped for a Cure, Officials Study How to Keep Prices From Falling in First Place—A Dollar Worth 98.4 Cents
Today, deflation no longer seems so remote.[11]

The Economist, February 1, 2003
In America, deflation looks a bigger risk than inflation.[12]

The Wall Street Journal, March 3, 2003
The Economy: Despite High Oil Prices, Deflation Fear Persists—Increase in Costs of Energy May Discourage Spending by Consumers, Businesses
Indeed, some notably bearish economists say global deflation is more of a worry now than it was before oil prices started rising. "The case for deflation actually looks more compelling than ever," says Morgan Stanley's chief economist.

Before oil prices rose on fears of war with Iraq, hitting a post-Gulf War high Thursday of nearly $40 a barrel before easing Friday to $36.60 a barrel for April delivery of U.S. light crude on the New York Mercantile Exchange, some economists worried that the sort of deflationary spiral now gripping Japan could spread around the world. Deflation already is a worry in China, parts of Europe and, according to some economists, the U.S.

"It would now take a fairly vigorous recovery in the global economy— several years of world GDP increasing in excess of 4%—to tilt the business cycle away from deflation," says Morgan Stanley's [ ]. "Yet precisely the opposite now seems to be in the cards."

[ ], head of research firm Independent Strategy, argues that deflation will pressure prices and corporate profitability throughout 2003. He says that pressure will be enough to prick what he sees as a "double bubble" of excessive consumer debt in the U.S. and the U.K. and inflated living standards in Europe, "either in a crash, or more likely in a slow, painful, grinding adjustment."[13]

The Economist, May 2003
The risk of falling prices is greater than at any time since the 1930s.[14]

ABC News, May 7, 2003
Fed's Remarks Show Deflation is Economy's New Worry[15]

The Wall Street Journal, May 7, 2003
In a Shift, Fed Signals Concern Over Deflation—Central Bank Leaves Rates Unchanged, but it Cites Possible "Fall in Inflation"[16]

USA Today, May 15, 2003
Price Slide Intensifies Fears About Deflation[17]

The Wall Street Journal, May 16, 2003
Leading the News: Producer Prices Show Sharp Drop—Report Backs Fed Warning on Deflation, as Other Data Offer a Few Bright Spots[18]

Los Angeles Times, May 17, 2003
Bond Yields Dive on CPI Data; Deflation Fears are Fanned by Prices Report; Key Stock Indexes End Modestly Lower.[19]

The Wall Street Journal, May 19, 2003
Having Defeated Inflation, Fed Girds for New War: Falling Prices
The continued slide in the rate of core inflation toward the zero mark increases the urgency for a pickup in activity to materialize before the next meeting of Fed policy makers, on June 24 and 25, said [ ], chief economist at RBS Greenwich Capital Markets in Greenwich, Conn. "Unless they can be reasonably comfortable that the economy has begun to improve, policy makers will most probably choose to pre-empt deflation in late June."

The market is "front-running the Fed," with prices rising as deflation fears mount and the market positions for possible Fed intervention, said [ ], portfolio manager at Waddell & Reed in Kansas City, Mo. If the economy can't rebound soon, "the next trick is for the Fed to start buying Treasurys," he said.

The Federal Reserve's historic shift from fighting inflation to resisting deflation didn't come a moment too soon.[20]

The Wall Street Journal, May 22, 2003
Federal Reserve Chairman Alan Greenspan said the threat of deflation is small, but the harm it could do is so serious that the central bank might have to lower interest rates to minimize the likelihood of it occurring.

The Federal Reserve said two weeks ago that the risks of inflation going too low now outweigh the risks of it going up. Investors took that to mean the Fed is on guard against deflation, or generally declining prices.

But he also conceded that growth in the current quarter "is going to be quite soft," and recent data have been "on the weak side." He fretted over high oil and natural-gas prices, and said there would be little downside risk to taking out "insurance" against weak spending—and thus deflation—with another rate cut.[21]

NO FEAR OF DEFLATION [F]
(Despite a low rate of change in the CPI)

The Wall Street Journal, July 16, 2003
The bond market suffered one of its biggest declines this year, and stocks slipped less markedly, after Federal Reserve Chairman Alan Greenspan called deflation a "remote" risk.[22]

Los Angeles Times, July 20, 2003
But bond owners also must consider the possibility that deflation fears have been overblown, and that inflation might be stabilizing at low levels or even poised to rise somewhat, should the economy accelerate.[23]

The Wall Street Journal, July 22, 2003
"Ever since Greenspan spoke, bonds have been getting crushed every day," Mr. Leone noted, referring to Federal Reserve Chairman Alan Greenspan's testimony to House and Senate committees last week. Investors concluded from the Fed chief's comments that he no longer is worried about deflation and that the Fed may not cut its target short-term rates further. Bond yields, which had gone to extreme lows on deflation fears, have been jumping ever since.[24]

Los Angeles Times, December 10, 2003
The Fed on Tuesday also changed its wording from recent statements, deemphasizing the risk of deflation, a broad-based decline in prices across the economy.

Stock investors, in theory, ought to be happy if deflation fears are waning, because that may signal better pricing power for many companies.

"The Fed kind of put 'deflation' in the dustbin," said [   ], managing director of equity strategy at brokerage RBC Dain Rauscher in Minneapolis. "I welcome that."[25]

The Wall Street Journal, December 10, 2003
Fed Leaves Rates at 1%, but Signals Shift on Inflation; In Upbeat Economic View, It Plays Down Deflation Risk; Improved Jobs Picture Cited
In its most upbeat economic assessment in at least a year, the central bank also said its concerns about deflation had all but disappeared.

Since May, the Fed has been saying that the possibility of already-low inflation falling too far—and risking deflation—exceeded the risk of rising inflation. Yesterday, it all but abolished its deflation concerns.... In addition, the Fed dropped its prior statement that the risk of falling inflation would be the dominant factor in its interest-rate decisions.[26]

The Wall Street Journal, January 5, 2004
"There's much less talk of deflation in recent months," Mr. [ ] said.[27]

Los Angeles Times, February 6, 2004
...Federal Reserve Gov. Ben Bernanke...said the risk of deflation, or falling prices, had "retreated very substantially."[28]

The Wall Street Journal, February 23, 2004
[ ], senior economist at Wachovia Securities said the two-decade process of falling inflation is ending. While inflation in services prices has slowed, "anecdotal reports are beginning to show a slight pickup in rents and even the hotel industry is doing a bit better," he said in a report, adding, "deflation in goods prices may also be coming to an end."[29]

The Wall Street Journal, February 26, 2004
In broader comments on the economy, Mr. Greenspan said the risk of deflation has faded considerably.

Mr. Greenspan said in response to a question that the probability of deflation, or generally declining prices, 'which was a year ago very low, is now much lower,' though not zero, citing the behavior of goods prices. Owing in part to the declining dollar, which pushes up the price of imports, and rising commodity prices, consumer-goods prices excluding food and energy were unchanged in January after 16 consecutive monthly declines.[30]

The Wall Street Journal, March 18, 2004
Consumer Prices Show Steady Gain; Core Costs Increased 0.2% In February, Easing Fears of Deflationary Pressures[31]

NO FEAR OF INFLATION [G]
(Despite an elevated rate of change in the CPI)

> *The Wall Street Journal*, June 13, 2004
> **Inflation Isn't All Bad for Investors**
> As long as inflation doesn't get out of hand, a rise in pricing power for corporations can be good for the market because it will help juice profits, bulls argue. "Inflation is coming back somewhat, but that can be a good thing," says [   ], chief investment officer at Wells Capital Management. "People forget that."[32]

> *The Atlanta Journal-Constitution*, June 16, 2004
> **Greenspan Downplays Inflation; Fed Chief Unfazed by Spurt in May**
> Just hours after the inflation numbers were announced, Federal Reserve Chairman Alan Greenspan reassured the Senate Banking Committee that "inflationary pressures are not likely to be a serious concern in the period ahead."[33]

> *The Washington Post*, June 16, 2004
> **Inflation Doesn't Worry Greenspan; Fed Chairman Says Threat is in Check—for Now—and Interest Rates Can Be Raised Gradually**
> Federal Reserve Chairman Alan Greenspan yesterday played down inflation concerns after a government report showed consumer prices rose in May at the fastest monthly rate in more than three years.
> "Our general view is that inflationary pressures are not likely to be a serious concern in the period ahead," he said in response to a question from committee Chairman Sen. Richard C. Shelby (R-Ala.).[34]

> *The Washington Post*, December 2, 2004
> **The End of the Age of Inflation**[35]

REFERENCES

[1] Adapted from Gorman, Wayne, "Social Mood Shapes Aggregate Opinion Regardless of Data," *The Elliott Wave Theorist*, May 17, 2005.

[2] "New Inflation Fears Roil Stocks; Wall St.: Strength in Some Tech Shares Lifts Nasdaq to Record, But Other Indexes Post Losses," *Los Angeles Times*, October 9, 1997, p. 3.

[3] Chandler, Clay, "Greenspan Warning on Economy, Stocks Again Roils Markets," *The Washington Post*, October 9, 1997, p. A.01.

4 Svaldi, Aldo, "Inflation Hawk Hoenig Weighs Deflation Threat," *Denver Business Journal*, August 7, 1998.

5 Egan, Mark, "Consumer Prices Edge Up but Set Off Few Alarms; Economy: Energy Costs Boost February Index 0.5%, But Core Prices Remain Tame. Modest Interest Rate Hike Expected Next Week," *Los Angeles Times*, March 18, 2000, p. 1.

6 "The Fed May Need New Tools," Editorial, *Los Angeles Times*, March 21, 2000, p. 6.

7 Zuckerman, Gregory, "Pessimism Hinders a Recovery in Bond Market," *The Wall Street Journal*, October 16, 2001, p. C.1.

8 Ip, Greg and Jacob M. Schlesinger, "Great Expectations: Did Greenspan Push High-Tech Optimism On Growth Too Far? — Some He Won Over at Fed Have Second Thoughts; At Stake: Interest Rates — Bank Took 'a Bit of a Risk,'" *The Wall Street Journal*, December 28, 2001, p. A.1.

9 Bailey, Ann, "Deflation's Days Are Numbered," *Grand Forks Herald*, January 24, 2002, p. B.2.

10 Ip, Greg, "The Economy: Labor Data Back Fed's Steady Course," *The Wall Street Journal*, October 7, 2002, p. A.2.

11 Ip, Greg, "Unsettling Scenario: Inside the Fed, Deflation Draws A Closer Look — Stumped for a Cure, Officials Study How to Keep Prices From Falling in First Place — A Dollar Worth 98.4 Cents," *The Wall Street Journal*, November 6, 2002, p. A.1.

12 Kilian, Lutz and Simone Manganelli, "Quantifying the Risk of Deflation," University of Michigan and CEPR, and European Central Bank, February 13, 2004, p. 2.; "Downhill Dollar," *The Economist*, February 1, 2003.

13 Day, Phillip, "The Economy: Despite High Oil Prices, Deflation Fear Persists — Increase in Costs of Energy May Discourage Spending By Consumers, Businesses," *The Wall Street Journal*, March 3, 2003, p. A.2.

14 Kilian, Lutz and Simone Manganelli, "Quantifying the Risk of Deflation." University of Michigan and CEPR, and European Central Bank, February 13, 2004, p. 2. "The Joy of Inflation," *The Economist*, May 17, 2003.

15 "Price Slide Intensifies Fears About Deflation." ABC News, May 7, 2003.

16 Ip, Greg, "In a Shift, Fed Signals Concern Over Deflation — Central Bank Leaves Rates Unchanged, but It Cites Possible 'Fall in Inflation,'" *The Wall Street Journal*, May 7, 2003, p. A.1.

17 Kirchhoff, Sue, "Price Slide Intensifies Fears About Deflation," *USA Today*, May 15, 2003.

18 Hilsenrath, Jon E., "Leading the News: Producer Prices Show Sharp Drop—Report Backs Fed Warning On Deflation, as Other Data Offer a Few Bright Spots," *The Wall Street Journal*, May 16, 2003, p. A.3.

19 "Bond Yields Dive on CPI Data; Deflation Fears Are Fanned by Prices Report. Key stock indexes end modestly lower," *Los Angeles Times*, May 17, 2003, p. C.3.

[20] Ip, Greg and Jon E. Hilsenrath, "Having Defeated Inflation, Fed Girds for New War: Falling Prices," *The Wall Street Journal*, May 19, 2003, p. A.1.

[21] Ip, Greg, "Greenspan Says U.S. Deflation Threat Is Small — Potential Harm Is Serious So Central Bank Might Act To Minimize the Jeopardy," *The Wall Street Journal*, May 22, 2003, p. A.2.

[22] McKay, Peter A., "Bond Prices Fall on Worries About Inflation," *The Wall Street Journal*, July 16, 2003, p. C1.

[23] Petruno, Tom, "For Bond Owners, Worries Add Up; As the Nation's Budget Deficit Swells, It Compounds Fears of Higher Interest Rates," *Los Angeles Times*, July 20, 2003, p. C.1.

[24] Browning, E.S., "Stocks Decline; Bonds Tumble As Rates Climb," *The Wall Street Journal*, July 22, 2003, p. C1.

[25] Gosselin, Peter G., "Fed Keeps Low Rate, Hints at Shift Coming; Central Bank Holds at 1% For Now, But Says Deflation Risk is 'Diminished,'" *Los Angeles Times*, December 10, 2003, p. C.1.

[26] Ip. Greg, "Fed Leaves Rates At 1%, But Signals Shift on Inflation; In Upbeat Economic View, It Plays Down Deflation Risk; Improved Jobs Picture Cited," *The Wall Street Journal*, December 10, 2003, p. A.1.

[27] Ip, Greg, "The Economy: Greenspan Sees Recovery as Vindication for Fed; Policy of Managing Risks Gets Credit for Success; Fresh Inflation Fears Lurk," *The Wall Street Journal*, January 5, 2004, p. A.2.

[28] "Markets; Stocks Rise on Fed Official's Upbeat Forecast; Nasdaq Adds 5 Points, Halting Previous Day's Tumble, and Dow Closes Up 25. Many Investors Await Today's Jobs Data," *Los Angeles Times*, February 6, 2004, p. C.4.

[29] Ip. Greg, "The Economy: Consumer Prices Rose in January, Driven by Energy," *The Wall Street Journal*, February 23, 2004, p. A.2.

[30] Ip, Greg, "The Economy: Greenspan Favors Entitlement Cuts; Fed Chief Sides With Bush In Opposing Tax Increases; Draws Fire From Democrats," *The Wall Street Journal*, February 26, 2004, p. A.2.

[31] Rebello, Joseph and Phil McCarty, "Consumer Prices Show Steady Gain; Core Costs Increased 0.2% In February, Easing Fears of Deflationary Pressures," *The Wall Street Journal*, March 18, 2004, p. A.2.

[32] Zuckerman, Gregory, "Inflation Isn't All Bad for Investors," *The Wall Street Journal*, June 13, 2004, p. 1.

[33] Geewax, Marilyn, "Greenspan Downplays Inflation; Fed Chief Unfazed by Spurt in May," *The Atlanta Journal-Constitution*, June 16, 2004, p. B1.

[34] Henderson, Neil, "Inflation Doesn't Worry Greenspan; Fed Chairman Says Threat Is in Check—for Now—and Interest Rates Can Be Raised Gradually," *The Washington Post*, June 16, 2004, p. E.01.

[35] Samuelson, Robert J., "The End of the Age of Inflation," *The Washington Post*, December 2, 2004, p. A.35.

Chapter 28

Social Mood Governs the Tone of Federal Reserve Board Meetings

Alan Hall

Many people view the Federal Reserve Board as being in charge of interest rates and the economy. If it were, soconomic theory would be suspect. Chapter 3 showed that the market, not the Fed, is in charge of interest rates, and we have argued that waves of social mood, not the Fed, are in charge of the economy. This study shows that waves of social mood are even in charge of mood at the Fed.

Since 1974, the Federal Open Market Committee (FOMC)—a group within the Federal Reserve that oversees the Fed's buying and selling of debt securities and sets the central bank's federal funds rate—has released five-year-delayed transcripts[1] of its meetings, which are held eight times per year. In November 1976, the transcripts began to include "[Laughter]" notations. As far as we can tell, the Daily Stag Hunt website in January 2012 was the first outlet to publish a chart showing a portion of the laughter data.[2] We have expanded on the idea by charting all "[Laughter]" notations and plotting them against the DJIA to assess how they align with social mood. Figure 1 shows our initial rendition, published in June 2012.

The first significant laughter notations occurred in 1979-1980, soon after Paul Volcker became Federal Reserve Chairman. Those chuckles immediately gave way to the longest dour spell in the data—a 17-month span marked at the bottom of the chart—which coincided with the interest rate extremes shown in Figure 3 of Chapter 3. Shortly afterward the Dow/PPI registered its major low of 1982.

A burst of laughter accompanied Alan Greenspan's August 11, 1987 appointment as Fed chairman. The Maestro arrived just two weeks before the August 25 peak in the stock market. The subsequent negative trend in social mood prompted the August-October stock market crash and cast a pall over the Fed's meetings.

As published on June 28, 2012, with DJIA wave labels omitted

SOCIAL MOOD GOVERNS THE
FOMC LAUGHTER INDEX
Laughter data through 2006
(5-year lag in reporting)

Sociometer
Dow Jones Industrial Average
monthly close, log scale
(left scale)

June 1981–Volcker sets
federal funds rate
to a record 19%

August 1979,
Volcker appointed
Chairman

Greenspan
Appointed
August 11, 1987

1982–Long-term
unemployment
highest since
Great Depression

9/1980-2/1982: Longest dour spell

February 1991,
"[Laughter/hoots]"

February 1999,
Ms Rivlin:
"Besides, nobody
can predict the
stock market."

October 2006,
record hilarity

Our
Forecast

Instances of Laughter
at FOMC Meetings
(right scale)

Two photos at left: Paul Volcker. Two photos at right: Alan Greenspan.

© June 2012 Socionomics Institute (www.socionomics.net)

Figure 1

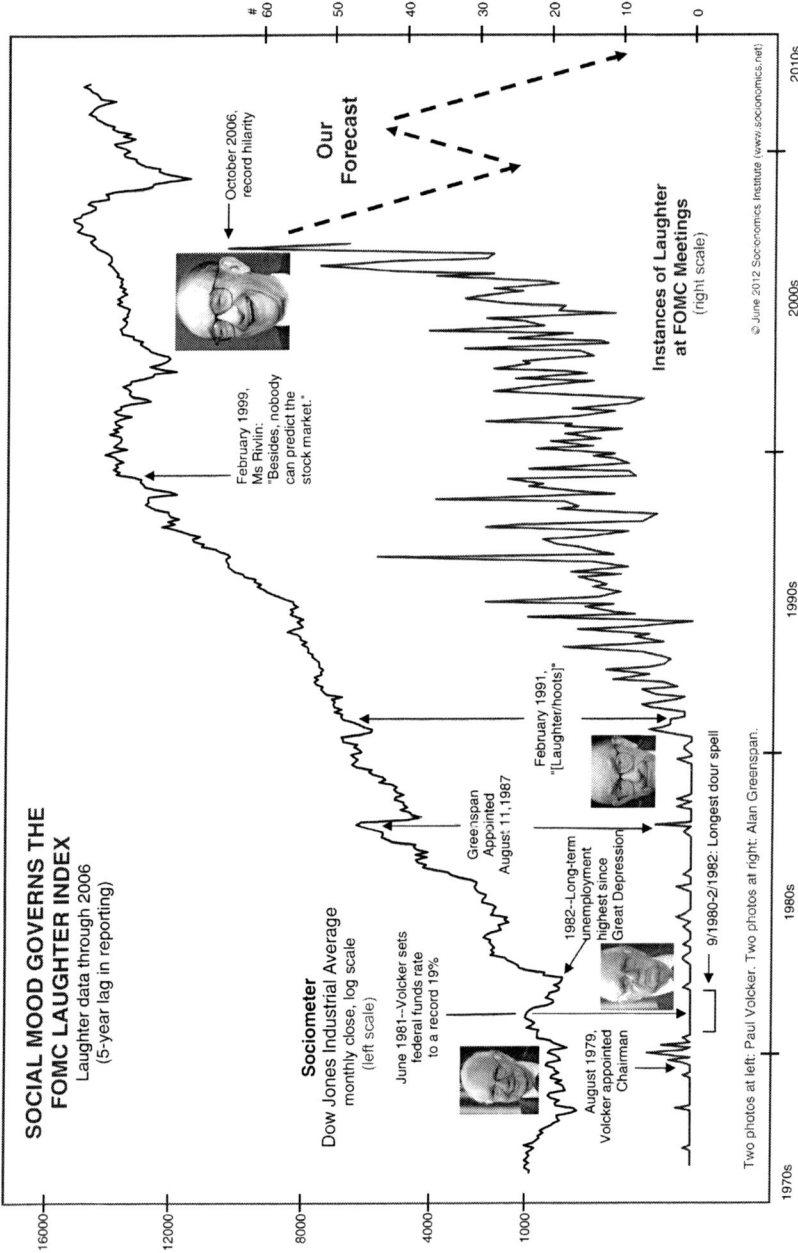

The transcript for February 1991 contains the only record of the FOMC committee "hooting" with laughter. As the economy remained mired in a recession at the time, the hooting would seem to have had little rational basis. Anyone trying to predict the Fed's mood using the conventional event-driven model would have forecast a somber meeting. But the stock market's correction of 1987 to 1990 (see the VLC graph in Figure 2) had ended four months earlier. A large-degree, positive trend in social mood had resumed, and the Dow was on its way to new all-time highs. The total amount of laughter was still low compared to what was coming, but in its way the committee was expressing society's emerging ebullience. Here is an excerpt from that meeting's transcript:

> MR. HOSKINS. You're probably all waiting for my stainless steel strip index, but I'm not going to give it to you because I've latched onto a new one: the Smuckers Index! I had a chance to talk with Paul Smucker, an elderly gentleman who has been through many business cycles and he told me that apple butter sales remain relatively soft and that's a good sign because during deep recessions apple butter sales soar. [Laughter] So, I'll be reporting to you on apple butter.
>
> CHAIRMAN GREENSPAN. It sounds to me as though business is in a jam! [Laughter/hoots][3]

The Fed's expressions of mirth expanded persistently for the next fifteen years, following the equally persistent, positive trend in social mood as indicated by a rising stock market.

In June 1999, seven months before the Dow's peak in 2000, chairman Greenspan predicted unequivocally that the economic expansion would continue. His extreme optimism—shared by America's corporate leaders—regarding a perceived positive, once-in-a-century "structural shift" in the economy was a socionomic signal that a reversal in the trend of social mood was nigh. His comments book-ended a joke about his own age, prompting laughter from his fellow committee members:

> CHAIRMAN GREENSPAN. We have no evidence at this stage of which I am aware, however, that indicates the acceleration in productivity has ended. All of our experience and courses in Econometrics 101 induce a visceral antipathy to such persistence in productivity gains, especially for me since I have the oldest gut in this room. [Laughter] What is increasingly evident is that something seems to be happening that none of us has ever witnessed before—perhaps a once-in-a-century structural shift in how goods and services are produced. People in the front lines of business operations, such as Jack

Welch of GE and Lou Gerstner of IBM say this is a true revolution. They have seen nothing like this in their experience. And I venture to say that if we get on the phone with a number of business people who have been around a long time, we are going to hear this view from all of them. No one is saying that this accumulative, technology-driven productivity growth is showing any signs of slowing.[4]

In August 1999, five months before the Dow's 2000 peak, FOMC member Alfred Broaddus, following Greenspan's lead, linearly extrapolated then-current economic conditions into the future. He, too, went for laughs:

> MR. BROADDUS. Mr. Chairman…we see relatively few signs of any deceleration in activity in our region. …Car sales remain at an exceptionally high level. One of our bank directors recently told us that new car loans at his bank were at an all-time high. …As you may know, BMW has a big new plant in Greenville, South Carolina. …people down there like to say that in South Carolina BMW stands for Bubba Makes Wheels! [Laughter][5]

Socionomic causality explains why the Fed was so jolly at these times.

The FOMC's laughter subsided after social mood began trending negatively in 2000-2002. Then it surged again as mood turned positive, supporting the new highs in both real estate and nominal stock prices in 2006-2007. Toward the peak of the housing bubble, the Fed was in an especially jovial and confident mood, unaware that huge plunges in stock and property prices lay immediately ahead. In the January 2006 meeting, Fed President William Poole thanked Alan Greenspan for his "extraordinary influence" on Poole's life and then made a recommendation:

> MR. POOLE. I have a suggestion for a title for your first book. … "The Joy of Central Banking." [Laughter] And I suggest that your second book be "More Joy of Central Banking." [Laughter]
>
> CHAIRMAN GREENSPAN. "How to Be a Joyous Central Banker, Even Though We Don't Have Hearts." [Laughter] …Thanks very much, Bill.

Later in that same meeting, the Chairman and Vice Chairman engaged in mutual appreciation and sappiness:

> VICE CHAIRMAN GEITHNER. Mr. Chairman, in the interest of crispness, I've removed a substantial tribute from my remarks. [Laughter]

CHAIRMAN GREENSPAN. I am most appreciative. [Laughter]

VICE CHAIRMAN GEITHNER. I'd like the record to show that I think you're pretty terrific, too. [Laughter] And thinking in terms of probabilities, I think the risk that we decide in the future that you're even better than we think is higher than the alternative. [Laughter][6]

A Nearly Completed Elliott Wave in FOMC Laughter in 2006

After examining these data, we reasoned that if social mood propels occurrences of FOMC laughter, and if social mood moves in Elliott waves, then the laughter data should produce some semblance of an Elliott wave.

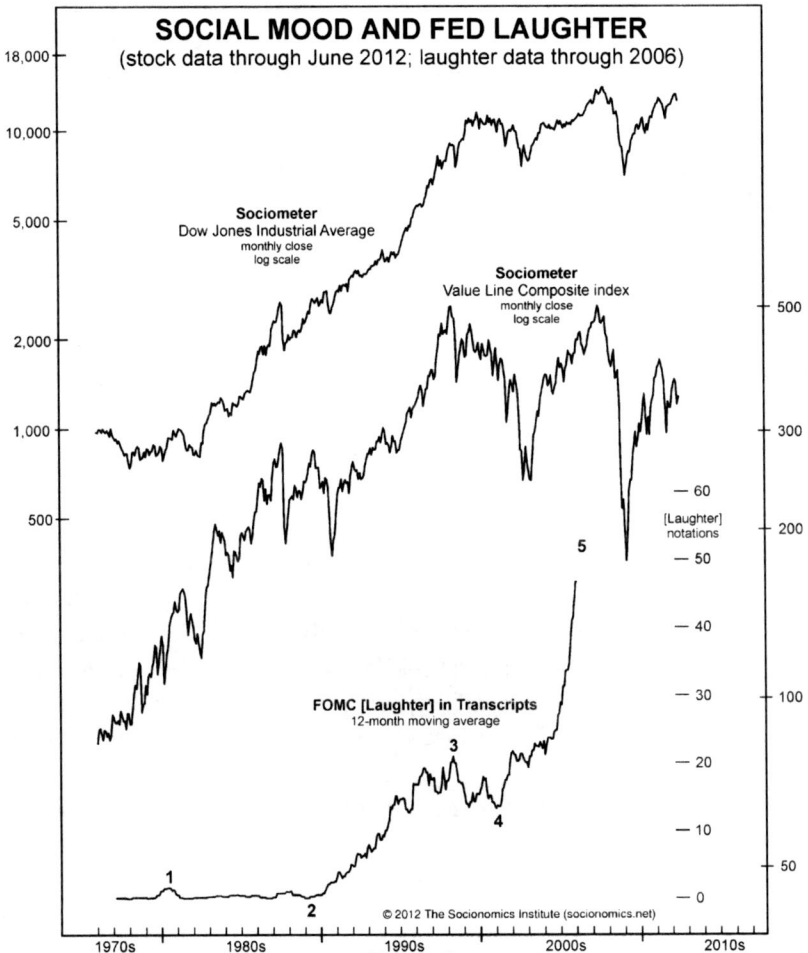

Figure 2

Indeed, we found that smoothing the data by plotting a centered, 12-month moving average revealed a nearly completed Elliott wave in Fed jocularity in 2006, as displayed in Figure 2. This pattern provided even more evidence that social mood was regulating the mood of the Federal Open Market Committee.

Our Forecast

After making all these observations in July 2012, we applied the socionomic insight to make the following forecast, shown graphically in Figure 1:

> Fed transcripts are released after a five-year delay. We have sketched a [Laughter] notation forecast in Figure 1 based on what we already know about the trend of social mood. Our forecast says that as post-2006 data become available, we will see fewer laughter notations until the first half of 2009, and levels may remain subdued into 2012 given the continued fall in real estate prices. If stocks continue to rise, there should be more laughter, though probably not reaching 2006-2007 levels, due to the completed Elliott wave form.[7]

Figure 3 updates the Dow through 2015 and the 12-month moving average of instances of Fed laughter through 2010, the last year for which these data have been released. As you can see, our socionomic forecast for the trend of the FOMC's jocularity—sketched originally in Figure 1—has worked out well.

Pawns on a Chessboard

Since the FOMC is so powerfully influenced by social mood, can one really expect central bankers to anticipate economic changes, regulate booms and recessions, and manage the economy? As the Laughter Index shows, and as Fed representatives' public comments unequivocally confirmed (see Chapter 5), the Fed in 2006 and 2007 possessed no knowledge whatsoever—and exhibited not an inkling of apprehension—about major financial and economic changes lying immediately ahead. As Prechter argued in *The Wave Principle of Human Social Behavior*, the Potent Directors Presumption is a myth.

Socionomic causality influences much more at central banks than the amount of laughter at their meetings. Social mood is in fact in charge of every aspect of central bankers' experience: (1) their feelings: when they feel comfortable or stressed; (2) their level of internal cooperation: when

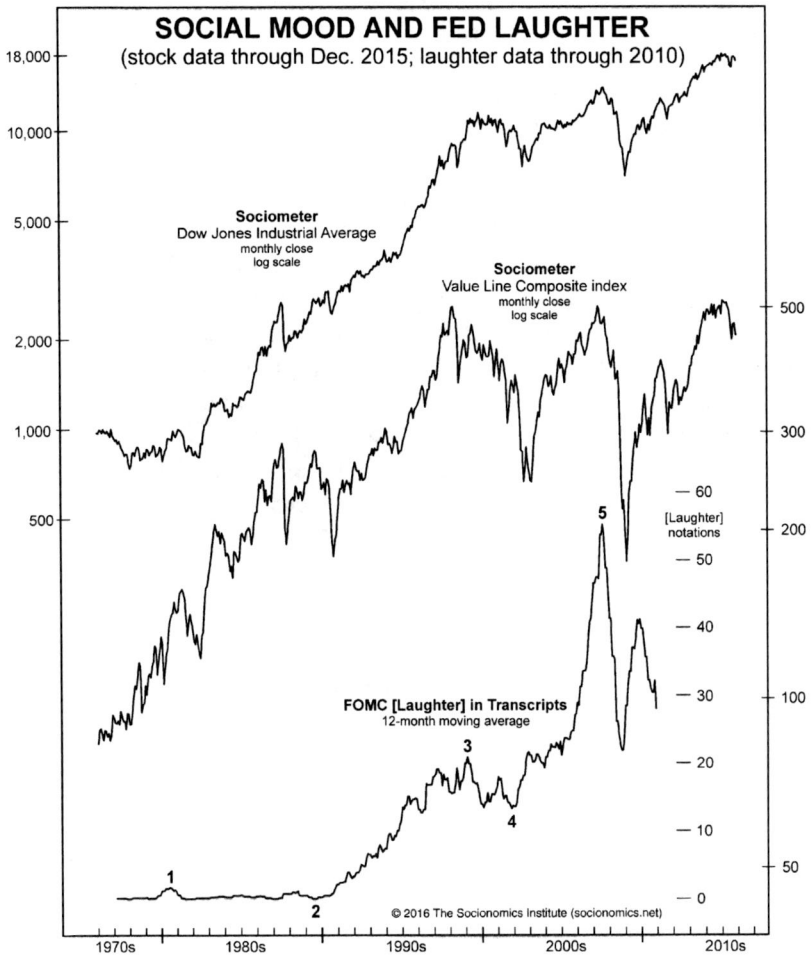

Figure 3

their members are harmonious or discordant; (3) their policies: when they act and don't act; (4) their reputations: when they are revered as successful and when they are reviled as failures; (5) and even the institution's very existence or non-existence (see Chapter 13 of *Pioneering Studies in Socionomics*). A severely negative social mood could someday foster anger among committee members, revolt within the institution, policy paralysis, and a bad reputation for the central bank. It could even induce combative political attitudes that lead to its demise, as proposed in Chapter 25.

NOTES AND REFERENCES

[1] Transcripts and other historical materials. Federal Open Market Committee. Board of Governors of the Federal Reserve System. Retrieved from http://www.federalreserve.gov.

[2] Akin, K. "The correlation of laughter at FOMC meetings," *The Daily Stag Hunt*, January 12, 2012. Retrieved from http://www.dailystaghunt.com.

[3] Meeting of the Federal Open Market Committee, February 5-6, 1991. Federal Reserve. Retrieved from http://www.federalreserve.gov.

[4] Meeting of the Federal Open Market Committee, June 29-30, 1999. Federal Reserve. Retrieved from http://www.federalreserve.gov.

[5] Meeting of the Federal Open Market Committee, August 24, 1999. Federal Reserve. Retrieved from http://www.federalreserve.gov.

[6] Meeting of the Federal Open Market Committee, January 31, 2006. Federal Reserve. Retrieved from http://www.federalreserve.gov.

[7] Hall, Alan, "Social Mood Governs the Tone of Federal Reserve Board Meetings," *The Socionomist,* June 2012 and *The Elliott Wave Theorist,* July 2012.

Chapter 29

Skepticism about "Potent Directors" Can Set You Apart from the Crowd

Brian Whitmer

The Breton Woods Agreement of 1944 fixed currency exchange rates. The fix fell apart in the early 1970s, and currencies were allowed to float.

The Swiss National Bank (SNB) tried the same thing in September 2011 when it tied the Swiss franc to the euro. The financial community thought it would work.

The Swiss National Bank's sudden decision on January 15, 2015 to end its 3⅓-year peg of the Swiss franc to the euro not only sent currency traders scrambling for the exit but also sent financial journalists running for the thesaurus. "Swiss Franc Shocker,"[1] read a *Barron's* headline. "Mayhem erupted,"[2] wrote *The Washington Post*. "Swiss currency brokers bleed,"[3] reported *CNN Money*. The announcement "sent shockwaves through equity and currency markets,"[4] said the *Financial Times*. According to Bloomberg, traders were "surprised," experts were "blindsided," and economists were "amazed that such a stoic central bank could end up abandoning such a long-held policy."[5]

Bloomberg[6] reported that exactly none of the 22 economists surveyed between January 4 and January 9, 2015 expected the SNB to abandon its cap anytime in that year. Another Bloomberg survey[7] found that "only one lone forecaster" among nearly fifty polled expected the Swiss franc to appreciate past the SNB's limit, and he had called for a mere 0.02-cent move to 1.18 francs per euro. Even Christine Lagarde, managing director of the International Monetary Fund, was so completely caught off guard that she expressed dismay that the SNB had failed to provide her with advance warning of the move.

Many experts[8] analyzed the SNB's decision after the fact. But as far as we know, Elliott Wave International is the only major forecasting firm that emphatically predicted that the currency cap would fail. Back in early

September 2011, four days before officials first enacted the peg, *The European Financial Forecast* (EFF) compared their policy plan to the failed Bretton Woods system: "Similarly to that time, a currency peg today would require a high level of international cooperation that a big bear market simply won't permit."

Our most crucial discussion of the SNB came on December 5, 2014. After illustrating a big rise in implied volatility (indicating waxing fear) as the euro descended toward 1.20, EFF flatly warned,

> A significant move may be fast approaching in the Swiss franc (CHF) relative to the euro. [T]he SNB will abandon its peg in an effort to protect whatever valuable assets it has left.

We published that forecast six weeks before the SNB's surprise decision. The before-and-after charts (Figures 1 and 2) display the dramatic results.

Our insight that moods and markets are stronger than policymakers allowed us to see what was invisible to nearly everyone else. When the SNB terminated its peg, the world of finance experienced brokerage shortfalls, insolvent firms and outright panic. Whoever acted on our insight either profited immensely or avoided all that pain.

THEN...

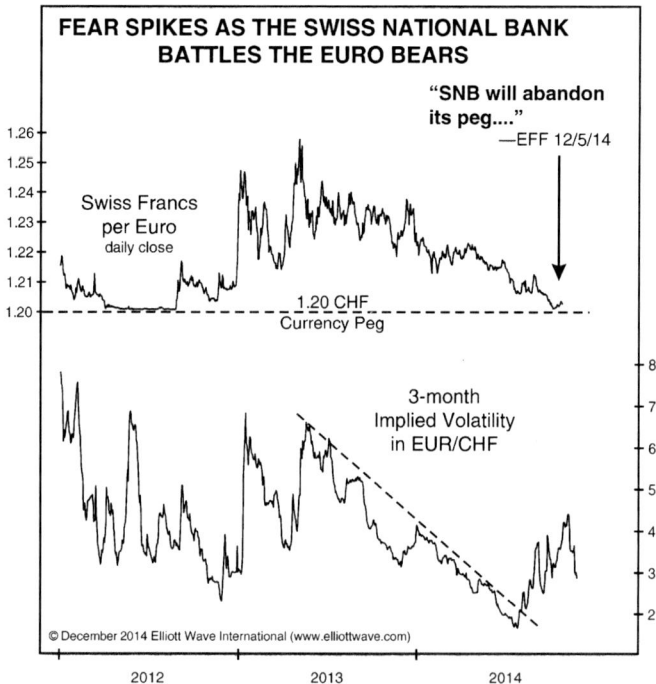

Figure 1

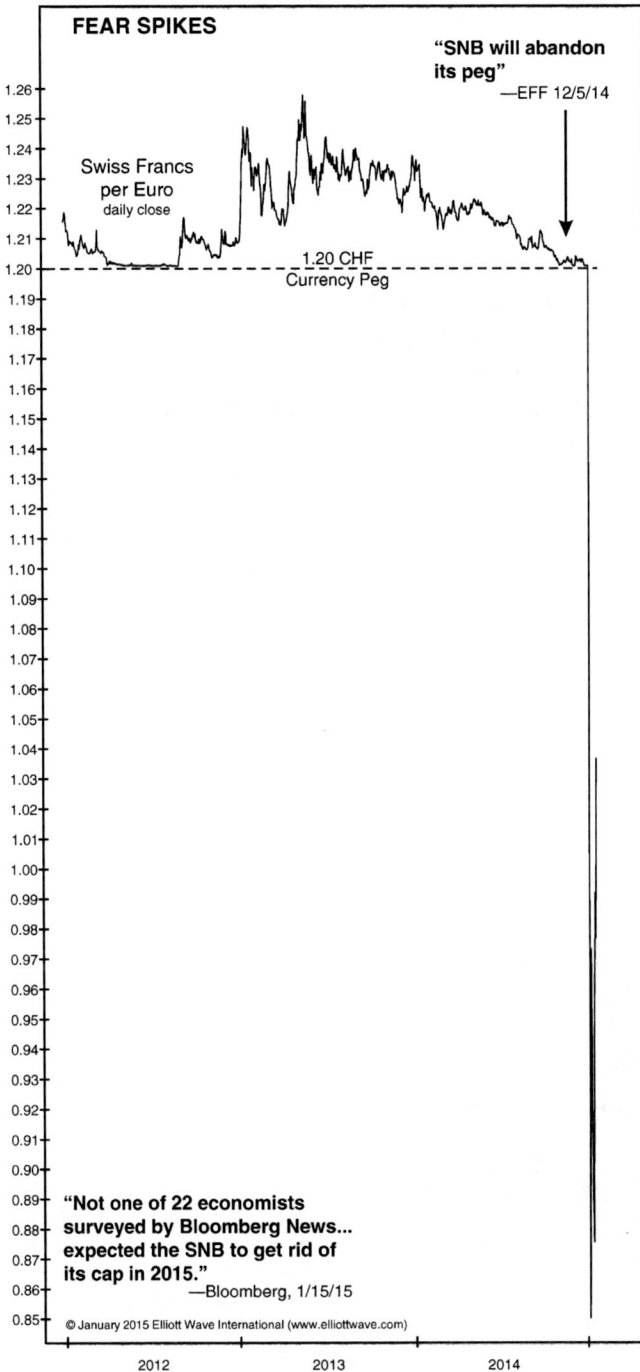

NOW...

FEAR SPIKES

"SNB will abandon its peg"
—EFF 12/5/14

Swiss Francs per Euro
daily close

1.26
1.25
1.24
1.23
1.22
1.21
1.20 —
1.19
1.18
1.17
1.16
1.15
1.14
1.13
1.12
1.11
1.10
1.09
1.08
1.07
1.06
1.05
1.04
1.03
1.02
1.01
1.00
0.99
0.98
0.97
0.96
0.95
0.94
0.93
0.92
0.91
0.90
0.89
0.88
0.87
0.86
0.85

1.20 CHF
Currency Peg

"Not one of 22 economists surveyed by Bloomberg News... expected the SNB to get rid of its cap in 2015."
—Bloomberg, 1/15/15

© January 2015 Elliott Wave International (www.elliottwave.com)

2012   2013   2014

Figure 2

REFERENCES

[1] Forsyth, Randall W., "Swiss Franc Shocker," *Barron's*, January 17, 2015.

[2] O'Brien, Matt, "Why Switzerland's Currency is Going Historically Crazy," *The Washington Post*, January 15, 2015.

[3] Petroff, Alanna, "Swiss Currency Brokers Bleed," *CNN Money*, January 16, 2015.

[4] "Forex Brokers Suffer Escalating Losses After Swiss Ditch Franc," *Financial Times*. January 16, 2015.

[5] Bosley, Catherine, "SNB Abandons Main Policy Tool as Jordan Goes for Shock Factor," *Bloomberg*, January 16, 2015.

[6] Bosley, Catherine, "Meet the Forecaster Who Saw Franc Gains Beyond SNB's Cap," *Bloomberg*, January 15, 2015.

[7] Meakin, Lucy, "SNB Unexpectedly Gives Up Cap on Franc, Lowers Deposit Rate," *Bloomberg*, January 15, 2015.

[8] See, for example, "Why the Swiss unpegged the franc," *The Economist*, January 18, 2015.

Chapter 30

A Proposed Relationship between Collective Approach-Avoidance Motivation and Social Mood

Kenneth Olson[1]

Social mood shapes a wide range of sociocultural phenomena. Research on a motivational construct that underlies many forms of animate life is consistent with the socionomic hypothesis and provides support for social mood as an important determinant of human social behavior.

The disposition to be motivated and live purposely is an evolutionary imperative "built into the most fundamental architecture of zoological organisms" (Klinger, 1998). Research from several fields suggests there are two basic motivational systems that regulate goal-directed approach and avoidance behaviors.

The avoidance system is commonly labeled the behavioral inhibition system, and the approach system is variously termed the behavioral activation system, behavioral facilitation system, behavioral approach system, and behavioral engagement system (see Olson, 2006). Influential research by Jeffrey Gray supported the existence of behavioral approach and inhibition systems that are based in the nervous system, are independent of each other, and represent appetitive and aversive motivation. Extensive research by Richard Davidson and colleagues concluded that neural substrates for behavioral approach and positive emotion are lateralized in the left anterior regions of the cerebral cortex, and that behavioral withdrawal and negative affect are lateralized in the right anterior cortical regions. Elliott and Thrash (2010) provided an overview of research and marshaled evidence that approach and avoidance temperaments are basic dimensions of personality.

The approach system facilitates the tendency to desire and seek rewards and goals, and it generates positive affect. In human studies it is empirically correlated with positive emotion. The avoidance system is sensitive to threats, punishment and aversive stimuli, is oriented toward avoiding and pre-venting harm and loss, and promotes vigilant attention to the environment. It is empirically correlated with negative emotion. Approach and avoidance motivation are associated with some, but not all, of the characteristics of positive and negative social mood identified by Prechter in Chapter 14 of *The Wave Principle of Human Social Behavior* (1999).

People differ from each other in the relative strength of their approach and avoidance tendencies. One might say that an individual with strong approach motivation sees the glass as half full, while an individual with strong avoidance motivation sees the glass as half empty (and worries about the glass tipping over).

I posit that social mood is associated with what I term collective approach-avoidance motivation. Collective approach motivation, the aggre-gate approach motivation of a group or society, is associated with positive social mood and leads to a societal focus on potential rewards and desirable outcomes. So, collective approach motivation stimulates collective goal-striving, risk-taking and achievement. Collective avoidance motivation, on the other hand, is associated with negative social mood and yields a societal emphasis on avoiding harm. It leads to collective caution, defensiveness and risk-aversion.

In the economic realm, collective approach/appetitive motivation is associated with positive social mood, which leads to confidence, investment and business expansion. Conversely, collective avoidance/aversive motiva-tion is associated with negative social mood, which contributes to anxiety, disinvestment and business contraction. Indeed, bull market psychology may be viewed as the collective motivation to *approach* risk and achieve gains, while bear market psychology is the collective motivation to *avoid* risk and prevent losses.<1> Similar to its use as an index of positive and negative social mood, the direction of the stock market is also a useful index of collective approach and avoidance motivation.

Approach and avoidance motivation are independent dimensions. The strength of collective approach motivation relative to collective avoidance motivation in a society varies over time. During bull markets, collective approach motivation is stronger than collective avoidance motivation. In bear markets, the opposite is true.

Avoidance motivation is correlated with negative emotions such as anger and rage, giving rise to the impulse to attack or destroy. For example, in response to perceived threat, the fight-or-flight response in animals and humans may lead to either self-protective withdrawal or violence.

Collective avoidance motivation may lead not only to social retrenchment and defensiveness but also to social protests and the desire to overthrow existing power structures that are viewed as threats.

Complex social phenomena typically have multiple influences. I am positing here a collective motivational system that is associated with social mood. This system fits the existing empirical evidence concerning the relations between approach-avoidance motivation and emotion, and it is conceptually consistent with the socionomic theory of motivational social mood.

REFERENCES

Elliott, A. J., & Thrash, T. M. (2010). Approach and avoidance temperament as basic dimensions of personality. *Journal of Personality, 78*, 1-42.

Klinger, E. (1998). The search for meaning in evolutionary perspective and its clinical implications. In P. Wong & P. Fry, (Eds.), *The Human Quest for Meaning*. Mahwah, N.J.: Lawrence Erlbaum & Associates, 1998, pp. 27-50

Olson, K. R. (2006). A literature review of social mood. *The Journal of Behavioral Finance, 7*, 193-2003.

EDITOR'S NOTES

[1] Kenneth Olson is Professor Emeritus of Psychology, Fort Hays State University.

<1> This formulation is fine, with the understanding that only objectively are speculators approaching risk. Subjectively, they perceive they are approaching reward, as Olson implies in the preceding paragraph. (See also Chapter 19.)

Chapter 31

This paper was financed by a grant from the forerunner of the Socionomics Foundation. Editor's notes, indicated in the text by numbers in <angle brackets>, are posted after the Author's Notes.

The Journal of Behavioral Finance
Vol. 6, No. 3, 2005, 144-160
Reprinted with permission

Social Mood and Financial Economics

John R. Nofsinger

The general level of optimism/pessimism in society is reflected by the emotions of financial decision-makers. Because these emotions are correlated across economic participants, our hypothesis leads to three important outcomes. First, social mood determines the types of decisions made by consumers, investors, and corporate managers alike. Extremes in social mood are characterized by optimistic (pessimistic) aggregate investment and business activity. Second, due to the efficient and emotional nature of stock transactions, the stock market itself is a direct measure or gauge of social mood. Third, since the tone and character of business activity follows, rather than leads, social mood, stock market trends help forecast future financial and economic activity. Specific predictions about stock market levels and trading volume, market volatility, firm expansion, leverage use, and IPO and M&A activity are also given.

Neoclassical financial economics, with a focus on general economic equilibrium, has tended to overlook the influence of social factors. In this,

John Nofsinger is Professor of Finance and Nihoul Faculty Fellow at Washington State University.

it has tended to follow the example of modern economics, which seems to see itself as an offshoot of physics, mechanics, or applied mathematics. One of the benefits enjoyed by these physical sciences, however, is the ability to study complete systems. That is, they can isolate the properties and characteristics of their theories in experiments.

Much of finance, on the other hand, is modeled in a Robinson Crusoe-type economy—isolated from the social system it belongs to. Yet viewing the economic system within the larger social system may have value. Economic dynamics can be considered an element of social dynamics, or, as Keynes [1955, p. 148] said,

> The theory of economic progress is more subordinate than are other portions of economic doctrine to general sociology.

In relating economic equilibrium to social equilibrium, Pareto [1963, pp. 1439–1440] said,

> States of the economic system may be regarded as particular cases of the general states of the sociological system.

The economy is not a physical system but a complex system of human interactions. The physics metaphor may examine stock market behavior from the perspective of economic "fundamentals," but what investors and corporate managers think is what drives their actions. And some psychologists would say that what people think derives from how they feel, which is influenced by their interactions with others.

In Prechter's [1999] "socionomic hypothesis," human interactions spread these emotions and characterize how people will act. When emotion or mood is correlated across society, the level of optimism (pessimism) affects financial decisions and can lead to marketwide phenomena. Several models have explored the effect of social mood on narrowly defined financial decisions. For example, DeLong et al. [1990] describe social mood as investor sentiment that influences stock market prices. Models of corporate finance decisions show the impact of optimism and overconfidence on capital budgeting and capital structure (e.g., Goel and Thakor [2002], Heaton [2002], and Gervais, Heaton, and Odean [2003]).

As we discuss later, researchers often explain the dilemmas surrounding merger waves, initial public offering (IPO) hot and cold markets, and business starts by blaming mass irrationality, sentiment, and optimism. The purpose of this paper is to connect these narrowly focused theories and reinterpret them as economic cases under the general sociological <1> state.

The recasting of individual optimism and investor sentiment as specific examples of a larger social mood is important, because it allows for new and more general hypotheses than the more focused models to date.

For example, consider that a high level of optimism in society implies more optimistic investors and corporate managers. This optimism may cause decision-makers to overestimate their probability of success and underestimate the riskiness of their decisions. Many investors will buy stock, trade, and respond to IPOs to excess. At the same time, corporate managers will choose to make more corporate investments, use more debt financing, and conduct more acquisitions.

The social mood is also reflected in consumer behavior. When society is optimistic, investors may be more willing to take on additional debt and increase spending. The social mood governing the activities of investors, corporate managers, and consumers drives the stock market up and increases the size of the economy. If social mood rises too high, however, the extreme overconfidence and euphoria can cause a stock market bubble and corporate overinvestment. Alternatively, when society is pessimistic, investors may tend to reduce their portfolio risk, stock markets may decline and become more volatile, and companies may make fewer capital expenditures. Therefore, social mood can be expected to govern the tone and character of financial and economic activity. Prechter [1999] posits this idea in his socionomic hypothesis.

A more general approach to social mood can predict the types and timing of economic activities that may manifest themselves. One financial decision that can be made and implemented quickly is the buy/sell/hold decision of stock market investors. Others, such as the decision to acquire other companies, conduct an IPO, or embark on bold capital budgeting projects, take time to unfold. Economists typically measure these activities after they are completed. Therefore, an improvement in social mood will result in more M&A activity, IPOs, and capital spending several months later.

Financial markets adjust to changes in mood faster than real markets. As Prechter [1999] argues, the influence of social mood on stock market participants is so strong and immediate that stock market activity and its movements are a good measure of social mood and its trends.

The next section reviews human interaction and decision-making. Particularly important is how society's mood and consensus opinions can influence the individual decision-maker. We define the characteristics and ramifications of "social mood," and explain its importance to stock market participants, asset prices, and corporate financial decisions.

Human Interaction and Economics

Human Interaction

Shiller [1995] points out that human society has had an evolutionary advantage in its ability to respond collectively because of our interpersonal communication skills. While communication was historically by speech, technology has developed innovations in writing, telecommunications, broadcasting, and, most recently, the internet. This conversation allows for a rapid exchange of information and opinion.

Economic models of this exchange are in the form of informational cascades (see Bikhchandani, Hirshleifer, and Welch [1992], Banerjee [1992], Elison and Fudenberg [1993]). However, interpersonal conversation seems to be more effective than the one-sided nature of the media (see McGuire [1985]) because it provides more interaction, which stimulates emotions. Along with conveying information, communicating emotion and mood also seem to be important.

For example, conversation is important to the stock market. Stockbrokers converse with clients and other brokers, analysts communicate with executives and managers, and they form local groups and associations to interact with each other. Institutional investors also form groups for sharing information, and individual investors may talk to family, neighbors, colleagues, and friends about investing.

Shiller and Pound [1989] surveyed institutional and individual investors about their patterns of communication, and found that direct interpersonal communications were very important to their investment decisions. Hong, Kubik, and Stein [2005] examine the portfolio holdings of money managers to test the premise that fund managers who work in the same city are more likely to exchange investment ideas by word of mouth. They find that managers in the same city are more likely to trade the same set of stocks. The results are robust to controls for local and familiarity biases. They conclude their evidence is consistent with information being spread via word of mouth.

Human interactions are how people share information and communicate emotion and mood. The cues we obtain from others influence our own opinions. A shared attitude, or social mood, is thus propagated. <2>

Emotions and Decision Making Under Uncertainty

Economists and psychologists who study the choices individuals make under risk and uncertainty characterize those decisions as an assessment of the consequences of the alternatives. From the expected utility perspective, people assess the severity and likelihood of the possible outcomes using subjective probabilities and some cognitive expectations-based equations to arrive at a decision.

More recently, psychologists and economists have examined the role of emotions in risky decision-making (e.g., Dowling and Lucey [2005], Elster [1998], Loewenstein [2000], Romer [2000], and Slovic et al. [2002]). Loewenstein et al. [2001] present a model in which influences unrelated to the cognitive evaluation at hand can affect the decision. This model is illustrated in Figure 1. Note that a person anticipates the outcomes of the alternatives and also anticipates the emotions of experiencing those outcomes. This process affects both the cognitive evaluation process and the current emotional state of the decision-maker. A person must also assess the subjective probabilities of each outcome. Lastly, other factors also affect the process. These include how clearly (or vividly) the outcomes are felt, the immediacy of the situation, and the background mood. We argue that this background mood can have an important influence on a risky decision.

Loewenstein et al.'s [2001] model also illustrates how emotions interact with the cognitive evaluation process to eventually form a decision. At times, emotional reactions diverge from cognitive evaluations and dominate the decision process. Forgas [1995] presents a model that measures to what extent people are likely to rely on emotions in decision-making. He argues that decision characteristics like risk and uncertainty are factors in whether

Risk as Feelings Perspective

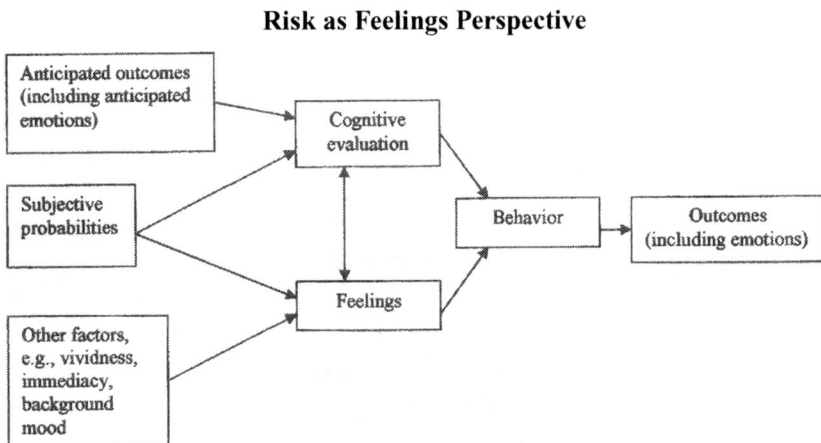

source: Loewenstein et al. (2001)

Figure 1

feelings play a role. The greater the complexity and uncertainty of a situation, the more emotions influence the decision.

Slovic et al. [2002] describe the affect heuristic, which has much in common with the Loewenstein et al. [2001] model and has similar outcomes. The term affect refers to subtle feelings of which people are often unaware. Pleasant (unpleasant) feelings motivate actions and thoughts to extend (avoid) the feelings. Using the affective impression to make decisions can be easier than weighing the pros, cons, and outcome probabilities. This is especially true when the decision is complex. Since the use of affect can be characterized as a mental shortcut, it is classified as a heuristic. The central question then becomes, what is the relative importance between affect and cognition in decision-making?

Slovic et al. [2002] argue that emotions play a large role in decision-making under uncertainty. In one example, they cite the patients of neurologist Antonio Damasio [1994], who had all suffered damage to the ventromedial frontal cortices of the brain. This damage leaves intelligence, memory, and the capacity for logic intact but impairs the ability to feel. Through various experiments, it is surmised that the lack of emotion in the decision-making process destroys the ability to make rational decisions (see Damasio, Tranel, and Damasio [1990]). Indeed, Damasio's patients became socially dysfunctional after their injuries. Damasio concludes that emotion is an integral component of reason.

Financial decisions are complex and include risk and uncertainty. Thus, the background mood of Loewenstein et al. [2001] and/or the affect heuristic of Slovic et al. [2002] may influence financial decisions. People often misattribute the mood they are in to the decision at hand. That is, people in a good mood may be more optimistic, and people in a bad mood more pessimistic.

Johnson and Tversky [1983] report that misattribution of mood can affect the evaluation of a risky decision. In other words, a person may make decisions partly because of emotional influences that have nothing to do with the situation. If someone is in a good mood, they may be more likely to be optimistic in evaluating an investment. Good (bad) moods will increase (decrease) the likelihood of investing in risky assets, like stocks. The misattribution bias has been tested in financial decisions in several ways. Equity returns are found to be affected by weather-induced moods (Saunders [1993]), sunshine (Hirshleifer and Shumway [2003]), the winter blues (Kamstra, Kramer, and Levi [2003]), and geomagnetic storm-induced moods (Krivelyova and Robotti [2003]). These investigations illustrate that investors misattribute their good/bad mood to perceived economic conditions and stock market prospects.

Social Mood

As the previous section illustrates, an individual's attitudes are not based solely on independent analysis. Interaction with others has a strong influence and leads to a shared emotion, or social mood.<3> Collectively shared opinions and beliefs shape individual decisions, which aggregate into social trends.

The economy is the sum of the economic interactions in society. One person's decision to, say, buy a car or risk the firm's capital on expansion may not affect the economy. But if the social mood fosters many people to buy cars and expand their businesses, then the economy expands. That is, the level of social mood affects the economy because participants interact.

Given the level of attention paid to the monthly consumer confidence data released by The Confidence Board, it appears the media, economists, and investors also find the relationship between mood and the economy important. We [socionomists] go one step further and propose that economic optimism is a subset of social optimism.

We also posit that a substantial change in the attitudes of society will lead to significant and important events in the society. Shiller [1984] models the diffusion of opinion, or mood, through a population using a general epidemic model, i.e., the spread of a mood is similar to the spread of a disease. The rate at which people are exposed to the changing attitudes and are persuaded equals the "infection rate." The parameters of the model can differ from one social movement to another, causing some to be long-lasting, while others are short-lived.

Prechter [1999] argues that changes in social mood cause people to make different decisions. A change in mood may begin with some people undergoing a substantial change or by most people undergoing a small change. These people make decisions and act on this change in mood. Their interaction and communication with others causes further mood swings in others. The collective decisions take time to appear in various ways. For example, a newfound optimism can be seen quickly in the stock market because it takes relatively little time and effort to trade. However, it takes longer for this optimism to be recorded in economic activity because of the additional time needed to plan and execute new business activity.

A Theory of Social Mood

Social mood changes through time. Positive moods lead to productive activities, while negative moods lead to unproductive ones. Consider the simple model of mood in Figure 2. Increasing mood is associated with emotions like optimism, happiness, and hope. These emotions become extreme

Social Mood Cycle and Phases

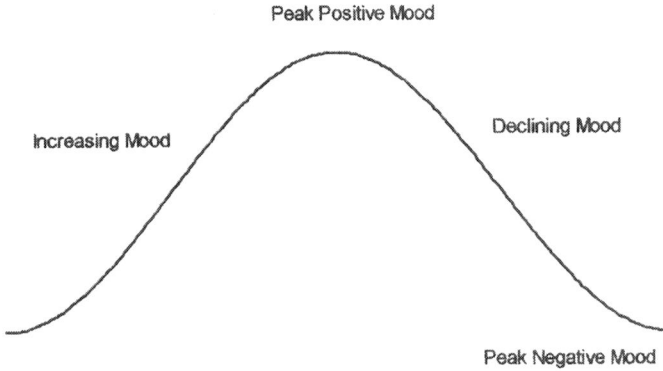

Figure 2

Emotional Characteristics at Each Phase of the Social Mood Cycle			
Increasing Mood	**Peak Positive Mood**	**Declining Mood**	**Peak Negative Mood**
Optimism	Overconfidence	Pessimism	Fear
Happiness	Euphoria	Sadness	Depression
Generous	Excess	Conservatism	Stinginess
Inclusion	Ambivalence	Exclusion	Segregation
Supportiveness	Graciousness	Defensiveness	Antagonistic
Hope	Trust	Suspicion	Mistrust

at the peak, leading to overconfidence, euphoria, and excess. A decreasing mood is associated with pessimism, conservatism, and suspicion. The lowest trough of social mood has strong emotions like fear, stinginess, and antagonism. These moods influence the decisions that create the resulting social activity. Therefore, social mood can be identified by collective behavior, varying from the type and tone of popular films (Prechter [2003]), to the character of laws being debated and enacted.

The level of social mood also determines the general attitude toward business and businesspeople. When social mood is high, corporate CEOs are treated like heroes and business is considered one of the most sacred and important institutions in society. When social mood is low, executives are considered greedy and companies are believed to be cheating the public. During periods of low social mood, these attitudes lead to more government intervention in business. Governments may become more active in antitrust activities (Prechter [2003]), and enact more regulations when social mood is declining. During optimistic times, however, the government may allow more mergers and deregulate industries.

For example, the positive mood periods of the 1920s and the 1990s saw repeals of the separation of commercial and investment banking (Nofsinger and Kim [2003] <4>). The 1990s brought limitations on the ability of investors to sue for corporate fraud. The low mood periods of the 1930s and early 2000s saw laws enacted to increase regulation, creating both the Securities and Exchange Commission and the Public Company Accounting Oversight Board.

Nofsinger and Kim [2003] <4> hypothesize that the changing social mood determines the nature of financial economic decisions, among other social actions. The implications of this theory are important to many areas of finance.

In the following sections, we illustrate how social mood impacts stock markets and corporate finance. For evidence of this hypothesis, we draw on dozens of studies across many areas of financial economics. We emphasize three main [socionomic] predictions:

(1) Social mood determines the types of decisions made by consumers, investors, and corporate managers alike.

(2) Due to the efficient and emotional nature of stock transactions, the stock market itself is a direct gauge of social mood.

(3) Since the tone and character of business activity follows rather than leads social mood, stock market trends help forecast future financial and economic activity.

Social Mood and the Stock Market

The stock market includes many participants who interact with each other and with society. The collective level of optimism or pessimism in society impacts investor decisions (the "social mood" of Prechter [1999], or the "background mood" of Loewenstein et al. [2001] and Slovic et al. [2002]).

Consider that an investor's decision to buy or sell a stock is based upon expectations. A rational expectations model assumes that investor expectations derive from using tools like fundamental analysis and modern portfolio theory. These tools require making certain assumptions about the future. What growth rate will the firm achieve over the next three years? What is its expected return, expected variance, and expected correlation with other assets? Even the most sophisticated investors do not agree about which methods produce the most accurate assumptions. The rational expectations model requires investors to resolve these uncertainties in an unbiased and rational way. Yet investor mood, influenced by social mood, may also impact these assumptions.

Au et al. [2003] examine foreign exchange trading decisions under different mood environments. They find that traders in a good mood environment tended to be overconfident, take unwarranted risks, make less accurate decisions, and perform poorly. Traders in a bad mood environment were more conservative and made more accurate decisions. We see that the general level of optimism in society affects the level of optimism in individuals, which in turn biases important investment opinions and assumptions.

Ivo Welch has implemented several surveys of financial economics professors that revealed interesting points about moods and financial decisions. The first series of surveys was implemented from 1997 through 1998; there was an additional survey in 1999 (Welch [2000]). Altogether, the surveys elicited 226 responses. Note that they were completed during a strong bull market. One question asked about the expected annual equity risk premium over the next thirty years. The median and mean response was 7% and 7.2%, respectively. In another question about stock market return mean reversion versus the random walk, the professors tended to believe that the stock market mean reverts.

Welch [2001] surveyed the profession again in 2001, when the market environment was much different. The S&P 500 had declined approximately 25% from its peak, and general social mood was declining. Given the earlier expression that stock returns may exhibit mean reversion, we expect respondents to predict a higher equity premium estimate after a market decline. However, the median and mean annual thirty-year premiums given were only 5% and 5.5%. 122 of the 510 total respondents had completed the earlier survey. While their updated estimates were about 2% lower, they reiterated their belief that stock returns are mean-reverting. Yet their estimates are not consistent with this belief. They are consistent with the hypothesis that social mood influences a person's predictions for the future. Predictions in periods of optimism lead to high stock return forecasts, and predictions in periods of pessimism lead to low stock return forecasts.

Most individual investors have a lower level of market valuation skills than finance professors, so we might expect their market forecasts to be influenced even more by the general social mood <5>. UBS Paine Webber hires The Gallup Organization to poll 1,000 U.S. individual investors every month to compute their sentiment index. In one question, the poll asks investors what overall annual rate of return they expect the market to earn over the next twelve months (UBS [2002]). On December 31, 1999, when the market was near its peak and the S&P 500 was at 1,469, the investor mean response was 15.3%. One year later, after the market had fallen 10% to 1,320, the investor mean response was 10.5%. The year 2001 closed with a 13% decline in the S&P 500 to 1,148. At the end of 2001, the investor mean response was 8.0%. Finally, after the Index fell another 23% in 2002 to 880, investors expected a market return of 5.9%. The 9.4 [percentage-point] difference in expectations over three years illustrates how the level of the stock market, and the social mood accompanying it, influences investor opinions about the future.

The hypothesis also proposes that forecasts will be the most positive at the peak of social mood, when euphoria is common. Consider that forecasts may be made purely by unbiased economic analysis, purely by emotion influenced by social mood, or via some other mixture. The influence of social mood is likely to be higher when it is at an extreme, like a peak or a bottom <6>. Dreman [2001] expresses this idea as follows:

> In reality, during periods of mania or panic, psychological influences are actually thought to play the biggest role in the decisions of most money managers and analysts. Cognitive, social and group psychologies all provide abundant experiments illustrating how psychological influences can divert decision-makers from purely rational decision-making.

Indeed, at the peak of the internet stock bubble, many analysts and financial pundits proposed that traditional valuation tools were no longer as helpful in analyzing the "new economy" firms.

Shiller [1984] recognizes that most investors do not understand data analysis, risk adjustments, and have no model (or a very incomplete one) of the behavior of stock prices. As they lack the necessary knowledge and skills for evaluating speculative assets, "the process by which their opinions are derived may be especially social." When social mood affects the attitudes and decisions of stock market participants, the stock market itself can be influenced.[1]

Shiller [1984] also mentions this link:

> Stock prices are likely to be among the prices that are relatively vulnerable to purely social movements because there is no accepted theory by which to understand the worth of stocks and no clearly predictable consequences to changing one's investments.

He presents a great deal of evidence that social movements are an important cause of stock price movements.

We argue that the stock market itself is a measure or gauge of social mood. Social movements like fads and cultural trends are results, not causes, of changes in social mood, as reflected by changes in aggregate stock prices. This perspective is consistent with the line of inquiry throughout this paper.

Equity Premium

Mehra and Prescott [1985] questioned whether rational investors with constant relative risk aversion (CRRA) utility could account for the high level of the equity risk premium. The rationality and CRRA assumptions fail to account for the time-varying properties of the observed risk premium. Recent models have departed from rational expectations and CRRA.

For example, Abel [2002] explores the impact of tendencies toward pessimism and doubt. His model predicts an equity risk premium closer to historical levels. Abel does not comment on the source of investor pessimism and doubt. Cecchetti, Lam, and Mark [2000] introduce both pessimistic and optimistic investor beliefs. Specifically, investors have relatively pessimistic (optimistic) beliefs about the persistence of the contraction (expansion) states of their endowment growth. By including these distorted beliefs in their model, Cecchetti, Lam, and Mark are able to match both the historical level of the equity risk premium and its volatility.

Mehra and Sah [2002] present a model where investors estimate two subjective parameters, the discount factor and the level of risk aversion. They propose that these estimates fluctuate over time, and that the fluctuations are positively correlated across investors. Introducing these fluctuations allows us to better explain the volatility of equity prices than models using both rational and CRRA assumptions. Mehra and Sah do not explore the source of what they call "mood fluctuations." However, the optimistic and/or pessimistic parameters used must be correlated across investors. Therefore, we argue that social mood is the source of these distorted beliefs.

Market Volatility

Stock market volatility has been a constant source of controversy among scholars. Two arguments stand out. First, markets become overvalued at times, causing a bubble and an eventual crash. We discuss market bubbles in the next section. Second, the stock market is more volatile than one would expect using rational expectations.

The debate about excess market volatility is summarized in Shiller [2003]. If markets are efficient, the aggregate stock market value must be an estimate of the underlying present value. As this process requires a forecast of future parameters, like dividend growth and discount rates, the market may be periodically wrong, either over- or undervalued. Under rational expectations theory and the efficient market hypothesis, deviations from fundamental value should not be systematic or predictable, however.

The key insight in this controversy is that the forecast must be less variable than what is being forecasted. Otherwise, high estimates would indicate positive forecast errors and low estimates would indicate negative forecast errors, and thus would be predictable. Therefore, Shiller [1981] and LeRoy and Porter [1981] argue that stock market volatility should be lower than the underlying fundamental value. They formulate variance bounds of the underlying fundamental value, and show that the stock market variance exceeds those bounds.

Shiller [2003] compares real stock prices with estimates of fundamental value, estimated as the present value of future dividends using various assumptions. No matter how fundamental value is computed, Shiller illustrates that real stock prices are more volatile than the underlying value. There are periods when the stock market is severely over- or undervalued. But socionomic theory posits that the stock market trends reflect social mood. The volatility of the stock market reflects changes in social mood.

Mood can strongly impact the valuation of an investor who uses present value methods, like the discounted dividend model. To illustrate, we proxy fundamental value using the constant discount rate version, $PV = D_1/(k-g)$. Market participants must predict this constant growth rate. Given the influence of social mood on risky and uncertain decisions, the expected value of the growth rate, $E(g)$, may become biased.[2] This in turn biases market value expectations and trading behavior. Market participants estimate their expected market value as $E(P) = D_1/(k - E(g))$.

Consider the deviation of expected market value from the investor's notion of fundamental value:

$$E(P) - PV = \frac{D_1}{k - E(g)} - \frac{D_1}{k - g} \tag{1}$$

Rearranging the variables in Equation (1) produces:

$$\frac{E(P)}{PV} = \frac{k - g}{k - E(g)} \tag{2}$$

Equation (2) illustrates how misvalued expectations develop. Consider an average annual market return of 11% and a long-term dividend growth rate of 5%. When the social mood is high, market participants may be convinced through the media that they are in a "new economy." In response, they overestimate the growth rate as 7%. Equation (2) then shows that the market may become overvalued by 50%, $E(P)/PV = 1.5$. On the other hand, if social mood is very pessimistic, investors may underestimate the growth rate as 3%. This would lead to the stock market being undervalued by 25%.[3]

The source of short-term volatility is another stock market puzzle. Schwert [1989] examines monthly stock volatility in relation to the volatility of macroeconomic variables from 1859 to 1987. Some of this analysis is also extended through the first half of 2001 in Schwert [2002]. Schwert [1989] summarizes his findings in several main points:

(1)   Stock market volatility is high during recessions and other periods of uncertainty such as wars (the Civil War, World War I, and World War II).

(2)   The market was most volatile during the Great Depression and has been very volatile recently.

(3)   Stock market volatility does not seem closely related to other measures of economic volatility, except that it is a predictor of macroeconomic volatility.

Schwert [1989] briefly suggested several rational expectations views of the high volatility during the Great Depression because he was "hesitant to cede all this unexplained behavior to social psychologists as evidence of fads or bubbles." Nevertheless, his findings do seem consistent with social mood. Pessimistic and declining social mood precedes disagreement of opinion, conflict, and strife. This disagreement manifests itself in the market through volatility. Surely, periods of recession, war, and depression would be considered times of negative social mood <7>.

In summary, the general volatility in the stock market seems too high to simply be caused by rational market decision-makers making unbiased forecasts of the present value of future dividends. Our explanation is that the level of social mood biases forecasts and causes the market to have historically high or low valuations for substantial periods of time. During periods of low (or declining) social mood, the increased general conflict within society is also reflected in stock market volatility.

Bubbles

Market bubbles and subsequent crashes are another expression of stock market volatility. Capital markets throughout history have experienced episodes of widespread euphoric speculation, followed by steady (and sometimes sharp) declines. Notable examples include the 17th century tulip mania, the roaring 1920s stock market, the Japanese stock market of the 1980s, and the most recent technology stock "irrational exuberance."

Both economists and sociologists have studied these manias. Economists tend to look at economic fundamentals for an explanation,[4] while sociologists study the "crowd mind." They tend to find that a stock market mania exhibits the same characteristics as amusement fads or clothing fashion (Visano [2002]). Indeed, they consider manias and panics to be periods when collective behavior and social mood subverts established individual guides of behavior (Turner and Killian [1987]).

Consider the Japanese stock market bubble and the U.S. technology bubble. The Japanese stock market experienced a dramatic rise in the 1980s. The Nikkei began 1984 near 10,000 and peaked in 1989 near 39,000. Then, in nine months, the market fell to 21,000. Three years after the peak, the market had fallen 56%. The market had not recovered even ten years later, when the Nikkei ended 2002 under 9,000. Shiller, Kon-Ya, and Tsutsui [1996] report that the fundamentals of the Japanese economy do not explain the bubble and crash. They posit that investor attitudes may be relevant.

The recent run-up and subsequent crash of technology stocks (particularly internet firms) is another example of a stock market bubble. As early as December 1996, Federal Reserve Bank Chairman Alan Greenspan warned investors about irrational exuberance. Many investors seemed to acknowledge that the stock market was experiencing a bubble, but they invested anyway. Fisher and Statman [2002a] surveyed investors in the late 1990s. Individual investor forecasts imply they believed the market was experiencing a bubble, but they thought it would continue to inflate. This seems to be an extreme in optimism.

Our [socionomic] view is that speculative bubbles are inflated by the unusually high optimism of investors. A positive social mood influences investor optimism. The peak of this social mood is characterized by emotional decisions, not rigorous evaluation. The cognitive evaluation analysis illustrates that stock prices have become too high, yet the emotion of optimism becomes a stronger influence in the decision-making process. Stories communicated from person to person seem to mollify the cognitive evaluation aspect of decision-making, allowing the emotional side to influence the outcome. A common phrase in a bubble is "We are in a new era, a new economy, in which the traditional views of economics just don't work." This was said about railroads in the 1870s, the Federal Reserve System in the 1920s, and the internet in the 1990s. So investors keep buying stocks and drive prices far above historical averages. Shiller [2002] argues that individuals inevitably wind up trusting this common view, even when it may be only superficially plausible. In other words, the optimism of others validates our own optimism.

Eventually, the euphoric social mood begins to decline. The previous degree of optimism proves unfounded. As the optimism bias fades, the cognitive evaluation aspect of the decision process becomes more influential. <8> Prices are viewed as too high; investors stop buying, or even sell. A stock market crash ensues. If social mood drops very low, pessimism will drive prices below historical averages. Thus, the mood in society influences the investor optimism/pessimism that drives speculative asset bubbles and crashes.

Investor and Consumer Sentiment

DeLong et al. [1990] model a class of investors whose expectations about asset returns are not warranted by fundamentals. These expectations are known as investor sentiment. When sentiment is correlated across investors, the model illustrates that strong optimistic (pessimistic) sentiment can cause stock prices to exceed (go lower than) fundamental value for long periods.

As an empirical test of the influence of investor sentiment on asset prices, Lee, Shleifer, and Thaler [1991] examine several puzzles. First, closed-end funds frequently trade at a discount from net asset value (NAV). While the average is around 10%, this discount can vary substantially over time. Also, both discounts and changes in discounts of all closed-end funds tend to be highly correlated with each other. Individual investors are the most active type of investor in closed-end funds, so Lee, Shleifer, and Thaler [1991] argue they are most likely to be sentiment investors. Individual investors are also active in small-company stocks and IPOs. They examine small-firm returns, discounts, and IPO activity, and find them to be highly correlated. When sentiment investors are optimistic, they are willing to take more risks and buy stocks. Their buying particularly influences closed-end fund prices, which decrease discounts. Their buying also moves small-company stock prices and encourages investment banks to take more firms public. Pessimistic sentiment causes selling, which can be seen in increasing discounts, falling stock prices, and lower IPO activity.

Lee, Shleifer, and Thaler [1991] also examine the relationships between monthly changes in discounts and macroeconomic factors. They conclude that monthly changes in discounts are not highly correlated with fundamentals. Therefore, the sentiment may originate outside the economy.

We [socionomists] argue that investor sentiment is actually a subset of the larger social mood. There is a popular belief that a link exists between how people behave as investors and how they behave as consumers. Consider, as we mentioned earlier, how much attention and importance is given to measures such as the consumer confidence data, as well as the Index of Consumer Expectations released by the University of Michigan's Survey Research Center. We refer to these types of measures as consumer sentiment.

The Index of Consumer Expectations is derived from questions about personal finances, business conditions, and buying conditions. The Center contends that consumer optimism, or pessimism, is an important predictor for the economy. The Center states,

> When many people change from an optimistic to a pessimistic view of economic prospects at the same time, it has been repeatedly found that a widespread shift toward postponement of expenditures follows.[5]

The U.S. Department of Commerce's Bureau of Economic Analysis also finds this measure of economic optimism important, and includes it in the composite Index of Leading Indicators. As we argue here, optimism in society leads to economic activities that will be later measured as economic expansion.

Fisher and Statman [2002b] illustrate the misperception that consumer sentiment follows the stock market. They show many instances where the media blames pessimistic attitudes on a declining stock market, and examine the relationship between consumer sentiment, investor sentiment, and stock market levels. They find that investor sentiment and consumer sentiment are highly correlated and move together. We argue that consumer sentiment and investor sentiment are mood outcomes that flow from the same dominant social mood. Fisher and Statman [2002b] also show that sentiment moves concurrently with the stock market.

Jansen and Nahius [2003] study the relationship between the stock market and consumer confidence in eleven European countries. They find that the strongest relationship is contemporaneous, not lead/lag, suggesting that both investor and consumer activities reflect social mood. However, the stock market is a better measure of social mood because it is measured instantaneously, while spending is measured with a time lag.[6]

Theory Assertions in Investments and Asset Pricing

Social mood affects the thoughts of stock market participants, and, therefore, stock prices. However, the effect is on aggregate valuation levels and occurs over time. This is not a cross-sectional prediction, although it can be considered consistent with Samuelson's [1998] dictum that the stock market is *micro* efficient, but *macro* inefficient.

Jung and Shiller [2002] explore this dictum. Essentially, the stock market is relatively efficient cross-sectionally.

Picking the stocks that will provide positive alphas in the near future is difficult at best. Yet the stock market is more predictable in the aggregate and over the long run. Due to changing social moods, long time-series waves of over- and undervaluations <9> occur for the aggregate market.

Positive social mood is characterized by investor and consumer optimism. The mood is quickly incorporated into stock market prices through a disposition toward higher-risk portfolios, stock buying, and greater levels of trading. The stock market rises and eventually becomes overvalued relative to historical averages. Negative social mood is characterized by pessimism and conflict. It coincides with stock price declines, higher volatility, and a flight toward safer portfolios. Lastly, stock market trends are useful measures of social mood trends.

Social Mood and Corporate Finance

This section examines the relationship between psychological and emotional bias in corporate finance decisions. Cognitive bias has a greater potential to influence decision-making in corporate finance than in the capital markets, because fewer individuals are making the decisions. In addition, due to asymmetric information, it is difficult for other stakeholders to assess the rationality of most decisions. But even if they do detect irrationality, most stakeholders do not have much recourse, because they have only limited ability to arbitrage suboptimal decisions. Or, as Heaton [2002] states, "there are larger arbitrage bounds protecting managerial irrationality than protecting security market mispricing."

An expanding literature describes how moods like optimism affect capital budgeting, capital structure, merger activity, and entrepreneurial activity. Most of this research investigates how the behavior of optimistic managers compares to that of rational managers.[7] At the end of this section, we recast these predictions for a social mood exhibiting time-varying properties.

Corporate Executive Behavior

March and Shapira [1987] examine corporate managers' perspectives on taking risk. They conclude that:

> Managers are quite insensitive to estimates of the probabilities of possible outcomes; their decisions are particularly affected by the way their attention is focused on critical performance targets, and they make a sharp distinction between taking risks and gambling.

These perceptions of risk are different from what we might expect from the classical rational expectations concept of risk-taking. In departing from this classical concept, research is examining the outcomes of corporate executives who may be susceptible to optimism or overconfidence. It is possible that many managers, who have achieved great success just to become top managers, may tend to overestimate their probability of success and underestimate the risk of their decisions. Goel and Thakor [2002] suggest that overconfident managers are more likely to take on riskier decisions because they underestimate the level of risk they are taking.

Since optimistic managers may overestimate the chance of a good performance, they may have a tendency to take on more capital budgeting projects (Heaton [2002]). Gervais, Heaton, and Odean [2003] posit that optimistic managers will believe that the expected net present value of potential projects is greater than it actually is. Their model predicts that optimistic and overconfident managers are more likely to undertake a project more quickly.

Hackbarth [2004] models the capital structure decisions of optimistic and overconfident managers. Specifically, these managers overestimate the growth rate of corporate assets, and underestimate their riskiness. His model predicts that optimism and overconfidence create a predisposition to issuing debt. Because the managers believe that equity is more underpriced than debt, they prefer to grow with internal capital first, debt second, and equity last.

Optimistic managers are more likely to accept more and riskier capital budgeting projects, thus creating a desire for additional capital. If the level of optimism in managers is correlated across the economy, it will be reflected in increasing business investment.

Mergers

The quantity of mergers and acquisitions over time has been somewhat of a puzzle. Financial economists have yet to find a consistent return to acquiring firms. At best, the literature suggests, mergers bring no value on average. At worst, the average merger destroys the acquirer's wealth. Yet Rappaport and Sirower [1999] report there were 12,356 announced mergers involving U.S. targets in 1998 alone.

One explanation for this large number comes from the idea that the managers of acquiring firms are optimistic or overconfident. Roll [1986], in his "hubris hypothesis," suggests that bidding firms irrationally fail to incorporate the winner's curse. Thus, they continue to bid in a takeover process that has a negative expected value. The bidding manager's decision is similar to the capital budgeting decision.

Malmendier and Tate [2003] model manager behavior using optimism and overconfidence characteristics similar to those discussed in the capital budgeting and capital structure discussion above. Overconfident CEOs are more likely to conduct mergers, because they overvalue the target firm's assets and overestimate the returns from potential synergies. Empirically, they find that overconfident CEOs are more likely to conduct a merger than rational CEOs. The resulting operations of the merged firm also support this hypothesis. In a sample of highly leveraged acquisitions, Kaplan and Ruback [1995] show that realized earnings end up lower, on average, in the first couple of years than acquiring managers forecasted.

Mitchell and Mulherin [1996] study mergers and conclude that (1) mergers occur in waves, and (2) within each wave, mergers cluster by industry. They posit that the merger waves are caused by unexpected industry shocks. Andrade, Mitchell, and Stafford [2001] argue that the most likely shocks are from deregulation. They identify the key industry deregulations of the past several decades and relate those industries to the merger waves. They conclude:

> The fact is that deregulation precipitated widespread consolidation and restructuring of a few industries in the 1990s, frequently accomplished through merger.

We argue that merger waves are due to the high social mood that causes more CEOs to be optimistic <10>. Merger waves are one result of a social mood cycle. In addition, the deregulation shock is not exogenous because it does not occur on its own. It happens because many participants in the industry want deregulation and lobby politicians for changes in the law. Deregulation itself is the result of the same changes in social mood that later result in the merger wave (Nofsinger and Kim [2003]).<4>

Rosen [2005] examines the short-term market reaction to merger announcements and the long-term performance of the bidder. He finds that merger announcements made during hot merger markets (or merger waves) have larger short-term market reaction than those made during cold merger markets. However, the positive short-term reaction is reversed by poor long-term performance. He concludes the evidence is consistent with the hypothesis that managerial irrationality (like overconfidence or hubris) plays a role in mergers. But he finds that investor optimism is also a factor. The paper concludes by stating:

> If investor sentiment affects the market reaction to a merger, then merger waves might reflect swings in investor optimism as much as the conditions of the merging firms or the economy.

Rosen therefore connects manager optimism with investor optimism. We argue that the optimism of the two groups is indeed correlated, because the general level of optimism in society affects both groups.

To illustrate, Figure 3 shows the stock market level graphed with the value of merger deals[8] each year. The level of optimism/pessimism between corporate mangers and investors appears highly correlated. Note that the M&A deals generally lag the market trends during increasing social mood and stock price periods. However, the lag does not appear to be as long in the decreasing mood and stock price periods. We argue this is because halting a deal in progress can be done more quickly than starting a new deal.

The M&A Deal Value and the Stock Market

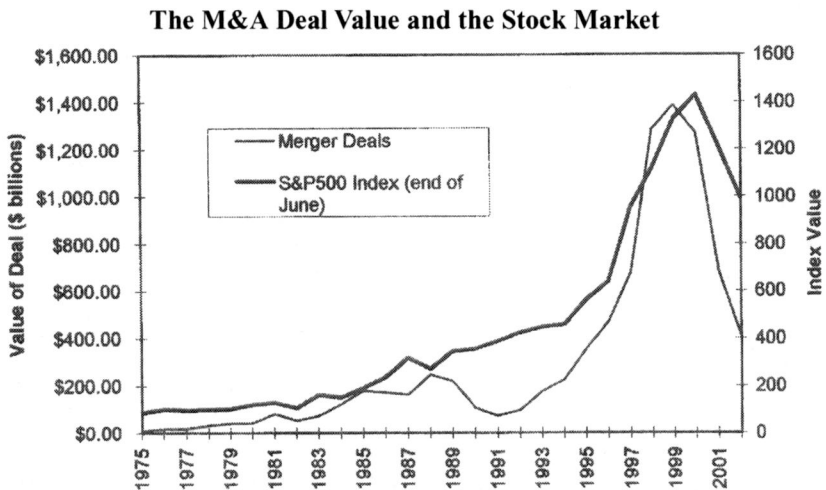

source: Mergerstat

Figure 3

Corporate mergers must comply with federal antitrust law. The Clayton Act forbids a firm to purchase the assets or the stock of another firm if the purchase might substantially lessen competition. The U.S. Department of Justice examines each merger and how it will affect competition, and [it] can block the merger. When social mood is high, few major mergers get blocked. Alternatively, mergers that would have been approved during high social mood periods frequently do get blocked during low social mood periods. In a high social mood period like the 1990s, megamergers that created oligopolies occurred in the cable, finance, publishing, and telecommunication industries, to name just a few. Alternatively, as the mood changed in 2000, the government blocked Worldcom's purchase of Sprint, the Heinz purchase of BeechNut Nutrition, and Burlington Northern Santa Fe's purchase of Canadian National Railway. Other mergers, like AOL and Time Warner, were allowed but received a great deal of scrutiny. <10>

Initial Public Offerings

The volume of IPOs has historically occurred in waves. For example, Lowry [2003] reports that 329 firms went public during the seven-year period from 1973 to 1979. In the next seven-year period starting in 1980, more than ten times the number of firms went public (3,805). Lowry investigates three hypotheses as to the cause of these waves: capital demands, information asymmetry, and investor sentiment hypotheses.

The capital demands explanation is that IPO volume varies with the business cycle. Private firms demand more capital during economic expansions, and going public is one way to access capital. The information asymmetry argument reflects a potential "lemons" problem during periods of uncertainty. Adverse selection costs vary over time and managers have an incentive to issue equity when a firm is overvalued. The investor sentiment hypothesis states that IPO volume is driven by investor optimism. <10> During some periods, investors are optimistic and more willing to buy stock (such as IPOs) in riskier firms.

Lowry finds that investor sentiment significantly affects IPO volume, supporting the evidence in Lee, Shleifer, and Thaler [1991] and Rajan and Servaes [1997]. She also finds that capital demand is an important factor in IPO volume. One measure of investor sentiment used is the discount on closed-end funds (discussed earlier). Lowry reports a puzzle for why the discount on closed-end funds is not important for the three quarters leading up to the IPOs, but is important one year before.

This evidence is consistent with our hypothesis. As mood improves, both investors and private firm owners become more optimistic, which is quickly reflected in the stock market. IPO initial returns will be high during a time of increased optimism. However, it takes time for private firms to find an underwriter and go through the registration process with the Securities and Exchange Commission. Therefore, social mood improvements today can be measured in investor sentiment today. But the resulting IPO issues will experience a time lag.

Lowry and Schwert [2002] find that more firms go public after observing high initial IPO returns for other firms. The lag between initial IPO returns and IPO volume is just another illustration of how both are influenced by social mood, but one takes longer to implement. Also, since social mood affects both investors and managers, we expect the managers to be more optimistic about capital projects, as previously discussed. Therefore, we would also expect the demand for capital to be highly correlated with investor sentiment. Because the source of investor optimism and manager optimism is the same, we expect both variables to predict IPO volume.

Investor sentiment measures will quickly reflect social mood decreases. With increasing pessimism, private firm owners will also be more pessimistic and not as interested in going public. Indeed, if the social mood turns negative quickly, some IPOs in the registration process will be cancelled. Note the asymmetry. Private firms can cancel an IPO halfway through the registration process, but cannot enter the process halfway through. Therefore, IPO volume should increase gradually during times of optimism, and decline more quickly during times of pessimism (similar to the M&A wave).

This is illustrated in the charts of IPO volume in Figure 4. Panel A shows the number of IPOs each quarter from 1960 to 2002. IPO volume is shown in relation to the preceding twelve-month return on the S&P 500, and it does appear to be related to the most recent stock market trends. Higher stock market returns lead to higher IPO volume. The declines in IPO volume seem to be sharper than the increases.

Panel B of Figure 4 shows the monthly IPO volume in Japan in relation to the level of the Nikkei 225 Index. The evidence from Japan also appears consistent with the social mood hypothesis. Stock market level and IPO activity are both outcomes of the general level of social optimism/pessimism. In this case, IPO volume is highly correlated with the stock market level (0.84). Declines in IPO volume appear sharper than increases.

Initial Public Offerings

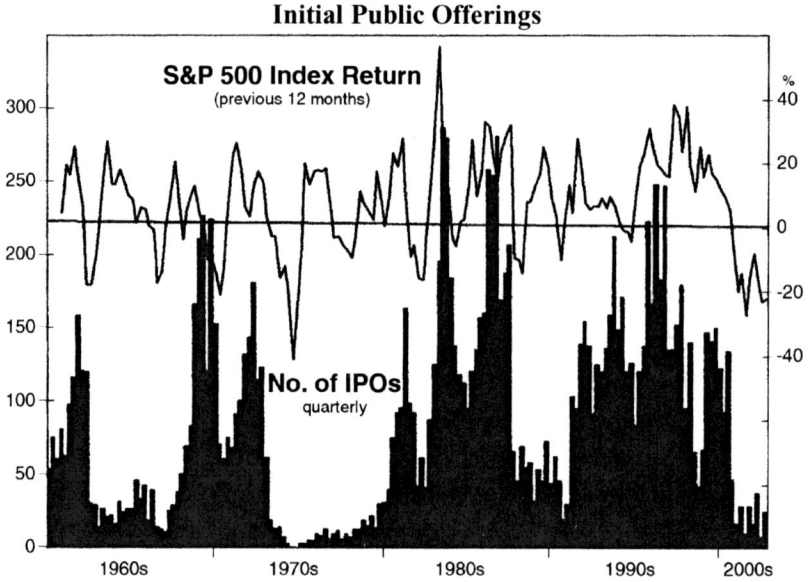

Panel A. Number of IPOs Each Quarter in the U.S. versus the Previous Twelve-Month Return on the S&P 500 Index (source of IPO volume is Ritter's website)

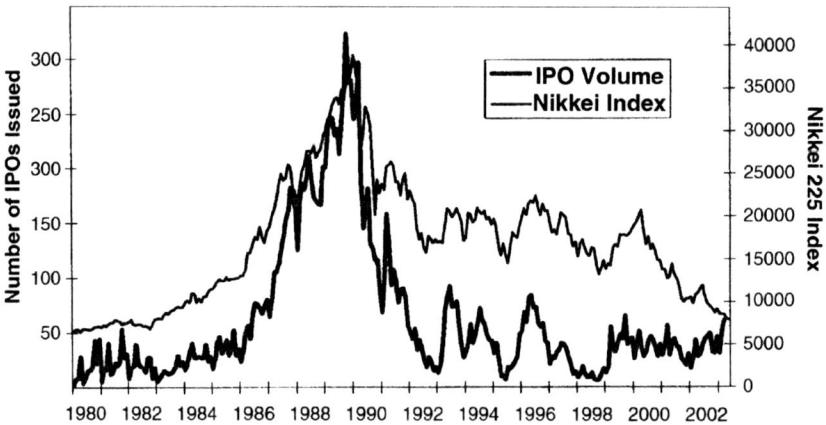

Panel B. Number of IPOs Each Month in Japan versus the Nikkei 225 Index

Figure 4

Entrepreneurs

Starting a new business is very risky. Cooper, Woo, and Dunkelberg [1988] summarize the failure rates computed in various studies. They conclude that 34% to 50% of new businesses fail within two years, and 50% to 71% fail within five years. Dunne, Roberts, and Samuelson [1988] estimated that nearly 62% of new entrants into manufacturing exited within five years. Nearly 80% exited within ten years. Yet, in the face of this high failure rate, entrepreneurs start more than 50,000 new businesses every month in the U.S.

Camerer and Lovallo [1999] and Manove [2000] propose that over-confidence in relative ability is one explanation for the high amount of business starts and failures. Surveys of entrepreneurs also illustrate their high levels of optimism. Cooper, Woo, and Dunkelberg [1988] surveyed 2,994 people who had recently started a business. 81% believed their odds of success were 7 out of 10 or better, and 33% believed their odds of success were certain, 10 out of 10! There is obviously a stark contrast between entrepreneurs' beliefs and their real chances of success as measured by the failure rates cited above. This high level of optimism probably plays a big part in driving people to start new businesses.

The social mood hypothesis predicts that when social mood is high, more people are optimistic, and some of these people will start businesses. When social mood is low, more people are pessimistic, and fewer will have the confidence to start a business. Therefore, the number of business starts reflects the level of social mood.

Theory Proposition in Corporate Finance

Previous papers on psychological bias and corporate finance mostly address cross-sectional issues. They examine the differences between investment activity and capital structure between firms with and without optimistic and overconfident managers. However, our [socionomic] propositions are different. As social mood changes over time, the percentage of managers and people who are optimistic also changes. Using that perspective, the proposition of this paper is that periods of optimistic social mood should lead to more corporate investment, higher debt financing, more mergers, higher IPO volume, and increased new business starts. Periods of pessimistic social mood should produce lower levels of these [financial and] economic activities. As social mood changes over time, the extent of corporate investment, debt offerings, M&A activity, equity offerings, and business starts should occur in correlated waves. There may also be lead/lag relationships between these activity measures because some of them take longer to implement.

The traditional rational expectations (RE) approach to finance may offer similar predictions. For example, RE predicts that the stock market will lead business activity because prices reflect the expectation of the activity. But this also implies lower volatility (Shiller [1981]) and greater market efficiency than is generally observed. Also, corporate managers may conduct more mergers, and the M&A may occur in waves because of better economic fundamentals. However, the RE approach is inconsistent with the evidence that acquiring firms do not generally obtain value from mergers.

Summary and Predictions

Social interaction is an important aspect of the decision-making process. People obtain information and opinions about a decision by communicating with one another. Psychologists believe emotion is a particularly important factor in making decisions under risk and uncertainty because emotions interact with cognitive evaluation in the decision process. In some circumstances, such as when there is a high degree of complexity and uncertainty, emotions have a strong influence on the decision made. But emotions exogenous to the decision at hand can also influence the action chosen. The general optimistic/pessimistic mood of society is transmitted through social interaction, and in turn influences all types of decision-makers, including financial ones.

Increasing mood is associated with emotions like optimism, happiness, and hope. At the peak, these emotions become extreme, leading to extreme overconfidence, euphoria, and excess. A decreasing mood is associated with pessimism, conservatism, and suspicion. The lowest levels of social mood are associated with strong emotions like fear, stinginess, and antagonism. We argue that when social mood is high, many financial decision-makers are optimistic (consumers, investors, and executives). Therefore, biased financial decisions tend to correlate across different types of financial decision-makers.

Social mood is most quickly propagated through investors to the stock market. Investor sentiment is impounded into stock prices. As a consequence, the stock market itself is a meter or register of social mood. The stock market reaches a high (low) when the social mood is high (low), and a rising (falling) stock market indicates an increasingly positive (negative) social mood trend.

Since the stock market is a measure of social mood, which influences economic activity, we are able to make more general economic predictions than the more narrow models of investor sentiment or corporate manager optimism. First, a rising (optimistic) mood is first measured by increases in stock market valuation. This rising mood influences (1) investors who seek higher-risk portfolios and increase trading, (2) consumers who spend more and take on more debt, and (3) business participants who increase their corporate investment, use more debt financing, conduct more mergers, take more firms public, and start more new businesses. The pro-business mood influences government as well. The government during high mood periods will be less likely to halt mergers and will conduct fewer antitrust activities. Congress may also be more likely to pass pro-business legislation. Many of these economic activities take time to complete, however. Thus, we may see a time lag between the rising stock market and the realization of this economic activity.

Second, declining stock valuation indicates a declining social mood. The pessimism and conflict associated with low levels of social mood cause more investor differences of opinion, higher market volatility, and a flight toward safer portfolios. Pessimistic consumers spend less and may concentrate more on paying down consumer debt. Business decision-makers spend less on capital projects, conduct less merger activity, issue fewer public offerings, and focus on cost-cutting rather than expansion. An anti-business environment is likely to arise and influence the government to pass investor protection legislation and attempt to protect consumers by initiating more anti-trust activities.

Third, since social mood changes over time, these investment and business activities occur in waves. The stock market changes quickly to reflect changes in social mood, but other financial actions take longer to unfold. For example, it will take time for the level of M&A activity and IPOs to increase. However, there is a shorter time lag between decreases in the stock market and decreases in business activity than in increases in mood and activity. This is because it is easier to stop mergers and public offerings than to initiate and complete them. So changes in the stock market lead business activity, but the time lag is asymmetric between increases and decreases in mood.

Fourth, extremely positive or negative social moods are associated with extreme behaviors. Emotions move to euphoria as social mood peaks, which can cause stock market bubbles. During this time, investors may be able to correctly evaluate that the market is overvalued, but their levels of optimism remain so high that they overcome reason, and investors continue to buy. The peaking mood fosters risk-seeking behavior and excesses. Consumers overextend themselves with credit, banks extend more generous terms, and businesses overinvest. As the euphoria wanes, social mood begins to decline and pessimism takes over. Lenders recall loans, corporate scandals are revealed, investors sell stocks, and companies lay off employees. The declining mood eventually bottoms. Many firms and people have declared bankruptcy, corporate investment is low, and unemployment is high. This sets the stage for the next rise in social mood and therefore the next business cycle.

Along with these predictions, it is appropriate to give a final comment on causality. A traditional rational expectations approach to the stock market and economic activity suggests that social events cause short and long-term market reactions. For example, the legislative activities of the government influence the direction of the stock market.

However, the socionomic hypothesis proposes the opposite. A positive or negative social mood is quickly reflected in the stock market, and eventually determines the tone and character of legislation. The standard assumption of causality is backward. It is not the actions of the Fed that drive the market—it is social mood that drives the market and business activity, and ultimately causes the Fed to act. Investors are not upset because the stock market has dropped—the market has dropped because people are upset, and so on.

Acknowledgments

I thank Kent Baker, Robert Folsom, Wayne Gorman, Gordon Graham, Mark Hirschey, James Montier, Paul Slovic, Dan Weaver, and seminar participants at Washington State University for providing helpful comments.

AUTHOR'S NOTES

[1] Even the popularity of the analytical methods used (momentum, value, etc.) are subject to social mood.

[2] Even if investors use the equation g = (1 − dividend payout ratio) x ROE to estimate the growth rate, they must predict the future return on equity.

[3] This analysis focuses only on a bias in estimating the growth rate. Overconfident people, however, tend to underestimate risk, while pessimists tend to overestimate risk. These biases would impact the estimation of the required rate of return k. This bias works in the same direction as that of the growth rate and magnifies our argument.

[4] For rational explanations based on economic fundamentals of the tulip, Mississippi, and South Sea bubbles, see Garber [1990].

[5] Survey of Research Center, "Surveys of Consumers," University of Michigan, undated, http://www.sca.isr.umich.edu/ main.php.

[6] Social mood might be measured by the popularity of different types of songs, movies, or fashion styles if they could be easily quantified [Prechter, 1999].

[7] See also Montier [2002, Ch. 7] for a review of psychology and corporate finance.

[8] Merger data come from Mergerstat (www.mergerstat.com).

EDITOR'S NOTES

<1> The more accurate word would be *socionomic.*

<2> Chapters 6 and 19 explain that social mood does not propagate but arises mutually; knowledge of ways to express social mood do propagate.

<3> A preferred construction would be "a shared, or social, mood."

<4> Expanding upon work by Elliott Wave International's Peter Kendall and reprinted as Chapter 33 in *Pioneering Studies in Socionomics.*

<5> See Chapters 12 and 17 of this book for a discussion of the homogeneity of participants in financial herding.

<6> Chapters 15 and 19 argue that the influence of social mood is constant, whether it induces calm or excitement.

<7> Under socionomic theory, trends toward negative social mood motivate actions that lead to these negative events, which may continue after negative mood abates. See Chapters 7 and 8.

<8> Under socionomic theory, objective pricing of stocks is impossible, so rational valuation is never dominant. It just seems that way at times.

<9> The preferred rendition would be "rising and falling valuations."

<10> Steven Hochberg and Peter Kendall introduced this idea and made predictions based upon it in *The Elliott Wave Financial Forecast*, 1999-present.

AUTHOR'S REFERENCES

Abel, Andrew B. "An Exploration of the Effects of Pessimism and Doubt on Asset Returns." *Journal of Economic Dynamics & Control*, 26, (2002), pp. 1075–1092.

Andrade, Gregor, Mark Mitchell, and Erik Stafford. "New Evidence and Perspectives on Mergers." *Journal of Economic Perspectives*, 15, 2, (2001), pp. 103–120.

Au, Kevin, Forrest Chan, Denis Wang, and Ilan Vertinsky. "Mood in Foreign Exchange Trading: Cognitive Processes and Performance." *Organizational Behavior and Human Decision Processes*, 91, (2003), pp. 322–338.

Banerjee, A.V. "A Simple Model of Herd Behavior." *Quarterly Journal of Economics*, 107, (1992), pp. 797–817.

Bikhchandani, S., D. Hirshleifer, and I. Welch. "A Theory of Fads, Fashion, Custom, and Cultural Change as Informational Cascades." *Journal of Political Economy*, 100, (1992), pp. 992–1026.

Camerer, Colin, and Dan Lovallo. "Overconfidence and Excess Entry: An Experimental Approach." *American Economic Review*, 89, (1999), pp. 306–318.

Cecchetti, Stephen G., Pok-sang Lam, and Nelson C. Mark. "Asset Pricing with Distorted Beliefs: Are Equity Returns Too Good to be True?" *American Economic Review*, 90, 4, (2000), pp. 787–805.

Cooper, Arnold, Carolyn Woo, and William Dunkelberg. "Entrepreneurs' Perceived Chances for Success." *Journal of Business Venturing*, 3, (1988), pp. 97–108.

Damasio, A. *Descartes' Error: Emotion, Reason, and the Human Brain*. New York: Avon, 1994.

Damasio, A., D. Tranel, and H. Damasio, "Individuals with Sociopathic Behavior Caused by Frontal Damage Fail to Respond Autonomically to Social Stimuli." *Behavioral Brain Research*, 41, (1990), pp. 81–94.

DeLong, J.B., A. Shleifer, L.H. Summers, and R.J. Waldmann. "Noise Trader Risk in Financial Markets." *Journal of Political Economy*, 98, (1990), pp. 703–738.

Dowling, Michael, and Brian Lucey. "The Role of Feelings in Investor Decision-Making." *Journal of Economic Surveys*, 90, 3, (2005), pp. 211–237.

Dreman, David. "The Role of Psychology in Analysts' Estimates." *Journal of Psychology and Financial Markets*, 2, (2001), pp. 66–68.

Dunne, Timothy, Mark J. Roberts, and Larry Samuelson. "Patterns of Firm Entry and Exit: U.S. Manufacturing Industries." *RAND Journal of Economics*, 19, 4, (1988), pp. 495–515.

Elison, G., and D. Fudenberg. "Rules of Thumbs for Social Learning." *Journal of Political Economy*, 101, (1993), pp. 93–126.

Elster, J. "Emotions and Economic Theory." *Journal of Economic Literature*, 36, 1, (1998), pp. 47–74.

Fisher, Kenneth L., and Meir Statman. "Blowing Bubbles." *Journal of Psychology and Financial Markets*, 3, 1, (2002a), pp. 53–65.

Fisher, Kenneth L., and Meir Statman. "Consumer Confidence and Stock Returns." Working paper, Santa Clara University, August 2002b.

Forgas, Joseph P. "Mood and Judgment: The Affect Infusion Model (AIM)." *Psychological Bulletin*, 117, 1, (1995), pp. 39–66.

Garber, Peter M. "Famous First Bubbles." *Journal of Economic Perspectives*, 4, 2, (1990), pp. 35–54.

Gervais, Simon, J.B. Heaton, and Terrance Odean. "Capital Budgeting in the Presence of Managerial Overconfidence and Optimism." Working paper, The Wharton School, July 2003.

Goel, Anand M., and Anjan V. Thakor. "Do Overconfident Managers Make Better Leaders?" Working paper, University of Michigan, August 2002.

Hackbarth, Dirk. "Managerial Traits and Capital Structure Decisions." Working paper, Indiana University, September 2004.

Heaton, J.B. "Managerial Optimism and Corporate Finance." *Financial Management*, 31, (2002), pp. 33–45.

Hirshleifer, D., and T. Shumway. "Good Day Sunshine: Stock Returns and the Weather." *Journal of Finance*, 58, 3, (2003), pp. 1009–1032.

Hong, Harrison, Jeffrey D. Kubik, and Jeremy C. Stein. "Thy Neighbor's Portfolio: Word-of-Mouth Effects in the Holdings and Trades of Money Managers." *Journal of Finance*, forthcoming, (2005).

Jansen, W. Jos, and Niek J. Nahius. "The Stock Market and Consumer Confidence: European Evidence." *Economic Letters*, 79, (2003), pp. 89–98.

Johnson, E.J., and A. Tversky. "Affect, Generalization, and the Perception of Risk." *Journal of Personality and Social Psychology*, 45, (1983), pp. 20–31.

Jung, Jeeman, and Robert J. Shiller. "One Simple Test of Samuelson's Dictum for the Stock Market." NBER Working Paper # 9348, November 2002.

Kamstra, M.J., L.A. Kramer, and M.D. Levi. "Winter Blues: A Sad Stock Market Cycle." *American Economic Review*, 93, 1, (2003), pp. 324–343.

Kaplan, Steven, and Richard Ruback. "The Valuation of Cash Flow Forecasts: An Empirical Analysis." *Journal of Finance*, 50, 4, (1995), pp. 1059–1093.

Keynes, J.M. *The Scope and Method of Political Economy*. New York: Kelley and Millman, 1955.

Krivelyova, Anya, and Cesare Robotti. "Playing the Field: Geomagnetic Storms and International Stock Markets." Working paper, Boston College, 2003.

Lee, Charles M., Andrei Shleifer, and Richard H. Thaler. "Investor Sentiment and the Closed-End Fund Puzzle." *Journal of Finance*, 46, 1, (1991), pp. 75–109.

LeRoy, Stephen, and Richard Porter. "Stock Price Volatility: Tests Based on Implied Variance Bounds." *Econometrica*, 49, (1981), pp. 97–113.

Loewenstein, George F. "Emotions in Economic Theory and Economic Behavior." *American Economic Review*, 90, (2000), pp. 426–432.

Loewenstein, George F., Elke U. Weber, Christopher K. Hsee, and Ned Welch. "Risk as Feelings." *Psychological Bulletin*, 127, 2, (2001), pp. 267–286.

Lowry, Michelle. "Why Does IPO Volume Fluctuate So Much?" *Journal of Financial Economics*, 67, (2003), pp. 3–40.

Lowry, Michelle, and William Schwert. "IPO Market Cycles: Bubbles or Sequential Learning?" *Journal of Finance*, 57, (2002), pp. 1171–1200.

Malmendier, Ulrike, and Geoffrey Tate. "Who Makes Acquisitions? CEO Overconfidence and the Market's Reaction." Working paper, Stanford University, December 2003.

Manove, Michael. "Entrepreneurs, Optimism and the Competitive Edge." Working paper, Boston University, November 2000.

March, James G., and Zur Shapira. "Managerial Perspectives on Risk and Risk Taking." *Management Science*, 33, 11, (1987), pp. 1404–1418.

McGuire, William J. "Attitudes and Attitude Change." In Lindzey Gardner and Elliott Aronson, eds., *Handbook of Social Psychology*. Reading, MA: Addison-Wesley, (1985), Vol. 2, pp. 233–346.

Mehra, Rajnish, and Edward Prescott. "The Equity Premium: A Puzzle." *Journal of Monetary Economics*, 15, 2, (1985), pp. 145–162.

Mehra, Rajnish, and Raaj Sah. "Mood Fluctuations, Projection Bias, and Volatility of Equity Prices." *Journal of Economic Dynamics & Control*, 26, (2002), pp. 869–887.

Mitchell, Mark L., and J. Harold Mulherin. "The Impact of Industry Shocks on Takeover and Restructuring Activity." *Journal of Financial Economics*, 44, (1996), pp. 193–229.

Montier, James. *Behavioural Finance: Insights into Irrational Minds and Markets*. West Sussex, England: John Wiley& Sons, 2002.

Nofsinger, John, and Kenneth Kim. *Infectious Greed: Restoring Confidence in America's Companies*. Upper Saddle River, NJ: Financial Times Prentice-Hall, 2003.

Pareto, V. *The Mind and Society*. New York: Dover Publications, 1963.

Prechter, Robert R. *The Wave Principle of Human Social Behavior and the New Science of Socionomics*. Gainesville, GA: New Classics Library, 1999.

Prechter, Robert R. *Pioneering Studies in Socionomics*. Gainesville, GA: New Classics Library, 2003.

Rajan, Raghuram, and Henri Servaes. "Analyst Following of Initial Public Offerings." *Journal of Finance*, 52, (1997), pp. 507–530.

Rappaport, Alfred, and Mark L. Sirower. "Stock or Cash? The Trade-Offs for Buyers and Sellers in Mergers and Acquisitions." *Harvard Business Review*, November 1, 1999.

Roll, Richard. "The Hubris Hypothesis of Corporate Takeovers." *Journal of Business*, 59, (1986), pp. 197–216.

Romer, P.M. "Thinking and Feeling." *American Economic Review*, 90, 2, (2000), pp. 439–443.

Rosen, Richard J. "Merger Momentum and Investor Sentiment: The Stock Market Reaction to Merger Announcements." *Journal of Business*, forthcoming, (2005).

Samuelson, Paul A. "Summing Up on Business Cycles: Opening Address." In Jeffrey C. Fuhrer and Scott Schuh, eds., Beyond Shocks: What Causes Business Cycles." Boston: Federal Reserve Bank of Boston, 1998.

Saunders, E.M. "Stock Prices and Wall Street Weather." *American Economic Review*, 83, 5, (1993), pp. 1337–1345.

Schwert, G. William. "Why Does Stock Market Volatility Change Over Time?" *Journal of Finance*, 44, 5, (1989), pp. 1115–1153.

Schwert, G. William. "Stock Volatility in the New Millennium: How Wacky is Nasdaq?" *Journal of Monetary Economics*, 49, (2002), pp. 3–26.

Shiller, Robert J. "Do Stock Prices Move Too Much to be Justified by Subsequent Changes in Dividends?" *American Economic Review*, 71, 3, 1981, pp. 421–436.

Shiller, Robert J. "Stock Prices and Social Dynamics." *Brookings Papers on Economic Activity*, (1984), Issue 2, pp. 457–498.

Shiller, Robert J. "Conversation, Information, and Herd Behavior." *American Economic Review*, 85, (1995), pp. 181–185.

Shiller, Robert J. "Bubbles, Human Judgment, and Expert Opinion." *Financial Analysts Journal*, 58, 3, (2002), pp. 18–26.

Shiller, Robert J. "From Efficient Market Theory to Behavioral Finance." *Journal of Economic Perspectives*, 17, 1, (2003), pp. 83–104.

Shiller, Robert J., Fumiko Kon-Ya, and Yoshiro Tsutsui. "Why Did the Nikkei Crash? Expanding the Scope of Expectations Data Collection." *Review of Economics and Statistics*, 78, (1996), pp. 156–164.

Shiller, Robert, and John Pound. "Survey Evidence on Diffusion of Interest and Information Among Investors." *Journal of Economic Behavior and Organization*, 12, 1, (1989), pp. 47–66.

Slovic, Paul, Melissa Finucane, Ellen Peters, and Donald MacGregor. "The Affect Heuristic." In T. Gilovich, D. Griffin, and D. Kahneman, eds., *Heuristics and Biases: The Psychology of Intuitive Judgment.* New York: Cambridge University Press, 2002, pp. 397–420.

Turner, Ralph L., and Lewis M. Killian. *Collective Behavior.* Englewood Cliffs, NJ: Prentice-Hall, 1987, 3rd ed.

UBS Report. "Index of Investor Optimism: Detailed Results." December 2002, http://www.ubs.com.

Visano, Brenda Spotton. "Financial Manias and Panics." *American Journal of Economics and Sociology*, 61, (2002), pp. 801–827.

Welch, Ivo. "Views of Financial Economists on the Equity Premium and on Professional Controversies." *Journal of Business*, 73, (2000), pp. 501–537.

Welch, Ivo. "The Equity Premium Consensus Forecast Revisited." Discussion Paper No. 1325, Cowles Foundation, September 2001.

Part VII:

METATHEORY AND STF'S RELATIONSHIP TO OTHER THEORIES

Chapter 32

The Metatheoretical Foundation
of Socionomics

Wayne D. Parker

A socionomist and a mechanist cannot understand each other at the most fundamental level, because their arguments have different metatheoretical foundations. My comments below attempt to spell out the differences.

While a mechanist might agree with a socionomist about certain properties of the socionomic system at the aggregate level of society, he would propose that they result from an additive process in which individual contributions sum to create the whole. But socionomics proposes a process in which there is cooperation between individual members of the group and the organizational structure under which they operate. The whole system is not reducible to a sum of independent, individual behaviors. The very nature of causality at the individual level is different from that at the social level. A mechanist would say that the hierarchical structure of social mood fluctuations cannot contribute to the cause but can only result from a mechanistic process that agents' individual actions bring about. It is almost impossible for a mechanist to understand the causative role of *mood* and *pattern* in socionomics, since these concepts relate to a metatheoretical difference, not merely a theoretical difference, between two worldviews.

The concept of *social mood* is a fundamental, explanatory principle related to the philosophical tradition of *contextualism* (see Stephen Pepper, *World Hypotheses*, 1942, and further discussion in Chapter 33). Socionomics is a context-specific paradigm, limited to the domain of human social systems in contexts of uncertainty. The Elliott wave pattern of constraint is also a fundamental explanatory principle, related to the philosophical tradition of *organicism*. Socionomic theory thus offers to the social sciences a model of causality in which organicism forms the context for contextualism so that contextualism at the individual level is nested inside organicism at the aggregate level in an progressing holistic structuralism.

Neither *mood* nor *pattern*, as articulated by socionomic theory, is reducible in reality or in principle to any "underlying" or "more fundamental" atoms or causes in the mechanistic sense. Thus, there is a categorical, metatheoretical distinction between mechanistic assumptions and socionomic assumptions about the nature of social causality and therefore all the hypotheses and predictions that flow logically from these two social-science paradigms. The two paradigms are *incommensurable* (per Pepper and Thomas Kuhn[1]). Until the difference is recognized, mechanists and contextualists/organicists are doomed to misunderstanding each other's terminology.

To clarify our idea of social mood under contextualism, it may be useful to think of mood as a type of *wish*. Mood is a predisposition to action, but it is not conceptually reducible either to the actions flowing from such wishes or to the actions of others preceding such wishes. The concept of *wish* subsumes both desires and fears, since a fear is merely a wish that something not happen. Contextualism implies something fundamentally different from mechanism about the nature of a human being, namely that a human being is irreducibly considered in the socionomic context to be an *active organism* rather than a *reactive organism,* meaning that a person has a fundamental capacity to turn wishes (positive desires or negative fears) into actions, without having such actions completely determined by factors external to those wishes, or by external causes of those wishes, as mechanism would have it.

(Willis Overton, Ralph Rosnow, and many other psychologists have contributed to an extensive literature in this area. Contextualist theories of psychology cover areas as diverse as visual perception as in Jerome Lettvin's "What the Frog's Eye tells the Frog's Brain,"[2] Kelly's "personal construct theory"[3] and topics in developmental psychology, to name a few.[4])

Sophisticated contextualist theories include a description of "bounded determinism" to explain realistic limits to human individuals' freedom. The paradigmatic assumption of contextualism is that there nevertheless remains in the definition of a human being some meaningful freedom of action and spontaneous self-organization. In contrast, the paradigmatic assumption of the mechanistic worldview is that a human is in principle a "reactive organism," meaning that his apparent freedom is merely an artifact that can be explained by determinism at the atomic level and below. His acts derive from hard-wired genetics, neurophysiology and brain-based "instincts," all of which are explained by a mechanistic version of evolutionary theory reduced to Skinnerian stimulus-response sequences in traditional behaviorism or conceived as some combination of such conditions.

These fundamental assumptions of contextualism and mechanism are (1) diametrically opposed to each other logically and thus incommensurable, and (2) empirically untestable and unverifiable. That is why they are not theoretical but metatheoretical. Respective beliefs about human nature and the nature of causality are the fundamental lenses through which each paradigm views its data, and no data can prove or disprove such lenses, since the assumptions built into each lens define the very meaning of what constitutes data and what counts as adequate "proof."

Socionomists and mechanists share a philosophical commitment to realism. Both readily agree that the Wave Principle does not exist as some kind of idealistic Platonic form, which would fall under Pepper's fourth metaphysical worldview, *formism*. A mechanist would argue that wave patterns are not as fundamental as individuals' actions. Socionomists argue—as Elliott himself first recognized[5]—that Elliott waves are categorically more causally fundamental than the individual actions taken within them. Both views are realistic under their respective metatheoretic bases.

Each side sees the other as succumbing to idealism. A mechanist would see the paradigm of contextualism/organicism as being equivalent to idealism, because that is the only conclusion his mechanistic worldview permits. A contextualist/organicist would consider mechanists' belief that all causality wells up from the attributes of the tiniest particle to be equally an idealistic article of faith.

For reductionistic mechanists, anything in the *explanandum* (the phenomenon to be explained) that is not as causally fundamental as the *explanans* (the concept by which the phenomenon is explained) is by definition a mere epiphenomenon, ontologically more in the lower category of appearances than in reality. This view is incommensurable with an organicist paradigm, where the theoretical goal is *synthesis*—as opposed to reductionistic *analysis*—of the complexity of the apparently real, thus preserving the ontological status of the *explanandum* at multiple levels of reality, all equally valid, interrelated in a specified manner per organicist/contextualist explanations, with no epiphenomenon to be explained away.

These distinctions can be discussed only at the philosophical level. A socionomist's assertion that the Wave Principle is a real constraint—even a law of nature as Elliott called it—is meaningful only within the context of socionomics' paradigm of organicism/contextualism. It is not that our assertion is untrue when viewed through the lens of the mechanistic worldview; it literally has no intelligible meaning from the mechanistic perspective. It is categorically incommensurable with the mechanistic assumption about reality, causality and the nature of human beings.

The socionomic model of causality is a holistic theory in which neither the individual level nor the aggregate level is dispensable. Under it (and in reality, in our opinion), one cannot discover an ultimate cause of changes in social mood via atomistic reduction. The structure of the system is a deterministic aspect of the causal model (synchronic aspect = pattern), but the impulses of the individuals in the herd prompt the creation of, and participate in the changes within, the unfolding pattern (diachronic aspect = change or elaboration of pattern). The relationship between the two levels of causality and the reciprocity of their interaction are integral to the ultimate expression of the system. Thus, the constraining form of patterned changes in social mood at the top, the individual brains that energize the system from the bottom, and the interactive relationship between them are all equally important to socionomic theory. The structure is our version of *organicism*, the impulses provide our version of *contextualism*, and the integration between them makes socionomic theory *holistic*, not reductionistic.

There are four key areas of metatheoretical disagreement between **socionomists** and mechanists:

1. Scientific model: **holism** vs. reductionism
2. Model of causality: **organicism and contextualism** vs. mechanism
3. Theoretical process: **synthesis** vs. analysis
4. Nature of human being: substantially **active organism** vs. entirely reactive organism.

Only pointless, confusing arguments can ensue when worldviews collide unless we take pains to define our terms and become conscious about the assumptive base of each paradigmatic lens. So, is there no point in discussion, if two camps do not share the same worldview? Are we doomed to failure in the scientific quest for truth?

Per logician-philosopher C.S. Peirce, the criterion of *usefulness* should help decide which lens to use in viewing human social behavior, and *predictive accuracy* is the best way to measure the usefulness of competing worldviews. Our claim for socionomics is that it has been and will continue to be the more useful paradigm for the social sciences on the basis of predictive power. Socionomics provides a far more effective basis for predicting financial market fluctuations and changes in the economy as well as social trends governing fads, fashions, finance, politics and history than the mechanistic worldview currently predominant. Since mechanists also value predictive power as a criterion by which to judge theories, perhaps our relative success in this area will at least open a dialogue about metatheory.

A mutual understanding of the issues discussed here will enhance our ability to communicate clearly to the world the radical new paradigm that socionomics offers to the social sciences. Our understanding of these issues helps us articulate the theoretical details of socionomics in a coherent, non-contradictory fashion that will eventually be understandable (even if not agreeable) to mechanists and non-mechanists alike.

Memo on Holism vs. Emergence[6]

To integrate our two interacting worldviews—contextualism at the individual level and organicism at the aggregate level—we initially pursued a theory of emergence that would link the two levels in a meaningful, non-contradictory fashion. The solution we eventually found does not provide a theory of emergence but rather obviates the need for it in a metatheoretically elegant way.

The solution came by looking closely at the implications of our metatheory: namely, the difference between the ontology implied by the mechanists and that implied by the interaction of organicism and contextualism. For the mechanists, a "thing ontology," under which only *objects* and *forces* are really real,[7] is more congenial to their way of thinking. This orientation works well for physics but not necessarily for biology and the actions of living human beings. For us, an "event ontology"[8] better fits with socionomics' proposed interaction between organicism and contextualism, since *processes* such as "choosing" and "unfolding patterns" are more fundamentally causal than objects. We recognize the existence of objects and do not exclude a role for them, but processes are more causally primary.

Searching for a theory of emergence with respect to social mood and WP was a red herring. It depended upon rules set by the old paradigm. Mechanists see the individual level of behavior and the aggregate level of behavior as two different *things* rather than one integrated, holistic *process*. If the levels are *not* two separate things, there can be no theory of emergence to connect them. This realization is compatible with Prechter's basic insight that there are no external causes for anything in the formological system regulating waves of social mood. His decision to draw boundaries with respect to contextual aspects of all human social behavior rather than between the stock market and "news" as an exogenous shock is the same insight that led me to resolve the emergence issue. Michael Polanyi's old *Science* article[9] about related matters certainly helped, but it was delving deeply into the metatheoretical implications of the socionomic insight that provided the solution.

One may still use variations on the term *emergent* but only in the already-established, occasionally used sense that "emergent properties" exist for the whole while not deriving from a sum of the parts. Scientists who already use the term in that way may thereby quickly relate to our ideas.

Ultimately, however, Prechter's term *formological* seems more appropriate in expressing our view of causality with respect to the organizing principle of Elliott waves of unconscious social mood and their results in social action. At the very least, formological thinking is indispensable for effective prediction, as demonstrated in Chapters 10, 21 and 22.

How Organicism and Contextualism Account for the Differences in News Interpretation[10]

Under socionomic theory, the very meaning of news is contextual. It can have an economic meaning in which rational reaction pertains, or a socionomic meaning in which pre-rational interpretation pertains. Which meaning matters depends upon the receiver's mental orientation toward that news.

In the financial context, news does not matter in the way the mechanists think it does. News is not an "exogenous shock" to a deterministic financial system that responds the same way to the same stimulus every time. Rather, news offers speculators a convenient referent to use in rationalizing feelings and actions involved in the endogenous herding process. The herd's assignment of meaning to news and the actions it takes either before or after any given bit of news depend upon the state of social mood within its organic pattern, which regulates the degree of the herd's optimism or pessimism. Here is an example of the difference:

Optimistic mood

Endogenous Impulse:	To *buy stocks*.
Action 1:	*Buy stocks*. The market goes up.
Rationalization A:	Happy days are here again; the economy and stock market are recovering.
(or) Action 2:	*Buy stocks*. The market goes up.
News:	**Jobs report comes in surprisingly high; lots of jobs created.**
(or) Action 3:	*Buy stocks*. The market goes up.
(or) Rationalization B:	Happy days are here again; the economy and stock market are recovering.
(or) Action 4:	*Buy stocks*. The market goes up.

Pessimistic mood

Endogenous Impulse:	To *sell stocks*.
Action 1:	*Sell stocks*. The market goes down.
Rationalization A:	The Fed will soon raise interest rates, which will hurt the recovery and the stock market.

(or) Action 2:	*Sell stocks.* The market goes down.
News:	**Jobs report comes in surprisingly high; lots of jobs created.**
(or) Action 3:	*Sell stocks.* The market goes down.
(or) Rationalization B:	The Fed will soon raise interest rates, which will hurt the recovery and the stock market.
(or) Action 4:	*Sell stocks.* The market goes down.

Observe that action 1, 2, 3 or 4 as well as rationalization A or B can either precede or follow the news and that the action can either precede or follow the rationalization. Impulsive commands are in charge, so the news is nothing more than a prop, which can be reported before or after the action and which can be referenced before or after the rationalization.

Chapter 2 offers real-life examples showing that news interpretation trumps news per se in financial narratives. Chapter 19 offers 22 more examples of widely utilized yet utterly contradictory news interpretations.

In each case, speculators view stock market action either before or after the news as confirming the meaning they assign to the news. But what actually happens is that social mood compatibly and contemporaneously prompts both the stock market action and speculators' interpretation of the news.

Socionomists do not consider news to be an exogenous cause of stock market activity, because events do not impact the stock market (per Chapter 1) and because most economic, political and cultural news items are just reports of human activity impelled previously by changes in social mood (see Chapters 7 and 8). Rather, social mood creates contexts of meaning within which news provides referents that speculators sometimes use for rationalizing actions taken in the process of herding.

Unfortunately for the mechanistic view of the causal relationship between news and the stock market, the same external event (a particular type of news) fails to lead to the same response each time. Variable outcomes from the same stimulus make no sense in the mechanistic worldview borrowed from physics, where the only really real entities are *objects* (such as "the stock market") and *forces* (such as "news") (nouns) that must have lawful relationships consistently producing the same results, per Hume's "constant conjunction." Socionomics' worldviews of organicism and contextualism produce no such problem. The ideas of *news interpretation in context* and *action by choice* make sense in its worldviews, which are congenial to an event ontology, where the really real includes objects but is primarily a matter of *processes* such as *choosing* and *assigning meaning* to events (verbs).

Ironically, for the very reason that most financial-market participants think mechanistically, they unconsciously default to rationalizing the news to fit their mood-induced predispositions, thus dooming them to herding. For the very reason that socionomists think organically and contextually, they avoid that trap.

Mechanistic Things vs. Organic Processes in a Holistic System[11]

Socionomics, consistently with its contextualism, posits a real and separable causal efficacy to human agency as opposed to such agency being reducible to reactions to exogenous causes. Mood describes an action capacity that exists in the neuroanatomical structures of the human brain and body. Socionomics allows that the individual agent may or may not act upon this potentiality, implying a degree of freedom in decision-making that is disallowed under the reactive-agent model assumed by mechanists.

Are these action potentialities *objects* or *processes*? It depends. Perhaps "objects" are most usefully conceptualized as "processes that persist over some period of time to be consistently observed to be identical from the perspective of some observer at some specified level of analysis." In this relativistic definition, if one loses either the persistence of the process, the consistency of the observation, the perspective of the observer, or the level of the analysis, one also loses the "object." From this epistemological stance, rooted in a process ontology, "objects" are only epiphenomena, dependent on processes of persistence in time, consistency of observation, and a multi-leveled analytic/synthetic theory of ontology and epistemology.

Is the human nervous system an *object* or a *process*? Individual action derives from an ensemble of millions of neuronal coordinations. Neurological research into the nature of neuroplasticity, including processes such as synaptic sprouting and pruning, suggest that during actions, the very structure of the nervous system, in the course of survival-oriented neuronal activity, is constantly co-evolving on a moment-by-moment basis with the individual's social environment. The nervous system, then, seems to be less of an object and more of a process in which action potentialities integrate with the environment toward the end of prompting or not prompting actions.

Aggregate structures affect or constrain individual behavior not in the mechanistic way of exogenous causes acting as deterministic forces upon individual agents ("objects") who are helplessly controlled by them but rather in a manner consistent with a blend of contextualist and organicist assumptions. Under socionomics, social mood produces only a positive or negative bias in the related *propensities* for social behavior. This is not the mechanistic "exogenous forces determine reactive behavior" formulation of neoclassicism. Social mood does not force all individuals in society to take specific actions. Rather, social mood is the causal mediator only of aggregate choices that adhere to the overall form constraining social behavior. This simultaneous mutual causation in the relationship between deterministic aggregate structure and flexible individual agency forges a qualitative difference between socionomics and neoclassical economic theory. If the causal relationship were one-sided, either from individuals to social aggregates (as in neoclassical economics), or from social aggregates to individuals (as in the approach of some institutionalists, especially after 1940, as discussed in Chapter 37), or if the mutual causation were sequential rather than simultaneous, the nature of causality in socionomic theory would reductionistically collapse into some variant of the mechanistic worldview: Either social institutions would control individuals exogenously, or individual choices would sum to create institutions in additive fashion, thereby justifying neoclassical economic theorists' search for supposed "microfoundations" of macroeconomics, per Figure 5 in Chapter 19. Holism dispenses with these myopic premises.

A Possible Neurophysiological Impediment to Holistic Theorizing

Why has the idea of simultaneous mutual causation between individuals and structures eluded economic theorists? Part of the reason may be humans' perception of their own nervous system. The human brain is vastly complex and redundantly interconnected through millions of neural pathways, but a person consciously perceives only the tiny percentage of the brain devoted to logical, sequential, rational thought. Thus, humans may be biased toward conceiving of linear, sequential, causal processes as opposed to simultaneous, mutually causal processes in constructing their theoretical models of human behavior. Even though "simultaneous, mutually causal processes" is the best description of what is happening all the time in the very human brains that think up theories, we are unable to perceive them as such. We certainly have the capacity to *imagine* such processes, just as we can imagine many aspects of visual perception in species with limitations that differ from our own. It just takes a little more mental effort.

Consider: If the processes inside human brains work holistically, would it not be reasonable for at least some of the products of cooperating human brains, such as our social institutions, also to take this form? Simultaneous, mutually causal processes may be harder to comprehend than unidirectional causal models, but they seem closer than mechanism to the way nature's living systems operate.

NOTES AND REFERENCES

[1] Kuhn, T.S. 1970. *The Structure of Scientific Revolutions.* 2nd ed. Chicago: University of Chicago Press. Stephen C. Pepper, (1942). *World Hypotheses: A Study in Evidence.* Berkeley: University of California Press.

[2] Lettvin, J.Y., H.R. Maturana, W.S. McCulloch, and W.H. Pitts. "What the Frog's Eye Tells the Frog's Brain." Ch. 7 in *The Mind: Biological Approaches to Its Functions*, William Corning and Martin Balaban, Eds., John Wiley & Sons, 233-58, 1968.

[3] Kelly, George A. *The Psychology of Personal Constructs.* 2 vols. New York: W.W. Norton, 1955.

[4] For a review of the ideas in Pepper's book as they relate to the study of psychology, see Hayes, Steven C., Linda J. Hayes, and Hayne W. Reese. "Finding the Philosophical Core: A Review of Stephen C. Pepper's *World Hypotheses: A Study in Evidence.*" Review of Pepper, Steven C. (1942). *World Hypotheses: A Study in Evidence.*" Berkeley: University of California Press. *Journal of the Experimental Analysis of Behavior*, Vol. 50, no. 1 (July 1988): 97-111. Editor's note: Parker identified "Skinnerian" ideas of stimulus and response as compatible with mechanism, whereas later in life Skinner himself gravitated toward a contextualist approach.

[5] See Green, Michael, "R.N. Elliott's Fundamental Challenge to Mechanistic Social Models," 2001, presented to the Fifth Congress of the International Society for the Interdisciplinary Study of Symmetry. Reprinted as Chapter 1 of *Market Analysis of a New Millennium*, 2002.

[6] Parker, Wayne D., "Emergence Problem Solved," email to Robert Prechter, July 2, 2004; edited by Prechter.

[7] Technically, one can have an "event ontology" combined with a mechanistic epistemology, but it doesn't work convincingly. Some might say that is why Whitehead's theories were never completely convincing.

[8] An alternative term to "event ontology" is "process ontology," a view of reality focused less on what presumably *is* in a static way and more on what *occurs* as well as ways of occurring. This perspective seems compatible with the regulatory principle of Elliott waves.

[9] Polanyi, Michael, "Life's Irreducible Structure," *Science*, vol 160, issue 3834, pp. 1308-1312, June 21, 1968.

[10] Parker, Wayne D., "Internal Working Document," July 2, 2004; edited by Prechter.

[11] Editor's note: The material in this section and the next originally appeared in Parker's paper, "Methodological Individualism vs. Methodological Holism" (2006), which is excerpted in Chapter 37; edited by Prechter.

Chapter 33

Excerpted and edited from *Intelligent Finance—A Convergence of Mathematical Finance with Technical and Fundamental Analysis** December 2004

Socionomics: A New and Metatheoretically Consistent Social Science Paradigm

Wayne D. Parker

Introduction

Prechter's first statement of socionomic ideas came in 1979 (see Prechter, 2003), and in the intervening years he has assembled much supporting evidence for these ideas. The socionomics paradigm runs counter to the mechanics paradigm prevailing in mainstream economic theory today, where basic principles of causality and beliefs about human nature differ greatly from those of socionomics.

Due to the way traditional economic paradigms have dominated much of the thinking in many of the social sciences in the Western world in recent decades, many people find it hard to accept socionomic theory, since it requires such a different way of thinking about human behavior. This paper provides a context for understanding both the historical development of economic thought and the main philosophical differences between socionomics and other paradigms.

*Heping Pan, Didier Sornette and Kenneth Kortanek, Editors, *Proceedings of the First International Workshop* (IWIF 1), published by the School of Intormation Technology and Mathematical Sciences, University of Ballarat, Mt Helen, Victoria Melbourne, Australia. Reprinted with permission.

Note: This chapter is Parker's portion of a co-authored paper. Prechter's portion is incorporated in "The Financial/Economic Dichotomy" by Prechter and Parker (2007), reproduced as Chapter 15 in this book. Some of Parker's material in this chapter appears in altered form in Chapter 15.

Kuhn (1970) defined a paradigm as a research program with fundamental assumptions about the nature of the phenomena under examination
that are qualitatively different from those of the research program that has
gone before. In the history of economic theory, there have been a number
of different paradigms (Kuhn, 1970) or research programs (Lakatos and
Musgrave, 1970). This paper will introduce another new paradigm, that of
socionomics (Prechter, 1999, 2003), which is a study of the laws of human
social behavior in contexts of uncertainty. The paper then briefly contrasts
socionomics with economic theories deriving from the competing paradigm.

Socionomics challenges both the mechanistic determinism and the
exogenous-cause, rational-reaction model of human behavior that underlie
much of current theory in finance and the social sciences. Socionomic theory
considers aggregate human behavior to be more like complex biological
phenomena than like the functioning of a machine or a computer. It is thus
more congruent with both the organicist and the contextualist worldviews
described by Pepper (1942) than with the mechanistic worldview. Furthermore, whereas mechanistic theories are failing to yield accurate predictions
of future events and trends in fields such as economics, sociology, political
science and social psychology, socionomics incorporates a model under
which aggregate human behavior is probabilistically predictable.

In Pepper's analysis of metatheoretical worldviews, his "root metaphor" method offered unique models of causality and theories of truth
for each of the separate worldviews he identified, namely organicism,
contextualism, mechanism and formism. The first two of these worldviews
are compatible with socionomics. The root metaphor for organicism is
the biological organism, and its theory of truth is the coherence theory of
truth, whereby facts are seen as part of an organic whole, made coherent
not just due to logical consistency (as in rationalism) but also to a self-
organizing integration of parts into a whole structure in a way that creates
its own pattern in reality through the organic growth of the whole system
being described. For Pepper, the root metaphor for contextualism is the
historic event created by human action in a meaningful context.[1]

Pepper saw these two worldviews as being possible to integrate
with each other as long as the combination was not applied to a scope
of phenomena too universal to be captured by its applicability. Though
socionomics pertains to the domains of many different social sciences, its
interdisciplinary focus is crosscutting in a specific manner and does not
claim unlimited scope for its *explanandum*. Its relevance is limited to the
domain of human social behavior resulting from decision-making in contexts
of uncertainty. The carefully circumscribed scope of socionomics is one of
its strengths in permitting the combination of contextualism and organicism

for its assumptive base. This clearly bounded scope of explanation also allows socionomics to offer a new theory of finance that is explicitly distinguishable from the primarily mechanistic causality that socionomic theory uniquely and realistically recognizes as substantially applicable only in the "microeconomic" domain of economic theory (Prechter and Parker, 2005 [Chapter 15]; also Chapters 12 and 13). Socionomics adopts its metatheoretical framework consciously in presenting a theory that is at once more coherent, consistent and systematic than much of institutionalist theory [see Endnote 3 and Chapter 37] but at the same time more powerfully predictive than the mechanistic financial and macroeconomic theories that it is attempting to replace.

Socionomics has four key elements. In human social settings,

(1) Shared unconscious impulses to herd in contexts of uncertainty lead to the emergence of mass psychological dynamics that manifest as social mood trends.

(2) These social mood trends conform to a hierarchical fractal pattern that takes a repetitive, self-affine form whose path is probabilistically predictable.

(3) This pattern of aggregate behavior is form-determined by an endogenous process rather than mechanistically determined by exogenous causes.

(4) These social mood trends determine the tenor and character of social actions and are their underlying source, both in financial markets and in other social contexts of uncertainty.

Putting these elements together, we can define the socionomic theory of social motivation as follows: Aggregated unconscious herding impulses under conditions of uncertainty produce endogenously regulated fluctuations in social mood, which in turn impel social actions, one of which is buying and selling in the stock market, whose fluctuations conform to a robust, self-affine, hierarchical fractal called the Wave Principle (see Elliott, 1938, 1946; Frost and Prechter, 1978/1998; and Prechter, 1999), whose path is probabilistically predictable. Because endogenous changes in social mood impel humans to take social actions that express their moods, we can apply a knowledge of the Wave Principle's pattern as well as knowledge of varying delays between initial decisions and ultimate actions to achieve some measure of success in forecasting the direction, extremity and character of financial, social, political, cultural and economic trends. Socionomics is a probabilistic science, not a strictly deterministic one. It allows socionomists to predict general trends of aggregates at times but not the specific acts of individuals, any one of whom is seen as at least partially free to vary at will from any social trend.

The metatheoretical assumptions of socionomics are incommensurable (Pepper, 1942) with those of the theories it aims to replace. If socionomics' predictive power proves to be more accurate than that of competing theories attempting to predict the same events, socionomics should inspire a revolutionary paradigm shift that will eventually necessitate a major revision of social causality theory as well as a metatheoretical reorientation in all the social sciences.

Traditional Theories of Finance and Asset Pricing

This brief paper cannot offer a complete historical review of theories of finance. (For good overviews of this literature, see Mishkin, 2003 and Mirowski, 1989.) The focus here is on a few highlights to illustrate that history, using several examples to make theoretical points about the new paradigm of socionomics as applied to finance.

Utility and Value Theory

Most economists see Adam Smith's *The Wealth of Nations* (1776) as the beginning of modern economic theory at its most general level. Financial theorists date the birth of their theoretical base to Daniel Bernoulli's *New Theory of Risk* (1738/1954). Not surprisingly, his version of utility theory is extremely simple, merely treating utility, money and pleasure as synonymous. Bernoulli's paper implicitly assumes that people's choices in risk-taking behavior are governed by rational principles of mathematically pristine logic. Modern economic theory has not made much progress with respect to that assumption since his paper was published in 1738.

Some of the earliest modern economists acknowledged that they were only temporarily making do with overly simplistic models borrowed from physics in order to get started with their new science. Alfred Marshall (1890/1920), one of the fathers of mathematical formalism in neoclassical economics, wrote:

> The Mecca of the economist lies in economic biology rather than in economic dynamics. But biological conceptions are more complex than those of mechanics; a volume on Foundations must therefore give a relatively large place to mechanical analogies; and frequent use is made of the term "equilibrium," which suggests something of statical analogy. This fact, combined with the predominant attention

paid in the present volume to the normal conditions of life in the modern age, has suggested the notion that its central idea is "statical," rather than "dynamical." But in fact it is concerned throughout with the forces that cause movement: and its key-note is that of dynamics, rather than statics. (p. 19)

The forces to be dealt with are however so numerous, that it is best to take a few at a time; and to work out a number of partial solutions as auxiliaries to our main study. Thus we begin by isolating the primary relations of supply, demand and price in regard to a particular commodity. We reduce to inaction all other forces by the phrase "other things being equal": we do not suppose that they are inert, but for the time we ignore their activity. This scientific device is a great deal older than science: it is the method by which, consciously or unconsciously, sensible men have dealt from time immemorial with every difficult problem of ordinary life. (p. 20)

The main concern of economics is thus with human beings who are impelled, for good and evil, to change and progress. Fragmentary statical hypotheses are used as temporary auxiliaries to dynamical— or rather *biological*—conceptions: but the central idea of economics, even when its Foundations alone are under discussion, must be that of living force and movement. (p. 22)

The manner in which the reasonings are to be combined depends on the nature of the problem. Sometimes the mere mechanical "composition of forces" suffices; more often allowance must be made for a quasi-chemical interaction of the various forces; while in nearly all problems of large scope and importance, regard must be had to *biological* conceptions of growth. (p. 23) (Marshall, 1890; emphases added)

Despite these good intentions, Marshall never got around to creating an economic theory based on "biological conceptions." While he formalized many aspects of the underpinnings of neoclassical theory, the first material mathematical advance on Bernoulli's work in utility theory came more than 200 years later, when von Neumann and Morgenstern presented a more elaborate, formalized, axiomatic version of the theory in their famous book, *Theory of Games and Economic Behavior* (1944). Their book not only established the essential formalisms of neoclassical theory but also created an entirely new field, game theory. Their book still provides foundational ideas for a major organizing set of theoretical tools used in economics, political science and other social sciences.

A 1948 paper by the great monetarist Milton Friedman and L.J. Savage is often cited as the most accurate and concise statement of neoclassical utility theory. Their paper incorporates many of the key theoretical points presented earlier in more daunting mathematical form by von Neumann and Morgenstern. It mentions Adam Smith and other classical economists' acknowledgment of humans' capacity for non-rational financial behavior before going on to reject those ideas in favor of an absolute allegiance to the rational-actor model, in which human beings of all social classes, levels of education and degrees of wealth are assumed to act with perfect rationality in all their financial decisions, even under very uncertain and risky conditions. Friedman and Savage acknowledged the existence of people who take unwise financial risks because of their "ignorance of the odds." They also cited Adam Smith's remarks on people taking irrational financial risks due to "their absurd presumption in their own good fortune" and quoted Alfred Marshall's comment on the financial risk-taking of "young men of an adventurous disposition [who] are more attracted by the prospects of a great success than they are deterred by the fear of failure" (Friedman and Savage, 1948, 280).[2] Yet Friedman and his co-author went on to make a case for using the perfect logic of von Neumann and Morgenstern even in their analysis of risky investment behavior. To their credit, after all their logical arguments they acknowledged in passing,

> It does not, of course, follow that there will exist a utility function that will rationalize in this way the reactions of individuals to risk. It may be that individuals behave inconsistently.... Further empirical work should make it possible to determine whether or not these implications conform to reality. (p. 282)

Near the end of their paper, the authors laid out a number of conditions under which rational utility theory would be falsifiable (pp. 303-304). Some of these conditions have already been met by recent work in behavioral finance. (For comprehensive reviews of this literature, see Kahneman et al., 1982, Camerer et al., 2004, and Vernon Smith's 2003 revision of his 2002 Nobel Prize lecture.) Yet most mainstream economists in academia have not abandoned their faith in neoclassical utility theory as applied to finance. Why?

Neoclassical studies of finance must make sweeping assumptions in order to make their favorite statistical tools useable. To that end, difficult conditions are simply assumed out of existence. For instance, Farrell's (1966) neoclassical study investigating whether speculation could be reliably profitable simply assumed the statistical independence of stock price changes. This assumption automatically ruled out any chance that his model would capture the herding dynamic incorporated in the socionomic theory of finance, much less the hierarchical fractal to which most socionomists believe it adheres.

Such assumptions are ubiquitous in neoclassical finance theory and produce circular arguments. They have also allowed neoclassical economists to avoid admitting that empirical research has falsified their theory. As Welty (1971) pointed out, difficult-to-model or "irrational" aspects of human behavior have often been assumed away and dismissed by the use of *ceteris paribus* clauses in neoclassical theory. When later empirical data do not confirm the theory, these same *ceteris paribus* clauses are invoked to excuse the discrepancy between theory and reality. This approach, as Welty demonstrated, began a century ago with Alfred Marshall's initial attempts to formalize utility theory mathematically, and it remains in practice. Unfortunately, that ubiquitous device renders neoclassical theory unfalsifiable and thus of dubious scientific merit. Penrose (1953, 608) criticized the infamous *ceteris paribus* device on that basis, and a half-century later Hodgson (2001, 232-247) issued an even more devastating critique meticulously exposing the non-falsifiability of neoclassical economics' utility theory.

An early precursor of the field of neuroeconomics was C. Reynold Noyes. As a Yale professor and chairman of the National Bureau of Economic Research, Noyes was frustrated with the unrealistic assumptions of neoclassical utility theory and developed his own neurophysiological theory of economic decision-making, which he called a "system of economic energetics." (See Wolfe, 1950, for a thoughtful review of Noyes' work.) Unfortunately, his theory attracted little interest and less support. His criticism of the incompatibility between financial realities and neoclassical equations were met with a "Ho hum, what else is new?" attitude by mainstream economists at the time. Wolfe dismissed Noyes' critique of the utility-maximizing model of finance and even went so far as to say, "No one in his senses has ever taken general equilibrium or the continuous curves of marginal analysis as precisely representative of reality" (Wolfe, 1950, 101).

The story of Noyes' frustrating failure to gain acceptance for his ideas points out a real danger currently embedded in the neuroeconomic approach. While he took pains to learn much about both economics and neurology, Noyes remained captive to the mechanistic *zeitgeist* of his era and unwittingly adopted many of the same assumptions about the nature of causality shared by the neoclassical economists he was attempting to overthrow. Though he did not acknowledge it as such, his theory of "economic energetics" embodied the fundamental elements of neoclassical utility theory in its

reliance on 19th-century thermodynamics and in its methodological commitment to mechanistic reductionism. Neurology's borrowing from the previous
century's physics was less blatant than economics' borrowing, but the same
metaphors powered both theoretical engines. (See Wolfe, 1950, for details
of Noyes' idea.) Noyes also invoked some elements of nonmechanistic
psychological theory, as Gestalt and field theory were popular in psychology at the time. This conflation served only to make his theoretical system
more eclectic and self-contradictory in its underlying assumptions and thus
less intelligible. As Pepper (1942) simply and memorably said of mixing
incommensurable philosophical worldviews, "Eclecticism is confusing."

Much of current theory in neuroeconomics is at risk due to the same
confusing metatheoretical eclecticism. Practitioners of both neuroeconomics
and behavioral finance are producing interesting and meaningful empirical
research, but their findings to date have resulted only in a scattered collection
of hypotheses. (See Glimcher, 2003, for an overview of neuroeconomics;
see Camerer et al., 2004, for a survey of behavioral finance.) Their work
can have a lasting impact if they get past this stage and find an overarching
theoretical and metatheoretical framework to help organize and guide their
neurophysiological and psychological research. Socionomics can provide
such a framework.

Specifically, socionomics resides within a coherent metatheoretical
framework involving the integration of contextualist assumptions about
a human being as an individual—emphasizing a non-reactionary, non-
exogenously determined, innate capacity to initiate action spontaneously
with enough freedom for meaningful choice—with organicist assumptions
about the nature of social causality, embodied in socionomic theory in its
depiction of waves of social mood and resulting social behavior.

Some of the institutionalists' ideas about the nature of human beings[3]
share socionomic theory's contextualist and organicist assumptions. Yet
unlike the theories of many institutionalists, socionomics' idea of a "formological" pattern of social mood and social behavior ruled by Fibonacci
mathematics and fractal geometry offers a quantified structuralism that
allows predictive ability at the aggregate level.

Keynes' is the most influential economic theory in the past century to
share elements of the contextualist and organicist worldviews. His oft-quoted
passage about the "animal spirits" of speculators in his *General Theory of
Employment, Interest, and Money* (Keynes, 1936/1997, 153-164) clearly
evokes contextualism's emphasis on human freedom from external determinism and from the bounds of perfect rationality. The organicist strand in
his thought is less well known, since his theory is at times colored by an

eclectic mix of organicist and mechanistic assumptions [see Chapter 25]. (See Hodgson, 2001, especially 63-64,169, and 215-231, for insights into expressions of organicism in Keynesian and institutionalist economic theory; also see Winslow, 1986, 1989, and Davis, 1989, for analysis of Keynesian organicism.) The clearest statement of organicist ideas in Keynes' work came in his biography of the neoclassicist Francis Edgeworth, where he criticized the latter's atomistic utility theory:

> The atomic hypothesis which has worked so splendidly in Physics breaks down in Psychics [here Keynes refers to psychological aspects of economic behavior, especially the "hedonism" implicit in neoclassical utility theory that Edgeworth had tried to mathematize]. We are faced at every turn with the problems of Organic Unity [organicism], of Discreteness, of Discontinuity—the whole is not equal to the sum of the parts, comparisons of quantity fail us, small changes produce large effects, the assumptions of a uniform and homogeneous continuum are not satisfied. (Keynes, 1972, 262, as quoted in Davis, 1989, 1166)

Unlike many economists who built their theories on organicist and/ or contextualist assumptions, Keynes did not believe that the uncertainty implicit in his version of these metatheoretical tenets made prediction impossible. His thoughts about "fundamental uncertainty" in financial markets led many critics to misunderstand his ideas and mistakenly think his theory was "nihilistic" in implying that financial behavior is unpredictable in principle. Yet a careful reading of Keynes reveals a different viewpoint, as described by Winslow:

> the conventional response [Keynes meant something akin to socionomics' "herding" concept by his use of this term] to fundamental uncertainty is the product of organic interdependence [organicism]. This enables [Keynes] to assume that conventional behavior is frequently sufficiently orderly and stable to be predictable. (Winslow, 1989, 1180)

Thus, Keynes implied a basic assumption of human freedom (see Winslow, 1989, 1177, and Lawson, 1985, 919), an essential part of contextualism, along with an organicist assumption about the predictability of human behavior in the aggregate due to its structure (see Winslow, 1989, 1180). Winslow noted that for Keynes, "The psychological structures which generate the [herding] response are the outcome of social relations within which the typical [investor] develops" (Winslow, 1989, 1180). These thin strands of organicism and contextualism in his theory are notable precursors of similar components in socionomics.

There are nevertheless important differences between the total body of Keynesian theory and socionomic theory. Keynes' theoretical eclecticism [see also Chapter 25] produced internal contradictions in his theory that ultimately sabotaged his ambition to create a coherent, well-integrated general theory of economics.

Unlike modern neoclassical economists' focus on the individual, many of the earliest utility theorists such as Jeremy Bentham (1952) in the late 1700s attempted to define "utility" in the service of a theory of ethics in society. They thought that if they could determine a way to measure utility at a broad level, summing up individual quantities of "good" in general to determine the greatest good for the greatest number of people, it would point the way toward the most ethical course of action in various situations. Over time, economic theory has moved away from such trains of thought. As economists realized that "cardinal utility," by which they might compare utility among individuals, was impossible to measure, they shifted to a search for a meaningful way to quantify "ordinal utility," or relative ranks of utility within an individual. In an attempt to become more objective, economists shifted from thinking of utility as a feeling-state of happiness or satisfaction to a concept of utility in which ordinal utility levels could theoretically be measured by observing people's preferences as revealed in their behavior. [See also Chapter 24's discussion of value-scale theory.] In order to make the system of preferences simple enough to calculate using available statistical methods, the neoclassical economists building mathematically formal models of economic behavior had to assume that all individuals would strive rationally to maximize the utility of their decisions all the time, including when making investing decisions.[4]

Utility theory's borrowing from physics to model the behavior of living human beings created theoretical problems, which Mirowski (1989) exposed in detail. There have been numerous mathematical challenges to the accuracy of its assumptions, and even its basic conceptual difficulties have been exposed over time. A central issue is that the utility theory that evolved into neoclassical economics was so elastic that it could not be proven wrong, no matter what the outcome of empirical studies examining its hypotheses. The most extreme example reported in Hodgson's critique is a study that purported to argue that even suicide could be seen—if the theorist is clever enough—as an example of utility-maximization (Hammermesh and Soss, 1974, reported in Hodgson, 2001, 243). [Rational-bubble theorists go to similar extremes to justify their rational-actor model; see Chapter 23.] Neoclassical utility theory has been increasingly characterized as merely an "empty black box" (Pettit, 1982), devoid of any compelling details of human thought and behavior other than imputed rationality, thus offering a hyper-elastic theory that could be "made compatible with both selfishness and altruism, with both calculative and unreflective behavior, with intelligence and stupidity" (Hodgson, 2001, 242). [For more on this theme, see Chapter 24.]

A full discussion of the problems inherent in utility theory is beyond the scope of this paper, but let us examine just one more of many logical flaws in its basic assumptions: the transitivity of preferences. This transitivity is simply assumed, as it must be for neoclassical equilibrium theory to use the models it borrowed from physics. Research shows that this assumption does not hold in the real world. Mirowski (1989) demonstrated how the failure of this assumption renders much of neoclassical utility theory invalid. If Sam likes A better than B, and likes B better than C, the neoclassicists assume he should like A better than C, but at times he perversely prefers C to A, thus defeating their axiom concerning the transitivity of preferences and taking down with it the entire mechanical structure of equilibrium theory.

Over the years, researchers have compiled a long list of "anomalies" for neoclassical theory in the form of empirical findings that defy the basic assumptions on which its usage of certain analytical tools depends. (For examples, see Kahneman and Tversky, 1979, De Bondt and Thaler, 1985, and Loewenstein and Thaler, 1989.) As these anomalies began to multiply, economists began first to challenge some of their assumptions, then to cast around for more predictive models. Some of the challengers were heads of the most prestigious professional associations of economists (see, for instance, MacDougall, 1974, and Leontief, 1971). Yet when some innovative economists announced theoretical breakthroughs that threatened to dethrone the neoclassical model from dominance, they often seemed to hedge their bets to avoid risking expulsion from the academy. This understandable cautiousness has resulted in an unfortunate situation in which the most basic assumptions of the neoclassical model—mechanistic causality, equilibrium, rational utility-maximizing, and the additive summing of individual agents to model aggregate dynamics—were not replaced with a significantly different paradigm. Rather, each new theorist would simply add his model as yet another factor in neoclassical equations, resulting in either the confusing eclecticism we have already discussed or the subsumption of any new ideas into the old framework, resulting in no significant advance in basic theory or predictive accuracy for the field as a whole.

One brief example may be illustrative. When Alchian published his paper "Uncertainty, Evolution, and Economic Theory" in 1950, making a bold announcement that he was going to eschew neoclassical theory's utility-maximizing assumption and base his model on biological notions such as evolution instead of physics models, many economists were excited and inspired. Alchian brashly trumpeted,

> [In markets] where foresight is uncertain, "profit maximization" is *meaningless* [emphasis in original] as a guide to specifiable action. The constructive development then begins with an introduction of the element of environmental adoption...of a posteriori most appropriate action according to the criterion of "realized positive profits." [Alchian later defines this process in biological, evolutionary terms, using examples from a new theory of the firm. He clarifies in a footnote that his new model is also applicable to individuals.] This is illustrated in an extreme, random-behavior model *without any individual rationality, foresight, or motivation whatsoever.* (p. 211; emphasis added)

Alchian committed himself to "reverting to a Marshallian type of analysis combined with the essentials of Darwinian evolutionary natural selection" (p. 213) and shocked neoclassical finance theorists by ascribing a central role to "sheer chance." This was a model that took uncertainty seriously. In his model, he calmly reported, "All individual rationality, motivation, and foresight will be temporarily abandoned..." to be replaced by evolutionary dynamics (p. 214). One element of this radical approach is another precursor to socionomic theory. Alchian offered "imitation" (cf. socionomic theory's "herding" concept in Prechter, 1999, pp. 147-177) as a key dynamic in his evolutionary finance theory:

> Many factors cause this motive to imitate patterns of action observable in past successes. [This is the aim of herding in socionomics.] Among these are (1) the absence of an identifiable criterion for decision-making [the context of uncertainty, which is essential for socionomic principles to operate], (2) the variability of the environment, (3) the multiplicity of factors that call for attention and choice, (4) the uncertainty attaching to all these factors and outcomes, (5) the awareness that superiority relative to one's competitors is crucial [like socionomics, Alchian links his theory to evolutionary survival considerations] and (6) the nonavailability of a trial-and-error process converging to an optimum position. In addition, imitation affords relief from the necessity of really making decisions and conscious innovations. [As with socionomic herding, Alchian's imitation is seen as at least partially unconscious.] (p. 218)

Alchian's evolutionary finance theory would seem to be very promising. What's wrong with it? While very influential and often cited (theorists of some strands of "evolutionary economics" still cite Alchian as one of their theoretical progenitors), Alchian could not, in the end, give up the basic elements of neoclassical methodology. He concluded, "In summary, I have asserted that the economist, using the present analytical tools developed in the analysis of the firm under certainty, can predict the more...viable types of economic interrelationships that will be induced by environmental change...." (p. 220) He gave little more than a promissory note for his explanation of how this task is to be done, but his loyalty to analytical tools similar to those in neoclassical theory is clear:

> It is straightforward...to start with uncertainty and nonmotivation and then to add elements of foresight and motivation in building an analytical model.... The existence of uncertainty and incomplete information is the foundation of the suggested type of analysis;...it motivates and rationalizes a type of adaptive imitative behavior; yet it does not destroy the basis of prediction, explanation, or diagnosis. It does not base its aggregate description on individual optimal action; yet it is *capable of incorporating such activity* [emphasis added] where justified. The formalization of this approach awaits the marriage of the theory of stochastic processes and economics.... (Alchian, 1950, 221)

Alchian thereby compromised his radical-sounding theory by offering to combine it in an additive fashion with the analytical tools of neoclassical finance theory. He failed to envision a formal model that was categorically different from that implied by the utility-optimizing assumption of the neoclassical theorists, rendering his theory hopelessly eclectic. (A more detailed but very incisive critique of the logical contradictions ensuing from Alchian's metatheoretical eclecticism may be found in Penrose, 1953.) Although his theory shares many general ideas with socionomics, it is ultimately unstructured and inapplicable to prediction, whereas the Elliott wave model gives socionomics a unique basis for explanation, analytical methodology and practical application (see Prechter, 1999, Chapters 2-7) that is congruent with both its metatheoretical assumptions and its theoretical depiction of the herding process.

The questions asked by traditional economists concerning value theory and utility theory have one thing in common with each other despite all their other theoretical differences: By asking "*What* do people value?" or "What is the value of this *thing*?" they are implicitly endorsing an *object ontology*, in which what matters most in depicting social reality is noun-like objects or substances, whether those noun-like things are theorized as money, pleasure, happiness, goods or financial assets. Efforts to shift to a theory of preferences in neoclassical theory have not escaped this object ontology but have only redirected the object of reification. The focus merely shifted from estimating the value imagined to be contained inside a good or asset to an attempt to quantify desire, which is seen as a thing to be measured inside each human. By contrast, socionomics uses an *event ontology* or *process ontology*,[5] seeing that what matters most in depicting reality is more verb-like than noun-like, being *dynamic relationships* in a *developing process*.[6] Thus, it focuses more on questions such as "What affects humans' valuing process?" and "How does social mood affect humans' process of valuing things?" The intuitive appeal of this new focus is readily apparent: When asked, "Do you like French food or Mexican food better?" most of us would honestly reply, "It depends on how I feel." In such cases, the value does not reside in the food but results from changeable feelings. Under socionomics, social mood determines changes in the feelings that regulate the aggregate valuing process for financial markets.

We wish to articulate clearly socionomic theory's ontological position, even in this brief paper. Some theorists are prone to misunderstand any statement of a "process ontology" as suggesting some type of solipsistic metaphysics that would imply that "objects" have no objective reality. (See Hodgson, 2001, 37-39, who responds to this confusion by offering a useful stance toward philosophical realism in economics.) It would be absurd to talk about reality as "process" without also presuming the reality—even if temporary or transitory—of objects that undergo processes. Any concept of "dynamic relationships" assumes the existence of objects among which there is a relationship. Rather, our ontological position is a statement about priority of emphasis. To understand and predict reality, it is more useful to emphasize dynamic processes rather than static reifications of phenomenology as primarily causal.

Asset Pricing Theory

Proponents of the "fundamental analysis" of stock prices are repre-sented by Graham and Dodd (1934). [See the discussion under the same subhead in Chapter 15. Identical text has been omitted here, leaving only the following concluding paragraph.]

Theories of fundamental analysis in asset pricing were more persuasive in earlier times when it seemed that economists were trying to place values on things such as factories, widgets, and hours of assembly-line labor. In recent years, however, there is a growing preponderance of firms in which 90% or more of their "fundamental" value is seen as residing in *nonmaterial* "things" such as intellectual capital, the likelihood (future value) of innovative technology finding a successful market, "business processes" that may now be patented and sold, and "goodwill" in important business relationships. The basic ontology of finance theory is breaking down—by shifting from "object ontology" to "process ontology"—making fundamental analysis of this sort less and less reliable.

Business Cycle Theory

A similar example of the incommensurability of socionomic theory and neoclassical economics is found in the area of business cycle theory. [Text identical to that in Chapter 15 has been omitted here as well.]

All the diverse theories—from Jevons to Schumpeter to the monetarists to Keynes—however different, share basic assumptions, especially their core faith in an equilibrium model derived from physics. (See Mankiw, 1989, for a sampling of business cycle theories within neoclassical economics.)

An exception to standard business cycle theories is the work of John Maurice Clark, an economist known as an institutionalist but whose theoretical work incorporated aspects of neoclassical theory along with aspects of institutionalism. His explanation of business cycles (see Adams, 1934, Hobson, 1937, and Clark, 1917) comprises eight factors, many of which are mechanistic but the last of which describes business cycles as "psychological swings from over-pessimism to over-optimism" (Adams, 1934, 308). Clark's inclusion of psychological motivations may be considered another precursor to socionomic theory's key idea of social mood as an endogenous type of causality. Overall, however, his approach to business cycles was thus highly eclectic, mixing assumptions from the competing models of equilibrium theory and institutionalism, so not much came of his work. Such errors among the institutionalists allowed hard-core neoclassical theory gradually to dominate the discussion.

A real problem arises in trying to contrast neoclassical business cycle theories with socionomics: Business cycles make sense in a mechanistic worldview only if one sees each significant change in the rate of economic growth (whether booms or busts) as an aberrant disequilibrium caused by some exogenous shock that knocks the economy out of equilibrium, to which it must return. When this simple idea proved false after much research, the creative neoclassicists invented ever-more-complicated theories of "multiple equilibria" [see Chapter 12] to try to explain why the economy never seemed to revert to its supposed original mean.

In contrast, the fractal nature of growth and retrenchment in the socio-nomic model suggests that no static equilibrium or multiple equilibria—and therefore no divergences therefrom—exist. There are only fractal oscilla-tions of positive and negative social mood, which inspire social actions that create the evolutionary path of progress and regress in humanity's financial, economic, political and social fortunes.

Neoclassical economic theories invoke metaphors from physics, while socionomics invokes biological metaphors. If you were studying the pen-dulum of a grandfather clock as well as the growth of an oak tree, would you ask the same questions in trying to explain changes you witness in both? It is easy to see why the simplicity of machines became so tempting for early economists to use for their first models. In the 17th century, the Italian philosopher Giambattista Vico (see Vico,1744/1999) explained why scientists defaulted to using metaphors drawn from certain objects made by humans—i.e., machines—in stating his principle of *verum factum* (loosely translated: "I made it, so I understand it"). But simple metaphors break down if they do not realistically fit the behaviors they are used to describe. Given the pervasive failure of these mechanical models to explain and predict so-cial change, socionomic theorists hope that social science is ready to adopt a more encompassing and realistic theoretical model that more naturally accounts for economic, financial and social behavior.

Herding and Decision-Making Under Uncertainty

In contrast to proponents of the efficient market hypothesis, two earlier theorists, Knight (1921) and Keynes (1921, 1936/1997), took uncertainty in financial markets seriously, thereby challenging neoclassical ideas. Knight, an early institutionalist, had a more "objective" theory about uncertainty, while Keynes, viewing the matter more psychologically, had a rather "subjective" interpretation of uncertainty. Knight's and Keynes' ideas were not very agreeable to the neoclassical finance theorists. In contrast to the probabilistic-knowledge version of uncertainty theory that was congruent with neoclassical equilibrium theory, Knight and Keynes posited that in some situations, rather than being uncertain about the exact nature of a financial dynamic that is determinate but only probabilistically knowable (what we may call "epistemological uncertainty"), one might actually have no way of even estimating probabilistically what the truth is, since the phenom-enon itself may be indeterminate (producing "ontological uncertainty" or Keynesian "fundamental uncertainty"). Here is how Keynes expressed the two types of uncertainty:

[By my term "uncertain knowledge" or "fundamental uncertainty," I] not only mean merely to distinguish what is known for certain from what is only probable. The game of roulette is not subject, in this sense, to uncertainty.... The sense in which I am using the term is that in which the prospect of a European war is uncertain, or the price of copper and the rate or interest twenty years hence...or the position of private wealth owners in the social system in 1970. About these matters there is no scientific basis on which to form any calculable probability whatever. We simply do not know. (Keynes, quoted in Rosser, 2001)

There are two points to be made about this more radical, ontological uncertainty. First, it is the context in which, according to socionomics, investors engage in herding. Second, in contrast to Keynesian theory, the possibility of prediction in socionomic theory does not rely upon knowledge of mechanistic determinism, so the lack of such knowledge does not thwart the possibility of prediction. On the contrary, socionomic causality affords form-determined probability to the social aggregate despite fundamental unpredictability at the level of individual participants. Under socionomics, predictability is primarily a higher-level property of the formological system.

While neoclassical economists see uncertainty as a temporary, unwanted aberration that distorts their equilibrium theory, socionomics sees uncertainty as both a real and a necessary feature in its dynamic event ontology. It is not something to be shunned and explained away but to be embraced and explained. Its very existence may provide the continuing impulse that generates growth in an economy. Perhaps without uncertainty there would be no herding, and without herding there would be no investment, and without investment there would be no prosperity.

Sornette (2003b, 27-36) provided an excellent summary of the growing literature concerning herding. It is interesting to see how early such a concept was mentioned in the economic literature. Pigou's (1903, 60-61) comments about people's desire to be "in the swim" (fashionable) presaged by a century Shiller's concept of "fads and fashions" (Shiller, 2000). Such expressions are loosely compatible with socionomics' concept of herding [see Chapter 34].

An even earlier precursor to socionomic ideas was Ellis (1892), who wrote,

a market knows its own present state...by the unconscious contribution of many minds to a daily growing opinion. That opinion grows

all wrong sometimes, and the swaying of opinion from wrong to right
and beyond—from excessive pessimism to immoderate optimism—is
the usual and immediate cause of fluctuations. (p. 110)

Facts tell, in the long run; the set of opinion is so strong, meanwhile,
as to disregard the facts of supply and demand for years. Hence
bubbles and manias and long periods of ensuing depression. (p. 116)
(Ellis, 1892)

These early notions of herding in contexts of uncertainty and especially the
idea of occasional supply-demand impotence—which socionomics wholeheartedly shares—defy the rational choice model of neoclassical economics.
    Socionomics more formally posits that the ontology behind financial
markets is specifically that of a psychological process—valuing and desiring under the influence of optimistic or pessimistic mood—rather than the
ontology of value residing in an external object waiting to be rationally
calculated. As Prechter wrote in 1999,

In just [the last] century, the Dow Jones Industrial Average...has been
valued as high as 5.6 times corporate book value...and as little as
0.5 times.... These huge differences are due to one thing: people's
opinion about the capital gain potential of stocks, i.e., the extent to
which they are bullish or bearish. Therefore, such valuations are a
direct measure of investors' optimism or pessimism.... (p. 359)

Some theoreticians construct models of what stocks "should" be
worth. Obviously, there is no such thing. Even if the premise of such
models were valid, the relentless uncertainty about what the naive
majority may do without regard for value is plenty enough to destroy
the utility of attempting to invest with respect to "intrinsic value."
(p. 360, Prechter, 1999)

From such an entirely different ontological perspective, the conclusions
of socionomics are bound to be incommensurable with those of neoclassical
finance theory. The theories are speaking two different languages that have
no mutual points of translation.

Summary of Literature Review

With this brief overview, we have seen that neoclassical finance theory—with respect to utility and value theory, asset pricing theory, business
cycle theory and financial decision-making under uncertainty—is a loosely
defined, physics-based model attempting reductionistically to compress the

complexity of individual and social reality into a static equilibrium. In doing so, it fails to model convincingly either the psychological dynamics of individuals' financial behavior or the aggregate results of speculators' choices in contexts of uncertainty. Indeed, the details of neoclassical utility theory are so under-specified that empirical research from this perspective seems close to useless when, as Hodgson pointed out, *"Any observed behavior can be fitted into the theory"* (2001, 237; emphasis his).

Conclusion

The new paradigm of socionomics is unique in eschewing previous theories' physics and machine metaphors and in being true to the psychological phenomenology of the biological organisms being studied. Socionomics differs from the old mechanistic model by describing and explaining the complex reality of financial and social behavior using integrated organicist and contextualist perspectives on the process of decision-making under uncertainty in a manner that captures the psychological reality of the individual while offering probabilistic prediction of the structure-determined developmental path of financial markets, economies and societies.

Socionomics and the competing macroeconomic paradigm are genuinely incommensurable, having fundamental ontological differences. The only basis for judging between these radically different approaches is the pragmatic one of predictive ability. Our research program includes empirically validating socionomic theory by comparing its predictions of human social behavior to those generated by other theories. [Our paper, "Social Mood, Stock Market Performance, and U.S. Presidential Elections: A Socionomic Perspective on Voting Results," reprinted in *Socionomic Causality in Politics* (2017) offers just such an example.] In time, especially if other scientists join us in exploring this exciting new paradigm of socionomics, we hope to craft additional tools to help us both explain our social past and to predict our social future more clearly than ever before.

NOTES

[1] [Editor's Note: This paragraph and part of the next originally appeared in this paper as part of Endnote 2. The bulk of the next paragraph was originally published in Parker (2006) (Chapter 36).]

[2] Two points in passing may be noted concerning these examples. Marshall's description applies exactly to Schumpeter's "entrepreneurs," whose irrational risk-taking he used to explain the great technical innovations that were the basis for his business cycle theory. Socionomics offers a different explanation for Schumpeter's business cycles. It posits that large-degree waves of positive social mood produce climates of optimism that inspire entrepreneurial types to have the confidence to take great risks in hopes of great rewards. Rather than fluctuations in business being the effect of the actions of solitary entrepreneurs, as Schumpeter held, waves of social mood arise endogenously from the total mass of people, causing the social conditions necessary for entrepreneurial motivation and success as well as alternating periods of retrenchment and failure.

[3] Some institutionalist ideas about economic man, from the American pragmatic philosophers John Dewey and Charles Sanders Peirce (see Hodgson, 2001, for an overview of this influence), imply contextualist assumptions. While institutionalism as a school of economic thought was once so diverse in its opinions that the only thing said to unify it was its opposition to neoclassical theory, the basic idea of institutionalism was to supplement neoclassical theory's myopic focus on reductionistic, methodological individualism [see Chapter 37] with an examination of the social dynamics of economic behavior, whether the "institution" within which those social dynamics operated was variously a static set of legal institutions of laws and treaties, constraints on individual liberties represented by social customs, habits and rules (down to and including those of family systems), or merely the "instituted" habits of thought within individuals related to their consideration of the social costs or benefits of seeking or losing their peers' approval or agreement. Too broad a focus threatens loss of coherence for any set of theories, but the institutionalists' common thread is in permitting methodological analysis of aggregates to enrich economic theory. This methodological approach need not be non-mechanistic, but historically the institutionalists since Veblen (the father of this approach to economics) have been more congenial to structuralist and contextualist thought than to mechanistic reductionism. Socionomics shares this metatheoretical and methodological choice, with its emphasis on aggregate analysis and its organicist/contextualist framework. An in-depth discussion of either the "old institutionalists" or the "neo-institutionalists" (see Hodgson, 2001, 2004) is beyond the scope of this paper but not beyond the scope of our future ambitions. [See Chapter 37.]

[4] This paragraph owes much to the general sources cited earlier.

[5] Editor's note: Greek philosopher Heraclitus was perhaps the first to argue that ever-present change is the essence of causality in the universe. He espoused the process version even of objects in his famous saying, "No man ever steps in the same river twice." Compatibly, WP depicts a process ontology—as opposed to an ontology of objects at equilibrium occasionally shocked by the impact of other objects—for human societies.

[6] See Mirowski, 1989 (especially pp. 142-144, 218-219, 238, 258-261, 280, 285, 342-345, 374-377, and 398-401) for a brilliant analysis of the philosophical implications of the evolving parallels between the metaphors used in theoretical models over the history of physics and those used in similar models in economic theory. His argument is that neoclassical economic theory is fundamentally flawed in leaving unresolved tension between conflicting ontological assumptions about reality related to its self-contradictory blend of a "substance theory of value" with a "field theory of value," which are incommensurable with each other in their mathematical assumptions. While Mirowski's arguments about physics-based models of reality make finer distinctions than our simple contrast between "object ontology" (which is most similar to his "substance theory of value") and the "process (or event) ontology" of socionomics, his overall analysis of the ontology of neoclassical economics, at the broadest level, may be seen as supportive of the present analysis.

We might also note that the phrase "process ontology" is mentioned in connection with Whitehead's philosophy, which some (for instance, Rosser, 2001) saw as having influenced Keynesian thought. The socionomic version of process ontology is vastly different from Whitehead's philosophy, however, as socionomics draws on an integration of contextualism and organicism for its metatheory, while Whitehead's philosophy appears to be a more eclectic, less integrated mix of the organicist and mechanistic worldviews. A full discussion of the implications of this difference, both for difficulties in Whitehead's ideas and for related contradictions within Keynesian theory [see Chapter 25], must await a lengthier treatment. In the meantime, one of the best discussions of aspects of ontological and epistemological differences in various economic theories is to be found in Hodgson (2001). The present discussion of the ontological differences between neoclassical value theory and socionomic theory is aided by his discussion of philosophical realism in economic theory (Hodgson, 2001, 37-39).

SOURCES AND REFERENCES

Adams, Arthur B. (Jun. 1934). "Strategic Factors in Business Cycles." *American Economic Review*, 24 (2), 306-308.

Alchian, Armen A. (June 1950). "Uncertainty, evolution, and economic theory." *Journal of Political Economy*, 58 (3), 211-221.

Bentham, Jeremy. (1952). *Jeremy Bentham's Economics Writings*, 3 vols., W. Stark, ed. London: Allen and Unwin.

Bernoulli, Daniel. (1738/1954). "Exposition of a new theory on the measurement of risk." *Econometrica*, 22 (1), 23-36.

Camerer, Colin F., George Lowenstein, and Matthew Rabin, eds. (2004). *Advances in Behavioral Economics*. Princeton: Princeton University Press.

Clark, J. Maurice. (Mar. 1917), "Business acceleration and the Law of Demand: A technical factor in economic cycles." *Journal of Political Economy*, 25 (3), 217-235.

Davis, John B. (Dec. 1989). "Keynes on Atomism and Organicism." *Economic Journal*, 99, 1159-1172.

De Bondt, Werner and Richard Thaler, (1985). "Does the stock market overreact?" *The Journal of Finance*, 40, (3), 793-805.

Elliott, R.N., *The Wave Principle* (1938) and *Nature's Law* (1946), reprinted in Prechter (ed.), *R.N. Elliott's Masterworks* (1993), New Classics Library.

Ellis, Arthur. (Mar. 1892). "Influence of opinion on markets." *Economic Journal*, 2 (5), 109-116.

Farrell, M.J. (May 1966). "Profitable speculation." *Economica*, New Series, 33 (130), 183-193.

Friedman, Milton, and L.J. Savage. (Aug. 1948). "The utility analysis of choices involving risk." *Journal of Political Economy*, 56 (4), 279-304.

Frost, Alfred John, and Robert R. Prechter (1978/1998). *Elliott Wave Principle— Key to Market Behavior*. Gainesville, GA: New Classics Library.

Gitman, Lawrence J., and Michael D. Joehnk. (1984). *Fundamentals of Investing*, 2nd ed. New York: Harper & Row.

Graham, Benjamin, and David Dodd (1934). *Securities Analysis*. New York: McGraw-Hill.

Hammermesh, Daniel S., and Neal M. Soss. (Jan.-Feb, 1974). "An Economic Theory of Suicide." *Journal of Political Economy*, 82 (1), 83-98.

Hobson, J.A., (Feb. 1937). "Review: Preface to Social Economics." *Economica*, New Series, 4 (13), 91-93.

Hodgson, Geoffrey M. (2001). *How Economics Forgot History: The Problem of Historical Specificity in Social Science*. New York: Routledge.

Glimcher, Paul W. (2003). *Decisions, Uncertainty, and the Brain: The Science of Neuroeconomics*. Cambridge, Massachusetts: The MIT Press.

Kahneman, Daniel, and Amos Tversky. (Mar. 1979). "Prospect theory: an analysis of decision under risk." *Econometrica*, 47 (2), 263-292.

Kahneman, Daniel, Paul Slovic, and Amos Tversky, eds. (1982). *Judgment under Uncertainty: Heuristics and Biases*. Cambridge: Cambridge University Press.

Keynes, John M. (1921). *The Treatise on Probability*. London: Macmillan.

Keynes, John M. (1936/1997). *The General Theory of Employment, Interest Rates, and Money*. New York: Prometheus Books.

Knight, Frank H. (1921). *Risk, Uncertainty, and Profit*. New York: Houghton Mifflin.

Kuhn, T.S. 1970. *The Structure of Scientific Revolutions*. 2nd ed. Chicago: University of Chicago Press.

Lakatos, I. and A. Musgrave, eds. (1970). *Criticism and the Growth of Knowledge*. Cambridge: Cambridge University Press.

Lawson, Tony. (Dec. 1985). "Uncertainty and economic analysis." *Economic Journal*, 95, 909-927. (1985)

Leontief, Wassily. (March 1971). "Theoretical assumptions and non-observed facts." *American Economic Review*, 61 (1), 1-7.

Loewenstein, George, and Richard H. Thaler. (Fall 1989). "Anomalies: Intertemporal Choice." *Journal of Economic Perspectives*, 3 (4), 181-193.

MacDougall, Donald. (Dec. 1974). "In praise of economics." *Economic Journal*, 84 (336), 773-786.

Mankiw, N. Gregory. (Summer 1989). "Real business cycles: a new Keynesian perspective." *Journal of Economic Perspectives*, 3 (3), 79-90.

Marshall, Alfred. (1890/1920). *Principles of Economics*, 8th ed. London: Macmillan and Co., Ltd. [Online at http://www.econlib.org/library/Marshall/marP.html.]

Mirowski, Philip. (1989). *More Heat than Light: Economics as Social Physics, Physics as Nature's Economics*. Cambridge: Cambridge University Press.

Mishkin, Frederic S. (2003). *The Economics of Money, Banking and Financial Markets*, 6th ed. New York: Addison Wesley.

Penrose, Edith T. (Sep. 1953). "Biological analogies in the theory of the firm: rejoinder." *American Economic Review*, 43 (4), 603-609.

Pepper, Stephen C. (1942). *World Hypotheses: A Study in Evidence*. Berkeley, California: University of California Press.

Pettit, Philip. (1982). "Rational choice, functional selection, and 'empty black boxes.'" In Maki, Uskali, ed., (2002). *Fact and Fiction in Economics: Models, Realism and Social Construction*. Cambridge: Cambridge University Press.

Pigou, A.C. (Mar. 1903). "Some remarks on utility." *Economic Journal*, 13 (49), 58-68.

Plosser, Charles I. (Summer 1989). "Understanding real business cycles." *Journal of Economic Perspectives*, 3 (3), 51-77.

Prechter, Robert R. (1999). *The Wave Principle of Human Social Behavior and the New Science of Socionomics*. Gainesville, GA: New Classics Library.

Prechter, Robert R. (2003). *Pioneering Studies in Socionomics*. Gainesville, GA: New Classics Library.

Rosser, J. Barkley, Jr. (Summer 2001). "Alternative Keynesian and post Keynesian perspectives on uncertainty and expectations." *Journal of Post Keynesian Economics*, 23 (4), 545-566.

Schumpeter, Joseph A. (1954). *History of Economic Analysis*. New York: Oxford University Press.

Shiller, Robert J. 2000. *Irrational Exuberance*. Princeton, New Jersey: Princeton University Press.

Smith, Vernon L. (June 2003). "Constructivist and ecological rationality in economics." *American Economic Review*, 93 (3), 465-508.

Sornette, D. (2003b). "Critical market crashes." *Physics Reports* 378 (1), 1-98.

Vico, Giambattista. (Anthony Grafton, trans.) (1744/1999). *New Science: Principles of New Science Concerning the Common Nature of Nations*. New York: Penguin Classics.

von Neumann, John, and Oskar Morgenstern. (1947). *Theory of Games and Economic Behavior*, 2nd ed. Princeton: Princeton University Press.

Welty, Gordon A. (1971). "Giffen's paradox and falsifiability." *Weltwirtschaftliches Archiv*, 107 (1), 139-146.

Winslow, E.G. (Oct.-Dec. 1986). "'Human Logic' and Keynes' economics." *Eastern Economic Journal*, 12, 413-430.

Winslow, E.G. (Dec. 1989). "Organic interdependence, uncertainty and economic analysis." *Economic Journal*, 99, 1173-1182.

Wolfe, A.B. (Apr. 1950). "Neurophysiological Economics." *Journal of Political Economy*, 58 (2), 95-110.

Chapter 34

Excerpted and edited from *Advances in Cognitive Economics: Proceedings of the International Conference on Cognitive Economics*, Sofia, Bulgaria August 2005

Herding: An Interdisciplinary Integrative Review from a Socionomic Perspective

Wayne D. Parker

Herding is one of the most important concepts in cognitive economics, especially as applied to financial markets. This paper presents an interdisciplinary integrative literature review of the herding concept, discusses the salient differences between ways of conceptualizing herding, and argues for the advantages of the perspective on herding provided by socionomics, a new theory that sees herding as a process having evolutionary, prerational and predictable aspects. The paper first summarizes the literature regarding diverse theoretical approaches to the concept of herding: social psychological approaches; information theory and cybernetic approaches; ethological and biological approaches; econophysics approaches; medical model approaches; and the socionomic model. The paper then categorizes these theories according to several theoretical distinctions:

Evolutionary component or not;
Assumes context of uncertainty or not;
Model of agents as homogeneous or heterogeneous;
Herding dynamics seen as endogenous or exogenous;
Conscious or unconscious processes;
Rational or other-than-fully-rational processes;
Assumes equilibrium theory or not;
Assumes utility-maximizing or not.

Finally, the paper offers the socionomic model of herding in contrast to other models.

656   THE SOCIONOMIC THEORY OF FINANCE

There has been an explosion of studies regarding herding in recent years as well as several excellent summaries of the growing herding literature (Devenow and Welch, 1996; Bikhchandani and Sharma, 2000; and Sornette, 2003b, 27-36). Most reviewers, however, have limited themselves to rather narrow theoretical confines. Some reviewers seem to have assumed that herding theories without a commitment to the rational choice model are not worth considering. One of them stated, "In this review, we do not discuss models of herd behavior by individuals who are not fully rational...."[1] (Bikhchandani and Sharma, 2000, 5).

This paper, in contrast, attempts to analyze a wider diversity of models of herding so that we can see the differences between socionomic theory and more established theories in this area. The literature reveals many theoretical approaches to herding, which tend to fall within the following categories:

(1) Social psychological approaches: imitation processes, fashions, fads, etc.

(2) Information theory and cybernetic approaches: information cascades, positive feedback, etc.

(3) Ethological approaches: flocking, migrating birds, swarming bees, ant recruitment, etc.

(4) Econophysics approaches: catastrophe theory, sandpile analogies, self-organized criticality, etc.

(5) Medical model approaches: disease and infection analogies such as contagion, epidemics, etc.

(6) The socionomic approach.

We categorize these theories in Table 1 according to eight salient dimensions. We have scored a theoretical model as "Yes" or "No" on theoretical dimensions on which the model takes a clear side on the issue, "Yes/No" if the model takes both sides of the issue, and "?" on those dimensions on which the model does not have a discernible stance. To facilitate comparisons, we have bolded the theoretical positions held in common with the positions taken by socionomics.

Social Psychological Theory of Herding

Shiller (1984, 1990, 2000, 2001) is perhaps the most representative proponent of the social psychological theory of herding. He has devoted much of his career to challenging economic theorists' assumption of the full rationality of investors.

Table 1: Summary of Positions of Theories of Herding on Eight Theoretical Dimensions								
	1. Evolutionary	2. Uncertainty	3. Homogeneous	4. Endogenous	5. Conscious	6. Rational	7. Equilibrium	8. Utility Maximization
Social Psychology	No	**Yes**	**Yes**	**Yes**/No	**Yes**/No	**Yes**/No	?	**Yes**
Medical Model	**Yes**	**Yes**	No	**Yes**	No	No	**Yes**/No	**Yes**
Ethological	**Yes**	**Yes**	**Yes**	**Yes**	No	No	?	**Yes**
Information theory	**Yes**/No	**Yes**	**Yes**/No	No	Yes	Yes	Yes	**Yes**
Econophysics	?	**Yes**	No	**Yes**/No	**Yes**/No	Yes	Yes	**Yes**
Socionomics	**Yes**	**Yes**	**Yes**	**Yes**	No	No	No	No

"Yes" means the theory named in the far-left column incoporates the quality named in the top row.
"No" means the theory named in the far-left column does not incoporate the quality named in the top row.
"?" means that theorists of the type indicated in the far-left column disagree or are silent about the quality named in the top row.
Bold indicates agreement with socionomic theory.

Many of Shiller's ideas overlap socionomic theory, especially his focus, echoing Keynes, on occasional waves of excessive optimism and pessimism, resulting in the emergence and dissolution of market "fads." Shiller describes the social dynamics of a stock market bubble as a combination of social enthusiasm, excessive optimism and selective attention: "The high demand for the asset is generated by the public memory of high past returns, and the optimism those high returns generate for the future." His "fads and fashions" model posits that "investors have over-confidence in a complex culture of intuitive judgments about expected future price changes, and an excessive willingness to act on these judgments" (Shiller, 2001, 3-4).

Though often lumped in with information-cascade theories of herding, papers about "reputational herding" (e.g., Hong, Kubik and Solomon, 1998) are also categorized here as social psychological theories of herding, since they rely on a simple process of "imitation for social advantage." Many of these theorists, moreover, cite social psychological research, such as Asch's early studies of conformity (cited, e.g., by Scharfstein and Stein, 1990). Other reputational herding papers include Zwiebel (1995) and Prendergast and Stole (1996).

Reputational herding is described as exogenous, conscious, rational and utility-maximizing. Papers on this topic typically do not mention equilibrium theory or assume an evolutionary source of the herding behavior, seeing it rather as a rational choice. Reputational herding theory usually offers a model of heterogeneous agents in interaction, with younger, inexperienced agents competing for a good reputation in society against older, more experienced agents who are assumed to have superior knowledge or skill. Scharfstein and Stein (1990) called their two groups "smart managers" and "dumb managers."

Medical-Model Theory of Herding

The medical model of herding has a long history, going back to classical economist David Ricardo (1815-1823/1951, as cited in Kelly and O'Grada, 2000). He first described market panics in terms of "social contagion" (p. 68) and ascribed the panic of 1797 to "the contagion of the unfounded fears of the timid part of the community." Thus, Ricardo saw such contagions as irrational, endogenous and heterogeneous.

A unique study serving as an exemplar of the medical model of herding is that conducted by Kelly and O'Grada (2000), using an analysis of historical banking data. In that study, factors such as individuals' size of bank account and years since immigration to the U.S. predicted some of the variance as to whether investors panicked and withdrew all their money during two bank runs in the 1850s, but by far the greatest part of the variance was predicted by an aspect of their "social network," namely their county of origin in Ireland. This social contagion study made sophisticated use of social network theory, which is often used by medical epidemiologists.

Another body of literature describing herding as social contagion draws heavily on the social psychological literature. (See Levy and Nail's 1993 review.) These contagion studies, however, are distinguished from social psychological studies by the fact that they draw their explanatory power primarily from unconscious processes, often involving the "infectiousness" of social mood, whereas social psychology theories primarily involve consciously imitative processes.

Many studies invoking the medical model expand the scope of herding effects by defining "financial contagion" as "the rapid spread from one market to another of declining prices, declining liquidity, increased volatility, and increased correlation associated with the financial intermediaries' own effect on the markets in which they trade" (Kyle and Xiong, 2001).

Ethological Theory of Herding

The study of animal behavior is the source of metaphors and analogies for the ethological model of herding. Diverse examples include those related to the work of Danchin et al. (2004), Okubo (1986), Saffre and Deneubourg (2002), and Viscido, Miller and Wethey (2002). The studies in this category are less unified theoretically than those in the other categories, since their primary commonality is a focus on animal behavior and its analogues in human behavior rather than on a single set of theoretical assumptions about the dynamics of herding.

Kirman (1993), a representative of this category, based his model on the process of "recruitment" seen in ant behavior. He claimed that his model of "stochastic recruitment...explains the 'herding' and 'epidemics' described in the literature on financial markets as corresponding to the equilibrium distribution of a stochastic process rather than to switching between multiple equilibria" (p. 137). Kirman approvingly cited studies in which herding behavior is depicted as "a source of endogenous fluctuations in the price level in asset markets." He felt that this "explanation is particularly appealing when...it does not rely on exogenous shocks to the system" (p. 138). Kirman's model does not endorse the equilibrium theory of neoclassical economics, since "there is no convergence to any particular state" (p. 147). Kirman also explained that while traditional models involving exogenous shocks cannot "detect the presence of periodically collapsing bubbles in asset prices," his ant recruitment model "will generate such bubbles" (p. 153).

Information Theory of Herding

The most frequently cited representatives of the informational model of herding, and perhaps the herding theorists most cited by economists, are Banerjee (1992) and Bikhchandani, Hirshleifer and Welch (1992) (referred to here as BHW). Banerjee (1992, 801) took pains to distinguish his informational model of herding from the reputational models such as that of Scharfstein and Stein (1990). BHW (p. 994) defined the essence of their model of herding: "An informational cascade occurs when it is optimal for an individual, having observed the actions of those ahead of him, to follow the behavior of the preceding individual without regard to his own information." The word "optimal" helps us see that this model assumes rational utility maximizing. The model also makes an assumption that neoclassical equilibrium theory is correct, likewise describing a fully rational, conscious process where causality is exogenous. Some studies related to Banerjee's or BHW's approach have modeled homogeneous agents in interaction, while others have modeled heterogeneous groups of agents. Herding models invoking a "positive feedback" process in their explanation are a subtype of the information theory model.

We include under information theory models of herding based on game theory. Some papers in this category mention evolutionary functions of herding behavior, while others do not. What they all share is a model of herding more closely aligned with neoclassical economics than any of the other five models we cover in this paper. Thus, this model is the most influential among traditional economists. See Hirshleifer and Teoh (2001) for a useful review of other papers using this model.

Econophysics Theory of Herding

UCLA geophysics professor Didier Sornette (2003a, 2003b) and his colleagues (Sornette and Andersen, 2002; Lux and Sornette, 2002) are exemplars of a model of herding that is even more mechanistic in its assumptions than the information theory model, since it models human herding behavior by comparing it to the behavior of nonliving systems.

Econophysics models have much in common with the information theory models of herding, which they often quote approvingly (e.g., Sornette and Andersen (2002, 172-173). The most significant difference is that most (but not all) econophysics models of herding have attempted to describe endogenous dynamics of "rational bubbles," while the information theory models incorporate only exogenous causality. Various versions of econophysics models describe homogeneous agents as well as heterogeneous agents, and econophysics papers vary as to whether the processes involved are conscious or not.

The econophysics models of herding include those based on catastrophe theory, self-organized criticality and the physics of sandpiles. While these variants on physics-based theory have important theoretical differences, they share the salient feature of mechanism.

Socionomic Theory of Herding

[Most of the material presented in this section, which was co-authored with Prechter, appears in substantially the same form in Prechter and Parker (2007) and Prechter and Parker (2004), which are reproduced as Chapters 15 and 33 in this book. To avoid redundancy, only the three paragraphs of additional material, as well as the inserted third and fourth paragraphs, originally published in Parker (2006) (Chapter 36), make up this section.]

The socionomic theory of herding (Prechter, 1999, 2001, 2003) is novel in describing a model of unconscious, prerational herding behavior that posits endogenous dynamics that have evolved in homogeneous groups of humans in contexts of uncertainty, while uniquely (see Table 1) eschewing the traditional economic assumptions of equilibrium and utility-maximization.

In separating financial behavior from economic behavior, socionomics both elucidates and resolves the conflict between endogenous and exogenous causal models of human social behavior. The Wave Principle suggests that social mood and financial pricing are endogenous and form-governed. Under the socionomic model of financial markets, prices are simply a record of the endogenous herding dynamic and do not regulate it [see Chapters 12 and 13]. Neoclassical economics, on the other hand, sees exogenous shocks as impacting financial prices, which in turn govern behavior via the law of supply and demand. Mirowski (1990, 296), following Mandelbrot's observation that "empirical [financial] time series of prices are not continuous functions," explained how it is inevitable that the "Marshallian 'law' of supply and demand is most certainly the primary victim of this reconceptualization." R.N. Elliott's (1938) discovery has long implied this very deduction, which socionomics has explicitly made and argued [see Chapter 12].

Under socionomics, cognitive uncertainty in survival-related situations is the context within which individuals shift from a rational basis for action to an instinctive, impulsive mode of unconscious herding. This shift necessitates the individual's reorienting away from his own information, valuation processes or plans and toward a focus primarily on the projected valuations of others as a guide to action, a reorientation that takes place unconsciously. Rationalization of the resulting action, whether pro or post hoc, completes this complex type of social action.

Basing the herding instinct in neurophysiology helps socionomic theory avoid the weakness of many versions of instinct psychology that are arbitrary or nonparsimonious in needlessly multiplying instincts for explanatory purposes without an empirical basis. (See Prechter and Parker, 2006 [Chapter 15; also Chapters 13 and 19] for some of the relevant neurological research related to socionomics.)

Socionomics has the added advantage of coherently differentiating between, and reconciling, a theory of economics governing decision-making where knowledge is relatively certain, and a theory of finance governing decision-making where knowledge is intrinsically uncertain. Socionomic theory recognizes the need both for accommodating reactive, exogenous, mechanistic causality in economic contexts of relative certainty, where rationality is the rule, and for assimilating active, endogenous, organic causality in social contexts of uncertainty, where herding is the rule. These Piagetian processes of accommodation and assimilation at the level of social behavior need not be in opposition conceptually if each process is understood in its proper context, a perspective socionomics affords. This unique feature makes socionomics the next step in the evolution of broader and more accurate, and therefore more powerful, theoretical models of human social behavior.

Impulsivity vs. Utility Maximization among Herding Models

The model of herding posited by socionomic theory differs on one or more theoretical dimensions from each of the other theories of herding covered in this paper. Financial behavior, as conceptualized in socionomic theory, derives from evolutionarily developed, endogenously regulated, unconscious, non-rational, non-utility-maximizing herding among homogeneous agents in contexts of uncertainty in which equilibrium does not apply. The socionomic theory of finance (STF) is especially at odds with financial models that share the prevailing neoclassical economics assumptions of utility maximization, equilibrium, rational pricing, mechanistic causality and exogenous shocks. Moreover, STF incorporates the only theory of herding to reject the utility-maximization assumption underlying all other herding theories covered in this paper.

We can benefit from a historical perspective on the conflict between these two radically different theoretical views. As Noelle-Neumann (1993, 116) documented,

> In the nineteenth and twentieth centuries, two views have repeatedly clashed—the view that stresses instinctual behavior and sees man as determined by herd instincts; and the view that assumes man reacts rationally to the experience of reality…. From one historical perspective it can be said that behaviorism has supplanted two different instinct theories, the one by the British biologist Wilfred Trotter [whose 1916 book first popularized the term "herd instinct"]… and the other one by McDougall [whose 1920 *The Group Mind* was about social behavior in the aggregate]…. The schools of thought that emphasized the rationality of man regarded imitation as a purposeful [conscious, rational] learning strategy. Because these schools clearly prevailed over the instinct theories, the subject of imitation [as instinctual herding]…fell into neglect.

In the evolution of social theory, the pendulum of history is beginning to swing back in the other direction. Thanks to behavioral finance and its identification of anomalies attending EMH (see, for example, Shiller, 1984, and Lo and MacKinlay, 1999), some economists are beginning to recognize the importance of the non-rational and instinctual aspects of human behavior. As this new wave of science comes into focus, we are moving past simplistic questions such as "Is human behavior instinctive or rationally determined?" toward the solution offered by socionomic theory under which the answer is: *both*. Socionomics poses a more sophisticated and more useful question:

"How do the dynamics of rational social behavior relate to the dynamics of impulsive social behavior?" Socionomic theory also provides an answer: Contexts of certainty vs. uncertainty activate humans' use of rational vs. impulsive behavior, creating the differences between economic vs. financial behavior.

EDITOR'S NOTE

[1] Consider a variant of that sentence: "In this review, we do not discuss models of herd behavior by lemmings who are not fully rational...." One wonders if a study of neoclassical researchers who herd only in the rational-herding direction would make the authors' cut.

SOURCES AND REFERENCES

Banerjee, Abhijit V. (Aug. 1992). "A simple model of herd behavior," *Quarterly Journal of Economics*, 107 (3), 797-817.

Bikhchandani, Hirshleifer and Welch (Oct. 1992). "A theory of fads, fashion, custom, and cultural change as informational cascades," *Journal of Political Economy*, 100 (5), 992-1026.

Bikhchandani, Sushil, and Sunil Sharma. (2000). "Herd Behavior in Financial Markets: A Review," (March 2000). IMF Working Paper No. 00/48. http://ssrn.com/abstract= 228343.

Bischoff-Grethe, A., M. Martin, H. Mao, and G.S. Berns. (2001). "The context of uncertainty modulates the subcortical response to predictability," *Journal of Cognitive Neuroscience*, 13 (7), 986-993.

Danchin, Etienne, Luc-Alain Giraldeau, Thomas J. Valone, and Richard H. Wagner (July 23, 2004). "Public information: From nosy neighbors to cultural evolution," *Science*, 305, 487-491.

Davis, John B. (Dec. 1989). "Keynes on atomism and organicism." *Economic Journal*, 99, 1159-1172.

Devenow, Andrea, and Ivo Welch (1996). "Rational herding in financial economics," *European Economic Review*, 40, 603-615.

Elliott, R.N., *The Wave Principle* (1938) and *Nature's Law* (1946), reprinted in Prechter (Ed.), *R.N. Elliott's Masterworks* (1993), New Classics Library.

Fama, Eugene F. (1970). "Efficient capital markets: A review of theory and empirical work," *Journal of Finance*, 25 (2), 383-417.

Frost, Alfred John, and Robert R. Prechter (1978/2005). *Elliott Wave Principle—Key to Market Behavior*. Gainesville, GA: New Classics Library.

Greenspan, Alan (August 29, 2003). Remarks at a symposium in Jackson Hole, WY, http://federalreserve.gov/board docs/speeches/2003/20030829/default.htm.

Graham, John R. (Feb. 1999), "Herding among investment newsletters: Theory and evidence," *Journal of Finance*, 54(1), 237-268.

Hirshleifer, David A. and Siew Hong Teoh. (Dec. 19, 2001). "Herd Behavior and Cascading in Capital Markets: A Review and Synthesis." Dice Center Working Paper No. 2001-20, http://ssrn.com/ abstract=296081.

Hong, Harrison, Jeffrey D. Kubik, and Amit Solomon (July 1998). "Security analysts' career concerns and herding of earnings forecasts," http://ssrn.com/abstract=142895

Kelly, Morgan, and Cormac O'Grada (Dec. 2000). "Market contagion: Evidence from the panics of 1854 and 1857," *American Economic Review*, 90 (5), 1110-1124.

Keynes, John M. (1921). *The Treatise on Probability*. London: Macmillan.

Keynes, John M. (1936/1997). *The General Theory of Employment, Interest Rates, and Money*. New York: Prometheus Books.

Kirman, Alan (Feb. 1993). "Ants, rationality, and recruitment." *Quarterly Journal of Economics*, 108 (1), 137-156.

Knight, Frank H. (1921). *Risk, Uncertainty, and Profit*. New York: Houghton Mifflin.

Kyle, Albert S., and Wei Xiong (Aug. 2001). "Contagion as a wealth effect," *Journal of Finance*, 56 (4), 1401-1440.

Levy, David A., and Paul R. Nail (May 1993). "Contagion: A theoretical and empirical review and reconceptualization," *Genetic, Social & General Psychology Monographs*, 119 (2), 235-284.

Lo, Andrew W., and A. Craig MacKinlay. (1999). *A Non-Random Walk Down Wall Street*. Princeton, New Jersey: Princeton University Press.

Lux, Thomas, and Didier Sornette. (Aug. 2002). "On rational bubbles and fat tails," *Journal of Money, Credit, and Banking*, 34 (3), 589-610.

Mirowski, Philip. (1989). *More Heat than Light: Economics as Social Physics, Physics as Nature's Economics*. Cambridge: Cambridge University Press.

Mirowski, Philip. (Oct 1990). "From Mandelbrot to chaos in economic theory." *Southern Economic Journal*, 57 (2), 289-307.

Noelle-Neumann, Elisabeth. (1993). *The Spiral of Silence: Public Opinion— Our Social Skin*, 2nd ed. Chicago: University of Chicago Press.

Okubo, Akira (1986). "Dynamical aspects of animal grouping: Swarms, schools, flocks, and herds," *Adv. in Biophysics*, 22, 1-94.

Olsen, R. (July/Aug. 1996). "Implications of herding behavior…" *Financial Analysts Journal*, 52 (4), 37-41.

Prechter, Robert R. (1999). *The Wave Principle of Human Social Behavior and the New Science of Socionomics*. Gainesville, GA: New Classics Library.

Prechter, Robert R. (2001). "Unconscious herding behavior as the psychological basis of financial market trends and patterns," *Journal of Psychology and Financial Markets [now Journal of Behavioral Finance]*, 2 (3), 120-125.

Prechter, Robert R. (2003). *Pioneering Studies in Socionomics*. Gainesville, GA: New Classics Library.

Prechter, Robert R., and Wayne D. Parker (2004). "The financial/economic dichotomy," in Heping Pan, Didier Sornette, and Kenneth Kortanek, Eds., *Intelligent Finance—A Convergence of Mathematical Finance with Technical and Fundamental Analysis*. Melbourne, Australia: International Workshop on Intelligent Finance (University of Ballarat).

Prendergast, Canice, and Lars Stole (1996). "Impetuous youngsters and jaded old-timers: Acquiring a reputation for learning," *Journal of Political Economy*, 104 (6), 1105-1134.

Saffre, F., and J.L. Deneubourg (2002). "Swarming strategies for cooperative species," *Journal of Theoretical Biology*, 214, 441-451.

Scharfstein, David S., and Jeremy C. Stein. (June 1990). "Herd behavior and investment," *American Economic Review*, 80 (3), 465-479.

Shiller, Robert J., Stanley Fischer, and Benjamin M. Friedman (1984). "Stock prices and social dynamics," *Brookings Papers on Economic Activity*, 1984 (2), 457-510.

Shiller, Robert J. (Spring 1990). "Speculative prices and popular models," *Journal of Economic Perspectives*, 4 (2), 55-65.

Shiller, Robert J. (2000). *Irrational Exuberance.* Princeton, New Jersey: Princeton University Press.

Shiller, Robert J. (May 2001). "Bubbles, human judgment, and expert opinion," Cowles Foundation Discussion Paper No. 1303, http://papers.ssrn.com/abstract_id=275515.

Sias, Richard W. (Spring 2004). "Institutional herding," *The Review of Financial Studies*, 17 (1), 165-206.

Sornette, D. (2003a). *Why Stock Markets Crash: Critical Events in Complex Financial Systems*, Princeton University Press.

Sornette, D. (2003b). "Critical market crashes." *Physics Reports* 378 (1), 1-98.

Sornette, D., and J.V. Andersen (2002). "A nonlinear super-exponential rational model of speculative financial bubbles." *International Journal of Modern Physics C*, 13 (2), 171-187.

Trueman, Brett. (Spring 1994). "Analyst Forecasts and Herding Behavior," *The Review of Financial Studies*, 7 (1), 97-124.

Viscido, Steven V., Matthew Miller, and David S. Wethey (2002). "The dilemma of the selfish herd: The search for a realistic movement rule," *Journal of Theoretical Biology*, 217, 183-194.

Welch, Ivo. (2000). "Herding among security analysts." *Journal of Financial Economics*, 58 (3), 369-396.

Winslow, E.G. (Dec. 1989). "Organic interdependence, uncertainty and economic analysis." *Economic Journal*, 99, 1173-1182.

Zetterberg, Hans L. (1993). "Elites: Vilfredo Pareto," ch. 3 in *European Proponents of Sociology Prior to WW I*. http://zetterberg.org/Books/b93e_Soc/b93eCh4.htm.

Zwiebel, Jeffrey (1995). "Corporate conservatism and relative compensation," *Journal of Political Economy*, 103 (1), 1-25.

Chapter 35

Olson's research links socionomic theory to hypotheses of psychology. Editor's notes, indicated in the text by numbers in <angle brackets>, are posted after the Author's References.

Journal of Behavioral Finance
2006, Vol. 7, No. 4, 193-203
Reprinted with permission

A Literature Review of Social Mood

Kenneth R. Olson

Emotions exert a significant influence on financial behavior. The "socionomic hypothesis" posits social mood, the collective mood of individuals, as a primary causal variable in financial and social trends. In order to provide a scientific basis for the study of social mood, this article reviews psychological research on major mood-related elements of personality: affect, motivation, and personality traits. We examine the structure and functions of these core personality dimensions, and discuss research on contagion processes by which individuals' moods spread and manifest in a collective social mood. We also address implications for financial and economic behavior. Social mood is rooted in empirically established personality dimensions that are fundamental to human nature, and can influence financial outcomes.

Acknowledgment

This research was supported in part by a grant from the Socionomics Foundation, Gainesville, Georgia. I wish to thank Wayne Parker for his helpful comments on a previous version of this article.

Kenneth Olson is a professor of psychology at Fort Hays State University.

Rational choice theory, a perspective that views people as "rational actors" who base economic decisions on logical calculations of their best interests, is strongly entrenched in the field of economics (Tetlock and Mellers [2002]). However, emotions, which are not taken into account in this theory, also exert a profound influence on human behavior, including economic behavior. In fact, every major problem faced by humanity involves emotion (Russell [2003]).

Modern economics explains agents' decisions and choices via the paradigm of utility maximizing. However, agents often exhibit irrational behavior that may decrease economic utility in order to achieve psychological satisfaction and subjective comfort (Gao and Schmidt [2005]).

The influence of emotion is present in both individual microeconomic decisions and aggregate trends in financial markets. In regard to individual economic choices, Lerner, Small, and Lowenstein [2004] demonstrated that emotions can have dramatic effects on economic transactions, even when they arise from a prior, irrelevant situation. A prime illustration can be found in the endowment effect—the tendency to ascribe a higher value to an item one already owns than one is willing to pay to acquire it today. Lerner, Small, and Lowenstein [2004] found that emotions such as disgust and sadness influenced both buying decisions and sellers' prices.

Another series of studies examined participants' intuitive understanding of the endowment effect and found that emotional states created an egocentric "empathy gap" between buyers and sellers. This resulted in very large discrepancies between [bidding] and offering prices and often led to a stand-off (Van Boven, Loewenstein, and Dunning [2003]).

On a broader scale, financial markets often fail to act as predicted by fundamental factors such as expected corporate earnings and economic variables such as interest rates and inflation levels. As Shiller [1984] noted, stock prices can be affected by social dynamics and mass psychology. Psychological factors and confidence levels are major contributors to market irrationality, which is most evident during financial bubbles and crashes (Shiller [2002]). It has been argued that financial market trends are caused by emotions that contribute to investors' tendency to act in concert and engage in unconscious herding behavior (Prechter [2001]).

Another phenomenon that can affect rational processing is information overload. The vast amounts of company, industry, market, and economic data that are available to both individual and professional investors can have a negative effect on the ability to reason (Dreman [2004]). When mental processing resources are reduced due to increasing memory load, greater reliance is placed on affect or emotion (Shiv and Fedorikhin [1999]).

Emotion adds to the complexity in predicting behavior because it does not conform to static models and patterns of linear causality (Mayne and Ramsey [2001]).

Social Mood

The results of the studies mentioned thus far imply that social mood may be a key factor in financial trends. The emotions of financial decision-makers reflect the overall mood of society. It has been argued that the stock market is a direct index of social mood, the collective level of optimism or pessimism in society at a given time (Elliott [1942], Prechter [1985, 1999], Green [2002]).

Prechter's [1999] "socionomic hypothesis" suggests that social mood determines various types of social actions in the areas of finance, culture, and macroeconomics. Nofsinger [2005] bolstered the case that social mood determines decisions made by consumers, investors, and corporate managers and that the level and nature of business activity follows rather than leads social mood. Social mood is considered an endogenous construct inherent in human psychology that can override external influences on economic outcomes.

A voluminous psychological literature exists on mood and individual emotion. However, psychologists have devoted less attention to the topic of social mood and its basis. Because social mood reflects the aggregate mood of individuals, a thorough understanding of collective social mood requires examining mood-related phenomena in individuals.

This article discusses research on the underlying structure of core mood-related personality dimensions: affect, motivation, and personality traits. We address functions of emotions, processes by which individuals' moods may become manifested in broader mass psychology, and implications for financial behavior. This research can provide a scientific foundation for the construct of social mood.

Affect

Although they are sometimes used interchangeably, we can distinguish between the closely related concepts of mood and emotion. In terms of duration, emotions tend to be shorter-term than moods. Moods appear to persist over longer periods of time (Ekman [1994]), but emotions fluctuate, and move around a mean level that exhibits a degree of stability over time and across situations (Diener and Lucas [2000]).

Also, an emotion is usually *about* something, e.g., love for a spouse, fear of an attacker. Philosophers note that emotion has a cognitive content, or an "intentional" object: fear *of* him, anger *at* her (Dennett [1987], Searle [1982]). The emotion is associated with someone or something.

Mood, on the other hand, is typically free-floating and unattached to any intentional object. Mood may be experienced in relation to no particular stimulus and directed at no specific target (Wood, Saltzberg, and Goldsamt [1990]). Social mood, therefore, may describe the characteristic affective condition of a population and is not necessarily tied to <1> any specific social event(s).

Structure of Emotion

Emotions as Discrete Entities

Several approaches have been suggested for determining the underlying structure of mood and emotion. One major model posits that there exist discrete, basic, universal emotions in all cultures (Ekman [1992]). Each emotion has unique patterns of physiological arousal, behavioral display, and unique functions such as motivation. These emotions likely developed during evolution to meet particular challenges in our early ancestral environments. Patterns that enhanced the ability to adapt and thrive led to survival and reproductive advantages and were therefore passed on. Those that did not died out.

However, there are a number of criticisms of this model. For example, how many discrete kinds of emotional experiences exist? Research on self-reported emotion has not settled on a number (Russell and Mehrabian [1977], Watson and Clark [1992]). It is also argued that distinctions between discrete emotions are the result of social construction, and are not inherent in the emotions themselves.

Positive Affect and Negative Affect

In contrast to the notion that emotions are discrete entities, an alternative concept posits a limited number of underlying dimensions as the basic structure of emotion. One important model emphasizes the importance of the dimensions of positive affect (PA) and negative affect (NA) (Tellegen,Watson, and Clark [1999], Watson and Tellegen [1985]). PA is defined by categories labeled pleasantness and emotional engagement. Specific emotions associated with PA include happiness, enthusiasm, and elation. NA is defined by unpleasant feelings such as sadness, anger, fear, and disgust.

There is evidence that PA and NA are somewhat independent dimensions of affect rather than opposite ends of a single bipolar dimension. One implication of this independence is that characteristics of PA and NA can coexist in an individual, and the presence of one type would not preclude the presence of the other. "Bittersweet" and other mixed feelings would be examples of emotions that include both positive and negative elements.

More recently, it has been suggested that PA and NA are the subjective components of two basic biobehavioral systems of activation (Watson et al. [1999]). These systems entail two broad, evolutionary motivational systems that promote adaptation and survival (we discuss this in more detail later).

At the individual level, PA and NA are a direct analog of positive and negative social mood at the collective level. Economic expansions, equity bull markets, and financial speculation are associated with positive feelings such as optimism and enthusiasm; economic contractions and bear markets reflect an increase in negative emotions such as pessimism, fear, and anger (Prechter [1999]).

PA and NA are major contributors not only to overall feelings of subjective well-being or dissatisfaction (Diener and Lucas [2000]) but also to perceptions of risk and benefit that influence investor behavior. During decision-making, emotional reactions to risk often differ from cognitive assessments of those risks. When such a divergence occurs, emotional reactions frequently end up driving behavior (Loewenstein et al. [2001]).

A number of empirical studies have found that mood influences reactions to risk. For example, people in a positive mood perceive choices as less risky, and the likely outcomes as more favorable. They are therefore more willing to take risks (Deldin and Levin [1986], Isen [1997], Nygren et al. [1996]). Williams [2004] similarly found that managers may be more willing to undertake risky business propositions when their own affective state is more positive.

Conversely, individuals in induced depressed moods <2> are significantly more conservative and less willing to take risks (Yuen and Lee [2003]). A negative mood can lead to a sense of deprivation (Kavanagh, Andrade, and May [2005]) and a greater desire for asset preservation and safety. Economic contraction due to reduced investment and spending may be fostered by the inclination toward risk aversion that is associated with negative affect.

Similarly, increased investment, spending, and economic expansion likely result from the perceptions of reduced risk and increased benefits associated with positive mood and confidence. Judgments of risk and benefit are inversely related: Actions judged to be low-risk tend to be judged as high in benefit, and vice versa (Alhakami and Slovic [1994]).

Personal trust can play an important role in stock market dynamics and can even contribute to market bubbles (Olsen [2004]). Affect and social mood influence trust levels: Positive emotions such as happiness and gratitude increase trust, while negative emotions such as anger decrease it (Dunn and Schweitzer [2005]). Thus, PA and positive social mood result in perceptions of trust, reduced risk, and increased benefits; NA and negative social mood lead to reduced trust and perceptions of greater risk and fewer benefits.

Valence Arousal Dimensions

Watson and Tellegen [1985] do not claim that PA and NA are the only basic affect dimensions. Evidence has been provided for a highly influential model that characterizes emotions as points plotted within a two-dimensional space (Russell [1980], Feldman Barrett and Russell [1998]). One dimension represents valence: pleasure versus displeasure, or pleasant versus unpleasant feelings (this is also referred to as hedonic value). The pleasure-displeasure axis ranges from one extreme (e.g., agony) to the opposite (ecstasy).

The second dimension is level of *arousal* (high or activated versus low or deactivated), which ranges from drowsiness, through various stages of alertness, to frenetic excitement. This dimension reflects feelings of mobilization and energy. High arousal states are preparations for action; low arousal states are periods of inaction. The combination of the valence and arousal dimensions, called core affect, describes moods and is always present (Russell [2003]).

A circumplex configuration is formed by the intersection of the axes for valence and arousal. Thus, the four quadrants of this circumplex are activated-pleasant, deactivated-pleasant, activated-unpleasant, and deactivated-unpleasant. Various emotions are located in each quadrant. Russell [2003] notes that a core affect of pleasure may qualify as the emotion of happiness, and a core affect of displeasure as sadness. The combination of pleasure and high arousal constitutes elation, and the combination of displeasure and high arousal constitutes anxiety. This model has received support in numerous studies that have replicated its two-dimensional structure (Feldman Barrett and Russell [1999]).

Prechter [1985, 1999] identified the emotions that characterize investors and society during the four stages of a stock market cycle: (1) *market uptrend*: calm, contented, at ease; (2) *market top* (peak positive mood): energetic, happy, enthusiastic; (3) *market downtrend*: sad, fatigued, inhibited, insecure; and (4) *market bottom* (peak negative mood): tense, hostile, angry, antagonistic. These four categories parallel the four categories formed by the affective dimensions of valence and arousal: (1) deactivated-pleasant (*market uptrend*); (2) activated-pleasant (*market top*); (3) deactivated-unpleasant (*market downtrend*), and (4) activated-unpleasant (*market bottom*). Thus the valence and arousal dimensions that characterize affect also reflect the predominant emotional tone of stock cycles. These fundamental dimensions of affect may be useful in identifying major stages of investment cycles.

Mild core affect is typically part of the background of consciousness rather than the focus of a person's conscious world. What causes changes in core affect is not fully understood, but it can change without any external stimulus. It can be influenced by endogenous factors like genetically based differences in volatility, the activity of immune cells, diurnal rhythms, and hormone changes (Russell [2003]). This aspect of core affect is consistent with the socionomic proposition that the fundamental causes of social mood are endogenous.

Recent psychological research indicates that core affect responds to unconscious information. Even people's goals and behavior are affected by stimuli outside conscious awareness (Bargh and Chartrand [1999]). Investment behavior may thus be influenced by emotions that (1) are outside conscious awareness, and (2) have endogenous causes that are not linked to external events. These characteristics of emotion may help explain why stock market cycles do not always concur with fundamental economic factors. The non-linear causal effects of emotion (Mayne and Ramsey [2001]) may reduce the accuracy of stock market predictions based solely on economic and financial variables.

Neural Systems in Emotion

Emotion also has a neuroanatomical basis. Several brain structures play a role in emotion. The amygdala has been consistently implicated in numerous studies of emotional processes and is a sort of "emotional computer" (LeDoux and Phelps [2000]). The amygdala influences many cortical areas, thus governing a variety of perceptual and higher-order mental processes.

Ochsner and Feldman Barrett [2001] view emotion as the product of an interaction between non-conscious, automatic processes, and deliberative, conscious processes. The amygdala's function is to automatically detect potential threats and associate them with corresponding physiological responses and appropriate actions. This system is associated with negative affect, and registers potentially threatening stimuli rapidly so we can respond immediately to the threat.

According to these researchers, another neural system, the basal ganglia, is associated with positive affect. Its function is to register possible rewards and encode sequences of action or thought that, over time, have led to a desired or positive outcome. This system operates more slowly. This makes sense, as adopting certain thoughts and behaviors would be useful only if they have led to a desirable end repeatedly and reliably over time.

Consistent with the differential speed of operation of the amygdala and basal ganglia is the frequently noted observation that stock prices fall more rapidly than they rise. Therefore, bear markets are typically shorter than bull markets. Investment lore commonly ascribes this tendency to the idea that fear is stronger than greed. A more precise explanation may be that the amygdala, which is associated with negative affect (bear markets), detects potential threats more rapidly, while the basal ganglia, associated with positive affect (bull markets), registers possible rewards more slowly.

This pattern is consistent with a robust psychological phenomenon termed the negativity bias, the propensity to react more strongly to negative than to positive stimuli (see Cacioppo, Gardner, and Berntson [1997]). This heightened sensitivity to negative information may have resulted from the process of natural selection because it is more difficult to reverse the consequences of an injurious or fatal assault than those of a missed opportunity (Cacioppo and Gardner [1999]).

Emotional Contagion

Social mood is the collective manifestation of individual mood. <3> But what dynamics link individual and social mood? In other words, by what process do individuals' moods spread and become enacted at a wider societal level? Studies of contagion effects, particularly emotional contagion, may provide an answer. <4> Studies of contagion share in common the finding that people's feelings and behavior are strongly affected by their observations of others. Psychological research has explored several types of contagion effects including goal contagion, social contagion of motivational orientations, and emotional contagion.

The goals of others are usually not communicated explicitly. However, research has found that people perceive others' behavior as goal-directed, and readily infer others' goals from their behavior (e.g., Heider [1958], McClure [2002]). Furthermore, people can make such inferences automatically, without conscious intent and awareness (Aarts and Hassin [2005]). This ability allows people to adjust adroitly to their social surroundings.

Aarts, Gollwitzer, and Hassin [2004] demonstrate experimentally that perception of others' behavior can lead to *"goal contagion*: the automatic adoption and pursuit of goals that others are perceived to strive for" (p. 24). Their results indicate that people may spontaneously take on the goals of others in an unconscious manner. These researchers noted that this may result in people becoming more similar in what they desire and strive for, and hence in their plans for the future. Thus, people and groups may orchestrate their goals and behaviors without much conscious thought. This mechanism may also account for what might be termed automatic social goal contagion, the tendency for us as a whole to non-consciously adopt and pursue collective goals at particular times.

Wild and Enzle [2002] review evidence for another form of contagion, social contagion of motivational orientations. This research suggests people's motivational orientations toward activities can spontaneously spread solely on the basis of their perceptions of others' motivations for engaging in an activity. Much of this research has focused on intrinsic and extrinsic motivation and the conditions under which intrinsic motivation is enhanced or undermined. These are key concepts in self-determination theory (see Deci, Koestner, and Ryan [1999]). Thus, people's goals and their reasons for pursuing those goals, i.e., their motivational orientations, are subject to contagion effects.

Contagion effects have also been studied in regard to emotion and mood. A broad working definition of emotional contagion is "the tendency to 'catch' (experience/express) another person's emotions"; this process "is relatively automatic, unintentional, uncontrollable, and largely unconscious" (Hatfield, Cacioppo, and Rapson [1992, p. 153]). For example, clinical research has found that depressed, anxious, and angry individuals tend to induce similar moods in people around them (Coyne [1976], Howes, Hokanson, and Lowenstein [1985]). Hatfield, Cacioppo, and Rapson [1992] suggest that emotional contagion is a universal human phenomenon.

In regard to theoretical bases for emotional contagion, Schacter's [1959] extension of social comparison theory (Festinger [1954]) posits that affiliating with others produces pressure to establish a common social reality. This theory suggests that one's emotional reactions to a situation are influenced by others' emotional states when one is aroused (e.g., under threat).

Another view of emotional contagion is conveyed by the theory of primitive emotional contagion (Hatfield, Cacioppo, and Rapson [1992, 1993]). This theory suggests emotional contagion occurs generally even when individuals are not aroused. Many studies have found that people spontaneously mimic the facial expressions, voices, postures, and body movements of affiliates, theoretically producing similar emotional states. The economic philosopher Adam Smith noted as early as 1759 that as people imagine themselves in another's situation, they display "motor mimicry."

Some research has supported a social comparison model of emotional contagion (Sullins [1991]); other studies of naturalistic threats have been more consistent with a primitive emotional contagion explanation (Gump and Kulik [1997], Kulik and Mahler [1987], Kulik, Moore, and Mahler [1993]). But all of these studies have established the operation of emotional contagion, with the majority suggesting it occurs regardless of the observer's emotional state.

Emotional contagion may help explain phenomena such as mass hysteria and social epidemics that multiply rapidly in an era of mass communication (Showalter [1997]). It may assist in understanding group behaviors that have shaped societies and history, such as Adolph Hitler's fanning of hate, Martin Luther King's message of love, the ways in which crowds behave, and the awesome power of mass media (Hatfield, Cacioppo, and Rapson [1993]). Direct human interaction was necessary for emotional contagion to occur in tribal societies. But in contemporary society, television, film, radio, newspapers, magazines, and the Internet provide vehicles for the rapid spread of contagion effects without direct person-to-person contact. The process of emotional contagion suggests how mood can spread throughout a society and become collectively manifested in widespread social mood.

Functions of Emotions

Why did emotions develop in humans (and animals) during the course of evolution? Some theorists hearken back to classical philosophers such as the Stoics, who believed emotions serve no useful functions. This position was renewed in the eighteenth century Enlightenment belief that the logic of reason should be the master of the unruly and unreliable passions (Solomon [1993]). This perspective considers emotions as disorganizing forces that disrupt rationality.

Functional accounts, on the other hand, typically assume that emotions are adaptations to problems of physical survival and social adjustment. For example, an evolutionary view suggests that emotions are a superordinate program of the mind and brain developed over thousands of years of natural selection. This emotional "uber-program" directs the activities and interactions of a very broad array of cognitive, behavioral, and physical subprograms of the individual (Cosmides and Tooby [2000]). The emotional system informs and motivates the organism to make choices and decisions in order to solve problems encountered in ancestral environments and promote its chances of adaptation and survival.

Functional theories generally emphasize the useful consequences of emotions, such as the value of fear in responding to threats (flight), and anger in motivating aggression (fight). Emotions serve important interpersonal and communicative purposes as well (e.g., Fridlund [1994]). Emotions regulate the distance between people, drawing them together or pushing them apart (Levenson [1999]). Emotions also perform significant intrapersonal functions. They facilitate mental functions of attention, perception, judgment, and memory retrieval (Russell [2003]). This cognitive utility is readily apparent in individuals with damage to parts of the brain involved in emotional processing: Their decision-making ability is fundamentally impaired so that they no longer have the ability to determine (feel) which choices and potential outcomes might be pleasant or unpleasant. Functional accounts generally imply that emotions are essential for coherent and purposeful human functioning.

An integrative view is that the positive and negative views of the effects of emotions are both partially true. Emotions sometimes disrupt or disorganize effective goal-directed behavior and rational thought. At other times, they facilitate organization and serve as "a master choreographer, the ultimate organizer of disparate response systems" (Levenson [1999, p. 495]). They perform in a unified manner in solving fundamental problems. Whether adaptive or disruptive, emotions are an integral element of human functioning that influence and pervade decision-making.

Motivation

Motives and traits are two fundamental and distinct elements of personality. The distinction between motives and traits is grounded in differing conceptions of human nature put forth by the ancient Greeks (Winter et al. [1998]). Motives refer to peoples' wishes and desires, the "why" of behavior (McClelland [1985, p. 4]). Traits refer to stylistic and habitual patterns of cognition and emotion, the "how" of behavior. Traits channel the ways in which motives are expressed (Winter et al. [1998]).

Regarding motivation, the disposition to be motivated and live purposely is an evolutionary imperative "built into the most fundamental architecture of zoological organisms" (Klinger [1998, p. 30]). Evidence from several literatures has centered around the idea that there are two basic motivational systems that mediate goal-directed approach and avoidance behaviors. The avoidance system is commonly labeled the *behavioral inhibition system* (e.g., Fowles [1987], Gray [1982]). The approach system has been variously labeled a *behavioral activation system* (Cloninger [1987], Fowles [1980]), a *behavioral approach system* (Gray [1981, 1990]), a *behavioral facilitation system* (Depue and Iacono [1989]), and a *behavioral engagement system* (Depue, Kraus, and Spoont [1987]). The approach system facilitates behavior and generates positive affect. This system directs organisms toward situations and experiences that are potentially pleasurable and rewarding. The avoidance system is sensitive to threats and aversive stimuli, and is responsible for behavioral inhibition or withdrawal and generating negative affect. The primary function of this system is to inhibit behavior that could lead to undesirable consequences such as pain or punishment (Watson et al. [1999]).

Elliot and Covington [2001] put forth several reasons why approach-avoidance motivation should be viewed as fundamental and basic to the study of human behavior. They noted that the approach-avoidance distinction has a long and rich intellectual history, ranging from Greek philosophy to its incorporation in many major and diverse psychological theories, including Freudian, Jungian, behavioral, cognitive, humanistic, and evolutionary. It is applicable not only to humans, but to other forms of animate life including organisms as simple as the single-cell amoeba (Schneirla [1959]).

Tooby and Cosmides [1990] argue that the decision to approach or withdraw has been the fundamental adaptive decision for organisms throughout evolutionary history. Zajonc [1998] suggests that all subsequent responses of an organism are based on the initial approach-avoidance discriminations, and these discriminations are the primary and most elemental reaction of organisms to environmental stimuli. A motivational system that can discriminate between hostile and hospitable stimuli is of primeval importance (Hunt and Campbell [1997]).

Elliot and Thrash [2002] provide empirical evidence that the approach-avoidance distinction is so conceptually central that it can organize and integrate seemingly disparate approaches to personality. An early and influential theory in this regard was developed by Gray [1976, 1991], who proposed individual differences in sensitivities of two conceptual nervous systems. The behavioral approach system (BAS) responds to incentives such as reward signals. This system stimulates movement toward goals, and is associated with positive feelings. The behavioral inhibition system (BIS) responds to threats, such as punishment signals. This system promotes vigilant attention to the environment and inhibits behavior; it is associated with negative feelings (Gray [1981, 1990]).

BAS and BIS are two independent systems representing appetitive and aversive motivation. As with affect, these systems differ as a function of valence (positive versus negative). BAS and BIS parallel and are statistically correlated with positive and negative affect, respectively (Gable, Reis, and Elliot [2000]).

Approach and avoidance motivation may play an integral role in financial behavior. Thus, the approach/appetitive motivation is associated with positive emotions that may lead to buying, investment, and business expansion. The avoidance/aversive motivation elicits negative emotions that contribute to caution, risk aversion, and business contraction. Indeed, bull market psychology may be viewed as the motivation to *approach* risk <5> and achieve gains, while bear market psychology is the motivation to *avoid* risk and prevent or minimize losses. Approach motivation would dominate during periods of positive social mood; avoidance motivation would dominate during periods of negative social mood.

BIS and BAS have different neural substrates. Gray's [1982, 1991] research suggests that the neural substrates of the BIS include the septo-hippocampal system, two sets of its ascending monaminergic neurons, and its neocortical projections in the frontal lobe. Although Gray has not specified the neural basis of the BAS as fully, a number of researchers believe dopaminergic pathways are centrally involved (Depue and Collins [1999], Gray et al. [1991], Stellar and Stellar [1985]).

Based on extensive research with his colleagues, Davidson [1992, 1995, 1998] concluded that specialized neural substrates for behavioral approach and positive affect are lateralized in the left anterior regions of the cerebral cortex, and behavioral withdrawal and negative affect are lateralized in the right anterior cortical regions.

Personality Traits

There are thousands of personality trait-related words in the English language. Since the beginning of the modern era of personality psychology in the 1930s, researchers have sought to identify the trait dimensions that are most fundamental and important. The most prominent solution that has emerged is the Five Factor Model (FFM), which posits that five major domains are the primary personality traits: Extraversion (versus Introversion), Agreeableness (versus Antagonism), Conscientiousness (versus Heedlessness), Emotional Stability (versus Neuroticism), and Openness to Experience (versus Closed to Experience). These are collectively referred to as the Big Five. The FFM indicates that traits are hierarchically ordered so that a variety of narrower, more specific traits are correlated with each of the five primary traits.

The FFM has been replicated in numerous studies with diverse populations and in many countries, and there is evidence that it may be a universal
structure of personality traits (McCrae and Costa [1997]). The FFM was
derived empirically and is atheoretical. Thus questions have been raised:
Why are these particular domains the fundamental dimensions of traits?
And are there higher-order dimensions of the Big Five?

In fact, two-factor analytic studies of the Big Five did find two higher-
order factors (Digman [1997], Carroll [2002]) that were interpreted quite
differently by their respective researchers. One was composed of Extraversion and Openness to Experience, and the other included Agreeableness,
Conscientiousness, and Emotional Stability. Other recent studies have also
found a two-factor structure (Saucier et al. [2005]).

Olson [2005] reinterpreted the data of Digman [1997] and Carroll
[2002] and suggested two factors uniting their results. This analysis posited
that Extraversion and Openness to Experience share the higher-order personality dimension of *Engagement* in common. The Engagement continuum
reflects social and experiential engagement, and ranges from engaged to
disengaged. At the high end of the Engagement continuum are traits such as
enthusiastic, active, energetic, curious, and involved. The low end includes
traits such as apathy, passivity, disinterest, detachment, and withdrawal.

As a fundamental trait dimension, Engagement would have evolutionarily adaptive benefits. Individuals must engage their environments in order
to obtain resources for nourishment, shelter, and growth. Engagement would
also facilitate exploration and pursuit of desirable incentives and goals that
would foster vital evolutionary tasks of survival and reproduction.

In regard to the second major factor, the Big Five traits of Emotional
Stability, Agreeableness, and Conscientiousness share in common the
dimension of *Self-Control*. Individuals with strong self-control are able to
restrain and control distressing emotions, antagonistic and antisocial interpersonal behaviors, and lackadaisical and irresponsible behaviors. Thus the
Self-Control dimension reflects interpersonal (Agreeableness), emotional
(Emotional Stability), and task-oriented (Conscientiousness) self-control.

Self-control traits also foster evolutionary survival. Inhibition of impulsive responses and rash actions help avoid exposure to dangers such as
predators, enemies, and disease. Careful planning and deliberation improves
chances of securing necessary resources such as food and shelter. Control of
negative emotional reactions such as rage and hostility facilitates formation
of cooperative and strategic alliances and successful mating.

A review of research has found that low scores on the three self-control
traits are associated with a wide spectrum of counterproductive work

behaviors such as absenteeism, stealing, drug and alcohol use, inappropriate customer service behaviors, and handling stress poorly. Conversely, high scores on self-control traits are related to stellar job performance (Ones and Viswesvaran [2001]). Low self-control traits are also correlated with a wide variety of diagnosable personality disorders (Olson [2005]). Deficiencies in self-control have been linked to numerous social and personal problems as well, including addiction, crime, domestic violence, bankruptcy, and academic failure (Tice, Bratslavsky, and Baumeister [2001]).

The foregoing analysis suggests Engagement and Self-Control constitute the fundamental dimensions of personality traits. They are also empirically related to affective dimensions. A number of studies have found that the Engagement traits of Extraversion and Openness to Experience are positively correlated with PA. The Self-Control traits of Agreeableness, Conscientiousness, and Emotional Stability are negatively correlated with NA (McCrae and Costa [1991], Watson and Clark [1992]). Negative emotions can be said to impair self-control (Tice, Bratslavsky, and Baumeister [2001]). Thus, Engagement is associated with positive emotions, and low Self-Control is associated with negative emotions.

Engagement and Self-Control are empirically related to PA and NA, respectively, and they are also conceptually related to positive and negative social mood. Researchers have debated the extent to which personality traits are fixed versus malleable across time. Recent empirical evidence indicates life experiences and social climate can cause changes in traits. Social influences from the domains of work, family, and social movements are associated with changes in personality traits in adulthood (Helson, Jones, and Kwan [2002], Roberts, Helson, and Klohnen [2002], Helson and Soto [2005]). Prechter [1999] has documented the extensive effects of social mood on numerous social and economic events and social climate. Thus, by affecting social climate, long-term changes in social mood may affect individual personality traits.

To the extent that traits are affected by social climate, and to the extent that Engagement traits are correlated with PA and positive social mood, individuals should tend to show greater trait Engagement during periods of positive social mood. The Engagement traits of energy, enthusiasm, curiosity, openness, and social involvement are the same characteristics that typify periods of positive social mood (Prechter [1999]). Similar to approach motivation, engagement is associated with positive emotions that stimulate buying and business expansion. *Engagement* in increased investment and risk-taking is a hallmark of bull market psychology.

During periods of negative social mood, individuals are more likely to display lower self-control. At an individual level, the characteristics of negative social mood identified by Prechter [1999] parallel the main features of the Big Five traits associated with low self-control: distressing emotions (neuroticism), greater antagonism and interpersonal discord (low agreeableness), and reduced interest in effort and achievement (low conscientiousness). Similar to avoidance motivation, the low self-control trait dimension is related to anxiety and other negative emotions that lead to the caution and risk aversion seen in bear market psychology.

At the societal level, the social problems associated with low self-control, such as addiction, crime, and bankruptcy (Tice, Bratslavsky, and Baumeister [2001]), are also more common during periods of negative social mood. So the level of low self-control traits and the problems associated with them should escalate when social mood becomes increasingly negative.

Conclusion

The aggregate emotional states of individuals comprise social mood. Social mood appears to be rooted in fundamental components of human personality that have been empirically established. The personality correlates of positive social mood include positive affect, approach motivation, and engagement-related traits. Negative social mood is related to negative affect, avoidance motivation, and traits associated with low self-control.

The fact that basic affect, motivation, and traits each appear to have a two-dimensional, bivariate structure implies that the core, underlying structure of basic personality is fundamentally bivariate in nature (Olson [2005]). Positive and negative social mood may be reflections at a collective level of this underlying two-dimensional personality structure.

Future research should examine empirical relationships between measures of investor and social mood, personality variables, and financial outcomes. Stock market indexes, a record of the cumulative buying and selling decisions of traders and investors, provide the broadest and most immediate reflection of investor mood. Measures of stock market sentiment such as surveys of institutional and individual investors (e.g., American Association of Individual Investors), market advisers (e.g., Investors Intelligence), and indices of market activity (e.g., put/call ratios of options, mutual fund inflows, mutual fund cash ratios) also reflect the cumulative mood of investors. Greater appreciation of the important influence of social mood should lead to a better ability to understand financial behavior and trends.

REFERENCES

Aarts, H., P.M. Gollwitzer, and R.R. Hassin. "Goal Contagion: Perceiving is for Pursuing." *Journal of Personality and Social Psychology*, 87, (2004), pp. 23–37.

Aarts, H., and R.R. Hassin. "Automatic Goal Inferences and Contagion: On Pursuing Goals One Perceives in Other People's Behavior." In J.P. Forgas, D.W. Kipling, and W. Von Hippel, eds., *Social Motivation: Conscious and Unconscious Processes*. New York: Psychology Press, 2005, pp. 153–167.

Alhakami, A.S., and P. Slovic. "A Psychological Study of the Inverse Relationship between Perceived Risk and Perceived Benefit." *Risk Analysis*, 14, (1994), pp. 1085–1096.

Bargh, J.A., and T.L. Chartrand. "The Unbearable Automaticity of Being." *American Psychologist*, 54, (1999), pp. 462–479.

Cacioppo, J.T., and W.L. Gardner. "Emotion." *Annual Review of Psychology*, 50, (1999), pp. 191–214.

Cacioppo, J.T., W.L. Gardner, and G.G. Berntson. "Beyond Bipolar Conceptualizations and Measures: The Case of Attitudes and Evaluative Space." *Personality and Social Psychology Review*, 1, (1997), pp. 3–25.

Carroll, J.B. "The Five-Factor Personality Model: How Complete and Satisfactory is It?" In H.I. Braun, D.N. Jackson and D.E. Wiley, eds., *The Role of Constructs in Psychological and Educational Measurement*. Mahwah, NJ: Lawrence Erlbaum Associates, (2002), pp. 97–126.

Cloninger, C.R. "A Systematic Method of Clinical Description and Classification of Personality Variants: A Proposal." *Archives of General Psychiatry*, 44, (1987), pp. 573–588.

Cosmides, L., and J. Tooby. "Evolutionary Psychology and the Emotions." In M. Lewis and J.M. Haviland-Jones, eds., *Handbook of Emotions*, 2nd ed. New York: Guilford Press, 2000, pp. 91–115.

Coyne, J.C. "Depression and the Response of Others." *Journal of Abnormal Psychology*, 85, (1976), pp. 186–193.

Davidson, R.J. "Anterior Asymmetry and the Nature of Emotion." *Brain and Cognition*, 20, (1992), pp. 125–151.

Davidson, R.J. "Cerebral Asymmetry, Emotion, and Affective Style." In R.J. Davidson and K. Hugdahl, eds., *Brain Asymmetry*. Cambridge, MA: MIT Press, (1995), pp. 361–387.

Davidson, R.J. "Affective Style and Affective Disorders: Perspectives from Affective Neuroscience." *Cognition and Emotion*, 12, (1998), pp. 307–330.

Deci, E.L., R. Koestner, and R.M. Ryan. "A Meta-Analytic Review of Experiments Examining the Effects of Extrinsic Rewards on Intrinsic Motivation." *Psychological Bulletin*, 125, (1999), pp. 627–668.

Deldin, P.J., and I.P. Levin. "The Effect of Mood Induction in a Risky DecisionTask." *Bulletin of the Psychonomic Society*, 24, (1986), pp. 4–6.

Dennett, D.C. *The Intentional Stance*. Cambridge, MA: MIT Press, 1987.

Depue, R.A., and P.F. Collins. "Neurobiology of the Structure of Personality: Dopamine, Facilitation of Incentive Motivation, and Extraversion." *Behavioral and Brain Sciences*, 22, (1999), pp. 491–569.

Depue, R.A., and W.G. Iacono. "Neurobehavioral Aspects of Affective Disorders." *Annual Review of Psychology*, 40, (1989), pp. 457–492.

Depue, R.A., S.P. Kraus, and M.R. Spoont. "A Two-Dimensional Threshold Model of Seasonal Bipolar Affective Disorder." In D. Magnusson and A. Ohman, eds., *Psychopathology: An Interactional Perspective*. Orlando, FL: Academic Press, 1987, pp. 95–123.

Diener, E., and R. Lucas. "Subjective Emotional Well-Being." In M. Lewis and J. M. Haviland-Jones, eds., *Handbook of Emotions*, 2nd edition. New York: Guilford Press, 2000, pp. 325–337.

Digman, J.M.. "Higher-Order Factors of the Big Five." *Journal of Personality and Social Psychology*, 23, (1997), pp. 1246–1256.

Dreman, D. "The Influence of Affect on Investor Decision-Making." *Journal of Behavioral Finance*, 5, (2004), pp. 70–74.

Dunn, J.R., and M.E. Schweitzer. "Feeling and Believing: The Influence of Emotions on Trust." *Journal of Personality and Social Psychology*, 88, (2005), pp. 736–748.

Ekman, P. "Facial Expressions of Emotions: New Findings, New Questions." *Psychological Science*, 3, (1992), pp. 34–38.

Ekman, P. "Strong Evidence for Universals in Facial Expressions." *Psychological Bulletin*, 115, (1994), pp. 268–287.

Elliot, A.J., and M.V. Covington. "Approach and Avoidance Motivation." *Educational Psychology Review*, 13, (2001), pp. 73–92.

Elliot, A.J., and T.M. Thrash. "Approach-Avoidance Motivation in Personality: Approach and Avoidance Temperaments and Goals." *Journal of Personality and Social Psychology*, 82, (2002), pp. 804–818.

Elliott, R.N.. "Educational Bulletin N: The Measurement of Mass Psychology." In R. Prechter, ed., *R.N. Elliott's Market Letters 1938–1946*. Gainesville, GA: New Classics Library, 1993, pp. 171–173.

Feldman Barrett, L., and J.A. Russell. "Independence and Bipolarity in the Structure of Current Affect." *Journal of Personality and Social Psychology*, 74, (1998), pp. 967–984.

Feldman Barrett, L., and J.A. Russell. "The Structure of Current Affect: Controversies and Emerging Consensus." *Current Directions in Psychological Science*, 8, (1999), pp. 10–14.

Festinger, L.A. "Theory of Social Comparison Processes." *Human Relations*, 7, (1954), pp. 117–140.

Fowles, D. "The Three-Arousal Model: Implications of Gray's Two-Factor Learning Theory for Heart Rate, Electrodermal Activity and Psychopathy." *Psychophysiology*, 17, (1980), pp. 87–104.

Fowles, D. "Application of a Behavioral Theory of Motivation to the Concepts of Anxiety and Impulsivity." *Journal of Research in Personality*, 21, (1987), pp. 417–435.

Fridlund, A.J. *Human Facial Expression*. San Diego, CA: Academic Press, 1994.

Gable, S.L., H.T. Reis, and A.J. Elliot. "Behavioral Activation and Inhibition in Everyday Life." *Journal of Personality and Social Psychology*, 78, (2000), pp. 1135–1149.

Gao, L., and U. Schmidt. "Self is Never Neutral: Why Economic Agents Behave Irrationally." *Journal of Behavioral Finance*, 6, (2005), pp. 27–37.

Gray, J.A. "The Behavioral Inhibition System: A Possible Substrate for Anxiety." In M. Feldman and A. Broadhurst, eds., *Theoretical and Experimental Bases of Behavior Modification*. London: Wiley, 1976, pp. 3–41.

Gray, J.A. "A Critique of Eysenck's Theory of Personality." In J.J. Eysenck, ed., *A Model for Personality*. Berlin: Springer-Verlag, (1981), pp. 246–276.

Gray, J.A. *The Neuropsychology of Anxiety: An Enquiry into the Functions of the Septo-Hippocampal System*. Oxford: Oxford University Press, 1982.

Gray, J.A. "Brain Systems that Mediate Both Emotion and Cognition." *Cognition and Emotion*, 4, (1990), pp. 269–288.

Gray, J.A. "Neural Systems, Emotion and Personality." In J. Madden, ed., *Neurobiology of Learning, Emotion and Affect*. New York: Raven Press, (1991), pp. 273–305.

Gray, J.A., J. Feldon, J. Rawlins, D.R. Hemsley, and A.D. Smith. "The Neuropsychology of Schizophrenia." *Behavioral and Brain Sciences*, 14, (1991), pp. 1–20.

Green, M.K. "R.N. Elliott's Fundamental Challenge to Mechanistic Social Models." In R. Prechter, ed., *Market Analysis for the New Millennium*. Gainesville, GA: New Classics Library, 2002.

Gump, B.B., and J.A. Kulik. "Stress, Affiliation, and Emotional Contagion." *Journal of Personality and Social Psychology*, 72, (1997), pp. 305–319.

Hatfield, E., J.T. Cacioppo, and R.L. Rapson. "Primitive Emotional Contagion." In M.S. Clark, ed., Review of Personality and Social Psychology: *Emotions and Social Behavior*, Vol. 14. Newbury Park, CA: Sage Publications, (1992), pp. 151–177.

Hatfield, E., J.T. Cacioppo, and R.L. Rapson. *Emotional Contagion*. Cambridge, England: Cambridge University Press, 1993.

Heider, F. *The Psychology of Interpersonal Relations*. New York: Wiley, 1958.

Helson, R., C. Jones, and V. Kwan. "Personality Change Over 40 Years of Adulthood: Hierarchical Linear Modeling Analyses of Two Longitudinal Samples." *Journal of Personality and Social Psychology*, 83, (2002), pp. 752–766.

Helson, R., and C.J. Soto. "Up and Down in Middle Age: Monotonic and Nonmonotonic Changes in Roles, Status, and Personality." *Journal of Personality and Social Psychology*, 89, (2005), pp. 194–204.

Howes, M.J., J.E. Hokanson, and D.A. Lowenstein. "Induction of Depressive Affect after Prolonged Exposure to a Mildly Depressed Individual." *Journal of Personality and Social Psychology*, 49, (1985), pp. 1110–1113.

Hunt, P.S., and B.A. Campbell. "Autonomic and Behavioral Correlates of Appetitive Conditioning in Rats." *Behavioral Neuroscience*, 111, (1997), pp. 494–502.

Isen, A.M. "Positive Affect and Decision Making." In W.M. Goldstein and R.M. Hogarth, eds., *Research on Judgment and Decision Making*. Cambridge, UK: Cambridge University Press, 1997, pp. 509–534.

Kavanagh, D.J., J. Andrade, and J. May. "Imaginary Relish and Exquisite Torture: The Elaborated Intrusion Theory of Desire." *Psychological Review*, 112, (2005), pp. 446–467.

Klinger, E. "The Search for Meaning in Evolutionary Perspective and Its Clinical Implications." In P. Wong and P. Fry, eds., *The Human Quest for Meaning*. Mahwah, NJ: Lawrence Erlbaum & Associates, 1998, pp. 27–50.

Kulik, J.A., and H.M. Mahler. "Effects of Preoperative Roommate Assignment on Preoperative Anxiety and Recovery from Coronary-Bypass Surgery." *Health Psychology*, 6, (1987), pp. 525–543.

Kulik, J.A., P.J. Moore, and H.I.M. Mahler. "Stress and Affiliation:Hospital Roommate Effects on Preoperative Anxiety and Social Interaction." *Health Psychology*, 12, (1993), pp. 118–124.

LeDoux, J.E., and E. Phelps. "Emotional Networks in the Brain." In M. Lewis and J.M. Haviland, eds., *Handbook of Emotions*, 2nd ed. New York: Guilford Press, 2000, pp. 157–172.

Lerner, J.S., D.S. Small, and G. Lowenstein. "Heart Strings and Purse Strings." *Psychological Science*, 15, (2004), pp. 337–341.

Levenson. "The Intrapersonal Function of Emotion." *Cognition and Emotion*, 13, (1999), pp. 483–504.

Loewenstein, G.F., E.U. Weber, C.K. Hsee, and N. Welch. "Risk as Feelings." *Psychological Bulletin*, 127, (2001), pp. 267–286.

Mayne, T., and J. Ramsey. "The Structure of Emotion: A Nonlinear Dynamic Systems Approach." In T.J. Mayne and G.A. Bonanno, eds., *Emotions: Current Issues and Future Directions*. New York: Guilford Press, (2001), pp. 1–37.

McClelland, D.C. *Human Motivation*. Glenview, IL: Scott, Foresman, 1985.

McClure, J.L. "Goal-Based Explanations of Actions and Outcomes." *European Review of Social Psychology*, 12, (2002), pp. 201–236.

McCrae, R., and P. Costa. "Adding Liebe and Arbeit: The Full Five-Factor Model and Well-Being." *Personality and Social Psychology Bulletin*, 17, (1991), pp. 227–232.

McCrae, R., and P. Costa. "Personality Trait Structure as a Human Universal." *American Psychologist*, 52, (1997), pp. 509–516.

Nofsinger, J.R., 2005. "Social Mood and Financial Economics." *Journal of Behavioral Finance*, 6, (2005), pp. 144–160.

Nygren, T.E., A.M. Isen, P.J. Taylor, and J. Dulin. "The Influence of Positive Affect on the Decision Rule in Risk Situations: Focus on Outcome (and Especially Avoidance of Loss) Rather Than Probability." *Organizational Behavior and Human Decision Processes*, 66, (1996), pp. 59–72.

Ochsner, K.N., and L. Feldman Barrett. "A Multiprocess Perspective on the Neuroscience of Emotion." In T.J. Mayne and G.A. Bonanno, eds., *Emotions: Current Issues and Future Directions*. New York: Guilford Press, 2001, pp. 38–81.

Olsen, R. "Trust, Complexity and the 1990s Market Bubble." *Journal of Behavioral Finance*, 5, (2004), pp. 186–191.

Olson, K.R. "Engagement and Self-Control: Superordinate Dimensions of Big Five Traits." *Personality and Individual Differences*, 38, (2005), pp. 1689–1700.

Ones, D., and C. Viswesvaran. "Personality at Work: Criterion-Focused Occupational Personality Scales Used in Personnel Selection." In B. Roberts and R. Hogan, eds., *Personality Psychology in the Workplace*. Washington, DC: American Psychological Association, 2001, pp. 63–92.

Prechter, R.R. "Popular Culture and the Stock Market." In R. Prechter, ed., *Pioneering Studies in Socionomics*. Gainesville, GA: New Classics Library, 1985, pp. 3–46.

Prechter, R.R. *The Wave Principle of Human Social Behavior and the New Science of Socionomics*. Gainesville, GA: New Classics Library, 1999.

Prechter, R.R. "Unconscious Herding Behavior as the Psychological Basis of Financial Market Trends and Patterns." *Journal of Psychology and Financial Markets*, 2, (2001), pp. 120–125.

Roberts, B.W., R. Helson, and E. Klohnen. "Personality Development and Growth in Women Across 30 Years: Three Perspectives." *Journal of Personality*, 70, (2002), pp. 79–102.

Russell, J.A. "A Circumplex Model of Affect." *Journal of Personality and Social Psychology*, 39, (1980), pp. 1161–1178.

Russell, J.A. "Core Affect and the Psychological Construction of Emotion." *Psychological Review*, 110, (2003), pp. 145–172.

Russell, J.A., and A. Mehrabian. "Evidence for a Three-Factor Theory of Emotions." *Journal of Research in Personality*, 11, (1977), pp. 273–294.

Saucier, G., S. Georgiades, I. Tsaousis, and L.R. Goldberg. "The Factor Structure of Greek Personality Adjectives." *Journal of Personality and Social Psychology*, 88, (2005), pp. 856–875.

Schacter, S. *The Psychology of Affiliation*. Stanford, CA: Stanford University Press, 1959.

Schneirla, T. "An Evolutionary and Developmental Theory of Biphasic Processes Underlying Approach and Withdrawal." Nebraska Symposium on Motivation. Lincoln: University of Nebraska Press, 1959, pp. 1–42.

Searle, J.R. *Intentionality: An Essay in the Philosophy of Mind*. Cambridge, MA: Cambridge University Press, 1982.

Shiller, R. "The Irrationality of Markets." *Journal of Psychology and Financial Markets*, 3, (2002), pp. 87–93.

Shiller, R.J. "Stock Prices and Social Dynamics." Brookings Papers on Economic Activity, 2, (1984), pp. 457–498.

Shiv, B., and A. Fedorikhin. "Heart and Mind in Conflict: Interplay of Affect and Cognition in Consumer Decision Making." *Journal of Consumer Research*, 26, (1999), pp. 278–282.

Showalter, E. *Hystories: Hysterical Epidemics and Modern Media*. New York: Columbia University Press, 1997.

Solomon, R.C. "The Philosophy of Emotions." In M. Lewis and J.M. Haviland, eds., *Handbook of Emotions*. New York: Guilford Press, (1993), pp. 3–15.

Stellar, J.R., and E. Stellar. *The Neurobiology of Motivation and Reward*. New York: Springer-Verlag, 1985.

Sullins, E.S. "Emotional Contagion Revisited: Effects of Social Comparison and Expressive Style on Mood Convergence." *Personality and Social Psychology Bulletin*, 17, (1991), pp. 166–174.

Tellegen, A., D. Watson, and L.A. Clark. "On the Dimensional and Hierarchical Structure of Affect." *Psychology Science*, 10, (1999), pp. 297–303.

Tetlock, P.E., and B.A. Mellers. "The Great Rationality Debate." *Psychological Science*, 13, (2002), pp. 94–99.

Tice, D., E. Bratslavsky, and R. Baumeister. "Emotional Distress Regulation Takes Precedence Over Impulse Control: If You Feel Bad, Do It!" *Journal of Personality and Social Psychology*, 80, (2001), pp. 53–67.

Tooby, J., and L. Cosmides. "The Past Explains the Present: Emotional Adaptions and the Structure of Ancestral Environments." *Ethology and Sociobiology*, 11, (1990), pp. 375–424.

Van Boven, L.V., G. Loewenstein, and D. Dunning. "Mispredicting the Endowment Effect: Underestimation of Owners' Selling Prices by Buyers' Agents." *Journal of Economic Behavior and Organization*, 51, (2003), pp. 351–365.

Watson, D., and L. Clark. "On Traits and Temperament: General and Specific Factors of Emotional Experience and Their Relation to the Five-Factor Model." *Journal of Personality*, 60, (1992), pp. 441–476.

Watson, D., and A. Tellegen. "Toward a Consensual Structure of Mood." *Psychological Bulletin*, 98, (1985), pp. 219–235.

Watson, D., D.Wiese, J. Vaidya, and A. Tellegen. "The Two General Activation Systems of Affect: Structural Findings, Evolutionary Considerations, and Psychobiological Evidence." *Journal of Personality and Social Psychology*, 76, (1999), pp. 820–838.

Wild, T.C., and M.E. Enzle. "Social Contagion of Motivational Orientations." In E. Deci and R. Ryan, eds., *Handbook of Self-Determination Research*. Rochester, New York: University of Rochester, 2002, pp. 141–157.

Williams, S. "The Impact of Mood on Managerial Perceptions." *Research and Practice in Human Resource Management*, 12, (2004), pp. 128–139.

Winter, D.G., O.P. John, A.J. Stewart, E.C. Klohnen, and L.E. Duncan. "Traits and Motives: Toward an Integration of Two Traditions in Personality Research." *Journal of Personality and Social Psychology*, 105, (1998), pp. 230–250.

Wood, J.V., J.A. Saltzberg, and L.A. Goldsamt. "Does Affect Induce Self-Focused Attention?" *Journal of Personality and Social Psychology*, 58, (1990), pp. 899–908.

Yuen, K.S.L., and T.M.C. Lee. "Could Mood State Affect Risk-Taking Decisions?" *Journal of Affective Disorders*, 75, (2003), pp. 11–18.

Zajonc, R., 1998. "Emotion." In D. Gilbert, S. Fiske, and R. Linzey, eds., *The Handbook of Social Psychology*, 4th ed. New York: McGraw-Hill, (1998), pp. 591–632.

EDITOR'S NOTES

<1> It would be better to say "caused by," because *future* social events are tied to social mood.

<2> Socionomists are wary of claims of induced mood and suspect that induced emotions are the more likely operant; see Chapter 19.

<3> Socionomic theory holds that social mood arises from an interactive process rather than being the sum of individuals' emotional states; see Chapters 6 and 19.

<4> Socionomic theory, while accepting the contagion model of referent-sharing, does not embrace the contagion model of mood sharing; see Chapters 6 and 19.

<5> Socionomic theory is more compatible with the earlier expressions in this chapter that buying in financial markets is related not to risk-approaching but to reward-approaching; also see Chapter 19.

Chapter 36

Conference of the Association for Heterodox Economics, London, England
July 2006

The Socionomic Theory of Finance and the Institution of Social Mood: Pareto and the Sociology of Instinct and Rationalization

Wayne D. Parker

Socionomics is a theory of human social behavior describing the causal relationship between social mood and social action. In finance theory, socionomics offers a new heterodox alternative to neoclassicism. The main principles of socionomics are that in human, self-organized complex systems, the following statements apply: (1) Shared unconscious impulses to herd in contexts of uncertainty lead to the emergence of mass psychological dynamics that manifest as social mood trends; (2) these social mood trends conform to hierarchical fractal patterns that take a repetitive, self-affine form and are therefore probabilistically predictable; (3) these patterns of aggregate behavior are form-determined due to endogenous processes rather than mechanistically determined by exogenous causes; and (4) these social mood trends determine the character of social actions and are their underlying cause, both in financial markets and in other social domains.

Socionomics posits that because contextual differences between economics and finance evoke different behavioral dynamics, the law of supply and demand, which is central to economics, is irrelevant to finance. In finance, uncertainty about valuations by other homogeneous agents serves as the context for unconscious, non-rational herding, which follows endogenously regulated fluctuations in social mood that in turn determine financial fluctuations.

Veblen distinguished between instincts, which are directed toward concrete ends, and habits, which are the flexible means by which one may reach such ends. One may view the concept of social mood in socionomics as a new type of unconscious social institution or affective habit, which has evolved to adapt to the context of other agents' uncertain social behavior. Socionomic theory, with its contextualist approach, posits that one of humanity's central purposes is embodied in the evolved instinct for herding in particular social contexts, those of uncertainty. Social mood may be a bridge between instinct and habit, between affective predisposition and context-specific cognition and action. Along with Hodgson, socionomics sees instinct as a bridge between biology and the social sciences that enables an evolutionary explanation of human social behavior (see also Cordes, 2005).

Aspects of socionomic theory echo Pareto's little-known sociological theory of residues and derivations. This paper explores similar ideas in socionomic theory about the relationship between unconscious instincts, likely mediated by the limbic system, and rationalizations for the resulting social behavior, which are cortically mediated. Pareto's postulation of an innate human instinct toward "sociability" is related to the socionomic conceptualization of a herding impulse (Pareto calls such instincts "residues"), while his concept of mental "derivations," the methods by which people justify their behavior, is related to socionomics' recognition of the role of rationalization in financial behavior. The role played by impulse and rationalization in the socionomic model of endogenous causality in an aggregate system of homogeneous agents differs both from the neoclassical theory of finance and from models of herding from other disciplines that invoke an assumption of heterogeneous agents and/or exogenous causality.

Note: All references to Pareto in this paper refer to Pareto (1916/1935). I am following the tradition of citing Pareto's sociological work by referring to section number and page number within each citation rather than giving volume and page number of the four-volume edition I used. The pagination is somewhat different in the Italian, English and French translations as well as in an abbreviated condensation of this voluminous work, but almost all versions cite the section numbers in the same fashion, so my doing so as well should facilitate further research and corroboration (or not) of my findings.

Introduction

Vilfredo Pareto (1916/1935) was a brilliant economic and sociological theorist. Best known for his work in creating and refining aspects of equilibrium theory in economics and for his economic concept of the "Pareto optimum," his later prolific work in sociological theory is all too often unknown or neglected. Ironically, some of the reasons for the relative neglect of Pareto's sociological work are themselves what Pareto would call "derivations"—nonlogical biases that even scientists have, disguised with a "varnish of logic," as he would say. One may say that Pareto was the first to do for sociological behavior what Freud (1900/1996) did for individuals' intimate, emotional behavior in laying bare its roots in unconscious motivations. Academics have neglected his theory in the past century due to several nonlogical factors:

(1)   After the publication of his sociological theory, some critics linked Pareto's name to fascism. Mussolini had apparently attended some of Pareto's sociological lectures in Lausanne, Switzerland, was greatly impressed, and used Pareto's theories to rationalize his brutal policies. Pareto was thereby branded a "fascist." There is no evidence that Pareto lent his support to Mussolini, and we know that Pareto declined Mussolini's offer of a position in his government. Many later reviewers of this controversy have called the charge "poppycock," and their assessment has had no reputable refutation. This slander nevertheless led many scientists to ignore Pareto's theory.

(2)   There is a natural human discomfort at hearing someone attribute people's behavior to factors beyond their conscious control and awareness, and many have felt this discomfort upon reading Pareto. Freud's theory about the nature of the unconscious mind and its motivation for a wide range of behaviors aroused the same discomfort and almost universal rejection initially, until its later application was found to be useful.

(3)   Readers have a certain discomfort with the lack of statistical tools required to make practical use of Pareto's concept of "mutual interdependencies" among various causal factors. Such a reaction is understandable, even if not a good reason to reject the theory as a whole.

(4)   Many have found his theory to be rather alienating to read, due to both its occasionally sarcastic style and the depressingly

pessimistic implications it has for the future of society. This is a stylistic or emotional objection.

Other reasons for the neglect of Pareto's sociology are entirely logical:

(1)   Many have found his exposition to be extremely and needlessly complex and difficult to read and understand.

(2)   His theory contains some internal contradictions and theoretical and metatheoretical inconsistencies (more about them later).

Why, then, should we read Pareto's sociology? What does it have to offer us? It has tremendous heuristic value, both as a precursor of modern systems theory and as an incisive social critique by a well-read theoretical gadfly. It prompts the reader to challenge widely held assumptions about the nature of causality, to reexamine the motivations for a wide range of human social behavior, and to evaluate more critically the myriad theories that Pareto takes insightfully to task for their nonlogical elements.

More relevant to our purposes, Pareto is an early forerunner, in several ways, of Prechter's socionomic theory. This paper attempts to sketch the primary similarities and differences between socionomics and Pareto's sociological theory, with the goals of elucidating both theories and offering evidence that socionomics provides many empirical, theoretical and metatheoretical improvements over Pareto's ideas. Both theorists aim to fashion a comprehensive theory of social dynamics based on the scientific principles of empirical observation and theoretical synthesis, but whereas no one had achieved a more comprehensive sociological theory than Pareto's at the time of its publication, Prechter's socionomic theory both delivers on the failed promise of many aspects of Pareto's work and provides a more scientific basis for social research.

Prechter and Pareto offer heterodox theories relevant to the social sciences, particularly economics, finance, sociology, history and political science; both theorists disavow the idea that the rational-choice model pertains to all sociological matters; both demonstrate the importance of nonrational and unconscious motivations for social behavior; and both offer nontraditional models of social causality. Despite these similarities, there are a number of ways in which the two theories differ.

This paper first briefly summarizes the key elements of socionomic theory and then presents an outline of Pareto's sociological theory. With that foundation, it describes their similarities and differences. Finally, it concludes with comments on the implications of this comparison.

Socionomic Theory of Herding

[This section is omitted here, because it mostly parallels that of the same title from "Herding: An Interdisciplinary Integrative Review," printed as Chapter 34 in this book. For cohesion, the three additional paragraphs previously appearing here have been transferred to Chapters 33 and 34.]

Summary of Pareto's Sociological Theory

Logical vs. Nonlogical Actions

Pareto describes *residues* as nonlogical actions manifesting underlying "sentiments" or "instincts," and *derivations* as post-hoc, pseudo-logical rationalizations that people use to explain their nonlogical behavior to themselves and others. Pareto (§296, p. 194, note 1) declares the formula underlying his theory as follows: "The fact, the nonlogical action, comes first, then the explanation of the fact, the logical varnish." First the residue, then the derivation. He makes his fundamental distinction between "logical" and "nonlogical" actions (§150, p. 77) in the following manner:

> Suppose we apply the term logical actions to actions that logically conjoin means to ends not only from the standpoint of the subject performing them, but from the standpoint of other persons who have a more extensive knowledge—in other words, to actions that are logical both subjectively and objectively in the sense just explained. Other actions we shall call nonlogical (by no means the same as "illogical").

An unusual aspect of this definition is the *contextualism*, or perspectivism, that it demonstrates. Pareto's very definition hinges on whether an action appears logical from the point of view of an observer. (Cf. the theory of *autopoiesis* by Maturana and Varela, 1992, in which the role of the observer is similarly crucial.) While Pareto in many passages sounds like a traditional positivist with his emphasis on scientifically verifiable methodology, elements of contextualism such as this separate him from the more mechanistic realists who predominated in the ranks of the positivists. His contextualism is useful heuristically if we consider how it differs from the standard mechanistic formulation, but his way of combining contextualism with mechanistic approaches created metatheoretical eclecticism in his theory, making it contradictory and confusing at times.

Role of Instinct

Pareto (§§156-158, pp. 82-84) discusses one category of nonlogical actions, those that are *instinctive*, by making comparisons to insect societies:

> Many, many human actions, even today among the most civilized peoples, are performed instinctively, mechanically, in pursuance of habit....

Again using animals for a comparison, he notes that instinctive behavior may occur "at times even contrary to the animal's interests." His comments here make it clear that he views instinctive behavior as a mix of conscious and unconscious action and at times as completely unconscious behavior. His relating of "instinct" to "habit" evokes similar concepts presented by later institutionalist theorists.

Pareto uses analogies from "animal societies" (§1506, p. 961) to argue for the role of instincts in human social behavior:

> Nor is it easy to see why the [social] contract should not hold just as well for animal societies such as the ants and the bees. If we assume that nothing but reasoning and logical thinking can hold human society together and prevent its dissolution, how [do we] explain the fact that the societies of ants and bees hold together and endure in time? But we say that such societies are grounded in instinct. How deny that that instinct plays its part in human societies as well?

While this logic is compelling, all varieties of "instinct psychology," including Pareto's, are vulnerable to a similar critique. It is quite tempting, once one starts explaining social phenomena by invoking some sort of instinct that prompts the behavior in question, to hypothesize a new instinct for every new category of social behavior that is observed but not otherwise easily explained. Such a careless approach is one reason instinct-related theories fell into disfavor early in the past century. Such overuse of the instinct concept for evolutionary psychologists may well threaten the validity of such an approach today. As Pareto remarked concerning social Darwinism, however, the approach of relating social behavior to its instinctive roots is not altogether without validity as long as one takes care to define the terms of such a theory very specifically and then to back up one's theoretical claims with empirical data.

After offering many examples of nonlogical actions in human social behavior, Pareto begins (§§217-218) to sketch his theory of residues and derivations. He inductively concludes that there are only a few different types of residues, and their appearance is constant, whereas the derivations are numerous and quite variable.

In the mode of a psychologist, Pareto takes seemingly incomprehensible behavior from the annals of history and analyzes it to discover the underlying "residue" whereby it becomes understandable (see §223, p. 149). Pareto (§249.2, p. 171) states his "need to do a thing of supreme importance for our purposes here—to tear off the masks nonlogical conduct is made to wear and lay bare the things they hide from view...to discover that the substantial element in the conduct lies in the things that underlie the logical exteriors."

In formulating his theory about the role of sentiments in motivating nonlogical conduct, Pareto (§285, pp. 188-189) clearly draws on the earlier work in this area by Spencer: "Herbert Spencer advances a theory that nonlogical actions alone influence society. 'Ideas do not govern and overthrow the world: the world is governed or overthrown by feelings, to which ideas serve only as guides.... All social phenomena are produced by the totality of human emotions and beliefs.'"

Evolutionary Component

Pareto seems to argue (§407, p. 247) for a theory of human social institutions related to an evolutionary theory in which human instincts themselves evolve to adapt to a changing environment:

> There are certain principles of nonlogical conduct from which human beings deduce their laws. Such principles of nonlogical conduct (or "residues"...) are correlated with conditions under which human beings live, and change with those conditions.

The translator noted that the Italian word translated here as "principle" could also be translated as "cause." It is also important to understand that for Pareto, "correlated" does not equate to "caused by." He posits a "mutual interdependency" between such things as unconscious sentiments and "conditions under which human beings live," seeing the process as a type of co-evolution. Such "conditions" were not limited to material conditions but also included cultural conditions such as those imposed by various social institutions.

Pareto notes (§2235, p. 1565, note 2), "But the power of sentiment and the influence of *habitual manners of reasoning* [emphasis added] are such that people disregard the force of logic entirely...." This wording is such that Pareto's residues and derivations may both be considered institutions in

the sense used by Veblen and other institutionalists if we include as institutions those "habits of thought" that influence or constrain social behavior.
(Similarly, one may view the fractal pattern of socionomic theory's aggregate
model of herding—the Wave Principle—as an institution that serves as a
probabilistic constraint on the path of development of a society.)

Pareto (§619, pp. 374-376) has a complex attitude toward evolutionary
theory, which he considers to have both scientific and unscientific versions:

> The "historical" method opened the door for experience to make its
> way into some of the sciences from which it had been barred, and so
> served as a transition, beneficial from the strictly logico-experimental
> point of view, for bringing sociology closer to the level already
> reached by the natural sciences. Curious the confusion still obtaining
> in the minds of many people as to the "historical" and "experimental"
> methods [recall that for Pareto, "experimental" can mean "observa-
> tional"]. The historical method, when it is—as seldom—genuinely
> historical and has no intermixture of metaphysical, sentimental,
> patriotic, and other similar reflections, is just a part of the experi-
> mental method. Its object is to study some of the relations arising in
> the experimental domain; in other words, it deals with "evolution,"
> with the manner in which certain facts succeed other facts in time.

This passage helps us understand why Pareto is often seen as having
been opposed to evolutionary theory. What he is actually opposed to is the
mixture of scientific versions of evolutionary theory with nonscientific,
sentimentally or politically inspired versions of "social Darwinism" or
"worshiping the God of Progress." He ridicules these "nonlogical" elements mercilessly. In addition, Pareto (§1770, pp. 1230-1231) rejects key
elements of Darwinian theory due to its causal reasoning, despite finding
some "element of truth" in its observations. He consistently rejects simple
mechanistic cause-and-effect explanations that have inadequate support in
empirical data and which may oversimplify a more complex set of causal
interdependencies.

Residues

Pareto has been justifiably criticized for his vague definition of
"residues" (§850, p. 501). Here, though, he clearly equates "residues" with
nonlogical instincts, and "derivations" with nonlogical cognition serving
post hoc to rationalize instinctive behavior:

Let us make the elements *a* and *b* our main concern. The element *a* [which Pareto later identifies with "residues"] corresponds, we may guess, to certain instincts of man, or more exactly, men, because *a* has no objective existence and differs in different individuals; and it is probably because of its correspondence to instincts that it is virtually constant in social phenomena. The element *b* [later identified with "derivations"] represents the work of the mind in accounting for *a*. That is why *b* is more variable, as reflecting the play of the imagination.

Pareto (§888, pp. 516-519) divides residues into six classes:

Class I   Instinct for combinations
Class II   Group-persistence (persistence of aggregates)
Class III   Need of expressing sentiments by external acts (activity, self-expression)
Class IV   Residues connected with sociality
Class V   Integrity of the individual and his appurtenances
Class VI   The sex residue.

The meaning of much of Pareto's terminology is unclear to the typical reader of English. His translator gives an extensive note on class I, the "instinct for combinations," explaining that the term translated as "combination" can mean "deal," "happy inspiration," "big idea," "scheme," etc., so that an "instinct for combinations" could mean "the inventive faculty," "ingeniousness," "originality," "imagination," etc.

Pareto calls his class II of residues "group-persistences" or "persistence of aggregates" (§991, pp. 596-598). A note from the translator clarifies what Pareto meant by his description of this class:

The Italian phrase is "*persistenza degli aggregati.*" The aggregate is an aggregate (combination, association, group) of *sensations*. The tendency to consolidate such groups of sensations and make them permanent in time Pareto regards as one of the great and fundamental forces in society…. The concept of "group-persistence" would be a definition of the ordinary concept of "habit" or "custom." The concept of "group-persistence" is basic in Pareto's theories of the social equilibrium and class-circulation, and in general in his whole conception of history. (p. 596)

In order to understand Pareto's theory, one must understand that this residue of "group-persistences"—the persistence of aggregates of sensations—operates at multiple levels. For instance, Pareto sees one's very concept of "the individual" or even one's own sense of identity as an example of this residue. At another level, concepts such as "Uncle Sam" or "Russia" or "God" are also examples of this residue, where (according to Pareto) one has unconsciously and sentimentally grouped a collection of sensations together in one's mind and then imagined that this grouping persists over time. It is strikingly original for Pareto to label this process a nonlogical action, but it would be challenging to assemble proof that his assertion is incorrect, that is, to falsify his claim.

At a yet higher level, the residue of group-persistences extends its influence into the maintenance of societal and cultural habits, customs and institutions (cf. Hodgson's 2004 discussion of "habit"). Pareto sets up this class II of residues in opposition to class I. He posits that in some domains of human social behavior the dynamic oscillation between the predominance of class I residues and class II residues plays itself out as the dynamic oscillation between societal forces for change vs. societal forces for conserving tradition. In other domains, the dynamic opposition of the motive forces generated by class I residues vs. class II residues explains for Pareto the "circulation of the elites."

Passing by class III for a moment, class IV of Pareto's hypothesized residues (§§1113-1125, pp. 659-664) is that of "residues connected with sociality" (elsewhere also called "sociability"). This class of residues, along with class II, is most directly related to the unconscious herding impulse that plays such an important role in socionomic theory. Pareto describes various subtypes in this class of residues, of which class IV-β1 is the most relevant to our purposes:

> *Voluntary conformity on the part of the individual.* Imitation is of that variety. Imitation plays an important role in social phenomena....
>
> The imitation may have a purpose: to attain some result that is beneficial, or is deemed beneficial, by means which have been seen to yield those results when used by others. But oftentimes no such purpose exists, at least no conscious purpose; and we then get nonlogical actions, which, as usual, come to be tinted with logical colourings. (p. 661)

Note that Pareto's "voluntary conformity" may be unconscious, and it may or may not be beneficial. The same is true of Prechter's herding impulse, which, like Pareto's conformity, is due to an unconscious instinct rather than a rational plan. The rationalizations for herding behavior are mere "logical colourings."

While Pareto does not directly address it, there is a strong connection between the instincts underlying the class IV residue of conformity and those underlying the class II residue of group-persistences. Obviously, one manifestation of group-persistences would be a person's desire to maintain his identity with a group of other individuals perceived to be like himself or that he wishes to emulate. We may characterize the distinction between class II and class IV residues as two aspects of the same instinct or as two closely related instincts. The class II aspect relates to the identity issue (perception of self as part of a group), while the class IV aspect relates to the concomitant behavior (herding). As Pareto often emphasizes, "All social phenomena are complex mixtures of many elements involving many residues" (§1165, p. 693). Pareto's discussion of the role of the class-IV conformity residue in the area of fashion (§1119, p. 661; cf. Shiller's 1984, 2000 and 2001 ideas about "fads and fashions" in finance) provides further confirmation that Pareto and Prechter are talking about the same social instinct.

Within class V, Pareto (§§1208-1216, pp. 727-731) posits a subtype he calls "sentiments of resistance to alterations." While much of his discussion of the instinct to "resist alterations in the social equilibrium" pertains to the domain of social or legal justice, the full discussion makes it clear that his "social equilibrium" is a much broader concept. For instance, he notes,

> The sentiment that inspires resistance to alterations of equilibrium places alterations in insignificant matters on a par with alterations in very important matters, and people regard as equally "just" a sentence condemning an anti-trinitarian to the stake and a sentence condemning a murderer to death. The mere wearing of clothes different from the common fashion clashes with the sentiment as violently as other far more important transgressions against the social order.

This subtype of class V residues also has some relationship to the herding instinct, the impulse to be sure one is acting as the others in one's perceived group. Pareto's comment (§1215, p. 730) about the sentiment of opposition to the disturbance of the social equilibrium confirms this observation: "That feeling, in human society, is somewhat analogous to the instinct in animals that makes them flee at perception of danger." Socionomic theory similarly hypothesizes that the dynamic of herding in contexts of uncertainty developed during evolution due to the survival value of such behavior: If one is uncertain of a source of danger, being sure to remain with the rest of the herd is perceived to enhance safety.

Thus, aspects of socionomic theory are related to classes I, II, IV and V of Pareto's residues. The other two classes of residues, class III (need of expressing sentiments by external acts) and class VI (the sex residue), are fairly self-evident aspects of human nature. While these residues do not appear to have any significant conceptual connection with the remainder of Pareto's theory (he rarely mentions them beyond their initial listing and description), they represent important components of socionomic theory, since mood impels social actions, including aggregate procreation (see Prechter, 1999b [and Chapter 10]). Thus, all six of Pareto's classes of residues are related to socionomic theory.

Derivations

Pareto defines "derivations" (§1397, p. 885) as "reasonings with which people try to make conduct that is nonlogical seem logical." The key element in this definition is the logical quality of the *conduct* that the derivations attempt to explain; the logical quality of the *reasoning* used in these explanations is not in question and may range from the patently absurd to the academically impressive. Some of the derivations Pareto identifies are related to accepted scientific theories, while others are more related to either religion or metaphysics, both of which Pareto considers to be worthless for science. Also recall that whether conduct is logical is judged not in accordance with some authority or with respect to some particular purpose (such as "survival value") but rather by the degree to which the connection between means and ends is judged to be logical by both the actor and observers. This standard is thus entirely atheoretical, a simple standard of "consensus" between actor and observer.

Pareto (§1419, p. 899) classifies derivations in the following categories:

Class I: Assertion
Class II: Authority
Class III: Accords with sentiments or principles
Class IV: Verbal proofs.

As with his classification of residues, many have criticized Pareto's classification of derivations for its arbitrariness and seemingly ad hoc nature. While such criticisms may be valid, this aspect of Pareto's system seems to be a function of his commitment to empirical observation and the inductive method. As much as possible, he sought not to impose any theoretical framework on his observations of the way in which people rationalize their nonlogical actions but rather simply to catalog their nonlogical reasonings. While Prechter's empirical approach led successfully to a comprehensive theory, that goal eluded Pareto. Nevertheless, if some other theorist were to take up the cause to construct a more coherent theoretical framework for derivations, he would do well to emulate Pareto's insistence on empirical validation.

Of course, a theory may share Pareto's ideas about humans' creative methods of rationalizing nonlogical actions without attempting to classify types of rationalizations that people's minds devise. Socionomics is such a theory. It proposes that the primary role of the neocortex in a context of uncertainty is to generate rationalizations justifying a person's unconsciously generated impulsive decisions, but it considers any effort to categorize the vast array of rationalizations that people use to be a tangential endeavor. [It does, however, list numerous examples; see Chapters 1, 2, 19 and 22.]

Similarities between Prechter's Socionomics and Pareto's Sociology

Role of Nonrational Aspects of Behavior

Both Pareto's sociological theory and Prechter's socionomic theory are at odds with rational choice theory, which assumes (1) methodological individualism [see Chapter 37], (2) optimality or utility-maximization and (3) exclusive focus on self-regard, the idea that individual action is exclusively seeking one's own welfare, not that of others (Abell, 2000). Both Prechter and Pareto posit that nonrational factors—"herding impulses" and "social mood" for Prechter, "sentiments" and "instincts" for Pareto—are central determinants for much, though not all, of human social behavior, whether they involve self-regard (as both reason and herding often do) or not.

As one example, under Prechter's theory of political change, unconscious shifts in nonlogical social mood underlie the impetus of the electorate either to oust incumbent political leaders or to re-elect them, regardless of objective factors such as the candidates' platforms or policies. Pareto has a similar notion in his "circulation of the elites" theory, in which nonlogical drives for change in the ruling class of society lead to a periodic replacement of "lions" by "foxes" among the elites and vice versa. Socionomic theory would agree—using Pareto's terms—that it is residues, not derivations or genuine logical thinking, that motivate the net voting behavior of the public.

Prechter's "socionomic hypothesis" states that social mood precedes and impels social actions, not the other way around, and that people rationalize such actions either before or after taking them. This depiction is compatible with, though not precisely identical to, Pareto's insight that residues precede and impel social behavior while derivatives come later in an attempt to justify those nonlogical actions.

Both Prechter and Pareto have highly original ideas about the distinction between logical and nonlogical thought, although other theorists have systematically developed this distinction at other times in the history of science. Compare, for instance, Freud's (1900/1996) distinction between "primary process" (nonlogical) and "secondary process" (logical) or Kahneman's (2003) "system 1" thinking vs. "system 2" thinking (see also Sloman, 1996).

Bi-Level Theories

Both theories have important theoretical components at the individual level and at the aggregate level. For Prechter, the unconscious impulse to herd in contexts of uncertainty functions at the individual level, while a fractal pattern of fluctuation in unconscious social mood functions at the aggregate level. For Pareto, residues and derivations function at the individual level, while the circulation of the elites functions at the aggregate level. Thus, the two theories speak to aspects of both agency and structure. Pareto's theory, however, does so mechanistically while Prechter's does so via a combination of contextualism and organicism [see Chapters 32 and 33].

Oversimplified responses to the agency/structure dichotomy in sociology are outdated. Modern sociologists are struggling to resolve this issue in a variety of creative ways. (For example, see Giddens' (1979) idea of "structuration.") Socionomic theory resolves this false dichotomy by setting its herding dynamic holistically in the context of a process ontology (Prechter and Parker, 2004 [Chapters 32 and 33]).

Ideas generally compatible with socionomics—such as "simultaneous mutual causation" and "autopoietic processes," which relate processes observed at the individual level to those observed at the aggregate level—likewise demonstrate a disavowal of linear, mechanistic, cause-and-effect analysis in favor of causal relationships that, in Prechter's words, "are neither linear nor nonlinear" but rather "proceed relentlessly according to form" (Prechter, 1999a, p. 400) at the societal level. In a similar vein, Pareto regards his ideas about "mutual interdependencies" among various social processes as crucial to his theory, resisting a reductionism to linear cause-and-effect relationships. These ideas were one of the tributaries to the later development of modern systems theory.

Potential for Voluntaristic Action

Prechter observes (1999a, p. 414), "collective systems do not possess or exercise free will, [but] the capabilities of an individual's independent, conscious mind include the potential to understand, recognize and to some degree mitigate or overcome some of the impulses of his unconscious mind." Similarly, Pareto comments (§1843, p. 1281), "The person who is able to free himself from the blind dominion of his own sentiments is capable of utilizing the sentiments of other people for his own ends." Thus, as Parsons (1937) perceived, there is room in Pareto's theory for elements of a "voluntaristic theory of action." In other words, as influential as the power of sentiments is over human social behavior, Pareto never sees these sentiments as entirely determining human choice. He leaves room for the human mind to stand against the influence of unconscious, internal sentiments as well as external influences and thereby to make choices that are not entirely predetermined. Socionomics contains this same element of individual agency alongside the probabilistic determinism of the aggregate pattern.

Thus, both theories imply a theory of action or agency that maintains a role for freedom of choice in decision-making at the individual level. They do not see such choices as being entirely determined by heredity, environment and exogenous forces. The roles of volitional agency and endogenous dynamics are explicit in socionomic theory, however, whereas Pareto's "mutual interdependency" between processes at individual and aggregate levels only hints at elements of voluntaristic agency.

In understanding the complexities of the relationships between individual agency and societal structure as described by both Prechter and Pareto, it is important to keep in mind another admonition from Alexander: "It is a nominalist error, associated with classical liberalism and neo-Kantian theory, to identify voluntarism with free will in the strong sense, that is, with the actions of a completely nonconstrained and nonsocialized actor" (p. 176). Neither Prechter nor Pareto show any sign of holding such a simplistic view of voluntarism; rather, they would both be comfortable with Alexander's observation, "There is a long tradition in social thought, most recently exhibited by Durkheim, Freud, and Piaget, which believes… that freedom depends, in part, on certain distinctive internal qualities which are produced only through association and internalization" (p. 176) and, we would add, the extent of one's conscious exploration of one's own unconscious impulses.

Endogenous vs. Exogenous Causality

As Rutherford (1998) pointed out, Veblen was like Schumpeter in seeing technological developments as explaining evolutionary changes in the "habits of thought" underlying institutional changes ("business cycles") in an economic system. Socionomics would charge that such explanations invoke technological change as a kind of exogenous *deus ex machina*. Socionomic theory differs in seeing changes in both technological innovation and prosperity as products—i.e., results, not causes—of fluctuations in social mood: Positive social mood is a primary source of the mental innovativeness and optimism that leads to technological breakthroughs and upswings in the financial markets and the economy, while negative social mood is a primary source of technological stagnation and financial and economic downturns.

Pareto's thinking about economic crises is at odds with orthodox economic theory but strikingly similar to Prechter's conceptualization of the same issue. Pareto states (§2338, p. 1689),

> A crisis must not be thought of as an accident interrupting a normal state of things. *The normal thing is the wave-movement* [emphasis added], economic prosperity bringing on depression, depression bringing on prosperity. In regarding economic crises as abnormal phenomena, the economist is making the mistake a physicist would be making in thinking of the nodes and internodes of a rod in vibration as accidents independent of the movements of the molecules of the rod....

> The "crisis" is just a particular case of the *great law of rhythm* [emphasis added] that prevails in all social phenomena.... The social system shapes the crisis; it does not affect its substance, which depends upon the nature of the human being and of economic problems in general.

While there are many metatheoretical crosscurrents in Pareto's work, and while some of the eclecticism in his thought yields contradictions, this passage gives us a view of his conception of society as an organic system, a structuralist view in which the general form of a society's progress, including its crises, are due to systemic processes rather than to exogenous shocks to an otherwise static and stable system. It is due to such passages that later theorists rank Pareto as one of the fathers of modern systems theory. Prechter (1999a, pp. 370-371; 399-400) likewise says,

> A variant of the approach that assumes society is a machine is the idea that the stock market is a machine. If it is running properly, the implied idea seems to go, then prices rise. If prices *fall*, the machine is broken. [But] to this day in evolutionary history, the emotional fragility of the human limbic system remains uncorrected. Until neocortexes evolve enough to dominate their primitive antecedents, the market shall ever rise, fall and occasionally crash.... the cause of a market's process is its form, [so] financial market movements

cannot result from a chain of incremental causes that trigger a reaction *because they follow the Wave Principle.*

Role of Instincts

Both theories see an important role for an element of "instinct psychology." Instinct theories are experiencing a renaissance in the social sciences (Pinker, 1994; Barkow, Cosmides and Tooby, 1992; Buss, 2003), though not in orthodox neoclassical economics. This increase in popularity should facilitate the acceptance of a theory such as socionomics, with its key component of unconscious herding.

Asso (2002, p. 3) saw Veblen's (1914/1990) definition of "instinct" as having four components: An instinct is an "(a) unlearned, (b) species-specific, (c) goal-directed and (d) organized pattern of behavior." Rutherford (1998, p. 465) noted that although "Veblen does not provide a precise definition of instincts...they are to be understood as determining the ends of action and not directly determining actions themselves." This distinction between the heritability of a structure for behavior rather than the heritability of the details of behavior is similar to the distinction Pinker (1994) made in describing what he called "the language instinct." He followed the Chomskyan approach to psycholinguistics whereby despite the "deep structure" of language, there is flexibility for social experience to modify the "surface structure" of linguistic behavior. It is also similar to what Prechter means by his "herding impulse," which is a deep structure to which changeable social circumstances—such as the modern context of financial speculation—conform. The socionomic view is that the herding impulse does not produce specific, automatic actions but is rather an innate, evolutionarily derived, goal-oriented inclination to herd in contexts of uncertainty. This concept leaves much flexibility for individuals to employ this impulse in a variety of contexts.

Waves within Waves

Both theories see society as undulating in a series of "waves inside waves." For Prechter, this is a specific fractal pattern (WP) with detailed aspects described by R.N. Elliott (1938, 1946) and Frost and Prechter (1978/2005). Pareto offers a similar concept of undulating waves inside waves but provides only a general impression rather than the detailed, comprehensive model subsumed under socionomic theory. Pareto concludes the abstract for his chapter on "The Social Equilibrium in History" (p. 1432) with two sentences that correspond to socionomic theory:

The trends toward crystallization and free initiative are mutually successive phenomena. That is just a particular case of the general law that social movements progress in waves.

If one were to substitute "negative social mood" or "corrective retrenchment" for "crystallization," and "positive social mood" or "impulsive growth" for "free initiative," one would have a general statement of the socionomic picture of social progress. Pareto asserts that assessing trends of "sentiments determining the social equilibrium" (Prechter's opposing phrase would be "social mood determining social dynamism") is difficult because of the fact that any such trends contain fluctuations inside fluctuations (§§1718-1719, pp. 1179-1182). Socionomics, in contrast, finds this quality helpful.

Though Mandelbrot had not yet coined the term "fractal," Pareto describes a concept similar to Elliott's undulating waves of various degrees over time. He illustrates his idea this way:

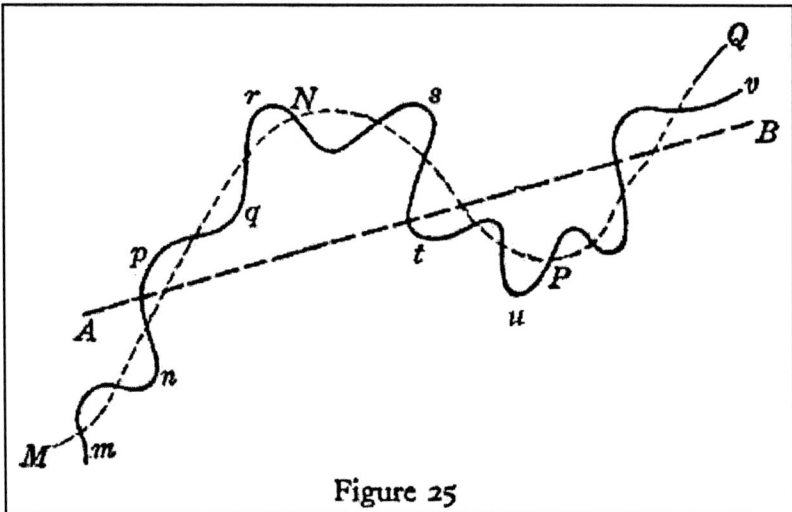

Figure 25

From Vilfredo Pareto, The Mind and Society, Vol. 3: Theory of Derivations, *1935 [orig. published in Italian in 1916], §1719, p. 1181. The original illustration inadvertently omitted the italic letter "u," which has been supplied here.]*

Pareto's footnote for his illustration of waves in society's development reads in part,

If the concrete development [in social trends] is represented (Figure 25) by *mnpqrstuv*, one observes: (1) That that line fluctuates about the undulatory line *MNPQ*; (2) that the latter in turn fluctuates about the line *AB*. In other words there are fluctuations of different amplitude, namely: 1. fluctuations of brief duration, represented by the line *mnpqrstuv*; 2. fluctuations of medium amplitude, represented by the line *MNPQ*; 3. fluctuations of maximum amplitude represented by the line *AB*; and so on.

By relating his illustration to social processes determined by "sentiments," Pareto presages Prechter's concept of waves of social mood and mood-inspired actions. Although Pareto postulates a rough version of WP, one element he misses is the self-similar form of these waves on varying time scales. Pareto's illustration, moreover, shows corrective waves as having five subwaves instead of WP's three, indicating that, like the Dow theorists, he approached in a primitive way the specifically delineated form that—as depicted in idealized form below—Elliott later discovered in financial prices and other data series, which he elucidated in 1938.

© 1978/1999 Robert R. Prechter

Fig. 1-3, from Robert R. Prechter (1999a). The Wave Principle of Human Social Behavior and the New Science of Socionomics. *Gainesville, Georgia: New Classics Library, p.26.*

Some Agreement on the Lack of Societal Progress

Pareto, disagreeing with many of the social Darwinists of his time, ridicules the assumption of progress in society, seeing waves of "elites" simply displacing each other over time. He famously remarks, "History is the graveyard of aristocracies." Pareto denies (§1681-1683, pp. 1112-1113) that theories in the social sciences show evidence of having produced cumulative progress toward truth, just as he denies that succeeding sets of elites in charge of government have produced cumulative progress, however one defines it, in society:

> And so it is, considering for the moment only one or two of such oscillations, that in a little more than a hundred years, and, specifically, from the close of the eighteenth to the beginning of the twentieth century, one witnesses a wave of Voltairean scepticism, and then Rousseau's humanitarianism as a sequel to it; then a religion of Revolution, and then a return to Christianity; then scepticism once more—Positivism; and finally, in our time, the first stages of a new fluctuation in a mystico-nationalistic direction. Leaving the natural sciences aside and keeping to social theory, there has been no notable progress in one direction or the other.

Pareto is both insightful and consistent (in contrast to his fellow economists) in realizing that his theory of social equilibrium implies (rather pessimistically, in the view of some critics) that real cumulative progress in cultural philosophies' ability to approximate truth does not take place over long spans of time. The "undulating" nature of small-degree social trends yields only the appearance of progress. Economists who espouse an equilibrium model of economic and social behavior nevertheless also generally hold an inconsistent (Pareto would say "nonlogical") belief in human progress, whether based on some poorly integrated version of evolutionary theory or on some simple, non-rational faith in the inevitability of progress. Although WP ultimately presents an optimistic view that long term progress occurs in at least certain aspects of the human experience (see discussion below), Prechter agrees with Pareto that socially shared beliefs about culture and politics have fluctuated but have failed to exhibit long range progress.

Socionomic theory, however, offers a different explanation for the lack of cumulative progress in socially held beliefs, including, for example, social theory itself [see Chapter 40]. The observed oscillations between different "fads" in cultural philosophy are due not to the opposition of the forces of "reality vs. utility" as Pareto speculates (for which he offers no evidence) but rather to the fluctuation of social mood between positive and negative valence. We have recently conducted an analysis of social theories (Parker, 2006 [Chapter 37]), looking at the alternation between the popularity of methodological individualism and methodological holism in the history of economic theory, which may also be somewhat correlated with positive and negative social mood, respectively. Even Pareto concludes that the key elements underlying this oscillation in social theory are "sentiments with which men could not dispense."

Pareto attempts to explain the "cyclical" and "undulating" form of the oscillation between protectionism and free trade primarily on the basis of his idea of the circulation of the elites (§§2215-2224, pp. 1549-1553), which in turn is based on his theory of the varying distribution of residues in different groups in society. We may thereby view his explanation for waves of protectionism alternating with free trade as being based on alternating waves of sentiment. Similarly, socionomic theory posits that periods of free trade are due to large-degree waves of positive social mood, which foster optimism about the outlook for prosperity as well as trust in the motivations of trading partners, while periods of protectionism are due to large-degree waves of negative social mood, which foster pessimism about the outlook for prosperity as well as distrust of trading partners. As both Pareto and Prechter would agree, ample evidence supports the fact that the alternation between positive and negative attitudes toward free trade over history is nonlogical. Free trade between countries is generally mutually advantageous, so if the choice were based on purely logical principles, the evidence of history would simply show more thoroughly embraced policies of free trade over the centuries. Political trends, then, provide an example of an area in which Prechter agrees with Pareto that societies are more prone to oscillate than to progress.

Differences between Prechter's Socionomics and Pareto's Sociology

Metatheoretical Assumptions

Pareto's theory is substantially mechanistic. Prechter's theory is instead compatible with contextualism and organicism (Pepper, 1942; Prechter and Parker, 2004 [Chapter 33; also Chapters 6 and 32]). While Pareto makes some statements that profess an intent to be holistic in his theory, the details of his theoretical explanations often contradict that stated intent. For instance, early in his treatise (§66, p. 32) he announces that his theory is holistic: "The fact that we deal with individuals by no means implies that a number of individuals taken together are to be considered a simple sum. They form compounds which, like chemical compounds, may have properties that

712 THE SOCIONOMIC THEORY OF FINANCE

are not the sum of the properties of their components." He is clearly alluding to emergent properties of the social aggregate. Yet the reductionistic, non-holistic aspects of Pareto's more mechanistic approach are evident not only in his announced intention to model his sociological theory in the style of classical mechanics but also in his analysis of the circulation of the elites, which involves a conceptualization of the class structure of society that is fully reducible to the personality variables of individuals in that society. In other words, for Pareto, compounds, classes and other such structures are epiphenomena that must be reduced to individual elements to be explained. Mechanistic reductionism does not recognize irreducible holistic processes as natural principles of structural organization. In contrast, the fractal pattern of WP in Prechter's theory is an irreducible organizational principle that regulates individual behaviors just as much as individual behaviors aggregate to express WP. Socionomics thereby integrates individual biology and behavior with the aggregate pattern, making Prechter's theory, like other organicist theories but in contrast to Pareto's, not mechanistic but holistic.

Heterogeneous vs. Homogeneous Agents

Pareto (§§2228-2236, pp. 1556-1566) develops a complex social theory involving the interactions of two different financial personality types: speculators or entrepreneurs (class S) and rentiers or savers (class R). While he offers no empirical evidence for this dichotomy, he speculates that class I residues (combination-instincts) predominate in class S personalities, while class II residues (group-persistences) predominate in class R personalities. His theory is thus one of heterogeneous agents interacting to produce the formal structure of society at the aggregate level.

While Pareto's theory (§1535, p. 982) posits interaction among heterogeneous agents to account for the circulation of the elites, Prechter's theory posits agents that are homogeneous relative to their possessing unconscious herding impulses, aggregations of which generate social mood. While Prechter's theory allows for (mostly quantitative) heterogeneity among agents with respect to secondary factors—e.g., levels of risk-aversion, short vs. long time-frames for decision-making, analytical approaches, degree of desire to conform, etc.—the theory's reliance on the homogeneity of agents with respect to its fundamentally causal aspect is rare among major theories of herding (see Parker and Prechter, 2005 [Chapter 34; see also Chapter 12]).

Thus there is a different emphasis in Pareto's theory as compared to Prechter's. The former accentuates differences between people and classes of people in society, while the latter accentuates an essential similarity among people with respect to herding impulses and therefore with respect to participating in social mood trends. Under socionomics, herding and mood-sharing motivate social actions of people of all social classes and all personality types, even if they differ from one another to some extent on less crucial quantitative dimensions. Prechter sees these supposedly separate types and classes not as divided groups but as poles of continua, a different perspective that accounts for much of the disagreement between socionomic theory and theories that invoke causal dynamics among heterogeneous groups.

Pareto claims (§2235, p. 1563),

> The two groups [class S and class R] perform functions of differing utility in society. The S group is primarily responsible for change, for economic and social progress. The R group, instead, is a powerful element in stability, and in many cases counteracts the dangers attending the adventurous capers of the S's. A society in which R's almost exclusively predominate remains stationary and, as it were, crystallized. A society in which S's predominate lacks stability, lives in a state of shaky equilibrium that may be upset by a slight accident from within or from without.

With respect to this formulation, Prechter's theory of homogeneous agents would seem to lend itself to more useful predictions about social trends and social change than Pareto's. Why? If the primary source of change vs. stability in a society were extremely stable (and heritable) factors such as personality traits, as Pareto has it, one would expect to see a very different world history, with more rigid differences between social behavior in one country vs. another than one in fact observes. Some countries, with a predominance of class S personality types, would lack stability almost all the time, while other countries, with a predominance of class R personality types, would be stable to the point of stagnation as the decades rolled by. This is not the record that history exhibits. While there certainly are significant differences in various countries' "national character," the path of history in every country shows periods of growth and development alternating with periods of stability, stagnation or deterioration. The reader is challenged to think of a single country that could serve as a counter-example over large-degree time spans. This historical record is more supportive of socionomic theory, in which—as the psychologist Harry Stack Sullivan once said in a related debate about the importance of different personality types—"People are more simply human than otherwise."

The Role of Equilibrium

Pareto's theory includes a key role for equilibrium. His thoroughly mechanistic version of equilibrium theory posits society as a type of homeostatic mechanism that seeks stability. His diverse statements about equilibrium include (1) allusions to different types of equilibria, (2) a "social equilibrium theory" that is based on "mutual interdependencies" among four sets of factors (residues, derivations, economic interests, and social heterogeneity and circulation) and (3) efforts to model all of these ideas after the equilibrium of physical processes in classical mechanics.

Pareto's concept of "social equilibrium" (§§1208-1212, pp. 727-729) is both complex and vaguely expressed. It is such a general concept—which he applies to many different dimensions and types of social phenomena—that one may question whether he is describing a unitary phenomenon. As a subtype of class V residues in his theory, Pareto posits "sentiments of resistance to alterations in the social equilibrium." Here is his vague definition:

> If an existing state of social equilibrium is altered, forces tending to re-establish it come into play—that, no more, no less, is what equilibrium means (§§2068 f.). Such forces are, in chief, sentiments that find their expression in residues of the variety we are here examining. On the passive side, they make us aware of the alteration in the equilibrium. On the active side, they prompt us to remove, repel, counteract, the causes of the alteration, and so develop into sentiments of the [vengeance] variety…. (§§1312 f.)

Prechter's theory, in contrast, clearly disavows the ideas of equilibrium and mean-reversion in social systems (Prechter and Parker, 2004 [Chapter 15; see also Chapter 12]). Under socionomic theory, there is only the ceaseless dynamism of social-mood waves regulating changes in aggregate sentiments and social actions.

Hierarchical Progress vs. Static Cycles

Both theories propose an endlessly fluctuating, wave-like form at the aggregate level, but Prechter sees aspects of society's progress and regress as conforming to a hierarchical fractal, whereas Pareto sees the process as cyclical. Thus, Pareto's theory has implications that are much more pessimistic than the implications one may draw from Prechter's theory. Pareto is very dubious that the pattern of history and evolution allow one to expect human social progress in any meaningful sense. Prechter's theory is ultimately positive about certain aspects of social progress. Although his model includes continual detours of recession and regression, there is net progress, for example, in the extent of knowledge of nature and how to exploit it, which expands the scale of human flourishing and achieving. WP's conformity to quantitatively elastic patterns of five waves upward followed by three waves downward is a "dance of progress": three steps forward, two steps back. In accommodating long-range social progress, Prechter's theory does not rely upon a vague feeling of optimism but on logical consistency uniting empirics and theoretical modeling.

Elliott insightfully observed that the fractal pattern he described for the stock market and other human activities is scale-invariant. As incorporated into socionomic theory, the same essential pattern describes the progress and regress of human society whether the time-frame under examination is years, decades, centuries or millennia. Since large-degree waves in this fractal pattern include corrective waves that may last hundreds of years, socionomic theory accounts for the occasional appearance of a dark age, but it always yields to another golden age thereafter.

Advantages of Socionomics

Socionomic theory offers heterodox economics and sociology a significant improvement over Pareto's sociology:

(1) Socionomics' model of social-mood-regulated herding among homogeneous agents explains many aspects of human social behavior that Pareto sought to understand (such as governmental regime changes) without invoking static ideas about class differences or personality differences among the people in a society. Socionomics can thus offer an explanation for some areas of social behavior that is more convincing than Pareto's theory, which relies at times either on a questionable dynamic interaction between the truth-value and the utility-value of ideas or on immutable class differences in societies.

(2) Socionomics offers a coherent contextualist theory of individual agency, rooted in neurophysiology in a logically consistent manner. Pareto's theory contains hints of a voluntaristic theory of agency but has internal contradictions due to a reliance on mechanistic assumptions about the nature of human beings.

(3) Socionomics offers an evolutionary theory incorporating aspects of instinct psychology in a manner that resolves conflicts in dichotomies that have previously represented great theoretical difficulty

to social theorists: the nature/nurture dichotomy and the structure/ agency dichotomy. Pareto's attempt to deal with these issues is less successful. His allegiance to a mechanistic metatheory predisposes him to treat structure in society reductionistically, as an epiphenomenon, rather than to integrate the dynamics of agency and structure; and this same allegiance predisposes him to struggle unsuccessfully to integrate an ad hoc list of instincts (nature) with a mechanistic view of constraining forces in society (nurture). While his concept of "mutual interdependencies" among various causal factors does prefigure more sophisticated versions of later systems theory, his model of causality is not fully developed. In contrast, socionomics' contextualism at the individual level and organicism at the social level integrates the challenging nature/ nurture and agency/structure dichotomies in a manner that not only produces theoretical consistency but also has a solid foundation in empirics. Evidence from financial, sociological and economic data support socionomics' claims about the structure of social mood and resulting social actions, and evidence from neurophysiological studies support its conceptualization of individual agency as related to unconscious mood.

(4)   The repetitive, self-affine, fractal form of the Wave Principle enhances the utility of socionomic theory at the aggregate level. Certain social trend changes are thereby probabilistically predictable under socionomic theory, whereas Pareto's theory offers no way to predict such trend changes.

Future Prospects for the Two Theories

Noelle-Neumann (1993, p. 116 [quoted in Chapter 15]) noted that for two centuries the view that social man is primarily rational has clashed with the view that social man is primarily instinctual. Instinct-related theories were popular at the time Pareto wrote. A prominent example is Trotter's *Instincts of the Herd in Peace and War* (1916). Other examples include the work of William James, William McDougall and C. Lloyd Morgan (see Asso and Fiorito, 2002, for an overview). In later decades, instinct psychology fell into disrepute as it was displaced by behaviorism in psychology and rational choice theory in economics and political science. With the rise of behaviorism in the 1930s, instinct theory became much less popular, first within psychology and then within institutionalism and economics as a whole (see Hodgson, 1998). The same trends that led popular opinion away from the influence of institutionalism in general after the 1930s most likely contributed to the neglect of Pareto's instinct-based theory as well. The current renaissance of instinct theory in the social sciences represents a significant trend change.

Fundamental views about instinct and rationality have cycled in and out of favor (Parker, 2006 [Chapter 37]), contributing to reasons why Pareto's sociology has been given such scant attention in the past half-century, during which time exclusively reason-based social theories have dominated the discussion. In the evolution of social theory, however, the pendulum of history is beginning to swing back in the other direction, toward theories incorporating instinctive behavior and less than fully rational decision-making.

The endogenous-cause model of socionomics charts a non-traditional course in the social sciences to which it applies. Its theory of finance is especially at odds with models of financial and macroeconomic behavior that share the prevailing neoclassical economic assumption of mechanistic causality and exogenous shocks. Neoclassical economic theory is useful as it relates to individuals' purely economic behavior [see Chapter 12], but finance and macroeconomics do not offer proper contexts for its application.

Looking back over the past century and looking forward to the future, how will history evaluate the two heterodox theories of Pareto and Prechter? Though Pareto's sociological theory has some heuristic usefulness, many of his specific hypotheses have not stood up well over time. For instance, Pareto sees two main factors determining the oscillations in a society's prosperity: the proportion of class I vs. class II residues in its governing elite, and variations in class-circulation in that society (§2417, pp. 1742-1743). Unfortunately, little evidence has accumulated in the century since he published these ideas to support their validity. His theory has inspired few followers to gather empirical evidence along these lines, both because his theoretical system is overly complex and hard to understand, even for willing students, and because there are significant measurement problems involved in detecting the relative predominance of "class I vs. class II residues" in a society. Though Pareto himself attempted to illustrate his theories with numerous lengthy anecdotal narratives from history, they have not inspired much useful research or prediction, despite having been available for nearly a century, whereas socionomic theory has already provided a basis for useful explanations and predictions of behavior in the realms of finance, economic trends, history, politics, culture, social health and other areas.

Some of the text of this essay has been rearranged and lightly edited for clarity.—Ed.

REFERENCES

Abell, Peter. (2000). Sociological theory and rational choice theory. In Bryan S. Turner, Ed., *The Blackwell Companion to Social Theory*, 2nd ed. Oxford: Blackwell, pp. 223-244.

Asso, Pier Francesco, and Luca Fiorito. (Dec. 2002). Human nature and economic institutions: Instinct psychology, behaviorism and the development of American institutionalism. Working paper #373, Universita degli Studi di Siena: Quaderni del Dipartimento di Economia Politica.

Barkow, Jerome H., Leda Cosmides, and John Tooby. (1992). *The Adapted Mind: Evolutionary Psychology and the Generation of Culture*. New York: Oxford University Press.

Buss, David M. (2003). *Evolutionary Psychology: The New Science of the Mind*, 2nd ed. Boston: Allyn & Bacon.

Cordes, Christian. (March 2005). Veblen's "Instinct of workmanship," its cognitive foundations, and some implications for economic theory. *Journal of Economic Issues*, *39*(1), pp. 1-20.

Elliott, R.N., The Wave Principle (1938) and *Nature's Law* (1946), reprinted in Prechter (Ed.), *R.N. Elliott's Masterworks* (1993), New Classics Library.

Freud, Sigmund. (1900/1996). *The Interpretation of Dreams*, trans. A.A. Brill. New York: Gramercy Books, 1996.

Frost, Alfred John, and Robert R. Prechter (1978/2005). *Elliott Wave Principle— Key to Market Behavior*. Gainesville, GA: New Classics Library.

Giddens, Anthony. (1979). *Central Problems in Social Theory: Action, Structure and Contradiction in Social Analysis*. Berkeley: University of California Press.

Graham, John R. (Feb. 1999), Herding among investment newsletters: Theory and evidence, *Journal of Finance*, 54(1), 237-268.

Hodgson, Geoffrey M. (Mar. 1998). The approach of institutional economics. *Journal of Economic Literature*, 36, 166-192.

Hodgson, Geoffrey M. (2004). Reclaiming habit for institutional economics. *Journal of Economic Psychology*, 25, 651-660.

Kahneman, Daniel. (Dec. 2003). Maps of bounded rationality: Psychology for behavioral economics. *American Economic Review*, 93(5), 1449-1475.

Keynes, John M. (1997). *The General Theory of Employment, Interest Rates, and Money*. New York: Prometheus Books. (Original work published in 1936.)

Lo, Andrew W., and A. Craig MacKinlay. (1999). *A Non-Random Walk Down Wall Street*. Princeton, New Jersey: Princeton University Press.

Maturana, Humberto R., and Francisco J. Varela. (1992). *The Tree of Knowledge: The Biological Roots of Human Understanding*. Boston: Shambhala.

Mirowski, Philip. (1989). *More Heat than Light: Economics as Social Physics,*

Physics as Nature's Economics. Cambridge: Cambridge University Press.

Mirowski, Philip. (Oct. 1990). From Mandelbrot to chaos in economic theory. *Southern Economic Journal*, 57, pp. 289-307.

Noelle-Neumann, Elisabeth. (1993). *The Spiral of Silence: Public Opinion— Our Social Skin*, 2nd ed. Chicago: University of Chicago Press.

Olsen, R. (July/Aug. 1996). Implications of herding behavior.... *Financial Analysts Journal*, 52(4), 37-41.

Pareto, Vilfredo. (1935). Arthur Livingston (Ed.), *Trattato di Sociologia generale* [The Mind and Society] (Andrew Bongiorno & Arthur Livingston, trans.), Vols. I-IV. New York: Harcourt, Brace and Company. (Original work published 1916.)

Parker, Wayne D. (2006). Methodological individualism vs. methodological holism: neoclassicism, institutionalism and socionomic theory. Paper presented at the joint annual congress of the International Association for Research in Economic Psychology (IAREP) and the Society for the Advancement of Behavioral Economics (SABE), Paris, France, July 5-8, 2006.

Parker, Wayne D., and Robert R. Prechter (2005). Herding: an interdisciplinary integrative review from a socionomic perspective. In Kokinov, Boicho, Ed., *Advances in Cognitive Economics: Proceedings of the International Conference on Cognitive Economics, Sofia, August 5-8, 2005*. Sofia, Bulgaria: NBU Press (New Bulgarian University), pp. 271-280. Also available online at http://papers.ssrn.com.

Parsons, Talcott. (1937). *The Structure of Social Action: A Study in Social Theory with Special Reference to a Group of Recent European Writers*, vol. I. New York: The Free Press.

Pepper, Stephen C. (1942). *World Hypotheses: A Study in Evidence*. Berkeley, California: University of California Press.

Pinker, Steven. (1994). *The Language Instinct: How the Mind Creates Language*. New York: HarperCollins Publishers.

Prechter, Robert R. (1979). What's going on? *The Elliott Wave Theorist*, August 3, 1979. Reprinted in Prechter (2003), p. 1.

Prechter, Robert R. (1999a). *The Wave Principle of Human Social Behavior and the New Science of Socionomics*. Gainesville, GA: New Classics Library.

Prechter, Robert R. (1999b). A socionomic view of demographic trends, or stocks & sex. *The Elliott Wave Theorist*, (Sept. 1999). Reprinted in Robert R. Prechter, Ed., *Pioneering Studies in Socionomics*. Gainesville, GA: New Classics Library, 2003, pp. 66-75.

Prechter, Robert R. (2001). Unconscious herding behavior as the psychological basis of financial market trends and patterns, *Journal of Psychology and Financial Markets* [now *Journal of Behavioral Finance*], 2(3), 120-125. Available at http://www.socionomics.org/pdf/Unconscious_Herding.pdf, 2001.

Prechter, Robert R., Ed. (2003). *Pioneering Studies in Socionomics*. Gainesville, GA: New Classics Library.

Prechter, Robert R., Deepak Goel, and Wayne D. Parker. (2002-2006). We know how you'll vote next November: social mood, financial markets and presidential election outcomes. Working paper, Socionomics Foundation, Gainesville, Georgia.

Prechter, Robert R., and Wayne D. Parker (2004). The financial/economic dichotomy. In Heping Pan, Didier Sornette, and Kenneth Kortanek, Eds., *Intelligent Finance—A Convergence of Mathematical Finance with Technical and Fundamental Analysis*. Melbourne, Australia: International Workshop on Intelligent Finance (University of Ballarat). Also available at http://www.socionomics.org/pdf/fin_econ_melbourne_us_REV.pdf, 2004.

Prechter, Robert R., and Wayne D. Parker (2006). The financial/economic dichotomy in social behavioral dynamics: The socionomic perspective. *Journal of Behavioral Finance*. http://papers.ssrn.com.

Rutherford, Malcolm. (1998). Veblen's evolutionary programme: a promise unfulfilled. *Cambridge Journal of Economics*, 22, 463-477.

Scharfstein, David S., and Jeremy C. Stein. (June 1990). Herd behavior and investment, *American Economic Review*, 80(3), 465-479.

Schumpeter, Joseph A. (1954). *History of Economic Analysis*. New York: Oxford University Press.

Shiller, Robert J., Stanley Fischer, and Benjamin M. Friedman (1984). Stock prices and social dynamics, *Brookings Papers on Economic Activity*, 1984(2), 457-510.

Shiller, Robert J. (Spring 1990). Speculative prices and popular models, *Journal of Economic Perspectives*, 4(2), 55-65.

Shiller, Robert J. (2000). *Irrational Exuberance*. Princeton, New Jersey: Princeton University Press.

Shiller, Robert J. (May 2001). Bubbles, human judgment, and expert opinion, Cowles Foundation Discussion Paper No. 1303, http://papers.ssrn.com.

Sias, Richard W. (Spring 2004). Institutional herding, *The Review of Financial Studies*, 17(1), 165-206.

Sloman, Steven A. (Jan. 1996). The empirical case for two systems of reasoning. *Psychological Bulletin*, 119(1), pp. 3-22.

Trotter, William. (1916). *Instincts of the Herd in Peace and War*. London: T. Fisher Unwin Ltd.

Trueman, Brett. (Spring 1994). Analyst forecasts and herding behavior, *The Review of Financial Studies*, 7(1), 97-124.

Veblen, Thorstein. (1914). *The Instinct of Workmanship and the State of the Industrial Arts*. New Brunswick, N.J.: Transaction Publishers, 1990 [originally published in 1914 by Macmillan Company].

Welch, Ivo. (2000). Herding among security analysts, *Journal of Financial Economics*, 58(3), 369-396.

Chapter 37

Excerpted and edited from *Congress of the International Association for Research in Economic Psychology and the Society for the Advancement of Behavioral Economics,* Paris, France
July 2006

Methodological Individualism vs. Methodological Holism and Their Resolution in Socionomic Theory

Wayne D. Parker

Historically, there has been tension between methodological individualism (MI) and methodological holism (MH) in economic theories. Rather than a steady accretion of progress toward more complete social knowledge, one sees an oscillation between the popularity of MI and MH. The new paradigm of socionomics offers a more complete theoretical synthesis of MI and MH than earlier constructs by nesting individual cognitive and affective processes within aggregate patterns of human social behavior.

Introduction

Almost all economic theories may be categorized according to whether methodological individualism (MI) or methodological collectivism or holism (MH) predominates. The MI/MH distinction has often been improperly confused or conflated with other theoretical polarities. Here I employ the admirably clear definitions for MI and MH given by Samuels (1972, p. 249):

By methodological individualism I mean the view which holds that meaningful social science knowledge is best or more appropriately derived through the study of individuals; and by methodological collectivism I mean the view which holds that meaningful social science knowledge is best or more appropriately derived through the study of group organizations, forces, processes and/or problems.

Though many economic theories manifest a blend of MI and MH, one or the other has almost always been predominant.

OVERVIEW OF HISTORY OF MI AND MH IN ECONOMIC THEORY

Early Modern Period

Mercantilists

The mercantilists, as described by Heckscher (as quoted by Keynes, 1936/1997, ch. 23) and as exemplified by such luminaries as the French minister of finance from 1665 to 1683, Jean-Baptiste Colbert, dominated economic thought during the early modern period for economics, roughly 1500-1776. As nation-states took form during this time, writers saw life as an economic struggle for survival in which money was viewed as a scarcity to be fought over in the course of international trade, an idea that led to self-defeating excesses of protectionism. Primitive as this thinking was, mercantilist theories were clearly MH, since their top-down theories addressed the competitive roles of nations rather than details of transactions among individuals.

Physiocrats

The timing of the physiocrats' publications, roughly 1756-1780, over-laps the period of Adam Smith's work. Unlike the mercantilists, whose ideas they rejected, these MI theorists examined the details of economic relations between individuals in society with different socioeconomic positions and roles. François Quesnay, the French surgeon and economist, created his famous *Tableau Economique*, published in 1758, to analyze the economic transactions of heterogeneous individuals. Smith (1776/1994) quoted Mirabeau saying that, along with writing and money, the *Tableau* was one of the three great inventions contributing most to social stability.

Modern Period

Classical Economists

Adam Smith (1776/1994) initiated the modern, classical period of economic thought with *The Wealth of Nations*. MI clearly characterizes most of his work, given its focus on the division of labor, although the MH of his famous "invisible hand" is briefly evident.

Original Institutionalists

"Institutionalists" (see Endnote 3 of Chapter 33) within the field of economics proposed that the top-down influence of institutional structures were causal to individuals' behavior. The "old," or original, institutionalist economists (OIEs) proposed their theories both as an attempt to solve the social and economic problems of their times and as a reaction against previous economic theories. OIE theorists were eager to emphasize their innovative MH ideas, though many of them tried to include both MI and MH concepts.

According to Boettke (2005, p. 148), Thorstein Veblen was one of first major critics of the MI emphasis on the concept of utility maximization, the related hedonistic theory of motivation, and the mechanistic "reactive organism" model of human action. He wrote,

> The hedonistic conception of man is that of a lightening calculator of pleasures and pains who oscillates like a homogeneous globule of desire and happiness under the impulse of stimuli that shift him about the area.... He is an isolated...human datum, in stable equilibrium except for the buffets of the impinging forces that displace him in one direction or another.... [The] hedonistic man is not a prime mover. He is not the seat of a process of living except that he is subject to... circumstances external and alien to him.

As Boettke further noted, from 1900 to 1935 the OIEs challenged the MI approach of the marginalists, and Keynes and his followers from the 1940s to the 1970s challenged some MI aspects of neoclassicism. Otherwise, however, the MI emphasis of neoclassical theory dominated economics for most of the twentieth century.

Mutual misunderstandings between the OIEs and their critics were inevitable, because both camps held prior commitments to worldviews that were incommensurable with each other. Most of the MI theorists bore allegiance (if only implicitly) to a mechanistic worldview in which the goals of science were implicitly assumed to be the *prediction* and *control* of human behavior, whereas most of the MH theorists among the OIEs were committed to nonmechanistic worldviews, either contextualism or organicism (Pepper, 1942), in which the goal of the social sciences was more related to the *description* and *understanding* of human behavior.

Neoclassicists

Hodgson (1998, p. 169) gave a useful definition of neoclassical theory:

Neoclassical economics...may be conveniently defined as an approach which (1) assumes rational, maximizing behavior by agents with given and stable preference functions, (2) focuses on attained, or movements toward, equilibrium states, and (3) excludes chronic information problems (such as uncertainty of the type explored by Frank Knight and John Maynard Keynes).

An MI approach is built into this definition due to its focus on utility maximizing by individual agents. The neoclassicists have been aggressive in claiming that the MI approach is the essence of science. One MI advocate, Jon Elster (quoted in Hodgson, 1997, p. 402), asserted,

The basic building block in the social sciences, the elementary unit of explanation, is the individual action guided by some intention.... Generally speaking, the scientific practice is to seek an explanation at a lower level than the explanandum.... The search for micro-foundations, to use a fashionable term from recent controversies in economics, is in reality a pervasive and omnipresent feature of science.

A commitment to MI has essentially been enforced in the economics profession. As James Tobin (quoted in Hodgson, 1997, p. 402) explained,

This [microfoundations] counter-revolution has swept the profession until now. It is scarcely an exaggeration to say that no paper that does not employ the "microfoundations" methodology can get published in a major professional journal, that no research proposal that is suspect of violating its precepts can survive peer review, that no newly minted PhD who can show his hypothesized behavioral relations are properly derived can get a good academic job.

Neither linear nor nonlinear versions of mechanistic financial modeling have succeeded in allowing practical prediction of financial, economic or social trends and events. This failure has prompted many economists to believe, as if by default, in the "random walk" model of price change in financial markets. This stance serves only as an admission of defeat in offering neither prediction nor explanation.

Burns (1931), arguing for the usefulness of institutionalism's MH approach over neoclassicism's MI approach, pointed out that even within its own theoretical domain, neoclassicism's assumptions about equilibrium sometimes produced unsuccessful predictions. Burns mused about why such failures did not lead neoclassicists to incorporate institutionalism as a useful set of complementary principles and concluded, "It may in part be due to psychological antipathy to embarking upon investigations likely to involve an important modification, if not abandonment, of the existing integrating structure and a dislike of the inevitable period of uncertainty during which the higher synthesis is in process of emergence" (pp. 84-85). As Kuhn (1970) pointed out, even clear falsification of a theory does not always cause its proponents to abandon it. This ubiquitous finding in the history of science suggests that socionomics is correct in postulating (see Chapter 40) that commitment to a particular view of causality or scientific methodology, such as MI or MH, is often more affectively inspired than rationally inspired.

A History of Oscillation

Now that we have a grounding in the difference between MI and MH, we may summarize the orientations of a few other schools of thought, as follows: the marginalists (MI), the monetarists (MI), the Austrians (MI), Keynes, Keynesians or New Keynesians (MI and MH, unsynthesized), the cycle theorists such as Kondratiev and Schumpeter (MH) and the New Classicals (MI).

This overview, though cursory, suggests that over the history of economic thought there has been not a steady accumulation of progress toward more a complete theory but rather an oscillation back and forth between MI and MH.

Attempts at Integration

Recent work by some of the new institutionalist economists (NIEs), expresses some awareness of the conflicts between MI and MH and has made an effort to blend these approaches. Hodgson (1998, pp. 180-181) pointed out that many of the OIEs made a serious attempt to integrate MI and MH:

> The thrust of the "old" institutionalist approach is to see behavioral habit and institutional structure as mutually entwined and mutually reinforcing: both aspects are relevant to the full picture.... A dual stress on both agency and structure is required, redolent of similar arguments in sociology and philosophy.... Both individuals and institutions are mutually constitutive of each other. Institutions mold, and are molded by, human action.

He added (p. 181) that this mutually causal relationship between agency (MI) and structure (MH) can be distorted by erring on either side. He charged that the NIEs err on the side of MI, since their approach "focuses primarily on the emergence of institutions out of the interactions of given individuals."

Due to incommensurability between the metatheoretical assumptions implicit in various aspects of the NIEs' theories, their attempts at synthesis to date have resulted in a confusing eclecticism rather than a genuinely coherent synthesis of prior analysis at the individual and aggregate levels. In the past, MI has been most closely related to the mechanistic worldview, whereas MH has been most closely related to either the organicist worldview via some type of structuralism in some institutionalists' writings, or to the contextualist worldview in the form of historicism in others. The categorical contradictions between the worldviews of mechanism and organicism/contextualism (Pepper, 1942) has caused the old ways of attempting to combine MI and MH to fail.

Socionomics Successfully Integrates MI and MH

Stark (1962, as reviewed by Martins, 1964) analyzed the history of MI and MH's connection to metatheory. He went back to Dilthey's discussion of three primary *Weltanschauung* in social theory and discussed their sociological relevance. Martins (pp. 77-78) summarized Stark's analysis:

> Not surprisingly, "mechanicism" (roughly, ontological or methodological individualism) and "organicism" (roughly, ontological and/or methodological collectivism) emerge as two of the basic thought-forms, logically prior to the third which can be seen as the sublation of the former. This third form...posits self and society as...aspects of the same thing, as ontologically equivalent: it is traced from Vico to Summer and Cooley.

By offering a process ontology under a combination of the contextualist and organicist worldviews, Prechter's socionomic theory has uniquely achieved this "third form" by successfully integrating MI and MH. Socionomics resolves the longstanding problem of synthesis, because it avoids the eclectic contradictions that result from attempts to combine mechanistic approaches to MI with organicist approaches to MH. Instead, socionomics non-mechanistically integrates a theory of unconscious mood at the MI level (via a contextualist theory) with a quantified structuralism at the MH level (a type of organicism).

Socionomic theory thus not only resolves the MI/MH conflict that has plagued the history of economic thought but also resolves the conflict between the goal of contextualist or organicist institutionalism (to understand) and the goal of mechanistic neoclassicism (to predict) by addressing both goals. Socionomics' singular synthesis allows one to understand numerous aspects of social and financial behavior at both the individual and aggregate levels, and WP's hierarchical-fractal structure makes probabilistic prediction possible for certain domains of human social behavior at the aggregate level.

Socionomics' integration of contextualism with organicism and its resulting integration of MI and MH without reliance on mechanistic assumptions is original. The socionomic theory of finance bases its MI component on a neurophysiological foundation and its MH component on an aggregate fractal pattern, linking them with theories of herding and mood-sharing under which individuals both contribute to and participate in the aggregate pattern. Socionomic theory is therefore irreducibly holistic in the way it depicts the relationship between MI and MH. The integration of MI and MH in socionomic theory involves a bi-level description of a single process that involves simultaneous, mutually causal relations between both the individual and the aggregate levels of activity. Socionomics thereby succeeds in moving social science away from theories based on analogies to 19th-century mechanics to achieve a synthesis of formerly antagonistic theoretical orientations toward the individual or the group, replacing them with a simultaneous orientation toward both.

Author's Note:

I am grateful for Robert Prechter's extensive edits of an earlier draft. For many of the ideas in this paper I also owe much to Hodgson (1997, 1998, 2004) and Findlay and O'Rourke (2001).

SOURCES AND REFERENCES

Boettke, Peter J., and Christopher J. Coyne. (2005). Methodological individualism, spontaneous order and the research program of the Workshop in Political Theory and Political Analysis. *Journal of Economic Behavior & Organization, 57,* 145-158.

Burns, E. M. (Mar. 1931). Does institutionalism complement or compete with "orthodox economics"? *American Economic Review,* 21 (1), 80-87.

DeQuech, David. (June 2002). The demarcation between the "old" and the "new" institutional economics: recent complications. *Journal of Economic Issues, 36* (2), 565-572.

Findlay, Ronald, and Kevin H. O'Rourke. (Nov. 2001). Commodity market integration, 1500-2000. Working Paper 8579, National Bureau of Economic Research, http://www.nber.org.

Giddens, Anthony. (1979). *Central Problems in Social Theory: Action, Structure and Contradiction in Social Analysis.* Berkeley: University of California Press.

Hodgson, Geoffrey M. (1997). Economics and the return to Mecca: the recognition of novelty and emergence. *Structural Change and Economic Dynamics, 8,* 399-412.

Hodgson, Geoffrey M. (Mar. 1998). The approach of institutional economics. *Journal of Economic Literature, 36,* 166-192.

Hodgson, Geoffrey M. (2004). Reclaiming habit for institutional economics. *Journal of Economic Psychology, 25,* 651-660.

Keynes, John M. (1997). *The General Theory of Employment, Interest Rates, and Money.* New York: Prometheus Books. (Original work published in 1936.)

Kuhn, T. S. (1970). *The Structure of Scientific Revolutions,* 2nd ed. Chicago: University of Chicago Press.

Martins, H. G. (Mar. 1964). The fundamental forms of social thought. *British Journal of Sociology,* 15 (1), 77-78.

Maturana, Humberto R., and Francisco J. Varela. (1992). *The Tree of Knowledge: The Biological Roots of Human Understanding,* rev. ed. New York: Shambhala.

Pareto, Vilfredo. (1935). Arthur Livingston (Ed.), *Trattato di Sociologia generale* [The Mind and Society] (Andrew Bongiorno & Arthur Livingston, trans.), Vols. I-IV. New York: Harcourt, Brace and Company. (Original work published 1916.)

Parker, Wayne D., and Robert R. Prechter (2005). Herding: An Interdisciplinary Integrative Review from a Socionomic Perspective. In Boicho Kokinov, Ed., *Advances in Cognitive Economics: Proceedings of the International*

Conference on Cognitive Economics, Sofia, August 5-8, 2005. Sofia, Bulgaria: NBU Press (New Bulgarian University), pp. 271-280. Also available online at http://papers.ssrn.com.

Parker, Wayne D., and Robert R. Prechter (2006). The socionomic theory of finance and the institution of social mood: Pareto and the sociology of instinct and rationalization. Paper presented at the meeting of the Association for Heterodox Economics, London, England, July 14-16, 2006.

Pepper, Stephen C. (1942). *World Hypotheses: A Study in Evidence.* Berkeley, California: University of California Press.

Prechter, Robert R. (1999). *The Wave Principle of Human Social Behavior and the New Science of Socionomics.* Gainesville, GA: New Classics Library.

Prechter, Robert R. (2001). Unconscious herding behavior as the psychological basis of financial market trends and patterns. *Journal of Psychology and Financial Markets* [now *Journal of Behavioral Finance*], 2(3), 120-125. Also available online at http://www.socionomics.org.

Prechter, Robert R., Ed. (2003). *Pioneering Studies in Socionomics.* Gainesville, GA: New Classics Library.

Prechter, Robert R., and Parker, Wayne D. (2004). The financial/economic dichotomy. In Heping Pan, Didier Sornette & Kenneth Kortanek (Eds.), *Intelligent Finance—A Convergence of Mathematical Finance with Technical and Fundamental Analysis.* Melbourne, Australia: International Workshop on Intelligent Finance (University of Ballarat). Also available online at http://www.socionomics.org.

Prechter, Robert R., and Parker, Wayne D. (2005). The financial/economic dichotomy in social behavioral dynamics: The socionomic perspective. *Journal of Behavioral Finance.* http://papers/ssrn.com.

Samuels, Warren J. (Aug. 1972). The scope of economics historically considered. *Land Economics, 48* (3), 248-268.

Shiller, Robert J., Stanley Fischer, and Benjamin M. Friedman. (1984). Stock prices and social dynamics. *Brookings Papers on Economic Activity, 1984*(2), 457-510.

Shiller, Robert J. (2000). *Irrational Exuberance.* Princeton, New Jersey: Princeton University Press.

Smith, Adam. (1994). *The Wealth of Nations* (Edwin Cannan, Ed.), New York: Modern Library (Random House). (Original work published 1776.)

Warsh, David. (2006). *Knowledge and the Wealth of Nations: A Story of Economic Discovery.* New York: W. W. Norton & Company.

Chapter 38

Socionomics Theorist
Wayne D. Parker, PhD, Dies at 61

Parker Played Key Role in Advancing
the Science of Socionomics

The Socionomist
November 2012

We are deeply saddened to report that Wayne D. Parker PhD (psychiatry), an esteemed colleague and friend who made important contributions to the field of socionomics, has died.

Dr. Parker served as director of the Socionomics Foundation from 2003 to 2009. He spoke at academic conferences around the world, co-authored landmark papers with Robert Prechter. His probing inquiries and dedication to consistency helped hone several key aspects of socionomic thought.

Dr. Parker co-authored three papers with Prechter:

- "Herding: An Interdisciplinary Integrative Review from a Socionomic Perspective" (2005), presented at the International Conference on Cognitive Economics, New Bulgarian University, Sofia, Bulgaria. Published in Boicho Kokinov, ed., *Advances in Cognitive Economics: Proceedings of the International Conference on Cognitive Economics*, Sofia, August 5-8, 2005. Sofia, Bulgaria: NBU Press, pp. 271-280 [Chapter 34 in this book];

- "The Financial/Economic Dichotomy in Social Behavioral Dynamics: The Socionomic Perspective" (2007), published in the *Journal of Behavioral Finance* [Chapter 15 in this book];

- "Social Mood, Stock Market Performance and U.S. Presidential Elections: A Socionomic Perspective on Voting Rights" (2012), with colleagues Deepak Goel and Matt Lampert, published in *SAGE Open* [republished in *Socionomic Causality in Politics*, 2017].

At the time of Dr. Parker's death, the presidential elections paper he co-authored with Prechter, Goel and Lampert had become the third most downloaded paper among the top 10,000 papers on SSRN.com, the website of the Social Science Research Network.

Dr. Parker also presented two conference papers:

- "The Socionomic Theory of Finance and the Institution of Social Mood: Pareto and the Sociology of Instinct and Rationalization" (2006), presented at the Conference of the Association for Heterodox Economics, London School of Economics, London, England [Chapter 36 in this book];

- "Methodological Individualism vs. Methodological Holism: Neoclassicism, Institutionalism and Socionomic Theory" (2006), presented at the Congress of the International Association for Research in Economic Psychology and the Society for the Advancement of Behavioral Economics, Paris, France. [excerpted in Chapter 37 of this book].

In 2006-2007, Parker contributed to a pilot study conducted by the American National Elections Survey (ANES), for which he composed survey questions designed to generate data on social mood. He also conducted a socionomically informed statistical analysis on ANES' previously employed questions.

Dr. Parker was born in 1951 in Montgomery, Alabama. He graduated magna cum laude from Yale University, where he was a member of the Whiffenpoofs, the world's oldest collegiate a cappella group. After receiving a PhD in Clinical Psychology from Temple University, he completed a postdoctoral fellowship in Child and Adolescent Psychology at the University of Texas Medical Branch in Galveston. He went on to receive training in neuropsychological testing at the University of Pennsylvania and was trained as a research analyst at the university's Wharton School. He later became an adjunct faculty member at the Emory University School of Medicine in the Department of Psychiatry and Behavioral Sciences.

As a marriage therapist for 35 years, Dr. Parker devoted a great deal of time to helping couples learn to love each other again. Since 1979, he was married to the love of his life, Miriam, with whom he raised three children.

Dr. Parker passed away November 26 after a two-year battle with carcinoid cancer. He will be greatly missed by those he loved and helped, and by those of us who knew him on a personal and professional basis. His dedication and service to the Socionomics Institute were an inspiration to those who served alongside him, and we are forever indebted to him for all he has done to advance the science of socionomics.

Part VIII:

AND FOR DESSERT...

Chapter 39

Brain Teaser:
Discounting Theory vs. Socionomic Theory

Robert R. Prechter

Take the time to go through this chapter step by step. The exercise may prove enlightening.

Suppose the economy were in a deep slump, and you lost your source of income. Fortunately, you get lucky and land a job as a lookout on an oil rig in the Gulf of Mexico. Your job is to observe approaching vessels and report any indication of hostile intent.

You share the post with another new recruit. Each of you works twelve hours on, twelve hours off, every day. On the night shift, floodlights illuminate the surrounding sea.

When you come to work one morning, your night-shift colleague has something fascinating to report. "Look through our telescope, and you'll see what appears to be a group of people out there, standing on the water!" You look through it, and sure enough, that's exactly what you see.

"Now look over there. See that barge?" Yes, you see it. "I've been watching that group of people and that barge all night. They both seem to be wandering over the ocean somewhat aimlessly. I can't make heads or tails of it."

You watch the two entities for a few minutes, but because they move so slowly you are unable to discern their paths of progress. You come up with a suggestion: "If you'll bring me some graph paper and a marker, I'll keep track of their movements all day. Then you can continue charting their movements during the night, and tomorrow morning we'll see what we have."

You spend the day, and your fellow lookout spends the night, plotting the movements of the two entities. The resulting graph is shown in Figure 1.

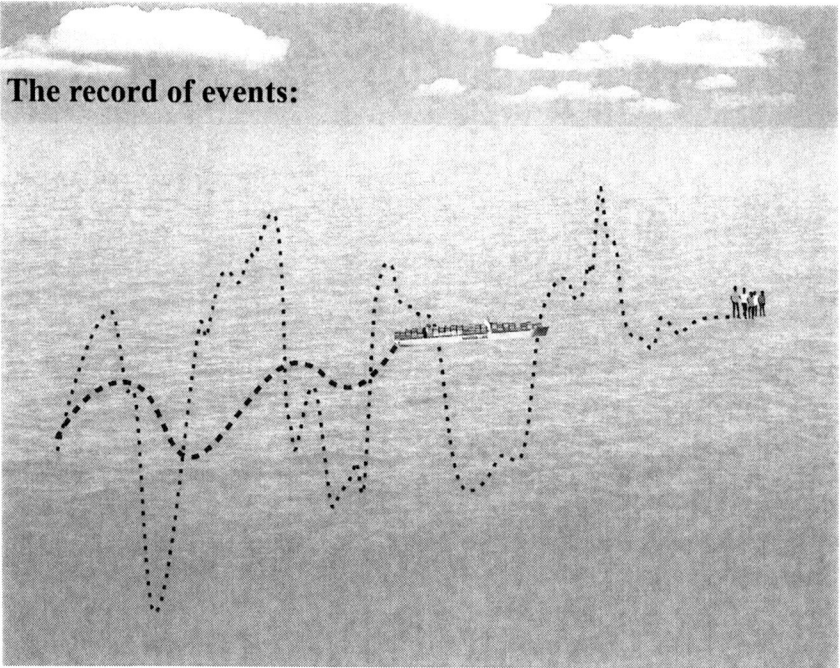

Figure 1

You and your friend study the graph. The barge, it seems, has slowly changed course only a few times over the 24-hour period, whereas the group of people changed course much more often, and its wanderings were more extreme. Nevertheless, over the past 24 hours, both entities ended up further toward the right.

"What do you think is going on?" you ask.

Your friend is ready with an answer. "I have been thinking about it all night, and here's my theory: The barge has an engine in it, and it's moving toward some destination. It's not moving in a straight line, though, so maybe the pilot is drunk or it's being steered by a computer on the fritz. But it seems to be charting its own course."

"OK," you say, "then what are the people doing?"

"From their actions, there is only one possibility: They're trying to anticipate the path of the barge. Sometimes they do it pretty well and sometimes not, but overall they get the general direction right."

You think for a moment and ask, "Your theory does seem to accommodate the facts. But there's one thing that bothers me: How could a group of people anticipate the general direction of a self-propelled barge?"

"All I can figure is that they're intuitive."

"You mean they're special people?"

"I don't think so. From what I can see through this telescope, they seem to be just everyday people. I figure the human population must have some ability to predict barge behavior, at least to a limited degree. The actions of these people prove it. The barge moves, and they move ahead of it, not perfectly but quite adequately. Their intuitive ability must be somewhat fuzzy."

Your friend takes out a marker and makes notes on the graph, as shown in Figure 2.

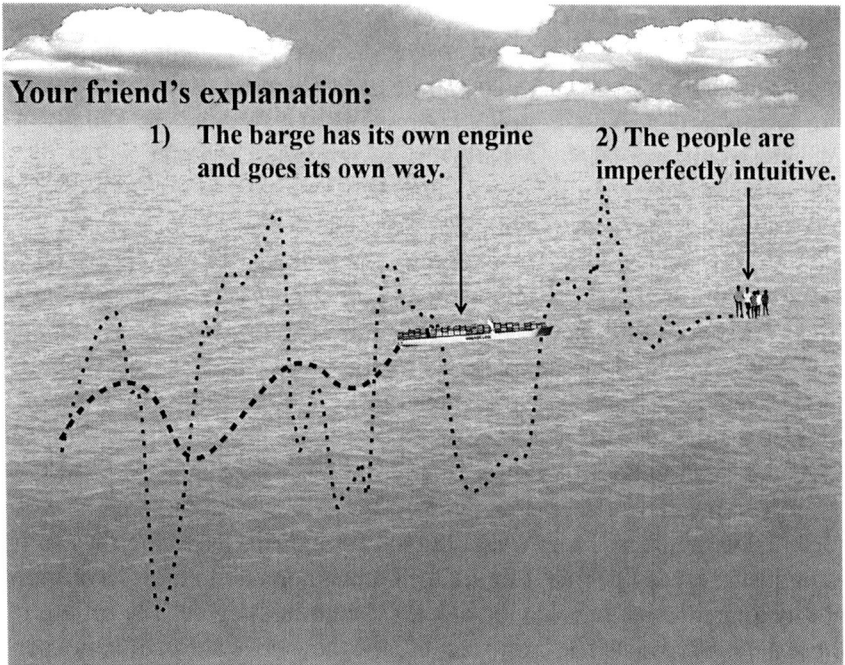

Figure 2

You study his depiction for a moment and say, "I have one last question. How are everyday people able to stand on water?"

"I don't know exactly," says your friend. "But it's quite magical."

You ruminate over your friend's theory. It seems to capture all the data. But does it properly *explain* it?

You don't have your own hypothesis yet, but you suspect his theory is wrong. Psychic powers are not on your list of likely causes for any observed phenomenon. Nor are magic abilities such as people standing on water. But how do you account for the striking events you see with your own eyes, without resorting to supernatural causes? Is there any way to explain it simply, directly, elegantly and magic-free?

You toss and turn for half the night. Finally an idea hits you. You fall into a contented sleep, looking forward to morning, when you can present an alternative hypothesis to your friend.

Do you have an explanation? Give it some thought. Don't continue reading until you've tried.

The next morning you bound up to the observation deck. Your friend is there, and he reports that the behavior of the two entities has stayed the same. "My theory still holds," he says. "The barge is still moving along, and the people are still standing on top of the water. All night long they have more or less successfully anticipated the barge's course. They wander a lot but always manage to figure out its general course ahead of time. When we get back to shore, I'm going to write a paper on this phenomenon and submit it to an academic journal. It's bound to be published."

"You might want to hold off on that idea," you say, "until you consider another explanation."

He looks annoyed. "What explanation?"

You pick up the marker and begin to draw on the graph. After thirty seconds, you're done. You step back and say nothing, because there is no need for words. Your depiction explains it all.

What have you drawn?

To see, turn the page and look at Figure 3.

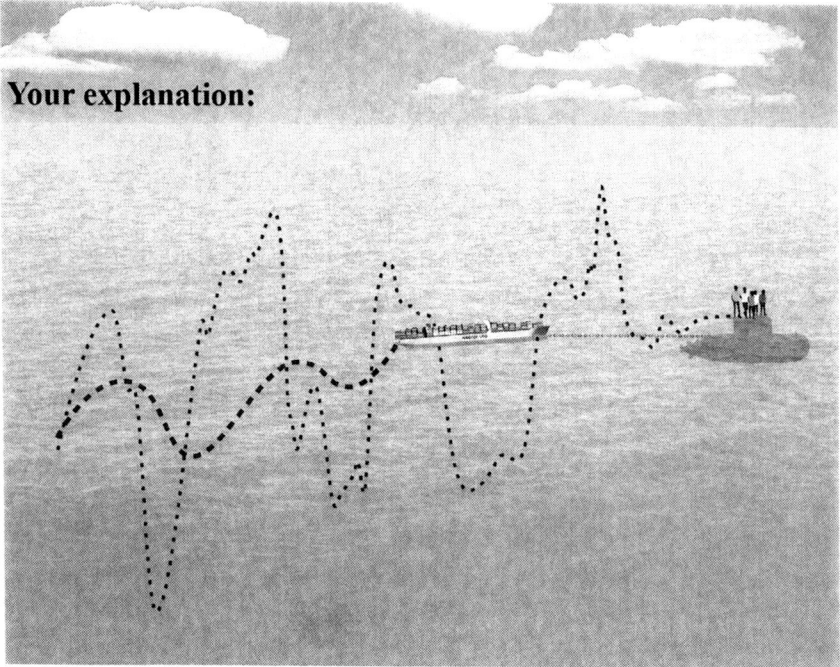

Figure 3

You summarize your hypothesis: "Forget psychic people. Forget walking on water. The existence of a submarine and a tow chain explains everything."

Your friend is silent, trying to take in your new hypothesis.

"See? The barge is just a barge. It has no engine. The submarine is the only powered vessel out there. The people aren't walking on water; they're standing on the deck of a sub. Where the sub goes, they go. The tow chain explains the difference in the paths of the two entities. The submarine shifts direction a lot, but the barge's turns are much slower and broader because of the long chain. I'll bet some simple math would provide the same result we are seeing out there on the water."

Your friend stays quiet, looking pensive.

"Well, what do you think?" you ask.

Exasperated, your friend protests, "But I can't see the submarine or the tow chain!"

"Well," you say, "neither can I, because they're under water. They constitute what scientists would call a hidden variable. We can't see it, but the observed data imply it and the limits of human thought and ability require it. It's there. We just can't observe it directly."

Your friend takes a deep breath and shakes his head. "I'm sticking with my theory. I figure the barge has an engine, so my theory is the only one that works."

"Wait. You say you don't believe the submarine exists because you can't see it. But you can't see the engine, either. So, why do you think *it* exists?"

"It makes more sense to me," he says, "to propose attributes of something I can see than something I can't see, and I can see the barge."

You pause for a while and finally ask, "You didn't start out as an oil-rig lookout. What was your profession before coming to work here?"

"Oh," he replies, "I'm an economist."

Suddenly all becomes clear. Your friend has simply transferred his causal ideas about stocks and the economy to your sea puzzle.

You draw Figure 4 for him. "This is what you believe, right?"

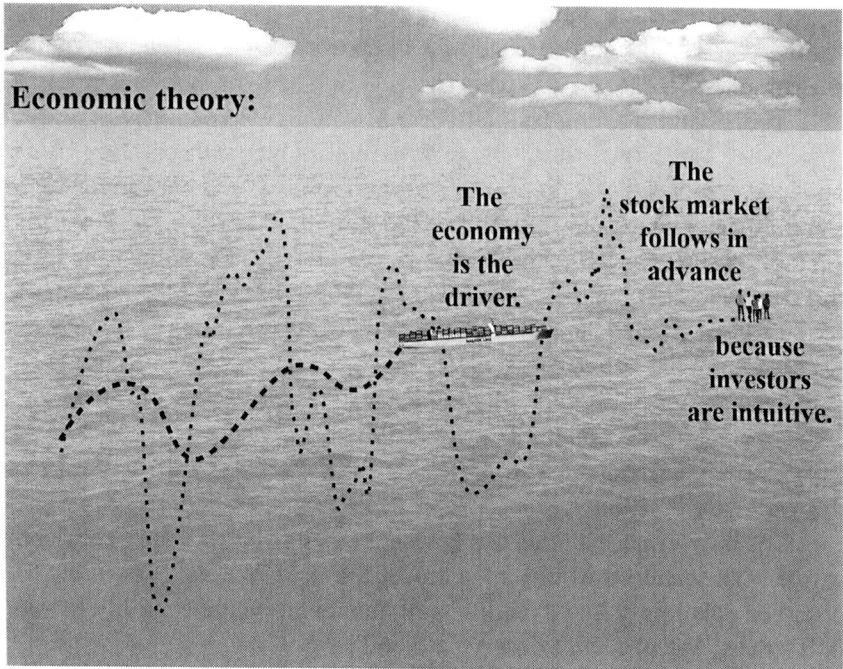

Figure 4

He confirms your suspicion: "Exactly! The economy drives itself. The stock market anticipates the path of the economy. It can do this trick because investors can see vaguely into the future, so they can discern fairly correctly where the economy will go. It's called *discounting*."

"I think," you reply, "that you should toss your whole explanation into the sea. No study shows that people can discern the future. On the contrary, they tend to be perfectly wrong about the future at every cusp of change. Even trained economists are notoriously unsuccessful at anticipating changes in the economy, so much so that their forecasts are typically six months to two years *behind* the economy, not ahead of it. If they can't predict the economy, why do you think everyday investors can do it?"

"Fine, but in your theory what is the driver, and how do you explain the fact that the economy follows the stock market?"

You begin writing on the graph the notes shown in Figure 5, talking as you go: "Simple. Social mood is a hidden driver, like the submarine. The economy is just a barge. Social mood takes stock investors for a ride, and the time delays involved in acting on mood-inspired business decisions pull the economy on a smoother path behind them."

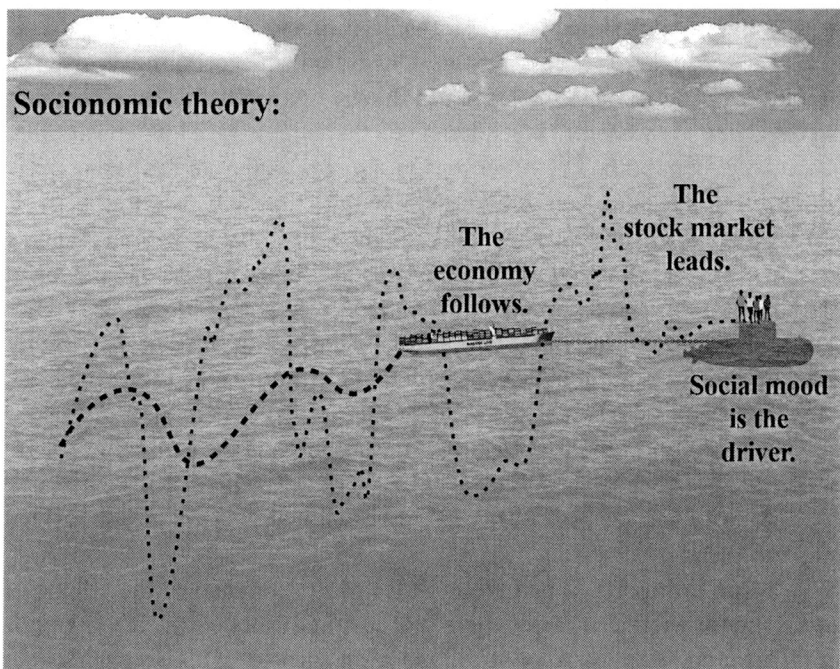

Figure 5

"I don't understand the time lag and the smoothing. Why doesn't the economy track social mood immediately as the stock market does?"

"People's decisions to buy and sell stocks can be carried out swiftly, so investors—like that group of people out there—express changes in the direction of social mood quite precisely. But business people's simultaneous decisions to expand or contract their businesses take time to effect. That time lag is like the tow chain, which transfers the volatile movements of the submarine into the smoother movements of the barge. Because of the varying time lags of actions based on individual business decisions, the shifts in social mood are likewise dampened into the lagging, less volatile movements of the economy."

"Why should someone choose your theory over discounting theory?"

"Under my explanation, there are no impossibilities such as psychic knowledge or people reacting to events that haven't happened yet. The causality is direct. The theory is simple, elegant and non-magical."

"So, how come nobody ever thought of this idea before?"

"I suppose there are two reasons. One is that when economists observe a relationship between variables A and B, they figure that one must be caus-ing the other. They haven't considered that there might be a hidden variable, C, causing them both. The other reason, I guess, is that my explanation is counter-intuitive. People's brains default to action and reaction when it comes to the stock market. They think the economy must be driving people's investment moods rather than the other way around. The bias is so powerful that they are more comfortable with a theory proposing mechanical reac-tion backwards in time than with a theory proposing direct causation by proaction forward in time, even though that is the only way time operates."

"But I can't *see* social mood."

"Well, I don't see intuitive investors anticipating the economic future, either."

"At last I can see both of my variables. One of yours is invisible. That puts me ahead on empirics."

"I don't think so. When we look for more evidence of the effects of social mood, we find it everywhere, not just in the economy. It's in trends in fashion, entertainment, politics, and even surprising places such as the frequency of nuclear-bomb testing and the timing of wars and epidemics. Social mood theory explains why all these trends broadly track each other."

"If these social-mood effects really are everywhere, how come other people don't recognize them as such?"

"For the same reason no one saw fractals until Mandelbrot pointed them out. After that, people began seeing them everywhere. My theory is just a new mental orientation. Once you cross that threshold, you'll never go back."

"I don't know. I'm not buying it. My theory has the benefit of longevity."

"That it does."

"Well, I'll think about it. So, you weren't always an oil-rig lookout. What was your profession?"

"Oh. I'm a socionomist."

Chapter 40

Using Socionomics To Predict Trends in the Popularity of Financial Theories

Robert R. Prechter

The Wave Principle of Human Social Behavior (1999) explained why socionomics offers a basis for predicting its own periods of popularity and unpopularity. We can use socionomics to forecast more broadly times of the relative acceptance or rejection of two basic types of financial theories: those based on rationality and human control, and those based on non-rationality and the lack of human control.

Waves of social mood regulate the popularity of these two types of financial theories. When the trend of social mood is toward the positive, causing the stock market to rise, academics and practitioners tend to espouse theories of exogenous cause and rational response, thereby justifying financial "engineering" and the like, and investors and observers embrace them. When the trend of social mood is toward the negative, causing the stock market to fall or go sideways, academics and practitioners lean more toward espousing theories of non-rational, endogenous cause, involving behavioral biases, herding, cycles, waves, etc., and investors and observers embrace them. Put succinctly: When the trend in social mood is positive, people tend to believe in theories of rational motivation and humans' power over trends. When the trend in social mood is negative, people tend to believe in theories of non-rational motivation and trends' power over humans. The reigning belief, then, oscillates between "We control cycles" and "Cycles control us."

Chapter 19 of *The Wave Principle of Human Social Behavior* described what we call the Potent Directors Presumption, the erroneous belief that agencies such as governments and banking monopolies can direct financial markets and overall economies. The idea that the economy has directors is a primitive notion that confers upon them the status of Greek gods. Primitive notions are especially susceptible to shifts in social mood, and this one is no exception. When social mood is strongly positive, people's faith in Potent Directors is as strong as any religion. When mood is deeply negative, people vilify them as fallen idols. Such expressions can be a good indicator of social mood.

The Wave Principle of Human Social Behavior also postulated that when the trends in stocks and the economy are positive, people feel that the machine of society is running properly thanks to rational human behavior. Economists and policy-makers are confident that things are as they should be, they know why they are so, and they accept credit for them. When the trends in stocks and the economy are negative, people feel as if the machine of society is broken, so they search for explanations other than rational human behavior to explain why they were caught off guard and why their efforts to prevent the setback failed. Their newly adopted ideas of causality offer the handy benefit of allowing them to deny blame for what happened. After all, rational humans would never make markets and the economy go down, would they? So, there must be some cause of social change that is beyond human control. The difference in explanations derives from a bias in human thinking that judges uptrends as good and downtrends as bad. Humans credit their own rational actions for "good" social uptrends and blame forces out of their control for "bad" social downtrends.

Socionomic theory, however, is steadfast in proposing that both up and down trends in economies are normal and that neither of them is consciously engineered but rather derives from unconsciously regulated waves of social mood. There is no need to change explanations every few decades.

Figure 1 shows that in times of increasingly positive social mood—such as the 1920s, the 1950s-1960s and the 1980s-1990s—people in the field of finance tend to believe in human rationality and humans' ability to control social trends. In times of increasingly negative social mood—such as the 1930s-1940s, the 1970s, and the first decade of the 2000s—there is a rebirth of interest in non-rational human behavior and the existence of cycles, waves and even extraterrestrial influences such as sunspots.

On September 5, 1929, two days after the Dow's all-time high for that era, *The New York Times* quoted Yale economist Irving Fisher saying, "Stock prices have reached a permanently high plateau." The same month, the President of the New York Stock Exchange announced, "It is obvious that we are through with business cycles as we have known them." Why? Because humans' enlightened institutions are in control. These are classic expressions of a high-degree extreme in positive social mood.

The sideways trend and net decline in real stock prices from 1929 to 1948 indicated a period of mostly negative social mood, during which time the nature of popular financial and economic hypotheses changed. The country's first major books on technical analysis, Richard Schabacker's *Technical Analysis and Stock Market Profits* and Robert Rhea's *The Dow Theory*, were published in 1932. Nicolai Kondratieff sent his paper, "Long Economic Cycles," to Harvard in 1935. R.N. Elliott's books on the Wave

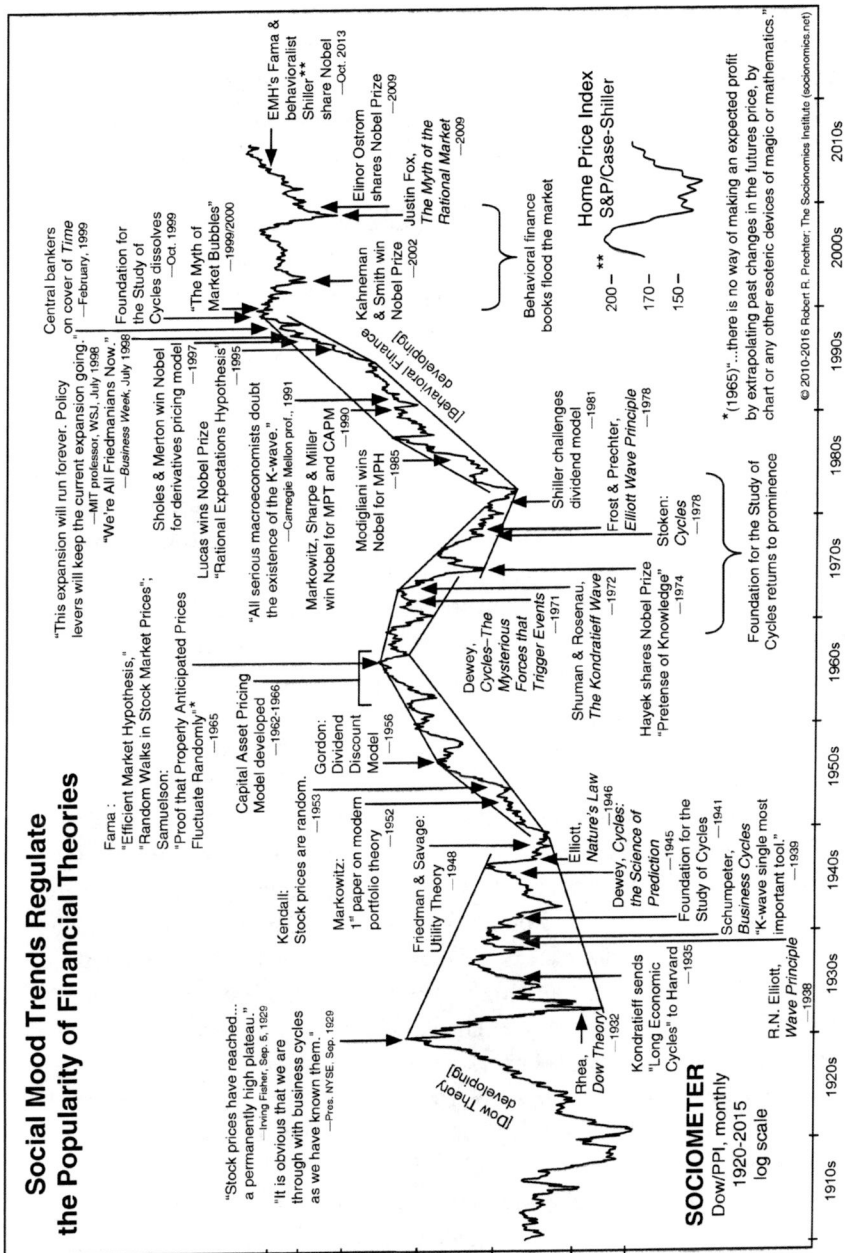

Social Mood Trends Regulate
the Popularity of Financial Theories

Figure 1

Principle came out in 1938 and 1946. In his 1939 book, *Business Cycles,*[1] Harvard professor Joseph Schumpeter championed the explanatory power of the Kondratieff cycle. In 1941, Edward Dewey formed the Foundation for the Study of Cycles, which was both suggested and funded by the U.S. government. He and Edwin Dakin published *Cycles: The Science of Prediction* in 1945.

When social mood and the stock market launched a positive trend that carried through the 1950s and 1960s, economists stopped believing in economic cycles. Freidman and Savage[2] in 1948 were early modelers of purely rational economic and financial agents (see Chapter 33). In 1952, Markowitz[3] introduced modern portfolio theory (MPT), under which mathematical formulas aim to optimize the mix of risk and return in a portfolio. In 1953, Kendall[4] proposed that stock-price changes are random. In 1956, Gordon and Shapiro developed the dividend discount model.[5] In 1958, Modigliani and Miller[6] proposed that in an efficient market the mode of corporate financing is irrelevant to company value. In the final four years of the bull market, Jack Treynor, William Sharpe, John Lintner and Jan Mossin independently developed the entirely mechanical Capital Asset Pricing Model in papers published from 1962 to 1966. Right at the peak of the Dow/PPI in 1965, Samuelson[7] cemented the random-walk model and Fama[8] published the first formulation of his efficient market hypothesis, which posits that perfect rationality determines randomly fluctuating stock prices. These ideas made emotional sense to academics at that time, because the trend in social mood had been strongly positive for seventeen years.

In the ensuing bear market period of the 1970s, cycle theories and technical analysis came back into vogue, at least among financial professionals and the public. The Foundation for the Study of Cycles flourished again throughout that decade, as did technically oriented financial newsletters. In 1973, technicians banded together to form a professional group, the Market Technicians Association. The Kondratieff cycle became the subject of several new books, and speakers discussed it at investment conferences. Frost's and my book, *Elliott Wave Principle*, was published in 1978. By 1979, Merrill Lynch's technical analysis enclave, the Market Analysis Department, had grown to a staff of fifteen. In 1981, the year between the respective multi-decade lows in Dow/gold and Dow/PPI, a paper by Robert Shiller[9] challenged the dividend-pricing model and by extension EMH. When Financial News Network debuted that same year, half of its interviewees were technicians.

In 1974, Friedrich Hayek—who had long argued that centrally planned economies are inferior to conditions of laissez-faire—won the Nobel Prize for economics. He delivered his Nobel lecture—"The Pretense of Knowledge"—

on December 11, two days after that era's low in the nominal Dow. He had to split the prize with Gunnar Myrdal, who advocated "planning" and "policy" to achieve economic and social goals. While this split lessened the degree of victory for the inability-to-control-the-economy viewpoint, it remains the case that at the nadir of social mood and stock prices in 1974, people on the Nobel committee felt that a hypothesis to the effect that economic planning had failed was worthy of the highest recognition.

The stock market turned up strongly in 1982 and climbed through 1999. During this time, books on cycles went out of vogue. In October 1985, three years into the new bull market, corporate financing theorist Franco Modigliani won the Nobel Prize in economics. In 1990, MPT developer Markowitz shared the Nobel Prize with corporate financing theorist Merton Miller and CAPM co-developer Sharpe. In 1991, a Carnegie Mellon professor echoed the consensus in saying, "All serious macroeconomists doubt the existence of the Kondratieff wave."[10] In 1995, Robert Lucas won the Nobel prize for refining the rational-expectations hypothesis. Fischer Black and Myron Scholes had issued "The Pricing of Options and Corporate Liabilities" back in 1973, the only year the Dow made a new all-time high between 1966 and 1982, and in 1997 Scholes and Robert Merton won the Nobel Prize for further developing their theme into a derivatives pricing model based on rational markets. (Befitting socionomic causality better than their mathematical modeling of rational markets, the pair's hedge fund, Long Term Capital Management, imploded the following year; Chapter 19 explains why.) By the late 1990s, Merrill Lynch's Market Analysis Department had slipped to one-third of its former size, and the vast majority of interviewees on CNBC were no longer technicians but economists, brokers, bankers and money managers, which is still the case. In November 1998, the headline of an ad in *The Wall Street Journal* read, "Timing is NOTHING." In June 1999, an article titled "The Myth of Market 'Bubbles'" was published (see Chapter 23). In late 1999, at the peak of society's celebration of financial rationality and economic engineering and its concomitant disdain for endogenous-cause theories, the Foundation for the Study of Cycles dissolved.

Meanwhile, monetary authorities were enjoying a heyday. In July 1998, three months after the Value Line Composite index registered a longstanding all-time high, an MIT professor of economics in an editorial in *The Wall Street Journal* offered the same view that Irving Fisher did in 1929: "This expansion will run forever."[11] He declared that business cycles were a thing of the past and argued that we need never have another recession because of "policy levers," "monetary and fiscal resources" and a "policy team that won't hesitate to use them for continued expansion."[12] In February 1999, just months before the all-time high in Dow/gold and a year before the all-time peak in the valuation of U.S. stock dividends, *Time* magazine celebrated this very policy team of lever-pullers. Its cover featured the nation's central-bank chairman and the government's top two financial authorities, elevating them to the pinnacle of adoration with the lofty title, *The Committee to Save the World.* This committee was supposedly so adept at fine-tuning the economy that it would never allow the country to suffer a recession again. If you look closely at the cover, you will see that these luminaries warranted more photo space than the president of the United States, the First

February 1999

Lady and Shakespeare combined. Once again, the business cycle supposedly had been slain.

At that time, the vast majority of economists were convinced that central bankers controlled the economy and that nothing but an impossible degree of blundering could alter the upward course of financial prices and economic progress. An embarrassing exception was the central bank of Japan, which, due to that country's deflation and stubbornly weak economy, experts quietly agreed was anomalously inept. The whole idea of waves, cycles and unconsciously motivated, non-rational financial and economic behavior appeared ridiculous.

In the month that magazine cover appeared, I was completing *The Wave Principle of Human Social Behavior*, which included this comment:

> The extremity of today's bemusement toward the outmoded idea of social cycles is yet another signal of an approaching major social mood reversal and the beginning of a trend back toward a general interest in patterns of social behavior.

Although I used an outlook for the stock market to help make this prediction, any socionomist—as demonstrated in Chapter 21—could have forecast an upsurge in the popularity of financial theories based on non-rationality by the appearance of *Time*'s magazine cover alone. If you understand socionomics, you know I was predicting this change not despite the ubiquity of the prevailing view but because of it.

In February 2000, *The Elliott Wave Theorist* added this observation:

The widespread acceptance of the idea that economic cycles are dead answers the question of why we have economic cycles. People's beliefs about trends are not scientific but emotional. When markets have gyrated, they believe in cycles. When they go down for a long time, they believe in doomsday. When they go up for a long time, they believe that cycles are dead and the only possible direction is up.

That quarter, the bull market ended and the S&P Composite index began its biggest bear market since 1929-1932. Over the ensuing decade, increasingly negative social mood brought stock values deeply lower and prompted a flood of new books about non-rational human behavior in the realms of finance and economics, as displayed in Figure 2.

During that time, the idea of endogenously regulated financial behavior enjoyed increasing respect. In 2002, Vernon Smith won a Nobel Prize for his reproduction in the lab of boom-and-bust investment cycles. He had conducted the initial studies for papers published in 1976 and 1982, during the 1966-1982 bear market. As the ensuing bull market raged for 18 years, social mood wasn't right for him to receive the award. He finally got the Nobel nod on October 9, 2002, the exact day of the closing low for the first wave of the bear market in U.S. stocks.

Just eight days after the ensuing low in the World Stock Index on March 12, 2003, a global financial authority issued a stunning report denying the efficacy of an entire half-century of its own actions:

IMF admits its policies seldom work

The International Monetary Fund, the Washington-based bank set up to police the financial globe and assist the Third World, yesterday made the startling admission that the policies it has been pursuing for the last 60 years do not often work. In a paper that will be seized on by IMF critics across the political spectrum, leading officials reveal they can find little evidence of their own success. Countries that follow IMF suggestions often suffer a "collapse in growth rates and significant financial crises," with open currency markets merely serving to "amplify the effects of various shocks." A recent study by the United Nations reported that the 47 poorest countries in the world—the biggest recipients of loans from the IMF and the World Bank—are poorer now than they were when the IMF was founded in 1944.

Loans in the last few years to Thailand, Indonesia, Korea, Russia and Argentina are widely regarded as having little positive effect. Activists in Bolivia last month blamed an IMF inspired tax increase for rioting that led to at least 20 deaths.

Books advocating a non-rational aspect to finance, 2001-2009

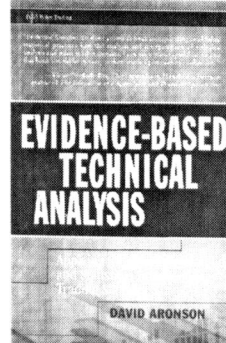

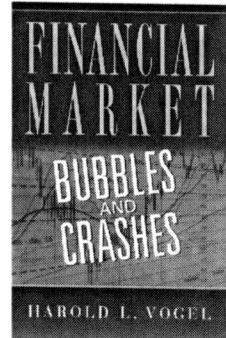

Figure 2

> A spokesman said the report should not be seen as an admission that the IMF itself had failed, but he admitted it was considering an overhaul of its practices.[13]

Soul-searching confessions among economists (see more in Chapters 2 and 5) tend to come at negative extremes in social mood, not when mood is strongly positive. Needless to say, as social mood turned positive thereafter, the IMF continued the same programs, and most people have forgotten its stunning admission.

In 2005, in an intra-correction environment of elevated social mood that fostered a boom in real estate and a new high in the Dow, brokerage firms fired prominent technicians. In February, Citigroup's Smith Barney dismissed the entirety of its ten-person technical analysis group, led by Louise Yamada, and in October, Prudential released Ralph Acampora and his group. (Morgan Stanley had already let three out of four technicians go in January 2002, at an interim peak in optimism.) In August 2007, right between the July/October peaks in social mood and stock prices, anonymous detractors successfully pressured Wikipedia into deleting its page on socionomics. Meanwhile, prominent economists, flushed with positive mood, were showering Potent Directors with credit. Here are excerpts from two editorials, appearing in the two most prominent newspapers in America, each written by a different Ivy-League-educated professor of economics who had served as an economic advisor to a former U.S. president:

(1) August 24, 2006, in *The Wall Street Journal*:

> Fed policy couldn't be better. The job the Fed has done has been flawless, nothing short of amazing. And the financial markets know it. Markets aren't so dumb after all.[14]

(2) December 23, 2007, in *The New York Times*:

> The truth is that the Fed governors, together with their crack staff of PhD economists and market analysts, are as close to an economic dream team as we are ever likely to see."[15]

These lofty assessments of the Fed's brainpower were surely accurate, making the outcome all the more pitiful. The first assessment appeared two months after a peak in real estate of epic proportion that led to a six-year implosion, during which stocks and commodities also plunged, and the second assessment appeared the very month the Great Recession commenced.

In April 2005, *The Elliott Wave Theorist* had responded as follows to the bank-owned brokerage firms' firing of technicians: "The cutback…is a great big sell signal for money-center banks and a buy signal for the field of technical analysis." The S&P banking index peaked in February 2007 and in just two years fell 89%, matching the Dow's record decline of 1929-1932, all while subscriptions to technical-analysis publications soared.

As related in Chapter 5, the financial implosion and Great Recession of 2006-2009 crushed the dream that economists could predict the economy, much less that they could control it. Ten years after *Time* magazine's cover featured those confident financial authorities, opinion had shifted 180 degrees, and the policy team's reputation was in tatters. In 2008-2009, numerous opinion papers from the profession itself, as quoted extensively in Chapter 5, excoriated economists and their theories. In April 2009 *Business Week* ran a cover asking, "What good are economists anyway?"[16] and in July 2009 *The Economist*[17] ran a cover showing that modern economic theory—which is based on equilibrium, perfect rationality, exogenous cause and the belief that authorities can direct the economy—had suffered a meltdown. These magazine covers and their accompanying articles— just as a socionomist would expect—were produced

April 2009

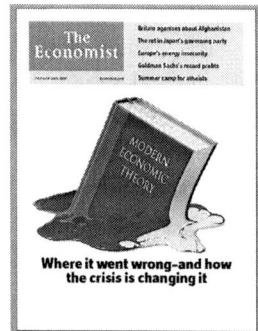

July 2009

Figure 3

respectively in April 2009, the month after stock prices bottomed, and in July 2009, the month after the recession ended, as we were informed much later by the National Bureau of Economic Research. Once again, prominent publications expressed the prevailing social mood, this time near a negative extreme.

In the same year of 2009, Elinor Ostrom shared the Nobel Prize in economics for a study showing that people naturally and peacefully self-organize to create workable arrangements for the use of "commons" property, which therefore need not be privatized or planned and regulated by authorities. The first books by outside authors on the subject of socionomics came out shortly thereafter: *Mood Matters* by John Casti and *Ahead of Change* by Constantin Malik, both from 2010—which were initiated in the bottoming year of 2009—and *Moods and Markets* by Peter Atwater, which was initiated the year Dow/gold bottomed in 2011 and came out the year of the real estate low of 2012. In another blow to the Potent Directors Presumption, a documentary from 2011 titled *The Flaw* went so far as to "paint Alan Greenspan as an embodiment of what went wrong with America."[18]

Since March 2009, social mood has trended positively for seven years so far, and efficient markets and central bankers have regained their halos. In 2013, Fama finally won a Nobel Prize for his efficient market hypothesis, formulated at the peak of a bull market nearly fifty years earlier. That he shared the prize with Shiller of "irrational exuberance" fame is socionomically incompatible with the elevated pricing of stocks at that time, but the market most closely related to Shiller's reputation is the real estate market, which had fallen a record amount from 2006 to 2012 (see inset in Figure 1), a year after which the committee finally extended him a share in the prize.

In the latest environment of elevated social mood, commentators have mostly forgotten that central bankers neither predicted nor prevented the Great Recession, and they have even credited them with stopping it. On December 16, 2014, the Official Monetary and Financial Institutions Forum named Fed Chairman Janet Yellen its "Person of the Year." In October 2015, former Fed Chairman Ben Bernanke's book, *The Courage to Act: A Memoir of a Crisis and Its Aftermath* and his op-ed for *The Wall Street Journal* titled "How the Fed Saved the Economy" claimed technocrats' victory over the forces of economic contraction. And so it goes.

Theoreticians tend to think that their explanations of financial and economic causality will change the prevailing view of social scientists forever. Kondratieff, Schumpeter and Dewey were sure their work on business cycles would change the practice of economic prediction. Kendall, Fama and Samuelson thought their theories of efficient markets and random walks would tie down the correct formulation of financial-market valuation for future generations. But each time the trend in social mood changes, previously popular theories of finance and economics fall out of favor and their opposites re-ascend. It seems unlikely that this oscillation will ever cease.

Socionomics is true, but humans' unconscious adoption of ideas amicable to their moods is too ingrained for most people to disregard. For the duration of positive-mood periods, most people will deem theories of rationality, exogenous cause and financial engineering to be obviously valid, and endogenous-cause theories will be widely dismissed and derided. Conversely, when the trend of social mood turns negative, theories of non-rationality, endogenous cause and uncontrollable waves and cycles will come into vogue. In each era, it seems hard to imagine that people could possibly return to the ideas then considered outmoded, but they always do.

Despite this inevitability, I hope to take advantage of a window of opportunity to establish the field of socionomics with enough durability that people who recognize it as the correct theory of social causality will have a home to call their own.

NOTES AND REFERENCES

[1] Schumpeter, Joseph A., *Business Cycles: A Theoretical, Historical, and Statistical Analysis of the Capitalist Process*, New York Toronto London: McGraw-Hill Book Company, 1939.

[2] Friedman, Milton, and L.J. Savage. (Aug. 1948). "The utility analysis of choices involving risk." *Journal of Political Economy.*

[3] Markowitz's first paper on MPT is Markowitz, H.M., "Portfolio Selection," *The Journal of Finance*, Vol. 7, No. 1, March 1952, pp. 77-91. Three other papers followed, in 1952, 1957 and 1959.

[4] Kendall, Maurice, and Bradford Hill, "The Analysis of Economic Time-Series-Part I: Prices," *Journal of the Royal Statistical Society. A (General).* Blackwell Publishing. (1953). Vol. 116, No. 1, pp. 11–34.

[5] Gordon, M.J and Eli Shapiro, "Capital Equipment Analysis: The Required Rate of Profit," *Management Science*, 3, 1, October 1956, pp. 102-110.

[6] Modigliani, Franco and Merton H. Miller, "The Cost of Capital, Corporation Finance and the Theory of Investment," *The American Economic Review*, June 1958.

[7] Samuelson, Paul, "Proof that Properly Anticipated Prices Fluctuate Randomly," *Industrial Management Review*, Vol. 6, Spring (1965) pp. 41-49.

[8] Fama, Eugene, "Random Walks In Stock Market Prices," *Financial Analysts Journal.* (September–October 1965), Vol. 21, No. 5, pp. 55–59

[9] Shiller, Robert, "Do Stock Prices Move Too Much to be Justified by Subsequent Changes in Dividends?" *The American Economic Review*, 1981, Vol. 71, Issue 3, pp. 421-36.

[10] Angrist, S.W., "Believers in One Wave Theory See U.S. in Deep Trough Soon," *The Wall Street Journal*, August 8, 1991, quoting Allen Meltzer, professor of political economy and public policy at Carnegie-Mellon University.

[11] Dornbusch, Rudi, "Growth forever," *The Wall Street Journal*, July 30, 1998.

[12] *Ibid.*

[13] English, Simon, "IMF Admits Its Policies Seldom Work," *The Telegraph*, March 20, 2003.

[14] Laffer, Arthur B., "The Flawless Fed," *The Wall Street Journal*, August 24, 2006.

[15] Mankiw, N. Gregory, "How to Avoid Recession? Let the Fed Work," *The New York Times*, December 23, 2007.

[16] *Business Week*, April 27, 2009.

[17] *The Economist*, July 18, 2009.

[18] Schneiderman, R.M, "Flawed Titan of the Fed," *Newsweek*, June 12, 2011.

Chapter 41

Setting the Record Straight about Socionomics

Mark Almand and Matt Lampert

April 13, 2011[1]

Five years ago, we were chatting with fellow socionomist Robert Prechter about the well-known progression of social attitudes toward breakthrough theories. We expressed the hope that when socionomics moved past the stage of being ignored to that of being criticized, it would be a shorter step from there to it being considered self-evident. With that progression in mind, all of us at the Socionomics Institute were glad to see a detailed essay critiquing socionomics,[2] hoping that it will spur a healthy dialogue.

The author of the essay seems well-meaning and in search of truth. We respond in that spirit. Following his lead, we have written this article with general readers in mind.

We will begin with the essay's main criticism of socionomics: that much of its published supporting evidence to date is derived through statistically informal methods. That is true. For now, much of the theory's evidence comes from graphical correlations and historical examinations. But in sum they show socionomics' compelling power to explain and in many cases predict financial, economic and cultural trends. These preliminary findings justify rigorously testing its hypotheses. As noted below, we have begun conducting statistical studies that support the tenets of socionomics. We will have more to say about observation, theory and statistics at the end of the article.

But first, we address the essay itself, which makes several crucial errors in explaining socionomics, its empirical support and its application to date. We hope our responses will equip readers to appreciate the significance of the socionomic perspective and make an informed decision about its potential uses.

Here are the most important portions of our critic's essay:

1. The essay reads,

The socionomics literature isn't clear at all on the issue of whether cultural trends as reflected in social phenomena such as television shows are predictive of stock market trends, or whether stock market trends are predictive of the cultural trends reflected in social phenomena such as television shows.

The literature offers neither of these formulations. The essence of socionomics is that a hidden variable—social mood—simultaneously motivates social actions of many types, including—to use the examples cited above—stock market trends *and* the popularity of various television shows.

The creative process for television shows is chaotic, and pilots are advanced all the time. Which ones become popular is a function of social mood. If shows compatible with social mood have already been developed, social mood will prompt viewers to embrace them, and if they haven't been developed, social mood will motivate producers to create them. So, some television shows become popular coincidentally with trends in the stock market and others arrive with a lag.[3]

2. The essay reads,

most available evidence points to the contrary thesis. Social mood actually tends to get darker after a bear market has been underway, not before. Likewise, social mood actually seems to get brighter after a bull market has been underway, not before.

Social mood gets "brighter" or "darker" not with a lag but slightly ahead of a bull or bear market. But the key issue is causality. Many people think that rising stock prices make society increasingly optimistic. Socionomics proposes that increasingly optimistic people make stock prices rise. So, the more positive social mood gets, the higher stock prices go; the more negative it gets, the lower stock prices go. This is why social mood is "brighter" after a bull market has been underway for some time. Mood does not reach maximum positivity the moment after a stock market bottom; it is simply a bit less negative. The converse is true at market tops.

By the way, the idea that a relationship exists between moods and stock prices is a key observation of socionomics and hardly self-evident. In fact, it is anathema to neoclassical economic theory and the efficient market hypothesis, under which stock prices reflect only objective-value criteria independently of people's moods.

The essay goes on to say,

> It wasn't until the economy started growing after 1983 and the stock market boomed that social mood turned around and Americans started feeling good about themselves again.

The first part of that statement is incorrect; the stock market turned up in August 1982, and the recession ended three months *later*. The lag occurred because increasingly optimistic investors could act almost instantly by bidding up the prices of stocks, whereas it took time for increasingly optimistic consumers to purchase new cars and houses, and for increasingly optimistic producers to get bank loans, hire employees, rent space, purchase materials, manufacture goods, design advertising campaigns, etc. Under socionomic theory, this is why the bottom of the recession lagged the bottom in the stock market [see Chapter 8].

The second part of his comment is fully compatible with socionomics. As the bull market began, people felt a bit less bad about themselves. By its midpoint, they were feeling good about themselves. By the peak in the stock market in 2000, when they proclaimed a "New Economy," they felt great about themselves.

The implicit assumption behind the author's statement, that events change social mood, is commonly believed yet challenged by socionomic theory. To extend this point a bit further: Prechter often comments, "No one asks where the booming economy came from in the first place." Socionomics both asks the question and provides an answer.

3. The essay claims,

> If you had invested based on any measurable gauge of social mood, there's little doubt that you would have bought stocks at the top of the bull market in late 1999 and early 2000.

It is important to understand at the outset that socionomics is not a market forecasting discipline but rather a theory describing the relationship between social mood and the tenor and character of social action. Nevertheless, socionomically informed investors understand better than others what an extreme in social mood implies for financial markets. So, the essay's statement is the opposite of what socionomically informed investors would do [for numerous cases in point, see Chapter 21]. Under the socionomic model, it is logical to buy stocks when social mood is depressed and to sell them when it is elevated. Measures of investors' actions show that most investors do the opposite; they buy when fundamentals—which socionomics recognizes as lagging actions brought about by social mood—look good (before and after a top) and sell when they look bad (before and after a bottom).

Furthermore, what socionomically minded analysts actually said at the 1999-2000 juncture is the opposite of our critic's portrayal, as evidenced by Elliott Wave International's market analysis from December 1999.[4] Its bearish conclusion was radically at odds with mainstream economists' published opinions at the time. A month later, the DJIA made an all-time high in real terms that has held for over a decade. The point here is not to claim anything about market forecasting accuracy, which can vary substantially. The point is that the author's charge against socionomics is incorrect. The objection is properly applicable only to non-socionomists.

The essay makes the same error later when it says,

> If you invested in stocks based on the social mood in the aftermath of 9/11 you would have sold stocks, right before one of the most powerful rallies in modern history.

That, too, is not only the opposite of what the theory would imply but also the opposite of how socionomically inclined forecasters applied it in real time in conjunction with the Elliott wave model. On the evening of September 11, 2001, as panic gripped the investment community, *The Elliott Wave Theorist* published a report[5] with charts and commentary calling for an impending stock-market bottom ("within days") and then the largest rally since the market's peak in 2000. The market bottomed five trading days later and took off in the largest rally since 2000. As far as we know, this is the only such forecast to be issued at that time.

4. The essay reads,

> Finally, social mood, by virtually any objective measure, was flying high right before the onset of the housing and financial crises in the 2007-2008 period. A person [who] had bought stocks based on such a reading of social mood would have been crushed by the most dramatic bear market since the Great Crash of 1929.

Contrary to the writers implication, analysts applying socionomics and the Elliott wave model during this period issued emphatic warnings about frothy peaks in real estate [see Chapter 21], stocks [see Chapters 13 and 21] and commodities [see Chapter 22], precisely because in each case market mood was historically elevated and ripe for a major reversal. Much of their commentary from 2002-2007 is documented in *The Mania Chronicles: A Real-Time Account of the Great Financial Bubble, 1995-2008.*[6]

5. The essay says,

> In all of these cases [as listed in points 3 and 4], the turn in social mood did not precede but followed a turn in the stock market, the economy or in broader social events (such as wars).

This statement is incorrect. When the real estate market topped in 2006, for example, no identifiable social event—no economic downturn, no war, no speech, no legislation—caused it. Rather, social mood, having reached a positive extreme, turned toward the negative, eroding creditors' confidence and depressing property prices and shortly thereafter stock prices, all of which led to an economic downturn a year and a half later. This sequence of events expressed socionomic causality all the way through, as did the other examples the author mentioned.

Part 2[7] of the essay also includes several important errors.

6. The critique reads,

> Super short miniskirts and stiletto heels were the hot trend according to market analyst Prieur du Plessis in June of 2008. Did that signal a bull market?

First, this statement gets socionomics backwards. Under socionomic theory, widespread enthusiasm for mini-skirts—which reflects a frisky attitude—should coincide with a peak in positive social mood, therefore implying an approaching bear market in stocks. Second, by mid-2008, stocks had rebounded in a countertrend rally (in "wave 2," per the Elliott wave model), and mini-skirts re-appeared on some fashion runways. But as mood soured thereafter, stocks fell to new lows, and long skirts [see Figures 6 and 7 in Chapter 10] became one of the year's notable fashion trends. Finally, socionomics does not claim that any particular fashion must ever be entirely adopted or rejected; there is always a degree of variety. Rather, it provides a guide for anticipating and assessing the relative popularity of those fashions.

7. The essay states that an econometric paper concluded as follows:

hemlines were neither leading nor coincident indicators of economic growth.

Other economists disagree. *Psychology Today* reported, "The econo-mists George Taylor (1926) and Paul Nystrom (1928) and more recently Helmut Gaus (1992) had noted that hemlines fluctuated in accordance with economic indicators."[8] George Taylor was a professor at the Wharton School of Business, where the George W. Taylor Professor of Management title is conferred in his honor; Nystrom was a professor at Columbia University who wrote "a large and scholarly work"[9] titled *The Economics of Fashion*; and Helmut Gaus is a professor of history at the University of Ghent.

Further, the essay here discusses the stock market and the economy as if they were the same thing. They are not. Socionomic theory posits that the stock market, where social mood is quickly registered, is a more sensitive sociometer than the economy. To support this case, four socionomists have completed a statistical paper showing that the stock market is superior to GDP, employment trends and inflation rates as a predictor of U.S. presi-dential reelection results. The paper is in the peer-review process now.[10] If reliable data over a sufficient period become available, it may be possible to complete a similar study regarding the relative degrees to which the stock market and the economy are statistically related to changes in hemline lengths and other fashion-related variables. Socionomics proposes that the stock market will have the edge.

8. The essay challenges the socionomic claim that negative trends in social mood, as indicated by bear markets in stocks, produce more intense horror films than do positive trends in social mood. The writer cites 13 titles that supposedly represent exceptions to socionomic expectations. They are: *The Shining, An American Werewolf in London, The Evil Dead, The Hitcher, Nightmare on Elm Street, Child's Play, Poltergeist, Scream, Candyman, The Blair Witch Project, Misery, Dead-Alive* and *Silence of the Lambs*. To follow this discussion, please refer to Figure 1, a chart published in Prechter's book, *Beautiful Pictures* (2003).[11]

Figure 1 delineates times that Elliott wave analysts have previously identified as Primary-degree bear market periods within the great Cycle-degree bull market of 1974-2000. The bear periods are **1977-1982** and **1987-1990**, with the resulting recession ending officially into **1991** but carrying through **1993** with respect to many economic statistics such as major job layoffs. Thus out of 26 years total, there are 13 years in which socionomists would expect horror movies to be, on average, more horrible, more numerous and more popular than in the other 13 years. Now observe the respective years of release for the 13 movies in Mr. Kostohryz's list of supposed exceptions: **1980, 1981, 1981,** 1986, 1984, **1988, 1982,** 1996, **1992,** 1999, **1990, 1992** and **1991**.

As Part 1 of the essay correctly stated, "Social mood was at its darkest point in modern American history in the late '70s and early '80s." This period includes 1980-1982, in which four of the 13 films on his list were released. Overall, nine of these 13 titles (69%) came out in the 13 bear market years, but just four of them (31%) came out in the 13 bull market years. The rate of issuance of these titles during the bear years, then, was more than twice that of the bull years. These titles fit nicely into the market template (Figure 1) that was published seven years earlier. And remember,

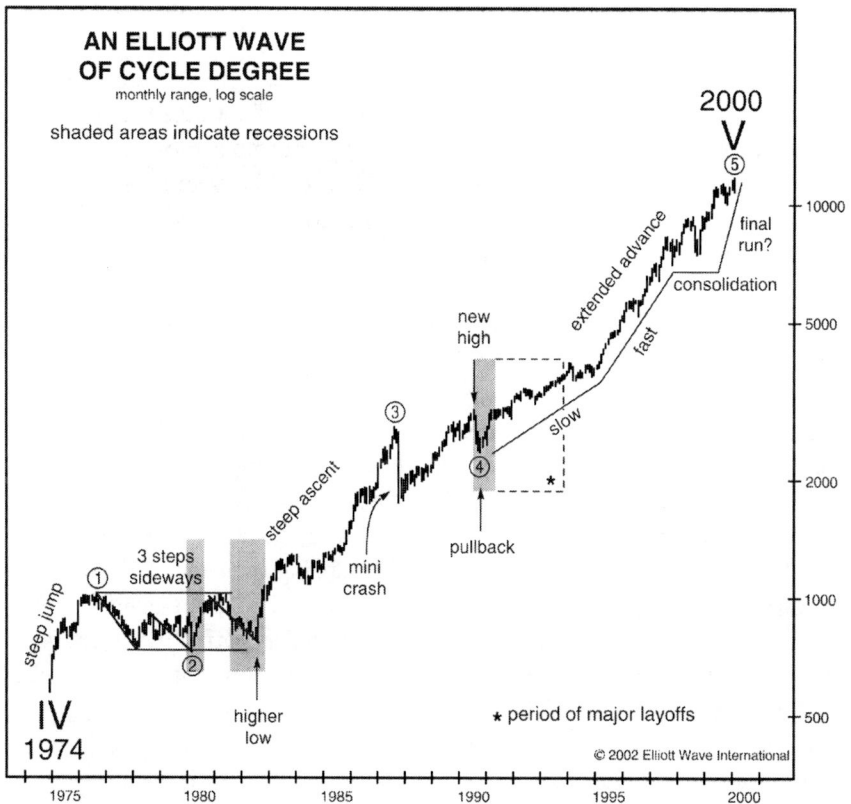

Figure 1

his critique lists only supposed *exceptions*. The rest of the horror films of that period presumably fit the mold. His list does not mention the truly ground-breaking slasher and zombie movies of the 1966-1982 bear market in inflation-adjusted terms nor the horrific "torture-porn" movies released after the stock market high in 2000. (If you can't feel the negative social mood expressed in those movies, you are a zombie!) We would welcome a statistical study analyzing the overall levels of intensity and popularity of horror films in relation to the stock market.

9. In discussing the coverage of warring in the video documentary *History's Hidden Engine*,[12] the essay reads,

> the film conspicuously omits mention of the Spanish-American War, World War I, and the Vietnam War.

That is true. The one-hour overview of socionomics necessarily high-lighted only the broadest, major points. Nevertheless, a socionomist did address all three of these wars, on page 269 of Prechter's 1999 book, *The Wave Principle of Human Social Behavior*. Figure 2, from Prechter's speech at the University of Cambridge in February 2010, illustrates the timing of major wars' occurrence, which dramatically supports socionomic theory. World War I was fought during the second half of a 28-year bear market in real stock prices (lasting from 1892 to 1920), the same period that produced the comparatively small Spanish-American War.

The Vietnam War, as stated in that 1999 book, is a partial exception to socionomic expectations in having simmered for years prior to the eight-year bear market that started in February 1966. But as the bear market progressed from that time forward, the nascent conflict became far more intense, as did the public's opposition to it, the latter culminating in the Kent State shootings at the stock market bottom of May 1970. (A former music critic at *Entertainment Weekly*, who is not a socionomist, recently wrote a piece[13] about the turmoil in popular music that occurred that same year.) Also consider the other mass killings during the bear market: Mao's Cultural Revolution, Cambodia's Killing Fields and the Soviet Union's Afghanistan War, all events reflecting the global negative trend in social mood of 1966-1982, as reflected by that period's decline in the Dow/PPI, as shown in Figure 2.

The socionomic view of causality, especially when married with an accurate stock market forecast, has special predictive value with respect to warring. *The Elliott Wave Theorist* predicted in 1982 that in concert with

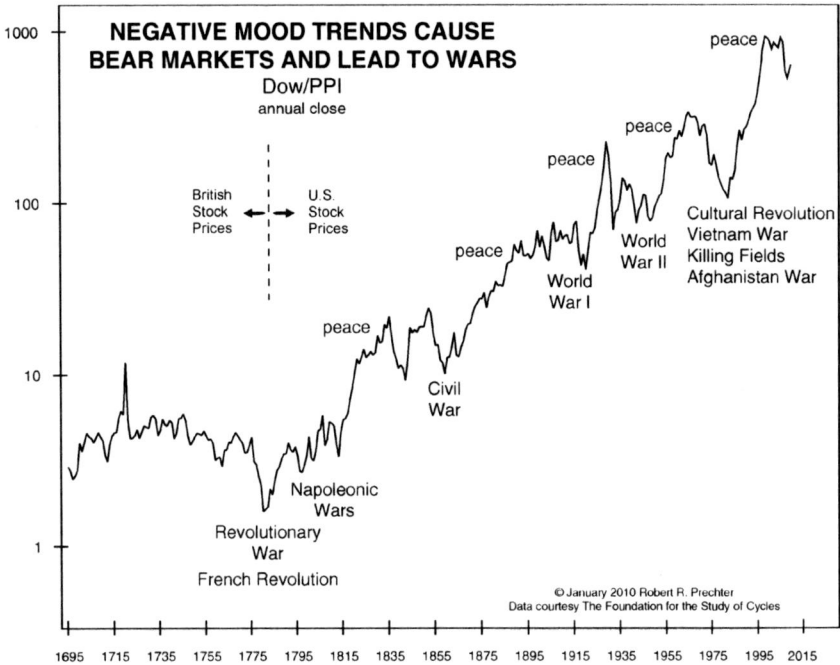

NEGATIVE MOOD TRENDS CAUSE
BEAR MARKETS AND LEAD TO WARS
Dow/PPI
annual close

Figure 2

a stock market boom there would be "no international war for at least ten years."[14] That outlook offered some comfort during the worrisome climate of that time. Two decades later, as the stock market turned down in 2000, socionomists correctly became concerned anew about war risk.

The essay continues,

And where was the multi-year decline in social mood leading up to the First Gulf War, the invasion of Afghanistan, the Iraq War, or the broader War on Terror? These military conflicts were all preceded by major multi-year bull markets and positive indicators of social mood generally.

These statements are erroneous on all four counts. The essay's examples in fact provide yet more compelling evidence that sizeable negative social mood trends lead to wars.

Figure 3

U.S. involvement in the Gulf War began within weeks of the end of the bear market of 1987-1990, as shown in Figure 3. The War on Terror began with the 9/11 attack on New York's Twin Towers, 18 months into a bear market that started in Q1 2000. Congress authorized the Iraq War on the bottom day in the stock market in October 2002, and U.S. forces launched their attack the very week of the ensuing low in the Dow, which was *the* low for that period in the World Stock Index, in March 2003. Socionomists have illustrated all three of these events in published literature, as summarized in Figure 4.

As for the Afghanistan conflicts, the Soviet Union attacked that country in 1979, near the bottom of a major negative-mood trend (see Figure 2), and the U.S. invaded Afghanistan on October 7, 2001, just sixteen days after the stock market bottomed for that year.

10. On the subject of popular music, the essay asks,

How can a documentary that claims to analyze the relationship of music to social mood and the stock market fail to analyze the social moods expressed in the music of Elvis and The Beatles even though these were arguably the two most important musical phenomena of their respective eras?

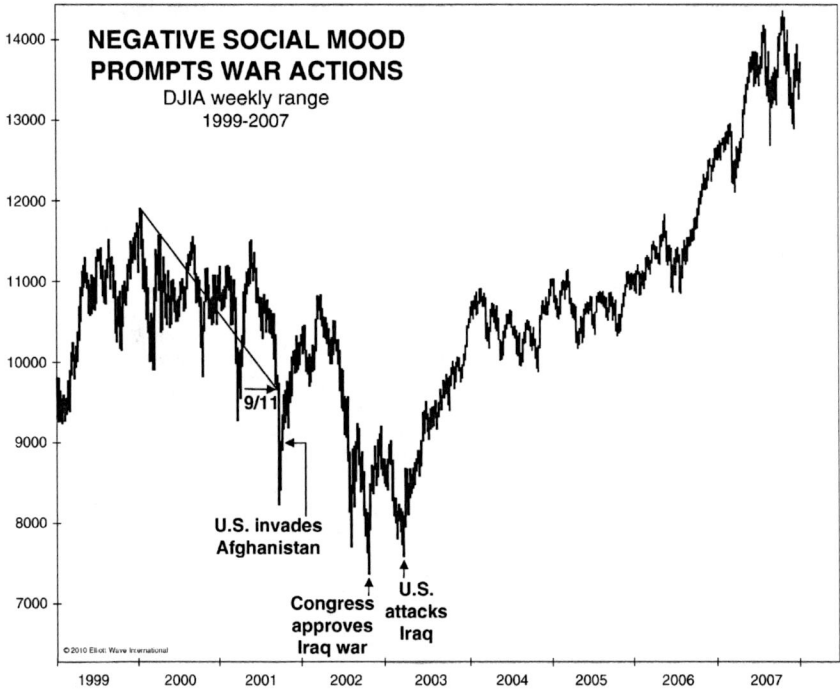

**NEGATIVE SOCIAL MOOD
PROMPTS WAR ACTIONS**
DJIA weekly range
1999-2007

9/11

U.S. invades
Afghanistan

U.S.
attacks
Iraq

Congress
approves
Iraq war

© 2010 Elliott Wave International

Figure 4

The question has four answers. First, our one-hour documentary does not make the claim the essay says it makes. Rather, it presents a brief overview of socionomic causality and its related manifestations, of which popular music is just one. Second, Elvis is represented in the film by the label "Rockabilly" on the film's accompanying graph, and the film includes an audio clip of the Beatles singing 'She Loves You' as an expression of elevated social mood. (The director of the documentary tells us, by the way, that it was not easy to get permission for that clip, and just try getting permission for an Elvis clip!) Third, page 251 of *The Wave Principle of Human Social Behavior* and its accompanying illustration, shown here as Figure 5, discussed and graphically illustrated the roles of Elvis Presley and the Beatles, along with three other popular music icons, in expressing positive social mood. Finally, in July 2010, Prechter's *Elliott Wave Theorist* offered a 40-page analysis of the Beatles' paths of progress and regress as they relate to rises and falls in the stock market. The report[15] was years in the making. It was published two weeks before the writer's critique was posted.

The essay similarly says,

As published in *The Wave Principle of Human Social Behavior*, 1999

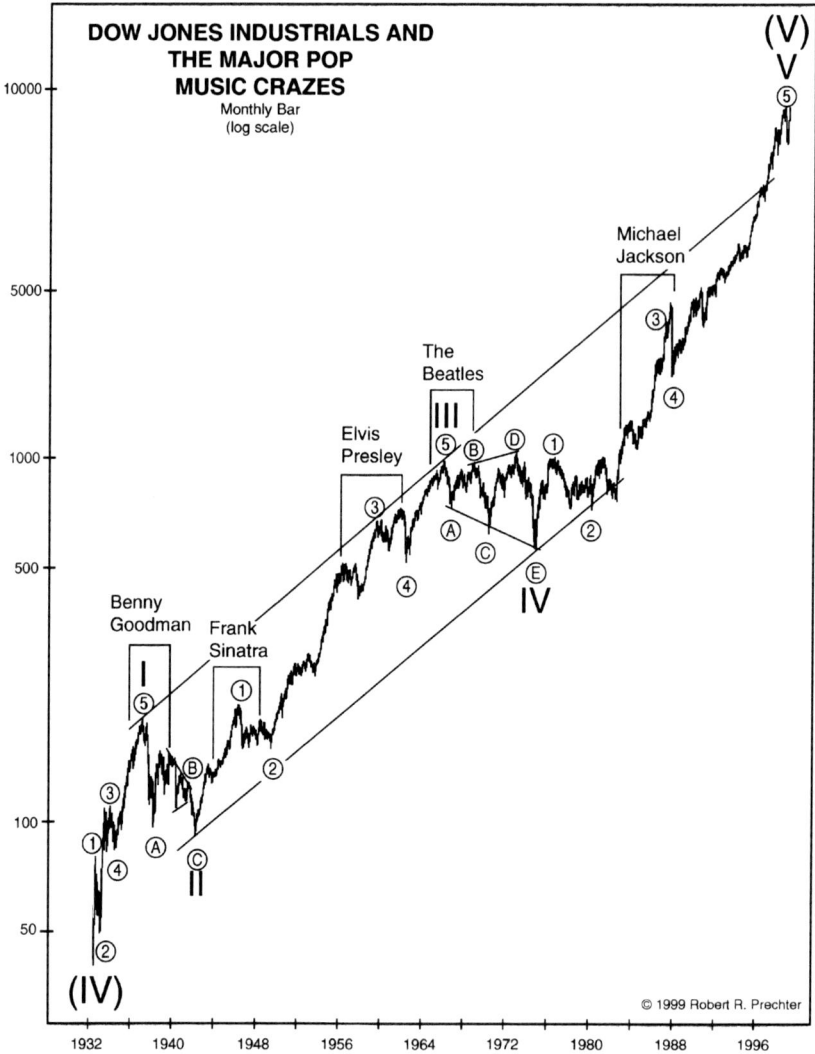

Figure 5

Another omission in the film is in regard to disco music in the late '70s. Disco is clearly very positive and upbeat in terms of lyrics and harmony, and yet stocks at this time were in a deep bear market.

Again, this one-hour introduction to socionomics necessarily omitted mention of several pop-music genres including disco, garage bands, comedy records and beat poetry. Over twenty years ago, however, Prechter's article, "Popular Culture and the Stock Market" (1985),[16] did discuss disco music and even illustrated its role graphically with respect to the divergent stock index trends of 1974-1979 as represented by the rising Value Line Composite index and the falling Dow/PPI.

Finally, the essay names a pop-music performer whose success supposedly contradicts socionomics because her negatively themed material was successful in a bull market. Socionomics proposes that the general character of overall popular music expression faithfully reflects social mood. It does not claim that any style of musical expression will completely disappear during any period; such a claim would be logically inconsistent with both theory and reality. The human social experience is complex. There is always a rich mix of music, fashion styles, film genres, etc. [see Chapters 6 and 8]. It is never all black or white, all upbeat or all downbeat, even on the very day of a major positive or negative extreme in social mood. Citing one seemingly contrary example does not refute the socionomic observation any more than a missed goal refutes the observation that Pelé was a good football player.

Conclusions

Socionomics proposes that changes in social mood influence the tenor and character of social actions. Practitioners are able to use this hypothesis of causality to forecast social change, a goal that frequently eludes social scientists. Failed social forecasting methods have yet to be supplanted, because a compelling theoretical alternative has been unavailable, until now.

The biggest breakthroughs of knowledge have typically come via new explanatory theories. People such as Copernicus, Darwin, Wegener and Watson & Crick developed new hypotheses for natural phenomena. Once they formulated their theoretical insights, scientific inquiry took over to test them. The articulators of heliocentricism, natural selection, continental drift and the structure of the double helix are not renowned for conducting statistical studies. Yet they certainly engaged in science, and their work initiated breakthroughs in understanding that led to many useful lines of inquiry. Empirics come first, hypotheses second and testing third. The first two phases are particularly difficult because they require meticulous observation and then a process of assimilation and induction to achieve a breakthrough in perspective. In the case of socionomics, Prechter has striven to formulate an internally and externally consistent theory. Wayne Parker has elucidated socionomics' metatheoretical context.[17] Other socionomists are constantly probing, leading to further refinements. The testing phase has only just begun.

Socionomists well understand the power and necessity of performing methodologically sound tests—both statistically and in the lab—of clearly articulated, falsifiable hypotheses [as offered in Chapter 11]. We at the Institute have already begun the laborious process of testing our ideas, per the elections study mentioned earlier and others underway.

Although literature on the subject has endeavored to explain socionomics clearly, it can be difficult for even bright individuals to grasp immediately. This is why we have taken the time to respond to our critic's essay in detail.

To readers: If you would like to learn more about socionomics and why people are talking about it, we suggest three books[18] and several DVDs[19] of Prechter's presentations to universities. He also has under development a new book on socionomics, which will flesh out the theory yet further [and here it is]. Theoreticians have covered much more ground than you might imagine. You may wish to attend our annual Socionomics Summit,[20] each of which has featured a stellar list of speakers from multiple disciplines.

The Socionomics Foundation,[21] a not-for-profit entity, makes funds available to scientists whose continuing research, we hope, will help advance socionomics from its current stage—as a comprehensive theory consistent both internally and with empirical observation—to a full-fledged social science discipline.

Again, we thank our critic for taking considerable time to pen his challenge. We hope that he will continue to avail himself of the socionomics literature and, perhaps, become one of a growing number of advocates.

The authors: *Mark Almand is Director of the Socionomics Institute in Gainesville, Georgia and Matt Lampert is the Socionomics Institute's Research Fellow at the University of Cambridge.*

NOTES AND REFERENCES

[1] Almand, Mark and Matt Lampert, "Setting the Record Straight About Socionomics," Minyanville.com, April 13, 2011. Lightly edited for clarity.

[2] Kostohryz, James, "The Failure of Socionomics, Part 1," Minyanville. com, August 4, 2010.

[3] This paragraph is new and replaces a paragraph on leading and lagging sociometers (covered in Chapter 7) and a paragraph on the Twitter and LiveJournal studies (covered in Chapter 9).

[4] Prechter, Robert, "Evidence at Cycle Degree" and "Evidence at Grand Supercycle Degree," *The Elliott Wave Theorist*, December 9, 1999. Reprinted in Prechter, Robert, *View From the Top of the Grand Supercycle*, 2000.

[5] Prechter, Robert, "Elliott Waves and Social Reality," *The Elliott Wave Theorist*, Special Report, September 11, 2001. Reprinted in Chapter 29 of *Pioneering Studies in Socionomics*.

[6] Kendall, Peter and Robert Prechter, *The Mania Chronicles: A Real-Time Account of The Great Financial Bubble (1995-2008)*, New Classics Library, 2009.

[7] Kostohryz, James, "The Failure of Socionomics, Part 2," Minyanville. com, August 4, 2010.

[8] Saad, Gad, "During Economic Crises Skirts Become Shorter," *Psychology Today*, April 23, 2009.

[9] "The Economics of Fashion by Paul Nystrom PhD 1928 1st," WorthPoint.com.

[10] The paper was published in the journal *SAGE Open* in 2012. It is available on SSRN.com and is reprinted in *Socionomic Causality in Politics,* 2017.

[11] Prechter, Robert, *Beautiful Pictures from the Gallery of Phinance*, New Classics Library, 2003.

[12] *History's Hidden Engine*, DVD, Socionomics Institute, 2006.

[13] Browne, David, "Rescuing 1970 from the Remainder Bin," The *New York Times*, August 15, 2010.

[14] Prechter, Robert, "Wave V Confirmed—Super Bull Market Underway," *The Elliott Wave Theorist*, Interim Report, October 6, 1982.

[15] Prechter, Robert, "Social Mood Regulates the Popularity of Stars, Cases in Point: The Beatles," *The Elliott Wave Theorist*, July 16, 2010. Reprinted in full as Chapter 2 of *Socionomics Studies of Society and Culture*, 2017.

[16] Prechter, Robert, "Popular Culture and the Stock Market," *The Elliott Wave Theorist*, Special Report, August 22, 1985. Reprinted as Chapter 2 of *Pioneering Studies in Socionomics*, 2003.

[17] See Chapters 32 and 33 of this book.

[18] Prechter, Robert, *The Wave Principle of Human Social Behavior and the New Science of Socionomics*, 1999; Prechter, Robert, Ed., *Market Analysis for the New Millennium*, 2002; and *Pioneering Studies in Socionomics*, 2003.

[19] Updated list of DVDs: Prechter, Robert, *Toward a New Science of Social Prediction: Robert Prechter at the London School of Economics*, 2009. *Robert Prechter at Oxford Cambridge and Trinity: Offering a New View of Financial and Social Causality*, 2013. *The Socionomic Theory of Finance: An Alternative to EMH and a Foundation for Technical Analysis*, 2015. Socionomics Institute.

[20] The Socionomics Institute continues to host the Socionomics Summit each April in Atlanta. For more information about the event, visit www.socialmoodconference.com. See also the lists of speakers at past summits noted in the Appendix to this book.

[21] For more information about the Foundation, visit www.socionomics.org.

Chapter 42

In the following exchange, excerpted and edited from the September 2010 issue of The Socionomist, *Dave Allman interviews John Casti, PhD (mathematics), scholar, speaker, entrepreneur and author of numerous books, including the well-received socionomics primer* Mood Matters.

A Well-Known Scholar
Embraces Socionomics

Dave Allman and John Casti

You were talking about "social behavioral patterns" back in 1989, for example in *Paradigms Lost*. What a great title!

That book was a collection of about six mini-books, each one addressing a major unsolved problem in modern science. One of the unsolved problems was the "nature-versus-nurture" question. That is, to what degree is human behavior genetically programmed as opposed to the dominant influence being the environment? In its more modern incarnation, the study of this question falls under the header of "evolutionary psychology." The book didn't come to any definitive conclusions. My objective was to look at these big questions of modern science and the competing paradigms and see who holds which positions and why. Just for fun and to make it easier to read, I structured each of the questions as a kind of jury trial. I presented the prosecution and the defense.

In *Mission to Abisko* (1997), another compilation, you touched on something that you do very well—the popularization of science, making it accessible to the public.

I have chosen most of my books' topics not because I am an expert on them. Instead, I wanted to understand those questions more deeply myself. I thought that one of the best ways I could come to understand them was to try to explain them to somebody else. Almost all the books I have written have that character. With socionomics, I received a lot of feedback on the manuscript from friends and so on. I kept sharpening my view of the whole topic. Eventually I was able to convey it with almost an outsider's inside perspective. It was especially difficult in the case of socionomics because, as you know yourself, you have to ask people to suspend their belief in the way the world works long enough to listen. That's a pretty tough requirement.

Especially for people who spent a small fortune to promote or to be indoctrinated into traditional economic thought.

Right. I must have given on the order of a hundred presentations about socionomics since my first article about it in *New Scientist* nine years ago [reproduced in *Pioneering Studies in Socionomics*]. I've spoken about it in pretty much every corner of the world. Almost without exception, the reaction is very encouraging and positive. I think Bob Prechter would probably tell you the same story. But, having people tell you, "Gee, it caused me to think differently about everything" is not the same thing as people declaring, "I changed my mind about this particular belief I once held." This notion that events drive social mood is so deeply wired into the human mindset that it's almost impossible for some people to abandon it. In fact, even though audiences on the whole have been receptive and encouraging, I have also had people in the audience who were so bothered and troubled by the idea that underlies socionomics—that mood is the motivator of events, not the other way around—that they were unable to even discuss the matter in a rational way. And these were academics, who are supposed to rely on scientific observation to arrive at their conclusions about the world. Some became angry and stomped out of the lecture room, slamming the door on the way out.

Yeah, I get that at home. Well, at least you know you were heard! So, do you think there are better sociometers than the stock market?

I do not think we will find any sociometers with all of the very useful properties the stock market has. Yet I do wish we could measure mood directly with brain probes, because it would make life infinitely easier for expositors of socionomics. Then nobody would imagine that *Mood Matters* is about financial markets. I wish I could have used all the same charts in *Mood Matters* but not labeled them as movements of the financial markets. I wish I could have just labeled the vertical axes "social mood." Then people would get the point more easily.

Iben Browning was a brilliant climatologist who had some very good forecasts—for example the San Francisco earthquake of 1989—and some great insights. But of course when the media finally built up a later earthquake forecast, it did not materialize. Thereafter they referred to Browning as the climatologist who forecast the earthquake that didn't happen. Are forecasters doomed whether or not they provide value?

These days, most of the people who are serious about forecasting do not put themselves in the position to get trapped. Even if you had a 100% surefire method of forecasting specific events, which no one does, you would then face bigger challenges. Number one, who do you tell? And number two, how do you get them to take action? These are not scientific questions. These are social, political and psychological issues that reside far outside the laboratory.

I am head of a project at our Institute that has the grand title of Extreme Events in Human Society. The focus of the project is to acquire insight into the likelihood of human-generated extreme events such as financial crises, terrorist attacks, political disturbances, revolutions, and so on. When I first set up this project I told my colleagues that we were not going to be in the business of making point-in-time forecasts such as, "This country is going to have a revolution at this time, and such-and-such a party is going to come into power." Such forecasts are lunacy; nobody can do that.

On the other hand, you *can* shed light on the environment within which events of a certain character are likely to unfold. You can predict that when the environment is in a certain state, it biases the likelihood or unlikelihood of events of a certain type. For example, you can say that a revolution or terrorist attack is more likely to take place in a period of negative social mood than at other times. This is why socionomics is so valuable.

The Socionomics Institute has a nascent service arm, Trendtelligence, Inc. The idea is to advise major corporations in areas such as the fashion industry and the auto industry—people who lay out half a million dollars for a 15-second spot during the Super Bowl—and say, "Here's the ad you should run because people are more likely to respond to it." They want to know: Should they be selling muscle cars or hybrids, Barbie dolls or Troll dolls? Aren't you also involved in the practical application of socionomics?

Yes. The projects I am heading in our X-Center Vienna institute involve a consortium of companies and government agencies. They want us to give them some insight into, for example, how things are likely to unfold in the economic and business arenas over the next twenty years.

What do you see as the major challenges for socionomics research?

Two things: First, understanding of how social mood shifts within a population. Here agent-based simulations could be of huge help. Second, determining more precisely the time lags in socionomic actions. This time-lag aspect is especially critical if you want to project the consequences of a sociometer into the future.

Chapter 43

Two Popular Science Magazines Review the Socionomic Hypothesis

Chuck Thompson
The Socionomist
October 8, 2010

John Casti's just-published book, *Mood Matters: From Rising Skirt Lengths to the Collapse of World Powers,* has helped bring sociononomics to the attention of the media. Two of the world's most prestigious science journals published lengthy reviews of Casti's presentation of the socionomic hypothesis in their September issues. One write-up was favorable toward Dr. Casti's book, the other less so.

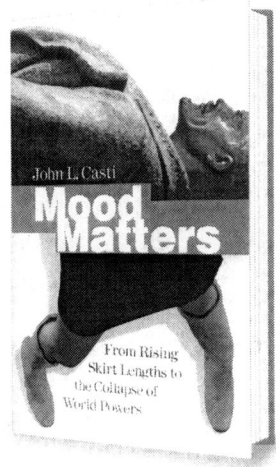

The first review appeared in *Nature,* the world's most highly cited interdisciplinary journal. In it, David Berreby, a science journalist and author, agreed that "reason [has been] dethroned as the ruling explanation for people's conduct" and that "the search is on for another framework in which human behavior can be modeled." Berreby applauded socionomists in their search for a new understanding. He correctly cited several key aspects of socionomic theory, including that "financial data are reservoirs of social information that can be tapped to predict crises."

But Berreby considered the idea of assigning "a single mood at a given time to a particular collective, whether that is the population of a city, country or even the world," to be untenable, because "each of us belongs to more than one social group, so how can we have one belief about the future?" For the record, Prechter addressed this idea over a decade ago in *The Wave Principle of Human Social Behavior and the New Science of Socionomics* (1999):

> Smaller aggregations are imbedded within larger ones. People can be members of several aggregations at once.... Together, all the [social-mood] waves of all the aggregations weave the fabric of social life.

Berreby further criticized *Mood Matters* by saying that its topic, socionomics, appears to be based only on examples and correlations. By necessity, Casti's summary book contains only a small fraction of the published research supporting the socionomic hypothesis. Statistical confirmation moreover, is already in progress [now published; see "Social Mood, Stock Market Performance and U.S. Presidential Elections: A Socionomic Perspective on Voting Results," *SAGE Open* (2012), reproduced in *Socionomic Causality in Politics* (2017)].

In his review for *Science*, which has the largest paid circulation of any peer-reviewed, general science journal in the world, University of Oregon physics professor Richard Taylor was unabashedly positive. He wrote that socionomics "presents an effective argument for why the financial market serves as the optimal choice of sociometer." He also lauded socionomists' "meticulous detective work of the time lines involved in major events," which reveal the "tell-tale manifestations of socionomics." Regarding socionomics' assertion that mood drives events and not the reverse, Taylor listed key examples of historic events that failed to affect the financial markets. He went on to write, "This unexpected insensitivity to world events addresses a historic puzzle: why the financial market traces out recognizable patterns as a function of time." He asked, rhetorically, that if we believe the conventional wisdom that the "market is driven by irregular and diverse events, why would these cumulate in a distinct pattern?"

Taylor commended Casti for wisely declaring early on—as Prechter did in his first book on socionomics—that his presentation is deliberately one-sided. That is as it should be, because the "purpose is to trigger a reaction against the established beliefs of the financial world," Taylor wrote. He concluded that by publicizing the relationship between events and social mood, *Mood Matters* "reveals the extent to which the latter determines our future."

Reviews such as these in *Nature* and *Science* suggest that socionomics may be moving beyond phase one—being ignored. Next is phase two—being debated. Eventually, if it makes it to the third and final phase, perhaps the theory will be accepted as self-evident.

Chapter 44

An Interview with Robert Prechter
on the Origin and Future of Socionomics

Q: This is your third book on socionomics, and two more are in the works for 2017. You have a flourishing Socionomics Institute (socionomics.net) and a Foundation (socionomics.org). The Institute has an established periodical called *The Socionomist*, and it has been hosting an annual conference on social mood titled the Socionomics Summit, which has attracted prominent speakers from academia. You have presented your ideas at MIT, the London School of Economics, the universities of Oxford, Cambridge and Trinity, two annual conferences hosted by the Academy of Behavioral Finance and Economics, and the annual symposium of the International Federation of Technical Analysts. The Institute has released DVDs of several of these presentations. Three outside authors have written books on socionomics, several socionomists have lectured for university classes, and five professors have incorporated socionomics into their courses. The Institute has produced and/or funded thirteen research papers, and its first research fellow is closing in on a doctorate at Cambridge. Socionomics seems to be gathering steam.

A: I always feel that it's taking too long for people to discover socionomics. But when you list these developments, it makes me realize that progress is happening. So thanks for the reminder.

To kick things off, what kind of education gave you a background to figure out socionomics?

I came into college as a physics major but quickly dropped the idea. I took freshman economics, thinking that would be my new future, but I found I disagreed with most of it, so that was out. I defaulted to a psychology degree because I had taken some courses and experienced a modicum of interest. Only twice do I recall being really excited about an upcoming course. Both times the subject was mass psychology, and both times the course was canceled. So even in the field that most strongly relates to socionomic theory, I was utterly untrained. Frankly, my passion for pop music was probably the most influential precursor. From there, I had to figure it out myself.

Then what brought you toward the socionomic way of thinking?

I was drifting toward it by early 1969, when I was 19 years old and wrote a college paper [reprinted in an Appendix to *Pioneering Studies in Socionomics*] assessing popular song lyrics for expressions of attitudes towards achievement and suggested they portended economic change. After graduating, I became a professional musician in the early 1970s and became interested in markets on the side.

You elected not to pursue a higher degree. Was that a good or bad decision?

I think it was both. PhD holders are automatically paid respect, and I never had that luxury. On the other hand, I didn't have to unlearn anything. Being independent of conventional economics allowed me to stay the course toward becoming an empiricist, practitioner and skeptic. I couldn't wait to get out into the real world, so that's what I did. As it turns out, the real world is a lab for socionomics.

How did you become a technician?

I started plotting financial prices in 1972 and taught myself technical analysis in 1973-1974, so I became a pure technician early. This was useful, because from the beginning I never adopted the idea that stock prices respond to conditions and news. All I could see were patterns, breadth, volume and trends in optimism and pessimism and how they corresponded to market action. Richard Russell was a huge early influence. My dad subscribed to *Dow Theory Letters*, and he would send me the issues after he'd read them. In the early 1970s, Russell began publishing Elliott wave analysis with input from A.J. Frost, which kicked off my interest in that area. When I was with Merrill Lynch in New York in the second half of the '70s, Bob Farrell and his team taught me a lot. They had great data, too, so you could do good research there.

You've told the story about how you got the initial insight about socionomics. What was that like?

The idea that the stock market and popular culture were linked crystallized in my mind in late 1975. I had just started in the Market Analysis Department at Merrill. I was perusing a wall chart of the stock market and thinking about tonal changes in Beatles records that occurred in 1965-1966. That led me to thinking about popular music in general, which I knew very well. I suddenly perceived that the musical styles I knew about had ebbed and flowed with the stock market. That's when I first had the feeling that I had perceived something important.

Were you instantly thrilled?

You know that hyper-alert feeling you get when you are introspecting and suddenly you get an insight? That's what I felt. But I didn't have the whole picture yet.

What happened next?

I studied Elliott waves and technical analysis in more depth and started applying them in reports for Merrill Lynch in 1976. As I watched the stock market confound fundamental analysts time and again, it became ever more obvious to me that news lags stock prices, not the other way around. During 1976-1978, I became completely committed to socionomic causality. I have a letter I sent to my dad in February 1979, where I wrote, "The state of business is a *consequence* of the changes in mood." I underlined the word *consequence* and used the term *mood*.

Did you run these ideas past your colleagues?

Not really. I realized I was the only one having these thoughts.

When did you start writing about socionomics?

In April 1979, I went independent and started a financial publishing company. In August of that year, I issued my first socionomic declaration. It's reprinted at the start of *Pioneering Studies*. I came to some other conclusions in the early 1980s, although during this period I was mostly focused on my new venture of publishing market commentary.

Then in August 1985, I wrote a long report titled "Popular Culture and the Stock Market" [also reprinted in *Pioneering Studies*], which was boiled down for a *Barron's* article. That sort of kicked things off.

Did you call it socionomics then?

I wrote that name on a file folder and put it away for the day when I would write my first book about it. I kept it to myself until 1999, when I finally gathered all my thoughts on the subject from the previous twenty years and came out with *The Wave Principle of Human Social Behavior and the New Science of Socionomics*.

Would you say you were you a pure socionomist from the start?

No, because socionomics is deeply counter-intuitive. I had to go through a long process of weeding out misconceptions from my mind that had taken root long ago. An early example was the idea that interest rates buffet the stock market. There are people who make a living on this idea. Economists are sure it's true. My professional colleagues were convinced of it. It makes sense. It's also wrong. If someone were to tell you the course of interest rates in advance, you couldn't predict stock prices. The stock market moves on waves of social mood. If you know that, you know more about stocks than the person who knows where interest rates are going. And, of course, no one knows where interest rates are going. Except that sometimes socionomists do know, because we study the history of waves and their attending social attributes.

What brought you to the finish line?

Heading into the late 1990s, I had become almost a complete purist. I was able to turn every exogenous-cause argument on its head. I would show it was wrong and then show that socionomic causality successfully explains the same data. But I still held a residual belief that the Federal Reserve had the power to control the money and credit supply and thereby move markets around. One day I realized that this idea, if it were true, challenged my whole model. I posed the same question I always did: How does the reverse order of causality re-form the question? So instead of asking how the Fed controls the markets, I asked how the mood behind the market controls the Fed. I discovered that people have created central banks at certain times in the wave structure [see Chapter 13 of *Pioneering Studies in Socionomics*]. I plotted interest rate data and saw that the Fed just follows the T-bill rate, which is set by the market [see Chapter 3]. I studied the Fed's historical actions and realized that the Fed does not act; it reacts [see Chapter 2]. Social mood pushes the economy around, and it also pushes the Fed around [see Chapter 28]. I realized if you know the trend of social mood you can predict what the Fed will do, but the Fed's behavior tells you nothing about what financial markets will do. That's when the whole Wizard of Oz image went up in smoke. That was my last bout with exogenous causality.

Were there additional breakthroughs along the way?

Realizing that the Elliott wave model described the structure of waves of social mood—not just financial pricing—was a key deduction. I also figured out that social mood is unremembered and that most financial thinking is rationalization, not reasoning. A big breakthrough was realizing that the causality attending economic behavior is completely different from that attending financial behavior. This is another idea that as far as I can tell no one had clearly proposed before. I wrote about it in Chapter 20 of my 1999 book and more thoroughly with Wayne Parker in a paper for the *Journal of Behavioral Finance* [see Chapter 15]. One evening in 2004, I drew a diagram [Figure 1 in Chapter 6] showing how all these ideas fit together.

Are you entirely averse to the idea of outside causes of social mood?

Yes. Well, except in the cosmic sense, where I retain an open mind. Some people have related climate, solar events and lunar and planetary cycles to movements in the stock market and economies. If advocates ever prove a relationship or establish causality, we might have to abandon the hypothesis that waves of social mood are internally regulated in favor of their being regulated by changes in the physical environment. It's a majestic vision to consider that human moods may collectively dance to a kind of music of the spheres. But advocates of this vision are nowhere near proving anything, and besides, I don't see how cosmic physics could create multiple, independent, social-mood trends shared by some people but not others. Endogenous causality still makes far more sense.

Has anyone ever shared an "aha moment" of their own regarding socionomics with you?

A fundamental insight came from Wayne Parker, who proposed a metatheoretical context for the theory [see Chapters 32 and 33]. Wayne taught me the metatheoretical difference between socionomic theory and mechanistic causality and pushed me to avoid eclecticism. He corrected my error of calling social mood a force, which was just another holdover from the old erroneous paradigm of mechanics. He and I also collaborated to come up with a socionomic version of the distinction between mood and emotions. Other people have expanded the scope of the field by conducting some excellent supportive studies, the best of which will be published in 2017 in *Socionomic Studies of Society and Culture* and *Socionomic Causality in Politics*.

When Brian Whitmer published his report predicting a Greek debt crisis, the media said nothing. There was no interest. Then a few months later when the Greek debt crisis occurred, it was too late for people to take action. This kind of thing happens regularly, doesn't it?

All the time. He did the same thing with the Swiss central bank's euro peg [see Chapter 29]. Socionomic insights are most useful precisely when most people are least inclined to pay attention to them. It is unfortunate and ironic, but socionomic theory explains why it is also axiomatic.

I would guess you guys disagree with most of the talk on financial television.

Oh, yeah. But what matters is not so much what people *say* on financial TV but the fact that there *is* financial TV. It's a consequence of highly elevated social mood at major degree. People think it's an innovation, here to stay. But during the next major trend toward negative social mood, it will go away.

I've never heard of anyone making your claims. All I ever read about the market is what caused what, or what *will* cause what.

Socionomics is not just a baby step in another direction. It's a total reformation.

What does STF mean for market technicians?

It's the basis for the whole profession.

What do you mean?

Economists have long judged technicians as delusional. I was told that for a long time the CFTC operated under an internal memo denoting technical analysis per se as fraud. And if economic theory pertained to finance, they would be right! Think of it this way: Wouldn't it be crazy to study past prices of shoes as if they meant anything about the future prices of shoes? That's how economists view technicians studying patterns of financial prices. Their view logically follows, because their premise is that stock pricing is no different from shoe pricing; they believe that economic and financial markets are fundamentally the same. But STF's financial/economic dichotomy erases that objection and justifies technicians' pursuits. Speculators are not reasoning but unconsciously herding, and unconscious processes aren't random; they proceed according to mental defaults. That's why financial markets display patterns such as persistent trends, head and shoulders formations, trend channels and Elliott waves. Of course, it is also possible for people to perceive patterns that don't exist. But economists are hardly immune to that problem. On the contrary, they're drowning in it!

So it's really economists trying to explain stock price movements in terms of outside causes who are delusional?

I would just say they are laboring under a misconception. They keep making statements contrary to the evidence because their arguments seem so *logical*—to hell with the data. They have to ignore data in order to keep believing in their paradigm of external causality. Chartists start by looking at data, which puts them a step ahead in the game.

But economists know a lot about their subject.

Definitely. But again, that's one of my points: Economics and finance are completely different fields. Economists are highly useful in their field, where the law of supply and demand applies. But in the field of finance, where the law of patterned herding rules, they are lost.

But technicians are often lost, too.

At the analytical level, sure. I've proved that one myself. Socionomic theory properly elucidates the obstacles that market analysts face and especially those that speculators face. But the big difference is that we are not existentially lost at the paradigm level, as economists are. We have the right map.

Technicians, along with the Graham-and-Dodd value analysts, have always operated under the belief that random walk is wrong. They both believe that the market provides buying and selling opportunities.

Yes, and now they have a coherent theory of market behavior to back them up. [See also Chapter 34 of *Pioneering Studies in Socionomics*.]

Didn't you use time cycles in your analysis at one time? How do they fit in?

Fixed-time cycles are temporary artifacts in market data that sometimes maintain for a while. I worked hard at applying the cycles model, but I rarely use it now, because cycles aren't the essence of market behavior. Not long after you notice them, they typically stop working, so they are more apt to throw you off then help. The market moves in waves, not cycles.

Might economists say that Elliott waves are just imaginary patterns imposed on price movements?

Some have said that. But it's ironic, because imposing imaginary causes is what economists do all day long. That's why their exogenous-cause and supply-demand models can't be used to predict changes in financial markets or even the economy.

Don't some studies show that people "see" patterns in random data?

Sure. But I think this fault is no more common in humans than missing real patterns that are right under their noses. People were surrounded by fractals in nature for thousands of years, but no one noticed them until Mandelbrot called attention to their form. Now they're obvious. R.N. Elliott catalogued the market's specific fractal forms, and the trained eye can see them, too.

Chapter 40 shows that financial authors expressed the negative social mood of 2000-2009 by writing a slew of books about non-rational markets. Your books on non-rational markets have come out at totally different times, namely in the extended, elevated bull markets of 1999 and now.

If my aim were to sell a lot of books right away, I would publish in the heart of a bear market, because that's when people are most receptive to this kind of message. That's what happened with *Conquer the Crash*, and it made the bestseller list. But I think it's better in the case of socionomics to publish when people are *not* thinking this way. It will probably hurt in terms of sales and reviews, but given my thesis I think it's important to demonstrate independence from prevailing fads. *Elliott Wave Principle* had a bullish message in 1978, late within a long bear market, so it hardly sold much at first. But interest in it spread once the bull market got going. For any hope of longevity, you have to be acting, not reacting. Whether that's smart or dumb in this case, I don't know.

Your 1999 book cited researchers who later became Nobel-Prize winners. You were ahead of that curve, what, three times?

Ha, yeah. There were two in that book and one later. I wrote up Vernon Smith because he had reproduced a boom-and-bust investment cycle in the lab even though his subjects were given access to fundamental data. I thought that study offered tremendous support for socionomics' hypothesis of endogenously regulated herding. He won the Nobel Prize in economics three years later, in 2002. He's at Chapman University now, along with a like-minded colleague, Terry Burnham, who wrote the excellent *Mean Markets and Lizard Brains* in 2008. Daniel Schectman's discovery of quasi-crystals intrigued me because their five-fold symmetry and spiral shape relate more to biological forms than to inanimate ones. I wrote about them in my 1999 book. Danny invited me to speak in Israel, but I was too busy to go. He finally won the Nobel in chemistry in 2011. In the April 2011 *Theorist*, I took the leap of referring to "Future Nobel Prize winning economist Robert Shiller." I thought he should win not because he was one of the early behavioral economists but because he was the only prominent economist talking about bubbles as they formed and applying sentiment gauges designed actually to anticipate financial-market changes. Two years later, he got it. I also cited Eugene Stanley's work throughout that book. He should be on their list, too.

Socionomics' connections to other fields are so wide-ranging.

I think so. Besides subsuming a large portion of the fields of finance, sociology, politics, history and the study of economic trends, I think socionomics will also prove meaningful to psychology, since social mood resides in individuals. It relates in important ways to biology and even has some connections to the physical sciences by way of quasi-crystals, DLA clusters and spiral galaxies, all of which I talked about in *The Wave Principle of Human Social Behavior and the New Science of Socionomics*. But it has little to add to microeconomics, which in my view *is* economics. So, as encompassing as socionomics is, it is quite apart from the field of economics as properly defined.

Books, videos, speeches, papers and a monthly publication. What are your other plans for getting the word out?

One of my long-time goals has been to get three papers published that would serve as pillars of support for further socionomic research. The first one would present the socionomic theory of finance, the next would contrast socionomic causality to standard causality statistically to provide a template for future researchers, and the third would be a comprehensive study validating the Elliott wave model. The first two are done [see Chapter 15 of this book and *Socionomic Causality in Politics*, 2017]. The third is in early development. Validation takes time, but we're making it happen.

Where do you see the science of socionomics heading next?

We need to keep testing all our ideas rigorously. We are doing so mostly on our own so far. The Socionomics Foundation offers grants to interested academics.

What is your biggest dream for socionomics?

I would like to see a socionomics journal. And departments of socionomics in universities.

Will they happen in your lifetime?

Depends on how long I live.

Appendix

KEY EVENTS IN SOCIONOMICS

Appendix

Key Events in Socionomics

1. **1938** — R.N. Elliott's book *The Wave Principle* introduces the idea that stock market prices move in waves, which take the form of a self-affine, hierarchical fractal.

2. **1940** — R.N. Elliott publishes "The Basis of the Wave Principle," a treatise elaborating on Charles Collins' observation that the numbers of waves in his empirically derived model conform to the Fibonacci number sequence.

3. **1946** — R.N. Elliott's second book, *Nature's Law—The Secret of the Universe*, includes additional discoveries and observations and is considered his definitive work on the Wave Principle.

4. **1969** — Nineteen-year-old Yale University student Robert R. Prechter edges toward the socionomic insight when in a college paper he contemplates the connection between song lyrics and trends in the economy.

5. **December 1975** — Shortly after becoming a technical analyst with Merrill Lynch in New York, Prechter realizes that there is a link between the character of popular music styles and the path of the stock market.

6. **November 1978** — A.J. Frost and Prechter's *Elliott Wave Principle— Key to Market Behavior* is published. It articulates socionomic principles on psychological aspects ("personalities") of waves and on the irrelevance, rationalization, lagging nature and parallel tenor of news.

7. **August 1979** — Prechter's first published statement on socionomic causality appears in *The Elliott Wave Theorist*: "changes in the mass emotional outlook [are] the cause of future events…affecting humanity both in and out of the market arena. Events do not shape the market; the forces behind the market shape events."

8. **October 1982** — *The Elliott Wave Theorist* makes its first socionomic forecast.

9. **August 1985** — Prechter writes a 20-page special report, "Popular Culture and the Stock Market," detailing manifestations of social mood in popular music, film and fashion.

10. **September 1985** — Prechter's socionomic insight reaches a national audience when his article, "Elvis, Frankenstein and Andy Warhol," becomes a cover story in *Barron's*.

11. **1988–1992** — Business journalist Peter Kendall begins analyzing cultural trends for several stock market and business journals. In 1992, Kendall joins Elliott Wave International and begins writing socionomic commentary for Prechter's monthly publication, *The Elliott Wave Theorist*.

12. **1997** — Elliott Wave International names Kendall director of the Center for Cultural Studies, an early precursor to the Socionomics Institute.

13. **November 1997** — Prechter presents the Wave Principle of social behavior in a talk titled "The Mathematical Basis of History" at the International Conference on the Unity of the Sciences in Washington, D.C.

14. **March 1999** — Jordan Kotick heads the new Socionomics Department at Elliott Wave International, the next precursor to the Institute.

15. **March 1999** — Prechter's book, *The Wave Principle of Human Social Behavior and the New Science of Socionomics,* is published.

16. **May 2000** — Prechter gives a presentation on socionomics to the Market Technicians Association's Annual Conference in Atlanta.

17. **July 2001** — Under a grant from the Socionomic Foundation's predecessor, philosophy professor Michael Green of the State University of New York (SUNY) at Oneonta presents "R.N. Elliott on Social Mood and Social Change" to the Fifth International Congress and Exhibition, sponsored by the International Society for the Interdisciplinary Study of Symmetry, Sydney, Australia. [Green's essay on philosophy and socionomics is available in *Market Analysis for the New Millennium*, 2002.]

18. **Fall 2001** — *The Journal of Psychology and Markets*—later renamed the *Journal of Behavioral Finance* (JBF)—publishes Prechter's "Unconscious Herding Behavior as the Psychological Basis of Financial Market Trends and Patterns" [Chapter 15].

19. **March 2002** — *Market Analysis for the New Millennium*, a collection of essays relating to Elliott waves and socionomics, is published.

20. **April 2002** — Prechter presents "Wave Theory of Social Behavior and Markets" to the Sixth Congress on the Psychology of Investing in Boston.

21. **August 2002** — John Casti's article on socionomics and Elliott waves is the cover story in the August 31, 2002 edition of *New Scientist*.

22. **September 2002** — Gordon Graham becomes director of the newly named Socionomics Institute, a division of Elliott Wave International (EWI).

23. **November 2002** — With guidance from Graham, John Nofsinger of Washington State University (WSU) and Kenneth Kim of SUNY-Buffalo conduct the first socionomic study by outside researchers. It reveals a relationship between social mood and the character of Congress' financial regulations [reprinted in *Pioneering Studies in Socionomics*, 2003].

24. **2003** — A forerunner of the Socionomics Foundation issues a grant to Nofsinger to write a research paper on social mood and corporate behavior [Chapter 31].

25. **February 2003** — Prechter and Graham meet neuroscientist Greg Berns of Emory University to discuss a way to test the socionomic proposition that herding and rational thought involve different areas of the brain.

26. **May 2003** — *Pioneering Studies in Socionomics*, a collection of essays and studies by socionomists, is published.

27. **September 2003** — Prechter briefly presents the socionomic hypothesis at the Neuroeconomics Conference in Martha's Vineyard, Massachusetts.

28. **September 2003** — Prechter presents "Fundamentals of Finance and Socionomics" to faculty and graduate students at MIT's Laboratory for Financial Engineering.

29. **September 2003** — Dr. Wayne Parker of the Emory University School of Medicine joins the Socionomics Institute as Director of Research.

30. **September 2003** — On September 18, Casti gives the first of his many presentations on socionomics, "How History Happens, or Why the Conventional Wisdom is Always Wrong," at the Complexity, Ethics and Creativity Conference at the London School of Economics and Political Science.

31. **2003-2008** — The Socionomics Foundation gives professor Green a series of grants to conduct and share socionomic research. Green produces thirteen conference presentations, several research papers and a book and obtains a residency at the University of Cambridge. Green adds aspects of socionomics to his course material.

32. **January 2004** — The not-for-profit Socionomics Foundation is officially incorporated, with Parker as Executive Director. Its purpose is to support education and research related to socionomics.

33. **March 2004** — Prechter delivers a two-hour lecture, "Socionomics: Social Mood Is the Engine of Social Activity," before a packed lecture hall at the London School of Economics.

34. **September 2004** — Marius Alexe, an MBA student at McGill University in Montreal, forms the world's first socionomics club.

35. **December 2004** — Prechter speaks at the International Workshop on Intelligent Finance in Melbourne, Australia. The conference proceedings include his and Parker's working paper, "The Financial/Economic Dichotomy."

36. **Spring 2005** — *JBF* publishes Nofsinger's paper, "Social Mood and Financial Economics" [Chapter 31].

37. **March 2005** — The Socionomics Foundation issues a research grant to Kenneth Olson, professor of psychology at Fort Hays State University, to conduct a review of social mood literature.

38. **August 2005** — Parker presents "Herding: An Interdisciplinary Integrative Review from a Socionomic Perspective" [Chapter 34] at the International Conference on Cognitive Economics in Sofia, Bulgaria.

39. **August 2005** — The journal *Biological Psychiatry* publishes Berns et al.'s "Neurobiological Correlates of Social Conformity and Independence During Mental Rotation."

40. **October 2005** — The Socionomics Institute is separately incorporated, with Robert Prechter as Executive Director.

41. **October 2005** — Prechter discusses "The Socionomic Model of Financial and Social Causality" at the annual conference of the Canadian Society of Technical Analysts in Montreal.

42. **November 2005** — Prechter presents "The Socionomic Model of Financial and Social Causality" at SUNY-Plattsburgh.

43. **2006** — Management cybernetics expert Constantin Malik teaches a course about socionomics at the University of Klagenfurt in Austria.

44. **March 2006** — A 60-minute documentary, *History's Hidden Engine,* by filmmaker David Edmund Moore, explains socionomics and its connection to changes in fashion, music, economics, politics and history. It features the views of Casti, Nofsinger, Parker, Hernán Cortés Douglas, Abraham G. Kocheril, Paul Macrae Montgomery, Donald Ratajczak, Didier Sornette and members of the Socionomics Institute.

45. **May 2006** — The Socionomics Foundation issues a grant to Julie Hall of Stanford University for brain imaging research. Hall finds that subliminal images of facial expressions generate activity in unconscious areas of the brain and affect traders' decisions. [See Chapter 19.]

46. **June 2006** — The American National Elections Survey (ANES) chooses Parker to compose polling questions designed to generate social mood data for a pilot study.

47. **July 2006** — Mark Galasiewski begins writing socionomics essays for *The Elliott Wave Theorist*. His study on car colors [republished in *Socionomic Studies of Society and Culture*, 2017] prompts discussion in *Radar Magazine.*

48. **July 2006** — Parker presents "The Socionomic Theory of Finance and the Institution of Social Mood: Pareto and the Sociology of Instinct and Rationalization" [Chapter 36] at The Eighth Annual Conference of the Association for Heterodox Economics in London, England.

49. **July 2006** — Parker presents "Methodological Individualism vs. Methodological Holism: Neoclassicism, Institutionalism and Socionomic Theory" [Chapter 37] at the Congress of the International Association for Research in Economic Psychology and The Society for the Advancement of Behavioral Economics in Paris, France.

50. **August 2006** — IMF economist, World Bank Economic Research Manager and Harvard University Luksic Scholar Hernán Cortés Douglas

argues on behalf of socionomics in "Toward a Revolution in Macroeconomics" [Chapter 36 of *Pioneering Studies in Socionomics*], presented at the 8th Biennial Alternative Perspectives on Finance Conference in Zakopane, Poland.

51. **Q4 2006** — *JBF* publishes Olson's review of social mood literature [Chapter 35].

52. **June 2007** — Prechter and Parker's "The Financial/Economic Dichotomy in Social Behavioral Dynamics: The Socionomic Perspective" is published in the *Journal of Behavioral Finance*.

53. **August 2007** — *The Sydney Morning Herald* publishes Economics Editor Ross Gittins' article, "The Herd's Suffering Mood Swings Again." It is the first mainstream news publication to explore the financial/economic dichotomy delineated in Prechter and Parker's 2007 *JBF* paper.

54. **August 2007** — Self-appointed censors using pseudonyms pressure Wikipedia.org to take down its page on socionomics. (As of Q1 2016, there is still no Wiki page on socionomics.)

55. **September 2007** — Marah Boyesen begins incorporating socionomics in her finance classes at a private high school in Pennsylvania.

56. **April 2008** — Elliott Wave International launches *The Asian-Pacific Financial Forecast*. Editor Galasiewski begins including socionomic commentary in his monthly market analysis.

57. **2008–2011** — Professors Johan Bollen, Eric Gilbert and Peter Gloor conduct research on the relationship between emotional expressions via social media and subsequent financial market activity. [See Chapter 9.]

58. **January 2009** — Casti and researcher Leena Ilmola launch the Extreme Events in Human Society exploratory program at the International Institute for Applied Systems Analysis (IIASA) in Vienna. They incorporate socionomics in their approach to social forecasting.

59. **February 2009** — Brian Whitmer becomes editor of *The European Financial Forecast* and begins including socionomics commentary in his monthly market analysis.

60. **April 2009** — The Institute launches *The Socionomist*, a monthly publication featuring socionomic analysis of history, current events and future trends.

61. **May 2009** — The Socionomics Institute releases *Toward a New Science of Social Prediction: Robert Prechter at the London School of Economics,* which captures Prechter's 2004 lecture on DVD.

62. **August 2009** — *New Scientist* covers Socionomics Institute researcher Euan Wilson's study on marijuana prohibition.

63. **September 2009** — Professors Robert Sizemore of Quinnipiac University and Meriem Chida of WSU incorporate socionomics into their classes.

64. **September 2009** — The Institute awards its first Research Fellowship to Matt Lampert to pursue post-graduate study at the University of Cambridge.

65. **November 2009** — *USA Today* introduces readers to the socionomic perspective in an article on the connection between social mood and popular music, television shows and movies.

66. **January 2010** — Rob Goodman, one of Chida's students, receives an undergraduate research grant from WSU's College of Agricultural, Human and Natural Resource Sciences to pursue his work on the relationship between social mood and fashion trends.

67. **February 2010** — Mark Almand is named director of the Socionomics Institute. In the next three years, the Institute grows to eight full-time staffers and several part-time contributors.

68. **February 2010** — Prechter presents "The Socionomic Theory of Finance" to students and faculty at the University of Cambridge.

69. **March 2010** — Three of Chida's students present their research on social mood and fashion trends at WSU's annual Academic Showcase.

70. **March 2010** — Professor Green wins the Susan Sutton Smith Prize for Academic Excellence due in part to research funded by the Socionomics Foundation.

71. **May 2010** — Copernicus Books publishes Casti's *Mood Matters: From Rising Skirt Lengths to the Collapse of World Powers*.

72. **July 2010** — Prechter introduces the fractal model of social-trend projection to the World Future Society in Boston at its annual conference.

73. **September 2010** — *Nature* and *Science* magazines review Casti's book, *Mood Matters*. [See Chapter 43.]

74. **October 2010** — *Time* magazine interviews Wilson about his research on social mood and the growing social acceptance of marijuana.

75. **November 2010** — Prechter presents "A New Perspective on Financial, Economic and Social Causality" to students and faculty at the University of Oxford and at Trinity College, Dublin.

76. **March 2011** — Campus Verlag publishes Constantin Malik's *Ahead of Change*, a book on socionomics, cybernetics and public policy.

77. **April 2011** — The Socionomics Institute hosts its inaugural Social Mood Conference at the Georgia Tech Conference Center in Atlanta. The conference features academics who study social mood and practitioners who apply it in business and finance. Presenters include Prechter, Casti, Bollen, Gilbert, Olson, Kendall, Lampert, Huina Mao and Kevin Depew.

78. **May 2011** — Lampert's presentation on socionomics wins "Best Presentation" at the University of Cambridge's Conference on Everything, sponsored by Churchill College.

79. **May 2011** — Lampert speaks about socionomics at the European Futurists Conference's Tipping Points Workshop in Mt. Pilatus, Switzerland.

80. **June 2011** — Lampert receives a National Academy of Sciences grant to contribute to Casti and Ilmola's work.

81. **September 2011** — Lampert presents socionomics to attendees at the Annual Meeting of the Academy of Behavioral Finance and Economics at the University of California-Los Angeles.

82. **October 2011** — Dennis Elam, accounting professor at Texas A&M-San Antonio, gives an on-campus socionomics presentation, "Cycling through History: How Social Mood Determines Your Career Success." He begins incorporating socionomics into his course material.

83. **January 2012** — Prechter, Deepak Goel, Parker and Lampert's paper, "Social Mood, Stock Market Performance and U.S. Presidential Elections: A Socionomic Perspective on Voting Results," is posted on the Social Science Research Network (SSRN). *The Washington Post*, the Associated Press, *The Hill* and other media outlets cover the paper.

84. **February 2012** — Adjunct professor and institutional financial consultant Peter Atwater begins teaching an honors colloquium on "Social Mood, Decision Making & Markets" at the University of Delaware.

85. **April 2012** — Three months after its posting, the Institutes's elections paper becomes one of SSRN's most-downloaded papers of the year.

86. **April 2012** — The Institute holds its second annual Social Mood Conference at the Georgia Tech Conference Center in Atlanta. Presenters include Terry Burnham, Richard L. Peterson, Kevin Coogan, Jose Carlos Carvalho, Ilmola, Kotick, Lampert, Mao, Atwater, Almand, Wilson and Prechter.

87. **July 2012** — Minyanville Media publishes Atwater's *Moods and Markets: A New Way to Invest in Good Times and in Bad*, a book on socionomics geared toward institutional asset managers.

88. **July 2012** — Prechter presents the Institute's elections paper and discusses the socionomic causality of trends in popular culture at FreedomFest in Las Vegas, Nevada.

89. **July 2012** — Lampert and Institute intern Idan Hodor introduce Elliotticity as a stylized fact of financial time series at the International Symposium on Forecasting in Boston, Massachusetts.

90. **August 2012** — *The Wall Street Journal* publishes Elam's letter on negative social mood and dark themes in popular entertainment.

91. **September 2012** — Prechter presents the Institute's elections paper at the Annual Meeting of the Academy of Behavioral Finance and Economics in Brooklyn, New York. A co-chairman of the conference observes, "The word *socionomics* is becoming part of the lexicon."

92. **September 2012** — Lampert presents the Institute's elections paper at the Elections, Public Opinion and Parties Conference at the University of Oxford.

93. **November 2012** — The Institute's elections paper is published in the peer-reviewed journal, *SAGE Open*. In line with the study's implications, incumbent U.S. president Barack Obama is re-elected following a 3½-year rally in stock prices.

94. **November 2012** — Lampert presents the Institute's elections paper at Churchill College, University of Cambridge.

95. **November 2012** — The Institute's elections paper becomes the third-most-downloaded paper for the preceding 12 months on SSRN.com.

96. **November 2012** — Dr. Wayne D. Parker, author and co-author of landmark papers about socionomics and founding Executive Director of the Socionomics Foundation, dies of carcinoid cancer at age 61.

97. **November 2012** — Casti presents "How the World Works: Why We Do What We Do—and Not Do Something Else" at TEDxVienna.

98. **January 2013** — Wilson presents the Institute's elections paper to the American Politics Group of the Political Studies Association Conference at the University of Leicester.

99. **March 2013** — Alan Hall, Lampert and Sebastian Di Cesare post their working paper, "Using Stock Market Indexes to Anticipate Elevated Public Health Risk: A Socionomic View of Epidemic Disease," to SSRN.com.

100. **April 2013** — HSBC's Murray Gunn completes the first independently conceived and executed socionomic study, "How Comparing Sectors Reveals Underlying Social Mood and Helps You Invest Better." A later study by Gunn, "Beyond The Redline: Socionomic Relationship Between Speed and Markets; 200mph Motorcycle Could Coincide with a Top," is published in the June 2015 *HSBC's Long Wave Outlook* [reprinted in *Socionomic Studies of Society and Culture*, 2017].

101. **April 2013** — The Institute hosts its third annual Social Mood Conference at the Georgia Tech Conference Center in Atlanta. Presenters include Michelle Baddeley, Mark Buchanan, Rishab Ghosh, Philip Maymin, Tobias Preis, Marah Boyesen, Jon Clifton, Kevin Armstrong, Gunn, Hall, Almand and Prechter.

102. **May 2013** — The Institute releases Prechter's presentations to Oxford, Cambridge and Trinity on DVD.

103. **June 2013** — Reuters quotes Prechter, Atwater, Burnham, Gunn and Peterson in an article on social mood and markets.

104. **June 2013** — Wilson connects social mood, the stock market and marijuana legalization on Yahoo! Finance's "Breakout" program.

105. **July 2013** — Hall presents the Institute's working paper on epidemics to the behavioral finance conference, SABE/IAREP/ICABEEP 2013, in Atlanta.

106. **August 2013** — Atwater presents "Confidence-Driven Decision Making," the first of two TEDx Talks on socionomics. (He delivers his second one at the College of William and Mary in April 2014.)

107. **September 2013** — Hall presents the Institute's research on social mood and epidemics at the Annual Meeting of the Academy of Behavioral Finance and Economics at DePaul University in Chicago.

108. **September 2013** — Hall introduces socionomics to faculty and students at the Stevens Institute of Technology in Hoboken, New Jersey.

109. **October 2013** — Kevin Armstrong's book, *Bulls, Birdies, Bogeys & Bears, The Remarkable and Revealing Relationship Between Golf & Investment Markets*, is published. He expands upon Kendall's socionomic insights on the history of golf in his study of the sport.

110. **October 2013** —Wilson presents "Much of How You're Taught to Think Is Wrong—An Introduction to Socionomics" at an event hosted by the Bryn Athyn College Business Club.

111. **November 2013** — Galasiewski's speech at the Irrational Economic Summit in La Jolla, California features socionomic commentary on the Asian-Pacific region.

112. **December 2013** — *Businessweek* interviews Wilson about the relationship between social mood and the drug war.

113. **April 2014** — The fourth annual Social Mood Conference at the Georgia Tech Conference Center in Atlanta features a keynote address by behavioral finance pioneer Werner DeBondt as well as presentations from Kenneth Kishida, Suzy Moat, Thomas Brudermann, Alan Brochstein, Mikko Ketovuori, Dave Allman, Atwater, Hall, Almand, Lampert and Prechter.

114. **May 2014** — Wilson gives an introductory lecture on socionomics at Golden Gate University.

115. **July 2014** — *Business Insider* publishes an article on Hall's 2007 socionomic study that had accurately forecast a major bear market in Russian stocks and a simultaneous military resurgence for the country. [Reprinted in *Socionomic Causality in Politics*, 2017.]

116. **September 2014** — Prechter presents his and Parker's 2007 *JBF* paper to the general session of the Annual Meeting of the Academy of Behavioral Finance and Economics in Los Angeles.

117. **October 2014** — At the height of an Ebola outbreak, Hall presents the socionomic view of epidemic disease at the annual Irrational Economic Summit in Miami.

118. **October 2014** — Prechter presents "The Socionomic Theory of Finance: An Alternative to EMH and a Foundation for Technical Analysis" at the annual conference of the International Federation of Technical Analysts (IFTA) in London.

119. **February 2015** — Elam addresses the American Association of Behavioral and Social Sciences Conference in Las Vegas. He discusses social mood's influence on accounting regulations in the United States.

120. **April 2015** — The fifth annual Social Mood Conference at Georgia Tech in Atlanta features presentations by Alex Bentley, Shikhar Agarwal, John Grable, Burnham, Whitmer, Lampert, Prechter, Hall and Elliott Prechter.

121. **September 2015** — Lampert presents "A Real-Time Case Study of Russia's Military Resurgence" at the Annual Meeting of the Academy of Behavioral Finance and Economics at Drexel University in Philadelphia.

122. **October 2015** — Elam's paper contrasting the socionomic theory of finance to traditional explanations for stock valuations is selected for publication in the Proceedings of the 23rd Annual Southwestern Business Administration Teaching Conference.

123. **October 2015** — Galasiewski presents a socionomic analysis of the Asian region at the annual conference of the International Federation of Technical Analysts in Tokyo.

124. **December 2015** — Hall introduces socionomics to the Inter-agency Health Leaders Roundtable at the National Defense University in Washington, D.C.

125. **January 2016** — Prechter's October 2014 presentation to IFTA is released on DVD.

126. **January 2016** — The University of Warwick's interdisciplinary two-day conference, "Mood—Aesthetic, Psychological and Philosophical Perspectives," lists "Robert Prechter's concept of mood in socionomics" as a topic of discussion.

127. **April 2016** — The Institute inaugurates audio versions of *The Socionomist*.

128. **April 2016** — Eugene Stanley, co-founder of econophysics, is the keynote speaker at the sixth annual Social Mood Conference at the Georgia Tech Conference Center in Atlanta. Prechter, Elam, Lampert, Kendall, Hall, Nerissa Brown, Jon Fassett, Alastair Macdonald and Robert Folsom round out the list of speakers.

129. **May 2016** — Lampert, Elam and Hall present at the University of Warwick's interdisciplinary conference on mood. Their topics are elections, social mood and epidemics, respectively.

130. **May 2016** — Four years after posting, the Institute's elections paper remains ranked among the top 2/100ths of 1% for download frequency among all 550,000 papers posted on the Social Science Research Network's website. It remains SSRN's most-downloaded paper of all time in both the Collective Decision-Making and Voting Behaviors categories.

LIST OF ILLUSTRATIONS

Chapter 1

Figure 1:   Good/Bad Economic News Headlines 3
Figure 2:   JFK Assassination, blank. 4
Figure 3:   JFK Assassination, with arrows. 5
Figure 4:   NYC Blackout, blank 6
Figure 5:   NYC Blackout, with arrows 7
Figure 6:   9/11 Attack, blank 7
Figure 7:   9/11 Attack, with arrows 8
Figure 8:   Hurricane Katrina & Oil Prices. 9
Figure 9:   Anthrax Attacks (fake) 11
Figure 10:   Anthrax Attacks (real) 12
Figure 11:   Greenspan Speech, intraday stock prices 17
Figure 12:   Fed Announcement, intraday stock prices 20
Figure 13:   Fed's Rate Increase, daily stock prices 21

Chapter 2

Figure 1:   Diagram: Exogenous-Cause Model of Stock Prices 24
Figure 2:   Rates & Stocks Fall 26
Figure 3:   Rates & Stocks Rise 27
Figure 4:   Rates Fall, Stocks Rise 28
Figure 5:   Rates Rise, Stocks Fall 29
Figure 6:   Oil Prices & S&P 500, 2003-6 30
Figure 7:   Oil Prices & S&P 500, 2008-11 31
Figure 8:   Oil & Stocks Lack of Correlation 34
Figure 9:   Trade Deficit vs. Stocks 37
Figure 10:   Earnings vs. Stocks, 1973-4 39
Figure 11:   GDP vs. DJIA 41
Figure 12:   World War I & Stocks 43
Figure 13:   World War II & Stocks 43
Figure 14:   Korean War & Stocks 43
Figure 15:   Vietnam War & Stocks 43
Figure 16:   Dow Rises in Peacetime, 1921-9 44
Figure 17:   Dow Falls in Peacetime, 1929-32 44
Figure 18:   Monetary Inflation vs. Gold & Silver Prices 47
Figure 19:   QE Ignored by DJIA 49
Figure 20:   QE Ignored by Commodities 50
Figure 21:   Gold & Silver Prices Fall after Fed Day, 12/12/12 51
Figure 22:   Gold & Silver Prices Fall during QE Era 53
Figure 23:   Central Banks' Gold Buying vs. Prices (fake) 54
Figure 24:   Central Banks' Gold Buying vs. Prices (real) 55
Figure 25:   Bailout Programs, blank 57
Figure 26:   Bailout Programs, with arrows 58
Figure 27:   Stocks Fall after Rescue Efforts, 2008 59
Figure 28:   Gold Prices Ignore Interest Rates 62

Chapter 3
Figure 1:   U.S. T-bill Rates Lead Fed Funds Rate, 2000-7 74
Figure 2:   U.S. T-bill Rates Lead Fed Funds Rate, 2000-12 74
Figure 3:   U.S. T-bill Rates Lead Fed Funds Rate, early 1980s 75
Figure 4:   Euro Bond Rate Leads ECB Rate 75
Figure 5:   UK Bond Rate Leads BOE Rate 76
Figure 6:   Australian RBA Rate Will Rise 77
Figure 7:   Australian T-bill Rate Leads RBA Rate 78
Figure 8:   Australian Stocks vs. Rates: No Correlation 79

Chapter 4
Figure 1:   French Stocks & Charlie Hebdo Attack 83

Chapter 6
Figure 1:   Diagram: Structure of Socionomic Theory 115
Table 1:   Expressions of Mechanical vs. Socionomic Causality 119
Figure 2:   Idealized Elliott Wave at Successive Degrees 122
Figure 3:   Idealized Elliott Wave, Five Degrees of Iteration 122

Chapter 7
Figure 1:   Timing among Immediate & Lagging Sociometers 142

Chapter 8
Figure 1:   Diagram: Quantity & Extremity of Social Mood 149
Figure 2:   Pivot Points in Idealized Elliott Waves 150
Figure 3:   Expressions of Social Mood, 1930-1932 151
Image: "500,000 Chicagoans Revel" Article, 1931. 153
Image: "500,000 Chicagoans Starve" Article, 1932 153
Image: Suicide News Reports, 1932 154
Figure 4:   Expressions of Social Mood, 1929-1933 155
Figure 5:   Expressions of Social Mood, 1973-1974 161
Figure 6:   Expressions of Social Mood, 2007-2012 164

Chapter 10
Figure 1:   Prosperity & Depression vs. Stocks 175
Figure 2:   U.S. GDP vs. Stocks 176
Figure 3:   U.S. Patents vs. Stocks 177
Figure 4:   Disney & Horror Movies vs. Stocks 178
Image: Smiling Monster Families. 179
Figure 5:   Annual Conceptions vs. Stocks 181
Figure 6:   Hemlines vs. Stocks 182
Figure 7:   Hemline Headlines vs. Stocks 183
Figure 8:   Presidential Incumbents' Fates vs. Stocks 184
Figure 9:   Nuclear Weapons Testing vs. Stocks .185
Figure 10:   Wars vs. Stocks 186
Figure 11:   Trade Deficit Forecast 188
Figure 12:   Trade Deficit Outcome 189
Figure 13:   Social Actions vs. Dow/Gold 190

Chapter 12
Figure 1:   History of Dividend Yields 204
Figure 2:   History of S&P Earnings 204

Figure 3:   History of Corporate Book Values 204
Figure 4:   History of Bond Yield/Stock Yield 204
Figure 5:   Japanese Dividend Payout & Bond/Stock Yield 206
Figure 6:   Computer Demand vs. Prices 210
Figure 7:   Number of Stock Owners vs. Prices 211
Figure 8:   Stock Ownership % vs. Prices 212
Figure 9:   Stock Trading Volume vs. Prices 213
Figure 10:   Diagram: Motivation to Buy/Sell vs. Price in Economics 214
Figure 11:   Diagram: Motivation to Buy/Sell vs. Price in Finance 214
Figure 12:   Diagram: Equilibrium from Producers and Consumers 228
Figure 13:   Diagram: Equilibrium in Economics 231
Figure 14:   Diagram: Dynamism in Finance 231

Chapter 13
Figure 1:   Economic vs. Financial Decisions in Human Brain 244
Figure 2:   Economics vs. Finance at Micro and Macro Level 247
Table 1:   Financial/Economic Dichotomy at Micro Level 254
Table 2:   Financial/Economic Dichotomy at Macro Level 255
Figure 3:   Boom-Bust Cycle in Real Estate Ownership 257
Table 3:   Tenets of STF vs. EMH 259

Chapter 14
Figure 1:   Economic-Socionomic Spectrum of Markets 266

Chapter 15
Figure 1:   History of Dividend Yield 280
Figure 2:   History of S&P Earnings 280
Figure 3:   History of Book Values 281
Figure 4:   History of Bond Yield/Stock Yield 281
Figure 5:   Computer Demand vs. Prices 286
Figure 6:   Stock Trading Volume vs. Prices 286
Figure 7:   Number of Stock Owners vs. Prices 287
Figure 8:   Stock Ownership % vs. Prices 287
Figure 9:   Correlation: Computer Demand vs. Prices 288
Figure 10:   Correlation: Trading Volume vs. Stock Prices 288
Figure 11:   Correlation: Number of Stock Owners vs. Prices 289
Figure 12:   Correlation: Stock Ownership % vs. Stock Prices 289
Table 1:   Correlation Statistics for Figures 9-12 290
Figure 13:   Volume in 1987 Crash 291
Figure 14:   Herding by Mutual Fund Managers 305
Figure 15:   Diagram: Price vs. Demand in Economics 308
Figure 16:   Diagram: Price vs. Demand in Finance 308
Figure 17:   Diagram: Law of Supply & Demand 309
Figure 18:   Diagram: Law of Patterned Herding 310
Table 2:   STF vs. EMH.......................................311

Chapter 16
Figure 1:   Herding by Institutions & Public 329

Chapter 17
Figure 1:   Herding by Individuals 338

Figure 2:   Herding by Futures Traders 338
Figure 3:   Herding by Financial Advisors 339
Figure 4:   Herding by Mutual Fund Managers 339
Figure 5:   Herding by Hedge Fund Managers 340
Figure 6:   Herding by Corporate Investors 340
Figure 7:   Herding by Wall Street Analysts 342
Figure 8:   Herding by Legislators 343
Figure 9:   Growth of CGM Focus Fund over 10 Years 348
Figure 10:   Investors' Return in CGM Focus Fund over 10 Years 349
Figure 11:   Projected Returns for Mutual Fund over 30 Years 350
Figure 12:   Best/Worst U.S. Stock Mutual Funds .350
Figure 13:   Buy/Sell Behavior of Novice Speculator 353
Figure 14:   Buy/Sell Behavior of Seasoned Speculator 354
Figure 15:   Buy/Sell Behavior of Sophisticated Speculator 354
Figure 16:   Buy/Sell Behavior of Contrarian Speculator 354

Chapter 18
Figure 1:   Economists Predict Higher Rates, June 1984 363
Figure 2:   Aftermath of June 1984 Peak in Bond Yield 364
Figure 3:   Bearish Consensus on Gold, February 2001 *Barron's* 365
Figure 4:   Consensus at Major Turning Points in Gold 366

Chapter 19
Figure 1:   Image, Lone Girl Listens to Headphones 387
Figure 2:   Image, Crowd Madness at Concert 387
Figure 3:   Image, Individuals Walking 387
Figure 4:   Image, Soldiers Marching in Step 387
Figure 5:   Image: Macroeconomic Equation 387
Figure 6:   Elliott Waves in Stocks and Oil Prices 406

Chapter 20
Figure 1:   Opinion Convergence in Crowds 416

Chapter 21
Figure 1:   Analysts' Forecasts Lag S&P Earnings 425
Figure 2:   Diagram: Linear Extrapolation w/ Idealized Elliott Wave 427
Figure 3:   GE Forecast 428
Figure 4:   Outcome of GE Forecast 429
Figure 5:   U.S. Dollar Index Forecast 430
Figure 6:   Outcome of U.S. Dollar Index Forecast 431
Figure 7:   Bearish Books at Stock Market Bottom 432
Figure 8:   Image: Bearish Books, 1966-1982 433
Figure 9:   Bullish Books at Stock Market Top 434
Figure 10:   Image: Bullish Books, 1998-2007 435
Figure 11:   Forecast for Fannie Mae 436
Figure 12:   Outcome of FNM Forecast 437
Figure 13:   Junk/Treasuries Yield Spread Forecast 437
Figure 14:   Outcome of Junk/Treasuries Yield Spread Forecast 438
Figure 15:   Fitness Trends & Positive/Negative Mood 439
Figure 16:   Bally's Stock Price vs. Dow/Gold 439

Figure 17:	Employment vs. Stocks	440
Figure 18:	Collectible Coins	444
Figure 19:	"New Economy" References	444
Figure 20:	Forecast for Homebuilding Stocks	445
Figure 21:	Outcome of Forecast for Homebuilding Stocks	446
Figure 22:	Images of Michael Jackson	448
Figure 23:	Gallup Poll of Global Warming Risk	449
Figure 24:	Bulls > Bears, Duration at Tops, 1929-2000	452
Figure 25:	Bulls > Bears, Duration at Tops, 1929-2007	453
Figure 26:	Crash in Earnings, 2008	455

Chapter 22

Figure 1:	World Oil Consumption vs. Production	458
Figure 2:	Price Turns vs. Production/Consumption	459
Figure 3:	Crude Oil Major Low Forecast, 1993	461
Figure 4:	Crude Oil Prices, 1859-1993	462
Figure 5:	Crude Oil Prices with Elliott Wave Labels, 1859-1993	462
Figure 6:	Elliott Wave Model & Oil Turn Dates, 1910-1993	463
Figure 7:	Crude Oil Low Forecast, 1998	464
Figure 8:	Crude Oil High Forecast, 2000	465
Figure 9:	Crude Oil Low Forecast, 2001	466
Figure 10:	Crude Oil Long Term Forecast	467
Figure 11:	Crude Oil Forecast at Kenos Conference, 2006	468
Figure 12:	Crude Oil High Forecast, 2006	468
Figure 13:	Image: Oil Crisis Books, 2005-2006	470
Figure 14:	Crude Oil Low Forecast, 2007	472
Figure 15:	Crude Oil Top Forecast, 2008	474
Figure 16:	Crude Oil Details of Final Rise	475
Figure 17:	Crude Oil Crash, 2008	476
Image:	"World without Oil" Article, 2005	471
Figure 18:	Details of 2008-9 Crude Oil Decline	477
Figure 19:	Peaks in CRB Index and Crude Oil, 2011	480
Figure 20:	Gasoline Prices vs. Expectations	482
Figure 21:	Crude Oil Forecast, May 2014	483
Figure 22:	Crude Oil Crash, 2014-15	485
Figure 23:	Details of Latest Decline in Crude Oil	486
Figure 24:	Crude Oil Rally Forecast, March 2016	487
Figure 25:	EWI Oil Calls, 1993-2016	488
Figure 26:	Idealized Elliott Wave w/ Oil Turns, 1998-2016	489
Figure 27:	Crude Oil Long Term Waves Since 1859	490
Figure 28:	Oil Price Rise Spurred U.S. Production	497
Figure 29:	Oil Price vs. Consumption/Production Ratio	498
Figure 30:	Stocks vs. Production/Consumption Ratio	500

Chapter 23

Figure 1:	Diagram: Valuation Behavior under BF & Bubble Theories	507
Figure 2:	An Elliott Wave in U.S. Auto Loans	512
Figure 3:	Diagram: Fifth-Wave Reversals of Increasing Degree	513
Figure 4:	Wave V Manias in U.S. Stocks Prices, 1780-2015	519

Chapter 26
Figure 1:   Uncertainty Spikes vs. Stock Prices 552
Figure 2:   Economic Policy Uncertainty vs. Events 553
Figure 3:   Economic Policy Uncertainty vs. Stocks 555
Figure 4:   NY Times Uncertainty Index vs. Stocks 555

Chapter 27
Figure 1:   Monetary Fears vs. CPI & Stock Market 558

Chapter 28
Figure 1:   Laughter at FOMC Meetings vs. Stocks 570
Figure 2:   Elliott Wave in Fed Laughter through 2006 573
Figure 3:   Fed Laughter vs. Stocks through 2010 575

Chapter 29
Figure 1:   Forecast: SNB Will Abandon Its Euro Peg 578
Figure 2:   Outcome: Swiss Francs per Euro Crash 579

Chapter 31
Figure 1:   Loewenstein Model of Risk as Feelings 589
Figure 2:   Phases of Social Mood Cycle 592
Figure 3:   Merger Deals Correlated to S&P 605
Figure 4:   IPO Volume Correlated to Stocks in U.S. & Japan 608

Chapter 34
Table 1:   Herding Models on Eight Theoretical Dimensions.......... 657

Chapter 36
Image: Pareto's Concept of Undulating Waves................... 708
Image: Idealized Elliott Wave 709

Chapter 39
Figure 1:   Barge & People 736
Figure 2:   Economist's Barge Hypothesis 738
Figure 3:   Socionomist's Submarine Hypothesis 740
Figure 4:   Barge Metaphor under Economic Theory 742
Figure 5:   Submarine Metaphor under Socionomic Theory 743

Chapter 40
Figure 1:   Financial Theories vs. Stocks 747
Image: "Committee to Save the World" *Time* Cover.............. 750
Figure 2:   Books on Non-Rational Finance, 2000-2009 752
Figure 3:   Image: Magazine Covers on Economic Theory at 2009 Low .. 754

Chapter 41
Figure 1:   Stock Market and Recessions 763
Figure 2:   Peace and War vs. Stocks 765
Figure 3:   1987-1990 Bear Market and Gulf War 766
Figure 4:   Terrorist Attacks vs. DJIA 767
Figure 5:   Pop Music Crazes vs. DJIA 768

Chapter 43
Image: *Mood Matters* book cover 777

INDEX

1929   61, 147, 150-7, 310, 404, 451-2, 746-9

1984 bottom, bonds   28, 73, 361-7

1987 crash, U.S. stocks   41-2, 45, 65, 89, 101, 147, 294, 300-1, 394, 451-3, 569, 766

1999 peak, U.S. stocks   175, 178, 190, 208, 368, 436, 442, 450, 503-4, 520, 559, 571-2, 648, 749-51, 759-64, 768, 787

2006 peak, real estate   85-7, 180, 187, 241-2, 256, 345, 369, 376, 383, 407, 435-45, 499, 515, 520, 549-51, 572-4, 753-5, 761

2007 peak, U.S. stocks   57, 64, 138, 147, 163-6, 176-82, 187-9, 343-7, 376, 435, 450-5, 574

2007-9 financial crisis   92-103, 138, 163, 176, 187, 347, 443, 516, 543

2008   10, 31, 35, 48-9, 56-61, 66-9, 74, 86-7, 96-7, 101, 163, 166, 170, 180, 205, 279, 344-7, 357, 368-9, 383, 400-9, 429-431, 435, 438, 451-3, 473-7, 484, 492-8, 516, 540-3, 754, 760-1, 787, 793-5

2009 bottom, U.S. stocks   39-40, 57, 87-103, 147, 163-6, 176, 179-82, 187, 337-41, 347-50, 368, 381, 406, 499, 520, 754-5

401K   344-5

9/11 attack   7-8, 11, 186, 383, 441, 554, 760, 766

A

A causing B   193, 542

Academy of Behavioral Finance & Economics   779, 797, 799, 800

affect, positive & negative (PA, NA)   411, 581, 670-4, 678-82

agent/agency   93, 125-6, 396-9, 628-9, 704-5, 715-6, 725-6

Alchian, Armen   642-3

Alexopoulos and Cohen   551-551

anecdotal evidence   173-4, 208, 233, 347

animal herding   408-9, 658-9, 696

Ant Recruitment Model   656, 659

anthrax attacks   11-2, 147, 403-4

Anxiety index   170

apparent learning   351-2

Apple Inc.   341-2

Approach-Avoidance   581-3 [Ch. 30], 677-82

art   269-72, 294

asset pricing theory   274, 277-9, 644-5, 649

Australia   77-80, 792-3

Austrian economics   523-537 [Ch. 24]

auto loans   512

autopoiesis   696-696

B

bailouts   56-60, 380, 400

Baker et al.   553

bank failures   509-511

Barron's   181, 366, 479, 577, 782

basal ganglia   245, 295, 325-6, 333, 674

basketball   389, 450

Beanie Babies   293, 512

bearish books   432-4

Beatles   376, 766-8, 781

behaviorism   310, 622, 662, 717

behavioral economics/finance (BE/BF)   260, 271, 274-5, 278, 308-310, 395, 399-402, 521, 636-8, 662, 721, 735, 798-9

benchmark sociometer   131-2, 144

Berkshire Hathaway   216-8

Bernanke, Ben   52, 87, 96-7, 516, 565

Berns, Greg   244-5, 792-3

Biggs, Barton   504-6

birth rates (see: conceptions)   136, 180-1

blackouts   5-7, 13

Bollen, John   169-70, 372, 795-6

bonds/bond yields   204-6, 281, 381, 563-4

book values   203-8, 533

boom-bust cycle   93, 252, 255-6, 265, 301, 327-8, 385, 751, 787

bottom-up   116, 124-6, 130, 401

bounded sociometer   133-6, 140, 144-5

brain   296, 590

branching   121-3, 128

Brock, William   65

bubbles   78, 86-7, 91, 99-100, 298, 306, 328, 348-51, 396, 443-5, 503-21 [Ch. 23], 561-2, 572, 587, 595-6, 599-600, 657, 761

bullish books   434-6

burn rate   208, 504

business cycle   96, 274, 279, 543, 562, 606, 612, 645-6, 648-50, 750

buybacks   222, 337, 341

C

CAC 40   81-3
Caldarelli et al.   301, 385
capital gains tax rate   66
Casti, John   372, 754, 773, 778, 793-8
Capital Pricing Asset Model (CAPM)   277-82, 600-2, 634, 644-5, 649, 748-9
central banks/bankers   54-64, 73-81 [Ch. 3], 540-2, 563-6, 574-7, 750
centrism/polarization   143
ceteris paribus   110, 277, 282, 386, 637
CGM Focus Fund   348-50
chaos theory   117-120, 260
Charlie Hebdo   81-4 [Ch. 4], 404
China   33, 38, 58, 144, 372, 377, 421, 423, 491, 562, 764
CNBC   163, 481, 749
Coca-Cola   216-8
coins   216-8
collectibles   268-72
commercials   257, 259, 356, 484
Commodity Futures Trading Commission   356, 785
communism/Marxism   423, 543
complex system/complexity   119, 126, 260, 586
computers: price vs. demand   209-10, 226, 284-8, 290
conception(s) (see: birth rates)   134, 136, 143, 180-1
Consumer Confidence Index (CCI)   133, 136
Consumer Price Index (CPI)   63, 89, 557-66
Consumer Sentiment Index (CSI)   133-133
contagion   111, 263, 384-5, 507, 656, 658, 667, 674-6, 690
contextualism   114, 294, 621-8, 632-3, 639-40, 695-7, 705, 712, 723, 726-7
corporate earnings   38-9, 89, 163, 203-4, 208, 328, 533, 668
corporate finance   586, 593, 602-9
corporate insiders   337, 340-1
credit default swaps (CDS)   100-100
Cutler et al.   42, 45, 64, 68-9, 167, 301-2
currencies   268, 271, 405, 428-30, 544, 577

D

data fitting   13, 48
DeBondt, Werner   799
deflation   31, 364, 371, 379, 501, 557-566 [Ch. 27], 750

democracy   421-2
depression   61, 66-8, 147, 156-8, 175, 187-90, 228, 327, 346, 404, 453, 499, 509, 598, 707
derivatives   91, 119, 511, 704, 749
discounting theory   79, 147, 491, 735-745 [Ch. 39]
Disney movies   177-80, 190, 197
dividend discount model   207, 277-9
dividends/dividend yield   25, 203-7, 250, 280, 343, 450-2, 504
dollar index   368, 429-31
dopamine   388
Dow/gold ratio   139, 175, 187, 343, 748-9
Dow/PPI (inflation-adjusted Dow)   139, 175, 178-9, 393, 406, 434, 450, 551, 748, 764
Dow/U.S. dollar (nominal Dow)   139, 175, 552-3, 749
dynamism   227-32, 251, 273, 292, 298, 306-9, 397, 400, 514, 709, 715

E

earnings   24, 38-42, 69, 89, 163, 203-8, 278-80, 305, 328, 425, 534
earthquakes   10, 166, 775
economic-socionomic spectrum   265-272 [Ch. 14]
econophysics   505, 655-7, 660, 800
efficient market hypothesis (EMH)   23, 24, 98, 230, 232, 236, 252, 255, 260, 273, 274, 275, 276, 277, 282, 283, 290, 293, 298, 304, 306, 308, 309, 311, 333, 358, 397, 399, 401, 516, 525, 532, 535, 543, 597, 646, 662, 748, 755
elections   183-4, 193-5, 731-2
Elliott, Ralph Nelson (R.N.)   64, 109, 114, 121, 123, 129, 232, 388, 402, 708-10, 716, 786, 791
Elliott Wave Principle (book)   113, 121, 262, 430, 432-4, 463, 473, 489, 748, 787, 791
Elliott wave model (EW)   112-4, 121-5, 149-50, 154, 160, 197, 232, 238, 251, 262-3, 426-434, 439, 442, 451, 460, 463, 467, 475, 478-9, 490-3, 503-521 [Ch. 23], 553, 643, 760-1, 783, 788
Elliott Wave Theorist (EWT)   30, 51, 150, 174-5, 185-191, 208, 244, 268, 361, 370, 429-431, 434, 442-3, 447-451, 467-483, 517, 750, 753, 760, 764, 767, 791-794
Ellis, George   125, 127

emergence   125-6, 333, 625, 712, 725
employment   40, 63, 192, 196, 199, 380, 440, 552-4, 638, 762
endogenous causality   110-119, 145, 196, 297, 301, 311-13, 426, 523, 539, 626-7, 633, 645, 655-661, 669-73, 691-2, 706-8, 717, 745, 749, 755, 783
Enron   18, 372, 394
epidemics   136, 189-91, 798-9
equilibrium theory   23-4, 227-33, 255, 271-83, 291-2, 298-300, 307-12, 402, 492, 495, 507, 512-4, 585-6, 641-663, 701-2, 709-715, 723-4
equity culture   518-518
ethological herding   655-8
European Central Bank   73, 76, 80
event/process ontology   298, 625-8, 644-651, 705, 726
evolutionary psychology   126-7, 295-7, 399, 408, 642-3, 655-60, 676-80, 695-9, 773
exogenous shock   3-85 [Part 1, Ch. 1-5], 88, 98, 109-10, 117-23, 137-8, 147, 166, 174, 180, 192, 196-9, 241, 263, 301-2, 311-3, 361-85 [Ch. 18] 394-9, 429, 539-42, 625-33, 659-62, 691-2, 706-8, 754-5, 782-6

F

falsifiability/falsifiable   195-200 [Ch. 11]
Fama, Eugene   98, 100, 274, 277, 356, 516, 755
Fannie Mae/Freddie Mac   56, 436
fashion   112, 132, 147-8, 182-3, 191-2, 256, 269-271, 276, 297, 306, 326, 375, 599, 624, 647, 656-7, 701, 744, 761-6, 769, 776, 791, 794, 796
fads   112, 265, 270, 276, 297, 301, 306, 326, 375, 596, 598-9, 624, 647, 656-7, 701, 710, 787
fat tails   403-403
federal funds rate   19-21, 73-6, 89, 426, 569
Fed laughter   Ch. 28, 238-9, 251, 255, 270, 274, 292-3, 303-13, 391, 463, 521, 785
Federal Reserve (FOMC)   13-20, 47-52, 57-66, 73-7, 86-9, 94-6, 138, 156-9, 429, 479, 516, 560-6, 569-75, 599-600, 626-7, 753-5, 782-3
feedback   116-20, 236, 260, 303
Fibonacci   114, 121, 128, 519, 638, 791
financial advisors   337-9, 346
Financial/Economic Dichotomy   117, 203-233 [Ch. 12], 244-6, 254, 272-313 [Ch. 15], 356, 417, 731, 793-5

Financial News Network (FFN)   181, 518, 748
fitness   438-9
Five Factor Model (FFM)   679-80
formism   114, 123, 623, 632
formological   117, 124, 130, 521, 625-6, 638, 647
Fractal Market Hypothesis   396-7
Fractal model/extrapolation   33, 70, 109, 112-4, 117, 121-3, 149, 313, 337-360 [Ch. 17], 385-6, 394-408, 421-455 [Ch. 21], 513-4, 519-21, 708-12, 716, 786, 791
Friedman, Milton   276, 304, 306, 540, 636
fundamental analysis   278-9, 300, 362, 398, 593, 631, 644-5
futurism/futurist   423, 427, 434, 442, 449

G

gasoline prices   209, 220, 243, 267, 284, 375, 479-82
GDP   23, 40-2, 63-5, 131-2, 135, 176
General Electric (GE)   428, 572
Glass-Steagall   442-442
Global Market Perspective (GMP)   460-6, 472, 486-490
global warming   448-450
gold   45-63, 158-9, 364-373, 381, 383, 405, 409, 443, 447
gorilla   52
government last to act   57-9, 342-6, 442, 611-2
Graham & Dodd   208, 278, 395, 644, 786
Great Depression   45, 61, 66-8, 187, 404, 434, 442, 453, 499, 509, 598
Great Recession   61, 86, 98, 147, 163, 180, 187, 346, 368, 443, 450, 753-755
Greek debt crisis   784-784
Green, Michael   388, 669, 792-3, 796
Greenspan, Alan   14-6, 89, 97, 293, 516, 539, 560-6, 571-2, 599, 754, 750
Gulf war (I and II)   337, 340
Guyon, Don   303

H

hedge funds, managers   248, 292, 313
hemlines   136, 181-3, 191, 762
herding theories   Ch. 34
heterogeneous/homogenous agency   215, 216, 217, 218, 230, 248, 254, 273, 292, 293, 298, 304, 306, 307, 313, 397, 399, 613, 639, 655, 657, 658, 659, 660, 662, 691, 692, 712, 713, 714, 715, 722, 723

hindcast 426
Hochberg/Kendall vi, 369, 428, 436-7, 442-446
holism/holistic 116, 123-5, 227, 235, 384-388, 409, 621, 624, 628-9, 711-2, 721-728 [Ch. 37], 732, 794
Home Building Index 445, 515
horror movies 177-80, 190-1, 198, 762-4
hurricane Katrina 9-10, 13, 457
hyperinflation, Germany 138

I

immigration 190, 376-7
incommensurability 622-3, 634, 638, 645, 648-651, 723, 726
incumbent 135, 183-4, 195, 197, 375, 441, 703, 798
Index of Consumer Expectations 601
Index of Economic Policy Uncertainty 551-555
induced mood 388-389
information theory (BHW) 655-60
instinct psychology 535-7, 695-7, 708, 717
institutionalism 645, 650, 717, 723-723, 725, 727
interest rates 13-7, 24-8, 56-8, 60-3, 73-80 [Ch.3], 86, 268, 361-5, 367, 372, 380, 561-6, 626-7, 782
intermediary markets 265, 270-2, 533
International Monetary Fund (IMF) 90, 542, 577, 751, 753
internet stocks 208, 595, 599-600, 645
intrinsic 93, 256, 293, 525-529, 648, 675
invisible hand 228, 252, 307, 722
Initial Public Offerings (IPOs) 471, 585-7, 600, 606-9
Iran hostage crisis 18
Iraq 186, 421, 562, 765-6
ISIS 187-187

J

Jackson, Michael 447-447
Japan 198, 206, 421, 599, 607-8, 750
JFK assassination 5, 13, 303
Joulin et al. 68
Journal of Behavioral Finance (JBF) 273, 585, 667, 783, 792-795
junk bonds 139, 268, 421, 437-9

K

Kindleberger, Charles 301, 306, 507-9
Keynes, John Maynard 279, 395, 508, 539-40, 586, 638-40, 645-7, 722-
King's Law of Prices 222-222
Knight, Frank 646, 724
Kondratieff Cycle 746-9, 755
Kuhn, Thomas 632, 725

L

labor unions 132, 136, 158
lagging/leading sociometer 133-5, 140-7, 150-65, 180, 191, 439-42
large speculators 356, 484, 496
law of patterned herding (LPH) 238-9, 251, 255, 270, 274, 292-3, 303-13, 391, 463, 521, 785
LeDoux, Joseph E. 243, 295-6, 299, 326, 673
legislation 342-3, 611-12
limbic system 245, 295, 300, 325-6, 330-2, 692, 707
linear extrapolation 343, 362, 367, 421-55 [Ch. 21]
LiveJournal 169-170
Lo, Andrew 92, 275, 400, 662
luxury goods 266-8

M

Maclean, Paul 295, 326, 330-2
macroeconomics vii, 90, 93, 95, 98, 109, 193, 198, 253, 385, 516, 629, 669, 717, 794
Malkiel, Burton 516
Mandelbrot, Benoit 232, 275, 709, 744, 786
mania 174, 180, 208, 262, 301, 383, 407, 503-6, 517-520, 595, 599, 648, 761
margin debt 450, 477, 506, 517
Market Technicians Association (MTA) 441, 748
Martingale model 275-275
mean reversion 227-32, 255, 298, 594
mechanical causality 17-18, 29, 65, 110-1, 119, 506-10, 521-3
mechanism 114, 123, 125, 285, 298, 305, 307, 382, 394, 517, 622-624, 629, 632, 675, 713, 726

mechanics paradigm 3-4, 19, 23, 40, 46-8, 56, 65, 68, 82-3, 87, 90, 110, 118, 127, 167, 171, 198, 227, 341, 359, 365, 372, 394, 403-4, 422, 446, 497, 515, 631
medical care 423-423
mercantilists 722-722
mergers and acquisitions (M&A) 585-7, 603-611
Merrill Lynch 88, 748-9, 780-1, 790
metatheory/metatheoretical 116, 123-5, 313, 384, 398, 541, 619-639 [Ch. 32], 643, 650-1, 694-5, 706, 711, 716, 726, 769, 784
methodological holism 712, 721-732 [Ch. 37], 794
methodological individualism 712, 721-732 [Ch. 37], 794
microeconomics 96, 101, 253, 385, 788
mimic 332, 384, 388
mini/maxi skirts 181-3, 191, 777
Mirowski, Philip 634, 640-1, 661
Mises, Ludwig 530-7
monetarist/monetarism 198, 539-545 [Ch. 25], 636
monetary policy 63, 67, 78, 293
money supply 46-8, 52, 495, 540
Montgomery, Paul 181, 295, 330, 422, 794
mood sharing 128, 131, 132, 133, 370, 388, 405-410, 727
mood vs. emotion 111, 114, 116, 169-71, 375-6
mortgages 100
motivation to buy 209, 214, 227, 236-7, 251, 255
mutual funds, managers 337, 339, 348-9

N

Ned Davis Research 15
neoclassical economic theory 23-4, 67-8, 101, 203, 232, 236, 252, 259-60, 271-84, 401, 532, 535, 629-51, 659-62, 723-4
neocortex 243, 295, 299-300, 325-6, 330-355, 358, 531, 704
neuroeconomics 637-8, 792
neurophysiology 318, 662, 661, 715
New Economy 368, 443, 504, 595, 598, 600, 759
Nikkei 599, 607, 608
Noelle-Neumann, Elisabeth 310, 662, 716
Nobel Prize 103, 355, 636, 748, 749, 751, 754, 755, 787

Nofsinger, John 342, 585, 593, 604, 669, 792, 794
Noyes, C. Reynold 637, 638
nuclear weapons testing 119, 147, 185, 190-1, 199, 744

O

Obama, Barack 165, 183
object ontology 298, 625, 643-5, 648, 651
objectivity 23, 199, 250, 268, 269, 528, 529
OCD/bipolar disorder 373
oil 9-10, 30-4, 60, 86-7, 198-9, 271-2, 368-72, 379-83, 406, 457-500 [Ch. 22], 562, 564
organicism 114, 124-6, 621-7, 632-3, 639-40, 651, 695, 705, 712, 723, 726-7
overreaction/underreaction model 394-5

P

paradox 52, 81, 94, 299, 359, 367, 373, 391, 516, 542
Pareto, Vilfredo 300, 586, 691-717 [Ch. 36]
Parker, Wayne 667, 769, 783-4, 793-4
patents 177, 190, 192, 193, 645
peace 24, 43, 44, 45, 63, 69, 83, 134, 135, 141, 143, 144, 148, 157, 185, 186, 190, 192, 195, 196, 302, 371, 382, 434, 441, 716, 754
Penrose, Edith 277, 637, 643
Pepper, Steven 116, 123, 129, 621, 622, 623, 630, 632, 634, 638, 711, 723, 726
physiocrats 722
Pigou, Arthur C. 284, 327, 647
pivot point 150, 152-7, 162, 469
pop music 768-9, 780
potent directors 574-579 [Ch. 29], 745, 753-4
praxeology 535-7
precious metals 18, 45, 46, 52, 60-3, 133, 270-1, 365, 405, 407, 430
predictive 98, 125, 145, 174, 179, 185, 192, 193, 197, 261, 262, 306, 386, 401, 451, 460, 498, 624, 633, 634, 638, 641, 649, 758, 764
Preis et al. 514, 798
pre-rational 110, 111, 112, 148, 238, 244, 245, 249, 250, 251, 252, 253, 255, 256, 269, 311, 341, 347, 355, 375, 396, 397, 399, 400, 402, 512, 513, 525, 531, 532, 533, 534, 536, 626

Presley, Elvis   766-7, 791
process ontology   628, 630, 644, 645, 645,
    651, 704, 726
Producer Price Index (PPI)   89, 138-9, 175,
    178-9, 193, 287-9, 394, 406, 432, 450,
    524, 553, 569, 748, 764, 769
protectionism   711, 722

Q

quantitative (quant)   70, 98, 130, 216, 218,
    306, 398, 405, 409, 508, 511-14, 712,
    713, 715
quantitative easing (QE)   48-53, 429

R

random walk/randomness   98, 121, 137,
    260, 275, 306, 355, 358, 370, 491, 516,
    594, 724, 748, 755, 786
rationalization   251-2, 257
rational bubble   298, 506, 640, 660
rational expectations (RE)   93, 593, 594,
    596, 597, 598, 603, 610, 612, 749
reactive   73, 76, 118, 260, 373, 399, 525,
    539, 622, 624, 628, 629, 661, 723
real estate   86-8, 180, 187, 241-2, 260, 268-
    72, 345, 369, 372, 407, 435-7, 440, 443-6,
    505, 515, 550-1, 572, 753-5, 760-1
recession   32-5, 57-61, 85-102, 119, 144,
    147, 162-3, 176-80, 187, 346, 368, 421,
    450-1, 499, 750-5, 759-62
reductionism   93, 388, 398, 624, 638, 650,
    704, 712
referents   111, 241, 263, 376, 382, 384, 385,
    559, 627, 690
reflexivity   398-399
regulation/deregulation   66, 127, 190, 255,
    295, 378, 379, 520, 521, 592, 593, 604, 799
residues   692, 692-705, 711-7
retirement funds   303, 342-5
risk models   298-9, 390-3, 582-3, 588-9
Rome   514
Rothbard, Murray   527, 532, 535

S

Samuelson, Paul   90, 91, 275, 602, 609,
    748, 755
savings rate   37, 388
scandals   18, 119, 190, 302, 372, 612

Schumpeter, Joseph   279, 645, 650, 705,
    725, 748, 755
sentiment indicators   208, 233, 424, 451,
    453, 454
Shiller, Robert   215, 216, 217, 218, 230,
    248, 254, 273, 292, 293, 298, 304, 306,
    307, 313, 397, 399, 613, 639, 655, 657,
    658, 659, 660, 662, 691, 692, 712, 713,
    714, 715, 722, 723
skyscrapers   136, 190
slope of hope   59, 171
smart money   304-306, 347
Smith, Adam   109, 228, 276, 307, 634, 636,
    675, 722
Smith, Vernon   301, 327, 328, 347, 385,
    411, 636, 751, 787
Social Mood Conference   796, 797, 798,
    799, 800
societal sociometer   132-7
sociology/sociological   23, 110, 126, 193,
    300, 586, 632, 691-8, 703, 704, 711, 712,
    715-718, 725, 726, 732, 788, 794
sociometer   113, 114, 131-148 [Chapter 7],
    169, 171, 180, 188, 191, 263, 404, 439-
    442, 449, 551, 557, 559, 762, 773, 774,
    776, 778
Socionomics Foundation   193, 281, 312,
    388, 675, 739, 770, 788, 792, 793, 794,
    796, 798
Socionomics Institute   183, 244, 273, 732,
    757, 770, 772, 776, 779, 792, 793, 794,
    795, 796
socionomics paradigm   110, 446, 623, 631
Sornette, Didier   298, 333, 523, 647, 656,
    660, 794
South Sea Bubble   306, 348, 518
sovereign wealth funds   446-7
space program   423-4
specialized sociometer   131, 132, 133, 135,
    405, 449
spontaneous command   114, 117, 237-9,
    250-5, 271-2, 492
standard of value/standards   203, 204, 205,
    208, 209, 250, 255, 395, 507
Stanley, Eugene   514, 788, 800
stimulus program   24, 542
structure of socionomic theory   109-128
    [Ch .6]
subliminal   333, 388, 794
submarine analogy   735-744

suicide rates   154, 190
supply and demand   218-238, 251-71, 366-9, 457-501 [Ch.22], 503, 533, 648, 661, 691, 785
Swiss franc   577-9
synthesis   101, 623, 624, 694, 721, 725, 726, 727

T

Tea Party   163
technicians   298, 347, 356-7, 395, 441, 748-53, 785-6, 792
technocratic theories   539-545 [Ch. 25]
technology bubble   208, 443, 504, 572, 599
terrorism   4, 10-3, 24, 69, 81-3, 87, 302, 404, 410, 441, 766, 775
tipping point hypothesis   508, 514
TIPS   368-9
tools   56, 92, 100, 103, 265, 267, 272, 276, 277, 298, 520, 593, 595, 635, 636, 641, 643, 649, 693
top-down   116, 124-7, 130, 386, 722-3
trade balance/deficit   34-8, 63, 69, 187-8, 198, 379-82
transitivity of preferences   641
Treasury bills   14, 73-7, 222-3, 367-8
triggers   23, 60, 64, 65, 86, 92, 301, 376, 417, 471, 507, 508, 509, 514, 515, 523, 539, 540, 560, 707, 778
triune brain   295, 326, 333
tulip bulbs   503, 505, 512, 599
Twitter   169-72, 372

U

U.S. Dollar Index   369, 429-31
U.S. Dollar   378, 429-31, 473
unbounded sociometer   133, 135-6, 140-1, 144-5, 171
unemployment (rate)   36, 39-40, 63, 67, 139, 143, 158, 160, 378, 380-1, 426, 612
unpredictable/unpredictability   97, 98, 162, 252, 311, 398, 539, 549, 550, 639, 647
utility (maximization)   213, 216, 227-228, 232, 238, 249, 251-4, 256-257, 259, 265, 269, 271, 277, 284, 285, 291, 307, 311, 503, 506, 527, 536, 637, 640-642, 655, 657, 659, 660, 662, 668, 703, 723, 724
utility theory   276-7, 634-49

V

Value Line Composite (VLC)   138, 139, 435, 499, 571, 749, 769
value scales   530, 531, 532, 533, 534, 640
valence   410, 411, 672, 673, 679, 711
Veblen, Thorstein   650, 692, 698, 705, 707, 723
VIX/VXO   17, 18, 171, 554
Vietnam War   18, 160, 764
Von Neumann and Morgenstern   276, 635, 636

W

war   18, 24, 42-4, 119, 134-8, 142-4, 160, 185-7, 381-3, 4040, 562-3, 598, 764-6
Wave Principle (WP)   112, 114, 120-123, 130, 149, 208, 251, 255, 271, 307, 309, 313, 388, 398, 399, 400, 401, 403, 442, 507, 508, 514, 515, 519, 521, 625, 651, 707, 709, 710, 712, 715, 727
Welty, Gordon   276, 277, 637
wisdom of crowds   415-419 [Ch. 20]
Wolfe, A.B.   637, 638
World Wars I and II   44, 458, 598, 764

Y

yield spreads   268, 437-8

CPSIA information can be obtained
at www.ICGtesting.com
Printed in the USA
LVOW09*0726230517

535429LV00018B/430/P